Alan Rogers

Europe

Quality camping & caravanning sites

2008

Compiled by: Alan Rogers Guides Ltd

Designed by: Paul Effenberg, Vine Design Ltd

Maps created by Customised Mapping (01769 540044)
contain background data provided by GisDATA Ltd
Maps are © Alan Rogers Guides and GisDATA Ltd 2007

© Alan Rogers Guides Ltd 2008

Published by: Alan Rogers Guides Ltd,
Spelmonden Old Oast, Goudhurst, Kent TN17 1HE
www.alanrogers.com Tel: 01580 214000

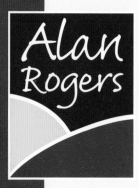

British Library Cataloguing-in-Publication Data:
A catalogue record for this book is available from the
British Library.

ISBN-13 978-1-906215-01-9

Printed in Great Britain by J H Haynes & Co Ltd

Contents

Contents

the Alan Rogers
approach

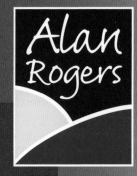

Last year we celebrated the publication of the fortieth editions
of the Alan Rogers Guides. Since Alan Rogers published the first
campsite guide that bore his name, the range has expanded to
six titles covering 27 countries. No fewer than 20 of the
campsites selected by Alan for the first guide are still featured
in our 2008 editions.

There are many thousands of campsites in Europe of varying
quality: this guide contains impartially written reports on
over 900 of the very finest, in no less than 24 countries. Each
one is individually inspected and selected. This guide does not
include sites in Britain and Ireland, for which we publish
a separate guide, and it contains only a limited selection of
sites in France, Italy, Spain & Portugal and the central Europe
countries as we also publish separate guides for these
destinations. All the usual maps and indexes are also included,
designed to help you find the choice of campsite that's right for
you. We hope you enjoy some happy and safe travels – and
some pleasurable 'armchair touring' in the meantime!

A question of quality

The criteria we use when inspecting and selecting sites are
numerous, but the most important by far is the question of
good quality. People want different things from their choice
of campsite so we try to include a range of campsite 'styles'
to cater for a wide variety of preferences: from those seeking
a small peaceful campsite in the heart of the countryside, to
visitors looking for an 'all singing, all dancing' site in a popular
seaside resort. Those with more specific interests, such as sporting
facilities, cultural events or historical attractions, are also
catered for.

The size of the site, whether it's part of a chain or privately
owned, makes no difference in terms of it being required to
meet our exacting standards in respect of its quality and it
being 'fit for purpose'. In other words, irrespective of the size
of the site, or the number of facilities it offers, we consider
and evaluate the welcome, the pitches, the sanitary facilities,
the cleanliness, the general maintenance and even the location.

" ...the campsites included in this book have
been chosen entirely on merit, and no payment
of any sort is made by them for their inclusion."

Alan Rogers, 1968

INSPECTED
SINCE 1968
& SELECTED

INSPECTED CAMPSITES & SELECTED

Expert opinions

We rely on our dedicated team of Site Assessors, all of whom are experienced campers, caravanners or motorcaravanners, to visit and recommend sites. Each year they travel some 100,000 miles around Europe inspecting new campsites for the guide and re-inspecting the existing ones. Our thanks are due to them for their enthusiastic efforts, their diligence and integrity.

We also appreciate the feedback we receive from many of our readers and we always make a point of following up complaints, suggestions or recommendations for possible new sites. Of course we get a few grumbles too – but it really is a few, and those we do receive usually relate to overcrowding or to poor maintenance during the peak school holiday period. Please bear in mind that, although we are interested to hear about any complaints, we have no contractual relationship with the campsites featured in our guides and are therefore not in a position to intervene in any dispute between a reader and a campsite.

HIGHLY RESPECTED BY SITE OWNERS AND READERS ALIKE, THERE IS NO BETTER GUIDE WHEN IT COMES TO FORMING AN INDEPENDENT VIEW OF A CAMPSITE'S QUALITY. WHEN YOU NEED TO BE CONFIDENT IN YOUR CHOICE OF CAMPSITE, YOU NEED THE ALAN ROGERS GUIDE.

- ☑ Sites only included on merit
- ☑ Sites cannot pay to be included
- ☑ Independently inspected, rigorously assessed
- ☑ Impartial reviews
- ☑ Over 40 years of expertise

Independent and honest

Whilst the content and scope of the Alan Rogers guides have expanded considerably since the early editions, our selection of campsites still employs exactly the same philosophy and criteria as defined by Alan Rogers in 1968.

'telling it how it is'

Firstly, and most importantly, our selection is based entirely on our own rigorous and independent inspection and selection process. Campsites cannot buy their way into our guides – indeed the extensive Site Report which is written by us, not by the site owner, is provided free of charge so we are free to say what we think and to provide an honest, 'warts and all' description. This is written in plain English and without the use of confusing icons or symbols.

Written in plain English, our guides are exceptionally easy to use, but a few words of explanation regarding the layout and content may be helpful. This guide is divided firstly by country, subsequently (in the case of larger countries) by region. For a particular area the town index at the back provides more direct access.

The Site Reports – *Example of an entry*

Site Number **Site name**
Postal Address (including county)
Telephone number. Email address

A description of the site in which we try to give an idea of its general features – its size, its situation, its strengths and its weaknesses. This section should provide a picture of the site itself with reference to the facilities that are provided and if they impact on its appearance or character. We include details on pitch numbers, electricity (with amperage), hardstandings etc. in this section as pitch design, planning and terracing affects the site's overall appearance. Similarly we include reference to pitches used for caravan holiday homes, chalets, and the like. Importantly at the end of this column we indicate if there are any restrictions, e.g. no tents, no children, naturist sites.

Facilities

Lists more specific information on the site's facilities and amenities and, where available, the dates when these facilities are open (if not for the whole season). Off site: here we give distances to various local amenities, for example, local shops, the nearest beach, plus our featured activities (bicycle hire, fishing, horse riding, boat launching). Where we have space we list suggestions for activities and local tourist attractions.

Open: Site opening dates.

Directions

Separated from the main text in order that they may be read and assimilated more easily by a navigator en-route. Bear in mind that road improvement schemes can result in road numbers being altered.

GPS: references are provided as we obtain them for satellite navigation systems (in degrees and minutes).

Charges 2008

Indexes

Our three indexes allow you to find sites by country, site number and name, by country and site name (alphabetically) or by the town or village where the site is situated. See also the handy Quick Reference sections at the back.

Campsite Maps

The maps of each country are designed to show the country in relation to others and will help you to identify the approximate position of each campsite. The colour of the campsite number indicates whether it is open all year or not. You will certainly need more detailed maps and we have found the Michelin atlas to be particularly useful.

Facilities

Toilet blocks

We assume that toilet blocks will be equipped with a reasonable amount of British style WCs, washbasins with hot and cold water and hot showers with dividers or curtains, and will have all necessary shelves, hooks, plugs and mirrors. We also assume that there will be an identified chemical toilet disposal point, and that the campsite will provide water and waste water drainage points and bin areas. If not the case, we comment. We do mention certain features that some readers find important: washbasins in cubicles, facilities for babies, facilities for those with disabilities and motorcaravan service points. Readers with disabilities are advised to contact the site of their choice to ensure that facilities are appropriate to their needs.

Shop

Basic or fully supplied, and opening dates.

Bars, restaurants, takeaway facilities and entertainment

We try hard to supply opening and closing dates (if other than the campsite opening dates) and to identify if there are discos or other entertainment.

Children's play areas

Fenced and with safety surface (e.g. sand, bark or pea-gravel).

Swimming pools

If particularly special, we cover in detail in our main campsite description but reference is always included under our Facilities listings. Opening dates, charges and levels of supervision are provided where we have been notified.

Leisure facilities

For example, playing fields, bicycle hire, organised activities and entertainment.

Dogs

If dogs are not accepted or restrictions apply, we state it here. Check the quick reference list at the back of the guide.

Off site

This briefly covers leisure facilities, tourist attractions, restaurants etc. nearby.

Charges

These are the latest provided to us by the sites. In those few cases where 2007 or 2008 prices are not given, we try to give a general guide.

Reservations

Necessary for high season (roughly mid-July to mid-August) in popular holiday areas (ie beach resorts). You can reserve via our own Alan Rogers Travel Service or through tour operators. Or be wholly independent and contact the campsite(s) of your choice direct, using the contact details shown in the site reports.

Telephone numbers

The numbers given assume you are actually IN the country concerned. If you are phoning from the UK remember that the first '0' is usually disregarded and replaced by the appropriate country code. For the latest details you should refer to an up-to-date telephone directory.

Opening dates

Are those advised to us during the early autumn of the previous year – sites can, and sometimes do, alter these dates before the start of the following season, often for good reasons. If you intend to visit shortly after a published opening date, or shortly before the closing date, it is wise to check that it will actually be open at the time required. Similarly some parks operate a restricted service during the low season, only opening some of their facilities (e.g. swimming pools) during the main season; where we know about this, and have the relevant dates, we indicate it – again if you are at all doubtful it is wise to check.

Some site owners are very laid back when it comes to opening and closing dates. They may not be fully ready by their stated opening dates – grass and hedges may not all be cut or perhaps only limited sanitary facilities open. At the end of the season they also tend to close down some facilities and generally wind down prior to the closing date. Bear this in mind if you are travelling early or late in the season – it is worth phoning ahead.

The Camping Cheque low season touring system goes some way to addressing this in that participating campsites are encouraged to have all key facilities open and running by the opening date and to remain fully operational until the closing date.

WHETHER YOU'RE AN 'OLD HAND' IN TERMS OF CAMPING AND CARAVANNING OR ARE CONTEMPLATING YOUR FIRST TRIP, A REGULAR READER OF OUR GUIDES OR A NEW 'CONVERT', WE WISH YOU WELL IN YOUR TRAVELS AND HOPE WE HAVE BEEN ABLE TO HELP IN SOME WAY.

WE ARE, OF COURSE, ALSO OUT AND ABOUT OURSELVES, VISITING SITES, TALKING TO OWNERS AND READERS, AND GENERALLY CHECKING ON STANDARDS AND NEW DEVELOPMENTS.

We wish all our readers thoroughly enjoyable Camping and Caravanning in 2008 – favoured by good weather of course!

THE ALAN ROGERS TEAM

have you visited www.alanrogers.com yet?

INSPECTED CAMPSITES & SELECTED

Alan Rogers

Our website has fast become the first-stop for countless caravanners, motorhome owners and campers all wanting reliable, impartial and detailed information for their next trip.

It features a fully searchable database of the best campsites in the UK & Ireland, and the rest of Europe: over 2,000 campsites in 26 countries.

Countries

Finland

Norway

Sweden

Denmark

Netherlands

Belgium

Luxembourg

Czech Republic

Slovakia

Germany

Austria

France

Hungary

Switzerland

Liechtenstein

Slovenia

Croatia

Andorra

Portugal

Italy

Greece

Spain

the Alan Rogers
awards

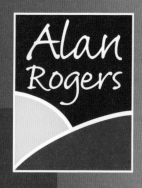

In 2004 we introduced the first ever Alan Rogers Campsite Awards.

Before making our awards, we carefully consider more than 2000 campsites featured in our guides, taking into account comments from our site assessors, our head office team and, of course, our readers.

Our award winners come from the four corners of Europe, from southern Portugal to the Czech Republic, and this year we are making awards to campsites in 14 different countries.

Needless to say, it's an extremely difficult task to choose our eventual winners, but we believe that we have identified a number of campsites with truly outstanding characteristics.

In each case, we have selected an outright winner, along with two highly commended runners-up.

Listed below are full details of each of our award categories and our winners for 2007.

Alan Rogers Progress Award 2007

This award reflects the hard work and commitment undertaken by particular site owners to improve and upgrade their site.

WINNER

AU0060 Natterersee, Austria

RUNNERS-UP

BE0712   Ile de Faigneul, Belgium

DE3672   Elbsee, Germany

Alan Rogers Welcome Award 2007

This award takes account of sites offering a particularly friendly welcome and maintaining a friendly ambience throughout reader's holidays.

WINNER

FR24090 Soleil Plage, France

RUNNERS-UP

IR9610   Mannix Point, Ireland

UK4640   Goosewood, England

Alan Rogers Active Holiday Award 2007

This award reflects sites in outstanding locations which are ideally suited for active holidays, notably walking or cycling, but which could extend to include such activities as winter sports or water sports

WINNER

DK2170 Klim Strand, Denmark

RUNNERS-UP

FR09060 Pre Lombard, France

DE3450   Munstertal, Germany

Alan Rogers Motorhome Award 2007

Motorhome sales are increasing and this award acknowledges sites which, in our opinion, have made outstanding efforts to welcome motorhome clients.

WINNER

PO8210 Campismo Albufeira, Portugal

RUNNERS-UP

IR9650   Woodlands Park, Ireland

FR29180 Les Embruns, France

Alan Rogers 4 Seasons Award 2007

This award is made to outstanding sites with extended opening dates and which welcome clients to a uniformly high standard throughout the year.

WINNER

CH9570	Eienwaldi, Switzerland

RUNNERS-UP

AU0440	Schluga, Austria
IT6814	Flaminio, Italy

Alan Rogers Seaside Award 2007

This award is made for sites which we feel are outstandingly suitable for a really excellent seaside holiday.

WINNER

ES8030	Nautic Almata, Spain

RUNNERS-UP

FR85210	Les Ecureuils, France
IT6036	Ca Pasquali, Italy

Alan Rogers Country Award 2007

This award contrasts with our former award and acknowledges sites which are attractively located in delightful, rural locations.

WINNER

UK1020	Oakdown, England

RUNNERS-UP

CZ4896	Camping Country, Czech Republic
NL5980	De Roos, Netherlands

Alan Rogers Rented Accommodation Award 2007

Given the increasing importance of rented accommodation on many campsites, we feel that it is important to acknowledge sites which have made a particular effort in creating a high quality 'rented accommodation' park.

WINNER

ES8480	Sanguli, Spain

RUNNERS-UP

NL5575	Scheldeoord, Netherlands
CR6736	Valdaliso, Croatia

Alan Rogers Unique Site Award 2007

This award acknowledges sites with unique, outstanding features – something which simply cannot be found elsewhere and which is an important attraction of the site.

WINNER

FR78040	Huttopia Rambouillet, France

RUNNERS-UP

FR80070	Ferme des Aulnes, France
UK1590	Exe Valley, England

Alan Rogers Family Site Award 2007

Many sites claim to be child friendly but this award acknowledges the sites we feel to be the very best in this respect.

WINNER

NL5985	Beerze Bulten, Netherlands

RUNNERS-UP

UK0170	Trevella, England
ES8540	Torre del Sol, Spain
IT6014	Villaggio Turistico Internazionale, Italy

Alan Rogers Readers' Award 2007

In 2005 we introduced a new award, which we believe to be the most important, our Readers' Award. We simply invited our readers (by means of an on-line poll at **www.alanrogers.com**) to nominate the site they enjoyed most. The outright winner for 2007 is:

WINNER

ES8530	Playa Montroig Resort, Spain

Alan Rogers Special Award 2007

A special award is made to acknowledge sites which we feel have overcome a very significant setback, and have, not only returned to their former condition, but has added extra amenities and can therefore be fairly considered to be even better than before. In 2007 we acknowledged two campsites, which have undergone major problems and have made highly impressive recoveries.

CH9510	Aareg, Switzerland
IT6845	San Nicola, Italy

Alan Rogers **.travel**

The Alan Rogers Travel Service was set up to provide a low cost booking service for readers. We pride ourselves on being able to put together a bespoke holiday, taking advantage of our experience, knowledge and contacts. We can tailor-make a holiday to suit your requirements, giving you maximum choice and flexibility: exactly what we have been offering for some 8 years now.

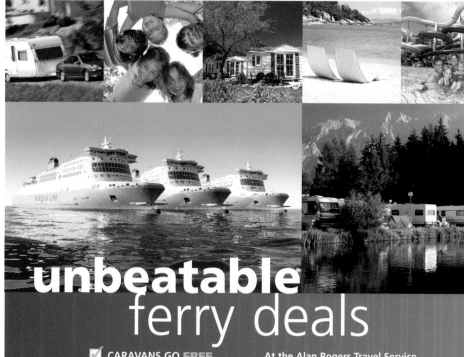

unbeatable
ferry deals

☑ CARAVANS GO FREE

☑ TRAILERS GO FREE

☑ MOTORHOMES PRICED AS CARS

ON CERTAIN ROUTES
- CONDITIONS APPLY

At the Alan Rogers Travel Service we're always keen to find the best deals and keenest prices. There are always great savings on offer, and we're constantly negotiating new ferry rates and money-saving offers, so just call us on

01580 214000

and ask about the latest deals.

or visit
Alan Rogers **.travel**

Whether you book on-line or book by phone, you will be allocated an experienced Personal Travel Consultant to provide you with personal advice and manage every stage of your booking. Our Personal Travel Consultants have first-hand experience of many of our campsites and access to a wealth of information. They can 'paint a picture' of individual campsites, check availability, provide a competitive price and tailor your holiday arrangements to your specific needs.

- Discuss your holiday plans with a friendly person with first-hand experience

- Let us reassure you that your holiday arrangements really are taken care of

- Tell us about your special requests and allow us to pass these on

- Benefit from advice which will save you money – the latest ferry deals and more

- Remember, our offices are in Kent not overseas and we do NOT operate a queuing system!

THE AIMS OF THE TRAVEL SERVICE ARE SIMPLE

- To provide convenience - a one-stop shop to make life easier.

- To provide peace of mind - when you need it most.

- To provide a friendly, knowledgeable, efficient service – when this can be hard to find.

- To provide a low cost means of organising your holiday – when prices can be so complicated.

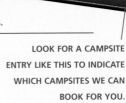

HOW IT WORKS

1 Choose your campsite(s) – we can book around 500 across Europe. Look for the yellow coloured campsite entries in this book. You'll find more info and images at www.alanrogers.travel.

Please note: the list of campsites we can book for you varies from time to time.

2 Choose your dates – choose when you arrive, when you leave.

3 Choose your ferry crossing – we can book most routes with most operators at extremely competitive rates.

Then just call us for an instant quote

01580 214000
or visit
www.alanrogers.travel

LOOK FOR A CAMPSITE ENTRY LIKE THIS TO INDICATE WHICH CAMPSITES WE CAN BOOK FOR YOU.

THE LIST IS GROWING SO PLEASE CALL FOR UP TO THE MINUTE INFORMATION.

Book The Best, **With The Best**

This Premier Selection is designed to offer a hand-picked range of sites, well-known to us, where you will find the best of everything that makes a great holiday.

PITCHES AND MOBILE HOMES

2008
The Premier Selection
40 Top French Campsites

The best sites in the most popular regions
all inspected & selected by Alan Rogers
BOOK WITH THE EXPERTS
PLUS: High spec mobile homes

FREE BROCHURE
01580 214000
www.**alanrogers.travel/premier**

Leave The Hassle To Us

- All site fees paid in advance (nominal local tourist taxes may be payable on arrival).
- Your pitch is reserved for you – travel with peace of mind.
- No endless overseas phone calls or correspondence with foreign site owners.
- No need to pay foreign currency deposits and booking fees.
- Take advantage of our expert advice and experience of camping in Europe.

Already Booked Your Ferry?

We're confident that our ferry inclusive booking service offers unbeatable value. However, if you have already booked your ferry then we can still make a pitch-only reservation for you (minimum 5 nights). Since our prices are based on our ferry inclusive service, you need to be aware that a non-ferry booking may result in slightly higher prices than if you were to book direct with the site.

The tiny independent principality of Andorra is situated high in the Pyrenees between France and Spain. With a diverse landscape of mountains, valleys, forests, lakes and hot springs, it is probably best known for skiing and duty-free shopping.

CAPITAL: ANDORRA LA VELLA

Tourist Office

Embassy of the Principality of Andorra
63 Westover Road, London SW18 2RF
Tel/Fax: 020 8874 4806 (visits by appointment only)
Internet: www.turisme.ad

Shopping and skiing aside, Andorra has plenty to offer the visitor in terms of leisure activities. One of the most unspoilt areas of the country is the hamlet of Llorts. Set amidst fields of tobacco overlooked by mountains, it's a great place for hiking. The enormous spa complex in Caldea offers the perfect place to relax. Fed by natural thermal springs, it houses lots of pools, hot tubs and saunas. Village festivals are a popular event with many Andorran towns and hamlets celebrating their heritage with music, dancing, wine and feasts. Most fall in the high season.

Administratively Andorra is divided up into seven parishes: Canillo, Encamp, Ordino, La Massana, Andorra la Vella, Sant Julià de Lòria and Escaldes-Engordany. The Principality of Andorra can be accessed by road from France through Pas de la Casa and the Envalira Pass and from Spain via Sant Julià de Lòria. The nearest main cities are Barcelona (185 km) and Lleida (151 km) on the Spanish side and Toulouse (187 km) and Perpignan (169 km) on the French side.

Population
66,500

Climate
The climate is temperate, with cold winters with a lot of snow and warm summers. The country's mountain peaks often remain snowcapped until July.

Language
The official language is Catalan, with French and Spanish widely spoken.

Telephone
The country code is 00 376.

Money
Currency: The Euro
Banks: Mon-Fri 09.00-13.00 and 15.00-17.00, Sat 09.00-12.00.

Shops
Mon-Sat 09.00-20.00, Sun 09.00-19.00.

Public Holidays
New Year's Day; Epiphany; Constitution Day, Mar 14; Holy Thursday to Easter Monday; Labour Day; Ascension; Whit Sunday; Whit Monday; St John's Day Jun 24; Assumption Aug 15; National Day Sep 8; All Saints' Day Nov 1; St Charles' Day; Nov 4; Immaculate Conception; Dec 8; Christmas Dec 24-26; New Year's Eve.

Motoring
There are no motorways in Andorra. Main roads are prefixed 'N' and side roads 'V'. Certain mountain passes may prove difficult in winter and heavy snowfalls could cause road closures. Expect traffic queues in the summer, with a high volume of motorists coming to and from France.

AN7143 Camping Xixerella

Ctra de Pals, Xixerella, La Massana
Tel: **836 613**. Email: **c-xixerella@campingxixerella.com**

Andorra is a country of narrow valleys and pine and birch forested mountains. Xixerella is attractively situated in just such a valley below towering mountains and beside a river. The site is made up of several sections of gently sloping grass, accessed by tarmac or gravel roads which lead to informal pitching. Electricity (3/6A) is available for most of the 150 places. Picnic area with barbecues and with bridge access to walks in the woods. Pleasant bar and restaurant with pool-side terrace. The site can be very busy from mid-July to mid-August, but otherwise it is usually quite peaceful. Do not forget to explore Andorra for that duty free shopping.

Facilities

The satisfactory main sanitary building is fully equipped, including British style WCs (no paper) and some children's toilets, some washbasins in cabins, showers with curtains. Laundry facilities. Further modern facilities in novel round building by the pool, including toilets, a laundry, baby bath and dishwashing sinks. Small shop, bar and restaurant (closed Oct). Swimming pool and paddling pool (mid-June - mid-Sept). Play area. Minigolf. Volleyball. Basketball. Table football. Electronic games. Disco in season. Torch useful. Off site: Riding 3 km. Skiing possible at Arinsal (5 km) or Pal (6 km).

Open: All year.

Directions

Site is 8 km. from Andorra la Vella on the road to Pal (this road can only be accessed on the north side of town), via La Massana.

Charges 2007

Per person	€ 5,00
child	€ 4,80
pitch	€ 9,80
electricity (3A)	€ 5,00

AN7145 Camping Valira

Avenida Salou, s/n, Andorra la Vella
Tel: **722 384**. Email: **campvalira@andorra.ad**

This small and unusual site is named after the river in the town of Andorra La Vella. It has a steep curving entrance which can become congested at peak times. You pass the pleasant restaurant and bar and the heated indoor pool as you enter the site. Maximum use has been made of space here and it is worth looking at the picture of the site in reception as it was in 1969. The 150 medium sized pitches are mostly level on terraces with some shading. One of the family will guide you to your place and this can be an interesting experience if the site is busy. All pitches have access to electricity, but some may need long leads. There are drinking water points around the site. As this is a town site there is some ambient noise but the site is ideal for duty free shopping. Some pitches at the south end of the site have a free 'birds eye' view of any event in the sports stadium.

Facilities

The facilities are modern and spotless, with provision for disabled campers, plus separate room with toddlers' toilet and good baby room. Two washing machines and dryer. The two blocks can be heated in winter. Bar/restaurant with good menu at realistic prices. Well stocked small shop. Small heated indoor pool. Paddling pool. Play area. Barrier closed 11 pm - 7 am. Off site: Town shops 10 minutes walk.

Open: All year.

Directions

Site is on the south side of Andorra La Vella, on left travelling south behind sports stadium. It is well signed off the N145. Watch signs carefully – an error with a diversion round town will cost you dear at rush hour.

Charges 2008

Per person	€ 5,75
child (1-10 yrs)	€ 5,00
pitch	€ 11,50
electricity (3-10A)	€ 3,75 - € 5,75

MAP 1

Austria is primarily known for two contrasting attractions: the capital Vienna with its fading Imperial glories, and the variety of its Alpine hinterland. It is an ideal place to visit year round, whether you want to admire the spectacular scenery and participate in winter sports or to visit historical sites and cultural attractions.

CAPITAL: VIENNA

Tourist Office

Austrian National Tourist Office (ANTO)
PO Box 2363, London W1A 2QB
Tel: 020 7629 0461
Fax: 020 7499 6038
Email: info@anto.co.uk
Internet: www.austria.info

Perhaps the best known area and the most easily accessible part of the country is the Tirol in the west. A charming region with picturesque valleys to explore, you'll be able to enjoy folk-lore entertainment year round. Situated in the centre is the Lake District and Salzburg. With its ancient castles, curative spas and salt mines to visit, Salzburg also has plenty of music, art and drama festivals to enjoy. Vienna, too, offers plenty of cultural pursuits with its museums, opera and famous choirs. The neighbouring provinces of Lower Austria, Burgenland and Styria, land of vineyards, mountains and farmland, are off the tourist routes, but provide good walking territory. Further south, in the Carinthia region, lakes and mountains dominate the landscape. The beautiful scenery and rural way of life offers a quieter retreat. There are a few large towns to explore, lots of pleasant villages and good, often uncrowded roads.

Population

8.1 million

Climate

Temperate, with moderately hot summers, cold winters and snow in the mountains.

Language

German

Telephone

The country code is 0043.

Money

Currency: The Euro
Banks: Mon, Tues, Wed & Fri 08.00-12.30 and 13.30-15.00. Thurs 08.00-12.30 and 13.30-17.30.

Shops

Mon-Fri 08.00-18.30, some close 12.00-14.00; Sat 08.00-17.00.

Public Holidays

New Year; Epiphany; Easter Mon; Labour Day; Ascension; Whit Mon; Corpus Christi; Assumption 15 Aug; National Day 26 Oct; All Saints 1 Nov; Immaculate Conception 8 Dec; Christmas 25, 26 Dec.

Motoring

Visitors using Austrian motorways and 'A' roads must display a Motorway Vignette on their vehicle as they enter Austria. Failure to have one will mean a heavy, on-the-spot fine. Vignettes are obtained at all major border crossings into Austria and at larger petrol stations. All vehicles above 3.5 tonnes maximum permitted laden weight are required to use a small device called the 'GO-Box' - see page 18.

AU0010 Alpencamping Nenzing

Garfrenga 1, A-6710 Nenzing (Vorarlberg)

Tel: **055 256 2491**. Email: **info@alpencampingnenzing.at**

Although best known for its skiing resorts, the forests and mountains of the Vorarlberg province make it equally suitable for a peaceful summer visit. Alpencamping Nenzing, is some 690 m. above sea level, set in a natural bowl surrounded by trees with some views across the pleasant countryside. Wind your way up from the main road or motorway, following a narrow road (exit by a different route). Some of the 168 level, small, touring pitches are in a flat area with others on neat terraces beyond. All have electricity and 105 have water, drainage, sewage, TV, gas and phone connections.

Facilities

The newer facilities are 'state of the art' and contain 20 free private bathrooms. Two older blocks remain and provide good facilities. Baby room. Facilities for disabled visitors. Motorcaravan services. Small shop. Bar. Restaurant. Heated pool (20 x 8 m). Play areas. Practice climbing wall. Sauna, solarium, massage. Internet access. Off site: Bicycle hire, riding, tennis and fishing near.

Open: All year excl. week after Easter - 30 April.

Directions

From A14 Feldkirch - Bludenz motorway take exit for Nenzing on B190 road and then follow small 'Camping' signs which have the site logo, a butterfly. GPS: N47:10.965 E09:40.929

Charges 2007

Per unit incl. 2 persons	€ 17,00 - € 29,00
child	€ 3,00 - € 4,00

No credit cards.

AU0015 Camping Grosswalsertal

Plazera 21, A-6741 Raggal (Vorarlberg)

Tel: **055 532 09**. Email: **info@camping-austria.info**

As we climbed up to this site we seemed to be above the clouds. We then descended into a beautiful green valley and saw the site on a flat plateau below. From almost every pitch there are the most fantastic views down the valley. On open grass, there are 55 slightly sloping and unmarked pitches all with 10A electricity. Plenty of sporting activities are available locally and there are many places to visit, as well as walks and bike rides in the immediate area.

Facilities

The modern sanitary block has ample and clean toilets, hot showers and washbasins. Washing machine and dryer. Small shop with essential supplies. Swimming pool (1/6-15/9). Play area. Bicycle hire. Off site: Fishing 2 km. Golf 14 km. Riding 2 km.

Open: 15 May - 30 September.

Directions

From the A14 take exit for Nenzing and Gr. Walsertal and proceed to Ludesch. Turn right (Raggal) and take left fork, pass supermarket and 2 km. downhill to the site. GPS: N47:12.951 E09:51.222

Charges 2007

Per unit incl. 2 persons	€ 14,50 - € 17,00
incl. electricity	€ 16,00 - € 18,50

No credit cards.

NOTE: From 1 January 2004, all vehicles above 3.5 tonnes maximum permitted laden weight using the Austrian network of motorways and expressways are required to attach a small device called the 'Go-Box' to their windscreen. The Go-Box uses the high frequency range to communicate with the around 400 fixed-installation toll points covering Austria, making it possible to effect an automatic toll deduction without slowing the flow of traffic. The on-board devices can be obtained for a one-off handling fee of Euro 5.00 at about 220 sales centres in Austria and in neighbouring countries or via the Internet. For further information visit the website at http://www.austria.info

KÄRNTEN
carinthia

| Life is sunny in the south. |

AU0232 Terrassencamping Sonnenberg

Hinteroferst 12, A-6714 Nüziders bei Bludenz (Vorarlberg)

Tel: 055 526 4035. Email: sonnencamp@aon.at

A friendly welcome awaits you at this well equipped site on the western end of Austria, at the junction of five alpine valleys. The views are captivating and ever changing. The site is mostly terraced with pitches for longer stay units having gravel hardstandings at one side of the site, while shorter stay units have an area closer to the entrance. A large car park area reduces the traffic congestion at peak times, and there are eight pitches designated for motorcaravans. There are 120 good sized pitches, all with electricity (13A), 40 are fully serviced. In the summer months these are all touring pitches. Traditional Tirolean musical evenings are a feature of this site, and on Sundays during the summer the men of the Dünser family, dressed in traditional costume, play the 'Alpenhorns'. The family also take parties of campers on guided walking tours, highly recommended, but do make sure that you are properly equipped, and reasonably fit. Good English is spoken.

Facilities

A superb new building contains high quality facilities. On the lower floor are WCs, spacious hot showers, and washbasins (some in cubicles), and a baby room. Drying room, laundry, and dishwashing upstairs. Motorcaravan service point. TV and cinema room. Sleeping loft for four campers (used in inclement weather). Shop. Baker calls daily in July/August. Playground. Only one dog per unit. Internet access. Seven studio apartments. Off site: Village with shops and ATM 500 m. Fishing 3 km. Riding and bicycle hire 4 km. Golf 8 km.

Open: 26 April - 6 October.

Directions

Nüziders is about 25 km. southeast of Feldkirch. From A14 exit 57 (Bludenz-Nüziders) turn north on road 190 and left at roundabout into village. Follow camping signs through village to site. GPS: N47:10.191 E09:48.448

Charges 2008

Per person	€ 5,00 - € 6,00
child (2-14 yrs)	€ 3,50
pitch	€ 6,00 - € 10,00
electricity (4 kWh/day)	€ 2,60
No credit cards.	

AU0045 Campingplatz Ötztal

Unterlangenfeld 220, A-6444 Längenfeld (Tirol)

Tel: 052 535 348. Email: info@camping-oetztal.com

Camping Ötztal, a family run site, is situated some 400 metres from the pretty village of Längenfeld, at the edge of a forest. Next door are the local sports centre and swimming pool and a restaurant. In summer the campsite is ideal for walking and cycling, as well as mountaineering tours. In the winter you can enjoy cross-country skiing right from the doorstep and a free bus shuttle operates to the Ötztal Ski arena. The site provides 200 level grass pitches of which 170 are for tourers. All pitches have electricity and 100 have also gas, water, drainage and TV point.

Facilities

Excellent sanitary facilities include 4 bathrooms to rent for private use. Baby room. Facilities for disabled people. Restaurant serves breakfast and takeaway. Sauna and solarium. Female hairdressing room. Dog shower. Washing machines and dryer. Ski room. Motorcaravan service point. WiFi. Bicycle hire. Off site: Längenfeld and Aqua Dome thermal spa facility.

Open: All year.

Directions

From the A12 take exit 123 and follow the 186 road along the Ötztal Valley towards Sölden for about 20 km. Site entrance is at the top of the hill in the centre of Längenfeld, to the right.

Charges 2007

Per person	€ 5,60 - € 7,40
pitch	€ 6,70 - € 11,60
electricity	€ 1,90
No credit cards.	

AU0035 **Camp Alpin Seefeld**

Leutascherstrasse 810, A-6100 Seefeld (Tirol)

Tel: **052 124 848**. Email: **info@camp-alpin.at**

Alpin Seefeld is a pleasant, modern campsite with very good facilities, set in an attractive setting some 1,200 metres high. With excellent views of the surrounding mountains and forests, there are 140 large, individual pitches arranged mainly on flat grass (plus a few hardstandings), all with gas, TV, electricity (16A) and waste water, with 10 water points around, but no shade. Some pitches at the back and edge of the site are terraced. This is a good base for both summer and winter activity, whether you wish to take a gentle stroll or participate in something more demanding, including skiing direct from the site.

Facilities

Excellent heated sanitary facilities include nine private bathrooms for hire, some private cabins. Washing machines and dryer. Sauna, Turkish bath and solarium. Infra-red cabin. Shop. Bar, snack bar and takeaway. Fishing. Play area. Bicycle hire. Off site: Sports centre with heated indoor and outdoor pools and restaurant are close. The popular Tirolean village of Seefeld 1 km. Golf 1.5 km.

Open: All year.

Directions

Seefeld is about 17 km. northwest of Innsbruck. The site is 2 km. from Seefeld on the road signed to Leutasch. It is well signed as you approach the town.

Charges 2007

Per person	€ 4,00 - € 9,90
child (3-14 yrs)	€ 3,00 - € 7,90
electricity	€ 0,70 - € 3,80
pitch	€ 5,00 - € 12,90

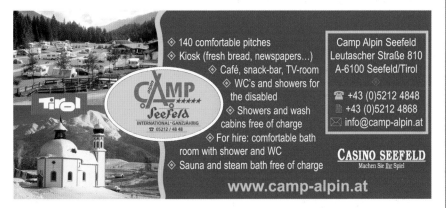

AU0040 **Ferienanlage Tiroler Zugspitze**

Obermoos 1, A-6632 Ehrwald (Tirol)

Tel: **056 732 309**. Email: **camping@zugspitze.at**

Although Ehrwald is in Austria, it is from the entrance of Zugspitzcamping that the cable car runs to the summit of Germany's highest mountain. Standing at 1,200 feet above sea level at the foot of the mountain, the 200 pitches (120 for tourists), mainly of grass over stones, are on flat terraces with fine panoramic views in parts. All have electricity connections (16A). The modern reception building at the entrance also houses a fine restaurant with a terrace which is open to those using the cable car, as well as those staying on the site. A further large modern building, heated in cool weather, has an indoor pool and fitness centre. This excellent mountain site, with its superb facilities, provides a good base from which to explore this interesting part of Austria and Bavaria by car or on foot. A trip up to the Zugspitze offers beautiful views and many opportunities for mountain walking.

Facilities

Two good sanitary blocks (cleaning may be variable) provide some washbasins in cabins and 20 private bathrooms for rent. Separate children's unit. Baby room. Unit for disabled people. Washing machines, dryers and dishwashers. Drying rooms. Motorcaravan service point. Shop. Bar. Restaurant. Indoor pool with sauna, whirlpool and fitness centre with solarium and massage room. Outdoor pool and children's pool with slide. Internet access. Bicycle hire. Play area. Organised activities in season. Off site: Hotel, souvenir shop and cable car station 100 m. Sports in Ehrwald 5 km.

Open: All year.

Directions

Follow signs in Ehrwald to Tiroler Zugspitzbahn and then signs to camp. GPS: N47:25.595 E10:56.486

Charges 2007

Per person	€ 10,00 - € 12,00
child (4-15 yrs)	€ 7,50 - € 8,50
pitch	€ 6,00 - € 8,00
electricity per kWh.	€ 0,80
dog	€ 4,00

Special seasonal weekly offers. Mastercard accepted.

AU0060 Ferienparadies Natterer See

Natterer See 1, A-6161 Natters (Tirol)

Tel: **051 254 6732**. Email: **info@natterersee.com**

Above Innsbruck, seven kilometres southwest of the town, this excellent site is in a quiet and isolated location around two small lakes. Founded in 1930, the site is renowned as one of Austria's finest campsites and last year the owners embarked on an ambitious improvement project with 40 large new 'super pitches'. Each with a minimum size of 110 sq.m, these pitches are all equipped with water, drainage and electricity. There are a further 210 individual pitches (180 for tourists) of varying size, either on flat ground by the lake or on higher, level terraces. All pitches have electricity (6A). Many are reinforced by gravel (possibly tricky for tents). Other projects include new roads, reception, café/bistro and a toilet block with private family bathrooms. There are many fine mountain views and a wide variety of scenic excursions. For the more active, signed walks start from the site. One of the lakes is used for swimming with a long 67 m. slide (free to campers, on payment to day visitors. For winter camping the site offers ski and drying rooms and a free ski-bus service. A toboggan run and langlauf have been developed with ice skating, ice hockey and curling on the lake. The excellent restaurant with a bar and a large terrace overlooking the lake has a good menu. The owners speak very good English.

Facilities

The large sanitary blocks have under-floor heating, some washbasins in cabins, plus excellent facilities for babies, children and disabled people. Laundry facilities. Motorcaravan services. Fridge box hire. Bar/restaurant (20/3-2/10). Pizzeria and takeaway. Good mini-market (20/3-2/10). Playgrounds. Children's activity programme. Child minding (day nursery) in high season. Sports field. Archery. Youth room with games, pool and billiards. TV room with Sky. Internet point and WiFi. Open air cinema. Mountain bike hire. 'Aquapark' (1/5-30/9). Surf-bikes and wind-glider. Canoes and mini sailboats for rent. Extensive daily entertainment programme (mid May - mid Oct). Dogs are not accepted in high season (2/7-27/8). Off site: Tennis, minigolf nearby. Riding 6 km. Golf 12 km.

Open: All year excl. 1 November - 14 December.

Directions

From Inntal autobahn (A12) take Brenner autobahn (A13) as far as Innsbruck-sud/Natters exit (no. 3) without payment. Turn left by garage onto the B182 to Natters. Turn first right and immediately right again and follow signs to site 4 km. Note: Care is needed when negotiating site entrance and there is a separate entrance for large units or vehicles over 3 m. high – ask at reception.
GPS: N47:14.258 E11:20.557

Charges 2007

Per person	€ 5,70 - € 7,80
child (under 13 yrs)	€ 4,40 - € 5,40
pitch	€ 7,80 - € 11,50
'de-luxe' pitch	€ 9,80 - € 14,00
dog (excl 2/7-27/8)	€ 3,00

Special weekly, winter, summer or Christmas packages. Camping Cheques accepted.

AU0055 Camping Arlberg

A-6574 Pettneu am Arlberg (Tirol)

Tel: **054 482 2266-0**. Email: **info@camping-arlberg.at**

This is an unusual site, located alongside, and lower than, the S16 autobahn, just a few kilometres to the east of the 13 km. long Arlberg toll tunnel. Inevitably there is some traffic noise. The site is unusual because it offers 145 pitches (out of 185) that are provided with an wooden cabin on the pitch housing the sanitary facilities, TV connection and 16A electricity. The grass and hardcore pitches are of medium size, fairly level and offer some views of the surrounding mountains. The other 40 pitches are near the reception building and offer electricity with a prepayment meter only (€ 1 coins). There are plenty of local opportunities for walking and cycling and skiing in the winter. The site is certainly well located for overnight stops en route.

Facilities

145 private bathrooms in wooden cabins, electrically heated with WC, washbasin and shower. (Electricity is metered). Chemical disposal point. Motorcaravan service point. Shop. Bar. Restaurant. Indoor pool. Play area. Fishing. Bicycle hire. Off site: Pettneu, swimming pool and the Tyrol. Skiing; ski bus operates in the season.

Open: All year.

Directions

From S16 (B316) take exit to Pettneu (not St Anton). Just at the end of the slip road between a swimming complex and a play area is the site entrance.
GPS: N47:08.705 E10:20.295

Charges 2007

Per unit incl. 2 adults and 2 children under 4 yrs	€ 18,00 - € 36,00
extra person	€ 7,00 - € 8,00
child (4-14 yrs)	€ 4,50
electricity per kWh	€ 0,45

No credit cards.
Camping Cheques accepted.

Your ★★★★★ Holiday Paradise in the Tirol Alps near Innsbruck...

full of life
Natterer See

8 convincing reasons for you to spend your holiday with us:

- the **unique scenic location** in the middle of unspoiled nature
- the **well-placed situation** - also perfect when en route to the South
- the **thrilling water experience** of our own swimming lake (average 22°C)
- the **guarantee for sports, amusement, fun and animation** - deal for all the family
- the **weekly discounted prices for senior citizens** and bargain hunters and our special mountain-bike-packages
- the comfortable **appartments and guest rooms** for friends and relatives
- the central position in the **„Olympia" ski region** Innsbruck / Seefeld / Stubaital
- the **high praise of ADAC** for the facilities at our site

Facilities • individual terraced pitches with electricity and telephone hook-up, partly water and drainage, sat-TV and Internet connection • motorhome service station • top quality sanitation facilities • mini-market • Pizzeria „da Giorgio" • restaurant with lake terrace • **comfortable guest rooms • holiday appartments** • mini-club • pool room • youth room • sport & games areas • streetball • beach volleyball • indian camp • **swimming lake** with 66 m giant waterslide • water-trampoline • windgliders • surfbikes • canoes • bumper boats • children's swimming bay • archery • tabletennis • open-air chess • mountainbike and cycle hire • **top animation programme** from May to September • attractive walks

ski and drying room • ice skating • ice hockey • curling and tobogganing on-site • cross country skiing • „Olympia" ski region • ski bus

Our news for you
- new and wider access road
- new central building with
  - reception • cafe bistro • lounge
  - supermarket • sanitary facilities
- luxury pitches 110 to 150 m²
- new and bigger „Kids-Club"
- new, bigger rooms for the young

finished in October 2007

Ask for our free CD-ROM !

DCC Europapreis

ADAC | Super-Platz 2007

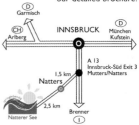

We will be pleased to send you our detailed brochure.

Garmisch (D)

(CH) Arlberg — INNSBRUCK — München Kufstein (D)

A 13 Innsbruck-Süd Exit 3 Mutters/Natters

1,5 km

Natters

2,5 km

Natterer See

Brenner (I)

Terrassencamping Natterer See
A-6161 Natters/Tirol/Austria

Tel. ++43(0)512/546732...
Fax ++43(0)512/54673216...

email: info@natterersee.com
http://www.natterersee.com

Servus in Österreich

TOP CAMPING AUSTRIA | **Tirol**

AU0070 Camping Hofer

Gerlosstrasse 33, A-6280 Zell-am-Ziller (Tirol)

Tel: 052 822 248. Email: info@campingdorf.at

Zell-am-Ziller is in the heart of the Zillertal valley at the junction of the B169 and B165 Gerlos Pass road and nestles round the unusual 18th century church noted for its paintings. Camping Hofer, owned by the same family for over 50 years, is on the edge of the village just five minutes walk from the centre on a quiet side road. The 100 pitches, all with electricity (6/10A), (long long leads may be needed) are grass on gravel. A few trees decorate the site and offer some shade.

Facilities

Good quality, heated sanitary provision is on the ground floor of the apartment building and has some washbasins in cabins. Baby room. Washing machines, dryers and irons. Gas supplies. Motorcaravan services. Restaurant with bar (closed 1/11-10/12 and 30/4-31/5). Shop opposite. Swimming pool (1/4-31/10). WiFi internet. Free organised entertainment and activities in high season. Ski room. Youth room. Appartments to rent. Off site: Town within walking distance.

Open: All year.

Directions

Site is well signed from the main B169 road at Zell-am-Ziller. Site is at southern end of town close to the junction of the B169 and B165. GPS: N47:13.724 E11:53.157

Charges 2008

Per person	€ 5,60 - € 6,60
child (under 14 yrs)	€ 3,00 - € 4,20
pitch incl. electricity	€ 9,00 - € 9,80

Special offers and winter packages.
No credit cards (debit cards accepted).
Camping Cheques accepted.

AU0085 Mountain Camp Pitztal

Niederhof 206, A-6474 Jerzens (Tirol)

Tel: 054 148 7571. Email: mountain-camp@aon.at

Mountain Camp Pitztal was opened in 2002 by Tobias Eiter and his wife and is the only site in the Pitztal valley. It is an ideal base for walks in the Tiroler Mountains or for mountain bike tours on the numerous paths through the woods and on the Schotterpiste or Wildspitze, the highest mountain in Tirol. Being a new site, the pitches are rather in the open, but all 38 have 13A electricity, water, waste water and gas supplies. The pitches are laid out on level, rectangular fields on a grass and gravel base, with gravel access roads. There are beautiful views of the mountains.

Facilities

One new, centrally located toilet block (heated) with toilets, washbasins (open style and in cabins) and free, controllable hot showers. Bathroom. Free washing machine. Dryer. Restaurant with bar. Fishing. Bicycle hire. Swimming pond with small beach. Activity programme in high season. Off site: Riding 2 km. Golf 25 km.

Open: All year exc. 2 May - 9 June.

Directions

From the A12, take exit 132 at Imst and continue south on minor road. Site is on the right, just before entering Jerzens. GPS: N47:08.552 E10:44.789

Charges 2007

Per unit with 2 persons	€ 18,00 - € 24,00
extra person	€ 4,00 - € 5,00
electricity (per kWh on meter)	€ 0,50

AU0090 Camping Zillertal-Hell

Gragering 212b, A-6263 Fügen (Tirol)

Tel: 052 886 2203. Email: info@zillertal-camping.at

The village of Fügen lies about six kilometres from the A12 autobahn at the start of the Zillertal, so is well placed for exploring the valley and the area around Schwaz. Easy to reach, Camping Zillertal-Hell is an attractive small site with excellent facilities and 170 marked pitches (140 for touring units) on flat grass. All have electricity (16A), 80 also have water and drainage and there are some hardstandings for motorcaravans. The site could make a good overnight stop or for a longer stay but, being on a main road, there is a little daytime road noise.

Facilities

New modern heated sanitary block of top quality has some washbasins in cabins, a children's wash room, and private bathrooms for hire. Unit for disabled campers. Washing machine, dryer and drying room. Motorcaravan service point. Attractive bar and small restaurant. Small shop. Heated swimming pool (20 x 10 m, 1/5-15/10). Solarium, sauna and steam room. Playground. Internet point. Organised activities and entertainment. Bicycle hire. Dogs not accepted. Off site: Fishing 500 m. Riding 2 km. Golf 15 km. Village 800 m.

Open: All year.

Directions

From the A12 Innsbruck - Worgl motorway take exit 39 and turn south on B169 towards Mayrhofen for 5 km. Turn into service road (on right) 1 km. north of Fugen (signed Gagering and site) and site entrance is on right. Note: this is a fast road, care is needed exiting site. GPS: N47:21.576 E11:51.128

Charges 2007

Per pitch incl. 2 persons and electricity	€ 22,40 - € 35,50
child (2-13 yrs)	€ 3,00 - € 4,50

Less for longer stays.

AU0065 Camping Seehof

Reintalersee, Moosen 42, A-6233 Kramsach (Tirol)

Tel: 053 376 3541. Email: info@camping-seehof.com

Camping Seehof, an excellent site in every respect, is situated in a marvellous, sunny and peaceful location on the eastern shores of the Reintalersee lake. Add to this that it is very much a family run site for families and you have almost perfection itself. It separates into two areas; a small area next to the lake, good for sunbathing, and a bigger one nearer the large excellent sanitary block. All the large pitches are served by good access roads and have electricity and TV point and many have waste water drains. Water points are conveniently located around the site. There are 40 new fully serviced pitches. Seehof provides an ideal starting point for walking, cycling or riding (with a riding stable nearby), and in the winter for cross-country skiing, ice skating and curling. A free shuttle bus operates from the site during the skiing season.

Facilities

New and refurbished sanitary facilities are first class and include ten bathrooms to rent for private use. Baby room. Facilities for disabled visitors. Medical room; including bed. Dog shower. Washing machine and dryer. Ski room. Motorcaravan service point. Small shop. Good restaurant. Playground and play room. WiFi. Bicycle hire. Fishing. Off site: Kramsach. Kristallwelten and the Swarovski Factory.

Open: All year.

Directions

From the A12 take exit 32 to Kramsach. At roundabout turn right and immediately turn left following signs for 'Zu den Seen' in village. After 3 km. turn right at camp sign. GPS: E11:54.429 N47:27.712

Charges 2008

Per person	€ 6,50
child (2-14 yrs)	€ 4,50
pitch with electricity	€ 9,50
electricity	€ 2,80

AU0080 Schloß-Camping

A-6111 Volders (Tirol)

Tel: 052 245 2333. Email: campingvolders@utanet.at

The Inn valley is not only central to the Tirol, but is a very beautiful and popular part of Austria. Volders, some 15 km. from Innsbruck, is one of the little villages on the banks of the Inn river and is perhaps best known for its 17th century Baroque Servite Church and monastery. Conveniently situated here is the very pleasant Schloss-Camping, dominated by the castle, from which it gets its name, that towers at the back of the site with mountains beyond. The 160 numbered grass pitches are on level or slightly sloping ground. Electricity connections throughout (16A), although long leads may be necessary.

Facilities

The small, old design, sanitary block is near the entrance and has some washbasins in cabins. Washing machine. Motorcaravan service point. Bar/restaurant. Snack bar with terrace. Shop for basics (all May - end Sept). Fenced and heated swimming pool (mid May-mid Sept). Minigolf. Playground. Car wash. Games and entertainment for children in high season. Off site: Supermarket 400 m. Bicycle hire 500 m. Golf and riding 7 km.

Open: 15 April - 15 October.

Directions

From A12 motorway, travelling east, leave at exit 68 for Hall, going west, take exit 61 for Wattens and follow the B171 and signs for Volders where site is signed. GPS: N47:17.231 E11:34.352

Charges 2008

Per person	€ 5,60 - € 6,50
pitch incl. car and electricity	€ 9,30 - € 10,50

No credit cards. Reductions for stays of 3 nights or more in low season.

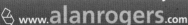

AU0100 Camping Seeblick Toni

Reintalersee, Moosen 46, A-6233 Kramsach (Tirol)

Tel: 053 376 3544. Email: info@camping-seeblick.at

Austria has some of the finest sites in Europe and Seeblick Toni Brantlhof is one of the best. In a quiet, rural situation on the edge of the small Reintalersee lake, it is well worth considering for holidays in the Tirol with many excursions possible. The surrounding mountains give scenic views and the campsite has a neat and tidy appearance. The 243 level pitches (215 for touring units) are in regular rows off hard access roads and are of good size with grass and hardstanding. All pitches have electricity (10A), 150 are fully serviced including cable TV and phone connections.

Facilities

Two quite outstanding (heated in cool weather) sanitary blocks. Facilities for disabled visitors and children. Baby room. Laundry facilities. Drying rooms. Motorcaravan services. Restaurant. Bar. Snack kiosk. Minimarket. Fitness centre. Playground. New indoor play area. Topi club, kindergarten and organised activities for children in high season. Youth room. Fishing. Bicycle hire. Riding. Internet point (July/Aug. only). Off site: Kramsach 3 km.

Open: All year.

Directions

Take exit 32 for Kramsach from A12 autobahn and turn right at roundabout, then immediately left following signs 'Zu den Seen' in village. After 3 km. turn right at sign. GPS: N47:27.673 E11:54.396

Charges 2007

Per person	€ 5,50 - € 8,00
pitch with electricity	€ 10,30 - € 15,70

Camping Cheques accepted.

AU0102 Seen Camping Stadlerhof

Seebühel 14, A-6233 Kramsach (Tirol)

Tel: 053 376 3371. Email: camping.stadlerhof@chello.at

This child friendly, family run site is in a beautiful location near the Krummsee. There are 130 sensibly sized pitches (99 for touring units) all with electricity hook-ups (10A). Many are individual and divided by hedges and shrubs, and some mature trees offer shade in parts. 50 multi-serviced pitches are available. The site has a heated outdoor pool complex with cafe and Wellness Centre as well as its own small lake, a panorama walk and a dog walk. Reasonable English is spoken.

Facilities

Spacious sanitary facilities include showers, some washbasins in cubicles, and 5 family bathrooms for rent. Laundry and dishwashing facilities. No dedicated facilities for disabled people. Small restaurant and bar. Basic provisions available. 'Wellness Centre', an outdoor heated stainless steel pool (12.5 m. x 6 m. and open in winter) with spa pool, children's pool and a cafe. Playground. TV room. Drying room, ski room. Off site: Kramsach is within walking distance. Reintalersee 3 km.

Open: All year.

Directions

Kramsach is approximately midway between Innsbruck and Kufstein. From A12 exit 32 turn right at roundabout and immediately left following signs for 'Zu den Seen' in village. Site is just outside village on left, after a right hand bend. GPS: N47:27.395 E11:52.886

Charges 2007

Per person	€ 4,60 - € 5,80
electricity per kWh	€ 0,65

No credit cards.

AU0110 Tirol Camp

Lindau 20, A-6391 Fieberbrunn (Tirol)

Tel: 053 545 6666. Email: office@tirol-camp.at

This is one of many Tirol campsites that caters equally for summer and winter (here seemingly more for winter, when reservation is essential and prices 50% higher). Tirol Camp is in a quiet and attractive mountain situation and has 280 pitches all on wide flat terraces, set on a gentle slope (193 for touring units). Marked out mainly by the electricity boxes or low hedges, they are said to be 80-100 sq.m. and all have electricity (10A), gas, water/drainage, TV and telephone connections.

Facilities

The original refurbished toilet block in the main building is excellent with some washbasins in cabins and some private bathrooms on payment. A splendid, modern heated block at the top end of the site has all washbasins in cabins. Facilities for disabled visitors. Laundry facilities. Motorcaravan services. Self-service shop and snacks. Restaurant (closed Oct, Nov and May). Outdoor pool (12 x 8 m; 1/6-30/9). Indoor pool and Wellness Centre. Sauna. Tennis. Lake fishing. Riding. Bicycle hire. Outdoor chess. Playground and children's zoo. Entertainment and activity programmes (July/Aug). Internet point.

Open: All year.

Directions

Site is on the east side of Fieberbrunn, which is on the B164 St Johann-Saalfelden road. Turn south off the B164, 2 km. east of Fieberbrunn and follow camp signs up the hill to the site. GPS: N47:28.095 E12:33.237

Charges 2008

Per person	€ 8,00 - € 12,00
child (4-14 yrs)	€ 5,00
pitch	€ 6,00 - € 13,00
electricity (per kWh on meter)	€ 0,75 - € 0,85

Camping Cheques accepted.

AU0170 **Camping Innsbruck-Kranebitten**

Kranebitter Allee 214, A-6020 Innsbruck (Tirol)

Tel: **051 228 4180**. Email: **campinnsbruck@hotmail.com**

This basic site is in a pleasant situation just outside Innsbruck. The 120 pitches are numbered, but not marked out, on mostly sloping grass, with good shade cover. There are three separate terraces for caravans and motorcaravans and all pitches have electricity (6A, long leads are on loan for some). By the side of the site, with access to it, is a large open field with a good playground and plenty of space for ball games. Being so near the attractive town of Innsbruck, the site makes an excellent base from which to visit the ancient city and also to explore the many attractions nearby. The 'Innsbruck-Card', available from the site, gives various discounts for attractions in the city, plus free travel on public transport (park-and-ride from the site, even if you don't stay overnight). A private taxi also runs a shuttle service to the city. Some road and aircraft noise may be heard. Good English is spoken.

Facilities

The large, toilet block shows signs of age, but is heated, clean and acceptable, with some washbasins in cabins and renovated showers. Washing machines and dryers. Motorcaravan services. Bar/restaurant (all year, but open times may vary). Internet point. Small shop. Playground with large play field adjoining. Games for children and barbecues in summer. Free mountain hiking and cycling tours in summer, free ski bus in winter. Bicycle hire. Off site: Swimming pool 2 km.

Open: All year.

Directions

From A12 Innsbruck - Arlberg motorway, take Innsbruck-Kranebitten exit 83 from where site is well signed, directly on B171 (Telfs-Innsbruck non-toll road). GPS: N47:15.821 E11:19.579

Charges 2007

Per person	€ 5,30 - € 5,40
child (4-14 yrs)	€ 3,50
pitch incl. car	€ 5,50 - € 6,80
electricity	€ 3,00 - € 3,30

Less 10% for stays over 10 days.
Special offers for sporting groups.

AU0120 **Erlebnis-Comfort-Camping Aufenfeld**

Aufenteldweg 10, A-6274 Aschau im Zillertal (Tirol)

Tel: **052 822 9160**. Email: **info@camping-zillertal.at**

This site is attractively situated in a mountain region with fine views and good facilities. The main area of the site is flat with pitches of 100 sq.m. on grass between good access roads, with further pitches on terraces at the rear. There are around 350 pitches (240 for touring units with 6A electricity) including around 40 with individual sanitary cubicles. The site can become full mid-July - mid-August and at Christmas, but usually has space at other times. Member of Leading Campings Group.

Facilities

Four well kept, heated sanitary blocks of excellent quality and size with a few washbasins in cabins for each sex, baby rooms and nine units for disabled people. Four additional units provide 40 private cabins for luxury pitches and several family bathrooms for rent. Laundry and drying room. Ski room. Motorcaravan services. New supermarket. Restaurant. General room. TV. Indoor pool, sauna and sunbeds. New wellness cente. Outdoor pool. Playground. Multisports court. Tennis. Riding. Fishing. Skateboard and rollerblade facilities. Trampolines. Bicycle hire. ATM. Western village. Mineral museum. Entertainment in high season includes line dancing, Western shows and archery. Off site: Walking and cycling in the Zillertall valley. Cross country skiing (winter).

Open: All year excl. 3 November - 8 December.

Directions

From A12 Inntal motorway, take exit 39 Zillertal, 32 km. northeast of Innsbruck. Follow road 169 to village of Aschau from which site is well signed. GPS: N47:15.800 E11:53.960

Charges 2007

Per person	€ 5,60 - € 9,90
child (under 12 yrs)	€ 4,00 - € 6,60
pitch incl. electricity and TV hook-up	€ 7,60 - € 12,50
with private sanitary cabin	€ 15,00 - € 23,00
dog	€ 3,50 - € 4,00

Winter prices are higher.

AU0130 Terrassen Camping Schloßberg Itter

Brixentaler Straße 11, A-6305 Itter bei Hopfgarten (Tirol)

Tel: 053 352 181. Email: info@camping-itter.at

With some 200 pitches this well kept site provides good facilities. It is suitable both as a base for longer stays and also for overnight stops, as it lies right by a main road west of Kitzbühel. The site is on a slight slope but most of the 200 numbered pitches are on level terraces. Some pitches are individual and divided by hedges and have electricity (8/10A) and cable TV connections, 150 have water and drainage. Space is usually available.

Facilities

The main sanitary facilities are heated and of very high standard. Units for families, with baby baths. Facilities for disabled visitors. Laundry. Motorcaravan services. Cooking facilities. Small shop, bar/restaurant (both closed Nov). Solar heated swimming pool (16 x 8 m). Sauna and solarium. Excellent playground and indoor playroom. Animation programme. Naturist sun deck. WiFi internet. Ski and drying rooms. Off site: Tennis, fishing, riding, bicycle hire within 2 km. Golf 10 km.

Open: All year excl. 16 - 30 November.

Directions

Site is 2 km. northwest of Hopfgarten. From A12 exit 17 (Worgl-Ost) turn right on B178 towards St Johann for 5 km. then take the B170 towards Hopfgarten for 2 km. Site is signed to left on a right hand bend opposite a Peugeot/Talbot garage.

Charges 2007

Per person	€ 4,00 - € 6,00
pitch	€ 4,00 - € 9,00
electricity	€ 2,00 - € 2,80

Prices higher for winter. No credit cards.

AU0140 Euro Camp Wilder Kaiser

Kranebittau 18, A-6345 Kössen (Tirol)

Tel: 053 756 444. Email: info@eurocamp-koessen.com

The village of Kössen lies to the south of the A8 Munich - Salzburg autobahn and to the east of the A93/A12 motorway near Kufstein. It is therefore well situated for overnight stops but even more for longer stays. Wilder Kaiser is located at the foot of the Unterberg with views of the Kaisergebirge (the Emperor's mountains) and surrounded by forests. Being about 2 km. south of the village, it is a quiet location, away from main roads. About 130 of the 190 pitches (grass over gravel) are available for touring units, plus an area for tents and a new area for motorcaravans.

Facilities

The heated, central sanitary block is of good quality with spacious showers, some washbasins in cubicles and a baby room. Washing machines and dryers. Motorcaravan services. Shop. Large restaurant/bar (closed Nov). Snack bar (high season). Club room with TV and play station. Heated swimming pool (May - Sept). Youth room. Sauna and solarium. Tennis. Large imaginative adventure playground. Club for children and other activities for all (high season). Off site: Bicycle hire 1 km. Golf 2 km. Fishing and Riding 4 km. Beach and boat launching 6 km.

Open: 13 December - 3 November.

Directions

From A8 (München - Salzburg), take Grabenstatt exit 109 and go south on B307/B176 to Kössen. Cross the river and at roundabout follow signs for 'Bergbahnen' and 'Euro Camp'. After 600 m. follow signs to site. From A93 (Rosenheim - Kufstein) take Oberaudorf exit and go east on B172 to Walchsee and Kössen. GPS: N47:39.222 E12:24.915

Charges 2007

Per person	€ 6,20 - € 7,20
pitch with electricity and TV	€ 6,30 - € 8,30
electricity	€ 0,65

AU0150 Camping Riffler

Bruggenfeldstraße 2, A-6500 Landeck (Tirol)

Tel: 054 426 4898. Email: lorenz.schimpfoessl@aon.at

This small, pretty site is almost in the centre of the small town of Landeck and, being on the main through route from the Vorarlberg to the Tirol, would serve as a good overnight stop. Square in shape it has just 40 pitches on level grass on either side of hard access roads. The main road lies on one side and the fast flowing River Sanna on the other edge. Trees and flowers adorn the site giving good shade and all pitches have electricity (10A). Activities in the area include walking, mountain biking, paragliding, kite flying, rafting, canoeing and climbing.

Facilities

The small toilet block has been rebuilt to a good standard. Washing machine and dryer. Basic motorcaravan services. Shop. Small general room. Fishing. Off site: Supermarket just outside the gate, other shops 100 m. Restaurants about 100 m. Bicycle hire and swimming pool 500 m. Reshen and Arlberg mountain passes within easy driving distance. Opportunities for watersports and hang-gliding.

Open: All year excl. May.

Directions

Take exit for Landeck-West from the A12 and turn left towards Landeck. Site is on the left just before town centre. GPS: N47:08.525 E10:33.665

Charges 2008

Per person	€ 7,20
pitch	€ 7,90 - € 9,10
electricity	€ 3,20

Winter prices slightly more. No credit cards.

AU0185 Campingplatz Seewiese

Tristachersee 2, A-9900 Lienz (Tirol)

Tel: 048 526 9767. Email: seewiese@hotmail.com

High above the village of Tristach and 5 km. from Lienz, this is a perfect location for a good campsite. When we arrived the owner said, 'This is a green paradise at the gateway to the Dolomites' – it did not take us long to agree totally with his assessment. The 110 pitches all have 6A electricity (long leads may be necessary) and the 11 pitches for motorcaravans near reception each have electricity, water and internet access. Caravans are sited on a gently sloping field which has level areas although pitches are unmarked and unnumbered. At the bottom of this field is a small lake.

Facilities

Toilet facilities are clean, heated and modern with free showers. Washing machine and dryer. Motorcaravan service point. Excellent restaurant/bar. Small play area. Internet access. Swimming in adjoining lake. Off site: Lienz 5 km.

Open: 11 May - 25 September.

Directions

In Lienz initially follow signs for Spittal and at traffic lights turn right towards Tristach. Go under the railway and over a small bridge then turn left, still towards Tristach. Go through Tristach and after 1.5 km. turn right to the site, which is at the top of a 1 km, 1:10 climb. GPS: N46:48.098 E12:48.172

Charges 2007

Per unit incl. 2 persons	€ 21,60
incl. electricity	€ 24,10

No credit cards. Camping Cheques accepted.

AU0155 Aktiv-Camping Prutz

Entbruck 70, A-6522 Prutz (Tirol)

Tel: 054 722 648. Email: info@aktiv-camping.at

Aktiv-Camping is a long site which lies beside, and is fenced off, from the River Inn. Most of the 110 individual level pitches are for touring and range in size from 70 to 90 sq.m. They all have 6A electrical connections. In the larger area the pitches fit together sideways and back to back so, at times, it can give the appearance of being quite crowded. There is a separate overnight area for motorcaravans. This is an attractive area with many activities in summer and winter for all age groups. You may well consider using this site not just as an overnight stop, but also for a longer stay.

Facilities

The sanitary facilities are of a high standard, with private cabins and good facilities for disabled visitors. Baby room. Washing machine. Dog shower. Small shop. Bar. Takeaway. Play room. Ski room. Skating rink. Internet point. Children's entertainment. Guided walks, skiing (free shuttle service). WiFi. Off site: Indoor pool at Feichten, Pilgrim's Church at Kaltenbrunn. Kaunertaler Glacier.

Open: All year.

Directions

Travelling west from Innsbruck on the E60/A12 for about 65 km. turn south onto the B180 signed Bregenz, Arlberg, Innsbruck and Fernpass for 11 km. to Prutz. Site is signed from the B180 over the bridge. GPS: N47:04.807 E10:39.564

Charges 2007

Per unit (summer) incl. electricity and 2 persons	€ 23,50
winter price (plus electricity on meter)	€ 21,50

Camping Cheques accepted.

AU0220 Øtztal Arena Camp Krismer

A-6441 Umhausen (Tirol)

Tel: 052 555 390. Email: info@oetztal-camping.at

This is a delightful site with lovely views, in the beautiful Øtz valley, on the edge of the village of Umhausen. Situated on a gentle slope in an open valley, it has an air of peace and tranquillity and is an excellent base for mountain walking, particularly in spring and autumn, skiing in winter or a relaxing holiday. The 98 pitches, some on individual terraces, are all marked and numbered and have electrical connections (12A); charges relate to the area available, long leads may be necessary. The reception building houses an attractive bar/restaurant and a new, fully equipped sauna.

Facilities

With under-floor heating, open washbasins, hairdressing room and showers on payment, the toilet facilities are of good quality. Sauna. Baby room. Washing machine and dryer, drying room. Basic motorcaravan services. Bar/restaurant (May-Sept, Dec-April). No shop, but bread can be ordered at reception. TV room. Ski room. Fishing. Bicycle hire. Basic playground. Off site: Shops in village 200 m. Play area 300 m. Golf 20 km. Riding 10 km.

Open: All year.

Directions

Take Øtztal Valley exit 123 from Imst - Innsbruck A12 motorway, and Umhausen is 13 km. towards Solden on the B186; site is well signed to south of village. GPS: N47:08.122 E10:55.951

Charges 2007

Per person	€ 5,80
child (2-13 yrs)	€ 4,30
pitch	€ 2,40 - € 8,00
electricity (per kWh)	€ 0,75

29

AU0225 **Romantik Camping Schloß Fernsteinsee**

Am Fernpaß Tirol, A-6465 Nassereith (Tirol)

Tel: **052 655 210**. Email: **hotel@fernsteinsee.at**

This is a secluded and attractive site in a sheltered location in the protected area of the Fernstein Lakes and part of the Schloss Fernsteinsee estate. There are 125 pitches, all for touring unts, in two separate areas and 80 have electricity (4/13A), water and waste water. The pitches are on level grass in front of the reception and services building on four shallow terraces divided by low rails or shrubs. A new area with flat, gravel pitches and all services has been developed at the bottom of the site. There is good shade here and gravel access roads.

Facilities

Modern heated facilities with a generous supply of controllable hot showers, washbasins (open style and in cabins) and facilities for disabled visitors. Laundry room. Small playground. Games room. Communal barbecue. Sauna and solarium. Fishing and boating on the lake. Off site: Hotel Schloss Fernsteinsee with bar and restaurant 500 m. Nassereith village 1.5 km.

Open: 15 April - 26 October.

Directions

Nassereith is 15 km. north of Imst, just south of the Fern Pass. From Imst take road 189 north for 13 km. then left on road 179 and continue past Nassereith, taking a tarmac entry road 500 m. before the river bridge (well signed). GPS: N47:20.258 E10:49.092

Charges 2007

Per unit incl. 2 persons	€ 18,00 - € 24,00
extra person	€ 5,60
electricity (plus meter)	€ 2,80

AU0227 **Comfort Camp Grän**

Engetalstr. 13, A-6673 Grän (Tirol)

Tel: **056 756 570**. Email: **comfortcamp@aon.at**

In a village location in the Tannheimer Tal, with panoramic mountain scenery, Comfort Camp Grän is a family run site with excellent heated sanitary facilities and a stylish modern indoor pool complex. It makes a good base for exploring this border region of Austria and Germany. The site has 210 pitches of 80-100 sq.m. (170 for touring units) all with 16A electricity, water (only for summer use) and waste water on fairly level grass, over gravel terrain with some shallow terraces. There are 14 private sanitary cabins for rent. The main services are grouped at the entrance.

Facilities

The main sanitary unit is impressive with superb facilities, spacious, light and airy. Controllable hot showers, washbasins in cubicles. Off site: Haldensee (lake) 3 km. Fishing 2 km. Riding 6 km. Beach 2 km. German Border 10 km. Walking trails and Ski Runs.

Open: 23 May - 2 November; 15 December - 18 April.

Directions

From Germany on the autobahn A7, turn off at exit 137, and turn south on road 310 to Oberjoch, then take road 308 (road 199 in Austria) east to Grän. At eastern end of village turn north signed Pfronten, and site is 1.5 km. GPS: N47:30.610 E10:33.050

Charges 2007

Per person	€ 7,00 - € 10,00
child (2-14 yrs)	€ 4,60 - € 8,00
pitch (electricity on meter)	€ 8,00 - € 12,50

AU0250 **AlpencampingMark**

Bundesstraße 12, Maholmhof, A-6114 Weer bei Schwaz (Tirol)

Tel: **052 246 8146**. Email: **alpcamp.mark@aon.at**

This pleasant Tirol site is neat and friendly with family owners who offer a warm welcome and a variety of outdoor activities. Formerly a farm, they now breed horses giving a free ride each day to youngsters and organising treks. Herr Mark junior (a certified alpine ski guide and ski instructor) runs courses for individuals or groups in climbing (there are practice climbing walls on site), rafting, mountain bike riding, trekking, hiking, etc. Set in the Inn valley, between mountain ranges, the site has 96 flat, grass pitches (71 for touring units) on either side of gravel roads, with 10A electricity.

Facilities

Good quality, modern, heated sanitary facilities are provided in the old farm buildings. Freezer. Washing machines and dryer. Caravan services. Small, cheerful bar/restaurant and shop (1/6-1/9). Small heated pool (15/5-15/9). Activity programme with instruction. Bicycle hire. Riding (free for children). Glacier tours. Large play area. Barn for use by children in wet weather. Off site: Imtal Valley, good for mountain biking.

Open: 1 April - 31 October.

Directions

Site is 200 m. east of the village of Weer on Wattens - Schwaz road no. B171 which runs parallel to the A12, just 10 km. east of Innsbruck. (If using A12 take exit 61 from west or 53 from east). GPS: N47:18.446 E11:38.875

Charges 2007

Per person	€ 4,50 - € 6,00
child (under 14 yrs)	€ 3,00 - € 4,00
pitch with electricity	€ 7,70 - € 9,70

AU0180 Sportcamp Woferlgut

Kroessenbach 40, A-5671 Bruck (Salzburg)

Tel: 065 457 3030. Email: info@sportcamp.at

The village of Bruck lies at the junction of the B311 and the Grossglocknerstrasse in the Hohe Tauern National Park. Sportcamp Woferlgut, a family run site, is one of the best in Austria. Although surrounded by mountains, the site is quite flat with pleasant views. The 350 level, grass pitches are marked out by shrubs (300 for touring units) and each has electricity (16A), water, drainage, cable TV socket and gas point. A high grass bank separates the site and the road. The site's own lake is used for swimming and fishing and is surrounded by a landscaped sunbathing area. The fitness centre has a fully equipped gym, whilst the other building contains a sauna and cold dip, Turkish bath, solarium (all free) massage on payment and a bar. In summer there is a free activity programme, evenings with live music, club for children, weekly barbecues and guided cycle and mountain tours. In winter a cross-country skiing trail and toboggan run lead from the site and a free bus service is provided to nearby skiing facilities. With Salzburg to the north and Innsbruck to the northwest, the management is pleased to advise on local attractions and tours, making this a splendid base for a family holiday. Good English is spoken. Used by tour operators (45 pitches).

Facilities

Three modern sanitary blocks (the newest in a class of its own) have excellent facilities, including private cabins, under-floor heating and music. Washing machines and dryers. Facilities for disabled visitors. Family bathrooms for hire. Motorcaravan services. Well stocked shop. Bar, restaurant and takeaway (all year). Small, heated outdoor pool and children's pool (28/4-30/9). Fitness centre. Two playgrounds, indoor play room and children's cinema. Tennis. Bicycle hire. Fishing. Watersports and lake swimming. Collection of small animals with pony rides for young children. Off site: ATM 500 m. Skiing 2.5 km. Golf 3 km. Boat launching and sailing 3.5 km. Hiking and skiing (all year) nearby.

Open: All year.

Directions

Site is southwest of Bruck. From road B311, Bruck by-pass, take southern exit (Grossglockner) and site is signed from the junction of B311 and B107 roads (small signs).

Charges 2008

Per person	€ 4,90 - € 7,90
child (under 10)	€ 4,00 - € 5,90
pitch with electricity	€ 9,40 - € 12,30
dog	€ 3,10 - € 4,30

Special offers for low season, longer stays.

AU0160 Seecamp Zell am See

Thumersbacherstrasse 34, A-5700 Zell-am-See (Salzburg)

Tel: 065 427 2115. Email: zell@seecamp.at

Zellersee, delightfully situated in the south of Salzburg province and near the start of the Grossglocknerstrasse, is ideally placed for enjoying the splendid southern Austrian countryside. Seecamp is right by the water about 3 km. from the town of Zell and with fine views to the south end of the lake. One is immediately struck by the order and neat appearance of the site, with 176 good level, mainly grass and gravel pitches of average size, all with electricity. About half have water, drainage and TV connections. Units can be close together in peak season.

Facilities

Excellent, heated sanitary facilities include facilities for disabled visitors and a baby room. Washing machines, dryers and irons. Motorcaravan services (access difficult for larger units). Restaurant (15/12-30/9). Shop (1/7-31/8 and 15/12-6/1). Play area. Play room. Fishing. Bicycle hire. 'Topi' Club and summer entertainment for children. Activity programme. Winter ski packages and free ski bus. Off site: Free entry to nearby lake beach, indoor pool and ice skating rink. Skiing 1.8 km. Golf and riding 2 km.

Open: All year.

Directions

From the north on the B311 take Thumersbach exit just before tunnel entrance (2 km. north of Zell-am-See town). After 500 m. turn left and site is 750 m. on the right. Note: 3.5 ton weight restriction but it is the only access to site. GPS: N47:20.384 E12:48.536

Charges 2008

Per person	€ 6,50 - € 7,10
pitch incl. electricity	€ 11,80 - € 14,10

Gas on meter. Less 20% in low season.
Special winter package prices.

AU0212 Panoramacamping Stadtblick

Rauchenbichl, Rauchenbichler Straße 21, A-5020 Salzburg (Salzburg)

Tel: 066 245 0652. Email: info@panorama-camping.at

With a panoramic view over the city of Salzburg this site is well named, and you can be sure of a warm welcome from the multi-lingual owner, Herr Wörndl. The site has 70 pitches all with electricity (4A) and water points, on grass over gravel terraces, plus 10 grassy tent pitches. They are reasonably sized for a city site location, and the view and the good value restaurant amply compensate for any shortcomings. This is an ideal site for a short stay to see all the sights of the city, with a bus stop within walking distance.

Facilities

The single sanitary unit is in the older style, but is neat, clean and well maintained. It provides some washbasins in cabins, controllable hot showers with limited changing space. No facilities for babies or disabled visitors. Laundry. Motorcaravan service point. Shop. Restaurant (May-Sept). TV lounge. Small playground. Off site: Golf 3 km. or 10 km. Bicycle hire 3 km. Swimming pool 3 km.

Open: 20 March - 5 November.

Directions

From A1 exit 288 (Salzburg Nord) turn south towards city. Approaching the first set of traffic lights get into the right hand lane, turn right here on a minor road (site signed) and continue to top of hill, and follow site signs. GPS: N47:49.708 E13:03.145

Charges guide

Per person	€ 6,50
pitch	€ 2,00 - € 7,00

AU0262 Oberwötzlhof Camp

Erlfeld 37, A-5441 Abtenau (Salzburg)

Tel: 062432698. Email: oberwoetzlhof@sbg.at

High up in the Lammertal Valley is this small farm site with amazing views of the surrounding mountains. Part of a working farm, it has a total of 70 pitches, of which 30 are for long stay units, leaving 40 places for tourers. All are serviced with 10A electricity hook-ups, water and drainage. Amateur astronomers will appreciate the lack of site lighting, but campers may find a torch useful. The small fenced swimming pool (10 x 5 m.) is unheated, and has paved surrounds. Despite the slightly dated facilities, we think that the friendly atmosphere and stunning location amply compensate for any shortcomings.

Facilities

New sanitary building. Laundry facilities, drying room. Solarium. No special facilities for babies or disabled campers. A new unit is under construction but it could be some time before it is finished. Restaurant open in winter only. Swimming pool. Internet terminal. Off site: Abtenau 2.5 km. (about 25 minutes walk). Skiing 2.5 km. Riding 8 km. Hallstättersee and salt mines 30 km.

Open: All year.

Directions

Abtenau is southeast of Salzburg. From A10 exit 28 (Golling), take B162 east for 14 km. and site is signed to the left about 2.5 km. before Abtenau. GPS: N47:35.171 E13:19.474

Charges 2008

Per person	€ 6,00
pitch (plus electricity on meter)	€ 9,00 - € 11,00

No credit cards.

AU0265 **Park Grubhof**

A-5092 Saint Martin bei Lofer (Salzburg)

Tel: **065 888 237**. Email: **camping@lofer.net**

Park Grubhof is a well organised, spacious site in a very scenic riverside location, once the pleasure park of the adjacent Schloss (now a hotel). The 200 pitches all with electricity hook-ups (10A), have been carefully divided into separate areas for different types of camper – dog owners, campers without children, young people, families and groups. There are now over 100 very large pitches, all with electricity, water and drainage, along the bank of the Saalach river. Parents of small children should be aware that the site is adjacent to the fast flowing river which is unfenced. Some areas are wooded with plenty of shade, others are more open and there are some very attractive log cabins which have been rescued from the old logging camps. Many of the possible activities are based around the river, where you will find barbecue areas, canoeing and white water rafting, fishing and swimming (when the river level reduces). Bordering the National Park of Berchtesgaden, The area is renowned for hiking, mountain climbing and cycling. Good English is spoken.

Facilities

Two attractive, modern sanitary units (one new in 2006), built with plenty of glass and wood, give a good provision of all facilities. Large showers. Some washbasins in cubicles. Separate facilities for canoeists. Motorcaravan service point. Shop, restaurant and bar. Playground. Games room. Watersports. Cabins to rent. Off site: Lofer 1 km. Gorges and caves 5-7 km. Salzburg 40 minutes drive. Many marked walking and cycling trails. Mountain climbing.

Open: 25 April - 5 October.

Directions

From A12 exit 17 take B178 east to St Johann in Tyrol, then continue on the B178 northwest to Lofer, and finally south on B311. Just past Schloss Grubhof at the northern edge of St Martin, turn left and follow lane to site. GPS: N47:34.474 E12:42.391

Charges 2007

Per person	€ 5,50 - € 6,20
child (under 15 yrs)	€ 3,50 - € 3,70
pitch incl. electricity	€ 4,40 - € 8,50
No credit cards.	

AU0345 Seecamping Gruber

Dorfstrasse 63, A-4865 Nußdorf am Attersee (Upper Austria)

Tel: 076 668 0450. Email: office@camping-gruber.at

The Attersee is the largest of a group of lakes just to the east of Salzburg in the very attractive Salzkammergut area. Seecamping Gruber is a small, often crowded site halfway up the western side of the lake. There are 150 individual pitches, with an increasing number of seasonal units taking the larger pitches. There are still some 60 pitches for tourers, all with 16A electricity and many with shade. Pitches tend to be small to medium size and the access roads are narrow making entrance and exit difficult and this is not helped by the seasonal visitors erecting fences to utilise every last inch of their pitches. Sadly the views across the lake to the hills beyond can only be seen from the swimming pool and the shallow children's play pool (both heated to 26 degrees and with sunbathing areas).

Facilities

Modern sanitary facilities offer some private cabins, washing machine and dryer, good unit for the disabled and baby room. Restaurant and takeaway. Shop. Play area. Swimming and paddling pools. Sauna, solarium and gym. Fishing. Off site: Windsurfing, sailing, both with courses. Mountain bikes, diving and balloon rides all available locally.

Open: 15 April - 15 October.

Directions

From the A1/E55/E60 between Salzburg and Linz, take exit 243 to Attersee and then south on the B151 to Nußdorf. Site is on the southern edge of the village.

Charges 2007

Per unit incl 2 persons and electricity	€ 22,90 - € 27,70
dog	€ 3,50

AU0340 Camping am See

Winkl 77, A-4831 Obertraun (Upper Austria)

Tel: 06131265. Email: camping.am.see@chello.at

It is unusual to locate a campsite so deep in the heart of spectacular mountain scenery, yet with such easy access. Directly on the shores of Halstattersee, near Obertraun and the Dachstein range of mountains, this 2.5 hectare, flat site, with 70 pitches is an excellent, peaceful holiday base which has been upgraded. The grass site is basically divided into two, with tents in a more shady area, whilst caravans and motorcaravans are more in the open. There are no specific pitches although the owners, within reason, control where you place your unit (only 36 electricity hook ups).

Facilities

Completely refurbished, fully equipped and modern, the toilet block includes a small baby room. Washing machine. Bar and limited restaurant with hot meals and wines to order. Basic daily provisions kept such as bread and milk. Playground. Off site: Activities nearby include walking for all ages and abilities, bird watching, fishing, mountain biking, rock climbing, scuba diving and much more. For naturists, 100 m. from the site is a delightful area designated as an FKK strand (naturist beach).

Open: 1 May - 30 September.

Directions

Due south from Bad Ischl on road B145, take road B166 to Hallstatt. After single carriageway tunnel, site is 4 km. on left on entering village of Winkl. Note: Road is a little narrow in places so care is needed. GPS: N47:32.927 E13:40.661

Charges 2007

Per unit incl. 2 persons	€ 21,80 - € 25,30
child (5-14 yrs)	€ 4,37
electricity	€ 3,00

No credit cards.

AU0350 Camp Mond See Land

Punz Au 21, A-5310 Mondsee (Upper Austria)

Tel: **062 322 600**. Email: **austria@campmondsee.at**

Mond See Land underwent an improvement programme in 2000 and now offers excellent facilities in a pleasant part of Austria, to the east of Salzburg, between the lakes of Mondsee and Irrsee. It is peacefully situated in a natural setting with mountain views, yet less than 10 minutes drive from the autobahn. There are 60 good sized, level touring pitches (80 long stay), set amongst the trees at the lower level and on terraces, each with water, waste water and 16A electricity. The heated swimming pool is covered and has a sunbathing terrace. There is a small fishing lake (unfenced) and a small children's playground. Good English is spoken.

Facilities

The sanitary facilities are in the reception and pool complex and offer first class facilities including some washbasins in cabins and a suite for disabled visitors. Laundry with washing machines and dryer. Kitchen with cooking and dishwashing. Motorcaravan service point. Shop and restaurant, both all season. Swimming pool (free). Playground. Riding. Off site: Mondsee is a popular large lake with many sporting opportunities. Golf 5 km.

Open: 1 April - 31 October.

Directions

From A1/E55 exit 265 (signed Straßwalchen) turn north onto B154. In 1.5 m. turn left at crossroads (by glassworks) and then 2 km. to site (signed). Note: Signs can be difficult to spot. GPS: N47:52.008 E13:18.379

Charges 2007

Per person	€ 4,90 - € 5,50
child (6-15 yrs)	€ 3,50 - € 3,80
pitch with electricity	€ 9,40 - € 10,40
dog	€ 2,90

Wiedlroither & Leidl KEG
Punz Au 21,
A-5310 Mondsee
Tel. +43(0)6232/2600
Fax +43(0)6232/27218
www.campmondsee.at
email: austria@campmondsee.at

When the children are happy, the parents have a holiday too!

Very modern site with 140 pitches, two holiday cabins in very tranquil countryside. Situated between Lake Mond and Lake Irr not far from Salzburg. Heated covered pool, fishing pond, Robinson-valley (adventure world for children), play area, ponies, very modern sanitary facilities, touring pitches with electricity, water and drainage. Newsagent, inn, kitchen and laundrette.

AU0240 Camping Appesbach

Au 99, A-5360 St Wolfgang (Upper Austria)

Tel: **061 382 206**. Email: **camping@appesbach.at**

St Wolfgang, a pretty little village on the lake of the same name which was made famous by the operetta 'White Horse Inn', is ringed round by hills in a delightful situation. The location of Appesbach, on the banks of the lake with a good frontage, is one of its main assets. The site has 170 pitches, with 100 for touring units (including 20 tent pitches) with some in regular rows and the rest on open meadows that could become full in high season. Pitches near the lakeside have higher charges. All have electricity (10A) with a mix of German and European sockets. The lake is used for all types of sailing and windsurfing and bathing is possible if it's not too cool. Also on site is a good value restaurant and takeaway.

Facilities

The two toilet blocks have been combined into one, extended and refurbished to a good standard. Motorcaravan service point. Good shop. Bar (1/5-31/8). Restaurant with TV (Easter-30/9). Snack bar with terrace (Easter-30/9). Small playground. Off site: Tennis nearby. Village 1 km. Many excursions possible including Salzburg 50 km.

Open: Easter - 31 October.

Directions

From B158 Salzburg-Bad Ischl road, turn towards St Wolfgang just east of Strobl and site is on the left 1 km. before St Wolfgang. GPS: N47:43.947 E13:27.826

Charges 2007

Per person	€ 4,10 - € 6,10
child (3-15 yrs)	€ 2,55 - € 3,55
pitch acc. to position and size of unit	€ 5,00 - € 13,00
electricity	€ 2,80
dog	€ 2,00

AU0280 Camping Stumpfer

A-3392 Schönbühel (Lower Austria)

Tel: 027 528 510. Email: office@stumpfer.com

This small, well appointed site with just 60 pitches is directly on the River Danube, near the small town of Schönbühel, and could make a convenient night stop being near the Salzburg - Vienna autobahn. The 50 unmarked pitches for touring units, all with electricity (16A), are on flat grass and the site is lit at night. There is shade in most parts and a landing stage for boat trips on the Danube. The main building also houses a Gasthof, with a bar/restaurant of the same name, that can be used by campers. This is very much a family run site.

Facilities

Part of the main building, the toilet block is of good quality with hot water on payment. Facilities for disabled visitors include ramps by the side of steps up to the block. Washing machine and dryer. Motorcaravan services. Small shop. Playground. Fishing. Off site: Swimming pool, bicycle hire or riding within 5 km.

Open: 1 April - 31 October.

Directions

Leave Salzburg - Vienna autobahn at Melk exit. Drive towards Melk, continue towards Melk Nord. Just before bridge turn right (Schönbühel), at T-junction turn right again and continue down hill. Turn right just before BP station (Schönbühel) and site is 3 km. on left with narrow entrance, next to the Gasthof Stumpfer. GPS: N48:14.233 E15:22.250

Charges 2007

Per person	€ 4,80
pitch incl. electricity	€ 6,70 - € 8,20

AU0290 Donaupark Camping Tulln

Donoulande 76, A-3430 Tulln (Lower Austria)

Tel: 022 726 5200. Email: camptulln@oeamtc.at

Donaupark Camping, owned and run by the Austrian Motor Club (OAMTC), is imaginatively laid out village-style with unmarked grass pitches grouped around six circular gravel areas. Further pitches are to the side of the hard road which links the circles and these include some with grill facilities for tents; 100 of the 120 touring pitches have electricity (3/6A) and cable TV sockets. Tall trees surrounding the site offer shade in parts. Tucked neatly away at the back of the site are 120 long stay caravans. Activities are organised in high season with guided tours around Tulln.

Facilities

Three modern, octagonal sanitary blocks can be heated. One is at reception (next to the touring area), the other two are at the far end of the site. Facilities for disabled visitors. Washing facilities. Cooking rings. Gas supplies. Bar and restaurant (1/5-15/9). Shop (15/5-15/9). Play areas. 'Topi' club (July/Aug). Tennis. Bicycle and canoe hire. Excursions. Internet access. Off site: Fishing 500 m. Bus service into Vienna 9/7-24/8. Half-hourly train service to Vienna. Steamer excursions.

Open: Easter - 31 October.

Directions

From Vienna follow south bank of the Danube on B14; from the west, leave A1 autobahn at Saint Christophen or Altenbach exits and go north on the B19 to Tulln. Site is on the east side of Tulln and is well signed.

Charges 2007

Per person	€ 6,50
pitch	€ 7,50 - € 11,00
electricity	€ 2,00
Camping Cheques accepted.	

AU0302 Aktiv Camping Wien Neue Donau

Am Kaisermuhlendamm 119, A-1220 Wien-Ost (Vienna)

Tel: 012 024 010. Email: neuedonau@campingwien.at

This is the sister site of Camping Wien-Sud and is located closer to Vienna. Near two busy motorways there is inevitably traffic noise, but it is perhaps easier to find and has similar facilities and standards. With 254 level touring pitches with electricity and a further 12 with water and drainage also, the site has a large and changing population. The site is close to the 'Donauinsel', a popular recreation area. The Neue Donau (New Danube), a 20 km. long artificial side arm of the Danube provides swimming, sports and play areas, while the Danube bicycle trail runs past the site.

Facilities

Modern toilet facilities are clean and well maintained with free showers. Facilities for disabled visitors. Washing machines and dryers. Motorcaravan service point. Campers' kitchen with cooking, fridges, freezers and TV. Shop. Small restaurant. Play area. Internet access. Barbecue areas. Bicycle hire and free guided bicycle tours. Off site: Vienna city centre 5 km. Prater Park 1 km.

Open: Easter - 15 September.

Directions

Site is close to the A23 and A22. From A23 heading east turn off at first exit after crossing the Donau (signed Lobau). At first traffic lights, near Shell station, turn left and after 200 m. turn right into site. GPS: N48:12.555 E16:26.669

Charges 2007

Per person	€ 5,90 - € 6,90
pitch	€ 5,50 - € 12,00

AU0306 Camping Wien West

Hüttelbergstrasse 80, A-1140 Wien (Vienna)

Tel: **019 142 314**. Email: **west@campingwien.at**

Opera, classical music, museums, shopping and the Danube; whatever it is you want in Vienna you are spoilt for choice. Wien West is an all year round site with good transport links to the city centre. It is the parent site of Wien Sud and Neue Donau and is inevitably busier. The site is located on the edge of the Vienna Woods with direct access to walking and mountain bike trails. There are 202 level and numbered pitches, all with 13A electricity. Buses to the metro stop right outside the gates and you can be in centre in 35 minutes. For somewhere different try the 'Black Camel' for a light lunch – it is easy to find from Stephensplatz – or perhaps the Danube cruise that will introduce you to the architecture of Freiderreich Hundertwasser. Whatever you do it will be a memorable visit to the Austrian capital.

Facilities

Three modern toilet blocks provide ample and clean toilets, hot showers and washbasins. Washing machine and dryer. Kitchen and dishwashing facilities. Motorcaravan services. Small shop for essentials. Restaurant (1/4-1/10). WiFi (free) and internet point. Games room. Playground. Bicycle hire. Off site: Vienna centre 8 km. Schönbrunn palace. Bicycle and walking trails. Tennis.

Open: All year (excl. February).

Directions

From the city centre follow signs to autobahn west and Linz. Site is well signed from the main roads. Coming from the A1 (Salzburg - Vienna) drive over the Bergmillergasse (bridge). Stay on this road to Huttelbergstraße after the first traffic lights. GPS: N48:12.554 E16:26.668

Charges 2007

Per person	€ 5,90 - € 6,90
child (4-15 yrs)	€ 3,50 - € 4,00
pitch	€ 5,50 - € 9,50
electricity	€ 3,00 - € 4,00

AU0304 Camping Wien-Sud

Breitenfursterstrasse 269, A-1230 Wien-Atzgersdorf (Vienna)

Tel: **018 673 649**. Email: **sued@campingwien.at**

This site, which is in a former Palace park and was closed for some years, reopened in 2003 with new facilities and new management. It is now probably the best site in the greater Vienna area, with good public transport links to the city centre and a friendly and welcoming atmosphere. There are 154 touring pitches with electricity (16A) and 42 with water and drainage. The site provides a good base for city sightseeing. With lots of mature trees and some shade you will find this a peaceful and quiet site. Walking and cycling are popular in the nearby Vienna woods. Right next door is a Merkur supermarket which is well worth a visit for storing up whichever way you are heading.

Facilities

Excellent modern toilet facilities are clean and well maintained with free showers. Facilities for disabled visitors. Washing machine and dryer. Some cooking facilities. Motorcaravan service point. Small play area. Tickets for Schloss Schönbrunn and other attractions sold at reception. Off site: Vienna 6 km.

Open: 1 June - 31 August.

Directions

From the A2 turn onto the A21 towards Linz (if you're heading north the slip is just past IKEA). Turn off the A21 at first exit (Brunn am Gebirge) and head north. Keep going on this road to site (well signed) on the right in Atzgersdorf. From the A23 (Süd-Ost Tangene) take Altmannsdorf exit and follow the signs.

Charges 2007

Per person	€ 5,90 - € 6,90
child (4-15 yrs)	€ 3,50 - € 4,00
pitch	€ 5,10 - € 17,00

AU0300 Camping Rodaun

Breitenfurter Straße 487, An der Au 2, A-1230 Wien-Südwest-Rodaun (Vienna)

Tel: 018 884 154

This good little site is within the Vienna city boundary and is a pleasant base for visiting this old and interesting world famous city. Just 9 km. from the centre, there is an excellent public transport system for viewing the sights as car parking is almost impossible in the city. Situated in a southern suburb, it has space for about 40 units on flat grass pitches or on concrete bases and an additional area for about 20 tents. With little shade, the pitches are not numbered or marked, either in the centre or outside the circular tarmac road running round the camping area, with 6A electricity provided.

Facilities

The toilet block has some washbasins in cabins and hot showers for which a token is needed (purchased at reception). Laundry service provided by Frau Deihs. Off site: Supermarket and restaurant within 250 m. Swimming pool 2 km.

Open: 15 June - 20 October.

Directions

Take Pressbaum exit from Westautobahn or Vosendorf exit from Sudautobahn and follow signs. Site is at 2 An der Au, which is a small side street leading off from Breitenfurter Strasse (a 16 km. long road).

Charges 2007

Per person	€ 6,50
pitch incl. car	€ 7,50 - € 9,00
electricty per kWh	€ 0,80

AU0330 Camping Central

Martinhofstraße 3, A-8054 Graz (Steiermark)

Tel: 067 637 85102. Email: guenther_walter@utanet.at

Although not as well known as Vienna, Salzburg and Innsbruck, Graz in the southern province of Styria, is Austria's second largest city. Camping Central is a quiet place which makes a good night stop when travelling from Klagenfurt to Vienna or a base from which to explore the region. The name is misleading as it is situated in the southwest of the town in the Strassgang district, some 6 km. from the centre. The 136 level touring pitches are either in regular rows either side of tarmac roads under a cover of tall trees or on an open meadow where they are not marked out. All have 6A electricity.

Facilities

The new, well built toilet block is of good quality and the other two blocks have been refurbished. Each can be heated in cool weather. Facilities for disabled visitors. Washing machines and dryer. Swimming pool with facilities including a special entry to the water for disabled people. Small restaurant at the pool. Tennis. Playground. Jogging track. Limited animation during high season. Off site: Two other restaurants within 300 m. Good shop about 400 m.

Open: 1 April - 31 October.

Directions

From the west take the exit 'Graz-west', from Salzburg exit 'Graz-sud' follow signs to Central and Strassgang and turn right just past traffic lights for site (signed).

Charges 2007

Per unit incl. 2 persons and electricity	€ 24,00 - € 28,00
extra person	€ 8,00
No credit cards.	

AU0502 Camping Im Thermenland

Bairisch Kölldorf 240, A-8344 Bairisch Kölldorf (Steiermark)

Tel: 031 593 941. Email: gemeinde@bairisch-koelldorf.at

Near both the Slovakian and Hungarian borders and set in the rolling countryside of southeast Austria, this is a real hidden gem. Not shown on many maps, but well worth the trip, if you want a good quiet site with modern amenities and excellent standards then come right here. There are 100 pitches of which 70 are for touring and all have electricity, water and drainage. The site is near numerous spas and thermal baths and close to Styrassic Park, a must for younger campers.

Facilities

Excellent toilet facilities are clean, well maintained and include free showers. Facilities for disabled visitors. Washing machine and dryer. Dog shower. Restaurant (all year). Unheated outdoor, but covered, swimming pool (May - Sept). Small play area. Off site: Styrassic Park 4 km. Fishing 100 m. Golf 3 km.

Open: All year.

Directions

Southeast of Graz. Leave A2 at exit 157 and head towards Feldbach on the 68. Continue on the 66 to Bad Gleichenberg, go straight over first roundabout and turn left at the second (supermarket). After 2.8 km. (just past fire station) turn left by a chapel and immediately right towards site in 600 m.

Charges 2007

Per person	€ 6,15
pitch	€ 7,25
electricity per kWh	€ 0,50
Camping Cheques accepted.	

AU0505 Camping Leibnitz

Rudolf Hans Bartsch-Gasse 33, A-8430 Leibnitz (Steiermark)

Tel: **034 528 2463**. Email: **stadtgemeinde@leibnitz.at**

Near the Slovakian border, close to the small town of Leibnitz, this site is set in the rolling wine-growing countryside of southeast Austria. A small site with only 52 pitches, it is set in a lovely park area and close to an excellent swimming pool complex which is available for campers to use (with access arrangements for disabled visitors). Minigolf and tennis facilities are nearby. All the pitches are of a good size, level and with 16A electricity connections, and some have shade.

Facilities

Excellent toilet facilities are clean and well maintained. Showers cost € 0.50. Facilities for disabled visitors. Washing machine. Small restaurant but many more within walking distance. Small play area. Off site: Leibnitz 500 m. Leisure centre with two heated outdoor swimming pools 100 m.

Open: 1 May - 30 September.

Directions

From the A9 take exit for Leibnitz, go straight over two roundabouts (through factory outlet centre), over traffic lights and after 300 m. turn left at site sign. Go straight over roundabout and enter Leibnitz, turn right and site is 500 m. on the left.

Charges 2007

Per person	€ 4,50
child (6-14 yrs)	€ 2,00
pitch incl. electricity	€ 8,30

AU0515 Katschtal Camping

Peterdorf 100, A-8842 Peterdorf (Steiermark)

Tel: **035 842 2813**. Email: **katschtalcamping@yahoo.de**

The small, quiet campsite with only 48 pitches is ideally located for exploring southwest Styria and the beautiful Mur valley, and the Niedere Tauern alps (highest point Greimberg 2472 m). To the north, snow capped Greimberg sits high above the site whilst in other directions you can see pine clad slopes and alpine pastures. Not too far away is Turracher Hohe, the small ski resort that nestles at an altitude of 1700 m. in the Nocky mountains, one of Austria's most scenic Alpine ranges between Styria and Carinthia. Walks and cycle routes abound or you can just sit and watch the countryside at work from your pitch. The level, unmarked pitches all have access to 6A electricity.

Facilities

The modern sanitary block provides ample and clean facilities including toilets, hot showers and washbasins. Washing machine. Chemical toilet disposal point. Kitchen with dishwashing facilities.

Open: All year.

Directions

From the Murau - Scheifling 96 road, turn north towards Katsch just west of Frojach. Follow this road up the valley towards and through Peterdorf to the site on the right set back from the road but clearly signed. GPS: N47:10.848 E14:13.003

Charges guide

Per unit incl. 2 persons	€ 13,50
electricity per kWh	€ 0,55

AU0520 Camping am Badesee

Hitzmonn Solorf 28, A-8822 Mühlen (Steiermark)

Tel: **035 862 418**. Email: **office@camping-am-badesee.at**

Set in a beautiful open alpine valley beside a lake in the southern part of the Steiermark region, this family run site will provide a warm welcome, and a relaxing holiday. The 60 good sized pitches are well spaced on open grassy terraces and with only 10 long stay units there should be around 50 available for touring units, all with electricity. From reception you can order bread, milk and eggs and basic requirements. A small cafe/snack bar with a terrace which overlooks the lake, serves regional dishes and drinks. The lake is used for swimming, fishing, canoes and non-powered craft.

Facilities

A modern heated sanitary unit provides spacious hot showers, some washbasins in cubicles, with child size showers and basins. Hairdressing and shaving areas. Dishwashing sinks outside under cover. Laundry room also has a baby bath. No dedicated facilities for disabled persons. Communal barbecue. Playground. Pets corner. Trampoline. Lake for swimming, fishing and boating. Bicycle hire. Off site: Two restaurants and services in Mühlen (15 minutes walk). Riding 1 km. Neumarkt (6 km.) has more comprehensive facilities. Golf 14 km.

Open: 1 May - 30 September.

Directions

From the west on the A10 take exit 104 (St Michael im Lungau) and head east on road 96 through Murau to Scheiffling. Turn right (south) on B317 to Neumarkt, and towards the end of village turn left on B92 to Mühlen. Site is 5.8 km. on the right. GPS: N47:02.225 E14:29.243

Charges 2007

Per unit with 2 persons and electricity	€ 16,00 - € 17,90
extra person	€ 4,50

10% reduction in May, June and September.

AU0400 Camping Arneitz

Seeuferlandesstrasse 53, A-9583 Faak am See (Carinthia)

Tel: **042 542 137**. Email: **camping@arneitz.at**

Directly on Faakersee, Camping Arneitz is one of the best sites in this area, central for the attractions of the region, watersports and walking. Family run, Arneitz led the way with good quality and comprehensive facilities. A newly built reception building at the entrance reflects the quality of the site and apart from reception facilities, has a good collection of tourist literature and three desks with telephones for guests to use. The 400, level, marked pitches are mainly of gravel, off hard roads, with electricity available. Some have good shade from trees. Grass pitches are available for tents.

Facilities	Directions
Splendid family washroom, large, heated and airy, with family cubicles around the walls and in the centre, washbasins at child height in a circle with a working carousel in the middle. Extra, small block nearer the lake. Washing machines. Motorcaravan services. Supermarket. Self-service restaurant, bar and terrace. General room with TV. Small cinema for children's films. Beauty salon. Massage. Large sauna/solarium. Minigolf. Playground. Fishing. Bicycle hire Off site: Riding 3 km. Golf 10 km. **Open:** 24 April - 30 September.	Site is southeast of Villach, southwest of Veldon. Follow signs for Faakersee and Egg rather than for Faak village. From A11 take exit 3 and head towards Egg, turn left at T-junction and go through Egg village. Just after leaving village, site is on right. GPS: N46:34.511 E13:55.996

Charges 2007

Per person	€ 6,80 - € 7,50
child (3-10 yrs)	€ 6,40 - € 7,00
pitch incl. electricity	€ 10,00 - € 13,00

AU0410 Strandcamping Turnersee Breznik

A-9123 St Primus (Carinthia)

Tel: **042 392 350**. Email: **info@breznik.at**

This neat and tidy site is situated in a valley with views of the surrounding mountains. The 275 marked and numbered pitches for touring units vary in size, on level grass terraces. Although there are many trees, not all parts have shade. All pitches have electricity (6A) and 50 also have water, drainage, TV and phone connections. At the lakeside is a large well mown grass area for sunbathing. A wooden decking area right next to the water provides steps down for swimming in the lake. It is very much a site for families where children really are catered for and it has a pleasant atmosphere.

Facilities	Directions
Four modern sanitary blocks include provision for young children and babies in the largest block. Facilities for disabled people. Large, central building housing well stocked shop. Pleasant restaurant with terrace, takeaway (9/5-25/9) and play room for small children. Good play areas and small zoo with goats and rabbits. 'Topi' club and organised activities for adults and children. Games room. Bicycle hire. Watersports. Internet access. Off site: Fishing and golf 1.5 km. Riding 3 km. Boat launching 5 km. **Open:** 3 April - 3 October.	Leave A2 motorway at exit 298 signed Grafenstien. Go east on road 70 for 5 km. and turn right for Tainach and St Kanzian. In St Kanzian keep bearing to the right, St Primas is signposted. Site is on left before St Primus. GPS: N46:35.127 E14:33.953

Charges 2007

Per person	€ 4,70 - € 7,80
pitch	€ 6,30 - € 10,50
incl. services	€ 8,00 - € 12,80
Camping Cheques accepted.	

AU0415 Camping Rosental Roz

Gotschuchen 34, A-9173 St Margareten im Rosental (Carinthia)

Tel: **042 268 1000**. Email: **camping.rosental@roz.at**

In the picturesque Drau valley, southeast of Flagenfurt, Rosental Roz has magnificent views along the valley and of the cliffs that form the Austrian southern border with Slovakia. The site is also close to Italy. With 430 pitches (all for touring) and 10 mobile homes to rent around a small swimming lake, all pitches have 6A electricity and 50 pitches have water and drainage. An active children's club provides lots to occupy the youngsters and guided walks for adults are organised from the campsite.

Facilities	Directions
Toilet facilities are clean and modern with free showers, 10 family washrooms and a large shower facility for young children. Washing machine and dryer. Facilities for disabled visitors. Restaurant/bar (1/5-30/9). Shop (1/6-15/9). Children's club (1/6-30/8). Playgrounds and large games area. Water slide. WiFi. Off site: Fishing 1 km. Riding 2 km. Many walks. Cycle rides. **Open:** Easter - 15 October.	Site is southeast of Klagenfurt. From the 91 road turn onto the 85 towards Feriach. Before reaching St Margareten, in the centre of the small hamlet of Gotschuchen turn left towards site. It is 1.5 km. but well signed (watch the overhanging gutters especially when passing another vehicle).

Charges 2007

Per person	€ 7,10
pitch	€ 8,20 - € 10,40

www.camping.woerthersee.com

Wörthersee • 4-Seental Keutschach

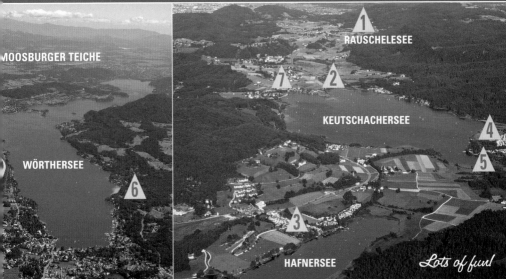

MOOSBURGER TEICHE

WÖRTHERSEE

RAUSCHELESEE

KEUTSCHACHERSEE

HAFNERSEE

Lots of fun!

Campsite Reichmann

uz 5, A-9074 Seental Keutschach, Tel. 00 43/463/281 452,
00 43/463/21 52 6-34, E-Mail: info@camping-reichmann.at,
w.camping-reichmann.at; Family run campsite, 12.000 m2, quietly located
e heart of unspoiled nature, located on the eastern bank of Lake Rauschele,
l site for families with children.

Strandcamping Süd

ja Hannelore Seger, A-9074 Seental Keutschach, Tel. 00 43/42 73/27 73,
00 43/42 73/27 73-4, Mobile phone from 6 pm: 00 43/699/12424403,
ail: info@strandcampingsued.at, www.keutschachsued.at
utiful family campsite, with direct lake access and at the forest edge,
rious facilities, large bathing area and play area, restaurant and Kidsclub.

Family campsite Hafnersee

our-Austria Hotelbetriebs GmbH, Plescherken 5,
074 Seental Keutschach, Tel. 00 43/42 73/23 75-0, Fax 00 43/42 73/23 75-16,
ail: info@hafnersee.at, www.hafnersee.at
dern and well equipped campsite, very child friendly,
n direct lake access, large pitches and play area.

Sabotnik Naturist campsite

ner Kaufitsch, Dobein 9, A-9074 Seental Keutschach,
00 43/42 73/25 09, Fax 00 43/42 73/26 05,
ail: info@fkk-sabotnik.at, www.fkk-sabotnik.at
ily friendly campsite in a tranquil setting, direct lake access,
ertainment programme, activities for children of all ages, sport
play areas, several spots for swimming, massage, mobile homes
hire, dog area, childrens' farm, internet café and wireless lan.

Müllerhof Naturist campsite

Family Safron, Dobein 10, A-9074 Seental Keutschach,
Tel. 00 43/42 73/25 17, Fax 25 17-5, Mobile phone: 00 43/664/33 55 425,
E-Mail: muellerhof@fkk-camping.at, www.fkk-camping.at
This site has been awarded by ADAC as a top class naturist site
since 1991. Located on Lake Keutschach. Mobile homes to rent at:
Fa. Gebetsroither GmbH., A-8940 Weißenbach/Liezen, Hauptstraße 6,
Tel. 00 43/3612/26300, Fax: 00 43/3612/26300 4,
E-Mail: office@gebetsroither.com, www.gebetsroither.com

Camping Weisses Rössl

Wörthersee-Süd, A-9220 Velden-Auen, Auenstr. 47,
Tel. 00 43/42 74/28 98, Fax 00 43/42 74/28 98-4,
E-Mail: weisses.roessl@aon.at, http://members.aon.at/weisses.roessl
Idyllic and quiet, located in an especially beautiful spot between
Velden and Maria Wörth. Private lake beach , two sanitary blocks
with free hot water in the showers and wash cabins. Children's play
areas, Children's play camp.

Strandcamping Brückler Nord

Gerhard Seger, A-9074 Seental Keutschach, Tel. 00 43/42 73/23 84,
Fax 00 43/42 73/210 80, E-Mail: camp.brueckler@aon.at,
www.brueckler.co.at
Family friendly Campsite, direct at the bank of Lake Keutschach.
We accept camping cheques.

mation: Wörthersee-Tourismus   Tel. 00 43/42 74/38 288   E-mail:info@woerthersee.com
20 Velden, Villacher Straße 19   Fax 00 43/42 74/38 288-19   woerthersee.com

Wörthersee

AU0490 Camping Terrassen Maltatal

Malta 6, A-9854 Maltatal (Carinthia)

Tel: 047 332 34. Email: info@maltacamp.at

Situated between two national parks in a mountain valley, this site offers spectacular views over the surrounding area especially from the pool which is over 300 sq.m. with a grassy sunbathing area and is open to all (free for campers). There are 220 grassy pitches on narrow terraces (70-100 sq.m.) mostly in rows on either side of narrow access roads. Numbered and marked, some separated with low hedges, all have electricity connections and 90 have water and drainage (the electricity boxes are often inconveniently located on the next terrace). The 'Kärnten-card' is available to purchase from the site which gives free travel on public transport and free entry to many attractions.

Facilities

Two toilet blocks, one with under-floor heating, have about half the washbasins in cabins and 10 family wash cabins. Facilities for babies and children. Washing machines, dryers and irons. Motorcaravan services. Only basic provisions kept. Restaurant (all season). Swimming pool (20/5-15/9). Sauna. Playground. Bicycle hire. Riding. Entertainment programme and many walks and excursions. Off site: Village 500 m. Fishing or golf 6 km. Malta High alpine road, Reisseck mountain railways and The Porshe Museum in Gmund are all nearby.

Open: Easter - 31 October.

Directions

Site is 15 km. north of Spittal. Leave A10 at Gmund exit (no. 129) . Pass through Gmund towards Malta. Site is on right 6 km. from autobahn exit.
GPS: N46:56.990 E13:30.576

Charges 2007

Per person	€ 4,70 - € 6,90
child (2-14 yrs)	€ 3,40 - € 4,50
pitch with electricity	€ 6,20 - € 9,10
incl. water and drainage	€ 8,80 - € 10,90
dog	€ 2,20 - € 2,60

Electricity included. Less for longer stays.
Camping Cheques accepted.

The campsite at 800 m altitude between the «Hohe Tauern» and «Nockberge» national parks, with amazing panoramic views.

Terrassencamping Maltatal

A-9854 Malta 5-6, Kärnten • Tel. 0043-4733-234 • Fax 0043-4733-23416 • www.maltacamp.at • info@maltacamp.at

AU0450 Naturpark Schluga Seecamping

A-9620 Hermagor (Carinthia)

Tel: 042 822 051. Email: camping@schluga.com

This site is pleasantly situated on natural wooded hillside. It is about 300 m. from a small lake with clean water, where the site has a beach of coarse sand and a large grassy meadow where inflatable boats can be kept. It also has a sunbathing area for naturists although this is not a naturist site. The 250 pitches for touring units are on individual, level terraces, many with light shade and all with electricity (10-16A). 124 pitches also have water, drainage and satellite TV and a further 47 pitches are occupied by a tour operator. English is spoken.

Facilities

Four heated modern toilet blocks are well constructed, with some washbasins in cabins and family washrooms for rent. Facilities for disabled people. Washing machines and dryer. Motorcaravan services. Shop (20/5-10/9). Restaurant/bar by entrance and takeaway (all 20/5-10/9). Playground. Room for young people and children. Films. Kiosk and bar with terrace at beach. Surf school. Pedalo and canoe hire. Aqua jump and 'Iceberg'. Pony rides. Bicycle hire. Fishing. Weekly activity programme with mountain walks and climbs. Internet point. Off site: Tennis (indoor and outdoor).

Open: 10 May - 20 September.

Directions

Site is on the B111 road (Villach - Hermagor) 6 km. east of Hermagor town.
GPS: N46:37.908 E13:26.802

Charges 2007

Per person	€ 4,90 - € 7,80
child (5-14 yrs)	€ 3,45 - € 5,20
pitch incl. electricity	€ 6,80 - € 9,40
dog	€ 1,90 - € 2,60

Camping Cheques accepted.

AU0440 Schluga Camping

Obervellach 15, A-9620 Hermagor-Pressegger See (Carinthia)

Tel: 04282 2051. Email: camping@schluga.com

Schluga Camping is under the same ownership as Schluga Seecamping, some four kilometres to the west of that site in a flat valley with views of the surrounding mountains. The 223 touring pitches are of varying size, 115 with water, drainage and satellite TV connections. Electricity connections are available throughout (10-16A). Mainly on grass covered gravel on either side of tarmac surfaced access roads, they are divided by shrubs and hedges. The site is open all year, to include the winter sports season, and has a well kept tidy appearance, although it may be busy in high seasons. English is spoken. A new bar and terrace have been added by the lake. Entertainment in high season includes a disco and cinema and a weekly programme sheet given to visitors details events at both Schluga sites and in the local area.

Facilities

Four sanitary blocks (a splendid new one, plus one modern and two good older ones) are heated in cold weather. Most washbasins in cabins and good showers. Family washrooms for rent. Baby rooms and suite for disabled people. Washing machines and dryers. Drying rooms and ski rooms. Motorcaravan services. Well stocked shop (1/5-30/9). Bar/restaurant with terrace (closed Nov). Heated swimming pool (12 x 7 m; 1/5-30/9). Playground. Youth games room. Bicycle hire. Sauna. Solarium. Steam bath. Fitness centre. TV room. Internet point. Kindergarten programme for small children. Off site: Tennis.

Open: All year.

Directions

Site is on the B111 Villach - Hermagor road (which is better quality than it appears on most maps) just east of Hermagor town.

Charges 2007

Per person	€ 4,90 - € 7,80
child (5-14 yrs)	€ 3,45 - € 5,20
pitch incl. electricity	€ 6,80 - € 9,40
dog	€ 1,90 - € 2,60

Check real time availability and at-the-gate prices...

www.alanrogers.com

AU0445 Alpencamp Kötschach Mauthen

A 9640 Kötschach Mauthen (Carinthia)

Tel: **047 154 29**. Email: **info@alpencamp.at**

The Lesachtal, the valley of a hundred watermills, bordered to the north by the Lienzer Dolomiten and to the south by the Karnische Alps, is one of Austria's most beautiful valleys. The watermills are no longer in use, although many of the wheels are still turned by falling water set against a backdrop of magnificent mountain scenery. Four years in the planning, Alpencamp is an environmentally friendly site where a fascinating combination of technology and tradition is used to preserve its beautiful setting. This family run site has 85 level pitches set on grass with some tree shade, all with electricity (13/16A).

Facilities

New sanitary blocks include washbasins in cabins and free hot showers. Laundry facilities. Motorcaravan service point. Small shop. Restaurant. Gym, steam bath, bio-sauna, solarium, massage, sun terrace and two adventure showers (storm in mountain effect with thunder, lightning and bird sounds). Play area. Bicycle hire. Off site: Town with entrance to 'Aquarena' with its indoor and outdoor swimming pools (free to site guests).

Open: 15 December - 15 October.

Directions

Coming from Villach on the 111, in town at the junction with the 110, turn left, then after 200 m. turn right and continue along the 111 in the direction of Lesachtal. After 500 m. site is to the left. GPS: N46:40.185 E12:59.477

Charges 2007

Per person	€ 4,10 - € 6,40
pitch	€ 4,40 - € 6,90
incl. electricity	€ 6,40 - € 8,90

AU0425 Seecamping Berghof

Ossiachersee Süduferstraße 241, A-9523 Villach Landskron (Carinthia)

Tel: **042 424 1133**. Email: **office@seecamping-berghof.at**

This surely must be the ultimate camping experience: a perfect location, excellent facilities, great pitches and a welcome to match. The Ertl family and their staff manage this 480 pitch site to perfection. Use of the natural topography means that you actually think you are in a small site wherever you camp. With lovely lake views from almost every spot, this is a great site to stop for a short or long stay. Constant improvements mean that slowly the number of pitches reduce as larger and more equipped places are provided. There are 190 pitches with water, electricity and drainage and many pitches have access to the internet.

Facilities

Five modern toilet blocks around the site, provide the usual facilities with special provision for young children and babies in two blocks. Facilities for disabled people. Good supermarket. Restaurant with terrace, takeaway and games room for older children. Play area and daily club for 4-11 year olds. Bicycle hire. Watersports including boat hire and windsurfing school. Minigolf. Swimming in the lake. Skateboard park. Off site: Fishing. Villach 5 km.

Open: 1 April - 20 October.

Directions

From A10 take exit 178, which travelling south is just after the tunnel. Head towards Ossiacher See and after 1 km. turn right towards Ossiacher See Sud. At traffic lights turn left and site is 3.5 km. on the left just after entering hamlet of Heiligengestade. GPS: N46:39.272 E13:55.768

Charges 2007

Per person	€ 5,00 - € 8,00
pitch	€ 7,50 - € 12,50

AU0405 Sommer & Winter Camping Ramsbacher

Gries 53, A-9863 Rennweg (Carinthia)

Tel: **047 346 63**

This is a beautiful small site set in a high alpine valley with great views in every direction. With 72 touring pitches, all with electricity, this is a great site for those seeking peace and quiet and the opportunity to explore the local area by either bike or on foot. The site is well placed in the Katschberg Mountains and close to the Pölital nature reserve. Cars are not allowed in the national park in the summer so entry is via a small 'train'.

Facilities

Toilet facilities are clean, heated and modern with free showers but a communal changing area. Washing machine, dryer and drying area. Attractive restaurant/bar. Small play area. Off site: Swimming pool, minigolf, tennis, beach volleyball, rollerskating and play area 25 m. Winter skiing with free shuttle bus.

Open: All year.

Directions

From A10 take exit 113 (just south of toll tunnel).and turn towards Rennweg. Turn right a little later in the village and then right again towards Oberdorf where site is well signed. From the A10 exit, climb the hill from the junction and then turn left down towards Oberdorf. GPS: N47:01.560 E13:35.430

Charges 2007

Per person	€ 5,20 - € 5,50
pitch	€ 6,50 - € 7,00
electricity	€ 2,00

AU0480 Komfort Campingpark Burgstaller

Seefeldstrasse 16, A-9873 Döbriach (Carinthia)

Tel: 042 467 774. Email: **info@burgstaller.co.at**

This is one of Austria's top sites in a beautiful location and with all the amenities you could want. You can always tell a true family run site by the attention to detail and this site oozes perfection. This is an excellent family site for winter and summer camping with a very friendly atmosphere, particularly in the restaurant in the evenings. Good English is spoken. The 600 pitches (560 for tourists) are on flat, well drained grass, backing onto hedges on either side of access roads. All fully serviced (including WiFi), they vary in size (45-120 sq.m.) and there are special pitches for motorcaravans. One pitch actually rotates and follows the sun during the course of the day! The latest sanitary block warrants an architectural award; all toilets have a TV and a pirate ship on the first floor of the children's area sounds its guns every hour. The site entrance is directly opposite the park leading to the bathing lido, to which campers have free access. There is also a heated swimming pool. Much activity is organised here, including games and competitions for children in summer with a winter programme of skiing, curling and skating. At Christmas, trees are gathered from the forest and there are special Easter and autumn events.

Facilities

Three exceptionally good quality toilet blocks include washbasins in cabins, facilities for children and disabled visitors, dishwashers and under-floor heating for cool weather. Seven private rooms for rent (3 with jacuzzi baths). Motorcaravan services. Good restaurant with terrace (May-Oct). Shop (May-Sept). Bowling alley. Disco (July/Aug). TV room. Sauna and solarium. Two play areas (one for under 6s, the other for 6-12 yrs). Bathing and boating in lake. Special entrance rate for lake attractions. Fishing. Bicycle hire. Mountain bike area. Riding. Comprehensive entertainment programmes. Covered stage and outdoor arena provide for church services (Protestant and Catholic, in German) and folk and modern music concerts. Off site: Mountain walks, climbing and farm visits all in local area.

Open: 1 January - 3 November.

Directions

Döbriach is at the eastern end of the Millstätter See about 15 km. south east of Spittal. Leave A10 at exit 139 (Spittal, Millstätter) then proceed alongside northern shore of lake through Millstätter towards Döbriach. Just before Döbriach turn right and after 1 km. site is on left. GPS: N46:46.208 E13:38.875

Charges 2007

Per person	€ 6,00 - € 9,00
child (4-14 yrs)	€ 4,00 - € 6,50
pitch	€ 4,70 - € 12,50
electricity	€ 1,90

Discounts for retired people in low season.

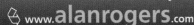

AU0460 Terrassen Camping Ossiacher See

Ostriach 67, A-9570 Ossiach (Carinthia)

Tel: 042 434 36. Email: martinz@camping.at

This gently sloping site has been partly terraced to provide good, level pitches. The site is protected by rising hills and enjoys lovely views across the lake to the mountains beyond. Trees, flowers, hedges and bushes abound, adding atmosphere to this neat, tidy site. The 530 pitches are in rows on the level grass terraces, separated by hard roads and some marked by hedges. There is shade in parts and electricity connections (4/6A) throughout. A separate area (25 pitches only) is provided for campers with dogs. Used by tour operators (28 pitches). Good English is spoken.

Facilities

Five well maintained sanitary blocks are heated in cool weather, some with washbasins in cabins. 10 family washrooms (charged), baby rooms and facilities for disabled campers. Washing machines, dryers and irons. Motorcaravan services. Restaurant (15/5-15/9). Well stocked supermarket. ATM. High season entertainment programme for children and adults. Playgrounds, games rooms and disco courtyard. Waterskiing and windsurfing schools and boats for hire. Tennis. Bicycle and moped hire. Fishing. Riding. Off site: Cycle path around lake. Hang-gliding possibilities in area.

Open: 1 May - 30 September.

Directions

Site is directly on the lake shore, 1.5 km. southwest of Ossiach village. Leave the A10 at exit 178 for Ossiachersee, turn left on road B94 towards Feldkirchen and shortly right to Ossiach Sud. The site is shortly before Ossiach. GPS: N46:39.825 E13:58.495

Charges 2007

Per person	€ 5,30 - € 7,90
child (3-12 yrs)	free - € 5,20
pitch acc. to season and location	€ 7,30 - € 11,70
small tent pitch	€ 4,30 - € 6,50

AU0475 Camping Brunner am See

Glanzerstraße 108, A-9873 Döbriach (Carinthia)

Tel: 042 467 189. Email: office@camping-brunner.at

This well appointed site at the eastern end of the Millstätter See, is the only site in the area with its own private beach directly accessible from the site. Consisting of fairly coarse sand, it is regularly cleaned. The 236 marked pitches (60-100 sq.m), all for touring units, are nearly all serviced with water, drainage and electricity hook-ups (4A) and are in rows on level grass with tarmac access roads. The site is fairly open with some shade from bushes and trees. There are three play areas for children. The site owns land on the opposite side of the road, which includes forest walks, a dog walk, a parking area and one of the playgrounds.

Facilities

A new building behind reception, houses the well appointed sanitary unit. Good facilities for disabled campers, especially handicapped children, plus a children's room with low level showers, basins, baby baths, changing deck etc. Family bathrooms (some for rent), some washbasins in cubicles, laundry facilities. Motorcaravan service point. Supermarket adjacent. Communal barbecue. Internet access. WiFi. Fishing. Watersports. Off site: Supermarket (May - Oct). Several restaurants. Tennis 100 m. Boat hire 200 m. Bicycle hire 300 m. with access to cycle route around Millstätter See. Riding 1.5 km. Golf 10 km. Skiing area 11 km.

Open: All year.

Directions

Döbriach is at the eastern end of the Millstätter See, about 15 km. south west of Spittal. Leave A10, exit 139 (Spittal, Millstätter), then proceed alongside northern shore of lake through Millstätter towards Döbriach. Just before Döbriach turn right and after 1.5 km. turn right at roundabout. Site is on right after 100 m. GPS: N46:46.060 E13:38.913

Charges 2007

Per person	€ 5,00 - € 7,50
child (4-18 yrs)	€ 3,50 - € 7,00
pitch incl. electricity	€ 7,00 - € 11,30
dog	€ 2,00 - € 3,00

Discounts for senior citizens (low season).

MAP 2

A small country divided into three regions, Flanders in the north, Wallonia in the south and Brussels the capital. Belgium is rich in scenic countryside, culture and history, notably the great forest of Ardennes, the historic cities of Bruges and Ghent and the western coastline with its sandy beaches.

CAPITAL: BRUSSELS

Tourist Office

Belgian Tourist Office Brussels & Wallonia,
217 Marsh Wall, London E14 9FJ
Tel: 0906 3020 245 Fax: 020 7531 0393
Email: info@belgiumtheplaceto.be
Internet: www.visitbelgium.com

Tourism Flanders-Brussels,
31 Pepper Street, London E14 9RW
Tel: 020 7867 0311 Fax: 020 7458 0045
Email: office@visitflanders.co.uk

Brussels is at the very heart of Europe and doubles as the capital of the European Union. A multi-cultural and multi-lingual city full of remarkable monuments, interesting museums and highly acclaimed restaurants. In the French speaking region of Wallonia lies the mountainous Ardennes, an area famous for its forests, lakes, streams and grottoes, making it a popular holiday destination, especially for those who like nature and walking. The safe, sandy beaches on the west coast run for forty miles. Here lies Ostend, a popular seaside resort with an eight kilometre long beach and a promenade coupled with a bustling harbour and shops. Bruges is Europe's best preserved medieval city and is certainly one of the most attractive, whether you want to relax on a boat trip along the canals, explore the narrow streets or visit one of the many churches and art museums.

Population
10.2 million

Climate
Temperate climate similar to Britain.

Language
There are three official languages. French is spoken in the south, Flemish in the north, and German is the predominant language in the eastern provinces.

Telephone
The country code is 00 32.

Money
Currency: The Euro
Banks: Mon-Fri 09.00-15.30.
Some banks open Sat 09.00-12.00.

Shops
Mon-Sat 09.00-17.30/18.00 hrs - later on Thurs/Fri; closed Sundays.

Public Holidays
New Year's Day; Easter Mon; Labour Day; Ascension; Whit Monday; Flemish Day 11 July; National Day 21 July; Assumption 15 Aug; French Day 27 Sept; All Saints 1, 2 Nov; Armistice Day 11 Nov; King's Birthday 15 Nov; Christmas 25, 26 Dec.

Motoring
For cars with a caravan or trailer, motorways are toll free except for the Liefenshoek Tunnel in Antwerp. Maximum permitted overall length of vehicle/trailer or caravan combination is 18 m. Blue Zone parking areas exist in Brussels, Ostend, Bruges, Liège, Antwerp and Gent. Parking discs can be obtained from police stations, garages, some shops.

BE0520 Camping de Blekker

Jachtwakersstraat 12, B-8670 Koksijde aan Zee (West Flanders)

Tel: 058 511 633. Email: camping.deblekker@belgacom.net

This family owned site, adjacent to a 186 hectare nature reserve on the Belgium coast, is divided into two sections: Blekker and Blekkerdal. De Blekker has 178 pitches with 75 allocated for touring units, all with 10A electricity. The pitches are grassy with some dividing hedges and trees. Visitors should drive to the Blekker reception but will be given a choice of where to park. Local attractions include the Koksijde annual Flower Market and Floral Pageant, National Fishery Museum and horseback shrimp fishing in Oostduinkerke, and Plopsaland (a small theme park) or Clown City in De Panne.

Facilities

Each section has a single modern sanitary unit including washbasins in cubicles. Facilities for babies and disabled persons (other than for washbasins, hot water is on payment throughout). Laundry. Small infirmary with bed. Bicycle hire. Internet access (in reception). English is spoken. Barbecues are not permitted in hot weather. Off site: Shop in nearest village 300 m. Restaurant and bars 0.4-3 km. Riding 1 km. Fishing and boat launching 1.5 km.

Open: 1 April - 15 November.

Directions

From A16 (E40) take ex 1A, then the N8 towards Koksijde. At roundabout take N396 towards Koksijde Dorp and then turn towards Koksijde-aan-zee. Follow small yellow camp signs. Site entrance road is on the right.

Charges 2007

Per unit incl. 4 persons	€ 19,00 - € 27,00

Special rates for bank holiday weekends.
10% discount on production of Alan Rogers Guide
Camping Cheques accepted.

BE0550 Kompas Camping Nieuwpoort

Brugsesteenweg 49, B-8620 Nieuwpoort (West Flanders)

Tel: 058 236 037. Email: nieuwpoort@kompascamping.be

Near Ostend, this large site with 952 pitches caters particularly for families. There are many on site amenities including a heated pool complex with two pools, a children's pool and a water slide, many sporting activities, and a children's farm. The numbered pitches, all with electricity, are in regular rows on flat grass. With 386 seasonal units and 71 caravan holiday homes, the site becomes full during Belgian holidays and in July/August. A network of footpaths links all areas of the site and gates to the rear lead to a reservoir. This is reserved for sailing, windsurfing and canoeing (canoes for hire) during certain hours only.

Facilities

Seven functional, clean and well maintained toilet blocks include washbasins in cubicles. The blocks are accessible to disabled people. Motorcaravan services. Supermarket, bakery, restaurant and café/bar (weekends and Belgian holidays outside July/Aug). Takeaway. Swimming pools with slide and pool games (1/6-10/9). Tennis. Adventure playground. Minigolf. Sports and show hall (stage shows, films). Entertainment programme (July/Aug). Off site: Fishing and bicycle hire within 500 m. Riding 3 km. Golf driving range 5 km. Nearest village 2 km. Beach 4 km.

Open: 21 March - 4 November.

Directions

From E40 take exit 4 (Middelkerke-Diksmuide). Turn towards Diksmuide following signs to Nieuwport. Pass through Sint-Joris and IC-Camping is on the right.

Charges 2008

Per family (max 6 persons)	
in Jul/Aug and B.Hs	€ 32,50
at other times	€ 22,00
electricity	€ 2,30

Largest unit accepted 2.5 x 8 m.
Less 10% with camping carnet.
Camping Cheques accepted.

BE0555 Recreatiepark Klein Strand

Varsenareweg 29, B-8490 Jabbeke (West Flanders)

Tel: **050 811 440**. Email: **info@kleinstrand.be**

In a convenient location, only 10 km. from Bruges, this site is in two distinct areas divided by an access road. The touring half of the campsite has 128 large pitches on flat grass and all with electricity. This central block of touring pitches is surrounded by semi-permanent caravans on the outer edges and it is a surprisingly relaxing area. The static half is closer to the lake and this area has most of the amenities. These include the main reception building, two restaurants, takeaways, bar, minimarket, and most of the sports facilities. This is a family holiday site with plenty of activities. A programme of activities and entertainment is provided in July/August. Water-ski shows take place on the lake (every Sunday in July and August at 17.00) and there is a water-ski school (charged for). The lake also has a swimming area with a slide, boat and kayak rental and beach volleyball area. In low season the site would also make a good base for sightseeing.

Facilities

A single modern, heated, toilet block in the touring area provides the usual facilities including good sized showers (charged) and vanity style open washbasins. Facilities for disabled campers. Laundry. Additional toilet facilities are located behind the touring field reception building and are opened for July/August. Motorcaravan service point. In high season a fun pool for small children and an adventure playground for older children. Barrier card deposit € 25. Off site: Golf 10 km. Riding 5 km.

Open: All year.

Directions

From Dunkirk take A10, then exit 6B signed Jabbeke. At roundabout take first exit signed for site. If missed, there is a second turn after a further 200 m. GPS: N51:11.071 E03:06.268

Charges 2007

Per unit incl. up to 6 persons and electricity	€ 15,00 - € 28,00
dog	€ 2,00

BE0530 Camping du Waux-Hall

Avenue Saint-Pierre 17, B-7000 Mons (Hainault)

Tel: **065 337 923**. Email: **ot1@ville.mons.be**

Waux-Hall is a useful and convenient site for a longer look at historic Mons and the surrounding area. It is a well laid out municipal site, close to the town centre and E42 motorway. The 75 pitches, most with electricity (10A), are arranged on either side of an oval road, on grass and divided by beds of small shrubs; the landscape maintenance is excellent. The pitches are small and manoeuvring could be difficult for larger units. A large public park with refreshment bar, tennis, a playground and a lake are adjacent, with direct access from the site when the gate is unlocked. Places to visit include the house of Van Gogh, the Fine Arts Museum, Decorative Arts Museum and the Collegiate church. The site has a new manager, Mme. Saucez.

Facilities

A single, heated toilet block is of older style, basic but clean, with most washbasins in cubicles for ladies. Washing machine and dryer. Soft drinks machine and ice cream. Bicycle hire. Tennis. Playground. Off site: Public park adjacent. Town centre shops and restaurants within easy walking distance. Fishing 300 m. Riding 2 km. Golf 4 km.

Open: All year.

Directions

From Mons inner ring road, follow signs for Charleroi, La Louviere, Binche, Beaumont. When turning off the ring road, keep to right hand lane, turning for site is immediately first right (signed Waux-Hall and camping).

Charges guide

Per unit incl. 1 person	€ 5,20 - € 6,10
extra adult	€ 3,35
child (0-12 yrs)	€ 2,15
electricity aftrer 2 nights (per Kw)	€ 0,15
No credit cards.	

BE0650 Camping Floreal Club Het Veen

Eekhoornlaan 1, B-2960 Sint Job in't Goor (Antwerp)

Tel: 036 361 327. Email: het.veen@florealclub.be

Floréal Club Het Veen is a modern, good value site, 20 km. from Antwerp. In a woodland area and with many sports facilities, it has good security and an efficient reception. There are 319 marked pitches (60 for touring units) on level grass, most with some shade and electricity (10A, long leads in some places) and also 7 hardstandings. Amenities include an indoor sports hall (charged per hour) and courts for tennis, football, basketball and softball are outside. Good opportunities for cycling and walking exist in the area. English is spoken.

Facilities

Four modern, spacious toilet blocks include a few washbasins in cubicles (only two are close to tourist pitches). Well equipped facilities for disabled people. Dishwashing and laundry facilities. Motorcaravan services. Well stocked shop. Restaurant, bar, café and takeaway (daily July/Aug. weekends only at other times). Tennis. Badminton. Volleyball. Softball. Basketball. Football. Table tennis. Boules. Exciting playgrounds and children's entertainment in season. Fishing. Canoeing. Bicycle hire. Off site: Riding and golf 8 km.

Open: 1 March - 31 October.

Directions

Sint Job In't Goor is northeast of Antwerp. From A1 (E19) exit 4, turn southeast towards Sint Job In't Goor, straight on at traffic lights and, immediately after canal bridge, turn left at campsite sign. Continue straight on for about 1.5 km. to site.

Charges 2007

Per person	€ 3,80
child (3-11 yrs)	€ 2,80
pitch incl. electricity	€ 9,40
hiker/cyclist and tent	€ 5,70
animal	€ 3,40

BE0565 Kompas Camping Westende

Bassevillestraat 141, B-8434 Westende (West Flanders)

Tel: 058 223 025. Email: westende@kompascamping.be

Part of the Kompas chain, Camping Westende is another large holiday site with 422 pitches. Of these 130 are taken by seasonal units and 5 chalets, leaving around 300 touring pitches. These are generally individual, on grass and with 10A electricity. There are 39 multi-service pitches with water, waste water drain and electricity. When we visited some pitches were looking rather well worn and untidy and would have benefited from a good clean up and reseeding. The rigid pitching policy dictates that caravans have to be placed on a specific side of the pitch, which may mean that you have to manhandle your UK built van into a nose in situation. All the main services are grouped around reception which can be a fair walk from the far end of the site.

Facilities

Four main toilet blocks are in modern style but suffer from heavy use and variable maintenance and cleaning. Facilities for children and disabled people at each block. Shop, bar, restaurant and takeaway (Easter - 14/11, but weekends only outside July/Aug. and certain public holidays). Adventure playground. Tennis. Boules. Children's entertainment and activities programme (July/Aug). Off site: Fishing 20 m. Golf 100 m. Beach 800 m. Bicycle hire 500 m. Riding and sailing 5 km. Markets in Nieuwpoort Friday, Middelkerke Thursday.

Open: Easter - 14 November.

Directions

Westende is 15 km. southwest of Ostende. From A18 (E40) take exit 3 to Nieuwpoort, turn right at traffic lights in town centre, and follow road round to the left, turning right at War Memorial, and left to Westende. Go along the main street, passing two sites on the right, turn left into Hovenierstraat. GPS: N51:09.487 E02:45.628

Charges 2008

Per unit incl. 4 persons	€ 22,00 - € 32,50
extra person	€ 5,00
electricity	€ 2,30
Camping Cheques accepted.	

BE0560 Camping De Lombarde

Elisabethlaan 4, B-8434 Lombardsijde Middelkerke (West Flanders)

Tel: 058 236 839. Email: info@delombarde.be

De Lombarde is a spacious, good value holiday site, between Lombardsijde and the coast. It has a pleasant atmosphere and modern buildings. The 380 pitches are set out in level, grassy bays surrounded by shrubs, all with electricity (16/20A, long leads may be needed). Vehicles are parked in separate car parks. There are many seasonal units and 22 holiday homes, leaving 180 touring pitches. There is a range of activities (listed below) and an entertainment programme in season. This is a popular holiday area and the site becomes full at peak times. A pleasant stroll takes you into Lombardsijde. There is a tram service to the town or the beach.

Facilities

Three modern heated, clean sanitary units are of an acceptable standard, with some washbasins in cubicles. Facilities for disabled people. Large laundry. Motorcaravan services. Shop (1/4-31/8). Restaurant/bar and takeaway (July/Aug. plus weekends and holidays 21/3-11/11). Tennis. Fishing lake. Entertainment for for children. Playground. Internet access. Torch useful. Off site: Beach 400 m. Riding and golf 500 m. Bicycle hire 1 km.

Open: All year.

Directions

Coming from Westende, follow the tramlines. From traffic lights in Lombarsijde, turn left following tramlines into Zeelaan. Continue following tramlines until crossroads and tram stop, turn left into Elisabethlaan. Site is on right after 200 m.

Charges 2007

Per unit incl. electricity	€ 15,50 - € 28,00
extra person	€ 2,80
dog (1 per pitch)	€ 2,60

BE0580 Camping Memling

Veltemweg 109, B-8310 Brugge (West Flanders)

Tel: 3250 35 58 45. Email: info@campingmemling.be

This traditional site is ideal for visiting Brugge. The 100 unmarked pitches (60 for touring units) are on slightly undulating grass, with gravel roads and trees and hedges that provide some shade. Electricity (6A) is available to 40 pitches. There is a separate area for tents. Bars, restaurants, local shops and supermarkets are within walking distance. Brugge itself has a network of cycle ways and for those on foot a bus runs into the centre from nearby. Visitors with large units should telephone in advance to ensure an adequate pitch. Necessary to make a reservation in July and August.

Facilities

Heated toilet facilities are clean and tidy, including some washbasins in cubicles. Facilities for disabled visitors. Laundry facilities. Freezer for campers' use. Club/TV room for 30 persons. Bicycle hire. Internet access. Off site: Municipal swimming pool (open all year) and park nearby. Supermarkets 250 m. The Maldegem Steam Centre and narrow gauge railway are 12 km. To the southwest of the town is the Boudewijn park and dolphinarium.

Open: All year.

Directions

From R30 Brugge ring road take exit 6 onto the N9 towards Maldegem. At Sint-Kruis turn right at traffic lights, where site signed (close to garage and supermarket, opposite MacDonald's).

Charges 2008

Per person	€ 5,00
child (under 15 yrs)	€ 4,00
pitch	€ 11,00 - € 25,00
electricity	€ 2,00

BE0570 Camping Jeugdstadion

Bolwerkstraat 1, B-8900 Ieper (West Flanders)

Tel: 057 217 282. Email: info@jeugdstadion.be

Camping Jeugdstadion is a small municipal close to the historic old town. At present there are only 21 caravan pitches, 12 on hardstandings and all with electricity (6A), plus a separate area for 15 tents. The barrier key also operates the lock for the toilet block. At the end of Leopold III Laan is the Menin Gate built in 1927, bearing the names of British and Commonwealth soldiers who lost their lives between 1914-1918. The last post is sounded below the gate at 8 pm. every evening in their honour.

Facilities

The modern, heated but fairly basic toilet block can struggle to cope in busy periods. It has cold water for washbasins and three sinks for dishwashing outside. Bicycle hire. Minigolf. Boules. Deposit required for barrier key. Off site: Sports complex adjacent. Indoor and outdoor swimming pools 500 m. Very large comprehensive playground. Minigolf. During school holidays these facilities are extensively used by local children and can therefore be fairly busy and lively.

Open: 16 March - 31 October.

Directions

Site is southeast of the city centre. From N336 (Lille) at roundabout by the Lille Gate, turn left on Picanolaan and take first right into Leopold III laan. Jeugdstadion entrance is on the right. Use roadside parking spaces and book in at 'Kantine' (08.00-19.00 hrs) on left inside gates. Alternatively go straight to the vehicle gate and walk through the site to book in.

Charges 2007

Per person	€ 3,00
caravan pitch incl. electricity	€ 4,50

BE0735 Camping Petite Suisse

Al Bounire 27, B-6960 Dochamps (Luxembourg)

Tel: 084 444 030. Email: info@petitesuisse.be

A member of the same group as Parc de la Clusure (BE0670), this quiet site is set in the picturesque countryside of the Belgium Ardennes, a region where rivers flow through valleys bordered by vast forests where horses are still usefully employed. Set on a southerly slope, the site is mostly open and offers wide views of the surrounding countryside. The 205 touring pitches, all with 10A electricity, are either on open sloping ground or in terraced rows with hedges between the rows and trees providing some separation. Gravel site roads provide access. To the right of the entrance barrier a large wooden building houses reception, a bar and restaurant and some sanitary facilities. Close by is an attractive outdoor pool with wide terraces surrounded by grass. Behind this is a large play area adjoining a small terrace. Although the site has many activities on offer the opportunity should not be missed to make excursions into the countryside with its hills and forests. The villages are filled with houses built from the local stone and small inviting bars and restaurants just waiting to be visited.

Facilities

All the facilities that one would expect of a large site are available. Showers are free, washbasins both open and in cabins. Baby room. Laundry room with washing machines and dryers. Shop. Restaurant, bar and takeaway. Swimming pool, paddling pool and slide. Sports field. Tennis. Bicycle hire. Playground and club for children. Entertainment programme (1/6-1/9). Varied activity programme, including archery, canoeing, climbing, abseiling and walking. Off site: La Roche en Ardennes 10 km. Golf 20 km.

Open: All year.

Directions

From E25/A26 autoroute (Liège - Luxembourg) take exit 50 then the N89 southwest towards La Roche. After 8 km. turn right (north) on N841 to Dochamps where site is signed. GPS: N50:13.832 E05:37.870

Charges 2007

Per pitch incl. 2 persons	€ 18,00 - € 25,00
extra person (over 4 yrs)	€ 4,00 - € 5,00
electricity	€ 3,50
dog	€ 4,00 - € 5,00

No credit cards.
Camping Cheques accepted.

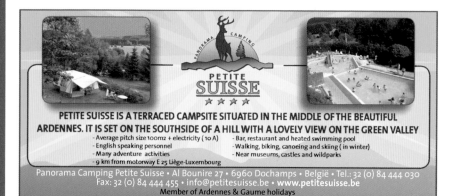

PETITE SUISSE IS A TERRACED CAMPSITE SITUATED IN THE MIDDLE OF THE BEAUTIFUL ARDENNES. IT IS SET ON THE SOUTHSIDE OF A HILL WITH A LOVELY VIEW ON THE GREEN VALLEY
- Average pitch size 100m2 + electricity (10 A)
- English speaking personnel
- Many adventure activities
- 9 km from motorway E 25 Liège-Luxembourg
- Bar, restaurant and heated swimming pool
- Walking, biking, canoeing and skiing (in winter)
- Near museums, castles and wildparks

Panorama Camping Petite Suisse • Al Bounire 27 • 6960 Dochamps • België • Tel.: 32 (0) 84 444 030
Fax: 32 (0) 84 444 455 • info@petitesuisse.be • www.petitesuisse.be
Member of Ardennes & Gaume holidays

BE0740 Camping l'Eau Rouge

Cheneux 25, B-4970 Stavelot (Liège)

Tel: 080 863 075. Email: info@eaurouge.nl

A popular, lively and attractively situated site, l'Eau Rouge is in a sheltered valley close to Spa and the Grand Prix circuit. There are 180 grassy pitches of 110 sq.m. on sloping ground either side of a central road (speed bumps) – 60 are taken by permanent units and 120 for touring units. The main building houses the busy reception, shop, bar and the main sanitary facilities. There are plenty of sporting activities in the area including skiing and luge in winter. The site is close to the motor race circuit at Spa Francorchamps and is within walking distance for the fit.

Facilities

There is a main block, a smaller unit serves the touring area. Good numbers of British WCs, mostly open washbasins, but fewer hot showers (free) – which could be stretched at times. Shop. Baker calls 08.30 in season. Takeaway (in summer). Bar. Archery (free lessons in high season). Playground. Entertainment in season. Off site: Bicycle hire 6 km. Riding 10 km.

Open: All year.

Directions

Site is 1 km. east of Stavelot on the road to the race circuit. Leave E42 exit 11 Malmédy. At roundabout follow signs for Stavelot. At end of road at T-junction turn right, then first right. GPS: N50:24.722 E05:57.190

Charges 2007

Per person	€ 2,25
pitch incl. electricity (10A)	€ 12,00

BE0578 Camping Ter Duinen

Wenduinesteenweg 143, B-8421 De Haan (West Flanders)

Tel: **050 413 593**

Ter Duinen is a large, seaside holiday site with 120 touring pitches and over 700 privately owned static holiday caravans. Pitches are laid out in straight lines each side of tarmac roads and the site has three immaculate toilet blocks. Other than a bar, a playing field and a little shop, the site has little else to offer, but it is only a 400 m. walk to the sea and next door to the site is a large sports complex with a sub-tropical pool and several sporting facilities. There are opportunities for riding and golf (18 hole course) close by.

Facilities

Three modern toilet blocks have good fittings, washbasins in cubicles (cold water only) and showers (€ 1.20). Baby bath. Facilities for disabled visitors. Two launderettes with two washing machines and a dryer, irons and ironing boards. Motorcaravan service point. Shop (closed Wed). Snack bar. Off site: Sea with sandy beach 400 m. Bicycle hire 400 m. Riding 1 km. Golf 3 km. Boat launching 6 km. A bus for Brugge stops 200 m. from the site, a tram for the coast 400 m.

Open: 16 March - 15 October.

Directions

On E40 in either direction take exit for De Haan and Jabbeke. In De Haan drive through centre and turn right in front of the station (don't cross the tramlines). Follow the Wenduinesteenweg to the site on the right.

Charges guide

Per unit incl. 2 persons and electricity	€ 15,00 - € 20,00
extra person	€ 2,25

Camping Cheques accepted.

BE0670 Camping Parc La Clusure

Chemin de la Clusure 30, B-6927 Bure-Tellin (Luxembourg)

Tel: **084 360 050**. Email: **info@parclaclusure.be**

Set in a river valley in the lovely wooded uplands of the Ardennes, known as the l'Homme Valley touring area, Parc La Clusure has 425 large marked, grassy pitches (350 for touring). All have access to electricity, cable TV and water taps and are mostly in avenues off a central, tarmac road. There is some noise from the nearby railway. There is a very pleasant, well lit riverside walk (the river is shallow in summer and popular for children to play in). The site's heated swimming pool and children's pool have a poolside bar and terrace. The site is used by a tour operator (the number of pitches varies). The famous Grottes of Han are nearby, also the Eurospace center and Lavaux St Anne castle . Those preferring quieter entertainment might enjoy the Topiary Park at Durbuy.

Facilities

Three sanitary units (one heated in winter) include some washbasins in cubicles facilities for babies and family bathrooms. Facilities for disabled persons. Motorcaravan services. Well stocked shop, bar, restaurant, snack bar and takeaway (all 21/3-2/11). Swimming pools (26/4-13/9). Bicycle hire. Tennis. New playgrounds. Organised activity programme including canoeing, archery, abseiling, mountain biking and climbing (Easter - Autumn). Caving. Fishing (licence essential). WiFi. Barrier card deposit (€ 20). Off site: Riding 7 km. Golf 25 km.

Open: All year.

Directions

Site is signed north at the roundabout off the Rochefort - St Hubert N803 road at Bure, 8 km. southeast of Rochefort with a narrow, fairly steep, winding descent to site.
GPS: N50:05.788 E05:17.230

Charges 2007

Per pitch incl. 2 persons	€ 19,00 - € 26,00
extra person	€ 4,00 - € 5,00
electricity (16A)	€ 3,50
dog	€ 4,00

Camping Cheques accepted.

Check real time availability and at-the-gate prices...

www.**alanrogers**.com

BE0590 Camping De Gavers

Onkerzelestraat 280, B-9500 Geraardsbergen (East Flanders)

Tel: 054 416 324. Email: gavers@oost-vlaanderen.be

Domein de Gavers is a modern, well organised holiday site in a peaceful location adjacent to a large sports complex, about 5 km. outside Geraardsbergen. A busy site in season, there is good security and a card operated barrier. Most of the 448 grassy, level pitches are taken by seasonal units but about 80 are left for touring units. Pitches are arranged on either side of surfaced access roads with some hedges and few trees to provide shade in parts, with electricity available to most. The site offers an extensive range of sporting activities and a full entertainment programme over a long season.

Facilities

Six modern, heated and well equipped sanitary buildings provide hot showers on payment (€ 0.50). Modern rooms for disabled people and babies. Launderette. No motorcaravan services. Shop (July/Aug). Restaurant and takeaway. Cafeteria and bars (daily 1/4-30/9, otherwise weekends). Heated indoor pool. Outdoor pool (1/5-31/8). Excellent playground. Tennis. Minigolf. Fishing. Sailing. Bicycle hire. Swimming and beach area at lake. Climbing. Off site: Bars and restaurants within 1.5 km.

Open: All year.

Directions

From E429/A8 exit 26 towards Edingen, take the N255 and N495 to Geraardsbergen. Down a steep hill, then left at site sign towards Onkerzele, through village and turn north to site. From E40/A10, exit at junction 17 on to N42, turn left onto the N495 and follow instructions as above.

Charges guide

Per unit incl. electricity	€ 10,00 - € 20,00
tent pitch	€ 10,00 - € 16,00

Discounts of 5-30% for longer stays.

BE0595 Kompas Camping Oudenaarde

Kortrijkstraat 342, B-9700 Oudenaarde (East Flanders)

Tel: 055 315 473. Email: oudenaarde@kompascamping.be

This is an extensive holiday site with 381 pitches, 179 of which are for touring. The remainder are occupied by 190 seasonal units, rental or private chalets, and a few pitches for a tour operator. Pitches are generally on grass all with 10A electricity hook-ups (31 also with water) and are of a reasonable size, some divided by hedges. The majority of the services are grouped around a central square close to reception, but some of the sporting facilities are at the far end of the site by the pool.

Facilities

Four toilet blocks all of a similar design include some facilities for babies and disabled campers. Block E has some washbasins in cubicles. Bar/restaurant and takeaway (30/3-11/11, weekends only outside July/August, public holidays). Shop. Swimming pool. Indoor playroom and several playgrounds for children. Boules. Tennis. Bicycle hire. Fishing. Children's entertainment and activities programme in July/August. Off site: Golf 3 km. Shops and other services in Oudenaarde 4 km. Riding 7 km.

Open: 30 March - 11 November.

Directions

Oudenaarde is 25 km. south of Ghent. From main N60 (Ghent - Ronse) road, take exit to Avelgem on N453. (just north of River Schelde). Continue west for 2.5 km. and follow rather small site signs to your right. GPS: N50:50.459 E03:34.476

Charges 2008

Per unit incl. 4 persons	€ 21,00 - € 29,50
extra person	€ 5,00
electricity	€ 2,30

Camping Cheques accepted.

BE0600 Camping Groeneveld

Groenevelddreef, Bachte-Maria-Leerne, B-9800 Deinze (East Flanders)

Tel: 093 801 014. Email: info@campinggroeneveld.be

Quiet and clean is how Rene Kuys describes his campsite. Groeneveld is a traditional site in a small village within easy reach of Gent. It has a friendly atmosphere and is also open over a long season. Although this site has 108 pitches, there is a fair number of seasonal units, leaving around 50 large touring pitches with electricity (10A). Hedges and borders divide the grassy area, access roads are gravel and there is an area for tents. Family entertainment and activities organised in high season include themed, musical evenings, barbecues, petanque matches, etc.

Facilities

Two clean sanitary units of differing age and design provide British style WCs, washbasins and free hot showers (new facilities are due in 2007/8). Motorcaravan services. Freezer (free). Bar/café (July/Aug. and weekends) with a good range of snacks, and a range of local beers. Small coarse fishing lake. Floodlit petanque. Adventure style play area. TV room. Internet access (at reception). Off site: Shops and restaurants. Golf 3 km.

Open: 26 March - 12 November.

Directions

From A10 (E40) exit 13, turn south on N466. After 3 km. continue straight on at roundabout and site is on left on entering village (opposite a large factory). Note: yellow signs are very small.

Charges 2008

Per unit incl. 2 persons & car	€ 17,50 - € 23,00
2 persons and tent	€ 13,00 - € 15,00

No credit cards.

BE0610 Camping Blaarmeersen

Zuiderlaan 12, B-9000 Gent (East Flanders)

Tel: **092 668 160**. Email: **camping.blaarmeersen@gent.be**

Blaarneersen is a comfortable, well managed municipal site in the west of the city. It adjoins a sports complex and a fair sized lake which together provide facilities for a variety of watersports, tennis, squash, minigolf, football, athletics track, roller skating and a playground. The 205 individual, flat, grassy touring pitches are separated by tall hedges and mostly arranged in circular groups; with electricity to 178. There are 40 hardstandings for motorcaravans, plus a separate area for tents with barbecue facility. Some noise is possible as the city ring road is close. There is a good network of paths and cycle routes around the city.

Facilities	Directions
Four sanitary units of a decent standard vary in size. Most of the 36 free hot showers are in one block. Showers and toilets for disabled people. Laundry. Motorcaravan services. Shop, café/bar (both daily March - Oct). Takeaway. Sports facilities. Playground. Fishing on site in winter, otherwise 500 m. Lake swimming. Off site: Bicycle hire 5 km. Riding and golf 10 km. **Open:** 1 March - 15 October.	From E40 take exit 13 (Gent-West) and follow dual carriageway for 5 km. Cross second bridge and look for Blaarmeersen sign, turning sharp right and following signs to leisure complex. In city avoid overpasses – most signs are on the lower levels. GPS: N51:02.833 E03:41.000

Charges 2007

Per person	€ 4,50
pitch	€ 5,50 - € 7,00
electricity	€ 1,25

BE0630 Camping Grimbergen

Veldkantsraat 64, B-1850 Grimbergen (Brabant)

Tel: **022 709 597**. Email: **camping.grimbergen@telenet.be**

A popular little municipal site with a friendly atmosphere, Camping Grimbergen has 90 pitches on fairly level grass, of which around 50 have electricity (10A). The site is not really suitable for large units, although four pitches for motorcaravans have been added. The municipal sports facilities are adjacent and the site is well placed for visiting Brussels. The bus station is by the traffic lights at the junction of N202 and N211, as well as 150 m. from the campsite and buses run into the city centre every 15 minutes. In Grimbergen itself visit Norbertine Abbey and the Sunday morning market.

Facilities	Directions
Immaculate sanitary facilities are heated in colder months. Separate facilities for disabled people. Motorcaravan services. Adventure playground. Off site: Fishing 800 m. **Open:** 1 April - 31 October.	From Brussels ring road take exit 7 (N202) to Grimbergen. After 2.5 km, turn right at traffic lights on N211 towards Vilvoorde (site signed), then left at second set of lights (slightly oblique turn). Site entrance is on right in 500 m. (watch for blue and white sign 'Lammekenshoeve').

Charges 2007

Per person	€ 4,50
pitch incl. electricity	€ 5,00 - € 10,00
No credit cards.	

BE0640 Camping Druivenland

Nijvelsebaan 80, B-3090 Overijse (Brabant)

Tel: **026879368**. Email: **info@campingdruivenland.be**

This small, peaceful site is within easy reach of Brussels and also close to 25,000 hectares of woodland where you can enjoy some of the best Belgian countryside by foot or by cycle. Neat and mature, the site is well looked after and family run. It has a large open touring field or further pitches available in the sheltered area of the static park. The pitches are slightly sloping but almost all have views over the countryside – in total there are 120 pitches, with 40 for touring units, all with electricity (16A).

Facilities	Directions
Fully equipped toilet block with some washbasins in cabins and toilets for children. Well laid out provision for disabled visitors (shower room and toilet/washroom). Washing machine and dryer. Kept extremely clean at all times, it is of a very high standard. Limited shop with some fresh food. Boules. Off site: Golf 3 km. **Open:** 15 March - 15 October.	From E411 Brussels - Namur road take exit 3 to Overijse (not exit 2). After 1 km. turn right signed Tombeek, Waver and Terlanen. Site is 1 km. on right.

Charges 2007

Per unit incl. 2 persons	€ 15,00 - € 17,00
extra person	€ 2,00
electricity	€ 2,00

BE0655 Camping De Lilse Bergen

Strandweg 6, Gierle, B-2275 Lille (Antwerp)

Tel: **014 557 901**. Email: **info@lilsebergen.be**

This attractive, quietly located holiday site has 503 shady pitches, of which 241 all with electricity (10A) are for touring units. Set on sandy soil among pine trees and rhododendrons and arranged around a large lake, the site has a Mediterranean feel. It is well fenced, with a night guard and comprehensive, well labelled, fire fighting equipment. Cars are parked away from units. The site is really child friendly with each access road labelled with a different animal symbol to enable children to find their own unit easily. An entertainment programme is organised in high season. The lake has marked swimming and diving areas (adult), a sandy beach, an area for watersports, plus a separate children's pool complex (depth 60 cm.) with a most imaginative playground. There are lifeguards and the water meets 'Blue Flag' standards. A building by the lake houses changing rooms, extra toilets and showers and a baby room. There are picnic areas and lakeside or woodland walks.

Facilities

Four of the six main toilet blocks have been fully refitted to a good standard and can be heated. Some washbasins in cubicles and good hot showers (on payment). Well equipped baby rooms. Facilities for disabled campers. Laundry. Barrier 'keys' can be charged up with units for operating showers, washing machine etc. First aid post. Motorcaravan service point. Restaurant (all year, weekends only in winter), takeaway and well stocked shop (Easter - 30/9; weekends only outside July/Aug). Tennis. Minigolf. Boules. Climbing wall. Playground, trampolines and skateboard ramp. Pedaloes, windsurfers and bicycles for hire. Children's electric cars and pedal kart tracks (charged for). Off site: Golf 1 km. Riding 1 km.

Open: All year.

Directions

From E34 Antwerp-Eindhoven take exit 22. On the roundabout take the exit for 'Lilse Bergen' and follow forest road to site entrance.
GPS: N51:17.345 E04:51.305

Charges 2007

Per unit incl. electricity (10A)	€ 18,00 - € 24,00
dog	€ 4,00

BE0700 Camping Spa d'Or

Stockay 17, B-4845 Sart-lez-Spa (Liège)

Tel: **087 474 400**. Email: **info@campingspador.be**

Camping Spa d'Or is set in a beautiful area of woodlands and picturesque villages, 4 km. from the town of Spa (the 'Pearl of the Ardennes'). The site is on the banks of a small river and is an ideal starting point for walks and bicycle trips through the forests. The Dutch owners have long term plans to upgrade the site which had been rather neglected. With 310 pitches in total, 240 are for touring (40 places are reserved for tents). The touring pitches have an open aspect, most are slightly sloping and all have 10A electricity connections.

Facilities

One new large, bright and cheerful sanitary block and one new smaller block (portacabin) both with all the usual facilities. Room for visitors with disabilities. Laundry. Shop (1/4-24/10). Bar, restaurant and takeaway (1/4-24/10). Outdoor heated swimming pool (1/5-15/9). Play area with good equipment. TV in bar. Goal posts and two boules courts. Entertainment during July and August. Off site: Fishing 2 km. Golf and riding 5 km. Maps for cycling and walking on sale at reception. Spa 4 km.

Open: All year.

Directions

From E42 take exit 9 and follow the signs to Spa d'Or. GPS: N50:30.455 E05:55.171

Charges 2007

Per unit incl. 2 persons	€ 16,50 - € 21,50
extra person (over 3 yrs)	€ 4,00 - € 4,50
tent incl. 2 persons.	€ 12,00 - € 15,00
electricity	€ 3,00
dog	€ 4,00

BE0660 Camping Baalse Hei

Roodhuisstraat 10, B-2300 Turnhout (Antwerp)

Tel: **014 448 470**. Email: **info@baalsehei.be**

The 'Campine' is an area covering three-quarters of the Province of Antwerp, noted for its nature reserves, pine forests, meadows and streams and is ideal for walking and cycling, while Turnhout itself is an interesting old town. Baalse Hei is a long-established, friendly site. It has 459 pitches including a separate touring area of 70 large pitches, all with 16A electricity, TV connections and a shared water point, on a large grass field, thoughtfully developed with young trees and bushes. Cars are parked away from the pitches. Large motorcaravans can be accommodated (phone first to check availability). There is also a fully equiped bungalow for rent. It is 100 m. from the edge of the field to the modern, heated, sanitary building. There is a small lake for swimming with a beach, a boating lake and a large fishing lake (on payment). Entertainment and activities are organised in high season. Walk in the woods and you will undoubtedly come across some of the many red squirrels or take the pleasant 1.5 km. riverside walk to the next village. Arrival after 16.00, departure before 12 noon.

Facilities

The toilet block provides hot showers on payment (€ 0.50), some washbasins in cabins and facilities for disabled visitors. Launderette. Motorcaravan services. Café/restaurant (daily 1/4-31/10, w/ends only other times, closed 16/11-25/1). Breakfast served in high season. Shop (all year). Club/TV room. Lake swimming. Fishing. Two tennis courts. Boules. Adventure play area. Bicycle hire. English is spoken. Off site: Riding 1.5 km. Golf 15 km.

Open: 16 January - 15 December

Directions

Site is northeast of Turnhout off the N119. From Antwerp on E34/A12 take Turnhout ring road to the end (not a complete ring) and turn right. There is a small site sign to right in 1.5 km. then a country lane. GPS: N51:21.280 E04:57.300

Charges 2008

Per unit all inclusive	€ 16,00 - € 24,00
electricity	€ 1,00
2 cyclists and tent	€ 10,00 - € 13,00
dog	€ 1,25
No credit cards.	

Baalse Hei offers a calm and quiet environment, boarding a nature reserve north of Turnhout. There are several lakes used for swimming, fishing and rowing. Football, volley- basket- and tennis facilities. A lot of cycling routes in the area. Caravans, Hikers' cabins and bicycle hire. Via E34/A12 Eindhoven-Antwerpen, exit n° 24. **Roodhuisstraat 10, 2300 Turnhout (Belgium) Tel. +32 (0)14 44 84 70 • Fax +32 (0)14 44 84 74 www.baalsehei.be • info@baalsehei.be**

BE0770 Camping le Vieux Moulin

Petite Strument 62, B-6980 La Roche-en-Ardenne (Luxembourg)

Tel: **084 411 380**. Email: **info@strument.com**

Located in one of the most beautiful valleys in the heart of the Ardennes, Le Vieux Moulin has 183 pitches and, although there are 127 long stay units at the far end of the site, the 60 touring pitches do have their own space. Some are separated by hedges, others for tents and smaller units are more open, all are on grass, and there are 50 electric hook-ups (6A). The 19th century water mill has been owned and operated by the owner's family for many years, but has now been converted into a small hotel and a fascinating mill museum.

Facilities

A newly constructed, centrally located toilet block is between the touring and long stay areas. It can be heated in cool weather and provides washbasins in cubicles and controllable hot showers on payment. Washing machine. No facilities for disabled persons. A further older unit is at the end of the mill building. Restaurant and bar with hotel (8 rooms). Mill museum. Off site: Town facilities 800 m.

Open: 1 April - 11 November.

Directions

From town centre take N89 south towards St Hubert, turning right towards Hives where site is signed. Site is 800 m. from the town centre. GPS: N50:10.417 E05:34.650

Charges 2007

Per person	€ 2,50
pitch	€ 8,50
electricity	€ 2,50
dog	€ 2,00

BE0675 Camping Spineuse

Rue de Malome 7, B-6840 Neufchâteau (Luxembourg)

Tel: **061 277 320**. Email: **info@camping-spineuse.be**

This Dutch-owned site lies about 2 km. from the town centre. It is on low lying, level grass, bordered by a river, with trees and shrubs dotted around the 87 grassy pitches. The main gravel access road can be dusty in dry weather. Seasonal units take 25 pitches leaving 62 for touring units, all with electricity (10/15A). There is also a separate area for tents. Parents of small children should be aware that there is unfenced water on site and a footbridge over the river with no guard rails. Reception is in the main building and keeps basic food items in July/August.

Facilities

Toilet facilities are in the central building and are looking dated with some cubicles small. Preset showers and open washbasins. No facilities for disabled campers. Washing machine and dryer. Extra facilities in a portacabin for July/Aug. Motorcaravan services. Bistro/bar (1/4-31/10). Small inflatable children's pool (1/6-30/9). Tennis. Boules. Small playground. Fishing. Off site: Riding 10 km.

Open: All year.

Directions

Site is 2 km. southwest of Neufchâteau on the N15 towards Florenville. There are three sites fairly close together, this is the last one on the left hand side.GPS: N49:49.899 E05:24.909

Charges 2007

Per person	€ 3,10
child (0-6 yrs)	€ 2,00
pitch incl. electricity	€ 11,25

BE0680 Camping Sud

Voie de la Liberté 75, B-6717 Attert (Luxembourg)

Tel: **063 223 715**. Email: **info@campingsudattert.com**

This is a pleasant family run site which would make a good base for a short stay and is also well sited for use as an overnight halt. The 86 touring pitches are on level grass with 6A electricity hook-ups and are arranged around an oval loop access road. There are 11 drive-through pitches especially for one-nighters, plus four hardstandings for motorcaravans and a tent area. The far end of the site is close to the N4 and may suffer from some road noise. On site facilities include a small restaurant/bar with takeaway facility and a shop for basics.

Facilities

A single building provides modern sanitary facilities including some washbasins in cubicles and baby areas. Showers are free in low season (€ 0.50 July/Aug). No facilities for disabled campers. Bar/restaurant and takeaway (1/4-25/10) TV in bar. Pool (May-Sept). Playground. Children's entertainment three afternoons per week during July/Aug. Off site: Supermarket, riding 5 km. Golf 8 km.

Open: 1 April - 25 October.

Directions

Attert is 8 km. north of Arlon. From N4 take Attert exit, continue east for 1 km. to Attert village, site entrance is immediately on your left as you join the main street. GPS: N49:44.894 E05:47.219

Charges 2007

Per person	€ 4,00
child (2-12 yrs)	€ 2,25
pitch with electricity	€ 10,25
No credit cards.	

BE0705 Camping l'Hirondelle

Château 1, B-4210 Oteppe (Liège)

Tel: **085 711 131**. Email: **info@lhirondelle.be**

This site is set in 20 hectares of woodland in the grounds of a castle that dates back to the 14th century. From the entrance, one gets a glimpse of the restaurant in one part of the castle. There are 800 pitches with 300 for tourers, all with 6A electricity. The pitches are arranged around a huge playground, basketball court and a building housing a games room, a supermarket and a bar. In high season the site offers a full programme of entertainment with film nights, sports tournaments, discos and contests. This is a pleasant site which has a lot to offer for children and teenagers.

Facilities

The two toilet blocks for tourers provide some washbasins in cabins, children's toilets and basins and a unisex baby room. Washing machine and dryer. Good provision for disabled visitors. Shop. Bar. Restaurant. Swimming pool (15 x 25 m). Huge adventure type playground. Boules. Playing field. Animation (5/7-21/8). Games room.

Open: 1 April - 31 October.

Directions

From Namen on the E42 take exit 10 towards Biewart then continue on the 80 to Burdinne. In Burdinne follow signs for Oteppe. The site is signed just before entering Oteppe.
GPS: N50:34.055 E05:07.031

Charges 2007

Per unit incl. 2 persons and electricity	€ 13,75 - € 21,00
extra person	€ 2,75 - € 4,00
extra small tent	€ 1,50

BE0710 Camping Colline de Rabais

Rue de Bonlieu, B-6760 Virton (Luxembourg)

Tel: **063 571 195**. Email: **info@collinederabais.be**

Colline de Rabais is a large site with an unusual layout. This comprises a circular road with smaller roads leading to circular pads with wedge shaped pitches. In a hill top setting, the site is surrounded by forest. The present Dutch owners took over in 1997 and are slowly revamping the site. There are around 250 pitches for touring units, all with 16A electricity (some long leads needed), plus 43 mobile homes and bungalows for rent and 22 tour operator tents. Various activities are organised throughout the season. A large sports complex is a walk away at the bottom of the hill offering tennis, fishing and much more. The forest is open to walkers and cyclists alike – you can go for ages without seeing another person.

Facilities

Three toilet blocks, one modernised with shower and washbasin cubicles and an en-suite room for disabled people. Cleaning and maintenance can be variable and not all blocks are open in low season. Washing machines and dryers. Motorcaravan service point. Bar/restaurant and shop (opening times vary). Small outdoor swimming pool (1/5-1/10) with wood decking for sunbathing. Bicycle hire. Off site: Fishing 1 km. Riding 3 km.

Open: All year.

Directions

From E25/E411 take exit 29 towards Etalle and Virton. Follow signs for Vallée de Rabais. Turn right at sports complex. At crossroads (with phone box) turn right and uphill to site at end of road. GPS: N49:34.809 E05:32.864

Charges 2007

Per unit incl. 2 persons	€ 17,50 - € 23,00
extra person (over 2 yrs)	€ 4,00 - € 4,50
electricity (16A)	€ 3,00
dog	€ 4,00 - € 5,00

Never knew that Belgium could be so surprising!

Colline de Rabais CAMPING

www.collinederabais.be

BE0711 Ardennen Camping Bertrix

Route de Mortehan, B-6880 Bertrix (Luxembourg)

Tel: **061 412 281**. Email: **bertrix@kompascamping.be**

Bertrix is located at the heart of the Belgian Ardennes, between the towns of Bastogne and Bouillon. This site has been recommended to us and we hope to undertake a full inspection in 2008. The site overlooks the hills of the Semois valley with many walking and cycle routes to explore. Pitches here are large and grassy, all have 10A electrical connections and some also offer water and drainage. Bertrix is close to the E411 and E25 motorways and this site may prove a useful overnight stop. However, the site is well equipped with a restaurant, snack bar and various leisure facilities including a swimming pool.

Facilities

Shop. Restaurant, snack bar and bar. Takeaway meals. Swimming pool. Paddling pool. Play area. Games room. Sports field. TV room. Volleyball. Bicycle hire. Entertainment and activity programme. Motorcaravan services. Mobile homes and chalets for rent. Off site: Canoeing. Fishing. Walking and cycle trails. Shops and restaurants in Bertrix.

Open: 14 March - 16 November.

Directions

Take exit 25 from the E411 motorway and join the N89 to Bertrix. After 6.5 km. join the N884 to Bertrix and upon arrival in the town, follow signs to site. GPS: N49:50.270 E05:15.145

Charges 2007

Per unit incl. 2 persons	€ 17,00 - € 22,00
extra person (over 2 yrs)	€ 4,00 - € 4,50
electricity (10A)	€ 3,50

Check real time availability and at-the-gate prices...

www.**alanrogers**.com

BE0712 Camping Ile de Faigneul

Rue de la Cherizelle 54, B-6830 Poupehan-sur-Semois (Luxembourg)

Tel: 061 466 894. Email: iledefaigneul@belgacom.net

Few campsites are in sole possession of an island, and when that island lies in a beautiful tree lined valley the site is likely to be something special. Camping Isle de Faigneul is! This quiet, peaceful site, surrounded by the River Semois, is near the small village of Poupehan in the picturesque Belgium Ardennes. The 130 level pitches, all with electricity, on this grass covered island are all for touring units. The site's friendly owners, Alouis and Daniella van Zon-Berkes, who speak good English, took over the site a few years ago and have worked hard to return it to its present state of natural beauty.

Facilities

The well appointed sanitary block is new and maintained to the highest standard. Ultra modern, it has preset showers operated by key (deposit € 25) and some washbasins in cabins. Facilities for disabled visitors, family shower room, baby changing area. Laundry room. Shop. Bar and restaurant. Canoe rental. Fishing. Playground. Special area beside river for campfires.

Open: 1 April - 30 September.

Directions

From A4/E411 towards Luxembourg take exit 25 then N89 southwest to Bouillon. In Bouillon follow signs for Poupehan. The twisting road passes through the forests. Left over stone bridge and right (site signed) and follow road, site is over bridge to the right. GPS: N49:48.963 E05:00.940

Charges 2007

Per unit incl. 2 person	€ 21,90
incl. electricity	€ 24,65
extra person	€ 3,00

BE0715 Camping de Chênefleur

Norulle 16, B-6730 Tintigny (Luxembourg)

Tel: 063 444 078. Email: info@chenefleur.be

This is a comfortable site with 223 pitches (196 for tourers), set beside the Semois river, close to Luxembourg and France. All pitches have 6A electricity and are separated by young trees. On the whole the site is open but there is some shade. One of the guests we spoke to, a first time visitor, was very pleased with the spacious pitches and the peace and quiet on site. The site is still being developed, but Fred, the owner, is very enthusiastic and hardworking. It has a swimming pool (also used by the locals) and in high season entertainment is organised.

Facilities

2 new fully refurbished sanitary blocks, 1 with childrens sanitary facilities. Washing machine and dryer. Shop. Bar. Restaurant. Swimming pool. Two new play areas. Full animation programme in season. Bicycle hire (1/4-1/10). Off site: Riding 4 km. Luxembourg City 40 km.

Open: 1 April - 31 October.

Directions

From Luik follow E25 towards Luxembourg and continue on E411. Take exit 29 Habay-La-Neuve and continue to Etalle. From Etalle follow N83 to Florenville. Drive through Tintigny and follow site signs. GPS: N49:41.098 E05:31.230

Charges 2007

Per unit incl. 2 persons	€ 17,50 - € 23,00
extra person (over 3 yrs)	€ 4,00 - € 4,50
electricity (6A)	€ 3,00
Camping Cheques accepted.	

BE0720 Camping Tonny

Tonny 35, B-6680 Amberloup (Luxembourg)

Tel: 061 688 285. Email: camping.tonny@belgacom.net

With a friendly atmosphere, this family campsite is in a pleasant valley by the River Ourthe. It is an attractive small site with 75 grassy touring pitches, with wooden chalet buildings giving a Tyrolean feel. The pitches (80-100 sq.m.) are separated by small shrubs and fir trees withelectricity available. Cars are parked away from the units. There is a separate meadow for tents. Surrounded by natural woodland, The main chalet has a café/bar, a freestanding fireplace, and a shady terrace for relaxing outside. Camping Tonny is ideal for outdoor activities.

Facilities

Two fully equipped sanitary units (both heated in cool weather) include dishwashing and laundry sinks (all hot water is on payment). Baby area and laundry. Freezer for campers use. Small shop. Cafe/bar. TV lounge and library. Sports field. Boules. Games room. Playgrounds. Skittle alley. Bicycle hire. Fishing. Canoeing. Cross country skiing.

Open: 15 February - 15 November.

Directions

From N4 take exit for Libramont at km.131 (N826), then to Amberloup (4 km.) where site is signed just outside of the southwest town boundary. GPS: N50:01.594 E05:30.770

Charges 2007

Per person	€ 4,00
pitch with electricity (4A)	€ 10,40 - € 10,90
Off season discounts for over 55s and longer stays.	

BE0780 Family Camping Wilhelm Tell

Hoeverweg 87, B-3660 Opglabbeek (Limburg)

Tel: 089 854 444. Email: receptie@wilhelmtell.com

Wilhelm Tell is a family run site that caters particularly well for children with its indoor and outdoor pools and lots of entertainment throughout the season. There are 128 pitches with 70 available for touring units, some separated, others on open fields. There are 60 electricity connections (10A) and, for winter use, 20 hardstandings. The super bar/restaurant has access for wheelchair users. M. Lode Nulmans has a very special attitude towards his customers and tries to ensure they leave satisfied and want to return. For example, in his restaurant he says 'it serves until you are full'. The Limburg region is a relaxing area with much to do, including shopping or touring the historic towns with a very enjoyable choice of food and drink!

Facilities

Toilet facilities are adequate. Facilities around the pool supplement at busy times. Baby room in reception area. Two en-suite units for disabled visitors. Laundry facilities. Motorcaravan service point. Fridge hire. Bar/restaurant and snack bar (times vary acc. to season). Outdoor heated pool with slide and wave machine (1/7-31/8) and indoor pool (all year) both well supervised. Play area.

Open: All year.

Directions

From E314 take exit 32 for Maaseik and follow 730 road towards As. From As follow signs to Opglabbeek. In Opglabbeek take first right at roundabout (Weg van Niel) then first left (Kasterstraat) to site. GPS: N51:01.711 E05:35.888

Charges 2008

Per person	€ 8,00
child	€ 4,00
pitch incl. electricity	€ 15,00

Less 30% in low season.
Camping Cheques accepted.

BE0725 Camping le Val de L'Aisne

Rue du TTA 1, B-6997 Erezee (Luxembourg)

Tel: 086 470 067. Email: info@levaldelaisne.be

From a nearby hill Château de Blier overlooks Camping Le Val de L'Aisne, a large site attractively laid out around a 1.5 hectare lake in the Belgium Ardennes. The site has 450 grass pitches with 150 for touring units, on level ground and with 10A electricity. Tarmac roads circle the site providing easy access. Trees provide some shade although the site is fairly open allowing views of the surrounding hills and the château. Activities play a large part on this site, ranging from quiet fishing in the lake to hectic quad bike tours in the surrounding hills.

Facilities

Three toilet blocks provide showers (paid for by token) and mainly open washbasins. Facilities for disabled people. Baby room. Washing machines and dryers. Motorcaravan service point. Bar/restaurant and snack bar with takeaway. Bread can be ordered in reception. On the lake: fishing, swimming, kayaks and pedal boats (to hire). Quad bike hire and tours arranged. Kayaks and mountain bike hire. Play area. Entertainment programme during summer and adventure games in the nearby wooded area. Off site: Riding, cycle and walking trails in the Ardennes woods.

Open: All year.

Directions

Leave the E411/A4 (Brussels - Luxembourg) motorway at exit 18 (Courière, Marche en Famenne), then southeast on the N4 to Marche. At Marche head northeast on N86 to Hotton, crossing bridge over the river. In Hotton follow signs for Soy and Erezée. Just west of Erezée at roundabout follow signs for La Roche. Site is 900 m. on the left.

Charges 2007

Per pitch incl. 2 persons and car	€ 18,00
extra person (over 3 yrs)	€ 3,00
electricity (3A)	€ 3,00

No credit cards. Reductions for longer periods of stay.

Belgium

BE0730 Camping Moulin de Malempré

1 Malempre, B-6960 Manhay (Luxembourg)

Tel: 086 455 504. Email: camping.malempre@cybernet.be

This pleasant countryside site, very close to the E25, is well worth a visit and the Dutch owners will make you very welcome (English is spoken). The reception building houses the office and a small shop, above which is an attractive bar and restaurant with open fireplace. The 140 marked touring pitches are separated by small shrubs and gravel roads on sloping terrain. All have 10A electricity, 40 have water and drainage as well and the site is well lit. There is a little traffic noise from the nearby E25 (not too intrusive). The star of this site is the main sanitary unit, an ultra-modern, two storey Scandinavian style building; this is complemented by a unisex unit.

Facilities

Modern toilet facilities include some washbasins in cubicles and family bathrooms on payment. The unisex unit can be heated and has a family shower room. Unit for disabled people. Baby room. Laundry. Motorcaravan services. Shop for basic provisions (15/5-31/8). Baker calls daily 08.30 - 09.15. Restaurant and bar (both 15/5-15/9 and weekends). Takeaway (15/5-15/9). Heated swimming pool and children's pools (15/5-15/9). TV. Boules. Playground. Off site: Bicycle hire 3 km. Riding 6 km. Fishing 10 km. Places to visit include the Hotton Grottoes, one of the prettiest Belgian caves (open daily April - Oct).

Open: 1 April - 31 October.

Directions

From E25/A26 (Liege-Bastogne) exit 49. Turn onto N651 (southwest) towards Manhay. After 220 m. turn sharp left (east) towards Lierneux. Follow signs for Malempré and site. GPS: N50:17.699 E05:43.390

Charges 2007

Per unit incl. 2 persons	€ 18,50 - € 22,00
extra adult	€ 4,00
child (3-12 yrs)	€ 2,75
electricity	€ 2,85
dog	€ 2,85

Less 20% in low season.

BE0732 Camping Floreal La Roche

Route de Holiffalize 18, B-6980 La Roche-en-Ardenne (Luxembourg)

Tel: 084 219 467. Email: camping.laroche@florealclub.be

Maintained to very high standards, this site is set in a beautiful wooded valley bordering the Ourthe river. Open all year, the site is located on the outskirts of the attractive small town of La Roche en Ardenne in an area understandably popular with tourists. The site is large with 600 grass pitches, of which 280 are for touring units. The pitches are on level ground and all have electricity. Amenities on site include a well stocked shop, a bar and restaurant and takeaway food. In the woods and rivers close by, there are plenty of opportunities for walking, mountain biking, rafting and canoeing.

Facilities

Six modern, well maintained sanitary blocks provide washbasins (open and in cabins), free preset showers. Facilities for disabled visitors. Baby room. Washing machines and dryers. Motorcaravan service point. Shop. Bar, restaurant, snack bar and takeaway. At Camping Floreal 1: outdoor heated swimming pool. Sports field. Tennis. Minigolf. Pétanque. Kayaks to rent. Off site: Indoor pool 800 m. Golf, riding and bicycle hire 1 km. Skiing 15 km.

Open: All year

Directions

From E25/A26 exit 50 take the N89 southwest to La Roche. In La Roche follow signs for Houffalize (beside Ourthe river). Floral Club Camping 1 is 1.5 km. along this road. N.B. Go to camping 1 not 2.

Charges 2007

Per person	€ 3,10
child (3-11 yrs)	€ 2,35
pitch	€ 7,90
pitch incl. electricity (4A)	€ 10,40
dog (max. 1)	€ 2,95

MAP 11

Croatia has thrown off old communist attitudes and blossomed into a lively and friendly place to visit. A country steeped in history, it boasts some of the finest Roman ruins in Europe and you'll find plenty of traditional coastal towns, clusters of tiny islands and mediaeval villages to explore.

Croatia

CAPITAL: ZAGREB

Tourist Office

Croatian National Tourist Office
2 The Lanchesters
162-164 Fulham Palace Road
London W6 9ER
Tel: 0208 563 7979 Fax: 0208 563 2616
Email: info@cnto.freeserve.co.uk
Internet: www.croatia.hr

The heart-shaped peninsula of Istria, located in the north, is among the most developed tourist regions in Croatia. Here you can visit the preserved Roman amphitheatre in Pula, the beautiful town of Rovinj with its cobbled streets and wooded hills, and the resort of Umag, well known for its recreational activities, most notably tennis. Islands are studded all around the coast, making it ideal for sailing and diving enthusiasts. Istria also has the highest concentration of campsites.

Further south, in the province of Dalmatia, Split is the largest city on the Adriatic coast and home to the impressive Diolectian's Palace. From here the islands of Brac, Hvar, Vis and Korcula, renowned for their lively fishing villages and pristine beaches, are easily accessible by ferry. The old walled city of Dubrovnik is 150 km south. At over 2 km. long and 25 m. high, with 16 towers, a walk along the city walls affords spectacular views.

Population
4.7 million

Climate
Predominantly warm and hot in summer with temperatures of up to 40°C.

Language
Croat

Telephone
The country code is 00 385.

Money
Currency: Kuna
Banks: Mon-Fri 08.00 - 19.00.

Shops
Mainly Mon-Sat 08.00-20.00, although some close on Monday.

Public Holidays
New Year's Day; Epiphany 6 Jan; Good Friday; Easter Monday; Labour Day 1 May; Parliament Day 30 May; Day of Anti-Fascist Victory 22 June; Statehood Day 25 June; Thanksgiving Day 5 Aug; Assumption 15 Aug; Independence Day 8 Oct; All Saints 1 Nov; Christmas 25, 26 Dec.

Motoring
Croatia is proceeding with a vast road improvement programme. There are still some roads which leave a lot to be desired but things have improved dramatically. Roads along the coast can become heavily congested in summer and queues are possible at border crossings. Tolls: some motorways, bridges and tunnels. Cars towing a caravan or trailer must carry two warning triangles. It is illegal to overtake military convoys.

Croatia

CR6720 Naturist Centre Ulika

Cervar, HR-52440 Porec (Istria)

Tel: 052 436 325. Email: mail@plavalaguna.hr

One of the many naturist campsites in Croatia, Ulika is run by the same concern as Zelena Laguna (CR6722) and Bijela Uvala (CR6724) and offers similar facilities. The site is well located, occupying a small peninsula of some 15 hectares. This means that there is only a short walk to the sea from anywhere on the site. The ground is mostly gently sloping with a covering of rough grass and there are 388 pitches with electricity connections. One side of the site is shaded with mature trees but the other side is almost devoid of shade and could become very hot. There are many activities on site (see below) and an excellent swimming pool. The reception office opens 24 hours for help and information. Single men are not accepted. All in all, this is a pleasant, uncomplicated site which is well situated, well managed and peaceful.

Facilities

Six toilet blocks provide mostly British style WCs, washbasins (half with hot water) and showers (around a third with controllable hot water). Facilities for disabled visitors. Dishwashing and laundry sinks (half with hot water). Laundry. Motorcaravan service point. Supermarket (seven days per week). Restaurant, pizzeria and snacks. Bicycle hire. Swimming pool. Fishing. Tennis. Table tennis. Minigolf. Water sports - water skiing, windsurfing, etc. Volleyball. Boating - marina on site. Off site: Bicycle hire 3 km. Riding 15 km. Porec the nearest town is 6 km. (a must to visit) with a regular bus service running from site reception.

Open: 19 March - 7 October.

Directions

Site is approx. 3 km. off the main Novigrad - Porec road, signed in village of Cevar.
GPS: N45:15.424 E13:35.027

Charges 2007

Per person	€ 3,80 - € 7,00
child (4-10 yrs)	free - € 4,90
pitch	€ 5,60 - € 13,20
electricity	€ 2,30 - € 3,20
dog	€ 3,10 - € 5,60

CR6722 Autokamp Zelena Laguna

HR-52440 Porec (Istria)

Tel: 052 410 101. Email: mail@plavalaguna.hr

A busy medium sized site (by Croatian standards), Zelena Laguna (green lagoon) is very popular with families and boat owners. Part of the Plava Laguna Leisure group that has eight other campsites and seven hotels in the vicinity, it is long established and is improved and modernised each year as finances permit. The 1,100 pitches (540 for touring units) are a mixture of level, moderately sloping and terraced ground and range in size from 40-120 sq.m. Slopes will be encountered on the site with quite a steep hill leading to the highest point allowing impressive views over the sea. Access to the pitches is by hard surfaced roads and shingle tracks which generally allow adequate space to manoeuvre. There are plenty of electrical hook-ups (10A); 42 super pitches are very popular and in other areas there are many water points. Like all others in the area, Zelena Laguna can get very crowded in late June, July and August and as it can get very hot in high summer (40°C), the pitches nearest the sea and therefore the sea breezes, are recommended (book ahead). The sea runs along two sides of the site and has mostly rocky beaches with Blue Flag status into which paved sunbathing areas have been inserted. At one end of the beach is an impressive marina where visitors may park their yachts. Approximately 25% of the beach area is reserved for naturists. There are many attractions to amuse you here or ample opportunity to just relax as it is quite peaceful.

Facilities

The sanitary blocks are good and some have been refurbished. The washbasins have hot water and there are free hot controllable showers in all blocks. Toilets are mostly British style and there are facilities for disabled campers. Supermarket and minimarket. Several restaurants and snack bars. Swimming pool. Sub-aqua diving (with instruction). Tennis (instruction available). Five-a-side football. Bicycle hire. Boat hire (motor and sailing). Boat launching. Beach volleyball. Riding. Aerobics. Animation programme for the family. Off site: Small market and parade of shops selling beach wares, souvenirs etc. immediately outside site. Regular bus service and also a small 'land train' known as the 'Bumble Zug' from the adjacent hotel complex into the centre of Porec (alternatively it is 15 minutes drive but parking tends to be somewhat chaotic). Supermarkets in Porec (4 km). Fishing 5 km. (permit required). Riding 300 m.

Open: 19 March - 7 October.

Directions

Site is between the coast road and the sea with turning 2 km. from Porec towards Vrsar. It is very well signed and is part of a large multiple hotel complex.

Charges 2007

Per person	€ 3,80 - € 7,00
child (4-9 yrs)	free - € 4,90
pitch	€ 5,60 - € 13,20
electricity	€ 2,30 - € 3,20
dog	€ 3,10 - € 5,60

CR6724 Camping Bijela Uvala

Bijela Uvala, Zelena Laguna, HR-52440 Porec (Istria)

Tel: **052 410 551**. Email: **mail@plavalaguna.hr**

Bijela Uvala is part of the Plava Laguna Leisure group and is a large friendly campsite with an extensive range of facilities. The direct sea access makes the site very popular in high season. The topography of the site is undulating and the gravelled or grass pitches are divided into zones which vary considerably. As the coastline winds along the site, the rocky and intermittently paved sea access increases with boat launching facilities, beach volleyball and various eateries dispersed along it. The 2,000 pitches, 1,476 for touring, are compact and due to the terrain some have excellent sea views and breezes, however as usual these are the most sought after so book early. They range from 60-120 sq.m. and all have electricity, 400 also have water connections. Some are formal with hedging, some are terraced and most have good shade from established trees or wooded areas. There are also very informal areas where unmarked pitches are on generally uneven ground. The smaller of the two pools is in a busy complex adjacent to the sea which includes a large entertainment area and a family style restaurant. There are many sporting facilities and fairground style amusements (some at extra cost). The adjoining campsite Zelena Laguna is owned by the same organisation and access to its beach (including a naturist section) and facilities is via a gate between the sites or along the beach. A large sports complex is also within walking distance. This site is very similar to Camping Zelena Laguna but with fewer permanent pitches.

Facilities

Eight sanitary blocks are clean and well equipped with mainly British style WCs. Free hot showers and hot water for dishwashing and laundry. Washing machines. Facilities for disabled visitors. Motorcaravan service point. Gas. Fridge boxes. Two restaurants, three fast food cafés, two bars and a bakery. Large well equipped supermarket and minimarket. Two swimming pool complexes, one with a medium size pool and the other a larger lagoon style with fountains. Tennis. Playground. Amusements. TV room. Animation centre. Off site: Zelena Laguna campsite facilities. Sports complex 100 m. Naturist beach 25 m.

Open: 19 March - 7 October.

Directions

The site adjoins Zelena Laguna. From the main Porec to Vrsar coast road turn off towards coast and the town of Zelena Laguna 4 km. south of Porec and follow campsite signs.

Charges 2007

Per person	€ 3,80 - € 7,00
child (4-9 yrs)	free - € 4,90
pitch	€ 5,60 - € 13,20
electricity	€ 2,30 - € 3,20
dog	€ 3,10 - € 5,60

CR6727 Camping Valkanela

Valkanela, HR-52450 Vrsar (Istria)

Tel: **052 445 216**. Email: **valkanela@maistra.hr**

Camping Valkanela is located in a beautiful green bay, right on the Adriatic Sea, between the villages of Vrsar and Funtana. It offers 1200 pitches, all with 6A electricity. Pitches near the beach are numbered, have shade from mature trees and are slightly sloping towards the sea. Those towards the back of the site are on open fields without much shade and are not marked or numbered. Most numbered pitches have water points close by, but the back pitches have to go to the toilet blocks for water. Unfortunately the number of pitches has increased dramatically over the years, many are occupied by seasonal campers and statics of every description, and parts of the site resemble a shanty town. Access roads are gravel. For those who like activity, Valkanela has four gravel tennis courts and opportunities for diving, water skiing and boat rental. There is a little marina for mooring small boats and a long rock and pebble private beach, with some lawns for sunbathing. It is a short stroll to the surrounding villages with their bars, restaurants and shops. There may be some noise nuisance from the disco outside the entrance and compared to most, the site looks overcrowded.

Facilities

Fifteen toilet blocks of varying styles and ages provide toilets, open style washbasins and controllable hot showers. Child-size toilets, basins and showers. Bathroom (free). Facilities for disabled visitors. Laundry with sinks and washing machines. Two supermarkets. Souvenir shops and newspaper kiosk. Bars and restaurants with dance floor and stage. Patisserie. Tennis. Minigolf. Fishing. Bicycle hire. Marina with boat launching. Boat and pedalo hire. Disco outside entrance. Daily animation programme for children up to 12 yrs. Excursions. Off site: Riding 2 km.

Open: 7 April - 30 September.

Directions

Follow campsite signs from Vrsar.
GPS: N45:09.913 E13:36.434

Charges 2007

Per person	€ 4,20 - € 6,40
child (5-11 yrs)	free - € 3,60
pitch incl. electricity	€ 6,40 - € 14,90
dog	€ 2,50 - € 6,00

CR6728 Camping Orsera

Sv. Martin 2/1, HR-52450 Vrsar (Istria)

Tel: **052 441 330**. Email: **valamar@riviera.hr**

Part of the Camping on the Adriatic group, this site is very close to the fishing port of Vrsar, with direct access from the site. The views of the many small islands are stunning. The site is proud of its beach's Blue Flag status and a safe rock pool has been created for children and a splash pool is at the base of a large flume in the beach area. This is a 30 hectare site with 833 pitches of which 593 are for touring units. Marked and numbered, the pitches vary in size with 90 sq.m. being the average. The sand and grass ground slopes towards the sea and there is some terracing. Ample shade is provided by mature pines and oak trees. Over 200 pitches have 16A electricity and water.

Facilities

Many of the toilet blocks have been renovated and one completely new block provides very good facilities. Mainly British style WCs, washbasins and showers, mostly with hot water. Some have facilities for disabled campers, private cabins, baby and children Off site: Golf 7 km. Riding 3 km. Excursions. Shops in Vrsar, although the nearest serious shopping centre is at Porec.

Open: 1 April - 8 October.

Directions

Site is on the main Porec (7 km) - Vrsar (1 km) road, well signed.

Charges 2007

Per person	€ 3,45 - € 6,15
child (4-10 yrs)	free - € 4,50
pitch incl. electricity	€ 5,75 - € 13,65
with water	€ 8,55 - € 14,65
Prices for pitches by the sea are higher.	

CR6725 Camping Porto Sole

Porto Sole, HR-52450 Vrsar (Istria)

Tel: **052 441 198**. Email: **portosole@maistra.hr**

Located near the pretty town of Vrsar and its charming marina, Porto Sole is a large campsite with 800 pitches and is part of the Maistra Group. The pitches vary; some are in the open with semi shade and are fairly flat, others are under a heavy canopy of pines on undulating land. There is some terracing near the small number of water frontage pitches. The site could be described as almost a clover leaf shape with one area for rental accommodation and natural woods, another for sporting facilities and the other two for pitches. There is a large water frontage and two tiny bays provide delightful sheltered rocky swimming areas. In peak season the site is buzzing with activity and the hub of the site is the pools, disco and shopping arcade area where there is also a pub and both formal and informal eating areas. The food is varied but simple with a tiny terrace restaurant by the water.

Facilities

Five completely renovated toilet blocks have mostly British style WCs and are clean and well maintained. The low numbers of showers (common to most Croatian sites) result in long queues. Facilities for disabled visitors and children. Washing machines and dryers. Dishwashing and laundry (cold water). Large well stocked supermarket (1/5-15/9). Small shopping mall. Pub. Pizzeria. Formal and informal restaurants. Swimming pools (1/5-29/9). Play area (alongside beach). Boules. Tennis. Table tennis. Minigolf. Massage studio. Disco. Animation in season. Miniclub. Scuba diving courses. Boat launching. Off site: Marina, sailing 1 km. Vrsar 2 km. Riding 3 km.

Open: 7 April - 29 September.

Directions

Follow signs towards Vrsar and take turn towards Koversada, then follow campsite signs.

Charges 2007

Per person	€ 4,60 - € 6,50
child (5-12 yrs)	free - € 4,20
pitch	€ 6,40 - € 12,80
dog	€ 3,10 - € 5,30

Camping Cheques accepted.

CR6731 Naturist Camping Valalta

Cesta Valalta-Lim bb, HR-52210 Rovinj (Istria)

Tel: **052 804 800**. Email: **valalta@valalta.hr**

This is a most impressive site for up to 6,000 naturist campers but there is a pleasant open feel about it. The passage through reception is efficient and pleasant and this feeling is maintained around the well organised site. A friendly, family atmosphere is to be found here. Single males are not admitted and continuous cautious monitoring within the site ensures the well being of all the naturist guests. An outer and inner reception adds to the security. All pitches are the same price with 16A electricity, although they vary in size and surroundings. The impressive lagoon-style pool has water features.

Facilities

Twenty high quality sanitary blocks of which four are smaller units of plastic 'pod' construction. Hot showers (coin operated). Facilities for disabled campers. Washing machines. Dryers. Supermarket. Four restaurants. Pizzeria. Two bars. Large pool complex. Beauty saloon. Fitness club. Massage. Minigolf. Tennis. Bocce. Sailing. Play area. Bicycle hire. Beach. Marina. Diving. Windsurfing. Internet. Animation all season. Kindergarten. Dogs not accepted.

Open: 24 April - 2 October.

Directions

Site is located on the coast 8 km. north of Rovinj. If approaching from the north turn inland (follow signs to Rovinj) to drive around the Limski Kanal. Then follow signs towards Valalta about 2 km. east of Rovinj. Site is at the end of the road.

Charges 2007

Per person	Kn 37,00 - 60,00
child (4-14 yrs)	Kn 19,00 - 30,00
pitch incl. electricity	Kn 55,00 - 100,00

CR6729 Naturist Camping Koversada

Koversada, HR-52450 Vrsar (Istria)

Tel: 052 441 378. Email: koversada-camp@maistra.hr

According to history, the first naturist on Koversada was the famous adventurer Casanova. Today Koversada is an enclosed holiday park for naturists with bungalows, 1,700 pitches (1438 for tourers, all with 6/8A electricity), a shopping centre and its own island. The main attraction of this site is the Koversada island, connected to the mainland by a small bridge. It is only suitable for tents, but has a restaurant and two toilet blocks. Between the island and the mainland is an enclosed, shallow section of water for swimming and, on the other side of the bridge, an area for mooring small boats. The pitches are of average size on grass and gravel ground and slightly sloping. Pitches on the mainland are numbered and partly terraced under mature pine and olive trees. Pitching on the island is haphazard, but there is also shade from mature trees. The bottom row of pitches on the mainland has views over the island and the sea. The site is surrounded by a long beach, part sand, part paved.

Facilities

Seventeen toilet blocks provide British and Turkish style toilets, washbasins and controllable hot showers. Child toilets and basins. Family bathroom (free). Facilities for disabled visitors. Dishwashing under cover. Laundry service. Supermarket. Several bars and restaurants. Playing field. Tennis. Minigolf. Fishing. Boats, surf boards, canoes and kayaks for hire. Paragliding. 'Tweety club' for children. Live music. Sports tournaments. Off site: Riding 2 km.

Open: 15 April - 30 September.

Directions

Site is just south from Vrsar. From Vrsar, follow site signs. GPS: N45:08.573 E13:36.316

Charges 2007

Per person	€ 4,70 - € 6,60
child (7-11 yrs)	free - € 3,30
child (12-18 yrs)	€ 3,20 - € 4,50
pitch	€ 6,20 - € 15,00
dog	€ 3,10 - € 5,30

Camping Cheques accepted.

Naturist park Koversada *Vrsar* — Istria Green Mediterranean.

New seaside lots! Children's clubs and playgrounds! ONLINE BOOKING

A Mediterranean paradise in a superb natural setting; the gentle climate and clean seas have made this a favourite summer holiday destination for many generations of naturists.

tel: +385 (0)52 441 378 / fax: 441 761 / koversada-camp@maistra.hr — www.maistra.hr — *maistra*

CR6730 Camping Amarin

Monsena bb, HR-52210 Rovinj (Istria)

Tel: 052 802 000. Email: ac-amarin@maistra.hr

Situated 4 km. from the centre of the lovely old port town of Rovinj this site has much to offer. The complex is part of the Maistra Group. It has 12.6 hectares of land and is adjacent to the Amarin bungalow complex. Campers can take advantage of the facilities afforded by both areas. There are 670 pitches for touring units on various types of ground and between 80-120 sq.m. Most are separated by foliage, 10A electricity is available. A rocky beach backed by a grassy sunbathing area is very popular, but the site has its own superb, supervised round pool plus a splash pool for children.

Facilities

Thirteen respectable toilet blocks have a mixture of British style and Turkish toilets. Half the washbasins have hot water. Some showers have hot water, the rest have cold and are outside. Some blocks have a unit for disabled visitors. Washing machines. Security boxes. Motorcaravan service point. Supermarket. Small market. Two restaurants, taverna, pizzeria and terrace grill. Swimming pool. Flume and splash pool. Watersports. Bicycle hire. Fishing (subject to permit). Daily animation. Barbecues are not accepted. Hairdresser. Massage. ATM. Off site: Hourly minibus service to Rovinj. Excursions. Riding nearby.

Open: 20 May - 23 September.

Directions

Follow signs towards Rovinj and if approaching from the north turn off about 2 km. before the town towards Amarin and Valalta. Then follow signs to Amarin and the campsite. Watch for a left turn after approx. 3 km. where signs are difficult to see.

Charges 2007

Per person	€ 4,20 - € 7,20
child (5-12 yrs)	free - € 3,60
pitch incl. electricity	€ 6,00 - € 11,60
dog	€ 3,10 - € 6,20

For stays less than 3 nights in high season add 10%.

CR6732 Camping Polari

Polari bb, HR-52210 Rovinj (Istria)
Tel: **052 801 501**. Email: **crs@maistra.hr**

This 60 hectare site has excellent facilities for both textile and naturist campers, the latter having a reserved area of 12 hectares called Punta Eva. Prime places are taken by permanent customers but there are some numbered pitches which are very good. An impressive swimming pool complex is child friendly with large paddling areas. The site, part of the Maistia Group has undergone a massive improvement programme and the results make it a very attractive option. There is something for everyone here to enjoy or you may prefer just to relax. Enjoy a meal on the huge restaurant terrace with panoramic views of the sea. Many of the pitches have also been thoughtfully upgraded and now a new pitch (100 sq.m) is offered with full facilities. Pitches are clean, neat and level and there will be shade when the young trees grow.

Facilities

All the sanitary facilities have been renovated to a high standard with plenty of hot water and good showers. Washing up and laundry sinks. Washing machines and dryers. Laundry service including ironing. Motorcaravan service point. Two shops, one large and one small, one restaurant and snack bar. Tennis. Minigolf. Children's animation with all major European languages spoken. Bicycle hire. Watersports. Sailing school. Off site: Riding 1 km. Five buses daily to and from Rovinj (3 km).

Open: 25 March - 30 September.

Directions

From any access road to Rovinj look for red signs to AC Polari (amongst other destinations). The site is 3 km. south of Rovinj.

Charges 2007

Per person	€ 3,80 - € 7,10
child (5-11 yrs)	free - € 4,20
pitch incl. electricity	€ 6,40 - € 14,90

For stays less than 3 nights in high season add 20%. Camping Cheques accepted.

Camping Polari *Rovinj*
Istria — Green Mediterranean.
NEW Children's clubs and playgrounds! Pitch with water supply and drain!
ONLINE BOOKING

A picturesque cove, ideal for all those who relish the pleasant shade of olive trees and the cleanest sea in the Mediterranean.

tel: +385 (0)52 801 501 / fax: 811 395 / e-mail: polari@maistra.hr   www.maistra.hr   *maistra*

CR6742 Camping Stoja

Stoja 37, HR-52100 Pula (Istria)
Tel: **052 387 144**. Email: **marketing@arenaturist.hr**

Camping Stoja in Pula, one of the famous little Istrian harbour towns, is on a little peninsula and therefore almost completely surrounded by the waters of the clear Adriatic. In the centre of the site is the old Fort Stoja, built in 1884 for coastal defence. Some of its buildings are now used as a toilet block or laundry and its courtyard is used by the animation team. The pitches here vary greatly in size (50-120 sq.m) and are marked by round, concrete, numbered blocks and separated by young trees. About half have shade from mature trees and all are slightly sloping on grass and gravel. Pitches close to the pebble and rock beach have beautiful views of the sea and Pula.

Facilities

Five toilet blocks with British and Turkish style toilets, open plan washbasins with cold water only and controllable hot showers. Child-size basins. Facilities for disabled visitors. Laundry and ironing service. Fridge box hire. Dishwashing under cover. Dog shower. Motorcaravan service point. Chemical disposal. Supermarket. Bar/restaurant. Miniclub and teen club. Bicycle hire. Water skiing. Boat hire. Boat launching. Surfboard and pedalo hire. Island excursions. Off site: Pula (walking distance).

Open: 24 March - 1 November.

Directions

From Pula follow signs to the site.
GPS: N44:51.583 E13:48.870

Charges 2007

Per person	€ 4,10 - € 7,20
child (4-12 yrs)	€ 2,80 - € 4,50
pitch	€ 5,00 - € 10,00
incl. electricity	€ 7,10 - € 14,90
dog	€ 2,50 - € 4,50

CR6733 Camping Vestar

HR-52210 Rovinj (Istria)

Tel: 052 800 250. Email: crs@maistra.hr

Camping Vestar, just 5 km. from the historic harbour town of Rovinj, is one of the rare sites in Croatia with a partly sandy beach. Right behind the beach is a large area, attractively landscaped with young trees and shrubs, with grass for sunbathing. The site has 750 large pitches, of which 600 are for tourers, all with 16A electricity (the rest being taken by seasonal units and 14 pitches for tour operators). It is largely wooded with good shade and from the bottom row of pitches there are views of the sea. Pitching is on two separate fields, one for free camping, the other with numbered pitches. The pitches at the beach are in a half circle around the shallow bay, making it safe for children to swim. Vestar has a small marina and a jetty for mooring small boats and excursions to the islands are arranged. There is a miniclub and live music with dancing at one of the two bar/restaurants in the evenings. The restaurants all have terraces, one covered with vines to protect you from the hot sun.

Facilities

Five modern and one refurbished toilet block with mainly Turkish style toilets and some British style, open washbasins and controllable hot showers. Child size basins. Family bathroom. Facilities for disabled people. Laundry service. Fridge box hire. Motorcaravan services. Shop. Two bar/restaurants. New large swimming pool. Playground. Tennis. Fishing. Boat hire. Miniclub (5-11 yrs). Excursions. Off site: Riding 2 km. Rovinj 5 km.

Open: 1 May - 1 October.

Directions

Follow site signs from Rovinj.
GPS: N45:03.259 E13:41.141

Charges 2007

Per person	€ 4,10 - € 7,90
child (7-11 yrs)	free - € 4,90

CR6745 Camping Bi-Village

Dragonja 115, HR-52212 Fazana (Istria)

Tel: **052 380 700**

Camping Bi-Village is large new holiday village, close to the historic town of Pula and opposite the Brioni National Park. The location is excellent and there are some superb sunsets. The site is landscaped with many flowers, shrubs and rock walls and offers 1,522 pitches, of which 922 pitches are for tourers, the remainder being taken by bungalows and chalets. The campsite is separated from the holiday bungalows by the main site road, that runs from the entrance to the beach. Pitches are set in long rows accessed by gravel lanes, slightly sloping towards the sea, with only the pitches at the bottom having shade from mature trees and good views over the Adriatic.

Facilities

Four modern toilet blocks with toilets, open plan washbasins and controllable hot showers. Child size washbasins. Baby room. Facilities for disabled visitors. Washing machine. Dishwashing under cover. Shopping centre. Several bars and restaurants. Bazaar. Gelateria. Pastry shop. Three swimming pools. Playground on gravel. Playing field. Tennis. Basketball. Trampolines. Minigolf. Fishing. Jet skis, motorboats and pedaloes for hire. Boat launching. Games hall. Sports tournaments and professional entertainment organised. Massage. Salsa lessons. Model making. Internet point. Off site: Historic towns of Pula and Rovinj are close.

Open: All year.

Directions

Follow no. 2 road south from Rijeka to Pula. In Pula follow site signs. Site is close to Fazana.

Charges 2007

Per person	€ 3,50 - € 9,00
child	free - € 4,50
pitch incl. electricity and water	€ 5,50 - € 18,00
dog	€ 2,00 - € 3,00

Camping Cheques accepted.

CR6650 Autocamp Korana

Rakovica, HR-53231 Plitvicka Jezera (Central)

Tel: **053 751 888**. Email: **info@np-plitvicka-jezera.hr**

For a visit to the famous Plitvice lakes in the far eastern part of the country, this site is a totally acceptable option for spending a night nearby. In a large, park-like environment, caravans and motorcaravans are placed on one of 540 unmarked tarmac hardstandings, with electricity available (16A). The toilet facilities are adequate and clean but other facilities are entirely missing: no washing machine, fridges, internet access, pools, sports or other forms of animation. A huge restaurant in the centre of the site tries hard to suggest it caters for groups only, but individual guests may find something here. Most people stay here for only one or two nights, so every morning and afternoon serious traffic jams arise. Leave early.

Facilities

The toilet blocks include facilities for disabled persons. Chemical disposal and motorcaravan service point. Shop is opened in the morning and afternoon and information about the national park can be found here. Off site: The wonderful (and expensive) National Park, but little else.

Open: May - end September.

Directions

Along the main road, pass entrances 1 and 2 of the National Park. Site is north of the park area just beyond the village of Seliste on the right (eastern) side and is signed. GPS: N44:57.019 E15:38.488

Charges 2007

Per person	€ 9,00
child (7-12 yrs)	€ 6,30
pitch incl. electricity	€ 6,00
dog	€ 3,00

CR6765 Camping Kovacine

HR-51557 Cres Island (Kvarner)

Tel: **051 573 150**. Email: **campkovacine@kovacine.com**

Camping Kovacine is located on a peninsula on the beautiful Dalmatian island of Cres, just 2 km. from the town of the same name. The site has 750 numbered, mostly level pitches, of which 750 are for tourers (300 with 12A electricity). On sloping ground, partially shaded by mature olive and pine trees, pitching is on the large, open spaces between the trees. Some places have views of the Valun lagoon. Kovacine is partly an FKK (naturist) site, which is quite common in Croatia, and has a pleasant atmosphere. Here one can enjoy Croatian camping with local live music on a stage close to the pebble beach (Blue Flag), where there is also a restaurant and bar. The site has its own private beach, part concrete, part pebbles, and a jetty for mooring boats and fishing. It is close to the historic town of Cres, the main town on the island, which offers a rich history of fishing, shipyards and authentic Dalmatian-style houses. There are also several bars, restaurants and shops.

Facilities

Five modern, comfortable toilet blocks (two refurbished) offer British style toilets, open plan washbasins (some cabins for ladies) and hot showers. Bathroom for hire. Facilities for disabled people (although access is difficult). Laundry sinks and washing machine. Fridge box hire. Dishwashing under cover. Motorcaravan service point. Dog shower. Car wash. Supermarket. Bar, restaurant and pizzeria. Playground. Daily children's club. Evening shows with live music. Boat launching. Fishing. Diving centre. Motor boat hire. Airport transfers. Off site: Historic town of Cres with bars, restaurants and shops 2 km.

Open: 16 April - 15 October.

Directions

From Rijeka take no. 2 road south towards Labin and take ferry to Cres at Brestova. Continue to Cres and follow site signs. GPS: N44:57.713 E14:23.790

Charges 2008

Per person	€ 4,80 - € 9,60
child (3-11 yrs)	€ 2,30 - € 3,50
pitch	€ 4,60 - € 8,40
dog	€ 1,00 - € 3,00

CR6768 Camping Slatina

Martinscica, HR-51556 Cres Island (Kvarner)

Tel: **051 574 127**. Email: **info@camp-slatina.com**

Camping Slatina lies about halfway along the island of Cres, beside the fishing port of Martinscica on a bay of the Adriatic Sea. It has 370 pitches for tourers, some with 10A electricity, off very steep, tarmac access roads, sloping down to the sea. The pitches are large and level on a gravel base and enjoy plenty of shade from mature laurel trees, although hardly any have views. Whilst there is plenty of privacy, the site does have an enclosed feeling. Some pitches in the lower areas have water, electricity and drainage. Like so many sites in Croatia, Slatina has a private diving centre, which will take you to the remote island of Lastovo. Lastovo is surrounded by reefs and little islands and the crystal clear waters of the Adriatic make it perfect for diving. Martinscica owes its name to the medieval church of the Holy Martin and has a Glagolite monastery, standing next to the 17th century castle, built by the Patrician Sforza. Both are well worth a visit.

Facilities

Two new and three refurbished toilet blocks provide toilets, open style washbasins and controllable hot showers. Facilities for disabled visitors. Laundry with sinks and washing machine. Fridge box hire. Dog shower. Car wash. Shop. Bar, restaurant, grill restaurant, pizzeria and fish restaurant. Playground. Minigolf. Fishing. Bicycle hire. Diving centre. Boat launching. Beach volleyball. Pedalo, canoe and boat hire. Excursions to the 'Blue Cave'. 'Pet projects'. Off site: Martinscica with bars, restaurants and shops 2 km.

Open: Easter - 30 September.

Directions

From Rijeka take no. 2 road south towards Labin and take ferry to Cres at Brestova. From Cres go south towards Martinscica and follow site signs. GPS: N44:49.400 E14:20.450

Charges 2007

Per person	€ 4,49 - € 7,31
child (3-12 yrs)	€ 1,35 - € 3,40
pitch	€ 3,74 - € 7,70

This is just a sample of the campsites we have inspected and selected in Central Europe. For more campsites and further information, please see the Alan Rogers Central Europe guide.

Shuttle service/Airport-
transfer: Airport Rijeka
– Cres and back:
only € 19,99/person

CAMP KOVAČINE

CRES-CHERSO

A crystal clear sea, beautiful beaches and pine and olive trees which provide plenty of shade, make Kovacine a unique holiday destination. The campsite is situated on the Cres peninsula and is close to the village with the same name. There are 1500 pitches which offer all the comfort you might wish. **Room (with breakfast), direct on the beach with sea view.**

Mobile homes – the freedom of camping with all the comforts of home. To book a pitch in advance possible!

We offer you a range of facilities:

- Bar, buffet, restaurant, Self service shop
- Modern, new sanitary facilities
- Boat mooring for your boat and boat crane

- Children's animation programme
- Various sport facilities
- First aid service on site

Camping »Kovačine« Cres • HR-51557 Cres • Tel. 00-385/51/573-150
Fax 00-385/51/571-086 • campkovacine@kovacine.com • www.camp-kovacine.com

CR6736 Camping Valdaliso

Monsena bb, HR-52210 Rovinj (Istria)
Tel: **052 815 025**. Email: **info@rovinjturist.hr**

Unusually Camping Valdaliso has its affiliated hotel in the centre of the site. The advantage for campers is that they can use the hotel and, as breakfast is served there but not in the restaurant, it may appeal to some. The fine Barabiga restaurant within the hotel offers superb Istrian and fish cuisine and the pool is also within the hotel. You are close to the beautiful old town of Rovinj and parts of this site enjoy views of the town. A water taxi makes exploring Rovinj very easy, compared with the impossible parking for private cars. A bus service is also provided but this involves considerable walking. The pitches are mostly flat with shade from pine trees and the site is divided into three sections all with 16A electricity. The choice of formal numbered pitches, informal camping or proximity to the sea impacts on the prices. The kilometre plus of beach has crystal clear water and a pebble beach. The animation programme is extremely professional and there is a lot to do at Valdaliso, which is aimed primarily at families. The variety of activities here and the bonus of the use of the hotel make this a great choice for campers

Facilities

Two large clean sanitary blocks have hot showers (coin operated), The northeastern block has facilities for disabled campers. Hotel facilities. Shop. Pizzeria. Restaurant. Table tennis. Volleyball. Basketball. Tennis. Fitness centre. Games room. Billiards. Children's games. Bicycle hire. Summer painting courses. Exchange. Water taxi. Bus service. Boat rental. Watersports. Boat launching. Fishing. Gym. Diving school. Internet in both receptions. Animals are not accepted. Off site: Town 1 km.

Open: 23 March - 15 October.

Directions

Site is 7 km. north of Rovinj on the main coast road between Vsrar and Rovinj. Watch for the signs to Monsena and the site.

Charges 2007

Per person	€ 3,90 - € 6,50
child (12-18 yrs)	€ 1,95 - € 3,25
child (under 12 yrs)	free
pitch	€ 5,50 - € 13,50

Camping VALDALISO * *Rovinj* Istria** Green Mediterranean. CROATIA

Your Family Holiday

Just in front of the old town of Rovinj, in the shadow of olive and pine trees lies the camping Valdaliso. With 1 mile of its own pebbles beach, with new modern toilet facilities, 2 restaurants, beach bar, grocery store, pizzeria, tennis, beach volley, surfing, table tennis and diving centre, a hotel with fitness, game room and rich day and evening animation entertainment programme and mobilhomes with air conditioning and SAT TV!

tel.: 00385 52 805 505 / fax: 00385 52 811 541 / e-mail: info@rovinjturist.hr   www.valdaliso.info   Rovinj

CR6761 Camping Zablace

E Geistlicha 38, HR-51523 Baska (Kvarner)
Tel: **051 856 909**. Email: **campzablace@campzablace.into**

Camping Zablace is at the southern end of the beautiful island of Krk, in the ancient ferry port of Baska. Like most sites in Croatia it has direct access to a large, pebble beach and from the bottom row of pitches one has views over the Adriatic and the little island of Kosljun with its Franciscan Monastery. The site has 500 pitches with 400 used for touring units. Zone 1 (nearest the beach) provides 200 individual pitches with electricity and water. The quietest zone, if further away (and across a public road that splits the site in two) has electricity and water taps. There is not much shade anywhere. There are few amenities on the site, but it is a five minute walk to the centre of Baska.

Facilities

Four toilet blocks (three new, one old) with toilets, open plan basins and hot showers (key access for the toilets nearest the beach; with deposit). Facilities for the disabled. Dishwashing under cover. Motorcaravan service point. Shop. Kiosks with fruit, drinks, tobacco, newspapers and beach wear. Fishing. Beach volleyball. Off site: Giant slide and games hall. Tennis. Minigolf 200 m.

Open: Easter - 15 October.

Directions

On Krk follow the no. 29 road south to Baska, then good signs to site. GPS: N44:58.001 E14:44.707

Charges 2008

Per person	Kn 30,00 - Kn 45,00
child (7-11 yrs)	Kn 15,00 - Kn 22,00
pitch with electricity	Kn 75,00 - Kn 130,00
dog	free - Kn 25,00
Camping Cheques accepted.	

CR6845 Camp Adriatic

Huljerat bb, HR-22202 Primosten (Dalmatia)

Tel: 022 571 223. Email: info@camp-adriatic.hr

As we drove south down the Dalmatian coast road, we looked across a clear turquoise bay and saw a few tents, caravans and motorcaravans camped under some trees. A short distance later we were at the entrance of Camping Adriatic. With 530 pitches that slope down to the sea, the site is deceptive and enjoys a one kilometre beach frontage which is ideal for snorkelling and diving. Close to the delightful town of Primosten (with a taxi boat service in high season) the site boasts good modern amenities and a fantastic location. Tour operators use some pitches on the sea front and there are seven caravans to rent. Most pitches are level and have shade from pine trees. There are 212 numbered pitches and 288 unnumbered, all with 10/16A electricity available.

Facilities

Four modern sanitary blocks provide clean toilets, hot showers and washbasins. Facilities for disabled visitors. Bathroom for children. Washing machine and dryer. Kitchen facilities. Small supermarket (15/5-30/9). Restaurant and bar (all season). Sports centre. Miniclub for children. Beach. Diving school. Sailing school and boat hire. Entertainment programme in July/Aug. Internet point.

Open: 1 May - 15 October.

Directions

Take the new A1 motorway south and leave at the Sibenik exit. Follow the 33 road into Sibenik and then go south along the coast road (no. 8), signed Primosten. Site is 2.5 km. north of Primosten. GPS: N43:36.391 E15:55.257

Charges 2007

Per person	Kn 31,00 - 43,00
child (5-12 yrs)	Kn 22,00 - 28,00
pitch	Kn 30,00 - 60,00

Camping Cheques accepted.

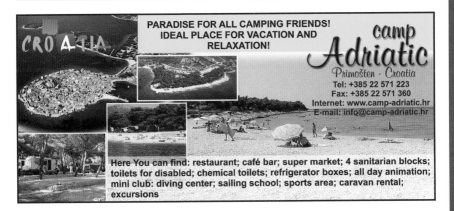

PARADISE FOR ALL CAMPING FRIENDS! IDEAL PLACE FOR VACATION AND RELAXATION!

camp Adriatic
Primošten - Croatia
Tel: +385 22 571 223
Fax: +385 22 571 360
Internet: www.camp-adriatic.hr
E-mail: info@camp-adriatic.hr

Here You can find: restaurant; café bar; super market; 4 sanitarian blocks; toilets for disabled; chemical toilets; refrigerator boxes; all day animation; mini club; diving center; sailing school; sports area; caravan rental; excursions

CR6850 Camp Seget

Hrvatskih zrtava 121, HR-21218 Seget Donji (Dalmatia)

Tel: 021 880 394. Email: kamp@kamp-seget.hr

Seget is a simple site which is pleasant and quiet with only 120 pitches, just 2 km. from the interesting old harbour town of Trogir. It is an ideal base for exploring this part of the Dalmatian Coast, or for visiting Trogir and Split. The site is set up on both sides of a tarmac access lane that runs down to the Adriatic Sea. Pitches to the left are off three separate, gravel lanes. They are fairly level and from most there are views of the sea. Pitches to the right are slightly sloping and mostly used for tents. Of varying sizes (80-100 sq.m) the pitches are on grass and gravel (firm tent pegs may be needed), mostly in the shade of mature fig and palm trees and some are numbered. All have access to 16A electricity (long leads may be necessary). To the front of the site a paved promenade gives access to the pebble beach. Via the promenade it is an easy five minute stroll to the first restaurants (we can recommend Frankie's) where you can enjoy good quality, good value meals.

Facilities

Two sanitary blocks (one half remaining a 'portacabin' style). British style toilets, washbasins and controllable, hot showers (free). Facilities for disabled visitors. Campers' kitchen. Fridge box hire. Dishwashing. Shop. Beach. Fishing. Boat rental. Barbecues permitted only on communal area. Off site: Bus at gate for touring. Golf, riding and bicycle hire 1 km. Boat launching 500 m.

Open: 15 April - 15 October.

Directions

Follow no. 8 coastal road south from Zadar towards Split and in Trogir look for prominent site signs, finishing in a sharp right turn.

Charges 2007

Per person	Kn 21,00 - 28,00
child (5-12 yrs)	Kn 14,00 - 17,00
pitch incl. car	Kn 43,00 - 81,00
electricity	Kn 16,50

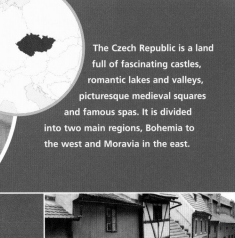

MAP 6

The Czech Republic is a land full of fascinating castles, romantic lakes and valleys, picturesque medieval squares and famous spas. It is divided into two main regions, Bohemia to the west and Moravia in the east.

CAPITAL: PRAGUE

Tourist Office

Czech Tourist Authority
95 Great Portland Street, London W1N 5RA
Tel. 020 7291 9925 Fax. 020 7436 8300
Email: ctainfo@czechcentre.org.uk
Internet: www.visitczech.cz

Although small, the Czech Republic is crammed with attractive places to explore. Indeed, since the new country first appeared on the map in 1993, Prague has become one the most popular cities to visit in Europe. Steeped in history with museums, architectural sights, art galleries, and theatres, it is an enchanting place. The beautiful region of Bohemia, known for its Giant Mountains, is popular for skiing, hiking and other sports. The town of Karlovy Vary, world famous for its regenerative waters, is Bohemia's oldest Spa town, with 12 hot springs containing elements that are said to treat digestive and metabolic ailments. It also has many picturesque streets to meander through and peaceful riverside walks. Moravia is quieter, the most favoured area Brno and from here it is easy to explore historical towns such as Olomouc and Kromeriz. North of Brno is the Moravian Karst, with around 400 caves created by the underground Punkya River. Some caves are open to the public, with boat trips along the river and out of the caves.

Population

10.3 million

Climate

Temperate, continental climate with four distinct seasons. Warm in summer with cold, snowy winters.

Language

The official language is Czech.

Telephone

The country code is 00420.

Money

Currency: The Koruna
Banks: Mon-Fri 0830-1630.

Shops

Mon-Fri 08.00-18.00, some close at lunchtime. Sat 09.00 until midday.

Public Holidays

New Year; Easter Mon; May Day; Prague Uprising 5 May; National Day 8 May; Saints Day 5 July; Festival (John Huss) Day 6 July; Independence Day 28 Oct; Democracy Day 17 Nov; Christmas 24-26 Dec.

Motoring

There is a good and well signposted road network throughout the Republic and, although stretches of cobbles still exist, surfaces are generally good. An annual road tax is levied on all vehicles using Czech motorways and express roads, and a disc can be purchased at border crossings, post offices and filling stations. Do not drink any alcohol before driving. Dipped headlights are compulsory throughout winter months. Always give way to trams and buses.

CZ4780 Autocamping Konopiste

CZ-25601 Benesov u Prahy (Stredocesky)

Tel: **317 729 083**. Email: **reserve@cckonopiste.cz**

Benesov's chief claim to fame is the Konopiste Palace, the last home of Archduke Franz Ferdinand whose assassination in Sarajevo sparked off the First World War in 1914. Autocamp Konopiste, now under new ownership, is part of a motel complex with excellent facilities situated in a very quiet, tranquil location south of Prague. On a hillside, rows of terraces separated by hedges provide 65 grass pitches of average size, 50 with electricity (10A). However, 34 are occupied all year by a tour operator's tents. One of the best Czech campsites, Konopiste has many different varieties of trees and much to offer those who stay there. A fitness centre and heated swimming pool are shared with motel guests. The whole complex has a well tended, cared for air.

Facilities

The good quality sanitary block is central to the caravan pitches. Washing machine and irons. Kitchen. Bar/buffet (high season) with simple meals and basic food items. Motel bar and two restaurants (all year). Pool (1/6-31/8). Tennis. Bicycle hire. Fitness centre. Playground. Club room with TV. Chateau and park. Off site: Shop 200 m. Fishing 1.5 km. Riding 5 km. Prague 48 km. (public transport).

Open: 1 May - 30 September.

Directions

Site is signed near the village of Benesov on the main Prague - Ceske Budejovic road no. 3/E55.

Charges 2007

Per person	CZK 90,00 - 120,00
child (6-15 yrs)	CZK 60,00 - 90,00
pitch incl. electricity	CZK 100,00 - 390,00
dog	CZK 50,00

CZ4820 Caravan Camp Valek

Chrustenice 155, CZ-26712 Lodenice (Stredocesky)

Tel: **311 672 147**. Email: **info@campvalek.cz**

Only 2.5 km. from the E50 motorway, this well maintained, family owned site creates a peaceful, friendly base enjoyed by families. Surrounded by delightful countryside, it is possible to visit Prague even though it is about 28 km. from the city centre. The medium sized, gently sloping grass site is divided in two by a row of well established trees (some shade) and the toilet block. Most pitches are relatively flat, in the open and not specifically marked. However this does not appear to cause overcrowding and generally there is plenty of space. Electricity (10A) is available. Some places have pleasant views of the sunbathing area in front of the pool with a pine-forested hillock as a backdrop.

Facilities

The single clean toilet block has limited numbers of toilets and showers, but during our visit in high season coped well. Small shop with fresh rolls daily. Waiter service restaurant with terrace has an extensive menu. Natural swimming pool (20 x 60 m; June - Sept). Live musical nights on Saturday. Tennis. Off site: Prague 28 km.

Open: 1 May - 30 September.

Directions

From E50 (D5) motorway take exit 10 for Lodenice. Follow camping signs and or Chrustenice. Site is 300 m. on right on leaving Chrustenice. GPS: N50:00.687 E14:09.033

Charges 2007

Per unit with 2 persons and electricity	CZK 480,00

Less 10% in May and Sept.

CZ4690 Camping Slunce

CZ-47107 Zandov (Severocesky)

Tel: **487 861 116**

Away from larger towns, near the border with the former East Germany, this is pleasant countryside with a wealth of Gothic and Renaissance castles. Zandov has nothing of particular interest but Camping Slunce is a popular campsite with local Czech people. There is room for about 50 touring units with 35 electrical connections (12A) on the level, circular camping area which has a hard road running round. Outside this circle are wooden bungalows and tall trees. The general building at the entrance houses all facilities including reception. A fairly basic site, but good value for money.

Facilities

The satisfactory toilet block is good by Czech standards. Kitchen with electric rings, full gas cooker and fridges. Restaurant (all year) but under separate management has live music during high season. Kiosk for basics (May - Sept). Tennis. Table tennis. Swimming pool. Mountain bike hire. Playground. Large, club room for games and TV. Barbecues are not permitted. Dogs are not accepted. Off site: Fishing 1 km. Riding 2 km.

Open: 15 May - 28 August.

Directions

Zandov is 20 km. from Decin and 12 km. from Ceske Lipa on the 262 road. Signed in the centre of Zandov village. GPS: N50:43.278 E14:24.179

Charges 2007

Per person	CZK 64,00
child	CZK 40,00
piitch incl. car	CZK 82,00 - 125,00
electricity per kWh	CZK 8,00

CZ4850 Camp Sokol Troja

Trojská 171A, CZ-17100 Praha (Prague)

Tel: **233 542 908**

This site is very close to the Vltava river although you cannot see it. It was subject to heavy flooding in 2002 and some of the facilities were washed away. There is clearly a continuing risk of flooding so care is needed when visiting this site. Nevertheless, it is only a 15 or 20 minute journey to the centre of the city by bus (stop in front of the site) or tram no. 17 (300 m. walk). Unlike many of the municipal sites near Prague, this site has few facilities and little entertainment. There are 75 touring pitches (10 with 16A electricity). The pitches are small (80-90 sq.m) and can become muddy with rain. The access road is narrow and manoeuvring space is limited so the site may be less suitable for large caravans and motorhomes. The site restaurant serves real Czech meals at very reasonable prices (many locals eat here) – you don't have to go to town for good value meals.

Facilities	Directions
The single, refurbished toilet block is a good provision with toilets, washbasins with hot and cold water and preset showers in cabins without curtain or door. Cleaning can be variable. Facilities for disabled people. Dishwashing and laundry sinks (free hot water). Campers' kitchen with hob. Good restaurant. Off site: Fishing 1 km.	From Dresden or Teplice, follow signs to the centre and turn right before the first bridge over the Moldau into the Kozlovka Pátkova, in the Troja district. Site is well signed from here. GPS: N50:07.010 E14:25.500

Open: All year.

Charges guide

Per person	CZK 105 - 120
pitch	CZK 120 - 200
electricity	CZK 100

CZ4840 Camping Oase Praha

Zlatniky-Liben, CZ-25241 Dolni Brezany (Prague)

Tel: **241 932 044**. Email: **info@campingoase.cz**

Camping Oase Praha is an exceptional site, only five kilometres from Prague and with easy access. You can take the bus (from outside the site) or drive to the underground stop (10 minutes). The site has 110 pitches, all around 100 sq.m, with 6A electricity and 55 with water and drainage, on level, well kept fields. The site is very well kept and has just everything one may expect, including a new Western style toilet block, a well maintained, heated pool, a restaurant and bar. The main attraction here is, of course, the Czech capital. However, this site will provide a relaxing environment to return to and another advantage is that Mr Hess, the helpful owner, speaks English.

Facilities	Directions
An outstanding, new toilet block includes washbasins (open style and in cabins) with hot and cold water, spacious, controllable showers and child size toilets. Facilities for disabled visitors. Laundry with washing machines and dryer. Campers kitchen with hob, fridge and freezer. Motorcaravan services. Restaurant and bar. Basic groceries are available in the shop. Swimming pool (9 x 15 m) and separate paddling pool with slide (both 15/5-20/9). New adventure style playgrounds. Minigolf. Internet point and WiFi. Bicycle hire. Off site: Fishing 2 km. Riding 3 km. Golf 10 km. Boat launching 15 km.	Go southeast from Prague on the D1 towards Brno and take exit 11 to Jesenice via road 101. At Jesenice turn right then immediately left, following camping signs to the site in Zlatniky where you turn left at the roundabout. Site is 700 m. after the village. GPS: N49:57.087 E14:28.510

Open: 20 April - 20 September.

Charges 2008

Per person	CZK 120,00
child (under 12 yrs)	CZK 90,00

Less 20% discount 15/4-31/5 and 1/9-30/9. Camping Cheques accepted.

CZ4795 Cisarska Louka Caravan Park

Cisarska Louka 599, CZ-15000 Praha 5 (Prague)
Tel: 257 318 681. Email: convoy@volny.cz

This city site on the Cisarská Louka Island is about the closest campsite you can get to the centre of Prague. Right behind the site, which is on the premises of the local Yacht Club, a ferry takes you across the Moldau River to the nearest metro station for the city centre (hourly until 22.00). This is a useful site for a visit to Prague if you can cope with the basic toilet facilities. The site is arranged on one large, well fenced field providing 50 touring pitches, 25 with electricity (10A). Pitching is rather haphazard off a gravel access road running half way up the site. Some pitches have views over the river and all have views of the attractive church on the opposite side of the water. Scattered around the site, mature trees provide useful shade after a hot day in the city.

Facilities

Basic toilet facilities with British style toilets, open washbasins and controllable hot showers (on payment). Facilities for disabled people. Dishwashing. Motorcaravan service point that also services as chemical disposal. River fishing. Boat launching. Off site: Two bar/restaurants close.

Open: All year.

Directions

Coming in from the west on the E50 continue alongside the river towards the town centre. Take a sharp right bend just before Shell petrol station. Site is the second site on the Cisacská Louka Island in the Moldau River. GPS: N50:03.745 E14:24.333

Charges 2007

Per person	CZK 95,00
child (0-15 yrs)	CZK 50,00
pitch incl. electricity	CZK 265,00 - 325,00

CZ4815 Triocamp Praha

Ustecka Ul, CZ-18400 Praha (Prague)
Tel: 283 850 795. Email: triocamp.praha@telecom.cz

This site on the northern edge of Prague is a great place to stay for a few days to visit the city. It has 70 pitches (all for tourers) with 6/15A electricity. Most are in the shade of mature trees, which can be very welcoming after a hard day sightseeing. The ground is slightly sloping but most pitches are level and access is off one circular, tarmac road, with cabins and pitches on both sides. There is one hardstanding for a motorcaravan. There is a bar/restaurant with a comprehensive menu and covered terrace attractively decorated with flowers. Toilet facilities are in good order and comfortable.

Facilities

Modern, comfortable toilet facilities provide British style toilets, open washbasins and free, pre-set hot showers. Facilities for disabled people. Laundry with washing machine. Motorcaravan services. Shop. Attractive bar/restaurant. Play area and children's pool. Off site: Prague is a few kilometres by public transport.

Open: All year.

Directions

On E55 in either direction, take exit 1 towards Zdiby and continue straight ahead on 608 road. Site is on right after about 3 km. GPS: N50:09.137 E14:27.019

Charges 2007

Per person	CZK 140,00 - 180,00
electricity	CZK 90,00
dog	free - CZK 80,00

CZ4845 Camping Busek Praha

U parku 6, CZ-18200 Praha 8 - Brezineves (Prague)
Tel: 283 910 254. Email: campbusekprag@volny.cz

No trip to the Czech Republic would be complete without a visit to the capital, Prague. At this site you can do just that without getting tangled up with the city traffic. Just about 8 km. from the centre, there is an excellent bus link from the site to the new metro station at Ladvi that is a part of the new integrated transport system. The site is part of a small motel complex and provides 20 level and unnumbered pitches, all with 10A electricity. It is on the edge of a small, rural village, which offers peace and quiet at the end of a long day's sightseeing; what more could you want!

Facilities

Modern sanitary block with clean toilets, hot showers and washbasins. Washing machine and dryer. Chemical disposal point. Kitchen and dishwashing facilities. Small restaurant (all year). Off site: Prague city centre only a bus and metro ride away. Outdoor swimming pool.

Open: All year.

Directions

From the Prague - Teplice (Dresden) motorway, the D8/E55, take exit to Brezineves and head towards the village. The site is before the village on the right. Turn towards the small fire station and the site is on the right. GPS: N50:09.844 E14:29.118

Charges 2008

Per person	CZK 80,00
pitch incl. electricity	CZK 110,00 - 220,00
No credit cards.	

CZ4590 Holiday Park Lisci Farma

Dolni Branna 350, CZ-54362 Vrchlabi (Vychodocesky)

Tel: **499 421 473**. Email: **info@liscifarma.cz**

This is truly an excellent site that could be in Western Europe considering its amenities, pitches and welcome. However, Lisci Farma retains a pleasant Czech atmosphere. The helpful young manager welcomes many Dutch visitors throughout the year, but in the winter months, when local skiing is available, snow chains are essential. The 260 pitches are fairly flat, although the terrain is slightly sloping and some pitches are terraced. There is shade. The site is well equipped for the whole family to enjoy with its adventure playground offering trampolines for children, archery, beach volleyball, Russian bowling and outdoor bowling court for older youngsters. A beautiful sandy, lakeside beach is 800 m. from the entrance. The more active amongst you can go paragliding or rock climbing, with experienced people to guide you. This site is very suitable for relaxing or exploring the culture of the area. Excursions to Prague are organised and, if all the sporting possibilities are not enough, the children can take part in the activities of the entertainment team, while you are walking or cycling or enjoying live music at the Fox Saloon.

Facilities

Two good sanitary blocks, near the entrance and another modern block next to the hotel, both include toilets, washbasins and spacious, controllable showers (on payment). Child size toilets and baby room. Toilet for disabled visitors. Launderette. Shop (15/6-15/9). Bar/snack bar. Games room. Swimming pool (6 x 12 m). Adventure style playground on grass. Tennis. Minigolf. Archery. Bowling. Paragliding. Rock climbing. Bicycle hire. Excursions. Shuttle bus for skiing. Off site: Fishing and beach 800 m. Riding 2 km. Golf 5 km.

Open: 1 December - 31 March, 1 May - 31 October.

Directions

Follow road no. 14 from Liberec to Vrchlabi. At the roundabout turn in the direction of Prague and site is about 1 mile on the right.
GPS: N50:36.516 E15:36.056

Charges 2008

Per person	CZK 115,00
child (4-14 yrs)	CZK 90,00
pitch incl. electricity	CZK 410,00 - 570,00
dog	CZK 90,00

Various discounts available in low season.
Camping Cheques accepted.

Active Holidays

Holiday Park Lišči Farma
www.liscifarma.cz
open all year TOP

Camping**** - Wintercamping**** - Hotel*** - Cottages - Restaurant - Swimmingpool
Tennis Court - Minigolf - Big Children's Playground - Adrenalin Sports - Music Nights
Ski school - Ski bus - Bustrips

Dolní Branná 350 - 543 62 - Vrchlabí - tel./fax.: 00420/ 499/ 421 656 E-mail: info@liscifarma.cz

CZ4860 Autocamping Orlice

P.O. Box 26, CZ-51741 Kostelec n Orlici (Vychodocesky)

Tel: **494 323 970**. Email: **orlice@wo.cz**

Kostelec does have a castle and a large Ferodo factory, although not a lot else to commend it, but is a good centre from which to explore the interesting town of Hradec Kralove, East Bohemia, the Orlicke Hory and other high districts near the Polish border. Autocamping Orlice, situated on the edge of town near the swimming pool, has a river running by and is in a quiet location with a pleasant appearance. Surrounded by tall trees, the grass pitches are of generous size although not marked or numbered, on each side of a concrete grid road which runs the length of this rectangular site. There is room for 80 units, half having electric points (16A) and with shade in parts.

Facilities

The central sanitary block includes hot water in washbasins, sinks and good showers – it is of a good standard for the Czech Republic. Chemical disposal point. Limited food supplies are in a bar/lounge during July/Aug. Café/bar (15/5-30/9). Off site: Town swimming pool near (15/6-31/8). Tennis 100 m. Fishing 500 m. Riding 5 km.

Open: 15 May - 30 September.

Directions

Site is signed from the centre of town.
GPS: N50:06.949 E16:13.010

Charges 2007

Per person	CZK 46,00 - 50,00
child (6-14 yrs)	CZK 22,00 - 26,00
pitch with electricity	CZK 157,00 - 225,00
electricity	CZK 65,00

CZ4880 Camping Roznov

Horni Paseky 940, CZ-75661 Roznov pod Radhostem (Severomoravsky)

Tel: **571 648 001**. Email: **info@camproznov.cz**

Roznov pod Radhostem is halfway up the Roznovska Becva valley amidst the Beskydy hills which extend from North Moravia into Poland in the extreme east of the Republic. It is a busy tourist centre which attracts visitors to the Wallachian open air museum and those who enjoy hill walking. There are 300 pitches (200 for touring units), some of which are rather small, although there are some new landscaped pitches of 90-100 sq.m. Arranged on flat grass and set amidst a variety of fruit and other trees, there are 120 electrical connections (16A) and shade in some parts.

Facilities

The good quality central toilet block has hot water in showers, washbasins and sinks. A further well equipped toilet block has washbasins and WCs en-suite for ladies and a washing machine. Only very basic food items available in shop (not always open). Swimming pool (25 m. open July/Aug). Tennis. Off site: Europlan Hotel 300 m. Fishing and golf 1 km. Riding 4 km.

Open: All year.

Directions

Site is at eastern end of Roznov on the main 35/E442 Zilina - Olomouc road opposite sports stadium. GPS: N49:27.977 E18:09.840

Charges 2007

Per person	CZK 55,00 - 90,00
child (3-15 yrs)	CZK 45,00 - 70,00
pitch	CZK 95,00 - 175,00
electricity	CZK 60,00 - 80,00

CZ4710 Camping Chvalsiny

Chvalsiny 321, CZ-38208 Chvalsiny (Jihocesky)

Tel: **380 739 123**. Email: **info@campingchvalsiny.nl**

Camping Chvalsiny is Dutch owned and has been developed from an old farm. It has been developed into real camping fields which are terraced and level. A newly built toilet block houses excellent facilities and everything looks well maintained. The 200 pitches are of average size but look larger because of the open nature of the terrain which also means there is little shade. Chvalsiny is a real family site and children are kept occupied with painting, crafts and stories. Older youngsters take part in soccer, volleyball and rafting competitions.

Facilities

Modern, clean and well kept toilet facilities include washbasins in cabins and controllable showers (coin operated). Family showers and baby room. Laundry. Dishwashing under cover. Kiosk (1/6-13/9) with bread and daily necessities. Snack bar (1/6-15/9). Play attic. Lake swimming. Climbing equipment and swings. Crafts, games, table tennis and soccer. Torches useful. Off site: Village restaurants close. Riding 10 km.

Open: 26 April - 15 September.

Directions

Take exit 114 at Passau in Germany (near the Austrian border) towards Freyung in the Czech Republic. Continue to Philipsreut and take no. 4 road towards Vimperk. Turn right on 39 road to Horni Plana and Cesky Krumlov. Turn left 4 km. before Cesky Krumlov on no. 166 to Chvalsiny and follow signs through village. GPS: N48:51.350 E14:12.510

Charges 2007

Per person	CZK 100,00
pitch incl. electricity	CZK 350,00
No credit cards.	

CZ4650 Autocamping Luxor

Plzenska, CZ-35301 Velká Hledsebe (Zapadocesky)

Tel: **354 623 504**. Email: **autocamping.luxor@seznam.cz**

An orderly site, near the German border, Luxor is adequate as a stopover for a couple of days. Now under new management, it is in a quiet location by a small lake on the edge of the village of Velká Hledsebe, 4 km. from Marianbad. The 100 pitches (60 for touring units) are in the open on one side of the entrance road (cars stand on a tarmac park opposite the caravans) or in a clearing under tall trees away from the road. All pitches have access to electricity (10A) but connection in the clearings section may require long leads. Forty bungalows occupy one side of the site.

Facilities

Toilet buildings are old and should be refurbished, but the provision is more than adequate. Cleaning could be better. No chemical disposal point. Restaurant with self-service terrace (1/5-30/9). Rest room with TV, kitchen and dining area. Small playground. Fishing. Bicycle hire. Off site: Very good motel restaurant and shops 500 m. in village. Riding 5 km. Golf 8 km.

Open: 1 May - 30 September.

Directions

Site is directly by the Stribo - Cheb road (no. 21), 500 m. south of Velká Hledsebe. GPS: N49:57.145 E12:40.100

Charges 2007

Per unit incl. 2 persons and electricity	CZK 160,00 - 250,00
extra person	CZK 60,00
No credit cards.	

Check real time availability and at-the-gate prices...

www.**alanrogers**.com

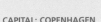

MAP 6

Denmark offers a diverse landscape all within a relatively short distance. The countryside is green and varied with flat plains, rolling hills, fertile farmland, many lakes and fjords, wild moors and long beaches, interrupted by pretty villages and towns.

CAPITAL: COPENHAGEN

Tourist Office

The Danish Tourist Board
55 Sloane Street, London SW1X 9SY
Tel: 020 7259 5959.
Fax: 020 7259 5955
Email: dtb.london@dt.dk
Internet: www.visitdenmark.com

Denmark is the easiest of the Scandinavian countries to visit, both in terms of cost and distance. There are many small islands but the main land masses that make up the country are the islands of Zeeland and Funen and the peninsula of Jutland, which extends northwards from the German border. Zeeland is the most visited region, its main draw being the capital, Copenhagen. This vibrant city has a beautiful old centre, an array of museums and art galleries plus a boisterous night life. Funen is the smaller of the two main islands and known as the Garden of Denmark, with its neat green fields and fruit and vegetable plots. Sandy beaches and quaint villages can be found here. Jutland has the most varied landscape ranging from heather-clad moors, dense forests to plunging gorges. It's also home to one of the most popular attractions in Denmark, Legoland, and the oldest town in Scandinavia, Ribe.

Population
5.3 million

Climate
Generally mild although changeable throughout the year.

Language
Danish, but English is widely spoken.

Telephone
The dialling code for Denmark is 00 45.

Money
Currency: Danish Krone
Banks: Mon-Wed & Fri 09.30-16.00, Thurs to 18.00. Closed Sat. In the provinces opening hours vary.

Shops
Hours may vary in the main cities. Regular openings are Mon-Thu 09.00-17.30, Fri 09.00- 19.00/20.00, and Sat 09.00-13.00/14.00.

Public Holidays
New Year's Day; Three Kings Day 6 Jan; April Fools Day 1 April; Maundy Thursday; Good Friday; Easter Monday; Queen's Birthday 16 April; Flag Day 18 April; Ascension; Whit Mon; Constitution Day 5 Jun; Valdemars 15 June; Mortens Day 11 Nov; Christmas 24- 26 Dec; New Year's Eve

Motoring
Driving is much easier than at home as roads are much quieter. Driving is on the right. Do not drink and drive. Dipped headlights are compulsory at all times. Strong measures are taken against unauthorised parking on beaches, with on the spot fines.

DK2015 Ådalens Camping

Gudenåvej 20, DK-6710 Esbjerg V-Sædding (Ribe)
Tel: **75 15 88 22**. Email: **info@adal.dk**

Owned and run by Britta and Peter Andersen, this superb site is in the northeast of Esbjerg and is a great starting point from which to tour the city with its harbour, museums and sea water aquarium. It is also convenient for those arriving on the ferry from Harwich (16 hours). From the attractive, tree lined drive, gravel lanes lead to large fields with well kept grass and good services. Ådalens has 193 pitches for touring visitors and 30 seasonal places. The pitches are split into groups of 5 or 10 by mature trees that provide some shade. There are 16 concrete hardstandings for large caravans or motorcaravans, 4 of which are fully serviced. Scattered around the site are a variety of newly planted shrubs and young trees. Ådalens is close to the beach but also has an attractive outdoor pool with waterfall, slide and paddling pool. Everything on this site is in pristine order, with amenities that will ensure a pleasant stay.

Facilities

Two modern toilet blocks with free hot showers. Special children's section in bright colours and family shower rooms (for rent). Excellent facilities for disabled visitors. Baby room. Laundry. Campers' kitchen. Motorcaravan services. Basics from reception (bread to order). Outdoor pool (15 x 10 m) with slide, waterfall, flume and paddling pool (1/6-1/9). Two new playgrounds. Animal farm. Giant chess. Minigolf. Internet access. TV room with library. Off site: Fishing, golf, bicycle hire and boat launching 5 km. City centre 5 km.

Open: All year.

Directions

From Esbjerg, take the 447 road northeast and continue along the coast. Turn right at sign for site and follow the signs. GPS: N55:30.778 E08:23.349

Charges 2007

Per person	DKK 69
child (1-11 yrs)	DKK 41

Camping Cheques accepted.

DK2020 Møgeltønder Camping

Sonderstregsvej 2, Møgeltønder, DK-6270 Tønder (Sønderjylland)
Tel: **74 73 84 60**. Email: **moegeltoender.camping@post.tele.dk**

This site is only five minutes walk from one of Denmark's oldest villages and ten minutes drive from Tønder with its well preserved old buildings and magnificent pedestrian shopping street. A quiet family site, Møgeltønder has 285 large, level, numbered pitches on grass, most with 10A electricity, divided up by new plantings of shrubs and small hedges. Only 35 pitches are occupied by long stay units, the remainder solely for touring units, and there are 15 cabins. The site also has an excellent outdoor heated swimming pool and children's pool, a good playground with bouncing cushion and a range of trolleys, carts and tricycles. From here you can visit the Schackenborg Castle Gardens (with guided tours) – the castle is owned by the Danish royal family and was built in 1283. The old town of Ribe is just 43 km. It is also convenient for the ferry ports.

Facilities

Two superb, modern, heated sanitary units include roomy showers (on payment), washbasins with either divider/curtain or in private cubicles, plus excellent bathrooms for families and disabled visitors. Baby room. Two kitchens with hobs (free). Laundry. Motorcaravan services. Shop for essentials (bread ordered daily). Swimming pool (10 x 5 m.) and paddling pool. Minigolf. Playground. TV and games rooms. Internet access. Off site: Golf and bicycle hire 10 km.

Open: All year.

Directions

Turn left off no. 419 Tønder - Højer road, 4 km. from Tønder. Drive through Møgeltønder village and past the church where site is signed. The main street is cobbled so drive slowly.

Charges 2007

Per person	DKK 56
child (0-12 yrs)	DKK 29
electricity	DKK 22
dog	DKK 5

DK2010 Hvidbjerg Strand Camping

Hvidbjerg Strandvej 27, DK-6857 Blavand (Ribe)

Tel: 75 27 90 40. Email: info@hvidbjerg.dk

A family owned, 'TopCamp' holiday site, Hvidbjerg Strand is on the west coast near Blåvands Huk, 43 km. from Esbjerg. It is a high quality, seaside site with a wide range of amenities. Most of the 570 pitches have electricity (6/10A) and the 130 'comfort' pitches also have water, drainage and satellite TV. To the rear of the site 70 new fully serviced pitches have been developed, some up to 250 sq.m and 16 with private sanitary facilities. Most pitches are individual and divided by hedges, in rows on flat sandy grass, with areas also divided by small trees and hedges. On site leisure facilities include an indoor suite of supervised play rooms, designed for all ages with Lego, computers, video games, television and more, plus an impressive, tropical style indoor pool complex. This includes stalactite caves and a 70 m. water chute, the 'Black Hole' with sounds and lights, plus water slides, spa baths, Turkish bath and a sauna. A Blue Flag beach and windsurfing school are adjacent to the site and the town offers a full activity programme during the main season (mid June - mid Aug). Member of Leading Campings Group.

Facilities

Five superb toilet units include washbasins (many in cubicles), roomy showers, spa baths, suites for disabled visitors, family bathrooms, kitchens and laundry facilities. The most recent units include a children's bathrooms decorated with dinosaur or Disney characters and racing car baths. Motorcaravan services. Supermarket. Café/restaurant. TV rooms. Pool complex, solarium and sauna. Play areas. Supervised play rooms (09.00-16.00 daily). Barbecue areas. Minigolf, football, squash and badminton. Riding (Western style). Fishing. Dog showers. ATM machine. Off site: Legoland 70 km.

Open: 31 March - 22 October.

Directions

From Varde take roads 181/431 to Blåvand. Site is signed left on entering the town (mind speed bump on town boundary).

Charges 2007

Per person	€ 10,34
child (0-11 yrs)	€ 7,59
pitch	€ 3,45 - € 16,55
electricity (6/10A)	€ 4,41 - € 4,97
dog	€ 3,72

DK2140 Jesperhus Feriecenter & Camping

Legindvej 30, DK-7900 Nykobing Mors (Viborg)

Tel: 96 70 14 00. Email: jesperhus@jesperhus.dk

Jesperhus is an extensive, well organised and busy site with many leisure activities, adjacent to Blomsterpark (flower park). It is a 'TopCamp' site with 662 numbered pitches, mostly in rows with some terracing, divided by shrubs and trees and with shade in parts. Many pitches are taken by seasonal, tour operator or rental units, so advance booking is advised for peak periods. Electricity (6A) is available on all pitches and water points are in all areas. The indoor and outdoor pool complex (daily charge) has three pools, diving boards, water slides with the 'Black Hole', spa pools, saunas and a solarium. With all the activities at this site an entire holiday could be spent here regardless of the weather, although Jesperhus is also an excellent centre for touring. Although it may appear to be just part of Jutland, Mors is an island in its own right surrounded by the lovely Limfjord. It is joined to the mainland by a fine 2,000 m. bridge at the end of which are signs to Blomsterpark (Northern Europe's largest flower park which also houses a Bird Zoo, Butterfly World, Terrarium and Aquarium) and the campsite – both under the same ownership. The flower park, situated well to the north of Denmark, is an incredible sight from early spring to late autumn, attracting some 4,000 visitors a day to enjoy over half a million flowering plants and magnificent landscaped gardens.

Facilities

Four good sanitary units are cleaned three times daily. Facilities include washbasins in cubicles or with divider/curtain, family and whirlpool bathrooms (on payment), suites for babies and disabled people. Free sauna. Superb kitchens and a fully equipped laundry. Supermarket (1/4-1/11) with gas. Restaurant. Bar. Café, takeaway. Pool complex with solarium. Bowling centre. Attractive minigolf. Tennis. Go-carts and other outdoor sports. Indoor sports hall and children's 'play-world'. Playgrounds. Pets corner. Golf. Fishing pond. Practice golf (3 holes). Off site: Riding 2 km. Bicycle hire 6 km. Beach 2 km.

Open: All year.

Directions

From south or north, take road no. 26 to Salling Sund bridge, site is signed Jesperhus, just north of the bridge. GPS: N56:45.049 E08:48.948

Charges 2007

Per person	DKK 75
child (1-11 yrs)	DKK 55
pitch	free - DKK 50
electricity	DKK 40

DK2022 Vikær Diernæs Strand Camping

Dundelum 29, Diernæs, DK-6100 Haderslev (Sønderjylland)

Tel: **74 57 54 64**. Email: **info@vikaercamp.dk**

The warm welcome at Vikær Diernæs will start your holiday off in the right way. This family site in Southern Jutland lies in beautiful surroundings, right on the Diernæs Bugt beaches – ideal for both active campers and relaxation seekers. The attractively laid out site has 330 grass pitches (210 for touring units), all with 10/16A electricity and separated by low hedges. Access is from long, gravel lanes. The upper part of the site provides 40 newly developed, fully serviced pitches with electricity, water, sewage, TV aerial point and internet. From these, and from the front pitches on the lower fields, there are marvellous views over the Diernæs Bugt. The site is next to a 'Blue Flag' beach providing safe swimming. For the active there are several routes for walking and cycling and, of course, sea fishing trips are possible. In the area are a newly developed swamp nature reserve, Schackenborg Castle and the battlefields of Dybbøl Banke.

Facilities

Three modern toilet blocks (one refurbished in 2007) with washbasins in cabins and controllable hot showers. Family shower rooms. Children's section. Baby room. En-suite facilities for disabled visitors. Laundry. Campers' kitchen. Motorcaravan services. Shop (Thursday - Sunday 7.30 - 21.00). Playground. Minigolf. Fishing. Archery. Watersports and boat launching. Petanque. New TV room. Play house with Lego and Play Station. Daily activities for children in high season. Torch useful. English is spoken. Off site: Golf 30 minutes. Riding 2 km.

Open: Week before Easter - mid October.

Directions

From German/Danish border follow E45 north. Take exit 69 and follow to Hoptrup. From Hoptrup follow to Diernæs and Diernæs Strand.

Charges 2007

Per person	DKK 67
child (under 12 yrs)	DKK 45
pitch	DKK 25 - 60
electricity	DKK 28
dog	DKK 10

DK2030 Sandersvig Camping & Tropeland

Espagervej 15-17, DK-6100 Haderslev (Sønderjylland)

Tel: **74 56 62 25**. Email: **sandersvig@dk-camp.dk**

An attractively laid out, family run site, Sandersvig offers the very best of modern facilities in a peaceful and beautiful countryside location, 300 metres from the beach. The 470 very large grassy pitches (270 for tourers) are divided by hedges, shrubs and small trees into small enclosures, many housing only four units, most with electricity (10A). The site is well lit, very quiet at night and there are water taps close to most pitches. The playground apparently boasts Denmark's largest bouncing cushion! Opposite the site, on the road to the beach, the site owners have planted new woodland. Sandersvig makes a very comfortable base for excursions. Visit nearby historic Kolding with its castle, museums and shops, the beautiful old town of Christiansfeld or the restored windmill at Sillerup. The drive to the island of Fyn takes less than an hour, with miles of country lanes around the site for cycling and walking.

Facilities

Four heated sanitary blocks offer some washbasins in cubicles and roomy showers (on payment). Suites for disabled visitors, 14 family bathrooms and baby rooms. Excellent kitchens with ovens, electric hobs. Very good laundry. Fish cleaning area. Motorcaravan services. Well stocked supermarket and fast food service, with dining room adjacent (Easter-15/9). Takeaway (15/6-15/8). Indoor heated pool with sauna, solarium, jacuzzi, whirlpool and slide (DKK 12.50). Solarium. Playground. Games room. TV lounge. Tennis. Boat launching. Off site: Riding 4 km. Bicycle hire 6 km. Fishing 7 km. Golf 16 km.

Open: 7 April - 17 September.

Directions

Leave E45 at exit 66 and turn towards Christianfeld. Turn right at roundabout onto 170 and follow signs for Fjelstrup and Knud village, turning right 1 km. east of the village from where site is signed.

Charges 2007

Per person	DKK 62
child (0-11 yrs)	DKK 36
pitch	DKK 15 - 40
electricity (10A)	DKK 25

DK2036 **Gammelmark Strand Camping**

Gammelmark 16, DK-6310 Broager (Sønderjylland)

Tel: **74 44 17 42**. Email: **info@gammelmark.dk**

The Siegers, a Danish/Dutch couple, have owned the site since 2001. Gammelmark has 289 level, grass pitches (200 for tourers), all with 13A electricity. From the new fully serviced pitches on the top terraces there are some great views of the Flensburger Förde. This site combines Danish hospitality with historical interest. In 1864 war was waged between the Danes and the Germans over the Flensburger Förde and this site organises excursions to the war museum in Dybbøl Banke where you can learn all about this devastating period in Danish history. It is useful as a stop over on your way to north, but also a good choice for the active camper.

Facilities

Modern, heated facilities include some washbasins in cabins and controllable hot showers (DKK 2). Facilities for babies, children and disabled visitors. Laundry. Shop. Activities organised. Playground. Animal farm. Fishing. Riding. Sailing. Diving. English is spoken. Off site: Bar and restaurant 2 km. Bicycle hire 6 km. Golf 10 km.

Open: Easter - 22 October.

Directions

From Flensburg take no. 7 road north and at exit 75 turn east towards Sønderborg. Take exit for Dynt and follow site signs.

Charges 2007

Per person	€ 9,03
pitch	€ 2,08 - € 5,76
electricity (plus meter)	€ 2,08

DK2040 **TopCamp Riis**

Osterhovedvej 43, DK-7323 Give (Vejle)

Tel: **75 73 14 33**. Email: **info@topcampriis.dk**

TopCamp Riis is a good quality touring site ideal for visiting Legoland (18 km) and Givskov Zoo (3 km). It is a friendly, family run 'TopCamp' site with 235 large touring pitches on sheltered, gently sloping, well tended lawns surrounded by trees and shrubs. Electricity (6A) is available to 205 pitches, 10 comfort pitches have electricity, water and waste water and there are 51 site owned cabins. The outdoor heated pool and water-slide complex and adjacent bar that serves beer, ice cream, soft drinks and snacks are only open in main season.

Facilities

Two excellent sanitary units (the older one now refurbished) include washbasins with divider/curtain and showers (on payment). Suites for babies and disabled visitors, family bathrooms (one with whirlpool bath, on payment) and solarium. Two excellent kitchens (on payment). Large sitting room with TV, plus a covered barbecue grill area. Cafe/bar. Laundry. Motorcaravan services. Shop. Pool complex. Minigolf. New playground. Train ride for children. Animal farm. Bicycle hire. WiFi internet. Off site: Fishing and golf 4 km. Beach 35 km.

Open: 31 March - 30 September.

Directions

Turn onto Osterhovedvej southeast of Give town centre (near Shell Garage) at sign to Riis and site. After 4 km. turn left into tarmac drive which runs through the forest to the site. Alternatively, turn off the 442 Brande-Jelling road at Riis village north of Givskud.

Charges 2007

Per person	DKK 69
child (0-11 yrs)	DKK 46
pitch	DKK 50 - 80
electricity	DKK 30

DK2044 **Hampen Sø Camping**

Hovedgaden 31, DK-7362 Hampen (Vejle)

Tel: **75 77 52 55**. Email: **info@hampen-soe-camping.dk**

If you are heading up towards Denmark to cross to Norway or Sweden, then this site in a natural setting close to lakes and moors could be a useful stopover. There are 230 pitches in total, with 80 seasonal units plus 34 cabins, but there will always be space for touring units. The pitches are arranged in large grassy bays taking around 15 units, and there are 10A electric hook-ups (some long leads may be needed). The nearby Hampen See lake is a pleasant walk through the forest and is said to be one of the cleanest lakes for swimming in Denmark.

Facilities

Three toilet blocks, one basic near the entrance, one central with new children's room and kitchen, and one at the far end with family shower rooms. Facilities for disabled visitors. Laundry. Good supermarket and restaurant (all year, w/ends in winter). Takeaway. Small outdoor pool (15/6-1/9). Covered minigolf. Play area. Race track for mini cars. Games and TV rooms. WiFi. Off site: Riding 500 m. Fishing 3 km. Golf 18 km.

Open: All year.

Directions

Site lies on road no.176, 500 m. southwest of its junction with road no.13 between Vejle and Viborg (around 50 km. south of Viborg). Look for Spar minimarket and camping signs.
GPS: N56:00.855 E09:21.856

Charges 2007

Per person	€ 8,97
electricity	€ 3,86

No credit cards. Camping Cheques accepted.

DK2046 Trelde Næs Colorcamp

Trelde Næsvej 297, Trelde, DK-7000 Fredericia (Vejle)

Tel: 75 95 71 83. Email: trelde@colorcamp.dk

Trelde Næs Color Camp is one of the larger Danish sites with 500 level and numbered pitches. The 400 touring pitches all have 10A electricity and there are 37 fully serviced pitches with electricity, water, wastewater and internet. Seasonal units take up the remaining pitches. Pitching is off tarmac access roads on well kept, grass fields with some shade from bushes at the rear. The toilet buildings are older in style but the fittings are good. At the front of the site is a heated, open air, fun pool with large slide, bubble bath, water curtain and play island. This is connected to a room with a sauna, Turkish baths and massage chairs, with play stations for children. The site is right next to the beach, but also close to the nature reserve of Trelde Næs which has been part of the Royal estates since the 14th century. City and culture lovers are well off too, for the historic town of Fredericia is close. Here we recommend you take the tour of the Walls, built by King Christian IV, and visit Den Historiske Miniby, a miniature model park of Fredericia.

Facilities

Four traditional toilet blocks have washbasins in cabins and controllable hot showers (card operated). Child size toilets and basins. Family shower room. Baby room. Laundry. Fun pool (10 x 20 m.) with island, large slide, Turkish bath, solarium and sauna. Shop. Takeaway. Several playgrounds. Minigolf. Fishing. Watersports. Full entertainment programme in high season for children. TV room. WiFi. Cabins and rooms to rent. Off site: Boat launching 7 km. Golf 6 km. Bicycle hire 6 km.

Open: All year.

Directions

From Fredericia follow road no. 28 north and take Trelde exit. Follow signs for Trelde and Trelde Næs.

Charges guide

Per person	DKK 66
child (0-11 yrs)	DKK 42
pitch	DKK 50
with services	DKK 30 - 70
electricity	DKK 25

Camping Cheques accepted.

DK2048 Fårup Sø Camping

Fårupvej 58, DK-7300 Jelling (Vejle)

Tel: 75 87 13 44. Email: faarup-soe@dk-camp.dk

This site was originally set up on the old farm woodlands of Jelling Skov where local farmers each had their own plot. Owned by the Dutch/Danish Albring family, this is a rural location on the Fårup Lake. Many of the trees have now been removed to give the site a welcoming, open feel. Fårup Sø Camping has 250 grassy pitches, mostly on terraces (from top to bottom the height difference is 53 m). The 35 newest terraced pitches provide beautiful views of the countryside and the Fårup lake. There are 200 pitches for touring units, most with 10A electricity, and some tent pitches without electricity. Next to the top toilet block is an open air barbecue area with a terrace and good views. A neighbour rents out water bikes and takes high season excursions onto the lake with a real Viking Ship which campers can join. During the last weekend of May the site celebrates the Jelling Musical Festival when it is advisable to book in advance. This family site is ideal for those who want to enjoy a relaxed holiday on the lakeside beaches or walking or cycling through the surrounding country. Some of Denmark's best known attractions such as Legoland and the Lion Park are nearby.

Facilities

One modern and one older toilet block have British style toilets, open style washbasins and controllable hot showers. Family shower rooms. Baby room. Facilities for disabled visitors. Laundry. Campers' kitchen. Motorcaravan services. Shop (bread to order). Outdoor swimming pool (15 x 5 m). New playgrounds. Minigolf. Games room. Pony riding. Lake with fishing, watersports and Viking ship. Animation, bread baking and campsite train for children (high season). Internet. Off site: Golf and riding 2 km. Lion Park 8 km. Boat launching 10 km. Legoland 20 km.

Open: 1 April - 30 September.

Directions

From Vejle take the 28 road towards Billund. In Skibet turn right towards Fårup Sø/Jennum/Jelling and follow the signs to Fårup Sô.
GPS: N55:44.159 E09:25.063

Charges 2007

Per person	DKK 61
child (3-11 yrs)	DKK 35
pitch	DKK 15 - 35
electricity	DKK 28

DK2080 Holmens Camping

Klostervej 148, DK-8680 Ry (Århus)

Tel: **86 89 17 62**. Email: **info@holmens-camping.dk**

Holmens Camping lies between Silkeborg and Skanderborg in a very beautiful part of Denmark. The site is close to the waters of the Gudensø and Rye Møllesø lakes which are used for boating and canoeing. Walking and cycling are also popular activities. Holmens has 225 grass touring pitches, partly terraced and divided by young trees and shrubs. The site itself is surrounded by mature trees. Almost all the pitches have 6A electricity and vary in size between 70-100 sq.m. A small tent field is close to the lake, mainly used by those who travel by canoe. The lake is suitable for swimming but the site also has an attractive pool complex. This comprises two circular pools linked by a bridge and a paddling pool with water canon. There are plenty of opportunities for activities including boat hire on the lake and for fishing (the site has its own fishing pond). Both Skanderborg and Silkeborg are worth a visit and in Ry you can attend the Skt. Hans party which takes place at midsummer.

Facilities

One traditional and one modern toilet block have washbasins (open and in cabins) and controllable hot showers (on payment). En-suite facilities with toilet, basin, shower. Baby room. Excellent facilities for disabled visitors. Laundry. Campers' kitchen. Small shop. Covered pool with jet stream and paddling pool with water canon. Finnish sauna, solarium, massage and fitness facilities (charged). Pool bar. Extensive games room. Playground. Tennis. Minigolf. Fishing. Bicycle hire. Boat rental. Large units are not accepted. Off site: Riding 2 km. Golf 14 km.

Open: 16 March - 29 September.

Directions

Going north on E45, take exit 52 at Skanderborg turning west on 445 road towards Ry. In Ry follow the site signs. GPS: N56:04.568 E09:45.601

Charges 2007

Per person	DKK 62 - 73
child (3-11 yrs)	DKK 35 - 40
pitch	DKK 20

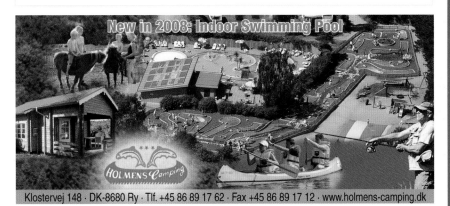

Klostervej 148 · DK-8680 Ry · Tlf. +45 86 89 17 62 · Fax +45 86 89 17 12 · www.holmens-camping.dk

DK2050 Terrassen Camping

Himmelbjergvej 9A, Laven, DK-8600 Silkeborg (Århus)

Tel: **86 84 13 01**. Email: **info@terrassen.dk**

Terrassen Camping is a family run site arranged on terraces, overlooking Lake Julso and the surrounding countryside. There are 260 pitches with good views, most with electricity (6/10A) and three hardstanding pitches for motorcaravans. A small area for tents (no electricity) is at the top of the site where torches may be required. There are also 29 seasonal units, and some site owned cabins. The solar heated pool has a paved terrace and is well fenced. This is a comfortable base from which to explore this area of Denmark where a warm welcome and good English will greet you.

Facilities

The main modern sanitary unit is heated and includes many washbasins in cubicles. Controllable showers (on payment). Family bathrooms. Facilities for disabled visitors. Kitchen. An older unit contains another kitchen, plus 4 more shower cubicles with external access. Motorcaravan services. Shop. Pool (8 x 16 m; 15/5-31/8). Games/TV rooms with internet. Adventure playground. Toddlers play room. Pets corner. Canoe hire. Bicycle hire. Riding. Off site: Fishing 200 m. Golf, sailing 5 km.

Open: 18 March - 18 September.

Directions

From the harbour in the centre of Silkeborg follow signs and minor road towards Sejs (5 km.) and Ry (20 km). Site lies on the northern side of the road at village of Laven (13 km). Note: Height restriction of 3 m. on railway bridge over this road.

Charges 2007

Per person	DKK 72
child (1-11 yrs)	DKK 48
pitch	free - DKK 40
electricity	DKK 30

DK2070 Fornæs Camping

Stensmarkvej 36, DK-8500 Grenå (Århus)

Tel: **86 33 23 30**. Email: **fornaes@1031.inord.dk**

In the grounds of a former farm, Fornæs Camping is about 5 km. from Grenå. From reception a wide, gravel access road descends through a large grassy field to the sea. Pitches to the left are mostly level, to the right slightly sloping with some terracing and views of the Kattegat. The rows of pitches are divided into separate areas by colourful bushes and each row is marked by a concrete tub containing a young tree and colourful flowers. Fornæs has 320 pitches of which 240 are for tourers, the others being used for seasonal visitors. All touring pitches have 10A electricity.

Facilities

Two toilet blocks have British style toilets, washbasins in cabins and hot showers (DKK 2). Child-size toilets. Family shower rooms. Baby room. Facilities for disabled people. Fully equipped laundry. Campers' kitchen. Motorcaravan service point. Shop. Café/grill with bar and takeaway (evenings). Pool (80 sq.m). Sauna and solarium. Adventure playground. Games room with TV. Minigolf. Fishing. Watersports. Off site: Golf and riding 5 km.

Open: 15 March - 20 September.

Directions

From Århus follow the 15 road towards Grenå and then the 16 road towards town centre. Turn north and follow signs for Fornæs and the site. GPS: N56:27.361 E10:56.464

Charges 2007

Per person	DKK 67 - 75
child (1-12 yrs)	DKK 38 - 42
electricity (10A)	DKK 28

Credit cards 5% surcharge.

DK2100 Blushoj Camping

Elsegårdevej 55, DK-8400 Ebeltoft (Århus)

Tel: **86 34 12 38**

This is a traditional type of site where the owners are making a conscious effort to keep mainly to touring units – there are only six seasonal units and four rental cabins. The site has 250 pitches on levelled grassy terraces surrounded by mature hedging and shrubs. Some have glorious views of the Kattegat and others overlook peaceful rural countryside. Most pitches have electricity (10A), but long leads may be required. There is a heated, fenced swimming pool (14 x 7 m.) with a water slide and terrace. The beach below the site provides opportunities for swimming, windsurfing and sea fishing.

Facilities

One toilet unit includes washbasins with dividers and showers with divider and seat (on payment). The other unit has a new kitchen with electric hobs, dining/TV room, laundry and baby facilities. Six very smart family bathrooms, and additional WCs and washbasins. Motorcaravan service point. Well stocked shop. Swimming pool (20/5-20/8). Minigolf. Play area. Games room. Beach. Fishing. Internet access. Off site: Riding, bicycle hire, boat launching and golf 5 km.

Open: 1 April - 15 September.

Directions

From road 21 northwest of Ebeltoft turn off at junction where several sites are signed towards Dråby. Follow signs through the outskirts of Ebeltoft turning southeast to Elsegårde village. Turn left for Blushøj and follow camp signs. GPS: N56:10.066 E10:43.843

Charges 2007

Per person	DKK 66 - 75
electricity	DKK 25

No credit cards.

DK2130 Hobro Camping Gattenborg

Skivevej 35, DK-9500 Hobro (Nordjylland)

Tel: **98 52 32 88**. Email: **hobro@dk-camp.dk**

This neat and very well tended municipal site is imaginatively landscaped and has 139 pitches on terraces arranged around a bowl shaped central activity area. Most pitches (100 for touring units) have electricity (10A) and there are many trees and shrubs. Footpaths connect the various terraces and activity areas. There are 30 seasonal units and 10 cabins. The reception building with a small shop and tourist information, has a covered picnic terrace behind, and a large TV lounge.

Facilities

The main heated sanitary building includes washbasins in cubicles and hot showers (on payment). Two family bathrooms. Facilities for disabled people. Baby room. Kitchen with hobs, sinks and free herbs. Washing machine and dryer. Motorcaravan services. Shop (order bread before 9 pm). Swimming pool (high season). Play areas. Minigolf. TV lounge with board games and library. Bicycle hire. Internet access. Off site: Town 500 m. Beach 1 km. Fishing 7 km. Golf 25 km.

Open: 1 April - 1 October.

Directions

From E45 exit 35, take road 579 towards Hobro Centrum. Site is well signed to the right, just after railway bridge. GPS: N56:38.083 E09:46.953

Charges 2007

Per person	DKK 60 - 70
child (0-11 yrs)	DKK 30 - 36
electricity	DKK 25

DK2150 Solyst Camping

Logstorvej 2, DK-9240 Nibe (Nordjylland)

Tel: **98 35 10 62**. Email: **soelyst@dk-camp.dk**

You will always be near the water in Denmark, either open sea or, as here, alongside the more sheltered waters of a fjord – Limfjord. Sølyst is a family run site providing 170 numbered pitches, of which 120 are for touring units. All have electricity (6A) and are arranged on gently sloping grass in fairly narrow rows separated by hedges. There are facilities for watersports and swimming in the fjord, the site also has a small heated swimming pool (8 x 16 m), slide and splash pool and a children's pool all with paved sunbathing area, and paddle boats can be rented. A little train provides rides for children. Good paths have been provided for superb, easy walks in either direction, and indeed right into the nearby town of Nibe. This is a delightful example of an old Danish town with picturesque cottages and handsome 15th century church. Its harbour, once prosperous from local herring boats, is now more concerned with pleasure craft.

Facilities

A central sanitary unit includes washbasins in cubicles, four family bathrooms, a baby room and facilities for disabled visitors. Good kitchen and small dining area. Fully equipped laundry. A second unit provides extra facilities. Hot water (except in washbasins) is charged for. Motorcaravan services. Shop. Snack bar and takeaway (main season). Swimming pool. Solarium. Play area. Minigolf. Boules. TV room. Games room. Fishing. Bicycle hire. Boat launching. Beach. Off site: Riding 1 km. Town of Nibe 1 km. Golf 4 km.

Open: All year.

Directions

Site is clearly signed from the no. 187 road west of Nibe town, with a wide entrance.
GPS: N56:58.332 E09:37.475

Charges 2007

Per person	DKK 67
child (under 12 yrs)	DKK 35
pitch	DKK 20
electricity	DKK 27

DK2165 Skiveren Camping

Niels Skiverenrej 5-7, DK-9982 Skiveren/Aalbæk (Nordjylland)

Tel: **98 93 22 00**. Email: **info@skiveren.dk**

This friendly seaside site, a member of the Danish 'TopCamp' organisation, is set up in 'maritime' style with the pitches separated by low wooden poles connected by a sailor's rope. Skiveren Camping has 670 pitches (595 for tourers), almost all with 6/10A electricity. Around the site are different varieties of low spruce and fir which give the site a pleasing appearance and atmosphere. The level pitches are of a good size (up to 120 sq.m), some having a picnic table and all are separated from the main tarmac access road by the low wooden fences. Toilet facilities look immaculate and the main block has an attractive, light blue children's section in maritime style again, with a lighthouse and a boat. The site has its own fitness centre with an outdoor pool, sauna, steam bath and solarium. This whole area is also great for a seaside holiday on the Ålbæk Bugt beaches. Other possibilities are walking and cycling on the surrounding moors or a visit to the interesting old harbour town of Skagen.

Facilities

Three immaculate toilet blocks include free family showers and private facilities with shower, toilet and basin for rent (DKK 40-60). Facilities for disabled visitors. Laundry. Campers' kitchen. Motorcaravan services. Supermarket. Strand Café for meals, drinks and takeaway. Outdoor pool (15 x 8 m) with whirlpool and sauna. Playground with area for toddlers. New indoor play hall. Multisports court. Tennis. Games room with wide screen TV. Bicycle hire. Children's club daily (from 16.00). Live music and dancing. Off site: Fishing 14 km. Golf 7 km. Riding 10 km.

Open: Easter - 30 September.

Directions

From the no. 40 road going north from Ålbæk, turn left at sign for 'Skiveren'. Follow this road all the way to the end. GPS: N57:36.997 E10:16.803

Charges 2007

Per person	DKK 55 - 73
child (1-11 yrs)	DKK 36 - 51
pitch	DKK 25 - 65
with water and drainage	DKK 45 - 95
electricity (6/10A)	DKK 27 - 37
Credit cards 4% surcharge.	

DK2170 Klim Strand Camping

Havvejen 167, Klim Strand, DK-9690 Fjerritslev (Nordjylland)

Tel: **98 22 53 40**. Email: **ksc@klim-strand.dk**

A large family holiday site right beside the sea, Klim Strand is a paradise for children. It is a privately owned 'TopCamp' site with a full complement of quality facilities, including its own fire engine and trained staff. The site has 560 numbered touring pitches, all with electricity (10A), laid out in rows, many divided by trees and hedges and shade in parts. Some 220 of these are fully serviced with electricity, water, drain and 18 channel TV connection. On site activities include an outdoor water slide complex, an indoor pool complex, tennis courts and pony riding (all free). A 'Wellness' centre is a recent addition. For children there are numerous play areas, an adventure playground with aerial cable ride and a roller skating area. There is a kayak school and a large bouncy castle for toddlers. Live music and dancing are organised twice a week in high season. Suggested excursions include trips to offshore islands, visits to local potteries, a brewery museum and bird watching on the Bygholm Vejle. Member of Leading Campings Group.

Facilities

Two good, large, heated toilet blocks are central, with spacious showers and some washbasins in cubicles. Separate children's room. Baby rooms. Bathrooms for families (some charged) and disabled visitors. Dog bathroom. Two smaller units are by reception and beach. Laundry. Well equipped kitchens and barbecue areas. TV lounges. Motorcaravan services. Supermarket. Pizzeria. Restaurant and bar. Sauna, solariums, whirlpool bath, hairdressing rooms, fitness room. Wellness centre. Internet cafe. TV rental. Pool complex. Play areas. Crèche. Bicycle hire. Cabins to rent. Off site: Golf 10 km. Boat launching 25 km.

Open: 1 April - 31 December.

Directions

Turn off Thisted-Fjerritslev no. 11 road to Klim from where site is signed. GPS: N57:08.000 E09:10.140

Charges 2007

Per person	DKK 75
child (1-11 yrs)	DKK 55
pitch	DKK 115
electricity	DKK 30

DK2180 Nordstrand Camping

Apholmenvej 40, DK-9900 Frederikshaven (Nordjylland)

Tel: **98 42 93 50**. Email: **info@nordstrand-camping.dk**

An excellent site, Nordstrand is 2 km. from Frederikshaven and the ferries to Sweden and Norway. It is another 'TopCamp' site and provides all the comforts one could possibly need with all the attractions of the nearby beach, town and port. The 430 large pitches are attractively arranged in small enclosures of 9-13 units surrounded by hedges and trees. Many hedges are of flowering shrubs and this makes for a very pleasant atmosphere. 250 pitches have electricity (10A) and drainage, a further 20 have water and there are 16 on hardstandings. There are 64 seasonal units, plus 23 site owned cabins. The roads are all paved and the site is well lit and fenced with the barrier locked at night. The reception complex also houses a café (high season), with a telephone pizza service available at other times. The beach is a level, paved 200 m. walk. On the roof of the indoor pool a small terrace gives views of the beach and the Ålbæk Bugt. There is much to see in this area of Denmark and this site would make a very comfortable holiday base.

Facilities

Centrally located, large toilet blocks provide spacious showers (on payment) and washbasins in cubicles, together with some family bathrooms, rooms for disabled people and babies. All are spotlessly clean. Laundry. Good kitchens at each block and some covered terraces. Motorcaravan services. Supermarket (all season). Café (15/6-15/8). Pizza service. Indoor swimming pool. Sauna. Solarium. 'Short' golf course. Minigolf. Tennis. Bicycle hire. Play areas. Internet access (free). Off site: Beach 200 m. Frederikshavn with shops 2 km.

Open: 1 April - 20 October.

Directions

Turn off the main no. 40 road 2 km. north of Frederikshaven at roundabout just north of railway bridge. Site is signed. GPS: N57:27.853 E10:31.653

Charges 2007

Per person	DKK 70
child (0-11 yrs)	DKK 50
pitch	DKK 50
electricity	DKK 29
dog	DKK 10

DK2200 Bøjden Strand Ferie Park

Bjden Landevej 12, Bjden, DK-5600 Fåborg (Fyn)

Tel: **63 60 63 60**. Email: **info@bojden.dk**

Bøjden is located in one of the most beautiful corners of southwest Fyn (Funen in English) known as the 'Garden of Denmark'. This is a well equipped site separated from the beach only by a hedge. Bøjden is a delightful site for an entire holiday, while remaining a very good centre for excursions. Arranged in rows on mainly level grassy terraces and divided into groups by hedges and some trees, many pitches have sea views as the site slopes gently down from the road. The 295 pitches (210 for touring units) all have electricity (10A) and include 65 new fully serviced pitches.

Facilities

The superb, central toilet block includes washbasins in cubicles, controllable showers, family bathrooms (some whirlpools and double showers), baby room and excellent facilities for disabled people. Well appointed kitchen and laundry. Motorcaravan services. Supermarket. Licenced restaurant. Takeaway. Indoor and outdoor swimming pools. Solarium. Toddler play area and separate adventure playground. TV and games rooms. Internet café and WiFi. Barbecue area. Fishing. Minigolf. Off site: Beach adjacent. Bicycle hire and riding 10 km. Golf 12 km.

Open: 14 March - 20 October.

Directions

From Faaborg follow road no. 8 to Bøjden and site is on right 500 m. before ferry terminal (from Fynshav). GPS: N55:06.317 E10:06.765

Charges 2007

Per person	DKK 67
child (0-11 yrs)	DKK 45
pitch	DKK 10 - 100
electricity	DKK 31

Credit cards accepted with 5% surcharge.
Camping Cheques accepted.

DK2205 Løgismosestrand Camping

Løgismoseskov 7, DK-5683 Hårby (Fyn)

Tel: **64 77 12 50**. Email: **info@logismose.dk**

A countryside site with its own beach and pool, Løgismosestrand is surrounded by picturesque villages and the owners are a friendly young couple. The 220 pitches here are arranged in rows and groups divided by hedges and small trees which provide a little shade. All the 221 pitches for touring units have 6/10A electricity points. A barbecue area has been developed with gas grills and there are swimming (8 x 14 m.) and paddling pools for which there is a small charge. Recent additions include an Asian restaurant, a new football pitch and ten cabins to rent.

Facilities

Heated toilet units, kept very clean, include washbasins in cubicles, roomy showers (on payment), baby room, bathrooms for families and disabled people. Good laundry facilites. Excellent kitchen (cooking facilities charged). Motorcaravan services. Well stocked shop. Restaurant. Takeaway (high season). Swimming pool (1/6-1/9). Minigolf. Bicycle and boat hire. Adventure playground. Games room. Off site: Riding 2 km. Golf 8 km.

Open: 20 March - 22 September.

Directions

Southwest of Hårby via Sarup and Nellemose to Løgismose Skov, site is well signed. Lanes are narrow, take care. GPS: N55:10.763 E10:04.434

Charges 2007

Per person	DKK 59
child (0-11 yrs)	DKK 35
pitch	free - DKK 40
electricity	DKK 26

Credit cards accepted with 4% surcharge.

DK2210 Bøsøre Strand Feriepark

Bøsørevej 16, DK-5874 Hesselager (Fyn)

Tel: **62 25 11 45**. Email: **info@bosore.dk**

A themed holiday site on the eastern coast of Fyn, the tales of Hans Christian Andersen are evident in the design of the indoor pool complex and the main outdoor children's playground at this site. The former has two pools on different levels, two hot tubs and a sauna and features characters from the stories, the latter has a fairytale castle with moat as its centrepiece. There are 300 pitches in total, and with only 25 seasonal units there should always be room for tourers out of the main season.

Facilities

Sanitary facilities are in one main central block and a smaller unit close to reception. They provide all usual facilities plus some family bathrooms, special children's section, baby rooms, facilities for disabled people. They could be stretched in high season. Laundry. Motorcaravan service point. Shop, bar/restaurant, pizzeria, takeaway. Kitchen (water charged). Solarium. Indoor pool complex. Games and TV rooms. Animal farm. Internet access and WiFi. Bicycle hire. Entertainment (main season).

Open: Easter - 22 October.

Directions

Site is on the coast about midway between Nyborg and Svendborg. From road no. 163 just north of Hesselager, turn towards coast signed Bøsøre Strand (5 km). GPS: N55:11.572 E10:48.318

Charges 2007

Per person	DKK 64
child (0-11 yrs)	DKK 43
pitch incl. electricity	DKK 53 - 98

Camping Cheques accepted.

DK2220 Helnæs Camping

Strandbakken 21, Helnæs, DK-5631 Ebberup (Fyn)

Tel: 64 77 13 39. Email: info@helnaes-camping.dk

Helnæs Camping is on the remote Helnæs peninsula to the southeast of Fyn, connected to the mainland by a small road. The site is adjacent to a nature reserve making it ideal for walkers, cyclists and bird spotters, or for those who enjoy sea fishing (this is a great location for sea trout). The road to the site takes you through a breathtaking environment with colourful flowerbeds on the Bobakkerne Wall to the north and large outer marches in the south. Helnæs Camping has 160 pitches, some terraced, on grassy fields sloping down towards to the sea.

Facilities

Two toilet blocks, one brand new, with washbasins in cabins and controllable showers. Baby room (heated). Facilities for disabled visitors. Laundry with washing machines and dryers. Campers' kitchen. Shop. Takeaway. Adventure type playground. Minigolf. Bicycle hire. Canoe hire. Watersports. In high season small circus for children. TV lounge. Internet access. Covered barbecue area. Off site: Sea fishing.

Open: 15 March - 1 September.

Directions

From Nørre Åby follow 313 road south to Ebberup. In Ebberup turn south to Helnæs and follow signs for Helnæs Strand. GPS: N55:07.970 E10:02.140

Charges 2007

Per person	DKK 55 - 67
child	DKK 30 - 36
electricity	DKK 25

No credit cards.
Camping Cheques accepted.

DK2235 Sakskøbing Grøn Camping

Saxes Allé 15, DK-4990 Sakskøbing (Lolland)

Tel: 54 70 47 57. Email: sax.groen.camp@mail.dk

This small, traditional style site provides a useful stop-over on the route from Germany to Sweden, within easy reach of the Puttgarden - Rødby ferry. There are 125 level grassy pitches, most with electricity (10A) and, although there are a fair number of seasonal units, one can usually find space. There is a pool at the nearby sports centre (100 m). The site has a well stocked shop, which is open long hours, but the attractive town centre is semi-pedestrianised, and has a good range of shops and a supermarket.

Facilities

Two sanitary units provide basic, older style facilities, including push-button free hot showers, some curtained washbasin cubicles and a baby room. Cooking and laundry facilities. Motorcaravan services. Shop. New play area. Off site: Town 100 m.

Open: 1 April - 30 September.

Directions

From E47, exit 46, turn towards town on road no. 9. Turn right at crossroads towards town centre (site is signed), cross railway and then turn right again, and site entrance is 250 m. on left. GPS: N54:47.905 E11:38.456

Charges 2007

Per person	DKK 65
child (0-14 yrs)	DKK 33
electricity	DKK 25

DK2257 Vesterlyng Camping

Ravnholtvej 3, DK-4591 Føllenslev (Sjælland)

Tel: 59 20 00 66. Email: info@vesterlyng-camping.dk

Vesterlyng is a pleasant, quiet site, close to Føllenslev and Havnsø on Sjælland. The ground slopes towards the sea and there are good views from some pitches. It is an open site but some mature trees provide shade. Vesterlyng has 181 mostly level touring pitches, 150 with 6/13A electricity. A further 100 pitches are used by mostly elderly, seasonal units. The pitches are on long, grassy meadows each taking 16-20 units, off tarmac access roads. Facilities on this site are basic, but clean. The local beaches are ideal for swimming and a relaxing beach holiday.

Facilities

Two traditional style toilet blocks include washbasins (open style and in cabins) and controllable hot showers. Family shower rooms. Basic facilities for disabled people. Washing machine and dryer. Small shop. Bar (daily). Swimming pool complex. Minigolf. Fishing. Riding trips. Bicycle hire. Water sports. WiFi. Boules. Animal enclosure and daily feeding. Live music nights. Off site: Fishing 1 km. Golf 15 km. Boat launching 1 km.

Open: 22 March - 21 October.

Directions

From Kalundborg follow road no. 23 east and exit on no. 155 road towards Svinninge. At Snertinge, continue north on road no. 255 for 2 km. Follow signs to site (6 km). From the west exit on road no. 225 towards Snertinge and folow signs after 2 km. GPS: N55:44.504 E11:18.540

Charges 2007

Per person	DKK 67
pitch incl. electricity	DKK 37 - 67

No credit cards.

DK2250 Hillerød Camping

Blytækkervej 18, DK-3400 Hillerod (Sjælland)

Tel: **48 26 48 54**. Email: **info@hillerodcamping.dk**

The northernmost corner of Sjælland is packed with interest, based not only on fascinating parts of Denmark's history but also its attractive scenery. Hillerød is also a fine base for visiting Copenhagen and is only 25 km. from the ferries at Helsingør and the crossing to Sweden. Centrally situated, the town is a hub of main roads from all directions, with this neat campsite clearly signed. It has a park-like setting in a residential area with five acres of well kept grass and some attractive trees. There are 100 pitches, of which 70 have electricity (10A) and these are marked. The site amenities are all centrally located in modern, well maintained buildings which are kept very clean. The town centre of Hillerød, like so many Danish towns, has been pedestrianised making shopping or outdoor refreshment a pleasure. Visit Frederiksborg Slot, a fine Renaissance Castle and home of the Museum of Danish national history.

Facilities

The bright, airy toilet block is older in style and includes washbasins with partitions and curtain. Facilities for babies can be used by disabled people. Campers' kitchen adjoins the club room and includes free new electric hot plates and coffee making machine. Laundry room (free iron). Motorcaravan services. Small shop. Comfortable club room with TV and children. Off site: Tennis and indoor pool 1 km. Riding 2 km. Golf 3 km. Excellent electric train service every 10 minutes (20 minutes. walk) to Copenhagen. The site sells the Copenhagen card.

Open: Easter - 16 September.

Directions

Follow road no. 6 bypassing road to south until sign for Hillerod S. Turn towards town at sign for 'Centrum' on Roskildvej road no. 233 and site is signed to the right. GPS: N55:55.436 E12:17.722

Charges 2007

Per person	DKK 60 - 67
child (2-11 yrs)	DKK 30 - 35
electricity	DKK 25 - 30
dog	free

DK2255 Topcamp Feddet

Feddet 12, DK-4640 Faxe (Sjælland)

Tel: **56 72 52 06**. Email: **info@feddetcamping.dk**

This interesting spacious site with ecological principles is located on the Baltic coast. It has a fine, white, sandy beach (Blue Flag) which runs the full length of one side, with the Præstø fjord on the opposite side of the peninsula. There are 413 pitches for touring units, generally on sandy grass, with mature pine trees giving adequate shade. All have 10/13A electricity and 20 are fully serviced (water, electricity, drainage and sewage). Two recently constructed sanitary buildings which have been specially designed, are clad with larch panels from sustainable local trees and are insulated with flax mats. They have natural ventilation, with ventilators controlled by sensors for heat, humidity and smell. Shaped blades on the roof increase ventilation on windy days. All this saves power and provides a comfortable climate inside. Heating is by a wood chip furnace, is CO_2 neutral and replaces many litres of heating oil annually. Rainwater is used for toilet flushing, but showers and basins are supplied from the normal mains, and urinals are water free. Water saving taps have an automatic turn off, and lighting is by low wattage bulbs with PIR switching. Recycling is very important here, with separate bins for glass, metal, paper, cardboard and batteries.

Facilities

Both sanitary buildings are impressive, equipped to very high standard. Family bathrooms (with twin showers), complete suites for small children and babies. Facilities for disabled people. Laundry. Kitchens, dining room and TV lounge. Excellent drive-over motorcaravan service point. Well stocked licensed shop. Licensed bistro and takeaway (1/5-20/10 but weekends only outside peak season). Minigolf. Games room. Indoor toddlers' playroom and several playgrounds for all ages. Event camp for children. Pet zoo. Bungee jump. WiFi. Gym, massage, reflexology and sun beds. Watersports. Fishing. Off site: Many other activities with guides or instructors, including Land Rover safaris, abseiling, Icelandic pony riding, educational courses, ocean kayaking, and seal watching in Fakse Bay. Indoor pool complex nearby. Amusement park.

Open: All year.

Directions

From south on E47/55 take exit 38 towards Præsto. Turn north on 209 road towards Fakse and from Vindbyholt follow site signs. From the north on E47/55 take exit 37 east towards Fakse. Just before Fakse turn south on 209 road and from Vindbyholt, site signs. GPS: N55:10.498 E12:06.122

Charges 2007

Per person	DKK 67
child (0-11 yrs)	DKK 46
pitch	DKK 25 - 95
electricity	DKK 30
dog	DKK 15

95

DK2260 DCU Nærum Camping

Ravnbakken, DK-2850 Nærum (Sjælland)

Tel: **45 80 19 57**. Email: **info@dcu.dk**

Obviously everyone arriving in Sjælland will want to visit 'wonderful, wonderful Copenhagen', but like all capital cities, it draws crowds and traffic to match. This sheltered site is near enough to be convenient but distant enough to afford peace and quiet (apart from the noise of nearby traffic) and a chance of relaxing after sightseeing. The 275 touring pitches are in two areas – in wooded glades taking about six units each (mostly used by tents) or on more open meadows where electricity is available. Nærum, a Danish Camping Union site, is only 15 km. from the city centre and very near a suburban railway that takes you there. The long narrow site covers a large area alongside the ancient royal hunting forests, adjacent to the small railway line and the main road. Power lines do cross the site but there is lots of grassy open space. This is a useful site to know for Copenhagen, but is also very near the interesting friendly shopping complex of Rødøvre and the amusement park at Bakken. Note: Should you wish to drive into the city, there is a useful car park on the quayside. It is within easy walking distance of the centre and is located where the Kalvebød Brygge meets the Langebrø bridge (suitable for motorcaravans and caravans).

Facilities

Two toilet blocks, one in the meadow area has been refurbished and includes partitioned washbasins. Good block at reception can be heated and also provides a laundry and a campers' kitchen. Good facilities for babies and disabled people. Four family bathrooms (free). Motorcaravan service point. Reception and shop for basics (closed 12.00-14.00 and 22.00-07.00). Club room and TV. Barbecue. Adventure playground. Off site: Sporting facilities nearby and café/restaurant within a few hundred metres. Train service to Copenhagen (400 m. on foot, change at Jaegersborg).

Open: 19 March - 25 September.

Directions

From E55/E47, take Nærum exit (no. 14), 15 km. north of Copenhagen. Turn right at first set of traffic lights (site signed), right on road 19 at second lights, cross bridge and turn left, following signs to site. GPS: N55:48.498 E12:31.865

Charges guide

Per person	DKK 62
child (0-11 yrs)	DKK 31
pitch	DKK 20
electricity	DKK 25

DK2265 Camping Charlottenlund Fort

Strandvejen 144B, DK-2920 Charlottenlund (Sjælland)

Tel: **39 62 36 88**. Email: **info@campingcopenhagen.dk**

On the northern outskirts of Copenhagen, this unique site is within the walls of an old fort which still retains its main armament of twelve 29 cm. howitzers (disabled, of course). There are 100 pitches on grass, all with 10A electricity hook-ups. The obvious limitation on the space available means that pitches are relatively close together, but many are quite deep. The site is very popular and is usually full every night, so we suggest that you either reserve or arrive well before midday. The site is only 6 km. from the centre of Copenhagen, with a regular bus service from outside the site. Alternatively you could use the excellent cycle network to visit the city. The fort was constructed during 1886-1887 and was an integral link in the Copenhagen fortifications until 1932. A restaurant in the fort (under separate management) has good sea views to Sweden and the spectacular Øresund bridge.

Facilities

Sanitary facilities located in the old armoury are newly rebuilt, well maintained and heated. Free showers. Kitchen facilities include gas hobs and a dining area. Laundry. Motorcaravan service point. Small shop in reception. Bicycle hire. WiFi. Beach. Off site: Riding 1.5 km. Golf 2 km. Copenhagen town centre 20 minutes by bus.

Open: 1 May - 14 September.

Directions

Leave E47/E55 at junction 17, and turn southeast on Jægersborgvej. After a short distance turn left (east) on Jægersborg Allé, follow signs for Charlottenlund (5 km.) and all the way to the end. Finally turn right (south) on to Strandvejen, and site entrance is on left after 500 m. GPS: N55:44.688 E12:35.123

Charges 2007

Per person	DKK 80
child (3-12 yrs)	DKK 35
pitch	DKK 25 - 45
electricity	DKK 5

MAP 8

Situated in the far north, Finland is a long and mainly flat county, dominated by huge dense forests and glorious lakes. The unspoilt wilderness of this country makes it a perfect place for relaxing in natural, peaceful surroundings.

CAPITAL: HELSINKI

Tourist Office

Finnish Tourist Board
PO Box 33213
London W6 8KX
Tel: 020 8600 5680
Fax: 020 8600 5681
Email: finlandinfo.lon@mek.fi
Internet: www.visitfinland.com

There is a considerable difference in the landscape between north and south, with the gently rolling, rural landscape of the south giving way to the hills and vast forests of the north and treeless fells and peat-lands of Lapland, where reindeer and moose run free. Forests of spruce, pine and birch cover three quarters of the country's surface and are inhabited by hares, elks and occasional wolves and bears.

The other outstanding feature of Finland is its thousands of post-glacial lakes and islands. The main Lake District is centred on the beautiful Lake Saimaa in the south east, where you can swim, sail and fish. In the south, the capital Helsinki retains a small town feel, with open air cafes, green parks, waterways and a busy market square surrounded by 19th century architecture and museums. The flat western coastal regions include Turku and the Åland islands, ideal for sailing and fishing.

Population

5.2 million

Climate

Temperate climate, but with considerable variations. Summer is warm, winter is very cold.

Language

Finnish

Telephone

The country code is 00 358.

Money

Currency: The Euro
Banks: Mon-Fri 09.15 - 16.15
(regional variations may occur).

Shops

Mon-Fri 09.00-17.00/18.00.
Sat 09.00-14.00/15.00, department stores usually remain open to 18.00. Supermarkets usually open to 20.00 Mon-Fri.

Public Holidays

New Year; Epiphany; Saints Day 16 Mar; Language Day 9 April; Good Friday; Easter Mon; May Day 30 Apr/1 May; All Saints Day 1 Nov; Independence Day 6 Dec; Christmas 25, 26 Dec.

Motoring

Main roads are excellent and relatively uncrowded outside city limits. Traffic drives on the right. Horn blowing is frowned upon. There are many road signs warning motorists of the danger of elk dashing out on the road. If you are unfortunate enough to hit one, it must be reported to police. Do not drink and drive, penalties are severe if any alcohol is detected.

FI2850 Rastila Camping

Karavaanikatu 4, FIN-00980 Helsinki (Uusimaa)
Tel: **093 216 551**. Email: **rastilacamping@hel.fi**

No trip to Finland would be complete without a few days stay in Helsinki, the capital since 1812. This all year round site has exceptional transport links with the metro; only five minutes walk from the campsite gates. It provides 165 pitches, 165 with electricity, plus an additional small field for tent campers. Shrubs have been planted between the tarmac and grass pitches. All visitors will want to spend time in the Capital and a 24 hour bus, tram and metro pass costs a little over € 6 and can be bought at the metro station. Once on the metro you are in the city centre within 20 minutes on this regular fast train service. Essential visits will include Senate Square, in the heart of the city, and Suomenlinna, a marine fortress built on six islands in the 1700s. This garrison town is one of the most popular sights in Finland and is the world's largest maritime fortress. Helsinki, on the other hand, is one of Europe's smallest capitals and walking around the centre and port is popular as well as visiting the market square alongside the ferry port. The city also has a wide variety of art galleries and museums, many of which are free with the Helsinki card.

Facilities

Four sanitary blocks (two heated) provide toilets and showers. Kitchens with cooking rings and sinks. Facilities for disabled visitors and babies. Laundry room. Saunas. Motorcaravan service point. Fully licensed restaurant. Playground. Games and TV room. Bicycles and kayaks for hire. Off site: Small beach adjacent. Golf 5 km. Tallinn the capital of Estonia is only 90 minutes away from Helsinki by fast jetliner ferry.

Open: All year.

Directions

Well signed from 170 or Ring I. From the 170, turn at Itakeskus shopping complex towards Vuosaari. After crossing bridge go up slip road to Rastila. At top of road turn left. Site is directly ahead. GPS: N60:12.395 E25:07.279

Charges 2007

Per pitch incl. 2 persons	€ 9,00 - € 15,00
electricity	€ 4,50

Discounts for weekly or monthly bookings.

Rastila Camping

City vacations and Camping athmosphere - Rastila Camping welcomes you to Helsinki. A seaside camping site only a metro trip away from the city centre of Helsinki, with caravan and tent pitches, diverse cabins and a modern summer hostel. Located beside a metro station. Open all year round.

Karavaanikatu 4 • 00980 Helsinki - Finland
T +358 (0)9 310 78517 • F +358 (0)9 310 36659
E rastilacamping@hel.fi
www.hel.fi/rastila   N 60°12'24" E 25°7'16"

FI2820 Tampere Camping Härmälä

Leirintäkatu 8, FIN-33900 Tampere (Häme)
Tel: **032 651 355**. Email: **harmala@lomaliitto.fi**

Härmelä is a lively campsite near Lake Pyhäjärvi. It is situated only 4 km. from Tampere city centre. You can chose from a large, unspecified number of unmarked pitches (about 180). The site has 111 cabins of various sizes and facilities. Amenities include a beach, saunas, playgrounds for children, a small shop and a pizzeria. The site seems a little run down but is acceptable for a couple of nights. Tampere is beautifully situated beside Lake Näsijärvi. A stroll along the harbour with its yachts and through the parks is a pleasant experience. Another must is the Sänkänniemi Adventure Park with its 168 m. high tower and revolving restaurant, zoo, aquarium and a amusements such as roller coasters and rapid rides.

Facilities

There are four sanitary blocks, one block is new, three are rather basic. Washbasins and showers have free hot water. Facilities for disabled visitors. Laundry room. Campers' kitchen with cooking rings, microwave. Chemical disposal and motorhome service point. Small shop. Pizzeria. Off site: Golf and riding 5 km.

Open: 17 May - 27 August.

Directions

Turn off the E12 and follow signs to the site. GPS: N61:28.318 E23:44.367

Charges guide

Per person	€ 4,00
child (0-14 yrs)	€ 2,00
pitch	€ 10,00 - € 11,50
electricity	€ 4,00

Check real time availability and at-the-gate prices...

www.**alanrogers**.com

FI2830 Camping Lakari

Lakarintie 405, FIN-34800 Virrat (Häme)

Tel: 034 758 639. Email: virtain.matkailu@phpoint.fi

The peace and tranquillity of the beautiful natural surroundings are the main attractions at this vast (18 hectares) campsite which is located on a narrow piece of land between two lakes. This site is a must if you want to get away from it all. There is a variety of cabins to rent, some with their own beach and jetty! Marked pitches for tents and caravans are beside the beach or in little meadows in the forest. You pick your own place. Site amenities include a café and a beach sauna. This is a spectacular landscape with deep gorges and steep lakeside cliffs. There is a nature trail from the site to the lakes of Toriseva or pleasant excursions to the Esteri Zoo and the village shop in Keskinen. The Helvetinjärvi National Park is nearby. Facilities at the site are rather basic but very clean and well kept. This is a glorious place for a nature loving tourist looking to relax.

Facilities

Two toilet blocks, basic but clean and well kept, include toilets, washbasins and showers. Free hot water. Chemical disposal and motorcaravan service point. Covered camper's kitchen with fridge, cooking rings and oven. Washing machine. Small shop and cafeteria. TV. Fishing. Bicycle hire. Off site: Golf 1 km. Riding 5 km.

Open: 1 May - 30 September.

Directions

Site is 7 km. south of Virrat on road 66. Follow signs. GPS: N62:12.589 E23:50.266

Charges guide

Per person	€ 2,00
child	€ 1,00
pitch	€ 12,00
electricity	€ 2,00

FI2922 Camping Taipale

Leiritie, FIN-78250 Varkaus (Kuopio)

Tel: 017 552 6644. Email: tuija.jalkanen@campingtaipale.inet.fi

Camping Taipale is situated right in the middle of an area of a thousand lakes, along the banks of Lake Haukivesi, which stretches to Savonlinna. Being at latitude of 62 degrees, daylight at Camping Taipale lasts for almost twenty four hours during the months of June and July. This site has 52 pitches, (all with electricity) in two lightly wooded areas, with a further grassy area for 90 tents and 16 log cabins to rent. To the south of the site there is a fine sandy beach and a small island with its own fishing dock for campers use. Savonlinna is the hub of the Lake Saimaa waterways traffic. The town is famous for its medieval castle Ovalinlinna, which is transformed each year for the world famous opera festival. To the north of the site is Kuopio, where Lake Kallavesi encircles the town centre. From the Puijo tower you can admire one of the most spectacular panoramas of Finnish lakes and forest while having lunch in the tower's revolving restaurant.

Facilities

Two sanitary blocks with good clean toilets and showers. The central block also provides a laundry with washing machines, driers, ironing facilities and good kitchen facilities. Two lakeside saunas (charged). Motorcaravan service point. Shop. Bar. Restaurant. Takeaway. Bicycle hire. Pedal boats. Beach volleyball. Minigolf. Trampoline. Off site: Old canal and museum within 1 km. The steamship 'Paul Wahl' has cruises on the lake. Varkaus 3 km. (home to the museum of mechanical music). Cruises from Kuopio.

Open: 26 May - 20 August.

Directions

Leave main road 5 at Varkaus and proceed through town. Site is about 7 km. from the route 5 junction. Turn at the traffic lights towards Taipale, then bear left. Site is on right about 1 km. further along.

Charges 2007

Per person	€ 4,00
child (2-15 yrs)	€ 1,00
pitch	€ 10,00

Check real time availability and at-the-gate prices...

www.alanrogers.com

FI2960 Koljonvirta Camping

Ylemmäisentie 6, FIN-74120 Iisalmi (Kuopio)

Tel: 017 825 252. Email: info@campingkoljonvirta.fi

Korljonvirta Camping is a large but quiet site located about 5 km. from the centre of Iisalmi. There are 200 marked grass pitches, 120 with electricity (16A). The site adjoins a lake and has a small beach and facilities for boating and fishing. Iisalmi town itself is on the northern edge of the Finnish Lake District and provides a good variety of shops, including some factory outlets, and an interesting variety of events during June, July and August. These vary from the world famous Wife Carrying World Championships to the Lapinlahti Cattle Calling Competition and the International Midnight Marathon.

Facilities

The sanitary blocks provide showers, toilets and a sauna in one block. Launderette. Shop. Snack bar. Fully licensed restaurant. Motorcaravan service point. Lake and small beach with facilities for boating and fishing. The site exhibits large wooden sculptures of animals. Off site: Riding 100 m. Golf 5 km.

Open: May - September.

Directions

From road 5 turn onto the 88 (towards Oulu) just north of Iisalmi. Go straight over the roundabout and the site is about 1 km. on the left. Follow signs. GPS: N63:35.649 E27:09.646

Charges 2007

Per person	€ 4,00
pitch	€ 9,00
electricity	€ 3,50

FI2970 Nallikari Camping

PL 55, FIN-90015 Oulun Kaupunki (Oulu)

Tel: 085 586 1350. Email: nallikari.camping@ouka.fi

This is probably one of the best sites in Scandinavia, set in a recreational wooded area alongside a sandy beach on the banks of the Baltic Sea, with the added bonus of the adjacent Eden Spa complex. Nallikari provides 200 pitches with electricity (some also have water supply and drainage), plus an additional 79 cottages to rent, 28 suitable for winter occupation. Oulu is a modern town about 100 miles south of the Arctic Circle that enjoys long, sunny and dry summer days. The Baltic however is frozen for many weeks in the winter and then the sun barely rises for two months.

Facilities

The modern shower/WC blocks also provide male and female saunas, kitchen and launderette facilities. Facilities for disabled visitors. Motorcaravan service point. Playground. New reception with café/restaurant, souvenir and grocery shop. TV room. WiFi. Bicycle hire. Off site: The adjacent Eden centre provides excellent modern spa facilities where you can enjoy a day under the glass-roofed pool with its jacuzzis, saunas, Turkish Baths and an Irish Bath. Fishing 5 km. Golf 15 km.

Open: All year.

Directions

Leave Route 4/E75 at junction with route 20 and head west down Kiertotie. Site well signed, Nallikari Eden, but continue on, just after traffic lights, cross a bridge and take the second on the right. Just before the Eden Complex turn right towards Lerike and new reception. GPS: N65:01.784 E25:25.076

Charges 2007

Per pitch incl. 2 persons	€ 9,00 - € 18,00
extra person	€ 4,00
child (under 15 yrs)	€ 1,00
electricity	€ 4,00 - € 6,00

FI2975 Manamansalo Camping

Teeriniemientie 156, FIN-88340 Manamansalo (Oulu)

Tel: 088 741 38. Email: manamansalo@kainuunmatkailu.fi

Manamansalo is a top class, 'Wild North' tourist centre on the island of Manamansalo in Lake Oulojärvi. You come by ferry or via a bridge from the mainland. This site is a real find if you are looking for peace and quiet and is also very good for families. It has 200 pitches, 140 with electricity, very attractively laid out in the forest with natural dividers of pine trees. The site stretches along the lake and has a long, narrow sandy beach. Nature lovers will appreciate the network of trails in the pine forest. Choose between walking and cycling or even skiing in spring.

Facilities

Three toilet blocks have toilets, washbasins and showers in cubicles with free hot water. Washing machines and dryers. Kitchen with sinks, cooking rings and ovens. Chemical disposal and motorcaravan service point. Fully licensed restaurant and small shop (from May). Playground. Canoes, pedaloes and rowing boats for hire. Fishing. WiFi.

Open: 1 March - 30 September.

Directions

Coming from the south on road 5/E63 turn at Mainau on road 28. At Vuottolahti turn on road 879 and follow signs to Manamansalo and site. From road 22 turn at Liminpuro or Melaillahti and follow signs. GPS: N64:23.365 E27:01.565

Charges guide

Per person	€ 4,00
pitch	€ 12,00 - € 14,00
electricity	€ 3,50

FI2980 Ounaskoski Camping

Jäämerentie 1, FIN-96200 Rovaniemi (Lapland)

Tel: 016 345 304

Ounaskoski Camping is situated almost exactly on the Arctic Circle, 66 degrees north and just 8 km. south of the Santa Claus Post office and village, on the banks of the Kemijoki River. The site has 153 marked touring pitches, (68 with electricity), plus a further a small area for tents. Rovaniemi attracts many visitors each year, especially in the weeks leading up to Christmas, who fly direct to the local airport and pay Santa Claus a visit. The town has much to offer with a good selection of shops and some restaurants. Reindeer meat is well worth trying! Not to be missed is the Artikum Museum where you will learn much of how people in the North live with nature and on her terms. Slightly further afield you can visit Vaattunkiköngäs and enjoy one of the many walks, which are suitable for everyone, from the 1 km. walk to the most challenging 9 km. path. Alternatively sit back and enjoy the summer sun on the riverbank.

Facilities

There are two sanitary buildings each providing toilets, showers, laundry and kitchen. One also houses a sauna. Facilities for disabled visitors. Motorcaravan service point. Café. Small shop. Playground. TV room. Fishing. Bicycle hire. Organised coach trips. Off site: Ranua Zoo. The Kemijoki, Finland's largest river, offers numerous opportunities for sightseeing by boat. Santa Claus village and Santa Park.

Open: 1 June - 15 September.

Directions

Ounaskoski Camping is on the banks of the Kemijoki River in the middle of Rovaniemi. From the 4/E75 go via the centre across the river and turn right. Site is between the Jatkankynttilasilta Bridge and the Rautatiesilta Bridge. GPS: N66:29.847 E25:44.594

Charges 2007

Per person	€ 4,50
child (under 15 yrs)	€ 2,50
pitch	€ 14,00
electricity (16A)	€ 3,90

FI2985 Camping Sodankylä Nilimella

Kelukoskentie 4, FIN-99600 Sodankylä (Lapland)

Tel: 016 612 181. Email: antti.rintala@naturex-ventures.fi

Camping Sodankylä Nilimella is a small, quiet site situated alongside the Kitinen River, just one kilometre from the centre of Sodankylä. The site is split into two areas by a small, relatively quiet, public road. The good sized pitches (80 in total) are clearly marked with hedges and 40 have 16A electricity. The reception area also serves drinks and snacks. Sodankylä town itself, at the junction of routes 4 and 5, is home to a small Sami community and is an important trading post, so you will find a variety of shops including supermarkets. The town is also home to the Geophysical Observatory, which constantly surveys the earth's magnetic field and measures earthquakes using seismic recordings. The Sodankylä Light Infantry Brigade, (the Finnish version of the SAS) which specialises in survival in cold climates is also based near here. This area is ideal for walking and bird watching; there are plenty of well marked paths to choose from. You can try the 4 km. Luosto Game trail or the 15 km. Kaares Fell hiking trail, which takes you right into the wilderness. There are many easier walks in the Urho Kekkonen National Park, which is close by, some 10 km. north of Vuotso.

Facilities

Two good sanitary blocks with toilets, hot showers and saunas. Facilities for disabled visitors. Campers' kitchen. Motorcaravan service point. Playground. River swimming, canoeing and water skiing. Off site: Shops and supermarkets in Sodankylä town.

Open: 1 June - 31 August.

Directions

Turn off Route 4 onto Route 5. The site is on the left just after you cross the river, it is well signed and easy to find. GPS: N67:25.053 E26:36.482

Charges 2008

Per unit incl. 2 persons and electricity	€ 21,50

FI2990 Camping Tenorinne

FIN-99950 Karigasniemi (Lapland)

Tel: **016 676 113**. Email: **camping@tenorinne.com**

This is probably the most northerly campsite in Finland and makes an excellent stop over on route to North Cape. This is a small site with space for 48 units, on three levels with a small access road sloping down to the river. Electricity points (16A) are available throughout the site but the pitches are unmarked. This area is still largely unpopulated, scattered with only small Sami communities and herds of reindeer. Karigasniemi is a slightly larger town as it is a border post with Norway and is close to both the Kevo Nature reserve and the Lemmenjoki National Park. Finland has 19 nature reserves covering an area of 1,520 square kilometres, Kevo takes up almost half of that area. The campsite is on the banks of the Tenojoki River and is an excellent base for walking and bird watching. A little further north you will find Nuvvus-Ailigas, the holy fell of the ancient sami, which rises to a height of 400 m. above the level of the Teno river. Karigasniemi is at the junction of the 970 with route 92 and is a good base to absorb all that Finnish Lapland has top offer.

Facilities	Directions
Sanitary block includes showers, toilets and sauna. Launderette. Kitchen. Reception with TV. **Open:** 1 June - 20 September.	If travelling south on the 970, site is on right as you enter town. If travelling west on the 92, turn right immediately before Norwegian customs point. Site shortly on left past petrol station. Entrance quite steep. GPS: N69:24.020 E25:50.670

Charges 2007	
Per person	€ 3,00
pitch incl. electricity	€ 15,00

FI2995 Ukonjarvi Camping

Ukonjärventi 141, FIN-99801 Ivalo (Lapland)

Tel: **016 667 501**. Email: **nuttu@ukolo.fi**

Ukonjärvi Camping lies on the banks of Lake Inari, situated in a forested area alongside a nature reserve. It is a quiet, peaceful site, ideal for rest and relaxation. 30 touring pitches have electricity and are surrounded by pine and beech trees. Cottages are available to rent. A bar and restaurant are located at reception; a range of local dishes are produced including reindeer casserole. There is also a barbecue hut, located in the centre of the site, if you prefer to cook your own food. A climb up to the nearby viewpoint offers spectacular views over the lake – you can even see over to Russia. The lake also provides plenty of opportunities for boating and fishing.

Facilities	Directions
Sanitary block includes toilets and showers. Laundry and campers' kitchen. Lakeside sauna (extra cost). Bar and restaurant. Barbecue hut with logs. Small beach. Fishing and boating on lake. TV room. WiFi. Off site: Tankavaaran kansainvalinen Kulamuseo, a gold mining experience where you can try gold panning – keeping what you find! The Northern Lapland Centre and the Sami Museum, displaying cultural and natural history exhibitions. **Open:** May - September.	Ukonjärvi Camping is 11 km. north of Ivalo on Route 4. Look for signs to Lake Inari viewpoint; site is about 1 km. down the narrow road (signed). GPS: N68:44.212 E27:28.612

Charges 2008	
Per person	€ 3,50
child	€ 2,50
pitch with electricity	€ 19,00

Widely regarded as the 'Bible' by site owners and readers alike, there is no better guide when it comes to forming an independent view of a campsite's quality. When you need to be confident in your choice of campsite, you need the Alan Rogers Guide.

☑ **Sites only included on merit**

☑ **Sites cannot pay to be included**

☑ **Independently inspected, rigorously assessed**

☑ **Impartial reviews**

☑ **40 years of expertise**

Check real time availability and at-the-gate prices...

www.**alanrogers**.com

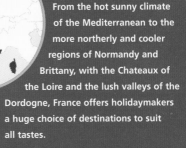

From the hot sunny climate of the Mediterranean to the more northerly and cooler regions of Normandy and Brittany, with the Chateaux of the Loire and the lush valleys of the Dordogne, France offers holidaymakers a huge choice of destinations to suit all tastes.

France

CAPITAL: PARIS

Tourist Office

The French Government Tourist Office (FGTO)
178 Piccadilly
London W1V 0AL
Tel: 0906 8244 123
Fax: 0207 493 6594
Email: info.uk@franceguide.com
Internet: www.franceguide.com

France boasts every type of landscape imaginable ranging from the wooded valleys of the Dordogne to the volcanic uplands of the Massif Central, the rocky coast of Brittany to the lavender covered hills of Provence and snow-capped peaks of the Alps. Each region is different and this is reflected in the local customs, cuisine, architecture and dialect. Many rural villages hold festivals to celebrate the local saints and you can also find museums devoted to the rural arts and crafts of the regions.

France has a rich architectural heritage with a huge variety of Gothic cathedrals, châteaux, Roman remains, fortresses and Romanesque churches to visit. Given the varied landscape and climate there is also great scope for outdoor pursuits with plenty of hiking and cycling opportunities across the country, and rock-climbing and skiing in the mountains. And of course a trip to France wouldn't be complete without sampling the local food and wine.

Population

60.2 million

Climate

France has a temperate climate but this varies considerably from region to region.

Language

French

Telephone

The country code is 00 33.

Money

Currency: The Euro
Banks: Mon-Fri 09.00-1200 and 14.00-16.00.

Shops

Mon-Sat 0900-1830. Some are closed between 1200-1430. Food shops are open 0700-1830/1930. Some food shops (particularly bakers) are open Sunday mornings. Many shops close Mondays.

Public Holidays

New Year; Easter Mon; Labour Day; VE Day 8 May; Ascension; Whit Mon; Bastille Day 14 July; Assumption 15 Aug; All Saints 1 Nov; Armistice Day 11 Nov; Christmas Day.

Motoring

France has a comprehensive road system from motorways (Autoroutes), Routes Nationales (N roads), Routes Départementales (D roads) down to purely local C class roads. Tolls are payable on the autoroute network which is extensive but expensive, and also on certain bridges.

FR22110 Camping les Madières

Le Vau Madec, F-22590 Pordic (Côtes d'Armor)

Tel: **02 96 79 02 48**. Email: **campinglesmadieres@wanadoo.fr**

Les Madières is well placed for exploring the Goëlo coast with its seaside resorts of St Quay-Portrieux, Binic and Etables-sur-Mer – ports used in the past by fishing schooners and now used by pleasure boats and a few coastal fishing boats. The young and enthusiastic owners here have already made their mark on this quiet campsite. With plenty of open spaces and set in the countryside, yet near the sea (800 m), it has 83 pitches of which 10 are used for mobile homes. There are no tour operators. The site has an outdoor swimming pool and some entertainment is organised in July and August by the welcoming and helpful owners.

Facilities

Two refurbished heated toilet blocks include facilities for disabled visitors. Basic provisions are kept all season. Bar, takeaway (all season) and newly refurbished restaurant. Swimming pool (1/6-20/9). Some entertainment (high season). Off site: Beach 800 m. Bus service nearby. Riding 2.5 km. Bicycle hire 3 km.

Open: 1 April - 31 October.

Directions

From St Brieuc ring-road (N12), turn north on D786 signed Paimpol (by the coast). Les Madières is at Pordic, 3 km. from the ring-road. Site is well signed from the D786. GPS: N48:34.944 W02:48.288

Charges 2007

Per person	€ 4,80
child (0-10 yrs)	€ 3,00
pitch incl. electricity (10A)	€ 11,00
dog	€ 2,00

Discounts outside July and August.

FR22210 Camping Bellevue

Route de Pléneuf Val-André, F-22430 Erquy (Côtes d'Armor)

Tel: **02 96 72 33 04**. Email: **campingbellevue@yahoo.fr**

Situated a mile from the beaches between Erquy and Pléneuf Val-André, Camping Bellevue offers a quiet country retreat with easy access to the cliffs of Cap Fréhel, Sables d'Or and St Cast. There are 140 pitches of which 120 are available for touring units, most with electricity (6/10A) and 15 with water and drainage. The site also has 20 mobile homes, chalets and bungalows to rent. Children are well catered for at this campsite – there are heated swimming and paddling pools, three play areas and minigolf, petanque and volleyball. Indoor entertainment for all includes theme evenings, Breton dancing and visits to a local cider house. There are numerous walks in the area and a vast range of aquatic sports at nearby Erquy. A 'Sites et Paysages' member.

Facilities

Two modern, unisex toilet blocks are of a high standard. Some washbasins in cubicles. Facilities for disabled visitors. Dishwashing and laundry facilities. Shop and bar (15/6-10/9). Restaurant and takeaway (12/6-31/8). Swimming and paddling pools (10/5-10/9). Play areas. Pool table. TV room. Table football, video games and library. Minigolf. Petanque. Volleyball. Entertainment and organised activities in high season. Off site: Beach and fishing 2 km. Golf 3 km. Bicycle hire and boat launching 5 km. Riding 6 km.

Open: 31 March - 30 September.

Directions

From St Brieuc road take D786 towards Erquy. Site is adjacent to the D786 at St Pabu and is well signed.

Charges 2007

Per unit incl. 2 persons	€ 15,20 - € 18,80
extra person	€ 4,00 - € 5,00
child (2-13 yrs)	free - € 4,40
electricity	€ 3,30
dog	€ 1,30 - € 1,70

This is just a sample of the campsites we have inspected and selected in France. For more campsites and further information, please see the Alan Rogers France guide.

Check real time availability and at-the-gate prices...

www.alanrogers.com

FR29010 Castel Camping le Ty-Nadan

Route d'Arzano, F-29310 Locunolé (Finistère)

Tel: 02 98 71 75 47. Email: infos@camping-ty-nadan.fr

Ty-Nadan is a well organised site set amongst wooded countryside along the bank of the River Elle. The 183 pitches for touring units are grassy, many with shade and 99 are fully serviced. The pool complex with slides and paddling pool is very popular as is the large indoor pool complex and an indoor games area with a climbing wall. There is also an adventure play park and a 'Minikids' park for 5-8 year olds, not to mention tennis courts, table tennis, pool tables, archery and trampolines. This is a wonderful site for families with children. Several tour operators use the site. An exciting and varied programme of activities is offered throughout the season – canoe and sea kayaking expeditions, rock climbing, mountain biking, aqua-gym, paintball, riding or walking – all supervised by qualified staff. A full programme of entertainment for all ages is provided in high season including concerts, Breton evenings with pig roasts, dancing, etc. Be warned, you will be actively encouraged to join in!

Facilities

Two older, split-level toilet blocks are of fair quality and include washbasins in cabins and baby rooms. A newer block provides easier access for disabled people. Washing machines and dryers. Restaurant, takeaway, bar and well stocked shop. Crêperie (July/Aug). Heated outdoor pool (17 x 8 m). New indoor pool. Small river beach (unfenced). Indoor badminton and rock climbing facility. Activity and entertainment programmes (high season). Bicycle hire. Boat hire. Fishing. Off site: Beaches 20 minutes by car. Golf 12 km.

Open: 1 April - 7 September.

Directions

Make for Arzano which is northeast of Quimperlé on the Pontivy road and turn off D22 just west of village at camp sign. Site is about 3 km.

Charges 2007

Per unit with 2 persons and electricity	€ 19,90 - € 45,90
child (under 7 yrs)	€ 1,70 - € 5,40
dog	€ 1,70 - € 5,40

Less 15-20% outside July/Aug.

Camping Cheques accepted.

Camping **** "Le Ty Nadan"

from the 31st of march for unforgettable holidays!

www.tynadan-vacances.fr

FR29030 Camping du Letty

F-29950 Bénodet (Finistère)

Tel: **02 98 58 62 82**. Email: **reception@campingduletty.com**

The Guyader family have ensured that this excellent and attractive site has plenty to offer for all the family. The site on the outskirts of the popular resort of Bénodet spreads over 22 acres with 493 pitches, all for touring units. Groups of four to eight pitches are set in cul-de-sacs with mature hedging and trees to divide each cul-de-sac. Most pitches have electricity, water and drainage. Although there is no swimming pool here, the site has direct access to a small sandy beach. At the attractive floral entrance, former farm buildings provide a host of facilities including an extensively equipped fitness room. There is also a modern nightclub and bar providing high quality live entertainment most evenings (situated well away from most pitches to avoid disturbance).

Facilities

Six well placed toilet blocks are of good quality and include mixed style WCs, washbasins in large cabins and controllable hot showers (charged). One block includes a separate laundry and dog washing enclosures. Baby rooms. Separate facility for disabled visitors. Launderette. Motorcaravan service points. Mini-market. Extensive snack bar and takeaway (21/6-31/8). Bar with games room and night club. Library/reading room with four computer stations. Entertainment room with satellite TV. Fitness centre (no charge). Saunas, jacuzzi and solarium (all on payment). Tennis and squash courts (charged). Play area. Entertainment and activities (July/Aug).

Open: 5 April - 5 November.

Directions

From N165 take D70 Concarneau exit. At first roundabout take D44 to Fouesnant. Turn right at T-junction. After 2 km. turn left to Fouesnant (still D44). Continue through La Forêt Fouesnant and Fouesnant, picking up signs for Bénodet. Shortly before Bénodet at roundabout turn left (signed Le Letty). Turn right at next mini-roundabout and site is 500 m. on left. GPS: N47:52.020 W04:05.270

Charges 2008

Per person	€ 4,00 - € 6,50
child (under 7 yrs)	€ 2,00 - € 3,25
pitch with electricity	€ 10,50 - € 13,00
car or motorcaravan	€ 2,00

FR29190 Camping les Prés Verts

B.P. 612, Kernous-Plage, F-29186 Concarneau Cedex (Finistère)

Tel: **02 98 97 09 74**. Email: **info@presverts.com**

What sets this family site apart from the many others in this region are its more unusual features which include its stylish pool complex with Romanesque style columns and statue, and its plants and flower tubs. The 150 pitches are mostly arranged on long, open, grassy areas either side of main access roads. Specimen trees, shrubs or hedges divide the site into smaller areas. There are a few individual pitches and an area towards the rear of the site where the pitches have sea views. Concarneau is just 2.5 km. and there are many marked coastal walks to enjoy in the area, plus watersports or boat and fishing trips available nearby. A 'Sites et Paysages' member.

Facilities

Two toilet blocks provide unisex WCs, but separate washing facilities for ladies and men. Pre-set hot showers and washbasins in cabins for ladies, both closed 21.00 - 8.00 hrs. Some child-size toilets. Laundry facilities. Pizza service twice weekly. Heated swimming pool (1/7-31/8) and paddling pool. Playground (0-5 yrs only). Minigolf (charged). Off site: Path to sandy/rocky beach (300 m.) and coastal path. Riding 1 km. Supermarket 2 km. Bicycle hire 3 km. Golf 5 km.

Open: 1 May - 22 September.

Directions

Turn off C7 road, 2.5 km. north of Concarneau, where site is signed. Take third left after Hotel de l'Océan.

Charges 2008

Per unit incl. 2 persons	€ 17,50 - € 22,00
extra person	€ 5,20 - € 6,50
child (2-7 yrs)	€ 3,40 - € 4,30
electricity (2-10A)	€ 3,20 - € 7,00
dog	€ 1,30 - € 1,60

Check real time availability and at-the-gate prices...

www.**alanrogers**.com

FR29050 Castel Camping l'Orangerie de Lanniron

Château de Lanniron, F-29336 Quimper (Finistère)

Tel: **02 98 90 62 02**. Email: **camping@lanniron.com**

L'Orangerie is a beautiful and peaceful, family site set in 10 acres of a XVIIth century, 42 acre country estate on the banks of the Odet river, formerly the home of the Bishops of Quimper. The site has 199 grassy pitches (156 for touring units) of three types varying in size and services. They are on flat ground laid out in rows alongside access roads with shrubs and bushes providing pleasant pitches. All have electricity and 88 have all three services. With lovely walks within the grounds, the restaurant and the gardens are both open to the public and in spring the rhododendrons and azaleas are magnificent. The site is just to the south of Quimper and about 15 km. from the sea and beaches at Bénodet. The family owner's five year programme to restore the park, the original canal, fountains, ornamental 'Bassin de Neptune', the boathouse, the gardens and avenues is very well advanced. The original outbuildings have been attractively converted around a walled courtyard. Used by tour operators (30 pitches). All facilities are available when the site is open.

Facilities

Excellent heated block in the courtyard and second modern block serving the top areas of the site. Facilities for disabled people and babies. Washing machines and dryers. Motorcaravan services. Shop (15/5-9/9). Gas supplies. Bar, snacks and takeaway, plus restaurant (open daily). Swimming pool (144 sq.m.) with paddling pool. New pool complex. Small play area. Tennis. Minigolf. Golf (9-hole) with academy and driving range. Fishing. Archery. Bicycle hire. General reading, games and billiards rooms. TV/video room. Karaoke. Outdoor activities. Large room for indoor activities. New putting green. Off site: Two hypermarkets 1 km. Historic town of Quimper under 3 km. Activities in the area include golf, cycling, walking, fishing, canoeing, surfing and sailing. Beach 15 km.

Open: 15 May - 15 September.

Directions

From Quimper follow 'Quimper Sud' signs, then 'Toutes Directions' and general camping signs, finally signs for Lanniron.

Charges 2008

Per person	€ 4,25 - € 7,10
child (2-9 yrs)	€ 2,75 - € 4,50
pitch (100 sq.m.)	€ 10,25 - € 17,70
with electricity (10A)	€ 13,25 - € 22,20
special pitch (120/150 sq.m.)	
with water and electricity	€ 17,00 - € 27,70
Less 15% outside July/Aug.	

Camping Cheques accepted.

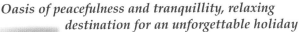
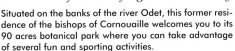

FR29340 Camping de la Côte des Légendes

Keravezan B.P. 36, F-29890 Brignogan-Plages (Finistère)

Tel: **02 98 83 41 65**. Email: **camping-cote-des-legendes@wanadoo.fr**

Located just behind a safe, sandy beach on the Bay of Brignogan and adjacent to a Centre Nautique (sailing, windsurfing, kayak), this site is ideal for a family seaside holiday. It is a quiet site with 147 level pitches arranged in rows and protected by hedges. There are a few mobile homes and chalets for rent but no tour operators. A shop, bar and takeaway are open in high season when activities are arranged for adults and children by the helpful owner (good English is spoken). The beach of fine sand can be reached directly from the site. The site is a good base for discovering the history behind the fables of the Côte des Légendes. Visit the nearby preserved fishing village of Meneham, set amongst spectacular random granite outcrops and boulders.

Facilities

Main toilet facilities are at the rear of the site in a large block that provides washbasins in cubicles, baby baths and facilities for disabled visitors. Dishwashing and laundry sinks. Motorcaravan service point. Games room. Further toilet facilities are at the reception building, also a laundry. Bar, small shop and takeaway (July/Aug). Playground and playing field. Off site: Watersports centre adjacent. Village 700 m. Bicycle hire 1 km. Riding 6 km.

Open: Easter - 1 November.

Directions

From Roscoff take the D58 towards Morlaix and after 6 km. turn right on the D10 towards Plouescat and then Plouguerneau. Turn right on the D770 to Brignogan-Plages. In the main street go straight on following signs for site and Club Nautique.

Charges guide

Per unit incl. 2 persons	€ 9,90 - € 12,50
extra person	€ 3,05 - € 3,75
electricity	€ 1,00 - € 3,10

FR29080 Camping le Panoramic

Route de la Plage-Penker, F-29560 Telgruc-sur-Mer (Finistère)

Tel: **02 98 27 78 41**. Email: **info@camping-panoramic.com**

This medium sized traditional site is situated on quite a steep, 10 acre hillside with fine views. It is personally run by M. Jacq and his family who all speak good English. The 200 pitches are arranged on flat, shady terraces, in small groups with hedges and flowering shrubs and 20 pitches have services for motorcaravans. Divided into two parts, the main upper site is where most of the facilities are located, with the swimming pool, its terrace and a playground located with the lower pitches across the road. Some up-and-down walking is therefore necessary, but this is a small price to pay for such pleasant and comfortable surroundings. This area provides lovely coastal footpaths. A 'Sites et Paysages' member.

Facilities

The main site has two well kept toilet blocks with another very good block opened for main season across the road. All three include British and Turkish style WCs, washbasins in cubicles, facilities for disabled people, baby baths, plus laundry facilities. Motorcaravan services. Small shop (1/7-31/8). Bar/restaurant with takeaway (1/7-31/8). Barbecue area. Heated pool, paddling pool and jacuzzi (1/6-15/9). Playground. Games and TV rooms. Tennis. Volleyball. Bicycle hire. Off site: Beach and fishing 700 m. Riding 6 km. Golf 14 km. Sailing school nearby.

Open: 1 June - 15 September.

Directions

Site is just south of Telgruc-sur-Mer. On D887 pass through Ste Marie du Ménez Horn. Turn left on D208 signed Telgruc-sur-Mer. Continue straight on through town and site is on right within 1 km. GPS: N48:13.428 W04:22.382

Charges 2008

Per person	€ 4,00 - € 5,00
child (under 7 yrs)	€ 2,40 - € 3,00
pitch	€ 9,60 - € 12,00
electricity (6-10A)	€ 3,10 - € 4,50
dog	€ 1,60

Less 20% outside July/Aug.

FR29090 Camping le Raguenès-Plage

19 rue des Iles, F-29920 Névez (Finistère)

Tel: 02 98 06 80 69. Email: info@camping-le-raguenes-plage.com

Madame Guyader and her family will ensure you receive a warm welcome on arrival at this well kept and pleasant site. Le Raguenès-Plage is an attractive and well laid out campsite with many shrubs and trees. The 287 pitches are a good size, flat and grassy, separated by trees and hedges. All have electricity, water and drainage. The site is used by one tour operator (60 pitches), and has 46 mobile homes of its own. A pool complex complete with water toboggan is a key feature and is close to the friendly bar, restaurant, shop and takeaway. From the far end of the campsite a delightful five minute walk along a path and through a cornfield takes you down to a pleasant, sandy beach looking out towards the Ile Verte and the Presqu'île de Raguenès.

Facilities

Two clean, well maintained sanitary blocks include mixed style toilets, washbasins in cabins, baby baths and facilities for disabled visitors. Laundry room. Motorcaravan service point. Small shop (from 15/5). Bar and restaurant (from 1/6) with outside terrace and takeaway. Reading and TV room, internet access point. Heated pool with sun terrace and paddling pool. Sauna (charged). Play areas, table tennis, games room and volleyball. Various activities are organised in July/Aug. Off site: Beach, fishing and watersports 300 m. Supermarket 3 km. Riding 4 km.

Open: 1 April - 30 September.

Directions

From N165 take D24 Kerampaou exit. After 3 km. turn right towards Nizon and bear right at church in village following signs to Névez (D77). Continue through Névez, following signs to Raguenès. Continue for 3 km. to site entrance on left (entrance is quite small and easy to miss).

Charges 2008

Per unit incl. 2 persons	€ 16,50 - € 28,80
extra person	€ 4,40 - € 5,80
child (under 7 yrs)	€ 2,20 - € 3,40
electricity (2-10A)	€ 3,20 - € 4,80
dog	€ 1,50 - € 2,50

FR29130 Camping des Abers

Dunes de Sainte Marguerite, F-29870 Landéda (Finistère)

Tel: 02 98 04 93 35. Email: camping-des-abers@wanadoo.fr

The location of this delightful 12 acre site is beautiful and the setting is ideal for those with younger children. Camping des Abers is set just back from the beach, the lower pitches sheltered from the wind by high hedges or with panoramic views from the higher places and the new orientation table. There are 180 pitches arranged in distinct areas, many partly shaded and sheltered by mature hedges, trees and flowering shrubs, all carefully tended over 30 years by the Le Cuff family.

Facilities

Three toilet blocks (recently refurbished) are very clean, providing washbasins in cubicles and roomy showers (token from reception € 0.80). Facilities for disabled visitors and babies. Laundry facilities. Motorcaravan services. Mini-market (25/5-22/9). Simple takeaway (1/7-31/8). Pizzeria and restaurant next door. Play area. Games room. Hairdresser. Massage. Live music. Breton dancing and cooking classes, and guided walks arranged. Direct access to beach with fishing and windsurfing. Torch useful. Off site: Miles of coastal walks. Riding 10 km. Golf 30 km. L'Aber Wrac'h with many restaurants.

Open: 28 April - 30 September.

Directions

From Roscoff (D10, then D13), cross river bridge (L'Aber Wrac'h) to Lannilis. Go through town taking road to Landéda and from there signs for Dunes de Ste Marguerite, 'camping' and des Abers. GPS: N48:35.584 W04:36.183

Charges 2008

Per person	€ 3,40
child (1-7 yrs)	€ 1,90
pitch with electricity	€ 8,50
dog	€ 1,80
Less 10% outside 15/6-31/8.	

Check real time availability and at-the-gate prices...

www.**alanrogers**.com

FR29180 **Camping les Embruns**

Rue du Philosophe Alain, le Pouldu, F-29360 Clohars-Carnoët (Finistère)

Tel: **02 98 39 91 07**. Email: camping-les-embruns@wanadoo.fr

This site is unusual in that it is located in the heart of a village, yet is only 250 metres from a sandy cove. The entrance with its code operated barrier and wonderful floral displays, is the first indication that this is a well tended and well organised site, and the owners have won numerous regional and national awards for its superb presentation. The 180 pitches (100 occupied by mobile homes) are separated by trees, shrubs and bushes, and most have electricity (10A), water and drainage. There is a covered, heated swimming pool, a circular paddling pool and a water play pool. It is only a short walk to the village centre with all its attractions and services. It is also close to beautiful countryside and the Carnoët Forest which are good for walking and cycling.

Facilities

Two modern sanitary blocks, recently completely renewed, include mainly British style toilets, some washbasins in cubicles, baby baths and good facilities for disabled visitors. Family bathrooms. Laundry facilities. Motorcaravan service point. Mini-market and restaurant by site entrance. Bar and terrace (1/7-31/8). Takeaway (20/6-5/9). Covered, heated swimming and paddling pools. Large games hall. Play area. Minigolf. Communal barbecue area. Daily activities (July/Aug). Off site: Nearby sea and river fishing and watersports. Bicycle hire 50 m. Beach 250 m. Riding 2 km.

Open: 4 April - 13 September.

Directions

From N165 take either 'Kervidanou, Quimperlé Ouest' exit or 'Kergostiou, Quimperlé Centre, Clohars Carnoët' exit and follow D16 to Clohars Carnoët. Then take D24 for Le Pouldu and follow site signs in village.

Charges 2008

Per unit incl. 2 persons	€ 10,50 - € 15,50
fully serviced pitch	€ 15,50 - € 29,90
extra person	€ 3,95 - € 5,50
child (under 7 yrs)	€ 2,60 - € 3,50
Less in low seasons.	
Use of motorcaravan services € 4.	

★★★★ *Les Embruns*

250 m from one of Brittany's sandy beaches Mr & Mrs Leguennou welcome you in their particularly well maintained campsite where you are assured of a good holiday.
• First class facilities and amenities in a green and floral environment • Mobile homes to let
• Motorcaravan service point • Covered heated swimming pool right from the opening •

LE POULDU - F-29360 CLOHARS-CARNOET
TEL: 0033 298 39 91 07 - FAX: 0033 298 39 97 87
www.camping-les-embruns.com
E-mail: camping-les-embruns@wanadoo.fr

FR35040 **Camping le P'tit Bois**

Saint Malo, F-35430 Saint Jouan des Guerets (Ille-et-Vilaine)

Tel: **02 99 21 14 30**. Email: camping.ptitbois@wanadoo.fr

On the outskirts of Saint Malo, this neat, family oriented site is very popular with British visitors, being ideal for one night stops or for longer stays in this interesting area. Le P'tit Bois provides 274 large level pitches with 114 for touring units. In two main areas, either side of the entrance lane, these are divided into groups by mature hedges and trees, separated by shrubs and flowers and with access from tarmac roads. Nearly all have electrical hook-ups and over half have water taps. Behind reception, an attractive, sheltered terraced area around the complex of heated indoor and outdoor pools provides a focus during the day along with a bar and snack bar.

Facilities

Two fully equipped toilet blocks, include washbasins in cabins. Baby baths. Laundry facilities. Simple facilities for disabled people. Motorcaravan service point. Small shop (from 5/4). Bar with entertainment in July-Aug. Snack bar with takeaway (from 5/4). Heated swimming pool, paddling pool and two slides (from 15/5). Heated indoor pool with Turkish Baths and Jacuzzi (from 5/4). Playground. Multisports court. Tennis. Off site: Beach, fishing 1.5 km. Buses 2 km. Bicycle hire or riding 5 km.

Open: 5 April - 13 September.

Directions

St Jouan is west off the St Malo - Rennes road (N137) just outside St Malo. Site is signed from the N137 (exit second exit St Jouan on the D4). GPS: N48:36.579 W01:59.270

Charges 2008

Per person	€ 5,00 - € 8,00
child (under 7 yrs)	€ 3,00 - € 6,50
pitch and car	€ 8,00 - € 19,00
electricity (10A)	€ 4,00
dog	€ 4,00 - € 6,00

Check real time availability and at-the-gate prices...

www.**alanrogers**.com

FR35080 Domaine du Logis

Le Logis, F-35190 La Chapelle-aux-Filtzméens (Ille-et-Vilaine)

Tel: **02 99 45 25 45**. Email: **domainedulogis@wanadoo.fr**

This is an attractive rural site, set in the grounds of an old château. The site's facilities are housed in converted barns and farm buildings, which although old, are well maintained and equipped. There are a total of 180 pitches, 90 of which are for touring. The grass pitches are level, of a generous size and divided by mature hedges and trees. All have 10A electricity connections. This site would appeal to most age groups with plenty to offer the active including a new fitness room with a good range of modern equipment or for those who prefer to relax, perhaps a quiet days fishing beside the lake. The site is well places for excursions to Mont Saint Michel, Dinard and Dinan.

Facilities

Two comfortable toilet blocks with washbasins and showers. Toilet and shower for disabled visitors. Dishwashing and laundry facilities. Shop in reception. Bar with TV (all season). Restaurant and takeaway (28/6-31/8). Outdoor swimming pool (15/5). Fitness and games rooms. BMX circuit. Bicycle hire. Lake fishing. Unfenced play areas. Children's club (high season). Internet access. Certain breeds of dogs are not accepted. Off site: Boating on the canal. Riding 10 km.

Open: 1 April - 27 October.

Directions

Turn south off N176 onto D795 signed Dol-de-Bretagne. Continue to Combourg and then take D13 to La-Chapelle-aux-Filtsmeens. Continue for 2 km. Site on right. GPS: N48:23.360 W01:50.080

Charges 2008

Per person	€ 4,50 - € 5,00
child (3-12 yrs)	€ 2,50 - € 3,50
pitch	€ 6,50 - € 18,00
electricity (10A)	€ 4,00

Camping Le Domaine du Logis****

35190 LA CHAPELLE AUX FILTZMEENS (Ille et Vilaine)
Tél.: 02 99 45 25 45 - Fax: 02 99 45 30 40 - E-mail: domainedulogis@wanadoo.fr - www.domainedulogis.com

FR35020 Castel Camping le Domaine des Ormes

Epiniac, F-35120 Dol-de-Bretagne (Ille-et-Vilaine)

Tel: **02 99 73 53 00**. Email: **info@lesormes.com**

This impressive site is in the northern part of Brittany, about 30 km. from the old town of Saint Malo, in the grounds of the Château des Ormes. In an estate of wooded parkland and lakes it has a pleasant atmosphere, busy in high season but peaceful at other times, with a wide range of facilities. The 800 pitches are divided into a series of different sections, each with its own distinctive character and offering a choice of terrain – flat or gently sloping, wooded or open. Only 150 pitches, all with electricity, are used for touring units and there is a large variety of other accommodation available to rent. A marvellous 'Aqua Park' with pink stone and palms and a variety of pools, toboggans, waterfalls and jacuzzi is set just above the small lake (with pedaloes and canoes for hire). A pleasant bar and terrace overlook the pools and a grass sunbathing area surrounds them.

Facilities

The toilet blocks are of fair standard, including washbasins in cabins and ample facilities for disabled people. Motorcaravan services. Shop, bar, restaurant, pizzeria and takeaway. Games room, bar and disco. Two traditional heated swimming pools and Aqua park. Adventure play area. Golf. Bicycle hire. Fishing. Equestrian centre with riding. Minigolf. Two tennis courts. Sports ground with volleyball, etc. Paintball. Archery. Cricket club.

Open: 19 May - 9 September, with all services.

Directions

Access road leads off main D795 about 7 km. south of Dol-de-Bretagne, north of Combourg.

Charges 2007

Per person	€ 4,25 - € 7,25
child (under 13 yrs)	free - € 4,00
pitch incl. vehicle	€ 17,75 - € 29,25
electricity 3/6A	€ 3,50 - € 4,30
water and drainage	€ 1,60 - € 2,00

Less 10% outside July/Aug.

111

FR44100 Sunêlia le Patisseau

29 rue du Patisseau, F-44210 Pornic (Loire-Atlantique)

Tel: **02 40 82 10 39**. Email: **contact@lepatisseau.com**

Le Patisseau is situated in the countryside just a short drive from the fishing village of Pornic. It is a relaxed site with a large number of mobile homes and chalets, and popular with young families and teenagers. The 115 touring pitches all with electrical connections (6A), are divided between the attractive 'forest' area with plenty of shade from mature trees and the more open 'prairie' area some are on a slight slope and access to others might be tricky for larger units. A railway runs along the bottom half of the site with trains several times a day, (but none overnight) and the noise is minimal. The Morice family works very hard to maintain a friendly atmosphere.

Facilities

The modern heated toilet block is very spacious and well fitted. Good facilities for disabled visitors and babies. Laundry rooms. Shop (15/5-8/9). Bar, restaurant and takeaway (1/7-31/9). Indoor heated pool with sauna, jacuzzi and spa (all season). Small heated outdoor pools and water slides (15/5-3/9). Play area. Multisport court. Bicycle hire. Off site: Fishing and beach 2.5 km.

Open: 8 April - 6 November.

Directions

Pornic is 19 km. south of the St Nazaire bridge. Access to site is at junction of D751 Nantes - Pornic road with the D213 St Nazaire - Noirmoutier 'Route Bleue'. Avoid Pornic town centre. GPS: N47:07.183 W02:04.397

Charges 2007

Per unit incl. 2 persons and electricity (6A)	€ 24,00 - € 39,00
extra person	€ 3,00 - € 7,00
child (1-7 yrs)	€ 2,00 - € 5,00
animal	€ 5,00

FR35000 Camping le Vieux Chêne

Baguer-Pican, F-35120 Dol-de-Bretagne (Ille-et-Vilaine)

Tel: **02 99 48 09 55**. Email: **vieux.chene@wanadoo.fr**

This attractive, family owned site is situated between Saint Malo and Mont Saint Michel. Developed in the grounds of a country farmhouse dating from 1638, its young and enthusiastic owner has created a really pleasant, traditional atmosphere. In spacious, rural surroundings it offers 199 good sized pitches on gently sloping grass, most with 10A electricity, water tap and light. They are separated by bushes and flowers, with mature trees for shade. A very attractive tenting area (without electricity) is in the orchard. There are three lakes in the grounds and centrally located leisure facilities include a restaurant with a terrace overlooking an attractive pool complex. In high season, some entertainment is provided, which is free for children.

Facilities

Three very good, unisex toilet blocks, which can be heated, include washbasins in cabins, a baby room and facilities for disabled people. Small laundry. Motorcaravan services. Shop, takeaway and restaurant (15/5-15/9). Heated swimming pool, paddling pool, slides (15/5-15/9; lifeguard July/Aug). TV room (satellite) and games room. Tennis court. Minigolf. Giant chess. Play area. Riding in July/Aug. Fishing. Off site: Supermarket in Dol 3 km. Golf 12 km. Beach 20 km.

Open: 31 March - 22 September.

Directions

Site is by the D576 Dol-de-Bretagne - Pontorson road, just east of Baguer-Pican. It can be reached from the new N176 taking exit for Dol-Est and Baguer-Pican. GPS: N48:32.972 W01:41.050

Charges 2007

Per person	€ 4,50 - € 5,75
child (under 13 yrs)	free - € 3,90
pitch with electricity	€ 10,00 - € 21,50
dog	€ 1,50

FR44090 Kawan Village du Deffay

B.P. 18 Le Deffay, Ste Reine de Bretagne, F-44160 Pontchâteau (Loire-Atlantique)

Tel: 02 40 88 00 57. Email: campingdudeffay@wanadoo.fr

A family managed site, Château du Deffay is a refreshing departure from the usual formula in that it is not over organised or supervised and has no tour operator units. The 142 good sized, fairly level pitches have pleasant views and are either on open grass, on shallow terraces divided by hedges, or informally arranged in a central, slightly sloping wooded area. Most have electricity. The facilities are located within the old courtyard area of the smaller château (that dates from before 1400). With the temptation of free pedaloes and the fairly deep, unfenced lake, parents should ensure that children are supervised. The landscape is natural right down to the molehills, and the site blends well with the rural environment of the estate, lake and farmland which surround it. For these reasons it is enjoyed by many. The larger château (built 1880) and another lake stand away from this area providing pleasant walking. The reception has been built separately to contain the camping area. Alpine type chalets overlook the lake and fit in well with the environment. The site is close to the Brière Regional Park, the Guérande Peninsula, and La Baule with its magnificent beach (20 km).

Facilities

The main toilet block could do with some updating but is well equipped including washbasins in cabins, provision for disabled people and a baby bathroom. Laundry facilities. Maintenance can be variable and hot water can take time to reach temperature in low season. Shop, bar, small restaurant with takeaway and solar heated swimming pool and paddling pool (all 15/5-15/9). Play area. TV. Animation in season including children's miniclub. Torches useful. Off site: Golf and riding 5 km.

Open: 1 May - 30 September.

Directions

Site is signed from D33 Pontchâteau - Herbignac road near Ste Reine. Also signed from the D773 and N165. GPS: N47:26.270 W02:09.350

Charges 2007

Per person	€ 3,10 - € 5,00
child (2-12 yrs)	€ 2,10 - € 3,40
pitch	€ 7,40 - € 11,30
with electricity (6A)	€ 10,70 - € 15,20
with 3 services	€ 12,50 - € 17,20

Camping Cheques accepted.

FR44180 Camping de la Boutinardière

Rue de la Plage de la Boutinardière, F-44210 Pornic (Loire-Atlantique)

Tel: 02 40 82 05 68. Email: info@laboutinardiere.com

This is truly a holiday site to suit all the family whatever their age, just 200 m. from the beach. It has 250 individual good sized pitches, 100-120 sq.m. in size, many bordered by three metre high, well maintained hedges for shade and privacy. All pitches have electricity available. It is a family owned site and English is spoken by the helpful, obliging reception staff. Beside reception is the excellent site shop and across the road is a complex of indoor and outdoor pools, paddling pool and a twin toboggan water slide. On site there are sports and entertainment areas. Facing the water complex, the bar, restaurant and terraces are new and serve excellent food, be it a snack or in the restaurant or perhaps a takeaway. This campsite has it all – 2 km from the beautiful harbour town of Pornic and 200 m. from the sea, together with the very best of amenities and facilities.

Facilities

Toilet facilities are in three good blocks, one large and centrally situated and two supporting blocks. Washbasins are in cabins, dishwashing is under cover. Laundry facilities. Shop (15/6-15/9). New complex of bar, restaurant, terraces (1/4-30/9). Three heated pools, one indoor (1/4-15/9), a paddling pool and slides (15/5-22/9). Games room. Playground. Minigolf. Off site: Sandy cove 200 m. Golf, riding, sea fishing, restaurants, fishing harbour, sailing and windsurfing, all within 5 km.

Open: 1 April - 30 September.

Directions

From north or south on D213, take Nantes D751 exit. At roundabout (with McDonalds) take D13 signed Bemarie-eb-Retz. After 4 km. site is signed to right. Note: do NOT exit for Pomic Ouest or Centre. GPS: N47:05.490 W02:03.080

Charges 2007

Per unit incl. 2 persons	€ 14,00 - € 31,00
extra person	€ 3,00 - € 6,00
child (under 8 yrs)	€ 2,00 - € 4,50
electricity (6-10A)	€ 3,50 - € 5,00

FR44210 Camping de l'Océan

F-44490 Le Croisic (Loire-Atlantique)

Tel: 02 40 23 07 69. Email: camping-ocean@wanadoo.fr

Camping de l'Océan is situated on the Le Croisic peninsula, an attractive part of the Brittany coastline. Out of a total of 400 pitches, just 80 are available for tourers with the remainder being taken by mobile homes either privately owned or for rent. Pitches are small, level and were rather worn when we visited. The leisure facilities however, which include a restaurant, bar and pool complex are of an excellent standard. This site, probably more suitable for families with young teenagers, can be very lively in high season with a wealth of activities and entertainment for all ages.

Facilities

Three toilet blocks are adequate although a little tired and include facilities for disabled visitors. Laundry facilities. Restaurant and bar. Takeaway. Shop. Motorcaravan service point. Swimming pool complex with indoor and outdoor pools and paddling pool. Tennis. Off site: Le Croisic for shops, bars and restaurants. Sailing, riding and golf.

Open: 9 April - 30 September.

Directions

From Le Pouliguen, travel west on N171 to Le Croisic. Site is well signed from here and found in approx. 1.5 km. GPS: N47:17.520 W02:32.090

Charges 2007

Per unit incl 2 persons and electricity (6A)	€ 16,50 - € 36,50
extra person	€ 3,00 - € 7,00

FR44220 Parc de Léveno

Route de Sandun, F-44350 Guérande (Loire-Atlantique)

Tel: 02 40 24 79 30. Email: domaine.leveno@wanadoo.fr

There have been many changes to this extensive site over the past three years and considerable investment has been made to provide some excellent new facilities. The number of mobile homes and chalets has increased, leaving just 47 touring pitches. However, these are mainly grouped at the far end where there is more the feel of a real French campsite. Pitches are divided by hedges and trees which offer good shade and all have electricity (10A). Access is tricky to some and the site is not recommended for larger units. Twin axle caravans and American motorhomes are not accepted.

Facilities

Main refurbished toilet block offers pre-set showers, washbasins in cubicles and facilities for disabled visitors. Laundry facilities. Small shop selling basics and takeaway snacks. Restaurant and bar (all July/Aug). Indoor pool. Heated outdoor pool complex (15/5-15/9). Fitness room. Play area. Programme of activities and events (high season). Off site: Large hypermarket 1 km. Fishing 2 km. Beach, golf and riding all 5 km. Boat launching 7 km.

Open: 5 April - 30 September.

Directions

Site is less than 3 km. from the centre of Guérande. From D774 and from D99/N171 take D99E Guérande by-pass. Turn east following signs for Villejames and Leclerc Hypermarket and continue on D247 to site on right. GPS: N47:19.987 W02:23.478

Charges 2007

Per unit incl. 2 persons, electricity and water	€ 10,80 - € 18,00
extra person	€ 3,60 - € 6,00

FR44190 Camping le Fief

57 chemin du Fief, F-44250 Saint Brévin-les-Pins (Loire-Atlantique)

Tel: **02 40 27 23 86**. Email: **camping@lefief.com**

If you are a family with young children or lively teenagers, this could be the campsite for you. Le Fief is a well established site only 800 metres from sandy beaches on the southern Brittany coast. It has a magnificent 'aqua park' with outdoor and covered swimming pools, paddling pools, slides, river rapids, fountains, jets and more. The site has 220 pitches for touring units (out of 413). Whilst these all have electricity (5A), they vary in size and many are worn and may be untidy. There are also 143 mobile homes and chalets to rent and 55 privately owned units. This is a lively site in high season with a variety of entertainment and organised activity for all ages. This ranges from a miniclub for 5-12 year olds, to 'Tonic Days' with aquagym, jogging and sports competitions, and to evening events which include karaoke, themed dinners and cabaret. There are plenty of sporting facilities for active youngsters.

Facilities

One excellent new toilet block and three others of a lower standard. Laundry facilities. Shop (15/5-15/9). Bar, restaurant and takeaway (15/4-15/9) with terrace overlooking the pool complex. Outdoor pools, etc. (15/5-15/9). Covered pool (all season). Play area. Tennis. Volleyball. Basketball. Pétanque. Table tennis. Archery. Games room. Internet access. Organised entertainment and activities (July/Aug). Off site: Beach, bicycle hire 800 m. Bus stop 1 km. Riding 1 km. Golf 15 km. Planète Sauvage safari park.

Open: 1 April - 15 October.

Directions

From the St Nazaire bridge take the fourth exit from the D213 signed St Brévin - L'Océan. Continue over first roundabout and bear right at the second to join Chemin du Fief. The site is on the right, well signed.

Charges 2007

Per pitch incl. 2 persons	€ 17,00 - € 37,00
extra person	€ 5,00 - € 9,00
child (0-7 yrs)	€ 2,50 - € 4,50
electricity	€ 5,00 - € 6,00
dog	€ 2,00 - € 5,00

Check real time availability and at-the-gate prices...

 www.**alanrogers**.com

FR56280 Airotel les Sept Saints

B.P. 14, F-56410 Erdeven (Morbihan)

Tel: **02 97 55 52 65**. Email: **info@septsaints.com**

One is attracted to this campsite on arrival, with a well-tended shrubbery and reception to the left of the entrance and a landscaped pool complex on the right. The 200 pitches are divided equally between mobile homes and touring pitches, arranged in three separate groups; 60 normal touring pitches with electricity (10A), mobile homes, and an area under the trees across the play area for tents. Touring pitches are separated by manicured hedges and are level grass. The heated swimming pool complex, with its slides, jacuzzi and padding pool, and overlooked by the bar terrace, provides a focal point. In July and August there are separate children's clubs for younger children and teenagers and a variety of entertainment in the evenings. The site offers a complete holiday within itself as well as access to the Brittany coast.

Facilities

Two modern toilet blocks include en-suite facilities for disabled visitors and attractive baby rooms. Two laundry rooms. Bar, takeaway and shop (10/6-9/9). Heated swimming pool with slides, Jacuzzi,and paddling pool with mushroom and baby slide (15/5-15/9). Excellent play areas. Multisports pitch. Boules. Grass area for ball games. Bicycle hire. Games room. TV room. Gas supplies. Internet. Off site: Fishing 1.5 km. Riding 3 km. Golf 3 km. Beach and sailing 3 km.

Open: 15 May - 15 September.

Directions

From N165 at Auray take exit for D768 to Carnac and Quiberon. At roundabout entering Plouharnel turn west on D781, following signs to Erdeven and L'Orient. Continue through Erdeven, turn left where site is signed after 1.5 km. and site is 150 m. on the right. GPS: N47:39.317 W03:10.307

Charges 2008

Per person	€ 4,00 - € 7,00
child (under 7 yrs)	€ 3,00 - € 5,50
pitch	€ 10,00 - € 18,00
electricity	€ 5,50

FR44150 Camping la Tabardière

F-44770 La Plaine-sur-Mer (Loire-Atlantique)

Tel: **02 40 21 58 83**. Email: **info@camping-la-tabardiere.com**

Owned and managed by the Barre family, this campsite lies next to the family farm. Pleasant, peaceful and immaculate, it will suit those who want to enjoy the local coast and towns but return to an 'oasis' for relaxation. It still, however, provides activities and fun for those with energy remaining. The pitches are mostly terraced and care needs to be taken in manoeuvring caravans into position – although the effort is well worth it. Pitches have access to electricity and water taps are conveniently situated. The site is probably not suitable for wheelchairs. A 'Sites et Paysages' member.

Facilities

Two good, clean toilet blocks are well equipped and include laundry facilities. Motorcaravan service point. Bar. Shop. Snacks and takeaway. Good sized covered swimming pool, paddling pool and slides (supervised). Playground. Minigolf. Table tennis. Volleyball and basketball. Half size tennis courts. Boules. Overnight area for motorcaravans (€ 13 per night). Off site: Beach 3 km. Sea fishing, golf, riding all 5 km.

Open: 1 April - 30 September.

Directions

Site is well signed, situated inland off the D13 Pornic - La Plaine sur Mer road.
GPS: N47:08.280 W02:09.110

Charges 2008

Per unit incl. 2 persons	€ 13,20 - € 25,90
extra person	€ 3,60 - € 6,20
child (2-9 yrs)	€ 2,70 - € 4,20
electricity (3/8A)	€ 3,10 - € 4,60
Camping Cheques accepted.	

FR14070 Camping de la Vallée

88 rue de la Vallée, F-14510 Houlgate (Calvados)

Tel: **02 31 24 40 69**. Email: **camping.lavallee@wanadoo.fr**

Camping de la Vallée is an attractive site with good, well maintained facilities, situated on one of the rolling hillsides overlooking the seaside resort of Houlgate. The original farmhouse building has been converted to house a good bar and comfortable TV lounge and billiards room overlooking the pool. The site has 373 pitches with around 100 for touring units. Large, open and separated by hedges, all the pitches have 4 or 6A electricity. Part of the site is sloping, the rest level, with gravel or tarmac roads. Shade is provided by a variety of well kept trees and shrubs. The town and its beach are only 900 metres walk. This is a popular site which is busy in high season with entertainment provided. It is used by tour operators (104 pitches), there are 150 mobile homes on site and around 40 seasonal units. The site has attractive chalets to rent in two areas of the site. English is spoken in season.

Facilities

Three good toilet blocks include washbasins in cabins, mainly British style toilets, facilities for disabled people and baby bathrooms. Laundry facilities (no washing lines allowed). Motorcaravan services. Bar. Snack bar with takeaway in season (from 15/5). Heated swimming pool (15/5-20/9; no shorts). Games room. Playground. Bicycle hire. Volleyball, football, tennis, petanque. Entertainment in Jul/Aug. Internet access. Off site: Riding 500 m. Beach, town, fishing 1 km. Golf 2 km.

Open: 1 April - 30 September.

Directions

From A13 take exit for Cabourg following signs for Dives/Houlgate. Go straight on at two roundabouts, then four sets of traffic lights. Turn left along sea front. After 1 km. at lights turn right, after 1 km. go over mini-roundabout – look for sign and flag poles on right. GPS: N49:17.644 W00:04.097

Charges 2007

Per unit incl. 2 persons and electricity (4A)	€ 21,00 - € 29,00
extra person	€ 5,00 - € 6,00
child (under 7 yrs)	€ 3,00 - € 4,00

Credit card minimum € 50.
Camping Cheques accepted.

www.campinglavallee.com
Tél. : +33 (0)2 31 24 40 69
88, rue de la Vallée
14510 HOULGATE

Authentic Normandy...
900 m away from the beaches

FR50050 Kawan Village le Cormoran

Ravenoville-Plage, F-50480 Sainte-Mère-Eglise (Manche)

Tel: **02 33 41 33 94**. Email: **lecormoran@wanadoo.fr**

This welcoming, family run site, close to Cherbourg (45 km) and Caen (96 km), is situated just across the road from a long sandy beach and is also close to Utah beach. It is ideally located for those wishing to visit the many museums, landing beaches and remembrance gardens. The site has 100 good size pitches on level grass, separated by mature hedges and all with electricity (6A). Extra large pitches are available. This is an ideal site which caters for both families and couples.

Facilities

Four toilet blocks of varying styles and ages but all maintained to a good standard. Dishwashing and laundry facilities. New shop, bar with snacks and takeaway. Swimming pool (heated 1/5-15/9, unsupervised). Play areas. Tennis. Boules. Entertainment, TV and games room. Bicycle and shrimp net hire. Communal barbecues. Off site: Beach 50 m. Golf 5 km.

Open: 1 April - 28 September.

Directions

From N13 take Ste Mère-Eglise exit and in centre of town take road to Ravenoville (6 km), then Ravenoville-Plage (3 km). Just before beach turn right and site is 500 m. GPS: N49:27.960 W01:14.104

Charges 2007

Per unit incl. 1 or 2 persons	€ 16,50 - € 27,00
extra person	€ 4,00 - € 7,00
child (3-10 yrs)	€ 2,00 - € 3,00
electricity (6A)	€ 4,00

Camping Cheques accepted.

FR27070 Camping de l'Ile des Trois Rois

1 rue Gilles Nicole, F-27700 Andelys (Eure)

Tel: **02 32 54 23 79**. Email: **campingtroisrois@aol.com**

One hour from Paris and 30 minutes from Rouen, L'Ile des Trois Rois has an attractive setting on the banks of the Seine, with a private fishing lake and is a haven of peace. It is overlooked by the impressive remains of the Château-Gaillard and would be ideal as an overnight stop or for longer. The site has been owned by the Francais Family for the past four years and they live on site. Within walking distance of the town and shops, the site has 300 spacious and partly shady grass pitches, 150 with electricity (long leads may be required for some). Water taps are rather scarce. There are also four mobile homes for rent and 50 pitches occupied by private mobile homes/seasonal units. The Medieval Festival in Les Andelys takes place on the last weekend in June. Bread and cakes are available from a vending machine.

Facilities

Four small, unheated toilet blocks have British style toilets (no seats), showers and washbasins all in cubicles, diswashing and laundry sinks. One has facilities for disabled people and another has a laundry. Motorcaravan service point. Two heated swimming pools (15/6-15/9). Fishing in the Seine or in the private lake. Fenced play area. Animation. Bar and restaurant. Evening entertainment (4/7-30/8). Bicycles and barbecues for hire. Internet access and satellite TV. Off site: Day trips to Paris and Rouen. Cycling and walking trails. Riding 5 km. Golf 9 km.

Open: 15 March - 15 November.

Directions

From the A13 motorway, take exit 17 and join the D316 to Les Andelys. In Les Andelys follow signs to Evreux, and the campsite is located just off the island before passing the bridge over the Seine.

Charges 2007

Per unit incl. 2 persons and electricity	€ 16,00
extra person	€ 5,00
child (under 3 yrs)	free

swimming pool opens during summer of 2007

L'Ile des Trois Rois

The park Ile des Trois Rois is situated in the most beautiful bend of the Seine nearby Castle Gaillard in Normandy and is a haven of peace. Paris is situated of less than than an hour and Rouen is half an hour driving from the camp site.
Facilities: two heated swimming pools, ping pong, camper service, bar and restaurant (high season) and play area

1, Rue Gilles Nicole - F-27700 Les Andelys - France
Tel. 0033 (0) 2 32 54 23 79 - Fax 0033 (0) 2 32 51 14 54 - Email campingtroisrois@aol.com

FR50080 Kawan Village Haliotis

Chemin des Soupirs, F-50170 Pontorson (Manche)

Tel: **02 33 68 11 59**. Email: **info@camping-haliotis-mont-saint-michel.com**

The Duchesne family have achieved a remarkable transformation of this former municipal site. Situated on the edge of the little town of Pontorson and next to the river Couesnon, Camping Haliotis is within walking, cycling and canoeing distance of Mont Saint Michel. The site has 152 pitches, including 118 for touring units. Most pitches have electricity and 34 really large ones also have water and drainage. The large, comfortable reception area has been developed to incorporate a bar and restaurant. You will receive a warm welcome from the family in their comfortable reception area where there is a pleasant bar that opens onto the swimming pool terrace, A good local bus service is available from close to the site entrance.

Facilities

Very clean, renovated and well-equipped toilet block. Laundry facilities. Bar where breakfast is served. Bread to order. Heated swimming pool. Sauna and solarium. Good fenced play area. Tennis. Bicycle hire. Fishing. Japanese garden and animal park. Club for children. Off site: Local services in Pontorson within walking distance. Riding 3 km. Golf 4 km. Fishing 25 km. Beach 30 km.

Open: 22 March - 5 November.

Directions

Site is 300 m. from the town centre, west of D976, alongside the river, and is well signed from the town. GPS: N48:33.424 W01:30.670

Charges 2007

Per person	€ 4,50 - € 6,00
pitch incl. electricity	€ 7,50 - € 10,00
Camping Cheques accepted.	

FR80060 Camping le Val de Trie

Rue des Sources, Bouillancourt-sous-Miannay, F-80870 Moyenneville (Somme)

Tel: **03 22 31 48 88**. Email: **raphael@camping-levaldetrie.fr**

Le Val de Trie is a natural countryside site in woodland, near a small village. The 100 numbered, grassy pitches are of a good size, divided by hedges and shrubs with mature trees providing good shade in most areas, and all have electricity (6A) and water. Access roads are gravel (site is possibly not suitable for the largest motorcaravans). It can be very quiet in April, June, September and October. If there is no-one on site, just choose a pitch or call at farm to book in. There are a few Dutch tour operator tents (5). This is maturing into a well managed site with modern facilities and a friendly, relaxed atmosphere. There are good walks around the area and a notice board keeps campers up to date with local market, shopping and activity news. English is spoken. The owners of Le Val de Trie have recently opened a new campsite nearby, Le Clos Cacheleux. This new site has 60 very large pitches (230 sq.m), all equipped with electricity (10A) and is located in the grounds of the 18th century Château de Bouillancourt. Visitors to this site are able to use the amenities at Le Val de Trie. We plan to undertake a detailed inspection of Le Clos Cacheleux during 2008.

Facilities

Two clean sanitary buildings include washbasins in cubicles, units for disabled people, babies and children. Laundry and dishwashing facilities. Motorcaravan services. Shop (from 1/4), bread to order and butcher visits in season. Bar with TV (1/4-15/10), snack-bar with takeaway (29/4-10/9). Room above bar for children Off site: Riding 14 km. Golf 10 km. Beach 12 km.

Open: 24 March - 15 October.

Directions

From A28 take exit 2 near Abbeville and D925 to Miannay. Turn left on D86 to Bouillancourt-sous-Miannay: site is signed in village. GPS: N50:05.038 E01:42.779

Charges 2008

Per unit incl. 2 persons	€ 14,60 - € 19,60
with electricity	€ 16,70 - € 23,60
extra person	€ 3,10 - € 4,90
child (under 7 yrs)	€ 1,90 - € 2,90
dog	€ 0,80 - € 1,30

Camping Cheques accepted.

Camping le Val de Trie ×××

Online reservation

Cottages to rent

Ideal spot for first or last night or longer stay
Situated at only 1 hour from Calais (A16) 12 km from the coast

Quiet and relaxing   Fishing pond   Swimming pools   Bar

BOUILLANCOURT sous MIANNAY   80870 MOYENNEVILLE
Tel : +33 3 22 31 48 88   Fax : +33 3 22 31 35 33
www.camping-levaldetrie.fr   raphael@camping-levaldetrie.fr

Camping le Clos Cacheleux   Route de Bouillancourt
80132 Miannay
raphael@camping-lecloscacheleux.com
www.camping-lecloscacheleux.com   tel.: +33 3 22 31 48 88

Online reservation

New

Ideal spot for first or last night or longer stay
1 hour from Calais (A16) 12 km from the coast

1 rue du Marais, Fresne-sur-Authie, F-80120 Nampont-St Martin (Somme)

Tel: **03 22 29 22 69**. Email: **contact@fermedesaulnes.com**

This peaceful site, with 120 pitches, has been developed on the meadows of a small, 17th century farm on the edge of Fresne and is lovingly cared for by its enthusiastic owner and his hard-working team. Restored outbuildings house reception and the facilities, around a central courtyard that boasts a fine heated swimming pool. A new development outside, facing the main gate, has 20 large level grass pitches for touring. There is also an area for tents. In the centre, a warden lives above a new facility building. The remaining 22 touring pitches are in the main complex, hedged and fairly level. From here you can visit Crécy, Agincourt, St Valéry and Montreuil (where Victor Hugo wrote Les Misérables). The nearby Bay of the Somme has wonderful sandy beaches and many watersports.

Facilities

Both sanitary areas are heated and include washbasins in cubicles with a large cubicle for disabled people. Dishwashing and laundry sinks. Shop. Piano bar and restaurant. Motorcaravan service point. TV room. Swimming pool (16 x 9 m; heated and with cover for cooler weather). Jacuzzi and sauna. Fitness room. Aqua gym and Balneo therapy. Playground. Beach volleyball, table tennis, boules and archery. Rooms with play stations and videos. Off site: River fishing 100 m. Golf 1 km. Riding 8 km.

Open: 22 March - 2 November.

Directions

From Calais, take A16 to exit 25 and turn for Arras for 2 km. and then towards Abbeville on N1. At Nampont St Martin turn west on D485 and site will be found in 2 km. GPS: N50:20.157 E01:42.740

Charges 2008

Per person	€ 7,00
child (under 7 yrs)	€ 4,00
pitch	€ 7,00
electricity (6/10A)	€ 6,00 - € 12,00

Camping Cheques accepted.

FR80040 Camping le Royon

1271 route de Quend, F-80120 Fort-Mahon-Plage (Somme)

Tel: **03 22 23 40 30**. Email: **info@campingleroyon.com**

This busy site, some two kilometres from the sea, has 300 pitches of which 100 are used for touring units. Of either 95 or 120 sq.m., the marked and numbered pitches are divided by hedges and arranged either side of access roads. Electricity (6A) and water points are available to all. The site is well lit, fenced and guarded at night (€ 30 deposit for barrier card). Entertainment is organised for adults and children in July/Aug when it will be very full. The site is close to the Baie de l'Authie which is an area noted for migrating birds. Nearby there are opportunities for windsurfing, sailing, sand yachting, canoeing, swimming, climbing and shooting.

Facilities

Slightly dated toilet blocks provide unisex facilities with British WCs and washbasins in cubicles. Units for disabled people. Baby baths. Dishwashing and laundry sinks. Shop. Mobile takeaway calls evenings in July/Aug. Clubroom and bar. Heated, covered pool (16 x 8 m). Open air children's pool and sun terrace. Playground. Table tennis, multicourt, tennis court and boules. Bicycle hire. Off site: Fishing, riding, golf within 1 km.

Open: 7 March - 1 November.

Directions

From A16 exit 24, take D32 around Rue (road becomes D940 for a while)then continues as the D32 (Fort-Mahon-Plage). Site is on right after 19 km. GPS: N50:19.980 E01:34.811

Charges 2007

Per pitch 95 sq.m. incl.	
electricity (6A) and 3 persons	€ 17,00 - € 27,50
extra person (over 1 yr)	€ 7,00
dog	€ 3,00

FR80090 Kawan Village Caravaning le Val d'Authie

20 route de Vercourt, F-80120 Villers-sur-Authie (Somme)

Tel: **03 22 29 92 47**. Email: **camping@valdauthie.fr**

In a village location, this well organised site is fairly close to several beaches, but also has its own excellent pool complex, small restaurant and bar. The owner has carefully controlled the size of the site, leaving space for a leisure area with an indoor pool complex. There are 170 pitches in total, but with many holiday homes and chalets, there are only 60 for touring units. These are on grass, some are divided by small hedges, with 6/10A electric hook-ups, and 10 have full services. The site has a fitness trail and running track, mountain bike circuit, and plenty of good paths for evening strolls. Ideas for excursions include the 15/16th century chapel and hospice and the Aviation Museum at Rue, a pottery at nearby Roussent, a flour mill at Maintenay, and the steam railway which runs from Le Crotoy to Cayeux-sur-Mer around the Baie de Somme.

Facilities

Good toilet facilities include some shower and washbasin units, washbasins in cubicles, and limited facilities for disabled people and babies. Facilities may be under pressure in high season and cleaning variable. Shop (not October). Bar/restaurant (4/4-12/10; hours vary). Swimming and paddling pools with lifeguards in July/Aug). Playground, club room with TV. Weekend entertainment in season (discos may be noisy until midnight, once weekly). Multicourt, beach volleyball, football, boules and tennis court. Internet room. Fitness room including sauna (charged).

Open: 29 March - 12 October.

Directions

Villers-sur-Authie is about 25 km. NNW of Abbéville. From A16 junction 24 take N1 to Vron, then left on D175 to Villers-sur-Authie. Or use D85 from Rue, or D485 from Nampont St Martin. Site is at southern end of village at road junction. GPS: N50:18.815 E01:41.729

Charges 2007

Per unit incl. 2 persons	€ 18.00
extra person	€ 6.00
child (under 7 yrs)	free - € 3.00
electricity (6/10A)	€ 5.00 - € 8.00
Camping Cheques accepted.	

FR77020 Camping le Chêne Gris

24 place de la Gare de Faremoutiers, F-77515 Pommeuse (Seine-et-Marne)

Tel: **01 64 04 21 80**. Email: **info@lechenegris.com**

This site is currently being developed by a new Dutch/Italian company. A new building which houses reception on the ground floor and an airy restaurant/bar plus a takeaway is of high quality. Of the 198 pitches, 65 are for touring many of which are on rough aggregate stone, the rest (higher up the hill on which the site is built) being occupied by over 100 mobile homes and 25 tents belonging to a Dutch tour operator. Terraces look out onto a heated leisure pool complex and an adventure play area for over-fives and the play area for under-fives is at the side of the bar with picture windows overlooking it. The site is next to a railway station with trains to Paris. Disneyland is 20 km.

Facilities

One basic toilet block with push-button showers, washbasins in cubicles and a dishwashing and laundry area. At busy times these facilities may be under pressure. A second block is to be added. Facilities for disabled visitors. Children's area with toilets and baby bath but showers at adult height! Bar, restaurant and takeaway. Pool complex (all season). Off site: Shops, restaurants and bars within walking distance. Fishing and riding 2 km.

Open: All year.

Directions

From A4 at exit 16 take N34 towards Coulommiers. In 10 km. turn south on D25 to Pommeuse; site on right after level-crossing. Also signed from south on D402 Guignes - Coulommiers road, taking D25 to Faremoutiers. GPS: N48:48.514 E02:59.530

Charges guide

Per unit incl. 2 persons, electricity	€ 29,00 - € 35,00
extra person	€ 2,00 - € 3,50
child (3-11 yrs)	€ 2,00 - € 3,00

FR77030 Camping International de Jablines

Base de Loisirs, F-77450 Jablines (Seine-et-Marne)

Tel: **01 60 26 09 37**. Email: **welcome@camping-jablines.com**

Jablines is a modern site which, with the leisure facilities of the adjacent 'Espace Loisirs', provides an interesting, if a little impersonal alternative to other sites in the region. Man-made lakes provide marvellous water activities. The 'Great Lake' as it is called, is said to have the largest beach on the Ile-de-France! The site itself provides 150 pitches, of which 141 are for touring units. Most are of a good size with gravel hardstanding and grass, accessed by tarmac roads and marked by fencing panels and shrubs. All have 10A electricity, 60 with water and waste connections also. The whole complex close to the Marne has been developed around old gravel workings. In season the activities at the leisure complex are supplemented by a bar/restaurant and a range of very French style group activities.

Facilities

Two toilet blocks, heated in cool weather, include push button showers, some washbasins in cubicles. Dishwashing and laundry facilities. Motorcaravan service (charged). Shop. Play area. Bar/restaurant adjacent at leisure centre/lake complex with watersports including 'water cable ski', riding activities, tennis and minigolf. Whilst staying on the campsite, admission to the leisure complex is free. Internet point. Ticket sales for Disneyland and Asterix. Off site: Golf 15 km.

Open: 29 March - 26 October.

Directions

From A4 Paris - Rouen autoroute turn north on the A104. Take exit 8 on D404 Meaux/Base de Loisirs Jablines. From A1 going south, follow signs for Marne-la-Vallée using A104. Take exit 6A Clay-Souilly on the N3 (Meaux). After 6 km. turn south on D404 and follow signs. GPS: N48:54.817 E02:44.051

Charges 2008

Per pitch incl. 2 persons and electricity (10A)	€ 21,00 - € 26,00
extra person	€ 6,00 - € 7,00
child (3-11 yrs)	€ 4,00 - € 5,00

Camping Cheques accepted.

FR52030 Kawan Village Lac de la Liez

Peigney, F-52200 Langres (Haute-Marne)

Tel: **03 25 90 27 79**. Email: **campingliez@free.fr**

Managed by the enthusiastic Baude family, this newly renovated lakeside site is near the city of Langres. Only 10 minutes from the A5, Camping Lac de la Liez provides an ideal spot for an overnight stop en route to the south of France. There is also a lot on offer for a longer stay. The site provides 131 fully serviced pitches, some with panoramic views of the 200 hectare lake with its sandy beach and small harbour where boats and pedaloes may be hired. Lake access is down steps and across quite a fast road (in total 150 m). With its old ramparts and ancient city centre, Langres was elected one of the 50 most historic cities in France.

Facilities

Two toilet blocks have all facilities in cabins (only one is open in low season). Facilities for disabled people and babies. Laundry facilities. Motorcaravan services. Shop, bar and restaurant (with takeaway food). Indoor pool complex with spa and sauna. Heated outdoor pool (15/6-15/9). Games room. Playground. Extensive games area and tennis court (free in low season). Off site: Lake with beach. Boat and bicycle hire and cycle tracks around lake. Fishing 100 m. Riding 5 km. Golf 40 km.

Open: 1 April - 1 November.

Directions

From Langres take the N19 towards Vesoul. After about 3 km. turn right, straight after the large river bridge, then follow site signs.
GPS: N47:52.440 E05:22.628

Charges 2008

Per person	€ 5,00 - € 7,00
child (2-12 yrs)	€ 3,00 - € 4,50
pitch	€ 6,00 - € 8,00
electricity	€ 3,50 - € 5,00
dog	€ 3,00

Camping Cheques accepted.

Camping du Lac de la Liez ★★

In the heart of the Champagne and Ardennes regions of France, Lac de la Liez is a top quality 4 star site, ideal for the whole family

Open 01st April - 01st November

Peigney, F-52200 Langres • tel 0033 (0)325 90 27 79 • fax 0033 (0)325 90 66 79
e-mail campingliez@free.fr • http://campingliez.free.fr

FR88130 Kawan Village Vanne de Pierre

5 rue du camping, F-88100 Saint Dié-des-Vosges (Vosges)

Tel: **03 29 56 23 56**. Email: **vannedepierre@wanadoo.fr**

La Vanne de Pierre is a neat and attractive site with 118 pitches, many of which are individual with good well trimmed hedges giving plenty of privacy. There are 13 chalets and mobile homes (for rent) and a few seasonal units, leaving around 101 tourist pitches, all multi-serviced with water, drain and electricity hook-up (6/10A). The reception building has been recently refitted and provides a well stocked small shop plus a restaurant/bar with a takeaway facility (all year but opening hours may vary). A 'Sites et Paysages' member.

Facilities

Main unit is heated with good facilities including washbasins in cubicles. Three family rooms each with WC, basin, and shower and two similar units fully equipped for disabled campers. Dishwashing and laundry rooms. A second, older unit (opened July/Aug). Shop. Bar/restaurant and takeaway. Swimming pool (1/4-30/9, weather permitting). Internet terminal. Gas supplies. Bicycle hire. Nordic walking is organised. Off site: Golf course, tennis courts, archery, riding all 1 km. Fishing. Supermarkets (some have 2.5 m. height barriers).

Open: All year.

Directions

St Dié is south east of Nancy. Site is east of town on north bank of river Meurthe and south of the D82 to Nayemont les Fosses. Site is well signed.
GPS: N48:17.160 E06:58.199

Charges 2007

Per unit incl. 2 persons	€ 15,00 - € 22,00
extra person	€ 4,00 - € 6,00
child (4-10 yrs)	free - € 4,00
electricity	€ 4,00 - € 5,00

Camping Cheques accepted.

FR88040 Kawan Village Lac de Bouzey

19 rue du Lac, F-88390 Sanchey (Vosges)

Tel: **03 29 82 49 41**. Email: **camping.lac.de.bouzey@wanadoo.fr**

Camping-Club Lac de Bouzey is eight kilometres west of Épinal, overlooking the lake, at the beginning of the Vosges Massif. The 125 individual 100 sq.m. back-to-back grass pitches are arranged on either side of tarmac roads with electricity (6-10A); 100 are fully serviced. They are on a gentle slope, divided by trees and hedging and some overlook the 130 ha. lake with its sandy beaches. Units can be close when site is busy. In high season there is lots going on for all ages, especially teenagers. Open all year, the site is much quieter in low season. English is spoken. 'Club' has been added to the name to indicate the number of activities organised in high season. Many water sports may be enjoyed, from pedaloes to canoes, windsurfing and sailing. The large, imposing building at the entrance to the site houses a restaurant and bar with terraces overlooking the lake. Two bars by the lake would indicate that the lakeside is popular with the public in summer but the camping area is quiet, separated by a road and well back and above the main entrance. It is well placed for exploring the hills, valleys, lakes and waterfalls of the south of Alsace Lorraine.

Facilities

Sanitary block includes a baby room and one for disabled people (there is up and down hill walking). In winter a small, heated section in main building with toilet, washbasin and shower is used. Laundry and dishwashing facilities. Motorcaravan service point. Shop. Bar and restaurant. Heated pool (1/5-30/9). Fishing, riding, games room, archery and bicycle hire. Internet access. Sound-proof room for cinema shows and discos (high season). Off site: Golf 8 km.

Open: All year.

Directions

Site is 8 km. west of Épinal on D460 and is signed from some parts of Épinal. Follow signs for Lac de Bouzey and Sanchey. GPS: N48:10.015 E06:21.594

Charges 2007

Per unit incl. 2 persons	€ 15,00 - € 25,00
extra person	€ 5,00 - € 9,00
child (4-10 yrs)	free - € 6,00
electricity (6-10A)	€ 5,00 - € 6,00

Camping Cheques accepted.

FR17030 Camping le Bois Roland

82 route Royan - Saujon, F-17600 Medis (Charente-Maritime)

Tel: **05 46 05 47 58**. Email: **bois.roland@wanadoo.fr**

This campsite is in an urban area on a busy N-road but, nevertheless, has some unique features. Over the past 30 years, M. Dupont, the owner, has planted a very large number of tree varieties to mark and separate the pitches and they provide some shade. The site has 88 pitches for touring units, mainly between 80-90 sq.m. All have electricity (some may need long leads) and access to water close at hand. The family run a bar and provide simple takeaway food in July and August and there is a welcoming swimming pool. The majority of the pitches are of good size and to return to them after a day in Royan may well be worth the drive. Royan, with all its noise and sophistication and well used beaches, is only 5 km. The village of Medis, with a variety of shops, is some 600 m. walk from the site.

Facilities

Two modernised toilet blocks contain a mixture of Turkish and British style toilets (no seats and no paper). Modern showers. Baby changing room. Special facilities for disabled campers. Dishwashing under cover. Laundry room with washing machines. Play area for young children. Off site: Buses pass the gate. Riding 1 km. Fishing 4 km. Bicycle hire 5 km. Golf 10 km. Supermarket with ATM 2 km. Beach 5 km.

Open: 23 April - 30 September.

Directions

Site is clearly signed on the west side of the N150, 600 m. north of the village of Medis (the N150 runs between Saujon and Royan).

Charges 2007

Per unit incl. 2 persons	€ 14,00 - € 17,50
extra person	€ 4,80
child (0-5 yrs)	€ 2,00 - € 3,50
electricity (5/10A)	€ 4,20 - € 4,90

Check real time availability and at-the-gate prices...

www.**alanrogers**.com

FR17010 Camping Bois Soleil

2 avenue de Suzac, F-17110 Saint Georges-de-Didonne (Charente-Maritime)

Tel: 05 46 05 05 94. Email: camping.bois.soleil@wanadoo.fr

Close to the sea, Bois Soleil is a fairly large site in three parts, with 165 serviced pitches for touring units and a few for tents. All touring pitches are hedged, and have electricity, with water and drainage between two. The main part, 'Les Pins', is attractive with trees and shrubs providing shade. Opposite is 'La Mer' with direct access to the beach, some areas with less shade and an area for tents. The third part, 'La Forêt', is for static holiday homes. It is best to book your preferred area and can be full mid June - late August. There are a few pitches with lockable gates. The areas are well tended with the named pitches (not numbered) cleared and raked between visitors and with an all-in charge including electricity and water. This lively site offers something for everyone, whether they like a beach-side spot or a traditional pitch, plenty of activities or the quiet life. The sandy beach here is a wide public one, sheltered from the Atlantic breakers although the sea goes out some way at low tide.

Facilities

Each area has one large sanitary block, and smaller blocks with toilets only. Heated block near reception. Cleaned twice daily, they include washbasins in cubicles, facilities for disabled people and babies. Launderette. Nursery. Supermarket, bakery (July/Aug). Beach shop. Restaurant and bar. Takeaway. Pool (heated 15/6-15/9). Steam room. Tennis. Bicycle hire. Play area. TV room and library. Internet terminal. Charcoal barbecues not permitted. Pets not accepted (24/6-2/9). Off site: Fishing, riding 500 m. Golf 20 km.

Open: 4 April - 2 November.

Directions

From Royan centre take coast road (D25) along the seafront of St Georges-de-Didonne towards Meschers. Site is signed at roundabout at end of the main beach. GPS: N45:35.130 W00:59.128

Charges 2008

Per unit incl. 2 persons, 6A electricity	€ 20,00 - € 37,00
tent incl. 2 persons	€ 15,00 - € 33,00

Less 20% outside July/Aug.
Camping Cheques accepted.

FR17140 Castel Camping Séquoia Parc

La Josephtrie, F-17320 Saint Just-Luzac (Charente-Maritime)

Tel: 05 46 85 55 55. Email: info@sequoiaparc.com

This is definitely a site not to be missed. Approached by an avenue of flowers, shrubs and trees, Séquoia Parc is a Castel site set in the grounds of La Josephtrie, a striking château with beautifully restored outbuildings and courtyard area with a bar and restaurant. Most pitches are 140 sq.m. with 6A electricity connections and separated by mature shrubs providing plenty of privacy. The site has 300 mobile homes and chalets, with 126 used by tour operators. This is a popular site with a children's club and entertainment throughout the season and reservation is necessary in high season. Member of Leading Campings Group. The site itself is designed to a high specification with reception in a large, light and airy room retaining its original beams and leading to the courtyard area where you find the bar and restaurant. The pool complex with water slides, large paddling pool and sunbathing area is impressive.

Facilities

Three spotlessly clean luxurious toilet blocks, include units with washbasin and shower and facilities for disabled visitors and children. Dishwashing sinks. New large laundry. Motorcaravan service point. Gas supplies. Large new supermarket. Restaurant/bar and takeaway. Impressive swimming pool complex with water slides and large paddling pool. Tennis, volleyball, football field. Games and TV room. Bicycle hire. Pony trekking. Organised entertainment all season. Off site: Fishing 5 km. Golf 15 km. Flying trips.

Open: 8 May - 14 September, with all services.

Directions

Site is 5 km. southeast of Marennes. From Rochefort take D733 south for 12 km. Turn west on D123 to Ile d'Oléron. Continue for 12 km. Turn southeast on D728 (Saintes). Site signed, in 1 km. on left. GPS: N45:48.699 W01:03.637

Charges 2008

Per unit incl. 2 persons and electricity	€ 18,00 - € 43,00
extra person	€ 7,00 - € 9,00
child (3-12 yrs)	€ 3,00 - € 5,00
dog	€ 5,00

Bois Soleil

Camping ★★★★
Charente-Maritime

Surrounded by pine trees and a sandy beach on the Atlantic Coast, with one direct access to the beach, Bois Soleil proposes to you many attractions like tennis, tabletennis, children playgrounds and entertainment. Shops, take-away and snack-bar with big TV screen.

Camping Qualité

Spring and Summer 2008

2, avenue de Suzac - 17110 ST GEORGES DE DIDONNE
Tel: 0033 546 05 05 94 - Fax: 0033 546 06 27 43
www.bois-soleil.com / e-mail: camping.bois.soleil@wanadoo.fr

FR17280 Camping la Grainetière

Route de Saint-Martin, F-17630 La Flotte-en-Ré (Charente-Maritime)
Tel: 05 46 09 68 86. Email: la-grainetiere@free.fr

A truly friendly welcome awaits you from the owners, Isabelle and Eric, at La Grainetière. It is a peaceful campsite set in almost three hectares of pine trees which provide some shade for the 65 touring pitches of various shapes and sizes. There are also 50 well spaced chalets for rent. Some pitches are suitable for units up to 7 metres (book in advance). There are no hedges for privacy and the pitches are sandy with some grass. Ample new water points and electricity (10A) hook-ups (Euro plugs) serve the camping area. The site is well lit.

Facilities	Directions
The unisex sanitary block is first class, with washbasins in cubicles, showers, British style WCs, facilities for children and people with disabilities. Shop (1/4-30/9). Takeaway (July/Aug). Swimming pool (heated 1/4-30/9). Bicycle hire. Fridge hire. TV room. Charcoal barbecues are not permitted. Off site: Beach and sailing 2 km. Fishing and boat launching 2 km. Riding 3 km. Golf 10 km. Bar and restaurant 2 km.	Follow camping signs from La Flotte, 1 km. from the village. GPS: N46:11.253 W01:20.696

Open: 1 April - 30 September.

Charges 2007

Per unit incl. 2 persons	€ 14,00 - € 24,00
extra person	€ 3,00 - € 7,00
child (0-7 yrs)	€ 2,00 - € 3,00
electricity (10A)	€ 4,00

La Grainetiere

Between St. Martin harbor and la Flotte. All kinds of shops at proximity. Isabelle and Eric welcome you in a wooded park. Friendly family atmosphere.

Route de Saint Martin - 17630 La Flotte - France - Tel: 0033 (0)5 46 09 68 86 - Fax: 0033 (0)5 46 09 53 13
lagrainetiere@free.fr - www.la-grainetiere.com

FR17340 Camping Port Punay

Allée Bernard Moreau, les Boucholeurs, F-17340 Châtelaillon-Plage (Charente-Maritime)
Tel: 05 46 56 01 53. Email: contact@camping-port-punay.com

Port Punay is a friendly, well run site just 200 metres from the beach and 3 km. from the centre of the resort of Châtelaillon-Plage. There are 166 touring pitches laid out on well trimmed grass, with many mature poplars and low shrubs. The site has a well stocked shop, open all season and a small bar and restaurant only open in high season. A heated swimming pool has a separate gated area for paddling. There is a good range of activities available and in high season some entertainment is arranged. This is a family run site (Famille Moreau) and the son of the family speaks excellent English, as does his Dutch wife.

Facilities	Directions
One large toilet block with good facilities including washbasins in cubicles and large shower cubicles. Facilities for disabled visitors and babies. Washing machines. Shop. Bar, restaurant and takeaway (1/7-31/8). Swimming pool. Games area. Play area. Bicycle hire. Internet access. WiFi. Off site: Châtelaillon-Plage 3 km. by road, 1.5 km. along the seafront on foot or bike. Buses to Rochefort and La Rochelle from outside site. Riding 2 km. Beach 200 m.	From N137 (La Rochelle - Rochefort) take exit for Châtelaillon-Plage. At the 1st roundabout follow the sign for the town centre. At the 2nd roundabout turn left. Follow signs to the site at the seaside hamlet of Les Boucholeurs. Here drive to the sea-wall then turn left through village to site. Take care, as the road has many traffic-calming measures and can be narrow in places.

Open: 1 April - 30 September.

Charges 2008

Per unit incl. 2 persons	€ 14,90 - € 22,00
extra person	€ 4,20 - € 5,50
child (0-3 yrs)	€ 3,20 - € 4,20
electricity (6/10A)	€ 4,00 - € 5,00

FR85480 Camping Caravaning le Chaponnet

Rue du Chaponnet N-16, F-85470 Brem sur Mer (Vendée)

Tel: 02 51 90 55 56. Email: campingchaponnet@wanadoo.fr

This well established family run site is within five minutes walk of Brem village and 1.5 km. from a sandy beach. The 80 touring pitches are level with varying amounts of grass, some with shade from mature trees. Pitches are separated by tall hedges and serviced by tarmac or gravel roads and have frequent water and electricity points (long leads may be required). Tour operators have mobile homes and tents on 70 pitches and there are 55 privately owned mobile homes and chalets. The swimming pool complex also has a jacuzzi, slides and a children's pool, together with a sauna and fitness centre.It is overlooked by the spacious bar and snack bar. Entertainment is provided for all ages by day and three or four musical evenings a week provide family fun rather than teenage activities.

Facilities

The six sanitary blocks are well maintained with washbasins in cubicles, some showers and basins have controllable water temperature. Facilities for babies and disabled people. Laundry facilities. Bar (15/5-6/9), snack bar and takeaway (1/6-30/9). No shop but bread and croissants available. Indoor (heated) and outdoor pools. Play area with space for ball games. Table tennis, tennis and bicycle hire. Indoor games room. Off site: Shops and restaurants. Beach 1.5 km. Fishing 5 km. Golf 12 km. Riding 10 km.

Open: 1 May - 15 September.

Directions

Brem is on the D38 St Gilles - Les Sables d'Olonne road. Site is clearly signed, just off the one-way system in centre of village.

Charges 2007

Per unit incl. 3 persons	€ 19,50 - € 30,00
with electricity	€ 23,80 - € 33,90
extra person	€ 4,10 - € 5,50
child (under 5 yrs)	€ 2,60 - € 3,70
dog	€ 3,00

FR85150 Camping la Yole

Chemin des Bosses, Orouet, F-85160 Saint Jean-de-Monts (Vendée)

Tel: **02 51 58 67 17**. Email: **contact@la-yole.com**

La Yole is an attractive and well run site, 2 kilometres from a sandy beach. It offers 278 pitches, the majority of which are occupied by tour operators and mobile homes to rent. There are 100 touring pitches, most with shade and separated by bushes and trees. A newer area at the rear of the site is more open. All the pitches are of at least 100 sq.m. and have electricity (10A), water and drainage. The pool complex includes an outdoor pool, a paddling pool, slide and an indoor heated pool with jacuzzi. Entertainment is organised in high season.

Facilities

Two toilet blocks include washbasins in cabins and facilities for disabled people and babies. A third block has a baby room. Laundry facilities. Shop. Bar, restaurant and takeaway (1/5-5/9). Outdoor pool and paddling pool. Indoor heated pool with jacuzzi. Play area. Ball games. Club room. Tennis. Table tennis, pool and video games. Entertainment in high season. Gas barbecues only. Off site: Beach, bus service, bicycle hire 2 km. Riding 3 km. Fishing, golf and watersports 6 km.

Open: 5 April - 26 September.

Directions

Signed off the D38, 6 km. south of St Jean-de-Monts in the village of Orouet. GPS: N46:45.383 W02:00.466

Charges 2007

Per unit incl. 2 persons,	
electricity	€ 16,00 - € 29,00
extra person	€ 3,70 - € 6,00
child (2-9 yrs)	€ 2,15 - € 4,50
baby (0-2 yrs)	free - € 3,30
dog	€ 4,00 - € 5,00

Camping Cheques accepted.

Camping La Yole ★★★★

Camping Cheque

Wake up to the sound of birdsong in a wooded park of 17 acres with four star comfort. Space, security, informal atmosphere: la yole, tucked away between fields and pine trees, only 2 km from the beach.

– Chemin des Bosses - Orouet - F 85160 Saint Jean de Monts –
– Tel: 0033 251 58 67 17 - Fax: 0033 251 59 05 35 –
– contact@la-yole.com / www.la-yole.com –

Check real time availability and at-the-gate prices...

www.alanrogers.com

FR85210 Camping les Ecureuils

Route des Goffineaux, F-85520 Jard-sur-Mer (Vendée)

Tel: **02 51 33 42 74**. Email: **camping-ecureuils@wanadoo.fr**

Les Ecureuils is a wooded site in a quieter part of the southern Vendée. It is undoubtedly one of the prettiest sites on this stretch of coast, with an elegant reception area, attractive vegetation and large pitches separated by low hedges with plenty of shade. Of the 261 pitches, some 128 are for touring units, each with water and drainage, as well as easy access to 10A electricity. This site is very popular with tour operators (103 pitches). Jard is rated among the most pleasant and least hectic of Vendée towns. The harbour is home to some fishing boats and rather more pleasure craft, and has a public slipway for those bringing their own boats.

Facilities

Two toilet blocks, well equipped and kept very clean, include baby baths, and laundry rooms. Small shop (bread baked on site). New snack-bar. Takeaway service (pre-order 1/6-15/9). Snacks and ice creams available from the friendly bar. Good sized L-shaped swimming pool and separate paddling pool (30/5-15/9). Indoor pool and fitness centre (all season). Two play areas for different age groups. Modern play area. Minigolf, table tennis and a pool table. Club for children (5-10 yrs) daily in July/Aug. Bicycle hire. Only gas barbecues are allowed. Dogs are not accepted. Internet access. Off site: Beach, fishing 400 m. Marina and town.

Open: 15 April - 27 September.

Directions

From Les Sables d'Olonne take the N949 towards Talmont St Hilaire. Keep right in the centre (D21 towards Jard). From la Roche sur Yon follow the D474 and the D49 towards Jard-sur-Mer. From the village follow the signs 'Autre campings' or 'Camping les Ecureuils'. Site is on the left. GPS: N46:24.683 W01:35.382

Charges 2007

Per person	€ 5,00 - € 6,70
child (0-4 yrs)	€ 1,50 - € 2,00
child (5-9 yrs)	€ 4,00 - € 4,50
per pitch with water and drainage	€ 13,00 - € 15,50
with electricity (10A)	€ 18,00 - € 22,20
Less 10% outside 30/6-1/9.	

FR85400 Camping Bois Soleil

Chemin des Barres, F-85340 Olonne-sur-Mer (Vendée)
Tel: 02 51 33 11 97. Email: camping.boissoleil@wanadoo.fr

A traditionally laid out site with 199 marked pitches, separated by hedges, on flat or gently sloping ground. There are just two tour operators and a scattering of mobile homes and chalets, leaving some 87 pitches for tourers and tents. All have electricity (6A, French style sockets) and water points adjacent and many also have waste water pipes. The main buildings house a small reception and tourist information room as well as the bar and attached shop. There is an excellent swimming pool complex with slides and an impressive flume, plus an indoor pool. In July and August a range of daily activities is organised for adults and children. This site has a very French feel, the majority of the population when we visited seeming to be French.

Facilities

The two toilet blocks have hot water, mainly British style toilets, with washbasins in cubicles in new block. Locked overnight, but basic toilet facilities provided. Dishwashing and laundry facilities. Shop (July/Aug) – 'eat in'/takeaway service; bread to order. Bar (28/6-31/8). Indoor and outdoor pools. Play area. Bicycle hire. Barbecues are not permitted. Off site: Bus service in Olonne-sur-Mer. Riding 400 m. Beaches 2.5 km. Fishing and golf 3 km.

Open: 5 April - 28 September.

Directions

Site is off D80 coast road between Olonne-sur-Mer and Brem-sur-Mer, clearly signed on the inland side.

Charges guide

Per unit incl. 2 persons	€ 15,00 - € 21,50
with electricity	€ 18,00 - € 24,50
extra person	€ 2,60 - € 3,70
child (under 7 yrs)	€ 2,10 - € 2,70
animal	€ 2,60

FR37050 Kawan Village la Citadelle

Avenue Aristide Briand, F-37600 Loches en Touraine (Indre-et-Loire)
Tel: 02 47 59 05 91. Email: camping@lacitadelle.com

A pleasant, well maintained site, La Citadelle is within walking distance of Loches, noted for its perfect architecture and its glorious history, at the same time offering a rural atmosphere in the site itself. Most of the 128 level, good-sized touring pitches (all with 10A electricity and 42 fully serviced) offer some shade from trees, although sun lovers can opt for a more open spot. The most recent addition is an on-site outdoor swimming pool with paddling pool (solar heated). Loches, its château and dungeons, is 500 m.

Facilities

Three sanitary blocks provide British and Turkish style WCs, washbasins (mostly in cabins) and showers. Dishwashing and laundry facilities. Motorcaravan service area. Two excellent baby units and provision for disabled people. Play equipment. Boules, volleyball and games room. Small bar and snack bar offering a variety of food and drink in a lively environment (15/6-13/9). Internet access and TV. Off site: Riding 3 km. Supermarket 3 km. Market on Wednesday and Saturday mornings. Golf 7 km.

Open: 19 March - 19 October.

Directions

From any direction take town bypass (RN143) and leave via roundabout at southern end (supermarket). Site signed towards town centre on right in 800 m. Do not enter centre. GPS: N47:07.382 E01:00.134

Charges 2007

Per pitch incl. 2 adults with electricity,	€ 13,90 - € 21,60
water and drainage	€ 18,70 - € 27,50
extra person	€ 3,90 - € 5,00
child (2-10 yrs)	€ 2,30 - € 3,50
dog	€ 1,50 - € 2,00
Camping Cheques accepted.	

FR37090 Camping du Château de la Rolandière

F-37220 Trogues (Indre-et-Loire)

Tel: **02 47 58 53 71**. Email: **contact@larolandiere.com**

This is a charming site set in the grounds of a château. The owners, Sabine Toulemonde and her husband, offer a very warm welcome. There are 30 medium sized, flat pitches, some gently sloping front to rear, separated by hedges. All but four have 10A electricity and water taps nearby and parkland trees give shade. The château and adjoining buildings contain rooms to let. The site has a pleasant swimming pool (14 x 6 m.) with a sunny terrace and paddling pool, minigolf through the parkland and an area for ball games, swings and slides. A 'Sites et Paysages' member. Situated on the D760 between Ille Bouchard and St Maure-de-Touraine, the site is 5 km. west of the A10, convenient for an overnight break or for longer stays to explore the châteaux at Chinon, Loches or Azay-le-Rideau and the villages of Richelieu and Crissay-s-Manse. There are interesting excursions to gardens and grottos. In nearby Azay-le-Rideau visit the wicker craftsmen's workshops.

Facilities

The toilet block is older in style but has been refurbished to provide adequte facilities with shower, washbasin, dishwashing and laundry areas around central British style WCs. Provision for disabled visitors. Bar with terrace and snacks/takeaway. Small shop for basics (July/Aug). Swimming pool (15/5-30/9). Minigolf (no children under 12 yrs). Play area. Fitness room. Bicycle hire 25 km. Off site: Fishing 1 km. to River Vienne. Restaurant 5 km.

Open: 15 April - 30 September.

Directions

Site is 5 km. west from exit 25 on A10 at St Maure-de-Touraine on D760 towards Chinon. Entrance is signed and marked by a model of the château. GPS: N47:06.460 E00:30.631

Charges 2007

Per person	€ 4,50 - € 6,00
child (under 10 yrs)	€ 2,50 - € 3,50
pitch incl. electricity	€ 10,50 - € 13,00

No credit cards.

FR37060 Kawan Village l'Arada Parc

Rue de la Baratière, F-37360 Sonzay (Indre-et-Loire)

Tel: **02 47 24 72 69**. Email: **info@laradaparc.com**

A good, well maintained site in a quiet location, Camping L'Arada Parc is a popular base from which to visit the numerous châteaux in this beautiful part of France. The 79 grass pitches all have electricity and 35 have water and drainage. The clearly marked pitches, some slightly sloping, are separated by trees and shrubs some of which are now providing a degree of shade. An attractive, heated pool is on a pleasant terrace beside the restaurant. Entertainment, themed evenings and activities for children are organised in July/August. A new site with modern facilities and developing well.

Facilities

Two modern toilet blocks provide unisex toilets, showers and washbasins in cubicles. Baby room. Facilities for disabled visitors (wheelchair users may find the gravel access difficult). Dishwashing and laundry facilities. Shop, bar, restaurant and takeaway (24/3-31/10). Swimming pool (no Bermuda style shorts; 1/5-13/9). Play area, games area. Boules, volleyball, badminton and table tennis. TV room. Bicycle hire. Internet access. Off site: Tennis 200 m. Riding 7 km. Fishing 9 km. Golf 12 km.

Open: 22 March - late October.

Directions

Sonzay is northwest of Tours. From the new A28 north of Tours take the exit to Neuillé-Pont-Pierre which is on the N138 Le Mans - Tours road. Then take D766 towards Château la Vallière and turn southwest to Sonzay. Follow campsite signs. GPS: N47:31.687 E00:27.180

Charges 2008

Per unit incl. 2 persons	€ 13,50 - € 17,50
extra person	€ 3,50 - € 4,50
child (2-10 yrs)	€ 2,75 - € 3,50
electricity (10A)	€ 3,50

Camping Cheques accepted.

Check real time availability and at-the-gate prices...

www.**alanrogers**.com

FR37030 Camping le Moulin Fort
F-37150 Francueil-Chenonceaux (Indre-et-Loire)
Tel: 02 47 23 86 22. Email: lemoulinfort@wanadoo.fr

Camping Le Moulin Fort is a tranquil, riverside site that has been redeveloped by British owners, John and Sarah Scarratt. The 137 pitches are enhanced by trees and shrubs offering some shade and 110 pitches have electricity (6A). The swimming pool (unheated) is accessed by a timber walkway over the mill race from the snack bar terrace adjacent to the restored mill building. Although not intrusive there is some noise from the railway across the river and a few trains run at night. The site is more suitable for couples and families with young children, although the river is unfenced. All over the campsite, visitors will find little information boards about local nature (birds, fish, trees and shrubs), about the history of the mill and fascinating facts about recycling. The owners are keen to encourage recycling on the site. The picturesque Château of Chenonceaux is little more than 1 km. along the Cher riverbank and many of the Loire châteaux are within easy reach, particularly Amboise and its famous Leonardo de Vinci museum.

Facilities

Two toilet blocks with all the usual amenities of a good standard, including washbasins in cubicles and baby baths. Shop (1/4-30/9). Bar, restaurant and takeaway (all 1/4-30/9). Swimming pool (15/5-30/9). Petanque. Minigolf. Games room and TV. Library. Regular family entertainment including wine tasting, quiz evenings, activities for children and light-hearted games tournaments. Motorcaravan service point. Fishing. Bicycle and canoe hire. Petanque. Live music events. Off site: Riding 12 km. Golf 20 km.

Open: 1 April - 30 September.

Directions

Site signed from D976 Tours - Vierzon road. From D40 (Tours - Chenonceaux), go through village and after 2 km. right on D80 to cross river at Chisseaux. Site on left just after bridge. GPS: N47:19.637 E01:05.358

Charges 2008

Per unit incl. 2 persons	€ 9,00 - € 22,00
extra person	€ 3,00 - € 5,00
child (4-12 yrs)	€ 2,00 - € 4,00
electricity (6A)	€ 4,00
dog	€ 2,00 - € 3,00

Check real time availability and at-the-gate prices...

www.alanrogers.com

FR41070 Kawan Village la Grande Tortue

3 route de Pontlevoy, F-41120 Candé-sur-Beuvron (Loir-et-Cher)

Tel: **02 54 44 15 20**. Email: **grandetortue@wanadoo.fr**

This is a pleasant, shady site that has been developed in the surroundings of an old forest. It provides 169 touring pitches the majority of which are more than 100 sq.m. 150 have 10A electricity and the remainder are fully serviced. The family owners continue to develop the site with a new multisport court already created. During July and August, they organise a programme of trips including wine/cheese tastings, canoeing and horse riding excursions. Used by tour operators. This site is well placed for visiting the châteaux of the Loire or the cities of Orléans and Tours.

Facilities

Three sanitary blocks offer British style WCs, washbasins in cabins and push button showers. Laundry facilities. Shop selling provisions. Terraced bar and restaurant with reasonably priced food and drink (15/4-15/9). Swimming pool and two shallower pools for children (1/5-30/9). Trampolines, a ball crawl with slide and climbing wall, bouncy inflatable, table tennis. New multisport court. Off site: Walking and cycling. Bicycle hire 1 km. Fishing 500 m. Golf 10 km. Riding 12 km.

Open: 9 April - 30 September.

Directions

Site is just outside Candé-sur-Beuvron on D751, between Amboise and Blois. From Amboise, turn right just before Candé, then left into campsite. GPS: N47:29.389 E01:15.515

Charges 2007

Per unit incl. 2 persons	€ 15,00 - € 26,00
incl. electricity	€ 19,50 - € 30,00
extra person	€ 5,00 - € 7,50
child (3-9 yrs)	€ 3,50 - € 5,50
animal	€ 3,70

Camping Cheques accepted.

FR41030 **Yelloh! Village le Parc des Alicourts**

Domaine des Alicourts, F-41300 Pierrefitte-sur-Sauldre (Loir-et-Cher)

Tel: 04 66 73 97 39. Email: info@yellohvillage-parc-des-alicourts.com

A secluded holiday village set in the heart of the forest and with many sporting facilities and a super new spa centre, Parc des Alicourts is midway between Orléans and Bourges, to the east of the A71. There are 490 pitches, 150 for touring and the remainder occupied by mobile homes and chalets. All pitches have electricity connections (6A) and good provision for water, and most are 150 sq.m. (min. 100 sq.m.). Locations vary from wooded to more open areas, thus giving a choice of amount of shade. All facilities are open all season and the leisure amenities are exceptional. Member of Leading Campings Group.

Facilities

Three modern sanitary blocks include some washbasins in cabins and baby bathrooms. Laundry facilities. Facilities for disabled visitors (shallow step to reach them). Motorcaravan services. Shop. Restaurant. Takeaway in bar with terrace. Pool complex. Spa centre. 7 hectare lake (fishing, bathing, canoes, pedaloes). 9-hole golf course. Play area. Tennis. Minigolf. Boules. Roller skating/skateboarding (bring own equipment). Bicycle hire. Internet access. Walk and cycle path.

Open: 30 April - 9 September.

Directions

From A71, take Lamotte Beuvron exit (no. 3) or from N20 Orléans to Vierzon turn left on to D923 towards Aubigny. After 14 km. turn right at camping sign on to D24E. Site signed in about 4 km.
GPS: N47:32.639 E02:11.516

Charges 2007

Per unit incl. 2 persons and electricity	€ 17,00 - € 41,00
extra person	€ 6,00 - € 9,00
child (1-17 yrs)	free - € 7,00

FR45010 **Kawan Village les Bois du Bardelet**

Route de Bourges, Poilly, F-45500 Gien (Loiret)

Tel: 02 38 67 47 39. Email: contact@bardelet.com

This attractive, lively family site, in a rural setting, is well situated for exploring the less well known eastern part of the Loire Valley. Two lakes (one for boating, one for fishing) and a pool complex have been attractively landscaped in 12 hectares of former farmland, blending old and new with natural wooded areas and more open field areas with rural views. Bois du Bardelet provides 260 pitches with around 130 for touring units. All are larger than 100 sq.m. and have electrical connections, with some fully serviced. The communal areas are based on attractively converted former farm buildings with a wide range of leisure facilities. A family club card can be purchased to make use of the many activities on a daily basis (some high season only). Various activities and excursions are organised, the most popular being to Paris on Wednesdays, which can be pre-booked.

Facilities

Two sanitary blocks (only one open outside 15/6-31/8) include washbasins in cabins. Facilities for disabled visitors and babies. Washing machines. Shop (1/4-30/9). Bar. Snack bar, takeaway, restaurant (all 1/4-14/9) and pizzeria (8/7-21/8). Outside pool (1/5-31/8). Indoor children's pool. Indoor pool, heated (with purchased club card). Aqua-gym, fitness and jacuzzi room. Games area. Archery. Canoeing and fishing. Tennis, minigolf, boules. Bicycle hire. Playground. Internet. Off site: Supermarket 5 km. Riding 7 km. Golf 25 km. Walking and cycling routes.

Open: 1 April - 30 September.

Directions

From Gien take D940 (Bourges). After 5 km. turn right and right again to cross road and follow site signs. From Argent sur Sauldre take D940 (Gien). Site signed to right after 15 km. Entrance is 200 m. past what looks like the first opening to site.
GPS: N47:38.497 E02:36.891

Charges 2008

Per unit incl. 2 persons and electricity	€ 18,50 - € 30,90
extra person (over 2 yrs)	€ 3,70 - € 6,20
Camping Cheques accepted.	

Check real time availability and at-the-gate prices...

www.**alanrogers**.com

FR49040 Camping de l'Etang

Route de St Mathurin, F-49320 Brissac (Maine-et-Loire)

Tel: **02 41 91 70 61**. Email: **info@campingetang.com**

At Camping de l'Etang many of the 124 level touring pitches have pleasant views across the countryside. Separated and numbered, some have a little shade and all have electricity with water and drainage nearby. 21 are fully serviced. A small bridge crosses the river Aubance which runs through the site (well fenced) and there are two lakes where fisherman can enjoy free fishing. The site has its own vineyard and the wine produced can be purchased on the campsite. Tour operators use 16 pitches. Originally the farm of the Château de Brissac (yet only 24 km. from the lovely town of Angers), this is an attractive campsite retaining much of its rural charm. The adjacent Parc de Loisirs is a paradise for young children with many activities including boating, pedaloes, pony rides, miniature train, water slide, bouncy castle and swings (free entry for campers). A 'Sites et Paysages' member.

Facilities

Three well maintained toilet blocks provide all the usual facilities. Laundry facilities. Baby room. Disabled visitors are well catered for. Motorcaravan service point. The farmhouse houses reception, small shop and takeaway snacks when bar is closed. A bar/restaurant serves crêpes, salads, etc (evenings June-August). Swimming pool (heated and covered) and paddling pool. Fishing. Play area. Bicycle hire. Wide variety of evening entertainment in high season. Off site: Golf and riding 10 km. Sailing 25 km.

Open: 1 May - 15 September.

Directions

Brissac-Quincé is 17 km. southeast of Angers on D748 towards Poitiers. Do not enter the town but turn north on D55 (site signed) in direction of St Mathurin. GPS: N47:21.560 W00:26.065

Charges 2008

Per unit incl. 2 persons	€ 15,00 - € 29,00
extra person	€ 5,00 - € 7,00
child (0-10 yrs)	free - € 4,00
electricity	free - € 3,00
dog	€ 3,00 - € 4,00

On the route of the châteaux of the Loire, 2 campsites welcome you

The same spirit of hospitality

Association de
Chantepie et de l'Etang
N° 2002/DRTEFP/280

CAMPING DE CHANTEPIE ★★★★
S¹-Hilaire-S¹-Florent - 49400 SAUMUR
Tél. +33 (0)2 41 67 95 34 - Fax +33 (0)2 41 67 95 85
e-mail : info@campingchantepie.com
www.campingchantepie.com

CAMPING DE L'ETANG ★★★★
Route de S¹-Mathurin
49320 BRISSAC
Tél. +33 (0)2 41 91 70 61 - Fax +33 (0)2 41 91 72 65
e-mail : info@campingetang.com
www.campingetang.com

FR49020 Camping de Chantepie

Saint Hilaire-St Florent, F-49400 Saumur (Maine-et-Loire)

Tel: **02 41 67 95 34**. Email: **info@campingchantepie.com**

On arriving at Camping de Chantepie with its colourful, floral entrance, a friendly greeting awaits at reception, set beside a restored farmhouse. The site is owned by a charitable organisation which provides employment for local disabled people. Linked by gravel roads (which can be dusty), the 150 grass touring pitches are level and spacious, with some new larger ones (200 sq.m. at extra cost, state preference when booking). All pitches have electricity and are separated by low hedges of flowers and trees offering some shade. This is a good site for families. A 'Sites et Paysages' member.

Facilities

The toilet block is clean and facilities are good with washbasins in cubicles, new showers (men and women separately) and facilities for disabled visitors. Dishwashing and laundry facilities. Baby area. Shop. Bar, terraced café and takeaway. Covered and heated pool, outdoor pool and paddling pool. Play area with apparatus. Terraced minigolf. Volleyball, TV, video games and table tennis. Pony rides. Bicycle hire. Internet access.
Off site: Fishing 500 m. Golf, riding 2 km. Sailing 7 km.

Open: 1 May - 15 September.

Directions

St Hilaire-St Florent is 2 km. west of Saumur. Take D751 (Gennes). Right at roundabout in St Hilaire-St Florent and on until Le Poitrineau and campsite sign, then turn left. Continue for 3 km. then turn right into site road.

Charges 2008

Per unit incl. 2 persons	€ 15,00 - € 29,00
extra person	€ 5,00 - € 7,00
child (3-10 yrs)	€ 3,00 - € 4,00
electricity (5/10A)	€ 3,00

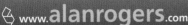

FR49060 Camping Parc de Montsabert

Montsabert, F-49320 Coutures (Maine-et-Loire)

Tel: 02 41 57 91 63. Email: camping@parcdemontsabert.com

This extensive site has recently been taken over by a friendly French couple who already have plans for improvements. It has a rural atmosphere in the shadow of Montsabert château, from where visiting peacocks happily roam in the spacious surroundings. The main features are the heated swimming pool (with cover) and the adjoining refurbished, rustic style restaurant. There are 96 large, well marked touring pitches, divided by hedges and all with water tap, drain and electricity (10A). Picnic tables are provided. Used by several small tour operators (30 pitches). Partially wooded by a variety of trees, this site offers the peace of the countryside and yet easy access to both Saumur and Angers. It is an ideal base for exploring the area, whether on foot, by bicycle or car.

Facilities

The main toilet block can be heated and has washbasins and bidets in cabins and a baby room. Laundry facilities. A second block serves the pool and another provides more WCs. Shop, bar and takeaway (31/5-31/8). Restaurant(14/6-23/8). Heated pool (no Bermuda style shorts) and paddling pool. Sports hall, minigolf, volleyball and basketball. Tennis. Play area. Bicycle hire. Entertainment (high season). Off site: Canoeing nearby. Fishing, riding 5 km. Golf 8 km.

Open: 12 April - 14 September.

Directions

Coutures is 25 km. southeast of Angers on the D751 to Saumur. From A11 take exit 14 and follow signs for Cholet/Poitiers, then Poitiers on D748. At Brissac-Quincé turn northeast on D55 and in 5 km. turn right to Coutures. Montsabert is north of village. GPS: N47:22.464 W00:20.709

Charges 2008

Per pitch incl. 2 persons	€ 16,00 - € 25,00
extra person	€ 4,00 - € 4,75
child (1-13 yrs)	€ 2,50 - € 3,20
electricity (5/10A)	€ 3,50 - € 4,20
dog	€ 3,30

PARC de MONTSABERT
www.parcdemontsabert.com
camping@parcdemontsabert.com

Spacious Pitches
25m heated Swimmingpool
Covered Pool, Childrenspool
Sportshall, Tennis, Tabletennis,
Volley, Soccer, Midget Golf, etc.
Bicycle rent, Walking- and
Cyclingroutes
Restaurant, Entertainment
English spoken
Holiday homes to let
Tel: (0033) 241 57 91 63

FR79020 Camping de Courte Vallée

F-79600 Airvault (Deux-Sèvres)

Tel: 05 49 64 70 65. Email: camping@caravanningfrance.com

This small and beautifully landscaped site is family run. Set in 10 acres of parkland close to the Thouet river, it is within walking distance of Airvault (the birthplace of Voltaire). In the heart of rural France and off the main tourist tracks, the site offers tranquility and a warm and friendly atmosphere in surroundings maintained to the highest standards. There are 64 grass pitches, many with electricity, water and drainage which makes the site ideal for a long stay to explore the area. Nearby are Puy du Fou, Fontevraud Abbey, Doué la Fontaine zoo and the châteaux of Saumur and Oiron.

Facilities

A modern unisex block has spacious cubicles for showers and washbasins, and shower and WC cubicles for disabled visitors, all kept to a very high standard of cleanliness. Washing machine and dryers. Reception sells 'frites', snacks, beers and wine and ice cream. Internet access. Swimming pool. Play area. Caravan storage. Wine tasting events and barbecues. Coffee bar. Off site: Airvault is a 10-15 minute walk. Fishing 300 m. Riding 8 km.

Open: All year.

Directions

From D938 (Parthenay-Thouars) take D725 Airvault. On approaching village turn left over bridge. At T-junction turn sharp left, second exit at roundabout, left at junction to site on left. GPS: N46:49.937 W00:08.909

Charges 2008

Per person	€ 7,00 - € 8,00
pitch incl. electricity	€ 14,00 - € 16,00
No credit cards.	

FR86040 Kawan Village le Futuriste

F-86130 Saint Georges-les-Baillargeaux (Vienne)

Tel: **05 49 52 47 52**. Email: **camping-le-futuriste@wanadoo.fr**

Le Futuriste is a neat, modern site, open all year and close to Futuroscope. With a busy atmosphere, there are early departures and late arrivals. Reception is open 08.00-22.00 hrs. There are 118 individual, flat, grassy pitches divided by young trees and shrubs which are beginning to provide some shelter for this elevated and otherwise rather open site (possibly windy). 82 pitches have electricity (6A) and a further 30 have electricity, water, waste water and sewage connections. All are accessed via neat, level and firmly rolled gravel roads. On raised ground with panoramic views over the strikingly modern buildings and night-time bright lights that comprise the popular attraction of Futuroscope, this site is ideal for a short stay to visit the park which is only 1.5 km. away (tickets can be bought at the site) but it is equally good for longer stays to see the region. Details of attractions are available from the enthusiastic young couple who run the site. Note: it is best to see the first evening show at Futuroscope otherwise you will find yourself locked out of the site – the gates are closed at 23.30 hrs.

Facilities

Excellent, clean sanitary facilities in two insulated blocks (can be heated). Those in the newest block are unisex. and include some washbasins in cabins and facilities for disabled people. Laundry facilities. Shop (bread to order), bar/restaurant (all 1/5-30/9). Snack bar and takeaway (1/7-31/8). Two heated outdoor pools, one with slide and paddling pool (1/5-30/9). Games room. TV. Boules. New multisports area. Lake fishing. Youth groups not accepted. Off site: Bicycle hire 500 m. Hypermarket 600 m. Golf 5 km. Riding 10 km.

Open: All year.

Directions

From either A10 autoroute or N10, take Futuroscope exit. Site is east of both roads, off D20 (St Georges-Les-Baillargeaux). Follow signs to St Georges. Site on hill; turn by water tower and site is on left. GPS: N46:39.928 E00:23.668

Charges 2008

Per pitch incl. 1-3 persons	€ 15,00 - € 20,00
extra person	€ 2,00 - € 2,80
electricity	€ 2,80 - € 3,70
animal	€ 1,90

Camping Cheques accepted.

Open all year. Panoramic view over the Futuroscope situated at 2 kms.
Heated swimming pool, pond, snack, bar, restaurant.
Chalets for hire.

86130 St-Georges les Baillargeaux
Tel.: 0033 549 52 47 52
Fax: 0033 549 37 23 33
www.camping-le-futuriste.fr

Check real time availability and at-the-gate prices...
www.**alanrogers**.com

FR71070 Kawan Village Château de l'Epervière

F-71240 Gigny-sur-Saône (Saône-et-Loire)

Tel: **03 85 94 16 90**. Email: **domaine-de-lepperviere@wanadoo.fr**

This site is peacefully situated in the wooded grounds of the 16th century Château, near the village of Gigny-sur-Saône, and within walking distance of the river where you can watch the river cruise boats on their way to and from Chalon-sur-Saône. There are 160 pitches in total, of which 45 are occupied by tour operators and 5 units are for rent. The 110 touring pitches, all with 10A electricity (30 fully serviced) are in two distinct areas. The original part, close to the Château and fishing lake, has semi-hedged pitches on level ground with shade from mature trees. The centre of the second area has a more open aspect, with large hedged pitches and mature trees offering shade around the periphery – birdwatchers will love this area. A partly fenced road across the lake connects the two areas. The main château's restaurant serves regional dishes. Gert-Jan and François, and their team enthusiastically organise many activities for visitors including wine-tasting in the cellars of the château. Don't forget, you are in the Maconnais and Chalonnaise wine areas and so close to the A6.

Facilities

Two well-equipped toilet blocks include washbasins in cabins, showers, baby rooms, dishwashing and laundry areas and facilities for disabled visitors. Washing machine and dryer. Basic shop (1/5-30/9). Second restaurant with basic menu and takeaway (1/4-30/9). Converted barn houses attractive bar, large TV and games room. Unheated outdoor swimming pool (1/5-30/9) partly enclosed by old stone walls. Smaller indoor heated pool, jacuzzi, sauna, paddling pool. Play area. Outdoor paddling pool. Fishing. Bicycle hire. Off site: Riding 15 km. Golf 20 km. Historic towns of Chalon and Tournus, both 20 km. The Monday market of Louhans, to see the famous Bresse chickens 26 km.

Open: 29 March - 30 September.

Directions

From the north, A6 exit Châlon-Sud, or Tournus from the south. Take N6 to Sennecey-le-Grand, turn east on D18 and follow site signs for 6.5 km.

Charges 2008

Per unit incl. 2 persons and electricity	€ 23,40 - € 32,20
extra person	€ 5,70 - € 7,70
child (under 7 yrs)	€ 3,50 - € 5,30
dog	€ 2,40 - € 3,00
Camping Cheques accepted.	

FR71140 Camping du Pont de Bourgogne

Rue Julien Leneveu, Saint Marcel, F-71380 Chalon-sur-Saône (Saône-et-Loire)

Tel: **03 85 48 26 86**. Email: **campingchalon71@wanadoo.fr**

This is a well presented site, useful for an overnight stop or for a few days if exploring the local area and you want a simple site without the frills. It does get crowded in the third week of July during the Chalon street theatre festival. There are 93 fairly small pitches with 6/10A electricity, 10 with a gravel surface. The new owners of the site plan to replace or improve the facilities in the near future, but when we visited there was a bar/restaurant with an outdoor terrace and serving a good selection of simple, inexpensive meals. Although alongside the Saône river, the site is well fenced. The staff are friendly and helpful.

Facilities

Three toilet blocks, two centrally located amongst the pitches and traditional in style and fittings, the third new and modern, alongside the reception building (including facilities for disabled visitors). Dishwashing facilities but no laundry. Modern bar/restaurant. No shop but essentials kept in the bar (bread to order). Simple play area. Bicycle hire arranged. Off site: Municipal swimming pool 300 m. Golf 1 km. Riding 10 km.

Open: 1 April - 30 September.

Directions

From A6 exit 26 (Chalon-Sud) bear right to roundabout and take N80 (Dole) straight on to roundabout at St Marcel. Turn left (fourth exit) and fork right into Les Chavannes. At central traffic lights turn right and under modern river bridge to site entrance.

Charges 2007

Per person	€ 4,30 - € 5,20
child (under 7 yrs)	€ 2,10 - € 2,80
pitch	€ 4,30 - € 5,90
electricity	€ 3,20 - € 3,90

Domaine du Château de l'Epervière

Camping caravaning - Locations ★★★★

Bourgogne du Sud

FRANCE

CAMPING DU Pont de BOURGOGNE

Chalon sur Saône - Bourgogne du Sud

FR25080 Camping les Fuvettes

F-25160 Malbuisson (Doubs)

Tel: **03 81 69 31 50**. Email: **lesfuvettes@wanadoo.fr**

High in the Jura and close to the Swiss border, Les Fuvettes is a well-established family site with a fine, lakeside setting on Lac Saint Point. The lake is large – over 1,000 hectares and a wide range of watersports are possible from the site, including sailing, windsurfing and pedaloes. Most equipment can be hired on site. Pitches here are grassy and of a reasonable size, separated by hedges and small trees. The new swimming pool is impressive with water slides and a separate children's pool. The site's bar/snack bar is housed in an attractive, steep roofed building and offers panoramic views across the lake. Walking and mountain biking are popular pursuits and many trails are available in the surrounding countryside. The Château de Joux is a popular excursion and the nearby Mont d'Or offers fine views towards the Alps. In high season, the site runs an entertainment and excursion programme, including a children's club.

Facilities

Three toilet blocks include facilities for babies and disabled people. Shop. Bar and snack bar. Swimming pool with waterslides and jacuzzi. Paddling pool. Play area. Minigolf. Archery. Beach volleyball. Bicycle hire. Sports pitch. Fishing (permit needed). Boat hire. Games room. Children's club in peak season. Entertainment and excursions (July/Aug). Mobile homes and chalets for rent. Off site: Sailing school. Tennis. Many cycling and walking trails. Restaurants and shops in Malbuisson (walking distance).

Open: 1 April - 30 September.

Directions

From Besançon, head south on the N57 and join the D437 beyond Pontarlier signed Lac St Point and Mouthe. This road runs along the easten shores of the lake and passes through Malbuisson. Site is at the end of the village on the right.

Charges 2007

Per unit incl. 2 persons and electricity	€ 19,00 - € 25,00
extra person	€ 3,40 - € 4,90
child (under 7 yrs)	€ 1,70 - € 2,70

CAMPING LES FUVETTES

F-25160 Malbuisson France

Tél.: 03 81 69 31 50
Fax: 03 81 69 70 46

les-fuvettes@wanadoo.fr

FR70020 Camping International du Lac

Avenue des Rives du Lac, F-70000 Vesoul-Vaivre (Haute-Saône)

Tel: **03 84 76 22 86**. Email: **camping-dulac@yahoo.fr**

This is one of the better examples of a town site and is part of a leisure park around a large lake. The campsite does not have direct access to the lake as it is separated by a security fence, but access is possible at the site entrance. There are 160 good sized, level, grass pitches, all with electricity (10A). Access is from hard roads and pitches are separated by shrubs and bushes. There is a large area in the centre of the site with a children's playground.

Facilities

Three good quality toilet blocks, one heated, are well spaced around the site and provide a mix of British and Turkish style WCs, washbasins and showers. Baby room. Two superb suites for disabled visitors. Washing machines and dryers. Motorcaravan service point. Baker calls daily (July/Aug); bread ordered from reception at other times. Animation (July/Aug). Bicycle hire. TV and games room. Boules. Internet access. Off site: Bar and restaurant adjacent. 9 km. velo-rail nearby. Riding 4 km.

Open: 1 March - 31 October.

Directions

On road D457 to west of Vesoul on route to Besançon, well signed around the town. GPS: N47:37.812 E06:07.700

Charges 2007

Per person	€ 3,40
child (under 7 yrs)	€ 1,50
pitch with electricity	€ 5,25
dog	€ 1,80

FR74070 Camping Caravaning l'Escale

F-74450 Le Grand-Bornand (Haute-Savoie)

Tel: 04 50 02 20 69. Email: contact@campinglescale.com

You are assured a good welcome from the Baur family at this beautifully maintained and picturesque site, situated at the foot of the Aravis mountain range. The 149 pitches, 122 of which are for touring, are of average size, part grass, part gravel and separated by trees and shrubs, giving a little shade. All pitches have electricity (2-10A) and 86 are fully serviced. Rock pegs are essential. The village (200 m. away) has all the facilities of a resort with activities for summer or winter holidays. In summer a variety of well signed footpaths and cycle tracks provide forest or mountain excursions. In winter the area provides superb facilities for down-hill and cross-country skiing.

Facilities

Good toilet blocks (heated in winter) have all the necessary facilities. Drying room for skis and boots. Superb complex with interconnected indoor (all season) and outdoor pools and paddling pools (10/6-31/8). Cosy bar/restaurant with local specialities (all season). Play area. Tennis. Table tennis. Torches essential. WiFi. Off site: Village (5 minutes walk), shops, bars, restaurants, archery, paragliding, hang-gliding. 150 km. of signed walks. Activities organised for children and adults. Ice skating, ice hockey in winter. Bicycle hire 200 m. Riding and golf 3 km.

Open: 15 December - 22 April, 20 May - 24 September.

Directions

From Annecy follow D16 and D909 towards La Clusaz. At St Jean-de-Sixt, turn left at roundabout D4 signed Grand Bornand. Just before village fork right signed Vallée de Bouchet and camping. Site entrance is on right at roundabout in 1.2 km. GPS: N45:56.412 E06:25.692

Charges 2007

Per unit incl. 2 persons	€ 16,00 - € 22,80
with services	€ 17,50 - € 25,80
extra person	€ 4,80 - € 5,80
electricity (2-10A)	€ 3,70 - € 8,50

Camping Cheques accepted.

FR73020 Camping Caravaneige le Versoyen

Route des Arcs, F-73700 Bourg-St-Maurice (Savoie)

Tel: 04 79 07 03 45. Email: leversoyen@wanadoo.fr

Bourg-St-Maurice is on a small, level plain at an altitude of 830 m. on the River Isère, surrounded by mountains. Le Versoyen attracts visitors all year round (except for a short time when they close). The site's 205 unseparated, flat pitches (180 for touring) are marked by numbers on the tarmac roads and all have electrical connections (4/6/10A). Most are on grass but some are on tarmac hardstanding making them ideal for use by motorcaravans or in winter. Trees give shade in some parts, although most pitches have almost none. Duckboards are provided for snow and wet weather. This is a good base for winter skiing, summer walking, climbing, rafting or canoeing, or for car excursions. For many years a winter ski resort, the area now caters for visitors all year round. The Parc National de la Vanoise is nearby, along with a wealth of interesting places.

Facilities

Two acceptable toilet blocks can be heated, although the provision may be hard pressed in high season. British and Turkish style WCs. Laundry. Motorcaravan service facilities. Outdoor and covered pools (July/Aug). Heated restroom with TV. Small bar with takeaway in summer. Free shuttle in high season to funicular railway. Off site: Fishing or bicycle hire 200 m. Tennis and swimming pool 500 m. Riding 1 km. Golf 15 km. Cross country ski track.

Open: All year (excl. 7/11-14/12 and 2/5-25/5).

Directions

Site is 1.5 km. east of Bourg-St-Maurice on the CD119 Les Arcs road. GPS: N45:37.324 E06:47.010

Charges 2007

Per unit incl. 2 persons and electricity	€ 16,10 - € 21,00
extra person	€ 4,00 - € 4,60
child (4-13 yrs)	€ 2,50 - € 4,40
dog	€ 0,50

FR33090 Flower Camping le Pressoir

Petit Palais et Cornemps, F-33570 Lussac (Gironde)

Tel: 05 57 69 73 25. Email: contact@campinglepressoir.com

The 100 large pitches at Le Pressoir are arranged on either side of a gravel road leading up a slight hill. Most are shaded by attractive trees, but almost all are sloping. They are over 100 sq.m. and equipped with electricity (blue EC plugs) and interspersed with 5 mobile homes for hire. The old barn has been converted into a stylish bar and a really charming, separate restaurant. A quiet, family site, Le Pressoir provides a comfortable base for a holiday in this area famous for good food and wine. Buried in the famous wine producing countryside of the Lussac, Pomerol and St Emilion areas north of Bordeaux, Le Pressoir is surrounded by fields of vines. The manicured entrance featuring attractive trees, shrubs and flowers, together with preserved equipment from its former role as a wine farm, welcomes one to the site.

Facilities

Fully equipped toilet block with facilities for disabled visitors, and washing machine. Bar and pleasant restaurant (all season). Swimming pool (15/5-15/9, no Bermuda shorts). Playground with timber equipment. Petanque, volleyball and table tennis. Mountain bike hire. Off site: Tennis nearby. Fishing 3 km. Riding and bicycle hire 9 km.

Open: All year.

Directions

From N89 Bordeaux - Périgueux at Saint Médard de Guizières turn south towards Lussac (D21). From Castillon-la-Bataille on D936 Libourne-Bergerac road, south of site, take D17 north towards St Médard then D21 through Petit Palais. Site signed. GPS: N44:59.824 W00:03.801

Charges 2008

Per person	€ 5,60 - € 7,50
child (2-6 yrs)	€ 3,30 - € 4,50
pitch	€ 13,00 - € 15,00
with 6A electricity	€ 13,00 - € 26,00

FR33080 Kawan Village Domaine de la Barbanne

Route de Montagne, F-33330 Saint Emilion (Gironde)

Tel: 05 57 24 75 80. Email: barbanne@wanadoo.fr

La Barbanne is a pleasant, friendly, family-owned site in the heart of the Bordeaux wine region, only 2.5 km. from the famous town of St Emilion. With 174 pitches, most for touring, the owners have created a carefully maintained, well equipped site. The large, level and grassy pitches have dividing hedges and electricity (long leads necessary). Twelve pitches for motorcaravans have tarmac surrounded by grass. The site owners run a free minibus service twice a day to St Emilion and also organise excursions in July and August to local places of interest, including Bordeaux.

Facilities

Two modern, fully equipped toilet blocks include facilities for campers with disabilities. Motorcaravan services. Well stocked shop. Bar, terrace, takeaway, restaurant (1/6-20/9). Two swimming pools, one heated with water slide (15/4-22/9). Enclosed play area with seats for parents, children's club (from 1/7). Evening entertainment (from 1/7). Tennis, boules, volleyball, table tennis, minigolf. The lake provides superb free fishing, pedaloes, canoes and lakeside walks. Bicycle hire. Off site: St Emilion and shops 2.5 km. Riding 8 km.

Open: 1 April - 22 September.

Directions

Site is 2.5 km. north of St Emilion. Caravans and motorhomes are forbidden through the village of St Emilion and they must approach the site from Libourne on D243 or from Castillon leave D936 and take D130/D243. GPS: N44:54.997 W00:08.513

Charges 2007

Per unit incl. 1 or 2 persons	€ 20,00 - € 30,00
extra person	€ 5,00 - € 8,00
child (under 7 yrs)	€ 3,50 - € 5,90
animal	free - € 3,00
Camping Cheques accepted.	

FR33130 Yelloh! Village les Grands Pins

Plage Nord, F-33680 Lacanau-Océan (Gironde)

Tel: **04 66 73 97 39**. Email: **info@yellohvillage-les-grands-pins.com**

This Atlantic coast holiday site with direct access to a fine sandy beach, is on undulating terrain amongst tall pine trees. A large site, with 600 pitches, 430 of varying sizes for touring units. One half of the site is a traffic free zone (except for arrival or departure day, caravans are placed on the pitch, with separate areas outside for parking). There are a good number of tent pitches, those in the centre of the site having some of the best views. This site is popular with an excellent range of facilities available for the whole season. Especially useful for tent campers are safety deposit and fridge boxes which are available for rent. Mobile homes (2 persons) are for hire. The large sandy beach is a 350 m. stroll from the gate at the back of the site.

Facilities

Four well equipped toilet blocks, one heated, including baby room and facilities for disabled people. Launderette. Motorcaravan services. Supermarket. Bar, restaurant, snack bar, takeaway. Heated swimming pool (lifeguard in July/Aug) with sunbathing surround. Jacuzzi. Free fitness activities. Games room. Fitness suite. Tennis. Two playgrounds. Adventure playground. Bicycle hire. Organised activities. WiFi in the bar (on payment). Only gas barbecues are permitted. Off site: Fishing, golf, riding and bicycle hire 5 km.

Open: 26 April - 20 September.

Directions

From Bordeaux take N125/D6 west to Lacanau-Océan. At second roundabout, take second exit: Plage Nord, follow signs to 'campings'. Les Grand Pins signed to right at the far end of road. GPS: N45:00.664 W01:11.602

Charges 2007

Per unit incl. 2 persons and electricity	€ 14,00 - € 43,00
extra person	€ 5,00 - € 9,00
child (2-12 yrs)	free - € 5,00
dog	€ 4,00

Half-board arrangements available.

Les Grands Pins
camping village ★★★★

Directly at the beach in the heart of an extensive pine forest, this is an ideal choice for family holidays, where you can relax in the open air. Discover Lacanau, the popular surfing spot, play golf, go cycling on one of the nice cycle tracks or choose a canoe trip on the lakes. For a full day excursion, visit a château in the famous Medoc Wine area, make a boat trip on the Bassin d'Arcachon or go shopping in the majestic town of Bordeaux.

NEW: weekend package €17,- per person in a fully equipped cottage
(including breakfast, bed linnen, towels and late departure time)

• **Pitch for 1 night from €14,-* • 1 night in a cottage for €29,-***

*between May 24th to May 30th 2008

Book your flight to Bordeaux-Mérignac Airport (45km)!

Yelloh! Village Les Grands Pins
33680 Lacanau Ocean
Tel: 0033 556 032 077
E-mail: reception@lesgrandspins.com

For information, special offers and online secure booking visit:
www.lesgrandspins.com

FR33110 Airotel Camping de la Côte d'Argent

F-33990 Hourtin-Plage (Gironde)

Tel: **05 56 09 10 25**. Email: **info@camping-cote-dargent.com**

Côte d'Argent is a large, well equipped site for leisurely family holidays. It makes an ideal base for walkers and cyclists, with over 100 km. of cycle lanes. Hourtin-Plage is a pleasant invigorating resort on the Atlantic coast and a popular location for watersports enthusiasts, The site's top attraction is its pool complex with wooden bridges connecting the pools and islands, with sunbathing and play areas plus indoor heated pool. There are 550 touring pitches, not clearly defined, under trees with some on soft sand. Entertainment takes place at the bar near the entrance (until 12.30). Spread over 20 hectares of undulating sand-based terrain and in the midst of a pine forest. There are 48 hardstandings for motorcaravans outside the site, providing a cheap stop-over, but with no access to site facilities. The site is well organised and ideal for children.

Facilities

Very clean sanitary blocks include provision for disabled visitors. Washing machines. Motorcaravan service points. Large supermarket, restaurant, takeaway, pizzeria bar. Four outdoor pools with slides and flumes. Indoor pool. Massage. Astronomy once a week. Tennis. Play areas. Miniclub, organised entertainment in season. Fishing. Riding. Bicycle hire. Internet. ATM. Charcoal barbecues are not permitted. Off site: Path to beach 300 m. Golf 30 km.

Open: 17 May - 14 September.

Directions

Turn off D101 Hourtin-Soulac road 3 km. north of Hourtin. Join D101E signed Hourtin-Plage. Site is 300 m. from beach. GPS: N45:13.381 W01:09.868

Charges 2008

Per unit incl. 2 persons and electricity	€ 25,00 - € 44,00
extra person	€ 3,00 - € 7,00

Camping Cheques accepted.

FR33260 Camping le Braou

Route de Bordeaux, F-33980 Audenge (Gironde)

Tel: **05 56 26 90 03**. Email: **info@camping-audenge.com**

The present owners, M. and Mme. Gharbi, were the wardens of this simple, former municipal site and now lease it from the town. They have funded several developments since they took over in 2003 including a small pool, a snack bar, play area and new electrical hook-ups. The site is flat with easy access, and the pitches are in avenues, separated by newly-planted small shrubs. There is no natural shade. The new electric hook-ups (on 116 of the 148 pitches) are 10A. Outside high season this is a pleasant, reasonably priced place to stay while exploring the Bassin d'Arcachon with its bird reserve, oyster-beds, way-marked walks and cycle tracks. As with many French sites nothing much happens here until the beginning of July. Audenge (800 m.) is a lovely little town with a good choice of shops and restaurants. The Gharbis are very proud of their site, and this shows in the welcome and the high standard of maintenance.

Facilities

The small toilet block would be stretched when the site is full, but adequate in low season. Washbasins are in cubicles on the ladies side, open for men. Showers are controllable for temperature, push button operated. Shop for basics. Bar and snack-bar (July/Aug). Small unheated swimming pool (1/6-31/8). Play area. Internet access. Motorhome service point and overnight pitches outside site. Mobile homes to rent. Off site: Town facilities 800 m. Beach and fishing 15 km. Riding 2 km. Golf 5 km.

Open: 1 April - 30 September.

Directions

From A63 take exit 22 onto A660 towards Arcachon. From A660 take exit 2 towards Facture, then D3 through Biganos to Audenge. Site is signed 'Camping Municipal' at lights in town.

Charges 2007

Per unit incl. 2 persons	€ 9,50 - € 16,50
extra person	€ 3,00 - € 5,00
child (0-13 yrs)	€ 3,00 - € 4,50
electricity	€ 3,50 - € 3,50

FR33220 Sunêlia le Petit Nice

Route de Biscarosse, F-33115 Pyla-sur-Mer (Gironde)
Tel: **05 56 22 74 03**. Email: **info@petitnice.com**

Le Petit Nice is a traditional seaside site, just south of the great Dune de Pyla (Europe's largest sand dune, and a genuinely remarkable sight). It is a friendly, if relatively unsophisticated, site with direct (steep) access to an excellent sandy beach. The 225 pitches are for the most part terraced, descending towards the sea. Many are quite small, with larger pitches generally occupied by mobile homes. For this reason it is likely to appeal more to campers and those with smaller motorcaravans and caravans. Most pitches are shaded by pine trees but those closest to the sea are unshaded. Unusually, the site also has a private hang-gliding and paragliding take-off strip (very popular activities here).

Facilities

Two refurbished toilet blocks include washbasins in cubicles, baby rooms and facilities for disabled people. New, very smart bar/restaurant. Well stocked shop. Games room. Attractive swimming pool with small slide, children's pool and jacuzzi. Good fenced play area. Tennis. Boules court.

Open: 1 April - 30 September.

Directions

The site is on the D218 (Arcachon - Biscarosse) south of the Dune de Pyla and is the fifth site you pass after the Dune. GPS: N44:34.339 W01:13.255

Charges 2007

Per pitch incl. 2 persons	€ 14,00 - € 28,00
with electricity (6A)	€ 17,00 - € 32,00
extra person	€ 4,00 - € 7,00
child (2-12 yrs)	€ 2,00 - € 6,00
Camping Cheques accepted.	

FR40190 Le Saint Martin Airotel Camping

Avenue de l'Océan, F-40660 Moliets-Plage (Landes)

Tel: **05 58 48 52 30**. Email: **contact@camping-saint-martin.fr**

A family site aimed mainly at couples and young families, Airotel St Martin is a welcome change to most of the sites in this area in that it has only a small number of chalets (85) compared to the number of touring pitches (575). First impressions are of a neat, tidy, well cared for site and the direct access to the beach is an added bonus. The pitches are mainly typically French in style with low hedges separating them plus some shade. Electric hook ups are 10-15A and a number of pitches also have water and drainage. Entertainment in high season is low key (with the emphasis on quiet nights) – daytime competitions and a miniclub, plus the occasional evening entertainment, well away from the pitches and with no discos or karaoke. With pleasant chalets and mobile homes to rent, and an 18-hole golf course 700 m. away (special rates negotiated), this would be an ideal destination for a golfing weekend or longer stay.

Facilities

Seven toilet blocks of a high standard and very well maintained, have washbasins in cabins, large showers, baby rooms and facilities for disabled visitors. Motorcaravan service point. Washing machines and dryers. Fridge rental. Supermarket. Bars, restaurants and takeaways. Indoor pool (22/3-1/11), jacuzzi and sauna (charged July/Aug). Outdoor pool area with jacuzzi and paddling pool (15/6-15/9). Multisport pitch. Play area. Internet access. Electric barbecues only. Off site: Excellent area for cycling, bicycle hire 500 m. Golf and tennis 700 m. Riding 8 km.

Open: 22 March - 1 November.

Directions

From the N10 take D142 to Lèon, then D652 to Moliets-et-Mar. Follow signs to Moliets-Plage, site is well signed. GPS: N43:51.145 W01:23.239

Charges 2008

Per unit incl. 2 adults, 1 child	€ 17,50 - € 39,00
with electricity	€ 21,00 - € 43,20
services	€ 24,00 - € 48,50
extra person	€ 6,00
dog	€ 3,50

Prices are for reserved pitches.

★ ★ ★ ★

Le Saint Martin

Airotel Camping
Caravaning

**Avenue de l'Océan
40660 Moliets-Plage**

Tél : (33) 05.58.48.52.30
Fax : (33) 05.58.48.50.73

www.camping-saint-martin.fr
contact @camping-saint-martin.fr

FR40240 Camping Mayotte Vacances

368 chemin des Roseaux, F-40600 Biscarrosse (Landes)

Tel: **05 58 78 00 00**. Email: **mayotte@yellohvillage.com**

This appealing site is set amongst pine trees on the edge of Lac de Biscarrosse. Drive down a tree and flower lined avenue and proceed toward the lake to shady, good sized pitches which blend well with the many tidy mobile homes that share the area. Divided by hedges, all the pitches have electricity (10A) and water taps. There may be some aircraft noise at times from a nearby army base. The pool complex is impressive, with various pools, slides and a jacuzzi, all surrounded by paved sunbathing areas. The excellent lakeside beach provides safe bathing with plenty of watersports available.

Facilities

Four good quality, clean toilet blocks (one open early season). Good facilities for visitors with disabilities. Unusual baby/ bathroom. Motorcaravan services. Laundry. Supermarket. Rental shop (July/Aug). Restaurant. Swimming pools (one heated). Play area. Bicycle hire. Watersports. Organised entertainment (July/Aug). No charcoal barbecues. ATM. Internet access. Off site: Golf 4 km. Riding 100 m. Beach 10 km. Town 2 km.

Open: 30 April - 24 September.

Directions

From the north on D652 turn right on D333 (Chemin de Goubern). Pass through Goubern and Mayotte Village. Take next right (signed to site) into Chemin des Roseaux. GPS: N44:26.097 W01:09.303

Charges 2007

Per unit incl. 2 persons	€ 17,00 - € 39,00
extra person	€ 3,50 - € 7,50
child (3-7 yrs)	free - € 3,50
dog	€ 3,00 - € 5,00

(149)

FR40100 Camping du Domaine de la Rive

Route de Bordeaux, F-40600 Biscarosse (Landes)

Tel: **05 58 78 12 33**. Email: **info@camping-de-la-rive.fr**

Surrounded by pine woods, La Rive has a superb beach-side location on Lac de Sanguinet. It provides mostly level, numbered and clearly defined pitches of 100 sq.m. all with electricity connections (6A). The swimming pool complex is wonderful with pools linked by water channels and bridges. There is also a jacuzzi, paddling pool and two large swimming pools all surrounded by sunbathing areas and decorated with palm trees. An indoor pool is heated and open all season. There may be some aircraft noise from a nearby army base. This is a friendly site with a good mix of nationalities. The latest addition is a super children's aqua park with various games. The beach is excellent, shelving gently to provide safe bathing for all ages. There are windsurfers and small craft can be launched from the site's slipway.

Facilities

Five good clean toilet blocks have washbasins in cabins and mainly British style toilets. Facilities for disabled visitors. Baby baths. Motorcaravan service point. Shop. Propane gas. Restaurant. Bar serving snacks and takeaway. Games room. Pool complex (supervised July/Aug). Play area. Tennis. Bicycle hire. Hand-ball, basketball. Table tennis, boules, archery and football. Fishing. Water skiing. Watersports equipment hire. Tournaments (June-Aug). Skateboard park. Trampolines. Miniclub for children. No charcoal barbecues on pitches. Off site: Golf 8 km.

Open: 1 April - 30 September.

Directions

Take D652 from Sanguinet to Biscarosse and site is signed on the right in about 6 km. Turn right and follow new tarmac road for 2 km. GPS: N44:27.607 W01:07.808

Charges 2008

Per pitch incl. 2 persons	
and electricity	€ 20,00 - € 42,00
with water and drainage	€ 23,00 - € 45,00
extra person	€ 3,40 - € 7,50
child (3-7 yrs)	€ 2,30 - € 6,00
dog	€ 2,10 - € 5,00

Camping Cheques accepted.

FR40060 Camping Club International Eurosol

Route de la Plage, F-40560 Vielle-St-Girons (Landes)

Tel: **05 58 47 90 14**. Email: **contact@camping-eurosol.com**

This attractive and well maintained site is set on undulating ground amongst mature pine trees giving good shade. The 405 pitches for touring are numbered and 209 have electricity with 120 fully serviced. Satellite reception is available in one area. A family site with multilingual entertainers, many games and tournaments are organised and a beach volleyball competition is held each evening in front of the bar. A third covered pool has recently been added to the smart, landscaped pool complex. A sandy beach 700 metres from the site has supervised bathing in high season.

Facilities

Four main toilet blocks and two smaller blocks are comfortable and clean with facilities for babies and disabled visitors. Motorcaravan services. Fridge rental. Well stocked shop and bar. Restaurant, takeaway (from 1/6). Stage for live shows arranged in July/Aug. Outdoor swimming pool complex. Tennis. Multisport court for basketball, handball and football. Bicycle hire. Charcoal barbecues are not permitted. Internet and WiFi. Off site: Riding school opposite. Fishing 700 m.

Open: 17 May - 13 September.

Directions

Turn off D652 at St-Girons on D42 towards St-Girons-Plage. Site is on left before coming to beach (4.5 km). GPS: N43:57.100 W01:21.087

Charges 2007

Per unit incl.1 or 2 persons	€ 13,00 - € 27,00
with electricity	€ 16,00 - € 31,50
with water and drainage	€ 16,00 - € 35,00
extra person (over 4 yrs)	€ 4,00
dog	€ 2,50

Domaine de La Rive

a Paradise for Children

www.larive.fr

Pool complex and a covered heated swimming pool

FR40200 Yelloh! Village le Sylvamar

Avenue de l'Océan, F-40530 Labenne-Océan (Landes)

Tel: **04 66 73 97 39**. Email: **info@yellohvillage-sylvamar.com**

Less than a kilometre from a long sandy beach, this campsite has a good mix of tidy, well maintained chalets, mobile homes and touring pitches. The 562 pitches (216 for touring) are level, numbered and mostly separated by low hedges. Most have electricity (10A), many also have water and drainage and there is welcoming shade. The swimming pool complex is superbly set in a sunny location. The pools are of various sizes (one heated, one not) with a large one for paddling. With four toboggans and a fast flowing channel for sailing down in the inflatable rubber rings provided, this is a haven for children. All are surrounded by ample sunbathing terraces and overlooked by the bar/restaurant.

Facilities	Directions
Four modern toilet blocks (one recently refurbished) have washbasins in cabins, and facilities for babies and disabled visitors. Washing machines. Shop. Bar/restaurant and takeaway. Internet access. Play area. Games room. Cinema and video room. TV room. Miniclub (July/Aug). Fitness centre. Tennis. Bicycle hire. Library. Extensive entertainment programme for all ages, incl. evening shows in the outdoor amphitheatre. Fridge hire. No charcoal barbecues. Internet access. Off site: Beach 900 m. Fishing, riding 1 km. Golf 7 km.	Labenne is on the N10. In Labenne, head west on D126 signed Labenne-Océan and site is on right in 4 km. GPS: N43:35.742 W01:27.383

Open: 26 April - 17 September.

Charges 2007

Per unit incl. 2 persons, electricity	€ 17,00 - € 38,00
extra person (over 7 yrs)	€ 3,00 - € 7,00
extra person (3-7 yrs)	free - € 5,00
dog	free - € 5,00

Le Sylvamar Avenue de l'Océan F-40530 - Labenne Océan - France
T [33] 05 59 45 75 16 - F [33] 05 59 45 75 16 - sylvamar@wanadoo.fr

Nestled in a 37-acre (15 hectares) pine forest, this village is paradise for nature lovers, beachgoers and marine activities. Located on the southern coast of France's Landes region, Sylvamar is right next to Basque country and Spain, between Biarritz and Hossegor. It's up to you to choose wether you'd like an active or relaxing vacation, with plenty of clean, fresh air to make the best of it.

A DREAM COME TRUE - THE AQUATIC AREA IS AT YOUR DISPOSAL:
Blue lagoon, quiet green, luxurious vegetation, natural surroundings. For aquatic fun, there are 2 heated pools, a play river and triple waterslide. For relaxation, use deck chairs to soak up sun, stroll about on bridges and whatever you feel like. It's all designed around games, having fun and taking it easy. Smiling children and parents and all in complete safety, with on-duty lifeguards.

FR40140 Camping Caravaning Lou P'tit Poun

110 avenue du Quartier Neuf, F-40390 Saint Martin-de-Seignanx (Landes)

Tel: **05 59 56 55 79**. Email: **contact@louptitpoun.com**

The manicured grounds surrounding Lou P'tit Poun give it a well kept appearance, a theme carried out throughout this very pleasing site. It is only after arriving at the car park that you feel confident it is not a private estate. Beyond this point an abundance of shrubs and trees are revealed. Behind a central sloping flower bed lies the open plan reception area. The avenues around the site are wide and the 168 pitches (99 for touring) are spacious. All have electricity (6/10A), many also have water and drainage and some are separated by low hedges. A 'Sites et Paysages' member. The jovial owners not only make their guests welcome, but extend their enthusiasm to organising weekly entertainment for young and old during high season.

Facilities	Directions
Two unisex sanitary blocks, maintained to a high standard and kept clean, include washbasins in cabins, a baby bath and provision for disabled people. Dishwashing sinks and laundry facilities with washing machine and dryer. Motorcaravan service point. Small shop (1/7-31/8). Café (1/7-31/8). Swimming pool (1/6-15/9) Play area. Games room, TV. Half court tennis. Table tennis. Off site: Bayonne 6 km. Golf 10 km. Fishing or riding 7 km. Sandy beaches of Basque coast ten minute drive.	Leave A63 at exit 6 and join N117 in the direction of Pau. Site is signed at Leclerc supermarket. Continue on N117 for 3.5 km. and site is clearly signed on right. GPS: N43:31.451 W01:24.730

Open: 31 May - 15 September.

Charges 2008

Per pitch incl. 2 persons and electricity	€ 21,50 - € 32,50
extra person	€ 6,00 - € 7,00
child (under 7 yrs)	€ 4,00 - € 5,00
dog	€ 3,50 - € 4,50

Check real time availability and at-the-gate prices...

www.**alanrogers**.com

FR64150 Airotel Résidence des Pins

Avenue de Biarritz, F-64210 Bidart (Pyrénées-Atlantiques)
Tel: **05 59 23 00 29**. Email: **lespins@free.fr**

This is a very pleasant, reasonably priced site which will appeal greatly to couples and young families. Set on a fairly gentle hillside, the top level has reception and bar. Slightly lower are the paddling and swimming pools in a sunny location with sunbeds. Next comes the well stocked shop, tennis courts and the rest of the pitches. Some pitches are behind reception and others, lower down, some slightly sloping, are under trees and separated by hydrangea hedges. Some have electricity (10A, long leads required). There is a varied entertainment programme in July and Aug. The site is not suitable for American motorhomes. It is used by tour operators and there are mobile homes around the outer edges of the site. Buses pass the gate. There is a little day-time road noise but not intrusive.

Facilities

The two toilet blocks have some washbasins and showers together. Washing machines, dryers, ironing boards and facilities for disabled people. Motorcaravan services. Shop and bar open all season, restaurant (1/6-10/9) and takeaway (1/7-31/8). Pool open all season. Games room. Table tennis. Tennis (charged in July/Aug). Play area (3-8 yrs). Bicycle hire. Off site: Lake 600 m. with fishing (no licence required). Golf 1 km. Riding 1 km. Beach with lifeguard 600 m.

Open: 8 May - 20 September.

Directions

Heading south on the A63 towards Spain, take exit J4 onto the N10 towards Bidart. At the roundabout straight after Intermarche turn right towards Biarritz. The site is on the right after 1 km.
GPS: N43:27.185 W01:34.425

Charges 2007

Per unit with 2 persons	€ 15,90 - € 24,50
extra person (over 2 yrs)	€ 3,30 - € 5,80
electricity	€ 3,30 - € 5,10
dog	free - € 2,50

Camping Cheques accepted.

FR40180 Camping le Vieux Port

Plage sud, F-40660 Messanges (Landes)

Tel: **01 72 03 91 60**. Email: **contact@levieuxport.com**

A well established destination appealing particularly to families with teenage children, this lively site has 1,406 pitches of mixed size, most with electricity (6A) and some fully serviced. The camping area is well shaded by pines and pitches are generally of a good size, attractively grouped around the toilet blocks. There are many tour operators here and well over a third of the site is taken up with mobile homes and another 400 pitches are used for tents. The heated pool complex is exceptional boasting five outdoor pools and three large water slides. There is also a heated indoor pool. The area to the north of Bayonne is heavily forested and a number of very large campsites are attractively located close to the superb Atlantic beaches. Le Vieux Port is probably the largest and certainly one of the most impressive of these. At the back of the site a path leads across the dunes to a good beach (500 m). A little train also trundles to the beach on a fairly regular basis in high season (small charge). All in all, this is a lively site with a great deal to offer an active family.

Facilities

Nine well appointed, recently renovated toilet blocks with facilities for disabled people. Motorcaravan services. Good supermarket and various smaller shops in high season. Several restaurants, takeaway and three bars (all open all season). Large pool complex (no Bermuda shorts) including new covered pool and Polynesian themed bar. Tennis, football, multisport pitch, minigolf. Bicycle hire. Riding centre. Organised activities in high season including frequent discos and karaoke evenings. Only communal barbecues are allowed. Off site: Fishing 1 km. Golf 8 km.

Open: 1 April - 30 September.

Directions

Leave RN10 at Magescq exit heading for Soustons. Pass through Soustons following signs for Vieux-Boucau. Bypass this town and site is clearly signed to the left at second roundabout. GPS: N43:47.863 W01:23.959

Charges 2008

Per unit incl. 2 persons	€ 12,00 - € 39,00
extra person	€ 3,50 - € 7,00
child (under 10 yrs)	€ 2,50 - € 5,00
electricity (6/8A)	€ 4,00 - € 7,00
animal	€ 2,00 - € 4,50

Camping Cheques accepted.

FR64110 Sunêlia Col d'Ibardin

F-64122 Urrugne (Pyrénées-Atlantiques)
Tel: 05 59 54 31 21. Email: info@col-ibardin.com

This family owned site at the foot of the Basque Pyrénées is highly recommended and deserves praise. It is well run with emphasis on personal attention, the friendly family and their staff ensuring that all are made welcome and is attractively set in the middle of an oak wood. Behind the forecourt, with its brightly coloured shrubs and modern reception area, various roadways lead to the 191 pitches. These are individual, spacious and enjoy the benefit of the shade (if preferred a more open aspect can be found). There are electricity hook-ups (4/10A) and adequate water points. From this site you can enjoy the mountain scenery, be on the beach in 7-10 km. or cross the border into Spain in approximately 14 km.

Facilities

Two toilet blocks, one rebuilt to a high specification, are kept very clean. WC for disabled people. Dishwashing and laundry facilities. Motorcaravan service point. Shop for basics and bread orders (15/6-15/9). Catering, takeaway service and bar (15/6-15/9). Heated swimming pool. New paddling pool. Playground and club (adult supervision). Tennis courts, boules, table tennis, video games. Bicycle hire. New multi-purpose sports area. Not suitable for American motorhomes. Off site: Supermarket and shopping centre 5 km. Fishing and golf 7 km. Riding 20 km.

Open: 21 March - 30 September.

Directions

Leave A63 autoroute at St Jean-de-Luz sud, exit no. 2 and join RN10 in direction of Urrugne. Turn left at roundabout (Col d'Ibardin) on D4. Site on right after 5 km. Do not turn off to the Col itself, carry on towards Ascain. GPS: N43:20.035 W01:41.077

Charges 2008

Per unit incl. 2 persons	
and electricity	€ 16,50 - € 34,00
extra person	€ 3,00 - € 6,00
child (2-7 yrs)	€ 2,00 - € 3,50
animal	€ 2,50

Camping Caravaning
Du Col D'Ibardin

Open 01 April – 30 September
Swimming pool ● Tennis ● Bar ● Children's Pool and Club
Launderette ● Hot Water ● Snacks ● Playground ● Bicycle Hire
● Little farm with animals for children
● Mobil-homes to rent

Tel: (0033) (0)559.54.31.21
Fax: (0033) (0)559.54.62.28
Site: www.col-ibardin.com
E-mail: info@col-ibardin.com
64122 URRUGNE
PAYS BASQUE

Check real time availability and at-the-gate prices...

 www.alanrogers.com

FR12080 Camping Club les Genêts

Lac de Pareloup, F-12410 Salles-Curan (Aveyron)

Tel: 05 65 46 35 34. Email: contact@camping-les-genets.fr

The 162 pitches include 80 grassy, mostly individual pitches for touring units. These are in two areas, one on each side of the entrance lane, and are divided by hedges, shrubs and trees. Most have electricity (6A) and many also have water and waste water drain. The site slopes gently down to the beach and lake with facilities for all watersports including water skiing. A full animation and activities programme is organised in high season, and there is much to see and do in this very attractive corner of Aveyron. This family run site is on the shores of Lac de Pareloup and offers both family holiday and watersports facilities. Used by tour operators (25 pitches).

Facilities

Two sanitary units with a suite for disabled people. The older unit has been refurbished. Baby room. Laundry. Well stocked shop. Bar, restaurant, snacks (main season). Swimming pool, spa pool (from 1/6; unsupervised). Playground. Minigolf, volleyball, boules. Bicycle hire. Pedaloes, windsurfers, kayaks. Fishing licences available. WiFi in bar. Not suitable for American motorhomes.

Open: 31 May - 11 September.

Directions

From Salles-Curan take D577 for about 4 km. and turn right into a narrow lane immediately after a sharp right hand bend. Site is signed at junction.

Charges 2007

Per unit incl. 1 or 2 persons and electricity (6A)	€ 11,00 - € 29,00
lakeside pitch	€ 11,00 - € 36,00
extra person	€ 4,00 - € 7,00

FR12120 Camping du Rouergue

Avenue de Fondiès, F-12200 Villefranche-de-Rouergue (Aveyron)

Tel: 05 65 45 16 24. Email: campingrouergue@wanadoo.fr

A spacious and well appointed site in the Vallée de l'Aveyron, Camping du Rouergue is adjacent to the municipal sports facilities. Now under new ownership, you will receive a helpful and friendly welcome. The site has 85 grassy individual touring pitches of varying sizes, served by tarmac roads, and all serviced with electricity (16A), water and drain. Some pitches are shady. A further 13 pitches are for mobile homes or tents for rental. Shops and restaurants are within walking distance along the riverside foot and cycle path. A smaller pool is also available on site. The site is ideally placed for exploring the many historical Bastides of the Rouergue and Aveyron.

Facilities

The modern spacious sanitary unit includes washbasins in cubicles. Facilities for babies and disabled persons. Washing machine. With two identical sections to the block, only one is open during low season. Motorcaravan service point outside entrance. Shop. Small bar, restaurant and takeaway (June - Aug). TV room. Swimming pool. Well equipped playground. Bicycle hire. Off site: Fishing 1 km. Riding 5 km.

Open: 15 April - 30 September.

Directions

Villefranche-de-Rouergue is about midway between Cahors and Rodez. Site is 1 km. southwest of town on D47 towards Monteils, follow signs from the D911 to campsite and 'Stade'.

Charges 2007

Per pitch incl. 2 persons	€ 11,00 - € 14,00
extra person (over 10 yrs)	€ 2,50
child (4-10 yrs)	€ 1,50
electricity	€ 3,00

FR24560 Domaine le Cro Magnon

Le Raisse, Allas-les-Mines, F-24220 Saint Cyprien (Dordogne)

Tel: 05 53 29 13 70. Email: contact@domaine-cro-magnon.com

Le Cro Magnon is pleasantly situated in the heart of the Dordogne valley in the Périgord Noir. The 160 spacious, mostly shady pitches are divided in two different types: tent pitches without electricity and serviced pitches (6A electricity hook up, water and waste water drain). The site also offers various accommodation for rent. The swimming complex includes two pools (one outdoor, one indoor), water slides, a jacuzzi and a sauna. Near the entrance are a snack bar, pizzeria, bar and a well stocked shop. From a viewpoint on the site there are incredible views over the Dordogne valley.

Facilities

Two toilet blocks provide the usual facilities including facilities for disabled visitors. Washing machines. Motorcaravan services. Shop. Bar with TV. Snack bar and takeaway. Swimming pools with slides, jacuzzi and sauna. Multisport court. Boules. Play area. Off site: Canoeing, walking and cycling. Fishing.

Open: 11 May - 30 September.

Directions

From the A20 (Limoges - Brive) take exit 55 for Souillac and Sarlat. In Sarlat take D57 to Vézac, then D703 to St Cyprien. In St Cyprien follow D703, then D50 (left) to Berbiguières and follow signs for site.

Charges 2007

Per person (over 4 yrs)	€ 3,40 - € 7,00
pitch	€ 5,00 - € 10,40
incl. services	€ 8,10 - € 17,10

FR24010 Kawan Village le Châteaux de Verdoyer

Champs Romain, F-24470 Saint Pardoux (Dordogne)

Tel: **05 53 56 94 64**. Email: **chateau@verdoyer.fr**

The 26 hectare estate has three lakes, two for fishing and one with a sandy beach and safe swimming area. There are 135 good sized touring pitches, level, terraced and hedged. With a choice of wooded area or open field, all have electricity (5/10A) and most share a water supply between four pitches. There is a swimming pool complex and in high season activities are organised for children (5-13 yrs) but there is no disco. This site is well adapted for those with disabilities, with two fully adapted chalets, wheelchair access to all facilities and even a lift into the pool. Le Verdoyer has been developed in the park of a restored château and is owned by a Dutch family. We particularly like this site for its beautiful buildings and lovely surroundings. It is situated in the lesser known area of the Dordogne sometimes referred to as the Périgord Vert, with its green forests and small lakes. The courtyard area between reception and the bar is home to evening activities, and provides a pleasant place to enjoy drinks and relax. The château itself has rooms to let and its excellent lakeside restaurant is also open to the public.

Facilities

Well appointed toilet blocks include facilities for disabled people and baby baths. Serviced launderette. Motorcaravan services. Fridge rental. Shop with gas. Bar, snacks, takeaway and restaurant, both open all season. Bistro (July/Aug). Two pools the smaller covered in low season, slide, paddling pool. Play areas. Tennis. Volleyball, basketball, badminton, table tennis, minigolf. Bicycle hire. Small library. Off site: Riding 5 km.

Open: 26 April - 6 October.

Directions

Site is 2 km. from Limoges (N21) - Chalus (D6bis-D85) - Nontron road, 20 km. south of Chalus and is well signed from main road. Site on D96 about 4 km. north of village of Champs Romain. GPS: N45:33.083 E00:47.683

Charges 2008

Per unit incl. 2 persons and electricity	€ 18,00 - € 29,00
full services	€ 18,00 - € 33,50
extra person	€ 5,00 - € 6,50
child (under 3-7 yrs)	€ 3,00 - € 4,50
dog	free - € 4,00

Between 9/7-20/8 stay 14 nights, pay for twelve. Camping Cheques accepted.

FR24090 Domaine de Soleil Plage

Caudon par Montfort, Vitrac, F-24200 Sarlat-la-Canéda (Dordogne)

Tel: 05 53 28 33 33. Email: info@soleilplage.fr

This site is in one of the most attractive sections of the Dordogne valley, with a riverside location. The site has 199 pitches, in three sections, around 104 are for touring units. The smallest section surrounds the main reception and other facilities. There are 59 mobile homes, 20 chalets and 17 bungalow tents. The site offers river bathing from a sizeable pebble or sand bank. All pitches are bounded by hedges and are of adequate size. Most pitches have some shade and have electricity and many have water and a drain. Various activities are organised during high season including walks and sports tournaments, and daily canoe hire is available from the site. Once a week in July and August there is a 'soirée' (charged for) usually involving a barbecue or paella, with band and lots of free wine – worth catching! The site is busy and reservation is advisable. Used by UK tour operators (42 pitches). English is spoken. The site is quite expensive in high season and you also pay more for a riverside pitch, but if you like a holiday with lots going on, you will like this one.

Facilities

Toilet facilities are in three modern unisex blocks (only two open). You will need to hire a plug (5 euro) for the baby bath. Washing machines and dryer (charged for). Motorcaravan service point. Pleasant bar with TV. Restaurant. Well stocked shop. Very impressive main pool, paddling pool, spa pool and two water slides. Tennis court and minigolf, (both charged in high season), table tennis, volleyball, football pitches. Playground. Fishing. Canoe and kayak hire. Bicycle hire. Currency exchange. Small library. Off site: Golf 1 km. Riding 5 km.

Open: 1 April - 30 September.

Directions

Site is 8 km. south of Sarlat. From A20 take exit 55 (Souillac) towards Sarlat. Follow the D703 to Carsac and on to Montfort. At Montfort castle turn left for 2 km. down to the river.
GPS: N44:49.510 E01:17.470

Charges 2007

Per person	€ 4,50 - € 7,00
child (2-9 yrs)	€ 2,50 - € 4,50
pitch with electricity	€ 9,00 - € 15,50
with full services	€ 12,00 - € 23,00

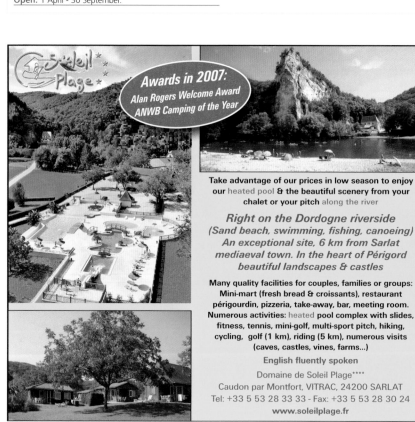

FR24130 Camping les Grottes de Roffy

Sainte Nathalène, F-24200 Sarlat-la-Canéda (Dordogne)

Tel: **05 53 59 15 61**. Email: **roffy@perigord.com**

A pleasantly laid out site, about 5 km. east of Sarlat, Les Grottes de Roffy has 162 clearly marked pitches, some very large. Set on very well kept grass terraces, they have easy access and good views across an attractive valley. Some have plentiful shade, although others are more open, and all have electricity (6A). The reception, bar, restaurant and shop are located within converted farm buildings surrounding a semi-courtyard. The campsite shop is well stocked with a variety of goods and a tempting charcuterie section (prepared on site) with plenty of ideas for the barbecue. Various entertainments and excursions are organised during high season. Conveniently located for Sarlat and all other Dordogne attractions, this is a good site for families. The site is used by tour operators (around 64 pitches).

Facilities

Two toilet blocks with modern facilities are more than adequate. Well stocked shop. Bar and restaurant with imaginative and sensibly priced menu. Takeaway (all amenities from 6/5). Good swimming pool complex comprising two deep pools (one heated), a fountain, children's pool and heated jacuzzi. Tennis, volleyball and badminton courts. Games room. Play area. Off site: Fishing 2 km. Bicycle hire 7 km. Riding 10 km. Golf 15 km.

Open: 26 April - 21 September.

Directions

Take D47 east from Sarlat to Ste Nathalène. Just before Ste Nathalène the site is signed on the right hand side of the road. Turn here, and the site is about 800 m. along the lane. GPS: N44:54.230 E01:16.920

Charges 2008

Per pitch with 2 persons	
and electricity	€ 20,80 - € 27,50
extra person	€ 5,50 - € 7,20
child (2-7 yrs)	€ 4,00 - € 5,80
dog	€ 2,00

les
Grottes
de
Roffy
c a m p i n g
c a r a v a n i n g
★ ★ ★ ★

Sainte-Nathalèle • 24200 Sarlat • France
E-mail roffy@perigord.com • Tél. +33 (0)5 53 59 15 61 • Fax +33 (0)5 53 31 09 11

FR24180 Camping Caravaning Saint Avit Loisirs

Le Bugue, F-24260 Saint Avit-de-Vialard (Dordogne)

Tel: **05 53 02 64 00**. Email: **contact@saint-avit-loisirs.com**

Although Saint Avit Loisirs is set in the middle of rolling countryside, far from the hustle and bustle of the main tourist areas of the Dordogne the facilities are first class, providing virtually everything you could possibly want without the need to leave the site. This makes it ideal for families with children of all ages. The site is in two sections. One part is dedicated to chalets and mobile homes, whilst the main section of the site contains 199 flat and mainly grassy, good sized pitches, 99 for touring, with electricity (6A), arranged in cul-de-sacs off a main access road. The café, shop and bar open onto a large terrace with pergola and hanging baskets, which overlooks the excellent pool complex. In high season a variety of activities and entertainments is organised.

Facilities

Three modern unisex toilet blocks provide high quality facilities, but could become overstretched in high season. Shop, bar, restaurant, cafeteria. Outdoor swimming pool, children's pool, water slide, 'crazy river', heated indoor pool with jacuzzi, fitness room. Sound-proofed disco. Tennis. Play area. Canoe trips and other sporting activities. Off site: Sarlat and Périgeux (markets and hypermarkets).

Open: 1 April - 27 September.

Directions

Site is 6 km. north of Le Bugue. From D710 Le Bugue - Périgueux road, turn west on narrow and bumpy C201 towards St Avit de Vialard. Follow road through St Avit, bearing right to site in 1.5 km. GPS: N44:57.082 E00:50.825

Charges 2007

Per person	€ 4,00 - € 9,70
child (under 4 yrs)	free
pitch incl. electricity	€ 10,10 - € 19,30

FR24220 Camping Domaine des Chênes Verts

Route de Sarlat, F-24370 Calviac en Périgord (Dordogne)

Tel: 05 53 59 21 07. Email: **chenes-verts@wanadoo.fr**

This peaceful countryside family campsite is set in a beautiful area of the Dordogne valley, and is complemented by the renovated Périgourdine farm buildings which house the amenities at the centre of the site. The spacious grounds which contain many trees provide 143 pitches on either side of the main buildings, of which 63 are for touring units. Most of the good sized, grassy pitches are shaded and all are separated by hedging. There is electricity (6A) to all pitches and water points nearby. The majority of pitches are large and level but some are gently sloping. The managers, who speak some English, are very helpful and friendly, and in high season they organise a range of entertainment and activities from wine tasting to canoeing expeditions and, of course, the obligatory boules tournaments.

Facilities

Two fully equipped unisex toilet blocks include washbasins in cabins, dishwashing and laundry areas. Washing machine. Small shop (fresh bread daily), bar, snack bar and takeaway. Motorcaravan service point. Fridge hire. Gas supplies. Medium sized swimming pool with large sunbathing area (15/6-15/9), covered, heated pool (1/4-20/9) and a paddling pool. Play area. Multisport court. Animation for children. TV and games room. Charcoal barbecues provided. Off site: Forest walks and cycle tracks lead from the site.

Open: 1 May - 28 September.

Directions

From D704 Sarlat - Gourdon road turn east on D704A towards Souillac and Calviac (this turning is about 3.5 km. from Sarlat). Site is about 5 km. along this road on the left. GPS: N44:51.794 E01:17.824

Charges 2007

Per person	€ 3,75 - € 4,70
child (under 7 yrs)	€ 2,15 - € 2,70
pitch incl. electricity	€ 11,70 - € 13,90
dog	€ 1,75 - € 2,20

FR24310 Camping Caravaning la Bouquerie

F-24590 Saint Geniès-en-Périgord (Dordogne)

Tel: 05 53 28 98 22. Email: **labouquerie@wanadoo.fr**

La Bouquerie is a well maintained site, situated within easy reach of the main road network in the Dordogne, but without any associated traffic noise. The main complex is based around some beautifully restored traditional Périgordin buildings. It includes a shop and a bar and restaurant overlooking the pool complex, with a large outdoor terrace for fine weather. The excellent restaurant menu is varied and reasonably priced. Of the 180 pitches, 91 are used for touring units and these are of varying size (80-120 sq.m.), flat and grassy, some with shade, and all with electrical connections (10A). The rest of the pitches are taken up by site owned mobile homes and a UK tour operator. In high season the site offers a range of tournaments and sporting activities (aquagym, archery, canoeing, walks etc) as well as a children's club each week day morning. La Bouquerie is ideally situated for exploring the Périgord region, and has something to offer families with children of all ages.

Facilities

Three well maintained toilet blocks with facilities for disabled visitors and baby rooms. Washing machines and covered drying lines. Small shop (15/05-15/09), takeaway food. Bar, restaurant (both 15/05-15/09). Paddling pool, large shallow pool (heated), large deep pool, sunbathing areas with loungers. Carp fishing in lake on site. Bicycle hire. Riding. Off site: Shops and restaurants, etc. in the nearby village of St Geniès.

Open: 19 April - 19 September.

Directions

Site is signed on east side D704 Sarlat - Montignac, about 500 m. north of junction with D64 St Geniès road. Turn off D704 at campsite sign and take first left turn signed La Bouquerie - site is straight ahead.

Charges 2008

Per pitch with 2 persons and electricity	€ 19,00 - € 25,50
extra person	€ 4,60 - € 6,50
child (under 7 yrs)	€ 3,20 - € 4,50

Check real time availability and at-the-gate prices...

 www.**alanrogers**.com

FR24160 Camping le Grand Dague

Atur, F-24750 Périgueux (Dordogne)

Tel: **05 53 04 21 01**. Email: **info@legranddague.fr**

Le Grand Dague is close to Périgueux, in a rural and tranquil setting. Built on a hillside, the site is clean, attractive and very spacious and 68 of the 93 pitches are for touring units. The pitches are only slightly sloping and are divided by tall, mature hedging (electricity 6A). There is a large field suitable for large motorhomes. Those with disabilities might find the roads quite steep. Several large, open grassy areas provide space for youngsters to play. Good range of equipment in the play area makes this an ideal site for young families.

Facilities

Excellent, part heated sanitary facilities include a baby room and facilities for people with disabilities. Small shop (15/6-15/9). Bar, attractive restaurant with appetising menu and takeaway (both from June). Swimming pool, water slide and paddling pool (from early May). Football, volleyball, badminton, petanque, minigolf and table tennis. Play area. Fishing. Off site: Paintball outside gate. Riding 5 km. Bicycle hire 8 km. Golf 10 km.

Open: 28 April - 15 September.

Directions

From the Bordeaux - Brive inner ring road in Périgueux take D2 south, signed Atur. Campsite signed. Turn east at roundabout just before entering Atur. Site is in 3 km. GPS: N45:08.880 E00:46.657

Charges 2007

Per person	€ 4,25 - € 6,50
child (0-7 yrs)	€ 2,75 - € 4,25
pitch with electricity	€ 8,45 - € 11,75
animal	€ 1,75

FR24170 Camping le Port de Limeuil

F-24480 Allés-sur-Dordogne (Dordogne)

Tel: **05 53 63 29 76**. Email: **didierbonvallet@aol.com**

At the confluence of Dordogne and Vézère rivers, opposite the picturesque village of Limieul, this delightful family site exudes a peaceful and relaxed ambience. There are 65 marked touring pitches on grass, some spacious and all with electricity (5A). The buildings are in traditional Périgourdine style and surrounded by flowers and shrubs. A sports area on a large open grassy space between the river bank and the main camping area adds to the feeling of space and provides an additional recreation and picnic area (there are additional unmarked pitches along the bank here). This is an ideal location for visiting the west central part of the Dordogne département, and is recommended for long stays. It is used fairly unobtrusively by a tour operator.

Facilities

Two clean, modern toilet blocks provide excellent facilities. Bar/restaurant with snacks and takeaway (all 20/5-5/9). Small shop. Swimming pool with jacuzzi, paddling pool and children's slide (1/5-30/9). Badminton, football, boules and volleyball. Mountain bike hire. Canoe hire - launched from the site's own pebble beach. WiFi in bar area. Off site: The pretty medieval village of Limeuil 200 m. Riding 1 km. Golf 10 km.

Open: 1 May - 30 September.

Directions

Site is 7 km. south of Le Bugue. From D51/D31E Le Buisson to Le Bugue road turn west towards Limeuil. Just before bridge into Limeuil, turn left (site signed), across another bridge. Site shortly on the right. GPS: N44:52.878 E00:53.444

Charges 2008

Per pitch incl. 2 persons	€ 14,00 - € 24,90
extra person	€ 4,50 - € 6,50
electricity (5A)	€ 2,50 - € 3,50

FR24330 **Camping de l'Etang Bleu**

F-24340 Vieux-Mareuil (Dordogne)

Tel: 05 53 60 92 70. Email: marc@letangbleu.com

There are 169 pitches, 151 for touring, with the remainder taken up by site owned mobile homes for rent. The pitches are a good size, flat and grassy, with mature hedging and trees providing privacy and plenty of shade. All pitches have water and 90 have electricity (10/16A). At the bottom of the site is a fishing lake stocked with carp (permit required) and various woodland walks start from the campsite grounds. The bright and cheerful 'bistro bar' provides good value food and drinks, and becomes a focal point for evening socialising on site. Set halfway between the historic towns of Perigueux and Angoulême, this is a tranquil countryside site in a mature woodland setting. It is run by enthusiastic British owners Mark and Jo Finch, who really are 'Living The Dream' as described in a BBC documentary about their site. This site is ideal for couples or families with young children who are looking for a quiet and relaxing holiday away from the hustle and bustle of the busiest tourist areas, but still within reach of some of the area's major towns.

Facilities

Modern well maintained toilet block provides facilities for babies and disabled people. Laundry. Small playground, paddling pool. Swimming pool, sun terrace. Bar with terrace (all season), restaurant (1/6-30/9), poolside bar. Takeaway (1/6-30/9). Small shop. Table tennis, boules, volleyball, badminton. Canoe and bicycle hire. Entertainments, sporting activities, excursions in high season. Off site: Restaurant 'Auberge de L'Etang Bleu' adjacent to campsite, small supermarket, post office etc. in Mareuil (7 km).

Open: Easter/1 April -18 October.

Directions

Site is between Angoulême and Périgueux. Leave D939 in Vieux Mareuil, take D93, and follow narrow road. Just after leaving village site signed on right, just past Auberge de L'Etang Bleu. Turn right, follow signs to site.

Charges guide

Per person	€ 3,75 - € 5,50
child (2-7 yrs)	€ 1,25 - € 2,00
pitch and car	€ 5,75 - € 7,25
with electricity	€ 7,75 - € 11,50

FR46040 **Camping Moulin de Laborde**

F-46700 Montcabrier (Lot)

Tel: 05 65 24 62 06. Email: moulindelaborde@wanadoo.fr

Based around a converted 17th century watermill, Moulin de Laborde has been created by the Van Bommel family to provide a tranquil and uncommercialised campsite for the whole family to enjoy. Bordered by woods, hills and a small river, there are 90 flat and grassy pitches, all of at least 100 sq.m. with electricity (6A). A variety of pretty shrubs and trees divide the pitches and provide a moderate amount of shade. A gate at the back of the site leads walkers onto a 'Grand Randonée' footpath which passes through the village of Montcabrier, 1 km. away. A small lake with rafts and rowing boats and an adventure-type play area with rope bridges and 'death slide' will keep children amused, whilst parents can relax in the charming courtyard area which houses the bar and restaurant.

Facilities

Well designed, clean toilet block, unit for disabled people. Washing machine, dryer. Basic shop (all season). Small bar, restaurant, takeaway. Swimming pool, sunbathing area, paddling pool (all season). Play area. Small lake, free rafts and rowing boats. Fishing. Volleyball. Badminton. Boules. Covered recreation area. Table tennis. Mountain bike hire. Rock climbing. Archery. No dogs. Off site: Riding 5 km. Golf 8 km. Tennis nearby and canoeing on the Lot. The Château of Bonaquil 6 km. Fumel 12 km.

Open: 25 April - 8 September.

Directions

Site is on the north side of the D673 Fumel - Gourdon road about 1 km. northeast of the turn to village of Montcabrier.

Charges 2007

Per person	€ 6,20
child (under 7 yrs)	€ 3,30
pitch	€ 8,40
electricity (6A)	€ 2,60

Less 20% outside July/August. No credit cards.

FR46010 Castel Camping le Domaine de la Paille Basse

F-46200 Souillac-sur-Dordogne (Lot)

Tel: 05 65 37 85 48. Email: paille.basse@wanadoo.fr

Set in a rural location some 8 km. from Souillac, this family owned site is easily accessible from the N20 and well placed to take advantage of excursions into the Dordogne. It is part of a large domain of 80 hectares, all available to campers for walks and recreation. The site is quite high up and there are excellent views over the surrounding countryside. The 262 pitches are in two main areas – one is level in cleared woodland with good shade, and the other on grass without shade. Numbered and marked, the pitches are a minimum 100 sq.m. and often considerably more. All have electricity (3/6A) with about 80 fully serviced. The site is well placed to take advantage of excursions into the Dordogne. A wide range of activities and entertainment are organised in high season. The site can get very busy in high season and is popular with three tour operators. If you like a livelier type of site, you will enjoy La Paille Basse.

Facilities

Three main toilet blocks all have modern equipment and are kept very clean. Laundry. Small shop. Restaurant, bar, terrace, takeaway. Crêperie. Main swimming pool, a smaller one, paddling pool (unheated), water slides. Sun terrace. Sound-proofed disco (three times weekly in season). TV (with satellite). Cinema below the pool area. Tennis (charged), football, volleyball, table tennis. Play area. Library. Massage. Off site: Golf 4 km.

Open: 15 May - 15 September.

Directions

From Souillac take D15 and then D62 roads leading northwest towards Salignac-Eyvignes and after 6 km. turn right at camp sign and follow steep and narrow approach road for 2 km.
GPS: N44:56.730 E01:26.450

Charges 2007

Per person	€ 5,40 - € 7,00
child (under 7 yrs)	€ 3,80 - € 5,00
pitch	€ 7,80 - € 10,80
incl. water and drainage	€ 9,80 - € 13,00
dog	€ 4,00

Less 20% outside 15/6-1/9.
Camping Cheques accepted.

Le Domaine de la Paille Basse, half way between Rocamadour and the caves of Lascaux, is an excellent base for excursions enabling you to visit the highlights of two régions. Situated at the top of a hill, La Paille Basse is a restored medieval village in the heart of 200 acres of wooded land. La Paille Basse has carefully combined architectural beauty and modernity, fitting its facilities within the original buildings.

Castel Camping La Paille Basse
★★★★
46200 Souillac
Tel: 0033 565 37 85 48
Fax: 0033 565 37 09 58

LES CASTELS
★★★★

Camping Cheque

163

FR46240 Camping Quercy Vacances

Mas de la Combe, F-46090 Saint Pierre Lafeuille (Lot)

Tel: 05 65 36 87 15. Email: quercy-vacances@wanadoo.fr

This clean and well run site is owned by a young, English speaking, French couple who are determined to improve the facilities and ambiance. It is only 4.5 km. from the A20 and is an ideal stopover site for holidaymakers travelling to and from Spain. However, it is better than just a stopover site and is worth staying a few extra days. It has 70 large unmarked touring pitches most of which have 6/10A hook-ups. The site facilities include a rustic bar and restaurant which has hand painted murals on the walls. The toilets and laundry are also housed in this single split-level building with the toilets located to the rear of the building on a lower level.

Facilities

Clean, modern toilet block, recently refurbished. Facilities for campers with disabilities are located in a separate building adjacent to the camping area. Small basic shop. Bar and takeaway. Restaurant serving specials like couscous and paella once per week. Large round swimming pool (20/6-15/9), unsuitable for young children, minimum depth 1.2 m. Live music, dancing (July/Aug). Small play area. Off site: Riding 5 km. Bicycle hire, fishing 10 km.

Open: 1 April - 31 October.

Directions

Leave A20 exit 57 (Cahors). Shortly turn left on N20 and then turn right on small un-named road (site signed) before reaching St Pierre Lafeuille (about 4.5 km. from the A20). Site on right in about 600 m. GPS: N44:31.889 E01:27.585

Charges 2007

Per person	€ 3,80 - € 5,00
child (3-9 yrs)	€ 3,00 - € 4,00
pitch	€ 5,00 - € 8,80
electricity (6/10A)	€ 3,30 - € 5,50

FR47150 Domaine de Guillalmes

Condat, F-47500 Fumel (Lot-et-Garonne)

Tel: 05 53 71 01 99. Email: info@guillalmes.com

Domaine de Guillalmes is a very attractive site and was until recently exclusively for chalets but the British owners have now added a 10 pitch touring caravan area. These pitches are all on hardstanding, divided by small hedges and with some shade from small trees. The pitches are very large and are ideal for very large outfits and American motorhomes. Each pitch has electricity (up to 16A) and there is a central motorcaravan service point. All facilities at this three hectare site are available to the touring units, including the magnificent pool and bar terrace. The site is on the banks of the river Lot and in the summer the river provides opportunities for water sports. The site is an ideal stopover for even the largest units and because of the facilities it is well worth staying longer.

Facilities

A shower and toilet are available 24 hours a day (more showers planned), plus dishwashing facilities. Other facilities including separate toilets, washbasins and facilities for disabled people are located in the restaurant area and are open 08.00 - 22.00. Large laundry room. Restaurant. Bar terrace and takeaway. Swimming pool (June - Oct) with jacuzzi. Play area. Tennis. Football. Volleyball. Boules. Canoeing. Table tennis. Badminton. Fishing. Boat slipway. Off site: Cycling and walking routes. Vineyards 2 km. Fummel, Rocamadour and Cahors.

Open: All year.

Directions

From Fumel, take D911 following signs to Cahors, then signs to Domaine de Guillalmes. The site is situated between Fumel and Soturac, 150 m. before Soturac (D911). GPS: N44:28.983 E01:00.562

Charges 2008

Per unit incl. 2 persons	€ 18,00 - € 22,00
extra person	€ 3,50 - € 5,50
child (under 7 yrs)	€ 2,50 - € 4,50
electricity (4/6A)	€ 5,00 - € 6,00

Domaine de Guillalmes

Owned and run by an English family, Domaine de Guillalmes is a perfect site whether you are looking for comfortable accomodation in a relaxing environment or large pleasant camping pitches.

Domaine de Guillalmes - Condat - 47500 Fumel - France - Tel: 0033 (0)553 71 01 99
Fax: 0033 (0)553 71 02 57 - info@guillalmes.com - www.guillalmes.com

FR47010 Kawan Village Moulin du Périé

F-47500 Sauveterre-la-Lemance (Lot-et-Garonne)

Tel: **05 53 40 67 26**. Email: **moulinduperie@wanadoo.fr**

Set in a quiet area and surrounded by woodlands this peaceful little site is well away from much of the tourist bustle. It has 125 reasonably sized, grassy pitches, all with 6A electricity, divided by mixed trees and bushes with most having good shade. All are extremely well kept, as indeed is the entire site. The attractive front courtyard is complemented by an equally pleasant terrace at the rear. Two small, clean swimming pools overlook a shallow, spring water lake, ideal for inflatable boats and paddling and bordering the lake, a large grass field is popular for games. The picturesque old mill buildings, adorned with flowers and creepers, now house the bar and restaurant where the food is to be recommended, as is the owner's extensive knowledge of wine that he is pleased to share with visitors. A quiet, friendly site with regular visitors – reservation is advised for July/Aug. Bergerac Airport is an hour away so would suit those choosing a mobile home or bungalow tent and wanting to travel light.

Facilities

Two clean, modern and well maintained toilet blocks include facilities for disabled visitors. Motorcaravan services. Fridge, barbecue, chemical toilet hire (book in advance). Basic shop. Bar/reception, restaurant, takeaway. Two small swimming pools (no Bermuda-style shorts). Boules, table tennis, outdoor chess. Playground. Trampoline. Small, indoor play area. Bicycle hire. Organised activities in high season; including canoeing, riding, wine tasting visits, sight seeing trips, barbecues, gastronomic meals. Winter caravan storage. Off site: Fishing 1 km. Small supermarket in village and larger stores in Fumel.

Open: 7 May - 20 September.

Directions

From D710, Fumel - Périgueux, turn southeast into Sauveterre-le-Lemance. Turn left (northeast) at far end on C201 signed campsite, Château Sauverre and Loubejec. Site is 3 km. on right.

Charges 2007

Per unit incl. 2 persons	€ 13,05 - € 21,85
with electricity	€ 16,95 - € 25,75
extra person	€ 4,20 - € 6,50
child (under 7 yrs)	€ 1,80 - € 3,45
animal	€ 2,15 - € 4,10

Camping Cheques accepted.

FR47110 Camping le Cabri

Route de Savignac, F-47120 Duras (Lot-et-Garonne)

Tel: **05 53 83 81 03**. Email: **holidays@lecabri.eu.com**

Le Cabri is delightfully situated in the heart of Lot-et-Garonne. This pleasantly wooded, terraced site with a pond is recently been acquired by Englishman James Cook and is currently undergoing development and expansion. There are currently 20 pitches which include 11 wooden chalets, 3 mobile homes and 6 touring pitches. One chalet is reserved disabled visitors with an en-suite shower and toilet. Previously known for its excellent chalet accommodation and fine restaurant, the expansion plans include a further 50 pitches with electricity and water and a much larger (160 sq.m.) swimming pool. The site is less than fifteen minutes walk from the château town of Duras with its many amenities, where you can shop, visit the weekly market, as well as hire bikes and canoes. You will receive a warm welcome and enjoy a comfortable stay.

Facilities

One sanitary block, with pre-set hot showers. Toilet for disabled visitors. Washing machine and dryer. Bar and restaurant with TV. Swimming pool. Minigolf. Boules. Play area and covered games area with range of children's toys. Off site: Riding 2 km. Golf (international course) 15 km. Tennis 1 km. Water sports 7 km. Canoeing 8 km. Aquatic park 45 minutes drive.

Open: All year.

Directions

From N113 southeast or northwest to Marmande, head through Marmande north on D708 to Duras for about 24 km. Look for the D203 through Duras and follow sign for site. It is less than 1 km. away.

Charges 2007

Per person	€ 4,00
child (under 7 yrs)	€ 2,00
pitch	€ 5,00
electricity (10A)	€ 4,00

FR15030 Camping Caravaning le Val Saint-Jean

F-15200 Mauriac (Cantal)

Tel: **04 71 67 31 13**. Email: **contact@revea-vacances.com**

Le Val Saint-Jean is set beside a lake in the heart of the département of Cantal. The campsite has 100 generously sized, slightly sloping, touring pitches (with 10A electricity), many with good views. It is organised for the maximum of privacy and you are never far from a sanitary block. Most of the activities are situated by the lake where you can use all the facilities of the leisure club (high season) including cycling, canoeing, kayaking and pedaloes. This less well known region is well worth exploring and the local gastronomy can be experienced in the village of Mauriac with its attractive architecture typical of the area. Salers, one of the most beautiful French towns is 20 km.

Facilities

The two toilet blocks are well equipped with hot water throughout, providing some washbasins in cabins, dishwashing sinks and a laundry room. Facilities for people with disabilities. Limited shop. Bar, snack bar and restaurant (all May - Sept). Play area, playing field and table tennis. Activities organised for children in July/Aug. Off site: Sandy beach. Lake fishing and swimming. Swimming pool (1/6-15/9). Golf course. Guided walks. Mauriac village 1.6 km. Riding 3 km.

Open: 26 April - 28 September.

Directions

Mauriac is 120 km. southwest of Clermont-Ferrand. Leave A89 autoroute at junction 23 (Ussel West), take D979 (Bort-les-Orgues) for 5 km. Turn right onto D982 (Mauriac) for 40 km. Follow site signs in town. GPS: N45:13.120 E02:18.953

Charges 2008

Per unit incl. 2 persons	€ 13,50 - € 19,50
extra person	€ 4,40 - € 5,40
child (2-7 yrs)	free - € 3,30
dog	€ 1,50
electricity (10A)	€ 3,60

Check real time availability and at-the-gate prices...

www.alanrogers.com

FR23010 Castel Camping le Château de Poinsouze

Route de la Châtre, B.P. 12, F-23600 Boussac-Bourg (Creuse)

Tel: **05 55 65 02 21**. Email: **info.camping-de.poinsouze@wanadoo.fr**

Le Château de Poinsouze is a well established site with pitches arranged on the open, gently sloping, grassy park to one side of the Château's main drive – a beautiful plane tree avenue. It is a well designed, high quality site. The 145 touring pitches, some with lake frontage, all have electricity (6-25A), water, drain and 66 have sewage connections. The site has a friendly family atmosphere, there are organised activities in main season including dances, children's games and crafts, family triathlons and there are marked walks around the park and woods. All facilities are open all season. This is a top class site with a formula which should ensure a stress-free, enjoyable family holiday. Boussac (2.5 km.) has a market every Thursday. The massive 12/15th century fortress, Château de Boussac, is open daily all year. The Château (not open to the public) lies across the lake from the site. Exceptionally well restored outbuildings on the opposite side of the drive house a new restaurant serving superb cuisine, other facilities and the pool area.

Facilities

High quality, sanitary unit, washing machines, dryer, ironing, suites for disabled people. Motorcaravan services. Well stocked shop. Takeaway. Bar, internet, two satellite TVs, library. Restaurant with new mini-bar for low season. Heated swimming pool, slide, children's pool. Fenced playground. Table tennis, petanque, pool table, table football. Bicycle hire. Free fishing in the lake, boats and lifejackets can be hired. Football, volleyball, basketball, badminton and other games. No dogs (7/7-21/8).

Open: 10 May - 14 September.

Directions

Site entrance is 2.5 km. north of Boussac on D917 (towards La Châtre). GPS: N46:22.356 E02:12.157

Charges 2007

Per unit incl. 2 persons with electricity (6A), water,	€ 13,00 - € 22,00
waste water	€ 19,00 - € 28,00
with electricity (10A), water, waste water, sewage connection	€ 24,00 - € 29,00
extra person	€ 3,00 - € 6,00

Camping Cheques accepted.

TO BOOK CALL **01580 214000**
Advice & low ferry-inclusive prices

TRAVEL SERVICE SITE

FR07140 Camping les Lavandes

Le Village, F-07170 Darbres (Ardèche)

Tel: 04 75 94 20 65. Email: sarl.leslavandes@online.fr

Situated to the northeast of Aubenas, in a quieter part of this region, Les Lavandes is surrounded by magnificent countryside, vineyards and orchards. The enthusiastic French owners, who speak good English, run a site that appeals to all nationalities. The 70 pitches (58 for touring) are arranged on low terraces separated by a variety of trees and shrubs that give welcome shade in summer. Electricity 6/10A is available to all. At the end of May the campsite trees are laden with luscious cherries. Organised activities include wine tasting, shows, musical evenings and children's games. A ride along the panoramic road to Mirabel is a must. Although slightly less sophisticated than some others in the region, this site should appeal to those seeking the real France for a pleasant family holiday. Traditional buildings house the reception (full of tourist information including a touch screen), shop, restaurant, takeaway and cosy bar offering excellent views over the swimming pool to the village (just a stroll away) and hillside beyond.

Facilities

Comprehensive and well maintained facilities, baby room, excellent facilities for disabled people. Washing machine. Small shop (1/7-31/8). Bar, terrace (1/6-31/8). Restaurant (5/6-31/8). Takeaway (15/4-31/8). Swimming and paddling pools, sunbathing areas, with super views. Play areas for younger children. Table games. Billiard room. Open air chess. No electric barbecues. Off site: Fishing 1 km. Riding 3 km. Tennis 5 km. Bicycle hire 15 km. Canoeing, carting. Caves, historical villages. Wonderful area for birds.

Open: 15 April - 30 September.

Directions

Site best approached from south. From Montélimar take N102 towards Aubenas. After Villeneuve, in Lavilledieu, turn right at traffic lights on D224 to Darbres (10 km). In Darbres turn sharp left by post office (care needed) and follow site signs.

Charges 2007

Per unit incl. 2 persons	€ 11,50 - € 17,00
extra person	€ 2,80 - € 3,50
electricity	€ 3,50

FR07150 Camping Domaine de Gil

Route de Vals-les-Bains, Ucel, F-07200 Aubenas (Ardèche)

Tel: 04 75 94 63 63. Email: info@domaine-de-gil.com

Under new ownership, this very attractive and well organised, smaller site in a less busy part of the Ardèche should appeal to couples and families with younger children. The 80, good sized, level pitches, 43 for touring, are surrounded by a variety of trees offering plenty of shade. All have 10A electricity. The focal point of the site is formed by the very attractive swimming pool, paddling pool and large sunbathing area, with the bar, restaurant and well appointed children's play areas all adjacent. A spacious sports area and shady picnic/play area are alongside the river Ardèche – an ideal spot to cool off on a hot day.

Facilities

Modern well appointed toilet block, washing machine and iron. Motorcaravan services. Basic shop. Bar/restaurant, takeaway (from June). Heated swimming pool, paddling pool. Two play areas. Volleyball, boules, minigolf, football, tennis. Canoeing, boating, fishing. Organised activities in high season. Only gas and electric barbecues. Off site: Shops at Vals-les-Bain 1.5 km. Interesting old town of Aubenas with larger range of shops, restaurants, bars 3 km. Organised canoe trips, canyoning on river Ardèche. Bicycle hire, riding 4 km.

Open: 14 April - 23 September.

Directions

Site north of Aubenas. From southeast (N102), after tunnel, turn right, roundabout (signed Ucel), cross river into Pont d'Ucel (3.5 tonne limit). Bear right and at roundabout, last exit (signed Ucel). Shortly turn left (signed Ucel D218), then right (Ucel D578B). Site is 2 km. GPS: N44:38.558 E04:22.775

Charges 2007

Per unit incl. 2 persons	€ 14,00 - € 29,00
extra person	€ 3,50 - € 5,75
child (under 10 yrs)	free - € 4,25
electricity	€ 4,00
animal	€ 2,00 - € 3,00

FR07120 Camping Nature Parc l'Ardéchois

Route touristique des Gorges, F-07150 Vallon-Pont-d'Arc (Ardèche)

Tel: 04 75 88 06 63. Email: ardecamp@bigfoot.com

This very high quality, family run site is within walking distance of Vallon-Pont-d'Arc. It borders the River Ardèche and canoe trips are run, professionally, direct from the site. This campsite is ideal for families with younger children seeking an active holiday. The facilities are comprehensive and of an extremely high standard, particularly the central toilet block. Of the 244 pitches, there are 225 for tourers, separated by trees and individual shrubs. All have electrical connections (6/10A) and 125 have full services. Forming a focal point is the bar and restaurant (good menus), with a terrace and stage overlooking the attractive heated pool. Member of Leading Campings Group. There is also a large paddling pool and sunbathing terrace. For children, there is a well thought out play area plus plenty of other space for youngsters to play, both on the site and along the river. Activities are organised throughout the season; these are family based – no discos. Patrols at night ensure a good night's sleep. Access to the site is easy and suitable for large outfits.

Facilities

Two well equipped toilet blocks, one superb with 'everything' working automatically. Facilities are of the highest standard, very clean and include good facilities for babies, those with disabilities, washing up and laundry. Four private bathrooms to hire. Washing machines. Well stocked shop. Swimming pool and paddling pool (no Bermuda shorts). Football, volleyball, tennis and table tennis. Very good play area. Internet access point. Organised activities, canoe trips. Only gas barbecues are permitted. Communal barbecue area. Off site: Canoeing, rafting, walking, riding, mountain biking, golf, rock climbing, bowling, wine tasting and dining. Vallon-Pont-d'Arc 800 m. Explore the real Ardèche on the minor roads and visit Labaume, Bazakuc and Largentière (market Tuesday).

Open: Easter - 30 September.

Directions

From Vallon-Pont-d'Arc (western end of the Ardèche Gorge) at a roundabout go east on the D290. Site entrance is shortly on the right.
GPS: N44:23.873 E04:23.929

Charges 2008

Per pitch incl. 2 persons and electricity	€ 42,00

FR26040 **Kawan Village le Couspeau**

F-26460 Le Poët Célard (Drôme)

Tel: **04 75 53 30 14**. Email: info@couspeau.com

As one approaches this site, a magnificent landscape of mountains and valleys unfolds. The site has 127 pitches with 83 for touring (6A electricity). Access to the older section of the site is reasonably easy and mature trees here provide some shade. The 30 fully serviced pitches on the lower section are large and separated by small hedges with little shade. Access is via a steep road but tractor assistance is available. Rock pegs are advised. The most direct approach to the site is via a steep road and with several hairpin bends to negotiate, care is required.

Facilities

Three sanitary blocks. Washing machines, dryer. Facilities for disabled campers (the site is not ideal with steep roads and steps). Shop (15/4-14/9). Bar (20/6-14/9). Restaurant and takeaway (25/6-25/8). Pool (1/6-30/8) and small, heated, covered, toddler's pool (14/4-14/9). Play area, organised activities. Tennis. Bicycle hire. Rafting, canoe trips (on River Drôme), riding, paragliding. Off site: Riding, fishing 5 km.

Open: 15 April - 14 September.

Directions

From A7, exit 16, take D104 towards Crest. At traffic lights on Crest bypass, turn right, D538 towards Bourdeaux. Before Bourdeaux turn right over bridge, D328B. Climb for 1.5 km. to T-junction, turn right. D328. Before Le Poët Célard turn left, D328A to site. GPS: N44:35.744 E05:06.680

Charges 2007

Per unit incl. 2 persons	€ 14,00 - € 28,00
child (under 12 yrs)	free - € 4,00
electricity (6A)	€ 3,00
Camping Cheques accepted.	

www.couspeau.com
+33 475 533 014

At the gates of Alps and Provence,
a great spot for your holiday !
Mobile homes and chalets, swimming pools, restaurant,
kids club, hiking and biking, quiet evenings...
camping ' ' ' ' opened from 15/05 to 30/09

FR26210 **Camping les Bois du Chatelas**

Route de Dieulefit, F-26460 Bourdeaux (Drôme)

Tel: **04 75 00 60 80**. Email: contact@chatelas.com

Located at the heart of the the Drôme Provencale, Les Bois du Chatelas is a smart, family run site which has undergone many recent improvements. The site is just 1 km. from the delightful village of Bourdeaux which offers a good range of shops, cafés, etc. There are 120 pitches here of which 69 are occupied by mobile homes. Although situated on a hillside, the pitches are level and of a good size. They all offer electricity, water and drainage. Les Bois du Chatelas is a particularly good choice for those seeking an active holiday. Member of Sites et Paysages de France. The long distance GR9 footpath passes through the site and there are very many walking and cycle routes close at hand. A popular aqua-gym is organised in the large outdoor pool in peak season. In the high season, a lively entertainment programme is organized as well as many cycling and walking excursions.

Facilities

Two heated toilet blocks (on upper and lower levels) with facilities for babies and disabled people (note: the site is hilly and may be unsuitable). Restaurant/pizzeria. Shop. Bar. Indoor swimming pool. Outdoor pool with water slide, waterfall and jacuzzi. Sports pitch. Archery. Play area. Bicycle hire. Entertainment and excursion programme (July/Aug). Mobile homes for rent. Off site: Rafting and canoe trips. Riding 5 km. Fishing 1 km. Vercors mountain range. Mediaeval villages.

Open: 7 April - 30 September.

Directions

From the north, leave A7 at exit 16 and join the eastbound D104 to Crest. Upon reaching Crest take D538 south to Bourdeaux and continue towards Dieulefit. Site is on the left 1 km. beyond Bourdeaux and is well signed.

Charges 2008

Per unit incl. 2 persons	€ 14,00 - € 24,00
extra person	€ 4,20 - € 5,00
child (1-7 yrs)	€ 2,70 - € 2,90
electricity (10A)	€ 4,30 - € 4,50

FR04030 Kawan Village Moulin de Ventre

Niozelles, F-04300 Forcalquier (Alpes-de-Haute-Provence)

Tel: 04 92 78 63 31. Email: moulindeventre@aol.com

This is a friendly, family run site in the heart of Haute-Provence, near Forcalquier, a bustling small French market town. Attractively located beside a small lake and 28 acres of wooded, hilly land, which is available for walking. Herbs of Provence can be found growing wild and flowers, birds and butterflies abound – a nature lovers delight. The 124 level, grassy pitches for tourists are separated by a variety of trees and small shrubs, 114 of them having electricity (6A; long leads may be necessary). Some pitches are particularly attractive, bordering a small stream. English is spoken. A 'Sites et Paysages' member. The site is well situated to visit Mont Ventoux, the Luberon National Park, the Gorges du Verdon and a wide range of ancient hill villages with their markets and museums etc.

Facilities

Refurbished toilet block. Facilities for disabled people. Baby bath. Washing, drying machines. Fridge hire. Bread. Bar/restaurant, takeaway (all season), themed evenings (high season). Pizzeria. Swimming pools (15/5-15/9). New playground. Bouncy castle. Fishing, boules. Some activities organised in high season. No discos. Only electric or gas barbecues. Internet access. Off site: Shops, local market, doctor, tennis 2 km. Supermarket, chemist, riding, bicycle hire 5 km. Golf 20 km. Walking, cycling.

Open: 5 April - 30 September.

Directions

From A51 motorway take exit 19 (Brillanne). Turn right on N96 then turn left on N100 westwards (signed Forcalquier) for about 3 km. Site is signed on left, just after a bridge 3 km. southeast of Niozelles. GPS: N43:56.100 E05:52.520

Charges 2008

Per unit incl. 2 persons and electricity	€ 17,20 - € 26,70
extra person (over 4 yrs)	€ 3,50 - € 5,50
child (2-4 yrs)	€ 2,00 - € 3,00
dog	€ 1,50 - € 3,00

No credit cards.
Camping Cheques accepted.

FR04020 Castel Camping le Camp du Verdon

Domaine du Verdon, F-04120 Castellane (Alpes-de-Haute-Provence)

Tel: **04 92 83 61 29**. Email: contact@camp-du-verdon.com

Close to the 'Route des Alpes' and the Gorges du Verdon. Two heated swimming pools and numerous on-site activities during high season help to keep non-canoeists here. Du Verdon is a large level site, part meadow, part wooded, with 500 partly shaded, rather stony pitches (390 for tourists). Numbered and separated by bushes, they vary in size, have 6A electricity, and 125 also have water and waste water. They are mostly separate from the mobile homes (60) and pitches used by tour operators (110). Some overlook the unfenced river Verdon, so watch the children. This is a very popular holiday area, the gorge, canoeing and rafting being the main attractions, ideal for active families. One can walk to Castellane without using the main road. Dances and discos in July and August suit all age groups – the latest finishing time is around 23.00 (after that time patrols make sure that the site is quiet). The site is popular and very busy in July and August.

Facilities

Refurbished toilet blocks include facilities for disabled visitors. Washing machines. Motorcaravan services. Restaurant, terrace, log fire for cooler evenings. New supermarket. Pizzeria/crêperie. Takeaway. Heated swimming pools, paddling pool with 'mushroom' fountain (all open all season). Organised entertainments (July and August). Playgrounds. Minigolf, table tennis, archery, basketball, volleyball. Organised walks. Bicycle hire. Riding. Small fishing lake. ATM. Room for games and TV. Internet access and WiFi. Off site: Castellane and the Verdon Gorge 1 km. Riding 2 km. Boat launching 4.5 km. Golf 20 km. Water sports.

Open: 15 May - 15 September.

Directions

From Castellane take D952 westwards towards Gorges du Verdon and Moustiers. Site is 1 km. on left.

Charges 2008

Per unit with 2 or 3 persons	€ 18,00 - € 32,00
incl. 6A electricity	€ 24,00 - € 38,00
extra person (over 3 yrs)	€ 7,00 - € 12,00
dog	€ 2,50

Camping Cheques accepted.

FR04100 Kawan Village International

Route Napoleon, F-04120 Castellane (Alpes-de-Haute-Provence)

Tel: **04 92 83 66 67**. Email: info@camping-international.fr

Camping International has very friendly, English speaking owners and is a reasonably priced, less commercialised site situated in some of the most dramatic scenery in France with good views. The 274 pitches, 130 good sized ones for touring, are clearly marked, separated by trees and small hedges, and all have electricity and water. The bar/restaurant overlooks the swimming pool with its sunbathing area set in a sunny location, and all have fantastic views. In high season English speaking young people entertain children (3-8 years) and teenagers. Access is good for larger units. On some evenings the teenagers are taken to the woods for campfire 'sing-alongs' which can go on till the early hours without disturbing the rest of the site. There are guided walks into the surrounding hills in the nearby Gorges du Verdon – a very popular excursion, particularly in high season. The weather in the hills here is very pleasant without the excessive heat of the coast.

Facilities

Small toilet blocks are of an older design. One newer block has modern facilities, including those for disabled visitors. Washing machines and dryer. Motorcaravan services. Fridge hire. Shop. Restaurant/takeaway (May-Sept). Swimming pool (1/5-30/9). Club/TV room. Children's animation, occasional evening entertainment (July/Aug). Play area. Boules. Internet access. WiFi free whole site. Off site: Riding 800 m. Castellane (1.5 km), with river, canyon and rapids, ideal for canoeing, rafting and canyoning etc. Walking, biking. Boat launching 5 km.

Open: 31 March - 1 October.

Directions

Site is 1 km. north of Castellane on the N85 'Route Napoleon'. GPS: N43:50.500 E06:30.420

Charges 2007

Per unit incl. 2 persons	€ 14,00 - € 19,00
extra person	€ 3,00 - € 4,00
electricity (6A)	€ 3,00 - € 4,00
dog	€ 2,00

Camping Cheques accepted.

Camping International
Route Napoléon
04120 Castellane
Tél : +33 492 836 667
Fax : +33 492 837 767
E-mail : info@campinginternational.fr
www.campinginternational.fr

Castel Camping Caravaning
Domaine du Verdon
04120 Castellane
Tél : +33 492 836 129
Fax : +33 492 836 937
E-mail : contact@camp-du-verdon.com
www.camp-du-verdon.com

Provence
Castellane
Canyon du Verdon

3 SEASONS ELITE

Camping Chèque

FR04010 Sunêlia Hippocampe

Route de Napoléon, F-04290 Volonne (Alpes-de-Haute-Provence)

Tel: **04 92 33 50 00**. Email: **camping@l-hippocampe.com**

Hippocampe is a friendly family run, 'all action' lakeside site, with families in mind, situated in a beautiful area of France. The perfumes of thyme, lavender and wild herbs are everywhere and the higher hills of Haute Provence are not too far away. There are 447 level, numbered pitches (221 for touring units), medium to very large (130 sq.m.) in size. All have electricity (10A) and 243 have water and drainage, most are separated by bushes and cherry trees. Some of the best pitches border the lake. The restaurant, bar, takeaway and shop have all been completely renewed. Games, aerobics, competitions, entertainment and shows, plus a daily club for younger family members are organised in July/August. A soundproof underground disco is set well away from the pitches and is very popular with teenage customers. Staff tour the site at night ensuring a good night's sleep. The site is, however, much quieter in low season and, with its good discounts, is the time for those who do not want or need entertaining. The Gorges du Verdon is a sight not to be missed and rafting, paragliding or canoe trips can be booked from the site's own tourist information office. Being on the lower slopes of the hills of Haute-Provence, the surrounding area is good for both walking and mountain biking. All in all, this is a very good site for an active or restful holiday and is suitable for outfits of all sizes. Used by tour operators (20 pitches). English is spoken.

Facilities

Toilet blocks vary from old to modern, all with good clean facilities that include washbasins in cabins. Washing machines. Motorcaravan service point. Bread available (from 26/4). Shop, bar, restaurant and pizzeria (26/4-7/9). Large, pool complex (open from 5/4, heated in early and late seasons). Tennis. Fishing. Canoeing. Boules. Several sports facilities (some with free instruction). Charcoal barbecues are not permitted. Off site: Village of Volonne 600 m. Bicycle hire 2 km. Riding 12 km. Various sporting opportunities.

Open: 22 March - 30 September.

Directions

Approaching from the north turn off N85 across river bridge to Volonne, then right to site. From the south right on D4, 1 km. before Château Arnoux. GPS: N44:06.366 E06:00.933

Charges 2008

Per unit with 2 persons	
simple pitch:	€ 13,00 - € 27,00
with electricity	€ 16,00 - € 32,00
with water/drainage 100 sq.m.	€ 16,00 - € 34,00
with water/drainage 140 sq.m.	€ 20,00 - € 39,00
extra person (over 4 yrs)	€ 3,00 - € 6,50

Special low season offers.
Camping Cheques accepted.

In the heart of the ALPS OF HAUTE PROVENCE, near VERDON and LUBERON, 12 km south of Sisteron. Relaxing holiday amidst olive and cherry orchards with a wide selection of activities.

Heated pools open from April 5th

Camping L'Hippocampe ★★★★

L'Hippocampe - Route Napoléon - 04290 VOLONNE
Tel: 00 33 492 33 50 00 - Fax: 00 33 492 33 50 49
http://www.l-hippocampe.com - e-mail: camping@l-hippocampe.com

Sunêlia
open style

Reservation required

Camping Cheque

FR84020 **Domaine Naturiste de Bélézy**

F-84410 Bédoin (Vaucluse)

Tel: **04 90 65 60 18**. Email: **info@belezy.com**

At the foot of Mt Ventoux, surrounded by beautiful scenery, Bélézy is an excellent naturist site with many amenities and activities and the ambience is relaxed and comfortable. The 238 marked pitches are set amongst many varieties of trees and shrubs. Electricity points (12A) are plentiful but long leads are necessary. So far as naturism is concerned, the emphasis is on personal choice, the only stipulation being the requirement for complete nudity in the pools and pool area. An area of natural parkland with an orchard, fishpond and woodland, has a good range of sports. facilities. The largest pool is for swimming and relaxation (you may enjoy a musical serenade) and the smaller pool (heated 22/3-9/10) is used for watersports and aquarobics. Near the pool area is the smart restaurant, with terrace, and the mellow old Mas (Provencal farmhouse) that houses many of the activities and amenities. There is a hydrotherapy centre to tone up and revitalise with qualified diagnosis, including steam baths, massage and seaweed packs, osteopathy, Chinese medicine (including acupuncture) and Bach therapies. Activities are arranged including painting, pottery courses and language lessons (not in July/Aug) and music (bring your own instrument). There are two children's clubs and a teenage club in holiday periods. Childrens farm. The emphasis is on informality and concern for the environment and during high season cars are banned from the camping area (supervised parking nearby).Member 'France 4 Naturisme'.

Facilities

Sanitary blocks differ – newer ones are excellent, with showers and washbasins in cubicles, others have hot showers in the open air, screened by stone dividers. One block has a superb children's section. Shop (22/3-21/9). Excellent restaurant and takeaway. Two swimming pools. Sauna. Tennis. Adventure play area. Activities in low season. Archery. Guided walks. Children's club. Hydrotherapy centre (1/4-30/9). Barbecues are prohibited. Pets are not accepted. Off site: Bédoin 1.5 km.

Open: 15 March - 5 October.

Directions

From A7 autoroute or RN7 at Orange, take D950 southeast to Carpentras, then northeast via D974 to Bédoin. Site is signed in Bédoin, being about 1.5 km. northeast of the village. GPS: N44:08.011 E05:11.247

Charges 2008

Per unit incl. 2 persons	€ 22,00 - € 36,50
extra person	€ 5,00 - € 8,50
child (3-8 yrs)	€ 5,50 - € 8,80
electricity (12A)	€ 4,50

Camping Cheques accepted.

FR84150 **Camping Flory**

Route d'Entraigues, F-84270 Vedéne (Vaucluse)

Tel: **04 90 31 00 51**. Email: **campingflory@wanadoo.fr**

Camping Flory is a traditional, country site in the heart of Provence and only ten minutes drive from the historic Papal town of Avignon. The area dedicated to camping is somewhat sloping, with shade provided by mature pine trees. There are 100 touring pitches, all with electricity (10A). Mobile homes occupy a separate area. Vedène lies in a low area not far from the confluence of the Rhône and Durance rivers, but the site is on a hillside and the danger of flooding is minimal with excellent precautions in place. An award-winning warm welcome is offered by owners, Ernest and Jeannine Guindos. Tourist destinations nearby include Avignon, Orange and Carpentras (all within 15-25 km) and, a little further east, Mont Ventoux (beloved by hill-climbing cyclists) and the spectacular Gorges de la Nesque.

Facilities

Three toilet blocks, two of the buildings are old but have been refurbished to a good standard, with some washbasins in cabins and pre-set showers. Very basic facilities for disabled visitors. Motorcaravan services. Small restaurant (1/7-30/8) with simple menu and takeaway. Shop providing basic supplies. Swimming pool (no shorts) with paddling pool. Play area. Boules. Table tennis. Some organised activities in high season. Off site: Golf 2 km. Riding 3 km. Bicycle hire and fishing 10 km. Wine tasting locally. Walking and cycling in area, including Mont Ventoux and the Nesque Gorge. Towns of Avignon, Orange, Carpentras.

Open: 15 March - 30 September.

Directions

From A7 Autoroute du Soleil, take exit 23 (Avignon Nord) and follow D942 towards Carpentras for 3 km then turn right at the second sign for Vedène. GPS: N43:59.260 E04:54.470

Charges 2007

Per unit incl. 2 persons	€ 15,00 - € 18,00
extra person	€ 4,00
child (under 7 yrs)	€ 2,50 - € 3,00
electricity (10A)	€ 4,50 - € 5,50

FR32010 Kawan Village le Camp de Florence

Route Astaffort, F-32480 La Romieu (Gers)

Tel: **05 62 28 15 58**. Email: **info@lecampdeflorence.com**

Camp de Florence is an attractive site on the edge of an historic village in pleasantly undulating Gers countryside. The 183 large, part terraced pitches (95 for tourers) all have electricity, 10 with hardstanding and 25 fully serviced. They are arranged around a large field (full of sunflowers when we visited) with rural views, giving a feeling of spaciousness. The 13th century village of La Romieu is on the Santiago de Compostela pilgrim route. The Pyrénées are a two hour drive, the Atlantic coast a similar distance. There are 20 tour operator pitches. It is run by the Mynsbergen family who are Dutch (although Susan is English) and they have sympathetically converted the old farmhouse buildings to provide facilities for the site. The collegiate church, visible from the site, is well worth a visit (the views are magnificent from the top of the tower), as is the local arboretum, the biggest collection of trees in the Midi-Pyrénées.

Facilities

Two toilet blocks. Washing machine, dryer. Motorcaravan services. Air-conditioned restaurant (open to the public) 1/5-30/9, barbecue. Takeaway. Bread. Swimming pool area with water slide. Jacuzzi, protected children's pool (open to public in afternoons). Adventure playground, games and pets areas. Games room, tennis, table tennis, volleyball, petanque. Bicycle hire. Video shows, discos, picnics, musical evenings. Excursions. Internet and WiFi. Off site: Shop 500 m. in village. Fishing 5 km. Riding 10 km. Walking tours, excursions and wine tasting.

Open: 1 April - 8 October.

Directions

Site signed from D931 Agen - Condom road. Small units turn left at Ligardes (signed), follow D36 for 1 km, turn right turn La Romieu (signed). Otherwise continue until outskirts of Condom and take D41 left to La Romieu, through village to site. GPS: N43:58.975 E00:30.091

Charges 2007

Per unit incl. 2 persons	
and electricity	€ 16,00 - € 30,90
extra person	€ 3,50 - € 6,90
child (4-9 yrs)	€ 2,60 - € 4,80

Camping Cheques accepted.

FR09020 Camping l'Arize

Lieu-dit Bourtol, F-09240 La Bastide-de-Sérou (Ariège)

Tel: **05 61 65 81 51**. Email: **camparize@aol.com**

The site sits in a delightful, tranquil valley among the foothills of the Pyrénées and is just east of the interesting village of La Bastide-de-Sérou beside the River Arize (good trout fishing). The river is fenced for the safety of children on the site, but may be accessed just outside the gate. The 70 large pitches are neatly laid out on level grass within the spacious site. All have 3/6A electricity and are separated into bays by hedges and young trees. An extension to the site gives 24 large, fully serviced pitches and a small toilet block.

Facilities

Toilet block includes facilities for babies and disabled people. Laundry room, dryer. Motorcaravan services. Small swimming pool, sunbathing area. Entertainment, high season, weekly barbecues and welcome drinks on Sundays. Fishing, riding and bicycle hire on site. Off site: Golf 5 km. Several restaurants and shops within a few minute's drive.

Open: 7 March - 12 November.

Directions

Site is southeast of the village La Bastide-de-Sérou. Take the D15 towards Nescus and site is on right after about 1 km. GPS: N43:00.109 E01:26.723

Charges 2008

Per pitch incl. 2 persons	
and electricity	€ 16,40 - € 31,60
extra person	€ 4,00 - € 5,40
child (0-7 yrs)	€ 3,00 - € 3,60

Discounts for longer stays in mid and low season.

FR31000 Camping le Moulin

F-31220 Martres-Tolosane (Haute-Garonne)

Tel: **05 61 98 86 40**. Email: **info@campinglemoulin.com**

Set in a 12 hectare estate of woods and fields, Camping Le Moulin is a family run campsite in the foothills of the Pyrénées, close to the interesting medieval village of Martres-Tolosane and situated on the site of an old mill on the bank of the River Garonne. There are 99 pitches (60 available for tourers) all of which have electrical connections. Most pitches are level and grassy, of a good size and with shade from mature trees. Some very large (150-200 sq.m.) 'super' pitches are also available and there are 34 chalets/mobile homes for rent.

Facilities

Large modern sanitary block with separate ladies and gents WC's. Communal area with showers and washbasins in cubicles. Heated area for disabled visitors with shower, WC and basin. Baby bath. Motorcaravan services. Outdoor bar with WiFi. Snackbar and takeaway (July/August). Daily bakers van (except Monday). Heated swimming pools (July/August). Tennis. Canoeing. Archery.Playground. Entertainment and children's club (high season). Off site: Martres-Tolosane 1.5 km.

Open: 22 March - 30 September.

Directions

From the A64 motorway (Toulouse-Tarbes) take exit 21 (Boussens) or exit 22 (Martres-Tolosane) and follow signs to Martres-Tolosane. Site is well signed from village.

Charges 2007

Per person	€ 4,20 - € 6,00
child (2-7 ys)	€ 2,10 - € 3,00
pitch	€ 5,95 - € 13,00
electricity (6/10A)	€ 2,45 - € 5,00

Less 20% outside July and August.

FR65060 Castel Camping Pyrénées Natura

Route du Lac, F-65400 Estaing (Hautes-Pyrénées)

Tel: **05 62 97 45 44**. Email: **info@camping-pyrenees-natura.com**

Pyrénées Natura, at an altitude of 1,000 metres, on the edge of the National Park is the perfect site for lovers of nature. The 60 pitches (46 for tourists), all with electricity, are in a large, level, open and sunny field. Around 75 varieties of trees and shrubs have been planted – but they do not spoil the fantastic views. The reception and bar are in a traditional style stone building with an open staircase. The small shop in the old water mill stocks a variety of produce, it is left unmanned and open all day and you pay at reception.

Facilities

First class toilet blocks include facilities for disabled visitors and babies. Washing machine and airers (no lines allowed). Motorcaravan services. Small shop, takeaway (15/5-15/9). Small bar (15/5-15/9), lounge area. Lounge, library, TV (mainly used for videos of the National Park). Sauna, solarium (free between 12.00-17.00). Music room. Play area for the very young. Small 'beach' beside river. Giant chess. Weekly evening meal in May, June and Sept. Internet. Off site: Village has two restaurants.

Open: 1 May - 20 September.

Directions

From Lourdes take N21 towards Argelès-Gazost. Exit 2, N2021/D21, into Argelès. Approaching town turn onto D918 towards Aucun. After 8 km. turn left, D13 to Bun, cross river, right on D103 to site (5.5 km). Narrow road, few passing places. GPS: N42:56.451 W00:10.631

Charges 2008

Per unit incl. 2 persons and electricity (3A)	€ 15,50 - € 24,50
extra person	€ 5,25

FR65080 Kawan Village du Lavedan

Lau-Balagnas, F-65400 Argelès-Gazost (Hautes-Pyrénées)

Tel: **05 62 97 18 84**. Email: **contact@lavedan.com**

Camping du Lavedan is an old established and very French site set in the Argelès-Gazost valley south of the Lourdes. It is beside the main road so there is some daytime road noise. The 105 touring pitches are set very close together on grass with some shade and all have electricity (2-10A). The area is fine for walking, biking, rafting and of course, in winter, skiing. There is a swimming pool which can be covered and a twice weekly event is organised in July/Aug, weekly in June.

Facilities

Acceptable toilet block. Baby room. Facilities for disabled visitors. Washing machines and dryer in separate block heated in winter. Restaurant with takeaway and terrace (1/5-15/9). Bar, TV (all year). No shop, bread delivery (1/5-15/9). Swimming pool (with cover), paddling pool. Excellent play area. Internet (July/Aug). Boules, table tennis. Off site: Fishing or bicycle hire 1 km. Supermarket or rafting 2 km. Riding 5 km. Golf 15 km.

Open: All year.

Directions

From Lourdes take the N21 (Voie rapide) south, exit 3 (Argelès-Gazost). Take N2021, D921 or D21 towards Luz-St-Sauveur for 2 km. to Lau-Balagnas. Site on right, southern edge of town. GPS: N42:59.293 W00:05.340

Charges 2008

Per unit incl. 2 persons	€ 15,00 - € 23,00
electricity (10A max)	€ 1,00

Camping Cheques accepted.

Check real time availability and at-the-gate prices...

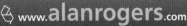 www.**alanrogers**.com

FR82010 Camping les Trois Cantons

F-82140 Saint Antonin-Noble-Val (Tarn-et-Garonne)

Tel: **05 63 31 98 57**. Email: **info@3cantons.fr**

Les Trois Cantons is a well established and very friendly family run with 100 pitches (85 for tourers) set among mature trees that give dappled shade. The pitches are of average size, reasonably level and all have electricity connections. The swimming pool is covered and heated in early and late season, with activities organised there in July and August. There are also walks, archery and boules, clay modelling plus wine tastings and a weekly dance. When the trees are bare early in the season, there could be a little road noise when the wind is in a certain direction.

Facilities

The two sanitary blocks include British and Turkish style WCs, showers, washbasins (some in cubicles) and facilities for disabled visitors, which have recently been refurbished. Laundry and dishwashing facilities. Very limited shop (bread daily). Bar serving snacks and takeaways. Swimming pool (heated from 15/5-30/9) and paddling pool. Games/TV room. Play area. Small farm area. Tennis. Volleyball. Boules. English spoken. Off site: Riding 1 km. Fishing 7 km. Many pretty medieval villages to visit.

Open: 15 April - 30 September.

Directions

From A20 or N20 at Caussade, take D926 signed Caylus and Septfonds. Site is signed to right 5 km. after Septfonds. Do not take the D5 towards St Antonin as it involves 5 km. of narrow road.

Charges 2008

Per pitch and 2 people	€ 14,50 - € 21,00
extra person	€ 4,55 - € 6,40
child (2-9 yrs)	€ 2,70 - € 4,20
electricity (2-10A)	€ 2,70 - € 6,80

Camping Cheques accepted.

FR11040 Camping le Martinet Rouge Birdie

F-11390 Brousses et Villaret (Aude)

Tel: **04 68 26 51 98**. Email: **campinglemartinetrouge@orange.fr**

Le Martinet Rouge provides a peaceful retreat in the Aude countryside to the north of Carcassonne. It is a small site where the owners have been working hard to improve the facilities. The most striking features of the site are the massive granite boulders (outcrops of smooth rock from the last ice age). The site offers 50 pitches for touring units, all with electricity (3/6A), in two contrasting areas – one is well secluded with irregularly shaped, fairly level, large pitches amongst a variety of trees and shrubs, while the other is on a landscaped gentle hill with mature trees.

Facilities

Four sanitary blocks of various ages, including facilities for disabled visitors, baby bathroom, laundry facilities. Swimming pool (15/6-15/9). Small shop (no others locally). Bar, terrace, TV (1/7-15/9). Snack bar (1/7-31/8). Barbecue area. Fitness room. Croquet, volleyball, half court tennis, table tennis, small play area. Internet access. Off site: Visit the paper mill in the village. Tennis, riding and fishing quite close.

Open: 1 April - 15 October.

Directions

Site is south of Brousses-et-Villaret, 20 km. northwest of Carcassonne. Best approached via D118. Turn onto D103 15 km. north of Carcassonne to Brousses-et-Villaret. Western outskirts of village turn south to site in 50 m. GPS: N43:20.350 E02:15.127

Charges 2007

Per unit incl. 2 persons	€ 12,50 - € 15,50
with electricity	€ 15,00 - € 18,00
extra person	€ 4,50 - € 5,50

No credit cards.

FR11050 Camping Rives des Corbières

Avenue du Languedoc, F-11370 Port Leucate (Aude)

Tel: **04 68 40 90 31**. Email: **rivescamping@wanadoo.fr**

Port Leucate is part of the major Languedoc development which took place during the sixties and seventies and it is now a thriving resort. The campsite is situated on the old coast road into Port Leucate between the Etang de Salas and the beach, 800 m. from the centre of the town and port and only 150 m. from the beach. A mixture of tall poplars and pine trees provide reasonable shade for the 305 pitches. On good-sized sandy plots, all have 6A electricity connections. About 90 are used for mobile homes. With no tour operators this is a good value site, essentially French.

Facilities

Four toilet blocks opened as required. Two have mainly Turkish toilets. Facilities for disabled people. Laundry room. Small supermarket, bar and takeaway (July/Aug). Swimming pools. Play area. Daytime games and tournaments and in the evening, live music, karaoke and dancing. Off site: Beach 150 m. (lifeguards July/Aug). Port 800 m.

Open: 1 April - 30 September.

Directions

From the A9 take exit 40 and follow signs for Port Leucate on D627 (passing Leucate village) for 14 km. Exit the D627 which is like a bypass into Port Leucate village. Go right into Avenue du Languedoc and site is 800 m. GPS: N42:50.009 E03:02.004

Charges 2007

Per unit incl. 2 persons and electricity	€ 16,30 - € 20,40

FR11070 Kawan Village les Mimosas

Chaussée de Mandirac, F-11100 Narbonne (Aude)

Tel: **04 68 49 03 72**. Email: **info@lesmimosas.com**

Six kilometres inland from the beaches of Narbonne and Gruissan, this site benefits from a less hectic situation than others by the sea. The site is lively with plenty to amuse and entertain the younger generation whilst offering facilities for the whole family. A free club card is available in July/Aug. to use the children's club, gym, sauna, tennis, minigolf, billiards etc. There are 250 pitches, 150 for touring, many in a circular layout of very good size, most with electricity (6A). There are a few fully serviced, with reasonable shade, mostly from 2 m. high hedges. There are also a number of mobile homes and chalets to rent. This could be a very useful site offering many possibilities to meet a variety of needs, on-site entertainment (including an evening on Cathar history), and easy access to popular beaches. Nearby Gruissan is a fascinating village with its wooden houses on stilts, beaches, ruined castle, port and salt beds. Narbonne has Roman remains and inland Cathar castles are to be found perched on rugged hill tops.

Facilities

Refurbished to a high standard sanitary buildings. Washing machines. Shop and 'Auberge' restaurant (open all season). Takeaway. Bar. Small lounge, amusements (July and Aug). Landscaped heated pool with slides and islands (open 1 May), plus the original pool and children's pool (high season). Play area. Minigolf. Mountain bike hire. Tennis. Volleyball. Sauna, gym. Children's activities, sports, entertainment (high season). Bicycle hire. Multi-sports ground. Off site: Riding. Windsurfing/sailing school 300 m. Gruissan's beach 10 minutes. Lagoon, boating fishing via footpath (200 m).

Open: 24 March - 31 October.

Directions

From A9 exit 38 (Narbonne Sud) take last exit on roundabout, back over the autoroute (site signed from here). Follow signs La Nautique and then Mandirac and site (6 km. from autoroute). Also signed from Narbonne centre.

Charges 2007

Per basic pitch	
incl. 1 or 2 persons	€ 13,50 - € 21,00
pitch with electricity	€ 17,00 - € 27,00
with electricity, water and waste water	€ 21,20 - € 31,00
extra person	€ 4,00 - € 5,90

Camping Cheques accepted.

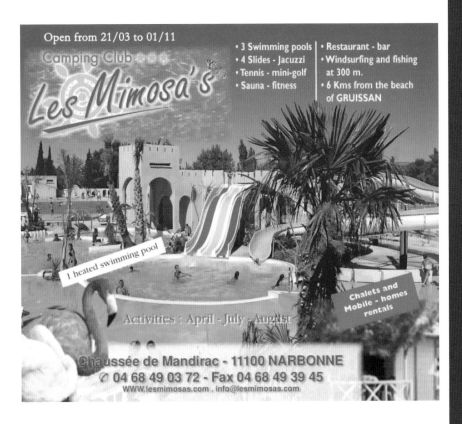

FR11080 Camping la Nautique

La Nautique, F-11100 Narbonne (Aude)

Tel: **04 68 90 48 19**. Email: **info@campinglanautique.com**

Owned and run by a very welcoming Dutch family, this well established site has pitches each with individual sanitary units. It is an extremely spacious site situated on the Etang de Bages, where flat water combined with strong winds make it one of the best windsurfing areas in France. La Nautique has 390 huge, level pitches, 270 for touring, all with 10A electricity and water. Six or seven overnight pitches with electricity are in a separate area. The flowering shrubs and trees give a pleasant feel. Each pitch is separated by hedges making some quite private and providing shade. Entertainments are organised for adults and children from Easter to September (increasing in high season), plus a sports club for surfing, sailing, rafting, walking and canoeing (some activities are charged for). The unspoilt surrounding countryside is excellent for walking or cycling and locally there is horse riding and fishing. English is spoken in reception by the very welcoming Schutjes family. This site caters for families with children including teenagers and is fenced off from the water for the protection of children. Windsurfers can have a key for the gate that leads to launching points on the lake.

Facilities

Each pitch has its own fully equipped sanitary unit. Specially equipped facilities for disabled visitors. Laundry, dishwashing sinks. Shop. Bar/restaurant, terrace, TV. Takeaway. All 1/5-30/9. Snack bar (1/7-31/8). Swimming pools, water slide, paddling pool, slide. Play areas, children Off site: Large sandy beaches at Gruissan 12 km and Narbonne Plage 20 km. Narbonne is only 4 km. Canoeing, sailing and windsurfing on the Etang.

Open: 15 February - 15 November.

Directions

From A9 take exit 38 (Narbonne Sud). Go round roundabout to last exit and follow signs for La Nautique and site, then further site signs to site on right in 2.5 km. GPS: N43:08.500 E03:00.140

Charges 2008

Per person	€ 5,00 - € 7,50
child (1-7 yrs)	€ 3,00 - € 5,50
pitch incl. electricity, water and sanitary unit	€ 9,50 - € 22,00

Private Sanitary facilities on every pitch.
Open from 15/02 till 15/11

www.campinglanautique.com

℡ (+33) 04 68 90 48 19

FR34470 Camping le Fou du Roi

Chemin des Codoniers, F-34130 Lansargues (Hérault)

Tel: **08 74 56 00 27**. Email: **contact@campinglefouduroi.com**

Beside the mellow stone village of Lansargues on the edge of the Camargue, Le Fou du Roi was taken over by the Brunel family two years ago. They have done much to update it with a new reception/bar area complete with an attractive Tahitian style construction which can be left open or closed depending on the weather. Altogether this a lovely little site. There are 82 pitches with 30 for touring units with 10A electricity, arranged in light shade amongst the vineyards. A small pool and play area for children make it a very comfortable site with a nice long season.

Facilities

Two toilet blocks, the first modern and fully equipped, the second not open when we visited. Facilities for disabled visitors. Washing machine and dryer. Motorcaravan service point. Small shop (July/Aug). Bar, simple snacks and takeaway (fully open July/Aug). Swimming pool (1/5-15/9). Play area. Only gas barbecues are permitted (communal area provided). Off site: Fishing and riding 3 km. Golf 4 km. Tennis in village. Village within easy walking distance with restaurants and shops.

Open: 30 March - 14 October.

Directions

From A9 exit 27 follow signs for Lunel and from there pick up D24 going south. Lansargues is 7 km. Do not take 'village centre' sign but continue past and pick up site sign just past village on right.

Charges 2007

Per unit incl. 2 persons	€ 13,00 - € 17,00
extra person	€ 3,00 - € 5,00
child (under 7 yrs)	free - € 2,50
electricity	€ 4,00

FR30100 Camping Naturiste de la Sablière

Domaine de la Sablière, Saint Privat de Champclos, F-30430 Barjac (Gard)

Tel: **04 66 24 51 16**. Email: **contact@villagesabliere.com**

Spectacularly situated in the Cèze Gorges, this naturist site with a surprising 497 pitches, 240 for touring, tucked away within its wild terrain offers a wide variety of facilities, all within a really peaceful, wooded and dramatic setting. The pitches themselves are mainly on flat stony terraces, attractively situated among a variety of trees and shrubs (some with a low overhang). Many are of a good size and have electricity (6/10A), very long leads may be needed. Nudity is obligatory only around the pool complex. You must expect some fairly steep walking between the pitches and facilities. Those with walking difficulties may not find this site appropriate, although cars can be used in low season and there is a minibus shuttle service in July and August. An excellent pool complex provides a children's pool area and two large pools, one of which is heated and can be covered by a sliding dome, sunbathing terraces, saunas and a bar. A large varity of activities is provided including book binding, pottery and yoga. This is a family run and orientated site and the owner, Gaby Cespedes, provides a personal touch that is unusual in a large site. Member France 4 Naturisme.

Facilities

Six good unisex sanitary blocks have excellent free hot showers in typical open plan, naturist style, washbasins (cold water), baby baths and facilities for people with disabilities. Laundry. Good supermarket. Bar (1/4-22/9). Excellent open air, covered restaurant and takeaway (1/4-22/9). Small café/crêperie. Swimming pool complex (all season). Fitness room. Tennis. Minigolf. Activity and entertainment programme. Torch useful. Barbecues are not permitted. Off site: Bicycle hire 8 km. Riding 10 km.

Open: 1 April - 1 October.

Directions

From Barjac take D901 east for 3 km. Turn right at site sign just before St Privat-de-Champclos and follow site signs along winding country lane to site entrance in 4 km. GPS: N44:16.021 E04:21.125

Charges 2007

Per pitch incl. 2 persons	€ 19,00 - € 37,00
extra person	€ 5,00 - € 7,00
child (4-8 yrs)	free - € 1,80

Camping Cheques accepted.

FR34450 Sunêlia Domaine de la Dragonnière

RN 112, F-34450 Vias-sur-Mer (Hérault)

Tel: **04 67 01 03 10**. Email: **dragonniere@wanadoo.fr**

La Dragonnière is a busy family site, located between the popular resorts of Vias and Portiragnes. There are no fewer than nine swimming pools here and a lively entertainment programme in high season. Many of the pitches are occupied by mobile homes and chalets but there are around 200 reasonably sized touring pitches, all offering some shade. The pitches all have electrical connections (6A) and many also offer water and drainage. La Dragonnière lies 5 km. from the nearest beach and a free shuttle operates in peak season. This is an ideal site for families with teenagers searching for a wide range of activities. The beach is doubtless the main appeal here but there is a great deal to visit in the area. Popular excursions include the nearby Canal du Midi, the Sigean animal reserve and the cities of Montpellier and Beziers. Alternatively, given the very impressive range of facilities, including a good supermarket, some may prefer to spend all their time on site.

Facilities

Well maintained toilet blocks include facilities for babies and disabled people. Laundry. Supermarket. Two swimming pool complexes with children's pools. Bar and restaurant complex, with good range of meals. Play area. Sauna and gym. Tennis. Multisport pitch. Excursions reserved at reception. Sports competitions, children's club and evening entertainment in high season, including talent shows, regular discos and cabaret evenings. Mobile homes and chalets for rent. Off site: Nearest beach 5 km. (free shuttle in peak season). Fishing 4 km. Golf 12 km.

Open: 15 March - 6 October.

Directions

Take the Beziers Est exit from the A9 autoroute. Follow directions to Villenevue, Serignan and Valras Plage. After 800 m. at the large roundabout, follow signs to Vias aéroport on the N112. After a further 7 km, the campsite can be found on the right.

Charges 2008

Per unit with 3 persons, water, waste water and electricity	€ 19,00 - € 42,00
extra person	€ 6,00 - € 7,00
dog	€ 5,50

FR34070 Yelloh! Village le Sérignan Plage

Le Sérignan Plage, F-34410 Sérignan (Hérault)

Tel: **04 66 73 97 39**. Email: **info@yellohvillage-serignan-plage.com**

A large, friendly, family-orientated site with direct access to superb sandy beaches, including a naturist beach. Those looking for 'manicured' sites may be less impressed, as its situation on 'the littoral' close to the beach makes it difficult to keep things neat and tidy. It has 273 mainly good sized, level touring pitches, including some (with little shade) actually alongside the beach, coupled with perhaps the most comprehensive range of amenities we've come across. Perhaps the most remarkable aspect is the cluster of attractive buildings which form the 'heart' of this site with courtyards housing many of the amenities. The hugely enthusiastic owners, Jean-Guy and Katy continually surprise us with new ideas and developments. New for 2004 was a superb 2800 sq.m. 'Spa Water Fitness centre' with more new pools, a fitness centre and jacuzzi. The amenities are just too extensive to describe in detail, but they include a pool complex, with slides surrounded by large grassy sunbathing areas with sun loungers and another indoor pool. Sérignan Plage exudes a strongly individualistic style which we find very attractive.

Facilities

Several modern blocks of individual design, with good facilities, including showers with washbasin and WC. Facilities for disabled people. Washing machines. Maintenance variable. Supermarket, bakery, newsagent, ATM. Poissonnerie, boucherie (7/6-8/9). Launderette. Hairdresser. Bars, restaurant, takeaway. Children's activities, evening entertainment. Heated indoor and outdoor pool with lifeguards in the main season (24/4-21/9). Sporting activities organised. Bicycle hire. Off site: Riding 2 km. Golf 10 km. Bicycle hire. Sailing and windsurfing school on beach (lifeguard in high season).

Open: 24 April - 21 September.

Directions

From A9 exit 35 (Béziers Est) follow signs for Sérignan, D64 (9 km). Before Sérignan, turn left, Sérignan Plage (4 km). At small sign (blue) turn right. At T-junction turn left over small road bridge and after left hand bend. Site is 100 m.

Charges 2008

Per unit incl. 1 or 2 persons and electricity (6A)	€ 14,00 - € 44,00
extra person	€ 5,00 - € 8,00
pet	€ 3,00 - € 4,00

Low season offers.
Discounts in low season for children under 7 yrs.

FR66130 Hotel de Plein Air l'Eau Vive

Chemin de St Saturnin, F-66820 Vernet-les-Bains (Pyrénées-Orientales)

Tel: **04 68 05 54 14**. Email: **info@leauvive.com**

Enjoying dramatic views of the Pic du Canigou (3,000 m.), this small site is 1.5 km. from the centre of Vernet-les-Bains in the Pyrénées. It is approached via a twisting road through a residential area. The 70 tourist pitches, with electricity (4/10A) and 45 fully serviced, are on a slight slope, part hedged and some terraced, with a separate tent field. Most pitches have some shade. Although there is no swimming pool, the site has a very attractive, natural pool with water pumped from the nearby stream, with a small beach. Well situated for touring this area of the Pyrénées and with comfortable amenities, this small site quickly becomes fully booked in season and advance reservation is essential. English is spoken by the welcoming Dutch owners, Ria and Gertjan, who will arrange walks, canoe and rafting trips or even 4x4 excursions up Mont Canigou. There is a central floating safety line across the pool but parents should keep an eye on children around the pool as there is no supervision or safety fence. Access to the bubbling mountain stream is possible.

Facilities

First class toilet facilities and provision for disabled people. Washing machine. Bread, main season. Bar/reception, pool table, library. Snack bar, takeaway (15/5-15/9). A 'meal of the day' can be ordered. Play area. Natural pool for children. Sports field. Basketball. Bicycle hire. Off site: Fishing 200 m. Swimming pool, thermal centre in village 1 km. Nearby medieval, walled town of Ville Franche de Conflent, Grottes des Canalettes, Fort Libena with its many steps are well worth visiting. Organised rafting, canoeing, hydrospeed trips.

Open: 16 December - 25 October.

Directions

Following N116 towards Andorra. At Ville Franche, turn south, D116, for Vernet-les-Bains. After 5 km, keep right avoiding town. Turn right over bridge towards Sahorre. Immediately turn right, Ave de Saturnin for about 1 km. beyond houses, site signed.

Charges 2007

Per unit incl. 2 persons	€ 12,50 - € 21,50
incl. electricity	€ 15,00 - € 25,00
extra person (over 4 yrs)	€ 1,50 - € 2,50
animal	€ 1,50 - € 2,50

Credit cards accepted 15/6-15/9 only.
Camping Cheques accepted.

Le Sérignan Plage

The magic of
the Mediterranean

Imagine – hot sunshine, blue sea, vineyards, olive and eucalyptus trees, alongside a sandy beach – what a setting for a campsite – not just any campsite either !

With three pool areas, one with four toboggans surrounded by sun bathing areas, an indoor pool for baby swimmers plus a magnificent landscaped, Romanesque spa-complex with half Olympic size pool and a superb range of hydro-massage baths to let you unwind and re-charge after the stresses of work.

And that's not all – two attractive restaurants, including the atmospheric "Villa" in its romantic Roman setting beside the spa, three bars, a mini-club and entertainment for all ages, all add up to a fantastic opportunity to enjoy a genuinely unique holiday experience.

Le Sérignan-Plage - F-34410 SERIGNAN
Tel: 00 33 467 32 35 33 - Fax: 00 33 467 32 26 36
info@leserignanplage.com - www.leserignanplage.com

FR66070 Yelloh! Village le Brasilia

B.P. 204, F-66141 Canet-en-Roussillon (Pyrénées-Orientales)

Tel: **04 66 73 97 39**. Email: **info@yellohvillage-brasilia.com**

An impressive family site beside the beach and well managed, Le Brasilia is pretty, neat and well kept with an amazingly wide range of facilities. There are 763 neatly hedged pitches all with electricity varying in size from 100-150 sq.m. Some of the longer pitches are suitable for two families together. With a range of shade from pines and flowering shrubs, less on pitches near the beach, there are neat access roads (sometimes narrow for large units). Over 100 of the pitches have mobile homes or chalets to rent. The sandy beach here is busy, with a beach club (you can hire windsurfing boards) and a naturist section is on the beach to the west of the site. There is also a large California type pool. The village area of the site provides bars, a busy restaurant, entertainment (including a night club) and a range of shops. In fact you do not need to stir from the site which is almost a resort in itself also providing a cash dispenser, exchange facilities, telephone, post office, gas supplies and even weather forecasts. It does have a nice, lively atmosphere but is orderly and well run – very good for a site with beach access. Although it is a large site it does not seem so. A 'Yelloh Village' member. Member of Leading Campings Group.

Facilities

Ten modern sanitary blocks are very well equipped and maintained, with British style WCs (some Turkish) and washbasins in cabins. Good facilities for children and for disabled people. Laundry room. Hairdresser. Bars and restaurant. Swimming pool with lifeguards (heated). Play areas. Sports field. Tennis. Sporting activities. Library, games and video room. Internet café. Daily entertainment programme. Bicycle hire. Fishing. Torches useful. Off site: Riding 5 km. Golf 12 km.

Open: 26 April - 27 September.

Directions

From A9 exit 41 (Perpignan Centre/Rivesalts) follow signs for Le Barcarès/Canet on D83 for 10 km, then for Canet (D81). At first Canet roundabout, turn fully back on yourself (direction Sainte-Marie) and watch for Brasilia sign almost immediately on right. GPS: N42:42.280 E03:02.090

Charges 2007

Per unit incl. 2 persons and electricity (6A)	€ 17,00 - € 43,00
extra person	€ 4,60 - € 8,00
child (1-4 yrs)	free - € 4,00

FR06080 Camping Caravaning les Cigales

505 avenue de la Mer, F-06210 Mandelieu-la-Napoule (Alpes-Maritimes)

Tel: **04 93 49 23 53**. Email: **campingcigales@wanadoo.fr**

It is hard to imagine that such a quiet, peaceful site could be in the middle of such a busy town and so near Cannes. The entrance (easily missed) has large electronic gates that ensure that the site is very secure. There are only 115 pitches (40 mobile homes) so this is quite a small, personal site. There are three pitch sizes, from small ones for tents to pitches for larger units and all have electricity (6A), some fully serviced. All are level with much needed shade in summer, although the sun will get through in winter when it is needed. The site is alongside the Canal de Siagne and for a fee, small boats can be launched at La Napoule, then moored outside the campsite's side gate. Les Cigales is open all year so it is useful for the Monte Carlo Rally, the Cannes Film Festival and the Mimosa Festival, all held out of the main season. English is spoken.

Facilities

Well appointed, clean, heated toilet blocks. Facilities for babies and disabled visitors. Washing machine. Motorcaravan services. Restaurant and takeaway (May - Oct). Heated swimming pool and large sunbathing area (April - Oct). Small play area. Table tennis. Two games machines. Canal fishing. Off site: Beach 800 m. The town is an easy walk. Two golf courses within 1 km. Railway station 1 km. for trains to Cannes, Nice, Antibes, Monte Carlo. Hypermarket 2 km. Bus stop 10 minutes.

Open: All year.

Directions

From A8, exit 40, bear right. Remain in right hand lane, continue right signed Plages-Ports, Creche-Campings. Casino supermarket on right. Continue under motorway to T-junction. Turn left, site is 60 m. on left opposite Chinese restaurant.

Charges 2007

Per person	€ 6,00
child (under 5 yrs)	€ 3,00
tent	€ 6,50 - € 13,50
caravan or motorcaravan	€ 14,00 - € 23,50

FR06140 Ranch Camping

Chemin Saint Joseph, F-06110 Le Cannet (Alpes-Maritimes)

Tel: **04 93 46 00 11**. Email: **dstallis@free.fr**

Ranch Camping is a well run 'French flavoured' site. The ambience here is calm and there is relatively little by way of entertainment or leisure amenities. The site is very well located for the beaches of Cannes just 2 km. away; a regular bus service runs past the site entrance. Despite its urban setting the site enjoys a tranquil position on a wooded hillside. There are 102 touring pitches which are generally level and well shaded, all with 6A electrical connections. The swimming pool is quite small and can be covered in low season. Other leisure facilities are nearby.

Facilities

Principal toilet block has been recently refurbished, whereas the second block is of 'portacabin' style. Both very clean and well maintained. Facilities for disabled people. Washing machines and dryers. Small shop. Swimming pool (covered in low season). Play area. Games room. Mobile homes, rooms to rent. Off site: Beach 2 km. Bus stop at site entrance (regular service to Cannes and beaches). Tennis 200 m. Fishing, bicycle hire 2 km. Golf 4 km.

Open: 1 April - 30 October.

Directions

From A8 exit 42 follow signs to Le Cannet, then L'Aubarède to the right (D809). Follow this road until signs for La Bocca and site is signed from here. GPS: N43:33.529 E06:58.396

Charges 2007

Per unit incl. 1 person	€ 11,00 - € 17,00
extra person	€ 6,00
child (5-10 yrs)	€ 3,00

FR83020 Castel Camping Caravaning Esterel

Avenue des Golf, F-83530 Saint Raphaël – Agay (Var)

Tel: **04 94 82 03 28**. Email: **contact@esterel-caravaning.fr**

Esterel is a quality caravan site east of St Raphaël, set among the hills at the back of Agay. The site is 3.5 km. from the sandy beach at Agay where parking is perhaps a little easier than at most places on this coast. It has 230 pitches for tourists, for caravans but not tents, all have electricity and water tap, 18 special ones have their own en-suite washroom adjoining. Pitches are on shallow terraces, attractively landscaped with good shade and a variety of flowers, giving a feeling of spaciousness. Some 'maxi-pitches' from 110-160 sq.m. are available with 10A electricity. Developed by the Laroche family for over 30 years, the site has an attractive, quiet situation with good views of the Esterel mountains. A member of 'Les Castels' group. Wild boar occasionally come to the perimeter fence to be fed by visitors. This is a very good site, well run and organised in a deservedly popular area. A pleasant courtyard area contains the shop and bar, with a terrace overlooking the attractively landscaped (floodlit at night) pool complex.

Facilities

Excellent refurbished, heated toilet blocks. Individual toilet units on18 pitches. Facilities for disabled people. Laundry room. Motorcaravan services. Shop. Gift shop. Takeaway. Bar/restaurant. Five circular swimming pools (two heated), one for adults, one for children, three arranged as a waterfall (1/4-30/9). Disco. Archery. Minigolf. Tennis. Pony rides. Petanque. Squash. Playground. Nursery. Bicycle hire. Internet access. Organised events in season. No barbecues. Off site: Golf nearby. Trekking by foot, bicycle or by pony in L'Esterel forest park. Fishing, beach 3 km.

Open: 1 April - 6 October.

Directions

From A8, exit Fréjus, follow signs for Valescure, then for Agay, site on left. The road from Agay is the easiest to follow but it is possible to approach from St Raphaël via Valescure. GPS: N43:27.253 E06:49.945

Charges 2007

Per unit incl. 2 persons,	
standard pitch	€ 23,00 - € 38,00
'maxi' pitch	€ 28,00 - € 47,00
deluxe pitch	€ 32,00 - € 51,00
extra person	€ 8,50
child (1-7 yrs)	€ 6,50

FR13060 Camping les Micocouliers

445 route de Cassoulen, F-13690 Graveson-en-Provence (Bouches du Rhône)

Tel: **04 90 95 81 49**. Email: **micocou@free.fr**

M. et Mme. Riehl started work at Les Micocouliers in 1997 and they have developed a comfortable site. On the outskirts of the town it is only 10 km. from St Rémy and Avignon. A purpose built, terracotta 'house' in a raised position provides all the facilities. The 65 pitches radiate out from here with the pool and entrance to one side. The pitches are on level grass, separated by small bushes, and shade is developing. Electricity connections are possible (4-13A). There are a few mobile homes. The popular swimming pool is a welcome addition. Bread can be ordered and in July and August a simple snack kiosk operates otherwise Mme. Riehl is most helpful in suggesting places to eat. She will also suggest places to visit with suggested itineraries for car tours. Each village in the area offers entertainment on different weeks so you are never short of experiencing the real France.

Facilities

Unisex facilities in one unit provide toilets and facilities for disabled visitors (by key), another showers and washbasins in cabins and another dishwashing and laundry facilities. Reception and limited shop (July/Aug) are in another. Swimming pool (12 x 8 m; 5/5-15/9). Paddling pool (1/7-31/8). Play area. Table tennis. Volleyball. Off site: Fishing 5 Km. Bicycle hire 1 km. Riding next door. Golf 5 km. Beach 60 km. at Ste Marie de la Mer.

Open: 15 March - 15 October.

Directions

Site is southeast of Graveson. From the N570 at new roundabout take D5 towards St Rémy and Maillane and site is 500 m. on the left.

Charges 2007

Per unit incl. 2 persons	€ 13,70 - € 17,30
extra person	€ 4,50 - € 5,70
child (2-12 yrs)	€ 2,50 - € 4,50
electricity	€ 3,50 - € 6,30

Camping Cheques accepted.

FR83030 Camping Caravaning Leï Suves

Quartier du Blavet, F-83520 Roquebrune-sur-Argens (Var)
Tel: 04 94 45 43 95. Email: camping.lei.suves@wanadoo.fr

This quiet, pretty site is a few kilometres inland from the coast, 2 km. north of the N7. Close to the unusual Roquebrune rock, it is within easy reach of St Tropez, Ste Maxime, St Raphaël and Cannes. The site entrance is appealing – wide and spacious, with a large bank of well tended flowers. Mainly on a gently sloping hillside, the 310 pitches are terraced with shade provided by the many cork trees which give the site its name. All pitches have electricity and access to water. A pleasant pool area is beside the bar/restaurant and entertainment area. It is possible to walk in the surrounding woods as long as there is no fire alert. A good number of the pitches are used for mobile homes.

Facilities

Modern, well kept toilet blocks include washing machines, facilities for disabled visitors. Shop. Good sized swimming pool, paddling pool. Bar, terrace, snack bar, takeaway (all 1/4-30/9). Outdoor stage near the bar for evening entertainment, high season. Excellent play area. Table tennis, tennis, sports area. Internet terminal. Only gas barbecues. Off site: Bus stop at site entrance. Riding 1 km. Fishing 3 km. Bicycle hire 5 km. Golf 7 km. Beach at St Aygulf 15 km.

Open: 1 April - 15 October.

Directions

Leave autoroute at Le Muy and take N7 towards St Raphaël. Turn left at roundabout onto D7 heading north signed La Boverie (site also signed). Site on right in 2 km. GPS: N43:28.677 E06:38.324

Charges 2008

Per unit incl. 2 persons	€ 19,00 - € 34,50
incl. 3 persons	€ 21,00 - € 37,00
extra person	€ 4,50 - € 7,50
electricity	€ 4,50

Check real time availability and at-the-gate prices...
www.alanrogers.com

FR83170 Camping Domaine de la Bergerie

Vallée du Fournel, route du Col du Bougnon, F-83520 Roquebrune-sur-Argens (Var)
Tel: **04 98 11 45 45**. Email: **info@domainelabergerie.com**

This excellent site near the Côte d'Azur will take you away from all the bustle of the Mediterranean to total relaxation amongst the cork, oak, pine and mimosa in its woodland setting. The 60 hectare site is quite spread out with semi-landscaped areas for mobile homes and, grassy avenues of 200 separated pitches for touring caravans and tents. All pitches average over 80 sq.m. and have electricity, with those in one area also having water and drainage. The restaurant/bar, a converted farm building, is surrounded by shady patios, whilst inside it oozes character with high beams and archways leading to intimate corners. Activities are organised daily and, in the evening, shows, cabarets, discos, cinema, karaoke and dancing at the amphitheatre prove popular (possibly until midnight). A superb new pool complex supplements the original pool adding more outdoor pools with slides and a river feature, an indoor pool and a fitness centre with jacuzzi, sauna, turkish bath, massage, reflexology and gym.

Facilities

Four toilet blocks (all refurbished in 2007) are kept clean and include washbasins in cubicles, facilities for disabled people and babies. Supermarket. Bar/restaurant. Takeaway. Pool complex (5/4-30/9) with indoor pool and fitness centre (body building, sauna, gym, etc). Tennis courts. Archery. Roller skating. Minigolf. English speaking childrens club. Mini-farm for children. Fishing. Only gas barbecues are permitted. Off site: Riding or golf 2 km. Bicycle hire 7 km. Beach, St Ayguif or Ste Maxime 7 km. Water skiing and rock climbing nearby.

Open: 25 April - 30 September.
Mobile homes 15 February - 15 November.

Directions

Leave A8 at Le Muy exit on N7 towards Fréjus. Go on for 9 km. then right onto D7 signed St Ayguif. Continue for 8 km. and then right at roundabout on D8; site is on the right.
GPS: N43:24.547 E06:40.481

Charges 2008

Per unit incl. 2 persons and electricity (6A)	€ 18,50 - € 40,00
2 persons and electricity, water and drainage	€ 24,00 - € 45,00
extra person	€ 5,00 - € 9,00
child (under 7 yrs)	€ 3,60 - € 6,50
electricity (10A)	€ 2,00 - € 3,00

FR83060 **Camping Resort la Baume – la Palmeraie**

Route de Bagnols, F-83618 Fréjus (Var)

Tel: **04 94 19 88 88**. Email: **reception@labaume-lapalmeraie.com**

La Baume is large, busy site about 5.5 km. from the long sandy beach of Fréjus-Plage, although with its fine and varied selection of swimming pools many people do not bother to make the trip. The pools with their palm trees are remarkable for their size and variety (water slides, etc.) – the very large 'feature' pool a highlight. Recent additions are an aquatic play area and two indoor pools with a slide and a spa area. The site has nearly 250 adequately sized, fully serviced pitches, with some separators and most have shade. Although tents are accepted, the site concentrates mainly on caravanning. It becomes full in season. Adjoining La Baume is its sister site La Palmeraie, providing self-catering accommodation, its own landscaped pool and offering some entertainment to supplement that at La Baume. There are 500 large pitches with mains sewerage for mobile homes. La Baume's convenient location has its 'downside' as there is some traffic noise on a few pitches from the nearby autoroute – somewhat obtrusive at first but we soon failed to notice it. It is a popular site with tour operators.

Facilities

Seven refurbished toilet blocks. Supermarket, several shops. Two bars, terrace overlooking pools, TV. Restaurant, takeaway. Six swimming pools (heated all season, two covered, plus steam room and jacuzzi). Fitness centre. Tennis. Archery (July/Aug). Organised events, daytime and evening entertainment, some English. Amphitheatre. Skateboard park. Discos all season. Children's club (all season). Off site: Bus to Fréjus passes gate. Riding 2 km. Fishing 3 km. Golf 5 km. Beach 5 km.

Open: 1 April - 30 September, with full services.

Directions

From west, A8, exit Fréjus, take N7 southwest (Fréjus). After 4 km, turn left on D4 and site is 3 km. From east, A8, exit 38 Fréjus and follow signs for Cais. Site is signed. GPS: N43:27.599 E06:43.229

Charges 2007

Per unit incl. 2 persons, 6A electricity, water and drainage	€ 18,00 - € 39,00
extra person	€ 4,00 - € 10,00
child (under 7 yrs)	free - € 6,00
dog	€ 4,00 - € 5,00
car	€ 4,00 - € 5,00

Min. stay for motorhomes 3 nights.
Large units should book.

FR83010 **Camping Caravaning les Pins Parasols**

Route de Bagnols, F-83600 Fréjus (Var)

Tel: **04 94 40 88 43**. Email: **lespinsparasols@wanadoo.fr**

Not everyone likes very big sites and Les Pins Parasols with its 189 pitches is of a comfortable size which is quite easy to walk around. It is family owned and run. Although on very slightly undulating ground, virtually all the pitches (all have electricity) are levelled or terraced and separated by hedges or bushes with pine trees for shade. There are 48 pitches equipped with their own fully enclosed, sanitary unit, with WC, washbasin, hot shower and dishwashing sink. These pitches naturally cost more but may well be of interest to those seeking extra comfort. The nearest beach is the once very long Fréjus-Plage (5.5 km) now reduced a little by the new marina, and adjoins St Raphaël. Used by tour operators (10%).

Facilities

Average quality toilet blocks (one heated) providing facilities for disabled people. Small shop with reasonable stocks, restaurant, takeaway (both 15/4-30/9). General room, TV. Swimming pool, attractive rock backdrop, separate long slide with landing pool, small paddling pool (heated). Half-court tennis. Off site: Bicycle hire or riding 2 km. Fishing 6 km. Golf 10 km. Bus from the gate into Fréjus 5 km. Beach 6 km.

Open: 5 April - 27 September.

Directions

From A8 take exit 38 for Fréjus Est. Turn right immediately on leaving pay booths on a small road which leads across to D4, then right again and under 1 km. to site.

Charges 2007

Per unit incl. 2 persons and electricity	€ 17,40 - € 26,10
pitch with sanitary unit	€ 22,00 - € 32,50
extra person	€ 4,40 - € 6,10
child (under 7 yrs)	€ 2,90 - € 3,70
dog	€ 1,80 - € 2,70

La Baume ★★★★
Camping - Caravaning

La Palmeraie ★★
Résidence de Tourisme

Fréjus Côte d'Azur

eated sanitary blocks, marked-out
ches, 6 swimming pools, covered
ated swimming pool, 6 water-slides.
kilometers from the sandy beaches of
éjus and Saint Raphaël.

On going entertainment
Cabaret, Show, Disco,
Children's club during the season

Le Sud Grandeur Nature

Heated swimming pool

1 covered
heated
swimming-pool

Provençal chalet,
mobil-homes 4/6 persons
and appartments 6 of 10 persons for hire

ecial rates in low season

FR83200 Kawan Village les Pêcheurs

F-83520 Roquebrune-sur-Argens (Var)

Tel: **04 94 45 71 25**. Email: **info@camping-les-pecheurs.com**

Les Pêcheurs will appeal to families who appreciate natural surroundings together with many activities, cultural and sporting. Interspersed with mobile homes, the 150 good sized touring pitches (electricity 6/10A) are separated by trees or flowering bushes. The Provencal style buildings are delightful, especially the bar, restaurant and games room, with its terrace down to the river and the site's own canoe station (locked gate). Across the road is a lake used exclusively for water skiing with a sandy beach, a restaurant and minigolf. This popular Riviera site has some new spa facilities including steam pool and sauna. Developed over three generations by the Simoncini family, this peaceful, friendly site is set in more than four hectares of mature, well shaded countryside at the foot of the Roquebrune Rock. Activities include climbing the 'Rock' with a guide. We become more and more intrigued with stories about the Rock and the Holy Hole, the Three Crosses and the Hermit all call for further exploration which reception staff are happy to arrange, likewise trips to Monte Carlo, Ventimigua (Italy) and the Gorges du Verdon, etc. The medieval village of Roquebrune is within walking distance.

Facilities

Modern, refurbished, well designed toilet blocks, baby baths, facilities for disabled visitors. Washing machines. Shop. Bar, restaurant, games room (all open all season). Heated outdoor swimming pool (all season), separate paddling pool (lifeguard in high season), ice cream bar. Spa facilities. Playing field. Fishing. Canoeing, water skiing. Activities for children and adults (high season), visits to local wine caves. Rafting and diving schools. Only gas or electric barbecues. WiFi in reception, bar/restaurant and pool area. Off site: Bicycle hire 1 km. Riding 5 km. Golf 5 km. (reduced fees).

Open: 1 April - 30 September.

Directions

From A8 take Le Muy exit, follow N7 towards Fréjus for 13 km. bypassing Le Muy. After crossing A8, turn right at roundabout towards Roquebrune-sur-Argens. Site is on left after 1 km. just before bridge over river.

Charges 2008

Per unit incl. 2 persons and electricity	€ 22,00 - € 40,00
incl. 3 persons	€ 24,50 - € 42,50
extra person	€ 4,00 - € 6,70
child (5-10 yrs)	€ 3,20 - € 5,50
dog (max. 1)	€ 3,10

Camping Cheques accepted.

FR83220 Kawan Village Cros de Mouton

P.O. 116, F-83240 Cavalaire-sur-Mer (Var)

Tel: 04 94 64 10 87. Email: campingcrosdemouton@wanadoo.fr

Cros de Mouton is a reasonably priced campsite in a popular area. High on a steep hillside, about 2 km. from Cavalaire and its popular beaches, the site is a calm oasis away from the coast. There are stunning views of the bay but, due to the nature of the terrain, some of the site roads are very steep (the higher pitches with the best views are especially so). There are 199 large, terraced pitches (electricity 10A) under cork trees with 73 suitable only for tents with parking close by, and 80 for touring caravans. English is spoken by the welcoming and helpful owners. The restaurant terrace and the pools share the wonderful view of Cavalaire and the bay. Olivier and Andre are happy to take your caravan up with their 4 x 4 Jeep if you are worried.

Facilities

Clean, well maintained toilet blocks have all the usual facilities including those for disabled customers (although site is perhaps a little steep in places for wheelchairs). Washing machine. Shop. Bar/restaurant, reasonably priced meals, takeaways. Swimming and paddling pools with lots of sun beds on the terrace and small bar for snacks and cold drinks. Small play area. Games room. Off site: Beach 1.5 km. Bicycle hire 1.5 km. Riding 3 km. Golf 15 km.

Open: 15 March - 9 November.

Directions

Take the D559 to Cavalaire-sur-Mer (not Cavalière 4 km. away). Site is about 1.5 km. north of the town, very well signed from the centre. GPS: N43:10.933 E06:30.966

Charges 2008

Per person	€ 6,30 - € 7,90
child (under 7 yrs)	€ 4,10 - € 4,30
pitch	€ 6,30 - € 7,90
electricity (10A)	€ 4,10 - € 4,50
dog	free - € 2,00

Camping Cheques accepted.

FR83240 Camping Caravaning Moulin des Iscles

Quartier La Valette, F-83520 Roquebrune-sur-Argens (Var)

Tel: 04 94 45 70 74. Email: moulin.iscles@wanadoo.fr

Moulin des Iscles is a small, pretty site beside the river Argens with access to the river in places for fishing, canoeing and swimming with some sought after pitches overlooking the river. The 90 grassy, level pitches have water and electricity (6A), A nice mixture of deciduous trees provides natural shade and colour and the old mill house is near the entrance, which has the security barrier closed at night. This is a quiet site with little on site entertainment, but with a pleasant restaurant. Handicapped visitors are made very welcome. It is a real campsite not a 'camping village'. A haven of peace and tranquillity, Moulin des Iscles is hidden down 500 m. of private, unmade road – an unusual find in this often quite hectic part of Provence. It is based around a former mill. The pitches radiate out from M. Dumarcet's attractive home which is where the restaurant and shop are situated.

Facilities

Fully equipped toilet block, plus small block near entrance, ramped access for disabled visitors. Some Turkish style toilets. Washbasins have cold water. Baby bath and changing facilities. Washing machine. Restaurant, home cooked dish-of-the-day. Well stocked shop. Library - some English books. TV, pool table, table tennis. Play area, minigolf, boules all outside the barrier. Internet terminal. Canoeing possible. Off site: Riding and golf 4 km. Bicycle hire 1 km. (cycle way to St Aygulf). Beach 9 km.

Open: 1 April - 30 September.

Directions

From A8, exit Le Muy, follow N7 towards Fréjus for 13 km. Cross over A8 and turn right at roundabout through Roquebrune sur Argens towards St Aygulf for 1 km. Site signed on left. Follow private unmade road for 500 m. GPS: N43:26.708 E06:39.470

Charges 2007

Per unit incl. 2 or 3 persons	€ 19,80
extra person	€ 3,20
electricity	€ 2,70

Camping Cheques accepted.

FR20040 Riva Bella Nature Resort & Spa

B.P. 21, F-20270 Alèria (Haute-Corse)

Tel: 04 95 38 81 10. Email: riva-bella@wanadoo.fr

This is a relaxed, informal, spacious naturist site alongside an extremely long and beautiful beach. Riva Bella is naturist camping at its very best, with great amenities. It offers a variety of pitches, situated in beautiful countryside and seaside. The site is divided into several areas with 200 pitches and bungalows, some alongside the sandy beach with little shade, others in a wooded glade with ample shade. The huge fish-laden lakes are a fine feature of this site. Although electricity is available in most parts, a long cable may be needed. The ground is fairly flat with terracing for tents. There is a 'balneotherapy' centre with the very latest beauty and relaxation treatments based on marine techniques (men and women). The owner Marie Claire Pasqual is justifiably proud of the site and the fairly unobtrusive rules are designed to ensure that everyone is able to relax, whilst preserving the natural beauty of the environment. There is, for example, a restriction on the movement of cars in certain areas (but ample free parking). An excellent naturist site.

Facilities

High standard toilet facilities. Provision for disabled people, children and babies. Laundry. Large shop (1/5-18/10). Fridge hire. Restaurant with lake views (all season) with reasonable prices. Excellent beach/snack bar. Bar. Watersports, sailing school, fishing, sub-aqua. Balneotherapy centre. Sauna. Volleyball, aerobics, table tennis, giant draughts, archery. Fishing. Mountain bike hire. Half-court tennis. Walk with llamas. Internet. WiFi. Professional evening entertainment programme. Off site: Riding 2 km.

Open: 1 April - 1 November.

Directions

Site is 12 km. north of Aleria on N198 (Bastia) road. Watch for large signs and unmade road to site and follow for 4 km.

Charges 2007

Per unit incl. 2 persons	€ 17,00 - € 32,50
extra person	€ 4,00 - € 8,50
child (3-8 yrs)	€ 2,00 - € 5,00
dog	€ 3,00 - € 3,00

Special offers and half-board arrangements available. Camping Cheques accepted.

Check real time availability and at-the-gate prices...

 www.alanrogers.com

FR20010 Camping Arinella Bianca

Route de la Mer, F-20240 Ghisonaccia (Haute-Corse)

Tel: **04 95 56 04 78**. Email: **arinella@arinellabianca.com**

Arinella is a lively, family oriented site on Corsica's east coast. The 415 level, grassy, good size, irregular shape pitches (198 for touring units) have a variety of trees and shrubs providing ample shade and 6A electricity (long leads needed). Some pitches overlook the attractive lakes which have fountains and are lit at night. The site has direct acess to a huge long beach of soft sand. The brilliantly designed resort style pools and paddling pool, overlooked by an attractive large restaurant, terraced bar and entertainment area, form the hub of Arinella Bianca. When we visited the area was buzzing with activity at night and appeared to delight everyone by incorporating excellent family entertainment. The extremely active children's club with an information point, boutique and supermarket complete the area. A huge range of sport and leisure facilities is also available. Evening entertainment starts at 21.00. Unfortunately a local disco can continue until the early hours. This site is a tribute to its owner's design and development skills as it appears to be in entirely natural glades where, in fact, these have been created from former marshland with a fresh water lake.

Facilities

Four open plan sanitary blocks provide showers, (some with dressing area), washbasins in cabins, mainly British style WCs. Open air dishwashing areas. Laundry, washing machines, ironing boards. Motorcaravan services. Shop, bar, terrace, restaurant, amphitheatre, snack bar (all 10/5-15/9). Swimming pool (from 1/5). Windsurfing. Canoeing. Fishing. Tennis. Riding. Children's miniclub. Play area. Disco. Good entertainment programme in the main season. Communal barbecue area. Off site: Sailing 500 m. Boat launching 2 km.

Open: Mid April - 30 September.

Directions

Site is 4 km. east of Ghisonaccia. From N198 in Ghisonaccia look for sign 'La Plage, Li Mare'. Turn east on D144 at roundabout just south of town. Continue for 3.5 km. to further roundabout where site is signed to right. Site is 500 m. Watch for speed bumps on approach road and on site.

Charges 2007

Per unit incl. 2 persons	€ 21,00 - € 36,00
extra person	€ 7,00 - € 9,80
electricity (6A)	€ 4,20

Camping Cheques accepted.

195

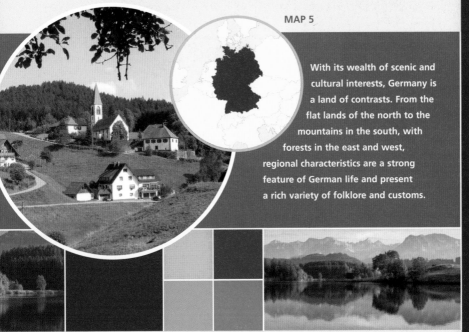

MAP 5

Germany

With its wealth of scenic and cultural interests, Germany is a land of contrasts. From the flat lands of the north to the mountains in the south, with forests in the east and west, regional characteristics are a strong feature of German life and present a rich variety of folklore and customs.

CAPITAL: BERLIN

Tourist Office

German National Tourist Office
PO Box 2695. London W1A 3TN
Tel: 020 7317 0908
Fax: 020 7495 6129
Email: gntolon@d-z-t.com
Internet: www.germany-tourism.co.uk

Each region in Germany differs greatly to the next. Home of lederhosen, beer and sausages is Bavaria in the south, full of charming forest villages, beautiful lakes, and towering mountains dotted with castles. In the southwest, Baden Württemberg is famous for its ancient Black Forest, with dense woodlands, medieval towns and scenic lakes, this region is a walker's paradise. Further west is the stunningly beautiful, Rhine Valley full of romantic castles, wine villages, woodland walks and river trails. Eastern Germany is studded with lakes and rivers, undulating lowlands that give way to mountains. The north has its lively ports such as Bremen and Hamburg and picturesque coastal towns, where watersports are a popular pastime in the North Sea. The capital city of Berlin, situated in the northeast of the county, is an increasingly popular tourist destination, with its blend of old and modern architecture and huge variety of entertainment on offer.

Population

83.2 million

Climate

Temperate climate. In general winters are a little colder and summers a little warmer than in the UK.

Language

German

Telephone

The country code is 00 49.

Money

Currency: The Euro
Banks: Mon-Fri 08.30-12.30 and 14.00-16.00. Late opening on Thurs until 18.00.

Shops

Mon-Fri 08.30/09.00 to 18.00/18.30.

Public Holidays

New Year's Day; Good Fri; Easter Mon; Labour Day; Ascension; Whit Mon; Unification Day 3 Oct; Christmas, 25, 26 Dec. In some areas: Epiphany 6 Jan; Corpus Christi 22 Jun; Assumption 15 Aug; Reformation 31 Oct; All Saints 1 Nov (plus other regional days).

Motoring

An excellent network of (toll-free) motorways (autobahns) exists in the 'West' and the traffic moves fast. Remember in the 'East' a lot of road building is going on amongst other works so allow plenty of time when travelling and be prepared for poor road surfaces.

DE3005 Camping Schnelsen Nord

Wunderbrunnen 2, D-22457 Hamburg (Hamburg)

Tel: **040 559 4225**. Email: **service@campingplatz-hamburg.de**

Situated some 15 km. from the centre of Hamburg on the northern edge of the town, Schnelsen Nord is a suitable base either for visiting this famous German city, or as a night stop before catching the Harwich ferry or travelling to Denmark. There is some traffic noise as the autobahn runs alongside (despite efforts to screen it out) and also some aircraft noise. However, the proximity of the A7 (E45) does make it easy to find. The 145 grass pitches for short-term touring are of about 100 sq.m. All have 6A electricity and are marked out with small trees and hedges.

Facilities

A deposit is required for the key to the single sanitary block, a well constructed modern building with good quality facilities and heated in cool weather. Good facilities for disabled visitors, with special pitches close to the block. Washing machines and dryers. Motorcaravan service point (for site guests only). Shop (basics only). Playground. Off site: Bus service, restaurants and shops 10 minutes walk. Swimming pool, tennis, golf and fishing.

Open: 1 April - 31 October.

Directions

From A7 autobahn take Schnelsen Nord exit. Stay in outside lane as you will soon need to turn back left; follow signs for Ikea store and site signs. GPS: N53:38.998 E09:55.736

Charges 2007

Per person	€ 6,00
child (3-13 yrs)	€ 3,50
pitch	€ 7,20 - € 11,50
electricity (6A)	€ 2,50

DE3010 Kur und Feriencamping Röders Park

Ebsmoor 8, D-29614 Soltau (Lower Saxony)

Tel: **051 912 141**. Email: **info@roeders-park.de**

Although near Soltau centre (1.5 km), Ebsmoor is a peaceful location, ideal for visits to the famous Luneburg Heath or as a stop on the route to Denmark. The site is run by the third generation of the Röders family who make their visitors most welcome and speak excellent English. There are 100 pitches (90 touring), all with 6A electricity and 85 with water and drainage. Some 40 pitches have satellite TV connections. Most have hardstanding and there is reasonable privacy between pitches. The central feature of the wooded site is a small lake crossed by a wooden bridge.

Facilities

Two modern, very clean sanitary blocks (one with under-floor heating) contain all necessary facilities. Excellent, separate unit (including shower) for wheelchair users. Private bathrooms for rent. Laundry room. Motorcaravan services. Gas supplies. Simple shop. Restaurant and takeaway (all Easter - Oct). Play area. Bicycle hire. Internet (free), WiFi (on payment). Off site: Thermal swimming pool 1 km. Fishing and riding 1.5 km. Golf 3 km. Bus service 100 m.

Open: All year.

Directions

From Soltau take B3 road north and turning to site is on left after 1.5 km. (opposite DCC camping sign) at yellow town boundary sign. GPS: N53:00.133 E09:50.317

Charges 2007

Per person	€ 5,50
child (4-14 yrs)	€ 4,00
pitch	€ 11,50

DE3021 Camping am Stadtwaldsee

Hochschulring 1, D-28359 Bremen (Bremen)

Tel: **042 184 10748**. Email: **contact@camping-stadtwaldsee.de**

This well designed and purpose built campsite overlooking a lake was opened in October 2005 and is ideally placed for those travelling to northern Europe and for people wishing to visit Bremen and places within the region. There is a bus stop outside the site. Of the 220 level pitches 168 are for touring units, standing on grass with openwork reinforcements at the entrances. All have electricity (16A), water and drainage. The pitches are positioned around the grass roofed sanitary block and are laid out in areas separated by young trees and hedges.

Facilities

Modern sanitary block with free hot showers, facilities for disabled people, five private bathrooms for rental. Washing machines and dryers. Kitchen. Children's play room. Lakeside café/restaurant. Small supermarket. Health centre with fitness courses. Play area. Lake swimming, FKK beach three minutes walk away. Windsurfing, fishing and scuba diving. Off site: Riding 8 km. Golf 10 km.

Open: All year.

Directions

From A27 northeast of Bremen take exit 19 for 'Universitat' and follow signs for University and camping. Site is on the left 1 km. after leaving the university area. GPS: N53:06.890 E08:49.948

Charges 2007

Per person	€ 6,50 - € 7,50
child (3-14 yrs)	€ 3,50 - € 4,50
caravan or motorcaravan	
with electricity (per kWh)	€ 9,00 - € 10,00

DE3025 Alfsee Ferien- und Erholungspark

Am Campingpark 10, D-49597 Rieste (Lower Saxony)

Tel: **054 649 2120**. Email: **info@alfsee.com**

Alfsee has plenty to offer for the active family and children of all ages. It is a really good base for enjoying the many watersports activities available here on the two lakes. The smaller one has a 780 m. water-ski 'tug' ski lift style (on payment) and there is also a separate swimming area here with a sandy beach. Improvements to this already well-equipped site continue. There are now over 800 pitches (many long stay but with 400 for tourers) on flat grass, 85 with 16A electricity, with some shade for those in the original area. A new camping area provides 290 large, serviced pitches. A little further along is a 600 m. go-kart track and a smaller track for youngsters. The Alfsee itself is a very large stretch of water with a sailing school, windsurfing, motor boats, row boats, canoes and pedaloes as well as fishing and a café/restaurant open daily. Member of Leading Campings Group.

Facilities

Three excellent sanitary blocks serve the original area with two new first class, heated buildings with family bathrooms (to rent), baby rooms and laundry facilities. Cooking facilities. Motorcaravan services. Gas supplies. Shop, restaurants and takeaway (high season). Pub (all year) with internet point. Watersports. Football practice field. Playground, new indoor play centre and entertainment for children. Entertainment hall. Grass tennis courts. Trampoline. Minigolf. Go-kart track. Games room with amusement machines. Fishing. Bicycle hire. Riding. Off site: Golf 10 km. Bus service 500 m.

Open: All year.

Directions

From A1 autobahn north of Osnabrück take exit 67 for Neuenkirchen and follow signs for Rieste, Alfsee and site. GPS: N52:29.158 E07:59.529

Charges 2007

Per person	€ 3,20 - € 6,20
child or student	€ 2,90 - € 4,20
pitch	€ 8,10 - € 12,50
electricity (once only, plus meter)	€ 1,00

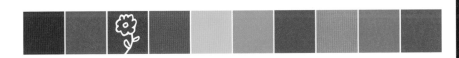

DE3055 Camping Prahljust

Lange Brüche 4, D-38678 Clausthal-Zellerfeld (Lower Saxony)

Tel: **053 231 300**. Email: **camping@prahljust.de**

In a woodland setting, 600 metres high and well away from main roads Camping Prahljust is a quiet site providing plenty of fresh air in an attractive location. The site slopes gently down to a lake which is used for swimming, boating, windsurfing and fishing or in winter ice skating. Of the 800 plus pitches 500 are reserved for tourists. These are arranged in larger open, grass areas separated by hedges with plenty of tree cover and all have electrical connections. The Oberharz is a winter sports region and January and February are the busiest months, with cross-country skiing from the site. During the rest of the year this attractive region has much to offer, rambling, mountain-biking and rock climbing are all popular and the list of interesting places to visit is almost unending. Early mining activity brought wealth to the region resulting in the development of many beautiful medieval towns with their half-timbered houses and impressive public buildings. The reception has a good selection of brochures on display; however the best tourist advice comes from the campsite owner, Rheinhardt Struve, who speaks excellent English.

Facilities

Three modern, heated toilet blocks are well maintained and hold all the usual facilities. Showers are free. Facilities for disabled people. Baby room. Washing machines, dryers, drying room and kitchen. Motorcaravan service point and chemical disposal facilities. Shop, restaurant and bar (closed November). Indoor, heated swimming pool (12 x 9 m; no shallow end). Sauna and solarium. Massage. Internet access. Fishing. Bicycle hire. Off site: Bus service 1.5 km. Riding 5 km.

Open: All year.

Directions

Leave Clausthal-Zellerfeld on the B242 towards Braunlage. After 1 km. site is signed. Turn south and site is a further 1.5 km. GPS: N51:47.066 E10:20.985

Charges 2007

Per person	€ 4,70
child	€ 4,20
pitch	€ 4,80
electricity (per kWh)	€ 0,55

Winter charges higher.
Camping Cheques accepted.

199

DE3065 Camping am Bärenbache

Bärenbachweg 10, Hohegeiss, D-38700 Braunlage (Lower Saxony)

Tel: 055 831 306. Email: info@campingplatz-hohegeiss.de

Pleasantly situated and over 600 metres high in the Harz, Campingplatz Bärenbache is a quiet, attractive, well run family site having direct access to the forests that surround it. This terraced site on a south facing slope reaps the maximum benefit from the sun throughout the year and offers views of the surrounding hills in an area known for its fresh air. Of the 140 pitches 90 are reserved for tourists all having 10A electrical connections. The level pitches are separated by hedges and are of various sizes, some suitable for one, others for several units. At the lower end of the site is a large, heated, outdoor swimming pool complex adjoined by a bar/restaurant. The Harz is a region steeped in geological, mythical, industrial and cultural history and the reception has a good selection of tourist information. In addition, the site owners are only too happy to give tourist advice. Roses, rambling, narrow gauge railways, witches, mines, mineral collections and medieval towns such as Goslar, all have their place in this fascinating region.

Facilities

As can be expected in a site that also has a winter season, all facilities are housed internally in the modern, well maintained and heated toilet block. Showers are free. Baby room. Washing machines, dryers and iron, drying room. Small kitchen with cooking rings. Bread to order. Bar/restaurant (all year) beside the pool. Large outdoor heated pool with two separate pools for children. Small playground. Bicycle hire. Off site: Village centre is only a few minutes walk. Riding 3 km. Fishing 10 km.

Open: All year.

Directions

The village of Hohegeiß is 10 km. southeast of Braunlage on the B4 road. Leaving Hohegeiss in the direction of Zorge, site is signed. Turn left before leaving village, 250 m. from the main road. GPS: N51:39.220 E10:40.080

Charges 2007

Per person	€ 4,30 - € 5,00
child (3-14 yrs)	€ 3,10 - € 3,50
pitch	€ 4,90
electricity (per kWh)	€ 0,53

DE3070 Südsee-Camp

Lindhorstforst 104, D-29649 Wietzendorf (Lower Saxony)

Tel: 051 969 80 116. Email: forst104@suedseecamp.de

Südsee-Camp in the Lüneburger Heide is a large well organised holiday centre where children are especially well catered for. Südsee has its own brochures that include walking, cycling and car tours. There are 1,100 touring pitches of varying types and sizes, all with electricity and most with fresh water, drainage and TV connection. Modern sanitary blocks are well maintained and contain all necessary facilities, including some areas specially built for children. Although centred around a large sandy shored lake, complete with shipwreck, the main swimming attraction is the South Sea Tropical swimming pool. This large, well designed glass roofed complex, has pools of different sizes with slides, whirlpools and a pirate ship, as well as a sauna, steam bath, sun benches and roof terrace. Adjoining is an outdoor pool. There is a full range of entertainment facilities and programmes for children of all ages. The campsite organises excursions to many interesting locations within the region. A riding school is adjacent to the site. Reception has a wide range of tourist information brochures and good English is spoken with the staff only too happy to help and advise. Member of Leading Campings Group.

Facilities

Thirteen, modern well maintained sanitary blocks with all the expected facilities, including facilities for disabled people and private bathrooms to rent. Hot showers need a token. Special areas for children ('Kinderland'), facilities for babies. Laundry rooms. Kitchens. Choice of bars, restaurants and snack bars. Tropical pool complex (on payment). Sound-proof disco. Fitness room. Bicycle and pedal car hire. Children's games room. Internet room. Off site: Riding adjacent. Fishing 2 km. Golf 10 km.

Open: All year.

Directions

From A7 autobahn take exit 45 towards Bergen and Celle on the B3 (campsite is signed). After 6 km. turn left (site again signed). GPS: N52:55.540 E09:57.550

Charges 2007

Per unit incl. 2 persons	€ 19,00 - € 34,50
extra person	€ 3,50 - € 4,50
child (2-18 yrs)	€ 2,00 - € 3,50
electricity (4-10A)	€ 1,50 - € 2,50

DE3080 Campingplatz am Hardausee

D-29556 Suderburg/Hosseringen (Lower Saxony)

Tel: 058 267 676. Email: info@camping-hardausee.de

The Hardausee site is evolving from a 'seasonal only' site into a site for touring units. When we visited, there were 80 touring pitches and 270 seasonal units, but as soon as a seasonal guest leaves, the pitch will be reallocated for touring. Hardausee is on sloping ground although the grassy, marked pitches are mostly level. Some pitches are numbered and most are 100 sq.m. or larger. The newer pitches have hardly any shade, but mature trees surround the older field. There are 45 serviced pitches with 16A electricity, water and drainage. It is an easy 300 m. walk to the Hardausee.

Facilities

Three heated toilet blocks provide washbasins in cabins and free, controllable hot showers. Washing machines and dryer. Motorcaravan services. Shop (for basics). Bar, restaurant and takeaway (April - Oct, closed Mondays). Large adventure playground. Cycling tours and excursions in the woods. Fishing. Lakeside beach. Off site: Bus service 200 m. Riding 1 km. Bicycle hire 300 m.

Open: All year.

Directions

From Uelzen, follow 4/191 road south towards Braunschweig. Take exit for Suderburg and follow signs for Hösseringen. Site is signed on the right 2 km. before Hösseringen. GPS: N52:52.475 E10:28.475

Charges 2007

Per person	€ 5,00
child (under 14 yrs)	€ 2,50
pitch incl. electricity	€ 5,00 - € 8,00

No credit cards.

DE3030 Regenbogen-Camp Tecklenburg

Grafenstrasse 31, D-49545 Tecklenburg-Leeden (North Rhine-Westphalia)

Tel: 054 051 007. Email: tecklenburg@regenbogen-camp.de

This is a well designed and attractive countryside site with lots of trees and hedges where modern buildings have been built in keeping with the traditional, half-timbered style of the region. There are 500 grass touring pitches arranged on large, open areas divided by tall hedges. Trees provide good shade and all pitches have electrical connections. Access from the A30 autobahn is convenient, although this is offset by the fact that some noise from the autobahn is evident in the touring pitch area. Facilities on this site are really good and include a modern pool complex and a bar/restaurant.

Facilities

Four modern, heated toilet blocks have free showers and provision for disabled visitors. Washing machines and dryer. Cooking facilities. Motorcaravan service point. Shop. Large traditional, timbered bar and restaurant (Easter - end Oct and Christmas). Excellent heated pool complex with indoor and outdoor pools, slide and paddling pool. Large play area. Minigolf. Off site: Riding 3 km. Golf 5 km. Fishing 6 km.

Open: All year.

Directions

Leave A30/E30 autobahn at exit 13 towards Tecklenburg. Between the autobahn exit and Tecklenburg, the site is signed at a roundabout. Leeden is a village to the east of Tecklenburg, site is 2 km. from the village.

Charges 2007

Per person	€ 6,30 - € 7,95
child (6-13 yrs)	€ 2,60 - € 3,10
pitch incl. electricity	€ 10,80 - € 16,50

DE3180 Camping Sonnenwiese

Borlefzen 1, D-32602 Vlotho (North Rhine-Westphalia)

Tel: 057 338 217. Email: info@sonnenwiese.com

Sonnenwiese is a first class, family run campsite where care has been taken to make everyone feel at home – there is even an insect hotel! The site is tastefully landscaped with lots of flowers, an ornamental pond crossed by a wooden bridge and large grass areas extending to the river. Situated between wooded hills and bordering the Weser river, this 400 pitch site offers 100 touring pitches, all with electricity and most also having water and drainage. There are special pitches with a private shower, toilet and washbasin unit. The site is particularly orientated towards families with children.

Facilities

The toilet block is modern and maintained to the highest standard. Showers are token operated. Baby room. Washing machines, dryer and ironing board. Cooking facilities. Supermarket. Panorama restaurant with good choice of dishes. Snack bar. Sauna, solarium and fitness room. Club room and room used for children's entertainment. Large adventure play area. Grass bordered lake for swimming. Fishing. Bicycle hire. Off site: Bus service from gate. Golf 4 km. Riding 5 km.

Open: All year.

Directions

Leave A2 autobahn at exit 31, 32 or 33 and head for Vlotho. In Vlotho, cross the Weser river and after 3 km. on the right are the entrances to two campsites. Sonnenwiese is on the left at the end of the entrance road. GPS: N52:10.250 E08:54.240

Charges 2007

Per person	€ 4,60
pitch	€ 8,00 - € 9,60
electricity (plus 0.40 kWh)	€ 0,50

No credit cards.

DE3182 Ferienpark Teutoburger Wald

Badeanstaltsweg 4, D-32683 Barntrup (North Rhine-Westphalia)

Tel: **052 632 221**. Email: **info@ferienparkteutoburgerwald.de**

Now under Dutch ownership, Ferienpark Teutoburger Wald is a long-established site which is rapidly undergoing redevelopment into a top-class site. The new toilet block has an ingenious system for water disposal, roomy showers and an attractive children's section. The site has 100 touring pitches, all 100-200 sq.m. and with 16A electricity. There are 8 with water, waste water and cable TV (Dutch and German channels) and a super new area with 9 fully serviced pitches. Although the site is on steep ground, most pitches are on level, grassy areas, with some shade from mature trees. Within walking distance of the site are the castle and attractive market square of Barntrup. This whole area thrives on the famous fairy tale about Hameln (every Sunday there is the 'Rattenfängerspiel' in Hameln). The Teutoburger Wald is an excellent area for walking and biking and the site has many maps available.

Facilities

Excellent, new heated toilet block with roomy showers (key) and open washbasins. Children's section. Family shower rooms (extra payment). Baby room. Facilities for disabled visitors planned. Dishwasher. Laundry facilities. Bread to order. Games room with TV and internet access. WiFi. Animation (high season). Children's disco. Walking tours. Chalets for rent. Off site: Tennis. Outdoor pool just outside gate. Mountain bike trails. Bad Pyrmont 12 km.

Open: 20 March - 30 September.

Directions

From Hanover, take the A2 west towards Osnabrück. At exit 35 continue on B83 road towards Hameln. In Hameln take the B1 road south towards Barntrup and follow signs. GPS: N51:59.209 E09:06.508

Charges 2007

Per pitch incl. 2 persons	
and electricity	€ 17,50 - € 23,00
incl. services	€ 25,00 - € 32,00
extra person	€ 4,75

DE3185 Campingplatz Münster

Laerer Werseufer 7, (Wolbecker Strasse), D-48157 Münster (North Rhine-Westphalia)

Tel: **025 131 1982**. Email: **campingplatz-muenster@t-online.de**

This is a first class site on the outskirts of Münster. Of a total of 570 pitches, 120 are touring units, each with electricity, water, drainage and TV socket. The pitches are level, most with partial hardstanding and others are separated into groups by mature hedges and a number of trees provide shade. The university city of Münster with its historical buildings and over 500 bars and restaurants, many offering local traditional dishes, is only 5 km. from the site. The city is the main attraction in this region and well worth visiting, especially on market days (Wednesdays and Saturdays). In the campsite reception there is a large range of tourist brochures, many in English, full of useful tips. Next to the reception desk is a small shop and adjacent is a comfortable bar/restaurant with a terrace. Bicycles are available for hire and there are cycle tour maps for the area. Just outside the campsite there is a bus stop. For those who wish to avoid the stress of driving in busy foreign cities and the even worse problem of finding a parking place, public transport offers a good solution.

Facilities

The two toilet blocks are well designed, modern and maintained to the highest standards. Controllable showers are token operated. Two units for disabled guests. Baby room. Cooking facilities. Laundry facilities. Sauna and solarium. Hairdressing salon. Motorcaravan service point. Shop. Bar/restaurant. Minigolf. Play area. Chess. Tennis. Playroom (under 8 yrs). Bicycle hire. Security barrier card deposit € 10. Off site: Public open air swimming pool adjacent. Canoeing and fishing. Bus stop 100 m.

Open: All year.

Directions

Site is 5 km. southeast of Münster city centre. Leave A1 autobahn at exit 78 (Münster Süd) and take B51 towards Münster. After 2 km. stay on the B51 in the direction of Bielefeld/Warendorf. After 5 km. turn south (right) towards Wolbeck. Follow site signs. GPS: N51:56.784 E07:41.467

Charges 2007

Per unit incl. 2 persons	
and electricity (1 night)	€ 24,00
extra person	€ 5,00

DE3202 Erholungszentrum Grav-Insel

Gravinsel 1, D-46487 Wesel (North Rhine-Westphalia)
Tel: 028 197 2830. Email: info@grav-insel.com

Grav-Insel claims to be the biggest family camping site in Germany, providing entertainment and activities to match, with over 2,000 permanent units as well as those for touring. It is a well maintained site, attractively situated on an island in the Rhine and is a good base for swimming (with a sandy beach by a quiet inlet), fishing and boating (with a boat park). A section for the touring units runs beside the water to the left of the entrance. The 500 pitches here are flat, grassy, mostly without shade and of about 100 sq.m. There are electricity boxes with multiple outlets (10/16A). A brand new building behind the modern reception is enormous and houses excellent sanitary facilities including some for disabled visitors, a restaurant with wheelchair access, terraces for a snack bar and ices, play rooms (including a large area for wet weather play) and a supermarket. However, these amenities are a long walk from some of the touring pitches. This is a busy, well managed site where the small zoo adds to the holiday atmosphere.

Facilities

Excellent, new sanitary facilities, augmented by older, very basic portacabin units in the touring area. Baby room. Launderette. Solarium. Supermarket (hours acc. to season). Restaurant (all year). Fishing. Swimming. Large play area on sand plus wet weather indoor area. Animation in high season. Boat park. Sailing. Off site: Bus service 500 m. The town of Xanten (reached by passenger ferry 5 km. north of site). Nord Park Duisburg, where an old steelworks has been turned into a leisure complex.

Open: All year.

Directions

Site is 5 km. WNW of the town of Wesel. From the A3 take exit 6 and B58 towards Wesel, then right towards Rees. Turn left at sign for Flüren, through Flüren and left to site after 1.5 km. If approaching Wesel from the west (B58), cross the Rhein, turn left at first traffic lights and follow signs Grav Insel and Flüren. GPS: N51:40.237 E06:33.360

Charges 2007

Per person	€ 2,00 - € 3,00
pitch incl. electricity	€ 6,00 - € 9,50

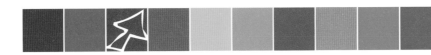

DE3205 Campingplatz der Stadt Köln

Weidenweg 35, D-51105 Köln-Poll (North Rhine-Westphalia)
Tel: 022 183 1966. Email: die-eckardts@netcologne.de

The ancient city of Cologne offers much for the visitor. This wooded park is pleasantly situated along the river bank, with wide grass areas (the manager takes great pains to keep it well) on either side of narrow tarmac access roads with low metal barriers separating it from the public park and riverside walks. Of 140 unmarked, level or slightly undulating touring pitches, 50 have 10A electricity and there is shade for some from various mature trees. Tents have their own large area. Because of its position close to the autobahn bridge over the Rhine, there is road and river noise. However, when we stayed the location and friendly atmosphere generated by the Eckhardt family, who have managed the site for 15 years, more than made up for it. Cologne has many museums (including the popular Museum of Chocolate), art galleries, opera and open-air concerts, as well as the famous Cathedral. The 'Phantasialand' theme park is close by at Brühl and the zoo and Rhine cruises are among other attractions.

Facilities

The small toilet block has fairly basic facilities, but is heated with free hot water (06.00-12.00, 17.00-23.00) in the washing troughs and by token in the showers. New facilities for disabled visitors. There is a large open-fronted room where you may cook and eat. Washing machine and dryer. Small shop for bread and basic supplies (mid May-Sept). Microwave evening snacks (March-Oct). Fishing. Bicycle hire. Drinks machine. Off site: Bar/café by entrance. Trams and buses to city centre 1 km. across the bridge. Golf 5 km. Riding 15 km.

Open: Easter - 17 October.

Directions

Leave A4 at exit 13 for Köln-Poll (just to west off intersection of A3 and A4). Turn left at first traffic lights and follow international site signs through a sometimes fairly narrow one-way system to the riverside, back towards the motorway bridge. GPS: N50:54.163 E06:59.440

Charges 2007

Per person	€ 5,50
child (4-12 yrs)	€ 3,00
pitch incl. car	€ 5,00 - € 6,50
electricity	€ 1,50

DE3210 Feriencamp Biggesee – Vier Jarheszeiten

Am Sonderner Kopf 3, D-57462 Olpe-Sondern (North Rhine-Westphalia)

Tel: 027 619 44111. Email: info@biggesee-sondern.com

Biggesee-Sondern is a high quality leisure complex and campsite, in an attractive setting on the shores of a large lake in the Südsauerland National Park, offering many leisure opportunities, as well as excellent camping facilities. It is therefore deservedly popular, and reservation is almost always advisable. There are 300 flat or sloping numbered pitches of 100 sq.m, of which about 250 are available for tourists, either in rows or in circles, on terraces, with 6A electricity and water points grouped throughout. The site is well managed, the same company also operating two other sites on the shores of the lake. Space may be available at these sites, which is useful as this area is also popular for short stays, being quite near the A45 and A4 roads. The leisure activities available are numerous. Watersports include diving, sailing and windsurfing, with lessons available. You may launch your own small boat, and also swim from the shore in a roped-off area.

Facilities

Excellent sanitary facilities are in two areas, heated when necessary (bring your own paper). Many washbasins in cabins and special showers for children. Facilities for babies and people with disabilities. Laundry. Motorcaravan services. Car wash area. Cooking facilities. Playroom and playground for smaller children. Skiing. Watersports. Walks around the lake. Fishing. Bicycle hire. Solarium and sauna. Entertainment and excursions. Off site: Train service 1 km. Tennis near. Riding 8 km. Golf 12 km. Restaurant and snacks 300 m. (Easter - 31/10).

Open: All year.

Directions

From A45 (Siegen-Hagen) autobahn, take exit 18 to Olpe (N), and turn towards Attendorn. After 6 km. turn right signed 'Erholungsanlage', then in another 100 m. turn right and follow site signs. GPS: N51:04.438 E07:51.390

Charges 2007

Per person	€ 4,05 - € 4,65
child (3-15 yrs)	€ 2,50 - € 2,60
pitch incl. electricity	€ 12,40 - € 14,45
dog	€ 2,50

No credit cards.

DE3002 Camping Park Schlei-Karschau

Karschau 56, D-24407 Rabenkirchen-Faulück (Schleswig-Holstein)

Tel: 046 429 20820. Email: info@campingpark-schlei.de

Schlei-Karschau is a pleasant, quiet site on the only Baltic Sea fjord in Germany. All you will hear is the wind from the sea and the calls of the birds. This site is ideal if you enjoy fishing or sailing, or you could visit one of the beaches on this coast, just 10 km. further on. The site has 160 open pitches, 100 for touring units, all with at least 6A electricity. There is no shop as yet, but bread can be ordered from a kiosk, and a restaurant with a bar and takeaway is open in high season. Students provide an entertainment programme for children in high season with painting and crafts for toddlers and sporting events for older youngsters. There is no evening entertainment for adults but, after a hard day fighting with large fish or sails at sea you may prefer to relax in the restaurant or bar. Relaxing in front of your caravan or tent is another possibility – you are likely to see many rabbits passing by.

Facilities

The single sanitary block includes controllable hot showers in cabins with washbasin, child size toilets and washbasins and facilities for disabled visitors. Washing machines and dryers. Campers' kitchen with fridge. Motorcaravan services. Restaurant and bar (daily in high season). New playground. Sports field. Children's activity programme six days a week in high season. River fishing (permits from reception). Bicycle hire. Motor boat hire. Off site: Golf 4 km. Riding 6 km. Beach 10 km.

Open: All year.

Directions

Follow the A7 from Hamburg north to Flensburg. Take exit Schleswig - Schuby onto B201 road towards Kappeln. Drive through Süderbrarup and turn right 5 km. after village to Faulück. Follow signs to site. GPS: N54:37.176 E09:53.049

Charges 2007

Per person	€ 4,00 - € 5,00
child (1-16 yrs)	€ 2,00 - € 3,00
pitch	€ 7,00 - € 9,00
electricity and water	€ 3,00
pet	€ 2,00

Discount (5-15%) for senior campers.
Camping Cheques accepted.

DE3003 Camping Wulfener Hals

D-23769 Wulfen auf Fehmarn (Schleswig-Holstein)

Tel: 043 718 6280. Email: camping@wulfenerhals.de

If you are travelling to Denmark or on to Sweden, taking the E47/A1 then B207 from Hamburg, and the ferry from Puttgarden to Rødbyhavn, this is a top class all year round site, either to rest overnight or as a base for a longer stay. Attractively situated by the sea, it is a large, mature site (34 hectares) and is well maintained. It has over 800 individual pitches of up to 160 sq.m. (half for touring) in glades and some separated by bushes, with shade in the older parts, less in the newer areas nearer the sea. There are many hardstandings and 552 pitches have electricity, water and drainage. A separate area has been developed for motorcaravans. It provides 60 extra-large pitches, all with electricity, water and drainage, and some with TV aerial points, together with a new toilet block. There is much to do for old and young alike at Wolfener Hals, with a new heated outdoor pool and paddling pool (unsupervised), although the sea is naturally popular as well. The site also has many sporting facilities including its own golf courses and schools for watersports. Member of the Leading Campings Group.

Facilities

Five heated sanitary buildings have first class facilities including showers on payment (€ 0.50) and both open washbasins and private cabins. Family bathrooms for rent. Facilities for disabled people. Laundry. Motorcaravan services. Shop, bar, restaurants and takeaway (all year). Swimming pool (May - Oct). Sauna. Solarium. Jacuzzi. Sailing, windsurfing and diving schools. Boat slipway. Golf courses (18 hole, par 72 and 9 hole, par 27). Riding. Fishing. Archery. Good play equipment for younger children. Bicycle hire. Catamaran hire. Only small dogs are accepted. Off site: Naturist beach 500 m. Village mini-market 2 km.

Open: All year.

Directions

From Hamburg take A1/E47 north to Puttgarden, cross the bridge onto the island of Fehmarn and turn right twice to Avendorf and follow the signs for Wulfen and the site. GPS: N54:24.386 E11:10.575

Charges 2007

Per unit incl. 2 persons	€ 11,60 - € 36,00
child (3-14 yrs)	€ 2,10 - € 5,30
electricity (6/10A)	€ 2,10 - € 2,90
water and drainage	€ 1,50
dog	€ 1,00 - € 7,50

Plus surcharges for larger pitches.
Many discounts available and special family prices.

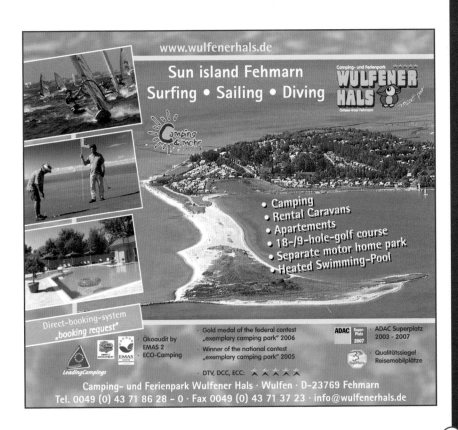

DE3008 Klüthseecamp Seeblick

Klüthseehof 2, D-23795 Klein Rönnau (Schleswig-Holstein)

Tel: 045 518 2368. Email: info@kluethseecamp.de

Klüthseecamp Seeblick is a modern, family run site situated on a small hill between two lakes. For those travelling on the A1 to Denmark it is a convenient overnight site, but additionally it is a useful base to explore the region. The large, open grass, touring part of the site is divided into smaller areas by some low hedges and young trees. There are 120 pitches on fairly level ground, all with electricity (10/16A) and 70 with water and drain. The site has two other parts, one accommodating permanent campers, the other for those who prefer camping in natural surroundings.

Facilities

Two cheerful, modern, heated sanitary blocks have washbasins (open or in cabins), six bathrooms to rent and free controllable showers. Facilities for disabled visitors. Attractive baby room. Gas supplies. Laundry room. Sauna (Finish and Bio) steam bath, massage. TV room with projector. Children's play room. Bicycle hire. Minigolf. Off site: Golf 6 km. Beach 25 km.

Open: All year.

Directions

Leave A1, exit 27, north towards Kiel on the A21 to exit 13 (Bad Segeberg Sud). Follow B432 (Hamburger Strasse) into Bad Segeberg and at T-junction with Ziegelstrasse turn left and continue on B432. 300 m. after Klein Rönnau turn right into Stripsdorferweg. Site signed. GPS: N53:57.661 E10:20.289

Charges 2008

Per person	€ 5,50
pitch incl. electricity	€ 8,00 - € 10,80

No credit cards.

DE3827 Camping Sanssouci-Gaisberg

An der Pirschheide, Templiner See 41, D-14471 Potsdam (Brandenburg)

Tel: 033 195 10988. Email: info@recra.de

Sanssouci is an excellent base for visiting Potsdam and Berlin, about 2 km. from Sanssouci Park on the banks of the Templiner See in a quiet woodland setting. Looking very attractive, reflecting the effort which has been put into its development, with modern reception, shop, takeaway, restaurant and bar. Of the 240 pitches, around 90 are seasonal but all the 150 touring pitches have electricity (6/10A), many also with their own water tap and drain. Tall trees mark out the tourist pitches, and access is good for larger units. There is a separate area for tents by the lake.

Facilities

Top class sanitary facilities are in two excellent, heated blocks containing hot showers, washbasins in cabins and facilities for babies. Very good facility for wheelchair users. New building with bathrooms to rent, kitchen, hairdresser and solarium. Laundry. Gas supplies. Motorcaravan services. Restaurant/bar. Shop. Boats for hire. Fishing. Swimming in the lake. Play area. Bicycle hire. Internet café and WiFi. Public transport tickets and discounts for many Berlin attractions. Off site: Leisure facilities at the Hotel Semiramis. Riding 3 km. Golf 10 km.

Open: 1 April - 4 November.

Directions

From A10 take Potsdam exit 22, follow B1 to within 4 km. of city centre then sign to right for site just before railway bridge. Or A10 exit 17 on the B2 into town and follow signs for Brandenburg and Werder. Site is southwest of Sanssouci Park. GPS: N52:21.514 E13:00.380

Charges 2007

Per person	€ 9,30
pitch incl. electricity	€ 8,90

Special low season offers. No credit cards.

DE3812 Seecamping Flessenow

Am Schweriner See 1A, D-19067 Flessenow (Mecklenburg-West Pomerania)

Tel: 038 668 1491. Email: info@seecamping.de

Seecamping Flessenow is owned and run by an enthusiastic, young Dutch couple. It is on the banks of the Schwerinner See and makes an ideal base for a beach holiday or for an active holiday on the water. There are 250 pitches (170 for touring units), arranged on two rectangular fields to one side of a hardcore access lane (which can become muddy with heavy rain) and on a newer field to the rear of the site. Some pitches have views over the lake and these have some shade from mature trees.

Facilities

Three toilet blocks (one older style) with open washbasins and controllable hot showers (token from reception). Baby room with shower. Washing machine and dryer. Motorcaravan services. Kiosk and takeaway (April - Oct; bread to order). Playground. TV room. Lake with beach. Fishing. Watersports. Riding. Bicycle hire. Boat launching. Sailing. Off site: Golf 20 km.

Open: April - October.

Directions

From Schwerin, take the A14 road north along the east side of the lake. At Schwerin Nord turn west towards Rampe and then north on a minor road towards Flessenow. Site is signed from there. GPS: N53:45.110 E11:19.780

Charges 2007

Per unit incl. 2 persons	€ 14,00 - € 22,00
electricity	€ 2,00

DE3820 Camping Park Havelberge am Woblitzsee

D-17237 Groß Quassow (Mecklenburg-West Pomerania)

Tel: 039 812 4790. Email: info@haveltourist.de

The Müritz National Park is a very large area of lakes and marshes, popular for birdwatching as well as watersports, and Havelberge is a large, well-equipped site to use as a base for enjoying the area. It is quite steep in places here with many terraces, most with shade, less in newer areas, with views over the lake. There are 400 pitches in total with 300 good sized, numbered touring pitches most with 10A electrical connections and 60 pitches on a newly developed area to the rear of the site with water and drainage. Pitches on the new field are level and separated by low hedges and bushes but have no shade. Over 170 seasonal pitches with a number of attractive chalets and an equal number of mobile homes in a separate areas. In the high season this is a busy park with lots going on to entertain families of all ages, whilst in the low seasons this is a peaceful base for exploring an unspoilt area of nature. Member of Leading Campings Group.

Facilities

Four sanitary buildings (one new and of a very high standard) provide very good facilities, with private cabins, showers on payment and large children's section. Fully equipped kitchen and laundry. Motorcaravan service point. Small shop and modern restaurant (April-October). The lake provides fishing, swimming from a small beach and non-powered boats can be launched - canoes, rowing boats, windsurfers and bikes can be hired. Play areas and animation in high season. Internet access. Off site: Riding 3.5 km.

Open: All year.

Directions

From A19 Rostock - Berlin road take exit 18 and follow B198 to Wesenberg and go left to Klein Quassow and follow site signs.
GPS: N53:18.310 E13:00.080

Charges 2008

Per person	€ 4,00 - € 6,30
child (2-14 yrs)	€ 2,70 - € 4,20
caravan and car	€ 6,90 - € 12,00

DE3833 Camping & Freizeitpark LuxOase

Arnsdorfer Strasse 1, Kleinröhrsdorf, D-01900 Dresden (Saxony)

Tel: **035 952 56666**. Email: **info@luxoase.de**

This is a pleasantly situated new park about half an hour from the centre of Dresden, in a very peaceful location with good facilities. It is owned and run by a progressive young family. On open grassland with views across the lake (access to which is through a gate in the site fence) to the woods and low hills beyond, this is a sun-trap with little shade at present. There are 138 large touring pitches (plus 50 seasonal in a separate area), marked by bushes or posts on generally flat or slightly sloping grass. All have 10/16A electricity and 100 have water and drainage. At the entrance is an area of hardstanding (with electricity) for late arrivals. The main entrance building houses the amenities and in front of the building is some very modern play equipment on bark. You may swim, fish or use inflatables in the lake. A wide animation program is organised for children in high season. There are many interesting places to visit apart from Dresden and Meissen, with the fascinating National Park Sächsische Schweiz (Saxon Switzerland) on the border with the Czech Republic offering some spectacular scenery. Boat trips on the Danube can be taken from the tourist centres of Königstein and Bad Schandau and Saxony is also famous for its many old castles, for which an English language guide is available. Bus trips organised to Prague. Member of Leading Campings Group.

Facilities

A well equipped building provides modern, heated facilities with private cabins, a family room, baby room, units for disabled visitors and two units for hire. Jacuzzi. Kitchen. Gas supplies. Motorcaravan services. Shop. Bar and restaurant (Apr - Oct). Bicycle hire. Lake swimming. Sports field. Fishing. Play area. Sauna. Train, bus and theatre tickets from reception. Internet point. Minigolf. Fitness room. Regular guided bus trips to Dresden, Prague etc. Off site: Riding next door (lessons available). Public transport to Dresden 1 km. Golf 7.5 km. Nearby Dinosaur park, zoo and indoor karting etc.

Open: 1 March - 7 November (phone in winter).

Directions

From A4 (Dresden - Görlitz) take exit 85 towards Radeberg, soon following signs to site via Leppersdorf and Kleinröhrsdorf.
GPS: N51:07.130 E13:58.480

Charges 2007

Per person	€ 5,00 - € 6,00
child (3-15 yrs)	€ 2,50 - € 4,00
motorcaravan or caravan/car	€ 7,50 - € 8,00
tent	€ 7,00 - € 7,50
electricity	€ 2,00

Various special offers in low season.

We are right in the middle:
Dresden- Elbsandstone-Mountains...

Familie Lux,
01900 Kleinröhrs-
dorf / Dresden
email: info@luxoase.de
www.luxoase.de
GPS: North 51° 07' 13",
East 13° 58' 48"

superb sanitary facilities - sauna - whirl-pool - minigolf - playgrounds - animation - fitnessroom - shop - sportfacilities - public transport nearby - swimming in the lake - roomy plots (>100 sqm, power/ water/sewage - horse riding - restaurant - organised bus-trips - new: W-LAN !

DE3836 Waldcamping Erzgebirgsblick

An der Dittersdorfer Höhe, D-09439 Amtsberg (Saxony)

Tel: **037 177 50833**. Email: **info@waldcamping-erzgebirge.de**

The Scheibner family first thought of opening a campsite when touring Canada in 1998, so it is not surprising to find reminders of their trip appearing in the site's buildings with pictures and Canadian names. They found their spot on land once belonging to the Stasi, the East German secret police, and turned it into a well kept and welcoming campsite. It has 90 touring pitches. either under mature pine trees in the woods or on open ground, partly separated by low bushes and shrubs, in front of reception and the sanitary block. All have 16A electricity and there are 12 with electricity, water, drainage and hardstanding.

Facilities

Excellent sanitary facilities with British style toilets, free, controllable hot showers and washbasins (1 cabin each for men and women). Washbasin and toilet for children. Baby room. Bathroom for rent. Washing machines, dryers, iron and board. Fully equipped kitchen, including fridge and dishwasher. Small shop in reception (bread to order). Lounge with dining table, TV and library. Playground. Bicycle hire. Small outdoor paddling pool. Off site: Fishing 5 km. Golf 5 km. Riding 2 km.

Open: All year.

Directions

From Chemnitz, take the B174 southeast towards Gronau. Site is well signed in Amtsberg, off the B174. Take care on the steep roads and the bumpy access road (which is only 100 m).
GPS: N50:45.960 E13:00.869

Charges 2008

Per person	€ 5,00
child (0-11 yrs)	free - € 11,00
pitch	€ 5,00 - € 7,00
electricity	€ 1,00

Necessary for Christmas and Whitsun.
No credit cards.

DE3847 Campingplatz Auensee

Gustav-Esche Strasse 5, D-04159 Leipzig (Saxony)

Tel: **034 146 51600**. Email: **info@camping-auensee.de**

It is unusual to find a good site in a city, but this large, neat and tidy site is one. It is far enough away from roads and the airport to be reasonably peaceful during the day and very quiet overnight and has 168 pitches, all for short-term tourers. It is set in a mainly open area with tall trees and attractive flower beds, with some chalets and 'trekker' huts for rent in the adjoining woodland, home to shoe-stealing foxes. The individual, numbered, flat grassy pitches are large (at least 100 sq.m), all with 16A electricity and five on hardstanding, arranged in several sections.

Facilities

Five sanitary buildings (mind your head if you are over 6 feet tall) have differing mixtures of equipment. Many washbasins in cabins and showers on payment (token). Well equipped rooms for babies and disabled visitors. Kitchen and laundry rooms. Motorcaravan service point. Bar/restaurant and snack bar. Entertainment rooms. Multisports court. Play areas. Bicycle hire. Barbecue area. Fishing. Off site: Public transport to the city centre every 10 minutes. Bicycle hire 6 km. Boat launching 12 km.

Open: All year.

Directions

Site is signed 3 km. from Leipzig centre on the B6 to Halle. From the A9 Berlin - Nurnberg take exit 16 at Schkeuditz onto the B6 towards Leipzig. Turn right to Auensee 3 km. before the centre of the town (just after the Church, if you pass the station you are too far). GPS: N51:22.185 E12:18.840

Charges 2007

Per person	€ 4,50
child (6-17 yrs)	€ 2,50 - € 3,50
pitch incl. car	€ 5,50 - € 10,00

DE3855 Oberhof Camping Oberhof

Am Stausee 09, D-99330 Frankenhain (Thuringia)

Tel: **036 205 76518**. Email: **info@oberhofcamping.de**

Beside a lake, at an altitude of 700 metres and quietly hidden in the middle of the Thüringer forest, Camping Oberhof has seen many changes since the departure of its former owners, the East German secret police. There are 150 touring pitches, all have 16A electricity and 100 with water and drainage. Access is now via a tarmac road replacing the former steeply descending forest track. From this fairly open site there are views of the surrounding forests and of the lake which is bordered by wide grass areas ideal for a picnic or for just lazing around and enjoying the view.

Facilities

New heated sanitary block with all usual facilities including free hot water, plus 15 bathrooms to rent. Facilities for disabled people. Baby room. Laundry. Motorcaravan services. Gas sales. Modern reception building with shop and attractive restaurant serving traditional dishes. Shop. TV room. Children's club room. Play area. On the lake: fishing (licence required), swimming and boating. Off site: Over 100 km. of way-marked paths from site. Bus 1.5 km. Riding 5 km.

Open: All year.

Directions

From A4 autobahn between Eisenach and Dresden take exit 42 (Gotha). Travel south on the B247 to Ohrdruf, then the B88 to Crawinkel and then Frankenhain. In Frankenhain follow Lütsche Stausee and Campingpark signs. GPS: N50:44.020 E10:45.400

Charges 2007

Per person	€ 6,00
pitch incl. electricity	€ 8,00
Camping Cheques accepted.	

DE3850 Camping Strandbad Aga

Reichenbacherstrasse 14, D-07554 Gera-Aga (Thuringia)

Tel: **036 695 20209**. Email: **info@campingplatz-strandbad-aga.de**

Strandbad Aga is a useful night stop near the A4/A9 and is within reach of Dresden, Leipzig and Meissen. It is situated in open countryside on the edge of a small lake, with 350 individual, fenced pitches, mostly fairly level, without shade. The 200 touring pitches all have 16A electricity – for stays of more than a couple of days, over-nighters being placed on an open area. The lake is used for swimming, boating and fishing (very popular with day visitors at weekends and with a separate naturist area) and there is a small playground on one side (close to a deep part of the lake).

Facilities

The sanitary building has some washbasins in cabins and hot showers on payment. Large (4 x 4 m.) room for wheelchair users. Laundry facilities. Motorcaravan services. Modern restaurant/bar open long hours. High season kiosk for drinks, ice creams, etc. Playground. Small lake used for inflatables, fishing, swimming and watersports. Entertainment in high season. Off site: Football 200 m. Shop in village (200 m). Riding and tennis 1 km.

Open: All year.

Directions

From A4/E40 Chemnitz - Erfurt autobahn take Gera exit (no. 58) then the B2 towards Zeitz, following Bad Köstritz signs at first then site signs. GPS: N50:57.232 E12:05.210

Charges 2007

Per person	€ 4,00
pitch incl. car	€ 6,00 - € 7,50
electricity plus meter	€ 1,50
No credit cards.	

DE3605 Camping Rangau

Campingstrasse 44, D-91056 Erlangen-Dechsendorf (Bavaria (N))

Tel: 091 358 866. Email: infos@camping-rangau.de

Run by the same family for many years now, this site makes a convenient stopover, quickly and easily reached from the A3 Würzburg - Nürnberg and A73 Bamberg - Nürnberg autobahns and is pleasant enough to stay a bit longer. It has 110 pitches which are mainly for tourists on flat ground, under trees, numbered and partly marked but only about 60-80 sq.m. so it can look cramped when busy. There are also 60 permanent units. There is usually space and, in peak season, overnight visitors can often be put on the adjacent football pitch.

Facilities

A satisfactory sanitary block, heated when cold, has well spaced washbasins (some cabins for ladies) and showers. Good facilities for disabled visitors. A new facility provides washbasins in cabins and WCs. Laundry facilities. Motorcaravan services. Gas supplies. Restaurant with terrace. Order bread from reception. Playground. Club/TV room Off site: Swimming 200 m. Erlangen centre 5 km.

Open: 1 April - 30 September.

Directions

Take exit for Erlangen-West from A3 autobahn, turn towards Erlangen but after less than 1 km. at Dechsendorf turn left and follow to site (site signed).

Charges 2007

Per person	€ 5,00
child (6-12 yrs)	€ 3,00
pitch incl. electricity (6A)	€ 7,00
dog	€ 2,00

DE3610 Knaus Campingpark Nürnberg

Hans Kalb Strasse 56, D-90471 Nürnberg (Bavaria (N))

Tel: 091 198 12717. Email: nuernberg@knauscamp.de

This is an ideal site for visiting the fascinating and historically important city of Nürnberg. There are 160 shaded pitches, 118 with 10A electrical connections and with water taps in groups. On mainly flat grass among the tall trees, some pitches are marked out with 'ranch' style boards, others still attractively 'wild', some others with hardstanding. There is sufficient space for them to be quite big and many have the advantage of being drive through. When there is an event at the Stadion there is a lot of noise and road diversions are in place. It is well worth checking before planning an arrival.

Facilities

A brand new heated sanitary building offers first class facilities including free showers. Washing machines and dryers. Cooking facilities. Unit for disabled visitors. Gas supplies. Motorcaravan services. Shop. Bar/bistro area with terrace and light meals served. Play area in woodland. Tennis. Large screen TV. Off site: Swimming pool (free entry for campers) and football stadium 200 m. Boat launching 2 km. City centre 4 km. (a 20 minute walk following signs takes you to the underground station).

Open: All year.

Directions

From the A9 (München - Bayreuth) east of Nürnberg, take Nürnberg-Fischbach exit. Proceed 3 km. on dual carriageway towards city then left at first traffic lights. From city follow 'Stadion-Messe' signs and site is well signed. The entrance road is not obvious. It is opposite a large office block and the sign 'Knaus Campingpark Zufahrt' is quite close to the ground. GPS: N49:25.389 E11:07.280

Charges 2007

Per person	€ 6,00
pitch incl. electricity	€ 12,50 - € 4,00
No credit cards.	

DE3625 Knaus Campingpark Frickenhausen

Ochsenfurter Strasse 49, D-97252 Frickenhausen (Bavaria (N))

Tel: 093 313 171. Email: frickenhausen@knauscamp.de

This is a pleasant riverside site with good facilities just south of Würzburg, situated towards the northern end of the 'Romantische Strasse' and not far from the A3 Frankfurt to Nürnberg. There are 115 fair sized, numbered touring pitches on generally flat grass, arranged in sections leading from tarred access roads with flowers around. Most have 6-16A electricity connections. About 80 long stay places are mostly separate nearer the river.

Facilities

Modernised, heated, sanitary facilities have washbasins (some private cabins) and dishwashing sinks. Laundry and cooking facilities. Gas supplies. Restaurant, café/wine bar and shop (1/12-31/10, weekends only in low season). Bread to order. Club room. TV. Small, free swimming pool (1/5-31/10). Play area on river island. Open air theatre. Bicycle hire. Fishing. Boat marina. Off site: Swimming pool 300 m. Riding 1 km. Golf and boat launching 15 km.

Open: All year excl. November.

Directions

From the A3 at Würzburg, take exit 71 (Ochsenfurt) and continue on the B13 towards Ochsenfurt and Ansbach. Do not cross the Main into town but follow signs for Frickenhausen and site which is shortly on the right. GPS: N49:40.176 E10:09.480

Charges 2007

Per person	€ 6,00
pitch with electricity	€ 8,00 - € 17,00
No credit cards.	

DE3632 Azur Camping Altmühltal

Am Festplatz 3, D-85110 Kipfenberg (Bavaria (N))

Tel: 084 659 05167. Email: kipfenberg@azur-camping.de

In the beautiful Altmühltal river valley, this Azur site is in pretty woodland, with lots of shade for much of it. On flat grassland with direct access to the river, one looks from the entrance across to the old Schloss on the hill. Outside the main entrance is a large, flat, grass/gravel field for 60 overnight tourers (with electricity). The main site has 277 pitches, of which 178 are for touring, plus two small areas for tents and one large one (at the end in an open area). Ranging in size up to 90 sq.m. they are generally in small groups marked by trees or bushes.

Facilities

The main sanitary facilities are good, with free hot water (no private cabins), baby room, unit for disabled visitors. Launderette. Kitchen with ovens and cooking rings. These facilities are mostly duplicated 'portacabin' style at the other end of the site (toilets only in low season). Motorcaravan services. Shop. Beer garden and snacks in July/Aug. Play area. Fishing. Off site: Bus service 50 m. Supermarket 100 m. Two restaurants within 300 m. Outdoor pool 200 m. Bicycle and canoe hire in town.

Open: All year.

Directions

From the A9/E45 (Munich - Nürnberg), take exit 59 Denkendorf or 58 Eichstätt and follow the signs to Kipfenberg. GPS: N48:56.904 E11:23.360

Charges guide

Per person	€ 5,50 - € 7,50
child (2-12 yrs)	€ 4,00 - € 6,00
pitch	€ 6,00 - € 9,00
electricity	€ 2,50
Camping Cheques accepted.	

DE3710 Azur Ferienpark Bayerischer Wald

Waldesruhweg 34, D-94227 Zwiesel (Bavaria (N))

Tel: 099 228 02595. Email: zwiesel@azur-camping.de

Bayerischerwald is a large site on the edge of town with views to the hills and a stream running through it. Pleasantly situated nearly 2,000 feet up (it can be cool at night) on a slight slope, there are around 500 pitches, just under 400 of which are individual numbered ones for tourers, but there is not much shade. There are various areas, with motorcaravans taken on a flat open, grassy section, whilst for caravans there are some flat and many sloping or undulating pitches, all with electricity (some 10A Euro, most 16A German) and water points along the central roadway.

Facilities

The two tiled sanitary blocks (one part-modernised) have some private cabins. Facilities for disabled visitors. Baby room. Bread orders at reception. Pleasant restaurant/bar (not open November). Laundry facilities. Off site: Indoor and outdoor pools adjacent. Ski lifts nearby.

Open: All year.

Directions

Site is on north side of Zwiesel. From autobahn A3 Regensburg-Passau, take Deggendorf exit and then B11 to Zwiesel. Take Zwiesel Nord exit and follow Azur signs. GPS: N49:01.530 E13:13.240

Charges 2007

Per person	€ 5,00 - € 6,50
pitch	€ 5,50 - € 7,00
No credit cards.	
Camping Cheques accepted.	

DE3739 Camping Katzenkopf

Am See, D-97334 Sommerach am Main (Bavaria (N))

Tel: 093 819 215

This is an excellent family run site, on the banks of the Main to the east of Wurzburg. For peace and quiet this site is likely to be at the top of the list. There are 270 pitches with some 170 for touring units. All pitches have electricity (6-16A) and 13 provide electricity, water, and drainage. English is spoken at reception which also houses a shop and good tourist information. Wurzburg is an important commercial and cultural centre that was substantially destroyed by bombing and has risen again from the ashes. The town is the home of the excellent Franconian wine.

Facilities

Excellent, modern toilet blocks include private cabins, free showers and facilities for disabled people and children. Laundry facilities. Motorcaravan service point. Shop, restaurant, bar and takeaway (all open all season). Fishing. Boat launching. Sailing courses. Dogs accepted in part of the site only. Off site: Sailing. Shops and vineyards.

Open: 31 March - 28 October.

Directions

From the A3 take Kitzingen exit and turn towards Schwarzach. After 4 km. turn right towards Sommerach. Just before the village turn left and site is well signed. GPS: N49:49.551 E10:12.334

Charges 2007

Per person	€ 5,70 - € 5,90
child (2-14 yrs)	€ 3,00 - € 3,30
pitch incl. electricity	€ 7,40 - € 8,40
No credit cards.	

DE3735 Spessart-Camping Schönrain

Schönrainstrasse 4-18, D-97737 Gemünden-Hofstetten (Bavaria (N))

Tel: **093 518 645**. Email: **info@spessart-camping.de**

Situated a short distance from the town of Gemünden, with views of forested hills beside the Main river, this is a very friendly, family run site, with excellent facilities. Frau Endres welcomes British guests and speaks a little English. There are 200 pitches, half of which are for touring. They vary in size from 70-150 sq.m. and most have 10A electricity, 20 also with water. Another area has been developed for tents. The site has an outdoor pool open from Whitsun to the end of September. A pleasant small restaurant and bar and a shop are on site with the local full-bodied Franconian wine and schnapps for sale. There are opportunities for walking and riding in the adjacent woods, excursions are organised in the main season and it is possible to hire a bicycle, ride to Würzburg and catch the pleasure boat back, or take a combined bus and cycle ride. Fishing and boating are both very popular in the locality.

Facilities

A superb new sanitary building has card operated entry – the card is pre-paid and operates the showers, washing machines and dryers, coffee machine, gas cooker, baby bathroom, jacuzzi etc. Two private bathrooms (complete with wine and balcony!) for rent. Motorcaravan services. General room with sections for very young children, a pool table and arcade games and a TV. Upstairs is a library and internet café, fitness room and solarium. Bar/restaurant (closed Tuesdays). Shop. Swimming pool. Playground. Bicycle hire. Excursions. New 'Beauty and Wellness' programme. Off site: Bus service 200 m. Menus for local restaurants held in reception with booking service and transport provided. Fishing 400 m. Canoeing, cycling and walking nearby. Drop off/pick up service for cyclists.

Open: 1 April - 30 September.

Directions

From Frankfurt - Würzburg autobahn, take Weibersbrunn-Lohr exit and then B26 to Gemünden. Turn over Main river bridge to Hofstetten. From Kassel - Wurzburg autobahn, leave at Hammelburg and take B27 to Gemünden, and as above.

Charges 2007

Per person	€ 6,10
child (under 14 yrs)	€ 3,80
pitch	€ 4,50 - € 10,30

Less 10% for stays over 14 days in mid and low seasons.

★★★★★
Spessart-Camping
Schönrain
www.spessart-camping.de

New: extensive beauty- and wellness program

In the heart of the MAIN SPESSART holiday area the ideal base for day trips, walks, cycling in the "Spessart Nature Park", the "Rhön Nature Park" and the "Fränkische Wine Area".

Experience & enjoy
a camping holiday with real comfort

Our camping ground is recommended as one of the most beautiful camping grounds of the region by leading camping guides, equipped with: ★ large pitches ★ outdoor swimming pool ★ solarium ★ whirlpool ★ family bath rooms ★ steam shower ★ fitness room ★ baby bath ★ campsite library and reading room ★ surfing point for Internetfreaks ★ playground ★ youth-, TV- and multipurpose room ★ cyclists transport service ★ shuttle-bus ★ bicycle hiring out ★ and many more
in the area: Gardens, castles, historic towns and villages to visit. Fishing, tennis, bowling and many other sports activities.

Spessart-Camping Schönrain, 97737 Gemünden Ortsteil Hofstetten
Tel. +49 (0)9351- 8645   info@spessart-camping.de   Fax +49 (0)9351- 8721

DE3750 Camping Schloss Issigau

Schloss Issigau, D-95188 Issigau (Bavaria (N))
Tel: 092 937 173. Email: info@schloss-issigau.de

This is an attractive, small family run site with very good facilities and of a type not often found in Germany with less than 50 pitches, all for tourers. Situated in northeast Bavaria, on the edge of a pretty village from where there are views of the surrounding fields and woods. Entering a large grass courtyard there are several sections, part terraced and with some old trees giving a little shade in places. As you go through the site it opens up to a largish, sloping tent area beside the small ponds, beyond which is a new play area. There are 45 pitches, around half individual and ranging up to 120 sq.m. All have 16A electricity, three also have water and waste water drain. There is a delightful café/bar and restaurant in the interesting old 'Schloss' (circa 1398 – a large fortified house is how we might describe it) with a museum of old armour.

Facilities

Satisfactory heated sanitary facilities are in an old building with some modern fittings and some washbasins in cabins. Laundry facilities. Baby room. Delightful café/bar and restaurant (open daily 12.00 - 22.00). Games room. Hotel accommodation. Off site: Bus service and small supermarket 300 m. Riding 1.5 km. Fishing 6 km. Golf 10 km. The Naturpark Frankenwald is on the doorstep to the southwest.

Open: 15 March - 31 October, 18 December - 9 January.

Directions

The village of Issigau is between Holle and Berg. From A9 (Berlin - Nürnberg) take exit 31 Berg/Bad Steben. Turn left and follow signs for Berg and then continue straight on towards Holle. Site is signed in Issigau. Go down a small slope and to the right (narrow in places). GPS: N50:22.451 E11:43.273

Charges 2008

Per person	€ 4,50
child (4-14 yrs)	€ 2,50
caravan or motorcaravan	€ 6,00
tent	€ 5,00 - € 6,00
dog	€ 1,50

DE3630 Camping Donau-Lech

Campingweg 1, D-86698 Eggelstetten (Bavaria (S))
Tel: 090 904 046. Email: info@donau-lech-camping.de

The Haas family have developed this friendly site just off the attractive 'Romantische Strasse' well and run it very much as a family site, providing a useful information sheet in English for their guests. The lake provides swimming and wildlife for children and adults to enjoy. Alongside it are 50 marked touring pitches with 16A electrical connections, on flat grass arranged in rows either side of a tarred access road. With an average of 120 sq.m. per unit, it is a comfortable site with an open feeling and developing shade. There are three pleasant, flat, grass areas near the entrance for people with tents with unmarked pitches. Long stay pitches are located beyond the tourers. Suitable not only as a night stop on the way south, the site is also not far from Augsburg and Munich. From the local railway station (3 km.) a family railcard costs about € 24 for both main line services and Munich city transport system.

Facilities

All amenities are housed in the main building at the entrance with reception. Sanitary facilities are downstairs with free showers and washbasins (no cabins), all of a good standard. Sauna. Washing machine and dryer. Motorcaravan services. Large area with terrace. Small shop for basics, bread to order (1/4-31/10). General room. Youth room. Play area. Health studio with massage, manicure and pedicure. Lake for swimming (own risk). Off site: Larger lake used for sailboarding 400 m. Golf course and driving range 1 km. Fishing 3 km. Restaurants and other amenities a short drive.

Open: All year excl. November.

Directions

Turn off main B2 road at site sign, about 5 km. south of Donauwörth at signs for Asbach-Bäumenheim Nord towards Eggelstetten, then follow signs for over 1 km. to site. GPS: N48:40.554 E10:50.450

Charges 2007

Per person	€ 5,00
child (2-15 yrs)	€ 2,50
pitch	€ 5,00 - € 7,80
electricity (plus meter)	€ 2,00
dog	€ 2,00

DE3635 Camping München-Obermenzing

Lochhausenerstraße 59, D-81247 München (Bavaria (S))

Tel: 089 811 2235. Email: campingplatz-obermenzing@t-online.de

On the northwest edge of Munich, this site makes a good stopover for those wishing to see the city or pass the night. The flat terrain is mostly covered with mature trees, giving shade to most pitches. Caravan owners are well off here as they have a special section of 130 individual drive-through pitches, mainly separated from each other by high hedges and opening off the hard site roads with easy access. These have 10A electricity connections and about 30 have water and drainage also. About 200 tents and motorcaravans are taken on quite large, level grass areas, with an overflow section, so space is usually available. There is a shop and rest room with TV and a drinks machine (including beer). There is some road noise, but we spent another reasonably undisturbed night here, helped by the new earth bank, and it is a very convenient site.

Facilities

The central sanitary block is large, having been extended, and together with a new 'portacabin' style unit, the provision should now be adequate. Cleaning is satisfactory and there is heating in the low season. Hot showers require tokens, as do some washbasins. Cooking facilities on payment. Washing machine and dryers. Gas supplies. Motorcaravan services. Shop (from May). Bar (from July). TV room. Charcoal barbecues not permitted. Off site: Baker and café nearby. Riding or golf 5 km. Bicycle hire 8 km. Public transport services to the city from very close by. By car the journey might take 20-30 minutes depending on the density of traffic.

Open: 15 March - 31 October.

Directions

Site is in the northwest of the city. From Stuttgart, Nürnberg, Deggendorf or Salzburg, leave A99 at 'Kreiss-West' for München-Lochhausen and turn left into Lochhausener Strasse. The site is a further 1.5 km. GPS: N48:10.489 E11:26.780

Charges 2007

Per person	€ 4,70
child (2-14 yrs)	€ 2,00
caravan and car	€ 10,50
motorcaravan	€ 7,50
electricity (plus meter)	€ 0,50

No credit cards.

Camping MÜNCHEN Obermenzing

A modern camping site located at the motorway A99, Cross West,
exit Munich-Lochhausen, in a 57,000 sq.m. park. Lavatory and shower for the disabled.
Resident propriertor: Andreas Blenck • Lochhausener Str. 59 • D-81247 München
Tel.: 0049 - 89 - 811 22 35 • Fax: 0049 - 89 - 814 48 07
• Ca. 20 min. to the city by car • Good connections by bus, tram or S-train
Bus stop directly at the campsite

DE3640 Camping Municipal München-Thalkirchen

Zentralländstraße 49, D-81379 München (Bavaria (S))

Tel: 089 723 1707. Email: munichtouristoffice@compuserve.com

This well cared for municipal site is pleasantly and quietly situated on the southern side of Munich in parkland formed by the River Isar conservation area, 4 km. from the city centre (there are subway and bus links) and tall trees offer shade in parts. The large city of Munich has much to offer and the Thalkirchen site becomes quite crowded during the season. There are 550 touring pitches, all with 10A electricity and shared water and waste water. The pitches are of various sizes (some quite small), marked by metal or wooden posts and rails. Like many city sites, groups are put in one area. and American motorhomes are accepted. The site is very busy (and noisy) during the annual Beer Festival (mid Sept - early Oct), but is well maintained and kept clean. Pleasant walks may be taken in the adjacent park and the world famous Munich zoo is just 15 minutes walk along the river from the site.

Facilities

There are five refurbished toilet blocks, two of which can be heated, with seatless toilets, washbasins with shelf, mirror and cold water. Hot water for showers and sinks is on payment. Facilities for disabled people. Washing machines and dryers. Shop. Snack bar with covered terrace. Drinks machine incl. beer. General room with TV pool and games. Good small playground. Maximum stay 14 days. Bicycle hire. Dormitory accommodation for groups (schools, scouts and guides etc.) Office hours 7 am - 11 pm. Off site: Restaurant 200 m. Adjacent parkland and Munich zoo.

Open: 15 March - end October.

Directions

From autobahns follow 'Mittel' ring road to SSE of the city centre where site is signed; also follow signs for Thalkirchen or the Zoo and site is close. Well signed now from all over the City. GPS: N48:05.471 E11:32.690

Charges guide

Per person	€ 4,40 - € 8,10
child (2-14 yrs)	€ 1,30
caravan and car	€ 10,00
motorcaravan (acc. to size)	€ 5,50 - € 7,00
electricity	€ 1,80

Credit cards only accepted for souvenirs.

DE3650 Camping Gitzenweiler Hof

Gitzenweiler 88, D-88131 Lindau-Oberreitnau (Bavaria (S))

Tel: **083 829 4940**. Email: **info@gitzenweiler-hof.de**

Gitzenweiler Hof has been developed into a really well-equipped, first-class site for a family holiday. In a country setting it has about 380 permanent caravans as well as about 450 places for touring units (it is advisable to book for July/Aug). In the tourist section many pitches are without markings with siting left to campers, the others in rows between access roads. There are 450 electricity connections (6/16A) and 56 pitches for caravans and motorcaravans with water, drainage and TV connections. A large open-air swimming pool has attractive surrounds with seats (free for campers). Lindau is an interesting town, especially by the harbour, and possible excursions include the whole of the Bodensee (Lake Constance), the German Alpine Road, the Austrian Vorarlberg and Switzerland. This is a pleasant, friendly, well-run site with a separate area just outside for overnight stops. Member of Leading Campings Group.

Facilities

The toilet blocks have been beautifully renovated and include some washbasins in cabins, a children's bathroom and baby bath. Washing machines, dryers and dishwasher. Motorcaravan services. Shop (limited hours in low season). Two restaurants with takeaway. Large swimming pool in summer (33 x 25 m). Two playgrounds and play room with entertainment in summer. Organised activities all year. Small animals and ponies for children. Free fishing in lake. Minigolf. Cinema. Club room with arcade games, library and internet points. American motorhomes accepted up to 10 tons.

Open: All year.

Directions

Site is signed from the B12 about 4 km. north of Lindau. Also from A96 exit 3 (Weißensberg), and from in and around Lindau.
GPS: N47:35.120 E09:42.385

Charges 2007

Per person	€ 6,30 - € 7,00
child (3-15 yrs)	€ 2,25 - € 4,50
pitch	€ 4,50 - € 9,00
serviced pitch	€ 7,50 - € 15,00

Discounts for stays over 14 days and in low season. Overnight hardstanding with electricity outside site barrier € 12.

DE3642 Lech Camping

Seeweg 6, D-86444 Mühlhausen bei Augsburg (Bavaria (S))

Tel: **082 072 200**. Email: **info@lech-camping.de**

Situated just north of Ausgburg, this beautifully run site is a pleasure to stay on. Gabi Ryssel, the owner, spends her long days working very hard to cater to every wish of her guests – from the moment you arrive and are given the key to one of the cleanest toilet blocks we have seen and plenty of tourist information, you are in very capable hands. The 40 level, grass and gravel pitches are roomy and have shade from pine trees. Electricity connections are available (10/16A). This is an immaculate site with a separate area for disabled people to park near the special facilities provided.

Facilities

The new toilet block (cleaned many times daily) provides British style WCs and good showers. Baby room. Separate family bathroom for rent. Facilities for disabled visitors. Laundry facilities. Motorcaravan service point. Small shop. Restaurant. Small playground (partially fenced). Bicycle hire. WiFi. Trampolines. Pedal boats and rowing boats for free. Off site: Bus service to city. Legoland 25 minute drive. Fishing 4 km. Golf 10 km. Riding 15 km.

Open: Easter - 15 September.

Directions

Site is northeast of Augsburg at the border of Muhlhausen. Leave E52/A8 (Munich - Stuttgart) at exit 73 and follow signs to Neuburg/Pöttmes. After 3 km. (past airport on right) on U49 you will see the Muhlhausen sign. Lech Camping is on right.

Charges 2007

Per person	€ 5,50
child (2-15 yrs)	€ 2,50
pitch incl. electricity	€ 9,10

DE3670 Camping Hopfensee

Fischerbichl 17, D-87629 Füssen im Allgäu (Bavaria (S))

Tel: 083 629 17710. Email: info@camping-hopfensee.com

Hopfensee is a high class site with excellent facilities, catering for discerning visitors, by a lake. It is well placed to explore the very attractive Bavarian Alpine region which, along with the architecture and historical interest of the Royal Castles at Hohenschwangau and the Baroque church at Wies, makes it a very popular holiday area. The 378 tourist pitches for caravans and motorhomes, most with shade, each have 16A electricity, water, drain and cable TV connections. They are marked, numbered and of a good size. At the centre of the site is a large building with an open village-like square in the middle, adorned with cascading flowers. It houses the exceptional sanitary facilities and, on the upper floors, a swimming pool, treatment and physiotherapy suites, a full spa centre, fitness centre, cinema and children's play room. There is direct access to the lake for sailing, canoeing etc. and a place for parking boats. Charges are high, but include the pool, super sports building, cinema, etc. Tents are not accepted. Member of Leading Campings Group.

Facilities

The exceptionally good, heated sanitary facilities provide free hot water in washbasins (some in cabins) and large showers. Baby and children's wash rooms. Some private units for rent. Motorcaravan services. Restaurant with terrace faces across the lake. Bar. Takeaway. Shop. Indoor pool and spa centre. Supervised courses of water treatments, massage, etc. Sauna, solarium and steam bath. Playground and kindergarten. Large games room. Bicycle hire. Tennis. Fishing. Ski school in winter. Small golf academy and green fee discounts for two local courses. No tents taken. Off site: Riding and boat launching 1 km.

Open: 15 December - 5 November.

Directions

Site is 4 km. north of Füssen. Turn off B16 to Hopfen and site is on the left through a car park. If approaching from the west on B310, turn towards Füssen at T-junction with the B16 and immediately right again for the road to Hopfen.
GPS: N47:36.167 E10:41.030

Charges 2008

Per person	€ 8,55 - € 9,75
child (2-12 yrs)	€ 5,15 - € 6,05
12-18 yrs	€ 6,65 - € 9,20
pitch with cable TV, electricity	€ 12,65 - € 14,00

No credit cards.

DE3680 Alpen-Caravanpark Tennsee

D-82494 Krün / Obb (Bavaria (S))

Tel: 088 251 70. Email: info@camping-tennsee.de

Tennsee is an excellent site in truly beautiful surroundings high up (1,000 m.) in the Karwendel Alps with super mountain views, and close to many famous places of which Innsbruck (44 km) and Oberammergau (26 km) are two. Mountain walks are plentiful, with several lifts close by. It is an attractive site with good facilities including 120 serviced pitches with individual connections for electricity (up to 16A and two connections), gas, TV, radio, telephone, water and waste water. The other 80 pitches also have electricity and some of these are available for overnight guests at a reduced rate. Reception and restaurants, bar, cellar youth room and a well stocked shop are all housed in attractive buildings. Many activities and excursions are organised to local attractions by the Zick family, who run the site in a very friendly, helpful and efficient manner.

Facilities

The first class toilet block has under-floor heating, washbasins in cabins and private units with WC, shower, basin and bidet for rent. Unit for disabled people with the latest facilities. Baby bath, dog bathroom and a heated room for ski equipment (with lockers). Washing machines, free dryers and irons. Gas supplies. Motorcaravan services. Cooking facilities. Shop. Restaurants with takeaway (waiter, self service and takeaway). Bar. Youth room. Solarium. Bicycle hire. WiFi. Playground. Organised activities and excursions. Bus service to ski slopes in winter. Off site: Fishing 400 m. Riding or golf 3 km.

Open: All year excl. 4 November - 15 December.

Directions

Site is just off the main Garmisch-Partenkirchen - Innsbruck road no. 2 between Klais and Krün, 15 km. from Garmisch watch for small sign 'Tennsee + Barmersee' and turn right there for site.

Charges 2007

Per person	€ 7,50 - € 8,00
1-3 children (3-15 yrs)	€ 4,00 - € 6,00
pitch	€ 8,50 - € 12,00
electricity per kWh	€ 0,65
dog	€ 3,30

Senior citizens special rates (not winter).

DE3672 Camping Elbsee

Am Elbsee 3, D-87648 Aitrang (Bavaria (S))

Tel: 083 432 48. Email: camping@elbsee.de

This attractive site, with its associated hotel and restaurant about 400 m. away, lies on land sloping down to the lake. This is not an area well known to tourists, although the towns of Marktoberdorf (14 km), Kaufbeuren (16 km) and Kempten (21 km) merit a visit. With this in mind, the owners have set about providing good facilities and a developing program of activities. All the 120 touring pitches have access to electricity (16A) and 78 also have their own water supply and waste water outlet. Some of the pitches restricted to tents slope slightly. In high season there are organised outings, musical performances on site or at the hotel, painting courses and children's activities. Next to the site is a supervised lake bathing area, operated by the municipality, with a kiosk selling drinks and snacks, a playground and an indoor play area. Entrance to this is at a reduced price for campers.

Facilities

Two clean, well appointed heated sanitary blocks include free showers, washbasins all in cabins, a children's bathroom and family bathrooms to rent. Facilities for disabled visitors. Dog shower. Motorcaravan service point. Shop (order bread for following day). New playground, indoor play area and activity rooms. TV, games and meeting rooms. Sports field. Fishing. Bicycle hire. Riding. Boat launching. Activity programme (20/7-31/8). Off site: At hotel, very good restaurant, takeaway and bar. Shop and ATM point 2 km. Golf 12 km.

Open: 15 December - 5 November.

Directions

From centre of Marktoberdorf, take minor road northwest to Ruderatshofen and from there minor road west towards Aitrang. Just south of Aitrang, site is signed to south of the road. The road (2 km.) is winding and narrow, but two caravans can just pass. GPS: N47:48.166 E10:33.206

Charges 2007

Per person	€ 5,30
child (4-14 yrs)	€ 3,00
pitch incl. car	€ 10,20 - € 14,70
electricity per kWh	€ 0,65

Camping Cheques accepted.

Holiday Paradise
in the centre of the Allgäu

★ summer and winter camping
★ sauna, fitness and wellness
★ natural lake with beach an boats for rent
★ families specially welcome
★ own restaurant
★ many interesting sights
★ many leisure activities

www.elbsee.de
Fam. Franz Martin | Am Elbsee 3, D-87648 Aitrang
Tel.: +49(0)8343-248 | Fax: +49(0)8343-1406
GPS: North 47° 48' 11,17" | East 10° 33' 14,76"

DE3685 Camping Allweglehen

D-83471 Berchtesgaden (Bavaria (S))

Tel: 086 522 396. Email: campingplatz.allweglehen@t-online.de

This all year site occupies a hillside position, with spectacular mountain views. The site access road is steep (14%), particularly at the entrance, but the proprietor will use his tractor to tow caravans if requested. There are 180 pitches (160 for touring), arranged on a series of gravel terraces, separated by hedges or fir trees and all with good views and electrical connections (16A). There is a separate area on a sloping meadow for tents. The pleasant restaurant, with terrace, offers Bavarian specialities at reasonable prices. This is a useful base for sightseeing or relaxing.

Facilities

Two adjacent older style toilet blocks near the restaurant can be heated. A further tiny unit serves the lowest terrace. Bathroom. Baby room. Cleaning and maintenance can be variable. Washing machines, dryers and iron. Motorcaravan services. Gas supplies. Restaurant. Kiosk for essentials (all year). Play area. Small heated pool (small charge, 15/5-15/10). Solarium. Minigolf. Fishing. Excursions. Internet access. Off site: Winter sports near. Walks. Riding 2 km. Bicycle hire 3 km. Golf 5 km.

Open: All year.

Directions

Easiest access is via the Austrian A10 autobahn (vignette necessary), Salzburg Sud exit and follow the B305 towards Berchtesgaden. Alternatively take the B305 from Ruhpolding (the pretty Alpenstrasse – winding and with 4 m. height limit), or the B20 from Bad Reichenhall. Site is 4 km. northeast of Berchtesgaden. GPS: N47:38.833 E13:02.387

Charges guide

Per person	€ 5,40
pitch	€ 7,50 - € 8,50
electricity per kWh	€ 0,50

DE3688 Panorama Camping Harras

Harrasser Strasse 135, D-83209 Prien am Chiemsee (Bavaria (S))

Tel: 080 519 04613. Email: info@camping-harras.de

Panorama Harras is a popular, friendly site on a small, wooded peninsula by the Chiemsee, with good views to the mountains across the lake. With some of them near the lake, the pitches vary in size (60-100 sq.m.) and most have electricity (6A). There are 80 numbered pitches marked by trees, but with no hedges, the site can look and feel crowded at busy times. A separate, all numbered section of gravel hardstanding is provided for motorhomes and an area for tents on grass and gravel. Sailing and windsurfing are very popular here and you can swim from the shingle beach.

Facilities

Toilet facilities include family shower rooms with washbasin and toilet (no paper). Push-button showers need a token. Baby room. Launderette. Good unit for disabled people. Well stocked shop. Restaurant with bar and takeaway (all open for the whole season). Bicycle hire. Off site: Bus services 1 km. in town. Boat trips on the lake. Golf and riding 5 km. Automobile museum 20 km.

Open: 6 April - 10 October.

Directions

The Chiemsee is north of the A8 (E52, E60) between Munich and Salzburg. Take exit 106 (Bernau) then north towards Prien. After 3 km, at the roundabout, turn east towards Harras (and Kreiskrankenhaus) following site signs. GPS: N47:50.450 E12:22.290

Charges 2007

Per person	€ 5,50 - € 6,50
pitch incl. car and electricity	€ 7,20 - € 9,20

Surcharge 15% for stays of less than 4 nights.
Camping Cheques accepted.

DE3686 Strandcamping

Am See 1, D-83329 Waging am See (Bavaria (S))

Tel: 086 815 52. Email: info@strandcamp.de

This is an exceptionally big site on the banks of a large lake fed by clear alpine streams. There are some 700 pitches for touring units out of a total of over 1,200. All the grass, level touring pitches have electricity (16A) with 86 also providing water and drainage. As you would expect with a site of this kind, there is a considerable range of sports facilities and an extensive games and entertainment programme during July and August. A small sandy beach offers facilities for swimming in the lake (lifeguards are in attendance in the high season).

Facilities

Good sanitary facilities include private cabins and free showers. Facilities for disabled people and children in the four modern blocks. 11 private bathrooms for rent. Laundry facilities. Motorcaravan service point. Shop and internet access at reception. Restaurant and bar. Lake beach. Windsurfing. Tennis. Archery. Minigolf. Fishing. Bicycle hire. WiFi. Dogs are not accepted between 20 June - 22 August. Off site: Golf 1 km.

Open: 1 April - 31 October.

Directions

From A8 take exit 112 and head towards Traunstein. Turn right on road no. 304 then left towards Waging. Just before bridge turn right and then right towards site. GPS: N47:56.565 E12:44.829

Charges 2007

Per person	€ 5,50 - € 6,90
child (3-15 yrs)	€ 2,50 - € 5,10
pitch	€ 6,20 - € 8,20
incl. services	€ 10,60 - € 11,60

DE3695 Dreiflüsse Camping

Am Sonnenhang 8, Donautat, D-94113 Irring b. Passau (Bavaria (S))

Tel: 085 466 33. Email: dreifluessecamping@t-online.de

Although the site overlooks the Danube, it is in fact some 9 km. from the confluence of the Danube, Inn and Ilz. Dreiflüsse Camping occupies a hillside position, well above high water level, to the west of Passau with pitches, flat or with a little slope on several rows of terraces. The 180 places for touring units are not all numbered or marked, although 16A electricity connection boxes determine where units pitch, and half have water and a drain. Trees and low banks separate the terraces which are of gravel with a thin covering of grass. There is some road and rail noise (24 hrs).

Facilities

The sanitary facilities are acceptable, if a little old, with two private cabins for women, one for men. Laundry. Motorcaravan services. Gas supplies. Pleasant, modern Gasthof restaurant with terrace at site entrance, where the reception, shop and sanitary buildings are also located. Shop all season. Small heated indoor swimming pool (May - 15 Sept on payment). Play area. Bicycle hire. Off site: Passau 9 km. Bus for Passau from outside site, or from Schalding 1.5 km. Riding 3 km. Golf 10 km.

Open: 1 April - 31 October.

Directions

From autobahn A3, take exit 115 (Passau-Nord) from where site is signed. Follow signs from Passau on road to west of city and north bank of Danube towards Windorf and Irring. GPS: N48:36.377 E13:20.750

Charges 2007

Per person	€ 4,50
pitch	€ 5,00 - € 9,50
electricity (plus kWh charge)	€ 2,50

No credit cards.

DE3697 Kur & Feriencamping Dreiquellenbad

Singham 40, D-94086 Bad Griesbach (Bavaria (S))

Tel: **085 329 6130**. Email: **info@camping-bad-griesbach.de**

This site is to the southwest of Passau, a town which dates back to Roman times and lies on a peninsula between the rivers Danube and Inn. Dreiquellenbad is an exceptional site in a quite rural area, with 200 pitches, all of which are used for touring units. All pitches have electricity, water, waste water and TV points. English is spoken at reception which also houses a shop and good tourist information. A luxury leisure complex includes indoor and outdoor thermal pools, a sauna, Turkish bath and jacuzzi (the use of which is free to campers). An adjoining building provides various beauty and complementary health treatments. Member of Leading Campings Group.

Facilities

Excellent sanitary facilities include private cabins and free showers, facilities for disabled visitors, special child facilities and a dog shower. Two private bathrooms for rent. Laundry facilities. Bar/restaurant. Motorcaravan services. Shop. Gym. Luxury leisure complex. Play area. Bicycle hire. Fishing. Internet. WiFi. Off site: Golf 2 km. Spa facilities of Bad Griesbach within walking distance.

Open: All year.

Directions

Site is 15 km. from the A3. Take exit 118 and follow signs for Pocking. After 2 km. turn right on B388. Site is in the hamlet of Singham - turn right into Karpfhan then left towards site. GPS: N48:25.204 E13:11.532

Charges 2007

Per person	€ 6,10
child (0-14 yrs)	€ 3,90
pitch	€ 9,90 - € 10,40
electricity (plus meter)	€ 1,00
dog	€ 2,20

Unique in Bavaria: Thermal Spring waters from the "Vital-Therme Reichersberg" on site !

LeadingCampings

Wellness, golf and fresh air in Bad Griesbach, Bavaria. ★ ★ ★ ★ ★

camping

The place to come for the 'cure', wellness and golf. Everything is on site: you are presented with a wide assortment of services such as regimens for rheumatic and joint illnesses, therapeutic baths, massages, sauna, solarium, jacuzzi or Turkish bath. And now the healthy spa water can be enjoyed directly in the campsite's pool. There is a doctor, an inn, apartments, holiday lettings, natural swimming lake, 'jungle garden', pitch & putt green, beautician and chiropodist, hairdresser etc: Bad Griesbach's thermal bath also nearby.

... all of this and Europe's Golf Centre and Academy!

W. Hartl´s Kur- und Feriencamping Dreiquellenbad e. K.
Singham 40 • D - 94086 Bad Griesbach / Bayern
tel: +49 85 32 / 96 13 - 0 • fax: +49 85 32 / 96 13 - 50
www.camping-bad-griesbach.de • info@camping-bad-griesbach.de

DE3720 Internationaler Campingplatz Naabtal

Sistelhausen 2, D-93188 Pielenhofen (Bavaria (S))

Tel: **094 093 73**. Email: **camping.pielenhofen@t-online.de**

International Camping Naabtal is an attractive riverside site in a beautiful tree-covered valley and makes an excellent base for exploring the ancient city of Regensburg on the Danube and other areas of this interesting part of Germany. It is also a good overnight site for those wishing to visit or pass through Austria or the Czech Republic. The best 130 of the 340 pitches are reserved for tourists and they are mainly located on the banks of the river on flat or gently sloping ground under willow and other trees. This is good walking and mountain biking country with many marked trails.

Facilities

Two original, heated toilet blocks are part of larger buildings and there is a newer block for the tent area. Some washbasins are in cabins, showers are on payment. First class unit for disabled people. Washing machines, dryers and irons. Gas supplies. Motorcaravan services. Sauna and solarium. Bar/restaurant (1/4-31/10 plus Xmas/New Year). Small shop (Easter - end Sept). Playground with imaginative apparatus. Large meeting room. Tennis. Bicycle hire. Fishing (permit required). Small boats on river. Off site: Shop and bus service in the village 1.5 km. Golf 15 km.

Open: All year.

Directions

From A3 (Nürnberg - Regensburg) take exit 97 (Nittendorf). Follow road to Pielenhofen and pass under the arch (Camping Naabtal is signed from exit). Cross river and turn right to site. Site is about 11 km. from autobahn exit. From A93 exit 39 onto B8 towards Nittendorf, then at Etterzhausen turn towards Pielenhofen. GPS: N49:03.547 E11:57.610

Charges 2007

Per person	€ 5,25
child	€ 3,25
pitch	€ 6,10
electricity (plus meter)	€ 0,50
No credit cards.	

DE3420 **Freizeitcenter Oberrhein**

D-79244 Rheinmunster (Baden-Württemberg)

Tel: **072 272 500**. Email: **info@freizeitcenter-oberrhein.de**

This large, well equipped holiday site provides much to do and is also a good base for visiting the Black Forest. To the left of reception are a touring area and a section of hardstanding for motorcaravans. The 285 touring pitches – out of 700 overall – all have electricity connections (mostly 16A, 3 pin, a few with 2 pin), and include 180 with water and drainage, but little shade. Two of the site's lakes are used for swimming (with roped-off areas for toddlers) and non-powered boating (the water was very clean when we visited), the third small one is for fishing. This site is well worth considering for a holiday, especially for families with young and early teenage children. Occasional live music is organised until late.

Facilities

Seven top quality, heated toilet buildings have free hot water and very smart fittings. Some have special rooms for children, babies and families. Excellent dog shower! Family wash cabins to rent. Motorcaravan services. Gas supplies. Shop (1/4-31/10). Lakeside restaurant; snack bar (both 1/4-31/10). Modern play areas on sand. Small zoo. Tennis. Bicycle hire. Minigolf. Windsurf school. Swimming and boating lakes. Fishing (charged). Off site: Supermarket 3 km. Riding 4 km. Golf 5 km.

Open: All year.

Directions

Leave A5/E35-52 at exit 51 and travel west in direction of Iffezheim. Turn south onto B36 passing through Hügelsheim to Stollhoffen where at the roundabout site is signed.
GPS: N48:46.346 E08:02.490

Charges 2007

Per person	€ 5,00 - € 8,50
child (6-16 yrs)	€ 3,00 - € 6,00
child (under 6 yrs)	€ 2,50 - € 4,50
pitch incl. car and electricity	€ 7,50 - € 10,50
dog	€ 2,50 - € 4,50

DE3406 **Camping Kleinenzhof**

D-75323 Bad Wildbad (Baden-Württemberg)

Tel: **070 813 435**. Email: **info@kleinenzhof.de**

In the northern Black Forest, a very good area for walking and cross-country skiing, this site runs along the sloping bank of a stream big enough to play in but small enough not to be dangerous. There are excellent facilities, which the owner is still working on improving. The land is terraced and accommodates around 200 seasonal pitches, and 100 touring pitches. All have 16A electricity and all but five have water and drainage. At the far end of the site is a hotel with a heated indoor pool and an outdoor pool which are free to campers. A full programme of activities is arranged, including walks, other outings, visits to the site's own distillery, films and communal barbecues at weekends, and a children's club every afternoon from May to September.

Facilities

Four sanitary blocks, all heated, are clean with many washbasins in cabins and showers. Facilities for disabled visitors. Baby changing. Children's bathroom. 12 free family bathrooms (many for rent). Dog shower. Laundry facilities. Motorcaravan service point. Gas. Shop. Bar and restaurant (at hotel). Indoor pool. Outdoor pool (May - Sept) and paddling pool. Playground. TV and games room. Internet. Bicycle hire. Off site: Fishing 3 km. Riding 8 km. Golf 25 km.

Open: All year.

Directions

From Pforzheim take B294 south through Birkenfeld and Neuenbürg to Calmbach (20 km.) From here do not go to Bad Wildbad. Continue on B294 to Kleinenzhof (about another 3 km).
GPS: N48:44.284 E08:34.626

Charges 2007

Per person	€ 6,40 - € 6,60
child (1-12 yrs)	€ 4,00 - € 4,10
pitch	€ 8,10 - € 8,30
electricity (per kWh)	€ 0,59
dog	€ 2,10

DE3415 **Camping Adam**

Campingstrasse 1, D-77815 Bühl (Baden-Württemberg)

Tel: **072 232 3194**. Email: **webmaster@campingplatz-adam.de**

This very convenient lakeside site is by the A5 Karlsruhe - Basel autobahn near Baden-Baden, easily accessed from exit 52 Bühl (also from the French autoroute A35 just northeast of Strasbourg). It is also a useful base for the Black Forest. Most of the touring pitches (180 from 490 total) have electricity connections (10A), many with waste water outlets too. Tents are positioned along the outer area of the lake. At very busy times, units staying overnight only may be placed close together on a lakeside area of hardstanding. Mobile homes are only available to rent 1/4-31/9. The site has a well tended look and good English is spoken. The lake is divided into separate areas for bathing or boating and windsurfing, with a long slide – the public are admitted to this on payment and it attracts many people on fine weekends. The shop and restaurant/bar remain open virtually all year (not Monday or Tuesday in low season), so this is a useful site to use out of season.

Facilities

Two heated sanitary buildings have mostly private cabins in the new block, hot showers on payment, facilities for babies and disabled people. Laundry and dishwashing sinks. Washing machine and dryer. Gas supplies. Motorcaravan services. Shop (1/4-31/10). Restaurant (1/3-30/10). Takeaway (1/5-31/8). Playground. Bicycle hire. Fishing. Off site: Riding or golf 5 km.

Open: All year.

Directions

Take A5/E35-52, exit 52 (Bühl), turn towards Lichtenau, go through Oberbruch and left to site. From French autoroute A35 take exits 52 or 56 onto D2 and D4 respectively then turn onto A5 as above. GPS: N48:43.590 E08:05.100

Charges 2007

Per person	€ 4,80 - € 7,00
child (3-16 yrs)	€ 2,50 - € 4,00
pitch with services	€ 4,80 - € 8,50
electricity	€ 2,20

DE3432 **Schwarzwald Camp**

Schiltacher strasse 80, D-77709 Wolfach-Halbmeil (Baden-Württemberg)

Tel: **078 348 59309**. Email: **info@schwarzwald-camp.com**

This site is set in a quiet position on the side of an attractive valley in the Black Forest. If you would like to dine or wake up to beautiful views across an alpine valley and watch herds of wild deer graze in the meadows opposite, then this is the site for you. Terraced but with little shade as yet, the site has fairly level pitches, many with electricity (16A), water and drainage, and an area which is used for tents. In front of the main building is an area of hardstanding for overnight visitors, also with electricity connections. Local attractions include the excellent waterfalls near Triberg which have been visited by, amongst others, Ernest Hemingway and Otto von Bismark.

Facilities

First class sanitary facilities include private cabins, large free showers including one multi-head, family bathrooms for hire, laundry and a kitchen, in the main building close to the entrance. It also houses reception with a small shop and the restaurant open daily all year. Off site: Wolfach 2 km. Outdoor swimming pool 5 km. Golf 20 km.

Open: All year.

Directions

From A5 Karlsruhe - Freiburg, take exit 55 Offenburg on B33/E531 to Haslach, then on 33/294 through Hausach and soon after left on 294 to Wolfach. Go through tunnel, stay on 294 for 3 km. to Halbmeil. Site on left at end of village. GPS: N48:17.467 E08:16.690

Charges 2008

Per person	€ 6,50
pitch	€ 3,50 - € 6,00
electricity (plus 0.5 kWh)	€ 1,00

DE3454 Kur und Feriencamping Badenweiler

Weilertalstrasse 73, D-79410 Badenweiler (Baden-Württemberg)

Tel: 076 321 550. Email: info@camping-badenweiler.de

Badenweiler is an attractive spa centre on the edge of the southern Black Forest, and is the site of the largest Roman baths north of the Alps. It is easily accessed from the A5 or B3, but far enough from them to be peaceful. This well kept, family run campsite with pleasant open views is on a hillside close to Badenweiler and the cure facilities. There are four terraces with 100 large, individual grass pitches, 96 for touring and all with electricity (16A), water and drain. Reception is part of a building which also houses a bar/café with takeaway snacks in the evenings in high season. Here too is a small shop and a children's room downstairs.

Facilities

Top quality sanitary facilities are contained in two fully tiled buildings, one with toilets and the other with free, controllable hot showers with full glass dividers and washbasins (cabins and vanity style). Family washrooms, facilities for babies and disabled visitors. Washing machines and dryers. Motorcaravan services. Gas supplies. Shop for basics. Play area and play room. Games room. Internet point and WiFi access throughout site. Off site: Municipal outdoor, heated swimming pool, free entry for campers at 200 m. Restaurants 200 m. Shop 300 m. Golf 12 km.

Open: All year excl. 16 January - 14 December.

Directions

From the A5 about midway between Freiburg and Basel take exit 65 onto the B378 to Müllheim, then the L131 signed to Badenweiler-Ost from where site is well signed. GPS: N47:48.592 E07:41.786

Charges 2008

Per person	€ 7,80
child (10-15 yrs)	€ 4,90
child (0-9 yrs)	€ 3,50
pitch	€ 9,00
dog	€ 2,50

No credit cards.

Familie Wiesler
Weilertalstr. 73 D-79410 Badenweiler
Tel. 07632/1550 • Fax 07632/5268
www.camping-badenweiler.de
info@camping-badenweiler.de

DE3437 Camping Hochschwarzwald

Oberhäuserstrasse 6, D-79674 Todtnau-Muggenbrunn (Baden-Württemberg)

Tel: 076 711 288. Email: camping.hochschwarzwald@web.de

Hochschwarzwald is a small, peaceful, quality site in an attractive wooded valley high up in the Black Forest. Of 85 marked pitches (some with shade), 50 are for tourers (all with 10A electricity) on level terraces of grass and gravel. There is an area at the entrance for overnight stays in high season.This is an extremely popular area, with many summer visitors enjoying walking and cycling, but it is also ideal for winter stays, with skiing from the site. At the back of the site, as well as being able to walk in the woods, you can paddle in a flat area of the stream which tumbles town the hill. There is an attractive barbecue area here with seating and table tennis tables.

Facilities

Two modern, heated sanitary buildings have good facilities with a few private cabins, a family room and a unit for disabled people. Washing machine and dryer. Small shop for essentials. Restaurant/bar (closed Mondays). Off site: Bus to Freiburg 50 m. Bicycle hire 5 km. Fishing 6 km. Riding 12 km. Golf 14 km. Walking and skiing directly from the site. Heated indoor pool, tennis court and ski school in Muggenbrunn. Todtnau waterfalls 3 km. Freiburg and Titisee both 25 km.

Open: All year.

Directions

Site is about 1 km. beyond Muggenbrunn on the road from Todtnau towards Freiburg. GPS: N47:51.934 E07:54.970

Charges 2008

Per person	€ 4,80 - € 5,30
child (2-12 yrs)	€ 2,80 - € 3,20
pitch	€ 5,90 - € 6,40
electricity per kWh	€ 0,50
dog	€ 1,50

No credit cards.
Camping Cheques accepted.

DE3440 Camping Kirchzarten

Dietenbacher Straße 17, D-79199 Kirchzarten (Baden-Württemberg)

Tel: **076 619 040910**. Email: **info@camping-kirchzarten.de**

There are pleasant views of the Black Forest from this municipal site which is within easy reach by car of Titisee, Feldberg and Todtnau, and 8 km. from the large town of Freiburg in Breisgau. It is divided into 496 numbered pitches with electricity, 380 of which are for tourists (some used by tour operators). Most pitches, which are side by side on level ground, are of quite reasonable size and marked out at the corners, though there is nothing to separate them and there are some hardstanding motorcaravan pitches. From about late June to mid-August it does become full. The fine swimming pool complex adjoining the site is free to campers and is a main attraction, with pools for diving, fun, swimming and children, surrounded by spacious grassy sunbathing areas and a children's play area on sand. It is only a short stroll from the site to the village centre, which has supermarkets, restaurants, etc.

Facilities

The new sanitary building is a splendid addition and includes a large, central children Off site: Tennis (covered court, can be booked from site). Adventure playground, fitness track, tennis and minigolf near. Riding 2 km. Golf 4 km.

Open: All year.

Directions

From Freiburg take B31 road signed Donaueschingen to Kirchzarten where site is signed (it is south of the village). GPS: N47:57.625 E07:57.050

Charges 2008

Per person	€ 9,50
child (4-16 yrs)	€ 4,90
pitch	€ 7,60
Every 15th day free.	

Caravan-hire!
Open all the year round!
Winter-camping!
Apply for information-prospekt

Our familiar lead camping-place is located at the foot of the southern Black-forest near by Freiburg. A very nice outdoor swimming-pool with four basins next to the camping-place, a children's playground, a new sanitary building, tenniscourts for indoor and outdoor, a riding-stable, mountainbike-routes and wonderful walking-tours leave no wish open. Attractions like the Steinwasen- and Europa-Park are easy to reach from here. We are looking forward to your visit.
Your family Ziegler

Free use of train and bus in the region.

Kirchzarten
Luftkurort im Schwarzwald

Tel. +49 (0)7661/9040910
Fax +49 (0)7661/61624
www.camping-kirchzarten.de
info@camping-kirchzarten.de

DE3442 Terrassen Campingplatz Herbolzheim

Im Laue, D-79336 Herbolzheim (Baden-Württemberg)

Tel: 076 431 460. Email: **s.hugoschmidt@t-online.de**

This well equipped campsite is in a quiet location on a wooded slope to the north of Freiburg. There are 70 touring pitches, all with electricity (16A) and grass surfaces, on terraces linked by hard access roads with a little shade for some. A separate meadow for tents is at the top of the site (with three cabin toilets) and some pitches are used by a tour operator. This is good walking country and with only occasional entertainment, this is a very pleasant place in which to relax between daily activities. It is useful as a night stop when travelling between Frankfurt and Basel, and is just 10 km. from Europa Park, only a short way from the A5 autobahn.

Facilities

The main toilet facilities are modern, with new facilities for babies and disabled visitors. Laundry and dishwashing facilities. Motorcaravan services. Bar/restaurant (Easter - Sept daily). Play area. Dogs are not accepted 15/7-15/8. Off site: Large open-air heated municipal swimming pool complex adjacent (1/5-15/9). Restaurants and shops in the village 3 km. Riding, bicycle hire 5 km. Local market on Friday mornings.

Open: 16 May - 3 October.

Directions

From A5 Frankfurt - Basel autobahn take exit 57, 58 or 59 and follow signs to Herbolzheim. Site signed south side of town near swimming pool. Go through pool car park and about 350 m. past the pool entrance. GPS: N48:12.966 E07:47.314

Charges 2007

Per person	€ 5,00
child (0-15 yrs)	€ 3,00
pitch	€ 7,00 - € 9,00
tent pitch	€ 6,00
electricity	€ 2,00
10% discount after 14 days.	

DE3427 Ferienparadies Schwarzwälder Hof

Tretenhofstr. 76, D-77960 Seelbach (Baden-Württemberg)

Tel: 078 239 60950. Email: **camping-rezeption@seelbach.org**

This site lies in a wooded valley, just south of the pleasant village of Seelbach in the Black Forest. The old buildings have been replaced by very attractive ones built in the old traditional style, but containing very modern facilities. There are 160 well drained touring pitches, either grass or hardstanding, all with electricity (10A), water supply and waste water outlet. There is also space for groups in tents. Just at the entrance is the family hotel with a restaurant. Besides a comprehensive general menu, there are also menus for children and older people with smaller appetites. A short walk from the site is a well-equipped municipal swimming pool and surrounding grass area. In July/August a good range of activities is organised for all ages, including a children's club. Fishing is possible in the stream which runs along the bottom of the site. The surrounding countryside is good for walking and cycling, and Europa Park is 30 km.

Facilities

Three sanitary blocks, all heated, clean and well maintained, include many washbasins in cabins and free showers. Facilities for wheelchair users. Family rooms (free). Baby room, superb children's bathroom, child size toilets and washbasins. Laundry facilities. Motorcaravan services. Gas supplies. Small shop. Restaurant, snacks and takeaway. TV and club room. Playground. Sauna (free after two night stay). Off site: Swimming 150 m. Bicycle hire 1 km. ATM in Seelbach 1 km. Riding 2 km. Golf 5 km.

Open: All year.

Directions

From A5/E35 autobahn, leave at exit 56 (Lahr). Follow road east through Lahr, until turn south to Seelbach. Go through Seelbach and the site is about 1 km. south. GPS: N48:17.983 E07:56.653

Charges guide

Per person	€ 8,70
child (3-15 yrs)	€ 5,70
pitch with services	€ 8,40 - € 9,90
electricity (plus 0.50 kWh)	€ 2,00
dog	€ 3,00

DE3455 Gugel's Dreiländer Camping

Oberer Wald 3, D-79395 Neuenburg (am Rhein) (Baden-Württemberg)

Tel: 076 317 719. Email: info@camping-gugel.de

Set in natural heath and woodland, Gugel's is an attractive site with 220 touring pitches either in small clearings in the trees, in open areas or on a hardstanding section used for single night stays. All have electricity (16A), and some also have water, waste water and satellite TV connections. Opposite is a meadow where late arrivals and early departures may spend the night. There may be some road noise near the entrance. The site may become very busy in high season and at Bank Holidays but you should always find room. There is a good atmosphere and can be recommended for both short and long stays. There is a social room with satellite TV where guests are welcomed with a glass of wine and a slide presentation of the attractions of the area. The Rhine is within walking distance. Neuenburg is ideally placed not only for enjoying and exploring the south of the Black Forest, but also for night stops when travelling from Frankfurt to Basel on the A5 autobahn. The site is winner of a prestigious environmental award. The permanent caravans set away from the tourist area, with their well-tended gardens, enhance rather than detract from the natural beauty.

Facilities

Three good quality heated sanitary blocks include some washbasins in cabins. Baby room. Facilities for disabled visitors. Laundry facilities. Motorcaravan services. Shop. Excellent restaurant. Takeaway (weekends and daily in high season). New state of the art wellness centre. Indoor pool. Boules. Tennis. Fishing. Minigolf. Barbecue. Beach Bar. Bicycle hire. Community room with TV. Activity programme (high season). Play areas. Off site: Riding 1.5 km. Golf 5 km. Neuenburg, Breisach, Freiburg, Basel and the Black Forest.

Open: All year.

Directions

From autobahn A5 take Neuenburg exit, turn left, then almost immediately left at traffic lights, left at next junction and follow signs for 2 km. to site (called 'Neuenburg' on most signs). GPS: N47:47.816 E07:33.000

Charges 2008

Per person	€ 6,40
child (2-15 yrs)	€ 3,00
caravan or tent	€ 5,80
small tent	€ 3,90
car	€ 4,30

Discount every 10th night, persons free.
No credit cards.

Germany

DE3428 Terrassen Camping Oase
Mühlenweg 34, D-77955 Ettenheim (Baden-Württemberg)
Tel: 078 224 45918. Email: info@campingpark-oase.de

This pleasant well run site lies on wooded land on the western edge of the Black Forest, a very good region for walking and cycling. The level area near the entrance holds the main facilities and 200 touring pitches, all with 6A electricity. Pitches for tents are on grass and there is grass or hardstanding for caravans and motorcaravans. On sloping land further away are 85 terraced seasonal pitches. Just outside the entrance is the family hotel/restaurant, which also has a playground, all open to campers. Europa Park is 7 km. away, and the city of Freiburg is 40 km. to the south. The site is only 5 km. from the A5/E35 autobahn, which makes it an ideal overnight stop on the way to Basel and Switzerland.

Facilities

Two sanitary blocks are heated, clean and well maintained. Many washbasins are in cabins. Showers are coin-operated. Facilities for wheelchair users. Baby changing room, children's bathroom. Dishwashing and laundry sinks. Motorcaravan services. Gas supplies. Shop. Restaurant and takeaway (at hotel). TV and club room. Off site: Leisure area. Tennis, riding and bicycle hire within 1 km. Fishing 2 km. Golf 5 km.

Open: Week before Easter - 4 October.

Directions

From A5/E35, exit 57A (Ettenheim), follow L103 road southeast to Ettenheim (about 2.5 km). From here site is signed, and is a further 1 km. along the same road. GPS: N48:14.862 E07:49.652

Charges 2007

Per person	€ 6,50
child (1-15 yrs)	€ 3,50
pitch	€ 6,00 - € 9,00
electricity	€ 2,00
dog	€ 1,50 - € 3,00

DE3439 Hirzberg Camping Freiburg
Kartäuserstrasse 99, D-79104 Freiburg (Baden-Württemberg)
Tel: 076 135 054. Email: hirzberg@freiburg-camping.de

Hirzberg Camping is a quiet city site backing onto meadows and wooded hills, yet within easy reach of Freiburg's old town quarter. To the right of the entrance is reception, a shop, the sanitary facilities and a children's room with a play area outside. Just opposite is a large convenient overnight parking area. The main part of the site is reached by a short climb passing a small reading room and flower decked sitting area. The upper part has 76 pitches, 60 for tourists almost all with 10A electricity connections. Hardcore roads lead to open grass pitches, many under mature trees. To the left of reception and conveniently reached through a gap in the hedge is a comfortable beer garden with tables spread out under tall trees. This belongs to a restaurant specialising in serving traditional meals. The site is ideally placed for visiting the city and there is easy access to the main road for visiting other regions. Reception holds plenty of tourist information material and the site owners, Herr and Frau Ziegler, both speak very good English and are most helpful with tourist advice.

Facilities

Modern heated, well maintained sanitary block provides free hot water, roomy adjustable showers and some washbasins in cabins. Washing machines and dryer. Kitchen with cooking rings on payment. Play room and play area for children. Reading room were daily weather report is on display. Small shop with essential supplies. Bicycle hire. WIFI internet over whole site. Off site: Bus service at entrance, tram 300 m. Golf 6 km. Riding 8 km.

Open: All year.

Directions

Site is in the eastern part of the city. To reach it without having to drive through the city, from the B31 take exit Freiberg Kappel (F. Kappel) which is well to the east of the city and follow camping signs. GPS: N47:59.514 E07:52.410

Charges 2007

Per person	€ 6,00
child (0-12 yrs)	€ 1,00 - € 2,50
pitch	€ 3,50 - € 4,50
electricity	€ 2,00
dog	€ 1,00

DE3450 Ferien-Campingplatz Münstertal

Dietzelbachstr. 6, D-79244 Münstertal (Baden-Württemberg)

Tel: 076 367 080. Email: info@camping-muenstertal.de

Münstertal is an impressive site pleasantly situated in a valley on the western edge of the Black Forest. It has been one of the top graded sites in Germany for 20 years and first time visitors will soon realise why when they see the standard of the facilities here. There are 305 individual pitches in two areas, either side of the entrance road on flat gravel, their size varying from 70-100 sq.m. All have electricity (16A) and 200 have drains, many also with water, TV and radio connections. The large indoor pool with sauna and solarium, and the outdoor pool, are both heated and free. There is a large, grass sunbathing area. The health and fitness centre provides a range of treatments, massages, etc. Children are very well catered for here with a play area and play equipment, tennis courts, minigolf, a games room with table tennis, table football and pool table and fishing. Riding is popular and the site has its own stables. The latest addition is an ice rink for skating and ice hockey in winter. There are 250 km. of walks, with some guided ones organised, and winter sports with cross-country skiing directly from the site (courses in winter – for children or adults and ski hire). The site becomes full in season and reservations, especially in July, are necessary. Member of Leading Campings Group.

Facilities

Three toilet blocks are of truly first class quality, with washbasins, all in cabins, showers with full glass dividers, baby bath, a unit for disabled visitors and individual bathrooms, some for hire. Dishwashers in two blocks. Laundry. Drying room. Motorcaravan services. Well stocked shop (all year). Restaurant, particularly good (closed Nov). Heated swimming pools, indoor all year, outdoor (with children's area) May-Oct. New health and fitness centre. Sauna and solarium. Games room. Bicycle hire. Tennis courses in summer Off site: Village amenities and train station near. Golf 15 km. Freiburg and Basel easy driving distances for day trips.

Open: All year.

Directions

Münstertal is south of Freiburg. From A5 autobahn take exit 64, turn southeast via Bad Krozingen and Staufen and continue 5 km. to the start of Münstertal, where site is signed from the main road on the left. GPS: N47:51.584 E07:45.825

Charges 2007

Per person	€ 6,80 - € 7,80
child (2-10 yrs)	€ 4,50 - € 4,95
pitch incl. services	€ 10,70 - € 13,70
dog	€ 3,30

Maestro cards accepted.

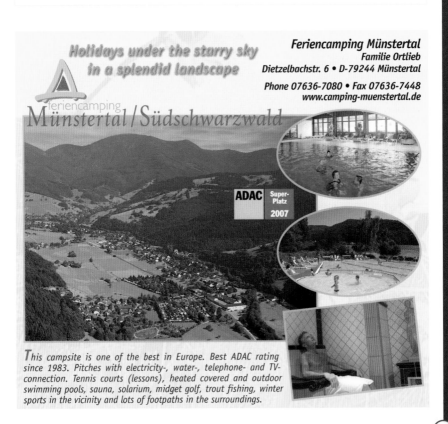

Holidays under the starry sky in a splendid landscape

feriencamping Münstertal / Südschwarzwald

ADAC Super-Platz 2007

Feriencamping Münstertal
Familie Ortlieb
Dietzelbachstr. 6 • D-79244 Münstertal
Phone 07636-7080 • Fax 07636-7448
www.camping-muenstertal.de

This campsite is one of the best in Europe. Best ADAC rating since 1983. Pitches with electricity-, water-, telephone- and TV-connection. Tennis courts (lessons), heated covered and outdoor swimming pools, sauna, solarium, midget golf, trout fishing, winter sports in the vicinity and lots of footpaths in the surroundings.

DE3436 Campingplatz Bankenhof

Bruderhalde 31, D-79822 Titisee (Baden-Württemberg)

Tel: **076 521 351**. Email: **info@bankenhof.de**

This peacefully located, fairly informal woodland site, with a friendly atmosphere, is situated just beyond the western end of Lake Titisee. The 190 pitches are on sparse grass and gravel, with some shade from a variety of trees, and 30 are occupied by seasonal units. The site is generally level, although there is a separate grassy area for tents which does have a slight slope. All pitches have electric hook-ups (16A), with gravel roads, and water taps for each area. Although there is some site lighting a torch might be useful for the darker areas under the trees. There is enough space for American RVs and other large units (welcomed, but booking is advised). Unusual features of the site are the glass walled technical area in the sanitary facilities, where the inquisitive can check the temperature of the water before taking their morning shower, and the totally separate sanitary unit with bright cheerful child-sized facilities for the under 10s. A popular bar and restaurant is open all year round (except November). Children also have an excellent fenced adventure playground. The lake and beach are only 300 m. via a direct path. This is an excellent site for exploring this part of the Black Forest and the Titisee area.

Facilities

Two sets of quality sanitary facilities plus three family bath/shower rooms for rent. Well equipped and heated, they include controllable hot showers and some washbasins in cubicles. A separate building houses facilities for disabled campers, and a unit for children (under 10 yrs). Kitchen (on payment). Laundry. Motorcaravan service point. Shop. Restaurant (excl. Nov). Fitness room. TV and cinema room. Adventure play area. Youth room. Bicycle, go-kart and buggy hire. Internet terminal. Off site: Free bus service 300 m. Fishing 500 m. Golf, riding and boat launching within 3 km. The Ski Museum at Hinterzarten 10 km. Railway Museum and steam trains at Blumberg or Germany's highest waterfall at Triberg both around 50 km.

Open: All year.

Directions

From Freiburg take road B31 east to Titisee. Pass through the town centre and continue for 2.5 km. following camping signs. The entrance to Bankenhof is on the left. GPS: N47:53.159 E08:07.842

Charges 2007

Per person	€ 5,80
child (3-16 yrs)	€ 2,90
pitch	€ 6,90
electricity per kWh	€ 0,50
dog	€ 2,00

DE3452 Terrassen Camping Alte Sägemühle

Badstrasse 57, D-79295 Sulzburg (Baden-Württemberg)

Tel: **076 345 51181**. Email: **info@camping-alte-saegemuehle.de**

This delightful site celebrated its 50th anniversary in 2005 and has erected a stone weighing several tons to commemorate the event. Situated beside a peaceful road leading only to a natural swimming pool (formerly the mill pond) and a small hotel, the site lies just beyond the picturesque old town of Sulzburg with its narrow streets. This attractive location is perfect for those seeking peace and quiet. Set in a tree-covered valley with a stream running through the centre, the site has been kept as natural as possible. It is divided into terraced areas, each surrounded by high hedges and trees. Electrical connections (16A) are available on 42 of the 45 large touring pitches, although long leads may be needed. The main building by the entrance houses reception, a small shop (which stocks a good selection of local wines) and the sanitary facilities. Run by the Geuss family (Frau Geuss speaks reasonable English) the site has won an award from the state for having been kept natural, for example, no tarmac roads, no minigolf, no playgrounds, etc. There are opportunities for walking straight from the site into the forest, and many walks and cycle rides are shown on maps available at reception. The tiny 500 year old Jewish Cemetery reached through the site has an interesting history.

Facilities

In the main building, facilities are of good quality with two private cabins, separate toilets, dishwashing, washing machine and dryer. Motorcaravan service point. Small shop for basics, beer and local wines (all year). Natural, unheated swimming pool adjacent (June - Aug) with discount to campers. Torch may be useful. New room for tent guests and motorcaravan service point. Off site: Public transport, restaurants and other shops in Sulzburg 1.5 km. Bicycle hire in Sulzburg. Riding 2 km. Bicycle hire 6 km. Fishing 8 km. Europa Park is less than an hour away.

Open: All year.

Directions

Site is easily reached (25 minutes) from autobahn A5/E35. Take exit 64 for Bad Krozingen just south of Freiburg onto the B3 south to Heitersheim, then on and up through Sulzburg, or if coming from the south, exit 65 through Müllheim, Heitersheim and Sulzburg. Reception is to the left of the road. GPS: N47:50.129 E07:43.402

Charges 2008

Per person	€ 6,00
child (1-15 yrs)	€ 3,00
pitch	€ 5,00 - € 7,50
electricity (plus meter)	€ 0,50
dog	€ 1,50

DE3445 Camping Belchenblick

Münstertäler strasse 43, D-79219 Staufen (Baden-Württemberg)

Tel: 076 337 045. Email: info@camping-belchenblick.de

This site stands at the gateway, so to speak, to the Black Forest. Not very high up itself, it is just at the start of the long road climb which leads to the top of Belchen, one of the highest summits of the forest. The site has 200 pitches (180 for touring units), all with electrical connections (10/16A), and 100 with TV and water. On site is a small heated indoor swimming pool and adjacent is a municipal sports complex, including an open-air pool and tennis courts. Reservation is necessary from early June to late August at this popular site. Charges include free hot water and the indoor pool. A little tractor will site your caravan if required. It is well situated for excursions by car to the best areas of the forest, for example the Feldberg-Titisee-Höllental circuit, and many excellent walks are possible nearby. Staufen is a pleasant little place with character.

Facilities

Three sanitary blocks are heated and have free hot water, individual washbasins (6 in private cabins), plus 21 family cabins with WC, basin and shower (some on payment per night for exclusive use). Washing machine. Gas supplies. Motorcaravan services. Shop (1/3-31/10). Bar (all year). Snacks and takeaway (1/3-31/10). Indoor and outdoor pools. Sauna and solarium. Tennis. Playground with barbecue section. Bicycle hire. Off site: Restaurant near. Fishing 20 Km. Riding 2 km.

Open: All year.

Directions

Take autobahn exit for Bad Krozingen, south of Freiburg, and continue to Staufen. Site is southeast of the town and signed, across an unmanned local railway crossing near the entrance. GPS: N47:52.307 E07:44.200

Charges 2007

Per person	€ 6,00 - € 7,50
child (2-12 yrs)	€ 4,00
pitch	€ 8,00
dog	€ 2,50
electricity (per kWh)	€ 0,60
No credit cards.	

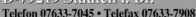

DE3465 Camping Wirthshof

Steibensteg 12, D-88677 Markdorf (Baden-Württemberg)

Tel: 075 449 627-0. Email: info@wirthshof.de

Lying 7 km. back from the Bodensee, 12 km. from Friedrichshafen, this friendly site with good facilities could well be of interest to Britons with young children. The 320 individual touring pitches have electrical connections (10A) and are of about 80 sq.m. on well tended flat grass, adjoining access roads. There are 100 larger pitches with water, waste water and electricity. No dogs are accepted in July/Aug. and there is a special section for campers with dogs at other times. Many activities are organised for children and adults over a long season.

Facilities

The three heated toilet blocks provide washbasins in cubicles, a unit for disabled people and a children's bathroom. Cosmetic studio. New beauty spa. Solar heated unit for dishwashing and laundry. Gas supplies. Motorcaravan services. Shop. Restaurant/bar with takeaway. Swimming pool (25 x 12.5 m; open 10/5-10/9). Sports field. Adventure playgrounds. Bicycle hire. Normal minigolf; also 'pit-pat', played at table height with billiard cues. Activity programme. Off site: Tennis near. Riding 8 km. Golf and fishing 10 km.

Open: 15 March - 30 October.

Directions

Site is on eastern edge of Markdorf, turn south off B33 Ravensburg road. The site is signed (but not named) from Markdorf. GPS: N47:42.869 E09:24.558

Charges 2007

Per person	€ 7,60
child (1-14 yrs)	€ 4,80
pitch incl. electricity	€ 12,50
No credit cards.	

DE3602 Camping Romantische Straße

Munster 67, D-97993 Creglingen-Münster (Baden-Württemberg)

Tel: 079 332 0289. Email: camping.hausotter@web.de

This popular tourist area can become very busy during the summer when this site would be much appreciated for its peaceful situation in a wooded valley just outside the small village of Münster. There are 100 grass touring pitches (out of 140), many level, others with a small degree of slope. They are not hedged or fenced, to keep the natural appearance of the woodland. All the pitches have electricity (6A), some shade, and are situated either side of a stream (fenced off from a weir at the top of the site). Good English is spoken by the friendly owners, who also own the restaurant.

Facilities

The main sanitary facilities are of good quality with free hot water. A small unit further into the site is not of the same quality. Launderette. Motorcaravan services. Small shop. Gas supplies. Large, pleasant bar/restaurant at the entrance (18/3-9/11, closed Mondays). Barbecue and sitting area. Heated indoor swimming pool (bathing caps required) and sauna. Minigolf. Play area. Bicycle hire. Rooms to let. Off site: Bus service 200 m. Lakes for swimming 100 m. and fishing 0.5 km. Riding 3.5 km.

Open: 15 March - 15 November.

Directions

From the Romantische Strasse between Rothenburg and Bad Mergentheim, exit at Creglingen to Münster (3 km). Site is just beyond this village.
GPS: N49:26.357 E10:02.520

Charges 2007

Per person	€ 4,80 - € 5,90
child (3-14 yrs)	€ 3,70 - € 3,90
pitch incl. electricity	€ 8,00 - € 9,00

No credit cards.
Camping Cheques accepted.

DE3627 Azur Camping Ellwangen

Rotenbacher Strasse, D-73479 Ellwangen (Baden-Württemberg)

Tel: 079 617 921. Email: ellwangen@azur-camping.de

In a quiet position on the edge of town, with the river Jagst along one side, this modern six hectare site, from which you can see the large hilltop castle, has a park-like appearance with mature trees giving some shade. The 95 large, flat, grassy pitches (8 hardstandings) are unmarked off tarmac access roads. Electricity is available for all the pitches from central boxes (16A). All the facilities are in one area to the left of the site entrance in modern units, with reception, the small shop for basic supplies and a bar/restaurant with a terrace open all year.

Facilities

Heated sanitary facilities provide some private cabins. Room for babies and disabled visitors. Laundry facilities. Gas supplies. Motorcaravan service point. Shop. Restaurant/bar. Play equipment on sand. Fishing is very popular. Off site: Cycle paths. Heated indoor municipal wave-pool 200 m. Numerous other local attractions.

Open: All year; 18 November - 28 February by reservation.

Directions

From A7 Ulm - Würzburg autobahn take exit 113 and go into Ellwangen from where site is signed on road to Rotenbach village. It is next to the Hallenbad, with a fairly tight left turn into the entrance road. GPS: N48:57.495 E10:07.240

Charges guide

Per person	€ 5,50 - € 7,50
child (2-12 yrs)	€ 4,00 - € 6,00
pitch incl. electricity	€ 8,50 - € 11,50

No credit cards.

DE3411 Campingplatz Heidehof

Heidehofstr 50, D-89150 Laichingen (Baden-Württemberg)

Tel: 073 336 408. Email: heidehof.camping@t-online.de

This site is at an altitude of 725 m. in the pleasant countryside of the Swabian Alb. Although there is an emphasis on permanent caravans, there are about 110 pitches for tourists. For overnight stays, these are in an area outside the barrier, and for longer stays pitches are inside the site. All have electricity connections (16A), and the overnight section also has an area for tents. A hotel/restaurant (open all year), although not actually in the campsite, is attached to it and immediately accessible from it. The city of Ulm and the recently opened Legoland are within easy reach.

Facilities

Five good quality toilet blocks, all heated and well maintained. 25 bathrooms to rent plus 3 for disabled visitors. Some washbasins are in cabins, and free showers. Facilities for disabled visitors. Baby rooms. Laundry facilities. Motorcaravan service point. Gas supplies. Shop with bakery. Bar and restaurant (at hotel). Swimming and paddling pools. Playgrounds. Children Off site: Riding 1 km. Fishing 6 km. Golf 10 km.

Open: All year.

Directions

Site is 6 km. from exit 61.A5/E52 Stuttgart - Ulm autobahn. Follow signs for Blaubeuren. Heidehof is about 2 km. south of the village of Machtolsheim. GPS: N48:28.659 E09:44.693

Charges 2007

Per person	€ 6,00
child (under 15 yrs)	€ 3,00
pitch	€ 5,00 - € 7,00
electricity (plus 0.5 per kWh)	€ 2,00

DE3490 Hegau Familien Camping

An der Sonnenhalde 1, D-78250 Tengen (Baden-Württemberg)

Tel: 077 369 2470. Email: info@hegau-camping.de

Located in the sunny southwest corner of Germany, this site, new in 2003, must be one of the best we have seen. It is ultra modern in design and exceptionally high standards are maintained. Located in meadowland in a quiet rural valley close to the Swiss border, it provides excellent opportunities for walking, cycling and sightseeing. All 170 touring pitches (out of a total of 200) have electricity (16A), water and drainage, although water points are shared. The pitches are grassy and level and of a good size. At the bottom of the site is an excellent heated swimming pool which also houses a sauna and Turkish bath. With the Swiss border only minutes away, it is well placed for visits to Schaffhausen and even as far afield as Zurich. It is also an excellent spot to rest from touring the southern Black Forest which is a drive of less than an hour to the west.

Facilities

New heated sanitary facilities include private cabins, showers, facilities for disabled visitors and for children. Laundry and dishwashing facilities. Three family shower rooms for rent (2 also have a bath). Motorcaravan service point. Restaurant, small shop and bar opposite reception. Swimming pool, sauna and Turkish bath (charged). Off site: Golf 20 km. Skiing for children possible in the adjoining meadows. Supermarket less than 1 km.

Open: All year.

Directions

From A81 take exit 42 on to B314. At roundabout in Tengen follow international camping signs. Turn right at supermarket on edge of village. From Kommingen follow camp signs turning left towards site at supermarket on edge of village.

Charges 2007

Per unit incl. 2 persons	€ 23,00 - € 30,00
extra person	€ 6,00
child (6-14 yrs)	€ 4,00
electricity per kWh	€ 0,60
dog	€ 4,00
Camping Cheques accepted.	

DE3467 Isnycamping

Lohbauerstr. 59-69, D-88316 Isny (Baden-Württemberg)

Tel: 075 622 389. Email: info@isny-camping.de

Isny is a delightful spot for families and for others looking for a peaceful stay in a very well-managed environment. The site has been developed to a high standard and lies just south of the village in a wood by a lake. In an open area there are 50 individual 100 sq.m. hardstanding pitches with a circular access road. A further area is on a terrace just above. A café with light snacks during the week and meals at the weekends is open long hours in high season. It has a terrace that overlooks the lake, which is used for swimming (unsupervised).

Facilities

The main sanitary unit is first class and has automatic toilet seat cleaning. There are cabins as well as vanity style washbasins, large controllable showers, with full curtain, token operated. Further facilities near the reception house showers, WCs, washbasins, and a good unit for disabled visitors. Laundry. Basic motorcaravan services. Café/bar. Reception keeps a few basic supplies. Bicycles to borrow. Off site: Tennis club. Recreation and play areas. Barbecue area. Restaurant and supermarket 1.5 km.

Open: 1 January - 30 October.

Directions

From the B12 between Lindau and Kempten, turn south at sign in Isny at traffic lights and follow signs up into the woods. GPS: N47:40.697 E10:01.821

Charges 2008

Per person	€ 6,50
child per year of age	€ 0,40
pitch	€ 9,50
electricity per kWh	€ 0,50
Special rates for senior citizens (low season).	

DE3280 Camping & Ferienpark Teichmann

An der B252, D-34516 Vöhl-Herzhausen (Hesse)

Tel: 056 352 45. Email: camping-teichmann@t-online.de

Situated by a six hectare lake (the Edersee) with tree-covered hills all around, this well cared for site blends in attractively with its surroundings. The 460 pitches (half for touring units) are mainly on flat grass, all with electricity and with some hardstandings. There is a separate area for tents with its own toilet block. Windsurfing, rowing boats, pedaloes, swimming and fishing are possible, all in different areas, and the site is also suitable for a winter sports holiday (with ski runs near). A good site for families, there are many activities (listed below) and a pitch can usually be found even for a one night stay. There are many local walks and the opportunity exists for taking a pleasure boat trip and riding home by bicycle. The many amenities include a mini-market and café. A very large open air model railway is a special attraction.

Facilities

Three good quality sanitary blocks can be heated and have some private cabins, with baby rooms in two with facilities for wheelchair users. Café and shop (both summer only). Restaurant by entrance open all day (closed Feb). Watersports. Boat and bicycle hire. Lake swimming. Football. Fishing. Minigolf. Tennis. Playground. Large working model railway. Sauna and solarium. High season disco. Off site: Riding 500 m. Golf 25 km. Cable car (you can take bikes), Aquapark, toboggan run, museums, boat trips and much else available in the Edersee area.

Open: All year.

Directions

From A44 Oberhausen - Kassel autobahn, take exit for Korbach. Site is between Korbach and Frankenberg on the B252 road, 1 km. to the south of Herzhausen, about 45 km. from the A44. GPS: N51:10.530 E08:53.440

Charges 2007

Per person	€ 3,50 - € 6,40
pitch	€ 8,00 - € 14,60
child (3-15 yrs)	€ 2,50 - € 3,80
electricity (10A)	€ 2,40
dog	€ 3,00 - € 3,60

DE3225 Naturpark Camping Suleika

Im Bodental 2, D-65391 Lorch am Rhine (Hesse)

Tel: **067 269 464**

On a steep hillside in the Rhine-Taunus Nature Park and approached by a narrow and steep system of lanes through the vineyards, this site is steeply arranged on small terraces up the side of the wooded hill with a stream flowing through – the water supply is direct from the springs. The surroundings are most attractive, with views over the vineyards to the river below. Of the 100 pitches, 50 are available for tourists. These are mostly on the lower terraces, in groups of up to four units. All have electricity and there are water points. Cars are parked away from the pitches near the entrance. There is a special area for younger campers. The site is popular for caravan rallies. A central block contains a very pleasant restaurant and small shop for basics (bread to order), with sanitary facilities alongside. With steep walks from most pitches to the facilities, this is probably not a site for visitors with disabilities; however, it is an attractive situation and reception staff are very friendly. This particular area is famous as it was briefly a 'Free State' (1919-23) and you will be able to taste and buy the site owner's wine and other items as souvenirs. The Riesling Walk footpath passes above the site. There are many local attractions (as well as the Lorelei) shown on a large map, and the helpful owner speaks good English.

Facilities

The excellent toilet block is heated in cool weather and provides some washbasins in cabins for each sex and a nicely furnished baby washroom, with WC, shower and bath. Laundry service. Motorcaravan services. Gas supplies. Restaurant (closed Mon. and Thurs.). Small shop (bread to order). Playground. Some entertainment in season. Off site: Bicycle hire. Fishing 300 m. Riding 4 km. The Riesling Walk footpath passes above the site.

Open: 15 March - 31 October.

Directions

Direct entrance road from B42 (cars only), between Rudesheim and Lorch, with height limit of 2.25 m. under railway bridge. Higher vehicles will find the site signed on the south side of Lorch. Site reached via a one-way system of lanes – follow signs. GPS: N50:01.047 E07:51.206

Charges 2008

Per person	€ 5,00
child	€ 2,00
pitch	€ 3,00 - € 7,00
electricity (plus meter)	€ 0,50 - € 1,00
dog	€ 2,00
No credit cards.	

DE3275 Camping Seepark

D-36275 Kirchheim (Hesse)

Tel: **066 281 525**. Email: **info@campseepark.de**

Kirchheim is just 5 km.from the A7 (50 km. south of Kassel) and also close to the Frankfurt to Dresden autobahns A5-A4 in eastern Hesse, which has the largest forested area in Germany. Pleasantly situated on the side of a valley, this is a large terraced site and is probably unique in offering a service for diabetics, with special food available and dialysis arranged in Bad Hersfeld hospital. There are 170 touring pitches (5 especially for people with disabilities) generally in their own areas (out of 370 altogether), varying in size from about 80 to 110 sq.m many marked with young trees in the corners. All have 16A electricity, just under half with water and drainage. They are mostly numbered in cul-de-sacs with access from tarmac roads leading up to an open area for larger vehicles and a tent field at the top. Thousands of bushes and trees have been planted over the years (but providing little shade for the pitches) and flowers are prominent around the service buildings. Opposite the entrance is a mainly sloping overnight area (including electricity and shower). This area of eastern Hesse has many areas of interest – Bad Hersfeld is an ancient town with an annual Festival of Drama and Opera from mid June to mid August, Fulda is an ecclesiastical centre and near it is Schloss Fasanerie, a good example of Baroque architecture with a fine collection of porcelain.

Facilities

The original sanitary facilities are in the complex at the entrance with further very good facilities at the modern restaurant building higher up the site (high season and holidays). They have under-floor heating and private cabins. The tent area is currently served by a portable unit. Launderette. Motorcaravan service point. Shop. Restaurant (breakfast available) open all year. Small free heated open air raised swimming pool (June-Aug; 1 m. deep). Tennis. Minigolf. Diabetic service. Play areas. Water-skiing. Barbecue area. Off site: Bus service 500 m. At the lake there is waterskiing, boat hire, adventure pool, roller skating rink, indoor tennis and fishing. Golf 4 km.

Open: All year.

Directions

From A7 Kassel - Fulda/Wurzburg take exit 87 for Kirchheim and follow signs to Seepark for 4.5 km. Site is on a minor road between the small villages of Rimboldshausen and Kemmerode, just west of the lake. GPS: N50:48.872 E09:31.070

Charges 2007

Per unit incl. up to 6 persons with electricity (plus meter)	€ 22,30
pet	€ 2,00

233

DE3265 Lahn Camping

Schleusenweg 16, D-65549 Limburg an der Lahn (Hesse)

Tel: 064 312 2610. Email: lahncamping@limburg-net.de

Pleasantly situated on the bank of the river Lahn (with direct access to it) between the autobahn and the town – both the autobahn viaduct and the cathedral are visible – this is a useful overnight stop for travellers along the Köln-Frankfurt stretch of the A3. The site is on level grass with 200 touring pitches (250 altogether) and 140 have 6A electricity (may need long cables). There are some trees but it is mainly open. It is very popular with many nationalities and can become crowded at peak times, so arrive early. There is road and rail noise.

Facilities

The main sanitary block is old and facilities are poor (showers need a token). A better quality, heated block at the other end of the site is a welcome addition. Washing machines, dryers, cookers. Gas supplies. Motorcaravan services. Bar/restaurant (evenings and Sundays) and takeaway. Small shop (not Sunday p.m.). Fishing (permit on payment). Play area. Bicycle and motorcycle hire. Off site: Swimming pool opposite. Riding 5 km. Pleasure cruises. Supermarkets, shops and restaurants in town.

Open: 23 March - 26 October.

Directions

Leave A3 autobahn at Limburg-Nord exit and follow road towards town and then signs for 'Camping-Swimming'. GPS: N50:23.357 E08:04.400

Charges 2007

Per person	€ 4,30
child (3-14 yrs)	€ 2,20
pitch incl. electricity	€ 10,10
dog	€ 1,30

No credit cards.

DE3220 Camping Burg Lahneck

Ortsteil Oberlahnstein, D-56112 Lahnstein (Rhineland Palatinate)

Tel: 026 212 765

The location of this site is splendid, high up overlooking the Rhine valley and the town of Lahnstein – many of the pitches have their own super views. It consists partly of terraces and partly of open grassy areas, has a cared for look and all is very neat and clean. One can usually find a space here, though from early July to mid-August it can become full. There are 100 individual touring pitches marked but not separated and mostly level, all with electricity (16A). Campers are sited by the management. Reception staff at the site are friendly and charges reasonable.

Facilities

The single central, heated toilet block is of a good standard, and well maintained and cleaned. There are some cabins. Showers are on payment. Washing machine and dryer. Motorcaravan services. Gas supplies. Small shop. Small playground. Off site: Cafe/restaurant adjoining site; meals also in Burg Lahneck restaurant. Town swimming pool (reduced charges for campers, 15/5-31/8). Tennis. Riding 500 m. Fishing 3 km. Bicycle hire 2 km.

Open: Easter/1 April - 31 October.

Directions

From B42 road bypassing the town, take exit for Oberlahnstein and follow signs 'Kurcentrum' and Burg Lahneck. GPS: N50:18.200 E07:36.460

Charges 2008

Per person	€ 6,00
caravan	€ 6,00
motorcaravan	€ 7,50 - € 8,50
electricity (plus meter)	€ 0,50

No credit cards.

DE3222 Camping Gülser Moselbogen

Am Gülser Moselbogen 20, Güls, D-56072 Koblenz (Rhineland Palatinate)

Tel: 026 144 474. Email: moselbogen@paffhausen.com

This site is set well above the river and has a pleasant outlook to the forested valley slopes. A large proportion of the 16 acre site is taken up by privately owned bungalows, but the touring section of 110 large individual pitches, is self contained and accessed by gravel paths leading off the main tiled roads. The flat pitches have little shade as yet, but all have connections for TV and 11/16A electricity and there are water points in each section. A new area of gravel hardstanding has been developed and RVs are accepted.

Facilities

Entry to the excellent, heated sanitary building is by a coded card that also operates the hot water to the showers (free to the washbasins, many of which are in cabins). Unit for disabled visitors. Baby room. Dishwashing and cooking rings (charged). Laundry. Gas supplies. Motorcaravan services. Shop. Café and bistro. Play area. Bicycle hire. Off site: Fishing 200 m. Special area for swimming in the Mosel 200 m. Restaurant 500 m. Güls village 1.5 km. Riding 3 km.

Open: All year.

Directions

Site is 1.5 km. west of village of Güls but easiest access is from the A61. Take exit 38 (Koblenz -Metternich). After 2 km. turn right at roundabout (Winningen). Keep on main road to Winningen until the B416 where you turn left towards Koblenz. Site is on right in 3.5 km. GPS: N50:19.954 E07:33.185

Charges 2008

Per person	€ 5,00
pitch	€ 5,00 - € 8,00
electricity (plus € 1,00 connection)	€ 1,50

DE3215 Camping Goldene Meile

Simrockweg 9-13, D-53424 Remagen (Rhineland Palatinate)

Tel: **026 422 2222**. Email: **info@camping-goldene-meile.de**

This site is on the banks of the Rhine between Bonn and Koblenz. Although there is an emphasis on permanent caravans, there are about 300 pitches for tourists (out of 500), most with 6A electricity and 100 with water and drainage. They are either in the central, more mature area or in a newer area where the numbered pitches of 80-100 sq. m. are arranged around an attractively landscaped, small fishing lake. Just 5 are by the busy river and there is likely to be some noise from the trains that run beside it. Access to the river bank is through a locked gate. Adjacent to the site is a large complex of open-air public swimming pools (campers pay the normal entrance fee). They claim always to find space for odd nights, except perhaps at B.Hs. This site is in a popular area and, although busy at weekends and in high season, appears to be well run.

Facilities

The main toilet block is heated and clean, with some washbasins in cabins, showers and facilities for wheelchair users. Shower and wash rooms locked 10 pm. A smaller block serves the newer pitches (no showers). Laundry and cooking facilities. Motorcaravan services. Gas. Shop, bar, restaurant and takeaway (all 1/4-30/10 and some weekends). Play areas and entertainment for children (July/Aug). Bicycle hire. Main gate locked at 22.00 (also 13.00 - 15.00). Off site: Swimming pool complex adjacent (May-Sept).

Open: All year.

Directions

Remagen is 23 km. south of Bonn on N9 road towards Koblenz. Site is on road close to the Rhine from Remagen to Kripp, signed from N9 south of Remagen. From A61 autobahn take Sinzig exit. GPS: N50:34.549 E07:15.085

Charges 2007

Per person	€ 5,70
child (6-16 yrs)	€ 4,70
pitch with electricity	€ 10,15 - € 11,65
dog	€ 1,60

Eurocards accepted.

DE3212 Landal Wirfttal

Wirftstraße, D-54589 Stadtkyll (Rhineland Palatinate)

Tel: **065 979 2920**. Email: **info@landal.de**

Peacefully set in a small valley in the heath and forest of the hills of the northern Eifel near the Belgian border, Wirfttal has 250 numbered pitches of which 150 are for tourers. They mostly back onto fences, hedges etc. on fairly flat ground of different levels (steel pegs are required for tents and awnings). The pitches (many on gravel) are 80 sq.m. or more, and all have electricity (8A) and TV aerial points with water points around. 5 individual pitches have their own water and waste water points. Also part of the site, but separate from the camping, is a large holiday bungalow complex.

Facilities

One main toilet block, and two small units, all heated. All ladies' washbasins and one for men in main block are in cabins. New shop. Restaurant and snacks. Swimming pool complex (discount for campers). Indoor pool (free) and sauna and solarium (on payment) Tennis. Riding. Fishing. Bicycle hire. Sports centre adjacent with squash hall. Play equipment. Adventure playground. Winter sports. Bicycle and sledge hire. Animation in season.

Open: All year.

Directions

Site is 1.5 km. south of Stadtkyll on road towards Schüller. Follow signs in Stadtkyll for Haus an der See). GPS: N50:20.326 E06:32.252

Charges 2008

Per unit incl. 2 persons and electricity	€ 14,00 - € 31,00
extra person	€ 3,00
dog	€ 3,00

Less in low season. Special 5, 8 or 10 day rates.

DE3233 Campingplatz Holländischer Hof

D-56820 Senheim (Rhineland Palatinate)

Tel: 026 734 660. Email: holl.hof@t-online.de

This campsite lies along a bend of the river Moselle, surrounded on three sides by hills, and on the other by the river. An arm of the river intrudes here and a harbour for small boats has been made. A road bridge passes over the very last pitches at one end of the site, but this did not seem to generate any noise nuisance. There are some seasonal pitches, but the site caters mostly for tourists. All 150 pitches have electricity points (6/10A). Dogs are not allowed on the site, but there are a dozen pitches outside the barrier for those who have dogs with them.

Facilities

Main sanitary block – washbasins (some in cubicles), showers (by token), unit for disabled visitors. Laundry facilities. Other toilet facilities in a 'portacabin' unit. Motorcaravan service point. Shop. Gas. Restaurant, snack bar, pizzeria and takeaway (with children's menu) and terrace. Playground. TV room. Games room. Sports field. River fishing. Off site: Tennis 300 m. Bicycle hire 2 km. ATM point 2 km. Golf 4 km.

Open: Easter - 1 November.

Directions

From Cochem (on the west bank) take B49 upstream (south). At Nehren, cross bridge towards Senheim. From the bridge the site is below on the left. If coming from upstream, take the B49 north from Alf. GPS: N50:04.931 E07:12.521

Charges 2008

Per person	€ 4,10
pitch	€ 7,15

No credit cards.

DE3237 Camping In der Enz

In der Enz 25, D-54673 Neuerburg (Rhineland Palatinate)

Tel: 065 642 660

This site is just outside the town, next to the municipal swimming pool complex, and the enthusiastic owners give a very warm welcome which makes this a very pleasant place to stay. The site is bisected by the unfenced River Enz which is little more than a stream at this point. The section nearest the road is occupied by 50 long stay units. The other half, on the other side of the river with its own access road and footbridge, is solely for tourists. This has 50 very large, open grass pitches, all with electricity (16A), of which 32 are multi-service with water and drainage.

Facilities

New sanitary block of very high quality with the usual facilities and provision for disabled visitors. Baby room. Kitchen and laundry. Family sauna room (extra charge). Play area. Bicycle hire. Internet point. The site is not suitable for American RVs. Off site: Swimming pool complex (May-Sept) and all year restaurant and bar (both adjacent). Fishing, riding and tennis within walking distance. Golf 13 km.

Open: 21 March - 31 October.

Directions

Neuerburg is about 50 km. northwest of Trier. From A60 (E29) take exit 6 and head south to Bitburg, then take road 50 west to Sinspelt. Finally turn north for 6 km. to Neuerburg, pass through town and site is 1.5 km. north of the town. GPS: N50:01.668 E06:16.613

Charges 2007

Per person	€ 3,00
pitch incl. car	€ 7,00 - € 9,00
electricity (per kWh)	€ 0,50

DE3242 Country Camping Schinderhannes

D-56291 Hausbay-Pfalzfeld (Rhineland Palatinate)

Tel: 06746 80280. Email: info@countrycamping.de

About 30 km. south of Koblenz, west of the Rhine and south of the Mosel, this site is set in a 'bowl' of land which catches the sun all day. With trees and parkland all around, it is a peaceful and picturesque setting. There are 150 permanent caravans in a separate area from 90 short stay touring pitches on hardstanding. For longer stays, an area around the lake has a further 160 numbered pitches. These are of over 80 sq.m. on grass, some with hardstanding and all with 8A electricity. You can position yourself for shade or sun.

Facilities

The sanitary buildings, which can be heated, are of a high standard with one section, in the reception/shop building, for the overnight pitches and the remainder close to the longer stay places. Facilities for disabled people. Laundry. Bar. Restaurant with takeaway. TV area. Skittle alley. Shop (all amenities 1/3-31/10 and Xmas). Tennis. Fishing. Play area. Rallies welcome. Torches useful. Barrier closed 22.00-07.00 hrs.

Open: All year.

Directions

From A61 Koblenz - Ludwigshafen road, take exit 43 Pfalzfeld (30 km. south of Koblenz) and on to Hausbay where site is signed. GPS: N50:06.358 E07:34.093

Charges 2008

Per person	€ 6,00
child (under 14)	€ 3,00
pitch incl. electricity	€ 8,00

Camping Cheques accepted.

DE3232 Family Camping

Wiesenweg 25, D-56820 Mesenich bei Cochem (Rhineland Palatinate)

Tel: **026 734 556**. Email: **info@familycamping.de**

Situated beside the River Mosel with views of forest and vineyard, this attractive, family run site is on a stretch of the river that is well away from the railway. The 94 touring pitches are among the vines, mainly level, with electric hook-ups (6/10A), separated by bushes and some with shade. There are 25 pitches with their own water tap and there are 35 tents for rent. The site roads are relatively narrow and are not suitable for larger units especially American RVs or twin axle caravans.

Facilities

Well equipped, heated toilet facilities provide good sized showers (on payment), washbasins mainly in cubicles or curtained. Good baby room. Laundry with washing machines and dryer. Shop, bar and restaurant (1/5-8/9). Takeaway (1/5-15/9). Swimming pools (1/6-15/9, weather dependant). Play area. Disco evenings and wine tours in July/Aug. River fishing (with permit). Dogs are not accepted in July/Aug. Off site: Bicycle hire 300 m. Golf 7 km. Riding 10 km. Wine museum. Cochem with its castle and leisure centre 15 km.

Open: 8 April - 8 October.

Directions

Mesenich is about 15 km. southwest of Cochem, on opposite side of the River Mosel. From B49 at Senheim, cross river and follow signs (Mesenich). Site in village on left. Or cross river at Cochem and follow L98 riverside road south to Mesenich. Or from scenic B421 Kirchberg to Zell road, turning to Senheim 15 km. after Kirchberg (winding, steep road at the end). GPS: N50:06.093 E07:11.628

Charges 2007

Per unit incl. 2 persons	€ 10,00 - € 14,00
extra person	€ 4,00

No credit cards.

DE3245 Landal Sonnenberg

D-54340 Leiwen (Rhineland Palatinate)

Tel: **065 079 3690**. Email: **info@landal.de**

With attractive views over the Mosel as you climb the approach road, 4 km. from the wine village of Leiwen and the river, this pleasant site is on top of a hill. It has a splendid free leisure centre incorporating an indoor activity pool with child's paddling pool, whirlpool, cascade and slides. Also in this building are tenpin bowling, a sauna, solarium and fitness room, tennis and badminton, plus a snack bar. Combining a bungalow complex (separate) with camping, the site has 150 large, individual and numbered grass/gravel pitches on terraces with electricity (6A) and TV connections.

Facilities

The single toilet block has under-floor heating, washbasins in cabins (all for women, a couple for men). It is stretched in busy times. Separate suite for disabled visitors. Laundry. Motorcaravan services. Shop. Restaurant, bistro, bar and snacks. Minigolf. Indoor leisure centre with activity pool, climbing wall, 10 pin bowling, tennis and badminton. Playground. Bicycle hire (high season). Disco, entertainment and excursions at various busy times. Deer park. Off site: Fishing 5 km. Riding or golf 12 km.

Open: 23 March - 3 November.

Directions

From A48/A1 (Trier - Koblenz) take new exit 128 for Bekond, Föhren, Hetzerath and Leiwen. Follow signs for Leiwen and in town follow signs for Ferienpark, Sonnenberg or Freibad on very winding road up hill 4 km. to site. GPS: N49:48.227 E06:53.554

Charges guide

Per unit incl. 2 persons and electricity	€ 22,00 - € 33,00
extra person	€ 3,00
dog	€ 3,00

DE3250 Landal Warsberg

In den Urlaub 1, D-54439 Saarburg (Rhineland Palatinate)

Tel: **065 819 1460**. Email: **info@landal.de**

On top of a steep hill in an attractive location, this site and the long winding approach road both offer pleasant views over the town and surrounding area. A large, well organised site, there are 461 numbered touring pitches of quite reasonable size on flat or slightly sloping ground, separated in small groups by trees and shrubs, with electrical connections (16A) available in most places. There are some tour operator pitches and a separate area with holiday bungalows to rent. This is a site with friendly reception staff, which should appeal to all age groups. July and August are very busy.

Facilities

Three toilet blocks of very good quality provide washbasins (many in private cabins) and a unit for disabled visitors. Large launderette. Motorcaravan services. Gas supplies. Shop. Restaurant and takeaway, games rooms adjacent. Swimming pool. Tennis. Minigolf. Bicycle hire. Playground. Entertainment in season. 530 m. long 'Rodelbahn' toboggan. Off site: Riding and fishing 5 km.

Open: 31 March - 30 October.

Directions

From Trier on road 51 site is well signed in the northwest outskirts of Saarburg off the Trierstrasse (signs also for 'Ferienzentrum'). Follow signs up hill for 3 km. GPS: N49:37.195 E06:32.609

Charges 2007

Per unit incl. 2 persons and electricity	€ 23,00 - € 31,00
extra person	€ 3,50

DE3255 Azur Camping am Königsberg

Am Schwimmbad 1, D-67752 Wolfstein (Rhineland Palatinate)

Tel: 063 044 143. Email: benspruijt@gmx.de

Situated in an area between the Rhine and Mosel rivers in a nature area at the foot of the Königsberg, this is a small attractive, well maintained site with plenty of facilities. Of the 100 pitches, 70 are reserved for tourists and most have electricity, fresh and waste water connections. The level, grass, mainly open pitches are easily reached by tarmac site roads. A large separate meadow is for tents and has a communal grill and covered eating area. Trees and hedges provide some shade and division of the site. A local railway with one train an hour, passes close to the site.

Facilities

Modern comfortable, heated sanitary block with all usual facilities including showers, free hot water and private cabins. Facilities for disabled people. Laundry room. Fridge rental. Shop. Bar/restaurant (all year). Takeaway. Play cabin, play area and games room for children with entertainment daily in summer. Minigolf. Bicycle hire. Fishing. Off site: Large swimming pool complex next to site, free to campers. Shops and other facilities in the village 300 m. Riding 2 km.

Open: All year.

Directions

Wolfstein is 20 km. northwest of Kaiserslautern on the B270. From A6 (Ludwigshafen - Saarbrücken) take exit 15 for Kaiserslauten West and head north towards Lauterecken. In Erfenbach left on B270 towards Lauterecken and Idar-Oberstein. Stay on the B270. Site is signed 300 m. south of the village of Wolfstein.

Charges guide

Per person	€ 5,50 - € 7,50
child (2-12 yrs)	€ 4,00 - € 6,00
pitch incl. electricity	€ 8,50 - € 11,50

DE3256 Azur Camping Hunsrück

Parkstrasse, D-54421 Reinsfeld (Rhineland Palatinate)

Tel: 065 039 5123. Email: reinsfeld@azur-camping.de

This quiet countryside site, spread over 20 hectares, is situated close to the French and Luxembourg borders. With 980 pitches (600 for touring units), the site is constructed with 29 circular grassed areas, each surrounded by trees, and containing no more than 25 pitches. This creates the impression of a smaller site, although you do have the facilities of a larger large site. A spacious central meadow opposite a lake is used for caravans and tents and is separated from a playing field by a tree lined stream. This is a quiet and relatively unknown comer of Germany.

Facilities

Six heated sanitary buildings with free hot showers, washbasins in cabins and family bathrooms to rent. Baby rooms. Facilities for disabled people. Laundry facilities. Motorcaravan service point. Gas supplies. Supermarket. Comfortable restaurant/bar with takeaway. Swimming pool. Tennis. Large play area and children

Open: All year.

Directions

Site is 20 km. southeast of Trier. Leave A1 at exit 132 (Reinsfeld) and follow sign for Reinsfeld. Continue through village and site is signed to the left. GPS: N49:68.612 E06:86.780

Charges 2007

Per person	€ 5,00 - € 7,00
child (2-12 yrs)	€ 3,00 - € 3,50
pitch with electricity	€ 8,70 - € 10,70

DE3260 Knaus Camping Park Bad Dürkheim

In den Almen 3, D-67098 Bad Dürkheim (Rhineland Palatinate)

Tel: 063 226 1356. Email: badduerkheim@knauscamp.de

This large site is comfortable and has some 550 pitches (about half occupied by permanent caravans) but, being the best site at this well known wine town, it is very busy in main season. However, with some emergency areas they can usually find space for everyone. The site is long with individual pitches of fair size arranged on each side of the central road, which is decorated with arches of growing vines. Growing trees provide some shade and electrical connections are available throughout (16A). There is some noise from light aircraft, especially at weekends.

Facilities

Three large sanitary blocks are spaced out along the central avenue. They are of a high standard (private cabins, automatic taps, etc) and are heated in cool weather. Laundry facilities. Gas supplies. Motorcaravan services. Cooking facilities. Shop. Restaurant. Sports programme. Tennis. Sports field. Playground. Sauna and solarium. Bathing and non-powered boat launching in lake. Activity programme (guided tours, biking, canoeing and climbing). Dogs are not accepted.

Open: All year excl. November.

Directions

Bad Dürkheim is on the no. 37 road west of Ludwigshafen. Site is on the eastern outskirts, signed from the Ludwigshafen road at traffic lights. GPS: N49:28.428 E08:11.502

Charges 2007

Per person	€ 6,00
child (4-14 yrs)	€ 3,00
pitch with electricity (plus meter)	€ 11,00 - € 18,00
No credit cards.	

DE3258 Camping Sägmühle

D-67705 Trippstadt (Rhineland Palatinate)

Tel: 063 069 2190. Email: info@saegmuehle.de

Camping Sägmühle has been in the same family for over 50 years, during which time it has undergone several major developments which have turned it into a first class site. It is peacefully situated beside a lake, in a wooded valley in the heart of the Palatinate Nature Park, and there are many kilometres of walks to enjoy, as well as castles to explore. The 200 touring pitches (half the total) are at least 80 sq.m. or more on flat grass, each with electricity (4A or more) and TV connections, with plenty of water points around. There are three separate areas of pitches. One area is close to the lake and it is a pleasant change to find a site that keeps the lakeside pitches for tourers. A first class restaurant offers you fine local wines, and there is plenty for younger children to enjoy with fishing, swimming and boating in the lake (pedaloes for hire), a fort, minigolf and tennis.

Facilities

Each area has its own sanitary facilities, those beside the lake and the back being first class, while those at the side have been renovated. Private cabins, baby bathroom, facilities for disabled people, launderette. Motorcaravan services. Restaurant serving local specialties and takeaway (lunchtime and evening). Bread available in high season. Solarium. Tennis. Play areas. Mountain bike hire. Boules. Minigolf. Lake fishing. Entertainment daily in high season. Off site: Shops and bus service 10 minutes walk in Trippstadt. Riding 4 km. Golf 25 km. Wilenstein Castle (12th century ruin) and the famous romantic Karls Valley Gorge are nearby.

Open: 1 January - 31 October, 12-31 December.

Directions

At Kaiserslautern on A6, take exit 15 (Kaiserslautern West) onto B270 towards Pirmasens. Turn left after 8 km. towards Karlstal/Trippstadt and follow site signs. From the A65 between Karlsruhe and Neustadt take exit 15 or 17 towards Annweiler on the B10. After Annweiler right on B48 to Rinnthal and on towards Kaiserslautern. After 20 km. left to Kaiserslautern and next left to Trippstadt. Follow site signs into the valley. GPS: N49:21.096 E07:46.862

Charges 2008

Per person	€ 6,20 - € 7,20
child (under 14 yrs)	€ 2,60 - € 3,20
pitch incl. electricity (4A)	€ 7,30 - € 9,30

Camping Cheques accepted.

DE3254 Camping Harfenmühle

An der Deutschen Edelsteinstrasse, D-55758 Asbacherhütte (Rhineland Palatinate)

Tel: 067 867 076. Email: mail@harfenmuehle.de

Harfenmühle is quietly situated in a wooded valley in the Naturpark Saar-Hunsrück, an attractive area of Germany just below the Mosel. The site has its own gourmet restaurant and wine cellar. It is a family-run, friendly, relaxed partly terraced site, with 100 mostly individual touring pitches. They range in size up to 150 sq.m. with 16A electrical connections and 20 pitches also have water and drainage. With a new, larger meadow for tents, there are also 60 seasonal units and 7 chalets.

Facilities

A new toilet block includes good shower cubicles (on payment), facilities for babies and disabled visitors. Further facilities in the main building. Launderette. Kiosk. Takeaway. Wine cellar/bar. Restaurant with terrace plus gourmet restaurant open Wed-Sun. Sauna and solarium. Swimming lake. Water play area. Off site: 1500 km. of marked walks through the Naturpark Saar-Hunsrück. Riding 3 km. Bicycle hire 5 km. Golf 10 km. Heated open air pool 12 km. Indoor pool 12 km. Nordic walking park.

Open: All year.

Directions

From the B41 Saarbrücken - Bad Kreuznach, exit north at Fischbach signed towards Herrstein and then on through Morschied to Asbacherhütte, with site entrance on right. GPS: N49:48.217 E07:16.167

Charges 2008

Per person	€ 5,00
child (2-15 yrs)	€ 2,50
pitch	€ 8,00
electricity per kWh	€ 0,50

No credit cards.

The Leading Campsites

in Europe

LeadingCampings – the pleasure of leisure.

We create that high level touring camping that you deserve for the most precious weeks of the year. 32 LeadingCampings throughout Europe guarantee first class vacations: in tent, caravan, motorcaravan or a wide range of rental accommodation. Enjoy also first class wellness spas, restaurants, sports and entertainment facilities. In this camping guide all entries of LeadingCampings are highlighted as 'member of the LeadingCampings'. Visit us on internet, order your personal LeadingCard and profit from all its benefits. You are welcome!

www.leadingcampings.com

LeadingCamping

MAP 12

Greece

The country's coastline offers huge variety – sheltered bays and coves, golden stretches of sand with dunes, pebbly beaches, coastal caves with steep rocks and volcanic black sand and coastal wetlands.

CAPITAL: ATHENS

Tourist Office

Greek National Tourism Organisation
4 Conduit Street, London, W1S 2DJ
Tel: 020 7495 9300 (Enquiries & Information)
Fax: 020 7287 1369
Email: info@gnto.co.uk
Internet: http://www.gnto.co.uk

Stretching from the Balkans in the north to the south Aegean, Greece shares borders with Albania, Macedonia, Bulgaria and Turkey.

It is above all a mountainous country – the Pindus range forms the backbone of mainland Greece, extending through central Greece into the Peloponnese and Crete. The majority of islands throughout the Aegean are in fact the mountain peaks of the now submerged landmass of Aegeis, which was once the link between mainland Greece and Asia Minor. Mount Olympus in the north of the country, known from Greek mythology as the abode of the gods, is the highest mountain (2,917 m).

Six thousand islands are scattered in the Aegean and Ionian Seas, a unique phenomenon on the continent of Europe; of these islands, only 227 are inhabited.

Population
10.9 million

Climate
Greece has a Mediterranean climate with plenty of sunshine, mild temperatures and a limited amount of rainfall.

Language
Greek, but most of the people connected to tourism and the younger generations currently practise English and sometimes German, Italian or French.

Telephone
The country code for Greece is 00 30.

Currency
Euro

Time
GMT + 2 (GMT + 3 from last Sunday in March to last Sunday in October).

Public Holidays
New Year's Day 1 Jan; Epiphany 6 Jan; Shrove Monday Orth. Easter; Independence Day 25 Mar; Easter: Good Friday, Easter Sunday and Easter Monday (Orthodox); Labour Day 1 May; Whit Sunday and Monday (Orthodox); Assumption Day 15 Aug; Ochi Day (National Fest) 28 Oct; Christmas 25/26 Dec.

Motoring
Speed limits are 100-120 km/h on highways unless otherwise posted; 50 km/h in residential areas unless otherwise marked. An international driver's licence is required. Road signs are written in Greek and repeated phonetically in English. Road tolls exist on two highways in Greece, one leading to Northern Greece and the other to the Peloponnese.

GR8120 Camping Poseidon Beach

Platamon-Pieria, GR-60065 Neos Panteleimonas (Central Macedonia)

Tel: **235 204 1654**

This site is located in a rural area at the foot of Mount Olympus, just off the motorway which follows the coast from Thessalonica to Athens. The area is known for its golden beaches and, as its name suggests, this campsite enjoys direct access. The 250 pitches are on level ground shaded by mature trees and a variety of shrubs and all have 16A electricity. There is a good restaurant, which is open for most of the season. The site is also close to the 10th century castle of Platamon, which is the principal attraction of the area. There may be some noise from the nearby railway and motorway.

Facilities

Two modern and one refurbished sanitary blocks with mainly British style WCs (one Turkish toilet per block), open washbasins and controllable showers. Chemical disposal. Laundry sinks, washing machines and dryers. Covered dishwashing area. Shop, bar and restaurant (all May - Sept). Fishing.

Open: 1 March - 31 October.

Directions

From E75 Thessaloniki - Athens motorway (toll road) turn left signed Neos Panteleimonas. Cross over railway bridge and turn left onto coastal road. In 500 m. turn right at campsite sign next to Camping Heraklia. Site is on right in 300 m. GPS: N40:00.778 E22:35.430

Charges guide

Per person	€ 4,40 - € 5,00
pitch incl. car and electricity	€ 9,30 - € 11,10

GR8145 Camping Areti

GR-63081 Neos Marmaras (Central Macedonia)

Tel: **237 507 1430**. Email: **info@camping-areti.gr**

If you imagine Greek campsites as being set immediately behind a small sandy beach in a quiet cove with pitches amongst the pine and olive trees which stretch along way back to the small coast road, then you have found your ideal site. Camping Areti is conveniently located just off the beaten track on the peninsula of Sithonia. It has 130 pitches, all for tourers (no static caravans are allowed). The olive groves at the rear provide hidden parking spaces for caravans and boats that can be brought to the site when the owner is present.

Facilities

Three excellent toilet blocks include showers, WCs and washbasins. Kitchen with sinks, electric hobs and fridges. Laundry with washing machines. Facilities for emptying chemical toilet. Small shop and restaurant. Sandy beach. Bungalows to rent. Fishing, sailing and swimming. Off site: Riding nearby. Sithonia, Mount Athos and the nearby Spalathronissia islands.

Open: 1 May - 31 October.

Directions

Although the postal address is Neos Marmaras the site is 12 km. south. So stay on the main coast road, go past the casino resort at Porto Carras and 5 km. further on turn right towards the site (signed). Then turn right again and go down to the coast where you must turn left and go for about 1.5 km. Turn right into site access road. Reception is about 700 m. GPS: N40:01.451 E23:48.957

Charges 2007

Per person	€ 8,10 - € 9,00
pitch incl. electricity	€ 13,90 - € 15,00
No credit cards.	

GR8235 Camping Kalami Beach

Plataria, GR-46100 Igoumenitsa (Epirus)

Tel: **266 507 1211**

A warm welcome awaits you on your arrival at Camping Kalami Beach. This family run site is ideally situated 8 kilometres from the ferry port of Igoumenitsa, where it is possible to take cruises to several islands and to Italy. The site is very well cared for with an attractive floral display around the reception building. There are 75 pitches of varying sizes with 10A electricity. Although the site is quite steep in places, the pitches themselves are level and well drained and those at the front of the site above the beach have panoramic views across the sea and to the mountains of Corfu.

Facilities

One sanitary block with British style WCs, washbasins and showers. Second block has showers and washbasins in cabins. Chemical disposal point. Laundry room with sinks and washing machines and dryer (token operated). Dishwashing area inside. Shop. Bar and restaurant, takeaway. Beach at site.

Open: 1 March - 31 October.

Directions

From Igoumenitsa head south on the E55 towards Preveza. In 8 km. site is on right, well signed. Entrance is 300 m. down a steep narrow lane. GPS: N39:28.427 E20:14.449

Charges 2007

Per person	€ 5,50
pitch incl. car and electricity	€ 10,30 - € 13,30
No credit cards.	

GR8285 Camping Hellas International

GR-38500 Kato Gatzea (Thessaly)

Tel: 242 302 2267. Email: camping-hellas@argo.net.gr

There is a warm welcome from the English speaking brother and sister team who own and run Camping Hellas. The campsite has been in the family since the sixties, when tourists first asked if they could camp overnight and use the facilities of the taverna. It is in a beautiful setting in a 500 year old olive grove, right next to the beach and the calm blue waters of the Pagasitikos gulf. Everything is kept spotlessly clean and the owners have many plans for further improvements. There are around 100 pitches all with 16A electricity. Pitch sizes vary and some parts are more level than others, but shade is plentiful thanks to the olive trees.

Facilities

One modern and one old sanitary block, both very clean with British style toilets and open washbasins. Very good facilities for disabled visitors. Laundry and dishwashing facilities. Shop has essentials from 15 April, fully stocked from May. Bar. TV room. Restaurant (from April). Boat launching. Dogs are not allowed on the beach. Off site: Fishing 5 km. Sailing 5 km. Riding 18 km. Bicycle hire 18 km. Pelion steam railway, boat trips to Skiathos.

Open: 15 March - 31 October.

Directions

From the north follow the E75 towards Lamia. Turn left at sign for Volos onto E92. Follow coastal road south towards Argalasti for 18 km. Site is off coastal road on right at Kato Gatzea.
GPS: N39:18.650 E23:06.546

Charges guide

Per person	€ 5,00 - € 6,00
child (4-16 yrs)	€ 3,00 - € 5,00
pitch incl. car and electricity	€ 9,90 - € 11,90

GR8330 Camping Ionion Beach

Glifa, GR-27050 Vartholomino Ilias (Western Greece)

Tel: 262 309 6395. Email: ioniongr@otenet.gr

This is a well kept site in a beautiful location by the Ionian Sea, created from former farmland by the Fligos family. Much has changed since they welcomed their first guests in 1982, when they still left plenty of space for growing potatoes. Now it is a modern site with a large pool and a paddling pool and two blocks of apartments to rent. Separated by a variety of trees and oleander bushes, there are 235 pitches with 16A electricity and of between 80 and 100 sq.m. Those at the front of the site have a view over the sea and the island of Zakynthos. The campsite has its own beach bar.

Facilities

Two modern sanitary blocks with British style WCs and showers with washbasins in cabins. Motorcaravan service point. Turkish style chemical disposal point. Laundry room with sinks and washing machine. Covered dishwashing area. Shop, bar, restaurant (15/4-15/11). Internet access in bar. Swimming pool and paddling pool (15/4-15/11). Caution is advised as there are no depth markings in the pool. Play area. Off site: Ferries to Zakynthos from Kilini, ancient city of Olympia, Frankish fortress of Chlemoutsi.

Open: All year.

Directions

From Patra head south on E55 towards Pyrgos. At sign for Vartholomio, turn right in town centre turn right at sign for Glyfa and Ionion Beach. In 15 km. campsite sign is on right. For those coming from the north of Greece, the there is a toll for the Korinthian gulf bridge toll (€ 15,50 each way when we visited). GPS: N37:50.197 E21:08.028

Charges 2007

Per person	€ 5,50 - € 6,00
pitch incl. car and electricity	€ 10,60 - € 16,60

GR8525 Chrissa Camping

Chrisso, GR-33054 Delphi (Central Greece)

Tel: 226 508 2050. Email: info@chrissacamping.gr

This well kept site is located close to Delphi which was once sacred to the god Apollo and is now the setting for some of the most important monuments of ancient Greek civilisation. The site's situation on a hill ensures stunning views across a vast olive grove to the Gulf of Corinth beyond. There are 60 pitches with electricity connections (16A). They are mainly arranged on terraces as the site is quite steep, which means that everyone can enjoy the views. As the site is in a conservation area, mobile homes are not permitted but there are some round wooden cabins to rent which blend in very well.

Facilities

Modern toilet block with British style WCs, open washbasins and controllable showers. Plastic seats available in showers. Motorhome service point. Chemical disposal point. Laundry facilities. Dishwashing room. Shop (1/4-30/10). Bar, restaurant and takeaway (weekends only in winter). Outdoor pool and paddling pool. Barbecues are not allowed. Internet. Off site: Beach 10 km. Skiing 18 km. Delphi.

Open: All year.

Directions

From Patra head west on E65 (48) towards Itea. Continue towards Delphi and 6 km. from Delphi, Chrisso is signed on the right. Site is directly opposite, clearly signed and entrance is 300 m. down a narrow lane. GPS: N38:28.346 E22:27.549

Charges 2008

Per person	€ 5,50 - € 6,50
pitch incl. car and electricity	€ 12,00 - € 13,00
Camping Cheques accepted.	

(243)

GR8565 Camping Kokkino Limanaki

GR-19009 Rafina (Attica)

Tel: 229 403 1604. Email: travelnet@otenet.gr

This site is an ideal base for visiting the famous ancient sites of Athens as it lies just 20 minutes away from the Acropolis. The site is located 100 m. above sea level, but also has access to the beach below. There are 100 pitches of various sizes on partly sloping ground some of which have views over the Aegean sea and nearby islands. All pitches have 16A electricity. The single sanitary block has unisex showers and may be stretched at busy times. A torch would be useful at night. The site has its own bar and restaurant with sea views from the terrace.

Facilities

Single toilet block with open style washbasins and unisex showers. Dishwashing sinks, washing machine and ironing board. Fridges for hire. Chemical disposal. Bar and restaurant. Takeaway (July and August). Off site: Fishing 1 km. Boat launching 4.5 km. Beach 200 m.

Open: 1 May - 30 September.

Directions

Travelling south on E75 towards Athens turn right onto slip road signed Varibobi. At traffic lights turn left and follow signs to Nea Makri. Enter town and follow signs to Rafina. 1.6 km. after leaving Nea Makri at traffic lights turn left (Kokkino Limanaki). Follow signs to site. GPS: N38:01.899 E24:00.095

Charges guide

Per person	€ 5,90 - € 6,50
child	€ 4,30
pitch incl. electricity	€ 8,60 - € 10,00

GR8640 Camping Kastraki

Assini, GR-21100 Nafplio (Peloponnese)

Tel: 275 205 9386. Email: sgkamania@kastrakicamping.gr

Ancient Assini, where Camping Kastraki is located, inspired the Nobel Prize winning poet, George Seferis, to write one of his most beautiful poems. This alone attracts the more romantic traveller to head for this wonderful coast. Others attracted by the magic of the shores of the Argolid will not be disappointed. Nearby Nafplio was the Capital of the newly formed Greek state from 1828 to 1834 when this role passed to Athens. Camping Kastraki, run personally by the owner, George Karmaniolas, offers 200 good pitches set amongst trees that border a narrow shingle beach.

Facilities

Refurbished toilet block includes showers, WCs and washbasins. Facilities for disabled visitors. Sinks for dishwashing. Gas hobs for cooking. Chemical toilet emptying point and motorcaravan service point. Washing machines. Small shop, bar and restaurant during high season. Flats to rent nearby. Slipway for small boats. Off site: Nafplio and Ancient Assini.

Open: 1 April - 20 October.

Directions

From Nafplio, head towards Tolo and go through the modern town of Assini. Shortly before Tolo, site is well signed on the left. From Drepano head towards Tolo and turn left at T-junction to site on the left. GPS: N37:31.680 E22:52.572

Charges 2007

Per person	€ 7,20 - € 8,00
child (4-10 yrs)	€ 4,30 - € 4,80
pitch incl. car and electricity	€ 14,20 - € 18,30

GR8700 Camping Erodios

Koroni, Gialova, GR-24001 Pylos (Peloponnese)

Tel: 272 302 8240. Email: erodioss@otenet.gr

This brand new site sets a standard not seen anywhere else in Greece! The owner, Efthinios Panourgias, has given great thought to what is needed and then provided it to the highest possible standard in an environmentally friendly way. He is constantly on the site ensuring these high standards are maintained and already has plans for further improvements. The 90 pitches have high reed screens to provide shade which is most welcome given the high temperatures even in the low season. There is direct access to the beach and the turquoise sea in a sheltered bay north of Pylos.

Facilities

Three excellent toilet blocks include showers, WCs and washbasins. Facilities for disabled visitors. Two kitchens include sinks, electric hobs and fridges. Laundry. Facilities for emptying chemical toilet. Motorcaravan service points. Very good shop. Bar/café with Internet. Excellent restaurant. Bicycle, car and motorbike rental. Barbecue. Play area for under 5s. Eight bungalows for rent. Off site: Pylos.

Open: 25 March - 31 October.

Directions

From Pylos head north on the main road and fork left towards Gialova. Once in the village turn left, signed to site and Golden Beach. Site is on the left in 700 m. From Gargaliari head south towards Pylos and in the village of Gialova turn right towards the site. GPS: N36:57.028 E21:42.030

Charges 2007

Per person	€ 5,00 - € 6,00
child	€ 3,00
pitch incl. electricity	€ 9,00 - € 14,00

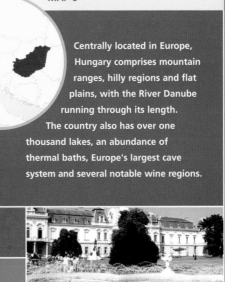

MAP 6

Hungary

Centrally located in Europe, Hungary comprises mountain ranges, hilly regions and flat plains, with the River Danube running through its length. The country also has over one thousand lakes, an abundance of thermal baths, Europe's largest cave system and several notable wine regions.

CAPITAL: BUDAPEST

Tourist Office

Hungarian National Tourist Office
46 Eaton Place, London SW1X 8AL
Tel: 020 7823 1032
Fax: 020 7823 1459
Email: htlondon@btinternet.com
Internet: www.hungarytourism.hu

An increasingly popular destination, Budapest is divided into two parts by the Danube, the hilly side of Buda on the western bank and the flat plain of Pest on the eastern bank. A cruise along the river will enable you to appreciate this picturesque city with its grand buildings, romantic bridges, museums and art galleries. It also has plenty of spas to tempt you. North of the city, the Danube Bend is one of the grandest stretches of the river, along the banks of which you'll find historic towns and ruins. Further afield in the north-eastern hills, the caves at Aggtelek are another firm favourite.

One of the largest in Europe, Lake Balaton covers an area of nearly 600 square miles and is great for swimming, sailing, windsurfing and waterskiing. It has two distinct shores, the bustling south with its string of hotels, restaurants and beaches, and the north offering a quieter pace with beautiful scenery and sights.

Population
10.2 million

Climate
There are four fairly distinct seasons – hot in summer, mild spring and autumn, very cold winter with snow.

Language
The official language is Magyar, but German is widely spoken.

Telephone
The country code is 00 36.

Money
Currency: Hungarian forints
Banks: Mon-Fri 09.00-14.00,
Sat 09.00-12.00.

Shops
Mon-Fri 10.00-18.00, Sat 10.00-14.00.
Food shops open Mon-Fri 07.00-19.00,
Sat 07.00-14.00.

Public Holidays
New Year; Revolution Day 15 March; Easter Mon; Labour Day; Whitsun; Constitution Day 20 Aug; Republic Day 23 Oct; All Saints Day 1 Nov; Christmas 25, 26 Dec.

Motoring
Dipped headlights are compulsory at all times but main beams should not be used in towns. Motorway stickers must be purchased for the M1 to Budapest, the M7 from Budapest to Lake Balaton and also on the M3 eastward. Also the full length of the M5 (Budapest - Kiskunfelegyhaza). Give way to trams and buses at junctions. Carrying spare fuel in a can is not permitted.

245

HU5070 Balatontourist Camping & Motel Kristof

H-8220 Balatonalmádi (Veszprem County)

Tel: 885 842 01. Email: ckristof@balatontourist.hu

This is a delightfully small site with just 33 marked pitches and many tall trees. Square in shape, the generously sized pitches are on either side of hard roads, on level grass. There is some shade and all pitches have electricity (6A). It is between the main road and railway line and the lake. Although there is no direct access to the lake, a public lakeside area adjoins the site, and site fees include the entry price. This is a neat little site with a kiosk with terrace for breakfast and dinner (steaks, etc) drinks, bread, milk and ice cream. Balatonalmádi is at the northern end of the lake and well placed for excursions around the lake or to Budapest. Kristof is suitable for anyone seeking a small, friendly site without the bustle of the larger camps. There are also 15 rooms for rent. Good English is spoken.

Facilities

The excellent, fully equipped toilet facility is part of the reception building. Laundry room with washing machine (small charge), kitchen and sitting room with TV. Motorcaravan service point. Café (12/5-19/9). Playground and entertainment daily except Sunday. Tennis. Paddling pool. Off site: Fishing and beach 50 m. Bicycle hire and boat launching 500 m. Supermarket 500 m. Riding 5 km.

Open: 12 May - 24 September.

Directions

Site is on road no. 71 at Balatonalmádi, between the railway line and the lake and is signed.
GPS: N47:01.507 E18:00.613

Charges 2007

Per person	HUF 620,00 - 1020,00
child (2-14 yrs)	HUF 460,00 - 870,00
pitch	HUF 1790,00 - 3620,00

HU5080 Balatontourist Diana Camping

H-8241 Aszófô (Veszprem County)

Tel: 874 450 13. Email: dianacamping@freemail.hu

Once a very large site of about 12 hectares, Diana was developed many years ago as a retreat for the 'party faithful'. Now just 8 hectares are used by Mr and Mrs Keller-Toth, who have leased it from the Balatontourist organisation and run it as a quiet, friendly site. There is a great feeling of space and much woodland around in which you may wander. There are 27 hedged pitches of 120 sq.m. (where two 60 sq.m. ones have been joined) on grass. Many have shade from trees including about 65 smaller individual ones. The remainder are amongst the trees which mark them out. There is no exact number of pitches, but about 150 units are taken, all with electrical connections (2 pin, 6 or 10A) on sloping ground. The fair-sized restaurant, open all season, has tables, benches and flowers in troughs outside. Animation is organised in high season with Hungarian musicians and animators, including occasional 'Diana days' with Hungarian folklore and goulash soup.

Facilities

Toilet facilities have been largely refurbished and are open 06.00-12.00 and 15.00-23.00 hrs. Very smart, new sections now provide large showers with private dressing for men and women and washbasins with hot water. Splendid, new children's washroom (key from reception), with 3 shower/baths, 2 designed for handicapped children. Washing machines, dryers and ironing (key from reception). Motorcaravan service point. Large kitchen with 3 cookers. Well stocked shop (open 08.00-17.00 low season or 22.00 high season). Restaurant (all season). Children's play area, with animation in high season. Volleyball. Tennis. Club room with video nights for adults at weekends. Off site: Many walking opportunities. Lake fishing 3 km. Riding or bicycle 5 km.

Open: 7 May - 17 September.

Directions

From road 71 on the north side of the lake, turn towards Azsófö just west of Balatonfüred, through the village and follow the signs for about 1 km. along access road (bumpy in places).
GPS: N46:56.368 E17:49.542

Charges 2007

Per pitch incl. electricity		HUF 1250,00 - 2000,00
person		HUF 800,00 - 1100,00
child (6-14 yrs)		HUF 600,00 - 800,00

Special rates for disabled persons and low season long stays.

This is just a sample of the campsites we have inspected and selected in Central Europe. For more campsites and further information, please see the Alan Rogers Central Europe guide.

HU5380 Balatontourist Camping Venus

H-8252 Balatonszepezd (Veszprem County)

Tel: 875 680 61. Email: venus@balatontourist.hu

For those who want to be directly beside Lake Balaton and would like a reasonably quiet location, Camping Venus would be a good choice and it is also possibly the best site in Hungary. Apart from the rather noisy train that regularly passes the site, this is a quiet setting with views of the lake from almost all the pitches. From the front row of pitches you could almost dangle your feet from your caravan in the warm water of the lake. There are 150 flat pitches all with at least 4/10A electricity. Varying in size (70-100 sq.m), almost all have shade. Given the small size of the site, Mária Ékes, the manager, gets to know every guest in person and she will make you very welcome. This is a well managed site with modern, well kept sanitary blocks and 24 hour security at the gate. Lake Balaton with its water temperature of about 25° Celsius in summer, is obviously the main attraction here, but you can also make several excursions, for example a trip to Budapest or a gipsy night in Riza.

Facilities

Two good sanitary blocks provide toilets, washbasins (open style and in cabins) with hot and cold water, pre-set showers, facilities for disabled people and child size toilets and basins. Launderette. Motorcaravan services. Shop for basics. Bar. Restaurant. Snack bar. Playground. Daily activity programme with pottery, fairy tale reading, horse shows, tournaments in Sümeg, trips over the lake and to Budapest. Canoe, pedalo, rowing boats and bicycle hire. Dogs are not accepted. Off site: Riding 3 km.

Open: 18 May - 9 September, with all services.

Directions

On the 71 road between Balatonfüred and Keszthely, site is in Balatonszepezd on the lake side of the road.

Charges 2007

Per person	HUF 670,00 - 1130,00
child (2-14 yrs)	HUF 510,00 - 820,00
pitch incl. electricity	HUF 1280,00 - 3470,00

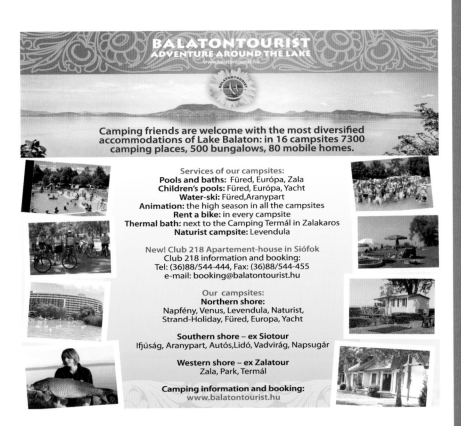

HU5090 Balatontourist Camping Füred

H-8230 Balatonfüred (Veszprem County)

Tel: **873 438 23**. Email: **cfured@balatontourist.hu**

This is a large international holiday village rather than just a campsite, pleasantly decorated with flowers and shrubs, with a very wide range of facilities and sporting activities. All that one could want for a family holiday can be found on this site. Directly on the lake with 800 m. of access for boats and bathing, it has a large, grassy lying out area, a small beach area for children with various watersports organised. There is also a swimming pool on site with lifeguards. Mature trees cover about two-thirds of the site giving shade, with the remaining area being in the open. The 944 individual pitches (60-120 sq.m), all with electricity (4-10A), are on either side of hard access roads on which pitch numbers are painted. Many bungalows are also on the site. Along the main road that runs through the site, are shops and kiosks, with the main bar/restaurant and terrace overlooking the lake. Other bars and restaurants are around the site. A water ski drag lift is most spectacular with its four towers erected in the lake to pull skiers around the circuit. Coach trips and pleasure cruises are organised. The site is part of the Balatontourist organisation and, while public access is allowed for the amenities, security is good. Some tour operators – Danish and German.

Facilities

Six fully equipped toilet blocks around the site include hot water for dishwashing and laundry. Private cabins for rent. Laundry service. Gas supplies. Numerous bars, restaurants, cafés, food bars and supermarket (all 15/4-15/10). Stalls and kiosks with wide range of goods, souvenirs, photo processing. Hairdresser. Excellent swimming pool with separate children's pool (20/6-25/9). Sauna. Fishing. Water ski lift. Windsurf school. Sailing. Pedaloes. Play area on sand. Bicycle hire. Tennis. Minigolf. Video games. Internet point. Dogs are not accepted. Off site: Riding 5 km. Close by a street of fast food bars, about 10 in all, offering a variety of Hungarian and international dishes with attractive outdoor terraces under trees.

Open: 15 April - 15 October.

Directions

Site is just south of Balatonfüred, on Balatonfüred - Tihany road and is well signed. Gates closed 1-3 pm. except Sat/Sun. GPS: N46:56.735 E17:52.626

Charges 2007

Per person	HUF 720,00 - 1530,00
child (2-14 yrs)	HUF 500,00 - 1130,00
pitch incl. electricity:	
120 sq.m.	HUF 3960,00 - 6500,00
100 sq.m.	HUF 2860,00 - 5100,00
70 sq.m.	HUF 2400,00 - 3880,00

Camping Cheques accepted.

HU5150 Fortuna Camping

Dózsa György út 164, H-2045 Törökbálint (Pest County)

Tel: **233 353 64**. Email: **fortunacamping@axelero.hu**

This good site lies at the foot of a hill with views of the vineyards, but Budapest is only 25 minutes away by bus. The owner, Csaba Szücs, will provide visitors with a map and instructions on how to see the town in the best way. The site is surrounded by mature trees and Mr Szücs will proudly name all 150 varieties of bushes and shrubs which edge some of the pitches. The site has a small restaurant with very reasonable prices but it is only open from 18.00-21.00. An open air swimming pool with flume will help you to cool off in summer with an indoor pool for cooler weather. Concrete and gravel access roads lead to terraces where there are 170 individual pitches most bordered with hedges, all with electricity (up to 16A, long leads needed), and 14 with water, on slightly sloping ground. A special field area provides for group bookings, and has separate facilities. Mr Szücs and his family will endeavour to make your stay a comfortable one. His daughter organises tours to Budapest or the surrounding countryside, and will also explain the mysteries of public transport in Budapest.

Facilities

One fully equipped sanitary blocks and two smaller blocks. Good facilities for disabled people. Dishwashing facilities, plus six cookers in sheltered area. Washing machine and dryer. Gas supplies. Motorcaravan services. Restaurant and bar (all year). Snack bar. Essentials from reception, (order bread previous day). Outdoor swimming pool with slide (15/5-15/9). Indoor pool. Small play area. Excursions. English spoken. Off site: Close to bus terminal for city centre 1 km. Riding 3 km. Fishing 4 km.

Open: All year.

Directions

From M1 Gyor - Budapest, exit for Törökbálint following signs for town and then site. Also accessible from M7 Budapest - Balaton road. GPS: N47:25.922 E18:54.066

Charges 2007

Per person	€ 6,00
child (4-14 yrs)	€ 4,00
pitch	€ 5,00
electricity	€ 2,00
dog	€ 2,00

No credit cards. Prices in Euros.

HU5180 Jumbo Camping

Budakalászi út 23-25, H-2096 Üröm (Pest County)

Tel: 263 512 51

Jumbo Camping is a modern, thoughtfully developed site in the northern outskirts of Budapest. The concrete and gravel access roads lead shortly to 55 terraced pitches of varying size, a little on the small size for large units, and some slightly sloping. Hardstanding for cars and caravan wheels, as well as large hardstandings for motorhomes. There is a steep incline to some pitches and use of the site's 4x4 may be required. All pitches have 6A electricity (may require long leads) and there are 8 caravan pitches with water and drain. They are mostly divided by small hedges and the whole area is fenced. Situated on a hillside 15 km. from Budapest centre, with attractive views of the Buda hills and with public transport to the city near, this is a pleasant and comfortable small site (despite the name) where you will receive a warm welcome. It is possible to park outside the short, fairly steep entrance which has a chain across. Reception, where you are given a comprehensive information sheet in English, doubles as a café/bar area.

Facilities

Sanitary facilities are excellent, with large showers (communal changing). Dishwashing under cover. Terrace with chairs and tables. Washing machine, iron and cooking facilities on payment. Motorcaravan services. Café where bread (orders taken), milk and butter available. Small, attractive swimming pool (10/6-10/9). Playground with covered area for wet weather. Barbecue area. English spoken and information sheet provided in English. Off site: Shop and restaurant 500 m. The 'Old Swabian Wine-Cellar' said to serve extremely good food. Bus to city 500 m. every 30 minutes. Fishing 8 km.

Open: 1 April - 31 October.

Directions

Site signed on roads to Budapest - nos. 11 from Szentendre and 10 from Komarom. If approaching from Budapest use 11 (note: site sign appears very quickly after sharp right bend; signs and entry are clearer if using road 10). Can also approach via Györ on M1/E60 and Lake Balaton on M7/E71. Turn into site is quite acute and uphill.
GPS: N47:36.093 E19:01.200

Charges 2007

Per person	€ 5,00
child (3-14 yrs)	€ 3,10
pitch acc. to size and season	€ 2,60 - € 6,40
electricity	€ 2,50

No credit cards (cash only). Prices in Euros.

HU5120 Gasthof Camping Pihenö

I-es föút, H-9011 Györszentivan-Kertváros (Gyor-Moson-Sopron County)

Tel: 965 230 08. Email: piheno@piheno_hu

This privately owned site makes an excellent night stop when travelling to and from Hungary as it lies beside the main no. 1 road, near the end of the motorway to the east of Györ. It is set amidst pine trees with pitches which are not numbered, but marked out by small shrubs, in a small clearing or between the trees. With space for about 40 touring units, all with electrical connections (6A), and eight simple, one roomed bungalows and four en-suite rooms. On one side of the site, fronting the road, is the reception, bar and pleasant restaurant with terrace (menu in English). The food is of excellent quality and very well priced (typical main course and coffee £3.50). The management offer a very reasonably priced package (if desired) which includes pitch and meals. A very friendly German speaking owner runs the site and restaurant with his wife and daughters who speak a little English.

Facilities

A single, small, basic toilet block has just two showers for each sex (on payment) and curtained, communal dressing space. Baby room. Room for washing clothes and dishes with small cooking facility. Washing machine. Bar. Restaurant with good menu and reasonable prices. Solar heated swimming and paddling pools (10 x 5 m, open June -Sept). Order bread at reception the previous evening. Off site: Gyor with shops and swimming pool.

Open: 1 April - 30 October.

Directions

Coming from Austria, continue through Györ following signs for Budapest. Continue on road no. 1 past start of motorway for 3 km. and site is on left. From Budapest, turn right onto road no. 10 at end of motorway, then as above.
GPS: N47:43.528 E17:42.883

Charges 2007

Per person	€ 4,40
pitch	€ 3,40
dog	€ 0,87
electricity	€ 1,50

Less 10% for stays over 4 days, 20% after 8 days. Prices in Euros.

Check real time availability and at-the-gate prices...

www.alanrogers.com

HU5025 Zalatour Thermal Camping

Gyogyfurdo 6, H-8749 Zalakaros (Zala County)

Tel: **933 401 05**. Email: **thermal@zalatour.hu**

Zalatour at Zalakaros has 280 attractively laid out, level pitches, all with 10A electricity and varying in size from 30-100 sq.m. (the larger pitches need to be reserved). There are 250 for touring units on grass and gravel (firm tent pegs may be needed) and around 10 hardstandings for larger units and motorcaravans. Mature trees provide useful shade and access roads are gravel. Zalatour attracts many elderly people who spend their day at the thermal spa 200 metres down the road – the waters are reputedly good for rheumatism and other joint problems. This site is good for rest and relaxation in the shade with the added benefit of the healing waters of the spa. Lake Balaton is close.

Facilities

Modern and comfortable toilet facilities with British style toilets, open washbasins and controllable, hot showers (free). Facilities for disabled visitors. Full-service laundry including ironing. Campers' kitchen. Motorcaravan service point. Shop. Bar/restaurant. Massage, acupuncture and pedicure. Sauna. Hairdresser. Bicycle hire. Off site: Fishing and beach 3 km. Golf 500 m. Riding 2 km.

Open: 1 April - 30 September.

Directions

On E71 travelling northeast from Nagykanisza, take exit for Zalakaros. Follow good site signs. GPS: N46:33.136 E17:07.556

Charges 2007

Per person	HUF 1000,00 - 1200,00
child (2-14 yrs)	HUF 500,00 - 600,00
pitch incl. electricity	HUF 1200,00 - 1650,00
tent	HUF 750,00 - 900,00

HU5210 Diófaház Accommodations

Ady Endre út 12, H-3348 Szilvásvárad (Heves County)

Tel: **363 555 95**. Email: **info@diofahaz.hu**

Diófaház is an ideal base in northeast Hungary for exploring this wooded part of the country, to visit the stud farm of the famous Lipizzaner horses (one of only five in the world) or to visit the town of Eger, world famous for its culture and red wine. The site is in private grounds on the edge of the village and provides a maximum of six pitches, all with electricity, which makes it quiet and peaceful. Gyöngyi Pap, the owner provides a warm welcome. There are plenty of opportunities for cycling or walking tours, or there is a lakeside beach within 6 km. Also close are the famous Szalajka waterfalls.

Facilities

The single, freshly painted toilet block includes washbasins in cabins with hot and cold water, controllable hot showers and sinks with free hot water. Fresh rolls to order every day with home made jam but no shop. Internet access. Discounts at four restaurants in the village if you show your campers card. Off site: Riding 200 m. Bicycle hire 500 m. Fishing 6 km.

Open: All year.

Directions

Take the no. 25 road from Eger north to Szilvásvárad. Site is signed when entering the village. GPS: N48:05.890 E20:23.040

Charges 2007

Per unit incl. 2 persons	€ 8,75 - € 10,50
extra person	€ 3,15
electricity pkWh	€ 0,18
Prices in Euros.	

HU5300 Kek-Duna Camping

Hösök Tere 23, H-7020 Dunafoldvar (Tolna County)

Tel: **755 411 07**. Email: **postmaster@camping_gyogyfurdo.axelero.net**

Dunafoldvár is a most attractive town of 10,000 people and you are in the heart of it in just two or three minutes by foot from this site, easily reached via the wide towpath on the west bank of the Danube. For a town site, Kék-Duna is remarkably peaceful. It is fenced all round and locked at night, with flat concrete access roads to 50 pitches. All have 16A electricity, the first half of the site being open, the remainder well shaded. Apart from the obvious attractions of the river, with a large island opposite and pleasant walks possible, the ancient town has a most interesting museum, the 'Burg', with a genuine dungeon and cells, Roman relics and with a panoramic view of the town and river.

Facilities

Modern, tiled sanitary building with nicely decorated ladies' section offers curtained showers with communal changing. The rest of the facilities are of above average standard. Dishwashing outside with cold water. Washing machine. Shop and café (from mid June), town shops close. Bicycle hire. Excursion information. German speaking receptionist. Off site: Tennis 50 m. Thermal swimming pool 200 m. (under the same ownership). Riding 5 km.

Open: All year.

Directions

From the roundabout south of Dunafoldvar turn towards the town centre. At the traffic lights turn right and go down as far as the Danube then turn left, under the green bridge and follow the towpath about 300 m. to the site.

Charges guide

Per person	HUF 500,00
pensioner, student or child	HUF 250,00
pitch incl. electricity	HUF 1100,00 - 1200,00
tent and car	HUF 550,00

MAP 7

Whether you want to explore historic cities, stroll around mediaeval hill towns, relax on sandy beaches or simply indulge in opera, good food and wine, Italy has it all. Roman ruins, Renaissance art and beautiful churches abound. For the more active, the Italian Alps are a haven for winter sports enthusiasts and also offer good hiking trails.

CAPITAL: ROME

Tourist Office

Italian State Tourist Board
1 Princes Street
London W1B 2AY
Tel: 020 7408 1254
Fax: 020 7399 3567
Email: italy@italiantouristboard.co.uk
Internet: www.enit.it

Italy only became a unified state in 1861, hence the regional nature of the country today. With 20 distinct regions, each one has retained its own individualism which is evident in the cuisine and local dialects.

In the north, the vibrant city of Milan is great for shopping and home to the famous opera house, La Scala, as well as Leonardo's Last Supper fresco. It is also a good starting-off point for the Alps; the Italian Lake District, incorporating Lake Garda, Lake Como and Lake Maggiore; the canals of Venice and the lovely town of Verona. Central Italy probably represents the most commonly perceived image of the country and Tuscany, with its classic rolling countryside and the historical towns of Florence, Siena, San Gimignano and Pisa, is one of the most visited areas. Further south is the historic capital of Rome and the city of Naples. Close to some of Italy's ancient sites such as Pompeii, Naples is within easy distance of Sorrento and the Amalfi coast.

Population

57.8 million

Climate

The south enjoys extremely hot summers and mild, dry winters, whilst the mountainous regions of the north are cooler with heavy snowfalls in winter.

Language

Italian. There are several dialect forms and some German is spoken near the Austrian border.

Telephone

The country code is 0039.

Money

Currency: The Euro. Banks: Mon-Fri 08.30-13.00 and 15.00-16.00.

Shops

Mon-Sat 08.30/09.00-13.00 and 15.30/16.00- 19.30/20.00, with some variations in larger cities.

Public Holidays

New Year; Easter Mon; Liberation Day 25 Apr; Labour Day; Republic Day 2 June; Assumption 15 Aug; All Saints 1 Nov; Unity Day 4 Nov; Immaculate Conception 8 Dec; Christmas 25, 26 Dec; plus some special local feast days.

Motoring

Tolls are payable on the autostrada network. If travelling distances, save time by purchasing a 'Viacard' from pay booths or service areas. An overhanging load, ie. bicycle rack, must be indicated by a large red/white hatched warning square. Failure to do so will result in a fine.

IT62490 Camping Continental Lido

Via 42 Martiri 156, I-28924 Fondotoce di Verbania (Piedmont)

Tel: **032 349 6300**. Email: **info@campingcontinental.com**

Continental Lido is a large, bustling site situated on the shore of the charming little Lake Mergozzo, about a kilometre from the better known Lake Maggiore. The 479 average-sized tourist pitches are back-to-back in regular rows on grass. All have electricity (6A) and there is shade from a variety of trees in some parts. There is a feeling of spaciousness here and the 185 mobile homes are not obtrusive. There is an impressive new swimming pool complex and a small sandy beach slopes gently into the lake where swimming and watersports can also be enjoyed (no powered craft may be used). Fir-clad mountains and a pretty village directly opposite the beach provide a pleasing, scenic background. An unusual feature here is the 9-hole golf course. There is a busy programme of activities from May to September. Under the same ownership as Isolino Camping Village, this site is managed by son Gian Paolo who speaks good English.

Facilities

Five high standard toilet blocks have free hot water, facilities for disabled visitors and washing machines and dryers. Mini-fridges. Well stocked shop and bar/restaurant with terrace and takeaway (all open all season). New swimming pool complex with children Off site: Riding 1 km. Sailing 5 km. 18-hole golf 12 km.

Open: 30 March - 24 September.

Directions

Verbania is 100 km. north west of Milan, on the western shore of Lake Maggiore. Site is off the SS34 road between Fondotoce and Gravellona, 200 m. west of junction with SS33.
GPS: N45:56.976 E08:28.835

Charges 2007

Per unit incl. 2 persons and electricity	€ 17,20 - € 29,50
extra person	€ 4,20 - € 7,00
child (3-11 yrs)	free - € 5,60

No credit cards.
Camping Cheques accepted.

IT62460 Camping Village Isolino

Via per Feriolo 25, I-28924 Verbania Fondotoce (Piedmont)

Tel: **032 349 6080**. Email: **info@isolino.com**

Lake Maggiore is one of the most attractive Italian lakes and Isolino is one of the largest sites in the region. Most of the 460 tourist pitches have shade from a variety of trees. Some are of a good size, many in long, angled rows leading to the beach. All have electrical connections (6A) and some have lake views. The bar and restaurant terraces and the very large, lagoon style swimming pool with its island sundeck area have stunning views across the lake to the fir-clad mountains beyond. The social life of the campsite is centred around the large bar which has a stage sometimes used for musical entertainment. A newly-constructed amphitheatre will provide a home for the programme of activities and entertainment which runs between May and mid-September. The extensive poolside terrace is outside the bar, takeaway and casual eating area. In the restaurant on the floor above some tables share the magnificent views across the lake. The site is well situated for visiting the many attractions of the region which include the famous gardens on the islands in the lake and at the Villa Taranto, Verbania. The Swiss mountains and resort of Locarno are quite near. The site is owned by the friendly Manoni family who also own Camping Continental Lido at nearby Lake Mergozzo and good English is spoken.

Facilities

Six well-built toilet blocks have hot water for showers and washbasins but cold for dishwashing and laundry. Baby room. Laundry facilities. Fridge box hire. Motorcaravan services. Supermarket, bar and takeaway (all season). Swimming pool (27/4-21/9). Ampitheatre. Football. Tennis. Fishing. Watersports. Bicycle hire and guided mountain bike tours. Long beach. Internet access. Off site: Golf 2 km. Sailing 5 km. Riding 12 km.

Open: 20 March - 21 September.

Directions

Verbania is 100 km. north west of Milan on the western shore of Lake Maggiore. From the A26 motorway, leave at exit for Stresa/Baveno, turn left towards Fondotoce. Site is well signed off the SS33 north of Baveno and 300 m. south of the junction with the SS34 at Fondotoce. GPS: N45:56.301 E08:30.005

Charges 2007

Per unit incl. 2 persons and electricity	€ 18,25 - € 32,85
extra person	€ 4,30 - € 7,30
child (3-11 yrs)	free - € 5,95
dog	€ 3,15 - € 7,30

ISOLINO camping village

The lightly leaning sandy beach is ideal for children - the campsite lies in a very quiet position with wonderful view • Bar • Pool bar • Restaurant • Supermarket • Free hot showers • Baby-room • Children's playground • facilities • Windsurfing school • Table tennis • We rent bicycles, pedalò, canoes, boats and surfboards • Bungalows, mobile homes and apartments for rent • **Animation • Internet Point • Internet Wireless.**

Pool of 1000 sq. m. open from 28.04. to 21.09.08 - animation from 28.04. to 08.09.08

Special Offer

FROM 5 NIGHTS :From 19.03. to 01.05. and from 13.09. to 22.09.08

FROM 7 NIGHTS: From 01.05. to 28.06. and from 30.08. to 13.09.08

Lago Maggiore

Dogs only on reservation from the 28.06 to the 30.08.08

NEW COVERED ARENA!

CHILDREN GRATIS 0-2 all the season long. 3-5 years till 05.07. and from 23.08.08

Via Per Feriolo, 25 • I-28924 Fondotoce di Verbania • Tel. 0039/0323496080 • Fax 0039/0323496414

info@isolino.com • www.isolino.it

IT62420 Camping Orta

Via Domodossola 28, I-28016 Orta San Giulio (Piedmont)

Tel: **032 290 267**. Email: **info@campingorta.it**

Lake Orta is a charming, less visited small lake just west of Lake Maggiore in an area with understated charm. The site is on a considerable slope, and most of the 70 touring pitches (all with 4A electricity) are on the top grassy terrace with spectacular views across the lake to the mountains beyond. There are some superb lakeside pitches across the main road (linked by a pedestrian underpass) although there is some traffic noise here. Amenities include a large games and entertainment room and a traditional Italian bar and restaurant serving good value family meals. Some English is spoken by the Guarnori family, who take pride in maintaining their uncomplicated site to a high standard. Book ahead to enjoy the lakeside pitches. If you are anxious about towing a large caravan to the top terraces, the owner will help out with his tractor!

Facilities	Directions
Three modern sanitary blocks are clean and well maintained providing mainly British style toilets, coin operated showers and an excellent unit for disabled visitors. Laundry facilities. Motorcaravan services. Excellent mini-market. Bar and restaurant with basic menu serving good value Italian family meals. Playground. Large games/TV room. WiFi internet access in reception/bar area. Fishing. Bicycle hire. Boat launching. Off site: Riding, golf and sailing all within 10 km.	Lake Orta is 85 km. north west of Milan and just west of Lake Maggiore. Site is on the SR229 between Borgomanero and Omega, 600 m. north of the turn to Orta San Giulio. There is a parking area for arrivals on the lake side of the road, but reception and main entrance are on the opposite side. GPS: N45:48.137 E08:25.216

Open: All year.

Charges 2007

Per person	€ 5,00 - € 6,50
pitch	€ 8,00 - € 15,00
electricity	€ 2,00

CAMPING ORTA

Loc. Bagnera

I-28016 Orta S.Giulio (NO)

Tel. and Fax 0039/032290267
E-mail: info@campingorta.it
Http: www.campingorta.it

On the shores of Orta Lake - 1,5 km from the village - the campsite enjoys a beautiful view on the quite neighborhood and on the lake. The right place for families with young children. Terraces up to the shores. Ideal starting point for visit to the interesting places of the lake and the surroundings, like villas, museums, cloisters and churches. Hot shower, electrical connection, supermarket, bar, restaurant, play area for children, pier, lighting on pitches. Services and toilettes for disabled people.
Open all year with great discounts from 01.01 to 30.06 and from 30.08 to 31.12.

IT62440 Camping Solcio

Via al Campeggio, I-28040 Solcio di Lesa (Piedmont)

Tel: **03227497**. Email: **info@campingsolcio.com**

Camping Solcio is a family run site on the lakeside and has lovely views over the lakes and of the green hills which surround some of the site. The neat pitches are 60-90 sq.m. in size with electricity (6A). Mostly shaded by trees, The 105 touring pitches are on flat sand and grass and access is easy. A very pleasant restaurant and a bar back onto a large building alongside the site, and there are some views of the lake from the terraces. You will have a view of the railway halfway up the hills alongside the site, so there is rail noise at times. The lakeside is good for safe swimming and, as the site is next to a large boat repair building plus its moorings, there is no through traffic in terms of fast boats. Many watersports are available here and the beach is of coarse sand. An ambitious entertainment programme is arranged for children in high season, and there is adventure sport for the over 10s. This is a pleasant site with modest facilities and it may suit those who do not seek the luxuries of the larger sites. English and Dutch are spoken and it is very popular with Dutch campers.

Facilities	Directions
One main central toilet block is smart and clean. Toilets here are British style. An older block nearer reception has mixed Turkish and British style toilets. Facilities for disabled visitors. Baby room. Washing machine. Restaurant and bar with terrace. Basic shop. Full animation programme in season. Play areas. Bicycle hire. Internet. Torches useful. Off site: Town facilities 1 km. Riding 5 km. Golf 10 km. Public transport 300 m. ATM 2 km.	Site is on the west side of Lake Maggiore. From the A4 (Milan - Torino) take the A8 to Castelletto Sticino. Then north on SS33 towards Stresa an look for site sign at km. 57 marker at town of Lesa. Take the narrow access road to the site.

Open: 1 April - 30 September.

Charges 2007

Per person	€ 5,00 - € 7,50
child (3-13 yrs)	€ 3,70 - € 5,50
pitch	€ 8,40 - € 21,00
electricity	€ 2,50 - € 2,60

IT62485 **Camping Conca d'Oro**

Via 42 Martiri, 26, I28835 Feriolo di Baveno (Piedmont)

Tel: **032328116**. Email: **info@concadoro.it**

Conca d'Oro is a delightful site with spectacular views across Lake Maggiore to the distant mountains. The first impression is one of spaciousness and colour. There are just a dozen mobile homes for rent, the remainder of the 210 grassy plots being good sized touring pitches. All with 6A electrical connections; they are marked by young trees and azalea bushes. The land slopes gently down to a sandy beach. An attractive restaurant serves a varied range of dishes and there is a good bar and pizzeria and a well stocked shop. The young owners Maurizio and Allesandra are sure to give you a warm welcome. The site is close to the lakeside town of Baveno from where boat trips are available to the three small islands on this part of Lake Maggiore. Fishing and boat launching are possible from the beach at the site, and sailing plus other watersports can be enjoyed from various points on the lake. There are nature reserves nearby and drives out into the surrounding mountains provide opportunities for walkers, cyclists and climbers.

Facilities

Three toilet blocks provide all necessary facilities kept in immaculate condition, including controllable showers and open style washbasins; some toilets with washbasins. En-suite unit for disabled visitors. Laundry room. Motorcaravan service point. Bar, restaurant, pizzeria and shop (all season). Swimming, fishing and boat launching from beach. Bicycle hire. Off site: Riding 700 m. Golf 1 km. Sailing 7 km. Shops, bars and restaurants nearby.

Open: 24 March - 23 September.

Directions

Baveno is 90 km. northwest of Milan on the western shore of Lake Maggiore. Site is off the SS33 road between Baveno and Fondotoce di Verbania, about 1 km. south of the junction with the SS34 and is well signed. GPS: N45:56.168 E08:29.209

Charges 2007

Per unit incl. 2 persons	€ 21,00 - € 37,50
extra person	€ 5,00 - € 7,00
child (2-13 yrs)	€ 3,50 - € 6,00
electricity	€ 2,50

Lago Maggiore

REGIONE PIEMONTE

CONCA D'ORO
C A M P I N G ★★★

Quiet campingsite, clean and proper, with sanitary blocks and pitches of 100 sqm. Conca d'Oro is situated directly on the lake in a area surrounded by nature. The campsite has a private sandy beach and is child friendly. Market, bar, restaurant, pizzeria, volley, ping-pong, canoa and cycling. Special offers in the low season. **www.concadoro.it**

This is just a sample of the campsites we have inspected and selected in Italy. For more campsites and further information, please see the Alan Rogers Italy guide.

IT64010 Camping Villaggio dei Fiori

Via Tiro a Volo 3, I-18038 San Remo (Ligúria)
Tel: **018 466 0635**. Email: **info@villaggiodeifiori.it**

Open all year round, this open and spacious site has high standards and is ideal for exploring the Italian Riviera or for just relaxing by the enjoyable, filtered sea water pools. Unusually all the pitch areas at the site are totally paved and there are some extremely large pitches for large units (ask reception to open another gate for entry). All pitches have electricity (3/6A), 50 also have water and drainage, and there is an outside sink and cold water for every four. There is ample shade from mature trees and shrubs, which are constantly watered and cared for in summer. The 'Gold' pitches and some wonderful tent pitches have pleasant views over the sea. There is a path to a secluded and pleasant beach with sparkling waters, overlooked by a large patio area. The rocky site surrounds are excellent for snorkelling and fishing with ladder access to the water. The friendly management speak excellent English and will supply detailed tourist plans. Activities and entertainment are organised in high season for adults and children. Excursions are offered (extra cost) along the Italian Riviera dei Fiori and the French Côte d'Azur, including night excursions to Nice and Monte Carlo. Buses run from outside the site to Monte Carlo, Nice, Cannes, Eze and many other places of interest. This is a very good site for visiting all the attractions in the local area.

Facilities

Three clean and modern toilet blocks have British and Turkish style WCs and hot water throughout. Baby rooms. Facilities for disabled campers. Laundry facilities. Motorcaravan services. Bar sells essential supplies. Large restaurant. Pizzeria and takeaway (all year). Sea water swimming pools (small extra charge in high season) and sophisticated whirlpool spa (June-Sept). Tennis. Play area. Fishing. Satellite TV. Internet access. Bicycle hire. Dogs are not accepted. Off site: Shop 150 m. Riding and golf 2 km.

Open: All year.

Directions

From SS1 (Ventimiglia - Imperia), site is on right just before San Remo. There is a sharp right turn if approaching from the west. From autostrada A10 take San Remo Ouest exit. Site is well signed. GPS: N43:48.070 E07:44.920

Charges 2007

Per unit incl. 4 persons	€ 27,00 - € 56,00
electricity (3A-6A)	€ 2,00 - € 4,00

Discounts for stays in excess of 7 days.
Discount for readers 10% in low season.
Camping Cheques accepted.

IT64030 Camping Baciccia

Via Torino 19, I-17023 Ceriale (Ligúria)
Tel: **018 299 0743**. Email: **info@campingbaciccia.it**

This friendly, family run site is a popular holiday destination. Baciccia was the nickname of the present owner's grandfather who grew fruit trees and tomatoes on the site. Tall eucalyptus trees shade the 120 tightly packed pitches which encircle the central facilities block. The pitches are on flat ground and all have electricity. There is always a family member by the gate to greet you, and Vincenzina and Giovanni, along with their adult children Laura and Mauro, work tirelessly to ensure that you enjoy your stay. The restaurant is informal and, as no frozen food is served, the menu is necessarily simple but is traditional Italian food cooked to perfection. The restaurant overlooks a large swimming pool and there are organised water polo and pool games, as well as a half size tennis court and boule. The private beach is a short walk (or free shuttle service) and the town has the usual seaside attractions but it is also worth visiting the tiny traditional villages close by. This site may suit campers looking for a family atmosphere and none of the brashness of large seaside sites. If you have forgotten anything by way of camping equipment the family will lend it to you.

Facilities

Two clean and modern sanitary blocks near reception have British and Turkish style WCs and hot water throughout. Laundry. Motorcaravan services. Restaurant/bar. Shop. Pizzeria and takeaway. Two swimming pools (20/3-31/10) and private beach. Tennis. Table tennis. Bowls. Play area. Bicycle hire. Wood-burning stove and barbecue. Internet point. Fishing. Diving. Entertainment for children and adults in high season. Excursions. Off site: Department store 150 m. Aqua Park 500 m. Riding and golf 5 km. Parachuting school 10 km. Ancient town (2000 years old) of Albenga 3 km.

Open: All year.

Directions

From the A10 between Imperia and Savona, take Albenga exit. Follow signs Ceriale/Savona and Aquapark Caravelle (which is 500 m. from site) and then site signs. Site is just south of Savona. GPS: N44:04.963 E08:12.964

Charges 2007

Per unit incl. up to 3 persons	€ 28,00 - € 47,00
extra person	€ 5,00 - € 9,00
half pitch	
incl. 2 persons, no car	€ 16,00 - € 32,00

Discounts for stays in excess of 7 days.
Discount for readers 10% in low season.

IT64190 Camping River

See advertisement on previous page.

Localitá Armezzone, I-19031 Ameglia (Ligúria)

Tel: 018765629. Email: info@campingriver.com

Ameglia, near La Spezia, is just south of the A12 autrostada and this site is just 5 km. from the Sarzana exit. Close to La Cinque Terre and on the banks of the Magna river, this popular site provides 100 touring pitches and about the same number for static caravans. With its own small marina and excellent swimming pools, the site provides a busy location for a short stop or a longer stay to explore Liguria. The narrow access road will stop larger motorhomes from gaining access, but when we visited there were several twin axle caravans on site. The river provides boat launching facilities and good fishing opportunities further up river. The site has direct access to the water and a small marina with docking facilities for visitors. A busy entertainment programme is provided from mid June.

Facilities

Two sanitary blocks provide toilets (some Turkish style), washbasins and unisex showers. Facilities for disabled campers. Motorcaravan service point. Restaurant and bar. Shop. Pizzeria. Swimming pool and sun deck. Boat launching. Fishing. Mobile homes and bungalows to rent. Off site: Tennis 200 m. Archery. Sailing. Scuba diving. La Spezia. La Cinque Terre.

Open: 1 April - 30 September.

Directions

Take Sarzana exit on the A12 (Genoa - Livorno) and follow signs towards Lerici. After 3 km. follow signs to Bocca di Magra and Ameglia where the site is signed off to the left. Access road is narrow with a tight bend. GPS: N44:04.552 E09:58.208

Charges 2007

Per person	€ 4,50 - € 9,20
pitch	€ 16,00 - € 45,80

No credit cards.

IT64120 Villaggio Camping Valdeiva

Localitá Ronco, I-19013 Deiva Marina (Ligúria)

Tel: 018 782 4174. Email: camping@valdeiva.it

A mature site three kilometres from the sea between the famous Cinque Terre and Portofino, Valdeiva is open all year. It is situated in a valley amongst dense pines so views are restricted. On flat ground and separated, most of the 140 pitches are used for permanent Italian units. There are 40 pitches for tents and touring units but in high season tourers can expect to be put onto a sloping 'overflow' area by the road with no shade. The touring pitches are in a square at the bottom of the site, some with shade, all with electricity (3A). Cars may be required to park in a separate area depending on the pitch and season. A small busy bar/restaurant offers food at realistic prices. There was late night noise from residents when we stayed in high season. The site does have a small pool, which is very welcome if you do not wish to take the free bus to the beach. The most interesting tourist option is a visit to Cinque Terre, five villages, some of which can only be reached by rail, boat or by cliff footpath. We see this as a transit site rather than for extended stays.

Facilities

The toilet block nearest the touring pitches provides cramped facilities. A new block is in the centre of the site. WCs are mainly Turkish, but there are some of British style. Washing machines and dryers. Shop (15/6-10/9). Bar/restaurant and takeaway (15/6-10/9). Small pool. Play area. Excursions. Free bus to the beach. Torches required. Bicycle hire. Internet access. WiFi. Off site: Beach 3 km.

Open: All year.

Directions

Leave A12 at Deiva Marina exit and follow signs to Deiva Marina. Site signs are clear at the first junction and site is on left 3 km. down this road. GPS: N44:13.482 E09:33.101

Charges 2008

Per person (over 6 yrs)	€ 6,00
pitch	€ 10,00 - € 23,00
small tent	€ 6,00 - € 12,00

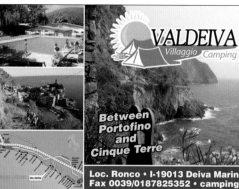

IT64110 Camping Miraflores

Via Savagna, 10, I-16035 Rapallo (Ligúria)

Tel: 0185 263 000. Email: camping.miraflores@libero.it

Camping Miraflores is located on the Ligurian coast, close to the famous resort of Portofino and the Cinque Terre. This site has been recommended by our Italian agent and we plan to undertake a full inspection in 2008. Pitches are mostly terraced with separate areas for tents (small pitches) and caravans or motor homes. There are also a number of mobile homes for rent. The site has recently added a small swimming pool. Rapallo is an attractive resort in its own right with an interesting old town centre. The A12 motorway (Rapallo exit) is close to the site and there may be some road noise.

Facilities

Bar. Shop. Pizzeria and takeaway meals. Games room. Playground. Swimming pool. Mobile homes for rent. Off site: Nearest beach 1.5 km. Tennis, riding, fishing, golf. Rapallo centre 1.5 km.

Open: 1 March - 31 January.

Directions

Site is located very close to the Rapallo exit from the A12 motorway. From this point, follow signs to Rapallo and the site is well signed. GPS: N44:21.552 E09:12.545

Charges 2007

Per person	€ 5,30 - € 6,00
child (under 9 yrs)	€ 3,00
pitch incl. electricity	€ 10,80 - € 13,30

IT62610 Camping Del Sole

Via per Rovato 26, I-25049 Iseo (Lombardy)

Tel: 030 980 288. Email: info@campingdelsole.it

Camping Del Sole lies on the southern edge of Lake Iseo, just outside the pretty lakeside town of Iseo. The site has 312 pitches, many taken up with chalets and mobile homes. The 180 touring pitches all have 3A electricity and some have fine views of the surrounding mountains and lake. Pitches are generally flat and of a reasonable size, but cars must park in the carpark. The site has a wide range of excellent leisure amenities, including a large swimming pool. There is a bar and restaurant with a pizzeria near the pool and entertainment area and a second bar by the lake. The site is near the delightful waterfront area of the town where you can enjoy classic Italian architecture, stroll around the shops or enjoy a meal in one of the many restaurants. There is a boat launching facility at the lakeside. There is a lively entertainment programme and excursions around the lake are organised, notably to Lake Iseo's three islands where you can sit at a street café or enjoy a walk while enjoying the magnificent scenery. Excursions are also organised to the wine cellars of Franciacorta.

Facilities

Sanitary facilities are modern and well maintained, including special facilities for disabled visitors. Washing machines and dryers. Bar, restaurant, pizzeria and snack bar. Supermarket. Motorcaravan service point. Bicycle and canoe hire. Swimming pool with children Off site: Golf 5 km. Riding 6 km.

Open: 1 April - 30 September.

Directions

From the A4 Milan - Venice autostrada take Rovato exit and at roundabout go north on SPX1 following signs for Lago d'Iseo for 12 km. Site is well signed to left at large roundabout. From Brescia on SS510, turn north before Iseo towards Rovato and turn right to site. GPS: N45:39.425 E10:02.244

Charges 2007

Per person	€ 4,50 - € 8,10
child	free - € 6,60
pitch incl. electricity	€ 8,50 - € 17,30
Camping Cheques accepted.	

IT62535 Camping du Parc

I-37017 Lazise sul Garda (Lake Garda)

Tel: **045 758 127**. Email: **duparc@camping.it**

Camping du Parc is a very pleasant, family owned site which resembles a Tardis, in that it extends and extends as you progress further through the site. Olive groves are interspersed with the pitch areas which gives an open and green feel. The site is set on a slope which goes down to the lakeside beach of soft sand. The 150 pitches are terraced, which takes out much of the slope, and all have 6A electricity and water. Units above 10 m. long will be challenged by some of the corners here. Pitches are separated by trimmed hedges and some have shade, others views of the lake. The restaurant is on the lower level with a terrace to catch the sunsets or alternatively the pizzeria also has a patio with sea views. Relax by the beach bar or in the pool whilst the children enjoy the slides and paddling pool. This is a very good site for those who prefer peace and quiet to the noisier atmosphere of the larger sites hereabouts. Buses stop by the gate to take you to Gardaland and other tourist attractions. As a site which caters for families, there is no disco or excessive noise and when we visited there were many happy customers. Animation takes place in the lower sports areas and is aimed mainly at children. All facilities are open the whole season. The beach, accessed through a security gate, is safe for swimming and there is a lifeguard.

Facilities

Four modern sanitary blocks are well placed and have free hot water throughout. Three blocks have facilities for disabled campers, one for children and babies. Washing machines and dryers. Motorcaravan services. Well stocked small supermarket. Restaurant with lake views. Pizzeria with terrace and views. Takeaway. Beach bar. Pool bar. Swimming pool. Large paddling pool with slides. Children's entertainment programme. Play area. Tennis. Multisport court. Fishing. Internet WiFi. Off site: Golf 10 km. Bicycle hire 500 m. Riding 1 km. Gardaland.

Open: 10 March - 30 September.

Directions

Leave A4 Venice - Milan autostrada by taking the Brennero exit to Lake Garda and then on to Lazise. At the lakeside in town turn left and follow signs for site. GPS: N45:29.917 E10:44.248

Charges 2007

Per person	€ 5,60 - € 8,20
child (1-5 yrs)	€ 1,50 - € 4,80
pitch	€ 10,90 - € 18,50
dog	€ 1,50 - € 4,90

Camping DU PARC — Lazise - Lago di Garda

I-37017 LAZISE SUL GARDA (Verona)
Tel. 0039/0457580127 • Fax 0039/0456470150
duparc@camping.it • www.campingduparc.com

IT62600 Camping Europa Silvella

Via Silvella 10, I-25010 San Felice del Benaco (Lake Garda)

Tel: **036 565 1095**. Email: **info@europasilvella.com**

This large, modern, lakeside site was formed from the merger of two different sites with the result that the 340 pitches (about 108 for tourists) are spread among a number of different sections of varying type. The marked pitches alongside the lake are in smaller groups and closer together; the main bar, restaurant and shop are located here. The main area is at the top of a steepish hill on slightly sloping or terraced grass and has slightly larger pitches. There is reasonable shade in many parts and all pitches have electricity. A large new swimming pool complex also provides a daytime bar and restaurant serving lunches. There is considerable tour operator presence (160 pitches) and there are 50 bungalows, mobile homes and log cabins to rent. The site has frontage to the lake in two places with a beach, jetty and moorings. The private beach is very pleasant, with all manner of watersports available. There is an animation programme with live entertainment in high season.

Facilities

Toilet blocks include washbasins in cabins, facilities for disabled visitors and a superb children's room with small showers. These are generally kept clean. Laundry. Shop. Bazaar. Restaurant/bars. Swimming pools (hats required). Fitness centre. Tennis courts. Volleyball and five-a-side soccer pitch. Table tennis. Playground. Bowling alley. Bicycle hire. Activities and entertainment (every night in season). Disco. Tournaments. Swimming and tennis lessons. Fishing and boat launching. First aid room. Off site: Golf 5 km. Riding 6 km.

Open: 23 April - 27 September.

Directions

San Felice is on western shore of Lake Garda at the southern end. From A4 Milan - Venice autostrada take Desenzano exit and head north on SS572 towards Saló for 14 km, turn right towards San Felice and follow brown tourist signs with site name (about 3 km). GPS: N45:34.471 E10:32.095

Charges 2007

Per person	€ 4,50 - € 8,50
child (1-4 yrs)	€ 3,50 - € 7,50
pitch incl. electricity	€ 9,50 - € 18,00
pitch with services	€ 11,00 - € 21,50
dog	€ 4,00 - € 7,50

EUROPA SILVELLA ★★★★

lago di garda

> New modern villas provide with all comforts: sat-tv, air conditioning, safe, kitchen with dishwasher and microwave, private terrace and green area! Modern Mobilhomes with air conditioning and sat-tv, chalets and bungalows.

> 345 pitches for caravans and tents, over 200 are provided with electricity, water and drainage. Several pitches are directly situated at the lakeside.

> An animationteam offers during the high season period all kind of games, sports, tournaments and shows, miniclub for children and group sports.

> Two swimmingpools for adults with a fitness area, whirlpool with sunloungers and laguna; swimmingpool for children with watergames especially studied for the smallest one's!

> New bar/restaurant exclusive for the pool- and solarium area.

> Footballfield, volley- and tenniscourt, bowls game, ping pong.

> Terrace/bar, restaurant, pizzeria direct on the lake, minimarket.

> Private beach with slides and floats (reservation necessary).

> We organize boattrips for our guests!

Via Silvella, 10 • I-25010 San Felice del Benaco (Brescia) • Tel. +39.0365.651095 • Fax +39.0365.654395 info@europasilvella.it • www.europasilvella.it • SKYPE: europasilvella.eliana • europasilvella.michela

261

IT62540 Camping Lido

Via Peschiera 2, I-37017 Pacengo (Lake Garda)

Tel: 045 759 0611. Email: info@campinglido.it

Camping Lido is one of the largest and amongst the best of the 120 campsites around Lake Garda and is situated at the southeast corner of the lake. There is quite a slope from the entrance down to the lake so many of the 683 grass touring pitches are on terraces which give lovely views across the lake. They are of varying size, separated by hedges, all have electrical connections and 57 are fully serviced. This is a most attractive site with tall, neatly trimmed trees standing like sentinels on either side of the broad avenue which runs from the entrance right down to the lake. A wide variety of trees provide shade on some pitches and flowers add colour to the overall appearance. Near the top of the site is a large, well designed pool with a paddling pool and slides into splash pools. A pool bar provides refreshment and there is a fitness centre for those who wish to stay in trim. The site has its own beach with a landing stage that marks off a large area for swimming on one side and on the other an area where boats can be moored. One could happily spend all the holiday here without leaving the site but with so many attractions nearby this would be a pity.

Facilities

Seven modern toilet blocks (three heated) include provision for disabled visitors and three family rooms. Washing machines and dryer. Fridge rental. Restaurant, bars, pizzeria, takeaway and well stocked supermarket. Swimming pool, paddling pool and slides. Superb fitness centre. Playground. Tennis. Bicycle hire. Watersports. Fishing. High season activities for children and adults. Shingle beach. Dogs are not accepted in high season (3/7-15/8). Off site: Bus service 200 m. Gardaland.

Open: 20 March - 15 October.

Directions

Leave A4 Milan - Venice motorway at exit for Peschiera. Head north on east side of lake on the SS249. Site on left after Gardaland Theme Park.

Charges 2007

Per person	€ 4,40 - € 6,70
child (3-5 yrs)	€ 2,80 - € 3,90
pitch incl. services	€ 9,40 - € 16,50

IT62560 Camping del Garda

Via Marzan 6, I-37019 Peschiera del Garda (Lake Garda)

Tel: 045 755 0540. Email: campingdelgarda@gardalake.it

Camping del Garda is directly on the lake with access through gates which provide security at night. This is one of the largest campsites around Lake Garda and is more of a self contained holiday village with many pitches used by tour operators, although they are generally separate from the touring pitches. The mature trees provide shade for the 659 grass pitches of which 337 are for tourers. Arranged in numbered rows, all have 4A electrical connections and hedges have been cleverly trimmed for maximum attractiveness. Hard roads give access. This is a well kept site with colour added by attractive flower beds. There is a very active animation programme throughout the season for all ages and two good pools with lifeguards. A huge range of sports activities including watersports is available and boat enthusiasts have boat launching close by. The picturesque little town of Peschiera is 1 km. over the bridges and the busy waterfront has pretty bars and restaurants.

Facilities

Eleven good quality toilet blocks have the usual facilities with free hot water. Facilities for disabled visitors in two blocks. Washing machines and dryers. Bars, restaurant and takeaway. Supermarket (all season). Swimming pools. Tennis courts and school. Minigolf. Watersports including windsurf school. Fishing. Playground. Organised activities in high season. Bowls. Dogs and motorcycles are not accepted. Off site: Gardaland, Zoo Safari, Verona, etc. Fishing 500 m. Golf and riding 2 km.

Open: 1 April - 30 September.

Directions

Leave the A4 (Milan - Venice) at Peschiera exit and travel through the town in the direction of Garda. After the second town bridge on Via Parcocatullo look for Via Marzan off the complex four road intersection. Campsite signs are small and difficult to see (campsite is on Via Marzan).

Charges guide

Per person	€ 4,00 - € 8,50
child (under 5 yrs)	free - € 5,00
pitch incl. electricity (4A)	€ 9,50 - € 17,50

I-37019 Peschiera (Verona)
Tel. 0039/0457551899
Tel. 0039/0457550540
Fax 0039/0456400711
campdelgarda@icmnet.net
www.campingdelgarda.it
www.camping-delgarda.com

VILLAGGIO TURISTICO
CAMPING DEL GARDA

Right on the lake. Quite, with shadow and beach, only 1 km from the village centre. 2 km from the highway exit Milan-Venice. Well equipped bathroom facilities, bar, self-service stores, pizzeria, market, camper-service, swimming pool, tennis, children's playground, table tennis, entertainment. Free of charge bus service to "Gardaland".

Friendliness and politeness is our slogan.

IT62520 Camping San Francesco

Strada Vicinale, I-25015 Rivoltella (Lake Garda)

Tel: 030 911 0245. Email: moreinfo@campingsanfrancesco.com

San Francesco is a large, very well organised site situated to the west of the Simione peninsula on the southeast shores of Lake Garda. The pitches are generally on flat gravel and sand and enjoy shade from mature trees. There are three choices of pitch of different sizes with either 3A or 6A electricity, 35 are fully serviced. They are marked by stones but there is no division between them. A wooded beach area of about 400 m. on the lake is used for watersports. There are delightful lake views from the restarant and terrace. There is also a new shopping mall with games area, bazaar and takeaway. The sports centre, pools and entertainment area are all located across a busy road away from the pitches and safely accessed by a tunnel. This is a good quality site which is great for families.

Facilities

Sanitary facilities are in two large, modern, centrally located buildings. Very clean when seen, they are well equipped. Excellent facilities for disabled campers. Shop. Restaurant. Bar. Pizzeria. Takeaway. In a separate area across the road: swimming pools (15/4-20/9) and jacuzzi, sports centre and tennis. Playground. Entertainment, activities and excursions. Bicycle hire arranged. Internet access. Off site: Riding 5 km. Golf 10 km.

Open: 1 April - 30 September.

Directions

From autostrada A4, between Brescia and Verona, exit towards Simione and follow signs to Simione and site. GPS: N45:27.921 E10:35.681

Charges 2007

Per person	€ 5,70 - € 10,00
child (under 6 yrs)	free - € 8,00
pitch incl. electricity	€ 12,00 - € 20,00
superior pitch	€ 13,50 - € 30,00
Camping Cheques accepted.	

IT62530 Camping Piani di Clodia

Localitá Bagatta, I-37017 Lazise (Lake Garda)
Tel: 045 759 0456. Email: info@pianidiclodia.it

Piani di Clodia is one of the best large sites on Lake Garda and it has a positive impression of space and cleanliness. It is located on a slope between Lazise and Peschiera in the southeast corner of the lake, with lovely views across the water to Sirmione's peninsula and the mountains beyond. The site slopes down to the water's edge and has over 950 pitches, all with electricity (6A), 250 with electricity, water and drainage, terraced where necessary and back to back from hard access roads. There is some shade from mature and young trees. The pool complex is truly wonderful with a range of pools, a pleasant sunbathing area and a bar. The whole area is fenced and supervised. At the centre of the site is a quality rooftop restaurant, a self service restaurant plus pizzeria and table service for drinks. From most of this area you will be able to enjoy the free entertainment on the large stage. The enthusiastic animation team provide an ambitious variety of entertainment. There is a fence between the site and the lake with access points to a private beach and opportunities for a variety of watersports. You are greeted at the gate by English speaking attendants who are keen to please, as are reception staff. The site is very close to several theme parks.

Facilities

Seven modern, immaculate sanitary blocks, well spaced around the site. British and Turkish style WCs. All have facilities for disabled visitors and one has a baby room. Washing machines, dryers and laundry service. Motorcaravan services. Shopping complex with supermarket, general shops for clothes, etc. Two bars. Self-service restaurant with takeaway and pizzeria and cream parlour. Swimming pools. Tennis. Gymnastics. Fishing. Bicycle hire. Large playground. Outdoor theatre with animation programme. Off site: Riding 6 km. Golf 12 km. Theme parks nearby.

Open: 20 March - 15 October.

Directions

Lazise is on the south-east side of Lake Garda about 30 km. west of Verona. From north on Trento - Verona A22 autostrada take Affi exit then follow signs for Lazise and site. From south on A4 Brescia - Venice motorway take Peschiera exit and site is 6 km. towards Lazise and Garda on SS249.
GPS: N45:28.963 E10:43.759

Charges 2007

Per person	€ 4,80 - € 9,70
child (1-9 yrs)	€ 3,10 - € 6,40
pitch with electricity	€ 9,80 - € 24,50
incl. electricity and water	€ 11,00 - € 26,50

IT63580 Camping Park Delle Rose

Localitá Vanon, I-37017 Lazise (Lake Garda)
Tel: 045 6471181. Email: info@campingparkdellerose.it

An orderly, well designed site with a feeling of spaciousness, Delle Rose is on the east side of Lake Garda, three kilometers from the attractive waterside village of Peschiera. The 396 pitches are of average size, most with grass and shade and laid out in 30 short, terraced avenues. The ratio of recreational area to pitches is unusually high, particularly for sites at Lake Garda. Unusually, reception is located one third of the way into the site. On approach one sees the attractive restaurant, gardens and comprehensive sporting facilities including the pool complex with its stylish terraced bar and animation area close by.

Facilities

Five very clean, modern sanitary blocks provide hot water throughout. Britiish style toilets, some in cabins with washbasins. Facilities for disabled visitors. Washing machines. Motorcaravan service point. Bar/restaurant, takeaway (all season), Shops. Swimming pool (mid April - Sept). Tennis. Archery. Minigolf. Play area and miniclub for children. Fishing (with permit). Beach. Watersports. Animation programme in high season. Excursions. Dogs are not accepted. Motorbikes are not accepted. Torches useful. Off site: Peschiera 2 km. Riding 8 km. Golf 6 km.

Open: 19 April - 30 September.

Directions

From A4 Milan - Venice autostrada take exit for Perschiera, west of Verona. Travel north towards Lazise. The campsite is on the southeastern lakeside about 2.5 km. north of Peschiera and well signed.

Charges 2007

Per person	€ 4,00 - € 8,00
child (1-7 yrs)	free - € 4,50
pitch	€ 9,00 - € 17,00

PIANI DI CLODIA
★ ★ ★ ★

Feel the emotion!

The Leading Camping
& Caravaning Parks of Europe

www.pianidiclodia.it

Località Bagatta - 37017 Lazise (Verona) Italy
T. +39 045 7590456 - F. +39 045 7590939
info@pianidiclodia.it

 GS 490 • Via Peschiera (Lazise)
• Località Bagatta (Lazise)

IT62550 Camping La Quercia

I-37017 Lazise sul Garda (Lake Garda)

Tel: 045 647 0577. Email: laquercia@laquercia.it

Celebrating its 50th anniversary in 2008, La Quercia is a spacious, popular site on a slight slope leading down to Lake Garda and is decorated by palm trees and elegantly trimmed hedges. Accommodating up to 950 touring units, pitches are mostly in regular double rows between access roads, all with electricity (6A). Most are shaded by mature trees, although those furthest from the lake are more open to the sun. Much of the activity centres around the impressive pool complex with its fantastic slides and the terrace bar, restaurant and pizzeria which overlook the entertainment stage. The daytime activities and evening entertainment are very professional with the young team working hard to involve everyone (some courses require enrolment on a Sunday). La Quercia has a fine sandy beach on the lake, with diving jetties and a roped-off section for launching boats or windsurfing (high season). Another restaurant serving traditional Italian food is located closer to the beach. The site is a short distance from the delightful lakeside towns of Lazise and Peschiera, which have a wide choice of restaurants, and is a short drive from Verona, one of Italy's finest cultural centres.

Facilities

Six toilet blocks are perfectly sufficient and are of a very high standard. Laundry. Supermarket. General shop. Bar, restaurant, self-service restaurant and pizzeria. Swimming pools (small charge). Tennis. Riding stables. Football. Aerobics and yoga. Scuba club. Playground with water play. Organised events (sports competitions, games, etc.) and free courses (e.g. swimming, surfboarding). Canoeing. Rollerblading. Archery, climbing, judo, multigym. Minigolf. Evening entertainment or dancing. Baby sitting service. Internet. ATM. Free weekly excursion. Medical service. Off site: Bicycle hire 300 m. Golf 10 km. Gardaland, Movieland and Caneva Aqua Park nearby.

Open: 10 days before Easter - 30 September.

Directions

Lazise is on the southeast side of Lake Garda about 30 km. west of Verona. From north on the Trento - Verona A22 autostrada take Affi exit then follow signs for Lazise and site. From south on the A4 Brescia - Venice motorway, take Peschiera exit and site is 7 km. towards Lazise and Garda on the SS249. GPS: N45:29.606 E10:43.969

Charges 2007

Per person	€ 5,30 - € 10,90
child (5-7 yrs)	free - € 7,20
pitch	€ 10,30 - € 29,10
dog	€ 3,50 - € 6,90

Low season discount for pensioners.

IT62750 Fornella Camping

Via Fornella 1, I-25010 San Felice del Benaco (Lake Garda)

Tel: 036 562 294. Email: fornella@fornella.it

Fornella Camping is one of the few campsites on Lake Garda still surrounded by farmed olive trees and with a true country atmosphere. Parts of the site have lake views, others a back drop of mountains and attractive countryside. The 180 touring pitches are on flat grass, terraced where necessary and most have good shade, all with electricity (6/10A); 42 have water and waste as well. The owners speak excellent English. This site has a superb new pool complex, a well appointed bar and restaurant, and top class facilities for boat owners, having recently purchased the adjoining marina. There are two separate lake accesses for boats and windsurfers. The pool complex includes a cloverleaf shaped swimming pool with a surface area of over 900 sq.m, a jacuzzi, water games and a paddling pool, all with lifeguard cover. A second pool is open for a longer period. There are 3,000 sq.m. of grassy pool gardens for sunbathing and a bar/café area. The owner describes animation here as 'soft' – lots of sport and activities with an emphasis on the environment and countryside, no loud speakers but live music in the evenings for campers. The bar and restaurant are located on the lakeside with a terrace offering splendid views over the lake.

Facilities

Three very clean, modern toilet blocks, well dispersed around the site, have mainly British type WCs and hot water in washbasins (some in cabins), showers and sinks. Facilities for disabled people. Washing machines, dryer and irons. Motorcaravan services. Bar/restaurant. Pizzeria and takeaway at certain times. Shop. Supervised swimming pools and paddling pool (15/5-15/9). Tennis. Table tennis. Two playgrounds and animation for children in season. Bicycle hire in high season. Beach. Fishing. Small marina, boat launching and repairs. Off site: Bicycle hire 4 km. Sailing 5 km. Golf 8 km. Riding 10 km.

Open: 29 April - 24 September.

Directions

San Felice is on western shore of Lake Garda at the southern end. From A4 Milan - Venice autostrada take Desenzano exit and head north on SS572 towards Salo for 13 km; turn right towards San Felice and follow signs. GPS: N45:35.098 E10:33.949

Charges 2007

Per person	€ 4,90 - € 8,50
child (3-7 yrs)	free - € 7,20
pitch incl. electricity (6A)	€ 9,50 - € 24,00

Charges acc. to season and pitch location. Various low season discounts.

Welcome!

Anniversario
1958-2008

Come and celebrate
the event of the year with us!
.. more parties, more freebies, more gifts for everyone!

Big competition: you can win a free staying for year 2009!

A COMPLETE HOLIDAY

...ady emplacements – Heated toilet bloks for both grown-up's and children – 24 hours Warm water – Restaurant – Pizzeria – Cocktail Bar – Funny ...ar on the beach – Swimmingpools with slides – Whirlpool – Full-comfort maxicaravans and bungalows for 4-5 persons with sight on the lake ...The widest sand beach on the lake – Theatre – Supermarket – Butcher's shop – Pastry- and bakers shop – Typical products of the lake – Fresh ...uit and vegetables every days – Tobacconist's shop – International newspaper kiosk – Rent a car service – Fax service – Professional animators ...Animation for children and teenagers – Tennis – Canoe – Archery – Surfing – Judo – Football – Fitness gym – Spinning – Horse-riding.

65500 SQUARE METRES OF CLEAN AND SAFE PRIVATE BEACH, JUST A FEW METRES AWAY FROM ALL THE AMENITIES

900 SHADY SPOTS IN BEAUTIFULLY-TENDED GROUNDS

18 AREAS WITH FACILITIES FOR SPORTS AND LEISURE ACTIVITIES

CAMPING ★★★★
LA QUERCIA
... more than a camping!

...formation and booking:

39.045.6470577

info@laquercia.it
www.laquercia.it

LAZISE SUL GARDA
VERONA - **ITALY**

IT62830 Camping La Rocca

Via Cavalle 22, I-25080 Manerba del Garda (Lake Garda)

Tel: **036 555 1738**. Email: **info@laroccacamp.it**

Set high on a peninsula, on the quieter western shore of Lake Garda, La Rocca is a very friendly, family-orientated campsite. With 180 attractive touring pitches enjoying shade from the tree canopy which also protects the campers from the summer heat, this is a 'real' campsite (20 pitches are on open terraces with lake views). It has the choice of two pebble lakeside beaches which can be accessed from the site, and a very nice pool complex. The site has all modern amenities without losing its distinctive Italian ambience. Nothing is too much trouble for the management. The owner Livio is charming and very engaging with his pleasant, halting English. Close to traditional Italian villages and modern theme parks there is something for everyone here.

Facilities

Two sanitary blocks with smart new units for disabled campers and baby changing areas which are kept in pristine condition at all times. Washing machines. Bar with terrace also offers basic meals. Small shop. Swimming pools. Tennis. Play area. Bicycle loan. Fishing (permit). Boat launching. Music in the evenings. Miniclub (high season). Torches required on beach steps and tunnel. Off site: Bars and restaurants a short walk away. Theme parks. Riding 3 km. Golf 5 km.

Open: 20 March - 28 September.

Directions

Manerba is on western shore of Lake Garda at the southern end. From A4 autostrada take Desenzano exit and follow SS572 towards Saló for about 11 km and look for campsite signs. Turn right off main road, then right along Via Belvedere and it is the second site on Via Cavalle. GPS: N45:33.615 E10:33.827

Charges 2007

Per person	€ 4,00 - € 7,50
child (3-11 yrs)	€ 3,00 - € 5,50
pitch with electricity	€ 9,00 - € 18,00
No credit cards.	

The camping site Rocca is situated directly on the lake, between the peninsula San Biagio and Rocca di Manerba. It provides 2 swimming pools, tennis court and beachvolleyball court, bar, minimarket, post service, telephone box, playground and table tennis. Reservations possible. **Opening: 15.03.-28.09.2008.**

Camping LA ROCCA
★★★★
Via Cavalle, 22
I-25080 MANERBA
LAGO DI GARDA (BRESCIA)
Tel. 0039/0365/551738
Fax 0039/0365/552045
Http: www.laroccacamp.it
E-mail: info@laroccacamp.it

Coordinates GPS:
North 45° 33' 440
East 10° 33' 530

IT63570 Campings Cisano & San Vito

Via Peschiera 48, I-37010 Cisano di Bardolino (Lake Garda)

Tel: **045 622 9098**. Email: **cisano@camping-cisano.it**

This is a combination of two sites and some of the 700 pitches have superb locations along the kilometre of shaded lakeside contained in Cisano. Some are on sloping ground and most are shaded but the San Vito pitches have no lake views. Both sites have a family orientation and effort has been taken in the landscaping to provide comfort even for the largest units. San Vito is the smaller and more peaceful location with no lakeside pitches. It shares many of the facilities of Cisano which is a short walk across the road. Each site has its own reception. A reader reports that a 2 m. fence separating the pitches from the beach and lake has been constructed at Cisano, with several gates, but only two that open at the moment, at the extreme ends of the beach. On the San Vito site there is a pleasant family style restaurant (some road noise). Excellent pools and play equipment, along with animation in high season are all here. The friendly efficient staff at both sites speak English.

Facilities

Plentiful, good quality sanitary facilities are provided in both sites (9 blocks at Cisano and 2 at San Vito). Facilities for disabled visitors. Fridge hire. Shop, bar, restaurant (open all season). Swimming pool. Play area. Fishing and sailing. Free windsurfing and canoeing. Internet access. Dogs are not accepted (cats are). Motorcycles not allowed on site (parking provided). Off site: Riding 15 km.

Open: 1 April - 1 October.

Directions

Leave A4 autoroute at Pescheria exit and head north towards Garda on lakeside road. Pass Lazise and site is signed (small sign) on left halfway to Bardolina.

Charges 2007

Per person	€ 4,00 - € 10,00
child	free - € 4,00
pitch	€ 9,00 - € 18,00
Camping Cheques accepted.	

IT62800 Camping Villaggio Weekend

Via Vallone della Selva 2, I-25010 San Felice del Benaco (Lake Garda)

Tel: **0365 43712**. Email: **info@weekend.it**

Created among the olive groves and terraced vineyards of the Chateau Villa Louisa, which overlooks it, this modern well equipped site enjoys some superb views over the small bay which forms this part of Lake Garda. On reaching the site you will pass through a most impressive pair of gates. There are 230 pitches, all with electricity, of which about 30% are taken by tour operators and statics. The touring pitches are in several different areas, and many enjoy superb views. Some pitches for larger units are set in the upper terraces on steep slopes and manoeuvring can be challenging. Although the site is 400 m. from the lake via a steep footpath, for many campers the views resulting from its situation on higher ground will be ample compensation for its not being an actual lakeside site. Being set in quiet countryside, it provides an unusually tranquil environment.

Facilities

Three sanitary blocks, one below the restaurant/shop, are modern and well maintained. Mainly British style WCs, a few washbasins in cabins and facilities for disabled people in one. Baby room. Laundry. Bar/restaurant (waiter service). Takeaway. Shop. Supervised swimming pool and paddling pool. Barbecues. Entertainment programme all season. Two playgrounds. First aid room. English spoken. Internet points. Off site: Fishing 2 km. Golf 6 km. Riding 8 km. Windsurfing, water skiing and tennis near.

Open: 19 April - 21 September.

Directions

From Milano - Venezia autostrada take Desenzano exit towards Saló and Localita Cisano - S. Felice. Watch for narrow right fork after Cunettone roundabout. Turn right towards San Felice for 1 km. Site is next left. GPS: N45:35.591 E10:31.853

Charges 2008

Per person	€ 5,75 - € 9,50
child (4-11 yrs)	€ 3,75 - € 6,50
pitch incl. electricity	€ 15,00 - € 31,00

Camping Cheques accepted.

IT62630 Camping Bella Italia

Via Bella Italia 2, I-37019 Peschiera del Garda (Lake Garda)

Tel: **045 640 0688**. Email: **bellaitalia@camping-bellaitalia.it**

Peschiera is a picturesque village on the southern shore of Lake Garda and Camping Bella Italia is an attractive, large, well organised and very busy site in the grounds of a former farm, just west from the centre of the village. Although over half of the 1200 pitches are occupied by the site's own mobile homes and chalets and by tour operators, there are some 500 tourist pitches, most towards the lakeside and reasonably level on grass under trees. All have electricity (6A) and are separated by shrubs. There are some fine views across the lake to the mountains beyond. The pitches are grouped in regular rows on either side of hard access roads (which are named after European cities) and the wide central road which leads to the shops and pleasant restaurants. The site slopes gently down to the lake with access to the water for swimming and boating and to the lakeside public path. A feature of the site is the group of pools of varying shapes and sizes with an entertainment area and varied sports provision nearby. A range of supervised activities is organised. Regulations are in place to ensure a peaceful site particularly during the afternoon siesta and during the hours of darkness. English is spoken by the friendly management.

Facilities

Six modern toilet blocks have British style toilets, washbasins and showers. Baby rooms and facilities for disabled visitors. Washing machines. Motorcaravan services. Shops. Bars. Waiter service restaurant and terrace and two other restaurants (one in the old farm building). Swimming pools. Tennis. Football. Volleyball. Basketball. Archery. Playgrounds (small). Games room. Watersports. Bicycle hire. Organised activities. Internet access. Dogs are not accepted. Off site: Fishing 1 km. Golf and riding both 5 km. Gardaland, Italy's most popular theme park is about 2 km. east of Peschiera.

Open: 8 March - 5 October.

Directions

Peschiera is 32 km. west of Verona. From A4 take exit for Peschiera del Garda and follow SS11 towards Brescia. Site is at the large junction at the western entrance to the village. GPS: N45:26.499 E10:40.752

Charges 2007

Per person	€ 6,00 - € 11,50
child (3-5 yrs)	free - € 5,00
pitch	€ 12,00 - € 21,00

Four charging seasons. No credit/debit cards. Camping Cheques accepted.

IT62660 Camping Gasparina

Via Gasparina 13, I-37010 Cavalcaselle (Lake Garda)

Tel: **045 7550775**. Email: **info@gasparina.com**

Gasparina is of average size for this area and of reasonable quality, but a little away from the towns around the lake. It is in a peaceful location and has the feeling of being in the countryside. As the site slopes gently towards the lake, levellers are needed in some parts. There are 430 grass tourist pitches in back-to-back rows separated by gravel roads. Many trees and flowers adorn the site, with shade in most parts. The pleasant swimming pools are separated from the restaurant terraces by a neat, well clipped hedge. Just beyond the site fence is a beach and pleasant promenade. Boats can be launched here. Near reception is the bar/restaurant with three terraces and good prices.

Facilities

Two refurbished and one new toilet block have the usual facilities with warm water in two blocks. Facilities for disabled visitors. Washing machines and dryer. Shop. Bar/restaurant with terrace. Swimming pool. Playground. Tennis courts. Watersports. Animation in high season. Dogs and other pets are not accepted. Off site: Bicycle hire 2 km. Riding 3 km.

Open: 1 April - 1 September.

Directions

Leave A4 Milan - Venice motorway at exit for Peschiera, go north on east side of lake on SS249 towards Lazise for entrance road on your left.

Charges guide

Per unit incl 4 persons	€ 15,00 - € 31,00
extra person	€ 3,00 - € 7,00
boat trailer	€ 10,00 - € 18,00

IT62860 Camping Baia Verde

Via Dell Edera 19, I-25080 Manerba del Garda (Lake Garda)

Tel: **0365651753**. Email: **info@campingbaiaverde.com**

Baia Verde is a new campsite located in the southwestern corner of Lake Garda. When we visited in late May 2007, construction was nearing completion and both the potential and the drawbacks were evident. The 69 touring pitches are in regular rows on flat, open ground where rough grass has been planted and young trees mark the corners of pitches; until these have grown there will be no shade. On the other hand, everything is being built to a very high standard and the restaurant block and the building housing all other facilities are in traditional style. All pitches are fully serviced and there are 12 super-pitches with private wash blocks. Heated swimming and paddling pools are attractively designed and nearby is a children's play area and sports pitch. The bar and restaurant will be open all season, as will the pool complex. The lake is just two minutes' walk away; this is the quieter, less commercialised side of Lake Garda, but popular attractions such as the Gardaland theme park and Caneva water park are an easy drive away.

Facilities

Full range of high quality sanitary facilities in an impressive 3-storey building in the style of an Italian villa. Baby and children's rooms, en-suite facilities for disabled visitors. Washing machines and dryers. Above will be a large television lounge and on the roof is a sunbathing area with jacuzzi. An entertainment and activity programme in high season is planned. Bicycle hire. Off site: Manerba del Garda 1 km. Beach with fishing, swimming and boat launching 400 m. Golf and riding 2 km.

Open: 26 May - 15 September.

Directions

Manerba is on western shore of Lake Garda at the southern end. From A4 Milan - Venice autostrada take Desenzano exit and head north on SS572 towards Saló for about 12 km; then turn right following signs to site. GPS: N45:33.680 E10:33.208

Charges 2007

Per unit incl. 2 persons	
and electricity	€ 19,00 - € 34,00
eextra person	€ 7,50
child (3-11 yrs)	€ 4,00

Camping Baia Verde - Via dell'Edera,19
I-25080 Manerba del Garda (BS)
Tel. +39 0365 651753 - Fax +39 0365 651809

info@campingbaiaverde.com

www.campingbaiaverde.com

- FIRST CLASS SANITARY BUILDING WITH PRIVATE BATHS
- SWIMMING POOL WITH JACUZZI, GAMES
- CHILDREN'S POOL
- SNACK BAR ON POOL PATIO
- MULTI-USE FIELD SUITABLE FOR BEACH VOLLEYBALL AND FOOTBALL
- CHILDREN'S PLAYGROUND
- PITCHES 80/90 M. SQ. WITH ELECTRICITY, WATER SUPPLY AND WASTE WATER OUTLET
- PITCHES "SUPERIOR" 90 M. SQ. WITH ELECTRICITY, WATER, DRAINAGE, PRIVATE BATHROOMS AND A KITCHENSINK FOR DISHWARE.
- SAT TV
- CAMPER SERVICE
- MOBILE HOMES WITH AIR CONDITIONING
- BOOKINGS WELCOME
- ROOF-SOLARIUM: SWIMMINGPOOL ON THE TERRACE, HEATED, WHIRLPOOL FOR 8 PERSONS.

272
Check real time availability and at-the-gate prices...
www.**alanrogers**.com

IT62840 Camping Belvedere

Via Cavalle 5, I-25080 Manerba del Garda (Lake Garda)

Tel: **036 555 1175**. Email: **info@camping-belvedere.it**

Situated along a promontory reaching into Lake Garda, this friendly, traditional campsite has been landscaped with terracing to give many of the 85 touring pitches a good vantage point to enjoy the wonderful views. They are mainly on hardstanding and all have 6A electricity. From the top of the terrace a long ramp (or 56 steps) takes you to the lakeside area with access to the long pebbly beach for a relaxing swim and for boat launching. The delightful restaurant and bar with pretty flowers is under shady trees at the water's edge. The site has grassy areas and attractive trees give many pitches a cool canopy. Italian villages with lots of atmosphere are close by as are the huge theme parks the area is known for. The landscaping and atmosphere are delightfully Mediterranean with charming Italian vistas. There are no facilities for disabled campers and really young children would require supervision as the terracing is unguarded in places.

Facilities

Five traditional sanitary blocks are well maintained and kept clean. Washing machine. Motorhome service point. Shop selling basics. Restaurant, bar and takeaway are all open most of the season. Play area. Full size tennis court. Music and TV in bar. Fishing. Torches useful. Mobile homes to rent. Off site: Golf and bicycle hire 2 km. Riding 4 km. Watersports nearby. Bars and restaurant a short walk away. Theme parks.

Open: 15 March - 5 October.

Directions

Manerba is on western shore of Lake Garda at the southern end. From A4 Milan - Venice autostrada take Desenzano exit and head north on SS572 towards Salo for about 11 km. and look for campsite signs. Turn right off main road, then right again along Via Belvedere. GPS: N45:33.724 E10:33.789

Charges 2007

Per person	€ 3,75 - € 6,75
child (3-11 yrs)	€ 3,00 - € 5,40
pitch with electricity	€ 8,50 - € 15,00
dog	€ 2,00 - € 4,00

On the shores of Lake Garda, in the suggestive gulf of Manerba, Camping Belvedere is the ideal place for a great relaxing holiday on the lakeside. Its unique position offers you s h a d y t e r r a c e d pitches with a fantastic view, 200 mt. Beach with private pear and buoys for boat anchorage in the calm and safe water of the gulf. A restaurant with a wide terrace on the beach, children-playground, swimming pools, boat-access, bar and mini-market are at disposal of the guests.

BELVEDERE

CAMPING BELVEDERE
Via Cavalle, 5 - 25080 MANERBA DEL GARDA (BS) ITALY
Tel. +39 0365 551175 - Fax +39 0365 552350
E-mail: info@camping-belvedere.it
www.camping-belvedere.it

IT61990 Camping Corones

I-39030 Rasun (Trentino - Alto Adige)

Tel: **0474496490**. Email: **info@corones.com**

Situated in pine forest clearing at the foot of the attractive Antholz valley in the heart of German speaking Südtirol, Corones is ideally situated both for winter sports enthusiasts and for walkers, cyclists, mountain bikers and those who prefer to explore the valleys and mountain roads of the Dolomites by car. There are 135 level pitches, all with electricity (16A) and many also with water and drainage and satellite TV. The Residence offers luxury appartments and tthere are authentic Canadian log cabins for hire. The bar/restaurant and small shop are open all season. From the site you can see slopes which in winter become highly rated skiing pistes. A short drive up the broad Antholz/Anterselva valley takes you to an internationally important Biathlon Centre. A not-so-young British couple who were on site when we visited had just driven up the valley and over the pass into Austria and then back via another pass. Back on site, a small pool and paddling pool could be very welcome. There is a regular programme of free excursions and occasional evening events are organised. Children's entertainment is provided in July and August.

Facilities

The central toilet block is traditional but well maintained and clean; it is gradually being refurbished. Additional facilities below the Residence are of the highest quality including individual shower rooms with washbasins, washbasins with all WCs, a delightful children's unit and an excellent facility for disabled visitors. Fully equipped private shower rooms for hire. Luxurious Wellness Centre with saunas, solarium, jacuzzis, massage, therapy pools and heat benches. Heated outdoor swimming and paddling pools (4/5-20/10). Play area. Internet facilities. Off site: Tennis 800 m. Bicycle hire 1 km. Riding and fishing 3 km. Golf (9 holes) 10 km. Canoeing 15 km.

Open: 6 December - 30 March, 4 May - 31 October.

Directions

Rasen/Rasun is 85 km northeast of Bolzano. From Bressanone/Brixen exit on A22 Brenner - Modena motorway, go east on SS49 for 50 km, then turn north (signed Razen/Antholz). Turn immediately west at roundabout in Niederrasen/Rasun di Sotto to site on left in 100 m. GPS: N46:46.551 E12:02.231

Charges 2007

Per unit incl 2 persons and electricity	€ 18,00 - € 25,50
extra person	€ 4,20 - € 7,20
child (3-15 yrs)	€ 3,00 - € 5,80

IT63590 Camping Serenella

Localitá Mezzariva, I-37011 Bardolino (Lake Garda)

Tel: 045 721 1333. Email: serenella@camping-serenella.it

Situated alongside Lake Garda, Serenella has 300 average size pitches, some with good lake views. Movement around the site may prove difficult for large units (look for the wider roads). The pitches are shaded and have 3A electricity. A long promenade with brilliant views of the mountains and lake runs the length of the campsite. It is dotted with grassy relaxation areas and beach bars where snacks are served and the atmosphere is charming. The pleasant pool complex is near an older style 'taverna' where delicious, sensibly priced food is served. There is some road noise at some of the amenities and the pool. There is an animation programme from May to September, a small market and a variety of tiny bungalows throughout the site. Serenella is a popular site.

Facilities

Five clean, well equipped sanitary blocks, include three that are more modern with laundry facilities. British style toilets, free hot water throughout. Facilities for disabled visitors. Washing machines and dryer. Freezer. Bar and restaurant, takeaway and shop (all season). Watersports. Animation programme for all in high season. Play area. Bicycle hire. Boat launching. Minigolf. Tennis. Satellite TV. Internet and WiFi. Dogs are not accepted. Motorcyles are not allowed. Off site: Beach with fishing and watersports. Golf 3 km. Riding 3.5 km. Town 3 km. Gardaland.

Open: Easter or 1 April - 22 October.

Directions

From E70 Milan - Venice autostrada take Pescheria exit and follow signs to Bardolino. Site is on lakeside between Bardolino and Garda, about 4 km. south of Garda.

Charges 2007

Per person	€ 4,00 - € 8,50
child (4-10 yrs)	free - € 4,00
pitch	€ 9,50 - € 16,50

IT60050 Villaggio Turistico Camping Europa

Via Monfalcone 12, I-34073 Grado (Friuli - Venézia Giúlia)

Tel: 043 180 877. Email: info@villaggioeuropa.com

This large flat, good quality site beside the sea and has 500 pitches, with 350 for touring units. They are all neat, clean and marked, most with shade and 6/10A electricity, 180 are fully serviced. The terrain is undulating and sandy in the areas nearer the sea, where cars have to be left in parking places. An impressive, large new Aquatic Park covers 1500 sq.m. with two slides (100 m. and 60 m. long and many other features. With many shallow areas it is very popular with children and there are lifeguards. A new pool bar is an attractive feature. There is direct access to the beach. The water recedes up to 200 m. from the beach, but leaves a natural paddling pool which is enjoyed by children when it is hot. A narrow wooden jetty gives acess to deeper water. This is a neat, well managed site which is probably the best in the area.

Facilities

Five excellent, refurbished toilet blocks are well designed and very clean. Mostly British style WCs and excellent facilities for disabled people. Washing machines. Motorcaravan services. Large supermarket, small general shop (all season). Large bar and restaurant with takeaway (all season). Swimming pools (May - Sept). Tennis. Fishing. Bicycle hire. Playground. Full entertainment programme in season. Internet access. Off site: Golf 500 m.

Open: 28 April - 22 September.

Directions

Site is 4 km. east of Grado on road to Monfalcone. Take the 35L road to Grado from west, continue through town to Grado Pineta on the beach road. Site is 2 km.

Charges 2007

Per person	€ 5,50 - € 10,00
child (3-11 yrs)	€ 3,50 - € 9,00
pitch incl. electricity	€ 8,00 - € 20,00

Less 10% for longer stays out of season.

IT60080 Camping Sabbiadoro

Via Sabbiadoro 8, I-33054 Lignano Sabbiadoro (Friuli - Venézia Giúlia)

Tel: **043 171 455**. Email: **campsab@lignano.it**

Sabbiadoro is a large, good quality site with a huge entrance and efficient reception. It has 1,215 pitches and is ideal for families who like all their amenities to be close by. This does mean that the site is busy and noisy with people having fun. Quite tightly packed, the pitches vary in size, are shaded by attractive trees and have electricity. You may wish to cover your car and unit to prevent sap covering it over time. The facilities are all in excellent condition and well thought out, especially the pool complex, and everything here is very modern, safe and clean. A second site close by is opened for younger customers in high season – they use the main site facilities. The local resort town is just 200 m. away and this too buzzes with activity in high season. The fine beach is 250 m. and is said to be safe for children.

Facilities

Well equipped sanitary facilities include superb facilities for disabled visitors. Washing machines and dryers. Motorcaravan service point. Huge supermarket (all season). Bazaar. Good restaurant and snack bar (15/5-28/9). Heated outdoor pool complex with separate fun pool area, slides and fountains (all season). Table tennis. Disco. TV room. Internet. Play areas. Tennis. Fitness centre. Small boat launching. Surgery. Entertainment in the main season. Off site: Shops, restaurants and bars. Riding, sailing and golf.

Open: 15 March - 28 September.

Directions

Leave A4 at Latisana exit, west of Trieste and head to Latisano. From Latisano follow road to Lignano, then Sabbiadoro. Site is well signed as you approach the town.

Charges 2008

Per person	€ 4,80 - € 9,00
child (3-12 yrs)	€ 3,00 - € 5,00
pitch	€ 7,20 - € 14,50
incl. electricity	€ 8,20 - € 15,50

IT62070 Camping Residence Sägemühle

Dornweg 12, I-39026 Prad am Stilfserjoch (Trentino - Alto Adige)

Tel: **047 361 6078**. Email: **info@campingsaegemuehle.com**

This small site in the countryside is alongside a little village and has attractive views of the surrounding mountains where skiing is popular in the winter. The grass pitches are neat and level, some have shade and most have water, electricity drainage and pretty views. For a tiny campsite there is a lot on offer here. The indoor pool area is welcoming for cooling off in the summer and relax in warm water after skiing in winter. The facilities are cleverly placed under the pool and include a tiny gymnasium, sauna and a TV/games room. The steps may prove difficult for those with mobility problems, although the facilities for disabled visitors are on ground level. Animation is provided in July and August and shared with a sister site. We visited in high summer season but the area is a renowned winter sports area. The friendly owners speak some English and Dutch.

Facilities

The main modern toilet block is under the pool complex. All WCs are British style and the showers are of high quality. 24 private cabins for hire. Facilities for disabled visitors. Children's facilities and baby baths, plus a new second play area. Washing machines. Restaurant and bar. Indoor swimming pool. Spa and sauna. Animation programme in season. Miniclub. Play area. Internet. Torches useful. Off site: Town facilities. Natural spring for paddling close by. Bicycle hire 300 m. Riding 800 m.

Open: All year excl. 7 November - 19 December.

Directions

Site is west of Bolzano. From A38/S40 west of Bolzano, take exit for Pso dello Stelvio/Stilfserjoch (also marked S38) and village of Prad am Stilfserioch. Site is well signed from here.

Charges 2008

Per person	€ 8,50 - € 9,50
child (11-15 yrs)	€ 6,20 - € 7,50
child (2-10 yrs)	€ 5,20 - € 5,90
pitch	€ 10,50 - € 12,00
electricity	€ 2,50

IT60020 Camping Aquileia

Via Gemina,10, I-33051 Aquileia (Friuli - Venézia Giúlia)

Tel: **043 191 042**. Email: **info@campingaquileia.it**

Aquileia is a UNESCO world heritage site and home to some of Italy's most important Roman remains. Camping Aquileia is a shady campsite, close to the town centre and just 10 minutes from the nearest beaches at Grado but claiming to be a tranquil antidote to the hustle and bustle of some busy coastal campsites. This site has been recommended by our Italian agent and we hope to undertake a full inspection in 2008. Pitches here are flat and a number of very large (140 sq.m). Camping Aquileia was the third site in Italy to be awarded the rigorous 'Ecolabel' which requires a keen awareness of environmental concerns and the implementation of a very sound environmental policy. In high season, excursions are organised to Aquileia'a archaeological sites, as well as boat trips on the Gulf of Trieste and the Laguna di Grado.

Facilities

Shop (opposite site entrance) Bar. Bicycle hire. Motorcaravan services.Swimming pool. Paddling pool. Play area. Excursion and activity programme. Mobile homes and chalets for rent. Off site: La Capannina restaurant (next to the site entrance, with discounts for campers). Aquileia centre 400 m. Bus stop at site entrance – buses to Grado, Gorizia and Trieste. Archaeological sites.

Open: 25 April - 15 September.

Directions

Leave the A4 (Venice - Trieste) motorway at the Palmanova exit and head south on the SS352 to Aquileia. Upon reaching Aquileia, turn left at the first traffic lights and the site is a further 400 m.

Charges 2008

Per 70 sq. m. pitch	
incl. 2 persons and electricity	€ 18,00 - € 24,50
140 sq. m. pitch	€ 26,00 - € 35,00
dog	€ 3,00 - € 4,50

IT62100 Camping Steiner

Kennedy Straße 32, I-39055 Laives (Bolzano) (Trentino - Alto Adige)

Tel: **0471950105**. Email: **info@campingsteiner.com**

Camping Steiner is very central for touring with the whole of the Dolomite region within easy reach. It has its share of overnight trade but, with much on site activity, one could spend an enjoyable holiday here, especially now the SS12 by which it stands has a motorway alternative. The 200 touring pitches, mostly with good shade and hardstanding, are in rows with easy access and all have electricity. There are also 30 chalets to rent. There is a family style restaurant, and indoor and outdoor pools. This friendly, family run site has a long tradition of providing a happy camping experience in the more traditional style – the owner remembers Alan Rogers who stayed here on many occasions. We met a British couple during our visit who had only intended to stay for one night but decided to stay for a week as it is so easy to get to different parts of the Dolomites.

Facilities

The two sanitary blocks are equipped to a high standard, one having been completely refurbished. They can be heated in cool weather. Bar/pizzeria/restaurant with takeaway service, (April - Oct). Cellar bar with taped music at times. Shop. Outdoor pool (April - Oct, heated in spring), with paddling pool, and a smaller covered heated pool (open all season, except July/Aug). Playground. Table tennis. Bicycle hire. No dogs in July and August.
Off site: Fishing 2 km. Riding 12 km. Golf 28 km.

Open: 28 March - 7 November.

Directions

Site is by the SS12 on northern edge of Leifers, 8 km. south of Bolzano. From north, at the Bolzano-Süd exit from A22 Brenner-Modena motorway follow Trento signs for 7 km; from south on motorway take Ora exit, then north on the SS12 towards Bolzano for 14 km. GPS: N46:25.773 E11:20.628

Charges 2007

Per person	€ 5,00 - € 7,00
child (0-9 yrs)	€ 3,00 - € 5,00
pitch incl. 6A electricity	€ 12,00 - € 14,00
Less 10% for 2 weeks or more.	

IT62000 Camping Gamp

Via Gries 10, I-39043 Chiusa (Trentino - Alto Adige)

Tel: **047 284 7425**. Email: **info@camping-gamp.com**

This is a little gem of a site in every respect but one. It is in the picturesque Isarco valley in the mountainous, Südtirol region of northern Italy. Across the valley from the site is a tree-clad hill rising to a cliff, topped by a picturesque convent. There are 80 pitches with full services including TV and internet connections. It is ideally located for a stopover on the A22 motorway, and therein lies its one drawback: the motorway passes above the site on a viaduct and there is inevitably a steady rumble of noise; more noticeable is the rattle of trains passing below the site. This aside, it is an ideal base from which to explore the mountains and valleys of this atttractive region. Back on site the amenities are modern and equipped to a high standard. Above the pitches is an associated Gasthof with a pleasant bar and terrace plus a restaurant with an interesting menu.

Facilities

Modern toilet block with excellent facilities, including controllable showers, baby room, and special children's washbasins. Hot water to dishwashing and laundry sinks. Motorcaravan overnight area with service point. Restaurant with takeaway, mini-market (April - Oct). Bar (closed Jan/Feb). Music and dancing. Off site: Bicycle hire 300 m. Fishing 1 km. Riding 5 km. Golf and skiing 12 km.

Open: All year.

Directions

Camping Gamp is only 800 m. away from the A22 motorway (Brenner - Verona). Take exit for Klausen/Grödental, turn left and then right in 700 m (site is well signed). GPS: N46:38.478 E11:34.406

Charges 2007

Per person	€ 5,50 - € 7,00
child (3-14 yrs)	€ 2,70 - € 4,90
pitch	€ 10,00 - € 14,00

IT62040 Camping Seiser Alm

Saint Konstantin 16, I-39050 Völs am Schlern (Trentino - Alto Adige)

Tel: **047 170 6459**. Email: **info@camping-seiseralm.com**

What an amazing experience awaits you at Seiser Alm! Elisabeth and Erhard Mahlknecht have created a superb site in the magnificent Sudtirol region of the Dolomite mountains. Catering for families and delightfully peaceful, towering peaks provide a magnificent backdrop when you dine in the charming, traditional style restaurant on the upper terrace. Here you will also find the bar, shop and reception. The 150 touring pitches are of a very high standard with 16A electricity supply, 120 with gas, water, drainage and satellite connections. Guests were delighted with the site when we visited, many coming to walk or cycle, some just to enjoy the surroundings. There are countless things to see and do here. Enjoy the grand 18 hole golf course alongside the site or join the plethora of excursions and organised activities. Local buses and cable cars provide an excellent service for summer visitors and skiers alike (discounts are available). In keeping with the natural setting, the majority of the luxury facilities are set into the hillside. Elisabeth's designs incorporating Grimm fairy tales are tastefully developed in the superb children's bathrooms that are in a magic forest setting complete with blue sky, giant mushroom and elves! A brilliant family adventure park with an enclosure of tame rabbits is at the lower part of the site where goats also roam. If you wish for quiet, quality camping in a crystal clean environment, then visit this immaculate site.

Facilities

One luxury underground block is in the centre of the site. 16 private units are available. Excellent facilities for disabled visitors. Fairy tale facilities for children. Infra red sensors, under-floor heating and gently curved floors to prevent slippery surfaces. Washing machines and large drying room. Sauna. Supermarket. Quality restaurant and bar with terrace. Animation programme five days a week. Miniclub. Children's adventure park and play room. Special rooms for ski equipment. Barbeques allowed. Torches useful. Off site: Riding alongside site. Golf 18 hole course (discounts) 1 km. Fishing 1 km. Bicycle hire 2 km. Lake swimming 2 km. ATM 3 km.

Open: All year excl. 5 November - 20 December.

Directions

Site is east of Bolzano. From A22-E45 take Bolzano Nord exit, then road for Prato Isarco/Blumau. Then follow road for Fie/Vols. Take care as the split in the road is sudden and if you miss the left fork as you enter a tunnel - you will pay a heavy price in extra kilometers. Enjoy the climb to Vols am Schlern and site is well signed approaching the village.

Charges 2008

Per person	€ 6,00 - € 8,50
child (2-16 yrs)	€ 3,40 - € 5,00
pitch	€ 5,00 - € 14,00
electricity	€ 0,60

Camping Cheques accepted.

IT62120 Camping Latsch an der Etsch

Reichstraße 4, I-39021 Laces-Latsch (Trentino - Alto Adige)

Tel: **047 362 3217**. Email: **info@camping-latsch.com**

Gasthof Camping Latsch is 640 m. above sea level between main road and the river, with splendid views across to the surrounding mountains. About 20 of the 100 tourist pitches are on a terrace by reception with the remainder on a lower terrace alongside the river. They are in regular rows which are separated by hedges with thin grass on gravel. All have electricity and 47 also have water, drainage and TV points. Trees provide shade to some parts. A large underground car park protects vehicles from winter snow and summer sun and, if used, gives a reduction in pitch charges. Another interesting feature is a water wheel which provides 3 kw of power and this is supplemented by solar heating. Although right by a main road, the Gasthof and terracing screen out most of the road noise. Mountain walkers will be in their element and several chairlifts give access to higher slopes. An enthusiastic reader's report on this site prompted a visit and we found, as suggested, a pleasant little campsite, whose friendly staff speak excellent English.

Facilities

The traditional but well maintained sanitary block is on two floors, has all the usual facilities and is heated in cool weather. Excellent private bathrooms (20 with basin, shower, toilet) for hire. No facilities for disabled visitors. Washing machine and dryer. Motorcaravan service point. Shop, bar and restaurant (all season). Small heated indoor pool, sauna, solarium and fitness room. Larger, irregularly shaped outdoor pool. Playground. Off site: Fishing 50 m. Bicycle hire 1 km. Riding 7 km. Skiing 30 km.

Open: 16 December - 8 November.

Directions

Latsch/Laces is 28 km. west of Merano on SS38 Bolzano-Silandro road. Site entrance by the Hotel Vermoi (keep on main road, don't turn off to village). GPS: N46:37.337 E10:51.870

Charges 2007

Per person	€ 6,40 - € 7,40
child (2-12 yrs)	€ 5,40 - € 6,40
pitch incl. electricity	€ 12,40 - € 14,90

Reduction on pitch fee if underground car park used.

IT62260 Camping Punta Lago

Via Lungo Lago, 42, I-38050 Calceranica al Lago (Trentino - Alto Adige)

Tel: **046 172 3229**. Email: **info@campingpuntalago.com**

There is something quite delightful about the smaller Italian lakes. Lago di Caldonazzo is in a beautiful setting about two kilometres from the historic village of Calceranica which has summer time markets. This well designed campsite has 140 level, shaded and grassy pitches. Of a good size, all have electricity (3/6A) and 50 are serviced with water and drainage. Access roads are paved and the sanitary facilities are of the highest quality. A small road separates the site from the grassy banks of the lake where all kinds of non-motorised water sports can be enjoyed.

Facilities

One central sanitary block has superb facilities with hot water throughout. Well designed bathroom and washbasin area. Excellent facilities for disabled campers and babies. Washing machines and dryer. Private units for rent, some with massage baths. Bar/snack bar and shop (all season). Fishing (with permit). Modern comprehensive play area. Freezer. Internet access. Cinema. TV. Five-a-side pitch. Volleyball. Off site: Town 1 km. and ATM. Watersports. Bicycle hire 1 km. Riding 3 km. Golf 20 km.

Open: 1 May - 15 September.

Directions

From A22 Bolzano - Trento autostrada take the SS47 towards Padova and then turn for Lago di Caldonazzo. Approaching town from the west beside the railway, continue along Via Donegani, turn left into Via al Lago and right at the lakeside into Via Lungolago. Site is on the right in 200 m.

Charges 2007

Per person	€ 6,00 - € 8,50
child	€ 5,00 - € 7,50
pitch incl. electricity	€ 9,00 - € 15,00

Valle di Ledro - Trentino • 0039.0464.508496
www.campingalsole.it • info@campingalsole.it

IT62320 Camping Al Sole

Via Maffei 127, I-38060 Molina di Ledro (Trentino - Alto Adige)

Tel: **046 450 8496**. Email: **info@campingalsole.it**

Lake Ledro is only 9 km. from Lake Garda, its sparkling waters and breathtaking scenery offering a low key alternative for those who enjoy a natural setting. The drive from Lake Garda is a real pleasure and prepares you for the treat ahead. This site has been owned by the same friendly family for over 40 years and their experience shows in the layout of the site with its mature trees and the array of facilities provided. Situated on the lake with its own sandy beach, pool and play area, the facilities were rebuilt in 2006 and now include an outstanding 'wellness' centre. The 'Chiva Som' centre provides a whirlpool, solarium, beauty therapies, aromatic showers and massage room. The sauna has panoramic views over the lake and mountains and there is a heated outdoor spa pool where one can relax under the stars at night. We are told this is a brilliant experience in the summer and even more spectacular when there is snow! Fully serviced pitches were also added in 2006. This is a very pleasant, peaceful site for extended stays or sightseeing. It came as no surprise to hear that many people choose to return to Camping al Sole year after year. The local community welcomes tourists and offers hiking programmes beginning with a Monday evening information night so that you can choose the most appropriate guided walks.

Facilities

Superb new facilities block (2006) with free hot water throughout. Well appointed facilities include 5 private bathrooms with shower, toilet, basin and safe. Excellent facilities for disabled people. Baby room. Laundry facilities. Freezer. Motorcaravan services. Small supermarket. Pleasant restaurant and pizzeria with outdoor terrace. Bar serving snacks and takeaway. Sun decks and snack bar at the lake. Wellness centre. Swimming pool. Play area. Bicycle hire. Boating, windsurfing, fishing and canoeing. Live music and dancing twice weekly in July/Aug. Children's club. TV room. Off site: Walk around the lake (10 km). Riding 2 km. Golf 20 km.

Open: Easter - 8 October.

Directions

From autostrada A22 exit for Lake Garda North to Riba del Garda. In Riva follow sign for Ledro valley. Site is well signed as you approach Lago di Ledra. GPS: N45:52.683 E10:46.064

Charges 2007

Per person	€ 5,50 - € 8,00
child (2-11yrs)	€ 4,50 - € 5,00
pitch incl. electricity	€ 8,00 - € 16,00
dog	€ 4,50

IT62290 Camping Lévico

Localitá Pleina, 5, I-38056 Lévico Terme (Trentino - Alto Adige)

Tel: **046 170 6491**. Email: **mail@campinglevico.com**

Sister site to Camping Jolly, Camping Levico is in a natural setting on the small, very pretty Italian lake also called Levico which is surrounded by towering mountains. The sites are owned by two brothers – Andrea, who manages Levico, and Gino based at Jolly. Both campsites are charming, with Levico having some pitches along the lake edge and a quiet atmosphere. There is a shaded terrace for enjoying pizza and drinks in the evening. Pitches are of a good size, most grassed, well shaded and with 6A electricity. Staff are welcoming and fluent in many languages including English and Dutch. There is a small supermarket on site and it is a short distance to the local village. The beautiful grassy shores of the lake are ideal for sunbathing and the crystal clear water is ideal for enjoying (non-motorised) water activities. This is a site where the natural beauty of an Italian lake can be enjoyed without being overwhelmed by commercial tourism. All the amenities at Camping Jolly can be enjoyed by traversing a very pretty walkway along a stream where we saw many trout.

Facilities

Four modern sanitary blocks provide hot water for showers, washbasins and washing. Mostly British style toilets. Single locked unit for disabled visitors. Washing machines and dryer. Ironing. Freezer. Motorcaravan service point. Bar/restaurant, takeaway and good shop (all season). Play area. Miniclub and animation (high season). Fishing. Satellite TV and cartoon cinema. Internet acess. Five-a-side soccer pitch. Kayak hire. Tennis. Billiards. Medical services. Torches useful. Off site: Town 2 km. with all the usual facilities and ATM. Bicycle hire 1.5 km. and bicycle track. Riding 3 km. Golf 7 km.

Open: 1 April - 5 October.

Directions

From A22 Verona - Bolzano road take turn for Trento on S47 to Levico Terme where site is very well signed. GPS: N46:00.700 E11:17.000

Charges guide

Per person	€ 5,00 - € 9,50
child (3-11 years)	€ 4,00 - € 6,00
pitch incl. electricity (6A)	€ 7,50 - € 18,00

IT62030 Caravan Park Sexten

Saint Josef Strasse 54, I-39030 Sexten (Trentino - Alto Adige)

Tel: **047 471 0444**. Email: **info@caravanparksexten.it**

Caravan Park Sexten is 1,520 metres above sea level and has 268 pitches, some very large and all with electricity (16A) and TV connections, and with water and drain in summer and winter (underground heating stops pipes freezing). Some pitches are in the open to catch the sun, others are tucked in forest clearings by the river. They are mostly gravelled to provide an ideal all-year surface. It is the facilities that make this a truly remarkable site; no expense or effort have been spared to create a luxurious environment that matches that of any top-class hotel. The brand new health spa has every type of sauna, Turkish and Roman baths, whirlpools, sunbeds, herbal baths, hairdressing and beauty treatment salons, relaxation and massage rooms and a remarkable indoor pool with children's pool, Kneipp therapy pool and whirlpools. The timber of the buildings is from 400 year old farmhouses and is blended with top quality modern materials to create amazing interiors and (mainly) authentically Tyrolean exteriors. The restaurant, bars and taverna are of equally high quality. Sexten is located in the Dolomites, in the German-speaking Südtirol, where the scenery is often spectacular. There is a wide variety of leisure activities on offer from gentle walking to extreme summer and winter sports.

Facilities

The three main toilet blocks are remarkable in design, fixtures and fittings. Heated floors. Controllable showers. Washbasins. Hairdryers. Luxurious private facilities to rent. Children and baby rooms. En-suite facilities for disabled visitors. Laundry and drying room. Motorcaravan services. Mini-market. New indoor pool, heated all season and heated outdoor pool (1/6-30/9). High quality health spa. Bars and restaurants with entertainment 2-3 nights a week. Good range of activities for all. Tennis. Bicycle hire. Rock climbing wall. Fishing. Adventure activity packages. Internet access and WiFi (whole site). Off site: Skiing in winter (free bus to 2 ski lifts within 5 km. Walking, cycling and climbing. Fishing. Riding, golf and villages nearby.

Open: All year.

Directions

Sexten/Sesto is 110 km. north east of Bolzano. From Bressanone/Brixen exit on A22 Brenner - Modena motorway follow the SS49 east for about 60 km. Turn south on SS52 at Innichen/San Candido and follow signs to Sexten. Site is 5 km. past village (signed). GPS: N46:40.059 E12:23.950

Charges 2007

Per person	€ 7,00 - € 11,50
child	€ 1,00 - € 10,00
pitch (80-280 sq.m.)	€ 4,00 - € 19,50
electricity per kWh (16A)	€ 0,70
dog	€ 2,00 - € 6,00

ADVENTURE IN THE DOLOMITES

Family Happacher · I-39030 Sesto / Moso (Alto Adige), Via San Giuseppe 54 · Tel. +39 / 0474 / 710 444
Fax +39 / 0474 / 710 053 · info@caravanparksexten.it · www.caravanparksexten.it

südtirol

IT62000 Camping Olympia

Camping 1, I-39034 Toblach (Trentino - Alto Adige)

Tel: **047 497 2147**. Email: **info@camping-olympia.com**

In the Dolomite mountains, Camping Olympia, always good, maintains its high standards and is constantly being upgraded. The 300 pitches have been relaid in a regular pattern and tall pine trees and newly planted shrubs and hedges make this a very pleasant and attractive site. There are hills on either side and craggy mountains beyond. The 238 touring pitches all have 6A electriciy and 16 are fully serviced with water, waste water, gas, telephone and satellite TV points. Some accommodation is available for rent, and there are 62 seasonal caravans which are mainly grouped at one end of the site. A little fish pond with a fountain and surrounded by flowers makes an attractive central feature, whilst on the far side of the site, a gate leads out into the woods where there is also a little play area and a few animals. The site is an ideal base from which to explore this part of German-speaking Südtirol on foot, by bicycle or by car – and Austria is just up the road!

Facilities

The main toilet block has been refurbished to a high standard. Rooms with WC, washbasin and shower to rent. Baby room. Facilities for disabled visitors. Two small blocks provide further WCs and showers. Motorcaravan service point. Shop. Bar, restaurant and pizzeria (all year). Second bar with grill and terrace by pool (10/6-30/9; 20/12-Easter). Heated swimming pool (20/5-15/9). Sauna, solarium, steam bath and whirl pools. Fishing. Bicycle hire. Play area. Activities and excursions. Entertainment in high season. Off site: Riding and golf 3 km.

Open: All year.

Directions

Site is west of the town. From A22 Innsbruck-Bolzano autostrada, take Bressanone exit and travel east on SS49 for about 60 km. Site signed to left just after a short tunnel. From Cortina take SS48 and SS51 northwards then turn west on SS49 for 1.5 km. GPS: N46:44.086 E12:11.638

Charges 2007

Per person	€ 8,00 - € 9,50
child (3-12 yrs)	€ 4,00 - € 7,50
pitch	€ 7,00 - € 11,50

INT. CAMPING OLYMPIA

www.camping-olympia.com

SÜDTIROL

I-39034 TOBLACH • DOBBIACO
Tel. +39 0474 97 21 47

IT62330 Camping Al Lago

Via Alzer 7/9, I-38060 Pieve di Ledro (Trentino - Alto Adige)

Tel: **046 459 1250**. Email: **mb.penner@libero.it**

Camping Al Lago is a small, unassuming site on the banks of the serene Lake Ledro, with towering hills of rock and forest on two sides. The 105 pitches (with electricity) are fairly tightly placed and the site has very limited facilities. It is very peaceful here and the friendly owner Mario will give help and guidance on what to do in the area including leading bicycle and walking tours. Only snacks are served in the bar behind reception but there is a choice of restaurants within 200 m. of the gate. A hire service for bicycles and kayaks is offered and the site has two sections with direct access to the lake. If you like very simple camping without the luxuries and amenities of the bigger sites and a sound night's sleep, this may be for you.

Facilities

A single toilet block provides a very limited number of showers and toilets that are mixed British and Turkish style. Facilities are extremely busy at peak periods. Provision for disabled campers. Washing machines and spin dryers. Bar with terrace. Snacks. Bicycle hire. Kayaking. Lakeside areas. Organised walking and cycling tours. Torches useful. Off site: Riding 2 km. Sailing 200 m. Town and supermarket 500 m.

Open: 25 April - 10 October.

Directions

Site is on the north side of Lake Ledro. From the A22 near Rovereto take S240 to Riva del Garda, then the S240 to Pieve di Lago. Site is well signed approaching the village.

Charges 2007

Per person	€ 5,50 - € 8,00
child (2-12 yrs)	free - € 5,50
pitch incl. electricity	€ 6,00 - € 10,00

IT60400 Camping Village Garden Paradiso

Via Baracca 55, I-30013 Cavallino-Treporti (Veneto)

Tel: **041 968 075**. Email: **info@gardenparadiso.it**

There are many sites in this area and there is much competition in providing a range of facilities. Garden Paradiso is a good seaside site which also provides three excellent, centrally situated pools, a fitness centre, minigolf, a train to the market and other activities for children. Compared with other sites here, this one is of medium size with 835 pitches. All have electricity (from 6A), water and drainage points and all are marked and numbered with hard access roads, under a good cover of trees. Flowers and shrubs abound giving a pleasant and peaceful appearance. The restaurant, with self-service at lunch time and waiter service at night, is near the beach with a bar/snack bar in the centre of the site. The site is directly on the sea with a beach of fine sand. Used by tour operators.

Facilities

Four brick, tiled toilet blocks are fully equipped with a mix of British and Turkish style toilets. Facilities for babies. Dishwashing and laundry sinks. Washing machines and dryers. Motorcaravan services. Shopping complex. Restaurant (23/4-30/9). Snack bar and takeaway. Swimming pools. Fitness centre. Tennis. Table tennis. Minigolf. Play area. Organised entertainment and excursions (high season). Bicycle hire. Dogs are not accepted. Off site: Riding 2 km. Fishing 2.5 km.

Open: 23 April - 30 September.

Directions

Leave Venice-Trieste autostrada either by taking airport or Quarto d'Altino exits; follow signs to Jesolo and Punta Sabbioni. Take first road left after Cavallino and site is a little way on the right.

Charges 2008

Per person	€ 4,50 - € 8,75
junior (3-5 yrs)	
or senior (over 60 yrs)	free - € 5,60
baby (0-2 yrs)	free
pitch with electricity, water and drainage	€ 9,90 - € 22,00

Less 10% for stays over 30 days (early), or 20 days (late) season.

This is just a sample of the campsites we have inspected and selected in Italy. For more campsites and further information, please see the Alan Rogers Italy guide.

IT62050 Camping International Dolomiti

Via Campo di Sotto, I-32043 Cortina d'Ampezzo (Veneto)

Tel: **043 624 85**. Email: **campeggiodolomiti@tin.it**

Cortina is a pleasant provincial town with many interesting shops and restaurants. A bus runs from the campsite gate to the town centre. The strength of this site is its beautiful mountain scenery and quiet location in a grassy meadow beside a fast flowing river (with a steep embankment but no fences). The site is dedicated to tourers with 390 good sized pitches, all with electricity (2A) and about half with shade. The site does not take reservations so arrive early in the day in the first three weeks of August to improve your chance of obtaining a pitch. There is a heated swimming pool on site, but otherwise this is a simple and uncomplicated site with fairly basic facilities which makes a good centre for touring the Dolomites. There are, of course, numerous opportunities for more energetic pursuits such as walking, cycling or mountain biking, and indeed for extreme mountain sports.

Facilities

The large central toilet block (only open in high season) is quite old but should now be refurbished. All WCs are British style. A smaller heated block is open all season and is well equipped and kept very clean. Facilities for disabled visitors. Washing machines. Bar and shop. Heated swimming pool (5/7-25/8). Playground. Off site: Restaurant 600 m. Supermarket 1 km. Fishing 1 km. Golf 2 km. Bicycle hire and riding 3 km.

Open: 1 June - 20 September.

Directions

Cortina is 60 km. north of Belluno. Site is 3 km. south of town off the SS51 from Toblach/Dobbiaco to Belluno and Veneto. Follow signs to site, turning right towards Campo from north or left in Zuel from south. GPS: N46:30.974 E12:08.160

Charges 2007

Per person	€ 4,50 - € 7,50
child (under 6 yrs)	€ 2,50 - € 4,00
pitch incl. electricity	€ 7,00 - € 9,00

IT62055 Camping Rocchetta

Via Campo 1, I-32043 Cortina d'Ampezzo (Veneto)

Tel: **043 650 63**. Email: **camping@sunrise.it**

Cortina d'Ampezzo is well known as one of Europe's most exclusive and smartest winter resorts. However, this is an enchanting area at any time and Camping Rochetta has been recommended to us by our Italian agent. We plan to undertake a full inspection in 2008. The site lies 20 minutes walk from the centre of Cortina and is the closest to the town. Pitches are generally flat and some offer shade. Electrical connections are available on most pitches. The site enjoys fine views of the mountains and the bar has a pleasant sun terrace. Although on site amenities are limited, Cortina offers a very wide range of shops and restaurants, and also hosts many festivals and exhibitions. Winter sports facilities are excellent with 30 chairlifts, with many of these also available in the summer months for exploration of the Dolomites.

Facilities

Heated toilet block and drying room. Play area. Shop. Bar. Motorcaravan services (all year). Minigolf. Off site: Cortina 1.5 km. (bus stop at site entrance). Winter sports. Ampezzo Valley and the Dolomite mountains. Walking and cycle trails.

Open: All year.

Directions

From the south (Venice), take the northbound A27. Beyond Belluno, take the exit towards Cadore and Cortina, joining the SS51. Continue on this road until you reach Cortina (passing the Olympic ski jump). Drive through town and follow signs for the campsite to the left. GPS: N46:31.350 E12:08.050

Charges 2007

Per person	€ 6,50 - € 7,50
pitch	€ 6,00 - € 9,00

IT60030 Centro Vacanze Pra' Delle Torri

P.O. Box 176, I-30021 Caorle (Veneto)

Tel: **042 129 9063**. Email: **torri@vacanze-natura.it**

Pra' delle Torri is another Italian Adriatic site which has just about everything! Pitches for camping, hotel, accommodation to rent, one of the largest and best equipped pool complexes in the country and a golf course where lessons for beginners are also available. Many of the 1,300 grass pitches (with electricity) have shade and they are arranged in zones – when you book in at reception you are taken by electric golf buggy to select your pitch. There are two good restaurants, bars and a range of shops arranged around an attractive square. Recent additions incude a crèche and a supervised play area for young children. The pool complex is the crowning glory with indoor (Olympic size) and outdoor pools with slides and many other features. Other super amenities include a large grass area for ball games, a good playground, a babies' car track, and a whole range of sports, fitness and entertainment programmes, along with a medical centre, skincare and other therapies. The site has its own sandy beach and Porto Santa Margherita and Caorle are nearby. One could quite happily spend a whole holiday here without leaving the site but the attractions of Venice, Verona, etc. might well tempt one to explore the area.

Facilities

Sixteen excellent, high quality toilet blocks with the usual facilities including very attractive 'Junior Stations'and units for disabled visitors. Motorcaravan service point. Large supermarket and wide range of shops, restaurants, bars and takeaways. Indoor and outdoor pools. Tennis. Minigolf. Fishing. Watersports. Archery. Diving. Fitness programmes and keep fit track. Crèche and supervised play area. Bowls. Mountain bike track. Wide range of organised sports and entertainment. Off site: Riding 3 km.

Open: 31 March - 29 September.

Directions

From A4 Venice - Trieste motorway leave at exit for Sto Stino di Livenze and follow signs to Caorle then Sta Margherita and signs to site.

Charges 2007

Per person	€ 3,75 - € 8,60
child (1-5 yrs)	free - € 6,30
senior (over 60 yrs)	€ 2,80 - € 7,35
pitch incl. electricity	€ 7,00 - € 40,00
tent pitch	€ 4,90 - € 15,45
Min. stay 2 nights.	

IT60360 Camping Ca'Pasquali

Via A. Poerio 33, I-30013 Cavallino-Treporti (Veneto)
Tel: **041 966 110**. Email: **info@capasquali.it**

Situated on the attractive natural woodland coast of Cavallino with its wide, safe, sandy beach, Ca'Pasquali is a good quality holiday resort with easy access to magnificent Venice. This is an ideal place for a holiday interspersed with excursions to Verona, Padova, the glassmakers of Murano, the local water park, pretty villages and many other cultural attractions. This is a large site affiliated with nos. IT60280 and IT60140. The detail is important here; there are superb pools, a fitness area, an arena for an ambitious entertainment programme and a beachside restaurant. The 400 pitches are shaded and flat (70-90 sq.m), some water and some with spectacular sea views. The fine sandy beach was alive with families playing games, flying kites and enjoying themselves when we watched from the thoughtfully renovated restaurant as the sun set. A family site with many extras, Ca'Pasquali has been thoughtfully designed to a high standard – it is ideal for families as a resort holiday or to combine with sightseeing.

Facilities

Three spotless modern units have excellent facilities and superb facilities for disabled campers and babies. Washing machines and dryers. Motorcaravan services. Restaurant. Pizzeria. Crêperie. Cocktail bar. Snack bar. Supermarket. Bazaar. Boutique. Superb pool complex with slides, fun pool and fountains. Fitness centre. Play areas. Bicycle hire. Canoe hire and lessons. Excellent animation. Amphitheatre. Mini-club. Internet access. Excursion service. Caravan storage. Dogs and other animals are not accepted. Off site: Golf and riding 5 km. Sailing 20 km. Fishing. Theme parks.

Open: 30 April - 18 September.

Directions

Leave autostrada A4 at Sant Dona Noventa exit and head for Sant Dona di Piave, Losolo and on to peninsula of Cavallino. Site is well signed shortly after town of Cavallino.

Charges 2007

Per person	€ 4,20 - € 8,80
child (1-10 yrs)	€ 3,50 - € 8,80
senior (over 60 yrs)	€ 2,90 - € 8,80
pitch	€ 7,20 - € 22,90

IT60140 Villaggio Turistico Internazionale

Via Colonie 2, I-30020 Bibione (Veneto)
Tel: **043 144 2611**. Email: **info@vti.it**

This is a large, professionally run tourist village which offers all a holidaymaker could want. The Granzotto family have owned this site since the 1960s and the results of their continuous improvements are impressive. There are 350 clean pitches, many fully serviced, shaded by mature trees and mostly on flat ground. The site's large sandy beach is excellent (umbrellas and loungers available for a small charge), as are all the facilities within the campsite where English speaking, uniformed assistants will help when you arrive. The tourist village is split by a main road with the restaurant, cinema and children's club on the very smart 'chalet' side. The professional hairdressing salon sets the luxury tone of the site. A comprehensive entertainment programme is on offer daily and the large pool provides a great flume and slides and a separate fun and spa pool. The local area is a major tourist resort but for more relaxation try the famous thermal baths at Bibione!

Facilities

Renovated apartments. Four modern toilet blocks house excellent facilities with mainly British style toilets. Excellent provision for children and disabled campers. Air conditioning in all accomodation. Washing machines and dryers. Motorcaravan service point. Supermarket. Bazaar. Good restaurant with bright yellow plastic chairs. Snack bar. New pool complex. Fitness centre. Disco. TV. Cinema and theatre. Internet. New childrens play areas. Football. Tennis. Volleyball. Billiards. Electronic games. Doctor's surgery. Off site: Bicycle hire 1 km. Riding 3 km. Golf 6 km. Fishing.

Open: 19 April - 28 September.

Directions

Leave A4 east of Venice at Latisana exit on Latisana road. Then take road 354 towards Ligmano, after 12 km. turn right to Beuazzana and then left to Bibione. Site is well signed on entering town. GPS: N45:38.600 E13:02.140

Charges 2007

Per person	€ 5,00 - € 9,50
senior	€ 3,50 - € 9,50
child (1-5 yrs)	free - € 7,00
pitch incl. electricity	€ 9,00 - € 18,50
with electricity and water	€ 12,00 - € 24,00

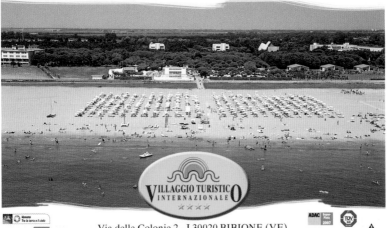

IT60280 Camping Vela Blu

See advertisement on previous page.

Via Radaelli 10, I-30013 Cavallino-Treporti (Veneto)
Tel: **041 968 068**. Email: **info@velablu.it**

Thoughtfully landscaped within a natural wooded coastal environment, the tall pines here give shade while attractive flowers enhance the setting and paved roads give easy access to the pitches. The 280 pitches vary in size (55-100 sq.m) and shape, but all have electricity (4/6A) and 80 have drainage. A sister site to nos. IT6036 and IT6014, Vela Blu is a relatively new, small, family style site and a pleasant alternative to the other massive sites on Cavallino. The clean, fine sand beach runs the length of one side of the site with large stone breakwaters for fun and fishing. The beach is fenced making it safer for children, access is via a gate and there are lifeguards in season. There are outdoor showers and footbaths. The hub of the site is the charming restaurant and brilliant play area on soft sand, both adjoining a barbecue terrace and entertainment area. A well stocked shop is also in this area. For those who enjoy a small quiet site, Vela Blu fits the bill. Venice is easy to access as is the local water park (there is no pool here as yet). The entrance can become congested in busy periods due to limited waiting space.

Facilities

Two excellent modern toilet blocks include baby rooms and good facilities for disabled visitors. An attendant is on hand to maintain high standards. Laundry facilities. Motorcaravan service point. Medical room. Shop. Bar. Gelateria. Restaurant and takeaway. Games room. Satellite TV room. Pedalo hire. Windsurfing. Fishing. Bicycle hire. Entertainment for children and adults. Off site: Bars, restaurants and shops. Ferry to Venice.

Open: 4 April - 15 September.

Directions

Leave A4 Venice - Trieste motorway at exit for 'Aeroporto' and follow signs for Jesolo and Punta Sabbioni. Site is signed after village of Cavallino.

Charges 2007

Per person	€ 3,90 - € 7,50
child (1-10 yrs)	free - € 7,30
seniors (over 60)	€ 2,90 - € 6,50
pitch with all services	€ 8,20 - € 16,20

Camping Cheques accepted

IT60320 Camping Village Cavallino

Via delle Batterie 164, I-30013 Cavallino-Treporti (Veneto)
Tel: **041 966 133**. Email: **info@campingcavallino.com**

This large, well ordered site is run by a friendly, experienced family who have other sites in this guide and offer tours between their sites. It lies beside the sea with direct access to a superb beach of fine sand, which is very safe and enjoys the cover of several lifeguards. The site is thoughtfully laid out with many unusually large pitches shaded by olives and pines. All 445 touring pitches have 6A electricity and there is a 10% tour operator presence. If you wish to visit Venice a bus service runs to the ferry at Punta Sabbioni, some 20 minutes away. You then catch an interconnecting ferry which, after a journey of 40 minutes, drops you directly at Saint Marco Square after negotiating its way around the gondolas. A late return will mean a 2 km. walk at the end of a different bus service, but the night views of Venice from the sea are wonderful. Be sure to pay independently at the ferry rather than using the supposedly cheap 'all-in' tickets which in fact are more expensive.

Facilities

Refurbished in 2007, the clean and modern toilet blocks are well spaced and provide a mixture of Turkish and British style WCs with facilities for disabled campers. Launderette. Motorcaravan services. Supermarket. Two restaurants, one with large terrace overlooking pools. Takeaway. Pizzeria. (all open all season). Swimming pools and whirlpool (May-Sept). Table tennis. Minigolf. Play area. Bicycle hire. Fishing. Ambitious animation programme aimed mostly at younger guests. ATM. Dogs are not admitted. Off site: Golf 1 km. Riding 2 km. Tours to all attractions. Bus at gate.

Open: 30 March - 21 October.

Directions

From Venice - Trieste autostrada leave at exit for airport or Quarto and Altino. Follow signs, first for Jesolo, then Punta Sabbioni. Site signs will be seen just after Cavallino on the left. GPS: N45:27.379 E12:30.055

Charges 2008

Per unit incl. 2 persons,	
water and electricity	€ 14,40 - € 44,40
extra person	€ 0,80 - € 7,20
child (3-9 yrs) or senior (over 60)	free - € 5,60

Min. stay in high season I week.

IT60220 Camping Village Portofelice

Viale dei Fiori 15, I-30020 Eraclea Mare (Veneto)

Tel: 042 166 411. Email: info@portofelice.it

Portofelice is an efficient and attractive coastal site with a sandy beach and plenty of well organised activity. There were many happy customers when we visited. It is unusual in being separated from the sea by a protected pine wood with a gravel path between the two. It is of medium size for this part of Italy with 532 touring pitches and 200 occupied by static caravans, bungalows and tour operators' accommodation. The pitches are arranged in rectangular blocks or zones in regular rows, separated by hedges from hard access roads and with either natural or artificial shade. Cars are parked separately. All pitches have electricity and 208 also have water, drainage and TV sockets. The social life of the site is centred around the stunning pool complex where the shops, pizzeria, bar, café and restaurant are also located. A wide range of entertainment and activities are organised for adults and children. If you can drag yourself away from the holiday village, you can explore the region by car with Venice, the Dolomites and the Italian Lakes within easy reach.

Facilities

Two modern sanitary blocks have the usual facilities with slightly more Turkish style toilets than British. Baby room and children's block (0-12 yrs). Facilities for disabled people. Supermarket. Pizzeria and takeaway. Restaurant with most tables on a covered terrace with waiter service. Three superb swimming pools. Playgrounds. Go-kart track. Pedaloes. Tennis. Sandy beach. Bicycle hire. ATM. Activity and entertainment programmes. Off site: Riding 200 m. Golf 6 km.

Open: 5 May - 16 September.

Directions

From A4 Venice - Trieste motorway take exit 'S Dona/Noventa' and go south through S Dona di Piave and Eraclea to Eraclea Mare where site is signed. GPS: N45:33.214 E12:46.051

Charges 2007

Per person	€ 3,40 - € 9,40
senior (over 60 yrs)	€ 2,40 - € 6,80
child (1-5 yrs)	free - € 6,80
pitch depending on type	€ 7,40 - € 20,70

IT60420 Camping Alba d'Oro

Via Triestina s.s.14, km 10, Ca'Noghera, I-30030 Mestre (Veneto)

Tel: 041 541 5102. Email: albadoro@tin.it

This well managed site is ideal for visiting Venice and the site's bus service takes you directly to the bus station on the west side of the city. There is always room here and on arrival you can select your own pitch. There is a separate area for backpackers and yet another for families. The 140 pitches, all with electricity, are of reasonable size and separated. The good sized pool is especially welcome after a hot day spent visiting Venice. The site is close to the airport and loud aircraft noise will be heard on some pitches especially to the east. However, as there is no night flying it is worth staying here to be close to the city rather than driving to Cavallino and having the long journey into Venice.

Facilities

The four modern sanitary blocks are kept very clean. One block has facilities for disabled campers. Launderette. Motorcaravan services. Supermarket. Restaurant with a most pleasant terrace overlooking the pool and serving good food at reasonable prices, is very busy every night. Part of the same complex, is a lively bar with entertainment in season. Pizzerias. Bicycle hire. Marina. Bus service 1 April - Oct. Shuttle bus to Verona.

Open: All year.

Directions

From Venice - Trieste autostrada leave at exit for airport and follow signs for Jesolo on the SS14. Site is on right at 10 km. marker.

Charges 2007

Per person	€ 7,00 - € 8,20
child (3-10 yrs)	€ 4,50 - € 5,60
pitch incl. car	€ 13,00 - € 14,40
dog	€ 2,00

IT60100 Camping Capalonga

Via della Laguna 16, I-30020 Bibione-Pineda (Veneto)

Tel: **043 143 8351**. Email: **capalonga@bibionemare.com**

A quality site right beside the sea, Capalonga is a large site with 1,350 pitches of variable size (70-90 sq.m). Nearly all marked out, all have electrical connections, some have water and drainage, and there is good shade almost everywhere. The site is pleasantly laid out – roads run in arcs which avoids the square box effect. Some pitches where trees define the pitch area may be tricky for large units. The very wide, sandy beach, which is cleaned by the site, shelves extremely gently so is very safe for children and it never becomes too crowded. A concrete path leads out towards the sea to avoid too much sand-walking and the water is much cleaner here than at most places along this coast. A large lagoon runs along the other side of the site where boating (motor or sail) can be practised and a landing stage and moorings are provided. There is also a swimming pool on site. Capalonga is an excellent site, with comprehensive facilities.

Facilities

Seven toilet blocks are well and frequently cleaned. Two newer blocks built side by side have facilities for disabled people and very fine children's rooms. British and some Turkish style toilets, some washbasins in private cabins. Launderette. Motorcaravan services. Large supermarket. General shop. Self-service restaurant and separate bar. Swimming pool (25 x 12-5 m; 19/5-15/9). Boating. Fishing. Playground. Free animation programme. First-aid room. Dogs are not accepted.

Open: 28 April - 30 September.

Directions

Bibione is about 80 km. east of Venice, well signed from afar on approach roads. 1 km. before Bibione turn right towards Bibione Pineda and follow camp signs. GPS: N45:37.830 E12:59.615

Charges 2008

Per person	€ 5,70 - € 10,50
child (1-4 yrs)	free - € 5,00
child (5-10 yrs)	free - € 8,00
pitch	€ 10,50 - € 24,00

IT60150 Camping Residence Il Tridente

Via Baseleghe 12, I-30020 Bibione-Pineda (Veneto)

Tel: **043 143 9600**. Email: **tridente@bibionemare.com**

This is an unusual site in that only half the area is used for camping. Formerly a holiday centre for deprived children, it occupies a large area of woodland stretching from the main road to the sea. It is divided into two parts by the Residence, an apartment block of first class rooms which are for rent. The 226 tourist pitches (483 in total) are located amongst tall pines in the area between the entrance and the Residence. Pitch size varies according to the positions of the trees (70-100 sq.m) and all have electricity connections (6/10A). Between the Residence and the sea is a pleasant open area used for sports facilities and the two excellent pools. The ground slopes gently from the main building to the beach of fine sand and this is used as the recreation area with two swimming pools, a 25 m. pool and a smaller children's pool – tennis courts, table tennis and sitting and play places. With thick woodland on both sides, Il Tridente is a quiet, restful site with excellent facilities.

Facilities

Three sanitary blocks, two in the main camping area and one near the sea, are of excellent quality. Mixed British and Turkish style WCs in cabins with washbasins and facilities for disabled people. Washing machines and dryers. Motorcaravan services. The Residence includes an excellent restaurant and bar. Huge new supermarket. Swimming pools. Playground. Tennis. Gym. Fishing. Internet access. Animation programme in high season. Dogs are not accepted. Off site: Bicycle hire 1 km. Riding 2 km. Boat launching 2 km. Golf 10 km.

Open: 12 April - 17 September.

Directions

From A4 Venice - Trieste autostrada, take Latisana exit and follow signs to Bibione and then Bibione Pineda and camp signs.

Charges 2008

Per person	€ 5,70 - € 10,00
child (1-4 yrs)	free - € 4,50
child (5-10 yrs)	free - € 6,50
pitch incl. electricity	€ 10,50 - € 19,00

Bibione PINEDA
VENEZIA ITALIA

EMAS
VERIFIED
ENVIRONMENTAL
MANAGEMENT
REG. NO. I-000091

Veneto
From Earth to Sky

BIBIONE PINEDA IS A PEACEFUL AND RELAXING SEASIDE RESORT LOCATED BETWEEN VENICE AND TRIESTE. ITS SILKY SAND BEACH STRETCHES ALONG THE COASTLINE FOR MORE THAN 3 KM AND IT IS 150 METERS WIDE. ITS MARINA, THE RESTAURANTS, CAFÉS, SHOPS, SPORT FACILITIES AND NIGHT CLUBS, ALL THIS IN A FANTASTIC PINE WOOD SETTING MAKES IT A PARTICULARLY DELIGHTFUL DESTINATION.

DISCOVER A NEW WAY OF HOLIDAYING!

THE "SUITE CARAVANS" AND "CHALET MOBIL" ARE ECO-FRIENDLY AS WELL AS COMFORTABLE. IN FACT, THEY ARE BUILT IN FINE WOOD AND ARE VERY WELL INSULATED. FURTHERMORE EACH UNITE CAN ACCOMODATE UP TO 6 PEOPLE, WITH A LARGE GREEN AREA AND PARKING AREA OUTSIDE. A VARIETY OF LOCATION SOLUTIONS ARE AVAILABLE AT THE 3 CAMPSITES: NEAR THE BEACH FACING THE SEA, IN THE GREEN PINEWOOD AREA, IN NO TRAFFIC AREAS FOR THE SAFE OF YOUR CHILDREN, OR EVEN FACING THE LAGOON NEXT TO YOUR BOAT MOORING.

CAMPING ★★★★ Capalonga

THE ONLY CAMPSITE IN EUROPE WITH 170 BOAT PLACES.
Tel. +39/0431438351
Fax +39/0431 438370
Tel. in winter +39/0431447190
+39/0431447198
Fax in winter +39/0431438986
e-mail capalonga@bibionemare.com

FLY & DRIVE
INFO
www.bibionemare.com

CAMPING-RESIDENCE ★★★★ IL TRIDENTE

ESPECIALLY THOUGHT TO SATISFY THE NEEDS OF FAMILIES WITH YOUNG CHILDREN.
Tel. +39/0431439600
Fax +39/0431446245
Tel. in winter+39/0431447393
Fax in winter+39/0431439193
e-mail tridente@bibionemare.com

★★★ Camping Lido

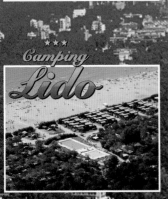

PERFECT FOR THOSE WHO LOVE NATURE AND WANT A PEACEFUL HOLIDAY. CLOSE TO THE SHOPPING CENTRE.
Tel. +39/0431438480
Fax +39/0431439292
Tel. in winter +39/0431447386
Fax in winter +39/0431439193
e-mail lido@bibionemare.com

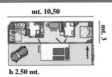

mt. 10,50
mt. 3
h 2.50 mt.

Air conditioning	Heating	New "Golden Suite" with clubwasher	Safe
Grill	Cycles	Private beach	Handycap

BIBIONE MARE S.P.A.
VIA DEI GINEPRI, 244
I-30020 BIBIONE PINEDA (VE)
www.bibionemare.com

VISA   booking online   MasterCard

IT60200 Camping Union Lido Vacanze

Via Fausta 258, I-30013 Cavallino-Treporti (Veneto)

Tel: **041 257 5111**. Email: **info@unionlido.com**

This amazing site is very large, offering everything a camper could wish for, is extremely well organised and it has been said to set the standard that others follow. It lies right beside the sea with direct access to a long, broad sandy beach which shelves very gradually and provides very safe bathing (there are lifeguards). The site itself is regularly laid out with parallel access roads under a covering of poplars, pine and other trees providing good shade. There are 2,600 pitches for touring units), all with 6A electricity and 1,684 also have water and drainage. Because of the size of the site there is an internal road train and amenities are repeated through the site. You really would not need to leave this site – everything is here, including a sophisticated Wellness centre. Overnight parking is provided outside the gate with electricity, toilets and showers for those arriving after 21.00. There are two aquaparks, one with fine sand beaches (a first in Europe) and both with swimming pools, lagoon pools for children, a heated whirlpool and a slow flowing 160 m. 'river'. A pool for hotel and apartment guests is open to others on payment. A huge selection of sports is offered, along with luxury amenities too numerous to list. Animation and fitness programmes are available in season. The golf 'academy' (with professional) has a driving range, pitching green, putting green and practice bunker, and a diving centre offers lessons and open water diving. Union Lido is above all an orderly and clean site, which is achieved by reasonable regulations to ensure comfortable, quiet camping and by good management. Member of Leading Campings Group.

Facilities

Fifteen well kept, fully equipped toilet blocks which open and close progressively during the season. Eleven blocks have facilities for disabled people. Launderette. Motorcaravan service points. Gas supplies. Comprehensive shopping areas set around a pleasant piazza (all open until late). Eight restaurants each with a different style. Nine pleasant and lively bars. Impressive aqua-parks (from 15/5). Tennis. Riding. Minigolf. Skating rink. Bicycle hire. Archery. Two fitness tracks in 4 ha. natural park with play area and supervised play for children. Golf academy. Diving centre and school. Windsurfing school in season. Boat excursions. Recreational events for adults and children, day and evening. Church service in English in July/Aug. Hairdressers. Medical centre. Internet cafés. ATM. Dogs are not accepted. Off site: Boat launching 3.5 km. Aqualandia (special rates).

Open: 1 May - 30 September, with all services.

Directions

From Venice - Trieste autostrada leave at exit for airport or Quarto d'Altino and follow signs first for Jesolo and then Punta Sabbioni, and site will be seen just after Cavallino on the left.

Charges 2007

Per person	€ 6,30 - € 9,60
child (under 3 yrs)	€ 3,60 - € 6,60
child (3-12 yrs)	€ 5,10 - € 8,20
pitch with electricity	€ 11,60 - € 21,00
pitch with water and drainage	€ 14,30 - € 25,00

Three different seasons:
(i) high season 29/6-31/8; (ii) mid-season 18/5-29/6 and 31/8-14/9, and (iii) off-season, outside these dates.

IT60210 Italy Camping Village

Via Fausta 272, I-30013 Cavallino-Treporti (Veneto)

Tel: **041 968 090**. Email: **info@campingitaly.it**

Italy Camping Village, under the same ownership as the better known Union Lido which it adjoins, is suggested for those who prefer a smaller site where less activities are available (although those at Union Lido may be used by guests here, charges applying). The 180 touring pitches are on either side of sand tracts off hard access roads under a cover of trees. All have 6A electricity connections and 70 are fully serviced. Being small (60-70 sq.m), they are impossible for large units, particularly in high season when cars are parked everywhere. There is direct access to a gently sloping sandy beach and a pleasant, heated, swimming pool which has slides and a whirlpool at one end. Strict regulations regarding undue noise here make this a peaceful site and with lower charges than some in the area, this would be a good choice for families with young children where it is possible to book in advance.

Facilities

Two good quality, fully equipped sanitary blocks include facilities for disabled visitors. Washing machines. Shop. Restaurant. Bar beside beach. Heated swimming pool (17 x 7 m). Small playground, mini-club and children's disco. Weekly dance for adults. Bicycle hire. Barbecues are only permitted in a designated area. Dogs are not accepted. Off site: Use of facilites at IT6020 Union Lido. Sports centre 500 m. Golf or riding 500 m.

Open: 21 April - 22 September.

Directions

From Venice - Trieste A4 autostrada leave at exit for airport or Quarto d'Altino and follow signs for Jesolo and Punta Sabbioni. Site on left after Cavallino.

Charges 2007

Per person	€ 4,70 - € 7,65
child (1-6 yrs)	free - € 5,90
pitch with electricity	€ 8,00 - € 18,50
pitch with electricity and water	€ 8,50 - € 19,90

Three charging seasons.

PARK & RESORT
CAMPING
LODGING
HOTEL
★ ★ ★ ★ www.unionlido.com

Union Lido Vacanze is situated on the green Cavallino Riviera, between the splendid Venetian lagoon and the Adriatic Sea.

Open from 24th April to 27th September.

- **Venice** and it's magnificent islands can be reached across water in approximately **30 minutes**.
- Spacious and well looked after pitches.
- The modern washrooms are constantly kept clean, complete with facilities for the disabled, and baby rooms for the smaller guests.

BUNGALOWS, MOBILE HOMES, MAXI CARAVANS COMPLETE WITH EVERY COMFORT.

- Rooms, villas and apartments at the high quality Park Hotel, the only 4 star hotel in the area, with it's own heated swimming pool, Jacuzzi and children's mini pool.
- The Gourmet Club Union Lido boasts 8 restaurants and 11 bars on site.
- 2 supermarkets and over 20 shops of various types.
- Exclusive beach 1km in length of fine sand and games for children.
- 2 Aqua Parks with pools for a total of 11.000 m²; Entrance to the parks is included in the price of your holiday.
- The Marino Club health Spa with sea view, salt water oasis with exclusive treatments.
- Entertainment for both children and adults. Diving school, surf school, golf academy, horse-riding, archery, rollerblade link. Excursions and trips to unforgettable destinations.

Visit our website **www.unionlido.com** for more information on our packages and super offers, check out the last minute offers too... ...for unrepeatable opportunities!

NEWS 2008

- New air-conditioning installations in our Bungalows Lido.
- Renewal of the successful Beach Card for sun-lounger and parasol hire on our beach.
- New security procedures on the campsite.
- 36 New Camping Home Patios, 40m², the maximum of comfort and technology to discover a new lifestyle.
- 200 pitches B and C that can be booked online.

30013 CAVALLINO VENEZIA - ITALIA
Camping Park & Resort
Tel. Camping +39 041 25 75 111
Tel. Park Hotel +39 041 96 80 43
Telefax +39 041 5 37 03 55
info@unionlido.com
booking@unionlido.com

Parco Turistico di Cavallino Treporti

Veneto From Earth to Sky

PROMOVE LR. 33/02

IT60450 Camping Marina di Venezia

Via Montello 6, I-30013 Punta Sabbioni (Veneto)

Tel: **041 530 2511**. Email: **camping@marinadivenezia.it**

This is a very large site (2,300 pitches) with much the same atmosphere as many other large sites along this appealing stretch of coastline. Marina di Venezia, however, has the advantage of being within walking distance of the ferry to Venice. It will appeal particularly to those who enjoy an extensive range of entertainment and activities, and a lively atmosphere. Individual pitches are marked out on sandy ground, most separated by trees or hedges. They are of an average size for the region (around 80 sq.m) and all are equipped with electricity and water. The site's excellent sandy beach is one of the widest along this stretch of coast and has a pleasant beach bar. The main pool is Olympic sized and there is also a very large children's pool adjacent. This is a well run site with committed management and staff.

Facilities

Ten modern toilet blocks are maintained to a high standard with good hot showers and a reasonable proportion of British style toilets. Good provision for disabled visitors. Washing machines and dryers. Range of shops. Several bars, restaurants and takeaways. Swimming pools (no slides). Several play areas. Tennis. Windsurf and catamaran hire. Kite hire. Wide range of organised entertainment. WiFi internet access in all bars and cafés. Church on site.

Open: 19 April - 30 September.

Directions

From A4 motorway, take Jesolo exit. After Jesolo continue towards Punta Sabbioni. Site is clearly signed to the left towards the end of this road, close to the Venice ferries. GPS: N45:26.250 E12:26.283

Charges 2007

Per person	€ 4,15 - € 8,25
child or senior (under 5 and over 60)	€ 3,50 - € 6,70
pitch with electricity and water	€ 10,50 - € 20,05

IT60460 Camping Miramare

Punta Sabbioni, I-30010 Cavallino-Treporti (Veneto)

Tel: **041 966 150**. Email: **info@camping-miramare.it**

This family owned site is well located, being one of the closest sites to the Punta Sabbione ferry and offering a free bus service to the ferry and the local beach. It has an unusually long season compared with others in the area. Miramare is ideally located for exploring Venice and its islands, as well as the Lido di Venezia. There are 130 level pitches here, all with 6A electricity. They intend to increase the numbers by 50% in 2008. The shop is superb for a small site and the restaurant is 50 m. out of the gate and is renowned for its excellent regional meals. An internet terminal is also here. Unusually, the site runs a free cycle loan scheme. The site is kept clean and most pitches have shade from mature trees and are level. Ask about the campsite logo – the 'Venetian iron'- very interesting, and the secret of the local flamingoes!

Facilities

Two toilet blocks (one heated in low season) with facilities for disabled people and babies. Motorcaravan service point. Bar, restaurant and pizzas from the oven in the restaurant. Takeaway. Excellent supermarket/shop. Play area. Internet point. Free bicycle hire. Dogs are not accepted. Free shuttle bus from Punta Sabbioni square (departure point for trips to Venice and the islands) and to the nearest beach on the Adriatic Coast. Off site: Fishing 2 km. Boat launching 1.5 km. Beach 1.8 km. Golf 8 km. Riding 8 km.

Open: Easter - early November.

Directions

Leave the A4 autostrada at exit for Venezia Mestre and follow signs to Noventa/San Dona

Charges 2007

Per person	€ 4,70 - € 7,00
child (1-10 years)	€ 3,00 - € 5,20
pitch	€ 9,60 - € 18,68

IT60530 Camping Fusina

Via Moranzani 79, I-30030 Fusina (Veneto)

Tel: **041 547 0055**. Email: **info@camping-fusina.com**

There are some sites that take one by surprise – this is one. This is old fashioned camping, but what fun, and we met English speaking people who have been coming here for 30 years. Choose from 500 well shaded, flat and grassy informal pitches or a position with views over the lagoon to the towers in Saint Mark's Square. With water on three sides there are welcoming cool breezes and fortunately many trees hide the industrial area close by. Those who don't wish to be disturbed by the lively bar can choose from the many informal waterside pitches on the far end of the site. The site owns a large ferry car park and a 700-boat marina which accepts and launches all manner of craft. A deep water channel carries huge ships close by and the water views are never boring. Fusina offers a very easy and comfortable, 20 minute ferry connection to the cultural heart of Venice, Accademia. Several site buildings, including some of the showers and toilets, were designed by the famous modern architect Scarpa. These are heritage listed and are visited by design students, although this listing makes development and improvement difficult. Many of the staff are mature Australian/New Zealand people and English is used everywhere.

Facilities	Directions
Modern, well equipped facilities include units for disabled visitors, along with some existing older units. Washing machines and dryers. Motorcaravan service point. Shop (15/3-31/10). Charming restaurant (no credit cards). Pizzeria. Lively bar entertainment. TV with satellite. Playground. Boat hire. Marina. London Cyber bus. ATM. Torches useful. Off site: Excellent public transport and ferry connections to Venice. **Open:** All year.	From SSII Padua - Venice road follow site signs on road east of Mira, turning right as signed. Site is in Fusina at end of peninsula and is well signed (also as 'Fusina parking'). GPS: N45:25.150 E12:15.416

Charges 2007

Per person	€ 8,00 - € 9,00
child (5-12yrs)	€ 4,50
pitch	€ 8,50 - € 14,00

IT60540 Camping Oasi

Via A. Barbarigo 147, I-30019 Sottomarina (Veneto)

Tel: **041 554 1145**. Email: **info@campingoasi.com**

Camping Oasi is a traditional, friendly, family site where many Italian families return for the summer – you could certainly practice your Italian language skills here. An excellent marina is just outside the site gates. The flat, grass pitches for tourers are in separate areas from the permanent units. Varying in size (65-80 sq.m.) with a choice of shade or sun, all have 6A electricity, 100 have water and drainage. Some overlook the pleasant pools, others have views over the harbour wall to the sea beyond. Through a rear gate there is a harbour wall walk to a soft sand beach.

Facilities	Directions
One sanitary block has been renovated (2007) and has mostly British style toilets and free hot showers. The second block is in the permanent area and has limited facilities for disabled campers and facilities for children and babies. They are both some way from the furthest touring pitches. Swimming pool and paddling pool with flumes. Play area. Sports area. Bicycle hire. Riding. Watersports. Fishing. Free WiFi. Off site: Choggia. **Open:** 22 March - 30 September.	Site is off the S309 south of Chioggia. Follow signs to Sottomaria, crossing Laguna del Lusenzo, then look for site signs. Site off this road (Viale Mediterranneo) to the right. Site is last along this narrow road. GPS: N45:10.888 E12:18.446

Charges 2007

Per person	€ 4,60 - € 7,50
pitch	€ 7,70 - € 16,50
Camping Cheques accepted.	

IT60550 Villaggio Turistico Isamar

Isolaverde, via Isamar 9, I-30010 Sa Anna di Chioggia (Veneto)

Tel: **041 553 5811**. Email: **info@villaggioisamar.com**

Many improvements have been made here over the years and these continue at this busy, well managed site. The largest camping area, which may be cramped at times, is under pines and grouped around the swimming pool, the large modern sanitary block and shops near reception. A smaller camping area is situated under artificial shade near the beach with an Olympic size, salt water swimming pool, paddling pool and four new pools, a covered entertainment section, pizzeria, bar/restaurant and a small toilet block. Between these sections are well constructed holiday bungalows. A third camping area has been developed mainly for the site's own accommodation. The pitches, on either side of hard access roads, vary in size and all have electrical connections. Although directly by the sea, with its own sandy beach, it is a fair way from the entrance to the sea. The site has a much higher proportion of Italian holidaymakers than many other sites. It is also popular with German and Dutch visitors and may become crowded in high season.

Facilities

The main toilet blocks are fully equipped and of good quality with British style WCs (small block has only Turkish style). Laundry. Motorcaravan services. Gas supplies. Fridge hire. Hairdresser. Supermarket and general shopping centre. Large bar/pizzeria and self-service restaurant. Swimming pools. Tennis. Playground. Disco. Games room. Riding. Bicycle hire. Extensive entertainment and fitness programme offered for adults and supervised play for children over 4 yrs old. Dogs are not accepted. Off site: Fishing 500 m.

Open: 13 May - 16 September.

Directions

Turn off main 309 road towards sea just south of Adige river about 10 km. south of Chioggia, and proceed 5 km. to site.

Charges 2007

Per person	€ 3,50 - € 9,80
child (2-5 yrs)	€ 2,50 - € 8,30
pitch with full facilities	€ 6,90 - € 23,00

Less 10% for stays in low season for over 2 weeks.

IT60370 Camping Jésolo International

Viale A. da Giussano, I-30016 Lido di Jésolo (Veneto)

Tel: **042 197 1826**. Email: **info@jesolointernational.it**

At this brilliant family resort style site with a focus on sporting activities, you can plan the cost of your holiday with confidence. The amazing array of on site activities is free and there are large discounts for some off site attractions. Jesolo International is located on a beautiful promontory with 700 metres of uncrowded white sandy beach and slowly shelving waters for safe swimming. As the site is narrow, all the pitches are close to the sea. There is a choice of three types of pitch, all flat, well shaded and with 10-20A electricity, water and drainage. Most also have a satellite TV connection supplying 26 free channels. The superb pool complex, where an excellent animation programme is presented each night, is centrally located and very spacious. The pool is open one night a week for a supervised pool party. The dynamic director Sergio Comino works long hours to maintain and improve this high quality family orientated site, to combine a unique holiday experience for guests, with real value for money. As the site is community owned, profits are returned to the guests in the form of facilities, sporting opportunities and entertainment. Cleanliness and security are high priorities. Electronic tags are given to guests to gain entrance and exit to the beach gates and this, combined with video surveillance of these key locations, allows guests to feel secure. Children's passes exclude them from accessing the beach alone or the hydro massage whirlpools reserved for adults alone A ferry service to Venice leaves from the marina adjoining the campsite and takes just 40 minutes to reach St Mark's Square in the heart of the city.

Facilities

Sanitary facilities include 72 modern, continually cleaned bathroom units (shower, toilet and basin), private bathrooms (extra cost) and baby rooms. Washing machines and dryers. Fridge boxes. Motorcaravan service point. Supermarket. Family style restaurant. Beach bar with snacks. Pool bar serving light lunches. Sports centre. Children's club and inflatable fun park on the beach. Indoor gym. Tennis courts and lessons (equipment provided). Golf (lessons, equipment and playing fees all free). Sailing with tuition and canoe courses. Introductory scuba dive lesson (followed by 50% discount on courses and excursions). Pedal boats. Language courses. Large grassy play area with adventure style equipment. Free medical service. Free internet. Dogs are not accepted. Off site: Golf 2 km. (free lesson and use of 18 hole course with equipment). Aqualandia 1.5 km. (30% discount). Ferry to Venice and Murano 200 m. Jesolo promenade with shops, restaurants and bars 500 m.

Open: 24 April - 30 September.

Directions

From A4 Venice - Trieste autostrada take Dona di Piave exit and follow signs to Jesolo then Punta Sabbioni. Turn off to Lido di Jesolo just before the Cavallino bridge where the site is well signed. GPS: N45:29.061 E12:35.319

Charges 2008

Per person (over 5 yrs)	€ 5,50 - € 11,00
child (1-5 yrs)	free - € 4,00
serviced pitch	€ 13,00 - € 25,50

IT60500 Camping Della Serenissima

Via Padana 334/a, I-30034 Oriago (Veneto)

Tel: **041 921 850**. Email: **camping.serenissima@shineline.it**

This is a delightful little site of some 155 pitches (all with 16A electricity) where one could stay for a number of days whilst visiting Venice (12 km), Padova (24), Lake Garda (135) or the Dolomites. There is a good service by bus to Venice and the site is situated on the Riviera del Brenta, a section of a river with some very large old villas. A long, narrow and flat site, numbered pitches are on each side of a central road. There is good shade in most parts with many trees, plants and lots of grass. The management is very friendly and good English is spoken. The site is used mainly by Dutch and British visitors, with some Germans, and is calm and quiet.

Facilities

Sanitary facilities are of a good standard with all facilities in private cabins. Facilities for disabled visitors. Motorcaravan services. Gas supplies. Shop (all season). Bar. Restaurant and takeaway (1/6-31/10). Play area. Fishing. Bicycle hire. Reduced price bus ticket to Venice if staying for 3 days. No entertainment but local markets, etc. all well publicised. Off site: Golf or riding 3 km.

Open: Easter - 10 November.

Directions

From the east take road S11 at roundabout SSW of Mestre towards Padova and site is 2 km. on right. From west, leave autostrada A4 at Dolo exit, follow signs to Dolo, continue on main road through this small village and turn left at T-junction (traffic lights). Continue towards Venice on S11 for site about 6 km. on left. GPS: N45:45.234 E12:18.333

Charges 2007

Per person	€ 6,50 - € 8,00
child (3-10 yrs)	€ 4,00 - € 5,50
pitch	€ 12,00 - € 13,00

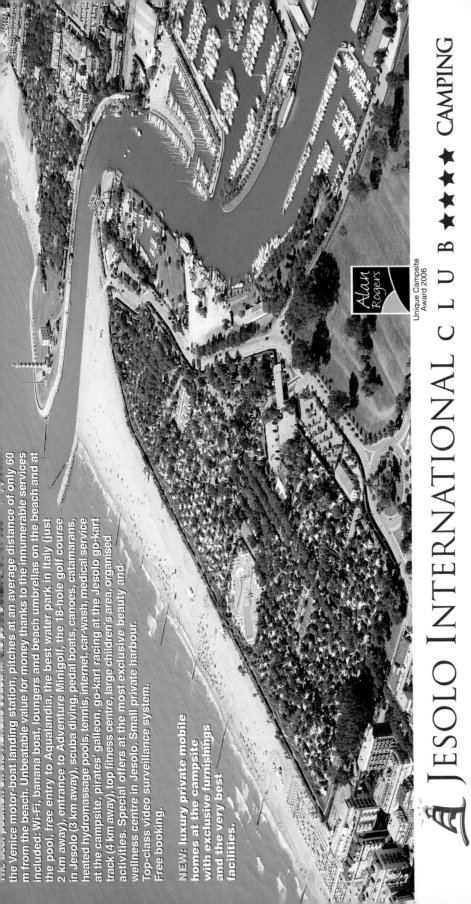

...the boat landing station, pitches at an average distance of only 60 m from the beach. Unbeatable value for money thanks to the innumerable services included: WI-FI, banana boat, loungers and beach umbrellas on the beach and at the pool, free entry to Aqualandia, the best water park in Italy (just 2 km away), entrance to Adventure Minigolf, the 18-hole golf course in Jesolo (3 km away), scuba diving, pedal boats, canoes, catamarans, heated hydromassage pools, tennis, internet, car-wash, medical service at the campsite, pirates' galleon, go-kart racing at the Jesolo go-kart track (4 km away), top fitness centre, large children's area, organised activities. Special offers at the most exclusive beauty and wellness centre in Jesolo. Small private harbour. Top-class video surveillance system. Free booking.

NEW! luxury private mobile homes at the campsite with exclusive furnishings and the very best facilities.

Å JESOLO INTERNATIONAL C L U B ★★★★ CAMPING

www.jesolointernational.it / info@jesolointernational.it / SOFORTIGE TELEFONRESERVIERUNGEN 0039 0421 971826

IT60470 Camping Scarpiland

I-30010 Treporti (Veneto)

Tel: 041 966488. Email: info@scarpiland.com

Scarpiland faces the Adriatic and has a fine sandy beach. This campsite is a most peculiar shape in that it is dissected by rows of accommodation to rent belonging to the site with long separating fences. This forces campers in the touring area to have long walks to the single beach access. It is a large site with the informal touring pitches under the shade of mature pines. Pitches, vary in size (70-90 sq m) with 6A electricity. The irregular tree placing will challenge some units and large units are not suitable here. The site has an attractive woodland setting but there is a very long walk to the two sanitary blocks. The first very small block is unisex and has all Turkish toilets, we have seen problems here at peak periods. The larger block is even further away but has British style toilets and hot showers. The only chemical disposal site is in this block. Few activities are on offer but much is available outside the site. The site's entertainment team organise activities for the children in a small staged area. All other amenities are worryingly situated on the main road which serves the site. All are open fronted and the games area and some shops are across the road so children must be carefully supervised. There is a selection of shops plus a bar and restaurant all open to the public.

Facilities

Two sanitary blocks one large one very small with Turkish style toilets only. Dated facilities for babies in the large block and one unit for disabled visitors. Newsagent. Supermarket. Butcher. Souvenir shop. Greengrocer and local produce (all on the main road). Restaurant/pizzeria. Ice cream parlour. Bicycle hire. Internet. Off site: Golf 3.4 km. Riding 3.4 km. Boat launching 5 km.

Open: 24 April - 22 September.

Directions

From Milan, take A4 autostrada to Venice and continue towards Trieste (Venezia-Trieste) as far as the A27 intersection, then follow signs to the airport. At the end of the bypass, follow signs to San Doná and Jesolo. When you reach Jesolo, follow directions to Lido del Cavallino and Punta Sabbioni. From here the site is clearly signed.

Charges guide

Per unit incl 2 persons and electricity	€ 14,90 - € 30,30
extra person	€ 3,90 - € 7,40
child (under 7 yrs)	free - € 4,30

IT60410 Camping Village Europa

Via Fausta 332, I-30013 Cavallino-Treporti (Veneto)

Tel: 041 96 8069. Email: info@campingeuropa.com

Europa has a great position with direct access to a fine sandy beach with lifeguards. There are 411 touring pitches, all with 8A electricity, some with water, drainage and satellite TV connections. There is a separate area for campers with dogs and some smaller pitches are available for those with tents. The site is kept beautifully clean and neat and there is an impressive array of restaurant, bars, shopping and leisure amenities. These are cleverly laid out along a long avenue and include a jeweller, a doctor's surgery, internet services and much more. Leisure facilities are arranged around the site. A professional team provides entertainment and themed 'summer parties'. Some restaurant tables have pleasant sea views. Venice is easily accessible by bus and then ferry from Punta Sabbioni.

Facilities

Three superb toilet blocks are kept pristine and have hot water throughout. Facilities for isabled visitors. Washing machines. Bars, restaurants, cafés and pizzeria. Large supermarket and shopping centre. Tennis. Football pitch. Games room. Playground. Children's clubs. Entertainment programme. Internet access. Direct access to the beach. Windsurf and pedalo hire. Mobile homes and chalets for rent. Off site: Riding and boat launching 1 km. Golf and fishing 2 km. ATM 500 m. Walking and cycling trails. Excursions to Venice.

Open: 24 March - 30 September.

Directions

From A4 autostrada (approaching from Milan) take Mestre exit and follow signs initially for Venice airport and then Jesolo. From Jesolo, follow signs to Cavallino from where site is well signed.

Charges 2007

Per person	€ 4,30 - € 7,70
child (2-5 yrs)	€ 2,90 - € 6,70
adult over 60 yrs	€ 3,30 - € 7,60
pitch	€ 7,95 - € 20,00
dog	€ 2,00 - € 4,35

VENETO TOURISM AND ENVIRONMENT MANIFESTO
CAVALLINO QUALITY CAMPING 2008

Operators in the Veneto have a unique and precious sensitivity
towards their Region. They have developed the "Veneto Tourism and Environment Manifesto"
protection initiative, which is the most concrete example
of eco-compatible tourism in Europe today.

IT60340 Camping Waikiki

Viale Oriente 144, I-30016 Lido di Jésolo (Veneto)

Tel: **042 198 0186**. Email: **info@campingwaikiki.com**

Waikiki is twinned with Camping Malibu Beach which is close by (see opposite page). This site also has direct access to a broad, soft sandy beach across a 300 m. grass area which has a boarded walkway. The beach shelves slowly so swimming is safe for children, there are sunshades and loungers to hire and lifeguards on the beach. The touring pitches here are shaded by pines and other trees, some close to the beach fence, but others with sea views. Relatively flat, all have 6A electricity and some have water. Amenities include an attractive swimming pool and paddling pool, both with lifeguard. An attractive restaurant/pizzeria with a very large terrace offers a good choice of reasonably priced food and there is a well stocked supermarket. Entertainment is provided daily. A regular bus service runs from the campsite to Jesolo, where there is an excellent selection of shops, bars and restaurants.

Facilities

Three good toilet blocks are smart and clean. Facilities for disabled visitors and children. Bar, restaurant/pizzeria, shop and bazaar. Games room. Fitness centre. Swimming and paddling pools (hats compulsory). Playground. Children's club. Entertainment programme. Direct access to the beach. Dogs are not accepted. Mobile homes and chalets for rent. Off site: Lido de Jesolo, excursions to Venice, Vicenza and Padova. Riding. Golf.

Open: 12 May - 11 September.

Directions

From A4 autostrada (approaching from Milan) take Mestre exit and follow signs initially for Venice airport and then Jesolo. From Jesolo, follow signs to Jesolo Pineta and site is well signed.

Charges 2007

Per person	€ 3,65 - € 6,80
child (2-7 yrs) or senior (over 65)	€ 2,80 - € 4,75
pitch with electricity	€ 8,75 - € 18,40

No credit cards. Minimum stay 2 nights.

IT60330 Villaggio Turistico Malibu Beach

Viale Oriente 78, I-30016 Lido di Jésolo (Veneto)

Tel: **042 136 2212**. Email: **info@campingmalibubeach.com**

This is a family site, twinned with Camping Wakiki nearby which has direct access to a beach. Malibu Beach has 407 pitches with 150 for touring units, all with 6A electricity. The touring pitches are set back from the beach, with the pitches in between being used for mobile homes and chalets. All are well shaded by pine trees and there are some fully serviced pitches with electricity and water. The beach is of soft sand, shelves gently and has lifeguards and the usual Italian sunshades and loungers for hire. central complex incorporates a bright, cheery bar/restaurant and a well stocked supermarket. Other amenities include a large swimming pool, plus a paddling pool with a slide and fountains. Everything around this site was clean and tidy and visitors we spoke to were happy. A professional team provides entertainment all season. Jesolo is nearby, along with all sorts of seaside entertainment, and the possibility of excursions to Venice.

Facilities

Three clean blocks provide good facilities, including for disabled visitors and children. Bar, restaurant and pizzeria. Shop. Games room. Fitness centre. Hairdresser. Massage. Swimming pool and paddling pool (hats compulsory). Playground. Children's club. Entertainment programme. Direct access to the beach. Fridge box hire. WiFi (at restaurant). Dogs are not accepted. Mobile homes and chalets for rent. Off site: Lido de Jesolo, excursions to Venice. Riding. Golf. Walking and cycling trails.

Open: 15 May - 13 September.

Directions

From A4 autostrada (approaching from Milan) take Mestre exit and follow signs initially for Venice airport and then Jesolo. From Jesolo, follow signs to Jesolo Pineta and site is well signed.

Charges 2007

Per person	€ 4,75 - € 7,75
child (2-7 yrs) and seniors over 65	€ 3,40 - € 6,30
pitch with electricity	€ 8,30 - € 21,20

No credit cards. Minimum stay 2 nights.

IT60350 Camping Mediterraneo

Via delle Batterie 38 Ca, I-30010 Cavallino-Treporti (Veneto)

Tel: **041 966 721**. Email: **mediterraneo@vacanze-natura.it**

This large site has been considerably improved in recent years and is near Punta Sabbioni from where boats go to Venice. Mediterraneo is directly on the Adriatic Sea with a 480 metre long beach of fine sand which shelves gently and also two large pools and a whirlpool. The 750 touring pitches, of which 500 have electricity (from 4A), water and drainaway, are partly in boxes with artificial shade, some larger without shade, with others in unmarked zones under natural woodland equipped with electric hook ups where tents must go. Tour operators use 145 pitches. This is an organised and efficient site. Sporting, fitness and entertainment programmes are arranged and sea swimming is supervised at certain times by lifeguards. Windsurfing and sailing schools are recent introductions.

Facilities

Eight modern sanitary blocks are of good quality with British type WCs and free hot water. Laundry facilities. Motorcaravan services. Commercial centre with supermarket and other shops with a restaurant, bars and a pizzeria near the pools. Swimming pool. Playground. Tennis court. Bicycle hire. Programme of sports, games, excursions etc. Dancing or shows 3 times weekly in main season. Windsurfing and sailing schools. Dogs are not accepted. Off site: Riding and golf 3 km.

Open: 22 April - 25 September.

Directions

Site is well signed from Jesolo-Punta Sabbioni road near its end after Ca' Ballarin and before Ca' Savio. Follow sitesigns, not those for Treporti as this village is some way from the site.

Charges guide

Per person	€ 4,00 - € 8,50
child (1-6 yrs) or senior (65 yrs+)	free - € 6,60
pitch with electricity	€ 7,60 - € 19,50
incl.water and drainage	€ 8,50 - € 21,30
tent pitch with electricity	€ 6,80 - € 17,50

Four rates.

This is just a sample of the campsites we have inspected and selected in Italy. For more campsites and further information, please see the Alan Rogers Italy guide.

(305)

IT60560 Camping Miramare

Via Barbarigo, 103, I-30019 Sottomarina di Chioggia (Veneto)

Tel: **041 490 610**. Email: **camping@tin.it**

Camping Miramare sits on both sides of the road leading to it; reception is on the beach side, along with most of the amenities, the other side is very peaceful with just sports amenities and a sanitary block. The touring pitches are separated from the permanent units. All have 6A electricity, some have water and drainage, Some have land views and others have shade. The beach is of soft sand with very safe bathing and a lifeguard. You can hire sunshades and loungers. The restaurant offers traditional food and a plethora of pizzas which can be enjoyed on the terraces. Some of these overlook the large safe paddling pool, children have several play areas and there is animation all season. The separated swimming pool is excellent, with two diving boards and a lifeguard. The site lies close to the ancient city of Chioggia, famous for its fishing and Venice like construction. It is well worth a visit on a bicycle as it has an amazing history. For those wishing to explore the region, there are many other opportunities. An excursion to Venice naturally holds a strong appeal, but other stunning cities are also close at hand, notably Padova, Vicenza, Treviso and, a little further afield, Verona. This is a pleasant, family oriented site which has a distinct Italian feel. English is spoken.

Facilities

Three identical, modern, clean blocks, one of which is in the area of the permanent campers. Pushbutton hot showers and primarily Turkish style toilets. Facilities for disabled guests. Baby room. Laundry rooms. Motorcaravan service point. Pleasant bar. Restaurant. Pizzeria and takeaway. Smart mini-market. Excellent swimming pool and separate paddling pool. Several great play areas. Multisport court. Entertainment and children's activities in high season. Mobile homes to rent. Dogs are not accepted. Off site: Bicycle hire 1 km. Fishing 1 km. Sailing 1 km. Riding 6 km. Golf 20 km. Visits to Choggia. Excursions to Venice and other cities.

Open: 5 April - 20 September.

Directions

Site is off the S309 south of Chioggia. Follow signs to Sottomaria, crossing the Laguna del Lusenzo, then look for site signs. Site is off Viale Mediterranneo road to the right. Site is the second of many along this narrow road. GPS: N45:11.417 E12:18.217

Charges 2007

Per person	€ 4,50 - € 7,40
child (under 6 yrs)	€ 2,25 - € 3,80
pitch	€ 7,50 - € 16,20

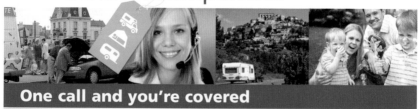

IT60900 Camping Arizona

Via Tabiano 42/A, I-43039 Tabiano di Salsomaggiore Terme (Emília-Romagna)
Tel: **052 456 5648**. Email: **info@camping-arizona.it**

Tabbiano and Salsomaggiore Terme are thermal springs dating back to the Roman era and the beneficial waters have given rise to attractive inland resort towns. The focus on water is developed within this family-run site. The complex of four large pools, long water slides, jacuzzi and play area are set in open landscaped grounds with good views and are also open to the public. Camping Arizona is a simple site set on steep slopes and is 500 metres from the town of Tabbiano. Access is easy to the lower pitches for even the largest of units. The 350 level pitches vary is size (50-90 sq.m), those on terraces enjoying shade from mature trees. Others have no shade, but all have access to electricity and water points are within 30 m. On site traffic is kept to a minimum during high season – with the exception of loading and unloading, vehicles must be parked in the large adjacent car park and golf trolleys are provided for use during your stay. Younger children will be entertained by the large, supervised play centre with bouncy castle, ball pool and other indoor and outdoor games.

Facilities

Sanitary facilities in four dated blocks are rather tired but kept clean. Mostly Turkish style WCs, open style washbasins and hot water throughout. Facilities for disabled visitors. Washing machines and dryers. Small well stocked shop. Restaurant/bar with patio. Swimming pools, slides and jacuzzi (18/5-15/9, also open to the public but free for campers). Tennis, boules and table tennis (charged). Play centre. Bicycle hire. Off site: Pub outside gate. Fidenza shopping village with designer outlets 8 km. Fishing 4 km. Golf 6 km.

Open: 20 March - 15 October.

Directions

From autostrada A1 take exit for Fidenza and follow signs for Tabiano. The site is on left 500 m. after Tabiano town centre. GPS: N44:48.400 E10:00.610

Charges 2007

Per person	€ 5,75 - € 8,00
child (2-9 yrs)	€ 4,00 - € 6,25
pitch	€ 6,50 - € 13,00
dog	€ 2,00 - € 2,50

No credit cards.

RELAX · SPORT · CULTURE

Camping Arizona

Tabiano - Salsomaggiore Terme
Tel. 0039/0524565648
Fax 0039/0524567589
e-mail: info@camping-arizona.it
www.camping-arizona.it

Imagine yourself in the wonderful countryside, with panoramic views. Tennis - 4 free of charge swimming pools - 2 waterslides - Football pitch - Basketball - Big playground. Restaurant with regional cooking - New Mobilhome with air conditioning - Cottage - Bungalows

IT60750 Camping Florenz

Viale Alpi Centrali, 199, I-44020 Lido degli Scacchi (Emília-Romagna)
Tel: **053 338 0193**. Email: **info@campingflorenz.com**

Popular with Italian families for over 30 years, Camping Florenz has many loyal campers who stay all season. The area which is most sought after by tourers is over the sand dunes along the seafront where there are good sized, shaded and level pitches with views of the water. The gently shelving beach has fine grey sand and lots of chairs and umbrellas. Away from the beach area there is heavy shade cover from pine trees. The pitches are mostly a mixture of sand and grass, of a good size and level, all with electricity (3A).

Facilities

Six mixed mostly old sanitary blocks with half British, half Turkish style toilets and pre-set showers. Some unisex showers at beach. Good facilities for disabled people. Motorcaravan service point. Good supermarket. Restaurant and bar with TV. Large outdoor pool. Activities and children's club in season. Good play area. Excellent beach for swimming and boat launching. Beach bar. Bicycle hire. WiFi. Off site: Small town 1 km.

Open: Easter - 20 September.

Directions

Site is at Lido di Scacchi just off the S309 running between Chioggia and Ravenna. Both Lido di Scacchi and site are well signed from the S309. GPS: N44:42.084 E12:14.324

Charges 2007

Per person	€ 4,20 - € 8,70
child (3-10 yrs)	free - € 5,40
pitch	€ 9,70 - € 24,00

Camping Cheques accepted.

IT60650 Camping Bungalow Park Tahiti

Viale Libia 133, I-44020 Lido delle Nazioni (Emília-Romagna)

Tel: **053 337 9500**. Email: **info@campingtahiti.com**

Tahiti is an excellent, extremely well run site, thoughtfully laid out less than 1 km. from the sea (a continuous small fun road-train link is provided). Flowers, shrubs, ponds and attractive wooded structures enhance its appearance and, unlike many campsites of this size, it is family owned and run. The 469 pitches are of varying size, back to back from hard roads and defined by trees with shade in most areas. There are 30 pitches with a private unit containing a WC and washbasin. Electricity is available throughout and 100 pitches also have water and drainage. They have thought of everything here and the manager Stefano is a dynamo who seems to be everywhere, ensuring the impressive standards are maintained. The staff are smart and attentive. As well as the swimming pool (25 x 12 m), there is a 'Atoll Beach' Caribbean style water play fun area with palms, plus a jacuzzi, bar and terrace (small extra charge for 'wet' activities). A new 'Thermal Oasis' offers health and beauty treatments. English is spoken by the friendly management, although the British have not yet really discovered this site, which is popular with other European campers. The site is very busy in season with much coming and going, but all is always under control – it is superb, especially for families with children. It is also keen on recycling and even has a facility for exhausted batteries.

Facilities

All toilet blocks are of a very high standard. British and Turkish style WCs. Baby room. Large supermarket. Two waiter service restaurants. Bar. Pizzeria. Takeaway. Swimming pools. Fitness and beauty centre. Several playgrounds and mini-club. Gym. Tennis. Floodlit sports area. Minigolf. Bicycle hire. Free transport to the beach. Entertainment and excursions (high season). 'Disco-pub'. Daily medical service. ATM. Internet. Torches needed in some areas. Dogs are not accepted. Off site: Fishing 300 m. Riding 500 m.

Open: 18 April - 23 September.

Directions

Turn off SS309 35 km. north of Ravenna to Lido delle Nazioni (north of Lido di Pomposa) and follow site signs.

Charges 2007

Per person	€ 4,90 - € 8,90
child (under 8 yrs)	free - € 6,60
pitch acc. to season and type and facilities	€ 8,90 - € 26,90
pitch with sanitary facility	€ 17,90 - € 52,90

IT66190 Numana Blu Camping Village

Via Costaverde, 37, I-60026 Numana (Marche)

Tel: 071 739 0993. Email: info@numanablu.it

Numana Blu lies on the Conero Riviera, south of Ancona, just 300 metres from the sea, and close to the town of Marcelli. Beneath the site's 12,000 trees there are 380 shady pitches, most offering electrical connections. Separate areas have a range of rentable accommodation, including chalets and bungalows. There's plenty to do here but the site retains a relaxed atmosphere. In peak season there are several children's clubs catering for different ages. The site also boasts an impressive array of leisure amenities including a large swimming pool, a restaurant/pizzeria and supermarket. This is a friendly site with multi-lingual reception staff. The beach is a short walk and offers private facilities. Numana is less than a kilometre away and has all the amenities of a typical Italian resort. The Sirolo National Park is very close and well worth a visit.

Facilities

Supermarket. Bar, restaurant/pizzeria and takeaway meals. Swimming pool and children's pool. Playground. Bicycle hire. Football pitch. Tennis. Children's clubs. Entertainment programme in high season. Off site: Beach 300 m. Conero Riviera, Monte Conero (at 572 m. the highest peak in the area) and Ancona. Riding. Cycle and walking trails. Golf.

Open: 1 May - 10 September.

Directions

Take the Loreto Porto Recanati exit from the A14 autostrada and follow signs to Numana. Site is south of Numana, 1.5 km. from the small town of Marcelli. GPS: N43:28.517 E13:37.751

Charges guide

Per person	€ 4,10 - € 9,10
child (under 6 yrs)	€ 2,70 - € 6,70
pitch	€ 9,80 - € 22,40
tent pitch	€ 6,55 - € 14,60
electricity	€ 2,80

IT66170 Camping Perticara

Via Serra Masini 10/d, Perticara, I-61017 Novafeltria (Marche)

Tel: 054 192 7602. Email: info@campingperticara.com

High in the Marche hills, not far from San Marino, Ravenna and Rimini, is Camping Perticara, a brand new, purpose built camping site with glorious views across a valley to the mountains and the nearby traditional village of Perticara. Its 80 pitches have water and drainage and are very large, all arranged on terraces to take advantage of the fabulous scenery. Good-sized trees have been planted to provide shade in the future. The shop, bar and restaurant area is attractively presented, with a terrace overlooking the swimming pool which shares the incredible vistas.

Facilities

Two immaculate modern units provide really excellent facilities with all the extras. Facilities are all in large luxury cabins with shower, toilet and basin. Units for disabled campers are of the same standard. Washing machine and dryers. Gas. Small shop. Restaurant (limited menu but good value). Snack bar. Swimming and paddling pools. Small play areas. Animation (miniclub) in high season. Torches useful. Off site: Bicycle hire 500 m. Fishing 10 km. Golf 25 km.

Open: 24 April - 1 October.

Directions

After Bologna on the A1 take A14 towards Ancona and take exit for Rimini Nord. After 200 m. turn right (San Leo), over five roundabouts (Montefeltro). At lights turn right to Novafeltria (32 km). At Novafeltria, 400 m. after lights, turn right (Perticara). Climb for 7 km. (under 12%) and at top turn left (Santa Agata Feltria). After 400 m. turn right to site.

Charges 2008

Per person	€ 5,50 - € 8,00
child (4-12 yrs)	€ 3,50 - € 6,00
pitch	€ 11,00 - € 15,00

IT65070 Camping Panorama

Strand Panorama, I-61010 Fiorenzuola di Focara (Marche)

Tel: 072 120 8145. Email: info@campingpanorama.it

Camping Panorama is a peaceful site located on a scenic coastal drive within a small national park (Parco del San Bartolo) and quite close to the delightful town of Pesaro. The site lies 100 metres above the sea and a pleasant path leads to the beach below. There are 150 pitches ranging in size from 45-100 sq.m. Most have electrical connections and all are well shaded. Leisure amenities include an attractive swimming pool (with smaller children's pool) and a sports court. This is a largely undeveloped area and has many opportunities for walking and mountain biking.

Facilities

Centrally located toilet block. Swimming pool and children's pool. Bar, pizzeria. TV room. Play area. Tourist information. Sports court. Off site: Riding. Golf. Nearest village is Fiorenzuola di Focara (2 km), a pretty village perched over the sea with bars, shops and restaurants. Pesaro 6 km. San Marino 42 km. Urbino 50 km. Mountain biking and walking.

Open: 21 April - 30 September.

Directions

From A14 (Bologna - Taranto) take Cattolica exit and join SS16 southbound towards Siligata. Here join the coast road (Strad Panoramico) towards Fionenzuola. Site is beyond this town and Fiorenzuola di Focara and before reaching Pesaro. GPS: N43:56.501 E12:50.751

Charges 2007

Per person	€ 6,00 - € 9,00
child (under 6 yrs)	€ 3,50 - € 5,50
pitch	€ 9,50 - € 13,00
electricity	€ 2,50

No credit cards.

IT66080 Camping Torre Pendente

Viale delle Cascine 86, I-56122 Pisa (Tuscany)

Tel: 050 561 704. Email: info@campingtorrependente.it

Torre Pendente is a most friendly site, well run by the Signorini family who speak good English and make everyone feel welcome. It is amazingly close to the famous leaning tower of Pisa and obviously its position means it is busy throughout the main season. It is a medium sized site, on level, grassy ground with some shade from trees and lots of artificial shade. There are 220 touring pitches, all with electricity. All site facilities are near the entrance including a most pleasant swimming pool complex with pool bar and a large terrace. Here you can relax after hot days in the city and enjoy drinks and snacks or find more formal fare in the restaurant with a la carte menu. This is a very busy site in high season with many nationalities discovering the delights of Pisa. It is ideal for exploring the fascinating leaning tower and other attractions.

Facilities

Three new toilet blocks are clean and smart with British style toilets with good facilities for disabled campers. Private cabins for hire. Hot water at sinks. Washing machines. Motorcaravan services. New supermarket. New restaurant, bar and takeaway. Swimming pool with pool bar, paddling pool and spa. Playground. Boules. Animation in high season. Internet access. Accommodation. Off site: Bicycle hire. Riding 3 km. Fishing 10 km. Golf 15 km.

Open: 15 March - 15 October.

Directions

From A12, exit at Pisa Nord and follow for 5 km. to Pisa. Do not take first sign to town centre. Site is well signed at a later left turn (Viale delle Cascine). GPS: N43:43.270 E10:22.590

Charges 2008

Per person	€ 8,00 - € 9,00
child (3-10 yrs)	€ 4,50 - € 5,00
pitch	€ 6,00 - € 15,00
dog	€ 1,60

Check real time availability and at-the-gate prices...

www.alanrogers.com

IT66060 Camping Europa

Viale dei Tigli - casella postale 115, I-55048 Torre del Lago Puccini (Tuscany)

Tel: 058 435 0707. Email: info@europacamp.it

Europa is a large, flat, rectangular site with roads on all four sides of the site. There are 400 pitches in 17 rows, several with well established permanent pitches, three with bungalows to rent. The site's facilities including a bar, shop and air conditioned reataurant, are in rows 5 and 6. The touring pitches in rows 12-17 are flat, very sandy and close together (55-70 sq.m). Some have shade from small trees or artificial cover and electricity (6A) is available. The site has been owned by the Morescalchi family since 1967 and they are very keen that you have an enjoyable stay. The pool and its separate paddling pool are pleasant (charged) and a jacuzzi is built into one end. A bicycle is a must for the beach 1 km. away, otherwise it is a brisk 20 minute walk through towering trees on a forest trail. However, once there, the sand is soft and the beach shelves gently into the water. Europa is conveniently situated for visiting many of the interesting places around such as Lucca, Pisa, Florence and the wealth of Puccini related historical items.

Facilities

Two sanitary blocks provide hot and cold showers (token from reception). Toilets are mixed Turkish and British style. Facilities for disabled visitors. Laundry facilities. Motorcaravan services outside gate. Bar/restaurant (air conditioned). Small shop. Good swimming pool (caps required). Play area. Entertainment. Miniclub. Bicycle hire. Internet access. Dogs are not accepted 4/7-25/8. Off site: Beach 1 km. Fishing. Golf 17 km. Riding 2 km.

Open: 22 March - 11 October.

Directions

From A11-12 to Pisa Nord take Viareggio exit. Turn south on Via Aurelia towards Pisa and then towards the sea for Marina di Torre Lago Puccini. Follow clear signs for site. GPS: N43:49.000 E10:16.430

Charges 2007

Per person	€ 4,00 - € 8,50
child (2-10 yrs)	€ 2,50 - € 4,50
pitch	€ 8,50 - € 12,00
car	€ 4,00 - € 8,00

IT66270 Camping Boschetto di Piemma

I-53037 San Gimignano (Tuscany)

Tel: 057 779 0352. Email: camping@selvadelletorri.com

The mediaeval Manhattan of San Gimignano is one of Tuscany's most popular sites. This new site lies just 2 km. from the town and there are 100 small pitches here, all with 10A electrical connections. The site is in a wood surrounded by olive groves and vineyards and has been developed with much care for the environment, using rain water for irrigation, for example. San Gimignano has been classified by UNESCO as a world heritage site and is best known for its towers, built by rival families, and which date back to the 11th century. An hourly bus service connects the site with the town.

Facilities

Excellent sanitary block and facilities for disabled visitors. Restaurant/pizzeria and bar. Mini-market (specialising in local produce). Swimming pool (15/5-15/9, small charge). Tennis (lessons available). Sports pitch. Playground. Entertainment and activity programme in high season. Apartments for rent. Off site: San Gimignano 2 km. Cycle and walking trails, riding, golf.

Open: 1 April - 30 October.

Directions

Take the Poggibonsi Nord exit from the Florence - Siena superstrada. Then follow signs to San Gimignano. At first roundabout follow signs to Volterra and then take first road to the left, signed Santa Lucia. Site is located close to the sports area. GPS: N43:27.196 E11:03.215

Charges 2007

Per person	€ 6,00 - € 7,80
child (3-11 yrs)	€ 4,00 - € 5,00
pitch incl. electricity	€ 6,00 - € 10,90

IT66110 Camping Il Poggetto

Via Il Poggetto 143, I-50067 Troghi - Firenze (Tuscany)

Tel: **055 830 7323**. Email: **info@campingilpoggetto.com**

This superb site has a lot to offer. It benefits from a wonderful panorama of the Colli Fiorentini hills with acres of the Zecchi family vineyards to the east adding to its appeal and is just 15 km. from Florence. The charming and hard working owners Marcello and Daniella have a wine producing background and you can purchase their fine wines at the site's shop. Their aim is to provide an enjoyable and peaceful atmosphere for families. All 106 pitches are of a good size and have electricity and larger units are welcome. On arrival you are escorted to view available pitches then assisted in taking up your chosen place. The restaurant offers excellent Tuscan fare including pizzas, pastas and delicate 'cucina casalinga' (home cooking). An attractive flower-bedecked terrace overlooks the two pools. Enjoy the views and revel in the choice of Chianti from the region. A bus runs directly from the site to the city. English is spoken at this delightful family site.

Facilities

Two spotless sanitary blocks with a mix of British and Turkish style WCs are a pleasure to use. Three private sanitary units for hire. Five very well equipped units for disabled campers. Baby room. Laundry. Motorcaravan services. Gas supplies. Shop. Bar. Restaurant. Takeaway. Swimming pools and jacuzzi (15/5-30/9). New fitness room. Bicycle and scooter hire. Playground and animation for children all season. Excursions and trekking. Internet point. Off site: Tennis 100 m. Fishing 2 km. Golf 12 km.

Open: 18 March - 14 October.

Directions

Exit A1 at Incisa Valdarno southeast of Florence and turn right onto the SS69. After about 4 km. turn left following 'Pian dell Isola' and follow the site signs. GPS: N43:42.083 E11:24.316

Charges 2007

Per person	€ 8,50
child (0-10 yrs)	€ 6,00
pitch	€ 14,50

Camping Village
Il Poggetto

Good bus-connection to Florence

Terraced place situated near Florence, it offers a wonderful view over Tuscany. Large pitches and sanitary facilities of high quality ensure a pleasant stay. At disposal are swimming pool with kids' basin, pizzeria, restaurant and bikes for rent. Ideal starting point for excursions to Florence (bus connection to the centre), Siena, Pisa and Arezzo. Taste the world-famous Chianti in one of the many wine properties. Private bathrooms, bungalows, bedrooms, maxi caravans and apartments. To reach us: motorway A1 Bologna-Rome, exit Incisa turn right and follow the road markings for 4 km. Turn left following the road markings for the campsite. **Open from 18.03. to 15.10.2008.**

GPS: N 43° 42' 05" - E 11° 24' 19"

REGIONE TOSCANA
TOSCANA   COMUNITÀ EUROPEA
Realizzato con il contributo regionale L.R. 28/97 ex art. 10 annualità 2007

TOSCANA Arte Mare Monti

Via Il Poggetto, 143 • I-50067 Troghi (FI) • Tel. and Fax 0039/0558307323
www.campingilpoggetto.com • info@campingilpoggetto.com

IT66310 Camping Mareblu

Localitá Mazzanta, I-57023 Cecina Mare (Tuscany)

Tel: **058 662 9191**. Email: **info@campingmareblu.com**

Mareblu is a well equipped family site with an impressive range of amenities, including a large swimming pool with an attractive terraced surround, and shopping complex incorporating a greengrocer, hairdressing salon, newsagent and internet centre. There is also a sandy beach 300 metres away, accessed through a pine wood. The pitches at Mareblu are well shaded and are all equipped with electrical connections (6A). Parking for all cars is in a dedicated area at the front of the site which ensures a pleasant traffic-free ambience within the site. The site is close to Cecina Mare, a popular resort with easy access to some of Tuscany's great cities, and the island of Elba.

Facilities

Five modern toilet blocks include facilities for disabled visitors. Shopping centre. Bar, restaurant and self-service cafeteria, pizzeria and takeaway. Swimming and paddling pools. Play area. Games field. Boules. Bicycle hire. Animation. Miniclub. Internet access. Direct access to beach. Off site: Tennis. Riding. Watersports and diving. Excursions.

Open: 20 March - 16 October.

Directions

Site is south of Livorno. From north, take A12 to Rosignano and then join the E80 to Vada, then to La Mazzanta. From here site is well signed. GPS: N43:19.105 E10:28.411

Charges 2007

Per person	€ 4,30 - € 8,10
child (0-10 yrs)	€ 3,20 - € 6,50
pitch incl. electricity	€ 5,50 - € 12,50

Camping Cheques accepted.

IT66000 Camping Barco Reale

Via Nardini 11-13, I-51030 San Baronto di Lamporecchio (Tuscany)

Tel: **057 388 332**. Email: **info@barcoreale.com**

Just forty minutes from Florence and an hour from Pisa, this site is beautifully situated high in the Tuscan hills close to the fascinating town of Pistoia. Part of an old walled estate, there are impressive views of the surrounding countryside. It is a quiet site of 15 hectares with 250 pitches with good shade from mature pines and oaks. Some pitches are huge with great views and others are very private. Most are for tourers, but some have difficult access (site provides tractor assistance). All 175 touring pitches have electricity and 50 have water and drainage. The site has an attractive bar, a smart restaurant with terraces (try the brilliant traditional dishes) and a leased shop. The pools have really stunning views to the west (on a clear day you may see the island of Capraia). Pleasant walks are available in the grounds of the estate. This is a most attractive and popular site, which will appeal to those who prefer a quiet site but with plenty to do for all age groups. Used by tour operators. Member of Leading Campings Group.

Facilities

Three modern sanitary blocks are well positioned and kept very clean. Good facilities for disabled people (dedicated pitches close by). Baby room. Laundry facilities. Motorcaravan services. Dog shower. Restaurant. Bar. Disco. Shop. Supervised and enlarged swimming pool (caps required; 1/5-30/9). Ice cream shop (1/6-31/8). Playgrounds. Bicycle hire. Internet point. Entertainment. Cooking lessons for Tuscan style food. Excursions. Off site: Village 1 km. Fishing 8 km. Golf 15 km.

Open: 1 April - 30 September.

Directions

From Pistoia take Vinci - Empoli - Lamporecchio signs to San Baronto. From Empoli signs to Vinci and San Baronto. Final approach involves a sharp bend and a steep slope. GPS: N43:50.514 E10:54.678

Charges 2008

Per person	€ 7,10 - € 9,90
child (3-11 yrs)	€ 3,80 - € 6,20
pitch	€ 10,00 - € 15,50

Credit cards accepted for amounts over € 155. Discounts for longer stays.

IT66450 **Parco Delle Piscine**

Via del Bagno Santo 29, I-53047 Sarteano (Tuscany)

Tel: **057 826 971**. Email: **info@parcodellepiscine.it**

On the spur of Monte Cetona, Sarteano is a spa, and this large, smart site utilises that spa in its very open environs. The site is well run with an excellent infrastructure and there is a friendly welcome from the English speaking staff. The 509 individual, flat pitches, are all of a good size and fully marked with high neat hedges giving real privacy. The novel feature is the three unique swimming pools fed by the natural thermo-mineral springs. These springs have been known since antiquity as 'del Bagno Santo' which flows at a constant temperature of about 24 degrees. Two of these pools (the largest is superb with water cascade and hydro-massage, and the other large shallow pool is just for children) are set in a huge park-like ground with many picnic tables. They are free to all those staying on the site. A third excellent pool is on the site itself and is opened in the main season for the exclusive use of campers. Delle Piscine is really good as a sightseeing base or as an overnight stop from the Florence - Rome motorway (it is 6 km. from the exit). The views from the town are unusual, over both Umbria and Tuscany.

Facilities

Two heated toilet blocks are of high quality with mainly British style WCs. Motorcaravan services. Restaurant/pizzeria with bar. Takeaway. Coffee bar. Swimming pools (one all season). Satellite TV room and mini-cinema with 100 seats and large screen. Tennis. Free guided cultural tours. Internet. Dogs are not accepted. Off site: Bicycle hire 100 m. Riding 3 km.

Open: 1 April - 30 September.

Directions

From autostrada A1 take Chiusi/Chianciano exit, from where Sarteano is well signed (6 km). In Sarteano follow camping/piscine signs to site. GPS: N42:59.249 E11:51.898

Charges 2007

Per person	€ 10,00 - € 14,00
child (3-10 yrs)	€ 6,00 - € 8,00
pitch incl. electricity	€ 14,50 - € 25,00

IT66290 **Camping Tripesce**

Via Cavalleggeri 88, I-57018 Vada (Tuscany)

Tel: **058 678 8167**. Email: **info@campingtripesce.com**

Neat and tidy, this family owned and run site has the great advantage of direct beach access through three gates (CCTV). The beach is of fine sand with a very gentle shelving – super for children, watersports and has a lifeguard in season. This great beach makes up for the lack of a pool on the site and the fairly small size of the 230 pitches. All have 4A electricity and 60 are serviced with water and drainage with some shade provided by young trees and artificial shade. The site is contained within a rectangle and bungalows for rent are placed near reception. Everything is kept spotlessly clean. The site has many German guests as demonstrated in the German language notices around the site. If you are a beach enthusiast this could be for you, especially the beachside pitches.

Facilities

Three clean, fresh toilet blocks provide hot and cold showers (water is solar heated and free). British and Turkish style toilets. Facility for disabled visitors. Washing machines. Motorcaravan service points. Bar/restaurant and takeaway. Shop (all season). Excellent beach. Play area (supervision required). Miniclub (high season). Internet terminals and WiFi. Fishing. Dogs are not accepted May - Sept. Off site: Bus service 300 m. Seaside town 1 km.

Open: Week before Easter - 20 October.

Directions

From S1 autostrada (free) between Livorno and Grosseto head south and take Vada exit. Site is well signed along with many others as you approach the town.

Charges 2007

Per person	€ 4,00 - € 7,00
child (0-7 yrs)	€ 2,50 - € 4,00
pitch incl. car and electricity	€ 11,00 - € 20,00
No credit cards.	

IT66380 Park Albatros Camping Village

Viale della Principessa, I-57027 San Vincenzo (Tuscany)

Tel: **056 570 1018**. Email: **parkalbatros@ecvacanze.it**

Camping Albatros is another venture for the Cardini/Vanucchi families and is situated on the historic Costa Degli Etruschi where natural parks abound. A group of conical buildings form the hub of the original, somewhat dated, infrastructure of Albatros. This theme of circles is continued through the peaceful new development in the form of round buildings and the placing of mobile homes in curves. The 300 new touring pitches (110 sq.m) are in a separate area on flat ground. All have water, drainage, 10A electricity and some shade from newly planted trees. The restaurant, bar and shopping complex are under natural pines at the hub. They provide a quality range of goods and services. There is also a vast new, air-conditioned supermarket and a new (2007) lagoon pool, bar and entertainment area. The new, architect designed, circular, bamboo covered toilet block on the touring side is amazing with brilliant children's rooms. Albatros aims to provide a wide range of services. Your visits to the local beach some 800 m. away will be assisted by site transport. There is much to see and explore in the area and a wide range of excursions and walks can be organized by the information point at reception.

Facilities

Two toilet blocks are on site. The new circular block is superb! All WCs are British style and the showers are really good, as are facilities for disabled visitors and children. Washing machines. Central area includes bar, restaurant and pizzeria with large terrace. Animation programme in season. Miniclub (4-12 yrs). Play areas. Lagoon pool complex. Bicycle hire. No barbecues allowed. Internet. Torches very useful. Off site: Beach 800 m. Riding 1 km. Vast choice of excursions and walks. Public transport at gate in high season.

Open: 24 April - 15 October.

Directions

Site is northwest of Grosseto and south of Livorno on the coast. From the SS1 take San Vincenzo exit. Site is well signed as you approach the village.

Charges 2008

Per person	€ 6,00 - € 12,00
child (2-12 yrs)	€ 4,00 - € 9,00
pitch	€ 8,50 - € 17,00
dog	€ 1,50 - € 3,50

IT66600 Camping Maremma Sans Souci

I-58043 Castiglione della Pescaia (Tuscany)

Tel: 056 493 3765. Email: info@maremmasanssouci.it

This delightful seaside site is owned and run by the Perduca family and sits in natural woodland on the coast road between Follonica and Grosseto. The minimum amount of undergrowth has been cleared to provide 370 individually marked and hedged, flat pitches for camping enthusiasts. This offers considerable privacy in individual settings. Some pitches are small and cars may not remain with tents or caravans but must go to a shaded and secure car park near the entrance. There is a wide road for motorcaravans but other roads are mostly narrow and bordered by trees (this is a protected area, and they cannot fell the trees). Access to some parts is difficult so each pitch is earmarked either for caravans or for tents. There are electrical connections for all caravan and motorhome pitches. A positive feature of this site is that there are no seasonal pitches. Only 3 km. from Castiglione della Pescaia, a lively holiday town with an old walled village and castle at the centre, the site is on a small cliff overlooking a marina. An excellent sandy beach is less than 100 m. from one end of the site.

Facilities

Five small, very clean, mature toilet blocks. Free showers. Three blocks have private cabins each with WC, basin and shower. Facilities for disabled campers. Motorcaravan services. Laundry. Shop. Excellent restaurant. Bar with snacks. Sailing school. Torches required in some areas. Dogs are not accepted 16/6-31/8.

Open: 1 April - 31 October.

Directions

Site is 2.5 km. northwest of Castiglione on road to Follonica on the S322. GPS: N42:46.406 E10:50.635

Charges 2007

Per person	€ 7,00 - € 11,00
child (2-6 yrs)	€ 5,00 - € 8,00
pitch and car	€ 9,00 - € 15,00

IT66610 Camping Toscana Village

Via Fornoli, 9, I-56020 Montopoli (Tuscany)

Tel: 057 144 9032. Email: info@toscanavillage.com

Five years ago a forest stood here and was part of the attractive medieval Tuscan village of Montopoli. Toscana Village has been thoughtfully carved out of the mature pines and it is ideal for a sightseeing holiday in this central area. The 150 level pitches (some large) are on shaded terraces and are carefully maintained. Some pitches have full drainage facilities and water, most have electricity (3A). The amenities are centrally located at the top of the hill in a pleasant modern building. English is spoken by the helpful reception staff. The restaurant has a terrace where there are views of the forest. For a swim or sunbathe and to relax, the unusually shaped pool is in a separate area of the site and will be a welcome break after touring the sights in Pisa, Florence and Lucca. This is a quality site tucked away from the hustle and bustle of the cities.

Facilities

One modern central block has excellent facilities including British style toilets, hot water at all the stylish sinks, private cabins and two large en-suite cubicles which may be suitable for disabled campers. Washing machines and dryer. Motorcaravan services. Shop. Gas. Restaurant with terrace (limited menu, evenings only). Takeaway. Bread to order. Swimming pool. Play area. Bicycle hire. Organised activities. Torches useful. Off site: Montopoli village 1 km. Fishing 6 km. Golf and riding 7 km.

Open: All year.

Directions

From A12 autostrada (Genova-Florence) take Pisa Centro exit. Take F1,P1,L1 and then Montopoli exit. Follow signs to Montopoli village. Look for cemetery on right. Opposite is Via Masoria leading to Via Fornoli and site.

Charges 2007

Per person	€ 4,90 - € 7,10
child (2-10 yrs)	free - € 5,00
pitch incl. electricity	€ 11,20 - € 14,90
Camping Cheques accepted.	

IT66750 Camping Cieloverde

Via della Trappola, 180, I-58046 Marina di Grosseto (Tuscany)

Tel: **056 432 1611**. Email: **info@cieloverde.it**

Cieloverde Camping Village lies in the heart of the Tuscan Maremma, between Marina di Grosseto and Principina, bordering the Maremma Natural Park. The huge site lies deep in a long-established pinewood, looking out onto the Costa d'Argento where a sandy beach slopes gently down to the sea. The 1000 touring pitches (all around 100 sq.m.) are in circular zones around sanitary blocks and all have 3A electricity and offer telephone hook-ups. Parking is in designated areas away from the camping area. A wide range of entertainment is organized here, including shows, dance events, open-air cinema and games. There is also a new adventure park, Tarzaland, where it's possible to explore the treetops thanks to a network of aerial walkways, ropes and swings. Surrounding the site is a large natural park where deer, sheep and other animals roam in freedom. The site restaurant and bars are centrally located and here you will find typical Maremma recipes.

Facilities

Modern toilet blocks. Shops, restaurant and takeaway. Pizzeria. Bars. Hairdresser. Play area. Games room. Archery. Cinema. Chapel. Volleyball. Football. 'Tarzaland' adventure park. Transport to the beach. Pets allowed in low season only. Off site: Watersports. Fishing (with licence). Marina di Grossetto. Riding 5 km. Golf 30 km.

Open: 12 May - 23 September.

Directions

The site is west of Grosseto on the coast. Take care here as Grosseto has only one way of crossing the railway for anything other than cars. Follow Grosseto signs from S1 (the Aurelia) and cross town following road to Castiglione della Pescaia until you connect with signs for Marina di Grosseto. Site signed.

Charges 2007

Per person	€ 5,00 - € 13,00
pitch	€ 6,90 - € 17,00

Camping Cheques accepted.

317

IT66710 Camping International Argentario

Localitá Torre Saline, I-58010 Albinia (Tuscany)

Tel: **056 487 0 302**. Email: **info@argentariocampingvillage.com**

Argentario is really two separate campsites with a large holiday villa complex, all sharing the common facilities. The pools, animation area and bar area, like the villa complex are new and elegantly designed. The large irregularly shaped pool and smaller circular paddling pool are very inviting. Entertainment is organised daily by the team where there is something for everyone, young and old. The 806 pitches with 300 for tourers are small but mostly flat and on a surface of dark sand and pine needles, all are shaded by tall pines. The area is quite dusty and many of the pitches are a very long way from the amenities. Motorcaravans are parked in a large separate open square. Some campers may find the long walks trying, especially as the older style facilities are tired and stressed during peak periods. A basic restaurant and pizzeria is remote from the touring section and has no views. The beach of dark sand has attractive views across to the mountains. We see this site more for short stays than extended holidays and as unsuitable for disabled campers.

Facilities

Three mature blocks have mostly Turkish style toilets, a few cramped showers with hot water and cold water at the sinks (showers are very busy at peak periods). Facilities for disabled campers but the sand surface and remoteness of some facilities are unsuitable. Washing machines. Motorcaravan service point. Shop. Restaurant, bar and takeaway. Swimming pools. Tennis. Boat hire. Minigolf. Tennis. ATM. Cars are parked in a separate car park in high season. Torches very useful. Dogs are not accepted. Off site: Bar and restaurant on the beach. Boat launching and riding 1 km. Golf 20 km.

Open: Easter/1 April - 30 September.

Directions

Site is south of Grosetto, off the SS1 at the 150 km. mark, signed Porto S. Stefano. Ignore the first 'combined' campsite sign and proceed 300 m. to the main entrance.

Charges guide

Per person	€ 7,00 - € 11,50
child (1-6 yrs)	€ 4,00 - € 7,00
pitch	€ 7,00 - € 11,50

IT6667 Camping La Finoria

Via Monticello 66, I-58023 Gavorrano (Tuscany)

Tel: **056 684 4381**. Email: **info@campeggiolafinoria.it**

An unusual site, primarily for tents, La Finoria is set high in the mountains with incredible views. It is a rugged site with a focus on nature. Italian school children attend education programmes here. The three motorcaravan pitches are at the top of the site for those who enjoy a challenge, with a dozen caravan pitches on lower terraces accessed by a steep gravel track. Under huge chestnut trees there is a very pretty terraced area for tents. These have a private natural feel which some might say is what camping is all about. Electricity (3A) is available to all pitches, although long leads may be needed. If you visit in November you can help collect the olives and make olive oil or in October gather chestnuts for purée, wild berries in May and make jam. Campers are invited to take part in the educational programmes in the 'LEA' building (Laboratario di Educazione Ambientale). The restaurant reflects the owner's attention to detail – the food here is wonderful and all the pasta is homemade. The views of Elba and the Gulf of Follonica from the terace by day and night are stunning. After an exhausting day communing with nature, or exploring the area, there is a large pool for a refreshing swim before enjoying the night views.

Facilities

Two blocks provide British and Turkish style toilets, hot showers and cold water at washbasins and sinks. Facilities for disabled campers. Washing machines. Quaint, small shop (closed Jan/Feb). Good restaurant and bar (closed Jan/Feb). Swimming pool (May - Sept). Tennis. Lessons on the environment. Excursions. Torches essential. Off site: Riding 2 km. Tennis 3 km. Village 3 km. Bicycle hire 6 km. Golf 8 km. Site's private beach for relaxing and fishing 12 km.

Open: All year.

Directions

From SS1 (Follonica - Grosseto) take Gavorrano exit, then Finoria road. This is a steady, steep climb for some 10 minutes. Start to descend and at junction (the only one), look left downhill for a large white sign to site. GPS: N42:55.350 E10:54.740

Charges 2007

Per person	€ 2,50 - € 10,00
child (1-6 yrs)	€ 2,00 - € 5,00
pitch	€ 4,00 - € 13,00

Toscana
Coste della Maremma • Costa d'Argento
Lazio

Pavilions • Bungalows • Caravans • Camping sites

TALAMONE
Camping Village

58010 TALAMONE (GR)
TEL 0564 / 88 70 26 FAX 0564 / 88 71 70
www.talamonecampingvillage.com
info@talamonecampingvillage.com

ARGENTARIO
Camping Village

58010 ALBINIA (GR)
TEL 0564 / 87 03 02 FAX 0564 / 87 13 80
www.argentariocampingvillage.com
info@argentariocampingvillage.com

IL GABBIANO
Camping Village

58010 ALBINIA (GR)
TEL 0564 / 87 02 02 FAX 0564 / 87 02 02
www.ilgabbianocampingvillage.com
info@il gabbianocampingvillage.com

CLUB DEGLI AMICI
Camping Village

01010 PESCIA ROMANA (VT)
TEL 0766 / 83 02 50 FAX 0766 / 83 17 49
www.clubdegli amicicampingvillage.com
info@clubdegliamicicampingvillage.com

CALIFORNIA
Camping Village

01014 MARINA DI MONTALTO (VT)
TEL 0766 / 80 28 48 FAX 0766 / 80 12 10
www.californiacampingvillage.com
info@californiacampingvillage.com

The Gitav group's establishments are situated along the coast, under secular pinewoods.
They are placed in a very popular area rich of natural, historical and archaeological appeals (oasis, natural parks and sea parks, medieval villages, Etruscan necropolis...).

Private beach
Sunshades
Deck chairs
Swimming pool
Paddle surfboards
Golf (practice range)
Whirlpool
Archery
Canoes
Kayaks
Mini football
Volleyball
Fitness
Tennis
Basketball
Sailing and diving
Entertainment
Miniclub
Dance school, ...

FORMULA CLUB ALL INCLUSIVE

TOSCANA
LAZIO

GITAV 6

CENTRO PRENOTAZIONI GITAV C.P. 71 I - 58010 ALBINIA (GR)
TEL 0039 - 0564 870068 FAX 0039 - 0564 870470 info@gitav.com

www.gitav.com

IT66730 PuntAla Camping Resort

I-58040 Punta Ala (Tuscany)

Tel: **056 492 2294**. Email: **info@campingpuntala.it**

This very large site was established some 35 years ago. Some of the original infrastructure remains and some has been renovated. The pitches vary tremendously in size and position relative to the amenities. With the size of the site some serious distances have to be covered from some areas to the amenities, most of which are near the entrance. There are 300 pitches for touring units on sand on a mainly flat site. All have 25A electricity (67 have water) and shade from very mature pines. Much hedging gives privacy and is quite extensive in parts. Bungalows and mobile homes are prevalent in the northern areas. More expensive, larger pitches are on offer to the north near the amenities and main beach access. We recommend avoiding a section adjacent to a huge treatment plan (alongside the fence)! The site is undergoing a refurbishment programme and we are told the sanitary blocks will all be updated to match the two new blocks. The site has direct access to a 900 m. soft sand beach which gently shelves into the sea (a long walk from some pitches). Watersports are available as are parasols and loungers (extra charge applies). The clientele is mainly Italian and the game here is to place your private brollie at the busy water's edge early in the morning to reserve your place.

Facilities

The nine blocks are a confusing mixture of facilities with some unisex facilities and many private cabins to hire. Two blocks have been rebuilt and these are popular (sometimes with long queues). The older blocks are less popular as they resemble old army blocks, and have mostly Turkish toilets. Unit for disabled campers (but site may be unsuitable due to the terrain). Washing machines and dryer near reception. Motorcaravan service point. Bars, restaurants and takeaway. Minimarket (all season). Animation programme all season. Play areas. WiFi. Bicycle hire. Beach. ATM. Animals are not accepted. Torches essential. Off site: Golf 14 km. Town 6 km.

Open: 1 April - 30 October.

Directions

From E80/S1/Aurelia superstrada take Follonica Nord exit onto S322 following signs for Punta Ala and Castiglione della Pescaia. Watch for district of Pian d'alma marked on maps – look for the Total petrol station on the right, go 450 m. past it and look for small white restaurant La Violina on the right. Site is now signed to the right along a narrow road. Watch for some nasty speed bumps. After 2 km. cross bridge and park on the left. Avoid town of Punta Ala – site is not on that road.

Charges 2007

Per person	€ 5,80 - € 17,30
child (2-9 yrs)	€ 4,10 - € 12,10
pitch	€ 5,50 - € 27,60

IT66770 **Camping Baia dei Gabbiani**

I-58020 Scarlino (Tuscany)

Tel: **0566 866158**. Email: **info@baiadeigobbiani.com**

Baia dei Gabbiani is a long and narrow site, situated between the busy S322 and the beach north of Puntino di Scarlino, 4 km. from the seaside resort of Follonica. The small pitches are on level ground and most have electrical connections. A range of amenities are on offer including a restaurant, bar and supermarket. The site has direct access to the beach and a lively activity programme is organised in peak season. Puntino is just 400 m. away and has a yachting harbour as well as a good selection of shops, bars and restaurants. The beach adjacent to the campsite has views towards Elba, and is popular for windsurfing, surfing and other water sports. The beautiful, unspoilt bays of Cala Violina and Cala Martina lie to the south and can be accessed on foot, by mountain bike or by boat.

Facilities

The sanitary block is old and provides mainly Turkish style toilets, washbasins and token operated showers. Restaurant and bar. Shop. Playground. Entertainment and activity programme in high season. Direct beach access. Chalets for rent. Off site: Puntino 400 m. Follonica 4 km. Siena, Florence and Pisa are all within 2 hours drive.

Open: 26 May - 16 September.

Directions

From Livorno take the southbound S1 Via Aurelia. Leave at Follonica Nord exit. Head initially towards Follonica and then towards Grosseto. Site is signed to the right on the S322, just before the small town of Scarlino. GPS: N42:53.599 E10:47.154

Charges 2007

Per person	€ 6,90 - € 11,70
child (3-7 yrs)	€ 5,20 - € 7,60
pitch incl. electricity	€ 9,70 - € 15,30

IT66810 **Camping Capalbio**

Strada Litoranea del Chiarone, Localitá Graticciaia, I-58010 Capalbio Scalo (Tuscany)

Tel: **056 489 0101**. Email: **mauro.ricci@ilcampeggiodicapalbio.it**

Camping di Capalbio is a coastal site in southern Tuscany. This site has been recommended by our Italian agent and we plan to undertake a full inspection in 2008. The site is next to a wide sandy beach and has a good range of amenities, including a bar, restaurant and supermarket. There are 175 shady pitches here including a number of mobile homes. Various activities are organised on the beach including volleyball and a number of games and competitions. This is a lively site in peak season with entertainment based around the beachside bar and restaurant. This part of southern Tuscany is sometimes overlooked given the wealth of places of interest further north. However, the ancient village of Capalbio and the beautiful Lago di Burano are both well worth discovering.

Facilities

Supermarket. Bar. Restaurant. Beach bar. Takeaway food. Motorcaravan services. Entertainment and activities in peak season.Direct access to beach. Play area. Mobile homes and chalets for rent. Off site: Capalbio 12 km. Lago di Burano Nature Reserve 4 km. Saturnia hot springs and thermal spa 30 km. Walking and cycle trails.

Open: 30 March - 23 September.

Directions

Head south from Livorno and Pisa on the SS1 (Via Aurelia). Shortly after passing the Lago di Burano, ignore sign to Capalbio to the left, but take the next road to the right (signed Chiarone Scalo). Site is well signed from here. GPS: N42:22.837 E11:26.848

Charges 2008

Per person	€ 6,00 - € 13,00
child (4-8 yrs)	€ 4,00 - € 8,00
pitch incl. electricity	€ 6,00 - € 15,00

IT66090 Camping Internazionale

Via San Cristofano 2, Bottai, I-50029 Firenze (Tuscany)

Tel: 055 237 4704. Email: internazionale@florencecamping.com

Camping Internazionale is set in the hills about 5 km. south of Florence, and 8 km. from the Duomo with its wonderful dome by Brunelleschi. There is a 800 m. walk to a bus stop which will take you into Florence. This is a well shaded, terraced site with 240 touring pitches set around the top of a hill. These all have electricity with water obtained from the laundry and kitchen areas or the motorhome service point only. The site is often lively at night with young people from tour groups enjoying themselves, however this area is located well away from the touring pitches. Although it is a very green site, the camping area is somewhat more open with two electricity pylons at the top of the hill and some noise from the busy motorway which is below and next to the site. The two toilet blocks are clean and well equipped with many washing machines and dryers. Although showers are a little small they are fully adjustable with free hot water. There is a kitchen area stocked with pots, pans etc, gas hobs and free use of refrigerators. Two good sized pools, one for children, are fenced with a nice playground adjacent. The inviting restaurant with its open bar area has a good menu. This site offers an easily accessible location to explore Florence and of the city sites, is probably the most family friendly.

Facilities

Two toilet blocks include free hot showers. Laundry. Kitchen facilities. Motorcaravan service point. Shop. Bar and restaurant. Evening entertainment. Two swimming pools. Playground. New bar and restaurant at the lower level. Off site: Florence 5 km.

Open: 1 April - 31 October.

Directions

From A1 take Firenza Certosa exit towards Florence. The turn to the site is just outside Bottai – turn left if coming from this direction (if you reach Galluzzo you have gone too far). From Florence take Via Senese (S2) through Galluzzo, turn right at site sign just before entering Bottai. Continue 500 m. to site. GPS: N43:43.425 E11:13.179

Charges 2007

Per person	€ 9,50
child (3-12 yrs)	€ 6,50
pitch	€ 6,00 - € 16,00

IT66430 Camping Village Europa

Localitá San Donato, 8, I-06065 Passignano sul Trasimeno (Umbria)

Tel: 075 827405. Email: **info@camping-europa.it**

The shores of Lake Trasimeno are dotted with a large number of campsites but we feel that Camping Village Europa has something different to offer. This is a high quality friendly site which, with just 100 pitches, is relatively small but which still manages to offer a wide range of amenities. The pitches are separated into four groups by clusters of mature trees, although shade on the pitches is quite limited. All the pitches offer 6A electrical connections. A regular bus service links the site with the nearby town of Passignano and its railway station. On site amenities include a swimming pool, bar, restaurant, pizzeria and well stocked shop. The site has its own private beach on Lake Trasimeno with a wide range of watersports available and beach parties in peak season.

Facilities

Three toilet blocks are maintained to a high standard with facilities for disabled users. Washing machines and dryers. Shop. Bar, restaurant, pizzeria and takeaway. Swimming pool. Play area. Children's club. Evening entertainment. Sports pitch. Direct access to lake and beach. Off site: Passignano 2 km. Perugia 30 km. Assisi 45 km. Riding, tennis, watersports.

Open: Easter - 10 October.

Directions

From Passignano take the road towards Perugia. Turn off this road after 1 km. and the site is clearly signed. GPS: N43:10.933 E12:09.900

Charges 2007

Per person	€ 5,50 - € 7,00
child (3-10 yrs)	€ 4,70 - € 6,00
caravan	€ 6,00 - € 7,00
motorcaravan	€ 6,50 - € 7,50
tent	€ 5,30 - € 6,30

IT66490 Camping Punta Navaccia

I-06069 Tuoro sul Trasimeno (Umbria)

Tel: 075 826 357. Email: **navaccia@camping.it**

Situated on the north side of Lake Trasimeno and run by friendly and welcoming owners, this is a large site with over 70,000 sq.m. and 400 touring pitches (200 with 4A electricity) and all with shade. The campsite has a long (stony) beach with facilities for mooring and launching your boat. There are 60 mobile homes with air conditioning for rent. The site is ideally located for exploring Umbria and its famous cities, such as Assisi and Perugia. Tuscany and its cities of Siena and Florence are also within easy reach and it is even possible to visit Rome for a day trip. The area surrounding the site also has a lot to offer, with an interesting historical past. It was here in 217BC that the historical battle of Tuoro del Trasimeno (battle of the Romans and Carthaginians) took place. The events of the battle can be retraced step by step. However, the main attraction here is of course the lake, ideal for swimming and a variety of watersports.

Facilities

Sanitary block with British style WCs, showers and some private cabins. Washing machine and dryer. Motorcaravan service point. Heated swimming and paddling pools. Shop. Restaurant and takeaway (April - Oct). Play area. Tennis. Table tennis. Large covered amphitheatre. Disco. Cinema screen. Miniclub. Animation is organised in high season (in Italian, English, German and Dutch). Boat launching. Daily boat trip around island (free). Off site: Sandy beach 200 m. Windsurfing, sailing and canoeing 200 m.

Open: 15 March - 31 October.

Directions

Going south on the A1 (Florence/Firenze - Rome), take exit for Val di Chiana to Perugia near Bettolle. After 15 km. take Tuoro sul Trasimeno exit. Site is well signed.

Charges 2007

Per unit incl. 2 persons	€ 17,00 - € 27,00
extra person	€ 5,50 - € 8,00
child (2-9 yrs)	€ 4,00 - € 6,00

IT66510 Camping Polvese

I-06060 S Arcangelo sul Trasimeno (Umbria)

Tel: 075 848 078. Email: cpolvese@interfree.it

Beside the lake, Polvese takes its name from the island which can be seen clearly from the site. The 80 tourist pitches (all with 6-10A electricity) are in two areas, generally separated from the very permanent pitches rented by Italian and German guests. On flat ground, the older pitches are reasonably sized, with some by the lake. Mature trees provide good shade. Children have a separate shallow pool in which to play and the adult pool is clean and pleasant. The restaurant has lake views and a pleasant terrace. It is run as a separate business. The very small bar doubles as a shop selling basics for campers. There is a miniclub in high season plus a little entertainment for adults in the evening, and a slightly tired outdoor cinema. Tours are organised along with tastings of the fare produced in Umbria. We see this as a site for short visits rather than extended stays.

Facilities

Modernised sanitary block with free hot showers. British and Turkish style toilets and cold water at all the sinks. Facilities for disabled campers. Washing machine. Motorcaravan services. Restaurant (not owned by site). Basic bar - doubles as shop. TV. Outdoor cinema (basic). Swimming pool. Bicycle hire. Barbecue area. Torches required. Off site: Riding 2 km. Golf (8 hole) 5 km.

Open: 1 April - 1 October.

Directions

Site is on south side of Lake Trasimino. From Florence - Rome autostrada take Magione exit and lakeside road south to S. Arcangelo. Site is well signed.

Charges 2007

Per person	€ 5,00 - € 6,00
child (3-10 yrs)	€ 3,50 - € 4,50
pitch and car	€ 6,00 - € 8,00
Camping Cheques accepted.	

I-06060 S. Arcangelo di Magione (PERUGIA)
Tel. 0039 075848078 • Fax 0039 075848050
E-mail: cpolvese@interfree.it • www.polvese.com

Polvese Campsite offers an attractive and peaceful setting with excellent resident services, and is ideal for a pleasant and enjoyable holiday for families and nature lovers. The mobile homes are set in the new part of the Camping Site, which lies right on the lake behind a chain of gentle hills with wonderful thick Mediterranean vegetation. Each mobile home has a bedroom with a double bed, a room for the children with 2-3 beds, a day room with a kitchen corner and a bathroom (with a shower, washbasins, WC); many also have air conditioning. Prices are "all-inclusive" (comprising electricity, gas, cleaning at the end of your stay and use of the Campsite's sports - and recreational facilities) and vary according to the period and number of people. Laundry is not included. 2 swimming pools, a children's play area, small football, tennis, beach-volley, bowls, table tennis. Restaurant, pizzeria for take-away pizzas, bar, mini-market, washing-machine, cold store, camper service, individual bathrooms. Animation and baby-club (July-August), excursions, bike hire, dancing, cinema, piano bar, maxi-screen, safe, credit cards, cash point.

IT66530 Camping Listro

Via Lungolago, I-06061 Castiglione del Lago (Umbria)

Tel: 075 951 193. Email: listro@listro.it

This is a simple, pleasant, flat site with the best beach on Lake Trasimeno. Listro provides 110 pitches all with electricity with 70% of the pitches enjoying the shade of mature trees. Younger campers are in a separate area of the site, ensuring no noise disturbance and some motorcaravan pitches are right on the lakeside giving stunning views out of your windows. Facilities are fairly limited with a small shop, bar and snack bar, and there is no organised entertainment. English is spoken and British guests are particularly welcome. If you enjoy the simple life and peace and quiet in camping terms, then this site is for you. The site's beach is private and the lake has very gradually sloping beaches making it very safe for children to play and swim. This also results in very warm water, which is kept clean as fishing and tourism are the major industries hereabouts. Listro is a few hundred yards north of the historic town of Castiglione and the attractive town can be seen rising up the hillside from the site.

Facilities

Two screened sanitary facilities are very clean with British and Turkish style WCs. Facilities for disabled visitors. Washing machine. Motorcaravan services. Bar. Shop. Snack bar. Play area. Table tennis. Fishing. Bicycle hire. Private beach. Off site: Town 800 m. Bars and restaurants nearby. Good swimming pool and tennis courts (discounts using the campsite card).

Open: 1 April - 30 September.

Directions

From A1/E35 Florence-Rome autostrada take Val di Chiana exit and join the Perugia (75 bis) superstrada. After 24 km. take Castiglione exit and follow town signs. Site is clearly signed just before the town. GPS: N43:08.000 E12:02.390

Charges 2007

Per person (over 3 yrs)	€ 3,80 - € 4,50
pitch	€ 3,80 - € 4,50
car	€ 1,30 - € 1,80
Less 10% for stays over 8 days in low season.	

IT66520 Camping Villaggio Italgest

Via Martiri di Cefalonia, I-06060 Sant Arcangelo Magione (Umbria)

Tel: **075 848 238**. Email: **camping@italgest.com**

Directly on the shore on the south side of Lake Trasimeno, which is almost midway between the Mediterranean and the Adriatic, Sant Arcangelo is ideally placed for exploring Umbria and Tuscany. The area around the lake is fairly flat but has views of the distant hills and can become very hot during summer. Villaggio Italgest is a pleasant site with 208 touring pitches on level grass and, except for the area next to the lake, under a cover of tall trees. All pitches have electrical connections and cars are parked away from the pitches. The site offers a wide variety of activities, tours are organised daily and there is entertainment for children and adults in high season, including Italian language and civilisation courses. The bar/disco remains open until 2 am. There is a good sized swimming pool area, one pool with slides, a smaller paddling pool and a whirlpool. The site has a marina for boats with a crane. Whether you wish to use this site as a base for exploration or as a place to relax, you will find this a most pleasant place to stay. English is spoken.

Facilities

The one large and two smaller sanitary blocks have mainly British style WCs and free hot water in the washbasins and showers. Facilities for disabled people. Motorcaravan services. Washing machines and dryers. Kitchen. Bar, restaurant, pizzeria and takeaway (all season). Mini-market. Swimming pool. Tennis. Play area. TV (satellite) and games rooms. Disco. Films. Watersports, motor boat hire and lake swimming. Fishing. Mountain bike and scooter hire. Internet point. Wide range of activities, entertainment and excursions. Off site: Golf, parachuting, riding, canoeing and sailing close.

Open: 23 March - 30 September.

Directions

Site is on the southern shore of Lake Trasimeno. Take Magione exit from the Perugia spur of the Florence - Rome autostrada, proceed southwest round the lake to S. Arcangelo where site is signed. GPS: N43:05.180 E12:09.230

Charges 2007

Per person	€ 6,00 - € 8,40
child (3-9 yrs)	€ 4,00 - € 6,00
pitch	€ 6,00 - € 9,50
small tent pitch	€ 5,00 - € 5,00
car	€ 2,00 - € 2,50

Camping Cheques accepted.

IT67850 Camping Internazionale Lago di Bracciano

Via del Pianolo 4, I-00069 Trevignano Romano (Lazio)

Tel: 069 985 032. Email: info@camping-inter-lagodibracciano.com

Lago di Bracciano, just 45 km. north of Rome, is of a size that provides excellent opportunities for watersports and is inevitably very popular with windsurfers. With some pitches alongside a little beach, the site provides 110 pitches of which about 50 are for tourers. Our pitch had a full view of the lake and the gentle breeze made the temperature at the end of June quite bearable. Some shade is provided by large trees. A bar and restaurant near the entrance are behind the site's small swimming pool and play area. The local bus has a regular service to Rome. There are opportunities for excursions that the site owners will be pleased to tell you about.

Facilities

The single toilet block is well equipped. Facilities for disabled visitors. Washing machine. Motorcaravan service point. Small shop. Bar and restaurant/pizzeria. Small swimming pool (15/5-15/9). Play area. Barbecue area (not allowed on pitches). Internet access. Mobile homes and bungalows to rent. Off site: Lago di Bracciano.

Open: 1 April - 30 October.

Directions

From the Rome GRA take exit 5 on SS2 towards Cassia. Turn left at Trevignano exit (km. 35) and follow SP4a towards the lake where you will find the site on the left. The access road and gate are max. 2.6 m. wide. GPS: N42:08.683 E12:16.119

Charges 2007

Per person	€ 6,00 - € 7,00
pitch incl. car	€ 11,00 - € 14,00

IT68100 Camping Seven Hills

Via Cassia 1216, I-00189 Roma (Lazio)

Tel: 063 031 0826. Email: info@sevenhills.it

Close to Rome, this site provides a quieter, garden setting in some areas, but has a very lively, busy atmosphere in others. It is situated in a delightful valley, flanked by two of the seven hills of Rome and is just off the autostrada ring road (GRA) to the north of the city. The site runs a bus shuttle service every 30 minutes in the mornings to the local station and one return bus to Rome each day. The 80 pitches for touring units (3A electricity to some) are not marked, but the management supervise in busy periods. Arranged in two sections, the top half, near the entrance, restaurant and shop consists of small, flat, grass terraces with two to four pitches on each, with smaller terraces for tents. Access to some pitches may be tricky. The flat section at the lower part of the site is reserved mainly for ready erected tents and cabins used by international tour operators who bring guests by coach. Consequently there may be a little extra noise, so choose your pitch carefully. The site is a profusion of colour with flowering trees and shrubs and a good covering of trees provides shade.

Facilities

Three soundly constructed sanitary blocks are well situated around the site, with open plan washbasins, and hot water in the average sized showers. Facilities for disabled campers. Well stocked shop. Bar/restaurant and terrace. Money exchange. Swimming pool at the bottom of the site with bar/snack bar and a room where the younger element tends to congregate (separate pool charge). Disco. Excursions. Bungalows to rent. Off site: Golf 4 km.

Open: 15 March - 1 November.

Directions

From autostrada ring road exit 3 take Via Cassia (signed SS2 Viterbo, NOT Via Cassia Bis) and look for site signs. Turn right after 1 km. and follow small road, Via Italo Piccagli for 1 km. to site. This narrow twisting road is heavily parked on during the day. GPS: N41:59.580 E12:25.011

Charges 2007

Per person (over 4 yrs)	€ 8,50 - € 9,50
pitch	€ 10,50 - € 12,00
No credit cards.	

IT68090 Camping Tiber

Via Tiberina km 1,400, I-00188 Roma (Lazio)

Tel: 063 361 0733. Email: **info@campingtiber.com**

An excellent city site with sound facilities and a dynamic approach to hosting visitors during their stay, Camping Tiber is also remarkably peaceful. It is ideally located for visiting Rome with an easy train service (20 minutes to Rome) a free shuttle bus every 30 minutes and trams for later at night. The 350 tourist pitches (with electricity) are mostly shaded under very tall trees and many have very pleasant views over the river Tiber. This mighty river winds around two sides of the site boundary (safely fenced) providing a cooling effect for campers. There is a new section with some shade, and bungalows to rent are in a separate area. A small but pleasant outdoor pool with a bar awaits after a busy day in the city. The excellent main bar, beer garden and restaurant all have terraces and, along with the takeaway, give good value. The site is extremely well run and especially good for campers with disabilities. Visiting the delights of Rome is easy from here.

Facilities

Fully equipped, very smart sanitary facilities include hot water everywhere, private cabins, a baby room and very good facilities for disabled campers. Laundry facilities. Motorcaravan service point. Shop. Bar, restaurant, pizzeria and takeaway. Swimming pool (hat required) and bar (15/3-31/10). Play area. Fishing. Internet access. Free shuttle bus to the underground station every 15 or 30 minutes according to season. Torches useful. WiFi. Off site: Local bars, restaurants and shops. Golf or riding 20 km.

Open: 15 March - 31 October.

Directions

From Florence, exit at Rome Nord Fiano on A1 and turn south onto Via Tibernia and site is signed. From other directions on Rome ring road (GRA) take exit 6 northbound on S3 Via Flaminia following signs to Tibernia. GPS: N42:00.570 E12:30.140

Charges 2007

Per person	€ 9,20 - € 10,50
child (3-12 yrs)	€ 6,40 - € 7,60
pitch	€ 7,00 - € 12,20

IT68110 I Pini Camping

Via delle Sassete 1/A, Fiano Romano, I-00065 Roma (Lazio)

Tel: **0765 453349**. Email: **ipini@ecvacanze.it**

The many years Roberto and his Australian born wife Judy have spent in the camping industry are reflected in this site, built only a few years ago. The 117 pitches are set on shaded grassy terraces with views of the nearby hills, access is easy for all units via tarmac roads, and everything is here, including a well stocked and reasonable supermarket. The beautifully designed restaurant with its high ceilings and wooden beams are typical of the thought that has gone into making I Pini a place where you can relax between exciting visits discovering the wonders of Rome or other nearby attractions. What could be more wonderful after several days or nights in Rome (travelling to and from I Pini by air conditioned bus) exploring all the amazing sights before returning to the cool breezes of this hillside site. Simone, Roberto's daughter is responsible for the restaurant and we recommend sampling the excellent menu on the large terrace with views and entertainment in high season. This is a family business with son Robbie also sharing in the task of making your stay enjoyable.

Facilities

The single excellent sanitary block is spotless and hot water is free in showers, washbasins and sinks. Two well equipped units for disabled visitors. Washing machines and dryers. Motorcaravan services. Bar. Restaurant. Snack bar and pizza oven. Pleasant market. Swimming pool. Tennis. Play area. Entertainment (1/6-30/8). Internet access. Buses to Rome daily. Off site: Fishing 3 km. Golf and riding 20 km.

Open: 15 March - 1 November.

Directions

From Rome ring road (GRA) take A1 exit to Fiano Romano. As you enter the town turn right along via Belvedere opposite an IP petrol station and follow camping signs - there is only the one site.
GPS: N42:09.360 E12:34.370

Charges 2007

Per person	€ 8,70 - € 10,50
child (3-12 yrs)	€ 5,60 - € 6,90
Electricity included.	

VIA DELLE SASSETTE, 11/A • 00065 • FIANO ROMANO (ROMA) • ITALY
TEL. +39 0765 453349 • FAX +39 0765 453057 • IPINI@ECVACANZE.IT •

IT68120 Camping Roma Flash

Via Settevene Palo km 19,800, I-00062 Bracciano (Lazio)

Tel: **069 980 5458**. Email: **info@romaflash.it**

This excellent site is in a superb location with magnificent views over Lake Bracciano, the source of Rome's drinking water. When we visited, although it was busy, it was still peaceful and relaxing. There are 275 pitches in total and facilities include a restaurant with a large terrace and small indoor area both overlooking the lake where you can enjoy a good menu and excellent pizzas. The owners Elide and Eduardo speak excellent English and happily go out of their way to ensure guests enjoy their holiday. Many of the visitors told us that they return year after year and some stay for several weeks at a time, enjoying all that the Lazio region has to offer.

Facilities

Two new large toilet blocks are very well appointed. Free hot water throughout and fully adjustable showers. Facilities for disabled visitors and a children Off site: Rome (40 minutes).

Open: 1 April - 30 September.

Directions

From E35/E45 north of Rome, take Settebagni exit. Follow GRA orbital road west to Cassia exit. Follow sign for Lago Bracciano to town of Bracciano. Site is well signed south east of town on the SP4A.
GPS: N42:07.896 E12:10.423

Charges 2007

Per person	€ 5,00 - € 7,50
child (3-10 yrs)	€ 3,00 - € 5,00
pitch incl. car	€ 9,00 - € 15,50
Camping Cheques accepted.	

IT68190 Camping Villaggio Settebello

Via Flacca km 3,6, I-04020 Salto di Fondi (Lazio)

Tel: 077 159 9132. Email: settebello@settebellocamping.com

The SS213 road hugs this beautiful coast line for many miles, running between small towns and villages and alongside the pine forests that are directly behind the beach. Settebello, an attractive and well managed site, is in a rural area but unfortunately the site straddles this busy road and inevitably there is traffic noise. The touring pitches are all on the beach side of the site in a wooded area. The ground rises before the beach and this is where many of the bungalows for rent have been built. With a total of 600 pitches about 260 are available for tourers. The remainder are used for seasonal caravans (225), mobile homes for rent (16) and bungalows (101). Given the site's popularity, it naturally provides many sporting and social activities. Being midway between Rome and Naples, it is a good point to break a journey when travelling, or perhaps for a longer stay in the low season.

Facilities

Five toilet blocks include showers, WCs (Turkish and British style) and washbasins. Facilities for disabled visitors. Motorcaravan service point. Small shop. Bar and restaurant. New swimming pool and children's pool (1/6-30/8). Skating. Tennis. Minigolf. Entertainment and children's club. Disco. Amphitheatre and cinema. Pets are not accepted. Bungalows and mobile homes to rent. Off site: Narrow public beach. Bicycle hire 2 km. Fondi 10 km. Riding 20 km. Watersports.

Open: 1 April - 30 September.

Directions

The Via Flacca is a comparatively short stretch of the SS213 between Sperlonga and Terracina. The site straddles this road at km. 3.6 which is close to Terracina. Turn towards the beach to find reception. GPS: N41:17.689 E13:19.190

Charges 2007

Per unit incl. 2 persons	€ 23,00 - € 52,00
extra person	€ 7,00 - € 14,00
child (3-12 yrs)	€ 6,00 - € 12,00

Camping Cheques accepted.

CAMPING VILLAGE

SETTEBELLO

www.settebellocamping.com

To the south of Rome, directly on the sea, 500 pitches, 100 modern bungalows, 14 mobile homes with private toilet and kitchenette for 2 to 6 people. Bed linen, electricity, gas, fridge, sun shade parasol, deck chair and deck chair in the internal solarium. Swimming pool, restaurant, pizzeria, market, bar, pub, shopping, newspaper kiosk, skate park, disco, sport fittings, internal car park.

Via Flacca - Km 3,600 - I-04020 Salto di Fondi (LATINA) - Tel. 0039/0771599132 - Fax 0039/077157635
settebello@settebellocamping.com

IT68130 Camping Porticciolo

Via Porticciolo, I-00062 Bracciano (Lazio)

Tel: 069 980 3060. Email: info@porticciolo.it

This small family run site, useful for visiting Rome, has its own private beach on the southwest side of Lake Bracciano. A pleasant feature is that the site is overlooked by the impressive castle in the village of Bracciano. There are 170 pitches (160 for tourers) split into two sections, some with lake views and 120 having electricity. Pitches are of average size and shaded by very green trees that are continuously watered in summer by a neat overhead watering system. The friendly bar has two large terraces, shared by the trattoria which opens for lunch and the pizzeria in the evenings.

Facilities

Three somewhat rustic, but clean, sanitary units with children's toilet and showers. Hot showers (by token). Laundry facilities. Motorcaravan services. Gas supplies. Shop (basics). Bar. Trattoria/pizzeria (15/5-5/9). Tennis. Play area. Bicycle hire. Fishing. Internet point and free WiFi. Torches required in some areas. Excursions 'Rome By Night' and nearby nature parks. Off site: Riding 2 km. Bus service from outside the gate runs to central Rome. Air conditioned train service from Bracciano (1.5 km) into the city - the site runs a connecting bus (09.00 daily).

Open: 1 April - 30 September.

Directions

From Rome ring road (GRA) northwest side take Cassia exit to Bracciano S493 (not 'Cassia bis' which is further northeast). Two kilometres before Bracciano village, just after going under a bridge follow site signs and turn along the lake away from Anguillara. Site is 1 km on the SP1f and has a steep entrance. GPS: N42:06.335 E12:11.167

Charges 2007

Per person	€ 4,70 - € 6,50
child (3-10 yrs)	€ 3,50 - € 4,50
pitch incl. electricity	€ 8,70 - € 15,50

329

IT68040 Camping Village Eurcamping

Lungomare Trieste Sud, I-64026 Roseto degli Abruzzi (Abruzzo)

Tel: **085 8993179**. Email: **eurcamping@camping.it**

Eurcamping is about two kilometers south of the small town of Roseto degli Abruzzi, on the small coastal road which runs parallel to the SS16. This is a quiet site, situated beside the sea, with a total of 358 small pitches (many under green screens) and all with electicity (3/6A). There is a small harbour and yacht club nearby and a small sandy section of the beach, about 75 m. away is solely for the use of visitors to the campsite. Accessing the site may be difficult for taller units as you have to pass under the coastal railway line and many of the bridges offer less than 2 m. headroom. There is some road noise but little noise from the railway. There are good facilities and some entertainment is provided for children in high season.

Facilities

Three sanitary blocks with free hot showers. Facilities for disabled people. Motorcaravan services. Laundry. Bar. Restaurant. Takeaway. Pizzeria. Shop. Swimming pools (hats must be worn) with solarium terrace. Play area and sports ground. Tennis. Bowling green. Internet point. Bicycle hire. Enterainment in high season. Clubs for children and teenagers. Pets are allowed only on assigned pitches. Off site: Beach. Canoe and pedalo hire.

Open: 1 April - 30 October.

Directions

From north or south on A14 motorway, take exit for Roseto degli Abruzzi. Turn on SS150 to Roseto degli Abruzzi. From Rome and L'Aquila on A24 take exit for Villa Vomano-Teramo, onto the SS150 (Roseto degli Abruzzi). GPS: N42:39.466 E14:02.116

Charges 2007

Per person	€ 4,00 - € 9,50
child (3-7 yrs)	€ 3,00 - € 6,00
pitch	€ 8,00 - € 16,50

SITUATED IN A QUIET AREA
BOOKING REQUIRED
358 GRASSY, NUMBERED AND GOOD SHADED EMPLACEMENTS (60-110 SM)
BUNGALOW

Lungomare Trieste Sud
64026 Roseto degli Abruzzi (TE)
tel. 085 8993179 • fax 085 8930552
www.eurcamping.it
eurcamping@camping.it

IT68000 Camping Europe Garden

via Belvedere 11, I-64028 Silvi (Abruzzo)

Tel: **085 930 137**. Email: **info@europegarden.it**

This site is 13 kilometres northwest of Pescara and, lying just back from the coast (2 km.) up a very steep hill, it has pleasant views over the sea. The 204 pitches, all with electricity, are mainly on good terraces – access may be difficult on some pitches. However, if installation of caravans is a problem a tractor is available to help. When we visited the site was dry but we suspect life might become difficult on some pitches after heavy rain. Cars stand by units on over half of the pitches or in nearby parking spaces for the remainder, and most pitches are shaded.

Facilities

Two good toilet blocks are well cleaned and provide mixed British and Turkish style WCs. Washing machines. Restaurant. Bar. Swimming pool (300 sq.m; caps compulsory), small paddling pool and jacuzzi. Tennis. Playground. Entertainment programme. Free weekly excursions (15/6-8/9). Free bus service (18/5-7/9) to beach. Dogs are not accepted.

Open: 27 April - 20 September.

Directions

Turn inland off S16 coast road at km. 433 for Silvi Alta and follow camp signs. From A14 autostrada take Pineto exit from north or Pescara Nord exit from the south. GPS: N42:34.043 E14:05.548

Charges 2007

Per person	€ 5,00 - € 10,00
child (0-3 yrs)	€ 4,00 - € 7,50
pitch	€ 10,00 - € 16,50
2-man tent	€ 6,00 - € 13,00
electricity	€ 2,50

No credit cards.
Discounts for longer stays outside high season.

Check real time availability and at-the-gate prices...

www.**alanrogers**.com

IT67915 Camping Le Foci

Via Fonte dei Cementi, I-67030 Opi (Abruzzo)

Tel: 0863 912233. Email: lefoci@tin.it

Le Foci has a fine setting high in the Abruzzo National Park. This site has been recommended by our Italian agent and we plan to conduct an inspection in 2008. There are 210 pitches here, of which 80 are reserved for tents and the balance for caravans or motorhomes. All pitches are equipped with electrical connections (5A). This is dramatic mountain country and the tranquility is disturbed only by cow bells. The delightful mountain village of Opi is close and from here the views are amongst the fnest in the National Park. The site was created by the Ferrazza family in 1980 with a desire to create a holiday centre in harmony with its beautiful environment. Since then, all development has been guided by the same principles. A new, low intensity lighting scheme is a good example of this. This is also a very rich area for walking and mountain biking and the site management will be pleased to recommend possible itineraries.

Facilities

Centrally located toilet block with token operated showers. Bar. Restaurant. Shop. TV room. Play area. Caravans for rent. Off site: Nearest town is Opi with bars, shops and restaurants 2 km. Covered swimming pool and tennis 6 km. Riding 2 km. Chair lift 6 km.

Open: All year.

Directions

From the A24 autostrada (Rome - Pescara) take Pescina exit. Join the SS83 following signs to the Abruzzo National Park. Pass through Pescasseroli and contune to Opi, from where the site is well signed.

Charges 2007

Per person	€ 5,00 - € 6,00
child (3-7 yrs)	€ 3,00 - € 4,00
pitch	€ 8,00 - € 9,00

The Camping Le Foci is situated in the middle of the national parc of Abruzzo at a height of 1200mt. In a fabulous pitoresque area surrounded by the impressive valleys and mountains protected by the highest and most affascinating tips of the mountain "Marsicano"

CAMPEGGIO - RISTORO

Camping offer 2008:
2 persons + camper or caravan or tent + electricity 10.00 euro from 01/01/2008 till 30/06/2008 and from 01/09/2008 till 31/12/2008.

Open all year

I - 67030 Via Fonte dei Cementi Opi (Aq) - Tel+Fax +39 0863 912233 - **www.lefoci.it - lefoci@tin.it**

IT68380 Camping Nettuno

Via A. Vespucci 39, Marina del Cantone, I-80061 Massa Lubrense (Campania)

Tel: 081 808 1051. Email: info@villaggionettuno.it

Situated in a protected area called the 'Punta Campanella', away from the busiest tourist areas of the Amalfi Coast, but not the appalling roads, this tiny campsite of only 42 pitches (4A) is a delight. Owned and run by the friendly Mauro family, who speak excellent English, it is nestled in the bay of Marina del Cantone between Positano and Capri. Pitches are informally arranged some with fabulous sea views (extra charge) and almost all with shade. Across a minor road up three flights of steps are about 50 mobile homes, a bar, excellent restaurant, small, well stocked shop and terrace where there is animation in the high season. The single small sanitary block is centrally located and newly refurbished with quality finishes. The site has two pathways to the nearby beach that, unusually for the area, involves little walking or steps. With their own diving centre, a designated BIZAC dive site this is a popular site for all divers.

Facilities

One clean and newly refurbished sanitary block with excellent facilities for disabled people (and access via a ramp to the beach). Washing machine. Motorcaravan service point. Gas supplies. Small shop. Delightful restaurant with sea views. Bar (lively at night). Dive centre. Excursions. TV in bar area. Small play area. Free tennis arranged at court next door. Off site: Small beach (pebbles) 5 m. from bottom of site. Excellent restaurants 100 m. Amalfi Coast, Capri, nature parks, walking etc.

Open: 1 March - 2 November.

Directions

From A3 motorway , take Castellamare di Stabia exit onto S145. Pass Castellamare, follow signs to Meta di Sorrento through Vico Equense bypass tunnel and turn off towards Positano in Meta. After 5 km. turn towards S. Agata dei due Golfi and to this village (6.5 km.) then follow signs to Nerano and finally Marina del Cantone. Site is well signed and entrance is 50 m. past the entrance to reception and dive centre. You will need to go on for 100 m. to turn round in order to enter site with its steep and narrow entrance. GPS: N40:34.996 E14:21.197

Charges 2007

Per person	€ 6,50 - € 9,00
child (3-10 yrs)	€ 4,00 - € 5,00
pitch	€ 7,50 - € 14,00
electricity	€ 2,50

Camping Cheques accepted.

(331)

IT68200 Baia Domizia Villaggio Camping

I-81030 Baia Domizia (Campania)

Tel: **082 393 0164**. Email: **info@baiadomizia.it**

This large, beautifully maintained seaside site is about 70 kilometres northwest of Naples, and is within a pinewood, cleverly left in its natural state. Although it does not feel like it, there are 750 touring pitches in clearings, either of grass and sand or on hardstanding, all with electricity. Finding a pitch may take time as there are so many good ones to choose from, but staff will help in season. Most pitches are well shaded, however there are some in the sun for cooler periods. The central complex is superb with well designed buildings providing for all needs (the site is some distance from the town). Restaurants, bars and a 'gelaterie' enjoy live entertainment and attractive water lily ponds surround the area. The entire site is attractive, with shrubs, flowers and huge green areas. Near the entrance is a new swimming pool complex complete with hydromassagepoints and a large sunbathing area. The supervised beach is 1.5 km. of soft sand and a great attraction. A large grassy field overlooking the sea is ideal for picnics and sunbathing. A wide range of sports and other amenities is provided. The site is very well organised with particular regulations (e.g. no dogs or loud noise), so the general atmosphere is relaxing and peaceful. Although the site is big, there is never very far to walk to the beach, and although it may be some 300 m. to the central shops and restaurant from the site boundaries, there is always a nearby toilet block. It is the ideal place to recover from the rigours of touring or to relax and allow the professionals to organise tours for you to Rome, Pompeii, Sorrento etc. Charges are undeniably high, but this site is well above average and most suitable for families with children. Member of Leading Campings Group.

Facilities

Seven new toilet blocks have hot water in washbasins (many cabins) and showers. Good access and facilities for disabled people. Washing machines, spin dryers. Motorcaravan services. Gas supplies. Supermarket and general shop. Large bar and restaurants with pizzeria and takeaway. Ice cream parlour. New pool complex. Playground. Tennis. Bicycle hire. Windsurfing hire and school. Disco. Excursions. Torches required in some areas. Dogs are not accepted. Off site: Fishing and riding 3 km.

Open: 28 April - 16 September.

Directions

The turn to Baia Domizia leads off the Formia
- Naples road 23 km. from Formia. From the Rome
- Naples autostrada, take Cassino exit to Formia. Site is to the north of Baia Domizia and well signed. Site is off the coastal road that runs parallel to the SS7. GPS: N41:12.432 E13:47.481

Charges 2007

Per person	€ 4,90 - € 10,60
child (1-3 yrs)	free - € 8,50
pitch incl. electricity (5A)	€ 10,90 - € 21,90
car	€ 4,00 - € 7,00
motorcaravan	€ 10,90 - € 21,90

IT68890 Villaggio Camping Costa Verde

Capo Vaticano di Ricadi, I-89865 San Nicolo di Ricadi (Calabria)

Tel: **096 366 3090**. Email: **tropea@costaverde.org**

The coast near Capo Vaticano is listed as one of the best 100 in the world and one of the top three in Italy. From our pitch the sandy beach was just five metres below, down a flight of steps, and we had an unobstructed view of the turquoise sea, the beach and beyond – what more can you ask for? Camping Costa Verde nestles in a small bay, almost hidden from the surrounding area. With its 80 shaded pitches, it offers all year round camping in a beautiful location. The nearby small town of Tropea is one of the most picturesque on the Tyrrhenian coast. Just a short ride away, the old town hangs on to a cliff facing a large rock which was once an island. The rock is topped by Santa Maria Dell'Isola, a former medieval Benedictine sanctuary.

Facilities

The toilet block includes showers, WCs and washbasins. Washing machine. Small shop (1/5-30/10). Bar/coffee shop and restaurant (1/5-30/10). Good sandy beach. Excursions arranged. Children's club in high season. Disco. Apartments to rent. Dogs are not accepted in July/Aug. Barbecues not permitted. Off site: Tropea and Capo Vaticano.

Open: All year.

Directions

From A3 (Naples - Reggio) take Rosarno exit and go through the town. Follow signs for Nicotera then Tropea. Before Tropea look for signs for Ricadi and at a fairly large junction, amongst others, for Costa Verde (if you reach the railway viaduct you have gone too far). Turn left here, then right for site. The last 400 m. is down a narrow, steep and winding road. We managed in our 7 m. camper but it will be difficult for larger outfits. GPS: N38:38.344 E15:50.056

Charges guide

Per person	€ 5,50 - € 11,00
pitch	€ 6,00 - € 11,00
car	€ 2,80 - € 5,50

IT68650 Camping Riva di Ugento

Litoranea Gallipoli, Santa Maria di Leuca, I-73059 Ugento (Puglia)

Tel: **083 393 3600**. Email: **info@rivadiugento.it**

There are some campsites where you can be comfortable, have all the amenities at hand and still feel you are connecting with nature. Under the pine and eucalyptus trees of the Bay of Taranto foreshore is Camping Riva di Ugento. Its 900 pitches are nestled in and around the sand dunes and the foreshore area. They have space and trees around them and the sizes differ as the environment dictates the shape of most. The sea is only a short walk from most pitches and some are at the water's edge. The buildings resemble huge wooden umbrellas and are in sympathy with the environment. There are swimming and paddling pools, although these are expensive to use in high season. The area is sandy but well shaded, and the sea breezes, scented with pine give the site a cool fresh feel. This site has an isolated, natural feel that defies its size. Cycling along the kilometre of beach, we enjoyed the tranquillity of the amazing pitches – shaded, private and inviting.

Facilities

Twenty toilet blocks all with WCs, showers and washbasins. New bathrooms. Bar. Restaurant and takeaway. Swimming and paddling pools. Tennis. Basketball. Volleyball. Watersports incl. windsurfing school. Cinema. TV in bar. WiFi. Entertainment for children. Bicycle hire. Off site: Fishing. Riding 500 m. Boat launching 4 km. Golf 40 km.

Open: 15 May - 30 September.

Directions

From Bari take the Brindisi road to Lecce, then the SS101 to Gallipoli, followed by the SR274 towards S. Maria di Leuca, and exit at Ugento. Site well signed and turn right at traffic lights on SS19. Bumpy approach road. GPS: N39:52.485 E18:08.467

Charges 2007

Per pitch incl. 2 persons	€ 18,00 - € 37,00
extra person (over 2 yrs)	€ 5,00 - € 9,00
Camping Cheques accepted.	

IT69190 Camping Scarabeo

I-97017 S Croce Camerina (Sicily)

Tel: **0932 918096**. Email: **info@scarabeocamping.it**

Scarabeo is a beautiful site located in Punta Braccetto, a little fishing port in Sicily's southeastern corner. It is a perfect location with exceptional facilities to match. Split into two separate sites (just 50 m. apart) with a total of 80 pitches, it is being constantly improved with care by Angela di Modica. All pitches are well shaded, some naturally and others with an artificial cane roof and have 3 or 6A electricity. Scarabeo lies adjacent to a sandy beach and the little village is close by. The site layout resembles a Sicilian farm courtyard and is divided into four principal areas. The Greek ruins of Kamerina and Caucana are just a few kilometres from the site and their ruins can be reached by bike. The Riserva Naturale at the mouth of the River Irminio is also a popular excursion.

Facilities

Exceptional sanitary blocks provide personal WC compartments (personal key access). Ample hot showers (free low season). Facilities for disabled visitors. Sinks for dishes and clothes washing. Washing machine. Direct access to beach. Playground. Entertainment programme in high season. Mobile homes for rent. Off site: Supermarket 4 km. Restaurant/café 500 m. Cycling and walking trails.

Open: All year.

Directions

Site is 20 km. southwest of Ragusa. From Catania, take S194 towards Ragusa and, at Comiso, follow signs to S Croce Camerina, then Punta Braccetto, from where site is well signed. Use second entrance for reception. GPS: N36:48.985 E14:27.962

Charges 2007

Per person	€ 4,00 - € 8,50
child (3-6 yrs)	€ 2,00 - € 5,00
pitch	€ 4,00 - € 11,00
Excellent long term discounts in low season.	

IT69300 Camping Villaggio Marinello

Via del Sol, 17, I-98060 Oliveri (Sicily)

Tel: **094 131 3000**. Email: **marinello@camping.it**

Camping Marinello is located alongside the sea with direct access to a lovely uncrowded sandy beach with an informal marina at one end and a spit of sand and natural pool areas at the other. The 160 gravel touring pitches here are shaded by tall trees. We enjoyed a delicious traditional meal in the excellent terraced restaurant with its lovely sea views. Tours are arranged to major sightseeing destinations such as Mount Etna, Taormina and the nearby Aeolian Islands. The Greco family have been here for over 30 years and work hard to ensure that their guests enjoy a pleasant stay. There is some noise from the coastal rail line which runs along the length of the site. The nearby resort area town has lots of attractions for the tourist and the site is easily accessible from the ferry at Messina.

Facilities

Two sanitary blocks with free hot showers, one is not currently used and is awaiting a much needed refurbishment and heating. Washing machines. Bazaar, market and supermarket. Bar with sea views. Restaurant and terraced eating area also with views. Electronic games. Piano bar in high season. Off site: Seaside resort style town of Oliveri.

Open: All year.

Directions

From A20 motorway take Falcone exit and follow signs to Oliveri. At the town turn north towards the beach (site sign), then turn west along the beach and continue 1 km. to site. You will need to make a right turn immediately before a small narrow bridge (2.2 m. high and 2.5 m. wide). GPS: N38:07.937 E15:03.263

Charges 2007

Per person (over 3 yrs)	€ 4,50 - € 9,00
pitch with electricity	€ 13,00 - € 21,00
tent	€ 4,50 - € 12,00
car	€ 3,00 - € 5,00

IT69250 Camping Il Peloritano

Contrada Tarantonio ss 113 dir., Rodia, I-98161 Messina (Sicily)

Tel: **090 348 496**. Email: **il_peloritano@yahoo.it**

Set in a 100 year old olive grove which provides shade for the 50 informally arranged pitches, Camping Il Peloritano is a quiet uncomplicated site, off the coast road, with excellent clean facilities. It is a 200 m. walk to the sandy beach and about 2 km. to the nearby village. The friendly owners, Patrizia Mowdello and Carlo Oteri, provide help and assistance to arrange excursions to the Aeolian Islands, Taormina and Mount Etna and will do everything to make your stay a pleasant one.

Facilities

Single refurbished toilet block provides hot showers (by token). Good facilities for disabled visitors. Washing machine. Motorcaravan service point. Small shop and bar. Meals can be ordered in from local restaurants. Excursions arranged. Sub aqua school and diving with guide. Bowls. Bicycle hire. Off site: Sandy beach 200 m. Small seaside village 2 km. Riding 2 km.

Open: 21 March - 31 October.

Directions

From Messina on the A20 motorway take Villafranca exit then follow 'Messina dir' and 'Tarantonio' for 2 km. From Palermo on the A20, take exit for Rometta and follow 'Messina - Tarantonio' for about 5 km. GPS: N38:15.559 E15:28.069

Charges 2007

Per person	€ 5,00 - € 7,00
child (3-7 yrs)	€ 3,00 - € 5,00
pitch incl. car and electricity	€ 8,50 - € 13,10

IT69350 Camping Rais Gerbi

Contrada Rais Gerbi, SS113, km 172.9, I-90010 Finale di Pollina (Sicily)

Tel: **092 142 6570**. Email: **camping@raisgerbi.it**

Rais Gerbi provides very good quality camping with excellent facilities on the beautiful Tyrrhenian coast not far from Cefalu. This attractive terraced campsite is shaded by well established trees and the good size pitches vary from informal areas under the trees near the sea to gravel terraces and hardstandings. Most have stunning views, many with their own sinks and with some artificial shade to supplement the trees. From the mobile homes to the unusual white igloos, everything here is being established to a high quality. The large pool with its entertainment area and the restaurant, like so much of the site, overlook the beautiful rocky coastline and aquamarine sea. Vincenzo Cerrito who speaks excellent English has been developing the site for many years and is continually upgrading and improving the resort style facilities. A frequently used rail line in a cutting, then a tunnel, divides part of the site. The cutting is well fenced and lined with trees but has some impact and one is unaware of the tunnel under the site.

Facilities

Excellent new sanitary blocks with British style toilets, free hot showers in generous cubicles. Small shop. Casual summer terrace and indoor (winter) restaurant. Animation area and pool near the sea. Tennis court and football field. High quality accommodation and tents for rent. Rocky beach at site. Off site: Small village of Finale 500 m. Larger historic town of Cefalu 12 km.

Open: All year.

Directions

Site is on the SS113 running along the east - north coast of the island, between km. 172 and 173, just west of the village of Finale (the turn into site is at end of the bridge on the outskirts of the village). It is 12 km. east of Cefalu and 11 km. north of Pollina. GPS: N38:01.397 E14:09.238

Charges 2007

Per person	€ 5,00 - € 10,00
pitch incl. car and electricity	€ 12,00 - € 26,00

IT69160 Sporting Club Village & Camping

Contrada Bocca Arena, I-91026 Mazara del Vallo (Sicily)

Tel: **0923 947 230**. Email: **info@sportingclubvillage.com**

Mazara del Vallo can be found on Sicily's southwestern coast. As the crow flies, Tunisia is not far, and the town has a distinct Arabic influence in its winding streets. Sporting Club Village has been recommended by our Italian agent and we plan to undertake a full inspection in 2008. The site is 2.5 km. from Mazara and boasts some good amenities including a large pool, surrounded by tall palm trees. Pitches here are grassy and generally well shaded. This is a lively site in high season with a wide range of activities and a regular entertainment programme. The nearest beach is 350 m. away and the site is also adjacent to a nature reserve.

Facilities

Good sports club with swimming pool, gymnasium, floodlit foot ball pitches, tennis and Volleyball. Restaurant, bar and large reception/function room. Off site: Beach 350 m. Mazara 2.5 km. Various excursions organised by the site, for example to the acropolis at Selinunte (25 km) or the island of Mozia.

Open: 1 April - 30 September.

Directions

From the A29 take the Mazara del Vallo exit and head towards the town. Go straight over the first roundabout and after about 1.5 km. turn right at the traffic lights toward the beach. At roundabout exit left and go straight on to site, not over the bridge.

Charges 2008

Per person	€ 4,50 - € 7,00
child (4-10 yrs)	€ 3,00 - € 4,50
pitch incl. car	€ 10,50 - € 21,00

IT69230 Camping Jonio

Via Villini a Mare, 2, Ognina, I-95126 Catania (Sicily)

Tel: **095 491 139**. Email: **info@campingjonio.com**

This is a small, uncomplicated and tranquil city site with the advantage of being on top of the cliff at the waters edge. The 70 level touring pitches are on gravel with shade from some tall trees and artificial bamboo screens. There are some clean high quality sanitary facilities (also some private facilities for hire). There is no pool but the views of the water compensate and there are delightful rock pools in the sea just a few steps from the campsite. A new attractive restaurant offers food in the summer high season.

Facilities

Sanitary facilities are in two blocks, one small block for men and another for women. Modern and clean. Laundry with roof top drying area. Motorcaravan services. Shop. Bar and restaurant. Basic old style playground (supervision recommended). Animation (high season). Diving school. Access to small gravel beach. Excursions. Dogs are not accepted in July/August. Off site: Large town of Catania, many historical sites and Mount Etna.

Open: All year.

Directions

From A18 motorway take Catania exit and follow signs to the SS114 coast road in the direction of Ognina. Site is off the SS114 (signed) on the northeast outskirts of town. Access to site is off the small one way system and via the site's separate car park. GPS: N37:31.939 E15:07.204

Charges 2007

Per person	€ 7,00 - € 10,00
pitch	€ 7,00 - € 14,00
car	€ 4,00 - € 6,00
electricity	€ 3,00

IT69960 Camping Mariposa

Via Lido 22, I-07041 Alghero (Sardinia)

Tel: **079 950 360**. Email: **info@lamariposa.it**

Mariposa is situated right by the sea with its own beach and the range of sports available here probably makes it best suited for active young visitors. Kite surfing, diving, windsurfing, sailing, surfing and paragliding courses are all available here on payment, whilst evening entertainment is provided free. Pitch size ranges from 50 to 80 sq.m. so they are also better suited for tents, although they do all have 6A electrical connections and caravans and motorcaravans are welcome. However, there are few marked pitches and the land is undulating and may be unsuitable for units which tend to park beside roads. Cars must be parked away from the pitches. Alghero (1.5 km) still has a strong Catalan flavour from its 400 year occupation by the Spanish. There are many small coves and the Neptune caves are well worth a visit.

Facilities

The sanitary facilities are fairly basic, open plan, with cold washbasins and troughs, dishwashing and laundry sinks and an equal amount of warm (token needed) and cold showers. Washing machines and dryer. Motorcaravan service point. Shop, self service restaurant and bar (all open 10/6-30/9). Bicycle hire. Dogs are not accepted in July and August.

Open: 1 April - 31 October.

Directions

Alghero is on the northwest coast, 35 km. southwest of Sassari. Mariposa is at the north of the town. Turn left at the main traffic lights towards the Lido and then left again at the T-junction, the site is on the right. GPS: N40:34.731 E08:18.752

Charges 2007

Per person	€ 8,00 - € 10,50
child (3-12 yrs)	€ 4,00 - € 8,50
pitch incl. car	free - € 18,00
electricity	€ 2,50

I-07041 ALGHERO (SS)
Tel. +39 079950360
+39 079950480

e-mail: info@lamariposa.it
www.lamariposa.it

la**Mariposa**
★★★ camping con bungalows
il gioco, ritrovarsi

Camping La Mariposa is very well equipped with bar, grocer's, market and private beach. It is well-known because of its care and hospitality. The camping site provides equipped pitches for tents, caravans and motorcaravans, but also double rooms, 4 bedded bungalows, 2/4 bedded caravans and 4 bedded mini-villas. Camping La Mariposa is looking forward to welcoming you for a pleasant holiday from 1st April till 30th October with booking facilities available all the year long.

IT69550 Camping Baia Blu La Tortuga

Pineta di Vignola Mare, I-07020 Aglientu (Sardinia)

Tel: **079 602 200**. Email: **info@baiablu.com**

In the northeast of Sardinia and well situated for the Corsica ferry, Baia Blu is a large, professionally run campsite. The beach with its golden sand, brilliant blue sea and pretty rocky outcrops is warm and inviting. The site's 350 touring pitches, and almost as many mobile homes, are of fine sand and shaded by tall pines with banks of colourful oleanders and wide boulevards providing good access for units. Four exceptionally good toilet blocks provide a good ratio of excellent facilities to pitches including some combined private shower/washbasin cabins for rent. This is a busy bustling site with lots to do and attractive restaurants.

Facilities

Four blocks with free hot showers, WCs, bidets and washbasins. Facilities for disabled people. Washing machines and dryers. Motorcaravan services. Supermarket. Gas. Bazaar. Bar. Restaurant, pizzeria, snack bar and takeaway (May-Sept). Gym. Hairdresser. Doctor's surgery. Playground. Tennis. Games and TV rooms. Windsurfing and diving schools. Entertainment and sports activities (high season). Excursions. Barbecue area (not permitted on pitches). Torches useful. Internet point. Massage centre. Off site: Disco 50 m. Riding 5 km.

Open: 30 March - 21 October.

Directions

Site is on the north coast between towns of Costa Paradiso and S. Teresa di Gallura (18 km.) at Pineta di Vignola Mare and is well signed. GPS: N41:07.463 E09:04.055

Charges 2008

Per unit incl. 2 persons and electricity		€ 14,40 - € 52,80
extra person		€ 0,80 - € 8,80
junior (3-9 yrs) or senior (over 60 yrs)		free - € 7,20
dog		€ 3,50 - € 8,00

Check real time availability and at-the-gate prices...

www.**alanrogers**.com

IT69720 Camping l'Ultima Spiaggia

Localitá Planargia, I-08042 Bari Sardo (Sardinia)

Tel: **078 229 363**. Email: **info@campingultimaspiaggia.it**

A great name for this campsite – 'the ultimate beach' – and the beach really is extremely good, along with the bright colourful décor and amenities. We think you will enjoy this clean and pleasant site, although little English is spoken. The 250 pitches are terraced on sand, some enjoying sea views, and are located at the end of the site. New mobile homes occupy the top of the site which slopes towards the sea. The good entertainment programme can be enjoyed from the terrace of the friendly restaurant which offers a reasonably priced menu which includes the local seafood specialities. Access to the fine beach (with lifeguard) and its watersports is gained through a security gate. Sub-aqua diving is extremely good hereabouts.

Facilities

Two toilet units include mainly Turkish style toilets and good facilities for disabled campers. Washing machines. Motorcaravan service point. Small supermarket. Restaurant and snack bar. Play areas. Windsurfing. Aerobics. Riding. Tennis. Minigolf. Canoeing. Bicycle hire. Miniclub. Entertainment. Excursions. Torches useful. Off site: Restaurants, bars and shops. Fishing.

Open: 20 April - 30 September.

Directions

Site is on east coast of Sardinia, well signed from SS125 in village of Bari Sardo. Note that the roads are very winding from the north – allow lots of time.

Charges 2007

Per person	€ 6,50 - € 13,50
child (1-6 yrs)	€ 3,50 - € 6,50
pitch	€ 6,00 - € 14,50
electricity	€ 3,00

The campsite is situated at the eastside with 13 km distance to the harbour of Arbatax. The Village is situated in the middle of a various pinewood with high trees which provide a lot of shadow, directly at the cristallblu sea. Quiet campsite, may, june and september, animation july and august, offers several accomodation possibilities of holiday with large pitches, caravan rental, mobilehomes with tv and airconditioning, bungalow and apartments at the seaside.

★★★★

Loc. Planargia · I-08042 Barisardo (NU) - Tel. 0039/078229363 - Fax 0039/078228963
Tel. invernale 0039/070381105   info@campingultimaspiaggia.it

www.campingultimaspiaggia.it - www.casevacanzerivamare.com

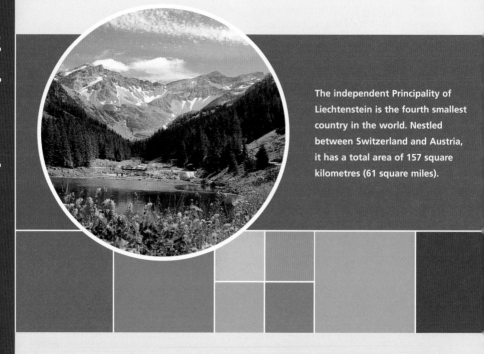

The independent Principality of Liechtenstein is the fourth smallest country in the world. Nestled between Switzerland and Austria, it has a total area of 157 square kilometres (61 square miles).

If you like clean mountain air and peaceful surroundings, then a visit to Liechtenstein would be worthwhile. The little town of Vaduz (the Capital) is where you will find most points of interest, including the world famous art collection (Kunstmuseum), which holds paintings by Rembrandt and other world famous artists. Above the town of Vaduz is the restored twelfth century castle, now owned by the prince of Liechtenstein (not open to the public). Take a walk up to the top of the hill, you can view Vaduz and the mountains stretched out below. Situated on a terrace above Vaduz is Triesenberg village, blessed with panoramic views over the Rhine Valley, a pretty village with vineyards and ancient chapels. Malbun is Liechtenstein's premier mountain resort, popular in both winter and summer, for either skiing or walking.

FL7580 Camping Mittagspitze

Sägastrasse 29, FL 9495 Triesen
Tel: **392 3677**. Email: **info@campingtriesen.li**

Camping Mittagspitze is attractively and quietly situated for visiting the Principality. Probably the best site in the region, it is on a hillside and has all the scenic views that one could wish. Extensive, broad, level terraces on the steep slope provide unmarked pitches (a reader tells us that spacing causes problems in high season) and electricity connections are available. There is little shade. Of the 240 spaces, 120 are used by seasonal caravans. Liechtenstein's capital, Vaduz, is 7 km, Austria is 20 km. and Switzerland 3 km.

Facilities

Two good quality sanitary blocks (the one near reception is new) provide all the usual facilities. Washing machine, dryer and ironing. Room where one can sit or eat with cooking facilities. Shop (1/6-31/8). Restaurant (all year). Small swimming pool (15/6-15/8), not heated but very popular in summer. Playground. Fishing. New TV room. Off site: Tennis and indoor pool nearby. Riding and bicycle hire 5 km.

Open: All year.

Directions

From A3 take Trübbach exit 10 and follow road towards Balziers. Then head towards Vaduz and site is 2 km. south of Triesen on the right. Site is signed. GPS: N47:05.193 E09:31.621

Charges 2008

Per person	€ 8,50
child (3-14 yrs)	€ 4,00
pitch	€ 8,00 - € 10,00
electricity (6A)	€ 5,00

MAP 2

The Grand Duchy of Luxembourg is a sovereign state, lying between Belgium, France and Germany. Divided into two areas: the spectacular Ardennes region in the north and the rolling farmlands and woodland in the south, bordered on the east by the wine growing area of the Moselle Valley.

Luxembourg

CAPITAL: LUXEMBOURG CITY

Tourist Office

Luxembourg National Tourist Office
122 Regent Street, London W1B 5SA
Tel: 020 7434 2800
Fax: 020 7734 1205
Email: tourism@luxembourg.co.uk
Internet: www.luxembourg.co.uk

From wherever you are in Luxembourg you are always within easy reach of the capital, Luxembourg-Ville, home to about one fifth of the population. The city was built upon a rocky outcrop, and has superb views of the Alzette and Petrusse Valleys. Those who love the great outdoors must make a visit to the Ardennes, with its hiking trails, footpaths and cycle routes that take you through beautiful winding valleys and across deep rivers, a very popular region for visitors. If wine tasting takes your fancy, then head for the Moselle Valley, particularly if you like sweet, fruity wines. From late spring to early autumn wine tasting tours take place in cellars and caves. The Mullerthal region, known as the 'Little Switzerland', lies on the banks of the river Sûre. The earth is mostly made up of soft sandstone, so through the ages many fascinating gorges, caves and formations have emerged.

Population
435,700

Climate
A temperate climate prevails, the summer often extending from May to late October.

Language
Letzeburgesch is the national language, with French and German also being official languages.

Telephone
The country code is 00 352.

Money
Currency: The Euro
Banks: Mon-Fri 08.30/09.00-12.00 and 13.30-16.30.

Shops
Mon 14.00-18.30. Tues to Sat 08.30-12.00 and 14.00-18.30 (grocers and butchers at 15.00 on Sat).

Public Holidays
New Year; Carnival Day mid-Feb; Easter Mon; May Day; Ascension; Whit Mon; National Day 23 June; Assumption 15 Aug; Kermesse 1 Sept; All Saints; All Souls; Christmas 25, 26 Dec.

Motoring
Many holidaymakers travel through Luxembourg to take advantage of the lower fuel prices, thus creating traffic congestion at petrol stations, especially in summer. A Blue Zone area exists in Luxembourg City and various parts of the country (discs from tourist offices) but meters are also used.

LU7610 Camping Birkelt

1 rue de la Piscine, L-7601 Larochette
Tel: **879 040**. Email: **info@camping-birkelt.lu**

This is very much a family site, the price representing the range of facilities provided. It is well organised and well laid out, set in an elevated position in attractive, undulating countryside. A tarmac road runs around the site with 424 large grass pitches, some slightly sloping, many with a fair amount of shade, on either side of gravel access roads in straight rows or circles. All pitches have 6A electricity. An all weather swimming pool complex is just outside the site entrance (free for campers) and entertainment for children is arranged in high season. The site is very popular with tour operators (140 pitches).

Facilities

Three modern sanitary buildings well situated around the site include mostly open washbasins (6 cabins in one block). Baby baths. Facilities for wheelchair users. Washing machines and dryers. Dishwashers (on payment). Motorcaravan service point. Shop. WiFi. Coffee bar. Restaurant with terrace. All weather swimming pool. Outdoor pool for toddlers. Massage. 4 Playgrounds. Minigolf. Tennis. Football ground. Riding. Balloon flights. Internet points. Bicycle hire. Off site: Golf and bicycle hire 5 km. Fishing and kayaking 10 km.

Open: 15 March - 2 November.

Directions

From N7 (Diekirch - Luxembourg City), turn onto the N8 at Berschblach (just past Mersch) towards Larochette. Site is signed on the right about 1.5 km. from Larochette. Approach road is fairly steep and narrow. GPS: N49:47.105 E06:12.620

Charges 2007

Per unit incl. 2 persons and electricity	€ 19,50 - € 30,75
extra person	€ 4,00

Less 25% in low season.
Camping Cheques accepted.

LU7620 Europacamping Nommerlayen

L-7465 Nommern
Tel: **878 078**. Email: **nommerlayen@vo.lu**

This is a top quality site in central Luxembourg with fees to match, but it has everything! A large, central building housing most of the services and amenities opens onto a terrace around an excellent swimming pool complex with two main pools (one heated 1/5-15/9) and an imaginative watery playground. The 396 individual pitches (70-120 sq.m.) are on grassy terraces, all have access to electricity (2/16A) and water taps. Interestingly enough the superb new sanitary block is called 'Badtemple' (its architecture suggesting this title as the entrance with colonnades supporting a canopy is reminiscent of a Greek temple). To gain entry to the sauna and to obtain hot water for washbasins, showers and sinks, one pays to have a cash equivalent charged into a triangular shaped plastic block which is then inserted into a slot. Member of Leading Campings Group.

Facilities

A large, high quality, modern sanitary unit provides some washbasins in cubicles, facilities for disabled people, and family and baby washrooms. The new block also includes special rooms for children and disabled visitors, plus a sauna. Twelve private bathrooms for hire. Laundry. Motorcaravan service point. Supermarket. Restaurant. Snack bar. Bar (all 23/3-1/11). Heated swimming pools (1/5-15/9). Solarium. Fitness programmes. Bowling. Playground. Large screen TV. Entertainment in season. Bicycle hire. Off site: Riding 1 km. Fishing and golf 5 km.

Open: 1 February - 1 December.

Directions

Take the 118 road between Mersch and Larochette. Site is signed 3 km. north of Larochette towards the village of Nommer on the 346 road. GPS: N49:47.097 E06:09.920

Charges 2007

Per unit incl. 2 persons and 2A electricity, acc. to pitch and facilities	€ 18,00 - € 36,00
extra adult	€ 4,40
child (under 18 yrs)	€ 3,85
dog	€ 2,75
electricity (16A) plus	€ 3,50

No credit cards.

LU7640 Camping Auf Kengert

L-7633 Larochette / Medernach

Tel: **837186**. Email: **info@kengert.lu**

A friendly welcome awaits you at this peacefully situated, family run site, 2 km. from Larochette, which is 24 km. northeast of Luxembourg city, providing 180 individual pitches, all with electricity. Some in a very shaded woodland setting, on a slight slope with fairly narrow access roads. There are also eight hardened pitches for motorcaravans on a flat area of grass, complete with motorcaravan service facilities. Further pitches are in an adjacent and more open meadow area. There are also site owned chalets and caravans. This site is popular in season, so early arrival is advisable. Alternatively, you can reserve a pitch.

Facilities

The well maintained sanitary block in two parts includes a modern, heated unit with some washbasins in cubicles, and excellent, fully equipped cubicles for disabled visitors. The showers, facilities for babies, additional WCs and washbasins, plus laundry room are located below the central building which houses the shop, bar and restaurant. Motorcaravan services. Gas supplies. Indoor and outdoor play areas. Solar heated swimming pool (Easter - 30/9). Paddling pool. Off site: Bicycle hire. Golf, fishing and riding 8 km.

Open: 1 March - 8 November.

Directions

From Larochette take the CR118/N8 (towards Mersch) and just outside town turn right on the CR119 towards Schrondweiler, site is 2 km. on right. GPS: N49:47.995 E06:11.890

Charges 2008

Per person	€ 11,00 - € 14,00
child (4-18 yrs)	€ 5,00 - € 7,00
electricity	€ 2,00
dog	€ 1,25

20% reduction for students, walkers and cyclists.

LU7650 Camping de la Sûre

23 route de la Sûre, L-9390 Reisdorf

Tel: **836 246**. Email: **ren2@pt.lu**

Camping de la Sûre is on the banks of the river that separates Luxembourg and Germany. It is a pleasant site close to Reisdorf with 180 numbered pitches (120 with 10A electricity). These are not separated but are marked with trees that provide some shade. There are caravan holiday homes in a fenced area towards the back of the site, leaving the prime pitches for touring units. Ongoing redevelopment is almost complete with new roads and a new toilet block.

Facilities

Modern, clean sanitary facilities recently refitted and extended, including some washbasins in cubicles. New block planned. Laundry. Small shop. Café/bar. Takeaway. Playground. Minigolf. Sports field. Canoeing. Fishing. Off site: Town centre within easy walking distance. Cycle ways abound. Bicycle hire 200 m. Golf 8 km.

Open: 1 April - 30 October.

Directions

From the river bridge in Reisdorf, take the road to Echternach, de la Sûre is the second campsite on the left. GPS: N49:52.202 E06:16.050

Charges 2007

Per person	€ 5,00
pitch	€ 5,50
electricity	€ 2,50
dog	€ 2,50

25% reduction in low season. No credit cards.

LU7660 Camping Kockelscheuer

22 route de Bettembourg, L-1899 Luxembourg

Tel: **471 815**. Email: **caravani@pt.lu**

Camping Kockelscheuer is 4 km. from the centre of Luxembourg city and quietly situated (although there can be some aircraft noise at times). On a slight slope, there are 161 individual pitches of good size, either on flat ground at the bottom or on wide flat terraces with easy access, all with 16A electricity. There is also a special area for tents. For children there is a large area with modern play equipment on safety tiles and next door to the site is a sports centre. Charges are very reasonable. There is a friendly welcome although little English is spoken.

Facilities

Two fully equipped, identical sanitary buildings, both very clean at time of visit. Washing machines. Motorcaravan services. Shop (order bread the previous day). Snack bar. Restaurant in adjacent sports centre also with minigolf, tennis, squash, etc. Rest room. No entry or exit for vehicles (reception closed) from 12.00-14.00 hrs. Off site: Bus 200 m. every 15 minutes to Luxembourg. Swimming pool 5 km.

Open: Easter - 31 October.

Directions

Site is SSW of Luxembourg city on the N13 to Bettembourg (this road is also known locally as the 186). From the south, exit A4 at junction signed Kockelscheuer onto N4. In 2 km. turn right (Kockelscheuer and campsite) and continue to follow the signs. GPS: N49:34.308 E06:06.540

Charges 2008

Per person	€ 3,75
child (3-14 yrs)	€ 2,00
pitch	€ 4,50
electricity (1 or 2 days)	€ 2,20

No credit cards.

Camping Kockelscheuer – Luxembourg

22, route de Bettembourg, L-1899 Luxembourg

Telephone 47 18 15 · Fax 40 12 43 · www.camp-kockelscheuer.lu

A modern campsite situated at Kockelscheuer's Leisure Centre, with an ice skating rink, tennis, walking trails, boules, bowling, sauna, solarium, whirlpool, restaurants. Spacious sanitairy facilities. Large pitches with electric hook-up.

Comfortable campers lounge with terrace. Camping shop.

LU7670 Camping des Ardennes

10 op der Héi, L-9809 Hosingen

Tel: **921 911**

A good value, small municipal site, Camping Ardennes is located on the edge of this attractive small town with an easy level walk to all amenities and parks and some floral arrangements to admire during the summer season. The 48 touring pitches are level, open and grassy. All have electricity (10A) and are arranged on either side of surfaced roads, with a few trees providing a little shade in places. Adjacent sports complex with tennis and football, etc. This site is useful as a stopover if travelling along the N7.

Facilities

The single well appointed, modern, clean sanitary block can be heated in winter and includes separate men's and women's facilities. Laundry facilities. Café/bar (opening variable). Barbecue. Playground. Skis and winter sports equipment for hire. English spoken. Rooms for rent (B&B).

Open: All year.

Directions

Hosingen is on the N7 21 km. north of Diekirch. Site and sports complex are signed in the village. 20 m. after leaving the main road turn right. Site is 100 m. on the left. GPS: N50:00.463 E06:05.410

Charges guide

Per person	€ 4,50
child (3-12 yrs)	€ 2,25
pitch	€ 4,50
electricity	€ 2,25
dog	€ 2,25

LU7680 Camping Kohnenhof

Maison 1, L-9838 Obereisenbach

Tel: **929 464**. Email: **info@campingkohnenhof.lu**

Nestling in a valley with the Our river running through it, Kohnenhof offers a very agreeable location for a relaxing family holiday. From the minute you stop at the reception you are assured of a warm and friendly welcome. Numerous paths cross through the wooded hillside so this could be a haven for walkers. A little wooden ferry crosses the small river across the border to Germany. The river is shallow and safe for children (parental supervision essential). A large sports field and play area with a selection of equipment caters for younger campers. During the high season, an entertainment programme is organised for parents and children. The owner organises special golf weeks with games on different courses (contact the site for details). The restaurant is part of an old farmhouse and, with its open fire to keep it warm, offers a wonderful ambience to enjoy a meal.

Facilities

Heated sanitary block with showers and washbasins in cabins. Motorcaravan service point. Laundry. Bar, restaurant, takeaway. Games and TV room. Baker calls daily. Sports field with play equipment. Boules. Bicycle hire. Golf weeks. Discounts on six local 18 hole golf courses. WiFi. Off site: Bus to Clervaux and Vianden stops (4 times daily) outside site entrance. Riding 5 km. Castle at Vianden 14 km. Monastery at Clervaux 14 km. Golf 15 km.

Open: 15 March - 10 November.

Directions

Take N7 north from Diekirch. At Hosingen, turn right onto the narrow and winding CR324 signed Eisenbach. Follow site signs from Eisenbach or Obereisenbach. GPS: N50:00.961 E06:08.160

Charges 2008

Per unit incl. 2 persons and electricity	€ 19,80 - € 25,40
child (under 12 yrs)	€ 3,00
dog	€ 2,80

Camping Cheques accepted.

LU7770 Camping Val d'Or

Um Gaettchen 2, L-9747 Enscherange

Tel: 920 691. Email: valdor@pt.lu

Camping Val d'Or is one of those small family-run countryside sites where you easily find yourself staying longer than planned. Set on lush meadowland under a scattering of trees, the site is divided into two by the tree lined Clerve river as it winds its way slowly through the site. Two footbridges go some way to joining the site together and there are two entrances for vehicles. There are 76 level grass touring pitches, all with electricity (4A). and with some tree shade. There are open views of the surrounding countryside with its wooded hills. The site's Dutch owners speak good English. Fred van Donk is active in the Luxembourg tourist industry. He is happy to give advice about this interesting, attractive and, to most people, less well known region of Europe which is within easy reach of the Channel ports and Holland. The friendly bar is a popular meeting point. Children have three playgrounds, two conventional and the third, beside the river, a water playground with pump, various waterways, waterwheel and a small pool. The site participates in the 'Wanderhütten' scheme providing wooden huts for rent to hikers. A local railway passes the site but it is not obtrusive and there are no night passenger services.

Facilities

Next to the reception is a heated sanitary block where some facilities are found, others including some showers are located, under cover, outside. Showers are token operated, washbasins open style. Laundry room. Gas supplies. Bar. Swimming or paddling in river. Three play areas. Bicycle hire. Off site: Fishing and golf 10 km.

Open: All year.

Directions

From A26/E25 (Liège - Luxembourg) exit 54 travel to Bastogne. From Bastogne take N84/N15 towards Diekirk for 15 km. At crossroads turn left (northeast) towards Wiltz following signs for Clervaux. Pass though Wiltz and entering Weldingen, 500 m. after a garage turn right. In Wilderwiltz follow signs for small village of Enscherange where site is signed. GPS: N50:00.012 E05:59.450

Charges 2007

Per person	€ 5,00
child (0-15 yrs)	€ 2,00
pitch incl. electricity	€ 10,00

No credit cards.

LU7780 Camping Woltzdal

Maison 12, L-9974 Maulusmühle

Tel: 998 938. Email: info@woltzdal-camping.lu

Set by a stream in a valley, Camping Wolzdal is one of the many delightful sites in the Ardennes, a region of wooded hills and river valleys that crosses the borders of Luxembourg, Belgium and France. The site has 83 touring pitches, set on grass amongst fir trees; all with 4A electricity. They are fairly open and have views of the surrounding wooded hills. A railway track passes the site on the far side of the stream, but there are only trains during the day and they are not disturbing. In the end this is a site of woods, water and wildlife. This is truly a family-run site where during the evenings in the small, friendly bar/restaurant, one brother cooks, the other serves the guests while their father runs the bar. In the surrounding hills there are kilometres of marked paths and mountain bike tracks for those wishing to enjoy the natural environment. For city life, a family ticket from the railway station close to the site is an economic and convenient way of visiting Luxembourg City with its museums, exhibitions and many other attractions. Details are available at reception.

Facilities

Tents to rent and 2 servicepoints for motorhomes. The heated sanitary block contains the usual facilities; showers are coin operated, washbasins open. Laundry room. Reception and small shop are in the large house at the entrance where there is also a restaurant/snack bar and a bar. Children's library/activity room. Internet cafe for guests. Play area. Boules. Mountain bike hire. Entertainment programme for children in high season. Small hikers' chalets to rent. Off site: Fishing and golf 6 km. Riding 20 km.

Open: 15 March - 1 November.

Directions

Site is 6 km. north of Clervaux on the CR335 road. Leave Clervaux in the direction of Troisvierge and site is signed in the 12 house village of Maulusmühle. GPS: N50:05.477 E06:01.670

Charges 2007

Per person	€ 5,90
child (4-12 yrs)	€ 2,95
pitch	€ 5,30
electricity (4A)	€ 1,80

LU7850 Camping Fuussekaul

4 Fuussekaul, L-9156 Heiderscheid
Tel: 268 8881. Email: info@fuussekaul.lu

Children who visit Fuusse Kaul (the name means fox hole) won't want to leave as there is so much for them to do. Apart from a fun pool, exciting play areas, and an entertainment programme, children and parents can bake their own pizzas in the open-air oven. Of the 370 pitches, 220 of varying sizes are for touring units, all with a 6A electricity connection. The touring area (separate from the chalets and seasonal pitches) is well endowed with modern facilities, although there is no provision for visitors with disabilities. An entertainment programme continues throughout the main holiday season. This includes mini shows and theatre productions, and various sporting activities. On the opposite side of the road (pedestrian access via an under-road passage) is a service and parking area for six motorcaravans. Each pitch has a hook-up, fresh water tap and waste water disposal point. There's also a drive-over service point for those not wishing to stay the night.

Facilities

Four excellent sanitary blocks provide showers (token € 0.50), washbasins (in cabins and communal) and children and baby rooms with small toilets, washbasins and showers. Laundry. Parking and service area for motorcaravans. Suite with sauna and sun beds etc. New beauty salon. Well-stocked shop, bar, restaurant and takeaway. Swimming pools. Playgrounds. Cross country skiing when snow permits. Bicycle hire. Children's club. Bowling centre. Off site: Bus stops outside site entrance. Riding 500 m. Fishing 3 km. Supermarket and shops in Ettelbruckk 7 km.

Open: All year.

Directions

Take N15 from Diekirch to Heiderscheid. Site is on left at top of hill just before reaching the village. Motorhome service area is signed on the right. GPS: N49:52.650 E05:59.570

Charges 2007

Per unit incl. 2 persons	€ 18,50 - € 32,00
extra person	€ 2,50
electricity	€ 0,40
dog	€ 2,00

LU7700 Camping Gaalgebierg

Boite Postale 20, L-4001 Esch-sur-Alzette
Tel: 541 069. Email: gaalcamp@pt.lu

Occupying an elevated position on the edge of town, near the French border, this pleasant good quality site is run by the local camping and caravan club. Although surrounded by hills and with a good variety of trees, not all pitches have shade. There are 150 pitches (100 for tourists), most on grass, (100 sq.m.) marked out by trees, with some on a slight slope. There is a gravel area set aside for one night stays, plus four all-weather pitches for motorcaravans although these are used mostly in the winter. All pitches have 16A electricity and TV points.

Facilities

Modern, well equipped toilet blocks can be heated and include some washbasins in cubicles, hot showers and excellent facilities for disabled people and babies. Laundry. Motorcaravan service point. Gas available. Shop for basics. Small bar and take-away on demand. TV room. Excellent playground. Bicycle hire. Entertainment and activities programme in high season. Off site: Restaurant within walking distance. Swimming pool and tennis.

Open: All year.

Directions

Site is well signed from centre of Esch, but look out as there are two acute right-handers on the approach to the site. GPS: N49:29.095 E05:59.194

Charges 2007

Per person	€ 3,75
child (3-12 yrs)	€ 1,75
pitch	€ 6,00
electricity (16A)	€ 1,50

LU7870 Camping de la Sûre

Route de Gilsdorf, L-9234 Diekirch

Tel: **809 425**. Email: **tourisme@diekirch.lu**

The municipal Camping de la Sûre is within walking distance of the centre of Diekirch, a town that is brimming with things to see and do. Located on the banks of the Sûre, this site offers 204 flat grass pitches, most with 10A electricity. One large building close to the entrance houses the reception and sanitary facilities, all of which were in pristine condition at the time of our visit. A path for walking and cycling runs alongside the campsite; maps are available in the Syndicat d'Initiative in the town centre. Diekirch, with a donkey as its mascot, is well worth a visit.

Facilities

New reception building with bar and attached heated modern facilities including showers and communal washbasins. Baby room and suite for disabled visitors. Laundry. Play area. Children's entertainment organised during July/Aug. Off site: Diekirch has leisure facilities within walking distance of the site. Large skateboard park and bicycle ramps . Walk/cycle path along site boundary.

Open: 1 April - 30 September.

Directions

Follow signs (only official camping signs, not site name) from centre of Diekirch. GPS: N49:52.002 E06:09.850

Charges 2007

Per person	€ 6,00
child (3-14 yrs)	€ 2,25
pitch	€ 5,00
electricity	€ 2,00

LU7880 Camping Trois Frontières

Hauptstrooss 12, L-9972 Lieler

Tel: **998 608**. Email: **camp.3front@cmdnet.lu**

On a clear day, it is possible to see Belgium, Germany and Luxembourg from the campsite swimming pool, hence its name: Les Trois Frontières. Martin and Esther Van Aalst own and manage the site themselves and all visitors receive a personal welcome and immediately become part of a large happy family. Most of the facilities are close to the entrance, leaving the camping area quiet, except for the play area. The restaurant/takeaway provides good quality food at reasonable prices, served either inside or on the pleasant terrace with flower borders and overlooking the pool (which the site reports is now covered and heated).

Facilities

Unisex facilities include excellent showers, washbasins in cabins, British-style WCs, suite for visitors with disabilities, plus baby bath and changing station. More WCs in second building (down some steps). Laundry. Swimming pool (1/4-31/10). Play area. Boules. Games room. Bicycle hire. Off site: Shops 2.3 km. Golf and riding 12 km. Clervaux 12 km.

Open: All year.

Directions

Take N7 northward from Diekirch. 3 km. south of Weiswampach turn right onto CR338 to Lieler (site is signed here). Site is on right as you enter the village. GPS: N50:07.404 E06:06.310

Charges 2007

Per pitch incl. 2 persons	€ 16,00 - € 21,00
extra person	€ 6,50 - € 7,00
electricity (4A)	€ 2,50

LU7890 Camping Haute Sûre

34 rue J. de Busleyden, L-9639 Boulaide

Tel: **993 061**. Email: **info@campinghautesure.com**

Located in a small village in a fairly remote area of the Grand Duchy, this site is very peaceful with some outstanding views over the Sûre valley. There are 87 pitches, 12 of which are used by a Dutch tour operator, plus 2 chalets for rent. The 73 large pitches for tourists are on well kept grass, generally with a slight slope, all have electricity hook-ups (6A) with a water tap serving four pitches. The emphasis at Haute Sûre is very much geared towards families, especially those with younger children, with an excellent adventure style playground.

Facilities

A modern building with under floor heating provides good facilities including spacious showers (pre-set to give 5 minutes use). Children's washbasins. Separate unisex baby room. Suite for disabled campers, with baby facilities. Laundry. Recycling. Shop, restaurant, bar and takeaway (15/4-15/9). Swimming and paddling pools (15/4-15/9). Games room. Adventure playground. Children's entertainment. Off site: Internet cafe 6 km. Fishing 3 km. Golf 30 km. Riding in village.

Open: 15 April - 15 September.

Directions

Boulaide is 15 km. northeast of Martelange on the Belgium border. From Bastogne take N4 south for 22 km. to Martelange. From Martelange take the N23 east and after about 4 km. turn north on minor road CR309, through Bigonville to Boulaide. Site is towards the northern end of village. GPS: N49:53.362 E05:48.899

Charges 2007

Per unit incl. 2 persons	€ 25,00
incl. 3 persons	€ 27,50
incl. 4 persons	€ 30,00

MAP 2

Netherlands

With vast areas of the Netherlands reclaimed from the sea, nearly half of the country lies at or below sea level. The result is a flat, fertile landscape, criss-crossed with rivers and canals. Famous for its windmills and bulb fields, it also boasts some of the most impressive coastal dunes in Europe.

CAPITAL: AMSTERDAM

Tourist Office

Netherlands Board of Tourism
15-19 Kingsway, 7th Floor, Imperial House
London WC2B 6UN Tel: 020 7539 7950
Fax: 020 7539 7953
Email: information@nbt.org.uk
Internet: www.holland.com/uk

There is more to the Netherlands than Amsterdam and the bulb fields. Granted, both are top attractions and no visitor should miss the city of Amsterdam with its delight of bridges, canals, museums and listed buildings or miss seeing the spring-time riot of colour that adorns the fields and gardens of South Holland. This is a country with a variety of holiday venues ranging from lively seaside resorts to picturesque villages, idyllic old fishing ports and areas where nature rules. The Vecht valley is an area of natural beauty which centres around the town of Ommen. Giethoorn is justly dubbed the 'Venice of the North'. The Alblasserwaard polder offers time to discover the famed windmills of Kinderdijk, cheese farms and a stork village. The islands of Zeeland are joined by amazing feats of engineering, particularly the Oosterschelde storm surge barrier. Island hopping introduces lovely old towns such as Middelburg, the provincial capital Zierikzee with its old harbour or the quaint old town of Veere.

Population

15.9 million

Climate

Temperature with mild winters and warm summers.

Language

Dutch. English is very widely spoken, so is German and to some extent French. In Friesland a Germanic language, Frisian is spoken.

Telephone

The country code is 00 31.

Money

Currency: The Euro
Banks: Mon-Fri 09.00-16.00/1700.

Shops

Mon-Fri 09.00/09.30-17.30/18.00.
Sat to 16.00/17.00. Later closing hours in larger cities.

Public Holidays

New Year; April Fools Day 1 April; Good Fri; Easter Mon; Queen's Birthday 30 April; Labour Day; Remembrance Day 4 May; Liberation Day 5 May; Ascension; Whit Mon; SinterKlaas 5 Dec; Kingdom Day 15 Dec; Christmas 25, 26 Dec.

Motoring

There is a comprehensive motorway system but, due to the high density of population, all main roads can become very busy, particularly in the morning and evening rush hours. There are many bridges which can cause congestion. There are no toll roads but there are a few toll bridges and tunnels notably the Zeeland Bridge, Europe's longest across the Oosterschelde.

Within a stone's throw of the city

www.citycamps.nl

CITYCAMPS

NL5500 Vakantiepark Pannenschuur

Zeedijk 19, NL-4504 PP Nieuwvliet (Zeeland)

Tel: **011 737 2300**. Email: **info@pannenschuur.nl**

This is one of several coastal sites on the narrow strip of the Netherlands between the Belgian frontier near Knokke and the Breskens ferry. Quickly reached from the ports of Ostend, Zeebrugge and Vlissingen, it is useful for overnight stops or for a few days to enjoy the seaside. A short walk across the quiet coast road and steps over the dike bring you to the open, sandy beach. Quite a large site, most of the 595 pitches are taken by permanent or seasonal holiday caravans but there are also 165 pitches for tourists mostly in their own areas. Mostly in bays of six or eight units surrounded by hedges, all have electricity (6A) and 100 also have water, drainage and cable connections. Cars are not parked by units but in separate parking areas. A star attraction is the recently updated complex that provides a super indoor heated pool with baby and children's sections, jacuzzi, sauna, Turkish bath and solarium. It also includes a full restaurant and bar, a shop and the reception, plus for children, a special restaurant (Pedro's Piratenship). Overall, this is a very good site.

Facilities

Five toilet blocks including two new, heated buildings, provide first class facilities including children's washrooms, baby rooms and some private cabins. Hot water is free (using a key - deposit € 11). Launderette. Motorcaravan services. Gas supplies. Supermarket. Restaurant, snack bar and takeaway. Swimming pool, sauna and solarium. All these amenities are closed 14/1-31/1. Large games room with soft drinks bar. Internet access. Playground and play field. Bicycle hire. Organised activities in season. Off site: Fishing 500 m. Riding 2 km. Golf 5 km.

Open: All year (all amenities closed 14/1-31/1).

Directions

At Nieuwvliet, on the Breskens - Sluis minor road, 8 km. southwest of Breskens, turn towards the sea at sign for Nieuwvliet-Bad and follow signs to site GPS: N51:23.013 E03:26.431

Charges 2007

Per unit (max. 5 persons)	
incl. electricity	€ 20,00 - € 40,00
extra person	€ 4,00

Rates available for weekly stays.

NL6925 Camping Weltevreden

Melsesweg, NL-4374 NG Zouteland (Zeeland)

Tel: **011 856 1321**. Email: **info@campingweltevreden.nl**

Camping Weltevreden is on Zeeland's 'Riviera', the area of the Dutch coast with the highest recorded annual hours of sunshine. It is a family site with a pleasant ambiance, located just behind the high, grassy dunes between Zoutelande and Westkapelle. This attractively landscaped site is only 100 m. from the sandy North Sea beaches. There are 144 pitches (50 for tourers) on well kept, grassy lawns, connected by narrow tarmac roads. Separated by a variety of low bushes and shrubs, all the touring pitches have 6A electricity, water and drainage. The site is divided into two areas divided by the toilet block and reception. As well as the beach, Zeeland's dunes here are excellent for walking and cycling.

Facilities

One central, modern toilet block with British style toilets, washbasins (open and in cabins), free hot showers, baby room and special children's section. Laundry with washing machines, dryer, spin dryer, iron and board. Shop. Boules. Basketball. Volleyball. Small play area. Dogs are not accepted. English is spoken. Off site: Fishing 100 m. Riding 3 km. Golf 6 km. Bicycle hire 1 km. Beach 100 m.

Open: April - October.

Directions

From Zoutelande, follow the coastal road towards Westkapelle. Site is on the left just outside Zoutelande. GPS: N51:30.545 E03:25.046

Charges 2007

Per unit incl. 2 persons	€ 12,50
incl. electricity	€ 20,00 - € 31,00
extra person	€ 5,00
child (0-5 yrs)	€ 2,75

NL6930 Camping Schoneveld

See advertisement on page 361

Schoneveld 1, NL-4511 HR Breskens (Zeeland)

Tel: **011 738 3220**. Email: **schoneveld@zeelandnet.nl**

This site is well situated within walking distance of Breskens and it has direct access to sand dunes. It has around 200 touring pitches and has many static vans, although these are kept apart. The touring pitches are behind reception, laid out in fields which are entered from long avenues that run through the site. There are also twelve car parking bays. One ultra modern and very clean toilet block serves this area. The complex at the site entrance houses reception, a restaurant and a recreation room. Also near the entrance are the indoor pool, tennis courts and a football field. The ferry link to Breskens from Vlissingen takes pedestrians and cyclists only, a tunnel is now open for motor vehicles. You could also visit the ancient towns of Brugge and Gent which are not too far away. A member of the Tulip Parc group.

Facilities

One large sanitary block provides showers, wash cubicles, child size toilets and washbasins, baby room, en-suite unit for disabled visitors. Motorcaravan service point. Restaurant. 'Fun Food Plaza' and takeaway (5/4-31/10). Bowling. Indoor pool. Tennis. Football field. Play area. Organised entertainment in July/Aug. Bicycle hire. WiFi internet access. Off site: Fishing 200 m. Boat launching 3 km. Golf or riding 10 km.

Open: All year.

Directions

From Breskens port follow N58 south for around 1 km. and turn right at camping sign. Site is 500 m. GPS: N51:24.064 E03:32.085

Charges 2007

Per unit incl. 2 persons	€ 19,50 - € 33,00
incl. 3 persons	€ 22,50 - € 36,00
incl. 5 persons	€ 28,50 - € 42,00
tent pitch incl. 1 or 2 persons	€ 15,00
extra person	€ 3,00

Weekly tariff and various discounts available. Camping Cheques accepted.

NL5510 Camping Groede

Zeeweg 1, NL-4503 PA Groede (Zeeland)

Tel: **011 737 1384**. Email: **info@campinggroede.nl**

Camping Groede is a friendly, fair-sized site by the same stretch of sandy beach as no. NL5500. Family run, it aims to cater for the individual needs of visitors and to provide a good all-round holiday. Campers are sited as far as possible according to taste – in family areas, in larger groups or on more private pitches for those who prefer peace and quiet. In total, there are 500 pitches for tourists (plus 380 seasonal units), all with electrical connections (4-10A) and 300 with water and drainage connections. A new field has been added with 63 fully serviced large pitches. Camping Groede is ideally sited for ferry stopovers (Breskens) and short stay visitors including hikers are very welcome, as well as long stay holiday makers. Access to the beach is good for wheelchairs and baby buggies. A nature reserve is being constructed adjacent to the site. Run by the family van Damme, who ask visitors to complete a confidential questionnaire to ensure that their site offers the best possible service and provide you with a comprehensive information booklet.

Facilities

Toilet facilities are excellent with a high standard of cleanliness, including some wash cabins, baby baths, family room and a dedicated unit for persons with disabilities. Motorcaravan services. Gas supplies. Shop, restaurant and snack bar (all weekends only in low seasons). Recreation room. Internet access. Sports area. Several play areas (bark base). Plenty of activities for children in peak season. Bicycle hire. Fishing. Off site: Riding 1 km. Golf 11 km

Open: 24 March - 31 December.

Directions

From Breskens take the coast road for 5 km. to site. Alternatively, the site is signed from Groede village on the more inland Breskens - Sluis road. GPS: N51:23.749 E03:29.263

Charges guide

Per pitch incl. 2 persons	€ 17,00 - € 24,00
with 4A electricity	€ 19,00 - € 26,00
with water and drainage	€ 23,00 - € 30,00
extra person	€ 2,50
dog	€ 2,10

No credit cards.

NL5570 Camping De Molenhoek

Molenweg 69a, NL-4493 NC Kamperland (Zeeland)

Tel: 011 337 1202. Email: molenhoek@zeelandnet.nl

This family-run site makes a pleasant contrast to the livelier coastal sites in this popular holiday area. It is rurally situated 3 km. from the Veerse Meer which is very popular for all sorts of watersports. Catering for 300 permanent or seasonal holiday caravans and 100 touring units, it is neat, tidy and relatively spacious. The marked touring pitches are divided into small groups with surrounding hedges and trees giving privacy and some shade, and electrical connections are available. A large outdoor pool is Molenhoek's latest attraction. Entertainment is organised in season (dance evenings, bingo, etc.) as well as a disco for youngsters. Although the site is quietly situated, there are many excursion possibilities in the area including the towns of Middelburg, Veere and Goes and the Delta Expo exhibition.

Facilities

Sanitary facilities in one fully refurbished and one newer block, include some washbasins in cabins. Toilet and shower facilities for disabled visitors and for babies. Laundry facilities. Motorcaravan services. Simple bar/restaurant with terrace and TV room. Restaurant/bar. Swimming pool (15/5-15/9). Playground. Bicycle hire. Off site: Tennis and watersports close. Riding 1 km. Shop 2 km. Fishing 2.5 km.

Open: 1 April - 28 October.

Directions

Site is west of the village of Kamperland on the 'island' of Noord Beveland. From the N256 Goes - Zierikzee road, exit west onto N255 Kamperland road. Site is signed south of this road. GPS: N51:34.704 E03:41.785

Charges 2007

Per unit incl. 2 or 3 persons and electricity	€ 21,00 - € 33,50
extra person	€ 3,50 - € 4,50
dog	€ 2,50 - € 3,00

No credit cards.

★★★★ **Familiecamping de Molenhoek**

✓ 4-stars familiecampsite – 9,5 hectare large
✓ Annual-, seasonal- and touring piches
✓ Well maintained toilet blocks
✓ Facilities for disabled – baby room
✓ Heated open air swimming pool
✓ Paddling pool for children
✓ Bar, restaurant and takeaway
✓ Caravans for rent
✓ First class animation in high season
✓ Dogs have a warm welcome!

info or direct booking 0113 371202 – e-mail: molenhoek@zeelandnet.nl – www.demolenhoek.com

NL5580 Camping De Veerhoeve

Veerweg 48, NL-4471 NC Wolphaartsdijk (Zeeland)

Tel: 011 358 1155. Email: info@deveerhoeve.nl

This is a family-run site near the shores of the Veerse Meer which is ideal for family holidays. It is situated in a popular area for watersports and is well suited for sailing, windsurfing or fishing enthusiasts, with boat launching 100 m. away. A sandy beach and recreation area ideal for children is only a five minute walk. As with most sites in this area there are many mature static and seasonal pitches. However, part of the friendly, relaxed site is reserved for touring units with 90 marked pitches on grassy ground, all with electrical connections. A member of the Holland Tulip Parcs group.

Facilities

Sanitary facilities in three blocks have been well modernised with full tiling. Hot showers are on payment. Laundry facilities including ironing. Motorcaravan services. Supermarket (all season). Restaurant and snack bar. TV room. Tennis. Playground and play field. Games room. Bicycle hire. Fishing. Accommodation for groups. Max. 1 dog per pitch. WiFi. Off site: Slipway for launching boats 100 m. Riding 2 km. Golf 5 km.

Open: 1 April - 30 October.

Directions

From N256 Goes-Zierikzee road take Wolphaartsdijk exit. Follow through village and signs to site (be aware - one of the site signs is obscured by other road signs and could be missed). GPS: N51:32.807 E03:48.807

Charges 2007

Per pitch incl. up to 4 persons with electricity (6A), water	€ 21,50 - € 24,50
and drainage	€ 22,50 - € 25,50
with TV connection	€ 24,00 - € 27,50

Camping Cheques accepted.

Check real time availability and at-the-gate prices...

www.**alanrogers**.com

NL6920 Camping Veerse Meer

Veerweg 71, NL-4471 NB Wolphaartsdijk (Zeeland)

Tel: **011 358 1423**. Email: **info@campingveersemeer.nl**

This well cared for family-run site is situated beside the Veerse Meer on the island of Noord Beveland in Zeeland. Not only is its location idyllic for watersports enthusiasts, it is also an excellent and picturesque setting for cyclists and walkers. Emphasis at this site is on a neat and tidy appearance, quality facilities and a friendly reception. The site spreads over both sides of the road. The area to the right provides 15 pitches with individual sanitary facilities (some are seasonal), fully serviced hardstanding pitches for motorcaravans and a tent field at the far end. The original part of the site is where you will find reception, a bar and the main toilet block (recently renovated to provide water heated by solar panels). There are 40 generous touring pitches in this area, many fully serviced and separated by hedging. A feature of this campsite is a narrow canal crossed by a bridge.

Facilities

The single updated toilet block has showers (token operated), open style wash areas, two wash cabins, child size WC and a baby bath. Dishwashing sinks. Laundry. Motorcaravan service point. Bar. WiFi. Play area. Organised events for all age groups in high season. Bicycle hire. Fishing.

Open: 1 April - 31 October.

Directions

From N256 Goes-Zierikzee road take Wolphaartsdijk exit. Follow through village and signs to site. GPS: N51:32.662 E03:48.769

Charges 2007

Per unit incl. 1 or 2 persons	€ 14,00 - € 20,50
incl. private sanitary facility	€ 23,00 - € 29,50
extra person	€ 2,50
No credit cards.	

NL6915 Camping Linda

Oostelijke kanaalweg 4, NL-4424 NC Wemeldinge (Zeeland)

Tel: **011 362 1259**. Email: **info@campinglinda.nl**

Camping Linda is a welcoming, family run site, situated on the shores of the Oosterachelde, with direct access to a small beach. The area is ideal for watersports enthusiasts and particularly popular with divers. Pitches are a good size, level and grassy, with 100 out of 350 places reserved for touring. Most of these are situated in the quieter part of the site, across a narrow country road and nearest to the beach access. Other pitches are closer to the reception area. All have electricity (6A), water and TV connection. In high season a comprehensive entertainment programme is organised.

Facilities

SiteFacilities Off site: Fishing from beach. Marina adjoining site. Nearby is the town of Goes with a wide variety of shops. Kapelle 3 km. with indoor and outdoor swimming pools. Golf 6 km.

Open: 1 April - 1 November.

Directions

From the south, take A58 towards Vlissingen. Leave at junction 35 and head north towards Kapelle. Continue on N670 to Wemeldinge. Site is next to Yacht Haven and is well signed.

Charges 2007

Per unit with 2 persons	
incl. electricity	€ 14,00 - € 19,50
extra person	€ 2,00 - € 4,00

NL5560 Camping De Wijde Blick

Lagezoom 23, NL-4325 CP Renesse (Zeeland)

Tel: **011 146 8888**. Email: **wijdeblick@ardoer.com**

The Van Oost family run this neat campsite in a pleasant and personal way. It is located on the outskirts of the village of Renesse in a quiet rural spot. Much redevelopment took place during 2005 and De Wijde Blick now has 316 pitches of which 234 are for touring units. These include 203 fully serviced pitches. There are private sanitary facilities and 31 attractively arranged motorcaravan pitches with hardstanding. All the touring pitches have 6/10A electricity and are 90-120 sq.m. in area. There are special 'bike and hike' pitches for those touring without a car. Those with cars must park away from the pitch areas. Children are welcomed by the campsite mascot, Billy Blick and will thoroughly enjoy the large playground, the indoor activity room or an evening at the theatre wagon. The newest toilet block is solar heated, with a special children's section and an interesting schedule of how the technology works. This is a real holiday area and there are restaurants and shops in the village (and a market on Wednesdays). The beach is 2 km. from the site.

Facilities

Three modern toilet blocks (one refurbished to very high standards and one) are first class, heated and with clean facilities including washbasins in cabins, controllable showers, facilities for disabled people, microwave and fridge. Bath (on payment). Laundry (with cartoons for children). Gas supplies. Motorcaravan services. Shop. Restaurant/bar (15/3-31/10). Swimming pool (1/5-15/9). WiFi internet access. Good playground. Bicycle hire. Activities for children. Dogs are not accepted. Off site: Tennis and minigolf. Riding and fishing 1.5 km. Golf 10 km. Beach 2 km.

Open: All year.

Directions

Renesse is on the island of Schouwen (connected to the mainland by a bridge and three dams). On the N57 from Middelburg take the Renesse exit. After 2 km. follow road 106 to the left and then site signs. Site is on the east side of the village. GPS: N51:43.106 E03:46.028

Charges 2008

Per unit incl. 2 persons	€ 15,00 - € 34,50
extra person	€ 4,50

CAMPING DE WIJDE BLICK - Lagezoom 23 - 4325 CP Renesse
T. +31 (0)111 468 888 - F +31 (0)111 468889 - E wijdeblick@ardoer.com - www.ardoer.com/wijdeblick

NL6950 Camping International Renesse

Scharendijkseweg 8, NL-4325 LD Renesse (Zeeland)

Tel: **011 146 1391**. Email: **info@camping-international.net**

Situated 300 metres from the beach at Renesse in Zeeland, this is a friendly, family run site. Its owners have set high standards, which is demonstrated by the immaculate and tastefully decorated sanitary facilities. There are 200 pitches, with 120 for touring units (80 have electricity connections 4-16A). These are generous size and laid out in bays and avenues surrounded by hedging. Around a courtyard area beyond reception is a supermarket and a bar which is attractively decorated with novel figures and the owner's personal memorabilia. Outside bench seating and umbrellas turns this corner of the camping into a popular meeting place.

Facilities

Two luxury sanitary blocks provide showers, washbasins (some in cabins) and a baby room. Dishwashing sinks (hot water on payment). Laundry room with washing machine, dryer and ironing board. Motorcaravan service point. Supermarket. Bar. Games room, TV and table tennis. Play area. Bicycle hire. Entertainment in high season for children and adults.

Open: 1 March - 31 October.

Directions

From Zierikzee follow N59 to Renesse for approx. 15 km. and turn right at roundabout (before town) onto local road signed R101. Continue for about 1 km. and turn left, then first right to site on right.

Charges 2007

Per unit incl. 2 persons and electricity	€ 23,50
extra person	€ 4,50
child (2-9 yrs)	€ 4,00

NL5630 Camping Koningshof

Elsgeesterweg 8, NL-2231 NW Rijnsburg (Zuid-Holland)

Tel: 071 402 6051. Email: info@koningshofholland.nl

This popular site is run in a personal and friendly way. The 200 pitches for touring units (some with hardstandings for larger units) are laid out in groups of four or twelve, divided by hedges and trees and all with electrical connections (10A). Cars are mostly parked in areas around the perimeter and 100 static caravans, confined to one section of the site, are entirely unobtrusive. Reception, a pleasant good quality restaurant, bar and a snack bar are grouped around a courtyard style entrance which is decorated with seasonal flowers. The site has a small outdoor, heated pool (13.5 x 7 m), with a separate paddling pool and imaginative children's play equipment. Recent additions are a recreation hall, an indoor swimming pool and a unique children's play pool with water streams, locks and play materials. The site has a number of regular British visitors from club connections who receive a friendly welcome, with English spoken. Used by tour operators (25 pitches). A very useful local information booklet (in English) is provided for visitors. A member of the Holland Tulip Parcs group.

Facilities

Three good toilet blocks, two with under-floor heating, with washbasins in cabins and provision for disabled visitors. Laundry facilities. Motorcaravan services. Gas supplies. Shop (1/4-15/10). Bar (1/4-1/11). Restaurant (1/4-10/9). Snacks and takeaway (1/4-1/11). Small outdoor pool (unsupervised; 15/5-15/9). Indoor pool complex (15/3-15/11). Solarium. Adventure playground and sports area. Tennis. Fishing pond (free). Bicycle hire. Entertainment in high season. Room for shows. One dog per pitch accepted in a limited area of the site. Off site: Riding or golf 5 km. Sandy beach 5 km. Den Haag 15 km. and Amsterdam 30 km.

Open: All year.

Directions

From N44/A44 Den Haag - Amsterdam motorway, take exit 7 for Oegstgeest and Rijnsburg. Turn towards Rijnsburg and follow camp signs GPS: N52:12.007 E04:27.374

Charges 2007

Per pitch incl. 2 persons	€ 21,50 - € 27,50
extra person (over 3 yrs)	€ 3,50
dog (see text)	€ 3,00
electricity (10A)	€ 4,50

Senior citizen discounts, group rates and special packages.
Camping Cheques accepted.

NL5600 Camping Delftse Hout

Korftlaan 5, NL-2616 LJ Delft (Zuid-Holland)

Tel: 015 213 0040. Email: info@delftsehout.nl

Pleasantly situated in Delft's park and forest area on the eastern edge of the city, this well run, modern site is part of the Koningshof group. It has 200 tourist pitches quite formally arranged in groups of 4 to 6 and surrounded by attractive young trees and hedges. All have sufficient space and electrical connections (10A). Modern buildings near the entrance house the site amenities. A good sized first floor restaurant serves snacks or full meals and has an outdoor terrace overlooking the swimming pool and pitches.

Facilities

Modern, heated toilet facilities include a spacious family room and children's section. facilities for disabled people. Laundry. Motorcaravan services. Shop for basic food and camping items (1/4-1/11). Restaurant and bar (1/4-1/10). Small outdoor swimming pool (15/5-15/9). Adventure playground. Recreation room. Internet access. Bicycle hire. Gas supplies Off site: Fishing 1 km. Riding or golf 5 km. Regular bus service to Delft centre.

Open: All year.

Directions

Site is 1 km. east of Delft. From A13 motorway take Delft - Pijnacker (exit 9), turn towards Pijnacker and then right at first traffic lights, following camping signs through suburbs and park to site. GPS: N52:01.060 E04:22.745

Charges 2007

Per unit incl. 2 persons	€ 21,50 - € 25,50
supplement for services	€ 8,50
extra person (3 yrs and older)	€ 2,00
electricity (10A)	€ 4,50

Camping Cheques accepted.

NL5640 Vakantiecentrum Kijkduinpark

Machiel Vrijenhoeklaan 450, NL-2555 NW Den Haag (Zuid-Holland)

Tel: 070 448 2100. Email: info@kijkduinpark.nl

This is now an ultra-modern, all year round centre and family park, with many huts, villas and bungalows for rent and a large indoor swimming pool complex. The wooded touring area is immediately to the left of the entrance, with 330 pitches in shady glades of bark covered sand. All pitches have electricity electricity 10A, water, waste water and cable TV connections. In a paved central area stands a supermarket, snack bar and restaurant. The main attraction here is the Meeresstrand; a long, wide sandy beach with flags to denote suitability for swimming.

Facilities

There are five modern sanitary blocks (key entry, € 20 deposit). Four private cabins for rent. Launderette. Snack bar. Shop. Restaurant. Supermarket (all year). Indoor pool. Sun beds. Tennis. Bicycle hire. Special golfing breaks. Entertainment and activities organised in summer. Internet. Off site: Beach, golf and fishing 500 m. Riding 5 km.

Open: All year.

Directions

Site is southwest of Den Haag on the coast and Kijkduin is well signed as an area from all round Den Haag. GPS: N52:03.581 E04:12.671

Charges 2007

Per unit incl. 5 persons	
and electricity	€ 19,00 - € 37,00
with electricity, water	
and drainage	€ 20,00 - € 48,25
extra person	€ 4,00

NL6970 Camping 't Weergors

Zuiddijk 2, NL-3221 LJ Hellevoetsluis (Zuid-Holland)

Tel: 018 131 2430. Email: weergors@pn.nl

A rustic style site built around old farm buildings, t'Weergors has a comfortable mature feel. At the front of the site is a well presented farmhouse which houses reception and includes the main site services. Around the courtyard area is one of the three sanitary blocks which is unsophisticated, but clean and functional. There are plans to replace this with a new reception and shop and build a new toilet block elsewhere. There are currently 100 touring pitches (plus seasonal and static places), with another field at the back of the site under development to provide a further 70 or 80 touring places.

Facilities

Three sanitary blocks have showers (by token), washbasins, some in cabins, child size WCs and a baby bath. Dishwashing sinks (token). Washing machine and dryer. Motorcaravan service point. Small shop (1/4-31/10). Restaurant and bar (all year). Snack bar. Tennis. Recreation room/TV. Internet access. Play area. Paddling pool. Organised entertainment in high season. Fishing. Bicycle hire. Rally field.

Open: 22 March - 31 October.

Directions

From Rotterdam join A15 west to Rozenburg exit 12 and join N57 south for 11 km. Turn left on the N497 signed Hellevoetsluis and follow site signs for 4.5 km. to roundabout. Turn right at roundabout to site 1.5 km. on right. GPS: N51:49.766 E04:06.971

Charges 2008

Per person	€ 3,50
pitch incl. car and electricity (6A)	€ 10,00

Camping Cheques accepted.

NL6980 Camping De Krabbeplaat

Oude Veerdam 4, NL-3231 NC Brielle (Zuid-Holland)

Tel: **0181 412 363**. Email: **info@krabbeplaat.nl**

Camping de Krabbeplaat is a family run site situated near the ferry port in a wooded, recreation area next to the 'Brielse Meer' lake. There are 510 spacious pitches, with 100 for touring units, each with electricity (10A) and cable connections and a water supply nearby. A separate field i used for groups of up to 450 guests. A nature conversation plan exists to ensure the site fits into with its natural environment. The lake and its beaches provide the perfect spot for watersports and relaxation and the site has its own harbour where you can moor your own boat. The beach is 7 km from the site for those who prefer the sea. Plenty of cultural opportunities can be found in the historic towns of the area. Because of the large range of amenities and the tranquil nature of the site, de Krabbeplaat is perfect for families and couples.

Facilities

One large and two smaller heated toilet blocks in traditional style provide separate toilets, showers and washing cabins. High standards of cleanliness, a dedicated unit for disabled persons and provision for babies. Warm water is free of charge. Launderette. Motorcaravan services. Supermarket and snack bar (1/4-1/10). Restaurant (July/Aug). Recreation room. Youth centre. Tennis court. Playground and play field. Animal farm. Bicycle and children's pedal hire. Canoe, surf, pedal boat and boat hire. Fishing. WiFi. Two cottages for hikers. Dogs are not accepted.

Open: 21 March - 19 October.

Directions

From the Amsterdam direction take the A4 road (Europoort), then the A15 (Europoort). Take exit for Brielle on N57 and, just before Brielle, site is signed.

Charges 2007

Per unit incl. 2 persons	
and electricity	€ 11,50 - € 21,00
extra person	€ 2,50 - € 2,90

Camping **De Krabbeplaat**

Op camping De Krabbeplaat bent u écht met vakantie

Facilities at ****Starlevel

- Tenniscourts
- Campsite harbour
- Holiday entertainment team
- Playground
- Beach
- Recreationroom

Dogs are not allowed

- Snack bar
- Small restaurant
- Youth centre
- Launderette
- Heated toilet blocks
- Wireless Internet
- Free Showers

- Supermarket
- Canoe, pedal boat, boat, bicycle and childeren's pedal car hire
- Freshwater and saltwater fishinggrounds

Oude Veerdam 4 | 3231 NC Brielle, Nederland | T +31(0)181 412 363 | F +31(0)181 12 093 | www.krabbeplaat.com

NL5680 Camping Noordduinen

Campingweg 1, NL-2221 EW Katwijk (Zuid-Holland)

Tel: **071 402 5295**. Email: **info@noordduinen.nl**

This is a large, well managed site surrounded by dunes and sheltered partly by trees and shrubbery, which also separate the various camping areas. The 200 touring pitches are marked and numbered but not divided. All have electricity (10A) and 45 are fully serviced with electricity, water, drainage and TV connection. There are also seasonal pitches and mobile homes for rent. Entertainment is organised in high season for various age groups. A new complex with indoor and outdoor pools, restaurant, small theatre and recreation hall provides a good addition to the site's facilities.

Facilities

The three sanitary blocks are modern and clean, with washbasins in cabins, a baby room and provision for people with disabilities. Hot water for showers and dishwashing is on payment. Laundry. Motorcaravan services. Supermarket with fresh bread daily. New pool complex, restaurant and bar and recreation room. Play area. Only gas barbecues are permitted. Fishing. No dogs are accepted. Off site: Beach (300 m) and Katwijk within walking distance. Riding 150 m.

Open: 31 March - 28 October.

Directions

Leave A44 at exit 8 (Leiden - Katwijk) to join N206 to Katwijk. Take Katwijk Noord exit and follow signs to site. GPS: N52:12.662 E04:24.587

Charges 2007

Per pitch incl. 2 persons	€ 15,00 - € 35,00
electricity (10A)	€ 4,50
extra person	€ 4,00

NL5690 Camping De Victorie

Broekseweg 75-77, NL-4231 VD Meerkerk (Zuid-Holland)

Tel: **018 335 2741**. Email: **info@campingdevictorie.nl**

Within an hour's drive of the port of Rotterdam you can be pitched on this delightful, spacious site in the 'green heart' of Holland. De Victorie, a working farm and a member of a club of small, 'green' sites, offers an alternative to the bustling seaside sites. A modern building houses reception, open plan office and space with tables and chairs, where the friendly owners may well invite you to have coffee. The 73 grass pitches (100-200 sq.m) are level and have 4A electricity supply. Everything about the site is surprising and contrary to any preconceived ideas. You can choose to be pitched in the shade of one of the orchards, or in the more open meadow area. The freedom of the farmland is especially enjoyed by children with farm animals and tractor rides. This is an ideal site for those seeking peace and quiet whilst still being close to the area's main attractions.

Facilities

The main sanitary block is kept spotlessly clean, tastefully decorated and fully equipped. Showers are on payment. Dishwashing area and laundry room. Additional sanitary facilities are around the site. Farm shop and small bar (once a week). Play area. Trampoline, and play field for football. Bicycle hire. Fishing. Riding. WiFi. Off site: Golf 15 km.

Open: 15 March - 31 October.

Directions

From Rotterdam follow A15 to junction with A27. Proceed 6 km. north on A27 to Noordeloos exit (no. 25) and join N214. Site is signed about 200 m. after roundabout at Noordeloos. GPS: N51:56.174 E04:57.449

Charges 2007

Per unit incl. 2 persons and electricity	€ 10,00 - € 12,00
extra person	€ 2,50

No credit cards. Special rates for longer stays. Large units may be charged extra.

NL5620 Vakantiepark Duinrell

Duinrell 1, NL-2242 JP Wassenaar (Zuid-Holland)

Tel: **070 515 5257**. Email: **info@duinrell.nl**

A very large site, Duinrell's name means 'well in the dunes' and the water theme is continued in the adjoining amusement park and in the extensive indoor pool complex. The campsite itself is very large with 1,150 tourist places on several flat grassy areas (60-80 sq.m) and it can become very busy in high season. As part of a continuing improvement programme, 950 marked pitches have electricity, water and drainage connections and some have cable TV. Amenities shared with the park include restaurants, a pizzeria and pancake house, supermarket and a theatre. Entry to the popular pleasure park is free for campers – indeed the camping areas surround and open out from the park. The 'Tiki' tropical pool complex has many attractions which include slides ranging from quite exciting to terrifying (according to your age!), whirlpools, saunas and many other features. There are also free outdoor pools and the centre has its own bar and café. Entry to the Tiki complex is at a reduced rate for campers. Duinrell is open all year and a ski school (langlauf and Alpine) with 12 artificial runs, is a winter attraction. There are now 425 smartly furnished bungalows to rent.

Facilities

Six heated toilet blocks serve the touring areas. Laundry facilities. Amusement park and Tiki tropical pool complex as detailed above. Restaurant, cafés, pizzeria and takeaways (weekends only in winter). Supermarket. Entertainment and theatre with shows in high season. 'Rope Challenge' trail and 'Forest Frisbee' trail. Bicycle hire. Bowling. Artificial ski slopes and ski school (winter). Diving experience package. All activities have extra charges. Off site: Beach 3.5 km. Riding 5 km. Golf 10 km.

Open: All year.

Directions

Site is signed from the N44/A44 (Den Haag - Amsterdam), but from the south the turning is about 5 km. after passing sign for start of Wassenaar town – then follow site signs. GPS: N52:08.785 E04:23.242

Charges 2007

Per person (over 3 yrs)	€ 4,95 - € 9,50
pitch	€ 8,50

Special package offers. Overnight stays between 17.00-10.00 hrs (when amusement park closed) less 25%.

Check real time availability and at-the-gate prices...

www.**alanrogers**.com

NL6960 **Recreatiepark De Klepperstee**

Vrijheidsweg 1, NL-3253 ZG Ouddorp (Zuid-Holland)

Tel: **018 768 1511**. Email: **info@klepperstee.com**

De Klepperstee is a good quality, family site. The site itself is peacefully located in tranquil countryside amid renowned nature reserves and just outside the village of Ouddorp in Zuid Holland. It offers excellent recreation areas that are spread over the centre of the site giving it an attractive open parkland appearance which is enhanced by many shrubs, trees and grass areas. The 338 spacious touring pitches are in named avenues, mostly separated by hedging and spread around the perimeter, together with the seasonal and static caravans. A variety of play equipment ensures hours of non-stop fun for children. There is even a special evening 'house' for older children with a television, etc. De Klepperstee would be ideal for a seaside holiday.

Facilities

One main sanitary block and a number of WC/shower units around the touring area provide hot showers (on payment), washbasins, some in cabins (hot water only), baby bath and shower, child size toilets and a unit for people with disabilities. Dishwashing (hot water on payment). Laundry. Motorcaravan service point. Supermarket. Restaurant, bar and takeaway. Small paddling pool. Play areas. Tennis. TV, pool and electronic games. Entertainment. Bicycle hire. No animals are accepted and no single sex groups.

Open: Easter - 31 October.

Directions

From Rotterdam follow A15 west to Rozenburg exit 12 and join N57 south for 22 km. Take exit for Ouddorp and follow signs for 'Stranden'. Site is on the left after about 3 km.
GPS: N51:48.961 E03:53.983

Charges 2008

Per unit incl. up to 4 persons	€ 10,00 - € 29,00
incl. 6A electricity	€ 12,50 - € 31,50
incl. 10A electricity	€ 17,50 - € 34,00
extra person	€ 2,75

NL5660 **Camping Het Amsterdamse Bos**

Kleine Noorddijk 1, NL-1187 NZ Amstelveen (Noord-Holland)

Tel: **020 641 6868**. Email: **info@campingamsterdamsebos.com**

Het Amsterdamse Bos is a large park to the southwest of Amsterdam, one corner of which has been specifically laid out as the city's municipal site and is now under family ownership. Close to Schiphol Airport (we only noticed little noise), it is about 12 km. from central Amsterdam. The site is well laid out alongside a canal, with unmarked pitches on separate flat lawns mostly backing onto pleasant hedges and trees, with several areas of new paved hardstandings. It takes 400 touring units, with 100 electrical connections (10A) and some with cable TV. An additional area is available for tents and groups.

Facilities

Two older style sanitary blocks rather let the site down, appearing somewhat small and well used. A third block is newer. Hot water is free to the washbasins but hot showers are on payment. Laundry facilities. Motorcaravan services. Gas supplies. Small shop with basics. Fresh bread from reception. Bicycle hire. Internet. Off site: Fishing, boating, pancake restaurant in the park. Riding 5 km.

Open: 15 March - 15 December.

Directions

Amsterdamse Bos and site are west of Amstelveen. From the A9 motorway take exit 6 and follow N231 to site (2nd traffic light).
GPS: N52:17.614 E04:49.378

Charges 2007

Per person	€ 5,00
child (4-12 yrs)	€ 2,50
pitch incl. car	€ 6,50 - € 8,50
electricity (10A)	€ 3,50
Group reductions.	

NL5670 Gaasper Camping Amsterdam

Loosdrechtdreef 7, NL-1108 AZ Amsterdam (Noord-Holland)

Tel: 020 696 7326

Amsterdam is probably the most popular destination for visits in the Netherlands, and Gaasper Camping is on the southeast side, a short walk from a Metro station with a direct 20 minute service to the centre. It is situated on the edge of a large park with nature areas and a lake with sailing facilities and swimming beaches. The site is well kept and neatly laid out on flat grass with trees and shrubs. There are 350 touring pitches in two areas – one open and grassy, mainly for tents (20 pitches with 10A connections), the other more formal with numbered pitches divided by shallow ditches or hedges. Hardstandings are available. All caravan pitches have electrical connections (10A).

Facilities

Three modern, clean toilet blocks (one unisex) for the tourist sections are an adequate provision. Six new cabins with basin and shower. Hot water for showers and some dishwashing sinks on payment. Facilities for babies. Laundry facilities. Motorcaravan services. Gas supplies. Supermarket (1/4-1/11). Café/bar plus takeaway (1/4-1/11). Shopping centre and restaurant nearby. Play area. Off site: Riding 200 m. Fishing 1 km. Golf 4 km.

Open: 15 March - 1 November.

Directions

Take exit No.1 for Gaasperplas - Weesp (S113) from the section of A9 motorway which is on the east side of the A2. Note: do not take the Gaasperdam exit (S112) which comes first if approaching from the west. GPS: N52:18.776 E04:59.489

Charges 2007

Per person	€ 4,75
child (under 12 yrs)	€ 2,25
pitch incl. car and electricity	€ 13,75 - € 14,75

NL5720 Camping Jachthaven Uitdam

Zeedijk 2, NL-1154 PP Uitdam (Noord-Holland)

Tel: 020 403 1433. Email: info@campinguitdam.nl

Situated beside the Markermeer which is used extensively for watersports, this large site has its own private yachting marina (300 yachts and boats). It has 200 seasonal and permanent pitches, many used by watersports enthusiasts, but also offers 260 marked tourist pitches (180 with 4/6A electricity) on open, grassy ground overlooking the water and 24 mobile homes to rent. There is a special area for campers with bicycles. Very much dominated by the marina, this site will appeal to watersports enthusiasts, with opportunities for sailing, windsurfing and swimming, or for fishing, but it is also on a pretty stretch of coast. Much construction was underway when we visited, but this was mainly in the seasonal areas. All the touring pitches have been upgraded with new drainage and there are new cabins for rent. Uitdam is 15 km. northeast of Amsterdam and is close to the ancient, small towns of Marken, Volendam and Monnickendam, which are well worth a visit. The views over the IJsselmeer from both ends of the touring fields are wonderful and this alone makes this site well worth visiting.

Facilities

Two good toilet blocks and one rather basic toilet block with toilets only. Good facilities include hot showers on payment, toilets, washbasins and a baby room. Dishwashing. Motorcaravan services. Gas supplies. Shop (1/4-1/10). Bar/restaurant (weekends and high season). TV room. Tennis. Playground and paddling pool. Bicycle hire. Fishing. Yacht marina (with fuel) and slipway. Watersports facilities. Entertainment in high season. Off site: Riding 4 km. Sailing 6 km. Golf 12 km.

Open: 1 March - 1 November.

Directions

From A10, take exit S116 onto the N247 towards Volendam. Then take Monnickendam exit south in direction of Marken on N518, then Uitdam. Site is just outside Uitdam. GPS: N52:25.668 E05:04.408

Charges 2007

Per unit incl. 2 persons	€ 22,50
tent incl. 2 persons	€ 15,50 - € 19,00
extra person (over 3 yrs)	€ 3,00
boat on trailer	€ 7,00

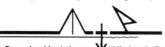

NL5700 Buitencentrum Molengroet

Molengroet 1, NL-1723 PX Noord-Scharwoude (Noord-Holland)
Tel: 022 639 3444. Email: info@molengroet.nl

Molengroet is a modern, pleasant site, close to a lake for watersports and 40 kilometres from Amsterdam. It is a useful stop on the way to the Afsluitdijk across the top of the Ijsselmeer or as an enjoyable stop for watersport enthusiasts. The 157 touring pitches are grouped according to services provided, ranging from simple pitches with no services, to those with electricity (4/10A), TV, water and waste water. Some have beautiful views over the lake and surrounding countryside. The bar and restaurant are open all season and there is a snack bar in high season. The nearby lake with surf school is an attractive proposition, particularly for those with teenagers. A site bus can take you to the local pool, the beach and Alkmaar with its famous cheese market. Friendly multi-lingual staff provide local information. An extensive animation programme is run in high season. A member of the Holland Tulip Parcs group.

Facilities

The best sanitary facilities, in a modern, heated building, are near the serviced pitches. Some private facilities for rent. Motorcaravan services. Gas supplies. Shop. Restaurant/bar. Bouncy castle. Fishing. Bicycle hire. Surfboards and small boats for hire. Entertainment is organised in high season and at weekends in a large tent. Off site: Watersports. Tennis, squash, sauna, and swimming nearby. Riding or golf 5 km.

Open: 1 April - 31 October.

Directions

From Haarlem on A9 to Alkmaar take N245 towards Schagen. Site is southwest of Noord Sharwoude on the N245, signed to west on road to Geestermerambacht. GPS: N52:41.673 E04:46.262

Charges 2007

Per unit incl. 2 persons and electricity	€ 19,00 - € 26,00

Reductions in low season and for longer stays.
Camping Cheques accepted.

NL5735 Camping Tempelhof

Westerweg 2, NL-1759 JD Callantsoog (Noord-Holland)

Tel: 022 458 1522. Email: info@tempelhof.nl

This first class site on the Dutch coast has 500 pitches with 250 for touring units, the remainder used by seasonal campers and a number of static units (mostly privately owned). All touring pitches have electricity (10/16A), water, drain and TV aerial point. The grass pitches are arranged in long rows which are separated by hedges and shrubs, with access from hardcore roads. There is hardly any shade. Tempelhof is close to the North Sea beaches (1 km), but the site has a heated indoor pool with a paddling pool, water slide and new gym. There are facilities for football, handball, volleyball and tennis and a climbing wall. In high season a full entertainment programme is arranged for children with water games, sports activities and music. Many of these activities take place in the new recreation hall with its stage. With all these activities, you may not want to leave the site other than to go to the beach. However, the site is close to the ferry port of Den Helder where you can catch a ferry to the largest Dutch Island – Texel. Tempelhof is also close to the cheese market in Alkmaar and only 60 km. or so from Amsterdam. Member of Leading Campings Group.

Facilities

Two toilet blocks have modern facilities including washbasins (open style and in cabins) and controllable hot showers (SEP key). Children's section and baby room with bath and changing mat. Private bathroom with shower, toilet and basin (€ 50 p/w). Facilities for disabled visitors. Fully equipped laundry. Motorcaravan services. Shop, restaurant and takeaway (1/4-1/11) and bar (all year). Swimming pool with paddling pool (charge). Recreation hall. Trim court. Play area. Extensive animation programme in high season. Wifi. Bicycle hire. Off site: Fishing 500 m. Beach 1 km. Golf 6 km. Riding 4 km. Boat launching 1 km.

Open: All year.

Directions

From Alkmaar take N9 road north towards Den Helder. Turn left towards Callantsoog on the N503 road and follow site signs.
GPS: N52:50.824 E04:42.915

Charges 2007

Per unit incl. 2 persons,	
electricity and services	€ 17,00 - € 35,00
extra person	€ 3,00
electricity per kWh	€ 0,35

NL6830 Recreatiecentrum Mijnden

Bloklaan 22A, NL-1231 AZ Loosdrecht (Utrecht)

Tel: 029 423 3165. Email: info@mijnden.nl

Recreatiecentrum Mijnden is located amidst typical Dutch countryside alongside the River Drecht and close to cities such as Amsterdam, Utrecht and Hilversum. The site has 120 level pitches for tourers, some on hardstanding, all with 4/10A electricity and 20 with water and drainage. There are also 80 seasonal pitches and 250 mobile homes. The pitches are on grassy fields and almost all provide lovely views over the lake. The site has recently undergone major changes, including the addition of an extra camping field overlooking the water providing 36 extra pitches (20 for tourers), some with their own landing stage for boats. Mijnden is in a central position in the Vechtstreek, one of the most beautiful parts of the Netherlands, and you can explore this area by car, bike or on foot. There are some famous country estates and several charming castles to visit. The site itself has much to offer with evening entertainment including live music, and activities including swimming, sailing, water skiing or boating. The site has its own boat slipway so you could bring your own boat and navigate the Loosdrechtse Plassen. The waterfront is not fenced or gated.

Facilities

Three modern, heated sanitary blocks with showers on payment, washbasins, toilets and facilities for disabled visitors. Launderette. Motorcaravan service point. Gas. Supermarket (1/4-15/9). Bar-café-restaurant 'Het Drechthuis' and snack bar (1/4-1/10). Room for teenagers. Zoo. New play area. Sports field. Boat slipway. Sailing and fishing competitions. Entertainment programme. Fishing. Bicycle hire. Caravan storage. Off site: Golf 10 km. Riding 5 km. Amsterdam and Utrecht 20 km. Loosdrechtse Plassen 100 m.

Open: 25 March - 1 October.

Directions

Take A2 from Utrecht towards Amsterdam. Exit for Hilversum and after bridge turn right. Drive through village of Loenen and turn left to site.
GPS: N52:12.156 E05:01.808

Charges 2008

Per unit incl. 2 persons,	
electricity	€ 19,00 - € 24,00
extra person	€ 4,00
small tent pitch incl. 2 persons	€ 12,50 - € 14,50

NL6870 Kennemer Duincamping De Lakens

Zeeweg 60, NL-2051 EC Bloemendaal aan Zee (Noord-Holland)

Tel: 023 541 1570. Email: delakens@kennemerduincampings.nl

De Lakens is part of de Kennemer Duincampings group and is beautifully located in the dunes at Bloemendaal aan Zee. This site has 940 reasonably large, flat pitches with a hardstanding of shells. There are 410 for tourers (235 with 16A electricity) and the sunny pitches are separated by low hedging. This site is a true oasis of peace in a part of the Netherlands usually bustling with activity. From this site it is possible to walk straight through the dunes to the North Sea. Although there is no pool, there is the sea.

Facilities

The six toilet blocks for tourers (two brand new) include controllable showers, washbasins (open style and in cabins), facilities for disabled people and a baby room. Launderette. Two motorcaravan service points. Bar/restaurant and snack bar. Supermarket. Adventure playgrounds. Bicycle hire. Entertainment program in high season for all ages. Dogs are not accepted. Off site: Beach and riding 1 km. Golf 10 km.

Open: 20 March - 1 November.

Directions

From Amsterdam go west to Haarlem and follow the N200 from Haarlem towards Bloemendaal aan Zee. Site is on the N200, on the right hand side. GPS: N52:24.338 E04:35.191

Charges 2007

Per pitch incl. 4 persons	€ 14,10 - € 27,45
incl. electricty	€ 18,40 - € 28,70
extra person	€ 4,20

NL6820 Camping Westerkogge

Kerkebuurt 202, NL-1647 MH Berkhout (Noord-Holland)

Tel: 022 955 1208. Email: info@camping-westerkogge.nl

Camping Westerkogge is near the A7 motorway, close to Hoorn and the Ijsselmeer. The 300 pitches (100 for touring units) are on grassy fields, surrounded by high trees and bushes that provide shade; 80 pitches have 6A electricity and 28 of these also have water and drainage. From this site you can cycle through the lovely West Friesland countryside, sail on the Ijsselmeer or visit the attractive old town of Hoorn. It is also a good base for visiting Amsterdam or the harbour of Den Helder. After that you could tour through the polder by boat or hire a canoe.

Facilities

Three toilet blocks include washbasins (open style and in cabins), child size washbasins and unisex showers. Facilities for disabled visitors. Laundry. Motorcaravan services. Shop (in reception). Café with bar and snacks. Covered pool (10 x 5 m) with separate paddling pool (also open to the public). Playground. Sports court. Tennis. Bicycle hire. Go-kart and canoe hire. Boat trips through the polder. Off site: Riding 10 km. Golf 15 km. Beach 30 km.

Open: 1 April - 30 October.

Directions

Follow the A7 from Amsterdam north towards Hoorn and take exit Berkhout - Hoorn. Follow signs for Berkhout and site. GPS: N52:58.341 E04:59.392

Charges guide

Per unit incl. 2 persons, 4A electricity	€ 18,80 - € 21,00
extra person	€ 2,10 - € 2,40
child (3-4 yrs)	€ 1,85
dog	€ 2,10 - € 2,40

NL6840 Camping Vogelenzang

2e Doodweg 17, NL-2114 AP Vogelenzang (Noord-Holland)

Tel: 023 584 7019. Email: camping@vogelenzang.nl

Camping Vogelenzang is a friendly site with 600 pitches, located 15 km. from the North Sea beaches. The cities of Haarlem and Amsterdam with their old streets are within reach. There are 300 pitches here for touring caravans and tents, about half with electricity connections. There is a separate area for tents. Arranged on flat grass, all the pitches are numbered and mature trees and hedges provide shade, but also give the site a somewhat enclosed feel. A family campsite, there is something for everyone. In high season, an activity program for children includes activities and games.

Facilities

Four modern and one older toilet block provide toilets, open washbasins with cold water, washbasins in cabins with hot and cold water, controllable showers (on payment), a family shower room and baby room. Motorcaravan service point. Shop (1/4-15/9). Bar and snack bar (1/4-15/9). Open air swimming pool (10 x 5 m) with separate paddling pool. Play area. Sports field. Extensive high season recreation programme. Dogs are not accepted. Off site: Beach 15 km.

Open: 1 April - 15 September.

Directions

From Haarlem on the N206 traveling south take exit for Vogelenzang and follow campsite signs through Vogelenzang and Hillegom. The entrance road is to the right on a bend just after leaving Hillegom. GPS: N52:19.204 E04:33.975

Charges 2007

Per unit incl. up to 6 persons	€ 14,75
tent pitch (4 persons)	€ 10,90
extra person	€ 4,45

NL6080 Camping De Zeehoeve

Westerzeedijk 45, NL-8862 PK Harlingen (Friesland)

Tel: **051 741 3465**. Email: **info@zeehoeve.nl**

Superbly located, directly behind the sea dyke of the Waddensea and just a kilometre from the harbour of Harlingen, De Zeehoeve is an attractive and spacious site. It has 300 pitches (125 for tourers), all with 10A electricity and 20 with water, drainage and electricity. There are 16 hardstandings for motorcaravans and larger units. Some pitches have views over the Harlingen canal where one can moor small boats. An ideal site for rest and relaxation, for watersports or to visit the attractions of Harlingen and Friesland. After a day of activity, one can wine and dine in the site restaurant or at one of the many pubs in the town. This splendid location allows one the opportunity to watch the sun slowly setting from the sea dyke. You can also stroll through Harlingen or take the ferry to Vlieland or Terschelling. It is possible to moor boats at Harlingen, to hire a boat or book an organised sailing or sea fishing trip.

Facilities

Hikers - cabins and boarding houses. Three sanitary blocks include open style washbasins with cold water only, washbasins in cabins with hot and cold water, controllable showers (on payment). Family showers and baby bath. Facilities for disabled people. Cooking hob. Launderette. Sinks with free hot water. Motorcaravan services. Bar/restaurant (1/7-31/8). Internet access. Play area. Bicycle hire. Pedalo and canoe hire. Fishing. Extensive entertainment programme in July/Aug. Off site: Beach 200 m. Riding 10 km.

Open: 1 April - 15 October.

Directions

From Leeuwarden take A31 southwest to Harlingen, then follow site signs. GPS: N53:09.742 E05:25.013

Charges 2007

Per unit incl. 2 persons and electricity	€ 16,10 - € 18,60
extra person	€ 3,80
child (4-11 yrs)	€ 3,30
tent (no car) incl. 2 persons	€ 13,60
pet	€ 3,00

CAMPING *DE ZEEHOEVE*   Beside the Waddenzee

Part of the famous Eleven-City skating route, "De Zeehoeve" is by the city of Harlingen, the only seaport in the beautiful, historical province of Friesland. You can make a day trip to Vlieland or Terschelling, two of the lovely Wadden Islands and our province has many places of interest, most close to the city itself - the Ald Faers Erf-route, Kazemattenmuseum, Technical Activity Centre Aeolus, the Planetarium in Franeker. You can rent bikes, canoe or use pedaloes, cycle, ramble or go sea fishing on the Waddensea - these are just some of the things to see and do in Friesland. The campsite is 1 km. south of Harlingen, with heated modern toilet facilities - launderette - animation in high season - an inland harbour with a trailer slip, and there is accommodation to hire.

Fam. Kleefstra, Westerzeedijk 45, 8862 PK Harlingen
Tel. +31 517-413465, fax +31 517-416971
E-mail: info@zeehoeve.nl www.zeehoeve.nl

Online direct booking

NL5710 Camping It Soal

Suderséleane 27, NL-8711 GX Workum (Friesland)

Tel: **051 554 1443**. Email: **info@itsoal.nl**

This is an attractive, child-friendly site with 800 metres of beach, situated directly beside the Ijsselmeer with a canal on one side. It is ideal for those who enjoy water sports as there are many activities on the lake, including windsurfing, sailing, swimming, fishing, or you can launch your own boat. There are 650 pitches here, of which 400 are good sized, individual, flat and grassy for tourers, with 4/6A electrical connections. A few pitches also have water and drainage. In separate areas, the other pitches are taken by seasonal guests and about 50 static units. Dogs are only allowed in one area and cars must be left in a car park.

Facilities

Sanitary facilities are clean and include toilets, washbasins (open and in private cabins) and free, controllable showers. Facilities for disabled visitors. Baby room. Laundry facilities. Shop, restaurant and takeaway (1/4-1/10). Play areas. Tennis. Bicycle hire. Fishing. Boat launching. Beach. Surfboards and sailing boats for hire. Entertainment. Off site: Riding 10 km. Golf 15 km.

Open: 1 April - 31 October.

Directions

From Groningen on the A7 (via Drachten, Joure and Sneek), exit just before Bolsward onto the N359 towards Workum, then exit Workum. Pass through village, follow sign (Ijsselmeer) and then site signs. GPS: N52:58.140 E05:24.863

Charges 2007

Per unit incl. 1 or 2 persons and electricity	€ 18,50 - € 27,00
extra person	€ 2,50

365

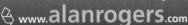

NL5760 Camping De Kuilart

Kuilart 1, NL-8723 CG Koudum (Friesland)

Tel: 051 452 2221. Email: info@kuilart.nl

De Kuilart is a well run, modern site by Friesland's largest lake and, with its own marina and private boating facilities, it attracts many watersports enthusiasts. The 450 pitches here are set in groups of 10 to 16 on areas of grass surrounded by well established hedges. There are 175 for touring units, all with electricity (6-16A), water, waste water, WiFi and TV connections, and 20 new pitches with private sanitary facilities. The restaurant provides good views of the lake and woodland. A children's 'house' is home to the entertainment team and there is an interesting Play Ship on the beach.

Facilities	Directions
Four modern, heated sanitary blocks with showers on payment and most washbasins (half in private cabins) have only cold water. Launderette. Motorcaravan services. Gas supplies. Restaurant/bar (22/3-26/10). Supermarket (21/4-2/9). Indoor pool (3 sessions daily, 31/3-29/10). Sauna and solarium. Sports field. Play areas. Tennis. Bicycle hire. Fishing. Recreation team (high season). Internet access. Lake swimming. Marina with windsurfing, boat hire and shop. Garage at harbour. Dogs accepted in certain areas (if booked). Off site: Riding or golf 4 km.	Site is southeast of Koudum, on the Fluessen lake. Follow the camping sign off the N359 Bolsward - Lemmer road GPS: N52:54.150 E05:27.972

Open: All year.

Charges 2007

Per unit incl. 2 persons,	
electricity	€ 16,50 - € 21,30
serviced pitch	€ 18,00 - € 22,90
'supercomfort' pitch	€ 23,00 - € 33,30
extra person	€ 3,85

Camping Cheques accepted.

NL6040 Recreatiecentrum Bergumermeer

Solcamastraat 30, NL-9262 ND Sumar (Friesland)

Tel: 051 146 1385. Email: info@bergumermeer.nl

Recreatiecentrum Bergumermeer's location beside the Bergum lake, makes it ideal for lovers of watersports, with sailing, surfing, water skiing and canoeing available, as well as swimming from two sandy beaches. There is also a large, heated indoor swimming pool, fun paddling pool and a solarium. The site provides 300 good sized, flat touring pitches for both caravans and tents, some having views over the Prinses Margrietkanaal and countryside, others with views over the lake. All pitches are fully serviced with electricity, water and drainage, and there are 10 large hardstandings.

Facilities	Directions
Three sanitary buildings offer private cabins, children's toilets, baby bath and facilities for disabled visitors. Children Off site: Riding 5 km. Golf 19 km.	From Amsterdam via the A7/E22, then Leeuwarden towards Drachten, or east via A6, onto A7 (Leeuwarden/Groningen), then on N31 (De Haven/ Drachten). In either case onto N356 towards Bergum following site signs. GPS: N53:11.476 E06:07.457

Open: 27 March - 16 October.

Charges guide

Per pitch incl. 2 persons,	
electricity (10A)	€ 17,50 - € 26,00
extra person	€ 4,25

NL6030 Recreatieoord Klein Vaarwater

Klein Vaarwaterweg 114, NL-9163 ME Buren (Friesland)

Tel: 051 954 2156. Email: info@kleinvaarwater.nl

Recreatieoord Klein Vaarwater is a bustling family holiday park on the interesting island of Ameland. The site is 800 m. from the North-Sea beaches and has its own indoor pool, with bars, restaurants, supermarket and party centre. Klein Vaarwater has 190 touring pitches, of which 130 have electricity, water, waste water and cable. Pitching is off hardcore access lanes, close to nature, on fields taking 6-10 units, on a grass and sand underground. There is some shade to the back from trees and bushes and level pitches are numbered and partly separated by young trees.

Facilities	Directions
Two older style toilet blocks (maintenance variable) with toilets, open style washbasins, pre-set hot showers (coin operated) and facilities for disabled people. Washing machines and dryers. Supermarket. Bar. Restaurants. Snack bar. Café. Boutique. Bicycle hire. Indoor pool (25 x 15 m.) with waterslide and paddling pool. Fitness programme. Playing field. Boules. Bowling alley. Minigolf. Animation. Off site: Beach 800 m. Buren 500 m.	From Leeuwarden, follow N357 all the way north to Holwerd and take the ferry to Ameland (reservations necessary in high season). On the island, follow the signs for Buren and then site signs. GPS: N53:27.215 E05:48.268

Open: April - October.

Charges guide

Per person	€ 3,65
pitch with electricity incl. car	€ 9,75

Camping Cheques accepted.

NL6090 Camping Lauwersoog

Strandweg 5, NL-9976 VS Lauwersoog (Groningen)

Tel: 051 934 9133. Email: info@lauwersoog.nl

The focus at Camping Lauwersoog is very much on the sea and watersports. One can have sailing lessons or hire canoes and, with a new extension, there is direct access to the beach from the site. There are 450 numbered pitches with 225 for tourers. Electricity (4/6A) is available at 200 pitches and 86 have water, drainage, electricity and cable connections. The pitches are on level, grassy fields (some beside the beach), partly separated by hedges and some with shade from trees. A new building, with beautiful views over the Lauwersmeer, houses a restaurant, bar, shop and laundry.

Facilities

The two toilet blocks for tourers provide washbasins (open style and in cabins), pre-set showers and child size toilets. Facilities for disabled people. Laundry. Campers' kitchen. Motorcaravan service. New restaurant, bar, snack bar and shop. Playground. Sailing school. Canoe hire. Surfing lessons (July/Aug). Bicycle and go-kart hire. Boules. Internet access. Extensive entertainment programme for all ages in high season. Torch useful. Off site: Riding 5 km.

Open: All year.

Directions

Follow N361 from Groningen north to Lauwersoog and then follow site signs.
GPS: N53:24.123 E06:13.039

Charges 2007

Per unit incl. 2 persons, 6A electrcity	€ 24,50
serviced pitch (125 sq.m)	€ 27,50
extra person	€ 4,00

Camping Cheques accepted.

NL6120 Camping 't Strandheem

Parkweg 2, NL-9865 VP Opende (Groningen)

Tel: 059 465 9555. Email: info@strandheem.nl

Camping Strandheem has 330 quite large, numbered pitches (110 sq.m.) some with hardstanding and suitable for motorcaravans. All with electricity, there are 180 used for touring units, partly separated by low hedges but without much shade. Of these, 34 pitches have water points, drainage and cable TV connections. The De Bruinewoud family will give you a warm welcome. A new reception building houses a bar, a full restaurant, a disco for teenagers and a shop. The site has a lot to offer with an entertainment programme in high season and water games in the lake adjacent.

Facilities

Two modern toilet buildings have washbasins (open style and in cabins), controllable showers, child size toilets and basins, a good baby room and fully equipped bathroom. Facilities for disabled people. Launderette. Motorcaravan service. Shop. Restaurant and bar. Café and snack bar. Covered swimming pool (5 x 5 m) with separate paddling pool, slide and sun terrace. Playgrounds. Covered play area with stage. Minigolf. Fishing. Bicycle hire. Extensive recreation program (July/Aug). Off site: Lake with beach 100 m. Riding 6 km. Golf 15 km.

Open: 1 April - 1 October.

Directions

Follow A7 west from Groningen towards Heerenveen and take exit 31. Follow campsite signs from there.
GPS: N53:09.167 E06:11.483

Charges 2007

Per unit incl. 2 persons	€ 17,00 - € 23,00
extra person	€ 3,75
private sanitary facility	€ 7,50
electricity (10A)	€ 2,00
dog	€ 3,75

Camping Cheques accepted.

NL5770 Camping Stadspark

Campinglaan 6, NL-9727 KH Groningen (Groningen)

Tel: 050 525 1624. Email: info@campingstadspark.nl

The Stadspark is a large park to the southwest of the city, well signed and with easy access. The campsite is within the park with many trees and surrounded by water. It has 200 pitches with 150 for touring units, of which 75 have 6A electricity and 30 are fully serviced with electricity, water and drainage. The separate tent area is supervised directly by the manager. Buses for the city leave from right outside and timetables and maps are provided by Mrs Van der Veer, the helpful, English speaking manager. Groningen is a very lively city with lots to do.

Facilities

Two sanitary blocks, one totally refurbished, provide hot water for showers and dishwashing is now free. Motorcaravan service point. Shop (15/3-15/10). Restaurant, café, bar and takeaway (1/4-15/9). Internet access in reception. Bicycle hire. Some play equipment and small paddling pool. Fishing. Canoeing. Off site: Riding and golf 5 km. Boat launching 6 km.

Open: 15 March - 15 October.

Directions

From Assen on A28 turn left on the A7. Turn on N370 and follow site signs (Stadspark, quite close).
GPS: N53:12.054 E06:32.142

Charges 2007

Per unit incl. 2 persons	€ 15,00
extra person	€ 2,50
electricity	€ 2,00

No credit cards.

NL6134 Camping Vorrelveen

Vorrelveen 10, NL-9411 VP Beilen (Drenthe)

Tel: 0593 527261. Email: info@campingvorrelveen.nl

In comparison with the larger (and justifiably popular) campsites in Drenthe, Camping Vorrelveen is a small, farm based site which reflects the pleasant countryside. The site is located within a working farm and enjoys beautiful views of the surrounding country. The pitches here are spacious and the owners do their best to ensure a very personal, tranquil atmosphere. For example, your bread for breakfast will be delivered to your pitch and, in the evening, you can order home made pizzas, prepared in the farm kitchen! This is a prime example of a small, uncomplicated rural campsite.

Facilities

Toilet block including a family shower (built in 2006). The same building houses a large room for meals and socialising. Play area with cable track and children's fort. Petanque. Motorcaravan services (with pitches on hardstanding). Tents (incl. breakfast) for rent.
Off site: Fishing. The museum villages of Orvelte and Kabouterland (Pixieland).

Open: April - October.

Directions

Take exit 30 from the A28 following signs to Smilde. Cross the third bridge and then immediately turn left. After a further 3 km you will find the campsite on the left.

Charges 2008

Per pitch incl. 2 persons	€ 10,50
child (2-12 yrs)	€ 2,25

NL5790 Rekreatiepark 't Kuierpadtien

Oranjekanaal NZ 10, NL-7853 TA Wezuperbrug (Drenthe)

Tel: 059 138 1415. Email: info@kuierpad.nl

Professionally run, this all year round site is suitable as a night stop, or for longer if you wish to participate in all the activities offered in July and August. The site itself is in a woodland setting on the edge of the village. The 525 flat and grassy pitches for touring units (with 653 in total) are of reasonable size. All have 4/6/10A electricity and 11 are fully serviced with electricity, TV aerial point, water and drainage. On-site activities encompass canoeing, windsurfing and a dry-ski slope, which is also open during the winter so that the locals can practise before going en-masse to Austria.

Facilities

Eight quite acceptable sanitary blocks, including a new one, with hot showers (17.30 - 10.00 in July/Aug). Laundry. Motorcaravan services. Supermarket (1/4-15/9) but bread all year. Restaurant and bar (all year). Takeaway. Indoor pool (all year). Outdoor pool (1/4-15/9). Sauna, solarium and whirlpool. Tennis. Dry ski slope. Play areas. Minigolf. Lake with beach. Boat rental.

Open: All year.

Directions

From N34 Groningen - Emmen road exit near Emmen onto N31 towards Beilen. Turn right into Schoonord where left to Wezuperbrug. Site is at beginning of village on the right.
GPS: N52:50.420 E06:43.620

Charges 2008

Per unit incl. 2 persons	€ 22,50 - € 39,50
extra person	€ 5,50

No credit cards.
Camping Cheques accepted.

NL6140 Camping De Valkenhof

Beilerstraat 13a, NL-9431 GA Westerbork (Drenthe)

Tel: 059 333 7546. Email: info@camping-de-valkenhof.nl

De Valkenhof is a spacious family site with 180 pitches, partly in the woods and partly on open fields without hedges to separate them. With 160 pitches for touring units, there are 143 with 4A electricity and 11 serviced pitches with electricity, water and drainage. Cars are not permitted on the campsite itself and this, together with the large pitches, provides for a really quiet holiday. Other than a recreation room for youngsters, a pool and sanitary buildings, the site has few amenities but you'll find all you need in the village.

Facilities

Two modern toilet blocks have washbasins (open style and in cabins, only one block with hot water at the basins), pre-set showers, toilets, showers and basins for children and a baby room. Facilities for disabled visitors. Motorcaravan services. Laundry. Basic provisions and some snacks from reception. Swimming pool with slide and paddling pool. Entertainment programme in high season for children. Games room. Only gas barbecues are permitted. Off site: Bicycle hire 2 km.

Open: 1 April - 1 October.

Directions

Travelling north from Zwolle on the A28, take exit for Beilen - Westerbork. Follow N31 eastwards and take exit for Westerbork. From there follow campsite signs.

Charges 2008

Per unit incl . 2 persons	€ 18,80 - € 23,50
extra person	€ 4,25
serviced pitch	€ 6,00

No credit cards.
Camping Cheques accepted.

NL6160 Camping Ruinen

Oude Benderseweg 11, NL-7963 PX Ruinen (Drenthe)

Tel: **052 247 1770**. Email: **info@camping-ruinen.nl**

Camping Ruinen is a large, spacious site with 344 pitches in the woods of Drenthe. All 276 touring pitches have electricity (4/10A) and include 55 serviced pitches with water, drainage, cable TV and electricity connections. The numbered pitches are over 100 sq.m. in size and are on large, grassy fields. They are separated by hedges and in the shade of trees and there are some hardstandings for camper vans. At this comfortable site you can relax by cycling or walking through the woods or over the moors, or join organised trips in groups on a regular basis.

Facilities

Four well-spaced toilet blocks provide washbasins (open style and in cabins), child-size toilets, bathrooms, child-size baths and a baby room. Facilities for disabled visitors. Laundry. Motorcaravan services. Shop. Restaurant with children Off site: Riding 400 m. Fishing 3 km. Golf 18 km.

Open: 1 April - 1 October.

Directions

From Zwolle follow A28 north and take Ruinen exit. Follow site signs from there.
GPS: N52:46.495 E06:22.196

Charges 2007

Per unit incl. 2 persons	€ 19,15 - € 25,00
extra person	€ 3,75

No credit cards.
Camping Cheques accepted.

NL6150 Vakantiepark Westerbergen

Oshaarseweg 24, NL-7932 PX Echten (Drenthe)

Tel: **052 825 1224**. Email: **info@westerbergen.nl**

Vakantiepark Westerbergen is beautifully situated in the picturesque region of Drenthe. The campsite is divided in two different areas, the campsite itself and the residential park. There are 391 pitches of which 293 are for touring campers. All pitches have electricity (6-16A) and 151 are equipped with water, drainage and cable TV connections. Mostly on a separate field, the marked pitches are of a good size. In the centre of the site there is a pond where children and adults can enjoy themselves when the weather is sunny and warm (the water quality of the pond is checked weekly by the local authority).

Facilities

Three good quality toilet blocks have British style toilets and individual washbasins. One block provides facilities for disabled people and for babies. Washing machines and dryer. Motorcaravan service point. Shop. Restaurant. Snack bar. Attractive bar and terrace. Two play areas, indoor and outdoor. Minigolf. Laser game. Archery. Quad track. Tennis. Bicycle hire. Fishing. Off site: Golf and riding 4 km.

Open: 21 March - 24 October.

Directions

From the A28 (Hoogeveen/Groningen) take exit for Zuidwolde and Echten (25). At crossing turn left towards Echten and at T-junction turn right (de Leeuweveenseweg), then left (de Echtenseweg) towards Echten. At the T-junction turn left and follow signs for site. In the village turn left and site is 1 km. GPS: N52:42.180 E06:22.584

Charges 2007

Per unit with up to 6 persons and electricity	€ 15,00 - € 27,50
dog	€ 5,00

NL6130 Camping De Vledders

Zeegersweg, NL-9469 PS Schipborg (Drenthe)

Tel: **050 409 1489**. Email: **info@devledders.nl**

Camping De Vledders is set in the centre of one of the most beautiful nature reserves in Holland, between the Drentsche Hondsrug and the Drentsche AA river. This attractive site is landscaped with many varieties of trees and shrubs. About one third of the site is aimed at tourers with pitching is on rectangular, grassy fields, separated by well kept hedges. There is some road noise. The level pitches are around 100 sq.m with some shade provided at the back from trees and hedges. Static units and seasonal pitches are on separate fields. In one corner of the site there is a lake with sandy beaches.

Facilities

Two toilet blocks with toilets, washbasins (open style and in cabins) and controllable hot showers. Family shower rooms. Baby room. En-suite facilities for disabled people. Shop for basics. Snack bar. TV in reception. Lake with fishing, boating, windsurfing. Football field. Riding. Nordic walking. Playground. Animation for children in season. Torch useful. Off site: Sub-tropical pool in Zuidlaren. Sprookjeshof theme park in Zuidlaren. City of Groningen.

Open: April - October.

Directions

From the A28 take exit 35 and continue towards Zuidlaren. Just before Zuidlaren follow signs for Schipborg and then site signs.
GPS: N53:04.756 E06:39.937

Charges 2007

Per unit incl. 2 persons and electricity	€ 20,25
extra person	€ 2,75
dog	€ 2,75

Allure Parks

Allure Parks are a group of seven well equipped sites, all of which can be found within the Utrechtse Heuvelrug National Park. This is a unique, natural area, relatively little known by visitors from the UK, but with a long and fascinating history, and ideal for exploration by cycle, on horseback or on foot. Aside from its attractive forested setting, there is a great deal to see here – many fascinating churches, museums, gardens, forts, windmills, castles and much more. We are featuring three Allure sites which we feel may be of interest. However, you may also wish to consider their site 't Eekhoornnest (NL6095) near the pretty town of Soest. This site has no touring pitches but offers an attractive range of chalets and apartments for rent, some even fitted out with dishwashers, fireplaces and jacuzzis! 't Eekhoornnest is a good base for visiting Amsterdam, Utrecht and Amersfoort, and the palace of the former Queen of the Netherlands is close by - well worth a visit! (www.eekhoornnest.nl)

NL6824 Allurepark Zeven Linden

Zevenlindenweg 4, NL-3744 BC Baarn (Utrecht)

Tel: **035 666 8330**. Email: info@dezevenlinden.nl

Zeven Linden was created in 1938 and since then has been a popular site for those seeking a peaceful holiday in a natural setting. There are 261 spacious touring pitches here spread over 13 separate fields. Unusually, the whole area is car-free, which goes a long way to ensuring peace and quiet, as well as improving safety for children around the site. The site is located on the northern fringe of the Utrechtse Heuvelrug, a heavily forested area. Within walking distance you can visit Drakensteyn castle, Soestdijk palace and the beautiful village of Lage Vuursche. Pitches are large and grassy, mostly with electrical connections. A unique feature here is the 'hut forest', where you can build your own bivouac or hut. The Utrechtse Heuvelrug stretches from Baarn in the north to Rhenen, its most southern point. Much of the forest has been designated as a National Park. Explorations by bicycle, on horseback or by foot are all popular. Well marked trails lead through a variety of different kinds of landscape including moorland, meadows, woodland and open fields.

Facilities

Modern, child friendly and spacious toilet blocks (two heated in low season). Two blocks have special family rooms with family showers and a separate children's area. Special facilities for disabled visitors. Washing machine and dryer. Small shop. Small field with animals. Football and volleyball pitch. 'Hut forest'. Off site: Recently renovated swimming pool 'Bosbad de Vuursche' 600 m.

Open: 31 March - 17 October.

Directions

Approaching from the west, site is well signed from the N415 Hilversum - Baarn road shortly before reaching the intersection with the N221.

Charges 2008

Per unit with 2 persons,
water and electricity   € 20,00 - € 29,00

NL6832 Allurepark Laag Kanje

Laan V. Laagkanje 1, NL-3951 KD Maarn (Utrecht)

Tel: **0343 441 348**. Email: **allurepark@laagkanje.nl**

Originally part of a great estate, Allurepark Laag Kanje has been developed into a top quality campsite over the last 40 years with the unusual, but attractive feature that cars are not allowed in the camping area. There are also mobile homes and chalets available to rent. This is a spacious site with a relaxed and tranquil atmosphere. The park is located at the heart of the forest, so sandy beaches may be the last thing you would expect here. However, there is a fine sandy beach alongside the site – ideal for swimming. In high season, there is an imaginative entertainment programme, including many activities for children, such as a Chinese lantern parade, puppet shows and forest hunts. Amersfoort, to the north, is a delightful city, with a network of canals and narrow streets.

Facilities

Modern toilet blocks with special facilities for children and disabled people. Three blocks are heated in the low season. Small restaurant and snack bar. Well stocked shop with fresh products available daily. Entertainment and activity programme for adults and children. Off site: Hiking and cycling. Utrecht, Amersfoort, Zeist, Lake swimming. Beach and woods adjacent.

Open: 1 April - 21 September.

Directions

Heading south from Amersfoort on the N227 towards Doorn, site is well signed shortly before arrival at the village of Maarn.

Charges 2008

Per unit with 2 persons and electricity	€ 19,50 - € 27,00
extra person (over 2 yrs)	€ 2,00 - € 2,95

NL6838 Allurepark De Krakeling

Woudenbergseweg 17, NL-3707 HW Zeist (Utrecht)

Tel: **030 691 5374**. Email: **krakeling@allurepark.nl**

Allurepark De Krakeling is a spacious (22 ha.) campsite with 350 touring pitches, spread over several grassy fields. All pitches are surrounded by hedges and are supplied with 6A electricity and a cable TV connection (additional charge). There are many mobile homes and chalets for rent. The site is attractively located in the middle of the Zeister forest and is a good choice for a family holiday with a wide range of facilities and a lively entertainment programme for young and old. The site enjoys a very pleasant natural setting, with innumerable routes for walking and cycling in the forest.

Facilities

Toilet block with facilities for babies and disabled visitors. Motorcaravan services. Restaurant/bar. Games room. Supermarket. Snack bar. Hairdresser. Off site: Forest walking and cycling routes. Visits to the Krommerijn and Gelderese valleys. Historic towns of Utrecht (12 km.) and Amersfoort (10 km.) and nearby town of Zeist with many shops, restaurants and cafés 3 km.

Open: 1 April - 1 October.

Directions

Take Zeist Oost exit from the A28 motorway (heading from Utrecht) and follow signs to Zeist. Site is well signed from the village.

Charges 2008

Per unit with 2 persons, water and electricity	€ 20,00 - € 24,70
extra person (over 2 yrs)	€ 1,00 - € 2,50

NL5810 Recreatiepark De Luttenberg

Heuvelweg 9, NL-8105 SZ Luttenberg (Overijssel)

Tel: **057 230 1405**. Email: **info@luttenberg.nl**

Considerable changes have been made to enhance this is a very smart woodland site which is well placed for either an active or peaceful holiday. It is a large park with 220 touring pitches (all with 10A electricity) in a central area off tarmac access roads. The large, individual pitches are numbered and separated, in rows divided by hedges and trees, with easy access. One area is a dog-free zone. There is a large bar and eating area with terrace and a small, separate restaurant.

Facilities

Good quality heated sanitary blocks with controllable showers give a good overall provision. An excellent new block has been built to a very high standard and includes a themed children Off site: Fishing 1.5 km. Riding 6 km.

Open: 31 March - 1 October.

Directions

From N35 Zwolle - Almelo turn on N348 Ommen road east of Raalte, then turn to Luttenberg and follow signs. From A1 (Amsterdam - Hengelo) take exit 23 at Deventer on N348, then as above. GPS: N52:25.698 E06:27.676

Charges 2007

Per unit incl. 2 persons and electricity	€ 17,50 - € 25,00
extra person	€ 4,00
Less 15% outside 15/7-1/9. No credit cards. Camping Cheques accepted.	

(371)

NL6470 Camping De Papillon

Kanaalweg 30, NL-7591 NH Denekamp (Overijssel)

Tel: 054 135 1670. Email: info@depapillon.nl

De Papillon is perhaps one of the best campsites in The Netherlands. The site is well thought through with an eye for detail and for nature and the environment. For example, at the toilet blocks, waste water from the showers is used to flush the toilets, all buildings are heated by solar energy and all rubbish is separated for recycling. The 320 touring pitches are spacious, averaging 110-120 sq.m. and all have electricity (4-10A). Arranged in small grassy fields surrounded by hedges and trees, each field provides a small play area. For more fun children can visit a large adventure style play area. This is located adjacent to the (covered) heated pool and not far from reception. In one area of the site the natural environment has been restored to the original heathland. It is not surprising that the owner has won various environmental prizes in recent years. This is a great destination for a holiday amongst nature. Highlights of this site are the large lake with its beach and, of course, the green countryside of the Twente region.

Facilities

Two large sanitary buildings with showers, toilets, washbasins in cabins, facilities for babies and for disabled visitors. This building is designed in the shape of a 'papillon' (butterfly). Laundry. Spacious reception area with supermarket, restaurant, bar and takeaway. Heated pool with children's pool and sliding roof. Lake swimming with sandy beach. New modern adventure play area and smaller play areas. Pétanque. Bicycle hire. Fishing pond. Tennis. Pets to stroke. Luxury bungalows to rent with views.

Open: 23 March - 1 October.

Directions

From the A1 take exit 32 (Oldenzaal - Denekamp) and continue to Denekamp. Pass Denekamp and turn right at village of Noord-Deurningen and follow signs to site.

Charges 2007

Per unit incl. 2 persons and 4A electricity	€ 24,75
with full services, plus	€ 3,25
extra person	€ 4,00

NL6480 Camping De Molenhof

Kleijsenweg 7, NL-7667 RS Reutum/Weerselo (Overijssel)

Tel: 054 166 1201. Email: info@demolenhof.nl

De Molenhof is a pleasant family site where you can enjoy the real hospitality of the people of the Twent region. It has 450 well laid out pitches of which 430 are for touring units, all with water, drainage, electricity (10A) and cable connections. This is a real family site with children under 12 particularly in mind rather than teenagers. Children will enjoy themselves in the covered, adventure playground or the two swimming pools (one outdoor, one covered) with a large slide on the outside. The entertainment team provides a full daily programme in high season.

Facilities

Four toilet blocks, three in 'fairy tale' style for children, provide washbasins (open style and in cabins), controllable showers, bathrooms and a baby room. Launderette. Motorcaravan service. Shop. Bar/restaurant. Pancake restaurant. Swimming pools. Playgrounds (1 covered). Sports court. Tennis (plans to replace the courts with a multi purpose all-weather sports area). Fishing. Bicycle and go-kart hire. Boules. Entertainment programme in high season. Off site: Beach and riding 6 km. Golf 8 km.

Open: 20 March - 28 September.

Directions

Follow A1 from Amsterdam east to Hengelo and take exit 31, Hengelo Noord. Go through Deurningen to Weerselo and from there the N343 towards Tubbergen and site signs. GPS: N52:21.928 E06:50.591

Charges 2007

Per unit incl. 2 persons	
incl. services	€ 18,50 - € 33,00
extra person	€ 5,00
Camping Cheques accepted.	

NL5980 Camping De Roos

Beerzerweg 10, NL-7736 PJ Beerze-Ommen (Overijssel)

Tel: **052 325 1234**. Email: **info@campingderoos.nl**

De Roos is a family run site in an area of outstanding natural beauty, truly a nature lover's campsite, immersed in an atmosphere of tranquillity. It is situated in Overijssel's Vecht Valley, a unique region set in a river dune landscape on the River Vecht. The river and its tributary wind their way unhurriedly around and through this spacious campsite (children should be supervised at all times as it is unfenced). It is a natural setting that the owners of De Roos have carefully preserved. Conserving the environment is paramount here and the 285 pitches and necessary amenities have been blended into the landscape with great care. Pitches, many with electricity hook-up (6A), are naturally sited, some behind blackthorn thickets, in the shadow of an old oak, or in a clearing scattered with wild flowers. For some there are lovely views over the Vecht river. De Roos is a car-free campsite during peak periods – vehicles must be parked at the car park, except on arrival and departure. Swimming, fishing and boating are possible in the river, or from an inlet that runs up into the site where there is a small beach. The enthusiastic owners have compiled walking and cycling routes which are written in English and follow the ever-changing countryside of the Vecht Valley.

Facilities

Four well maintained sanitary blocks are kept fresh and clean. The two larger blocks are heated and include baby bath/shower and wash cabins. Launderette. Motorcaravan services. Gas supplies. Health food shop and tea room (1/5-1/9). Bicycle hire. Boules. Several small playgrounds and field for kite flying. River swimming. Fishing. Dogs are not accepted (and cats must be kept on a lead!). Torch useful. Off site: Riding 6 km. Golf 10 km.

Open: 6 April - 30 September.

Directions

Leave A28 at Ommen exit 21 and join N340 for 19 km. to Ommen. Turn right at traffic lights over bridge and immediately left on local road towards Beerze. Site on left after 7 km. just after Beerze village sign. GPS: N52:30.647 E06:30.922

Charges 2007

Per pitch incl. 2 persons	€ 15,75
extra person (over 3 yrs)	€ 3,40
electricity	€ 2,40

www.campingderoos.nl

NL5990 Camping De Vechtstreek

Grote Beltenweg 17, NL-7794 RA Rheeze-Hardenberg (Overijssel)

Tel: **052 326 1369**. Email: **info@sprookjescamping.nl**

It would be difficult for any child (or adult) to pass this site and not be curiously drawn to the oversized open story book which marks its entrance. From here young children turn the pages and enter the exciting world of Hannah and Bumpie, two of the nine characters around which this site's fairy-tale theme has been created. There are 270 touring pitches mostly laid out in bays which accommodate around 12 units. In the centre of each is a small play area. The area at the back of the site has been upgraded with new hook-ups, a gravel road and attractive lighting.

Facilities

Three modern, well equipped and heated toilet blocks include a baby room, separate child sections and family showers. Excellent laundry room. Sauna, solarium and jacuzzi. Well stocked supermarket. Restaurant, snack bar and takeaway (all season). Play areas. Fairy-tale water play park (heated). Daily activity club. Internet access. Football field. Theatre. Access to a fishing, swimming and boating recreation area at rear of site (200 m).

Open: 1 April - 15 September.

Directions

From Ommen take N34 Hardenberg road for 9 km. Turn right on N36 and proceed south for 3.5 km. Turn left at crossroads and after 200 m. left again on local road towards Rheeze. Site clearly is signed to the left in 2 km. GPS: N52:32.764 E06:34.249

Charges 2007

Per unit incl. 2 persons and electricity	€ 29,50 - € 39,00
extra person	€ 5,75

NL5985 Kampeercentrum De Beerze Bulten

Kampweg 1, NL-7736 PK Beerze/Ommen (Overijssel)

Tel: 052 325 1398. Email: info@beerzebulten.nl

Kampeercentrum De Beerze Bulten is a large holiday park with all amenities one could think of. Beside reception is a large, partly underground 'Rabbit Hole' providing a large indoor playground for children, a theatre for both indoor and outdoor shows and a buffet. De Beerze Bulten has over 500 pitches, all for touring units. In the shade of mature trees in woodland, all the pitches are level and numbered, all with 6/10A electricity, water, drainage and cable. To the back of the site is large lake area with a sandy beach and adventure play equipment. Centrally located on the site is a full 'wellness' spa centre. As well as heated indoor and outdoor pools, a fun paddling pool, jet stream, several different saunas and a water playground, this also offers full fitness facilities and a special 'salt cave' treatment for those suffering from asthma or skin troubles. De Beerze Bulten will provide a relaxing and active family holiday and if the site doesn't offer enough, there is always the extensive surrounding woodland for walking and cycling.

Facilities

Several toilet blocks, well placed around the site, with toilets, washbasins in cabins and hot showers (key). Laundry. Shop. Bar and restaurant with open air terrace. Snack bar. Heated indoor and outdoor pool complex and spa centre. Multi-sports court. Bicycle hire. Indoor playground and theatre. Playgrounds. WiFi internet. Full animation team in season and school holidays. Dogs only allowed on some fields.

Open: All year.

Directions

From A28, take exit 21 for Ommen and continue east towards Ommen. From Ommen, follow N34 northeast and turn south on N36 at crossing. Site is signed from there.

Charges 2007

Per unit incl. 2 persons and full service pitch	€ 25,50 - € 39,50
extra person	€ 3,50 - € 4,50
dog	€ 3,50

NL6000 Vechtdalcamping Het Tolhuis

Het Lageveld 8, NL-7722 HV Dalfsen (Overijssel)

Tel: 052 945 8383. Email: tolhuis@gmx.net

Vechtdalcamping Het Tolhuis is a pleasant, well established site with 145 pitches. Of these, 70 are for tourers, arranged on well kept, grassy lawns off paved and gravel access roads. All touring pitches have 4/10A electricity, water, waste water, cable and WiFi internet. Some arshaded of mature trees and bushes, others are more in the open. The touring pitches are located apart from static units. To the rear of the site is an open air pool (25 x 8 m. and heated by solar power) with a small paddling pool for toddlers. Along the lane running from reception to the back of the site is a takeaway for drinks and snacks.

Facilities

Two heated toilet blocks, one immaculate new one to the front and an older one to the back, with toilets, washbasins (open style and in cabins) and controllable hot showers (key). Special, attractive children's section. Family shower rooms. Baby room. Laundry. Small shop (bread to order). Café for snacks and drinks. Open air pool with paddling pool. Playing field. Playground and trampoline. Animation team for children in high season. ATM point. Internet. Off site: Restaurant 2 km. Fishing 5 km.

Open: 1 April - 1 October.

Directions

From the A28 take exit 21 and continue east towards Dalfsen. Site is signed in Dalfsen.

Charges 2007

Per unit incl. 2 persons and electricity	€ 16,50 - € 24,70
extra person	€ 1,50 - € 2,75
dog (not high season)	€ 3,00

NL6004 Vakantiepark Het Stoetenslagh

Elfde Wijk 42, NL-7797 HH Rheezerveen-Hardenberg (Overijssel)

Tel: **0523 638 260**. Email: **info@stoetenslagh.nl**

Arriving at Het Stoetenslagh and passing reception, you reach the pride of the campsite: a large natural lake with several little beaches. Many hours can be spent swimming, canoeing or sailing a dinghy here. Spacious grass pitches (100 sq.m) are divided between several fields, arranged around clean sanitary buildings. Each field also has a small volleyball area and climbing frames. You may choose between 'nature' pitches, standard pitches or comfortable serviced pitches with water, drainage, 6/10A electricity and cable connection. There are climbing frames for children, much space for playing, a children's club and, particularly popular with little ones, a small animal farm. Teenagers are also very welcome and the site provides a range of activities, including sports, outdoor camping trips, discos and more, all organized by a special animation team. When the weather takes a turn for the worse, there are indoor activities such as curling, bowling or archery.

Facilities

Five toilet blocks include private cabins, baby facilities, family showers and facilities for disabled visitors. Beach shower. Washing machines and dryers. Motorcaravan service point. Restaurant with bar. Snack bar with takeaway. Disco, bowling, curling and archery (all indoor). Natural pool with sandy beaches. Canoeing. Play areas. Activities for children and teenagers. Bouncy castle. Tennis. Volleyball.

Open: 21 March - 31 October.

Directions

On the N34 travel towards Ommen and go through town. At TINQ petrol station follow signs for 'Stoetenslagh' following 'Het Zwarte Pad'. After about 3 km after Rheezerveen, follow signs for 'Stoetenslagh' right. Site is on right after 3 km.

Charges 2007

Per serviced pitch	
incl. 2 persons	€ 19,00 - € 32,00
extra person	€ 3,00

NL5780 Camping De Zanding

Vijverlaan 1, NL-6731 CK Otterlo (Gelderland)

Tel: **031 859 6111**. Email: **info@zanding.nl**

De Zanding is a family-run, highly-rated site that offers almost every recreational facility, either on site or nearby, that active families or couples might seek. Immediately after the entrance, a lake is to the left where you can swim, fish, sunbathe or try a two-person canoe. There are many sporting options and organised high season programmes for all ages. There are 463 touring pitches spread around the site (all with 4/6/10A electricity), some individual and separated, others in more open spaces shaded by trees. Some serviced pitches are in small groups between long stay units and there is another area for tents.

Facilities

First class sanitary facilities are housed in five modern blocks that are clean, well maintained and well equipped. Good provision for babies and people with disabilities. Laundry. Kitchen. Motorcaravan services. Gas supplies. Supermarket. Restaurant/bar (30/3-28/10). Lake swimming. Fishing. Tennis. Minigolf. Boules. Five play areas. Bicycle hire. Organised activities.

Open: 21 March - 28 October.

Directions

Leave A12 Utrecht - Arnhem motorway at Oosterbeek at exit 25 and join N310 to Otterlo. Then follow camping signs to site, watching carefully for entrance. GPS: N52:05.586 E05:46.654

Charges 2007

Per unit incl. 2 persons and 4A electricity	€ 18,00 - € 29,00
Camping Cheques accepted.	

NL5950 Rekreatiecentrum Heumens Bos

Vosseneindseweg 46, NL-6582 BR Heumen (Gelderland)

Tel: **024 358 1481**. Email: **info@heumensbos.nl**

The area around Nijmegen, the oldest city in the Netherlands, has large forests for walking or cycling, nature reserves and old towns to explore, as well as being quite close to Arnhem. The site covers 16 ha. and is open over a long season for touring families (no groups of youngsters allowed) and all year for bungalows. It offers 165 level, grass pitches for touring units, all with electricity (6A) and cable TV connections. Numbered but not separated, in glades of 10 and one large field, all have easy access with cars parked elsewhere. One small section for motorcaravans has some hardstandings. The restaurant, which offers a good menu and a new terrace, is close to the comfortable bar and snack bar. An open air swimming pool with a small children's pool is maintained at 28 degrees by a system of heat transfer from the air. Mr Van Velzen and his sons took over this site in 2002 and are planning new buildings and an internet point.

Facilities

The main, high quality sanitary building, plus another new block, are modern and heated, providing showers on payment. Rooms for families and disabled people. Another smaller building has acceptable facilities. Smart launderette. Motorcaravan services. Gas supplies. Shop. Bar, restaurant and snack bar (all season). Heated swimming pool (from 1/5). Bicycle hire. Tennis. Boules. Glade area with play equipment on sand and grass, Activity and excursion programme (high season). Large wet weather room. Off site: Riding 300 m. Fishing 2 km. Golf 10 km.

Open: 1 April - 1 November.

Directions

From A73 (Nijmegen - Venlo) take exit 3 (4 km. south of Nijmegen) and follow site signs.
GPS: N51:46.149 E05:49.230

Charges 2007

Per pitch incl. 2 persons, caravan or tent	€ 16,00 - € 25,00
dog (max. 1)	€ 4,00
electricity	€ 2,50

Special low season weekends (incl. restaurant meal) and special deal for persons over 55 yrs.

NL5870 Camping De Vergarde

Erichemseweg 84, NL-4117 GL Erichem (Gelderland)

Tel: **034 457 2017**. Email: **info@devergarde.nl**

Situated north of 's Hertogenbosch and west of Nijmegen and Arnhem, De Vergarde has been developed on a former orchard with a beautiful old farmhouse at its entrance. The site is in two sections on either side of a lake. Static holiday caravans are on the left, with the 207 touring pitches to the right. About a third of these are taken by seasonal units. Arranged in sections, access is good. Pitches are numbered on flat grass and include 225 with 6A electricity, water, drainage and TV connections. There are trees all around the perimeter (but not much shade on the pitches).

Facilities

Good sanitary facilities in three blocks include family showers and baby bathrooms. Most, but not all, hot water is on payment. Washing machines. Motorcaravan services. Heated swimming pool and attractive paddling pool (1/5-1/9). Shop (1/5-1/10). Restaurant (1/5-1/10). Play area and large indoor games room. Pony riding. Pets corner. Horse drawn wagons. Minigolf. Bicycle hire. Games room. Two tennis courts. Fishing.

Open: 1 March - 30 October.

Directions

From A15 Dordrecht - Nijmegen road exit at Tiel West (also MacDonald's) and follow signs to site.
GPS: N51:53.939 E05:21.646

Charges 2007

Per unit incl. 2 adults with electricity, water	€ 13,00 - € 20,00
and drainage	€ 13,80 - € 23,00
with satellite TV	€ 15,00 - € 25,00
extra person (over 2 yrs)	€ 2,50 - € 3,50
dog (max. 1)	€ 2,00 - € 3,00

NL6285 Camping De Wildhoeve

Hanendorperweg 102, NL-8166 JJ Emst-Gortel (Gelderland)
Tel: **057 866 1324**. Email: **info@wildhoeve.nl**

Camping De Wildhoeve is a welcoming, privately owned site with many amenities of the type one would normally find on larger holiday camps. The well maintained site is located in woodland and has 400 pitches with 330 for tourers. Pitching is in several areas, mostly in the shade of mature conifers. Partly separated by trees and bushes, the level pitches are numbered and all have 6/12A electricity, water and drainage. Behind reception is an octagonally shaped sub-tropical pool with a large water slide and fun paddling pool. Next to reception is a water adventure playground. To the front of the site are tennis courts and next to that is an open air pool with a large slide. Here also are a shop, bar/restaurant with TV and games room with electronic games and a snack bar. Many activities are organised for children, including open air theatre, and for adults there are craft workshops. The toilet facilities on this site are excellent and include one block that has a special children's section with an area for children with disabilities.

Facilities

Four well placed, heated blocks with toilets, washbasins (open style and in cabins) and free, pre-set hot showers. Special children's section with showers, basins and toilets. Baby room. Family shower room. Facilities for disabled children. Laundry with washing machines and dryers. Shop. Bar/restaurant with TV. Snack bar. Indoor and outdoor pools with slides and paddling pool. Water adventure playground. WiFi internet. Bicycle hire. Tennis. Open air theatre. Craft workshops. Dogs not accepted.

Open: April - October.

Directions

From the A28, take exit 15 (Epe/Nunspeet). Continue east towards Epe and at traffic lights, turn south towards Emst. Continue straight ahead at roundabout in Emst. Turn right at church, into Hanendorperweg. Site is on the right after 3.5 km. GPS: N52:18.829 E05:55.652

Charges 2007

Per unit incl. 2 persons	€ 19,00 - € 34,25
3 persons	€ 22,50 - € 38,75
4 persons	€ 26,00 - € 43,25

NL5850 Camping De Hooge Veluwe

See advertisement on page 361

Koningsweg 14, NL-6816 TC Arnhem (Gelderland)
Tel: **026 443 2272**. Email: **info@dehoogeveluwe.nl**

Its situation at the entrance to the Hoge Veluwe National Park with its moors, forests, sand drifts, walking routes and cycle paths, makes this a highly desirable holiday base. The site itself is well managed and laid out in an orderly fashion, with 260 touring pitches, including 85 fully serviced places of 300 sq.m. All have electricity (4/6A), are numbered and laid out in small fields which are divided by hedging. Some are traffic free which means cars must be left in a nearby car park. There is some road noise. Mobile homes are discreetly placed mostly in the centre of the site.

Facilities

Five excellent, heated sanitary blocks with all facilities, are easily identified by colourful logos. Launderette. Motorcaravan services. Gas supplies. Supermarket. Restaurant. Takeaway. All facilities open all season. TV room. Heated outdoor and indoor pools, and a paddling pool. Several small play areas. Recreation hall. Football pitch, tennis, cycle track, basketball, minigolf, etc. Bicycle hire. Organised activities Off site: Riding 50 m. Golf 6 km. Beach 12 km.

Open: 26 March - 30 October.

Directions

Leave A12 motorway at exit 25 (Oosterbeck) and follow signs for Hooge Veluwe. Site is on right in 6 km. From the A50, take exit 21 to Schaarsbergen and follow signs. GPS: N52:01.861 E05:52.008

Charges 2007

Per unit incl. 2 persons and electricity	€ 19,00 - € 28,00
extra person	€ 2,00 - € 4,00

377

NL6290 Camping Eiland van Maurik

Rijnbandijk 20, NL-4021 GH Maurik (Gelderland)

Tel: 034 4691502. Email: info@eilandvanmaurik.nl

Camping Eiland van Maurik is beside a lake in the centre of an extensive nature and recreation park in the Nederrijn area. These surroundings are ideal for all sorts of activities – swimming, windsurfing, waterskiing or para-sailing, relaxing on the beach or fishing. There is even an animal farm for the children. The site has 365 numbered, flat pitches, with 155 for touring units, all with 10A electricity and cable TV connections and 64 also with water and drainage. You could enjoy pancakes in the 'Oudhollandse' restaurant and the views over the water. There is direct access to the lakeside beach.

Facilities

The three toilet blocks for tourers include washbasins (open style and in cabins), controllable showers and a baby room. Launderette with iron and board. Shop. Bar/restaurant (1/4-1/10). Play areas (one indoors). Play field. Tennis. Minigolf. Bicycle hire. Go-karts. Water skiing. Sailing and motorboat hire. Para-sailing. Animal farm. Entertainment in high season (incl. riding). Gate key deposit € 50. Off site: Shop, restaurant and bar nearby. Golf 9 km.

Open: 1 April - 1 October.

Directions

From the A2 (Utrecht - 's Hertogenbosch) take the Culemborg exit towards Kesteren and follow signs for 'Eiland Maurik'. From the A15 (Rotterdam - Nymegen) take exit 33 Tiel towards Maurik and follow signs as above. GPS: N51:50.586 E05:15.511

Charges 2007

Per unit incl. 2 persons and electricity	€ 17,50 - € 25,00
extra person (under 2 yrs free)	€ 3,50

No credit cards. Camping Cheques accepted.

NL6310 Recreatiepark Arnhem

Kemperbergerweg 771, NL-6816 RW Arnhem (Gelderland)

Tel: 026 443 1600. Email: arnhem@holiday.nl

Recreatiepark Arnhem is a wooded site in the Veluwe region of the Netherlands, close to the 'Hooge Veluwe' National Park. The 750 pitches are partly in the sun and partly in the shade of tall trees and there are 500 for touring units, some with hardstanding. This is a perfect base for visiting the National Park, the Kroller Muller museum or the outdoor museum. You could also go riding or play golf nearby or experience the silence high up in the air in a glider from Terlet airport. There is also plenty to do on the site including tennis and minigolf.

Facilities

Modern sanitary blocks provide free hot showers, facilities for disabled visitors and a baby room. Fully equipped launderette. Motorcaravan services. Supermarket. Café. Bar. Tennis. Minigolf. Table tennis. Sports field. Open air theatre. Playgrounds. Adventure pond. Swimming pool and paddling pool. Entertainment programme in high season. Bicycle hire. Off site: Arnhem for shopping. Burgers Zoo. Kroller Moller museum. Airborne museum.

Open: 1 April - 26 October.

Directions

From the A50 take exit 21 for Schaarsbergen. Go to Schaarsbergen and follow the camp signs. GPS: N52:01.430 E05:51.576

Charges guide

Per unit incl. 2 adults, 2 children and 4A electricity	€ 12,00 - € 32,00

Camping Cheques accepted.

NL5960 Camping De Wielerbaan

Zoomweg 7-9, NL-6705 DM Wageningen-Hoog (Gelderland)

Tel: 031 741 3964. Email: info@wielerbaan.nl

This family run park has an interesting history and a natural setting at a point where the Veluwe, the valley of Gelderland and the picturesque area of Betuwe meet. Translated 'Wielerbaan' means 'cycle race track' which still stands in the heart of this site. The present owners have utilised this area to accommodate recreation facilities which include an indoor swimming pool. Touring pitches in a meadow setting are serviced with water, electricity and drainage. Planned cycles routes are available at reception, or maps to choose your own way. It is possible to go by boat to Arnhem.

Facilities

Four toilet blocks of a reasonable standard provide wash cabins, showers and a baby room. Launderette. Gas supplies. Shop. Small restaurant. Snacks and takeaway. Library. Swimming pool. Minigolf. Boules. Ten small play areas. Organised entertainment in high season. Off site: Golf 500 m. Fishing 5 km. Boat launching.

Open: All year.

Directions

Leave A12 at exit 24 towards Wageningen and continue for 4.5 km. to second roundabout, where site is clearly signed. Follow signs to site, 1.5 km. from the town. GPS: N51:59.199 E05:47.275

Charges 2008

Per unit incl. 2 persons and electricity	€ 10,50 - € 31,00
extra person	€ 7,00 - € 8,00
dog (max. 2)	€ 3,00

NL6425 **Recreatiecentrum De Twee Bruggen**

Meenkmolenweg 13, NL-7109-AH Winterswijk (Gelderland)

Tel: **0543 565 366**. Email: **info@detweebruggen.nl**

De Twee Bruggen is a spacious recreation park set in the countryside. The pitches are divided between several fields of varying sizes. Although the fields are surrounded by tall trees, the ground is open and sunny. Indoor and outdoor swimming pools can be enjoyed by children and adults. At the indoor pool there is a covered terrace and, for relaxation, a sauna and jacuzzi. Adjacent to the pool is a small, open air theatre, where shows are staged in high season. The restaurant at the entrance of the campsite is of high quality and also attracts many outside visitors. A small shopping centre, including a supermarket and more is beside reception. Fresh bread is baked each morning. A variety of mobile homes and chalets is for rent. The German border is within 20 minutes of the site.

Facilities

Three modern, well maintained sanitary buildings include showers and washbasins in private cabins. Facilities for disabled visitors. Washing machines and dryers. Bar and restaurant (all year). Takeaway. TV room. Supermarket. Heated swimming pool (30/4-7/9). Heated indoor pool (all year). Paddling pool. Sauna. Jacuzzi. Two tennis courts. Bicycles hire. Table tennis. Minigolf. Bowling. Playground. Bouncy castle. Deer field.

Open: All year.

Directions

Take the A18 towards Varsseveld will turn onto the N18. In Varsseveld follow signs for Aalten (N318). In Aalten follow signs for Winterswijk. Drive through Aalten and site is signed after about 4 km.

Charges 2008

Per unit with 2 persons	€ 16,00 - € 37,00
extra person	€ 1,00 - € 2,00

NL6190 Rekreatiepark Hazevreugd

Vormtweg 9, NL-8321 NC Urk (Flevoland)

Tel: **052 768 1785**. Email: **info@hazevreugd.nl**

Recreatiepark Hazevreugd, set in the Urkerbos on the former island Urk, is a true family site with lots of sporting facilities. You can hire go-karts and bikes, go surfing from the beaches of the Ijsselmeer or go riding in the woods. The site has 220 pitches, 192 for tourers, all with shade and 6A electricity. There are also 63 serviced pitches with water, electricity and drainage and separate pitches for motorcaravans, which will become hardstandings. In high season an entertainment team organises sports competitions, scouting expeditions and entertainment evenings.

Facilities

Two modern toilet blocks have washbasins (open style and in cabins), pre-set showers, child size toilets, family showers and a baby room. Facilities for disabled visitors. Laundry. Motorcaravan services. Shop (bread to order). Bar/restaurant and snack bar. Outdoor pool (40 sq.m.) with paddling pool. Playground. Sports court. Bicycle and go-kart hire. Recreation hall with games. Satellite TV. Off site: Fishing, boat launching and beach 2 km.

Open: April - September.

Directions

Follow the A6 from Almere to the north and take exit 13 to Urk (N352). Site is next to the Urkerbos and well signed.

Charges guide

Per unit incl. 2 persons	€ 15,00 - € 19,50
extra person	€ 2,50

No credit cards.

NL5540 Camping De Katjeskelder

Katjeskelder 1, NL-4904 SG Oosterhout (Noord-Brabant)

Tel: **016 245 3539**. Email: **kkinfo@katjeskelder.nl**

This site is to be found in a wooded setting in a delightful area of Noord Brabant. It is well established and offers extensive facilities with a new and impressive ultra-modern reception area. Around the 25 hectare site there are many bungalows and 102 touring pitches, all with electricity and water, plus 13 fully serviced pitches. Motorcaravans are now accepted (on hardstandings near the entrance), as well as tents and caravans. The site has a 'cat' theme, hence the cat names including that of the restaurant, the 'Gelaarsde Kat' (Puss in Boots) which is situated in the 'Tropikat' complex.

Facilities

One modern, heated sanitary block (may be stretched in high season) includes a family shower room and provision for disabled people. Laundry. Supermarket. Restaurant, bar, snack bar, pizzeria and takeaway. Indoor pool. Outdoor pools. Play field. Tennis. Bicycle hire. Minigolf. Play areas. Large adventure playground. Entertainment for children all season. Off site: Oosterheide nature park.

Open: All year.

Directions

From A27 Breda - Gorinchem motorway take Oosterhout Zuid exit 17 and follow signs for 7 km. to site GPS: N51:37.799 E04:49.926

Charges 2007

Per unit incl. up to 5 persons, electricity, water and TV connections	€ 22,00 - € 39,00
extra person	€ 4,00

NL5910 Vakantiecentrum De Hertenwei

Wellenseind 7-9, NL-5094 EG Lage Mierde (Noord-Brabant)

Tel: **013 509 1295**

Set in the southwest corner of the country quite close to the Belgian border, this relaxed site covers a large area. In addition to 100 quite substantial bungalows with their own gardens (some residential, 30 to let and 32 mobile homes), the site has some 335 touring pitches. These are in four different areas on oblong meadows surrounded by hedges and trees, with the numbered pitches around the perimeters. There is a choice of pitch size (100 or 150 sq.m.) and all have 6A electrical connections, water and drainage, and even a cable TV connection as well.

Facilities

Four toilet blocks are of slightly differing types, all of quite good quality and well spaced around the site. Virtually all washbasins in private cabins and the blocks can be heated in cool weather. Units for disabled people. Launderette. Gas supplies. Motorcaravan services. Supermarket (Easter - end Oct). Bar. Indoor pool (13 x 6 m, charged). Three outdoor pools, the largest 25 x 10 m. (26/4-31/8). Restaurant, snack bar. Disco. Tennis. Play areas. Sauna. Solarium. Jacuzzi. Bicycle hire. Off site: Supermarket 2 km. Bus to Tilburg or Eindhoven. Fishing and riding 4 km.

Open: All year.

Directions

Site is by N269 Tilburg - Reusel road, 2 km. north of Lage Mierde and 16 km. south of Tilburg GPS: N51:25.130 E05:08.250

Charges 2008

Per unit incl. 2 persons and electricity	€ 20,50 - € 35,25

Less 25-40% in low seasons.

NL5970 Camping De Paal

Paaldreef 14, NL-5571 TN Bergeyk (Noord-Brabant)

Tel: **049 757 1977**. Email: **info@depaal.nl**

A first class campsite, De Paal is especially suitable for families with young children. Situated in 42 hectares of woodland, there are 530 touring pitches of up to 150 sq.m. (plus 70 seasonal pitches). The pitches are numbered and separated by trees, with cars either parked on the pitch or in a dedicated parking area. All have 6A electricity, TV, water, drainage and a bin. There are 40 pitches with private sanitary facilities which are partly underground and attractively covered with grass and flowers. With child safety in mind, there is a play area on each group of pitches.

Facilities

High quality sanitary facilities are ultra modern, including wash cabins, family rooms and baby baths, all with lots of space. Facilities for disabled visitors. Launderette. Motorcaravan services. Underground supermarket. Restaurant (high season), bar and snack bar (all season). Indoor pool. Outdoor pool (May - Sept). Bicycle hire. Tennis. Play areas. Theatre. WiFi internet access. Bicycle storage room. Off site: Tennis complex (Sept - May). Riding and covered wagons for hire 500 m. Fishing 4 km.

Open: Easter/1 April - 31 October.

Directions

From E34 Antwerpen-Eindhoven road take exit 32 (Eersel) and follow signs for Bergeyk and site (2 km. from town). GPS: N51:20.147 E05:27.302

Charges guide

Per pitch incl. 2 persons and services	€ 26,00 - € 38,00
extra person (over 1 yr)	€ 5,00
cyclist	€ 9,00
dog	€ 5,00

NL5880 Vrijetijdspark Vinkeloord

Vinkeloord 1, NL-5382 JX Vinkeloord (Noord-Brabant)

Tel: **073 534 3536**. Email: **vinkeloord@libema.nl**

Run by the same group as Beekse Bergen (NL5900), Vinkeloord is a large site with motel accommodation and a bungalow park, in addition to its 500 camping pitches. These are divided into several grassy areas, many in an attractive wooded setting. There are 381 for touring units, all with electrical connections 4-10A and some with full services (water taps and TV connections). A small, landscaped lake has sandy beaches. Some of the touring pitches overlook the water. Campers are entitled to free entry to the adjacent 'Autotron' attraction.

Facilities

Eight toilet blocks are well situated with a mixture of clean and simple facilities (some unisex) with some warm water for washing and some individual washbasins. Baby room. Supermarket. Bar. Restaurant. Snack bar/takeaway (high season). Free outdoor heated swimming pools (1/6-1/9). Indoor pool (charged). Ten-pin bowling. Minigolf. Bicycle hire. Pedaloes. Fishing. Play areas. Organised activities in season. Max. 1 dog per pitch.

Open: 29 March - 3 November.

Directions

Site is signed from the N50/A50 road between 's Hertogenbosch and Nijmegen, about 10 km. east of 's Hertogenbosch at Vinkel.

Charges 2007

Per unit incl. 2 persons and electricity	€ 13,00 - € 17,00

NL5900 Beekse Bergen Safari Camping

Beekse Bergen 1, NL-5081 NJ Hilvarenbeek (Noord-Brabant)

Tel: **013 549 1100**. Email: **beeksebergen@libema.nl**

Beekse Bergen is a large impressive leisure park set around a very large, attractive lake near Tilberg. The park offers a range of amusements, including water based activities, a small amusement park and much more. On the far side of the lake, there are two distinct campsites – one on flat meadows near the lake, the other in a more secluded wooded area reached by a tunnel under the nearby main road. The 420 pitches are about 100 sq.m. and all have electricity and cable connections (4/6A). There are 62 with full services. There is a 'typical safari environment' and a viewpoint over the Safari Park.

Facilities

Sanitary facilities are quite adequate and include some washbasins in private cabins. Launderettes. Restaurants, cafés and takeaway (weekends only in low seasons). Supermarket. Playgrounds. Indoor pool. Beaches and lake swimming. Rowing boats (free) and canoe hire. Tennis. Minigolf. Fishing. Recreation programme. Bicycle hire. Riding. Twin axle caravans not accepted. Bungalows and tents to rent. Off site: Golf 5 km.

Open: 28 March - 26 October.

Directions

From A58/E312 Tilburg - Eindhoven motorway, take exit to Hilvarenbeek on the N269 road. Park and campsite are signed Beekse Bergen.

Charges 2007

Per unit incl. 2 persons and electricity	€ 18,00 - € 22,00
Discounts for weekly stays, camping packages available.	

NL6790 Camping De Kienehoef

Zwembadweg 35-37, NL-5491 TE Sint-Oedenrode (Noord-Brabant)

Tel: **041 347 2877**. Email: **info@kienehoef.nl**

Camping de Kienehoef is at Sint Oedenrode in Noord Brabant, which boasts many historical sights, including two castles. This site is well cared for and attractively laid out with reception to the right of the entrance and the site facilities to the left. Behind this area is a heated swimming pool. The generous pitches are mostly laid out in bays and placed between trees and shrubs to the right of a long avenue through the site. The touring pitches are on three separate fields amongst pitches used for caravan holiday homes. There are some 40 serviced pitches (electricity, water and drainage).

Facilities

Two modern, clean and well maintained toilet blocks include pre-set showers and some shower/wash cubicles, also family and baby rooms. Laundry area with iron and board. Motorcaravan services. Shop, restaurant/bar and snacks (all 1/5-15/9). Heated outdoor pool (1/5-15/9). Lake fishing. Bicycle hire. Sports field. Tennis. Dogs and pets are not accepted. Off site: Golf 1 km. Riding 15 km.

Open: 28 March - 28 October.

Directions

Leave A2 s'Hertogenbosh - Eindhoven motorway at exit 27 and follow signs to Sint Oedenrode. Site is well signed from village.
GPS: N51:34.653 E05:26.809

Charges 2007

Per unit incl. 2 persons and electricity	€ 24,00 - € 29,00

Camping Cheques accepted.

NL5890 Kampeercentrum Klein Canada

Dorpstraat 1, NL-5851 AG Afferden (Limburg)

Tel: **048 553 1223**. Email: **info@kleincanada.nl**

Following the war, the family who own this site wanted to emigrate to Canada – they didn't go, but instead created this attractive site with the maple leaf theme decorating buildings, pool and play equipment. There are three touring areas, one on an island surrounded by an attractive, landscaped moat used for fishing, the other on flat ground on the other side of the entrance. They provide 195 large, numbered pitches, all with electricity (6-10A), water, drainage and TV connections. Some places have hardstanding for motorcaravans. The newest area offers 80 pitches, each with its own sanitary unit and car park space.

Facilities

Mixed toilet facilities are partially refurbished and include some with washbasins in cubicles, family facilities in a tiled and heated room and a separate children's section. Some pitches have individual units. Motorcaravan services. Gas supplies. Supermarket, Bar, restaurant, snack bar and takeaway (all 1/4-31/10). Outdoor pool (May - Sept). Indoor pool (all year). Sauna and solarium. Tennis. Fishing. Playground. Animals enclosure. Bicycle hire. Off site: Golf 3 km. Riding 5 km. Boat launching 15 km.

Open: All year.

Directions

Afferden is on the N271 between Nijmegen and Venlo, just south of the A77/E31 motorway into Germany. Site is on the N271 and is signed.
GPS: N51:38.309 E06:00.228

Charges 2007

pitch incl. 6A electricity, water and TV	€ 20,50 - € 29,00
Per person	€ 4,50
dog	€ 3,00

Camping Cheques accepted.

NL6530 Terrassencamping Gulperberg Panorama

Berghem 1, NL-6271 NP Gulpen (Limburg)

Tel: **043 450 2330**. Email: **info@gulperberg.nl**

Gulperberg Panorama is just three kilometres from the atttractive village of Gulpen. Pitches are large and flat on terraces overlooking the village on one side and open countryside on the other. Many have full services. English is spoken in the reception, although all written information is in Dutch (ask if you require a translation). Gulperberg Panorama is a haven for children. During the high season there is a weekly entertainment programme to keep them occupied. The site is not suitable for visitors with disabilities. Dogs are restricted to one section of the campsite.

Facilities

Four modern sanitary blocks have excellent facilities. Family shower room and baby room. Laundry. Shop (27/4-31/8). Bar. Takeaway. New restaurant with terrace. Swimming pool (29/4-15/9). Three play areas. Giant 'air-cushion'. TV and games room. Entertainment programme. Off site: Golf and bicycle hire 3 km. Fishing 4 km. Riding 5 km. Further afield are caves, museums and Maastricht with its large variety of shops. Beach 15 km.

Open: Easter - 31 October.

Directions

Gulpen is east of Maastricht. Take N278 Maastricht - Aachen. Site signed as you enter Gulpen at traffic lights. Turn right. Follow signs for approx. 3 km.

Charges 2007

Per unit incl. 2 persons	€ 15,10 - € 19,75
with electricity (6A)	€ 16,90 - € 22,50
with services	€ 20,90 - € 26,50
extra person (over 2 yrs)	€ 2,40 - € 3,50

Camping Cheques accepted.

NL6520 Camping BreeBronne

Lange Heide 9, NL-5993 PB Maasbree (Limburg)

Tel: **077 465 2360**. Email: **info@breebronne.nl**

One of the top campsites in the Netherlands, BreeBronne is set in a forest region beside a large lake. There are 370 pitches, of which 220 are for touring units. They are at least 80 sq.m. in size and all have electricity (10A), water, waste water and cable TV connections. Touring pitches are separated from the static units. The lake provides a sandy beach with water slide and many opportunities for swimming, sailing and windsurfing. Alternatively, you can swim in the heated open air pool or the 'sub-tropical' heated indoor pool with its special area for children. Sanitary facilities are excellent here and include private bathrooms for rent. Member of Leading Campings Group.

Facilities

The sanitary facilities are top class with a special section for children, decorated in fairy tale style, and excellent provision for disabled visitors and seniors. Launderette. Dog shower. Solarium. Private bathrooms for hire. 'De Bron' restaurant with regional specialities. Bar. Takeaway. Shop. Outdoor swimming pool (May - Aug). Indoor pool April - Oct). Play area. Play room. Internet. Tennis. Animation.

Open: All year.

Directions

Breebronne lies between Sevenum and Maasbree. From autobahn A67 towards Venlo take exit 38 and fork right. After 3 km. turn for Maasbree, then left (Maasbree). On to roundabout, take third exit. BreeBronne is signed. Go through town and fork right after 2 km. to site on left. GPS: N51:22.488 E06:03.657

Charges 2008

Per unit incl 4 persons	€ 27,70 - € 45,40
extra person	€ 4,80
private bathroom	€ 11,80

NATURAL ENJOYMENT...

BREEBRONNE

Leisureparc BreeBronne | Lange Heide 9, NL-5993 PB Maasbree | Tel: +31 (0)77 - 465 23 60 | i: www.breebronne.nl | e: info@breebronne.nl

NL6510 Camping De Schatberg

Midden Peelweg 5, NL-5975 MZ Sevenum (Limburg)

Tel: **077 467 7777**. Email: **info@schatberg.nl**

In a woodland setting of 86 hectares, this family run campsite is more reminiscent of a holiday village, with a superb range of activities that makes it an ideal venue for families. Look out for the wallabies and the deer! The 600 touring pitches, with electricity (6/10A), cable, water and drainage, average 100 sq.m. in size and are on rough grass terrain mostly with shade, but not separated. Four pitches have private sanitary facilities and some pitches have been renewed. A range of rented and private accommodation is unobtrusively placed in separate areas and includes some very smart, brick-built bungalows for rent.

Facilities

Five modern, fully equipped toilet blocks, supplemented by three small wooden toilet units to save night time walks, receive heavy use in high season and maintenance can be variable. Family shower rooms, baby baths and en-suite units for disabled visitors. Laundry facilities. Motorcaravan service point. Supermarket. Restaurant, bar and takeaway. Pizzeria. Pancake restaurant. Indoor and outdoor pools. Tennis. Minigolf. Trampoline. Play areas. Fishing. Watersports. Bicycle hire. Mini-train. Games room. Internet access. Bowling, casino, underground disco, entertainment in high season. Off site: Golf 4 km.

Open: All year.

Directions

Leave A67 Eindhoven - Venlo motorway at Helden exit 38 and follow signs for 1 km. to site. GPS: N51:22.953 E05:58.575

Charges 2008

Per unit incl. up to 4 persons	€ 19,00 - € 35,50
extra person (over 3 yrs)	€ 5,00
dog	€ 5,00
Camping Cheques accepted.	

NL6540 Camping Rozenhof

Camerig 12, NL-6294 NB Vijlen-Vaals (Limburg)

Tel: **043 455 1611**. Email: **info@campingrozenhof.nl**

Camping Rosenhof is a friendly, family run site and its hillside location offers views over a valley that has won awards for its natural beauty. This partially wooded, hilly region is popular with countryside lovers, ramblers and cyclists. Rosenhof has 101 pitches arranged on a series of small terraced, hedged meadows. There are 82 used for touring units, some with hardstanding and all with electricity, water and drainage. A number of mature trees afford some shade. A rustic restaurant, to the left of the wide entrance has a large terrace and, as the site's name suggests, roses and plants are much in evidence. With its own stables, a small swimming pool, playground and a pets corner, there is ample provision for younger children when they are not out and about enjoying the countryside. In reception a range of tourist information brochures is available, including a detailed map of the immediate area showing footpaths. During June, July and August a tourist bus passes the site several times a day. Well worth a days outing are the nearby cities of Maastricht and Aachen.

Facilities

To the rear of reception, the heated modern sanitary unit houses all the usual facilities including controllable showers, washbasins open and in cabins. Facilities for disabled people. Baby room and family shower room. Washing machines and dryers. Shop. Restaurant/bar and takeaway. Gas supplies. Playground, play room and pets corner for children. Riding. Bicycle hire. Off site: Fishing 5 km. Golf 9 km.

Open: All year.

Directions

Leave A76/E314 at Knooppunt Bochtolz (not exit for Bocholtz town) and follow N281 southwest towards Vaals for 3 km. to T-junction with N278. Turn left, then first right (Mamelisserweg) to Vijlen. In Vijlen second road to the right (Vijlen Berg) and straight on for 4 km. to T-junction at the other side of the forest. Turn right and comtinue for 300 m. the site is to the right. GPS: N50:46.189 E05:55.705

Charges 2008

Per unit incl. 2 persons	€ 17,00
extra person (over 3 yrs)	€ 2,00
electricity (4A)	€ 2,50

NL6580 Recreatieterrein De Gronselenput

Haasstao 3, NL-6321 PK Wijlre (Limburg)

Tel: **043 459 1645**. Email: **gronselenput@paasheuvelgroep.nl**

Camping Gronselenput is a small, quiet, countryside site located at the end of a tree lined lane. Family run, it has 60 grassy level pitches 55 of which are for tourists, 40 having 6A electricity. With a peaceful location between a wooded hill and the river Geul (fishing allowed with permit), it is popular with visitors with younger children and those seeking a quiet site. Cars are parked separately from the camping area thus ensuring vehicle free space. The site is set out in a series of small hedged meadows with pitches tending to be located around the edges. Three gravel pitches are reserved for motorcaravans. This region of Holland, with small villages set in lush green valleys surrounded by woods and hills, is extremely popular with walkers and cyclists. Within the region there are lots of attractive bars and restaurants, The Monte Verde garden is 15 km. from the site and the towns of Maastricht and Aachen are within easy reach and well worth visiting. The railway station is only a 30 minute walk from the campsite and on certain days there are steam train rides.

Facilities

In the sanitary block hot water for showers is free. Entry to the toilets is directly from outside. Two baby areas. Washing machines and spin dryer. Gas supplies. Shop (excellent English spoken). Bar selling pizzas with a partly covered terrace facing one of the playgrounds. Large room used for organised children's activities. Off site: Riding and bicycle hire 15 km. Golf 25 km.

Open: 1 April - 31 October.

Directions

Site is near village of Wijlre, 10 km. northwest of Aachen. Leave A4/E314/A76 at Knooppunt Bocholtz 2 km. northwest of the German border (not exit for Bocholtz town). Follow N281 southwest for 5 km. and at junction turn right (northwest) to Wittem on the N278. In Wittem, at traffic lights turn right on N595 to Wijlre. Just after entering Wijlre site is signed to the left. GPS: N50:50.530 E05:52.649

Charges 2007

Per unit incl. 2 persons	€ 14,40 - € 20,20
incl. electricity	€ 16,90 - € 22,70
extra person	€ 2,50
dog	€ 3,20

NL6515 Camping Oolderhuuske

Oolderhuuske 1, NL-6041 TR Roermond (Limburg)

Tel: **0475 588 686**. Email: **info@oolderhuuske.nl**

This unusual site is located on an island in the river Maas and provides 200 pitches, some right beside the water. All the pitches within 60 m. of the water. The site has a beach where the water is of tested daily to ensure it is safe for swimming. On request one can have a pitch near the camping jetty or at the harbour. Whichever pitch you choose, you will always have a beautiful view. The spacious pitches are arranged in rows and all have electricity and cable TV hook-ups. There are 15 overnight pitches outside the barrier. The campsite forms part of the Resort Marina Oolderhuuske which also offers villas to rent on the water and much more.

Facilities

Two 'portacabin' style units provide toilets, showers (free), washbasins and outside dishwashing and laundry sinks. All the facilities of the Marina (not all free): restaurant with terrace, snacks (takeaway) indoor swimming pool, sport fields, tennis courts, playgrounds, and entertainment during high season. Many possibilities for boating, sailing, swimming and fishing.

Open: 1 April - 31 October.

Directions

Coming from Maastricht on the A2 (Maastricht - Eindhoven) take exit for Roermond and Maasbracht and continue to Roermond (centrum). In Roermond follow signs for Eindhoven and, just after the Muse river bridge (Maasbrug)s turn right to Hatenboer/de Weerd. Follow brown signs to Marina Oolderhuuske.

Charges 2007

Per unit incl. up to 2 persons and electricity	€ 22,00 - € 25,00
dog	€ 3,00

MAP 8

A land full of contrasts, from magnificent snow capped mountains, dramatic fjords, vast plateaux with wild untamed tracts, to huge lakes and rich green countryside. With nearly one quarter of the land above the Arctic Circle it is not surprising that Norway has the lowest population density in Europe.

CAPITAL: OSLO

Tourist Office

Norwegian Tourist Board
Charles House, 5 Lower Regent Street
London SW1Y 4LR
Tel: 0207 839 6255
Email: infouk@ntr.no
Internet: www.visitnorway.com

Norway is made up of five regions. In the heart of the eastern region and the oldest of the Scandinavian capitals, Oslo is situated among green hills and vast forest areas, rich in Viking folklore and traditions. If your main reason for visiting Norway is to see the fjords then head to the west. They are magnificent, with waterfalls and mountains that plunge straight down into the fjords. Trondheim, the third largest city, is in the heart of central Norway, steeped in history with a mixture of old wooden houses and modern architecture. Southern Norway sees the most sun, a popular holiday destination for the Norwegians, with a coastline ideal for swimming, sailing, scuba diving and fishing. The north is the 'Land of the Midnight Sun', where the sun never sets in summer and in winter it fails to rise. The scenery is diverse with forested valleys, stark mountains and lush valleys, and there are also coastal cities to explore, including Tromsø, which boasts the world's most northerly brewery.

Population
4.4 million

Climate
Weather can be unpredictable, although less extreme on the west coast. Some regions have 24 hours of daylight in summer but none in winter.

Language
Norwegian, but English is widely spoken.

Telephone
The country code is 00 47.

Money
Currency: Norwegian Krone
Banks: Mon-Fri 09.00-15.00.

Shops
Mon-Fri 09.00-16.00/17.00, Thu 09.00-18.00/20.00 and Sat 09.00-13.00 /15.00.

Public Holidays
New Year's Day; King's Birthday 21 Feb; Holy Thursday; Good Friday; Easter Monday; May Day; Liberation Day 8 May; Constitiution Day 17 May; Ascension; Whit Monday; Queen's Birthday 4 July; Saint's Day 19 July; Christmas 25, 26 Dec.

Motoring
Roads are generally uncrowded around Oslo and Bergen but be prepared for tunnels and hairpin bends. Certain roads are forbidden to caravans or best avoided (advisory leaflet from the Norwegian Tourist Office). Vehicles must have sufficient road grip and in winter it may be necessary to use winter tyres with or without chains. Vehicles entering Bergen on week-days must pay a toll and other tolls are also levied on certain roads.

NO2610 **Neset Camping**

N-4741 Byglandsfjord (Aust-Agder)

Tel: **37 93 42 55**. Email: **post@neset.no**

On a semi-promontory on the shores of the 40 km. long Byglandsfjord, Neset is a good centre for activities or as a stop en route north from the ferry port of Kristiansand (from England or Denmark). Neset is situated on well kept grassy meadows by the lake shore with the water on three sides and the road on the fourth and provides 200 unmarked pitches with electricity and cable TV available. The main building houses reception, a small shop and a restaurant with fine views over the water. This is a well run, friendly site where one could spend an active few days. Byglandsfjord offers good fishing (mainly trout) and the area has marked trails for cycling, riding or walking in an area famous for its minerals.

Facilities	Directions
Three modern sanitary blocks which can be heated, all with comfortable hot showers (some on payment), washing up facilities (metered hot water) and a kitchen. Restaurant and takeaway (15/6-15/8). Shop (1/5-1/10). Campers' kitchen. Playground. Lake swimming, boating and fishing. Excellent new barbecue area and hot tub. Bicycle, canoe and pedalo hire. Climbing, rafting and canoeing courses arranged (including trips to see beavers and elk). Cross-country ski-ing possible in winter. Off site: Rock climbing wall. Marked forest trails.	Site is on route 9, 2.5 km. north of the town of Byglandsfjord on the eastern shores of the lake. GPS: N58:41.309 E07:48.079

Charges guide

Per person	NOK 10
child (5-12 yrs)	NOK 5
pitch	NOK 160
electricity	NOK 30

Camping Cheques accepted.

Open: All year.

Neset Camping

**4741 Byglnadsford
Aust-Agder
Norway
Tel: +47 37934050
post@neset.no
www.neset.no**

Open all year

NO2600 **Rysstad Feriesenter**

N-4748 Rysstad (Aust-Agder)

Tel: **37 93 61 30**. Email: **post@rysstadferie.no**

Setesdal is on the upper reaches of the Otra river which runs north from the southern port of Kristiansand and right up to the southern slopes of Hardangervidda. The small village of Rysstad is named after the family who has developed camping in this area. The site occupies a wide tract of woodland between the road and the river towards which it shelves gently, affording a splendid view of the valley and the towering mountains opposite. The site is in effect divided into two sections; one is divided by trees and hedges into numbered pitches, some occupied by chalets, the other is an adjacent open field and 20 electrical connections are available (6 with satellite TV).

Facilities	Directions
Sanitary facilities have showers on payment, washbasins in cubicles, dishwashing sinks and a cooker. Laundry facilities. Play area and amusement hut. Sports field. Fishing, swimming and boating (boats for hire). Fitness track. Bicycle hire. Centre includes café, mini shop and restaurant. Handicraft shop. Area on the river's edge for barbecues and entertainment with an arena type setting. New 5 room motel, open all year. Off site: Village within walking distance. Bank, shop, petrol station.	Site is about 1 km. south of junction between route 9 (from Kristiansand) and route 45 (from Stravanger). GPS: N59:05.464 E07:32.434

Charges 2007

Per person	NOK 20
child (4-12 yrs)	NOK 10
caravan or tent	NOK 130
hiker	NOK 60
electricity	NOK 25

Open: 1 May - 1 October.

NO2590 Sandviken Camping

N-3650 Tinn Austbygd (Telemark)

Tel: **35 09 81 73**. Email: **kontakt@sandviken-camping.no**

Sandviken is a remote, lakeside site, in scenic location, suitable for exploring Hardangervidda. With its own shingle beach, at the head of Tinnsjo Lake, it provides 150 grassy, mostly level, pitches. In addition to 50 seasonal units and 12 cabins, there are 85 numbered tourist pitches with electricity (10/16A), plus an area for tents, under trees along the waterfront. The office/reception kiosk also sells sweets, soft drinks, ices etc. and a baker calls daily in July. A 1 km. stroll takes you to the tiny village of Tinn Austbygde which has a mini-market, bakery, café, bank, garage and post office.

Facilities

Tidy heated sanitary facilities includes some washbasins in cubicles, showers on payment, sauna, solarium and a dual-purpose disabled/family bathroom with ramped access and baby changing mat. Kitchen and laundry rooms (hot water on payment). Motorcaravan services. Kiosk (20/6-1/9). Playground. TV/games room. Minigolf. Fishing. Watersports. Boat hire. Off site: Handicraft exhibition 5 km. Riding 15 km.

Open: All year.

Directions

Easiest access is via the Rv 37 from Gransherad along the western side of the lake. GPS: N59:59.352 E08:49.069

Charges 2007

Per person	NOK 15
child (4-18 yrs)	NOK 10
caravan or motorcaravan	NOK 110 - 150
tent and car	NOK 95 - 115

NO2660 Preikestolen Camping

Jørssangvegen 265, Preikestolvegen 97, N-4100 Jørpeland (Rogaland)

Tel: **51 74 97 25**. Email: **info@preikestolencamping.com**

Taking its name from one of Norway's best known attractions, the Preikestolen (Pulpit Rock) cliff formation, Preikestolen Camping is situated in the beautiful region of Rogaland, surrounded by high mountains and deep fjords. This is a site where you easily could stay a few days to explore the beautiful region. The friendly owners are happy to help with maps and guidance. The site is laid out in a relaxed way with an open, level grass area where trees and bushes create pleasant little 'rooms' for your tent, caravan or motorcaravan. There are 100 pitches, 56 with electricity (10/16A), water tap and waste water drainage.

Facilities

The modern heated sanitary block has showers, washbasins in cubicles and facilities for disabled visitors. Washing facilities. Motorcaravan service point. Freezer. Shop and craft shop (15/5-15/9). Restaurant and takeaway (15/5-15/9). Fishing. Internet (WiFi). Off site: Preikestolen. Stavanger. Lysefjordsentret salmon park in Oanes. Rock carvings at Solbakk. Golf 500 m. Riding 15 km. Helicopter sightseeing.

Open: 1 March - 1 December.

Directions

Site is on road 13, 3 km. south of Jörpeland. Follow signs to site. GPS: N58:59.933 E06:05.530

Charges 2007

Per person	NOK 30
child	NOK 20
pitch	NOK 150
electricity	NOK 30

NO2315 Ringoy Camping

N-5780 Kinsarvilk (Hordaland)

Tel: **53 66 39 17**

Although the village of Ringoy is quiet and peaceful, it occupies a pivotal position, lying not only midway between two principal ferry ports of Upper Hardangerfjord (Kinsarvik and Brimnes), but also near the junction of two key roads (routes 7 and 13). This site is basically a steeply sloping field running down from the road to the tree-lined fjord with two flat terraces and the shore area for camping. The owners, the Raunsgard family are particularly proud of the site's remarkable shoreside barbecue facilities. On arrival you find a place as there is no reception – someone will call.

Facilities

The toilet block is small and simple (with metered showers), but well designed, constructed and maintained. It is possibly inadequate during peak holiday weeks in July. Rowing boat (free). Off site: Supermarket, bank and other facilities in Kinsarvik 10 km.

Open: 15 May - 15 September.

Directions

Site is on route 13, midway between Kinsarvik and Brimnes.

Charges 2007

Per person	NOK 10
pitch	NOK 100
electricity (10A)	NOK 20

No credit cards.

NO2330 Eikhamrane Camping

N-5776 Nå (Hordaland)

Tel: **53 66 22 48**

About halfway along the western shore of Sørfjord is Eikhamrane Camping. Arranged on a well landscaped and partly terraced field which slopes alongside the road to a pebbly lakeside beach, it was formerly part of an orchard which still extends on both sides of the site. There is room for 40 units on unmarked, well kept grass with 20 electrical hook ups (10A). There are attractive trees and good gravel roads, with areas of gravel hardstanding for poor weather. Many pitches overlook the fjord where there are also picnic benches.

Facilities	Directions
Two small timber toilet blocks, one for toilets with external access, the other for washbasins (open) and showers (on payment). Both are simple but very well kept. Small kitchen with dishwashing facilities (hot water on payment) and two laundry sinks outside, under cover. Some supplies kept at reception office in the old farmhouse, home of the owner (bread and milk to order). Watersports (sailing, canoeing and rowing), and fishing in fjord. Off site: Digranes nature reserve (birdwatching) nearby.	Site is on road 550 about 8 km. south of the village of Nå, on the western shore of Sørfjord, 32 km. south of Utne and 16 km. north of Odda. GPS: N60:10.984 E06:33.104

Open: 1 June - 31 August only.

Charges 2007

Per person	NOK 10
child (4-12 yrs)	NOK 5
pitch	NOK 100
electricity	NOK 25

No credit cards.

NO2350 Espelandsdalen Camping

N-5736 Granvin (Hordaland)

Tel: **56 52 51 67**. Email: **post@espelandsdalencamping.no**

If one follows Hardangerfjord on the map and considers the mighty glacier which once scooped away the land along its path, it is easy to imagine that it started life in Espelandsdalen. For generations farmers have struggled to make a living out of the narrow strip of land between water and rock. One of these farmers has converted a narrow, sloping field bisected by the road (572) into a modest lakeside campsite taking about 50 units. The grassy meadow pitches below the road run right down to the lake shore. There are 30 electrical hook ups (10A). Campers come here for the fishing and walking, or just to marvel at the views of the valley and its towering mountain sides.

Facilities	Directions
A newly refurbished sanitary block consists of a washing trough with hot water, a shower on payment and WCs. Some basic foodstuffs are kept in the office. Swimming, fishing and boating in lake. Boat hire. Off site: Pleasant walk to local waterfall.	The northern loop of the 572 road follows Espelandsdalen and the campsite is on this road, about 6 km. from its junction with route 13 at Granvin. GPS: N60:35.545 E06:48.390

Open: 1 May - 31 August.

Charges 2007

Per person	NOK 15
pitch incl. electricity	NOK 125

No credit cards.

NO2320 Odda Camping

Borsto, N-5750 Odda (Hordaland)

Tel: **41 32 16 10**. Email: **post@oppleve.no**

Bordered by the Folgefonna glacier to the west and the Hardangervidda plateau to the east and south, Odda is an industrial town with electro-chemical enterprises based on zinc mining and hydro-electric power. This site has been attractively developed on the town's southern outskirts. It is spread over 2.5 acres of flat, mature woodland, which is divided into small clearings by massive boulders. There are 55 tourist pitches including 36 with electricity. The site fills up in the evenings and can be crowded with facilities stretched from the end of June to early August.

Facilities	Directions
A single timber building at the entrance houses the reception office and the simple, but clean sanitary facilities which provide, for each sex, 2 WCs, one hot shower (on payment) and 3 open washbasins. New building provides additional unisex toilets, showers and laundry facilities. Small kitchen with dishwashing facilities. Mini shop. Off site: Town facilities close.	Site is on the southern outskirts of Odda, signed off road to Buar, with a well marked access. GPS: N60:03.192 E06:32.628

Open: All year.

Charges 2007

Per person	NOK 10
pitch	NOK 110- 130
electricity	NOK 40

No credit cards.

NO2360 Ulvik Fjord Camping

N-5730 Ulvik (Hordaland)

Tel: **91 17 96 70**. Email: **camping@ulvik.org**

Ulvik was discovered by tourists 150 years ago when the first liners started operating to the head of Hardangerfjord, This pretty little site is 500 m. from the centre of the town and occupies what must once have been a small orchard running down to the fjord beside a small stream. There is room for about 80 units on undulating ground which slopes towards the fjord, with some flat areas and 32 electrical connections and 6 cabins. Access is by winding roads, either along the side of the fjord or up a steep narrow road behind the town – probably not to be recommended for caravans. To this day, a regular stream of cruise liners work their way into the very heartland of Norway.

Facilities

New facilities in a small wooden building which houses reception and the well kept sanitary facilities. For each sex there are 2 open washbasins, WCs and 2 modern showers on payment. Kitchen with cooker and dishwashing sink. Washing machine. Bicycle hire. Boat slipway, fishing and swimming in fjord. Jetty with rowing boat (free). Large barbecue area and hot tub. Off site: Hotel opposite, shops and restaurants in town.

Open: 1 May - 15 September.

Directions

Ulvik is reached by road no. 572; the site is on the southern side of the town, opposite the Ulvikfjord Pension. There is a ferry from road no. 7 at Brimnes. Cars and caravans can also connect with road 7 via a tunnel. GPS: N60:33.908 E06:54.487

Charges 2007

Per pitch	NOK 130
electricity	NOK 20

NO2460 Prinsen Strandcamping

Gåseid, N-6015 Ålesund (Møre og Romsdal)

Tel: **70 15 21 90**. Email: **post@prinsencamping.no**

Prinsen is a lively, fjordside site, five kilometres from the attractive small town of Alesund. It is a more attractive option than the more crowded sites closer to town, even so, this is mainly a transit and short-stay site. Divided by trees and shrubs, and sloping gently to a small sandy beach with views down Borgundfjord, the site has 100 grassy pitches, 34 cabins and 7 rooms, 110 electricity connections (16A) and 75 cable TV hook-ups. Fresh baked bread can be ordered daily.

Facilities

The main heated sanitary unit in the reception building is fully equipped with mostly open washbasins, showers on payment and a sauna. Kitchen with cooker and sinks. Laundry facilities. Additional older facilities mainly serving rooms and cabins, but include multi-purpose bathroom for disabled people, families and baby changing. Motorcaravan service point. Kiosk (1/6-1/9). TV room. Barbecue areas. Playground. Slipway and boat hire. Fishing. Off site: Restaurant 800 m. Supermarket 1 km.

Open: All year.

Directions

Turn off E136 at roundabout signed to Hatlane and site. Follow signs to site. GPS: N62:27.509 E06:15.192

Charges 2007

Per pitch	NOK 200

NO2490 Skjerneset Brygge Camping

Ekkilsoya, N-6530 Averoy (Møre og Romsdal)

Tel: **71 51 18 94**. Email: **info@skjerneset.com**

The tiny island of Ekkilsøya lies off the larger island of Averøy and is reached via a side road and bridge from road 64 just south of Bremsnes from where the ferry crosses to Kristiansund. At Skjerneset Camping there is space for 30 caravans or motorcaravans on gravel hardstandings around a rocky bluff and along the harbour's rocky frontage and all have electricity (10/16A). A small grassy area for 5 tents is under pine trees in a hollow on the top of the bluff together with 5 fully equipped cabins. Note: this is a working harbour with deep unfenced water very close to the pitches.

Facilities

Unisex sanitary facilities are heated, but basic and include washbasins in cubicles. Two new sanitary blocks. Kitchen and dishwashing sinks. Small laundry. Motorcaravan service point. Kiosk for basic packet foods, crisps, ices, sweets, postcards etc. Satellite TV. Motor boat hire. Organised sea-fishing or sightseeing trips in the owner's sea-going boat, and for non-anglers who want a fish supper, fresh fish are usually available on site.

Open: All year.

Directions

Site is on the little island of Ekkilsøya which is reached via a side road running west from the main Rv 64 road, 1.5 km. south of Bremsnes. GPS: N63:04.881 E07:35.767

Charges 2007

Per person	NOK 150
pitch	NOK 250 - 500
electricity	NOK 25
No credit cards.	

NO2452 Trollveggen Camping

Horgheimseidet, N-6300 Åndalsnes (Møre og Romsdal)

Tel: **71 22 37 00**. Email: **post@trollveggen.no**

The location of this site provides a unique experience – it is set at the foot of the famous vertical cliff of Trollveggen (the Troll Wall), which is Europe's highest vertical mountain face. The site is pleasantly laid out in terraces with level grass pitches. The facility block, the four cabins and the reception are all very attractively built with grass rooves. Beside the river is an attractive barbecue area where barbecue parties are sometimes arranged. This site is a must for people who love nature. The site is surrounded by the Troll Peaks and the Romsdalshorn Mountains with the rapid river of Rauma flowing by. Here in the beautiful valley of Romsdalen you have the ideal starting point for trips to many outstanding attractions such as 'The Troll Road' to Geiranger or to the Mandalsfossen waterfalls. In the mountains there are nature trails of various lengths and difficulties. The campsite owners are happy to help you with information. The town of Åndalsnes is 10 km. away and has a long tourism tradition as a place to visit. It is situated in the inner part of the beautiful Romsdal fjord and has a range of shops and restaurants.

Facilities

One heated toilet block provides washbasins, some in cubicles, and showers on payment. Family room with baby bath and changing mat, plus facilities for disabled visitors. Communal kitchen with cooking rings, small ovens, fridge and sinks (free hot water). Laundry facilities. Motorcaravan service point and chemical disposal point. Barbecue area (covered). Playground. Duck pond. Off site: Climbing, glacier walking and hiking. Fjord fishing. Sightseeing trips. The Troll Road. Mardalsfossen (waterfall). Geiranger and Åndalsnes.

Open: 10 May - 20 September.

Directions

Site is located on the E136 road, 10 km. south of Åndalsnes. It is signed. GPS: N62:29.674 E07:45.500

Charges 2007

Per unit incl. 2 persons	NOK 130 - 140
electricity	NOK 40
Camping Cheques accepted.	

NO2450 Bjolstad Camping

N-6445 Malmefjorden (Møre og Romsdal)

Tel: **71 26 56 56**. Email: **post@bjolstad.no**

This is a delightful small, rural site, which slopes down to Malmefjorden, a sheltered arm of Fraenfjorden. Bjølstad has space for just 55 touring units on grassy, fairly level, terraces either side of the tarmac central access road. A delight for children is a large, old masted boat which provides hours of fun playing at pirates or Vikings. At the foot of the site is a waterside barbecue area, a shallow, sandy, paddling area for children and a jetty. Both rowing and motorboats (with lifejackets) can be hired, one can swim or fish in the fjord.

Facilities

The very basic, clean, heated sanitary unit includes two showers per sex (on payment), plus washbasins with dividers. Small campers' kitchen with two dishwashing sinks and hot-plate. Laundry service at reception. Playground. Boat hire. Fjord fishing and swimming. Dogs are not accepted in cabins. Off site: Riding 9 km. Golf 12 km.

Open: 1 June - 30 September (earlier on request).

Directions

Turn off Rv 64 on northern edge of Malmefjorden village towards village of Lindset (lane is oil bound gravel). Site is 1 km. GPS: N62:48.875 E07:13.518

Charges 2007

Per pitch	NOK 120 - 150
electricity	NOK 60

NO2370 Botnen Camping

N-5961 Brekke (Sogn og Fjordane)

Tel: **57 78 54 71**. Email: **joker.brekke@ngbutikk.net**

For those setting forth north on E39 from Bergen there are suprisingly few attractive sites until one reaches the southern shore of mighty Sognefjord. At Brekke is a well known tourist landmark, the remarkable Breekstranda Fjord Hotel, a traditional turf-roofed complex which tourist coaches are unable to resist. A mile or two beyond the hotel, also on the shore of the fjord, is the family run Botnen Camping. This simple site slopes steeply towards the fjord, providing wonderful views to distant mountains from individual, mostly level pitches. It has its own jetty and harbour, with motor boats and canoes for hire.

Facilities	Directions
Toilet block with washbasins and showers (on payment). Small kitchen with microwave, hotplate and washing machine. Small shop. Play area. Swimming, fishing and boating in fjord. Boats and canoes for hire. Off site: Hiking, fishing and boating.	Site is on the coast road west of Brekke, 11 km. from E39.

Open: 1 June - 31 August.

Charges 2007

Per person	NOK 15
caravan or motorcaravan	NOK 90
tent	NOK 80
electricity	NOK 20

NO2380 Tveit Camping

N-6894 Vangsnes (Sogn og Fjordane)

Tel: **57 69 66 00**. Email: **tveit@online.no**

Located in the district of Vik on the south shore of Sognefjord, 4 km. from the small port of Vangsnes, Tveit Camping is part of a small working farm and it is a charming neat site. Reception and a kiosk open most of the day in high season, with a phone to summon assistance at any time. Three terraces with wonderful views of the fjord provide 35 pitches with 30 electricity connections (10A) and there are also site owned cabins. On the campsite you will find a restored Iron Age burial mound dating from 350-550AD, whilst the statue of 'Fritjov the Intrepid' towers over the landscape at Vangsnes.

Facilities	Directions
Modern, heated sanitary facilities provide showers on payment, a unit for disabled visitors, kitchens with facilities for dishwashing and cooking, and a laundry with washing machine, dryer and iron (hot water on payment). Motorcaravan services. Kiosk (15/6-15/8). TV rooms. Playground. Harbour for small boats, slipway and boat/canoe hire. Fishing. WiFi is planned. Off site: Shop, café and pub by ferry terminal in Vangsnes 4 km. Riding 15 km.	Site is by Rv 13 between Vik and Vangsnes, 4 km. south of Vangsnes.

Open: Mid March - mid November.

Charges 2007

Per person (over 5 yrs)	NOK 15
pitch	NOK 120
electricity	NOK 25
No credit cards.	

NO2385 PlusCamp Sandvik

Sandvik Sor, N-6868 Gaupne (Sogn og Fjordane)

Tel: **57 68 11 53**. Email: **sandvik@pluscamp.no**

Sandvik is a compact, small site on the edge of the town of Gaupne close to the Nigardsbreen Glacier. It provides 60 touring pitches, 48 with electrical connections (8/16A), arranged on fairly level grassy terrain either side of a road. A large supermarket, post office, banks, etc. are all within a level 500 m. stroll. A café in the reception building is open in summer for drinks and meals and the small shop sells groceries, ices, soft drinks, sweets, etc.

Facilities	Directions
The single, fully equipped, central sanitary unit includes washbasins with dividers and two hot showers per sex (on payment). Multi-purpose unit for families or disabled people with facilities for baby changing and a further WC, basin and shower with ramp for access. Small campers' kitchen. Dishwashing facilities. tables, chairs and TV. Separate laundry. Playground. Boat hire. Fishing. Bicycle hire. Off site: Nigardsbreen (glacier). Sognefjellet.	Signed just off Rv 55 Lom-Sogndal road on eastern outskirts of Gaupne. GPS: N61:24.032 E07:18.029

Open: All year.

Charges 2007

Per pitch incl. up to 4 persons	NOK 140
electricity	NOK 30

NO2375 Lærdal Ferie & Fritidspark

N-6886 Lærdal (Sogn og Fjordane)
Tel: **57 66 66 95**. Email: **info@laerdalferiepark.com**

This site is beside the famous Sognefjord, the longest fjord in the world. It is ideally situated if you want to explore the glaciers, fjords and waterfalls of the region. The 100 pitches are level with well trimmed grass and connected by tarmac roads and are suitable for tents, caravans and motorcaravans. There are 80 electrical hook-ups. The fully licensed restaurant serves traditional meals as well as snacks and pizzas. The pretty little village of Laerdal, only 400 m. away, is well worth a visit. A walk among the old, small wooden houses is a pleasant and interesting experience. You can hire boats on the site for short trips on the fjord. Guided hiking, cycling and fishing trips are also available. The site also provides cabins, flats and rooms to rent, plus a brand new motel, all very modern and extremely tastefully designed.

Facilities

Two modern and well decorated sanitary blocks with washbasins (some in cubicles), showers on payment, and toilets. Facilities for disabled visitors. Children's room. Washing machine and dryer. Kitchen. Dishwashing sinks. Motorcaravan services and chemical disposal point. Small shop. Bar, restaurant and takeaway (20/5-5/9). TV room. Playground. Motorboats, rowing boats, canoes, bicycles and pedal cars for hire. Bicycle hire. Fishing. Internet (WiFi) at reception. Off site: Cruises on the Sognefjord 400 m. The Norwegian Wild Salmon Centre 400 m. The Flåm railway 40 km. Riding 500 m. Golf 12 km.

Open: All year.

Directions

Site is on road 5 (from the E16 Oslo - Bergen road) 400 m. north of Laerdal village centre. GPS: N61:09.999 E07:47.090

Charges 2007

Per unit incl. 2 persons	NOK 140
with electricity	NOK 175
extra person	NOK 48
child (4-18 yrs)	NOK 24 - 36

Camping Cheques accepted.

Laerdal Ferie & Fritids Parks

P.O. Box 7
6886 Laerdal

E-mail: info@laerdalferiepark.com
Internet: www.laerdalferiepark.com

Tel: 0047 57 66 66 95
Fax: 0047 57 66 87 81

NO2400 PlusCamp Jolstraholmen

Postboks 11, N-6847 Vassenden (Sogn og Fjordane)
Tel: **57 72 89 07**. Email: **jolstraholmen@pluscamp.no**

This family run site is situated on the E39 between Sognefjord and Nordfjord. It is located between the road and the fast-flowing Jolstra River (renowned for trout fishing), 1.5 kilometres from the lakeside village of Vassenden, behind the Statoil filling station, restaurant and supermarket complex which is also owned by the family. The 35 pitches (some marked) are on grass or gravel hardstanding all with electricity (10A), five also have water and waste points and some have TV connections. A river tributary runs through the site and forms an island on which some pitches are located.

Facilities

The main heated sanitary facilities, fully equipped in rooms below the complex, include showers on payment plus one family bathroom per sex. Small unit located on the island. Two small kitchens provide dishwashing and cooking facilities (free of charge). Laundry. Supermarket and café. Restaurant. Garage. Covered barbecue area. Playground. Water slide (open summer, weather permitting). Rafting. Fishing. Guided walks. Boat hire. Off site: 9-hole golf course 50 m. Ski-slopes within 1 km.

Open: All year.

Directions

Site is beside the E39 road, 1.5 km. west of Vassenden, 18 km. east of Førde. GPS: N61:29.420 E06:04.820

Charges 2007

Per unit incl. 1-4 persons	NOK 135 - 175
small tent incl. 2 persons	NOK 80 - 120
electricity	NOK 40

NO2570 Fossheim Hytte & Camping

N-3550 Gol (Buskerud)

Tel: **32 02 95 80**. Email: **foshytte@online.no**

Centred on the country town of Gol is one of Norway's favourite camping areas, Hallingdal. This small touring site lies just four kilometres west of the town, on the banks of the Hallingdal river bank, shaded by elegant tall birch trees. From reception downstream there are mini rapids. There are 50 grassy touring pitches, with electricity (10/16A) available to 40 and cable TV connections for some. Most overlook the river. In addition there are 10 cabins and 4 rooms for rent. Static caravans are not accepted. Trout fishing with a specially constructed wooden walkway and platform.

Facilities

A modern heated toilet unit includes some washbasins in cubicles, separate unit for disabled people and a sauna for each sex. Small kitchen and laundry rooms provide for dishwashing and cooking (free of charge), plus a washing machine and dryer. Shop with basic provisions and bread to order (1/6-31/8). TV lounge overlooking the river. Motorcaravan services. Play area. Canoe hire. Fishing. Hiking trails from site. Off site: Riding 18 km. Golf 18 km.

Open: 15 May - 15 September.

Directions

Site is 4 km. west of Gol on route Rv 7 leading to Geilo. GPS: N60:41.012 E08:52.485

Charges 2007

Per unit incl. 2 persons	NOK 135 - 190
electricity	NOK 40

NO2510 Håneset Camping

Osloveien, N-7374 Roros (Sør Trøndelag)

Tel: **72 41 06 00**

At first sight Håneset Camping is neither promising, lying between the main road and the railway, nor is the gritty sloping ground of the site very imaginatively landscaped – for grass, when it grows up here, is rather coarse and lumpy. However, as we soon discovered, it is the best equipped campsite in the town, and ideal to cope with the often cold, wet weather of this bleak 10 m. high plateau. The 50 unmarked touring pitches all have access to electricity, and most facilities are housed in the main building. People flock from all over Europe to visit this remarkably well preserved mining town.

Facilities

Heated sanitary facilities provide three separate rooms for each sex, fully equipped with showers on payment. Washing machine and two clothes washing sinks. Kitchen. Huge sitting/TV room and two well equipped kitchens which the owners, the Moen family, share fully with their guests, plus 9 rooms for rent. Off site: Town 20 minutes walk.

Open: All year.

Directions

Site is on the Rv 30 leading south from Røros to Os, 3 km. from Røros. GPS: N62:34.047 E11:21.118

Charges guide

Per pitch incl. 4 persons	NOK 160
electricity	NOK 30
No credit cards.	

NO2515 Gjelten Bru Camping

N-2560 Alvdal (Hedmark)

Tel: **62 48 74 44**

Located a few kilometres west of Alvdal, this peaceful little site, with its traditional turf roof buildings, makes an excellent base from which to explore the area. The 50 touring pitches are on level neatly trimmed grass, served by gravel access roads and with electricity (10A) available to all. Some pitches are in the open and others under tall pine trees spread along the river bank. Across the bridge on the other side of the river and main road, the site owners also operate the local, well stocked market and post office. The UNESCO World Heritage town of Røros is 75 km. to the northeast of this charming little site, and the Dovrefjell National Park is also within comfortable driving distance.

Facilities

Heated toilet facilities are housed in two buildings. One unit has been refurbished, the other is of newer construction. There is a mix of conventional washbasins and stainless steel washing troughs, and hot showers on payment. Separate unit for disabled visitors. Two small kitchens. Laundry facilities. TV room. Swings. Fishing. Shop. Off site: Supermarket and post office nearby. Bicycle hire 5 km.

Open: All year.

Directions

On the road 29 at Gjelten 3.5 km. west of Alvdal. Turn over the river bridge opposite village store and post office, and site is immediately on right. GPS: N62:07.871 E10:34.126

Charges 2007

Per pitch	NOK 140
electricity	NOK 20

NO2390 Kjørnes Camping

N-6856 Sogndal (Sogn og Fjordane)

Tel: 57 67 45 80. Email: camping@kjornes.no

Kjørnes Camping is idyllically situated on the Sognefjord, 3 km. from the centre of Sogndal. The site has 100 pitches for camping units (90 with electricity), 9 cabins and 2 apartments for rent. Located at the very centre of the 'fjord kingdom' by the main no. 5 road, this site is the ideal base from which to explore the Sognefjord. You are within a short drive (a maximum of one hour) from all the major attractions including the Jostedal glacier, the Nærøyfjord, the Flåm Railway, the Urnes Stave Church and Sognefjellet. The site occupies a long open meadow which is terraced down to the tree lined waterside. This site is ideal for those who enjoy peace and quiet, lovely scenery or a spot of fishing. Access is via a narrow lane (that does have passing places) which drops down towards the fjord 3 km. from Sogndal.

Facilities

The heated sanitary unit is basic but clean, providing open washbasins, and 2 showers pr sex (on payment). Baby room. Facilities for disabled visitors. A new block and motorcaravan services are planned. New building with kitchen with cooking facilities, dishwasher, dining area overlooking the fjord, and laundry facilities. Small shop (20/6-20/8). Satellite TV, WiFi and internet. Off site: Hiking, glacier walks, climbing, rafting, walking around Sognefjord. Details from reception.

Open: 1 May - 1 October.

Directions

Site is off the Rv 5, 3 km. east of Sogndal, 8 km. west of Kaupanger. GPS: N61:12.674 E07:07.263

Charges 2007

Per person	NOK 30
child (4-12 yrs)	NOK 10
pitch	NOK 100
electricity	NOK 30

NO2436 Byrkjelo Camping

N-6826 Byrkjelo (Sogn og Fjordane)

Tel: 91 73 65 97. Email: byrkjelocamping@sensewave.com

This neatly laid out and well equipped small site offers 25 large marked and numbered touring pitches, all with electrical connections (10A) and 15 with gravel hardstandings. It is a good value site in a village location with neatly mown grass, attractive trees and shrubs with a warm welcome from the owners. Fishing is possible in the river adjacent to the site. Reception and a small kiosk selling ices, sweets and soft drinks, are housed in an attractive cabin and there is a bell to summon the owners should they not be on site when you arrive.

Facilities

The good heated sanitary unit includes 5 shower rooms each with washbasin, on payment. Facilities for families with babies and disabled visitors, incorporating a WC, basin and shower with handrails, etc. Campers' kitchen with dishwashing sinks, hot-plates and dining area. Laundry facilities. Motorcaravan services. Kiosk. TV room. Minigolf. Small playground. Fishing. Swimming pool and children's pool (20/6-20/8), both heated (fee charged). Off site: Riding 4 km. Golf 15 km. Ideal base for Nordfjord and Jostedalsbreen. Rafting.

Open: 1 May - 1 October.

Directions

Site is beside the E39 in the village of Byrkjelo, 19 km. east of Sandane. GPS: N61:43.826 E06:30.507

Charges 2008

Per person	NOK 10
child	NOK 5
pitch	NOK 125
electricity	NOK 30

NO2525 Østrea Æra Camping

N-2460 Osen (Hedmark)

Tel: **62 44 49 11**. Email: **info@ostre-aera-camping.com**

This all year site is located on the banks of the Osa river, where you can catch trout and prepare it in the site's barbecue hut for dinner. The site has 90 pitches (including 60 seasonal), all with 10A electricity and on level grass. There are also 20 cabins for rent. A swimming pool is heated during peak season and has a 50 m. slide. Visit in winter for ice fishing in the Osa lake or good ski facilities in Trysil and Reva, cross country as well as downhill. The small town of Rena is 25 km. away, located in the centre of Norway's largest forest and mountain area. This region is ideal for canoeing, fishing, walking and the only limit is your imagination.

Facilities

Two toilet blocks, one small and unheated. Washbasins with dividers and showers on payment. Facilities for disabled visitors. Laundry. No kitchen. Small shop. TV room next to reception. Heated pool with 50 m. slide. Football field. Playground. Barbecue hut. WiFi. Fishing.

Open: All year.

Directions

Site is on road no. 215, 25 km. northeast of Rena, and is signed. GPS: N61:14.148 E11:39.748

Charges 2007

Per unit incl. electricity	NOK 125 - 195

NO2545 Plus Camp Rustberg

N-2636 Oyer (Oppland)

Tel: **61 27 77 30**. Email: **rustberg@online.no**

Conveniently located beside the E6, 23 km. from the centre of Lillehammer, this attractive terraced site provides a comfortable base for exploring the area. Like all sites along this route it does suffer from road and train noise at times, but the site's facilities and nearby attractions more than compensate for this. There are 70 pitches with 30 available for touring units, most reasonably level and with some gravel hardstandings available for motorcaravans. There are 70 electrical connections (16A). A small open air, heated swimming pool has a water slide.

Facilities

Heated, fully equipped sanitary facilities include washbasins in cubicles, showers on payment and free saunas. Two good family bathrooms. Unit for disabled people. Campers' kitchen and dining room with dishwashing, microwave oven and double hob. Separate laundry. Motorcaravan services. Restaurant. Solarium (on payment). Kiosk for basics. Swimming pool and slide (1/6-31/8, weather permitting). Billiard golf. Playground. New reception and cafe. Off site: Forest walks directly from site. Fishing in the nearby river, day licence from reception. Golf 7 km. Children's farm and pony riding.

Open: All year.

Directions

Site is well signed from the E6, 20 km. north of Lillehammer (North) exit. GPS: N61:16.815 E10:21.657

Charges 2007

Per pitch incl. electricity	NOK 175 - 200

NO2415 Kautokeino Fritidssenter & Camping

Suonpatjavri, N-9520 Kautokeino (Finnmark)

Tel: **78 48 57 33**

This is a friendly, lakeside site, 8 km. south of Kautokeino. The 50 pitches are not marked but are generally on a firm sandy base amongst low growing birch trees, with 20 electric hook-ups (16A) available. There are also cabins and motel rooms for rent. Although the grass is trying to grow, the ground is frozen from September until May so there are mainly hardstandings with some grass areas. The site is 35 km. north of the Finnish Border and is one day's drive from North Cape.

Facilities

The modern sanitary building is heated and well maintained, with 2 British style WCs, 2 open washbasins and 2 showers (on payment) per sex. Small kitchen with cooker, dishwashing sinks and refrigerator. Laundry with washing machine, dryer and ironing facilities. Separate bathroom for disabled people, also containing baby facilities. Football. Canoes, boats and pedalos for hire. Free fishing available in lake. Off site: Kautokeino (Sami Museum), Juhl's Silver Gallery.

Open: 1 June - 30 September.

Directions

Site is 8 km. south of Kautokeino on road Rv 93. GPS: N68:56.841 E23:05.376

Charges guide

Per pitch	NOK 140
electricity	NOK 20

NO2615 Olberg Camping

Sandsveien 4, Olberg, N-1860 Trogstad (Østfold)

Tel: 69 82 86 10. Email: froesol@online.no

Olberg is a newly developed, delightful small farm site, close to Lake Øyeren and within 70 km. of Oslo. There are 35 large, level pitches and electricity connections (10-16A) are available for 28 units located on neatly tended grassy meadow with trees and shrubs. The reception building also houses a small gallery with paintings, glasswork and other crafts. A short drive down the adjacent lane takes you to the beach on Lake Øyeren, and there are many woodland walks in the surrounding area. Please bear in mind that this is a working farm.

Facilities	Directions
Excellent, heated sanitary facilities are fully equipped and include a ramp for wheelchair access and one bathroom for families or disabled visitors. Dishwashing under cover with hot and cold water. Washing machine, tumble dryer and ironing board. Small kitchenette with full size cooker and food preparation area. Kiosk. Snacks available. Craft gallery. Playground. Off site: Fishing 3 km. Golf, tropical pool and spa 18 km.	Site is signed on Rv 22, 20 km. north of Mysen on southern edge of Båstad village. GPS: N59:41.296 E11:17.575

Charges 2008

Per unit incl. 2 persons	NOK 175
tent incl. 2 persons	NOK 175

Open: 1 May - 1 October, other times by arrangement.

NO2435 Solvang Camping

Box 1280, N-9505 Alta (Finnmark)

Tel: 78 43 04 77. Email: solvangcamp@hotmail.com

This is a restful little site with a welcoming atmosphere. It is set well back from the main road, so there is no road noise. The site overlooks the tidal marshes of the Altafjord, which are home to a wide variety of birdlife, providing ornithologists with a grandstand view during the long summer evenings bathed by the Midnight Sun. The 30 pitches are on undulating grass amongst pine trees and shrubs, and are not marked, although there are 16 electric hook-ups (16A). The site is run by a church mission organisation.

Facilities	Directions
New block with reception and floor-heated sanitary facilities with wash basins in cubicles, showers and a family room. Facilities for disabled visitors. Sauna. New kitchen with cooker, sinks and dining area. Washing machine and dryer. Chemical disposal point. Large TV room. Football field. Children's playground. Off site: Alta Museum. Rock carvings.	Site is signed off the E6, 10 km. north of Alta. GPS: N69:58.781 E23:28.085

Charges guide

Per pitch incl. 2 persons and electricity	NOK 150

Open: 1 June - 10 August.

NO2425 Kirkeporten Camping

Box 22, N-9763 Skarsvag (Finnmark)

Tel: 78 47 52 33. Email: kipo@kirkeporten.no

This is the most northerly mainland campsite in the world (71/06) and considering the climate and the wild unspoilt location it has to be one of the best sites in Scandinavia, and also rivals the best in Europe. The 40 pitches, 22 with electricity (16A), are on grass or gravel hardstanding in natural 'tundra' terrain beside a small lake, together with 16 rental cabins and 5 rooms. We advise you pack warm clothing, bedding and maybe propane for this location. Note: Although overnighting at Nordkapp Centre is permitted, it is on the exposed carpark with no electric hook-ups or showers. Sea fishing and photographic trips by boat can be arranged and buses run 4 times a day to Honningsvåg or the Nordkapp Centre. We suggest you follow the marked footpath over the hillside behind the campsite, from where you can photograph Nordkapp at midnight if the weather is favourable.

Facilities	Directions
Excellent modern sanitary installations in two under-floor heated buildings. They include a sauna, two family bathrooms, baby room, and excellent unit for disabled visitors. Laundry. Kitchen, with hot-plates, sinks and a dining area. Motorcaravan service point. Reception, restauarant and mini shop at the entrance open daily. Off site: North Cape, Kirkeporten.	On the island of Magerøya, from Honningsvåg take the E69 for 20 km. then fork right signed Skarsvåg. Site is on left after 3 km. just as you approach Skarsvåg. GPS: N71:06.456 E25:48.761

Charges guide

Per person	NOK 20
pitch	NOK 150
electricity	NOK 20

Open: 20 May - 1 September.

397

NO2428 Andenes Camping

Storgata 53, N-8483 Andenes (Nordland)

Tel: **76 14 12 22**. Email: **erna.strom@norlandia.no**

This extremely popular exposed site at sea level with picturesque mountain backdrop, is only 3 km. from the base of 'Whalesafari'. This company is deemed the world's largest, most successful Arctic whale watching operation for the general public. The site is also an exceptional location for the midnight sun. Lying on the west coast of Andøy between the quiet main road (82) and white sandy beaches, an area of uneven ground provides space for an unspecified number of touring units and you park where you like. The ground is mainly of grass with some hardstanding. Twenty units only can access 16A electricity and you are highly advised to arrive by mid-afternoon.

Facilities

The reception building houses clean separate sex sanitary facilities providing for each 2 toilets, 2 showers (NOK 10 for 5 minutes). with curtain to keep clothes dry and 3 washbasins. Small kitchen. Motorcaravan service point. Off site: Well stocked supermarket 250 m. From the nearby village of Bleik (8 km), trips for deep sea fishing and visits to Bleiksøya one of Norway's most famous bird cliffs.

Open: 1 June - 30 September.

Directions

Travelling north on road 82, site is on left 3 km. before Andenes.

Charges guide

Per unit	NOK 120
incl. electricity	NOK 130
tent	NOK 90

NO2455 Ballangen Camping

N-8540 Ballangen (Nordland)

Tel: **76 92 76 90**. Email: **ballcamp@c2i.net**

Ballangen is a pleasant, lively site conveniently located on the edge of a fjord with a small sandy beach, with direct access off the main E6 road. The 150 marked pitches are mostly on sandy grass, with electricity (10/16A) available to all. There are a few hardstandings, also 54 cabins for rent. A TV room provides tourist information, a coffee machine and games machines, and there is a heated outdoor pool and waterslide (charged), free fjord fishing, and boat hire.

Facilities

Toilet facilities include some washbasins in cubicles. Facilities for disabled visitors, sauna and solarium. Kitchen with dishwashing sinks, 2 cookers and covered seating area. Laundry. Motorcaravan services. Well stocked shop. Café and takeaway (main season). TV/games room. Swimming pool and waterslide (charged). Minigolf. Fishing. Golf. Boat and bicycle hire. Pedal car hire. Mini zoo. Playground. Off site: Riding 2 km. Ballangen 4 km. has supermarket and other services. Narvik 40 km.

Open: 1 March - 31 December.

Directions

Access is off the E6, 4 km. north of Ballangen, 40 km. south of Narvik. GPS: N68:20.333 E16:51.468

Charges 2007

Per pitch	NOK 170
electricity	NOK 40

NO2465 Lyngvær Lofoten Bobilcamping

N-8310 Kabelvag (Nordland)

Tel: **76 07 87 81**. Email: **relorent@c2i.net**

Some camping sites on Lofoten are very basic with extremely limited facilities but Lyngvaer is in complete contrast. This established site is very popular, with many customers returning. In the centre of Lofoten alongside a tidal fjord with mountains all around, the setting and location is quite idyllic. Large terraces provide fine views for most of the 200 pitches, mainly grass, some with hardstanding, with electricity for 110 (10/16A). Fresh water, waste water and chemical disposal is free for guests (otherwise waste disposal and fresh water NOK 50).

Facilities

Toilet facilities are spotlessly clean with showers in small cubicles (NOK 10 for 6 minutes). Extra unisex showers and toilets are beside reception. Communal kitchen. Large sitting area with satellite TV. Play areas. Boat hire. Fishing (fish cleaning area). Off site: Within a reasonable distance, manufacturing of metal birds, glass blowing, Viking museum, aquarium and the capital of Lofoten, Svolvaer.

Open: 1 May - 30 September.

Directions

On disembarking the ferry (Skutvik - Svolvaer) turn southwest on E10 signed Lofoten. Site is on left in 18 km. (There is a campsite about 6 km. from Skutvik on the left on approach, details unknown).

Charges guide

Per unit incl. 1 person	NOK 100
extra person	NOK 5
electricity	NOK 20

NO2475 Saltstraumen Camping

Bok 85, N-8056 Saltstraumen (Nordland)

Tel: **75 58 75 60**. Email: **saltstraumen@pluscamp.no**

On a coastal route, this extremely popular site, in a very scenic location with a magnificent backdrop, is close to the largest Maelstrom in the world. It is an easy short walk to this outstanding phenomenon. As well as 20 cabins, the site has 60 plain touring pitches mostly on level, gravel hardstandings in rows, each with electricity. A few 'softer' pitches are available for tents. The site is 33 km. from Bodø and 50 km. from Fauske. You are advised to arrive by late afternoon.

Facilities

Basic but heated sanitary facilities are clean and fully equipped. Separate shower areas for men and women have dividers, shower curtains and communal changing (free). Kitchen with two full cookers, fish cleaning area and fish freezer. (free). Laundry with washing machine and dryer. Motorcaravan service point. TV room. Playground. Minigolf. Fishing. Off site: Well stocked mini supermarket and snack bar outside site entrance. Hotel and cafeteria nearby. This area is said to be the fourth best location in the world for diving.

Open: All year.

Directions

Travelling from the south: Before Rognan take Rv 812 signed Saltstraumen. At junction with Rv 17 turn right. Site on left immediately after second bridge. From the north: From Rv 80 (Fauske -Bodø) turn south on Rv 17, site is 12 km. at Saltstraumen on right immediately before bridge.

Charges guide

Per unit incl. 2 persons	NOK 90 - 120
extra person	NOK 15
electricity	NOK 30

NO2485 Krokstrand Camping

Krokstrand, Salt Jellveien 1573, N-8630 Storforshei (Nordland)

Tel: **75 16 60 02**

This site is a popular resting place for all nationalities on the long trek to Nordkapp and it is only 18 km. from the Arctic Circle with its Visitor Centre. There are 45 unmarked pitches set amongst birch trees with electrical connections (10A) for 28 units. In late spring and early summer the river alongside, headed by rapids is impressive with the possibility of mountains close by still being snow-capped. The small reception kiosk is open 08.00-10.00 and 15.00-22.00 hrs in high season, otherwise campers are invited to find a pitch and pay later.

Facilities

Well maintained, spotlessly clean, small sanitary unit includes two showers per sex (on payment). Laundry with washing machine and dryer. Small kitchen with double hot-plate and dishwashing sink. Motorcaravan services. Brightly painted children's playground with trampoline, well maintained. Minigolf. Fishing. Off site: Hotel with café/restaurant just outside site entrance (same ownership as the site) with good meals, snacks and very basic provisions. Souvenir shop.

Open: 1 June - 20 September.

Directions

Entrance is off E6 at Krokstrand village opposite hotel, 18 km. south of the Arctic Circle. GPS: N66:28.072 E15:04.594

Charges 2007

Per person	NOK 15
child	NOK 10
pitch	NOK 110
electricity	NOK 30
No credit cards.	

NO2495 Vegset Camping

N-7760 Snasa (Nord-Trøndelag)

Tel: **74 15 29 50**. Email: **mveg@online.no**

This small, basic but pleasant site is seven kilometres south of Snåsa, directly beside the E6 road on the banks of Lake Snåsavatn. It consists of ten site owned chalets, a number of static units and a small area for about 20 touring units on slightly sloping ground. There are 10A electricity connections available. For those travelling to or from Northern Norway, Vegset provides a good resting point or night halt. Snåsa is a centre for the South Lapp people who have their own boarding school, museum and information centre there. The Bergasen Nature Reservation is close to the village and is famous for its rare flora, especially orchids. The Gressamoen National Park is also near.

Facilities

The satisfactory toilet block provides showers (NOK 10), plus a shower with toilet suitable for disabled people. Kitchen. Kiosk selling emergency groceries doubles as a TV room (end June - mid Aug). Swimming, boat hire and fishing (licence from site).

Open: Easter - 10 October.

Directions

Site is just off the E6 road, 7 km. south of Snåsa.

Charges guide

Per pitch	NOK 110
electricity	NOK 30

NO2500 Tråsåvika Camping

Orkanger, N-7354 Viggja (Sør Trøndelag)
Tel: **72 86 78 22**. Email: **jowiggen@start.no**

On a headland jutting into the Trondheimfjord some 40 km. from Trondheim, Trasavika commands an attractive position. For many, this compensates for the extra distance into town. The 65 pitches (some slightly sloping) are on an open grassy field at the top of the site, or on a series of terraces below, which run down to the small sandy beach, easily accessed via a well designed gravel service road. There are 48 electricity connections (10A). To one side, on a wooded bluff at the top of the site, are 14 cabins (open all year), many in traditional style with grass rooves.

Facilities

The neat, fully equipped, sanitary unit includes two controllable hot showers per sex (on payment). Hot water on payment in kitchen and laundry which have a hot-plate, dish and clothes washing sinks, washing machine and dryer. Shop. Café (20/6-30/8). TV/sitting room. Play area. Jetty and boat hire. Free fjord fishing with catches of good sized cod from the shore.

Open: 1 May - 10 September.

Directions

Site is to the west of Viggja with direct access from the E39 between Orkanger and Buvik, 21 km. from the E6 and 40 km. west of Trondheim. There is a new E39 from Bersa or Orkanger.

Charges 2007

Per pitch	NOK 170
electricity	NOK 40

NO2432 Harstad Camping

Nesseveien 55, N-9411 Harstad (Troms)
Tel: **77 07 36 62**. Email: **postmaster@harstad-camping.no**

For those visiting or exiting Lofoten and Vesterålen, this well established, popular site close to Harstad, provides an excellent stopping point on Hinnøya, the largest island in Norway. In a delightful setting with fine views, the campsite has space for 120 units as it slopes down to Vågsfjorden. Pitches are not marked but by the waters edge a flat area provides most of the 33 electricity hook-ups (16A). This part of the site is sought after and we advise a mid-afternoon arrival for the possibility of a level pitch and/or electricity connection.

Facilities

Good facilities include British style WCs, washbasins and showers (two for each sex, NOK 10 for 4 minutes). Room for disabled visitors. Laundry room (hot water NOK 5). Kitchen with hot plates (free), tables and chairs. Chemical disposal point. Reception (manned 08.00-23.00 high season) has a small selection of soft drinks, ices, sweets, crisps, some tinned foods and postcards (no bread or milk). Off site: Supermarket and garage at 2 km.

Open: All year.

Directions

Travelling north on road 83, site is on right 3 km. before Harstad. After turning right, turn immediate left and site is 1 km. along firm unmade road (site signed from either direction).

Charges 2007

Per unit	NOK 175
incl. electricity	NOK 200

NO2505 Magalaupe Camping

Engan, N-7340 Oppdal (Sør Trøndelag)
Tel: **72 42 46 84**. Email: **camp@magalaupe.no**

This is a rural, good value, riverside site in a sheltered position with easy access from the E6. Fairly simple facilities are offered but there are a host of unusual activities in the surrounding area. The 52 unmarked and grassy touring pitches (42 with 16A electricity) are in natural surroundings amongst birch trees and rocks and served by gravel access roads. There are also 8 attractive and fully equipped site owned cabins. As the site rarely fills up, the simple facilities should be adequate at most times. Activities in the area include caving, canyoning, rafting, gold panning, mineral hunting, and musk oxen, reindeer and elk safaris. In winter the more adventurous can also go snow-moiling or skiing in the high Dovrefjell National Park.

Facilities

Small, clean, heated sanitary unit fully equipped and the showers are on payment. Extra WC/washbasin units in reception building. Small kitchen with hot-plate, fridge and freezer, plus a combined washing/drying machine. Kiosk for ices, soft drinks, etc. Bar (mid June - Aug). TV lounge. Fishing. Bicycle hire. Off site: Supermarkets and other services in Oppdal (11 km). Riding or golf 12 km.

Open: All year.

Directions

Site is signed on E6, 11 km. south of Oppdal. GPS: N62:29.822 E09:35.121

Charges guide

Per pitch	NOK 100
tent	NOK 80
electricity	NOK 20

No credit cards.

MAP 13

Situated in the heart of Europe, Poland is a country rich in culture and heritage. Having transformed itself after years of invasions and interference from its neighbours, it has now become an ideal place for those looking for something a little different.

CAPITAL: WARSAW

Tourist Office

Poland National Tourist Office
Remo House, 310-312 Regent St,
London W1B 3AX
Tel: 020 7580 8811 Fax: 020 7580 8866
E-mail: info@visitpoland.org
Internet: www.visitpoland.org

The northern part of Poland is varied, well-forested and gently undulating, with the coastline providing miles of sandy beaches, bays, cliffs and dunes. The flat central plain is the main agricultural area and heading south the terrain rises, with the mountainous regions being dominated by two big ranges, the Sudetens in the west and the Carpathians in the south. Poland also has over 9,000 lakes; the majority located in the north east in the Pomeranian and Masurian Lake districts. These lakes offer many opportunities for water sports enthusiasts, anglers, nature lovers and bird watchers.

Completely ravaged by the Second World War, Warsaw has been rebuilt and developed into a thriving capital, with plenty of churches, palaces, galleries and museums to visit. Unlike the capital, Kraków still retains its original character and wealth of architecture, having come through the war unscathed to become one of the world's twelve most significant historic sites as listed by UNESCO.

Population

38.6 million

Climate

Temperate climate, with warm and sunny summers, cold winters with large snowfalls. Hottest and sunniest days are in June and July but these months also seem to have more rainfall than at any other time of year - be prepared!

Language

Polish

Telephone

The country code is 00 48.

Money

Currency: The Zloty

Shops

Mon-Fri 6.00/7.00 - 18.00/19.00. Sat: 7.00 -13.00. Supermakets usually stay open until 21.00/22.00.

Public Holidays

New Year; Easter Mon; Womens' Day 8 Mar; April Fool's Day 1 April; Labour Day; Constitution Day 3 May; Corpus Christi; Assumtion, All Saints; Independence Day 11 Nov; Christmas 25, 26 Dec.

Motoring

International Driving Permit is required. Between October and March it is compulsory to have headlights switched on at all times while driving. Be aware that some of the roads and motorway surfaces are badly rutted - drive with caution. Motorcyclists must keep their lights on all year round.

Poland

PL3050 Camping Tramp Nr. 33

Ul. Kujawska 14, PL-87-100 Torun (Kujawsko-Pomorskie)

Tel: **056 654 7187**. Email: **tramp@mosir.torun.pl**

Camping Tramp has a pleasant appearance and lies in a basin below the level of the roads which run on both sides of the site. A variety of trees cover part of the site where pitches (with electric hook-ups) mingle with holiday bungalows. The other, larger field is an open meadow, where half the pitches have electricity. The 100 pitches, reached from hard access roads, are neither marked nor numbered but the position of electric boxes define where to go. Some pitches are separated by low hedging. The main E75 runs along one side of the campsite just before a busy junction and river bridge resulting in continuous traffic noise. Torun, a Gothic jewel built originally by the Teutonic Knights and now listed by UNESCO as a world heritage site, like so many Polish towns has a long, interesting and troubled history. Famous as the birth place of Copernicus, it is today a prosperous university city on the wide River Wisla. The old walled town is worth a visit in its own right, and with a major part of it pedestrianised, walking over the Wisla bridge from the campsite is a perfect way to enjoy your visit. Inevitably the town has a planetarium which has two shows a day in English. Whilst we would not recommend this as a 'holiday' base, it makes a good night stop when travelling between Germany and the Baltic coast or to visit Torun.

Facilities

One refurbished and fully tiled, traditional style toilet block with toilets, hot showers and washbasins. Clean and smelling fresh when visited but without dressing space. Washing Machine. Dishwashing sinks. Facilities for disabled visitors (ramped access). Welcoming bar/restaurant (good value) with basic food supplies. Basketball. Playing field. Fishing. Off site: Town with restaurants and shops 2 km. Riding 5 km. Golf 10 km.

Open: 1 May - 30 September.

Directions

From the south approaching the town you have a choice – fork left for a restricted height route (max 3.2 m) or straight on. If you fork left go under the bridge and turn right immediately to site 300 m. on left. If straight on, follow blue truck signs for 1 km, then turn back towards main bridge. Site access on right before river crossing. From the north go over the Wisla bridge and turn left before railway to site in 300 m. on left. GPS: N53:00.016 E18:36.451

Charges 2007

Per person	PLN 8,00
child (under 10 yrs)	PLN 4,00
pitch	PLN 5,00 - 26,00
electricity (10A)	PLN 8,00

PL3300 Camping Polana Sosny Nr. 38

Os. Na Polenie Sosny, PL-34-441 Niedzica (Malopolskie)

Tel: **018 262 9403**. Email: **dworek@pro.onet.pl**

The small village of Niedzica is south of the Pieniny mountain range in the Dunajec valley and about 40 km. northeast of Zakopane. This excellent little campsite is right alongside the Dunajec dam and the river, at the eastern end of the Czorsztynskie lake. With 35 level touring pitches, all with electricity, it is a good short or long stay. Adjacent is the Dwor restaurant which is open from 10.00 to 22.00 all the year. The raft ride on the river that flows through the limestone mountain gorges is one of the best known tourist attractions in Poland.

Facilities

The small sanitary block near reception has toilets and showers and two good sets of facilities for disabled visitors. Chemical toilet disposal. Small campers' kitchen with sinks and electric rings. Bar, restaurant and takeaway (all season). Off site: Village park adjacent with children

Open: All year.

Directions

From Nowy Targ head east on the 969. In village of Debno turn right towards Niedzica (17 km). The Czorsztynskie lake is on the left and Czorsztyn Castle is ahead. After the castle continue through Niedzica-Zamek towards Niedzica. Just before the second Dunajec dam bridge turn right and site is on the left. GPS: N49:24.246 E20:19.963

Charges 2007

Per person	PLN 5,00
pitch	PLN 15,00 - 30,00

PL3320 Auschwitz Centre

Ul. M. Kolbego 1, PL-32-602 Oswiecim (Malopolskie)

Tel: **033 843 1000**

Oswiecim is a name that many foreigners will not have heard, but any mention of the German equivalent, Auschwitz, evokes fear in almost everyone. Founded in 1992 this centre gives the outward appearance of being a first class hotel. Its aim is to create a venue for meetings, exchanges, education, reflection and prayer for all those who visit Auschwitz and are moved by what happened here. To further this aim campers are welcome to use the landscaped gardens with tents, motorcaravans or caravans and use the centre's facilities. Electricity has been provided (6A) with 20 pitches either on the grass or on the large parking area. The state museum in Oswiecim (Auschwitz/Birkenau), now a UNESCO World Heritage site, is only a few minutes walk away, and is open almost every day of the year. No visitor can leave unmoved. Entrance is free and guided tours are available in English; alternatively you could buy the English guide book and walk around on your own.

Facilities

Showers and toilets are provided and are clean and well maintained. The restaurant in the centre may be used by campers. Off site: Oswiecim and the museums of Auschwitz and Birkenau.

Open: All year.

Directions

The centre is 600 m. from the Auschwitz museum on the road to the south running parallel to the road that serves the museum. It is on the 950/933 and is situated between a roundabout and a large electricity substation. It appears to be a first class hotel from the outside and has facilities to match.
GPS: N50:01.412 E19:11.879

Charges 2007

Per person	PLN 23,00

PL3090 Kemping Nr. 19 Kamienny Potok

Ul. Zamkowa Góra 25, PL-81-713 Sopot (Pomorskie)

Tel: **058 550 0445**

Kamienny Potok is set back from the beach in Sopot and, by Polish standards, is a large site with 288 touring pitches, some back to back on either side of concrete access roads, others in open meadows. Places are numbered but not marked out, of grass on sand and 150 pitches have electricity (6-10A). With well mown grass, the site was neat and tidy. There are many tall trees around the site, although not much shade in camping areas. It is an easy 25 minute train ride from the site to Gdansk and the station is only 500 m. walk. Dutch clubs rally here and the whole campsite has a pleasant quiet atmosphere, although there is some road and train noise near the entrance. Sopot is a popular seaside resort on the Gulf of Gdansk with a sandy beach, promenade and pier against a background of wooded hills. There are many attractions nearby including 'Opera-in-the-Woods' with 5,000 seats, an annual pop concert and centres of historic interest. From the pier a ferry service departs for Gdansk, Gdynia or to Hel on the Baltic Sea peninsula and it is possible to travel from Gdansk to Finland.

Facilities

Three toilet blocks (all refurbished to high standards) with toilets, open style washbasins, hot showers and sinks for dishwashing. Facilities for disabled visitors. Motorcaravan service point. Washing machine. Open air bar with food service. Playgrounds. Fishing. Volleyball. Basketball. TV room. Billiard club with electronic dart boards (also sells drinks). Off site: Swimming pool complex with giant slide 200 m. Beaches 500 m. Riding 1 km. Bicycle hire 1.5 km. Boat launching/hiring 2 km. Shell garage with basic food supplies. Ferry service to Gdansk, Gdynia and Hel 1 km.

Open: 1 May - 30 September.

Directions

Site is 2 km. north of Sopot on main road behind Shell garage. Take the exit for the Sopot Aqua Park and immediately turn left.
GPS: N54:27.702 E18:33.311

Charges 2007

Per person	PLN 12,00
child (4-15 yrs)	PLN 6,00
pitch	PLN 5,00 - 9,00
electricity (10A)	PLN 9,00

Check real time availability and at-the-gate prices...

www.alanrogers.com

PL3100 Camping Przy Plazy Nr. 67

Ul. Bitwy pod Plowcami 73, PL-81-731 Sopot (Pomorskie)

Tel: **058 551 6523**. Email: **camping67@sopot.pl**

This is a large site for Poland, with 180 unmarked pitches, 160 with electricity (16A). There is shade from mature trees and direct access to the beach. Some road nooise can be heard as the Gdansk - Gdynia coast road runs past the site. Sopot is Poland's most popular seaside resort and one of the large sandy beaches is only 25 m. from this site, with the town only a short walk away. The town was first established as a sea bathing centre in 1824 and its heyday came in the interwar years when it attracted the richest people in Europe. The pier and the main street contain many bars, restaurants and cafes and is a pleasant place to enjoy a beer and the sea air.

Facilities

Each sanitary block has toilets and showers and is a little worn. Motorcaravan drain down available. Small covered campers' kitchen with sinks. Small shop and buffet. Play area. Off site: Sopot with numerous shops, bars and restaurants. Beach, sailing, bicycle hire and riding within 1 km.

Open: 15 June - 31 August.

Directions

Sopot is between Gdansk and Gydnia on Poland's Baltic coast. To find this site you need to be on the coastal road between Sopot and Gdansk. The site is next to the new Novotel at the southern end of the town and is well signed.

Charges 2007

Per person	PLN 11,00
child (7-16 yrs)	PLN 8,90
pitch incl. electricity	PLN 16,00 - 21,00

PL3280 Korona Camping Nr. 241

Ul. Myslenicka 32, PL-32-031 Gaj (Slaskie)

Tel: **012 270 1318**. Email: **biuro@camping-korona.com.pl**

This attractively landscaped site, with direct access from the main road, is 10 km. from Krakow. It is down a slope, some 100 m. back from the road, so is not noisy and it has lovely views over the village. The site is terraced, but caravans and motorcaravans tend to use a flat area near the toilet block. Tent pitches are slightly sloping. It is a family run site that takes about 100 units, all with 6A electricity, and pitches are separated by young trees. To the back of the site is a large pond for fishing (well fenced) and a large, covered barbecue area. Mrs Trepizynska has fresh bread rolls available each morning and cooks a delicious stroganoff soup. There are buses from the main road into Krakow, but each evening Mr Trepizynska will ask if anyone wishes to make the trip and if he finds ten people, will take them in his own minibus for a small charge. Similarly he will take people to the Wieliczka salt mines (16 km.). Ausschwitz is 64 km. and impressive enough to spend a day.

Facilities

One modern toilet block (could be under pressure in high season) with hot showers (temperature can be variable), washbasins and toilets, all clean and well maintained. Baby bath in both sections. Dishwashing under cover. Shop. Bar with open air terrace and some basics. Fishing pond. Playing field. Volleyball. Playground. WiFi and internet access. Trips to Kraków and the Wieliczka salt mines. Off site: Bus stop outside site. Bar/restaurant 500 m. Tennis 2 km. Riding 3 km. Kraków 10 km. Beach 20 km.

Open: May - September.

Directions

Site is 10 km. south of Kraków off the E77 Kraków - Zakopane road. Take care because access to the site is directly off the motorway and is particularly difficult when coming from Zakopane because one has to cross the motorway.
GPS: N49:57.760 E19:53.412

Charges 2007

Per person	PLN 15,00
child (5-10 yrs)	PLN 10,00
pitch incl. car	PLN 14,00 - 24,00
electricity	PLN 8,00

PL3160 Camping Echo

PL-11-511 Rydzewo (Warminsko-Mazurskie)
Tel: 087 421 1186. Email: echo@mazury.info

This is a very good, small family campsite run by the welcoming owner, Barbara Nowakowska. With only space for about 40 pitches, all with 6A electricity, it would be a good choice for a short or medium term stop while you explore and enjoy the Mazurian Lakes. It is on the eastern banks of Lake Neogocin which is popular with watersports enthusiasts and swimmers alike. The Mazurian Lakes area is a very popular holiday spot but despite this the countryside remains unspoiled with many rare plants and birds thriving here. The district is also a paradise for ramblers.

Facilities

The small sanitary block has toilets and hot showers which are immaculate. Washing machine. Chemical disposal point. Bread to order. Gas. Small restaurant and bar. Fishing. Bicycle hire. Beach. Boat trips on the lake. Boat launching possible. Off site: Mazurian Lakes and not far away the Wolfslair, Hitler's bunker.

Open: 1 May - 30 September.

Directions

Rydzewo is south of Gizycko and the site is easy to find just on the northern outskirts of the village. It is on the eastern banks of Lake Neogocin. Coming from Mikolajki, turn right after Kamin towards Pratski, cross the river and continue north towards Rydzebo.

Charges 2007

Per person	PLN 12,00
child (3-16 yrs)	PLN 8,00
pitch incl. car and electricity	PLN 28,00

PL3170 Camping Pension Galindia Mazurski Eden

Bartlewo 1, PL-12-210 Ukta (Warminsko-Mazurskie)
Tel: 087 423 1416. Email: galindia@galindia.com.pl

Mazurski Eden is in the centre of the beautiful Mazurian Lake District, surrounded by the interesting flora and fauna of the Piska forest. It is a quite amazing place approached by a 1.5 km. sand road, easily negotiable by caravans, with the entrance flanked by tall pine posts of carved figures. Wood carvings abound with statues by the water's edge, on buildings and inside the hotel. The camping area, with room for 100 units, is grass on sand under tall trees which serve to determine the pitches, with electrical connection boxes topped with lamps for night illumination. A wealth of activities includes organised photographic safaris, canoeing and hiking trips, cycle excursions and visits to the Kadzidlowo nature reserve with its wolves, bison, beavers and other wildlife. Sailing and other watersports are arranged and even fishing under the ice in winter. Parties, picnics and barbecues are organised with dancing and folk bands. Various national days are noted, with open air workshops for painters and sculptors and church festivals are celebrated in a family atmosphere. The manager has a great interest in the social history of the ancient people of this area and this is reflected in the entertainment offered to group conferences being held in the hotel, to which campers are invited.

Facilities

Good tiled sanitary block (caveman style) with toilets, basins and showers. Dishwashing sinks with free hot water. Laundry service in the hotel. Motorcaravan service point. Kayaks, canoes, sailing boats and pedaloes for hire. Beach. Boat mooring. 'Cave men' festivities. Bar in cave under the pension with billiards. Open air bar near the lake. 'Cave men style' restaurant. Lounge with TV with English and German channels. Cave men style events organised with 'Chief Galindia'. Off site: Skiing and sailing.

Open: All year.

Directions

Take 609 road from Mikolajki to Ukta and turn off towards Iznota (signed Iznota 3 km.) on sand road. Pass through Nowy Most to Iznota and follow camp signs. GPS: N53:44.049 E21:33.794

Charges 2007

Per person	PLN 15,00
pitch	PLN 13,00 - 26,00
electricity	PLN 20,00

Check real time availability and at-the-gate prices...
www.alanrogers.com

MAP 9

Portugal is a relatively small country occupying the southwest part of the Iberian peninsula, bordered by Spain in the north and east, with the Atlantic coast in the south and west. In spite of its size, the country offers a tremendous variety in both its way of life and traditions.

Portugal

CAPITAL: LISBON

Tourist Office

ICEP Portuguese Trade & Tourism Office
2nd Floor 22/25a Sackville Street
London W1S 3LY
Tel: 0845 3551212
E-mail: info@visitportugal.com
Internet: www.visitportugal.com

Most visitors looking for a beach type holiday head for the busy Algarve, with its long stretches of sheltered sandy beaches, and warm, clear Atlantic waters, great for bathing and watersports. With its monuments and fertile rolling hills, central Portugal adjoins the beautiful Tagus river that winds its way through the capital city of Lisbon, on its way to the Altantic Ocean. Lisbon city itself has deep rooted cultural traditions, coming alive at night with buzzing cafes, restaurants and discos. Moving southeast of Lisbon the land becomes rather impoverished, consisting of stretches of vast undulating plains, dominated by cork plantations. Consequently most people head for the walled town of Evora, an area steeped in two thousand years of history. The Portuguese consider the Minho area in the north to be the most beautiful part of their country, with its wooded mountains and wild coastline, a rural and conservative region with picturesque towns.

Population

10 million

Climate

The country enjoys a maritime climate with hot summers and mild winters with comparatively low rainfall in the south, heavy rain in the north.

Language

Portuguese

Telephone

The country code is 00 351.

Money

Currency: The Euro
Banks: Mon-Fri 08.30-11.45 and 13.00-14.45. Some large city banks operate a currency exchange 18.30-23.00.

Shops

Mon-Fri 09.00-13.00 and 15.00-19.00.
Sat 09.00-13.00.

Public Holidays

New Year; Carnival (Shrove Tues); Good Fri; Liberty Day 25 Apr; Labour Day; Corpus Christi; National Day 10 June; Saints Days; Assumption 15 Aug; Republic Day 5 Oct; All Saints 1 Nov; Immaculate Conception 8 Dec; Christmas 24-26 Dec.

Motoring

The standard of roads is very variable, even some of the main roads can be very uneven. Tolls are levied on certain motorways (auto-estradas) out of Lisbon, and upon southbound traffic at the Lisbon end of the giant 25th Abril bridge over the Tagus. Parked vehicles must face the same direction as moving traffic.

PO8210 Parque de Campismo Albufeira

EN 125 Ferreiras - Albufeira, P-8200-555 Albufeira (Faro)

Tel: **289 587 629**. Email: **campingalbufeira@mail.telepac.pt**

The spacious entrance to this site will accommodate the largest of units (watch for severe speed bumps at the barrier). One of the better sites on the Algarve, it has pitches on fairly flat ground with some terracing, trees and shrubs giving reasonable shade in most parts. There are some marked and numbered pitches of 50-80 sq.m. Winter stays are encouraged with many facilities remaining open including a pool. An attractively designed complex of traditional Portuguese style buildings on the hill, with an unusually shaped pool and two more for children, forms the central area of the site. It has large terraces for sunbathing and pleasant views and is surrounded by a variety of flowers, shrubs and well watered lawns, complete with a fountain. The 'á la carte' restaurant, impressive with its international cuisine, and the very pleasant self-service one; both have views across the three pools. A pizzeria, bars and a soundproofed disco are great for younger campers.

Facilities

The toilet blocks include hot showers. Launderette. Very large supermarket. Tabac (English papers). Waiter and self-service restaurants. Pizzeria. Bars. Satellite TV. Soundproof disco. Swimming pools. Tennis. Playground. Internet access. First aid post. Car wash. ATM. Car hire. Off site: Site bus service from gate to Albufeira every 45 minutes (2 km). Theme parks nearby. Beaches.

Open: All year.

Directions

From N125 coast road or N264 (from Lisbon) at new junctions follow N395 to Albufeira. Site is about 2 km. on the left.

Charges 2007

Per person	€ 5,20
child (4-10 yrs)	€ 2,60
pitch	€ 5,60 - € 11,95
electricity (10A)	€ 2,85

PO8202 Camping Turiscampo

EN 125, Espiche, Luz, P-8600 Lagos (Faro)

Tel: **282 789 265**. Email: **info@turiscampo.com**

This site is being thoughtfully refurbished and updated to include most of the existing infrastructure since it was purchased by the friendly Coll family, who are known to us from their previous Spanish site. Work was still in progress when we visited but the site does show great promise and will become a quality site. The site provides 206 pitches for tourers mainly in rows of terraces, all with electricity and some with shade. They vary in size (70-120 sq.m). The upper areas of the site are being developed and are mostly destined for bungalows (which are generally separate from the touring areas). A new, elevated Californian style pool plus a children's pool have been constructed and the supporting structure is a clever water cascade and surround. There is a large sun lounger area on astroturf. One side of the pool area is open to the road. The restaurant/bar has been tastefully refurbished and Giovanni and staff are delighted to use their excellent English to provide good fare at most reasonable prices (bargain menu of the day for € 6.50). The restaurant has two patios one of which is used for live entertainment and discos in season and the other for dining out. The sea is 2 km. and the city of Lagos 4 km. with all the attractions of the Algarve within easy reach. When complete this will be a very good site for families and for 'Snowbirds' to over-winter.

Facilities

The two existing toilet blocks have been refurbished and a new block added containing modern facilities for disabled campers. The site reports a new, heated block added in 2007. Hot water throughout. Facilities for children. Washing machines. Shop (all year). Gas supplies. Restaurant/bar (all year). Swimming pool (March - Oct) with two new terraces. Bicycle hire. Internet. Cable TV. Entertainment in high season on the bar terrace. Playground on sand. Adult art workshops, aqua gymnastics and mini-club (5-12 yrs) in season. Bungalows to rent. Petanque. Archery. Sports field with basketball, volleyball etc. WiFi on payment. Off site: Bus to Lagos and other towns from Praia da Luz village 1.5 km. Fishing and beach 2 km. Golf 4 km. Riding 10 km. Sailing 5 km. Boat launching 5 km.

Open: All year.

Directions

Take exit 1 from the N125 Lagos-Vila do Bispo. The impressive entrance is about 3 km. on the right.

Charges 2008

Per person	€ 3,00 - € 5,80
child (3-10 yrs)	€ 1,60 - € 2,90
pitch with electricity	€ 7,90 - € 16,70
dog	€ 1,00 - € 1,50
Camping Cheques accepted.	

PO8220 Orbitur Camping Quarteira

Estrada da Fonte Santa, avenida Sá Cameiro, P-8125-618 Quarteira (Faro)

Tel: **289 302 826**. Email: **info@orbitur.pt**

This is a large, busy attractive site on undulating ground with some terracing, taking 795 units. On the outskirts of the popular Algarve resort of Quarteira, it is 600 m. from a sandy beach which stretches for a kilometre for the town centre. Many of the unmarked pitches have shade from tall trees and there are a few small individual pitches of 50 sq.m. with electricity and water for reservation. There are 680 electrical connections. Like others along this coast, the site encourages long winter stays. There is a large restaurant and supermarket which have a separate entrance for local trade. The swimming pools (free for campers)are excellent, featuring pools for adults (with a large flume) and children (with fountains).

Facilities

Five toilet blocks provide British and Turkish style toilets, washbasins with cold water, hot showers plus facilities for disabled visitors. Washing machines. Motorcaravan services. Gas supplies. Supermarket. Self-service restaurant (closed Nov). Separate takeaway (from late May). Swimming pools (April - Sept). General room with bar and satellite TV. Tennis. Open air disco (high season). Off site: Bus from gate to Faro. Fishing 1 km. Bicycle hire (summer) 1 km. Golf 4 km.

Open: All year.

Directions

Turn off N125 for village of Almancil. In the village take road south to Quarteira. Site is on the left 1 km. after large, official town welcome sign.

Charges 2008

Per person	€ 3,10 - € 5,50
child (5-10 yrs)	€ 1,70 - € 3,00
caravan and car	€ 6,90 - € 13,00
electricity	€ 2,50 - € 3,10
Off season discounts (up to 70%).	

PO8230 Camping Olhão

Pinheiros de Marim, P-8700 Olhão (Faro)

Tel: **289 700 300**. Email: **parque.campismo@sbsi.pt**

This site, with around 800 pitches, is open all year. It has many mature trees providing good shade. The pitches are marked, numbered and in rows divided by shrubs, although levelling will be necessary and the trees make access tricky on some. There is electricity for 102 pitches (6A) and a separate area for tents. Permanent and long stay units take 20% of the pitches, the touring pitches filling up quickly in July and August, so arrive early. There is some noise nuisance from an adjacent railway. The site has a relaxed, casual atmosphere. Amenities include very pleasant swimming pools and tennis courts, a reasonable restaurant/bar and a café/bar with TV and games room. All are very popular with the local Portuguese who pay to use the facilities. The large, sandy beaches in this area are on offshore islands reached by ferry and are, as a result, relatively quiet; some are reserved for naturists. This site can get very busy in peak periods and maintenance can be variable. There was a large, low season British contingent when we visited, enjoying the low prices.

Facilities

Eleven sanitary blocks are adequate, clean when seen, and are specifically sited to be a maximum of 50 m. from any pitch. One block has facilities for disabled visitors. Laundry. Excellent supermarket. Kiosk. Restaurant/bar (all year). Café and general room with cable TV. Playgrounds. Swimming pools (April - Sept) and tennis courts (fees for both). Bicycle hire. Internet at reception. Off site: Bus service to the nearest ferry at Olhão 50 m. from site. Indoor pool 2 km. Riding 1 km. Fishing 2 km. Golf 20 km.

Open: All year.

Directions

Just over 1 km. east of Olhão, on EN125, take turn to Pinheiros de Marim. Site is back off the road on the left. Look for very large, white, triangular entry arch as the site name is different on the outside wall.

Charges guide

Per person	€ 2,20 - € 4,00
child (5-12 yrs)	€ 1,20 - € 2,20
pitch	€ 3,45 - € 10,80
electricity	€ 1,50

Less for longer winter stays.

Camping Olhão ★★★ Open All Year

Tennis
Football
Bar
Swimming Pool
Restaurant
Bungalows
Mobile Homes

parque.campismo@sbsi.pt
Algarve - Portugal
www.sbsi.pt/camping
351 289 700 300

PO8430 Orbitur Camping Sagres

Cerro das Moitas, P-8650-998 Sagres (Faro)

Tel: **282 624 371**. Email: **info@orbitur.pt**

Camping de Sagres is a pleasant site at the western tip of the Algarve, not very far from the lighthouse in the relatively unspoilt southwest corner of Portugal. With 960 pitches for tents and 120 for tourers, the sandy pitches, some terraced, are located amongst pine trees that give good shade. There are some hardstandings for motorhomes and electricity throughout. The fairly bland restaurant, bar and café/grill provide a range of reasonably priced meals. This is a reasonable site for those seeking winter sun, or as a base for exploring this 'Land's End' region of Portugal.

Facilities

Three spacious toilet blocks are showing some signs of wear but provide hot and cold showers and washbasins with cold water. Washing machines. Motorcaravan services. Supermarket (all year). Restaurant/bar and café/grill (all Easter and June-Oct). TV room. Satellite TV in restaurant. Bicycle hire. Barbecue area. Playground. Fishing. Medical post. Car wash. Off site: Buses from village 1 km. Beach and fishing 2 km. Boat launching 8 km. Golf 12 km.

Open: All year.

Directions

From Sagres, turn off the N268 road west onto the EN268. After about 2 km. the site is signed off to the right.

Charges 2008

Per person	€ 2,50 - € 4,50
child (5-10 yrs)	€ 1,30 - € 2,50
caravan and car	€ 5,60 - € 10,20
electricity (6A)	€ 2,50 - € 3,10

Off season discounts (up to 70%).

PO8200 Orbitur Camping Valverde

Estrada da Praia da Luz, Valverde, P-8600-148 Lagos (Faro)

Tel: 282 789 211. Email: info@orbitur.pt

A little over a kilometre from the village of Praia da Luz and its beach and about 7 km. from Lagos, this large, well run site is certainly worth considering for your stay in the Algarve. It has 600 numbered pitches, of varying size, which are enclosed by hedges. All are on flat ground or broad terraces with good shade in most parts from established trees and shrubs. The site has a swimming pool with a long slide and a paddling pool (under 10s free, adults charged). This is an excellent site with well maintained facilities and good security.

Facilities

Six large, clean, toilet blocks have some washbasins and sinks with cold water only, and hot showers. Units for disabled people. Laundry. Motorcaravan services. Supermarket (all year), shops, restaurant and bar complex with both self-service and waiter service in season (closed November). Takeaway. Coffee shop. Swimming pool (April - Sept). Playground. Tennis. Satellite TV in bar. Disco. Pub. Excursions. Off site: Bus service from site gate. Beach and fishing 1.5 km. Bicycle hire 3 km. Golf 10 km.

Open: All year.

Directions

From Lagos on N125 road, after 7 km. turn south to Praia da Luz. At the town follow Orbitur camping signs. The beach road is narrow and cobbled and is very challenging in a large unit.

Charges 2008

Per person	€ 2,90 - € 5,40
child (5-10 yrs)	€ 1,50 - € 3,00
caravan and car	€ 6,80 - € 12,00
electricity	€ 2,50 - € 3,10

Off season discounts (up to 70%).

PO8410 Parque de Campismo de Armacao de Pêra

P-8365 Armacão de Pêra (Faro)

Tel: 282 312 296. Email: camping_arm_pera@hotmail.com

A modern site with a wide attractive entrance and a large external parking area, the 1,200 pitches are in zones on level grassy sand. They are marked by trees that provide some shade, and are easily accessed from tarmac and gravel roads. Electricity is available for most pitches. The facilities are good. The self service restaurant, bar and supermarket should cater for most needs, and you can relax around the pools. The disco near the entrance and café complex is soundproofed which should ensure a peaceful night for non-revellers. The site is within easy reach of Albufeira and Portimão.

Facilities

Three modern sanitary blocks provide British and Turkish style WCs and showers with hot water on payment. Facilities for disabled campers. A reader reports that maintenance can be variable. Laundry. Supermarket. Self-service restaurant. Three bars (one all year). Swimming and paddling pools (May - Sept; charged per day; no lifeguard). Games and TV rooms. Play area. ATM. Off site: Bus to town. Fishing, bicycle hire and watersports.

Open: All year.

Directions

Turn off N125/IC4 road in Alcantarilha, taking the EN269-1 towards the coast. Site is on left before Armação de Pêra. There are sites with similar names in the area, so be sure to find the right one.

Charges guide

Per person	€ 2,50 - € 5,50
pitch	€ 4,00 - € 7,50
electricity (6A)	€ 2,50 - € 4,00

Min. stay 3 nights 1 June - 31 Aug.

PO8170 Parque de Campismo São Miguel

São Miguel, Odeceixe, P-7630-592 Odemira (Beja)

Tel: 282 947145. Email: camping.sao.miguel@mail.telepac.pt

Nestled in green hills near two pretty white villages, 4 km. from the beautiful Praia Odeceixe (beach) is the attractive camping park São Miguel. Unusually the site works on a maximum number of 700 campers, you find your own place (there are no defined pitches) under the tall trees, there are ample electrical points, and the land slopes away gently. Wooden chalet style accommodation to rent is in a separate area, but some mobile homes share the two traditional older style but clean sanitary blocks. The main building is built around two sides of a large grassy square.

Facilities

Two older style toilet blocks with British style WCs and free hot showers. Washing machines. Toilets and basins for disabled campers but no shower. Shop (June -Sept). Self-service restaurant (March-Oct). Bar, snacks and pizzeria (June-Sept). Satellite TV. Playground. Tennis (charged). Swimming pool (charged). Dogs not accepted. Torches useful. Off site: Bus service from gate. Beach, fishing and sailing 4 km. Riding 20 km.

Open: All year.

Directions

Between Odemira and Lagos on the N120 just before the village of Odeceixe on the main road well signed. GPS: N37:26.321 W08:45.341

Charges 2007

Per person	€ 3,50 - € 5,50
child (5-10 yrs)	€ 2,00 - € 3,00
pitch	€ 3,50 - € 10,00
electricity	€ 2,75

Plus 7% VAT.

PO8150 Orbitur Camping Costa da Caparica

Avenida Alfonso de Albuquerque, Quinta de Ste Antonio, P-2825-450 Costa da Caparica (Setubal)

Tel: 212 901 366. Email: info@orbitur.pt

This is very much a site for 600 permanent caravans but it has relatively easy access to Lisbon (just under 20 km.) via the motorway, by bus or even by bus and ferry if you wish. It is situated near a small resort, favoured by the Portuguese themselves, which has all the usual amenities plus a good sandy beach (200 m. from the site) and promenade walks. There is a small area for touring units which includes some larger pitches for motorcaravans. We see this very much as a site to visit Lisbon rather than for prolonged stays.

Facilities

The three toilet blocks have mostly British style toilets, washbasins with cold water and some hot showers - they come under pressure when the site is full. Facilities for disabled visitors. Washing machine. Motorcaravan services. Supermarket. Large bar/restaurant (not Nov.). TV room (satellite). Playground. Gas supplies. Off site: Bus service from site gate. Fishing 1 km. Riding 4 km. Golf 5 km.

Open: All year.

Directions

Cross the Tagus bridge (toll) on A2 motorway going south from Lisbon, immediately take the turning for Caparica and Trafaria. At 7 km. marker on IC20 turn right (no sign) – the site is at the second roundabout. GPS: N38:39.220 W09:14.330

Charges 2008

Per person	€ 2,70 - € 4,80
child (5-10 yrs)	€ 1,40 - € 2,50
caravan and car	€ 6,70 - € 11,30
electricity	€ 2,50 - € 3,10
Off season discounts (up to 70%).	

PO8130 Orbitur Camping Guincho

EN 247, Lugar da Areia - Guincho, P-2750-053 Cascais (Lisbon)

Tel: 214 870 450. Email: info@orbitur.pt

Although this is a popular site for permanent Portuguese units with 1,295 pitches, it is nevertheless quite attractively laid out among low pine trees and with the A5 autostrada connection to Lisbon (30 km), it provides a useful alternative to sites nearer the city. This is viewed as an alternative for visiting Lisbon, not a holiday site. There is a choice of pitches (small – mainly about 50 sq.m.) mostly with electricity, although siting amongst the trees may be tricky, particularly when the site is full. Located behind sand dunes and a wide, sandy beach, the site offers a wide range of facilities.

Facilities

Three sanitary blocks, one refurbished, are in the older style but are clean and tidy. Washbasins with cold water but hot showers. Facilities for disabled visitors. Washing machines and dryers. Motorcaravan services. Gas. Supermarket. Restaurant, bar and terrace (all year). General room with TV. Tennis. Playground. Entertainment in summer. Chalets to rent. Off site: Bus service from gate. Excursions. Riding 500 m. Beach 800 m. Fishing 1 km. Golf 3 km.

Open: All year.

Directions

Approach from either direction on N247. Turn inland 6.5 km. west of Cascais at camp sign. Travelling direct from Lisbon, the site is well signed as you leave the A5 autopista. GPS: N38:43.270 W09:28.000

Charges 2008

Per person	€ 2,70 - € 4,80
child (5-10 yrs)	€ 1,40 - € 2,50
caravan and car	€ 6,70 - € 11,30
electricity	€ 2,50 - € 3,10

PO8450 Parque de Campismo Colina do Sol

Serra Dos Mangues, P-2465 Sao Martinho do Porto (Leiria)

Tel: 262 989 764. Email: parque.colina.sol@dix.pt

Colina do Sol is a well appointed site with its own swimming pool and near the beach. Only 2 km. from the small town of S. Martinho do Porto, it has around 350 pitches marked by fruit and ornamental trees on grassy terraces. Electricity (6A) is available. The attractive entrance with its beds of bright flowers, is wide enough for even the largest of outfits, and the surfaced roads are very pleasant for manoeuvring. There is a warm welcome and good English is spoken. The beach is at the rear of the site, with access via a gate which is locked at night.

Facilities

Two large, clean and modern toilet blocks provide British style WCs (some with bidets), washbasins with hot water. Dishwashing and laundry sinks are outside but covered. Motorcaravan services. Supermarket. Bar and restaurant (1/7-31/8). Satellite TV. Swimming pool (1/7-10/9). Off site: Bus from gate to nearby towns. Shop, restaurant and bar within 200 m. Beach (no lifeguard).

Open: All year excl. 25 December.

Directions

Turn from EN 242 (Caldas - Nazaré) road northeast of San Martinho do Porto. Site is clearly signed. GPS: N39:31.370 W09:07.380

Charges guide

Per person	€ 3,65 - € 4,30
child (4-10 yrs)	€ 1,79 - € 2,10
pitch	€ 6,92 - € 9,85
electricity	€ 2,60

PO8110 Orbitur Camping Valado

Rua dos Combatentes do Ultramar, 2, Valado, P-2450-148 Nazaré (Leiria)

Tel: **262 561 111**. Email: **info@orbitur.pt**

This popular site is close to the old, traditional fishing port of Nazaré which has now become something of a holiday resort and popular with coach parties. The large sandy beach in the town (about 2 km. steeply downhill from the site) is sheltered by headlands and provides good swimming. The campsite is on undulating ground under tall pine trees, has 503 pitches and, although some smallish individual pitches with electricity and water can be reserved, the bulk of the site is not marked out and units are close together during July/August. About 375 electrical connections are available.

Facilities

The three toilet blocks have British and Turkish style WCs, washbasins (some cold water) and 17 hot showers, all very clean when inspected. Laundry. Motorcaravan services. Gas supplies. Supermarket (all season). Bar, snack bar and restaurant with terrace (Easter and June-Oct). TV/general room. Playground. Tennis. Off site: Bus service 20 m. Fishing and bicycle hire 2 km.

Open: 1 February - 30 November.

Directions

Site is on the Nazaré - Alcobaca N8-5 road, 2 km. east of Nazaré.

Charges 2008

Per person	€ 2,30 - € 4,10
child (5-10 yrs)	€ 1,20 - € 2,10
caravan and car	€ 5,10 - € 9,30
electricity	€ 2,50 - € 3,10

Off season discounts (up to 70%).

PO8480 Orbitur Camping Foz do Arelho

Rua Maldonado Freitas, P-2500-516 Foz do Arelho (Leiria)

Tel: **262 978 683**. Email: **info@orbitur.pt**

This is a large and roomy ex-municipal site and improvements are still taking place. It is 2 km. from the beach and has a new central complex with a most impressive swimming pool and separated children's pool with lifeguard. Pitches are generally sandy with some hardstandings. They vary in size and are unmarked on two main levels with wide tarmac roads. There is some shade and all touring pitches have electricity (5/15A). The large two storey building contains all the site's leisure facilities but has no ramped access and there are no sanitary facilities anywhere on site for disabled campers.

Facilities

Four identical modern sanitary buildings (solar heating) with seatless British and Turkish style WCs and free showers. Washing machine in one. No facilities for disabled campers. No chemical disposal point. Supermarket (all year). Bar/snacks and restaurant. (closed November). Children's club. Games room. Small new amphitheatre. Playground - supervision needed. Bus service. Doctor's room. Torches useful. Off site: Bus 500 m. Seaside town 2 km. Fishing 2 km.

Open: All year.

Directions

Site is north of Lisbon and west of Caldos la Rainha. From the A8 take N360 to Foz de Arelho. Site is well signed. GPS: N39:25.840 W09:12.050

Charges 2008

Per person	€ 2,70 - € 4,80
child (5-10 yrs)	€ 1,40 - € 2,50
caravan and car	€ 6,70 - € 11,30
electricity	€ 2,50 - € 3,10

PO8100 Orbitur Camping São Pedro de Moel

Rua Volta do Sete, P-2430 São Pedro de Moel (Leiria)

Tel: **244 599 168**. Email: **info@orbitur.pt**

This quiet and very attractive site is situated under tall pines, on the edge of the rather select small resort of São Pedro de Moel. This is a shady site which can be crowded in July and August. The 525 pitches are in blocks and unmarked (cars may be parked separately) with 404 electrical connections. A few pitches are used for permanent units. Although there are areas of soft sand, there should be no problem in finding a firm place. The large restaurant and bar are modern as is the superb swimming pool, paddling pool and flume (there is a lifeguard).

Facilities

Four clean toilet blocks have mainly British style toilets (some with bidets), some washbasins with hot water. Hot showers are mostly in one block. Laundry. Motorcaravan services. Gas supplies. Supermarket (all year). Large restaurant and bar with terrace (closed in November). Swimming pools (31/3-30/9). Satellite TV. Games room. Playground. Tennis. Off site: Bus service 100 m. Beach 500 m. Fishing 1 km.

Open: All year.

Directions

Site is 9 km. west of Marinha Grande, on the right as you enter São Pedro de Moel. GPS: N39:45.450 W09:01.600

Charges 2008

Per person	€ 2,70 - € 4,80
child (5-10 yrs)	€ 1,40 - € 2,50
caravan and car	€ 6,70 - € 11,30
electricity	€ 2,50 - € 3,10

Off season discounts (up to 70%).

PO8460 Camping Caravaning Vale Paraíso

EN 242, P-2450-138 Nazaré (Leiria)

Tel: **262 561 800**. Email: **info@valeparaiso.com**

A pleasant, well managed site, Vale Paraiso improves every year, with the latest additions being new reception buildings and pool areas. The owners are keen to welcome British visitors and English is spoken. The site is by the main N242 road in eight hectares of undulating pine woods. There are 650 shady pitches, many on sandy ground only suitable for tents. For other units there are around 250 individual pitches of varying size on harder ground with electricity available. A large range of sporting and leisure activities includes an excellent outdoor pool and paddling pool with sunbathing areas. The adventure playground is very safe with new equipment. There is a pleasant bar, innovative takeaway selling roasts and a lower level restaurant/bar. Several long beaches of white sand are within 2-15 km. allowing windsurfing, sailing, surfing or body-boarding. Animation for children and evening entertainment is organised in season. Nazaré is an old fishing village with narrow streets, a harbour and marina and outdoor bars and cafés, with a lift to Sitio. There is much of historical interest in the area although the mild Atlantic climate is also conducive to just relaxing.

Facilities

Spotless sanitary facilities have hot water throughout. Nearly all WCs are British style. Modern facilities for disabled people. Baby baths. Washing machine and dryers. Motorcaravan services. Supermarket (1/5-30/9). Restaurant (March - Sept). Café/bar with satellite TV (all year). Brilliant takeaway. Tabac. Swimming and paddling pools (March - Sept; free for under 11s). Petanque. Leisure games. Amusement hall. Bicycle hire. Safety deposit. Gas supplies. E-mail and fax facilities. Apartments to rent. Off site: Bus service from gate. Fishing 2 km. Boat launching 2 km. Riding 6 km. Golf 40 km.

Open: 1 January - 19 December, 25-31 December.

Directions

Site is 2 km. north of Nazaré on the EN242 Marinha Grande road. GPS: N39:37.131 W09:03.230

Charges 2008

Per person	€ 3,20 - € 4,50
child (3-10 yrs)	€ 1,60 - € 2,30
electricity (4-10A)	€ 2,50

Credit cards accepted for amounts over € 150. Camping Cheques accepted.

vale paraíso camping

Apartments Bungalows Chalets

NATURE • SEA • CULTURE

Reservations on-line - www.valeparaiso.com
Estrada Nacional 242
2450-138 Nazaré-PORTUGAL
Tel. 351 262 561 800 Fax. 351 262 561 900
info@valeparaiso.com

PO8050 Orbitur Camping São Jacinto

EN 327 km 20, São Jacinto, P-3800-909 Aveiro (Aveiro)

Tel: **234 838 284**. Email: **info@orbitur.pt**

This small site is in the Sao Jacinto nature reserve, on a peninsula between the Atlantic and the Barrinha, with views to the mountains beyond. The area is a weekend resort for locals and can be crowded in high season – it may therefore be difficult to find space in July/Aug, particularly for larger units. This is not a large site, taking 169 units on unmarked pitches, but in most places trees provide natural limits and shade. Swimming and fishing are both possible in the adjacent Ria, or the sea, 20 minutes walk from a guarded back gate.

Facilities

Two toilet blocks, very clean when inspected, contain the usual facilities. Dishwashing and laundry sinks. Washing machine and ironing board in a separate part of the toilet block. Motorcaravan services. Shop (all season). Restaurant, bar and snack bar (Easter and June-Oct). Playground. Five bungalows to rent. Off site: Bus service 20 m. Fishing 200 m. Bicycle hire 10 km.

Open: 1 February - 31 October.

Directions

Turn off N109 at Estarreja to N109-5 to cross bridge over Ria da Gosta Nova and on to Torreira and São Jacinto. From Porto go south N1/09, turn for Ovar on the N327 which leads to São Jacinto.

Charges 2008

Per person	€ 2,30 - € 4,10
caravan and car	€ 5,10 - € 9,30
electricity	€ 2,50 - € 3,10

PO8060 Camping Costa Nova

Quinta dos Patos, Costa Nova do Prado, P-3830 Gafanha da Encarnação (Aveiro)

Tel: 234 393 220. Email: info@campingcostanova.com

This campsite has been recommended by our agent and we plan to undertake a full inspection in 2008. Camping Costa Nova is situated between a river (Ria de Aveiro) and the sea with direct access to a large sandy beach via a wooden walkway. The 300 grassy pitches are provided with electricity hook ups (10A). This site is ideal for those who enjoy watersports and the surroundings offer plenty of sites of interest for exploration. The site boasts a large bar/restaurant and a café with TV and internet access. English speaking visitors are welcomed and this sheltered site also attracts many for winter stays. Apartments are available for let.

Facilities

Sanitary facilities with free hot water. Laundry room. Restaurant. Bar. Takeaway food. Snack bar. Shop. Games room. Disco. TV. Play area. Internet access. Off site: Beach 500 m. Fishing.

Open: 1 February - 31 December.

Directions

On the IP5 travelling from Aveiro east towards Barra, cross the bridge. At roundabout take third exit and site is well signed.

Charges 2007

Per unit incl.electricity	€ 6,30 - € 8,70
person	€ 3,70
child (under 10 yrs)	€ 1,80
dog	€ 1,50

Costa Nova - Ilhavo

PO8400 Campismo O Tamanco

Casas Brancas II, P-3105-158 Outeiro do Lourical (Leiria)

Tel: 236 952 551. Email: campismo.o.tamanco@mail.telepac.pt

O Tamanco is a peaceful countryside site, with a homely almost farmstead atmosphere; you will have chickens and ducks wandering around and there is a Burro here. The young Dutch owners, Irene and Hans, are sure to give you a warm welcome at this delightful little site. The 75 good sized pitches are separated by cordons of all manner of fruit trees, ornamental trees and flowering shrubs, on level grassy ground. There is electricity (6/16A) to 72 pitches and 5 pitches are suitable for large motorhomes. The site is lit and there is nearly always space available.

Facilities

The single toilet block provides very clean and generously sized facilities including washbasins in cabins, with easy access for disabled visitors. As facilities are limited they may be busy in peak periods. Hot water throughout. Washing machine. Bar/restaurant. Roofed patio with fireplace. TV room/lounge (satellite). Internet access. Swimming pool. Off site: Bus service 1 km. Lake 2 km. Beach 11 km. Market in nearby Lourical every Sunday.

Open: All year.

Directions

From the A17 Lisboa-Porto, take exit 10 for Carrico, turn right at the roundabout and O Tomanco is on the left. GPS: N39:59.500 W08:47.310

Charges 2007

Per person	€ 3,45
child (up to 10 yrs)	€ 1,85
pitch	€ 2,55 - € 6,25
electricity (6-16A)	€ 2,25 - € 3,50

Winter discounts up to 40%.
No credit cards.

PO8370 Parque de Campismo de Cerdeira

P-4840 Campo do Gerês (Braga)

Tel: **253 351 005**. Email: **info@parquecerdeira.com**

Located in the National Park of Peneda Gerês, amidst spectacular mountain scenery, this excellent site offers modern facilities in a truly natural area. The National Park is home to all manner of flora, fauna and wildlife, including the roebuck, wolf and wild boar. The well fenced, professional and peaceful site has some 600 good sized, unmarked, mostly level, grassy pitches in a shady woodland setting. Electricity is available for most pitches, though some long leads may be required. A very large timber complex, tastefully designed with the use of noble materials, granite and wood, provides a superb restaurant with a comprehensive menu.

Facilities

Four very clean sanitary blocks provide mixed style WCs, controllable showers and hot water. Dishwashing and laundry sinks under cover. Laundry. Gas supplies. Minimarket. Restaurant/bar (15/4- 30/9, plus weekends and holidays). Playground. Bicycle hire. TV room (satellite). Medical post. Good tennis courts. Minigolf. Car wash. Barbecue area. Torches useful. English spoken. Attractive bungalows to rent. Dogs are not accepted in July/August. Off site: Fishing and riding 800 m. Off site: Fishing and riding 800 m.

Open: All year.

Directions

From north, N103 (Braga-Chaves), turn left at N205 (7.5 km. north of Braga). Follow N205 to Caldelas Terras de Bouro and Covide where site is clearly marked to Campo do Geres. An eastern approach from the N103 is for the adventurous but will be rewarded by magnificent views over mountains and lakes. GPS: N41:45.811 W08:11.330

Charges 2008

Per person	€ 3,20 - € 4,60
child (5-11 yrs)	€ 2,00 - € 3,10
pitch incl. electricity (6/10A)	€ 6,80 - € 11,70

PO8030 Orbitur Camping Rio Alto

EN 13 km 13, Rio Alto-Est, Estela, P-4570-275 Póvoa de Varzim (Porto)

Tel: **252 615 699**. Email: **info@orbitur.pt**

This site makes an excellent base for visiting Porto which is some 35 km. south of Estela. It has around 700 pitches on sandy terrain and is next to what is virtually a private beach. There are some hardstandings for caravans and motorcaravans and electrical connections to most pitches (long leads may be required). The area for tents is furthest from the beach and windswept, stunted pines give some shade. There are arrangements for car parking away from camping areas in peak season. There is a quality restaurant, snack bar and a large swimming pool plus across the road from reception.

Facilities

Four refurbished and well equipped toilet blocks have hot water. Washing machines and ironing facilities. Facilities for disabled campers. Gas supplies. Shop (1/6-31/10). Restaurant, bar, snack bar (1/5-31/10). Swimming pool (1/6-30/9). Tennis. Playground. Games room. Surfing. TV. Medical post. Car wash. Evening entertainment twice weekly in season. Off site: Fishing. Golf. Bicycle hire. Riding (all within 5 km).

Open: All year.

Directions

From A28 in direction of Porto, take exit 18 signed Fão/Apuila. At roundabout take N13 towards Pavoa de Varzim/Porto for 2.5 km. At Hotel Contriz, turn right on narrow cobbled road. Site signed in 2 km.

Charges 2008

Per person	€ 2,90 - € 5,40
child (5-10 yrs)	€ 1,50 - € 3,00
caravan and car	€ 6,80 - € 12,00
electricity (5/15A)	€ 2,50 - € 3,10

Off season discounts (up to 70%).

MAP 14

Forests cover over one quarter of the country and the fauna is one of the richest in Europe including bears, deer, lynx, chamois and wolves. Whilst driving through Transylvania it is easy to get caught up in the Dracula tale.

CAPITAL: BUCHAREST (BUCURESTI)

Tourist Office

Romanian Tourist Office
22 New Cavendish Street,
London W1M 7LH.
Tel: (020) 7224 3692
Fax: (020) 7935 6435
E-mail: infouk@romaniatourism.com
Internet: www.romaniatourism.com

Romania features splendid mountains, beautiful rolling hills, fertile plains and numerous rivers and lakes. The Carpathian Mountains traverse the centre of the country bordered on both sides by foothills and finally the great plains of the outer rim. The legendary Danube River ends its journey through eight European countries at the Black Sea by forming one of the most interesting wetlands in the world, the Danube Delta.

Romania's history has not been as peaceful as its geography. Over the centuries, various migrating people invaded Romania. The provinces of Wallachia and Moldova offered furious resistance to the invading Ottoman Turks, while Transylvania was successively under Hapsburg, Ottoman or Wallachian rule. Romania's post WWII history as a communist-block nation is more widely known. In 1989 a national uprising led to the overthrow of the dictator, Ceausescu and the 1991 Constitution established Romania as a republic.

Population

22.5 million (2005 est.)

Climate

Temperate, four distinct seasons: pleasant temperatures during spring and autumn, hot summers, cold winters.

Language

Romanian; German and Hungarian are spoken in some provinces.

Telephone

The country code for Romania is +40.

Currency

The Leu (pl. Lei), with its fractional coin, the ban. On 1 July 2005, Romania will drop four zeros from its national currency (e.g. 27,700 Romanian lei (ROL) will equal 2.77 (new) (2 lei (RON) and 77 bani (bah-nee). Both old and new coins and banknotes will be in circulation until 31 December 2006. American Express, MasterCard and Visa are accepted in the main cities. It is advised to travel with some Euros in cash in case of difficulty using credit cards or Travellers' cheques.

Public Holidays

New Year 1, 2 Jan; Monday following Orthodox Easter; Labour Day 1 May; National Day 1 Dec; Christmas 25-26 Dec.

Motoring

Driving in the mountains can be a challenge in poor weather conditions. Make sure to have plenty of fuel as filling stations can be few and far between outside the major cities. Parking is allowed only on the right side of the street and cars must be parked in the direction of traffic.

RO7070 **Camping Aurel Vlaicu**

Strada Principale 155, RO-335401 Aurel Vlaicu (Jud. Hunedoara)

Tel: **025 424 5541**. Email: **aurelvlaicu@email.ro**

The town of Aurel Vlaicu is named after the famous Romanian aviator of the same name who was born here in 1882. A small museum near the campsite details his life and most towns in Romania have a street and a school named after him. He is also depicted on the new 50 Lei note. The village is typically Romanian – one made up street, a stork's nest, geese and ducks walking around in family groups and the locals sitting outside watching the world pass by. This Dutch owned campsite is small but has good views across open farmland to the mountains beyond. The front entrance has restricted access but an alternative is available to deal with larger units. There are 30 level and marked pitches, all with 10A electricity.

Facilities

The modern sanitary block has clean toilets, hot showers and washbasins. Washing machine. Chemical toilet disposal point. Dishwashing facilities. Restaurant. Off site: Aurel Vlaicu Museum (300 m). Corvinestilor Castle and much more within an easy drive.

Open: 15 April - 30 September.

Directions

Aurel Vlaicu is north of the 1/E68 between Sebes and Deva and east of Orastie. Drive slowly through the village to the site, which is signed. GPS: N45:54.896 E23:16.765

Charges 2008

Per person	€ 4,00
child (3-12 yrs)	€ 2,00
pitch	€ 2,00 - € 3,50

Prices in Euros. No credit cards.

RO7040 **Complex Turistic International**

Aleea Padurea Verde 6, RO-300310 Timisoara

Tel: **025 620 8925**. Email: **campinginternational@yahoo.com**

This large tourist complex provides 124 touring pitches (67 with 6A electricity) in a heavily wooded site next to a busy and noisy main road (24 hours). There are 17 places for motorcaravans or caravans with hardstanding, water and drainage, but the access road is narrow and there are low stone walls which impede access. The very tall trees mean you have no views whatsoever. However, Timisoara is close at hand and as Romania's fourth largest city, known by the locals as Primul Oras Liber (First Free Town), it is somewhere you may wish to visit. It was here that the first anti-Ceausecu protests took place that prompted his downfall from power. There is much to see in the old town and every October the town hosts the national beer festival.

Facilities

The reasonable sanitary block provides sufficient clean toilets, hot showers and washbasins. Chemical toilet disposal point. Restaurant with terrace. Café. Play area. Wooden cabins to rent. Barbecues are not permitted. Dogs are not accepted. Off site: Forest walks. The city of Timisoara.

Open: All year.

Directions

Site is on the north side of the 6/E70 just east of Timisoara. GPS: N45:46.144 E21:15.975

Charges 2007

Per person	RON 10,00
pitch	RON 10,00
tent (per person)	RON 10,00
car	RON 20,00

Camping Cheques accepted.

Check real time availability and at-the-gate prices...

www.alanrogers.com

RO7090 Camping de Oude Wilg

Strada Prundului 311, RO-557070 Carta

Tel: 072 318 6343. Email: de-oude-wilg@yahoo.com

The pretty and typically Romanian village of Carta (or Cirta as it is spelt on some old Russian-era road signs) is almost in the centre of Romania, north of the Fagaras mountains (highest peak Moldoveanu 2544 m.) in a broad valley. Manette Twilt, who gives you a warm welcome at any time, runs this small campsite owned by a Romanian-Dutch couple. To reach the site you have to cross a small, flat, concrete bridge so those with very large units and those over 3.5 tonnes will find it difficult. However, for a chance to see Romanian rural life at its best you should plan to visit this delightful village and campsite. The site has 30 level pitches, 12 with 6A electricity connections. The town of Sibiu is about 30 minutes away and is worthy of a visit.

Facilities

Modern sanitary block with clean toilets, hot showers and washbasins. Washing machine and dryer. Chemical toilet disposal point. Small restaurant.

Open: All year.

Directions

Carta (Cirta) is 3 km. north of the 1/E68 road between Sibiu and Fagaras and 1 km. east of the junction with the 7C. As you go through the village turn left on an unmade road towards this small site. GPS: N45:47.032 E24:33.990

Charges 2007

Per person	€ 3,15
child (over 4 yrs)	€ 2,00
pitch incl. car	€ 3,40 - € 4,50
electricity	€ 2,50

RO7130 Camping Eldorado

RO-407310 Gilau

Tel: 026 437 1688. Email: info@campingeldorado.com

If you cross the border into Romania near Oradea this could well be the first campsite you will encounter. You will not be disappointed! Dutch owned but locally managed, it offers excellent facilities and good pitches, although its proximity to the route 1 road does mean there is some background traffic noise. There are 144 level pitches, unmarked but with some shade and all with 8A electricity connection possible. At the edge of the Transylvanian basin, you will have passed the small mountainous area and can now enjoy the rolling countryside with its extensive views. The site offers an excellent base from which to explore the area. The nearby city of Cluj-Napoca has little to offer but it will always be remembered as the home of one of Eastern Europe's most successful pyramid schemes in the early 1990s and its consequences are still felt today. Doomed to collapse, it ended in 1994 and has ingrained the have/have not system in the area and throughout Romania.

Facilities

The modern sanitary block provides ample and clean facilities including toilets, hot showers and washbasins. Dishwashing facilities. Laundry. Chemical toilet disposal point. Small shop with essentials. Restaurant. Play area. Small wooden cabins to rent. Free WiFi internet. Off site: Guided walks in July and August. Fishing, hunting and riding.

Open: 15 April - 15 October.

Directions

The site is easily found on route 1/E60, the road from Oradea to Cluj-Napoca, just after the village of Capusu Mare and about 1 km. before the village of Gilau. GPS: N46:46.022 E23:21.170

Charges 2008

Per person	€ 3,50
child (4-16 yrs)	€ 2,00
pitch incl. car	€ 4,00
electricity	€ 2,50
Prices in Euros.	

Check real time availability and at-the-gate prices...

www.**alanrogers**.com

RO7150 Camping Vasskert

Strada Principala 129, RO-3295 Sovata

Tel: 026 557 0902. Email: vasskert@szovata.hu

Sovata has been a popular resort from the early 19th century. Five lovely lakes surround the town all with reputed curative powers. The most popular is the salt water Lacu Usru for its supposed ability to cure infertility. It is impossible to sink in this lake with 150 grams of salt per litre. A 40 cm. thick layer of fresh water covers the lake and maintains warm temperatures year round. This quiet small family run campsite is just 2 km. from Lacu Ursu and is within walking distance of the small town centre where there are shops, cash exchange facilities and restaurants. There are 20 level un-numbered pitches with some shade and all with 6A electricity. In northern Transylvania you are surrounded by beautiful countryside and lots of places to visit, from the salt mine at Praid to the renowned potteries selling their green, brown and cobalt blue wares, on the road south towards Odorheiu Secuiesc.

Facilities

Ample and clean, the modern sanitary block provides toilets, hot showers and washbasins. Dishwashing facilities. Small wooden cabins to rent.

Open: 1 May - 30 September.

Directions

From Targu Mures take the 13/E60 road south. After 24 km. turn left on the 13a towards Sovata. At the village take the left fork, signed Sovata Bai and go towards the village centre. The site is 2 km. from the fork on the right. GPS: N46:35.442 E25:04.388

Charges 2007

Per person	€ 3,50
child (4-24 yrs)	€ 1,50
pitch	€ 1,50 - € 2,50
dog	€ 1,00
Prices in Euros.	

RO7160 Vampire Camping

Sohodol Street 77c, RO-2229 Bran

Tel: 062 508 3909. Email: info@vampirecamping.com

Bran Castle, most commonly known as Dracula's Castle, was not built by Vlad Tepes (father of Vlad the Impaler) upon whom the novelist Bram Stoker is (incorrectly) supposed to have based his vampire, Count Dracula. The castle, perched atop a 60 metre peak in the village centre, was built by Saxons from Brasov in 1382 to defend the Bran Pass from Turks. Whatever its history, the castle makes an interesting visit since it was occupied for many years by the Romanian Royal Family as a summer residence. Inevitably the entrance is surrounded by souvenir stalls but there are some good restaurants locally as well. Ideally located, Vampire Camping is a very good, Dutch owned, but locally managed, site opened in 2004. There are 40 pitches, all with 6A electricity, plus a separate area for tents. Tony speaks very good English and is very conscientious and helpful.

Facilities

The modern toilet block is very well maintained and provides hot showers, WCs and washbasins. Washing machine. Sinks for dishwashing and food preparation. Ice cream, wine, beer and soft drinks available at reception. Off site: Bran Castle and village only 800 m.

Open: 1 April - 31 October.

Directions

Bran is 30 km. south of Brasov on the 73/E574. Entering the village from Brasov site is signed and is just after supermarket and a petrol station, on the right. GPS: N45:31.715 E25:22.221

Charges 2007

Per person	RON 15,00
pitch	RON 11.00 - 22,00
electricity (6A)	RON 12,00
Camping Cheques accepted.	

RO7170 Camping Dârste

Strada Calea bucuresti 285, RO-2200 Brasov

Tel: 026 833 9967. Email: camp.dirste@dettanet.ro

Brasov, Romania's second most visited city, lies north of the Prahova valley and was first colonised by the Saxons in the 12th century. Nowadays, the pedestrianised Str Republicii provides respite from the traffic that detracts from the rest of the old town. There is plenty to see and do in the surrounding countryside. Saxon fortresses can be found at Prejmer, Harman and Rasnov and of course Bran, and you can easily visit the mountain resort of Poiana Brasov. Camping Dârste is probably the best equipped site you will find in Romania (at the present time) and is good for short or long stays. There are 84 level, numbered and marked pitches and all have 6A electricity, drainage and a water supply.

Facilities

Two modern, clean toilet blocks provide ample toilets, hot showers and washbasins. A third block has Turkish style toilets and more hot showers. Washing machine. Chemical toilet disposal point. Kitchen and dishwashing facilities. Bar and restaurant. Off site: Brasov 8 km.

Open: 20 April - 30 October.

Directions

From Brasov take the N1/E60 towards Ploiesti. About 8 km. out of Brasov, just past the junction with the 1A road and on a right hand bend, the site is on the left adjacent to a BMW agent. Look for Motel signs.

Charges 2007

Per unit incl. 2 persons and electricity	RON 48,00
tent (per person)	RON 10,00

RO7190 Camping Casa Alba

Aleea Privighetorilor 1-3, Baneasa-Bucuresti

Tel: 012 305 203. Email: info@casaalba.ro

If you want to visit the Romanian capital then this site near Bucharest airport is the only one available and that is a shame. Attached to the Casa Alba restaurant, it is primarily an enclosure in a wood for 50 cabins to rent. If you want to camp with a caravan or motorcaravan then you have to park on a gravel area in the centre around three large willow trees. Electricity is available. When we were there after continuous rain deep puddles covered the whole area. The cabins seem to be occupied by groups of young people and the noise from music and shouting went on till after 01.00. Bucharest is not far away by bus, but we didn't think we would leave our motorcaravan here unattended.

Facilities

A refurbished toilet block includes showers, WCs and washbasins. Sinks for dishwashing (not very clean). Electric hobs for cooking. Manhole available for emptying chemical toilet. Restaurant. Off site: Bucharest 8 km.

Open: All year.

Directions

From N1 Ploiesti - Bucuresti road turn east at traffic lights just north of airport. Go past police academy and turn left where tree canopy gets very dense. The site is 50 m. GPS: N44:31.040 E26:05.564

Charges 2007

Per unit incl. 2 persons	RON 17,00 - 40,00

Widely regarded as the 'Bible' by site owners and readers alike, there is no better guide when it comes to forming an independent view of a campsite's quality. When you need to be confident in your choice of campsite, you need the Alan Rogers Guide.

☑ Sites only included on merit

☑ Sites cannot pay to be included

☑ Independently inspected, rigorously assessed

☑ Impartial reviews

☑ 40 years of expertise

Check real time availability and at-the-gate prices...

www.alanrogers.com

MAP 6

Slovakia

Slovakia is a small scale country in the heart of Europe, consisting of a narrow strip of land between the spectacular Tatra Mountains and the river Danube. Picturesque, there are historic castles, evergreen forests, rugged mountains, cave formations, and deep lakes and valleys.

CAPITAL: BRATISLAVA

Tourist Office

Czech & Slovak Tourist Centre
16 Frognal Parade
Finchley Road
London NW3 5HG
Tel: 020 7794 3263 Fax: 020 7794 3265
E-mail: info@czechtravel.co.uk
Internet: www.slovakiatourism.sk

Slovakia has much to offer the visitor with an abundance of year round natural beauty. Its terrain varies impressively; the Carpathian Arc Mountains take up nearly half the country and include the Tatra Mountains, with their rugged peaks, deciduous forests and lakes. Southern and eastern Slovakia is mainly a lowland region and home to many thermal springs, with several open to the public for bathing. Many Hungarians have moved to this area and there is a strong Hungarian influence.

Slovakia has over four thousand registered caves, twelve are open to the public and vary from drop stone to glacial; each one claims to have healing benefits for respiratory disorders. The capital, Bratislava is situated on the river Danube and directly below the Carpathian Mountains. Although it may not be as glamorous as Prague, it contains many fascinating buildings from nearly every age and is a lively cheerful city.

Population
5.4 million

Climate
Cold winters and mild summers. Hot summers and some rain in the eastern lowlands.

Language
Slovak

Telephone
The country code is 00 421.

Money
Currency: The Koruna
Banks: Mon-Fri 08.00-13.00 and 14.00-17.00.

Shops
Mon-Fri 09.00-12.00 and 14.00-18.00. Some remain open at midday. Sat 09.00-midday.

Public Holidays
New Year; Easter Mon; May Day; Liberation Day 8 May; Saints Day 5 July; Festival Day 5 July; Constitution Day 1 Sept; All Saints 1 Nov; Christmas 24-26 Dec.

Motoring
A full UK driving licence is acceptable. The major route runs from Bratislava via Trencin, Banska, Bystrica, Zilina and Poprad to Presov. A windscreen sticker which is valid for a year must be purchased at the border crossing for use on certain motorways. Vehicles must be parked on the right.

Slovakia

SK4900 Autocamping Trusalová
SK-03853 Turany (Zilina)

Tel: 043 4292 636. Email: autocampingtrusalova@zoznam.sk

Autocamping Trusalová is situated right on the southern edge of the Malá Fatra National Park, northeast of the historic town of Martin which has much to offer to tourists. The town is perhaps best known for the engineering works which produced most of the tanks for the Warsaw Pact countries, but is now the home of Volkswagen Slovakia. Paths from the site lead into the Park, it's an ideal base for walkers and serious hikers who wish to enjoy this lovely region. The site is in two halves, one on the left of the entrance and the other behind reception on a slight slope. Surrounded by trees with a stream rushing along one side, pitches are grass from a hard road with room for about 150 units and there are some bungalows.

Facilities
Each half has its own old, but clean and acceptable, toilet provision including hot water in basins, sinks and showers. Motorcaravan service point. Each section has a covered barbecue area with raised fire box, chimney, tables and chairs. Volleyball. TV lounge. Playground. Outdoor chess board. Bicycle hire. Off site: Bar just outside site. Restaurants 500 m. or 1 km. Village 3 km.

Open: 1 June - 15 September.

Directions
Turn north between the Auto Alles car dealer and the Restaurica of the same name on road no. 18/E50 near the village of Turany to campsite. GPS: N49:08.300 E19:03.000

Charges 2008
Per person	SKK 100,00
pitch incl. electricity	SKK 200,00 - 270,00

No credit cards.

SK4905 Autocamping Stara Hora
Oravska Priehrada, SK-02901 Namestovo (Zilina)

Tel: 043 55 22 223. Email: camp.s.hora@stonline.sk

Stara Hora has a beautiful location on the Orava artificial lake. It is in the northeast of Slovakia in the Tatra Mountains and attracts visitors from all over Europe which creates a happy and sometimes noisy atmosphere. The site has its own pebble beach with a large grass area behind it for sunbathing. The lake provides opportunities for fishing, boating and sailing and the area is good for hiking and cycling and in winter, it is a popular skiing area. Autocamping Stara Hora is on steeply sloping ground with 160 grassy pitches, all for touring units and with 10A electricity. The lower pitches are level and have good views over the lake, pitches at the top are mainly used by tents.

Facilities
The modern toilet block has British style toilets, open washbasins and controllable hot showers (free). It could be pressed in high season and hot water to the showers is only available from 07.00-10.00 and 19.00-22.00. Shop for basics. Bar and lakeside bar. Small restaurant. Basic playground (new playground planned). Pedalo, canoe and rowing boat hire. Waterskiing. Fishing (with permit). Torch useful. Off site: Slanica Island.

Open: May - September.

Directions
From Ruzomberok take E77 road north towards Trstena. Turn left in Tvrdosin on the 520 road towards Námestovo. Site is on the right. GPS: N49:23.135 E19:31.657

Charges 2007
Per person	€ 2,42
child	€ 1,21
pitch incl. electricity	€ 5,75

SK4910 Autocamping Turiec
Kolonia hviezda 92, SK-03608 Martin (Zilina)

Tel: 043 428 4215. Email: recepcia@autocampingturiec.sk

Turiec is situated in northeast Slovakia, 1.5 km. from the small village of Vrutky, 4 km. north of Martin, at the foot of the Lucanska Mala Fatra mountains and with castles nearby. This good site has views towards the mountains and is quiet and well maintained. Holiday activities include hiking in summer, skiing in winter, both downhill and cross-country. There is room for about 30 units on grass inside a circular tarmac road with some shade from tall trees. Electrical connections are available for all places. A wooden chalet by the side of the camping area has a TV rest room and a small games room. You will receive a friendly welcome from Viktor and Lydia Matovcik.

Facilities
One acceptable sanitary block to the side of the camping area, but in winter the facilities in the bungalow at the entrance are used. Cooking facilities. Restaurant/snack bar in summer. Badminton. Volleyball. Swimming pool 1.5 km. Rest room with TV. Small games room. Covered barbecue. Off site: Shop outside entrance.

Open: All year.

Directions
Site is signed from E18 road (Zilina - Martin) in the village of Vrutky, 3 km. northwest of Martin. Turn south on the bend and follow signs to Martinské Hole.

Charges 2007
Per unit incl. 2 persons and electricity	SKK 430,00

SK4915 Autocamping Liptovsky Trnovec

SK-03222 Liptovsky Trnovec (Zilina)

Tel: **044 55 98 458**. Email: **atc.trnovec@atctrnouec.sk**

This is a good Slovakian site beside the Liptovská Mara reservoir, also close to the Tatra Mountains which are popular for climbing, hiking and mountain biking. The site is close to the historic cities of Liptovsky Mikulás (6 km), Vlkolinec (on the UNESCO World Heritage list) and Pribylina. There are 250 pitches, all used for touring units and with 14A electricity. With tarmac access roads, the level pitches are on a circular, grassy field and as pitching is rather haphazard, the site can become crowded in high season. Mature trees provide some shade, but in general this is an open site. There are several bars with snack and takeaway services on site with a restaurant nearby (300 m).

Facilities

Two good modern toilet blocks have British style toilets, washbasins in cabins and showers. Facilities for disabled visitors. Washing machines. Campers' kitchen. Bar with covered terrace and takeaway service. Basic playground. Minigolf. Fishing. Bicycle hire. Canoe hire and boat rental. Games room. Beach. Off site: New Tatralandia Aqua Park nearby. Walking in the Lower Tatra Mountains, or real climbing in the Higher Tatra Mountains.

Open: 1 May - 15 October.

Directions

From E50 road take exit for Liptovsky Mikulás and turn left towards Liptovsky Trnovec on 584 road. Continue alongside the lake to site on the left. GPS: N49:06.668 E19:37.767

Charges 2007

Per person	SKK 70,00 - 110,00
child (4-15 yrs)	SKK 25,00 - 60,00
pitch incl. car	SKK 105,00 - 220,00

SK4920 Autocamping Trencin

Na Ostrove, P.O. Box 10, SK-91101 Trencin (Trencin)

Tel: **032 743 4013**. Email: **autocamping.tn@mail.pvt.sk**

Trencin is an interesting town with a long history and dominated by the partly restored castle which towers high above. The small site with room for 30 touring units (all with electricity) and rooms to let, stands on an island about one kilometre from the town centre opposite a large sports complex. Pitches occupy a grass area surrounded by bungalows, although when the site is busy, campers park between and almost on top of the bungalows. The castle is high on one side and woods and hills on the other. There is some rail noise. This is a very neat, tidy friendly site.

Facilities

Toilet block is old but tiled and clean with hot water in the washbasins (in cabins with curtains) and showers (doors and curtains) under cover but not enclosed. Hot water for washing clothes and dishes. Electric cookers, fridge/freezer, tables and chairs. Little shade. Bar in high season. Boating and fishing in river. Off site: Restaurants 200 m. Shops 300 m. Tennis, indoor and outdoor swimming pools within 400 m.

Open: 1 May - 15 September.

Directions

Initially you need to follow signs for 61 Zilina and having crossed the river, bear left. Turn left at first main traffic lights, under the railway and left again. Then turn right after the stadium. Site is over the canal, on the left. GPS: N48:52.996 E18:02.440

Charges 2007

Per person	SKK 170,00 - 200,00
pitch	SKK 50,00 - 150,00
electricity	SKK 100,00

No credit cards.

SK4925 Camping Lodenica

Slnava 1, SK-92101 Piestany (Trnava)

Tel: **033 76 26 093**

This site is 1.5 km. south of the most important spa in the Slovak Republic and lies in a quiet forest setting on the shores of the Sinava lake, close to the town of Piestany. The site is only 4 km. from the main motorway between Bratislava and Trencin and therefore useful as a night stop when travelling between Poland and Hungary or the Czech Republic. Lodenica is divided into three main camping areas with 250 pitches (150 with electricity).

Facilities

One traditional toilet block with toilets, open style washbasins (cold water only) and hot showers. Laundry with 5 sinks. Campers' kitchen with gas hob and oven. Good value bar/restaurant. Playing field. Rowing boats, canoes and surfboards for hire at the lake. Waterskiing. Bicycle hire. Off site: Fishing and beach 200 m. Piestany town with shops, hot food, bars, indoor and outdoor pools 1.5 km. Riding 5 km.

Open: 1 May - 30 September.

Directions

Take motorway form Bratislava towards Trencin and exit at Piestany. At first main junction turn right at traffic lights and go south. Turn left at the hospital towards site. GPS: N48:39.450 E17:49.442

Charges 2007

Per person	SKK 90,00
pitch	SKK 120,00
electricity	SKK 80,00

No credit cards.

Slovakia

SK4950 Autocamping Zlaté Piesky

Senecka cesta c 2, SK-82104 Bratislava (Bratislava)

Tel: **024 445 0592**. Email: **kempi@netax.sk**

Bratislava undoubtedly has charm, being on the Danube and having a number of interesting buildings and churches in its centre. However, industry around the city, particularly en-route to the camp from the south, presents an ugly picture and gives no hints of the hidden charms. Zlate Piesky (golden sands) is part of a large, lakeside sports complex which is also used during the day in summer by local residents. The site is on the northeast edge of the city with 200 touring pitches, 120 with electrical connections, on level grass under tall trees. Twenty well equipped and many more simple bungalows for hire are spread around the site. An attractive lakeside recreation area also has pedaloes for hire and fitness area in the park, plus water skiing/boarding where you are propelled by something akin to a ski lift. For a night stop or a short stay, this might suit.

Facilities

Four toilet blocks, two for campers and two for day visitors, are good and clean. Two restaurants, one with waiter service, the other self service. Many small snack bars. Shops. Lake for swimming and watersports with large beach area. Table tennis. Minigolf. Play areas. Room with billiards and electronic games. Disco. Off site: Tesco supermarket nearby.

Open: 1 May - 15 October.

Directions

From E75 Bratislava - Trencin motorway exit towards Zlate Piesky just north of the airport. Head towards Bratislava on the 61/E571 and immediately after the footbridge turn left at the traffic lights. The site is a little way ahead on the left.

Charges 2007

Per person	SKK 100,00
child (4-15 yrs)	SKK 50,00
pitch	SKK 110,00 - 160,00
electricity	SKK 90,00
dog	SKK 40,00

No credit cards.

SK4980 Autocamping Levocská Dolina

Kovásvá vila 2, SK-05401 Levoca (Presov)

Tel: **053 451 2701**. Email: **rzlevoca@pobox.sk**

According to the owner, Mr Rusnák, this campsite is one of the top ten sites in Slovakia and we agree. The site forms part of a restaurant and pension business and the good value restaurant is welcoming. The entrance is attractively landscaped with varieties of shrubs and colourful flowers and the whole site looks well cared for. There are 60 pitches (all for tourers) and 27 electricity connections. On grassy fields with views of the mountains, there is some terracing. The main road runs steeply uphill and then continues on grass roads. This may cause larger units some difficulty in bad weather. This is a good base from which to explore the Tatra Mountains or visit the Ice Caves.

Facilities

Well renovated toilet block with British style toilets, open washbasins and controllable, hot showers (free). Campers' kitchen. Sauna. Whirlpool. Bar/restaurant. Basic playground. Torch useful. Off site: Lake with pedalo hire 300 m. Dobsinska Ice Caves and Slovakian Paradise. Town of Levoca.

Open: All year.

Directions

From Liptovsky Mikulás, take E50 road east towards Levoca. In Levoca follow site signs. Site is 3 km. north of the town. GPS: N49:02.939 E20:35.210

Charges 2007

Per person	SKK 85,00
child	SKK 45,00
pitch	SKK 40,00 - 150,00

This is just a sample of the campsites we have inspected and selected in Central Europe. For more campsites and further information, please see the Alan Rogers Central Europe guide.

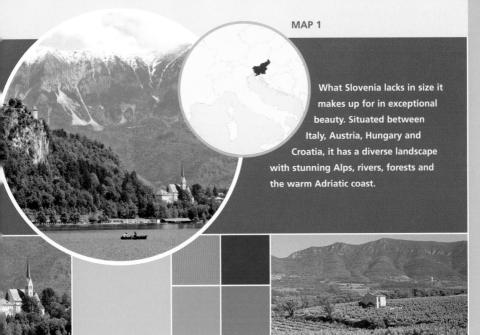

MAP 1

What Slovenia lacks in size it makes up for in exceptional beauty. Situated between Italy, Austria, Hungary and Croatia, it has a diverse landscape with stunning Alps, rivers, forests and the warm Adriatic coast.

Slovenia

CAPITAL: LJUBLJANA

Tourist Office

Slovenian Tourist Office
South Marlands, Itchingfield,
Horsham RH13 0NN
Tel: 0870 225 5305 Fax: 0208 5842 017
E-mail: slovenia.tourism@virgin.net
Internet: www.slovenia-tourism.info

With its snow capped Julian Alps and the picturesque Triglav National park that include the beautiful lakes of Bled and Bohinj, and the peaceful Soca River, it is no wonder that the northwest region of Slovenia is so popular. Stretching from the Alps down to the Adriatic coast is the picturesque Karst region, with pretty olive groves and thousands of spectacular underground caves, including the Postojna and Skocjan caves. Although small, the Adriatic coast has several bustling beach towns such as the Italianised Koper resort and the historic port of Piran, with many opportunities for watersports and sunbathing. The capital Ljubljana is centrally located, with Renaissance, Baroque and Art Nouveau architecture, you will find most points of interest are along the Ljubljana river. Heading eastwards the landscape becomes gently rolling hills, and is largely given over to vines (home of Lutomer Riesling). Savinja with its spectacular Alps is the main area for producing wine.

Population

2 million

Climate

Warm summers, cold winters with snow in the Alps.

Language

Slovene, with German often spoken in the north and Italian in the west.

Telephone

The country code is 386.

Money

Currency: The Euro
Banks: Mon-Fri 8.30-16.30 with a lunch break 12.30-14.00, plus Saturday mornings 8.30-11.30.

Shops

Shops usually open by 8am sometimes 7am. Closing times vary widely.

Public Holidays

New Year; Culture Day 8 Feb; Easter Monday; Resistance Day 27 Apr; Labour Day 1-2 May; National Day 25 Jun; Peoples' Day 22 July; Assumption; Reformation Day 31 Oct; All Saint's Day; Christmas Day; Independence Day 26 Dec.

Motoring

Small but expanding network of motorways radiating from Ljubljana (there may be tolls). Secondary roads often poorly maintained. Tertiary roads are often gravel (known locally as 'white roads' and shown thus on road maps). Road markings and signs are generally good.

SV4150 **Kamp Kamne**

Franc Voga, Dovje 9, SLO-4281 Mojstrana

Tel: **045 891 105**. Email: **info@campingkamne.com**

For visitors proceeding down the 202 road, from Italy or the Wurzen Pass, towards the prime attractions of the twin lakes of Bled and Bohinj, a delightfully informal little site is to be found just outside the village of Mojstrana. For those arriving via the Karavanke Tunnel the diversion along the 202 is very well worth it. Owner Franc Voga opened the site as recently as 1988, on a small terraced orchard. He has steadily developed the facilities, adding a small pool, two tennis courts and improved all other facilities. The little reception doubles as a bar where locals wander up for a beer and a chat.

Facilities

The small excellent sanitary block is of a high quality and well maintained. Reception/bar. Small swimming pool. Two tennis courts. Table tennis. TV room. Mountain bike hire. Franc's English is good and his daughter Anna is fluent. Twice weekly excursions to the mountains (free) in July and August. Two new apartments and bungalows now available to rent. Off site: Walking trails.

Open: All year.

Directions

Site is well marked on north side of the 202 4 km. from Jesenice, just to west of exit for Mojstrana. Site is 4 km. from the Karawanken tunnel. GPS: N46:27.872 E13:57.472

Charges 2008

Per person	€ 7,00 - € 6,00
child (7-17 yrs)	€ 4,50 - € 5,00
electricity	€ 2,00 - € 2,50

SV4210 **Camping Sobec**

Sobceva cesta 25, SLO-4248 Lesce

Tel: **045 353 700**. Email: **sobec@siol.net**

Sobec is situated in a valley between the Julian Alps and the Karavanke Mountains, in a pine grove between the Sava Dolinka river and a small lake. It is only 3 km. from Bled and 20 km. from the Karavanke Tunnel. There are 500 unmarked pitches on level, grassy fields off tarmac access roads (450 for touring units), all with 16A electricity. Shade is provided by mature pine trees and younger trees separate some pitches. Camping Sobec is surrounded by water – the Sava river borders it on three sides and on the fourth is a small, artificial lake with grassy fields for sunbathing.

Facilities

Three traditional style toilet blocks (two refurbished, one old) with mainly British style toilets, washbasins in cabins and controllable hot showers. Child size toilets and basins. Well equipped, baby room. Facilities for disabled visitors. Laundry facilities. Dishwashing under cover. Motorcaravan service point. Supermarket, bar/restaurant (all open all season) with stage for live performances. Playgrounds on grass and stone. Rafting, canyoning and kayaking organised. Miniclub. Off site: Golf and riding 2 km.

Open: 21 April - 30 September.

Directions

Site is off the main road from Lesce to Bled and well signed just outside Lesce. GPS: N46:21.364 E14:08.995

Charges 2007

Per person	€ 9,70 - € 11,50
child (7-14 yrs)	€ 7,30 - € 8,60
electricity (16A)	€ 3,00
dog	€ 3,00

SV4235 **Kamp Klin**

Lepena 1, SLO-5232 Soca

Tel: **053 889 513**. Email: **kampklin@volja.net**

Kamp Klin is next to the confluence of the Soca and Lepenca rivers and is surrounded by mountains. The park is close to the Triglavski National Park and from here it is only a short drive to the highest point of Slovenia, the Triglavski mountain and its beautiful viewpoint with marked walking routes. Being next to two rivers, the site is also a suitable base for fishing, kayaking and rafting. Kamp Klin is privately owned and there is a 'pension' next door, all run by the Zorc family, who serve the local dishes with 'compe' (potatoes), cottage cheese, grilled trout and local salami in the restaurant. The campsite has only 50 pitches, all for tourers and with electricity, on one large, grassy field, connected by a circular, gravel access road.

Facilities

One modern toilet block and a 'portacabin' style unit with toilets and controllable showers. Laundry with sinks. Dishwashing (inside). Bar/restaurant. Play field. Beach volleyball. Fishing (permit required). Torch useful. Off site: Riding 500 m. Bicycle hire 10 km.

Open: All year.

Directions

Site is on the main Kranjska Gora - Bovec road and is well signed in Soca. Access is via a sharp turn from the main road and over a small bridge that may be difficult for larger units. GPS: N46:19.804 E13:38.640

Charges guide

Per person	€ 5,50 - € 7,20
electricity	€ 2,40

SV4200 **Camping Bled**

Kidriceva 10c, Sl, SLO-4260 Bled

Tel: 045 752 000. Email: info@camping.bled.si

On the western tip of Lake Bled is Camping Bled. The waterfront here is a small public beach immediately behind which gently runs a sloping narrow wooded valley. Pitches at the front, used mainly for over-nighters, are now marked, separated by young trees and enlarged, bringing the total number down to 280. In areas at the back, visitors are free to pitch where they like. Unlike at many other Slovenian sites the number of statics (and semi-statics) here appears to be carefully controlled with touring caravans, motorcaravans and tents predominating. Some visitors might be disturbed by the noise coming from trains as they hurtle out of a high tunnel overlooking the campsite on the line from Bled to Bohinj. But this is a small price to pay for the pleasure of being in a pleasant site from which the lake, its famous little island, its castle and its town can be explored on foot or by boat.

Facilities

Toilet facilities in five blocks are of a high standard (with free hot showers). Two blocks are heated. Solar energy used. Backpackers' kitchen. Washing machines and dryers. Chemical disposal point. Motorcaravan services. Gas supplies. Fridge hire. Supermarket. Restaurant. Play area and children's zoo. Table tennis. Games hall. Beach volleyball. Trampolines. Organised activities in July/Aug. including children's club, excursions and sporting activities. Mountain bike tours. Live entertainment. Fishing. Bicycle hire. Internet access. Off site: Riding 3 km. Golf 5 km. Within walking distance of waterfront and town.

Open: 1 April - 15 October.

Directions

From the town of Bled drive along south shore of lake to its western extremity (some 2 km) to the site. GPS: N46:21.693 E14:04.845

Charges 2007

Per person	€ 8,50 - € 11,50
child (7-13 yrs)	€ 5,95 - € 8,05
electricity	€ 3,00
dog	€ 1,50 - € 2,50

Less 10% for stays over 6 days.
Camping Cheques accepted.

CAMPING BLED

Come and find yourself...

Camping Bled, Kidričeva 10c, 4260 Bled, Slovenija
Tel: +386 (0) 4 575 20 00
Fax: +386 (0) 4 575 20 02
www.camping-bled.com
E-mail: info@camping.bled.si

SV4100 **Autocamp Spik**

Jezerci 21, SLO-4282 Gozd Martuljek

Tel: 045 877 100. Email: recepcija.spik@hitholidays-kg.si

Most British motorists enter Slovenia on the E55 from Villach through the easy Karawanka tunnel. On the Slovenian side they will join national route 202 and could proceed to Kransjska Gora, this pleasant resort town being the main northern gateway for the Julian Alps. Close to Kransjska Gora is the small village of Gozd Martuljek and here, directly on route 202, is Kamp Spik, named after the peak which dominates the spectacular view from the site of the jagged Julian Alps skyline. This is the highest site in Slovenia at an altitude of 750 m. (nearly 2,500 ft). It is large and flat, covering eight hectares of spruce woodland, with 200 touring pitches, all with electricity (6A). The site is shared with the modern Spik Hotel and the facilities are extensive. As a result of its spectacular location and its extensive facilities many of the pitches are occupied by caravans which may not be statics but which are clearly not tourers.

Facilities

Two toilet blocks include open plan washbasins (cold water only) and controllable hot showers. Motorhome service point. Supermarket. Tennis. Beach volleyball. Fishing. Bicycle hire. Climbing school. Mountaineering. Off site: Riding 6 km.

Open: All year.

Directions

Site is well signed on the 202 just outside Gozd Martuljek. GPS: N46:28.887 E13:50.235

Charges guide

Per person	€ 5,84 - € 9,60

Less 5% for stays over 7 days
and 10% for 10 days or longer.

SV4250 Camping Danica Bohinj

Triglavska 60, SLO-4265 Bohinjska Bistrica

Tel: 045 747 820. Email: info@camp-danica.si

For those wanting to visit the famous Bohinj valley, which stretches like a fjord right into the heart of the Julian Alps, an ideal site is Danica Bohinj which lies in the valley 3 km. downstream of the lake. Danica was set up in 1989 to supplement the camping accommodation then only available at Zlatorog. Danica occupies a rural site that stretches from the main road leading into Bohinj from Bled (25 km. away), to the bank of the newly formed Sava river. It is basically flat meadow, broken up by lines of natural woodland. This excellent site has 165 pitches, 145 for touring units, all with 10A electricity and forms an ideal base for the many sporting activities the area has to offer.

Facilities

Two good toilet blocks with toilets, open plan washbasins and hot showers. Facilities for disabled visitors. Laundry with washing machines and dryers. Ironing board. Chemical disposal point. Motorcaravan service point. Volleyball. Football. Tennis. Small shop. Café. Fishing. Bicycle hire. Organised excursions in the Triglavski National Park. Off site: Riding 6 km. Canoeing, kayaking, rafting and numerous walking and mountain bike trails.

Open: May - September.

Directions

Driving from Bled to Bohinj, the well signed site lies just behind the village of Bohinjska Bistrica on the right-hand (north) side of the road.
GPS: N46:16.401 E13:56.921

Charges 2007

Per person	€ 7,00 - € 10,00
child (7-14 yrs)	€ 5,60 - € 7,50
electricity	€ 2,50

Less 10% for stays over 7 days.

SV4265 Lazar Kamp

Gregorciceva, SLO-5222 Kobarid

Tel: 053 885 333. Email: edi.lazar@siol.net

This new campsite high above the Soca river has a good location and is ideally situated for the many sporting activities this region of Slovenia has to offer. However, the road to the site from the Napoleon Bridge is narrow, twisting and unmade and is not really suitable for most modern motorcaravans or larger caravans. The owner of the site does insist that larger rigs do get down there, but I certainly was not going to try. The site is very suitable for tents and those with small outfits and offers 50 pitches (all with electricity) and good facilities. Kobarid is a delightful town and has much to offer the interested visitor.

Facilities

The sanitary block is of a good standard and includes facilities for disabled visitors. Dishwashing sinks. Fridge. Washing machine. Bar. Crêperie and grill with terrace area. Internet access. Ranch style clubroom. Excursions and lots of local sporting activities.

Open: 1 April - 31 October.

Directions

Site is on a side road leading east out of Kobarid towards Bosec, just beyond the so-called Napoleon's Bridge. It is not well signed but follow Kamp Koren signs to the bridge then the site is straight on down the narrow unmade road.

Charges 2007

Per person	€ 8,00 - € 10,00
electricity	€ 2,00

SV4270 Kamp Koren Kobarid

Drenzniske Ravne 33, SLO-5222 Kobarid

Tel: 00386 53 891 311. Email: info@kamp-koren.si

The campsite, run to perfection by Lidija Koren, occupies a flat, tree-lined meadow on a wide ledge which drops down sharply to the Soca river and a new, terraced area behind reception. A small, site with just 60 pitches, it is deservedly very popular with those interested in outdoor sports, including paragliding, canoeing, canyoning, rafting and fishing. Equally, a pleasant atmosphere is generated for those seeking a quiet and relaxing break. The Julian Alps and in particular the Triglav National Park is a wonderful and under-explored part of Slovenia that has much to offer.

Facilities

Two attractive log-built toilet blocks are of a standard worthy of a high class private sports club. Facilities for disabled visitors. Laundry facilities. Chemical disposal point. Motorcaravan services. Shop (March - Nov). Café dispenses light meals, snacks and drinks apparently without much regard to closing hours. Sauna. Play area. Bowling. Fishing. Bicycle hire. Canoe hire. Climbing walls for adults. Off site: Riding 5 km. Golf 20 km. Town within walking distance.

Open: 15 March - 1 November.

Directions

Site is on a side road leading east out of Kobarid towards Bosec, just beyond the so-called Napoleon's Bridge, well signed on the left.
GPS: N46:15.045 E13:35.195

Charges 2007

Per person	€ 7,50 - € 9,00
child (7-13 yrs)	€ 3,75 - € 4,50
electricity	€ 3,00

SV4330 Camping Pivka Jama

Veliki Otok 50, SLO-6230 Postojna

Tel: 057 203 993. Email: autokamp.pivka.jama@siol.net

Postojna is renowned for its extraordinary limestone caves which form one of Slovenia's prime tourist attractions. Among campers it is also renowned for the campsite situated in the forest only four kilometres from the caves. Pivka Jama is a most convenient site for the visitor, being midway between Ljubljana and Piran and only about an hour's pleasant drive from either. This good site is deep in what appears to be primeval forest, cleverly cleared to take advantage of the broken limestone forest bedrock. The 300 pitches are not clustered together but nicely segregated under trees and in small clearings, all connected by a neat network of paths and slip roads. Some level, gravel hardstandings are provided. The facilities are both excellent and extensive and run with obvious pride by enthusiastic staff.

Facilities

Two toilet blocks with very good facilities. Washing machines. Motorcaravan service point. Chemical disposal point. Campers' kitchen with hobs. Supermarket. Bar/restaurant. Swimming pool and paddling pool. Volleyball. Basketball. Tennis. Table tennis. Bicycle hire. Daytrips to Postojna Caves and other excursions organised. Off site: Fishing 5 km. Riding or skiing 10 km. Golf 30 km.

Open: March - October.

Directions

Site is 5 km. from Postojna. Take the road leading east from Postojna and then north west towards the Postojna Cave. Site is well signed 4 km. further along this road. GPS: N45:48.320 E14:12.274

Charges 2007

Per person	€ 9,50 - € 10,30
child (7-14 yrs)	€ 7,50 - € 8,10
electricity	€ 3,70

SV4405 Camping Menina

Varpolje 105, SLO-3332 Recica ob Savinji

Tel: 035 835 027. Email: info@campingmenina.com

The Menina site is in the heart of the 35 km. long Upper Savinja Valley, surrounded by 2,500 m. high mountains and unspoilt nature. It is being improved every year by the young, enthusiastic owner, Jurij Kolenc and has 200 pitches, all for touring units, on grassy fields under mature trees and with access from gravel roads. All have 6-10A electricity. The Savinja river runs along one side of the site, but if its water is too cold for swimming, the site also has a lake which can be used for swimming as well. This site is a perfect base for walking or mountain biking in the mountains (a wealth of maps and routes is available from reception). Rafting, canyoning and kayaking, or visits to a fitness studio, sauna or massage salon are organised.

Facilities

The traditional style toilet block has modern fittings with toilets, open plan basins and controllable hot showers (incl. 8 new) and the site reports that a new second block is ready. Chemical disposal point. Motorcaravan service point. Bar/restaurant with open air terrace (evenings only) and open air kitchen. Sauna. Playing field. Fishing. Mountain bike hire. Giant chess. Russian bowling. Excursions (52). Live music and gatherings around the camp fire. Indian village. Hostel. Off site: Fishing 2 km. Recica and other villages with much culture and folklore are close. Indian sauna at Coze.

Open: 1 April - 15 November.

Directions

From Ljubljana take A1 towards Celje. Exit at Trnava and turn north towards Mozirje. Follow signs Recica ob Savinj from there. Continue through Recica to Nizka and follow site signs.
GPS: N46:18.701 E14:54.548

Charges 2008

Per person	€ 8,00
child (5-15 yrs)	€ 5,00
electricity	€ 2,50
dog	€ 2,50

Paying too much for your mobile home holiday?

Spain

One of the largest countries in Europe with glorious beaches, a fantastic sunshine record, vibrant towns and laid back sleepy villages, plus a diversity of landscape, culture and artistic traditions, Spain has all the ingredients for a great holiday.

CAPITAL: MADRID

Tourist Office

Spanish National Tourist Office,
22/23 Manchester Square, London W1U 3PX
Tel: 020 7486 8077
Email: info.londres@tourspain.es
Internet: www.spain.info

Spain has a huge choice of beach resorts. With charming villages and attractive resorts, the Costa Brava boasts spectacular scenery with towering cliffs and sheltered coves. There are plenty of lively resorts, including Lloret, Tossa and Calella, plus several quieter ones. Further along the east coast, the Costa del Azahar stretches from Vinaros to Almanzora, with the great port of Valencia in the centre. Orange groves abound. The central section of the coastline, the Costa Blanca, has 170 miles or so of silvery-white beaches. Benidorm is the most popular resort. The Costa del Sol lies in the south, home to more beaches and brilliant sunshine, whilst in the north the Costa Verde is largely unspoiled, with clean water, sandy beaches and rocky coves against a backdrop of mountains.

Beaches and sunshine aside, Spain also has plenty of great cities and towns to explore, including Barcelona, Valencia, Seville, Madrid, Toledo and Bilbao, all offering an array of sights, galleries and museums.

Population

39.5 million

Climate

Spain has a very varied climate. The north is temperate with most of the rainfall; dry and very hot in the centre; subtropical along the Mediterranean.

Language

Castilian Spanish is spoken by most people with Catalan (northeast), Basque (north) and Galician (northwest) used in their respective areas.

Telephone

The country code is 00 34.

Money

Currency: The Euro
Banks: Mon-Fri 09.00-14.00.
Sat 09.00-13.00.

Shops

Mon-Sat 09.00-13.00/14.00 and 15.00/16.00-19.30/20.00. Many close later.

Public Holidays

New Year; Epiphany; Saint's Day 19 Mar; Maundy Thurs; Good Fri; Easter Mon; Labour Day; Saint's Day 25 July; Assumption 15 Aug; National Day 12 Oct; All Saints Day 1 Nov; Constitution Day 6 Dec; Immaculate Conception 8 Dec; Christmas Day.

Motoring

The surface of the main roads is on the whole good, although secondary roads in some rural areas can be rough and winding. Tolls are payable on certain roads and for the Cadi Tunnel, Vallvidrera Tunnel and the Tunnel de Garraf on the A16.

ES80200 Camping Internacional de Amberes

Playa de la Rubina, E-17487 Empúria-brava (Girona)

Tel: **972 450 507**. Email: info@inter-amberes.com

Situated in the 'Venice of Spain', Empuria Brava is interlaced with inland waterways and canals, where many residents and holidaymakers moor their boats directly outside their homes on the canal banks. Internacional Amberes is a large friendly site 50 m. from the wide, sandy beach, which is bordered on the east and west by the waterway canals. Amberes is a surprisingly pretty and hospitable site where people seem to make friends easily and get to know other campers and the staff. The site has 657 touring pitches, most enjoying some shade from strategically placed trees. All have electricity and water connections. The restaurant and bar are close to the site entrance and the cuisine is so popular that locals use it too. Unusually the swimming pool is on an elevated terrace, raised out of view of most onlookers with sunbathing areas and a small children's pool adjoining.

Facilities

Toilet facilities are in five fully equipped blocks. Washing machines. Motorcaravan services. New supermarket, bakery and shop. Restaurant/bar. Takeaway. Pizzeria. Watersports – windsurfing school. Organised sports activities, children's programmes and entertainment. Swimming pool. Playgrounds. Football. Table tennis. Tennis. Volleyball. Internet and WiFi. Apartments. Off site: Beach 200 m. Fishing 300 m. Bicycle hire and boat launching 500 m. Riding 1 km. Golf 12 km.

Open: 1 April - 15 October.

Directions

Empuria Brava is north of Girona, east of Figueres on the coast. From AP7/E15 take exit 3 going south or exit 4 north (note there is no exit 3 north) and then N11 to the C260 towards Roses. At Empuria Brava follow camping signs to site. GPS: N42:15.160 E03:07.902

Charges 2007

Per person over 3 yrs	€ 3,20 - € 3,40
pitch incl. electricity (55 sq.m.)	€ 9,90 - € 22,80
pitch (acc. to size)	€ 10,90 - € 29,50

Less 20% for pensioners for stays of 15 days or over in low seasons.

ES80800 Camping El Delfin Verde

Ctra de Torroella de Montgri, E-17257 Torroella de Montgri (Girona)

Tel: **972 758 454**. Email: info@eldelfinverde.com

A large, popular and high quality site in a quiet location, El Delfin Verde has its own long beach stretching along its frontage. A prime feature of the site is an attractive large pool in the shape of a dolphin with a total area of 1,800 sq.m. This is a large site with 1420 touring pitches and around 6,000 visitors at peak times. It is well managed by friendly staff. Level grass pitches nearer the beach are marked and many are separated by small fences and hedging. All have electrical connections (5/6A) and access to water points. A stream runs through the centre of the site. There is shade in some of the older parts and a particularly pleasant area of pine trees in the centre provides marked but not separated pitches (sandy and not so level).

Facilities

Six excellent large and refurbished toilet blocks plus a seventh smaller block, all with resident cleaners, have showers using desalinated water and some washbasins in cabins. Laundry facilities. Motorcaravan services. Supermarket and shops. Swimming pools (with lifeguard). Two restaurants, grills and pizzerias. Three bars. 'La Vela' barbecue and party area. Large sports area. 2 km. exercise track. Dancing and floor shows weekly in season. Excursions. Bicycle hire. Minigolf. Playground. Fishing.Gas supplies. Internet access. Dogs are not accepted in high season (11/7-14/8). Off site: Golf 4 km. Riding 4 km.

Open: 8 April - 15 October.

Directions

Torroella de Montgri is close to the coast east of Girona. From A7/E15 exit 6 take C66 (Palafrugell). Then the GI 642 east to Parlava and turn north on C31. GPS: N42:00.718 E03:11.284

Charges 2007

Per person	€ 4,00 - € 4,50
child (2-9 yrs)	€ 3,50 - € 4,00
pitch incl. electricity	€ 13,00 - € 39,00
dog (excl 11/7-14/8)	€ 3,50

All plus 7% VAT. Special offers on long stays in low season.

This is just a sample of the campsites we have inspected and selected in Spain & Portugal. For more campsites and further information, please see the Alan Rogers Spain & Portugal guide.

ES80350 Camping l'Amfora

2 avenida Josep Tarradellas, E-17470 Sant Pere Pescador (Girona)

Tel: **972 520 540**. Email: **info@campingamfora.com**

This is a superb spacious and friendly family site with a Greek theme, which is manifested mainly in the restaurant and pool areas. The site is spotlessly clean and well maintained and the owner operates in an environmentally friendly way. There are 830 pitches (730 for touring), all with 10A electrical connections and most with a water tap, on level grass with trees and shrubs. Of these, 64 pitches are large (180 sq.m.), made for two units per pitch and each with an individual sanitary facility (toilet, shower and washbasin). In addition to the individual units, three main sanitary blocks (one heated) offer free hot water, washbasins in cabins, hairdryers and baby rooms. There is extra provision near the pool area. Access is good for disabled visitors. An inviting terraced bar and self-service restaurant overlook four large swimming pools (one for children) with two water slides. Ambitious evening entertainment (pub, disco, shows) and children's animation are organised in season and a choice of watersports activities is available on the beach.

Facilities

Three main toilet blocks, one heated, provide washbasins in cabins and free showers. Baby rooms. Laundry facilities. Motorcaravan services. Supermarket. Terraced bar, self service and waiter service restaurants. Takeaway. Restaurant and bar on the beach with limited menu (high season). Disco-bar. Swimming pools (1/5-30/9). Gymnasium. Petanque. Tennis. Bicycle hire. Minigolf. Playground. Entertainment and activities. Windsurfing. Boat launching and sailing. Fishing. Exchange facilities. Games and TV rooms. Internet room and WiFi. Car wash. Torches required in beach areas. Off site: Riding 4 km. Golf 15 km.

Open: 5 April - 30 September.

Directions

Sant Pere Pescadore is south of Perpignan on the coast between Roses and L'Escala. From the AP7/E15 take exit 4 onto N11 north towards Figueres and then C31 towards Torroella de Fluvia. Take the Vilamacolum road east and continue to Sant Pere Pescadore. Site is well signed in town. GPS: N42:18.181 E03:10.403

Charges 2008

Per person	€ 3,60 - € 4,80
child (2-9 yrs)	free - € 3,80
pitch (100 sq.m.)	€ 15,60 - € 39,00
pitch with individual sanitary arrangements	€ 27,00 - € 61,00

Electricity (10A) included. Plus 7% VAT.
No credit cards. Camping Cheques accepted.

Check real time availability and at-the-gate prices...

www.alanrogers.com

ES80300 Camping Nautic Almata

Ctra St Pere Pescador, km 11.6, E-17486 Castelló d'Empúries (Girona)

Tel: 972 454 477. Email: info@almata.com

In the Bay of Roses, south of Empuria Brava and beside the Parc Natural dels Aiguamolls de l'Empordá, this is a site of particular interest for nature lovers (especially bird watchers). Beautifully laid out, it is arranged around the river and waterways, so will suit those who like to be close to water or who enjoy watersports and boating. It is worth visiting because of its unusual aspects and the feeling of being on the canals, as well as being a high quality beachside site. A large site, there are 1,109 well kept, large, numbered pitches, all with electricity and on flat, sandy ground. There are some pitches right on the beach. As you drive through the natural park to the site watch for the warning signs for frogs on the road and enjoy the wild flamingos alongside the road. The name no doubt derives from the fact that boats can be tied up at the small marina within the site and a slipway also gives access to a river and thence to the sea. Throughout the season there is a varied entertainment programme for children and adults. The facilities on this site are impressive. Some tour operators use the site.

Facilities

Toilet blocks of a high standard include some en-suite showers with basins. Good facilities for disabled visitors. Washing machines. Gas supplies. Excellent supermarket. Restaurant and bar. Two separate bars by beach where discos held in main season. Water-ski, diving and windsurfing schools. 300 sq.m. swimming pool. Tennis, squash, volleyball and 'fronton' (all free). Minigolf. Games room. Extensive riding tuition with own stables and stud. Children's play park (near river). Fishing (licence required). Car, motorcycle and bicycle hire. Hairdresser. Torches are useful near beach. Off site: Canal trips 18 km. Aquatic Park 20 km.

Open: 3 May - 14 September, including all facilities.

Directions

Site is signed at 26 km. marker on C252 between Castello d'Empuries and Vildemat, then 7 km. to site. Alternatively, on San Pescador - Castello d'Empuries road head north and site is signed. GPS: N42:12.750 E03:05.166

Charges 2008

Per pitch incl. up to 6 persons	€ 21,40 - € 42,80
extra person (over 3 yrs)	€ 2,15 - € 4,30
dog	€ 4,60 - € 6,00
boat or jetski	€ 8,50 - € 11,50

All plus 7% VAT. No credit cards.

ES80400 Camping Las Dunas

Ctra San Marti - Sant Pere, E-17470 Sant Pere Pescador (Girona)

Tel: 972 521 717. Email: info@campinglasdunas.com

Las Dunas is an extremely large, impressive and well organised site with many on site activities and an ongoing programme of improvements. It has direct access to a superb sandy beach that stretches along the site for nearly a kilometre with a windsurfing school and beach bar. There is also a much used swimming pool with large double children's pools. Las Dunas is very large, with 1,700 individual hedged pitches (1,479 for tourers) of around 100 sq.m. laid out on flat ground in long, regular parallel rows. All have electrical connections and 180 also have water and drainage. Shade is available in some parts of the site. Pitches are usually available, even in the main season. Much effort has gone into planting palms and new trees here and the results are very attractive. The large bar and restaurant have spacious terraces overlooking the swimming pools and you can enjoy a very pleasant more secluded cavern styled pub. A magnificent disco club is close by in a soundproof building (although people returning from this during the night can be a problem for pitches in the central area of the site). With free quality entertainment of all types in season and positive security arrangements, this is a great site for families with teenagers. Everything is provided on site so you don't need to leave it during your stay. Member of Leading Campings Group.

Facilities

Five excellent large toilet blocks (with resident cleaners 07.00-21.00) have British style toilets, controllable hot showers and washbasins in cabins. Excellent facilities for youngsters, babies and disabled people. Laundry facilities. Motorcaravan services. Extensive supermarket and other shops. Large bar with terrace. Large restaurant. Takeaway. Ice cream parlour. Beach bar in main season. Disco club. Swimming pools. Playgrounds. Tennis. Minigolf. Sailing/windsurfing school and other watersports. Programme of sports, games and entertainment, partly in English (15/6-31/8). Exchange facilities. ATM. Safety deposit. Internet café. WiFi. Dogs taken in one section. Torches required in some areas.

Open: 19 May - 2 September.

Directions

L'Escala is northeast of Girona on coast between Palamos and Roses. From A7/E15 autostrada take exit 5 towards L'Escala on GI 623. Turn north 2 km. before reaching L'Escala towards Sant Marti d'Ampurias. Site well signed. GPS: N42:09.659 E03:08.087

Charges 2007

Per person	€ 3,00 - € 4,25
child (2-10 yrs)	€ 2,50 - € 3,00
standard pitch incl. electricity	€ 13,00 - € 41,00
water and drainage	€ 15,00 - € 46,00
dog	€ 3,00 - € 4,00

All plus 7% VAT.

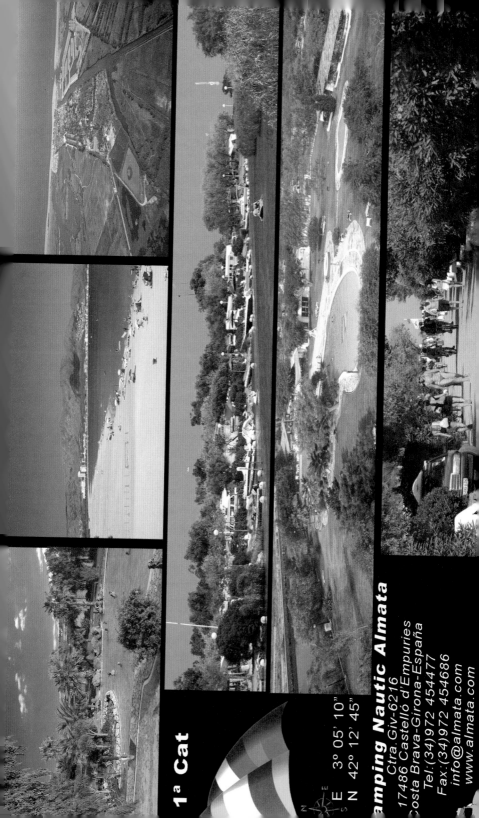

1ª Cat

E   3° 05' 10"
N   42° 12' 45"

Camping Nautic Almata
Ctra.Giv-6216
17486 Castelló d'Empuries
Costa Brava-Girona-España
Tel:(34)972 454477
Fax:(34)972 454686
info@almata.com
www.almata.com

Ctra Figueres - Roses km 38, E-17486 Castelló d'Empúries (Girona)
Tel: **972 454 175**. Email: **info@campingmasnou.com**

Some two kilometres from the sea on the Costa Brava, this is a surprisingly tranquil site in two parts on either side of the access road. One part contains the pitches and toilet blocks, the other houses the impressive leisure complex. There are 450 neat, level and marked pitches on grass and sand, a minimum of 70 sq.m. but most 80-100 sq.m and 300 with electricity (10A). The leisure complex is across the road from reception and features a huge L-shaped swimming pool with a paddling area. A formal restaurant has an adjoining bar, pleasant terrace crêperie and rotisseria under palms. A barbecue/rotisseria in another part of the site offers takeaway meals (in season). The site owns the large souvenir shop on the entrance road. There are many traditional bargains here and it is worth having a good look around as the prices are extremely good. Lots of time and money goes into the cleanliness of this site and it is good very for families. Ask about the origin of the site coat of arms. The Bay of Roses and the Medes islands have a natural beauty and a visit to Dali's house or the museum (the house is fascinating) will prove he was not just a surrealist painter.

Facilities

Three excellent, fully equipped sanitary blocks include baby baths, good facilities for disabled visitors. Washing machines. Supermarket and other shops. Bar/restaurant. Takeaway. Swimming pool with lifeguard (from 1/5). Tennis. Minigolf. Miniclub (July/Aug). Play area. Electronic games. Off site: Riding 1.5 km. Fishing or bicycle hire 2 km. Beach 2.5 km. Aquatic Park. Romanica tour of famous local churches.

Open: 15 March - 28 September.

Directions

From A7 use exit 3. Mas Nou is 2 km. east of Castelló d'Empúries, on the Roses road, 10 km. from Figueres. Do not turn left across the main road but continue to the roundabout and return. GPS: N42:15.935 E03:06.150

Charges 2008

Per person	€ 2,50 - € 4,70
child (4-11 yrs)	free - € 3,30
pitch	€ 14,40 - € 27,30
electricity	€ 3,10 - € 4,40
dog	free - € 2,10

All plus 7% VAT.
Camping Cheques accepted.

CÀMPING
masnou
✳ ✳ ✳

Crta. de Figueres a Roses, Km. 38
Tel. (0034) 972 45 41 75
Fax (0034) 972 45 43 58
17486 CASTELLÓ D'EMPÚRIES - (Girona)
info@campingmasnou.com

www.campingmasnou.com

You will experience a whole world of sensations

ES80150 Camping Caravaning La Laguna

Apdo 55, E-17486 Castelló d'Empúries (Girona)

Tel: **972 450 553**. Email: **info@campinglaguna.com**

La Laguna is a relaxed, spacious site on an isthmus within a Catalan national maritime park, on the migratory path of many different birds. It has direct access to a sandy beach and the estuary of the river Muga. The owners continue to spend much time and effort on improvements. The double lagoons are a most attractive feature. The 780 pitches (with just 10 mobile homes) are shaded and clearly marked on grass and sand, all with 6/10A electricity. There are also 33 fully serviced pitches. An attractive bar/restaurant overlooks the lagoons and there are two swimming pools (one is heated in low season). A disco operates across the road from reception, keeping the noise away from the main site. A large riding school operates (May - Sept) and there are many other activities. The beach frontage is large and has a sailing school. It is said to be possible to cross over to Empuria Brava when the tide is out. There are many pleasant walks in this area and this a good site for family holidays.

Facilities

Five toilets blocks, placed to avoid long walks. All have been completely rebuilt and provide solar heated water. Laundry room. Bar, restaurant and takeaway (all 13/3-26/10). New supermarket. Swimming pools (1/4-26/10). Basketball. Football. Tennis (free in low seasons). ATM. Minigolf. Windsurfing and sailing schools (July/Aug). Fishing. Miniclub. New play area. Bicycle hire. Riding. Animation programme and competitions. Satellite TV. Internet access and WiFi. Off site: Boat launching. Golf 15 km. Birdwatching.

Open: 13 March - 26 October.

Directions

Castello d'Empuries is north of Girona and east of Figueres on the coast. From AP7/E15 take exit 3 south or exit 4 north (note there is no exit 3 north) and then N11 to the C260 towards Roses. At Castello d'Empuries follow camping signs and a 4 km. unmarked road will take you to the site. GPS: N42:14.238 E03:07.284

Charges 2007

Per person	€ 4,50 - € 7,90
child (3-10 yrs)	€ 3,65 - € 5,85
pitch	€ 4,50 - € 15,80

Discounts for longer stays and pensioners in low season. No credit cards.

ES80600 Camping La Ballena Alegre 2

E-17470 San Pere Pescador (Girona)

Tel: **902 510 520**. Email: **infb2@ballena-alegre.com**

La Ballena Alegre 2 is partly in a lightly wooded setting, partly open, and has some 1,800 m. of frontage directly onto an excellent beach of soft golden sand (cleaned daily). They claim that none of the 1,531 touring pitches is more than 100 m. from the beach. The grass pitches are individually numbered and there is a choice of size (up to 100 sq.m). Electrical connections (5/10A) are available in all parts and there are 91 fully serviced pitches. It is a great site for families.

Facilities

Seven well maintained toilet blocks are of a very high standard. Facilities for children, babies and disabled campers. Launderette. Motorcaravan services. Gas supplies. Supermarket. New 'Linen' restaurant. Self-service restaurant and bar. Pizzeria and beach bar in high season. Swimming pool complex. Jacuzzi. Tennis. Watersports. Fitness centres. Bicycle hire. Playgrounds. Organised activities, sports and entertainment. WiFi. Off site: Go-karting. Fishing 300 m. Riding 2 km.

Open: 12 May - 24 September.

Directions

From A7 Figueres - Girona autopista take exit 5 to L'Escala Gl 623 for 18.5 km. At roundabout take sign to Sant Marti d'Empúries and follow camp signs. GPS: N42:09.194 E03:06.749

Charges 2007

Per person	€ 3,50 - € 3,75
child (3-9 yrs)	€ 2,50 - € 3,00
pitch incl. electricity	€ 14,90 - € 41,00

All plus 7% VAT. No credit cards.

ES80080 Camping Joncar Mar

Ctra Figueres s/n, E-17480 Roses (Girona)

Tel: **972 256 702**. Email: **info@campingjoncarmar.com**

Family owned since 1977, Jonca Mar is a mature, all year site with basic facilities. Its strength is its location with the beach promenade just outside the gate, and the many resort leisure facilities and local cultural attractions readily available to customers. The site is divided by a minor road and most leisure facilities are positioned on one side of the site. There are no views and the site has some apartment blocks around the periphery. Pitches are small (60 sq.m.) with 6A electricity, and the mobile home area in one corner of the site is extremely cramped. Some pitches require long electricity leads and long stay customers have arranged unpleasant systems of hoses draining into road drains. The modest swimming pool has a shallow area at right angles at one end for children, but no barrier separating it from deeper water, so small children will need supervision, especially as there is no lifeguard. The pool is overlooked by a restaurant area offering an uncomplicated 'eat all you can' fixed evening buffet menu, which is open to the street and thus non-camping customers. The site offers a very basic, no frills service which will only appeal to a limited number of campers.

Facilities

Two dated, refurbished toilet blocks are well positioned on the main side of the site and the third very tired block on the other side is due for refurbishment. No formal facilities for disabled visitors but one toilet/shower with a wider door. One washing machine. Small shop. Small bar and buffet restaurant. Swimming pool. Basic play area. TV in bar. Limited animation programme. Internet. Torches useful. Off site: Nearest beach 50 m. Bicycle hire 100 m. Riding 3 km. Golf 20 km.

Open: All year.

Directions

Roses is north of Girona and east of Figueres on the coast. From AP7/E15 take exit 3 south or exit 4 north (there is no exit 3 northbound) and then the N11 to the C260 and on to Roses. Site is well signed before you enter the town – follow camping signs initially.

Charges 2007

Per person	€ 5,30 - € 5,50
child (under 10 years)	€ 3,55 - € 3,65
pitch	€ 6,35 - € 11,15
electricity (10A)	€ 3,55 - € 3,65

Wi Fi ZONE

Camping

JONCAR MAR

BUNGALOWS

A holiday site with all facilities, situated in Roses and next to a beautiful sandy beach. NEW BUNGALOWS. 50% reduction alter 7 days (1.4 – 30.6 and 1.9 – 30.10)

Camping Caravaning **JONCAR MAR** Str. Figueras, s/n • Postadr. Apartado 483 E-17480 ROSES
Costa Brava • Tel./Fax: 0034 972 25 67 02 • www.campingjoncarmar.com • info@campingjoncarmar.com

ES80500 Camping Aquarius

Playa s/n, E-17470 Sant Pere Pescador (Girona)

Tel: **972 520 003**. Email: **camping@aquarius.es**

A smart and efficient family site, Aquarius has direct access to a quiet sandy beach that slopes gently and provides good bathing (the sea is shallow for quite a long way out). One third of the site has good shade with a park-like atmosphere. There are 435 pitches with electricity (6/16A). Markus Rupp and his wife are keen to make their visitors experience a happy one. The site is ideal for those who really like sun and sea, with a quiet situation.

Facilities

Attractively tiled, fully equipped, large toilet blocks provide some cabins for each sex. Excellent facilities for disabled people, plus baths for children. Superb new block has under-floor heating and family cabins with showers and basins. Laundry facilities. Gas supplies. Motorcaravan services. Supermarket. Restaurant and bar. Takeaway. Children's play centre. 'Surf Center'. Minigolf. Bicycle hire. ATM. Internet access. WiFi. (No pool). Off site: Fishing and boat launching 3 km.

Open: 15 March - 31 October.

Directions

From the AP7/E15 take exit 4 onto N11 north towards Figueres and then C31 towards Torroella de Fluvia. Take Vilamacolum road east and continue to Sant Pere Pescador. Site well signed in town. GPS: N42:10.614 E03:06.478

Charges 2007

Per person	€ 2,85 - € 3,50
pitch acc. to season and facilities	€ 7,15 - € 36,10
electricity	€ 2,90 - € 5,80

All plus 7% VAT. No credit cards.

ES81020 Camping-Resort Mas Patoxas Bungalow-Park

Ctra C31 Palafrugell - Pals km 339, E-17256 Pals (Girona)

Tel: **972 636 928**. Email: **info@campingmaspatoxas.com**

This is a mature and well laid out site for those who prefer to be apart from, but within easy travelling distance, of the beaches (5 km.) and town (1 km). It has a very easy access and is set on a slight slope with wide avenues on level terraces providing over 400 grassy pitches of a minimum 72 sq.m. All have electricity (5A) and water; many have drainage as well. There are some very pleasant views and shade from a variety of mature trees. Both bar and restaurant terraces give views over the pools and distant hills. The air-conditioned restaurant/bar provides both waiter service meals and takeaway food to order (weekends only mid Sept - April) and entertainment takes place on a stage below the terraces during high season. The restaurant menu is varied and very reasonable. We were impressed with the children's miniclub activity when we visited. There is a large, supervised irregularly shaped swimming pool with triple flume, a separate children's pool and a generous sunbathing area at the poolside and on the surrounding grass.

Facilities

Three modern sanitary blocks provide controllable hot showers, some washbasins with hot water. Baby bath and three cabins for children. No specific facilities for disabled people. Laundry facilities. New supermarket (15/3-30/9). Restaurant/bar, pizzeria and takeaway (all 15/3-30/9). Swimming pool (1/5-30/9). Tennis. Entertainment in high season. Fridges for rent. Gas supplies. Torches useful in some areas. Off site: Bus service from site gate. Bicycle hire or riding 2 km. Fishing or golf 4 km.

Open: 12 January - 16 December.

Directions

Site is east of Girona and approx. 1.5 km. south of Pals at km. 339 on the C31 Figueres-Palamos road, just north of Palafugel. GPS: N41:57.311 E03:09.478

Charges 2008

Per unit incl. 2 persons and electricity	€ 15,00 - € 42,00
extra person	€ 3,60 - € 5,75
child (1-7 yrs)	€ 3,00 - € 4,00
dog	€ 2,10 - € 3,20

Plus 7% VAT. Special low season offers.

ES81030 Camping El Maset

Playa de Sa Riera, E-17255 Begur (Girona)

Tel: **972 623 023**. Email: **info@campingelmaset.com**

A delightful little gem of a site in lovely surroundings, El Maset has 116 pitches, of which just 20 are slightly larger for caravans or motorcaravans, the remainder suitable only for tents. The owner of some 40 years, Sr Juan Perez is delightful and his staff are very helpful. The site entrance is steep and access to the caravan pitches can be quite tricky. However, the owner's son will tow your caravan to your pitch. All these pitches have electricity, water and drainage with some shade. Tent pitches are more shaded on attractive rock-walled terraces on the hillside. Access to these seems quite straightforward, with parking for cars not too far away – of necessity the pitches are fairly small. All steep terraced pitches are safely fenced for children. For a small site the amenities are quite extensive, including an unusual elliptical shaped swimming pool. A bar and very homely restaurant offering excellent food, with a terrace giving very pleasant views over the pool and towards the other side of the valley. This small site provides the standard of service normally associated with the very best of the larger sites. It is situated in the tiny resort of Sa Riera with access to the beach (300 m.) in a beautiful protected bay with traditional fishing boats taking up one end of the sand. There is a naturist beach (via a longer uphill path). Begur, with its beautiful, small, quite unspoilt bay and beach, is 10 minutes by car.

Facilities

Good sanitary facilities in three small blocks are kept very clean. Baby facilities. Washing machines and dryers. Unit for disabled campers but the ground is steep. Bar/restaurant, takeaway (all season). Shop (from May). Swimming pool (all season). Solarium. Play area. Area for football and basketball. Excellent games room. Internet access. Dogs are not accepted. Off site: Fishing 300 m. Golf and bicycle hire 1 km. Riding 8 km.

Open: Easter - 24 September.

Directions

From the C31 Figueres - Palamos road south of Pals, north of Palafrugell, take GI653 to Begur. Site is 2 km. north of the town; follow signs for Playa de Sa Riera and site (steep entrance). GPS: N41:58.116 E03:12.601

Charges 2007

Per person	€ 4,70 - € 6,70
child (1-10 yrs)	€ 3,00 - € 4,70
pitch incl. car	€ 6,30 - € 14,00
electricity	€ 3,50 - € 4,70

Plus 7% VAT. Discount in low season for 7 day stay.

ES80730 Camping L'Empordá

E-17258 L'Estartit (Girona)

Tel: **972 75 06 49**. Email: **info@campingemporda.com**

L'Empordá is a fairly small, family site located 1 km. from the resort of L'Estartit and a similar distance from the nearest beach. This site has been recommended by our Spanish agent and we hope to undertake a full inspection in 2008. Pitches here are of a good size and generally grassy. There are also chalets available for rent. The main appeal of this site will no doubt be the fine beach, 5 km. long, gently shelving and with great views towards the beautiful Medes islands. L'Empordá has a good range of amenities, including a good sized swimming pool and separate children's pool. In high season, the site organises a variety of activities, including aerobics, aquagym and evening entertanment including karaoke and discos.

Facilities	Directions
Bar. Restaurant. Takeaway. Shop. Play area. Swimming pool. Children's pool. Entertainment and activities in peak season. Children's club. Chalets for rent. Off site: Nearest beach 1 km. L'Estartit 1 km. Minigolf. Tennis. Fishing. **Open:** 15 March - 28 September.	From the AP7 take Palamos exit and take the C66 towards Palamos. Then take the GI 642 towards Parlava and the GI 643 towards Torroella de Montgri. Lastly, the GI 641 towards L'Estartit and site is well signed shortly before arriving at the resort centre.

Charges 2008

Per unit with 2 persons and electricity	€ 16,00 - € 26,40
extra person	€ 2,80 - € 5,30
child (3-10 yrs)	€ 1,80 - € 3,90

CAMPING L'EMPORDÀ

Our camp site is small, quiet and familiar. It is situated at 1 km from the village l'Estartit and at the same distance from a fine sandy beach of 5 km, where you can enjoy a fabulaous view on the isles of Medas.

Road Torroella-l'Estartit, km 4,8
E- 17258 L'ESTARTIT
(Girona) COSTA-BRAVA
Tel.: 0034 972 75 06 49
Fax: 0034 972 75 14 30
www.campingemporda.com
info@campingemporda.com

ES80690 Camping Neus

Cala Montgó, E-17130 L'Escala (Girona)

Tel: **972 770 403**. Email: **info@campingneus.com**

Camping Neus is a mature site which is undergoing an ongoing renovation programme. It is set on the edges of a forest under mature pines with 190 pitches arranged on sets of terraces. The pitches vary in size and 160 have 4A electricity. The site facilities are mainly close to the reception building. A small pool with a circular paddling pool is welcome after a hot days sightseeing and other site amenities include a tennis court and bar/restaurant. The nearest beach at Cala Montgó is 850 m. away and easily accessible on foot. A range of activities is on offer there, including sea kayaking and diving (introductory courses available in the site's pool).

Facilities	Directions
Bar. Restaurant. Takeaway. Shop. Play area. Swimming pool. Children's pool. Entertainment and activities in peak season. Club for children. Off site: Nearest beach 850 m. Fishing. Kayaking. Diving. **Open:** 30 May - 14 September.	Take exit 5 from the AP7 and the GI623 to L'Escala. Continue to Riells and Montgó. Site is on the right shortly before reaching Cala Montgó. GPS: N42:06.306 E03:09.502

Charges 2008

Per unit with 2 persons and electricity	€ 20,00 - € 38,50
extra person	€ 3,00 - € 5,00
child (5-10 yrs)	€ 1,00 - € 3,00

ES81700 Camping Valldaro

Apdo 57, avenida Castell d'Aro 63, E-17250 Platja d'Aro (Girona)

Tel: **972 817 515**. Email: **info@valldaro.com**

Valldaro is 600 m. back from the sea at Platja d'Aro, a small, bright resort with a long, wide beach and plenty of amusements. It is particularly pleasant during out of peak weeks and is popular with British and Dutch visitors. Like a number of other large Spanish sites, Valldaro has been extended and many pitches have been made larger, bringing them up to 85 sq. m. There are now 1,200 pitches with 650 available for tourers. The site is flat, with pitches in rows divided up by access roads. You will probably find space here even at the height of the season. The newer section has its own vehicle entrance (the nearest point to the beach) and can be reached via a footbridge; it is brought into use at peak times. It has some shade and its own toilet block, as well as a medium-sized swimming pool of irregular shape with a grassy sunbathing area and adjacent bar/snack bar and takeaway. The original pool (36 x 18 m.) is adjacent to the attractive Spanish-style restaurant which also offers takeaway fare. There are 400 permanent Spanish pitches and 150 mobile homes and chalets to rent, but these are in separate areas and do not impinge on the touring pitches.

Facilities

Four sanitary blocks are of a good standard and are well maintained. Child-size toilets. Washbasins (no cabins) and adjustable showers (temperature perhaps a bit variable). Two supermarkets and general shops. Two restaurants. Large bar. Swimming pools. New outdoor jacuzzi. Tennis. Minigolf with snack bar. Playgrounds. Sports ground. Children's club. Organised entertainment in season. Hairdresser. Internet. WiFi area (charge to use). Satellite TV. Gas supplies. Off site: Fishing, bicycle hire and golf 1 km. Riding 4 km.

Open: 14 March - 28 September.

Directions

Platja d'Aro is on the coast southeast of Girona. From Girona on the AP7/E15 take exit 7 to Sant Feliu on C65. On C65 at km. 313 take exit to Platja d'Aro (road number changes here to C31). In 200 m. at roundabout take GI 662 towards Platja d'Aro. Site is at km. 4 marker. If approaching from Palomas, access is via Platja d'Aro centre, exit on the GI 662 as the GI 662 cannot be accessed from the C31 southbound. GPS: N41:48.856 E03:02.622

Charges 2008

Per unit incl. 2 persons	€ 19,30 - € 43,00
extra person	€ 3,90 - € 6,50
child (3-12 yrs)	€ 2,60 - € 3,70
dog	€ 2,70

All plus 7% VAT. Discounts in low seasons.
No credit cards.
Camping Cheques accepted.

ES81010 Camping Playa Brava

Avenida del Grau 1, E-17256 Platja de Pals (Girona)

Tel: **972 636 894**. Email: **info@playabrava.com**

This is a pleasant site with an open feel which has access to a large sandy beach (200 m.) and a freshwater lagoon. On both you can enjoy watersports and you may launch your own boat. The ground is level and very grassy with shade provided for the 500 pitches by a mixture of conifer and broad-leaf trees. Electricity is provided (5A) and about a third of the pitches (75-85 sq. m.) have water and drainage. The air of spaciousness continues around the large swimming pool. There are no fences but huge grass sunbathing areas, the whole being overlooked by the restaurant terrace. The restaurant is very pleasant and offers a most reasonable menu of the day including wine. An energetic entertainment programme runs during July and August. There are many interesting things to explore in the area including La Bisbal – famous for the ceramics, Dali's Museum, the Roman ruins at Empuries Girona and many more. A green and pleasant family site.

Facilities

Five modern, fully equipped toilet blocks include facilities for disabled visitors. Washing machines and dryers. Motorcaravan service point. Bar/restaurant. Takeaway. Supermarket. Swimming pool. Tennis. Volleyball. 5-a-side soccer. Minigolf. Play area on grass. Fishing. Watersports on river and beach, including sheltered lagoon for windsurfing learners. Internet access. Satellite TV. ATM. Gas supplies. Torches required in some areas. Dogs are not accepted. Off site: Two 18-hole golf courses 1 km. Bicycle hire 3 km. Riding 5 km.

Open: 14 May - 18 September.

Directions

Platja de Pals is southeast of Girona on the coast. From the AP7/E15 at Girona take exit 6 towards Palamos on the C66. This road changes number to the C31 near La Bisbal. 7.5 km. past La Bisbal, exit to Pals on the GI 652. Follow signs for Platja de Pals. At El Masos take the 6502 east to the coast. Travel through Sa Piera (site signed). Site on left just before road ends at beach car park. GPS: N42:00.106 E03:11.621

Charges 2007

Per person	€ 2,00 - € 3,00
child (2-9 yrs)	free - € 2,00
senior (over 60 yrs)	free - € 3,00
pitch incl. electricity	€ 23,00 - € 38,00

All plus 7% VAT. Discount for longer stays in low season. No credit cards.

ES81000 Camping Inter-Pals

Avenida Mediterrania, E-17256 Platja de Pals (Girona)

Tel: **972 636 179**. Email: **interpals@interpals.com**

Set on sloping ground with tall pine trees providing shade and about 500 metres from the beach, Inter-Pals has 625 terraced pitches. It is sister site to no. ES8170 Valldaro. Arranged on level terraces, mostly with shade, some of the terraced pitches have views of the sea through the trees. The main entrance and its drive resembles a pretty village street as the bungalows are set on both sides of the street which is lined with traditional lamp posts. Continuing the village theme is a row of shops where you will find most camper's needs. The formal restaurant with good value menu and choice of takeaway overlooks the pools. The site is close to Platja de Pals which is a long sandy unspoilt stretch of beach, a discreet area, part of which is now an official naturist beach. The pretty town of Pals is close by along with a good golf course. The site will assist with touring plans of the area.

Facilities

Three well maintained toilet blocks include facilities for disabled campers. Laundry facilities. Gas supplies. Fridge/TV rental. Shops. Restaurant/bar. Pizzeria with dancing and entertainment area. Café/bar by entrance. Swimming pool. Tennis. Playground. Organised activities and entertainment in high season. Excursions. Watersports arranged. ATM. Internet access. Some breeds of dog are excluded (check with site). New mini adventure park. Medical centre. Torch useful. Off site: Fishing 200 m. Bicycle hire 500 m. Golf 1 km. Riding 10 km.

Open: 19 March - 2 October.

Directions

Site is on the road leading off the Torroella de Montgri-Bagur road north of Pals and going to Playa de Pals (Pals beach). GPS: N41:58.520 E03:11.590

Charges 2008

Per person	€ 4,00 - € 6,10
child (3-12 yrs)	€ 2,90 - € 3,60
pitch	€ 18,50 - € 32,10
small tent and car	€ 10,90 - € 16,00

Plus 7% VAT. Discounts for long stays in low season. No credit cards.
Camping Cheques accepted.

ES80900 Camping Cypsela

Ctra de Pals - Platja de Pals, E-17256 Platja de Pals (Girona)

Tel: **972 667 696**. Email: **info@cypsela.com**

This impressive, de-luxe site with lush vegetation and trees is very efficiently run. The main part of the camping area is pinewood, with 569 clearly marked touring pitches of varying categories on sandy gravel, all with electricity and some with full facilities. The 228 'Elite' pitches of 120 sq.m. are impressive. The site has many striking features, one of which is the sumptuous complex of sport facilities and amenities near the entrance. If you wish to travel to the beach there is a regular free bus service from the site. Cypsela is a busy, well administered site, only two kilometres from the sea, which we can thoroughly recommend, especially for families. The site has good quality fixtures and fittings, all kept clean and maintained to a high standard. All your needs will be catered for here. The gates are closed at night. Several tour operators use the site (257 pitches).

Facilities

Four sanitary blocks are of excellent quality with comprehensive cleaning schedules and solar heating. Three have washbasins in cabins and three have amazing children's rooms. Superb facilities for disabled people. Serviced launderette. Supermarket and shops. Restaurant, cafeteria and takeaway. Bar. Hairdresser. Swimming pools. Tennis. Squash. Football. Minigolf. Skating rink. Fitness room. Solarium. Air conditioned social/TV room. Barbecue and party area. Children's club. Comprehensive animation programme in season. Organised sports and games activities. Games room. Business and internet centre. Medical centre. Gas supplies. ATM. Dogs not accepted. Off site: Bicycle hire 150 m. Golf 1 km. Fishing 2 km.

Open: 15 May - 21 September.

Directions

Platja de Pals is southeast of Girona on the coast. From the AP7/E15 at Girona take exit 6 towards Palamos on the C66. This road changes number to the C31 near La Bisbal. 7.5 km. past La Bisbal, exit to Pals on the GI 652. Follow signs for Platja de Pals. At El Masos take the 6502 for 1 km. The main entrance is on the left between white metal fencing.

Charges 2008

Per person	€ 6,00
child (2-10 yrs)	€ 4,60
pitch acc. to season and services	€ 22,80 - € 61,50

ES80720 Camping Les Medes

Paratge Camp de L'Arbre, E-17258 L'Estartit (Girona)

Tel: **972 751 805**. Email: **campinglesmedes@cambrescat.es**

Les Medes is different from some of the 'all singing, all dancing' sites so popular along this coast and the friendly family of Pla-Coll are rightly proud of their award winning site and provide a very warm welcome. With just 172 pitches, the site is small enough for the owners to know their visitors and, being campers themselves, they have been careful in planning their top class facilities and are aware of environmental issues. The level, grassy pitches range in size from 60-80 sq.m. depending on your unit. All have electricity (5/10A) and the larger ones (around half) also have water and drainage. All are clearly marked in rows, but with no separation other than by the deciduous trees which provide summer shade. Set back from busy L'Estartit itself, it is only 800 m. to the nearest beach and a little train runs from near the site (June-Sept) to the town.

Facilities

Two modern spacious sanitary blocks can be heated and are extremely well maintained. Washbasins in cabins, top class facilities for disabled people and baby baths. Laundry facilities. Motorcaravan services. Bar with snacks. Good value restaurant (1/4-31/10). Shop. Outdoor swimming and paddling pools (15/6-15/9). Indoor pool with sauna, solarium (15/9-15/6). Masseur. Play area. TV room. Internet access and WiFi. Excursions (July/Aug). Diving activities arranged. Boules. Bicycle hire. Dogs only accepted at certain times - check with the site. Torches are useful. Off site: Riding 400 m. Fishing 800 m. Beach 800 m. Medes Natural Reserve 1.5 km. Strait 2 km. Golf 8 km.

Open: All year excl. November.

Directions

Site is signed from the main Torroella de Montgri - L'Estartit road GE641. Turn right after Camping Castel Montgri, at Joc's hamburger/pizzeria and follow signs. GPS: N42:02.900 E03:11.273

Charges 2007

Per person	€ 6,70
child (0-10 yrs)	€ 4,75
pitch	€ 15,00
electricity	€ 3,90

All plus 7% VAT. Discounts outside high season and special offers for low season longer stays. No credit cards.

This is just a sample of the campsites we have inspected and selected in Spain & Portugal. For more campsites and further information, please see the Alan Rogers Spain & Portugal guide.

ES81040 Camping Begur

Ctra d'Esclanya km 2, E-17255 Begur (Girona)

Tel: **972 623 201**. Email: **info@campingbegur.com**

The owners here have made a massive investment in making the site a pleasant place to spend some time. There are some good supporting facilities including a pleasant swimming pool at its centre. The bar and snack bar are part of this new pool complex and it has been well designed with terraces and sunbathing area. The touring areas are protected from the sun by mature trees which are all numbered and protected. The 317 pitches are informally arranged on sloping sandy ground (chocks useful). Most pitches have electricity (10A), water and drainage. A few mobile homes and apartments are scattered around the slopes. Environmental activities are encouraged including visits to the revolutionary water cleansing plant deep in the woods. There are many sporting facilities including a well equipped weight training room (free). A huge supermarket is just outside the gate, used by locals and on site there is a restaurant and a very pleasant outdoor café and bar overlooking the pool. The bays of the Costa Brava are just 1.5 km. away.

Facilities

Two modern toilet blocks are fully equipped and include really large showers. Excellent facilities for disabled campers. Baby bath. Washing machines and dryers. Motorcaravan services. Bar and snacks. Swimming pools (June-Sept). Table tennis. Boules. Weight training room. Play area. Some animation in high season. Children's entertainment in high season. Little farm with ponies, goat and chickens. Internet access. Off site: Restaurant and supermarket just outside gate. Village and beaches 1.5 km. Fishing 3 km. Golf 10 km. Riding 15 km.

Open: 1 April - 30 September.

Directions

From Girona take road east to La Bisbal and Palafrugell then Begur. Turn south towards Fornells, the site is well signed 3 km. south of Begur.

Charges 2007

Per person	€ 3,00 - € 5,70
child (3-10 yrs)	€ 1,40 - € 3,10
pitch with electricity	€ 8,80 - € 16,70
fully serviced	€ 10,70 - € 18,90

No credit cards.

CRA. D'ESCLANYÀ KM.2, 17255 BEGUR-COSTA BRAVA-SPAIN TEL. 972 623 201-FAX. 972 624 566 EMAIL: INFO@CAMPINGBEGUR.GPS:41.9404°N-3.1989° E

WWW.CAMPINGBEGUR.COM

ES81600 Camping Cala Gogo

Ctra S Feliu - Palamós km 46.5, Platja d'Aro, E-17251 Calonge (Girona)

Tel: **972 651 564**. Email: **calagogo@calagogo.es**

Cala Gogo is a large traditional campsite with a pleasant situation on a wooded hillside with mature trees giving shade to most pitches. The 917 shaded touring pitches varying in size are in terraced rows, some with artificial shade, all have 10A electricity and 250 have water and drainage. There may be road noise in eastern parts of the site. Some pitches are now right by the beach, the remainder are up to 800 m. uphill, but the 'Gua gua' tractor train, operating all season, takes people between the centre of site and beach and adds to the general sense of fun.

Facilities

Seven toilet blocks are of a high standard and are continuously cleaned. Some washbasins in private cabins. New laundry room. Motorcaravan services. Gas supplies. Supermarket. Shop. Restaurants and bars. Swimming and paddling pools (lifeguards). New playground. Crèche and babysitting (charged). Sports centre. Entertainment. Bicycle hire. Kayaks. Fishing. Internet and WiFi. Dogs not accepted mid June - end Aug. Off site: Bicycle hire and golf 4 km. Riding 10 km.

Open: 29 April - 24 September.

Directions

Sant Antoni de Calonge is southeast of Girona. Leave the AP7/E15 at exit 6. Take C66 towards Palomos which becomes the C31. Use the C31 (Girona - Palomos) to avoid Palomas town. Take the C253 coast road. Site is at km. 46.5 and 4 km. south of Palomas. GPS: N41:49.850 E03:04.948

Charges 2007

Per person	€ 3,30 - € 6,25
pitch incl. electricity (5A)	€ 10,20 - € 27,15

All plus 7% VAT. No credit cards.

ES81200 Kim's Camping

Font d'en Xeco, E-17211 Llafranc (Girona)

Tel: **972 301 156**. Email: **info@campingkims.com**

This attractive, terraced site (to which the owner has been welcoming guests for 50 years) is arranged on the wooded slopes of a narrow valley leading to the sea and there are many trees including huge eucalyptus. There are 350 grassy and partly shaded pitches, all with electricity (5A). Many of the larger pitches are on a plateau from which great views can be enjoyed. The terraced pitches are connected by winding drives, narrow in places. This is a pleasant place for holidays where you can enjoy the bustling atmosphere of the village and beach, while staying in a quieter environment. The site has an excellent swimming pool (with lifeguard) and children's pool, a bar, and a pleasant restaurant with 'al fresco' eating. An entertainment programme is provided. The site is under 1 km. from the resort of Llafranc. There is an outstanding view along the coastline and of the Pyrenees from Cap Sebastian close by. English and Dutch is spoken by the very friendly management and staff.

Facilities

All sanitary facilities are spotlessly clean and include a small new block and excellent toilet facilities for disabled visitors. Laundry facilities. Motorcaravan services. Gas supplies. Well stocked shop. Bar. Bakery and croissanterie. Cafe/restaurant (15/6-10/9). Swimming pools. Play areas and children's club. TV room. Excursions arranged – bus calls at site. Visits arranged to sub-aqua schools for all levels of diving (high season). Torches required. WiFi. Off site: Beach, fishing, sailing and bicycle hire 500 m. Llafranc 1 km. Riding 4 km. Golf 9 km.

Open: Easter - 30 September.

Directions

Llafranc is southeast of Palafrugell. Turn off the Palafrugell - Tamariu road at turn (GIV 6542) signed 'Llafranc, Club de Tennis'. Site is on right 1 km. further on. GPS: N41:54.032 E03:11.361

Charges 2007

Per person	€ 2,50 - € 6,00
child (3-10 yrs)	€ 1,00 - € 3,00
pitch incl. electricity	€ 12,00 - € 26,00

Plus 7% VAT. Discounts for long stays and for senior citizens.

1st. CATEGORY E-17211 LLAFRANC
Tel: (34) 972 30 11 56 and 61   Fax: (34) 972 61 08 94
Internet: http://www.campingkims.com E-mail: info@campingkims.com

One of the most beautifully situated campsites on the Costa Brava in a landscaped green zone belt, at only 500 metres from the sea, with two swimming pools, children's playground, bar, restaurant, supermarket. Only 325 sites (60-70-120 sq.m) on a surface of 62,500 sq.m. Bungalows and mobile homes for hire

Open: Easter – 30.9

1ᴬ CATEGORIA ★★★

ES81300 Camping Internacional de Calonge

Ctra San Feliu/Guixols - Palamós, E-17251 Calonge (Girona)

Tel: **972 651 233**. Email: **info@intercalonge.com**

This spacious, well laid out site has access to the fine beach by a footbridge over the coast road, or you can take the little road train as the site is on very sloping ground. Calonge is a family site with two good sized pools on different levels, a paddling pool plus large sunbathing areas. The site's 800 pitches are on terraces and all have electricity (5A) with 167 available for winter use. A large proportion are suitable for touring units (the remainder for tents) being set on attractively landscaped terraces. Access to some pitches may be a little difficult.

Facilities

Generous sanitary provision in new or renovated blocks include some washbasins in cabins. One block is heated in winter. Laundry facilities. Motorcaravan services. Gas supplies. Shop, Bar/restaurant, Patio bar (pizza and takeaway)(all 15/3-19/10). Swimming pools (15/3-12/10). Playground. Electronic games. Rather noisy disco two nights a week (but not late). Bicycle hire. Tennis. Hairdresser. ATM. Internet. Torches necessary in some areas. Off site: Fishing 300 m. Golf 3 km. Riding 10 km. Supermarket 500 m.

Open: All year.

Directions

Site is on the inland side of the coast road between Palamos and Platja d'Aro. Take the C31 south to the 661 at Calonge. At Calonge follow signs to the C253 towards Platja d'Aro and on to site which is well signed. GPS: N41:50.000 E03:05.050

Charges 2008

Per person	€ 3,65 - € 7,55
child (3-10 yrs)	€ 1,85 - € 4,25
pitch for caravan or motorcaravan with electricity and water	€ 14,80 - € 33,25

All plus 7% VAT. No credit cards.

ES80740 Camping Paradis

Avenida de Montgó 260, E-17130 L'Escala (Girona)

Tel: **972 770 200**. Email: **info@campingparadis.com**

If you prefer a quieter site out of the very busy resort of L'Escala then this site is an excellent option. This large, family run site has a dynamic owner Marti, who speaks excellent English. The site is divided by the beach access road and has its own private access to the very safe and unspoilt beach. There are 358 pitches, all with electricity (10A), some on sloping ground although the pitches themselves tend to be flat. Established pine trees provide shade for most places with more coverage on the western side of the site. Non-stop maintenance ensures that all facilities at this site are of a high standard. There are three swimming pools, the largest with an idyllic and most unusual setting on the top of a cliff overlooking the Bay of Roses. A CCTV security system monitors the pools and general security from a purpose built centre.

Facilities

Modern, fully equipped sanitary blocks are kept very clean. Washing machines and dryers. Shop, extensive modern complex of restaurants, bars and takeaways (all open all season). Swimming pools (1/5-20/9). Pool bar. Play areas. Fishing. Kayak hire. Organised activities for children in high season. ATM machine. Private access to beach. Off site: Cala Montgo beach 100 m. with a charming bay of soft sand offering all manner of watersports, pretty restaurants and a disco in season. Road train service to town centre from outside site. Riding 2 km. Golf 10 km.

Open: 18 March - 15 October.

Directions

Leave autopista A7 at exit 5 heading for Viladimat, then L'Escala. Site is well signed from town centre. Follow signs for Montgo and site is south of town beside the coast.

Charges 2007

Per person	€ 2,80 - € 5,00
child (3-10yrs)	€ 2,00 - € 3,50
pitch	€ 10,70 - € 23,60
electricity	€ 3,40

Plus 7% VAT. No credit cards.

ES82100 Camping Tucan

Ctra de Blanes - Lloret, E-17310 Lloret de Mar (Girona)

Tel: **972 369 965**. Email: **info@campingtucan.com**

Situated on the busy Costa Brava near Lloret de Mar, Camping Tucan is well placed to access all the attractions of the area. Views over the mountains are mixed with views of the nearby town. The 250 good size pitches all have electricity, and are laid out in a herring-bone pattern with areas dedicated to singles, families with young children and couples who enjoy the quiet. Pitches are on terraces, flat surfaced with gravel and many are shaded. Tucan is a lively site with a variety of activities including an animation programme for children and modest entertainment at night. Activities on the site centre around the pleasant pool, bar, restaurant and terrace all of which are close to reception. There is a separate, largely independent area with facilities for young people at the rear of the site.

Facilities

Two modern toilet blocks include washbasins with hot water and facilities for disabled visitors, although access is difficult. All very clean when seen. Washing machine. Gas supplies. Shop. Busy bar and good restaurant. Takeaway. Swimming pools and indoor solarium. Playground and fenced play area for toddlers. TV in bar. Bicycle hire. Animation in high season. Miniclub. Off site: Town 500 m. Nearest beach 600 m. Riding 1 km. Golf 4 km.

Open: 1 April - 30 September.

Directions

From A7/E4, A19 or N11 Girona - Barcelona roads take an exit for Lloret de Mar. Site is 1 km. west of the town, well signed and is at the base of the hill off the roundabout. The entrance can get congested in busy periods. GPS: N41:41.832 E02:49.310

Charges 2007

Per person	€ 4,40 - € 6,95
child (1-9 yrs)	€ 3,30 - € 4,70
pitch	€ 4,40 - € 6,95
electricity	€ 3,40 - € 4,40
animal	€ 1,80

ES82000 Camping Cala Llevadó

Ctra GI-682 de Tossa a Lloret, pk. 18,9, E-17320 Tossa de Mar (Girona)

Tel: **972 340 314**. Email: **info@calallevado.com**

For splendour of position Cala Llevadó can compare with almost any in this book. A beautifully situated cliff-side site, it has fine views of the sea and coast below. It is shaped something like half a bowl with steep slopes. High up in the site with a superb aspect, is the attractive restaurant/bar with a large terrace overlooking the pleasant swimming pool. There are terraced, flat areas for caravans and tents (with electricity) on the upper levels of the two slopes, with a great many individual pitches for tents scattered around the site. Some of these pitches have fantastic settings and views. There is usually car parking close to these pitches, although in some areas cars may be required to park separately. The steepness of the site would make access difficult for disabled people or those with limited mobility. One beach is for all manner of watersports within a buoyed area and there is a sub-aqua diving school. Some other pleasant little coves can also be reached by climbing down on foot (with care!). Cala Llevadó is luxurious and has much character and the atmosphere is informal and very friendly. Many of the 577 touring pitches are available for caravans with 10A electricity. There are a few tour operator pitches (45) and 26 bungalows. The site is peacefully situated but only five minutes away from the busy resort of Tossa – take a look at the town where the castle is beautifully lit by night or if you visit in July enjoy the many lively fiestas. The botanic garden on the site is charming with many of the plants, flowers and trees of the region and includes an historic windmill.

Facilities

Four very well equipped toilet blocks are immaculately maintained and well spaced around the site. Baby baths. Laundry facilities. Motorcaravan services. Gas supplies. Fridge hire. Large supermarket. Restaurant/bar (5/5-28/9). Swimming and paddling pools. Three play areas. Botanic garden. Entertainment for children (4-12 yrs). Sailing, water ski and windsurfing school. Fishing. Excursions. Internet access and WiFi. Torches definitely needed in some areas. Off site: Bicycle hire 3 km. Large complex adjacent for sports, activities and swimming.

Open: 1 May - 30 September, including all amenities.

Directions

Cala Llevadó is southeast of Girona on the coast. Leave the AP7/E15 at exit 7 to the C65 Sant Feliu road and then take C35 southeast to the GI 681 to Tossa de Mare. Site is signed off the GI 682 Lloret - Tossa road at km. 18.9, about 3 km. from Tossa. Route avoids difficult coastal road. GPS: N41:42.769 E02:54.374

Charges 2007

Per person	€ 5,00 - € 7,50
child (4-12 yrs)	€ 3,50 - € 5,00
pitch incl. car	€ 7,50 - € 13,50
Plus 7% VAT.	

sènia

Good campings.
Good people.

CALIDAD TURISTICA

Sant Pere Pescador

Girona

Rupit

Lloret de Mar

Pineda de Mar

arcelona

Online Booking < < <

w w w . s e n i a . b i z

CAMPING CABALLO DE MAR

CAMPING TUCAN

CAMPING RUPIT

CAMPING RIU

Passeig Marítim, s/n	Ctra. de Blanes a Lloret	Ctra. de Vic a Olot
Apdo. Correos 3	Apdo. Correos 1171	08569 Rupit
08397 Pineda de Mar	17310 Lloret de Mar	Barcelona • Spain
Barcelona • Spain	Girona • Spain	tel. +34 938 522 153
tel. +34 937 671 706	tel. +34 972 369 965	fax +34 937 671 615
fax +34 937 671 615	fax +34 972 360 079	
info@caballodemar.com	info@campingtucan.com	info@rupit.com
www.caballodemar.com	www.campingtucan.com	www.rupit.com

Ctra. de la Platja, s/n
17470 Sant Pere Pescador
Girona • Spain
tel. +34 972 520 216
fax. +34 972 550 469

info@campingriu.com
www.campingriu.com

GPS			
N	41°	37'	02"
E	02°	40'	39"

GPS			
N	41°	41'	832"
E	02°	49'	310"

GPS			
N	42°	01'	51"
E	02°	27'	53"

GPS			
N	42°	11'	247"
E	03°	05'	340"

ES83920 Camping El Garrofer

Ctra 246 km 39, E-08870 Sitges (Barcelona)

Tel: **938 941 780**. Email: **info@garroferpark.com**

This large, pine covered site, alongside fields of vines, is 800 m. from the beach, close to the pleasant town of Sitges. It has over 500 pitches of which 380 with 6A electricity are for tourers, including 28 with water used for large motorcaravans. Everything is kept clean and the pitches are tidy and shaded. The amenity buildings are along the site perimeter next to the road which absorbs most of the road noise. The permanent pitches are grouped in a completely separate area. A varied menu is offered in the cosy restaurant with a small terrace. Everything is cooked to perfection and complemented with the wines of the Penedes DO made hereabouts (the restaurant has a local reputation and is used by non campers – the menu of the day is great value). A traditional bar is alongside and from here you can see the pretty mosaic clad play area (the 'Gaudi touch' which is also evident elsewhere). An ambitious animation programme is conducted for children in summer. Late evening Salsa classes were offered for adults when we visited. A small swimming pool with sunbathing areas is welcome on hot summer days or you can walk to the very pleasant beach.

Facilities

Two of the three sanitary blocks have been refurbished and provide roomy showers and special bright facilities for children. Separate baby room with bath. Good facilities for disabled campers. Laundry. Bar/restaurant. Shop (reception in low season). Swimming pool. Golf packages. Practice golf. Tennis. Play area for older children and fenced play area for toddlers. Bicycle hire. Boules. Off site: Bus from outside site to Barcelona. Golf, riding and fishing 500 m.

Open: 17 January - 17 December.

Directions

Sitges is 30 km. southwest of Barcelona. From A16/C32 autopista take exit 26 towards Vilanova and St Pere Ribes. From Tarragona, go under autopista, around roundabout and back to roundabout on the other side to pick up site sign (towards Sitges). Look for the flags.

Charges 2007

Per person	€ 2,78 - € 4,89
child (1-9 yrs)	€ 1,89 - € 3,78
pitch incl. electricity	€ 14,92 - € 19,27
Plus 7% VAT.	

CAMPING EL GARROFER

C-31 (ex C-246a) km.39
E-8870- Sitges
Open: 17.1-17.12
Direct access to the sea (10 min)
Special area for motorhome with water connection and outlet
Mobile home for handicaped
Direct bus connection to Barcelona, every hour
Airport-Sitges
Tel. (34) 938941780 - Fax. (34) 938110623
www.garroferpark.com
info@garroferpark.com

BUNGALOWS DISCOUNT FOR PENSIONERS except. july and august

ES84820 Camping La Pineda de Salou

Ctra Costa Tarragona - Salou km 5, E-43481 La Pineda (Tarragona)

Tel: **977 373 080**. Email: **info@campinglapineda.com**

La Pineda is just outside Salou towards Tarragona and this site is just 300 m. from the Aquapark and 2.5 km. from Port Aventura. There is some noise from this road. The site has a fair-sized swimming pool adjoining a smaller, heated one, open from mid June, behind large hedges close to the entrance. A large terrace has sun loungers, and various entertainment aimed at young people is provided in season. The 366 flat pitches are mostly shaded and of about 70 sq.m.

Facilities

Sanitary facilities are mature but clean with baby bath, dishwashing and laundry sinks. Facilities for disabled visitors. Washing machines. Gas supplies. Shop, restaurant and snacks, swimming pools (all 1/7-31/8). Bar (all season). Small TV room. Bicycle hire. Games room. Playground. Entertainment (1/7-30/8). Torches may be required. Off site: Beach and fishing 400 m. Golf 12 km.

Open: All year.

Directions

From A7 exit 35 just southwest of Tarragona follow signs to La Pineda and Port Aventura then campsite signs appear. GPS: N41:05.310 E01:10.947

Charges 2007

Per person	€ 4,60 - € 6,70
child (1-10 yrs)	€ 3,10 - € 5,00
pitch incl. car and electricity	€ 15,10 - € 34,20
All plus 7% VAT.	

ES83900 Camping Vilanova Park

Ctra de l'Arboc km 2.5, E-08800 Vilanova i la Geltru (Barcelona)

Tel: **938 933 402**. Email: **info@vilanovapark.es**

Sitting on the terrace of the bustling but comfortable restaurant at Vilanova Park, it is difficult to believe that in 1908 this was a Catalan farm and then, quite lacking in trees, it was known as 'Rock Farm'. Since then imaginative planting has led to there being literally thousands of trees and gloriously colourful shrubs making a most attractive, large campsite, with an impressive range of high quality amenities and facilities open all year. There are 248 marked pitches for touring units in separate areas. All have 6A electricity, 133 also have water and some larger pitches (100 sq.m.) also have drainage. The terrain, hard surfaced and mostly on very gently sloping ground, has many trees and considerable shade. At present there are 865 pitches with a significant proportion occupied by bungalows and chalets carefully designed to fit into the environment. The site is used by tour operators (106 pitches). The really good amenities include a new second pool higher up in the site with marvellous views across the town to the sea and an indoor pool, sauna, jacuzzi and gym. Here there is also a second, more intimate restaurant for that special romantic dinner overlooking the twinkling evening lights. The original pool has water jets and a coloured floodlit fountain playing at night time, which complement the dancing and entertainment taking place on the stage in the courtyard overlooking the pool. An unusual attraction is a Nature Park and mini-zoo with deer and bird life, which has very pleasant picnic areas and views. There is a good excursion programme. There is also a transfer service from both Barcelona and Reus airports should you fancy taking advantage of the off season offers in the site's own accommodation.

Facilities

All toilet blocks are of excellent quality, can be heated and have washbasins (over half in cabins) with free hot water, and others of standard type with cold water. Serviced laundry. Motorcaravan services. Supermarket. Restaurants. Bar with simple meals (all year). Swimming pools (outdoor 1/4-15/10, indoor all year). Wellness centre including sauna, jacuzzi and gym. Play areas. Sports field. Games room. Bicycle hire. Tennis. ATM and exchange facilities. Off site: Fishing 4 km. Golf 5 km. Buses hourly in the main season. Vilanova town and beach are 4 km.

Open: All year.

Directions

Site is 4 km. northwest of Vilanova i la Geltru towards L'Arboc (BV2115). From the A7 Tarragona - Barcelona take exit 29 onto C15 to Vilanova, then C31 El Vendrell road (Km. 153) then onto BV2115.

Charges 2008

Per pitch incl. caravan/tent, car and electricity	€ 17,15 - € 28,70
with water	€ 20,15 - € 31,50
extra person	€ 3,50 - € 6,30
child (4-12 yrs)	€ 2,10 - € 3,85

Camping Cheques accepted.

Situated in a very quiet area, 50 km south of Barcelona in the wine and cava region of Catalonia. Very modern installations. 2 enormous swimming pools (1.000 m²) and paddling pools. Multicolouredfountain with water jets. Excellent restaurant in old Catalan mansion. Al facilities of a first class site. Children programmes and organised leisure. Private pine trees and palm covered park (40 ha). Ideal climate. Bus service to the beach. Golf at 1 km.

Special offers for old age pensioners from September till June on sites and Bungalows (100 with air-cond.).

Highway Barcelona-Tarragona, AP-7 exit 29; coming from Tarragona to Barcelona exit 31, direction Barcelona C-32, exit 16.

GOLF TOURNEMENT 1KM. IN VILANOVA PARK
YACHT HARBOUR IN VILANOVA I LA GELTRÚ
COVERED SWIMMING POOL AND SPA
OPEN THROUGHOUT THE YEAR

Wi Fi ZONE

Apartado 64 · E-08800 Vilanova i la Geltrú (Barcelona) · Tel.: (34) 93 893 34 02 · Fax: (34) 93 893 55 28
www.vilanovapark.es · info@vilanovapark.es · reservas@vilanovapark.es

Check real time availability and at-the-gate prices...
www.**alanrogers**.com

ES84810 Camping Cambrils Park

Avenida Mas Clariana s/n., E-43850 Cambrils (Tarragona)
Tel: 977 351 031. Email: mail@cambrilspark.es

This is a superb site for a camping holiday providing for all family members, whatever their age. A drive lined with palm trees and flowers leads from a large, very smart round reception building at this impressive modern site. Sister site to no. ES8480, it is set 500 metres back from the excellent beach in a generally quiet setting with outstanding facilities. The 684 slightly sloping, grassy pitches of around 90 sq.m. are numbered and separated by trees. All have 10A electricity, 55 have water and waste water connections, some having more shade than others. The marvellous central lagoon pool complex with three pools and water slides is the main focus of the site with a raised wooden 'poop deck' sunbathing area with palm surrounds that doubles as an entertainment stage at night. There is a huge bar/terrace area for watching the magnificent floodlit spectacles, along with an excellent restaurant in the old farmhouse with an adjacent takeaway. By day there is a small bar at a lower level in the pool where you can enjoy a cool drink from submerged stools, plus a dryer version on the far side of the bar or just relax on the spacious grass sunbathing areas. There are a number of tour operator pitches and attractive thatched chalets. A fabulous jungle theme children's pool is nearer the entrance – they love it, especially the elephants! An extra pool for adults has been added here, along with a snack bar.

Facilities

Four excellent sanitary buildings provide some washbasins in cabins, superb units for disabled visitors and immaculate, decorated baby sections. Dishwashing and laundry sinks. Huge serviced laundry. Motorcaravan services. Car wash. Restaurant. Takeaway. Huge supermarket, souvenir shop and 'panaderia' (fresh-baked bread and croissants). Swimming pools with lifeguards. Minigolf. Tennis. Multi-games court. Petanque. Animation and entertainment all season. Miniclub. Internet café. Medical centre. ATM. Gas supplies. Dogs are not accepted. Off site: Beach 500 m. Fishing, bicycle hire 400 m. Riding 3 km. Port Aventura theme park 4 km. Golf 7 km.

Open: 7 April - 8 October.

Directions

Site is about 1.5 km. west of Salou. From the A7 take exit 35 and at roundabout take signs for Cambrils. Follow new dual carriageway around the back of Salou and site is signed at last roundabout towards Cambrils. GPS: N41:04.584 E01:06.527

Charges 2007

Per person	€ 6,00
child (4-12 yrs)	€ 4,00
pitch incl. electricity	€ 13,00 - € 41,00
pitch with water and waste water	€ 15,00 - € 43,00

All plus 7% VAT. Special offers, plus low season discounts for pensioners.
Camping Cheques accepted.

ES84700 Camping La Siesta

Calle Ctra Norte 37, E-43840 Salou (Tarragona)
Tel: 977 380 852. Email: info@camping-lasiesta.com

The palm bedecked entrance of La Siesta is only 250 m. from the pleasant sandy beach and close to the life of the resort of Salou. The site is divided into 470 pitches which are large enough and have electricity (10A), with smaller ones for tents. Many pitches are provided with artificial shade and within some there is one box for the tent or caravan and a shared one for the car. There is considerable shade from the trees and shrubs that are part of the site's environment. In high season, the siting of units is carried out by the friendly management. Young campers are located separately to the rear of the site. The town is popular with British and Spanish holidaymakers and has just about all that a highly developed Spanish resort can offer. For those who do not want to share the busy beach, there is a large, free swimming pool which is elevated above pitch level. The restaurant, which overlooks the good-sized pool, has a comprehensive menu and wine list, competing well with the town restaurants. A bar is alongside with TV and a large terrace, part of which is given over to entertainment in high season. A surprisingly large supermarket caters for most needs in season.

Facilities

Three bright and clean sanitary blocks provide very reasonable facilities. Motorcaravan services. Supermarket. Various vending machines. Self-service restaurant and bar with cooked dishes to take away. Dancing some evenings till 11 pm. Swimming pool (300 sq.m. open all season). Playground. Medical service daily in season. ATM point. Torches may be required. Off site: Many shops, restaurants and bars near. Port Aventura is close. Bicycle hire 200 m. Fishing 500 m. Riding and golf 6 km.

Open: 14 March - 3 November.

Directions

Leave A7 at exit 35 for Salou. Site is signed off the Tarragona/Salou road and from the one way system in the town of Salou. The site is in the town so keep a sharp eye for the small signs.

Charges 2007

Per person	€ 4,15 - € 7,90
child (4-9 yrs)	€ 3,10 - € 4,10
pitch	€ 3,10 - € 15,80
electricity	€ 2,90 - € 3,40

All plus 7% VAT. No credit cards.

Cambrils • Costa Daurada • Espanya

The only luxury camping on the Costa Daurada

CAMPING RESORT
Cambrils Park ★★★★★ LUXE

Av. Mas Clariana s/n • CAMBRILS
📞 Camping   +34 977 35 10 31
📞 Bungalow +34 977 38 90 04
   Fax   +34 977 35 22 10

@ mail@cambrilspark.es
   www.cambrilspark.es
✉ Apartat de Correus 123
   43840 SALOU • Tarragona • España

Online   Booking   —   www.cambrilspark.es

ES85080 Camping Poboleda

Placa de les Casetes s/n, E-43376 Poboleda (Tarragona)

Tel: **977 827197**. Email: **poboleda@campingsonline.com**

Time stands still at this unique site hidden away in a corner of the village, watched over by La Morera de Montsant, a peak of the Serra del Montsant. Situated among olive groves, yet almost in the heart of the lovely old village of Poboleda, it is an idyllic site for tents, small caravans and motorcaravans. Large units may have problems negotiating the narrow village streets. The 151 pitches of 80 sq.m. are set under olive and almond trees. Fairly level and 70 with 4A electricity, they provide a peaceful haven broken only by the peal of church bells or bird song. The young manager is enthusiastic and proud of the facilities offered which are quite unexpected and special. Behind the modern reception is a traditional, comfortably furnished room with piano and TV, which doubles as a peaceful cool area for relaxing if it is too hot on the terrace. Here you can have breakfast or order a drink. The village is on the doorstep for other needs. The mellow terraced pool area is a lovely surprise and very welcome, as is the tennis court. There is plenty to do, walking or climbing, visiting the region's vineyards and enjoying the local cuisine. A must to visit is the monastery of Poblet nearby.

Facilities

One small block, open all year, is fully equipped, as is a larger block open for high season. Shower for children. Facilities for disabled people (key). Dishwashing and laundry sinks. Laundry service. Breakfast can be ordered. Bar. Swimming pool (24/6-11/9). Tennis. Boules. Reception has tourist information, postcards and basic bits and pieces. Off site: Beach and Port Aventura 30 km. Bicycle hire 10 km. Fishing 12 km.

Open: All year.

Directions

Bypass Reus (west of Tarragona) on N420. After Borges del Camp pick up C242, signed Alforja. Continue over Coll d'Alforja. Watch for left turn (T702) for Poboleda. Continue for 6 km. to village. Watch for signs and through narrow village streets. Not for large units. GPS: N41:14.000 E00:50.410

Charges 2007

Per person	€ 5,00
child (under 10 yrs)	€ 4,50
pitch incl. car and electricity	€ 14,00 - € 15,00

C∧mping
Poboleda

Plaça les Casetes, s/n
Tel./Fax: (34) 977 827 197
E-43376 Poboleda
(PRIORAT- TARRAGONA)

Quietly situated site in the picturesque village Poboleda (region of the Priorato wines). At the foot of the mountain Montsant, near Scala Dei and near the monastery of Poblet. At 30 km from Port Aventura. 80 m² sites, petanque, tennis etc.

Landscape – nature – climbing
adventure sports - culture – gastronomy and good wines

ES84830 Camping Tamarit Park

N340 km 1172, Tamarit, E-43008 Tarragona (Tarragona)

Tel: **977 650 128**. Email: **tamaritpark@tamarit.com**

This is a marvellous, beach-side site, attractively situated at the foot of Tamarit castle at one end of a superb one kilometre long beach of fine sand. Parts are landscaped with lush Mediterranean palms and shrubs; other areas have natural pine shade, all home to mischievous red squirrels. The 694 pitches, 50 of which are virtually on the beach, are marked out on hard sand and grass and some are attractively separated by green vegetation which provides good shade. There are about 120 tour operator pitches, a number of seasonal pitches and about 120 bungalows. All have 6A electricity.

Facilities

Sanitary blocks (one heated) provide good facilities. The showers have push button control for hot water with tap controlled cold. Private bathrooms to rent. Laundry facilities. Motorcaravan services. Gas supplies. Shop, bar/restaurant and takeaway. Swimming pool (15/5-15/10). Tennis. Minigolf. Playground. Animation in season. Fishing. Internet. Barbecues not permitted on pitches. Off site: Riding 1 km. Bicycle hire 2 km. Golf 8 km.

Open: 30 March - 15 October.

Directions

From A7 take exit 32 (Tarragona) and continue for 4.5 km. At roundabout (km. 1172 marker) turn back towards Atafulla/Tamarit and after 200 m. turn right to Tamarit. Take care over railway bridge, then sharp right. Site 1 km. GPS: N41:07.943 E01:21.652

Charges 2007

Per person	€ 4,50 - € 5,00
pitch acc. to size and season	€ 17,00 - € 48,00
All plus 7% VAT.	

ES84100 Camping Playa Bara

Ctra N340 km 1183, E-43883 Roda de Bará (Tarragona)

Tel: **977 802 701**. Email: **info@barapark.es**

This is a most impressive, family owned site near the beach, which has been carefully designed and developed. On entry you find yourself in a beautifully sculptured, tree-lined drive with an accompanying aroma of pine and woodlands and the sound of waterfalls close by. Considering its size, with over 850 pitches, it is still a very green and relaxing site with an immense range of activities. It is well situated with a 50 m. walk to a long sandy beach via a tunnel under the railway (some noise) to a new promenade with palms and a quality beach bar and restaurant. Much care with planning and in the use of natural stone; palms and flowering plants gives a pleasing tropical appearance to all aspects of the site. The owners have excelled themselves in the design of the impressive terraced Roman-style pool complex, which is the central feature of the site. This complex is really amazing. Sunbathe on the pretty terraces or sip a drink whilst seated at the bar stools submerged inside one of the pools or enjoy the panorama over the sea from the rooftop spa or the upper Roman galley bar surrounded by stylish friezes. An extremely well equipped gym with a dedicated instructor and a massage service. A separate amphitheatre seats 2,000 and is used to stage very professional entertainment in season. Pitches vary in size and are being progressively enlarged; the older ones terraced and well shaded with pine trees, the newer ones more open, with a variety of trees and bushes forming separators. All have electricity (5A) and a sink with water.

Facilities

Excellent, fully equipped toilet blocks include private cabins and excellent facilities for children and new block for disabled visitors. Private facilities to hire. Superb launderette. Motorcaravan service points. Supermarket and several other shops. Full restaurant. Large bar with simpler meals and takeaway. Three other bars and pleasant bar/restaurant on beach. Swimming pools. Jacuzzi/hydro-massage. Fronton and tennis (floodlit). Junior club. Sports area. Windsurfing school. Gym. Massage. Petanque. Minigolf. Fishing. ATM. Hairdresser. Internet room. Flights and excursions booked. WiFi. Off site: Bicycle hire 2 km. Riding 6 km. Golf 8 km.

Open: 7 March - October, with all amenities.

Directions

From the A7 take exit 31. Site entrance is at the 1183 km. marker on the main N340 just opposite the Arco de Bara Roman monument from which it takes its name. GPS: N41:10.200 E01:28.100

Charges 2007

Per person	€ 3,00 - € 9,40
child (1-9 yrs)	€ 2,00 - € 6,60
pitch	€ 3,50 - € 9,40
electricity	€ 3,20

All plus 7% VAT. Low season reductions for pensioners and all sports charges reduced by 90%. No credit cards.

ES84800 Camping & Bungalows Sanguli

Prolongacion Calle, Apdo de Correos 123, E-43840 Salou (Tarragona)

Tel: **977 381 641**. Email: **mail@sanguli.es**

Sanguli is a superb site boasting excellent pools and ambitious entertainment. Owned, developed and managed by a local Spanish family, it provides for all the family with everything open when the site is open. There are 1,041 pitches of varying size (75-90 sq.m.) and all have electricity. About 155 are used by tour operators and 205 for bungalows. A wonderful selection of trees, palms and shrubs provides natural shade. The good sandy beach is little more than 100 metres across the coast road and a small railway crossing (a little noise). Although large, Sanguli maintains a quality family atmosphere due to the efforts of the very keen and efficient staff. The owners are striving to achieve the 'Garden of Eden' that is their dream. There are three very attractive pool areas, one (heated) near the entrance with a grassy sunbathing area partly shaded and a second deep one with water slides that forms part of the excellent sports complex (with fitness centre, tennis courts, minigolf and football practice area). The third pool is the central part of the amphitheatre area at the top of the site which includes an impressive Roman style building with huge portals, containing a bar and restaurant with terraces. An amphitheatre seats 2,000 campers and treats them to very professional free nightly entertainment (1/5-30/9). All the pools have adjacent amenity areas and bars. A real effort is made to cater for the young including teenagers with a 'Hop Club' (entertainment for 13-17 year olds), along with an internet room. Located near the centre of Salou, the site can offer the attractions of a busy resort while still being private and it is only 3 km. from Port Aventura. This is a large, professional site providing something for all the family, but still capable of providing peace and quiet for those looking for it.

Facilities

The quality sanitary facilities are constantly improved and are always exceptional, including many individual cabins with en-suite facilities. A new block also has excellent facilities for babies. All are kept very clean. Launderette with service. Motorcaravan services. Bars and restaurant with takeaway. Swimming pools. Jacuzzi. Fitness centre. Sport complex. Fitness room (charged). Playgrounds including adventure play area. Miniclub, teenagers club. Internet room. Upmarket minigolf. First-aid room. Gas supplies. Off site: Fishing and bicycle hire 100 m. Riding 3 km. Golf 6 km. Resort entertainment.

Open: 14 March - 2 November.

Directions

On west side of Salou about 1 km. from the centre, site is well signed from the coast road to Cambrils and from the other town approaches.

Charges 2007

Per person	€ 6,00
child (4-12 yrs)	€ 4,00
pitch incl. electricity	€ 13,00 - € 37,00
incl. water	€ 13,00 - € 43,00

All plus 7% VAT. Less 25-45% outside high season for longer stays.
Special long stay offers for senior citizens.

ES85360 Camping Caravanning Ametlla Village Platja

Apdo 240, Paraje Santes Creus, E-43860 Ametlla de Mar (Tarragona)

Tel: **977 267 784**. Email: **info@campingametlla.com**

This site within a protected area has been well thought out and is startling in the quality of service provided, the finish and the materials used in construction. The 373 pitches are on a terraced hillside above colourful coves with shingle beaches and two small associated lagoons (with a protected fish species). The many bungalows here have been tastefully incorporated. There are great views, particularly from the friendly restaurant. There is some train noise. The site is used by tour operators (30 pitches). It is a very good site for families or for just relaxing.

Facilities

Three really good toilet blocks. Some private cabins with WC and washbasin, plus others with WC, basin and shower. Motorcaravan services. Gas supplies. Supermarket (21/3-30/9; small shop incl. bread at other times). Good restaurant with snack menu and bar with TV (21/3-30/9). Swimming pool. Sub-aqua diving. Kayaking. Fishing. Children's club and play area. Fitness room. Bicycle hire. Entertainment (July/Aug). Barbecue area. Fishing. Off site: Boat launching 3 km. Golf 15 km. Riding 20 km. Theme parks.

Open: All year.

Directions

From A7/E15 (Barcelona - Valencia) take exit 39 for L'Ametlla de Mar. Follow numerous large white signs on reaching village and site is 2.5 km. south of the village.

Charges 2008

Per person	€ 2,37 - € 5,64
child (under 10 yrs)	€ 1,94 - € 4,61
pitch incl. electricity	€ 9,54 - € 20,19

All plus 7% VAT. Less for longer stays, especially in low season.

Paseo Miramar–Plaza Venus • SALOU
Camping +34 977 38 16 41
Bungalow +34 977 38 90 05
Fax +34 977 38 46 16
@ mail@sanguli.es
www.sanguli.es
Apartat de Correus 123
43840 SALOU • Tarragona • España

Online Booking: www.sanguli.es

Luxurious holidays at the Costa Daurada

Salou • Costa Daurada • España

ES85300 Playa Montroig Camping Resort
See advertisement on the back cover.

Aptdo 3, N340 km 1136, E-43300 Montroig (Tarragona)

Tel: **977 810 637**. Email: **info@playamontroig.com**

What a superb site! Playa Montroig is about 30 kilometres beyond Tarragona set in its own tropical gardens with direct access to a very long soft sand beach. The main part of the site lies between the sea, road and railway (as at other sites on this coast, there is some train noise) with a huge underpass. The site is divided into spacious, marked pitches with excellent shade provided by a variety of lush vegetation including very impressive palms set in wide avenues. There are 1,950 pitches, all with electricity and 330 with water and drainage. Some 48 pitches are directly alongside the beach. Member of Leading Campings Group. They are somewhat expensive and extremely popular. The site has many outstanding features: there is an excellent pool complex (one heated for children). The restaurant serves traditional Catalunian fare (seats 150) and overlooks an entertainment area where you may watch genuine Flamenco dancing and buffet food is served (catering for 1,000). A large terrace bar dispenses drinks or if you yearn for louder music there is a disco and smaller bar. If you prefer international food there is yet another eating option in a very smart restaurant (seats 500). Above this is the 'Pai-pai' Caribbean cocktail bar where softer music is provided in an intimate atmosphere. Activities for children are very ambitious – there is even a ceramics kiln (multi-lingual carers). 'La Carpa', a spectacular open air theatre, is an ideal setting for daily keep fit sessions and the professional entertainment provided. If you are 5-11 years old you can explore the 'Tam-Tam Eco Park', a 20,000 sq.m. forest zone where experts will teach about the natural life of the area. You can even camp out for a night (supervised) to study wildlife (a once weekly activity). This is an excellent site and there is insufficient space here to describe all the available activities. We recommend it for families of all ages and there is much emphasis on providing activities outside the high season.

Facilities

Fifteen sanitary buildings, some small, but of very good quality with toilets and washbasins, others really excellent, air conditioned larger buildings housing large showers, washbasins (many in private cabins) and separate WCs. Facilities for disabled campers and for babies. Several launderettes. Motorcaravan services. Shopping centre. Restaurants and bars. The 'Eurocentre' for entertainment (air conditioned). Fitness suite. Eco-park. TV lounges. Beach bar. Playground. Free kindergarten with multilingual staff. Skate-boarding. Jogging track. Sports area. Minigolf. Pottery and gardening classes. Windsurfing and water skiing courses. Surfboard and pedalo hire. Boat mooring. Hairdressers. Bicycle hire. Internet café. Gas. Dogs are not accepted. Off site: Riding and golf 3 km.

Open: 1 March - 31 October.

Directions

Site entrance is off main N340 nearly 30 km. southwest from Tarragona. From motorway take Cambrils exit and turn west on N340 at 1136 km. marker.

Charges 2007

Per unit incl 2 persons and electricity	€ 14,00 - € 32,00
premium pitch	€ 27,00 - € 99,00
extra person	€ 5,00 - € 6,00
child (1-9 yrs)	free - € 5,00

All plus 7% VAT.
Discounts for longer stays and for pensioners.

ES85350 Camping-Pension Cala d'Oques

Via Augusta s/n, E-43890 Hospitalet del Infante (Tarragona)

Tel: **977 823 254**. Email: **caladoques@tinet.org**

This peaceful and delightful site has been developed with care and dedication by Elisa Roller over 30 years or so and she now runs it with the help of her daughter Kim. Part of its appeal lies in its situation beside the sea with a wide beach of sand and pebbles, its amazing mountain backdrop and the views across the bay to the town and part by the atmosphere created by Elisa, and staff – friendly, relaxed and comfortable. There are 255 pitches, mostly level and laid out beside the beach, with more behind on wide, informal terracing.

Facilities

Toilet facilities are in the front part of the main building. Clean and neat, there is hot water to showers (hot water by token but free to campers - a device to guard against unauthorized visitors from the beach). New heated unit with toilets and washbasins for winter use. Additional small block with toilets and washbasins at the far end of the site. Motorcaravan service point. Restaurant/bar and shop (1/4-30/9). Play area. Kim's kids club. Fishing. Internet point. Gas supplies. Torches required in some areas Off site: Village facilities, incl. shop and restaurant 1.5 km. Bicycle hire or riding 2 km.

Open: All year.

Directions

Hospitalet del Infante is south of Tarragona, accessed from the A7 (exit 38) or from the N340. From the north take first exit to Hospitalet del Infante at the 1128 km. marker. Follow signs in the village, site is 2 km. south, by the sea.
GPS: N40:58.666 E00:54.203

Charges 2007

Per unit incl. 1 person	€ 11,05 - € 26,75
extra person	€ 4,55 - € 8,25
electricity	€ 3,30 - € 3,90
dog	€ 2,35 - € 2,95

No credit cards.

ES85400 Camping La Torre del Sol

Ctra N340 km 1136, E-43300 Montroig (Tarragona)

Tel: **977 810 486**. Email: **info@latorredelsol.com**

A pleasant banana tree-lined approach road gives way to avenues of palms as you arrive at Torre del Sol, sister site to Templo del Sol (ES8537). Torre del Sol is a very large site occupying a good position with direct access to the clean, soft sand beach, complete with a beach bar. Strong features here are 800 m. of clean beach-front with a special Mediterranean type of pitch, and the entertainment that is provided all season. There is a separate area where the 'Happy Camp' team will take your children to camp overnight in the Indian reservation, plus they can amuse them two days a week with other activities. The cinema doubles as a theatre to stage shows all season. A complex of three pools, thoughtfully laid out with grass sunbathing areas and palms has a lifeguard. There is good shade on a high proportion of the 1,500 individual, numbered pitches. All have electricity and are mostly of about 70-80 sq.m. There is wireless internet access throughout the site. There is usually space for odd nights but for good places between 10/7-16/8 it is best to reserve (only taken for a stay of seven nights or more). Part of the site is between the railway and the sea so there is train noise. We were impressed with the provision of season-long entertainment and to give parents a break whilst children were in the safe hands of the animation team who ensure they enjoy the novel 'Happy Camp' and various workshops.

Facilities

Four very well maintained, fully equipped, toilet blocks include units for disabled people and babies. Washing machines. Gas supplies. Large supermarket, bakery, and souvenir shops. Full restaurant. Takeaway. Bar with large terrace where entertainment held daily all season. Beach bar. Coffee bar and ice cream bar. Pizzeria. Disco. Swimming pools (two heated). Solarium. Sauna. Jacuzzi (35 people). Tennis. Squash. Minigolf. Sub-aqua diving. Bicycle hire. Fishing. Windsurfing school; sailboards and pedaloes for hire. Playground, crèche and Happy Camp for children. Fridge hire. Library. Hairdresser. Business centre. Car repair and car wash. No animals permitted. No jet skis.

Open: 15 March - 20 October.

Directions

Entrance is off main N340 road by 1136 km. marker, about 30 km. from Tarragona towards Valencia. From motorway take Cambrils exit and turn west on N340.

Charges 2007

Per unit incl. 2 persons and electricity	€ 19,70 - € 58,80
extra person	€ 3,25 - € 9,00
child (0-10 yrs)	free - € 7,15

All plus 7% VAT.
Discounts in low season for longer stays.
Camping Cheques accepted.

ES84790 Camping Playa Cambrils – Don Camilo

Ctra Cambrils - Salou km 1.5, E-43850 Cambrils (Tarragona)

Tel: **977 361 490**. Email: **camping@playacambrils.com**

Almost completely canopied by trees which provide welcome shade on hot days, the site is 300 m. from the beach across a busy road. It is mature and has had some recent renovations. The small (60 sq.m.) pitches are on flat ground, divided by hedges. There are many permanent pitches and half the site is given up to chalet style accommodation. Large units are placed in a dedicated area where the trees are higher. The pool complex includes a functional glassed restaurant and bar with a distinct Spanish flavour reflected in the menu and tapas available all day. As this is a popular site with Spanish families it is a good place to practice your language. The pool is long and narrow with separate children's pool and a large paved area for soaking up the sun. Entertainment for children is organised by a good animation team. A big building at one end of the site consists of the supermarket, an attended electronic games room and a large play room.

Facilities

One modern sanitary building, and one large plus one small refurbished block offer reasonable facilities with British style WCs and free showers in separate buildings. Facilities for disabled campers. Laundry facilities. Supermarket (April-Sept). Bar/snacks and separate restaurant (April-Sept). Swimming pool. Playground. Animation in high season. Miniclub. Huge electronic games room. Torches useful. Off site: Resort town has a range of shops, bars and restaurants. Bicycle hire 500 m. Fishing and golf 1 km. Riding 1.5 km.

Open: 15 March - 12 October.

Directions

Leave AP7 autopista at exit 37 and head for Cambrils and then to the beach. Turn left along beach road. Site is 1 km. east of Cambrils Playa and is well signed as you leave Cambrils marina.

Charges 2008

Per person	€ 2,50 - € 4,80
child (under 9 yrs)	€ 1,70 - € 3,65
pitch	€ 11,60 - € 27,60

No credit cards.

ES85590 Azahar Residencial Camping & Bungalow Park

Ptda. Villarroyos, s/n, E-12598 Peñiscola (Castelló)

Tel: **964 475 480**. Email: **info@campingazahar.com**

Set inland from the popular coastal resort of Peniscola, Camping Azahar is set amongst the orange groves. This development of luxury residential and holiday park homes also provides 110 level touring pitches. All have electricity (6/10A), water and a drain, and are accessed by wide, gravel roads. Shade is provided by young palms, pines and plane trees. The pitches are not separated and large units can be accommodated. Recent developments include a spa with saunas, a steam room, sun beds, jacuzzi, hydrotherapy and massage. The sea and a 15 km. stretch of sandy beaches are nearby.

Facilities

Two modern toilet blocks include showers, open washbasins and separate toilets. Facilities for disabled visitors. Laundry facilities. Shop. Bar/restaurant. Outdoor swimming pool (Easter - Oct). Spa centre. Gym. Play area. Minigolf. Bicycle hire. Internet access. Activity programme, excursions, Spanish lessons, games, competitions. Animals not accepted July/Aug. Cabins, mobile homes, apartments to rent. Off site: Shopping and entertainment complex 1 km. Irta mountains and nature reserve 3 km. Peniscola 3 km. Fishing and golf 5 km. Beach and sailing 5 km.

Open: All year.

Directions

From A7 (Barcelona - Valencia) take exit 43 and N340 towards Peniscola which will direct you onto the Cv141. Approaching outskirts of the town turn left signed Camping Azahar and follow signs. GPS: N40:40.168 E00:38.074

Charges 2007

Per unit	€ 16,55 - € 24,15
extra person	€ 3,00 - € 4,00
child (3-10 yrs)	€ 2,50 - € 3,50

ES85800 **Bonterra Park**

Avenida de Barcelona 47, E-12560 Benicasim (Castelló)

Tel: **964 300 007**. Email: **info@bonterrapark.com**

If you are looking for a town site which is not too crowded and has very good facilities, this one may be for you, as there are few quality sites in the local area and this is open all year. It is a 300 m. walk to a good beach – and parking is not too difficult. The site has 320 pitches (70-90 sq.m.) all with electricity (6/10A) and a variety of bungalows. Bonterra has a clean and neat appearance with reddish soil, palms, grass and a number of trees which give good shade. There is a little road and rail noise. The site has an attractive pool complex including a covered pool for the winter months. The beach is good for scuba diving or snorkelling – hire facilities are available at Benicasim. This is a well run, Mediterranean style site useful for visiting local attractions such as the Carmelite monastery at Desierto de las Palmas, six kilometres distant or the historic town of Castellon.

Facilities

Four attractive, well maintained sanitary blocks provide some private cabins, washbasins with hot water, others with cold. Baby and dog showers. Facilities for disabled campers. Laundry. Motorcaravan services. Restaurant/bar. Shop (all year). Swimming pool, covered pool and children's pool. Playground (some concrete bases). Tennis. Multi-sport court. Gymnasium. Disco. Bicycle hire. Miniclub. Satellite TV. Internet access (WiFi). Off site: Town facilities. Sandy beach and fishing 500 m. Riding 3 km. Boat launching 5 km. Golf 10 km. Nature Park.

Open: All year.

Directions

Site is about 1 km. east of Benicasim village with access off the old main N340 road running parallel with the coast. The road re-numbering here is very confusing but there are many blue signs to the site with the campsite name so it is not difficult to find. Coming from the north, turn left at sign 'Benicasim por la costa'. On the A7 from the north use exit 45, from the south exit 46. GPS: N40:03 W00:04.46

Charges 2008

Per person	€ 3,50 - € 5,15
child (3-9 yrs)	€ 3,00 - € 4,20
pitch acc. to type and season	€ 8,15 - € 35,80

All plus 7% VAT. Less in low season and special long stay rates excl. July/Aug.

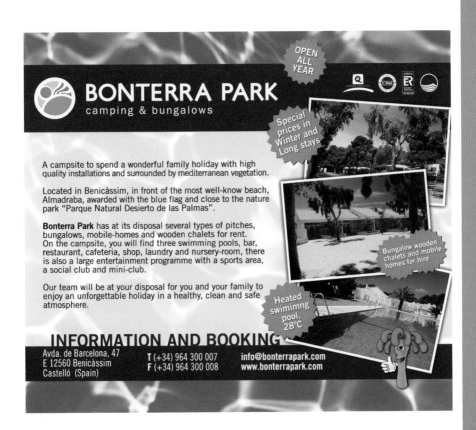

ES85600 Camping Playa Tropicana

Playa Tropicana, E-12579 Alcossebre (Castelló)

Tel: **964 412 463**. Email: **info@playatropicana.com**

Playa Tropicana is a unique site which will strike visitors immediately as being very different. It has been given a tropical theme with scores of 'Romanesque' white statues around the site including in the sanitary blocks. The site has 300 marked pitches separated by lines of flowering bushes under mature trees. The pitches vary in size (50-90 sq.m.), most are shaded and there are electricity connections throughout (some need long leads). 50 pitches have water and drainage. It has a delightful position away from the main hub of tourism, alongside a good sandy beach which shelves gently into the clean waters. To gain access to this it is necessary to cross a pretty promenade in front of the site, which also has statues. It is in a quiet position and it is a drive rather than a walk to the centre of the village resort. The theme extends into an excellent restaurant where, in high season, you may dine on the upper terrace with uninterrupted sea views. A variety of entertainment is provided and there is also a children's club and social room with films and soft drinks bar in high season. The site has several large water features by the high quality restaurant (some are very cheeky!). Aviaries are housed in a corner of the site.

Facilities

Three sanitary blocks delightfully decorated, fully equipped and of excellent standard, include washbasins in private cabins. Baby baths and facilities for disabled people. Washing machine. Motorcaravan services. Gas supplies. Large supermarket. Superb restaurant, a little expensive. (Easter - late Sept). Swimming pool (18 x 11 m.) and children's pool. Playground. Bicycle hire. Children's club. Fishing. Torches necessary in some areas. No TVs allowed in July/Aug. Dogs are not accepted. Off site: Fishing and watersports on the beaches. Riding and boat launching 3 km. Golf 40 km.

Open: All year.

Directions

Alcoceber (or Alcossebre) is between Peniscola and Oropesa. Turn off N340 at 1018 km. marker towards Alcossebre on CV142. Just before entering town proceed through the traffic lights to main road. At next junction, turn right and follow coast road to site in 2.5 km. The sliding gate is on the coast road and a bell is on the right side.

Charges 2008

Per unit incl 2 persons and electricity	€ 19,00 - € 63,00
extra person	€ 4,00 - € 8,00
child (1-10 yrs)	€ 3,00 - € 7,00

Electricity and VAT included.
Many discount schemes out of season.
Camping Cheques accepted.

A really recommendable site, something very different and at the beach

CAMPING CARAVANING

PLAYA TROPICANA

ALCOSSEBRE (CASTELLÓN)

Tel.: (34) 964 41 24 63 and 964 41 24 48 · Fax: (34) 964 41 28 05
www.playatropicana.com · info@playatropicana.com

erkende camping
ANWB

Tropical atmosphere. Far from any noise. Open all year (except for the restaurant).
Consult our special fees in low season and winter.
FORBIDDEN: Dogs throughout the year and TV in July and August).
Sites of 80 - 100 sqm with free electr. (6 Amp), some with water and ablution.
APPARTMENTS AND BUNGALOWS RIGHT BY THE BEACH TO LET
250 km south of Barcelona (20 km south of Peñiscola).
A-7 exit 44, follow 3 km on the N340 northwards, at km 1018 turn towards the sea.
GPS: long. 0: 0° 16' 09'' - lat. N: 40° 13' 2''

BUNGALOWS

Extraordinary social room with complete activity programme, movies, internet, etc.

Also a **social room for children** with activities (July and Aug.)

ES86150 Kiko Park Oliva

E-46780 Oliva (Valencia)

Tel: **962 850 905**. Email: **kikopark@kikopark.com**

Kiko Park is a smart site nestled behind protective sand dunes alongside a 'blue flag' beach. There are sets of attractively tiled steps over the dunes or a long boardwalk near the beach bar (good for prams and wheelchairs) to take you to the fine white sandy beach and the sea. The 180 large pitches all have electricity and the aim is to progressively upgrade all these to serviced 'super' pitches. There are plenty of flowers, hedging and trees adding shade, privacy and colour. A new outdoor pool complex with a spa, whirlpool, solarium, gym and a pool bar was added in 2006. An award-winning restaurant with architecture that reminds one of a ship is near the tropical style beach bar, both overlooking the marina, beautiful beach and sea. This is an excellent site for watersport enthusiasts, as it is beside a marina for boat launching. A wide variety of entertainment is provided all year and Spanish lessons are taught along with dance class and aerobics during the winter. The site is run by the second generation of a family involved in camping for 30 years and their experience shows. They are brilliantly supported by a friendly, efficient team who speak many languages. The narrow roads leading to the site can be a little challenging for very large units but it is worth the effort.

Facilities	Directions
Four modern sanitary blocks are very clean with large showers, washbasins (a few in cabins), British style WCs and excellent facilities for disabled visitors. Laundry facilities. Motorcaravan services. Gas supplies. Supermarket (all year). Restaurant. Bar with TV. Beachside bar and restaurant. Swimming pools and gym. Playground. Watersports. Entertainment for children from mid June. Petanque. Bicycle hire. Off site: Footpath to the marina leads to town. Golf 5 km. Riding 7 km.	From A7 north of Benidorm take exit 61 to the town and then the beach; site is at the northwest end.

Open: All year.

Charges 2007

Per person	€ 2,90
child (under 10 yrs)	€ 2,40
pitch acc. to services and season	€ 10,20 - € 27,00
dog	€ 0,70
electricity (per kWh)	€ 0,35

ES86250 Kiko Park Rural

Ctra Embalse Contreras km 3, E-46317 Villargordo del Cabriel (Valencia)

Tel: **962 139 082**. Email: **kikoparkrural@kikopark.com**

Approaching Kiko Park Rural, you will see a small hilltop village appearing in a landscape of mountains, vines and a jewel-like lake. Kiko was a small village and farm and the village now forms the campsite and accommodation. Amenities are contained within the architecturally authentic buildings, some old and some new. The 76 pitches (with 6A electricity and water) all have stunning views, as do the swimming and paddling pools. Generous hedge plantings provide some privacy.

Facilities	Directions
Three toilet blocks include excellent facilities for disabled people. Motorcaravan services. Gas. Shop. Excellent restaurant. Bar. Swimming and paddling pools. Bicycle hire. Playground. Animation in high season. Many activities can be arranged (white water rafting, gorging, orienteering, trekking, bungee, riding). Off site: Fishing, canoeing and windsurfing on the lake. Village 3 km.	From autopista A7/E15 on Valencia ring road (near the airport) take A3 to west. Villagordo del Cabriel is 80 km. towards Motilla. Take the village exit and follow signs through village and over a hill – spot the village on a hill 2 km. away. That is the campsite!

Open: All year.

Charges 2007

Per person	€ 4,60 - € 5,75
pitch	€ 6,30 - € 13,00

463

ES87540 Camping Jávea

Ctra Cabo de la Nao km 1, Aptdo de Correos No. 83, E-03730 Jávea (Alacant)

Tel: 965 791 070. Email: info@camping-javea.com

The 200 metre long access road to this site is a little unkempt as it passes some factories, but all changes on the final approach with palms, orange and pine trees, the latter playing host to a colony of parakeets. English is spoken at reception. The boxed hedges and palms surrounding this area with a backdrop of hills dotted with villas presents an attractive setting. Three hectares provides space for 214 numbered pitches with 183 for touring units. Flat, level and rectangular in shape, the pitches vary in size 60-80 sq.m. (not advised for caravans or motorhomes with an overall length exceeding 7 m). All have a granite chip surface and 8A electricity. Being a typical Spanish site, the pitches are not separated so units may be close to each other. Some pitches have artificial shade, although for most the pruned eucalyptus and pepper trees will suffice. The area has a large number of British residents so a degree of English is spoken by many shopkeepers and many restaurants provide multi language menus. Besides being popular for a summer holiday, Camping Jávea is open all year and could be of interest to those that wish to 'winter' in an excellent climate. Discounts can make an extended stay extremely viable.

Facilities

Two very clean, fully equipped, sanitary blocks include two children's toilets plus a baby bath. Two washing machines. Fridge hire. Small bar and restaurant where in high season you purchase bread and milk. Large swimming pool with lifeguard and sunbathing lawns. Play area. Boules. Electronic barriers (deposit for card). Caravan storage. WiFi. Tennis. Off site: Sandy beach 3 km. Old and New Jávea within easy walking distance with supermarkets and shops catering for all needs.

Open: All year.

Directions

Exit N332 for Jávea on A134, continue in direction of Port (road number changes to CV 734). At roundabout (with supermarket) turn right signed Cabo de la Nao. Straight on at next roundabout to camping sign and slip road in 100 m.
GPS: E00:10.190 N38:47.000

Charges 2008

Per person	€ 5,22 - € 5,80
child	€ 4,50 - € 5,00
pitch incl. electricity	€ 15,92 - € 19,50

ES86810 Camping Villasol

Avenida Bernat de Sarria, E-03503 Benidorm (Alacant)

Tel: 965 850 422. Email: camping-villasol@dragonet.es

Benidorm is increasingly popular for winter stays and Villasol is a genuinely good, purpose built modern site. Many of the 309 well separated pitches are arranged on wide terraces which afford views of the mountains surrounding Benidorm. All pitches (80-85 sq.m.) have electricity and satellite TV connections, with 160 with full services for seasonal use. Shade is mainly artificial. Reservations are only accepted for winter stays of over three months (from 1 Oct). There is a small indoor pool, heated for winter use, and a very attractive, large outdoor pool complex (summer only).

Facilities

Modern toilet blocks provide free, controllable hot water to showers and washbasins and British style WCs. Good facilities for disabled campers. Laundry facilities. Good value restaurant. Bar. Shop. Swimming pools, outdoor and indoor. Playground. Evening entertainment programme. Dogs are not accepted. Off site: Fishing and bicycle hire 1.3 km. Golf 8 km.

Open: All year.

Directions

From autopista exit 65 (Benidorm) and turn left at second set of lights. After 1 km. at lights turn right, then right again at next lights. Site is on right in 400 m.

Charges guide

Per person	€ 5,00 - € 6,50
pitch incl. car and electricity	€ 14,00 - € 21,80
All plus 7% VAT.	

ES87550 Camping Caravanning Moraira

Camino Paellero 50, E-03724 Moraira-Teulada (Alacant)

Tel: 965 745 249. Email: campingmoraira@campingmoraira.com

This small hillside site with some views over the town and marina is quietly situated in an urban area amongst old pine trees and just 400 metres from a sheltered bay. Terracing provides shaded pitches of varying size, some really quite small (access to some of the upper pitches may be difficult for larger units). Some pitches have water and drainage and a few have sea views. There are electricity connections. An attractive irregularly shaped pool with paved sunbathing terrace is below the small bar/restaurant and terrace. The pool has observation windows where you can watch the swimmers, and is used for sub-aqua instruction. The site runs a professional diving school for all levels (the diving here is good and the water warm, even in winter). A sandy beach is 1.5 km. A large, painted water tower stands at the top of the site. The reception building is being extended to provide a range of new facilities.

Facilities

The high quality toilet block, with polished granite floors and marble fittings, is built to a unique and ultra-modern design with extra large free hot showers. Washing machine and dryer. Motorcaravan services. Bar/restaurant and shop (1/7-30/9). Small swimming pool (all year). Sub-aqua with instruction. Tennis. Torches may be required. Off site: Shops, bars and restaurants within walking distance. Beach 1.5 km. Fishing 400 m. Bicycle hire 1 km. Golf 8 km.

Open: All year.

Directions

Site is best approached from Teulada. From A7 exit 63 take N332 and in 3.5 km. turn right (Teulada and Moraira). In Teulada fork right to Moraira. At junction at town entrance turn right signed Calpe and in 1 km. turn right into road to site on bend immediately after Res. Don Julio. Do not take the first right, as the signs seem to indicate, otherwise you will go round in a loop.

Charges guide

Per person	€ 4,70
pitch incl. car	€ 10,50 - € 12,60
electricity	€ 3,20

All plus 7% VAT. Less 15-60% in low season.

ES86830 Camping Benisol

Avenida de la Comunidad Valenciana s/n, E-03500 Benidorm (Alacant)

Tel: 965 851 673. Email: campingbenisol@yahoo.es

Camping Benisol is a well developed and peaceful site with lush, green vegetation and a mountain background. Mature hedges and trees afford privacy to each pitch and some artificial shade is provided where necessary. There are 298 pitches of which around 115 are for touring units (60-80 sq.m). All have electrical hook-ups (4/6A) and 75 have drainage. All the connecting roads are now surfaced with tarmac. Some daytime road noise should be expected. The site has an excellent restaurant serving traditional Spanish food at great prices, with a terrace overlooking the pool.

Facilities

Modern sanitary facilities, heated in winter and kept very clean, have free, solar heated hot water to washbasins, showers and sinks. Laundry facilities. Gas supplies. Restaurant with terrace and bar (closed 1 day a week). Shop. Swimming pool (Easter - Nov). Small play area. Minigolf. Jogging track. Tennis. Golf driving range. ATM. Off site: Riding 1 km. Bicycle hire 3 km. Fishing (sea) 3 km.

Open: All year.

Directions

Site is northeast of Benidorm. Exit N332 at 152 km. marker and take turn signed Playa Levant. Site is 100 m. on left off the main road, well signed.

Charges 2007

Per person	€ 4,95 - € 5,25
child (1-10 yrs)	€ 4,00 - € 4,40
pitch incl. electricity	€ 16,05 - € 20,90

All plus 7% VAT. No credit cards.

ES87430 Yelloh! Village Le Marjal

Ctra N332 km 73.4, E-03140 Guardamar del Segura (Alacant)

Tel: 04 66 73 97 39. Email: info@yellohvillage-marjal.com

Marjal is located beside the estuary of the Segura river, alongside the pine and eucalyptus forests of the Dunas de Guardamar natural park. The fine sandy beach can be reached through the forest (800 m). This is a new site with a huge lagoon-style pool and a superb sports complex. There are 212 pitches on this award winning site, all with water, electricity, drainage and satellite TV points, the ground covered with crushed marble, making the pitches clean and pleasant. There is some shade and the site has an open feel with lots of room for manoeuvring. Reception is housed within a delicately coloured building complete with a towering Mirador, topped by a weather-vane depicting the 'Garza Real' (heron) bird which frequents the local area and forms part of the site logo. The large leased restaurant overlooks the pools and the river that leads to the sea in the near distance. This situation is shared with the taperia (high season) and bar with large terraces fringed by trees, palms and pomegranates. The impressive pool/lagoon complex (1,100 sq.m.) has a water cascade, an island bar plus bridge, one part sectioned as a pool for children and a jacuzzi. The extensive sports area is also impressive with qualified instructors who will customise your fitness programme whilst consulting the doctor. No effort has been spared here, the quality heated indoor pool, light-exercise room, sauna, solarium, beauty salon, fully equipped gym and changing rooms, including facilities for disabled visitors, are of the highest quality. Aerobics and physiotherapy are also on offer. All activities are discounted for campers. A programme of entertainment is provided for adults and children in season by a professional animation team.

Facilities

Three excellent heated toilet blocks have free hot water, elegant separators between sinks, spacious showers and some cabins. Each block has high quality facilities for babies and disabled campers, modern laundry and dishwashing rooms. Car wash. Well stocked supermarket. Restaurants. Bar. Large outdoor pool complex (1/6-31/10). Heated indoor pool (low season). Fitness suite. Jacuzzi. Sauna. Solarium. Aerobics and aquarobics. Play room. Minigolf. Floodlit tennis and soccer pitch. Bicycle hire. Games room. TV room. ATM. Business centre. Internet access. Off site: Beach 800 m. Riding or golf 4 km.

Open: All year.

Directions

On N332 40 km. south of Alicante, site is on the sea side between 73 and 74 km. markers. GPS: N38:06.560 W00:39.280

Charges 2008

Per person	€ 6,00 - € 8,00
child (4-12 yrs)	€ 3,00 - € 5,00
pitch	€ 20,00 - € 35,00
electricity	€ 2,00 - € 3,00
All plus 7% VAT.	

ES86890 Camping Playa del Torres

Partida Torres Norte 11, Apdo. Correus 243, E-03570 Villajoyosa (Alacant)

Tel: 966 810 031. Email: into@playadeltonnes.com

Jacinto and Mercedes have a pretty beachside site with the lower part set under eucalyptus trees. Reception is placed in one of the site's tasteful wooden buildings close to the beach (excellent English is spoken). If you prefer a smaller site away from the 'high rise' and bustle of Benidorm offering high quality this could be for you. The 85 lower pitches, some large, are on flat ground with shade. 10 good pitches are right alongside the beach fence (book early). All have electricity (16A), some are fully serviced and there are ample water fountains around the site along with efficient, modern lighting. The upper levels of the site have chalets and mobile homes. A modestly sized pool with a sunbathing area is set in the centre part of the site between the building housing the bar, cafeteria and shop and the separate clean sanitary block (a short walk from the beachside pitches). Boats can be launched from the sand and shingle beach, sub-aqua diving and other watersports can be organised. Benidorm with its beaches is close, along with many tourist activities including the Fuentes del Algar waterfall and the huge exciting new 'Terra Mittica' theme park.

Facilities

The sanitary building is of a high specification, as are the fittings within, including excellent showers. Laundry. Bar. Cafeteria. Shop. Swimming pool. Children's play area. Petanque. Fishing. Barbecues. Freezer. Satellite TV. Reception will assist with all tourist activities. Off site: Riding 100 m. Golf 18 km. Serious or recreational walking and climbing is possible about 20 minutes away from the site. Benidorm is very close.

Open: All year.

Directions

From Villajoyosa on N332, site is 1 km. east of the town. Look for clear site signs towards beach. From Benidorm on N332, site is 3 km. on the left, but a left turn is prohibited. Proceed 400 m. to traffic lights to turn, then proceed as above.

Charges guide

Per person	€ 4,90
child (4-13 yrs)	€ 3,80
pitch	€ 4,90 - € 35,00
electricity (plus meter)	€ 3,97
Plus 7% VAT.	
Less 5-50% for low season stays of 7 days or more.	

ES86850 Camping Caravaning El Raco

Avenida Doctor Severo Ochoa, 19, E-03503 Benidorm (Alacant)

Tel: 965 868 552. Email: info@campingraco.com

This purpose built site with good facilities and very competitive prices provides about 425 pitches (90 for touring units). There is wide access from the Rincon de Loix road. The site is quietly situated 1.5 km. from the town, Levante beach and promenade. It has wide tarmac roads and pitches of 80 sq.m. or more, separated by low cypress hedging and some trees which provide some shade. Satellite TV connections are provided to each pitch and 94 have all services including 10A electricity. The good value restaurant, bar and pools are some distance from the touring pitches.

Facilities

Four large toilet blocks are well equipped. Facilities for disabled people. Dishwashing sinks. Laundry facilities. Gas supplies. Motorcaravan services. Restaurant. Bar. Well stocked shop. Busy bar with TV also open to public and good value restaurant. Outdoor swimming pool, no slides or diving board (1/4-31/10). Indoor heated pool (1/11-31/3). Playground. ATM. Off site: Beach 1 km. Bicycle hire 2 km. Golf 6 km. Theme parks.

Open: All year.

Directions

From autopista exit 65 (Benidorm, Levante) at second set of traffic lights turn left on the N332 (Altea, Valencia). After 1.5 km. turn right (Levante Playa), then straight on at next lights for 300 m. to site on right. From north on N332 follow signs for Playa Levante (or Benidorm Palace). At lights turn left (Playa Levante).

Charges 2007

Per person	€ 5,20 - € 6,00
pitch incl. electricity	€ 15,00 - € 21,60

VAT included. No credit cards.

ES86870 Camping Cap Blanch

Playa de Cap Blanch 25, E-03590 Altea (Alacant)

Tel: 965 845 946. Email: capblanch@ctv.es

This well run, small site has plenty of character. It is open all year and is very popular for winter stays. Alongside the beach road, it has direct access to the pebble beach and is within a few hundred yards of all Albir's shops and restaurants. The 250 pitches on flat, hard gravel are of a good size and well maintained with 5A electricity. The site tends to be full in winter and is very popular with several nationalities, especially the Dutch. For winter stays, it would pay to get there before Christmas as January and February are the peak months.

Facilities

The refurbished sanitary block can be heated and provides good facilities including some washbasins in cabins, baby facilities and a room for disabled visitors. Motorcaravan services. Gas supplies. Laundry. Bar and restaurant. Takeaway. Playground. Tennis. Fitness centre. Organised entertainment. ATM. Off site: Restaurants and commercial centre. Golf 500 m. Bicycle hire 1 km. Riding 5 km.

Open: All year.

Directions

Site is on the Albir - Altea coast road and can be reached from either end. From N332, north or south, watch for sign Playa del Albir and proceed through Albir to the coast road. Site is on north side of Albir.

Charges guide

Per person	€ 3,50 - € 5,50
pitch incl. car and electricity	€ 11,50 - € 28,50

VAT included. Low season and long stay discounts.

ES87450 Camping La Fuente

Camino de La Bocamina, E-30626 Banos de Fortuna (Murcia)

Tel: 968 685 125. Email: info@campingfuente.com

Located in an area known for its thermal waters since Roman and Moorish times and with just 87 pitches and 6 bungalows, La Fuente is a gem. The main attraction here is the huge hydrotherapy centre where the water is constant at 36 degrees all year. The pool can be covered in inclement weather. The site is in two sections, one where pitches are in standard rows and the other where they are in circles around blocks. The hard, flat pitches are on shingle (rock pegs advised), have 10A electricity and 53 have their own mini-sanitary unit.

Facilities

All pitches have their own facilities including a unit for disabled campers. Washing machines and dryers. High quality restaurant shared with accommodation guests. Snack bar by pool. Supermarket. Bicycle hire. Communal barbecues. New jacuzzi. Off site: Spa town, massage therapies, hot pools 500 m. Fortuna, shops, bars, restaurants 3 km. Golf and riding 20 km.

Open: All year.

Directions

From A7/E15 Alicante - Murcia road take C3223 to Fortuna then follow signs to Banos de Fortuna. The site with its bright yellow walls can be easily seen from the road and is very well signed in the town. GPS: N38:12.409 W01:06.439

Charges 2007

Per person	€ 3,25
pitch incl. electricity	€ 9,50 - € 11,50

Pitch prices discounted after five days.

ES87420 Camping Internacional La Marina

Ctra N332 km 76, E-03194 La Marina (Alacant)

Tel: **965 419 200**. Email: **info@campinglamarina.com**

Efficiently run by a friendly Belgian family, La Marina has 381 pitches of seven different types and size ranging from about 50 sq.m. for tents to 100 sq.m. with electricity (10A), TV, water and drainage. Artificial shade is provided and the pitches are extremely well maintained on level, well drained ground with a special area allocated for tents in a small orchard. The lagoon swimming pool complex is absolutely fabulous and has something for everyone (with lifeguards). William Le Metayer, the owner, is passionate about La Marina and it shows in his search for perfection. A magnificent new, modern building houses some superb extra amenities. Member of Leading Campings Group. These include a relaxed business centre with internet access, a tapas bar decorated with amazing ceramics (handmade by the owner's mother) and a quality restaurant with a water fountain feature and great views of the lagoon. There is also a conference centre and an extensive library, with the whole of the lower ground floor dedicated to children with a play area and a 'cyber zone' for teenagers. With a further bar and a soundproofed disco, the building is of an exceptional, eco-friendly standard. A fine fitness centre and covered, heated pool (14 x 7 m.) are close by. A pedestrian gate at the rear of the site gives access to the long sandy beach through the coastal pine forest that is a feature of the area. We recommend this site very highly whatever type of holidaying camper you may be.

Facilities

The elegant sanitary blocks offer the very best of modern facilities. Heated in winter, they include private cabins and facilities for disabled visitors. Laundry facilities Motorcaravan services. Gas. Supermarket. Bars. Restaurant (all year). Swimming pools (1/4-15/10). Indoor pool. Fitness centre. Sauna. Play rooms. Extensive activity and entertainment programme. Sports area. Tennis. Huge playground. Hairdresser. Off site: Fishing 500 m. Boat launching 5 km. Golf 7 km. Bicycle hire 8 km. Riding 15 km. Hourly bus service from outside the gate. Theme parks.

Open: All year.

Directions

Site is 2 km. west of La Marina. Leave N332 Guardamara de Segura - Santa Pola road at 75 km. marker if travelling north, or 78 km. marker if travelling south. Site is well signed. GPS: N38:07.474 W00:38.598

Charges 2007

Per person	€ 5,00 - € 7,56
child (under 10 yrs)	€ 3,50 - € 5,04
pitch incl. electricty,	
acc. to type and season	€ 19,10 - € 39,06
dog	free - € 2,00

Plus 7% VAT. Seven grades of pitch. Less in low season, plus good discounts for longer stays 16/9-14/6, excluding Easter.

Check real time availability and at-the-gate prices...

www.**alanrogers**.com

ES87530 Caravaning La Manga

Autovia Cartagena - La Manga Salida 11, E-30370 La Manga del Mar Menor (Murcia)

Tel: **902 021 352**. Email: **lamanga@caravaning.es**

This is a very large well equipped, 'holiday style' site with its own beach and both indoor and outdoor pools. With a good number of typical Spanish long stay units, the length of the site is impressive (1 km.) and a bicycle is very helpful for getting about. The 1,000 regularly laid out, gravel touring pitches (84 or 110 sq. m.) are generally separated by hedges which also provide a degree of shade. Each has 10A electricity supply, water and the possibility of satellite TV reception. This site's excellent facilities are ideally suited for holidays in the winter when the weather is very pleasantly warm. If you are suffering from aches and pains try the famous local mud treatment. Reception will assist with bookings. November daytime temperatures usually exceed 20 degrees. La Manga is a 22 km. long narrow strip of land, bordered by the Mediterranean on one side and by the Mar Menor on the other. There are sandy bathing beaches on both sides and considerable development in terms of hotels, apartments, restaurants, night clubs, etc. in between – a little reminiscent of Miami Beach! The very end of the southern part is great for 'getting away from it all' (take a picnic for the beach and be sure to go over the little bridge for privacy). The campsite is situated on the approach to 'the strip' enjoying the benefit of its own semi-private beach with impressive tall palm trees alongside the Mar Menor which provides shallow warm waters, ideal for families with children.

Facilities

Seven clean toilet blocks of standard design, well spaced around the site, include washbasins (with hot water in five blocks). Laundry. Gas supplies. Large well stocked supermarket. Restaurant. Bar. Snack bar. Pool complex (April - Sept). Indoor pool, gym, sauna, jacuzzi and massage. Open air cinema (April - Sept). Tennis. Petanque. Minigolf. Play area. Watersports school. Internet café (also WiFi). Off site: Golf, bicycle hire and riding 5 km.

Open: All year.

Directions

Use exit (Salida) 11 from MU312 dual carriageway towards Cabo de Palos, signed Playa Honda. Cross bridge and double back. Site entrance is clearly visible beside dual carriageway with flags flying.

Charges 2008

Per pitch incl. 2 persons	€ 8,15 - € 18,85
extra person	€ 2,70 - € 3,85
child	€ 2,30 - € 3,30

Camping Cheques accepted.

ES87520 Camping Naturista El Portus

El Portus, E-30393 Cartagena (Murcia)

Tel: **968 553 052**. Email: **elportus@elportus.com**

Set in a secluded south facing bay fringed by mountains, El Portus is a fairly large naturist site enjoying magnificent views and with direct access to a small sand and pebble beach. There are some 400 pitches, 300 for tourers, ranging from 60-100 sq.m. and all but a few having electricity (6A). They are mostly on fairly level, if somewhat stony and barren ground. El Portus has a reasonable amount of shade from established trees and nearly every pitch has a view.

Facilities

Five acceptable toilet blocks, all unisex, are of varying styles. Unit for disabled visitors, key from reception. Washing machines. Motorcaravan services. Shop. Bar with TV and library. Restaurants (beach restaurant is closed in low season). Swimming pools. Play area. Tennis. Petanque. Yoga. Scuba-diving (high season). Windsurfing. Entertainment (high season). Off site: Golf 28 km.

Open: All year.

Directions

Site is on the coast, 10 km. west of Cartagena. Follow signs to Mazarron then take E22 to Canteras. Site is well signed for 4 km.
GPS: N37:35.100 W01:04.030

Charges 2007

Per person	€ 6,60
pitch incl. 6A electricity	€ 20,75

Plus 7% VAT. Camping Cheques accepted.

ES87480 Camping Los Madriles

Ctra de la Azohia km 4.5, E-30868 Isla Plana (Murcia)

Tel: **968 152 151**. Email: **camplosmadriles@terra.es**

An exceptional site with super facilities, Los Madriles is run by a hard working team, with constant improvements being made. Twenty kilometres west of Cartegena, the approach to the site and the surrounding area is fairly unremarkable, but the site is not. A fairly steep access road leads to the 311 flat, good to large size terraced pitches, each having electricity, water and a waste point. Most have shade from large trees with a number with panoramic views of the sea and the mountains.

Facilities

Four sanitary blocks and one small toilet block provide excellent facilities, including services in one block for disabled campers. Private wash cabins. Washing machines and dryers. Motorcaravan services. Car wash. Restaurant/snack bar. Bar. Supermarket. Swimming pools with jacuzzi. Boules. Play areas. Bicycle hire. ATM. Dogs and other animals are not accepted. Torches useful. Off site: Town close by. Fishing 800 m. (Licence required, purchase in Puerto Mazarron). Boat launching 3 km. Riding 6 km. Golf 20 km. Beach 800 m.

Open: All year.

Directions

From E15/A7 take exit 627 signed MU602, Cartagena and Fuente Alamo. After 5 km. turn right on MU603 signed Mazarron. Continue towards Puerto Mazarron and take N332 (Cartagena). On reaching coast continue with N332 (Cartagena and Alicante). Shortly after at roundabout turn right towards Isla Plana and La Azohia. Site is signed and on the left in 5 km. GPS: N37:34.410 W01:11.470

Charges 2008

Per person	€ 4,50 - € 5,50
pitch incl. electricity	€ 17,00 - € 20,00

ES87630 Camping Cabo de Gata

Ctra Cabo de Gata s/n, Cortijo Ferrón, E-04150 Cabo de Gata (Almería)

Tel: **950 160 443**. Email: **info@campingcabodegata.com**

Since this medium sized site opened in 1993, it has strived continually to make improvements and today can be regarded as a very pleasant, all year campsite offering facilities to a good standard. Very popular with British visitors through the winter, it is located within the Cabo de Gata-Nijar natural park and set in open farmland, yet is only a 1 km. walk from a fine sandy beach. The 250 gravel pitches are level and of a reasonable size, with 6/16A electricity and limited shade from maturing trees or canopies. There are specific areas for very large units and 7 chalets for rent. A modern, airy reception is adjacent to internet facilities, whilst the nearby irregularly shaped swimming pool in close proximity to the bar/restaurant are both first class. To the west, Salinas de Acosta and the lighthouse at Faro de Gata (fine views). The salinas are renowned for their bird life and from one of the hides you will see large flocks of pink flamingo and many other species. Almeria has many quality shops and the Alcazaba (955 AD) and the white washed village of Nijar.

Facilities

Two, well-maintained, clean toilet blocks provide all the necessary sanitary facilities. including British type WCs, washbasins and free hot showers. Facilities for disabled campers. Restaurant, bar and shop (open all year). Swimming pool. Tennis court. Small playground. Library. Bicycle hire. English spoken. Entertainment programme. Off site: Nearest beach 1 km. Bus 1 km. Fishing 1 km. Golf 10 km. Riding 15 km.

Open: All year.

Directions

From A7-E15 take exit 460 or 467 and follow signs for Retamar via N344 and for Cabo de Gata. Site is on the right before village of Cabo de Gata. The final stretch of road is in a poor state of repair due to restrictions imposed within the natural park.

Charges 2008

Per person	€ 5,50
child (3-10 yrs)	€ 5,00
pitch incl. electricity	€ 16,80

Camping Cheques accepted.

471

ES92900 Camping El Balcon de Pitres

Ctra Orgiva - Ugijar km 51, E-18414 Pitres (Granada)

Tel: **958 766 111**. Email: **info@balcondepitres.com**

A simple country site perched high in the mountains of the Alpujarras, on the south side of the Sierra Nevada, El Balcon de Pitres has its own rustic charm. Many thousands of trees planted around the site provide shade. There are stunning views from some of the 175 level grassy pitches (large units may find pitch access difficult). The garden is kept green by spring waters, which you can hear and sometimes see, tinkling away in places. The Lopez family have built this site from barren mountain top to cool oasis in the mountains in just fifteen years.

Facilities

Two toilet blocks provide adequate facilities but the steeply sloping site is unsuitable for disabled campers and thus there are no facilities for them. Snack bar. Bar. Shop (closed Tuesdays). Swimming pools (extra charge, € 2.40 adult € 1.50 child). Bicycle hire. Torches useful. Off site: Fishing. Canyoning. Trekking. Parascending. Quad bikes. Sports centre for football.

Open: All year.

Directions

Site is 30 km. northeast of Motril. Heading south on A44 (E902) exit 164 (Lanjaron) onto E348 towards Orgiva. Fork left at sign (A4132) Pampaneira 8 km. Continue to Pitres (7 km). Site signed (steep and winding roads). GPS: N36:55.911 W03:19.961

Charges 2007

Per person	€ 5,00
child	€ 4,50
pitch incl. car and electricity (2A)	€ 13,50 - € 17,50

ES92850 Camping Las Lomas

Ctra de Sierra Nevada, E-18160 Güejar-Sierra (Granada)

Tel: **958 484 742**. Email: **laslomas@campings.net**

This site is high in the Güéjar Sierra and looks down on the Patano de Canales reservoir. After a wonderful drive to Güéjar-Sierra, you are rewarded with a site boasting excellent facilities. It is set on a slope but the pitches have been levelled and are quite private, with high separating hedges and many mature trees giving good shade (some pitches are fully serviced, with sinks and most have electricity). The large bar/restaurant complex and pools have wonderful views over the lake and a grassed sunbathing area runs down to the fence (safe) looking over the long drop below.

Facilities

Pretty sanitary blocks (heated in winter) provide clean facilities. First class facilities for disabled campers and well equipped baby room (key at reception). Spa for hire. Motorcaravan services. Good supermarket. Restaurant/bar. Swimming pool. Play area. Table tennis. Minigolf. Basketball. Many other activities including parascending. Barbecue. Internet access. Torches useful. Off site: Buses to village and Granada (15 km). Tours of the Alhambra organised. Useful site for winter skiing.

Open: All year.

Directions

Heading south towards Granada on A44 (E902 Jaén - Motril) take exit 132 onto A395 (Alhamba/Sierra Nevada). After 4 km. marker, exit 5B (Sierra Nevada). At 7 km. marker, exit right onto slip road. At junction turn left (Cenes de la Vega/Güéjar-Sierra). In 200 m. turn right on A4026. In 1.6 km. turn left (Güéjar-Sierra). Drive uphill, past dam. Site on right in 2.8 km.

Charges guide

Per person	€ 4,00 - € 5,00
pitch	€ 10,00 - € 12,00

ES92800 Camping Sierra Nevada

Avenida Madrid 107, E-18014 Granada (Granada)

Tel: **958 150 062**. Email: **campingmotel@terra.es**

This is a good site either for a night stop or for a stay of a few days while visiting Granada and for a city site it is surprisingly pleasant. It has an open feeling and, to encourage you to stay a little longer, an irregular shape pool with a smaller children's pool open in high season. There is some traffic noise around the pool as it is on the road boundary. With 148 pitches for touring units (10/20A electricity), the site is in two connected parts with more mature trees and facilities to the northern end.

Facilities

Two very modern sanitary blocks, with excellent facilities, including cabins, very good facilities for disabled people and babies. Washing machines. Motorcaravan services. Gas supplies. Shop (15/3-15/10). Swimming pools with lifeguards and charge of € 1.50 (15/6-15/9). Bar/restaurant by pool. Tennis. Table tennis. Petanque. Large playground. Doctor lives on site. Off site: Fishing 10 km. Golf 12 km. Bus station 50 m. from site gate.

Open: 1 March - 31 October.

Directions

Site is just outside the city to north, on road to Jaén and Madrid. From autopista, take Granada North - Almanjayar exit 123 (close to central bus station). Follow road back towards Granada and site is on the right, well signed. From other roads join the motorway to access the correct exit. GPS: N37:12.241 W03:37.022

Charges 2007

Per person	€ 5,50
pitch incl. electricity (10A)	€ 16,35
VAT included.	

ES88000 Camping Marbella Playa

Ctra N340 km 192,8, E-29600 Marbella (Málaga)

Tel: **952 833 998**. Email: **recepcion@campingmarbella.com**

This large site is 12 kilometres east of the internationally famous resort of Marbella with public transport available to the town centre and local attractions. A sandy beach is about 150 metres away with direct access. There are 430 individual pitches of up to 70 sq.m. with natural shade (additional artificial shade is provided to some), and electricity (10/20A) available throughout. Long leads may be required for some pitches. The site is busy throughout the high season but the high staff/customer ratio and the friendly staff approach ensures a comfortable stay. A large swimming pool complex with a restaurant/bar provides a very attractive feature.

Facilities

Four sanitary blocks of mixed ages, are fully equipped and well maintained. Three modern units for disabled visitors. Laundry service. Large supermarket with butcher and fresh vegetable counter. Bar, restaurant and café. Supervised, free swimming pool (April - Sept). Playground. Children Off site: Bus service 150 m. Fishing 100 m. Golf and bicycle hire 5 km. Riding 10 km. Beach 200 m.

Open: All year.

Directions

Site is 12 km. east of Marbella with access close to the 193 km. point on the main N340 road. Signed Elviria, then follow camping signs. GPS: N36:29.476 W04:45.795

Charges 2007

Per person	€ 3,05 - € 5,05
pitch incl. electricity	€ 8,00 - € 18,20
All plus 7% VAT.	

ES88020 Camping Cabopino

Ctra N340 km 194.7, E-29600 Marbella (Málaga)

Tel: **952 834 373**. Email: **info@campingcabopino.com**

This large mature site is alongside the main N340 Costa del Sol coast road, 12 km. east of Marbella and 15 km. from Fuengirola. The Costa del Sol is also known as the Costa del Golf and fittingly there is a major golf course alongside the site. The site is set amongst tall pine trees which provide shade for the sandy pitches (there are some huge areas for large units). The 300 touring pitches, a mix of level and sloping (chocks advisable), all have electricity (10A), but long leads may be required for some. There is a separate area on the western side for groups of younger guests.

Facilities

Five mature but very clean sanitary blocks provide hot water throughout (may be under pressure at peak times). Washing machines. Bar/restaurant and takeaway. Shop. Swimming pools (indoor open all year). Play area. Some evening entertainment. Excursions can be booked. ATM. Torches necessary in the more remote parts of the site. Off site: Beach 600 m. Fishing, bicycle hire and riding within 1 km. Golf 7 km.

Open: All year.

Directions

Site is 12 km. from Marbella. Approaching Marbella from the east, leave the N340 at the 194 km. marker (signed Cabopino). Site is off the roundabout at the top of the slip road.

Charges 2007

Per unit incl. 2 persons and electricity	€ 18,05 - € 28,60
extra person	€ 3,65 - € 5,86
Plus 7% VAT. Camping Cheques accepted.	

ES90810 Camping Villsom

Ctra Sevilla - Cadiz km 554.8, E-41700 Sevilla (Sevilla)

Tel: **954 720 828**

This city site was one of the first to open in Spain and it is still owned by the same pleasant family. The administrative building consists of a peaceful and attractive bar with patio and satellite TV (where breakfast is served) and there is a pleasant, small reception area. It is a good site for visiting Seville with a frequent bus service to the centre. Camping Villsom has around 180 pitches which are level and shaded. A huge variety of trees and palms are to be seen around the site and in summer the bright colours of the flowers are very pleasing.

Facilities

Sanitary facilities require modernisation in some areas. Some washbasins have cold water only. Laundry facilities. Small shop selling basic provisions. Bar with satellite TV (open July/Aug). Swimming pool (June-Sept). Putting. Table tennis. Drinks machine. Off site: Bus stop close. Most town facilities including restaurant, supermarket, cinema and theatre.

Open: All year.

Directions

On main Seville - Cadiz NIV road travelling from Seville take exit at km. 553 signed Dos Hermanos - Isla Menor. Go under road bridge and immediately right (Isla Mentor) to site 80 m. on right. From Cadiz take same exit. At roundabout take fourth exit over main road, then down slip road to go under bridge, then as above. GPS: N37:16.641 W05:56.210

Charges 2007

Per person	€ 4,00
pitch incl. car and electricity	€ 8,50 - € 11,20

ES88590 **Camping Roche**

N340 km 19,5, Carril de Pilahito, E-11140 Conil de la Frontera (Cádiz)

Tel: **956 442 216**. Email: **info@campingroche.com**

Camping Roche is situated in a pine forest near white sandy beaches in the lovely region of Andalusia. It is a clean and tidy, welcoming site. Little English is spoken but try your Spanish, German or French as the staff are very helpful. A family site, it offers a variety of facilities including a sports area and swimming pools. The restaurant has good food and a pleasant outlook over the pool. Games are organised for children. A recently built extension provides further pitches, a new toilet block and a tennis court. There are now 240 pitches which include 104 bungalows to rent. There are pleasant paths in the area for mountain biking and this is an ideal base for visiting the cities of Seville and Cádiz.

Facilities	Directions
Three toilet blocks are traditional in style and provide simple, clean facilities. Washbasins have cold water only. Washing machine. Bar and restaurant. Supermarket. Swimming and paddling pools. Sports area. Tennis. Play area. Off site: Bus stops 3 times daily outside gates.	From the N340 (Cádiz - Algeciras) turn off to site at km. 19,5 point. From Conil, take El Pradillo road. Keep following signs to site. From CA3208 road turn at km. 1 marker and site is 1.5 km. down this road on the right.

Open: All year.

Charges 2007

Per person	€ 5,80
child	€ 4,80
pitch	€ 10,70
electricity	€ 4,70
VAT included.	

Situated in a pine forest, in a peaceful area of the Costa de la Luz in Conil, Cadiz, Andalusia, near a lot of beaches of white and fine sand. Familiar atmosphere. Comfortable bungalows, large plots, free cool water and sports area, swimming pools and games for children. Nice paths for mountain biking, and well communicated to visit the wonderful cities of Sevilla and Cadiz.

CAMPING ROCHE

Ideal to spend the winter

www.campingroche.com

E-11149 Conil de la Frontera (Cádiz)-A-48 salida 15 (Conil Norte) N-340 Km.19,2-Tel.:[34]956442216/956232319

ES88650 Camping Playa Las Dunas de San Anton

Paseo Maritimo, Playa de la Puntilla s/n, E-11500 El Puerto de Santa Maria (Cádiz)

Tel: **956 872 210**. Email: **info@lasdunascamping.com**

This site lies within the Parque Natural Bahia de Les Dunes and is adjacent to the long and gently sloping golden sands of Puntilla beach. This is a pleasant and peaceful site (though very busy in August) with some 400 separate marked pitches, 260 for tourers, with much natural shade and ample electrical connections (5/10A). Motorcaravans park in an area called the Oasis which is very pretty. The tent and caravan pitches, under mature trees, are terraced and separated by low walls. This is a spacious site with a tranquil setting and popular with people who wish to 'winter over' in peace.

Facilities

Immaculate modern sanitary facilities with separate facilities for disabled campers and a baby room. Laundry facilities are excellent. Gas supplies. Bar/restaurant (all year). Supermarket (high season). Very large swimming pool (supervised) and toddlers pool (high season). Play areas. Night security all year. Off site: Fishing 500 m. Riding and golf 2 km. Municipal sports centre close by offers all manner of sporting activities and the beach provides additional free sports facilities such as volleyball. Local buses for town and cities visits and a ferry to Cádiz.

Open: All year.

Directions

Site is 5 km. north of Cádiz off N1V route. Take road to Puerto Santa Maria, site is very well signed throughout the town (small yellow signs high on posts). From south, turn left into town just after large bridge. Keeping sea inlet on your left, follow road for about 1 km. Site on right opposite beach.

Charges 2007

Per person	€ 3,94 - € 4,38
child	€ 3,37 - € 3,74
pitch	€ 3,94 - € 6,29
electricity (5A)	€ 4,99

ES88730 Camping La Aldea

El Rocio, E-21750 Almonte (Huelva)

Tel: **959 442 677**. Email: **info@campinglaaldea.com**

This impressive site lies just on the edge of the Parque Nacional de Donana, southwest of Sevilla on the outskirts of El Rocio. The town hosts a fiesta at the end of May with over one million people attending the local shrine. They travel for days in processions with cow drawn or motorized vehicles to attend. If you want to stay this weekend book well in advance! The well planned, modern site is well set out and the 246 pitches have natural shade from trees or artificial shade and 10A electricity. There are 52 serviced pitches with water and sewerage. There are also pitches for tents and bungalows for rent. The facilities are new, large and very clean. A beautiful waiter service restaurant (where the Spanish eat) provides lovely local food. The staff are welcoming and helpful with plenty of tourist information to hand. Expeditions on horseback or by 4x4 vehicle can be arranged in the national park.

Facilities

Two sanitary blocks provide excellent facilities including provision for disabled visitors. Motorcaravan service point. Swimming pool (May - Oct). Restaurant and bar in separate new complex. Shop. Internet connection. Playground. Off site: Bus stop 5 minutes walk. Huelva and Sevilla are about an hour's drive. Beach 15 km.

Open: 6 January - 25 December.

Directions

From main Huelva - Sevilla road E1/A49 take exit 48 and drive south through Almonte to outskirts of El Rocio. Site is on left just past 25 km. marker. Go down to the roundabout and back up to be on the right side of the road to turn in.

Charges guide

Per person	€ 4,00 - € 5,00
child	€ 3,00 - € 4,00
pitch incl. car and electricity	€ 11,00 - € 15,00
Less 10-15% for low season stays over 3 days.	

Camping La Aldea
Road El Rocio, km 25. Apdo. Correos 1
E-21750 El Rocio-Almonte (Huelva)
Tel.: (34) 959 442 677
Fax: (34) 959 442 582
www.campinglaaldea.com
info@campinglaaldea.com

Situated in El Rocio, at the gate of the national Park Donana and only 15 min. from the beach of Matalascanas. Excursions to the famous religious pilgrimage place of Almonte, Lugares Colombinos and Seville. The camp site is open all year. Swimming pool, supermarket and all facilities of a good holiday site.

ES90800 Camping Municipal El Brillante

Avenida del Brillante 50, E-14012 Córdoba (Córdoba)

Tel: **957 403 836**. Email: **elbrillante@campings.net**

Córdoba is one of the hottest places in Europe and the superb pool here is more than welcome. If you really want to stay in the city, then this large site is a good choice. It has 120 neat pitches of gravel and sand, the upper pitches covered by artificial and natural shade but the lower, newer area with little. The site becomes very crowded in high season. The entrance is narrow and may be congested so care must be exercised – there is a lay-by just outside and it is easier to walk in initially.

Facilities

The toilet blocks include facilities for babies and disabled people. Motorcaravan services. Gas supplies. Bar and restaurant (1/7-30/9). Shop (all year). Swimming pool (15/6-15/9). Play area. Off site: Bus service to city centre from outside site. Commercial centre 300 m. (left out of site, right at traffic lights).

Open: All year.

Directions

Site is on the north side of the river. From the NIV/E25 road from Madrid, take exit at km. 403 and follow signs for Cathedral into city centre. Pass it (on right) and turn right onto the main avenue. Continue and take right fork where the road splits, and follow signs for campsite and/or green signs for El Brillante district. Site is on right up slight hill on this avenue.

Charges 2007

Per unit incl. 2 persons	€ 18,50
electricity	€ 3,50

No credit cards.

ES90270 Camping Parque Natural de Monfrague

Ctra Plasencia - Trujillo km 10, E-10680 Malpartida de Plasencia (Cáceres)

Tel: **927 459 233**. Email: **contacto@campingmonfrague.com**

Situated on the edge of the Monfrague National Park, this well managed site owned by the Barrado family, has fine views to the Sierra de Mirabel and delightful surrounding countryside. Many of the 130 good-sized pitches are grassed on slightly sloping terraced ground. Scattered trees offer a degree of shade, there are numerous water points and electricity is rated at 10A. It would prove difficult to find a more suitable location for those that savour peace, quiet, study of yesteryear, flora and fauna. On rare occasions a goods train travels along the nearby railway line. Used by locals, the air-conditioned restaurant provides good quality food at very acceptable prices. An evening meal on the veranda as the sun sets will provide fond memories of a rewarding holiday. Created as a National Park in 1979, Monfrague is now recognised as one of the best locations in Europe for anyone with any degree of interest in birdwatching. Nearby Plasencia has a medieval aqueduct, fine cathedral (14th C.) and the town's original twin ring of walls containing 68 towers.

Facilities

Large modern toilet blocks, fully equipped, are very clean. Facilities for disabled campers and baby baths. Laundry. Motorcaravan service point. Supermarket/shop. Restaurant, bar and coffee shop. TV room with recreational facilities. WiFi. Swimming and paddling pools (June - Sept). Play area. Tennis. Bicycle hire. Riding. Animation for children in season. Barbecue areas. Guided safaris into the Park for birdwatching at an acceptable price. Off site: Large supermarket at Plasencia.

Open: All year.

Directions

On the N630, from the north take EX-208 (previously C524); site on left in 6 km. From the south turn right just south of Plasencia on EX-108 (previously C511) to Malpartida de Plasencia. Right at main junction onto EX-208 to site. GPS: W06:05.040 N39:56.370

Charges 2008

Per person	€ 4,00
child (3-12 yrs)	€ 3,50
pitch	€ 7,00 - € 7,50

VAT included. Camping Cheques accepted.

ES90890 Camping Despenaperros

Ctra Infanta Elena, E-23213 Santa Elena (Jaén)

Tel: **953 664 192**. Email: **info@campingdespenaperros.com**

This site is on the edge of Santa Elena in a natural park with shade from mature pine trees. This is a good place to stay en route from Madrid to the Costa del Sol or to just explore the surrounding countryside. The 116 pitches are fully serviced including a satellite TV/internet link. All rubbish must be taken to large bins outside the site gates (a long walk from the other end of the site). The site is run in a very friendly manner where nothing is too much trouble. Reception has a monitor link with tourist information and access to the region's sites of interest.

Facilities

Two traditional, central sanitary blocks have Turkish style WCs and well equipped showers. One washing machine (launderette in town). Shop. Excellent bar (all year) and charming restaurant (12/3-20/10). Swimming pools (15/6-15/9). Tennis. First aid room. Caravan storage. Night security. Off site: Walking, riding and mountain sports nearby. The main road gives good access to Jaén and Valdepenas.

Open: All year.

Directions

Travelling north towards Madrid on A4 (E5) take exit 259 (Santa Elena). Drive through town and site is on right up steep slope (alternative entrance for tall vehicles – ask reception). Travelling south towards Bailén take exit 257 and as above. GPS: N38:20.584 W03:32.117

Charges guide

Per person	€ 3,27 - € 3,50
child	€ 2,52 - € 2,70
pitch incl. car	€ 5,47 - € 5,85
electricity	€ 3,27 - € 3,50
All plus 7% VAT.	

ES90860 Cáceres Camping

Ctra N630 km 549.5, E-10005 Cáceres (Cáceres)

Tel: **927 233 100**. Email: **info@campingcaceres.com**

Recommended by our agent in Spain, we plan to conduct a full inspection of this all-year site in 2008. Cáceres Camping is quite a small site, located to the west of the interesting city of Cáceres, a World Heritage site. There are 130 pitches here, and, unusually, each has a chalet providing a shower, washbasin and toilet. The pitches are of a reasonable size (80 sq.m.) and are well shaded. A range of leisure facilities is provided, including a swimming pool and a separate children's pool. Cáceres is a city with much interest, and a fascinating history – cave paintings on the city outskirts date back 30,000 years! The city is capital of High Extremadura and close by, the Montanchez mountain range offers many opportunities for walking and cycling.

Facilities

Individual wash blocks. Bar, restaurant, cafeteria and takeaway meals. Supermarket. Swimming pool. Off site: City centre 2 km. Golf, walking and cycling opportunities.

Open: All year.

Directions

From the east (E90 motorway) take the N521 to Cáceres. Continue on this road to the west of the city. At the large roundabout,

Charges 2008

Per person	€ 4,00
child	€ 3,00
pitch	€ 12,00
electricity	€ 3,20

ES90280 Camping Las Villuercas

Ctra Villanueva, E-10140 Guadalupe (Cáceres)

Tel: **927 367 139**

This rural site nestles in an attractive valley northwest of Guadalupe. The 50 pitches are level and of a reasonable size; although large units may experience difficulty in getting into the more central pitches. With an abundance of mature trees most pitches offer some degree of shade. There are 25 pitches with 10A electricity. A river runs alongside the site and the ground can be muddy in wet periods. The site is co-located with hostel accommodation. The restaurant provides excellent food at low prices and leads to a patio with vines and potted plants allowing elevated views of the pools.

Facilities

The single toilet block is older in but very clean, one area for women and one for men, providing British type WCs, washbasins and showers (hot water is from a 40 litre immersion heater which could be overwhelmed in busy periods). Facilities for disabled visitors. Laundry facilities. Restaurant. Bar. Swimming pools. Shop. Tennis. Small playground. Barbecue area. Safe deposit. Medical post. No English spoken. Off site: Riding 2 km. Fishing 3 km.

Open: 1 March - 30 November.

Directions

From NV/E90 exit at Navelmoral de la Mata. Follow south to Guadalupe on CC713 (83 km). Site is 2 km. from Guadalupe (near Monastery). From further southwest take exit 102 off main E90/NV (northeast of Merida). Follow signs (Guadalupe). Go through villages and near 72 km. marker turn left to site.

Charges guide

Per person	€ 3,00
pitch incl. electricity	€ 7,50 - € 8,00

No credit cards.

ES90870 Camping Mérida

Ctra NV Madrid-Port, km 336.6, E-06800 Mérida (Badajoz)

Tel: **924 303 453**. Email: **proexcam@jet.es**

Camping Mérida is situated alongside the main N-V road to Madrid, the restaurant, café and pool complex separating the camping site area from the road where there is considerable noise. The site has 80 good sized pitches, most with some shade and on sloping ground, with ample electricity connections (long leads may be needed) and hedges with topiary. No English is spoken, but try out your Spanish. Reception is open until midnight. Camping Mérida is ideally located to serve both as a base to tour the local area or as an overnight stop en route when travelling.

Facilities

The central sanitary facility includes hot and cold showers, British style WCs. Gas supplies. Small shop for essentials. Busy restaurant/cafeteria and bar, also open to the public. Medium sized swimming and paddling pools (May - Sept). Bicycle hire. Play area (unfenced and near road). Caravan storage. Torches useful. Off site: Town 5 km.

Open: All year.

Directions

Site is alongside NV road (Madrid-Lisbon), 5 km. east of Mérida, at km. 336.6. From east take exit 334 and follow camping signs (doubling back). Site is actually on the 630 road that runs alongside the new motorway. GPS: N38:56.143 W06:18.306

Charges guide

Per person	€ 3,15
pitch incl. car and electricity	€ 9,30

All plus VAT.

ES90900 Camping El Greco

Ctra CM-4000 km 0,7, Puebla de Montalban, E-45004 Toledo (Toledo)

Tel: **925 220 090**

Toledo was the home of the Grecian painter and the site that bears his name boasts a beautiful view of the ancient city from the restaurant, bar and superb pool. The friendly, family owners make you welcome and are proud of their site which is the only one in Toledo (it can get crowded). The 150 pitches are of 80 sq.m. with electrical connections and shade from strategically planted trees. Most have separating hedges giving privacy, with others in herring bone layouts making interesting parking in some areas. The river Tagus stretches alongside the site which is fenced for safety.

Facilities

Two sanitary blocks, both modernised include facilities for disabled campers and everything is of the highest standard and kept very clean. Laundry. Motorcaravan services. Swimming pool (15/6-15/9; charged). Restaurant/bar (1/4-30/9) with good menu and fair prices. Small shop in reception. Playgrounds. Ice machine. Off site: Fishing in river. Golf 10 km. Riding 15 km. An hourly air-conditioned bus service runs from the gates to the city centre, touring the outside of the walls first.

Open: All year.

Directions

Site is on C4000 road on the edge of the town, signed towards Puebla de Montelban; site signs also in city centre. From Madrid on N401, turn off right towards Toledo city centre but turn right again at the roundabout at the gates to the old city. Site is signed from the next right turn.

Charges 2007

Per person	€ 5,79
pitch incl. electricity (6A)	€ 14,09 - € 14,75

Plus 7% VAT.

ES90980 Camping Rio Mundo

Ctra Comarcal 412, km 205, Mesones, E-02449 Molinicos (Albacete)

Tel: **967 433 230**. Email: **riomundo@campingriomundo.com**

This typically Spanish site is situated in the Sierra de Alcaraz (south of Albacete), just off the scenic route 412 between Elche de la Sierra and Valdepenas. The drive to this site is through beautiful scenery (well worth the drive) and although from the west the main road is winding in some places, it should cause no problems if driven carefully. Shade is provided either by trees or by artificial means for the 100 pitches and electricity is supplied to the centre ones. It is a beautiful setting with majestic mountains and wonderful countryside which begs to be explored.

Facilities

One toilet block provides clean modern facilities. Basic toilet facilities for disabled people. Washing machine. Small shop for basics. Outside bar serving snacks with covered seating area. Another bar by the swimming pool. Playground. Petanque. Barbecue area.

Open: 18 March - 12 October.

Directions

Site is just off the 412 road which runs west to east, between the A30 and 322 roads south of Albacete. Turn at km. 205 on the 412, 5 km. east of village of Riopar and west of Elche de la Sierra. From here follow signs to site. The road narrows to one lane for a few hundred yards but keep straight on for 1-2 km. to site. GPS: N38:29.347 W02:20.781

Charges 2007

Per person	€ 3,60 - € 4,75
child	€ 2,50 - € 3,20
pitch incl. car	€ 8,00 - € 10,60
electricity	€ 2,95

ES92100 Camping Pico de la Miel

Ctra NI Madrid - France, km 58, E-28751 La Cabrera (Madrid)

Tel: **918 688 082**. Email: **pico-miel@picodelamiel.com**

Pico de la Miel is a very large site 60 kilometres north of Madrid. Mainly a long-stay site for Madrid, there is a huge number of very well established, fairly old statics. There is a small separate area with its own toilet block for touring units. The pitches are on rather poor, sandy grass, some with artificial shade. Others, not so level, are under sparse pine trees and there are yet more pitches for tents (the ground could be hard for pegs). The noise level from the many Spanish customers is high and you will have a chance to practice your Spanish! Electricity connections are available. Tall hedges abound and with the trees, make it resemble a giant maze. No internal signs are provided and the long walk to the pool can be a challenge. The site is well signed and easy to find, two or three kilometres southwest off the main N1 road, with an amazing mountain backdrop.

Facilities

Dated but clean tiled toilet block, with some washbasins in cabins. It can be heated. En-suite unit with ramp for disabled visitors. Motorcaravan services. Gas supplies. Shop. Restaurant/Bar and takeaway (1/6-30/9). Excellent swimming pool complex (15/6-15/9). Tennis. Playground. Off site: Bicycle hire and riding 200 m. Fishing 8 km.

Open: All year.

Directions

Site is well signed from the N1. Going south or north use exit 57 and follow site signs. When at T-junction, facing a hotel, turn left. (Exit 57 is closer to site than exit 60). GPS: N40:51.547 W03:37.034

Charges 2007

Per person	€ 5,60
child (3-9 yrs)	€ 4,80
pitch	€ 5,40 - € 8,90
car	€ 4,80
electricity	€ 4,00
All plus 7% VAT. Less 10-25% for longer stays.	

ES90910 Camping Internacional Aranjuez

Soto del Rebollo, s/n (antigua N-IV km. 46.8), E-28300 Aranjuez (Madrid)

Tel: **918911395**. Email: **info@campingaranjuez.com**

Aranjuez, supposedly Spain's version of Versailles, is worthy of a visit with its beautiful palaces, leafy squares, avenues and gardens. This useful, popular and unusually well equipped site is therefore excellent for enjoying the unusual attractions or for an en-route stop. It is 47 km. south of Madrid and 46 km. from Toledo. The site is alongside to the River Tajo in a park-like situation with mature trees. There are 178 touring pitches, all with electricity (10A), set on flat grass amid tall trees. The site has recently been acquired by the owners of La Marina (ES8742) who are working hard to improve the pitches and the site. Two little tourist road trains run from the site to the palaces daily. You can visit the huge, but slightly decaying Royal Palace or the Casa del Labrador (translates as farmer's cottage) which is a small neo-classical palace in unusual and differing styles. It has superb gardens commissioned by Charles II. Canoes may be hired from behind the supermarket and there is a lockable moat gate to allow access to the river. There is good security backed up with CCTV around the river perimeter.

Facilities

The largest of three modern, good quality sanitary blocks is heated in winter and well equipped with some washbasins in cabins. Laundry facilities. Gas supplies. Small shop, bar and restaurant (all year) with attractive riverside patio (also open to the public). Takeaway. TV room. Swimming and paddling pools (15/6-15/9). Play area. Bicycle hire. Canoe hire. Torch useful. Off site: Within easy walking distance of palace, gardens and museums. Riding 5 km. Golf 20 km.

Open: All year.

Directions

From the M305 (Madrid - Aranjuez) look for 8 km. marker on the outskirts of town. Then follow campsite signs (back onto M305 going north now) and site is signed right at 300 m. on the first left bend. Follow signs down the narrow road for 400 m.

Charges 2007

Per person	€ 4,00 - € 5,50
pitch incl. electricity	€ 11,50 - € 21,50

Plus 7% VAT. Discounts for groups or long stays. Camping Cheques accepted.

Visit Aranjuez, the Spanish Versailles!

Camping Internacional Aranjuez
C/ Soto del Rebollo, s/n
E-28300 Aranjuez (Madrid) SPAIN
Telf.: (+34) 91 891 13 95
Fax: (+34) 91 892 04 06
info@campingaranjuez.com
www.campingaranjuez.com

ES92000 Caravanning El Escorial

Apdo 8, Ctra M600, km 3.5, E-28280 El Escorial (Madrid)

Tel: **918 902 412**. Email: **info@campingelescorial.com**

There is a shortage of good sites in the central regions of Spain, but this is one (albeit rather expensive). El Escorial is very large, there are 1,358 individual pitches of which about 600 are for touring, with the remainder used for permanent or seasonal units, but situated to one side of the site. The pitches are shaded (ask for a pitch without a low tree canopy if you have a 3 m. high motorcaravan). There are another 250 pseudo 'wild' spaces for tourists on open fields, with good shade from mature trees (long cables may be necessary for electricity).

Facilities

One large toilet block for the touring pitches, plus two smart, small blocks for the 'wild' camping area, are all fully equipped with some washbasins in cabins. Baby baths. Facilities for disabled campers. The blocks can be heated. Large supermarket (1/3-31/10). Restaurant/bar and snack bar (all year; w/ends only in low season). Disco-bar. Swimming pools (15/5-15/9). Three tennis courts. ATM. Off site: Town 3 km. Riding or golf 7 km.

Open: All year.

Directions

From the south go through town of El Escorial, and follow M600 Guadarrama road. Site is between the 2 and 3 km. markers north of the town on the right. From the north use A6 autopista and exit 47 to M600 towards El Escorial town. Site is on the left.

Charges 2007

Per person	€ 6,00
pitch incl. electricity	€ 22,00

VAT included. No credit cards.

ES90190 Camping La Pesquera

Ctra de Caceres - Arrabal, E-37500 Ciudad Rodrigo (Salamanca)

Tel: **923 481 348**

This modest site has just 54 pitches and is located near the Rio Agueda looking up to the magnificent fortress ramparts of Ciudad Rodrigo. Entry to the site is through a municipal park with a large play area. Whilst the site is small it can take even the largest units, the centrally located facilities have all been refurbished to a high standard, the pitches are flat and grassy and the roads are well maintained gravel. The pitches are shaded by trees by day and there is site lighting at night although you may find torches useful due to the tree canopy.

Facilities

Attractive ochre stone sanitary building with British WCs and free hot showers. Facilities for disabled campers. Washing machine. Basics sold from bar in high season. Bar/snacks (April - Sept). Playground outside gates. Barbecue outside gate. Torches useful. Off site: River fishing 1 km. Riding 5 km. Superb walking area.

Open: 25 April - 30 September.

Directions

Site is southwest of Salamancar close to Ciudad Rodrigo. From the E80 N260, any direction, take the 526 to Coria. Site is alongside river directly off the road and well signed.

Charges guide

Per person	€ 3,20
pitch incl. car and electricity	€ 6,20 - € 12,40

ES90260 Camping El Burro Blanco

Camino de las Norias s/n, E-37660 Miranda del Castañar (Salamanca)

Tel: **923 161 100**. Email: **el.burro.blanco@hotmail.com**

Set on a hill side, within the Sierra Peña de Francia and with views of the romantic walled village of Miranda del Castañar and its charming, crumbling castle. This site has been developed by a Dutch team; husband and wife Jeff and Yvonne and their friend Paul. You are welcomed at the gate and are walked around the facilities. There are 31 level touring pitches, all between 80 and 120 sq.m. and 25 have electricity. They are beautifully set in 3.5 hectares of attractive natural woodland.

Facilities

One central modern sanitary facility, fully equipped includes a baby bath. Two washbasins have hot water. Out of season part of the unit is closed and therefore facilities are unisex. Launderette. Gas supplies. Library with book swap and small bar. Off site: Restaurants, bars, shops and ATM in village 600 m. Municipal swimming pool nearby, river swimming and fishing 1.5 km.

Open: 1 April - 1 October.

Directions

From east - west direction take Bejar - Ciudad Rodrigo road turning south towards Cepeda/Coria. The road to Miranda del Castañar is 7 km. northeast of the village of Cepeda. Turn off main road signed Miranda. After 1.2 km. going downhill towards town look for left turn onto a concrete road. Follow road for 1.1 km. (a short stretch unmade) and site is on right. GPS: N40:28.488 W05:59.931

Charges 2007

Per person	€ 4,80
pitch incl. electricity (2-10A)	€ 9,50 - € 12,80
Plus 7% VAT. No credit cards.	

ES92420 Camping El Acueducto

Avenida D. Juan de Borbón, 49, E-40004 Segovia (Segovia)

Tel: **921 425 000**. Email: **informacion@campingacueducto.com**

Located right on the edge of the interesting city of Segovia with lovely views across the open plain with mountains in the background, this is a family run, typically Spanish site. The grass pitches are mostly of medium size, although a few pitches near the gate would have room for larger motorcaravans. The owner is helpful and speaks good English. El Acueducto is well positioned for discovering Segovia. About three miles away, Segovia is deeply and haughtily Castilian, with squares and mansions from its days of Golden Age grandeur, when it was a royal resort.

Facilities

Two traditional style toilet blocks provide basic facilities, a laundry room and dishwashing sinks, all of which are clean. Small shop for basics. Bar. Two swimming pools. Table tennis. Large play area. Off site: Large restaurant nearby. Bus service into city centre. Madrid is within driving distance.

Open: 1 April - 30 September.

Directions

From the north on N1 (Burgos - Madrid) take exit 99 on N110 towards Segovia. On outskirts of city take third exit on N603 signed Madrid. Pass one exit to Segovia and take second signed Segovia and La Granja. At roundabout turn right towards Segovia. Site is 500 m. on right beside the dual carriageway.

Charges guide

Per person	€ 4,50 - € 5,00
pitch	€ 14,00 - € 15,50

ES90230 Camping Camino de Santiago

Casco Urbano, E-09110 Castrojeriz (Burgos)

Tel: **947 377 255**. Email: **campingcastro@eresmas.com**

This tranquil site lies to the west of Burgos on the outskirts of Castrojeriz, a small unspoilt Spanish rural town. In a superb location, almost in the shadow of the ruined castle high on the hillside, it will appeal to those who like peace and a true touring campsite without all the modern trimmings, and at a reasonable cost. The 50 marked pitches are level, grassy and divided by hedges, with electricity (5A) and drainage available to all. There is also a number of permanent pitches. Mature trees provide shade and there is a pretty orchard in one corner of the site.

Facilities

Adequate sanitary facilities with showers, British and Turkish style WCs, and washbasins with cold water only. These facilities are in older style, but are well maintained and clean. Washing machine. Bar (serving coffee and soft drinks). Games room. Tennis. Play area. Bicycle hire. Barbecue area. Note: the present owner is looking to sell the site so things may change.

Open: 1 March - 30 November.

Directions

From N120/A231 (Leon - Burgos), turn onto the BU404 (Castrojeriz). Turn left at crossroads on southwest side of town, then left at site sign. From A62 turn north at Vallaquirán on Bu400/401 to Castrojeriz. GPS: N42:17.484 W04:07.899

Charges guide

Per person	€ 3,75
pitch incl. electricity	€ 6,50 - € 8,00

ES90290 Camping El Astral

Camino de Pollos 8, E-47100 Tordesillas (Valladolid)

Tel: **983 770 953**. Email: **info@campingelastral.es**

The site is in a prime position alongside the wide River Duero (safely fenced). It is homely and run by a charming man, Eduardo Gutierrez, who has excellent English and is ably assisted by brother Gustavo and sister Lola. The site is generally flat with 154 pitches separated by thin hedges. They vary in size from 60 - 200 sq.m. with mature trees providing shade. There is an electricity pylon tucked in one corner of the site but this is hardly noticeable.

Facilities

One attractive sanitary block including two cabins with WC, bidet and washbasin. Some facilities for disabled campers, including ramps. Baby room in ladies' area. Washing machines. Motorcaravan services. Supermarket. Bar. Restaurant frequented by locals. Swimming and paddling pools (1/6-15/9). Playground. Tennis (high season). Minigolf. Internet point and WiFi. Animation daily in high season. Torches are useful.

Open: 15 April - 30 September.

Directions

Tordesillas is 28 km. southwest of Valladolid. From all directions, leave the main road towards Tordesillas and follow signs to campsite or 'Parador' (a hotel opposite the campsite). GPS: N41:29.779 W05:00.312

Charges 2008

Per person	€ 4,20 - € 6,40
pitch	€ 7,10 - € 9,70
electricity (5A)	€ 3,50

ES89420 Camping Los Manzanos

Avenida de Emilia Pardo Bazan, E-15179 Santa Cruz (A Coruña)

Tel: **981 614825**. Email: **info@camping-losmanzanos.com**

Los Manzanos has a steep access drive down to the site, which is divided by a stream into two sections linked by a bridge. Pitches for larger units are marked and numbered, 85 with electricity (12A) and, in one section, there is a fairly large, unmarked field for tents. Some aircraft noise should be expected as the site is under the flight path to La Coruña (but no aircraft at night). The site impressed us as being very clean, even when full, which it tends to be in high season. Some huge interesting stone sculptures create focal points and conversation pieces.

Facilities

One good toilet block provides modern facilities including free hot showers. Small shop with fresh produce daily (limited outside June-Sept). High quality restaurant/bar (July/Aug). Swimming pool with lifeguard, free to campers (15/6-30/9). Playground. Barbecue area. Bungalows for rent. Off site: Bus service at end of entrance drive. Beach and fishing 800 m. Bicycle hire 2 km. Golf and riding 8 km.

Open: Easter - 30 September.

Directions

Exit AP9 at junction 7, signed O Burgo. Carry on through town. At roundabout (signed airport to left), go straight ahead. Continue and immediately at entry to underpass take slip road and turn right into N-V1. Take next left (Santa Cristina/Santa Cruz) and follow AC173. In Santa Cruz turn right and follow sign to site for 0.8 km. Site on left. GPS: N43:29.960 W08:20.140

Charges 2007

Per person	€ 5,30
pitch incl. car and electricity	€ 14,35 - € 14,95
All plus 7% VAT.	

ES90240 Camping As Cancelas

Rue do 25 de Xullo 35, E-15704 Santiago de Compostela (A Coruña)

Tel: **981 580 476**. Email: **info@campingascancelas.com**

The beautiful city of Santiago has been the destination for European Christian pilgrims for centuries and they now follow ancient routes to this unique city, the whole of which is a national monument. The As Cancelas campsite is excellent for sharing the experiences of these pilgrims in the city and around the magnificent cathedral. It has 125 marked pitches (60-90 sq.m.) arranged in terraces and divided by trees and shrubs. On a hillside overlooking the city, the views are very pleasant, but the site has a steep approach road and access to most of the pitches can be a challenge for large units. Electrical hook-ups (5A) are available, the site is lit at night and a security guard patrols. There are many legendary festivals and processions here, the main one being on July 25th, especially in holy years (when the Saint's birthday falls on a Sunday). Examine for yourself the credibility of the fascinating story of the arrival of the bones of St James at Compostela (Compostela translates as 'field of stars'), and also discover why the pilgrims dutifully carry a scallop shell on their long journey. There are many pilgrims' routes, including one commencing from Fowey in Cornwall.

Facilities

Two modern toilet blocks are fully equipped, with ramped access for disabled campers. The quality and cleanliness of the fittings and tiling is good. Laundry with service wash for a small fee. Small minimarket. Restaurant. Bar with TV. Well kept, unsupervised swimming pool and children's pool. Small playground. Internet access. Off site: Huge commercial centre (open late and handy for off season use) 20 minutes walk downhill (uphill on the return!).

Open: All year.

Directions

From motorway AP9-E1 take exit 67 and follow signs for 'Casco Historico' and 'Centro Ciudad' then follow site signs. GPS: N42:53.360 W08:31.450

Charges 2007

Per person	€ 4,00 - € 5,25
child (up to 12 yrs)	€ 2,50 - € 4,00
pitch	€ 8,00 - € 11,30
electricity	€ 3,60

All plus VAT.

ES89400 Camping Los Cantiles

Ctra N634 km 502,7, E-33700 Luarca (Asturias)

Tel: **985 640 938**. Email: **cantiles@campingloscantiles.com**

Luarca is a picturesque little place with a pretty inner harbour and two sandy beaches, and Los Cantiles is two kilometres to the east of town on a cliff top that juts out into the sea, giving excellent views from some pitches and the sound of the waves to soothe you to sleep. The site is well maintained and is a pleasant place to stop along this under-developed coastline. The 150 pitches, 105 with electricity, are mostly on level grass, divided by huge hedges of hydrangeas and bushes. Some pitches have gravel surfaces. There is a separate area for late arrivals in high season.

Facilities

Two modern, fully equipped sanitary blocks (one in low season which is heated in winter) are kept very clean. Facilities for disabled people and babies. Laundry. Freezer service. Gas supplies. Small shop for basics. Bar with hot snacks (1/7-15/9). Day room for backpackers with seating and cooking facilities (own gas). Playing field. Torches helpful after midnight. English is spoken. Off site: Indoor swimming pool, sauna and fitness centre, bar/restaurant and shop 300 m. Luarca 2 km. Beach and fishing 700 m.

Open: All year.

Directions

Luarca is 85 km. west of Gijon. From A8 Oviedo - La Coruña exit at 467 onto N634 for Luarca. After km. 502 east of Luarca, turn right at petrol station and follow signs to site for 2.5 km. Last 150 m. is narrow. GPS: N43:32.953 W06:31.459

Charges 2007

Per person	€ 4,00
child (under 10 yrs)	€ 3,50
pitch incl. electricity (3/6A)	€ 9,50 - € 11,50

Plus 7% VAT. No credit cards.

ES89450 Camping Lagos de Somiedo

Valle de Lago, E-33840 Somiedo (Asturias)

Tel: **985 763 776**. Email: **campinglagosdesomiedo@hotmail.com**

This is a most unusual small site in the Parque Natural de Somiedo. Winding narrow roads with challenging rock overhangs, hairpin bends and breathtaking views (for 8 km.) finally bring you to the lake and campsite at an elevation of 1,200 m. This is a site for 4 x 4s, powerful small campervans and cars – not for medium or large motorhomes, and caravans are not accepted. It is not an approach for the faint hearted! There are 210 touring pitches available (just 4 with electricity hook-up), undefined in two open meadows.

Facilities

There are British style toilets and free hot water to clean hot showers and washbasin. Facilities for babies and children. Washing machine. Combined reception, small restaurant, bar and reference section. Shop for bread, milk and other essentials, plus local produce and crafts. Horses for hire, trekking. Lectures on flora, fauna, history and culture. Fishing (licence required). Barbecue area. Small play area. Gas supplies. Off site: The very small village is 500 m. and it maintains the Spanish customs and traditions of this area.

Open: Easter - 15 October.

Directions

From N634 via Oviedo turn left at 442 km. marker on AS-15 signed Parque Natural de Somiedo. At 9 km. marker past village of Longoria, turn left on AS-227. At 38 km. marker, turn left into Pol de Somiedo, signed Centro Urbano. Follow signs for Valle de Lago and El Valle; 8 km. of hairpin bends from Pola, passing Urria on the left, brings you to the valley. Site is signed on the right. GPS: N43:04.320 W06:02.110

Charges guide

Per person	€ 4,50
pitch incl. car	€ 7,00

ES89550 Camping Caravaning Arenal de Moris

A8 Salida 337, E-33344 Caravia Alta (Asturias)

Tel: **985 853 097**. Email: **camoris@teleline.es**

This smart, well run site is close to three fine sandy beaches so gets very busy at peak times. It has a backdrop of the mountains in the nature reserve known as the Sueve which is important for a breed of short Asturian horses, the 'Asturcone'. The site has 330 grass pitches (269 for touring units) of 40-70 sq.m. and with 200 electricity connections available (5A). With little shade, some pitches are terraced with others on an open, slightly sloping field with views of the sea.

Facilities

Three sanitary blocks provide comfortable, controllable showers (no dividers) and vanity style washbasins, laundry facilities and external dishwashing (cold water). Supermarket. Bar/restaurant. Swimming pool. Tennis. Play area in lemon orchard. English is spoken. Off site: Fishing 200 m. Golf 5 km. Riding, bicycle hire and sailing 10 km. Bar and restaurants in village 2 km. Beach 200 m.

Open: 1 June - 17 September.

Directions

Caravia Alta is 50 km. east of Gijón, Leave the A8 Santander - Oviedo motorway at km. 337 exit, turn left on N632 towards Colunga and site is signed to right in village, near 16 km. marker. GPS: N43:28.349 W05:10.999

Charges guide

Per person	€ 5,00
pitch incl. car and electricity	€ 10,80 - € 14,07

ES89610 Camping El Helguero

Ctra Santillana - Comillas, E-39527 Ruiloba (Cantabria)

Tel: **942 722 124**. Email: **reservas@campingelhelguero.com**

This site, in a peaceful location surrounded by tall trees and impressive towering rock formations, caters for 240 units (of which 100 are seasonal) on slightly sloping ground. There are many marked pitches on different levels, all with access to electricity (6A), but with varying amounts of shade. There are also attractive tent and small camper sections set close in to the rocks and some site owned chalets. The site gets very crowded in high season, so it is best to arrive early if you haven't booked.

Facilities

Three well placed toilet blocks, although old, are clean and all include controllable showers and hot and cold water to all basins. Facilities for children and disabled visitors. Washing machines and dryers. Motorcaravan services. Small supermarket (July/Aug). Bar/snack bar plus separate more formal restaurant. Swimming pool (caps compulsory). Activities and entertainment (high season). Playground. ATM. Torches useful in some places. Off site: Bus service 500 m. Bar/restaurants in village.

Open: 1 April - 30 September.

Directions

From A8 take km. 249 exit (Cabezón and Comillas) and turn north on Ca135 towards Comillas, At km. 7 turn right on Ca359 to Ruilobuca and Barrio la Iglesia. After village turn right up hill on Ca358 to site on right (signs refer to 'Camping Ruiloba'). GPS: N43:22.973 W04:14.880

Charges 2008

Per person	€ 4,00 - € 4,70
pitch incl. electricity	€ 8,40 - € 13,60
Camping Cheques accepted.	

ES89620 Camping La Isla Picos de Europa

Picos de Europa, E-39570 Potes-Turieno (Cantabria)

Tel: **942 730 896**. Email: **campicoseuropa@terra.es**

La Isla is beside the road from Potes to Fuente Dé, with many mature trees giving good shade and glimpses of the mountains above. Established for over 25 years, a warm welcome awaits you from the owners (who speak good English) and a most relaxed and peaceful atmosphere exists in the site. The 121 unmarked pitches are arranged around an oval gravel track under a variety of fruit and ornamental trees. Electricity (6A) is available to all pitches, although some need long leads.

Facilities

Single, clean and smart sanitary block retains the style of the site. It includes washbasins with cold water. Washing machine. Gas supplies. Freezer service. Small shop and restaurant/bar (all season). Small swimming pool (caps compulsory; 1/5-30/9). Play area. Barbecue area. Fishing. Bicycle hire. Riding. Off site: Shops, bars and restaurants plus Monday morning market in Potes 4 km. Fuente Dé and its spectacular cable-car ride 18 km.

Open: 1 April - 30 October.

Directions

From A8/N634 (Santander - Oviedo) take exit for Unquera (km. 272, end of motorway section). Take N621 south to Panes and up spectacular gorge (care needed if towing) to Potes. Take CA165 to Funte Dé and site is on the right, 3 km beyond Potes.

Charges 2007

Per person	€ 3,75 - € 4,05
pitch incl. electricity	€ 6,15 - € 13,80

All plus VAT. Low season reductions.

ES90000 Camping Playa Joyel

Playa de Ris, E-39180 Noja (Cantabria)

Tel: **942 630 081**. Email: **playajoyel@telefonica.net**

This very attractive holiday and touring site is some 40 km. from Santander and 80 km. from Bilbao. It is a busy, high quality, comprehensively equipped site by a superb beach providing 1,000 well shaded, marked and numbered pitches with 3A electricity available. These include 80 large pitches of 100 sq.m. Some 250 pitches are occupied by tour operators or seasonal units. This well managed site has a lot to offer for family holidays with much going on in high season.

Facilities

Six excellent, spacious and fully equipped toilet blocks include baby baths. Large laundry. Motorcaravan services. Gas supplies. Freezer service. Supermarket (all season). General shop. Kiosk. Restaurant and takeaway (1/7-31/8). Bar and snacks (all season). Swimming pools (20/5-15/9). Entertainment organised (July-Aug). Gym park. Tennis. Playground. Riding. Fishing. Natural animal park. Torches necessary in some areas. Dogs and other animals are not accepted. Off site: Sailing and boat launching 10 km. Riding and golf 20 km.

Open: Easter - 30 September.

Directions

From A8 (Bilbao - Santander) take km. 185 exit and N634 towards Beranga. Almost immediately turn right on Ca147 to Noja. In 10 km. turn left at multiple campsite signs and go through town. At beach roundabout turn left and continue to site at end of road. GPS: N43:29.369 W03:32.220

Charges 2007

Per person	€ 3,70 - € 5,50
pitch incl. electricity	€ 15,00 - € 25,00

All plus 7% VAT. No credit cards.
Camping Cheques accepted.

ES90350 Camping Portuondo

Ctra Gernika - Bermeo, E-48360 Mundaka (Bizkaia)

Tel: **946 877 701**. Email: **recepcion@campingportuondo.com**

This well kept site has a lovely retaurant, bar and terrace taking full advantage of the wonderful views across the ocean and estuary. Set amongst gardens, the pitches are mainly for tents and smaller vans, but there are eight large pitches at the lower levels for caravans and motorhomes. The access to these is a little difficult as the road is very steep and there is no turning space. In high season (July/August) it is essential to ring to book your space. English is spoken.

Facilities

Two fully equipped toilet blocks can be heated and include mostly British WCs and a smart baby room. Washing machines and dryers. Shop (15/6-15/9). Bar and two restaurants, all open to public (28/1-14/12). Takeaway (15/6-15/9). Swimming pools (15/6-15/9). Barbecue area. Torches may be useful. Off site: Fishing 100 m. Beaches 500 m. bracing walk. Surfing on Mundaka beach 500 m. Boat launching 1 km. Shops, bars and restaurants 2 km. Riding 8 km. Bicycle hire 10 km. Golf 40 km. Buses to Bilbao and Gernika (every 30 mins) 300 m.

Open: 28 January - 16 December.

Directions

Mundaka is 35 km. northeast of Bilbao. From the A8 (San Sebastián - Bilbao) take exit 18 and follow signs for Gernika on Bi635. Continue on the Bi2235 towards Bermeo. Site is on right approaching Mundaka. Care is needed as a wide approach may be necessary as this is a sharp right turn with a steep access. Road signs do not permit turning laft to site. GPS: N43:23.951 W02:41.766

Charges 2007

Per person	€ 4,90 - € 5,50
pitch incl. electricity	€ 13,90 - € 14,70

ES90430 Camping Caravanning Errota el Molino

E-31150 Mendigorria (Navarra)

Tel: **948 340 604**. Email: **info@campingelmolino.com**

This is an extensive site set by an attractive weir near the town of Mendigorria, alongside the river Arga. It takes its name from an old disused water mill (molino) close by. The site is split into separate permanent and touring sections. The touring area is a new development with good-sized flat pitches with electricity and water for tourers, and a separate area for tents. Many trees have been planted around the site but there is still only minimal shade. The chirpy owner Anna Beriain will give you a warm welcome. Reception is housed in the lower part of a long building along with the bar/snack bar which has a cool shaded terrace, a separate restaurant and a supermarket. The upper floor of this building is dormitory accommodation for backpackers. The site has a sophisticated dock and boat launching facility and an ambitious watersport competition programme in season with a safety boat present at all times. There are pedaloes and canoes for hire. The site is very busy during the festival of San Ferm'n (bull running) in July in Pamplona (28 km). Tours of the local bodegas (groups of ten) to sample the fantastic Navarra wines can be organised by reception.

Facilities

The well equipped toilet block is very clean and well maintained, with cold water to washbasins. Facilities for disabled campers. Washing machine. Large restaurant, pleasant bar. Supermarket (Easter - Sept). Superb new swimming pools for adults and children. Bicycle hire. Riverside bar. Weekly animation programme (July/Aug) and many sporting activities. Squash courts. Internet access. Pleasant river walk. Torches useful. Off site: Bus to Pamplona 500 m. Riding 15 km. Golf 35 km.

Open: All year.

Directions

Mendigorria is 30 km. southwest of Pamplona. From A15 San Sebastian - Zaragoza motorway, leave Pamplona bypass on A12 towards Logon. Leave at km. 23 on NA601 to hill top town of Mendigorria. At crossroads turn right towards Larraga and down hill to site. GPS: N42:37.497 W01:50.533

Charges 2007

Per person	€ 4,50
pitch incl. car and electricity	€ 12,30

Camping Cheques accepted.

ES90420 Camping Etxarri

Paraje Dambolintxulo s/n, E-31820 Etxarri-Aranatz (Navarra)

Tel: **948 460 537**. Email: **info@campingetxarri.com**

Situated in the Valle de la Burundi the site is a peaceful oasis with superb views of the 1,300 m. high San-Donator Mountains. The approach to the constantly improving site is via a road lined by huge 300 year old oak trees, which are a feature of the site. Reception is a purpose built chalet with a touring reference library (mostly in Spanish). There are 100 average sized pitches on flat ground, 50 for tourers, with 6A electricity to all and water to 25. The site is well placed for fascinating walks in unspoilt countryside and is close to three recognised nature walks.

Facilities

The single toilet block has good facilities including baby bath. Laundry. Gas supplies. Essential supplies kept in high season. Bar (1/4-30/9). Restaurant and takeaway (1/6-15/9). Large swimming pool with children's pool (15/6-15/9) also open to the public and can get crowded. Bicycle hire. Minigolf. Play area. Off site: Bus and trains nearby. Bars, restaurants and shops 2 km. Golf, fishing, riding all 20 km. Pamplona 40 km.

Open: 1 April - 1 October.

Directions

Etxarri-Aranatz is 40 km. northwest of Pamplona. From A8 (San Sebastian - Bilbao) take A15 towards Pamplona, then 20 km. northwest of Pamplona, take A10 west towards Vitoria/Gasteix. At km. 19 take NA120 to and through town following site signs. Turn left after crossing railway to site at end of road.

Charges 2008

Per person	€ 4,70
pitch incl. electricity	€ 9,35 - € 12,60

ES90470 Camping Ezcaba

E-31194 Eusa (Navarra)

Tel: **948 33 03 15**. Email: **info@campingezcaba.com**

Camping Ezcaba is a small site located 5 km. north of Pamplona, on the banks of Ulzama river. This all year site has been recommended by our Spanish agent and we hope to undertake a full inspection in 2008. Pitches here are large and grassy and there is a number of mobile homes available for rent. The site becomes very busy for the Festival of San Fermin in Pamplona, possibly Spain's most famous fiesta and best known for the running of the bulls through the city's narrow streets. The site has a swimming pool and a restaurant specialising in local cuisine. Ezcaba is well located for exploring the magnificent Navarra countryside and maybe sample some of its fine wines.

Facilities

Bar. Restaurant. Takeaway food. Shop. Play area. Swimming pool. Entertainment and activities in peak season. Mobile homes and chalets for rent.
Off site: Pamplona 7 km. Parque Natural de Bertiz 38 km. Fishing. Walking and cycle trails.

Open: All year.

Directions

From Pamplona take the northbound N121A towards Irun and the French border. Shortly after leaving the city, turn left to join the NA4210 and then the NA4211 to Eusa. Site is clearly signed from here.

Charges 2007

Per person	€ 4,20 - € 4,49
child	€ 3,65 - € 3,91
pitch	€ 4,45 - € 7,38
electricity	€ 3,85 - € 4,12

ES90600 Camping Peña Montañesa

Ctra Ainsa - Francia, km 2, E-22360 Labuerda (Huesca)

Tel: **974 500 032**. Email: **info@penamontanesa.com**

A large site situated quite high up in the Pyrenees near the Ordesa National Park, Peña Montañesa is easily accessible from Ainsa or from France via the Bielsa Tunnel (steep sections on the French side). The site is essentially divided into three sections opening progressively throughout the season and all have shade. The 288 pitches on fairly level grass are of about 75 sq.m. and 10A electricity is available on virtually all. Grouped near the entrance are the facilities that make the site so attractive, including a fair sized outdoor pool and a glass-covered indoor pool with jacuzzi and sauna.

Facilities

A newer toilet block, heated when necessary, has free hot showers but cold water to open plan washbasins. Facilities for disabled visitors. Small baby room. An older block in the original area has similar provision. Washing machine and dryer. Bar. Restaurant. Takeaway. Supermarket. Outdoor swimming pool (1/4-31/10). Indoor pool (all year). Playground. Boules. Bicycle hire. Riding. Rafting. Only gas barbecues are permitted. Torches required in some areas. Off site: Fishing 100 m. Skiing in season. Canoeing near.

Open: 1 March - 10 December.

Directions

Site is 2 km. from Ainsa, on the road from Ainsa to France. GPS: N42:26.112 E00:08.171

Charges 2007

Per person	€ 3,50 - € 6,60
child (1-9 yrs)	€ 3,00 - € 5,60
pitch	€ 12,50 - € 21,00
electricity	€ 5,00
All plus 7% VAT.	

ES91250 Camping Lago Barasona

Ctra N123a km 25, E-22435 La Puebla de Castro (Huesca)

Tel: **974 545 148**. Email: **info@lagobarasona.com**

This site, alongside its associated ten room hotel, is beautifully positioned on terraces across a road from the shores of the Lago de Barasona (a large reservoir), with views of hills and the distant Pyrenees. The very friendly, English speaking owner is keen to please and has applied very high standards throughout the site. The grassy, fairly level pitches are generally around 100 sq.m. with 35 high quality pitches of 110 sq.m. for larger units. All have electricity (6/10A), many are well shaded and some have great views. Water skiing and other watersports are available in July and August.

Facilities

Two toilet blocks in modern buildings have high standards and hot water throughout including cabins (3 for ladies, 1 for men). Bar/snack bar and two excellent restaurants (all season). Shop (1/4-30/9). Swimming pools (1/6-30/9). Tennis. Mountain bike hire. Canoe, windsurf, motor boat and pedalo hire. Miniclub (high season). Lake swimming, fishing, canoeing, etc. Walking (maps provided). Money exchange. Mini-disco. Off site: Riding 4 km.

Open: All year.

Directions

Site is on the west bank of the lake, close to km. 25 on the N123A, 6 km. south of Graus (about 80 km. north of Lleida/Lerida). Travelling from the south, site is on the left off a newly built roundabout and slip road. GPS: N42:08.498 E00:18.915

Charges 2008

Per person	€ 4,00 - € 5,80
child (2-10 yrs)	€ 3,30 - € 4,85
pitch incl. car and electricity	€ 9,00 - € 16,60

Plus 7% VAT. Camping Cheques accepted.

ES91050 Camping Lago Park

Ctra Alhama de Aragon - Nuevalos, E-50210 Nuevalos (Zaragoza)

Tel: **976 849 038**

Lago Park is situated in an attractive area which receives many visitors for the Monasterio de Piedra just 3 km. distant and it enjoys pleasant views of the surrounding mountains. This site is suitable for transit stops or if you wish to visit the monasterio as it is the only one hereabouts and appears to make the most of that fact. It is not recommended for extended stays. Set on a steep hillside, the 280 pitches (260 for tourers) are on terraces. Only the lower rows are suitable for large caravans. These pitches are numbered and marked by trees, most having electricity (10A).

Facilities

The single very clean sanitary block has British style WCs. washbasins with hot water and controllable hot showers (no dividers). Restaurant/bar (June-Sept). Shop (all season). Swimming pool (late June-Sept). Play area. Gas supplies. Torches needed in some areas. Off site: Fishing 300 m. Riding 2 km.

Open: 1 April - 30 September.

Directions

From Zaragoza (120 km.) take fast A2/N11/E90 road and turn onto C202 road beyond Calatayud to Nuévalos (25 km). From Madrid, exit A2 at Alhama de Aragón (13 km). Follow signs for Monasterio de Piedra from all directions.

Charges 2007

Per person	€ 5,60
pitch incl. car and electricity	€ 10,30 - € 14,60

ES90620 Camping Boltaña

Ctra N260 km 442, E-22340 Boltaña (Huesca)

Tel: **974 502 347**. Email: **info@campingboltana.com**

Nestled in the Rio Ara valley, surrounded by the Pyrenees mountains and below a tiny but enchanting, historic hill top village, is the very pretty and thoughtfully planned Camping Boltaña. Generously sized, grassy pitches have good shade from a variety of trees and a stream meanders through the campsite. The landscaping includes ten charming rocky water gardens and a covered pergola doubles as an eating and play area. A stone building houses the reception, social room and supermarket. Opposite is a terrace for tapas, listening to music, casual eating, animation and games.

Facilities

Two modern sanitary blocks include facilities for disabled visitors and laundry facilities. Casual restaurant and bar and a more formal restaurant (18/3-21/9). Supermarket. Swimming pools (22/3-30/9). Playground. Barbecues. Animation for children (high season). Petanque. Guided tours, plus hiking, canyoning, rafting, climbing, mountain biking and caving. Torches useful in some parts. Off site: Local bus service.

Open: 15 January - 20 December.

Directions

South of the Park Nacional de Ordesa, site is about 50 km. from Jaca near Ainsa. From Ainsa travel northwest on N260 toward Boltaña (near 443 km. marker) and 1 km. from Boltaña turn south toward Margudgued. Site is well signed and is 1 km. along this road. GPS: N42:25.811 E00:04.729

Charges 2008

Per person	€ 4,96 - € 6,20
pitch	€ 5,23 - € 11,78
car	€ 5,23 - € 6,53

VAT included. Camping Cheques accepted.

Check real time availability and at-the-gate prices...

www.alanrogers.com

MAP 8

With giant lakes and
waterways, rich forests,
majestic mountains and
glaciers, and vast, wide open
countryside, Sweden is almost
twice the size of the UK but with
a fraction of the population.

CAPITAL: STOCKHOLM

Tourist Office

Swedish Travel and Tourism Council
Swedish House, 5 Upper Montagu Street
London W1H 2AG
Tel: 020 7870 5600
Fax: 020 7724 5872
Email: info@swetourism.org.uk
Internet: www.visit-sweden.com

The beautiful southwest region, otherwise
known as the 'Swedish Lake and Glass
country', is easily accessible by ferry or
overland from Norway. The area is
dominated by two great lakes, Vänern and
Vättern, Europe's second and third largest
lakes. There are also many fine beaches
with picturesque harbours and historic
ports such as Gothenburg, Helsingborg and
Malmö, which is now linked by a bridge
to Copenhagen. Stockholm, the capital,
is a delightful place built on fourteen
small islands on the eastern coast. It is an
attractive, vibrant city, with magnificent
architecture, fine museums and historic
squares. Moving northwards into central
and northern Sweden, you'll discover
beautiful forests and around 96,000 lakes,
which are perfect for ice skating (in winter!)
and you may even see moose and reindeer.
Today Sweden enjoys one of the highest
standards of living in the world
and a quality of life to go with it.

Population

9 million

Climate

Sweden enjoys a temperate climate thanks
to the Gulf Stream. There is generally less
rain and more sunshine in the summer than
in Britain.

Language

Swedish. English is fairly widely spoken.

Telephone

The country code is 00 46.

Money

Currency: The Krona
Banks: Mon-Fri 09.30-15.00. Some city
banks stay open until 17.30/18.00 on
Thursdays (regions may vary).

Shops

Mon-Fri 09.00-18.00.
Sat 09.00-13.00/16.00. Some department
stores remain open until 20.00/22.00.

Public Holidays

New Year; Epiphany; Easter Mon; Labour
Day; Ascension; Whit Sun; Constitution Day
June 6; Mid-summer Festival; All Saints;
Christmas Dec 24-26.

Motoring

Roads are generally much quieter than in
the UK. Dipped headlights are obligatory.
Away from large towns, petrol stations
rarely open 24 hours but most have self
service pumps (with credit card payment).
Buy diesel during working hours, it may not
be available at self service pumps.

sw2706 Lisebergs Camping Askim Strand

Marholmsvagen, S-436 45 Askim (Hallands Län)

Tel: **031 286 261**. Email: **askim.strand@liseberg.se**

Within easy reach of the city, this is a very pleasantly located site, close to a long gently sloping beach which is very popular for bathing. As a result the area behind the campsite is populated by many holiday homes and cabins. A very open site with very little shade, it has 266 mostly level, grassy pitches all with 10A electricity, plus two areas for tents. Many pitches are fairly compact, although there are some larger ones. The key card entry system operates the entrance barrier and access to the buildings and there is a night security guard (June-Aug). Reception has a range of tourist information, and can provide details of reductions on bus and taxi fares to the city, also selling the Göteborg Card.

Facilities

Two heated sanitary buildings, the larger one fairly new, the smaller recently refitted. Both are maintained to a high standard and provide all the usual facilities, including a good suite for small children, dishwashing sinks, laundry, kitchens with cooking facilities, and a unit for disabled visitors. Hot water is free. Motorcaravan services. Snack bar (July). Playground. TV room. Bicycle hire. Off site: Small shop just outside the site. Göteborg city. Golf 2 km.

Open: 20 April - 2 September.

Directions

About 10 km. south of Göteborg, take exit signed Mölndal S and ports (Hamnar). Take the Rv 159 towards Frolunda, and watch for a slip road to the right. After 200 m. turn left at the roundabout, signed Askim, and follow signs to campsite. GPS: N57:37.699 E11:55.231

Charges 2007

Per pitch	SEK 165 - 345

Only pitches with electricity available for high season.

sw2640 First Camp Båstad-Torekov

Flymossa Vagen 5, S-260 93 Torekov (Skåne Län)

Tel: **043 136 4525**. Email: **torekov@firstcamp.se**

Part of the Kronocamping chain, this campsite is 500 m. from the fishing village of Torekov, 14 km. west of the home of the Swedish tennis WCT Open at Båstad on the stretch of coastline between Malmö and Göteborg. Useful en route from the most southerly ports, it is a very good site and worthy of a longer stay for relaxation. It has 510 large pitches (390 for touring units), all numbered and marked, mainly in attractive natural woodland, with some on more open ground close to the shore. Of these, 300 have electricity (10A) and cable TV, 77 also having water and drainage. The modern reception complex is professionally run and is also home for a good shop, a snack bar, a restaurant and a pizzeria. The spacious site covers quite a large area and there is a cycle track along the shore to the beach with bathing. Games for children are organised in high season and there is an outdoor stage for musical entertainment and dancing (also in high season). This well run site is a pleasant place to stay.

Facilities

Three very good sanitary blocks with free hot water and facilities for babies and disabled visitors. Laundry. Cooking facilities and dishwashing. Motorcaravan service point. Bar. Restaurant, pizzeria and snack bar with takeaway (15/-5/8). Shop and kiosk. Minigolf. Sports fields. Play areas and adventure park for children. Bicycle hire. TV room. Beach. Fishing. WiFi on 50% of pitches. Off site: Tennis close. Golf 1 km. Riding 3 km. Games, music and entertainment in high season.

Open: 11 April - 28 September.

Directions

From E6 Malmö - Göteborg road take Torekov/Båstad exit and follow signs for 20 km. towards Torekov. Site is signed 1 km. before village on right. GPS: N56:25.858 E12:38.433

Charges 2007

Per unit incl electricity and TV connection	SEK 200 - 340
tent pitch	SEK 155 - 255

Camping Cheques accepted.

Check real time availability and at-the-gate prices...

www.**alanrogers**.com

SW2630 Röstånga Camping & Bad

Blinkarpsvägen 3, S-260 24 Röstånga (Skåne Län)

Tel: 043 591 064. Email: nystrand@msn.com

Beside the Söderåsen National Park, this scenic campsite has its own fishing lake and many activities for the whole family. There are 100 large, level, grassy pitches with electricity (10A) and a quiet area for tents with a view over the fishing lake. The tent area has its own service building and several barbecue places. A large holiday home and 14 pleasant cabins are available to rent all year round. A pool complex adjacent to the site provides a 50 metre swimming pool, three children's pools and a water slide, all heated during peak season. A one day visit is free for campers. Activities are arranged on the site in high season, including a children's club with exciting activities such as treasure hunts and gold panning, and for adults aqua-aerobics, Nordic walking and tennis. The Söderåsen National Park offers hiking and bicycle trails. The friendly staff will be happy to help you to plan interesting excursions in the area.

Facilities

Four good, heated sanitary blocks with free hot water and facilities for babies and disabled visitors. Laundry with washing machines and dryers. Kitchen with cooking rings, oven and microwave. Motorcaravan service point. Small shop at reception. Bar, restaurant and takeaway. Minigolf. Tennis. Fitness trail. Fishing. Canoe hire. Children's club. Off site: Swimming pool complex adjacent to site (one visit free for campers). Many golf courses nearby. Motor racing track at Ring Knutstorp 8 km.

Open: 31 March - 29 October.

Directions

From Malmö: drive towards Lund and follow road no. 108 to Röstånga. From Stockholm: turn off at Østra Ljungby and take road no. 13 to Röstånga. In Röstånga drive through the village on road no. 108 and follow the signs. GPS: N55:59.795 E13:16.803

Charges guide

Per pitch	SEK 130 - 165
electricity	SEK 35
Camping Cheques accepted.	

SW2645 Camping Mölle

S-260 42 Mölle (Skåne Län)

Tel: 042 347 384. Email: molle@firstcamp.se

FirstCamp Mölle is a family campsite with a fine location at the foot of the Kullaberg, which marks the point where the Atlantic divides into the Kattegatt and Øresund. The site is open all year. There are 250 pitches, generally of a good size and 220 with electrical connections. The nearby Kullaberg Nature Park is dramatic and well worth a visit. The region is also well known for its ceramics and many potters and artists have settled in the area. On-site amenities include a heated paddling pool and water games complex. The nearest beach is 1.5 km. away and is popular for kayaking and fishing.

Facilities

Two modern sanitary blocks with free hot water and facilities for disabled visitors. Family shower rooms. Laundry with washing machines and dryers. Kitchen with cooking rings and microwave. Motorcaravan services. Restaurant with bar and cafeteria. Shop. Minigolf. Sports pitch. Heated paddling pool. Entertainment and children's activity programme (high season). Bicycle hire. TV room. WiFi. Cabins for rent. Off site: Nearest beach 1.5 km. Kayaking 2 km. Golf 4 km. Kullaberg Nature Park 1 km. Mölle lighthouse 6 km. Höganäs ceramics 8 km.

Open: All year.

Directions

From Helsingborg take the E4 north and then join road 111 towards Höganäs. Pass through this town and follow signs to Mölle and site. From the north take exit 33 on E6 towards Höganäs. Follow signs to site.

Charges 2007

Per pitch	SEK 150 - 285
electricity	SEK 45
tent pitch	SEK 110 - 240

SW2650 Skånes Djurparks Camping

Jularp, S-243 93 Höör (Skåne Län)

Tel: **041 355 3270**. Email: **info@grottbyn.se**

This site is probably one of the most unusual we feature. It is next to the Skånes Djurpark – a zoo park with Scandinavian species – and has on site a reconstructed Stone Age Village. The site is located in a sheltered valley and has 110 large, level grassy pitches for caravans and motorhomes all with 10A electricity and a separate area for tents. The most unusual feature of the site is the sanitary block – it is underground! The fully air-conditioned building houses a superb and ample complement of facilities. Well placed for the Copenhagen - Malmo bridge or the ferries, this is also a site for the discerning camper who is looking for something distinctly different. The site also has a number of underground, caveman style, eight bed (dormitory type) holiday units which can be rented by families or private groups (when not in use by schools on educational trips to the Stone Age Village). They open onto a circular courtyard with a barbecue and camp fire area and have access to the kitchens and dining room in the sanitary block. There are good walks through the nature park and around the lakes, where one can see deer, birds and other wildlife.

Facilities

The underground block includes roomy showers, two fully equipped kitchens, laundry and separate drying room and an enormous dining/TV room. Facilities for disabled people and baby changing. Cooking facilities. Laundry. A small new block and motorcaravan service point are planned. Small shop and café (15/6-15/8). Small heated family swimming pool (15/6-15/8). Playground. Stone Age Village. Off site: Restaurant just outside the entrance. Fishing 1.8 km. Bicycle hire 5 km. Riding and golf 8 km.

Open: All year (full services 15/6-10/8).

Directions

Turn off no. 23 road 2 km. north of Höör (at roundabout) and follow signs for Skånes Djurpark. Campsite entrance is off the Djurpark car park. GPS: N55:57.222 E13:32.289

Charges 2007

Per unit	SEK 160
electricity	SEK 40 - 50

Skånes Djurparks Camping
Jularp, S-243 93 Höör
Tel: 0046 413 55 32 70 • e-mail: info@grottbyn.se

SW2655 Tingsryds Camping

Mårdslyckesand, S-362 91 Tingsryd (Kronobergs Län)

Tel: **047 710 554**. Email: **tingsryd.camping@swipnet.se**

A pleasant, well managed site by Lake Tiken, Tingsryds Camping is well placed for Sweden's Glass District. The 200 large pitches are arranged in rows divided by trees and shrubs, with some along the edge of a lakeside path (public have access). All have electricity (10/16A) and there is shade in parts. The facilities are housed in buildings near the site entrance, the reception building having the restaurant, café, bar and a shop. Adjacent to the site is a small beach, grassy lying out area, playground and lake swimming area and three tennis courts.

Facilities

Heated sanitary facilities are in two well maintained buildings, one including showers, mostly with curtains (on payment, communal undressing), the other a kitchen with hobs and dining area. Facilities for disabled people. Laundry. Motorcaravan services. Shop (1/5-15/9). Restaurant and cafe (1/5-15/9). Minigolf. Playground. Lake swimming. Canoe hire. Fishing. Bicycle hire. Off site: Golf 15 km.

Open: 5 April - 20 October (full servics 24/5-19/8).

Directions

Site is 1 km. from Tingsryd off road no. 120, well signed around the town. GPS: N56:31.723 E14:57.688

Charges 2007

Per unit	SEK 120 - 195
incl. electricity	SEK 160 - 235

sw2705 Lisebergsbyn Karralund

Olbersgatan 9, S-416 55 Göteborg (Västra Götalands Län)

Tel: 031 840 200. Email: karralund@liseberg.se

Well positioned for visiting the city, this busy, well maintained site has 190 marked pitches, 152 with electricity (10A) and cable TV, 42 hardstandings, and several areas for tents. Pitches do vary in size, some are fairly compact and there are no dividing hedges, consequently units can be rather close together. Additionally there are cabins for rent, a budget hotel and a youth hostel. All this makes for a very busy site in the main season, which in this case means June, July and August. An advance telephone call to check for space is advisable.

Facilities

Two heated sanitary buildings, the larger one fairly new, and a smaller, older one with limited facilities, are well maintained and cleaned. They provide all the usual facilities, with controllable hot showers, a good suite for small children, dishwashing sinks and a laundry, kitchens with cooking facilities, and a complete unit for disabled visitors. Motorcaravan services. Shop. Playground. TV room. Off site: Göteborg city with Liseberg amusement park.

Open: All year (full services 9/5-28/8).

Directions

Site is about 2.5 km. east of city centre. Follow signs to Lisebergsbyn and campsite symbol from the E20, E6 or Rv 40. GPS: N57:42.293 E12:01.790

Charges 2007

Per pitch	SEK 190 - 245
electricity	SEK 50
tent and car	SEK 225

Only pitches with electricity available in high season.

sw2665 Jönköping Swecamp Villa Björkhagen

Friggagatan 31, S-554 54 Jönköping (Jönköpings Län)

Tel: 036 122 863. Email: villabjorkhagen@swipnet.se

Overlooking Lake Vättern, Villa Björkhagen is a good site, useful as a break in the journey across Sweden or visiting the city during a tour of the Lakes. It is on raised ground overlooking the lake, with some shelter in parts. There are 280 pitches on well kept grass which, on one side, slopes away from reception. Some pitches on the other side of reception are flat and there are 200 electrical (10A), 100 cable TV and 40 water connections available.

Facilities

Heated sanitary facilities include hot showers on payment (some in private cubicles) and a sauna, plus provision for disabled visitors and babies. Laundry. Dishwashing facilities. Motorcaravan services. Gas supplies. Well stocked mini-market (all year). Restaurant (1/5-30/9). Playground. TV room. Minigolf. Off site: Pool complex 500 m. Fishing 500 m. Golf 1 km. Riding 7 km.

Open: All year (full services 1/5-30/9).

Directions

Site is well signed from the E4 road on eastern side of Jönköping. Watch carefully for exit on this fast road. GPS: N57:47.221 E14:13.077

Charges 2007

Per unit incl. all persons	SEK 180 - 230

Prices may be increased if there is a local exhibition. Camping Cheques accepted.

sw2670 Grännastrandens Familjecamping

Box 14, S-563 21 Gränna (Jönköpings Län)

Tel: 039 010 706

This large, lakeside site with modern facilities and busy continental feel, is set below the old city of Gränna. Flat fields separate Gränna from the shore, one of which is occupied by the 25 acres of Grännastrandens where there are 450 numbered pitches, including a tent area and some seasonal pitches. The site is flat, spacious and very regularly laid out on open ground with only a row of poplars by the lake to provide shelter, so a windbreak may prove useful against any onshore breeze. About 230 pitches have electricity (10A).

Facilities

The large, sanitary block in the centre of the site has modern, well kept facilities including British style WCs, some with external access, washbasins, and free hot showers, some in private cubicles. Dishwashing sinks. Laundry facilities. Provision for disabled people. A further small, older block is by reception. Cooking facilities. Motorcaravan services. Shop (15/6-20/8). TV room. Playground. Lake swimming area. Boating and fishing. Off site: Café outside site (1/5-31/8) or town restaurants close. Bus stop nearby. Golf 6 km.

Open: 1 May - 30 September.

Directions

Take Gränna exit from E4 road (no camping sign) 40 km. north of Jönköping. Site is signed in the centre of the town, towards the harbour and ferry. GPS: N58:01.657 E14:27.482

Charges guide

Per pitch	SEK 160
incl. electricity and TV connection	SEK 200

sw2675 Västervik Lysingsbadet

Lysingsvägen, S-593 53 Västervik (Kalmar Län)

Tel: **049 088 920**. Email: **lysingsbadet@vastervik.se**

One of the largest sites in Scandinavia, Lysingsbadet has unrivalled views of the 'Pearl of the East Coast' – Västervik and its fjords and islands. There are around 10 large, mostly marked and numbered pitches, spread over a vast area of rocky promontory and set on different plateau, terraces, in valleys and woodland, or beside the water. It is a very attractive site, and one which never really looks or feels crowded even when busy. There are 83 full service pitches with TV, water and electrical connections, 163 with TV and electricity and 540 with electricity only, the remainder for tents. Reception is smart, efficient and friendly with good English spoken. An hourly bus service to Västervik runs from the site entrance from June to August. On site facilities include a full golf course, minigolf, heated outdoor pool complex with water slide and poolside café, sauna and solarium, playgrounds, boat hire, tennis, basketball, volleyball and fishing. For children, Astrid Lindgren's World theme park at Vimmerby is an easy day trip away and for adults the delights of the old town of Västervik and its shopping.

Facilities

Ten modern toilet blocks of various ages house a comprehensive mix of showers, basins and WCs. All are kept very clean. Several kitchens with dishwashing sinks and cookers. Four laundry rooms. All facilities and hot water are free. Key cards operate the barriers and gain access to sanitary blocks, pool complex and other facilities. Motorcaravan services. Supermarket (15/5-31/8). Restaurant and café/takeaway (12/6-138). Swimming pool complex (1/6-31/8). Golf. Minigolf. Bicycle and boat hire. Fishing. Entertainment and dances in high season. Play areas. Quick Stop service. Bus service.
Off site: Riding 10 km.

Open: All year.

Directions

Turn off E22 for Västervik and follow signs for Lysingsbadet. GPS: N57:44.294 E16:40.119

Charges 2007

Per pitch	SEK 17 - 30
incl. electricity	SEK 22 - 36
incl. electricity/TV connection	SEK 24 - 38

sw2680 Krono Camping Saxnäs

S-386 95 Färjestaden (Kalmar Län)

Tel: **048 535 700**. Email: **saxnas@kronocamping-oland.se**

Well placed for touring Sweden's Riviera and the fascinating and beautiful island of Øland, this family run site, part of the Krono group, has 420 marked and numbered touring pitches. Arranged in rows on open, well kept grassland dotted with a few trees, all have electricity (10A), 320 have TV connections and 112 also have water. An unmarked area without electricity can accommodate around 60 tents. The site has about 130 long stay units and cabins for rent. The sandy beach slopes very gently and is safe for children. Reception is efficient and friendly with good English spoken. In high season children's games are organised and dances are held twice weekly, with other activities on other evenings. Nearby attractions include the 7 km. long Øland road bridge and the 400 old windmills on the island (in the 19th century there were 20). The southern tip of Øland, Ottenby, is a paradise for bird watchers. Kalmar and its castle, museums and old town on the mainland, Eketorp prehistoric fortified village, Øland Djurpark. The Swedish Royal family's summer residence, Solliden, is well worth a visit.

Facilities

Three heated sanitary blocks provide a good supply of roomy shower cubicles, washbasins, some washbasin/WC suites and WCs. Facilities for babies and disabled visitors. Well equipped laundry room. Good kitchen with cookers, microwaves and dishwasher (free), and sinks. Hot water is free. Gas supplies. Motorcaravan services. Shop (1/5-30/8). Pizzeria, licensed restaurant and café (all 1/5-30/8). Bar (1/7-31/7). Playgrounds. Bouncy castle. Boules. Fishing. Canoe hire. Bicycle hire. Minigolf. Family entertainment and activities. Football.
Off site: Golf 500 m. Riding 2 km.

Open: 17 April - 11 September.

Directions

Cross Øland road bridge from Kalmar on road no. 137. Take exit for Øland Djurpark/Saxnäs, then follow campsite signs. Site is just north of the end of the bridge. GPS: N56:41.236 E16:28.909

Charges 2007

Per pitch	SEK 110 - 235
incl. electricity	SEK 160 - 285
incl. electricity/TV connection	SEK 170 - 295
Weekend and weekly rates available.	

SW2690 Kronocamping Böda Sand

S-380 75 Byxelkrok (Kalmar Län)

Tel: **048 522 200**. Email: **bodasand@kronocampingoland.se**

Kronocamping Böda Sand is beautifully situated at the northern end of the island of Øland and is one of Sweden's largest and most modern campsites. Most of the 1,300 pitches have electricity (10/16A) and TV connections, 130 have water and waste water drainage. The pitches and 123 cabins for rent are spread out in a pine forest, very close to the fabulous 10 km. long, white sand beach. Here you will also find a restaurant, kiosks, toilets and beach showers, and a relaxation centre with an indoor/outdoor pool. The reception, toilet blocks and services are excellent and comprehensive.

Facilities

Seven heated sanitary blocks provide good roomy shower cubicles, washbasins, some washbasin suites and WCs. Facilities for babies and disabled visitors. Well equipped laundry rooms. Excellent kitchens with cookers, ovens, microwaves and dishwashers (free). Motorcaravan services. Supermarket and bakery. Pizzeria, café, pub and restaurant. Takeaway. Bicycle hire, pedal cars and pedal boat hire. WiFi. Minigolf. 9-hole golf course. Swimming pool (on the beach). Family entertainment and activities.

Open: 1 May - 1 October.

Directions

From Kalmar cross the Øland road bridge on road no. 137. On Øland follow road no. 136 towards Borgholm and Byxelkrok. Turn left at the roundabout north of Böda and follow the campsite signs to Kronocamping Böda Sand.

Charges 2007

Per pitch	SEK 155 - 235
incl. electricity	SEK 195 - 285

SW2710 Lidköping SweCamp Kronocamping

Läckögatan, S-531 54 Lidköping (Västra Götalands Län)

Tel: **051 026 804**. Email: **info@kronocamping.com**

This high quality, attractive site provides 423 pitches on flat, well kept grass. It is surrounded by some mature trees, with the lake shore as one boundary and a number of tall pines have been left to provide shade and shelter. There are 374 pitches with electricity (10A) and TV connections and 91 with water and drainage also, together with 60 cabins for rent. The site takes a fair number of seasonal units. There is a small shop (a shopping centre is very close) and a fully licensed restaurant with conservatory seating area in the reception complex.

Facilities

Excellent, modern sanitary facilities are in two blocks with under-floor heating. Free hot water. Make up and hairdressing areas, baby room and facilities for disabled people. Private cabins. Dishwashing sinks outside. Good kitchens with cookers and microwaves. Motorcaravan services. Shop. Restaurant. Minigolf. Playgrounds. TV room. Games room. Bicycle hire. Lake swimming, fishing and watersports. Off site: Swimming pool adjacent. Riding 4 km. Golf 6 km.

Open: All year (full services 8/6-15/8).

Directions

From Lidköping town junctions follow signs towards Läckö then pick up camping signs and continue to site. GPS: N58:30.889 E13:08.390

Charges 2007

Per pitch	SEK 170 - 210
with electricity/TV connection	SEK 190 - 250

SW2715 Gröne Backe Camping & Stugor

Södra Moränvägen, S-66832 Ed (Västra Götalands Län)

Tel: **053 410 144**. Email: **gronebackecamping@telia.com**

In the heart of the beautiful Dalsland region, this pleasant, well shaded (mostly pine) site is open all year. It is well laid out, mostly overlooking the Lilla Le lake, and there is easy access from road no. 164. There are 180 pitches for caravans or motorcaravans, most with electricity (10A) and special areas for tents. Also on the site are 11 cabins for rent and 40 seasonal pitches. At small shop and café are at the reception building. Canoes, rowing boats and bicycles may be hired.

Facilities

Three heated toilet blocks, two in the centre, one at reception, provide washbasins, both vanity type and in cubicles. Showers (on payment). Baby rooms. Facilities for disabled visitors. Laundry. Cooking facilities and dishwashing (free hot water). Motorcaravan services. Small shop. Café. Internet and WiFi. Playground. Minigolf. Sports field. Canoes, rowing boats, bicycles and pedal cars for hire. Beach. Off site: Village nearby. Moose ranch. Canodal (large canoe centre).Tresicklan National Park.

Open: All year.

Directions

Site is on road no. 164 at Ed, and is well signed. GPS: N58:53.965 E11:56.092

Charges guide

Per unit	SEK 135 - 230

495

sw2720 Tidaholm-Hökensås Semesterby och Camping

Hakangen, S-522 91 Tidaholm (Västra Götalands Län)

Tel: 050 223 053. Email: info@hokensas-semesterby.com

Hökensås is located just west of Lake Vättern and south of Tidaholm, in a beautiful nature reserve of wild, unspoiled scenery. This pleasant campsite is part of a holiday complex that includes wooden cabins for rent. It is relaxed and informal, with over 200 pitches either under trees or on a more open area at the far end, divided into rows by wooden rails. These are numbered and electricity (10A) is available on 135. Tents can go on the large grassy open areas by reception. This site is a find for all kinds of people who enjoy outdoor activities. The park is based on a 100 km. ridge, a glacier area with many impressive boulders and ice age debris but now thickly forested with majestic pines and silver birches, with a small, brilliant lake at every corner. The forests and lakes provide wonderful opportunities for walking, cycling (gravel tracks and marked walks) angling, swimming and when the snow falls, winter sports.

Facilities

The original sanitary block near reception is supplemented by one in the wooded area, both refurbished. Hot showers in cubicles with communal changing area are free. Separate saunas for each sex and facilities for disabled visitors and babies. Campers' kitchen at each block with cooking, dishwashing and laundry facilities. Small, but well stocked shop. Very good angling shop. Fully licensed restaurant with takeaway. Playground. Minigolf. Sauna. Lake swimming. Fishing. Off site: The town of Tidaholm and Lake Hornborga. Fishing 2 km. Riding 10 km. Bicycle hire 15 km.

Open: All year (full services 20/6-11/8).

Directions

Approach site from no. 195 western lake coast road. at Brandstorp, about 40 km. north of Jönköping, turn west at petrol station and camp sign signed Hökensås. Site is about 9 km. up this road. GPS: N58:05.890 E14:04.480

Charges 2008

Per pitch	SEK 125 - 140
(more for Midsummer celebrations)	
electricity	SEK 20 - 21,45

sw2725 Hafsten Swecamp Resort

Hafsten 120, S-451 96 Uddevalla (Västra Götalands Län)

Tel: 052 264 4117. Email: info@hafsten.se

This privately owned site on the west coast is situated on a peninsula overlooking the magnificent coastline of Bohuslän. Open all year, it is a lovely terraced site with a beautiful, shallow and child-friendly sandy beach and many nature trails in the vicinity. There are 180 touring pitches, all with electricity (10A), 70 of them with water and drainage. In all, there are 300 pitches including a tent area and 60 cottages of a high standard. There are plenty of activities available including, canoeing, fishing, horse riding, minigolf, tennis, clay pigeon shooting, water slide and a paddling pool (charged), boat and motor boat hire. Troubadour evenings are arranged during the summer. Almost any activity can be arranged on the site or elsewhere by the friendly owners if they are given advance notice. Amenities include two clean and well maintained service buildings, a pub, a fully licensed restaurant with wine from their own French vineyard, a takeaway and a well stocked shop.

Facilities

Two heated sanitary buildings provide the usual facilities. Showers are on payment. Kitchen with good cooking facilities and dishwashing sinks, dining room. Laundry facilities. Units for disabled visitors. Motorcaravan services. Shop. Restaurant, takeaway and pub. Troubadour evenings. TV room. Relaxation centre with sauna and jacuzzi (charged). Water slide (charged). Internet access (WiFi). Riding. Minigolf. Tennis. Playground. Off site: Nordens Ark (animal park) 40 km. Havets hus (marine museum) 30 km. Golf 13 km. Shopping centre 13 km.

Open: All year.

Directions

From the E6, north Uddevalla, at Torpmotet exit take the 161 road towards Lysekil. At the Rotviksbro roundabout take the 161 road towards Orust. The exit to the site is located further on road 2 km. on the left. Follow the signs for 4 km. It is a narrow, one way road for motorcaravans and caravans. GPS: N58:18.881 E11:43.400

Charges 2007

Per pitch	SEK 150
incl. electricity	SEK 195
No credit cards.	

sw2730 Ekuddens Camping

Strandbadet, S-542 00 Mariestad (Västra Götalands Län)

Tel: **050 110 637**. Email: **a.appelgren@mariestad.mail.telia.com**

Ekuddens occupies a long stretch of the eastern shore of Lake Vänern to the northwest of the town, in a mixed woodland setting, and next door to the municipal complex of heated outdoor pools and sauna. The lake, of course, is also available for swimming or boating and there are bicycles, tandems and canoes for hire at the tourist information office. The spacious site can take 350 units and there are 230 electrical hook-ups (10A). Most pitches are under the trees but some at the far end of the site are more exposed with good views over the lake. The site becomes very busy in high season.

Facilities

Sanitary facilities are in three low wooden cabins, all clean and well maintained. Facilities for disabled visitors with good access and baby changing rooms. Kitchens with dining facilities. Shop. Bar. Takeaway (high season). Playground. Minigolf. TV room. Lake swimming, boating and fishing. Entertainment in high season. Off site: Pools adjacent. Golf 4 km. Bicycle 3 km. Riding 7 km.

Open: 1 May - 15 September (full services 15/6-15/8).

Directions

Site is 2.5 km. northwest of the town and well signed at junctions on the ring road. From the E20 motorway take exit for Mariestad S. and follow signs in the direction of Marieholm. GPS: N58:42.943 E13:47.723

Charges 2007

Per pitch	SEK 120 - 160
electricity	SEK 40

sw2735 Daftö Feriecenter

S-452 97 Strömstad (Västra Götalands Län)

Tel: **052 626 040**. Email: **info@dafto.com**

This extremely high quality, open all year site, is beautifully situated on the west coast, 5 km. south of the small 'summer town' of Strömstad. A very large site, some parts are terraced, other areas are open, some parts are shady. In total there are 650 pitches with 350 for touring, all with electrical hook-ups (10A, CEE plugs). In addition there are 125 modern, very well equipped chalets of various sizes. Daftö Feriecenter is a family campsite with all kinds of activities for children such as beach volleyball, theatre, competitions, treasure hunting and a 'Jolly Roger' playground.

Facilities

Four excellent toilet blocks with washbasin cubicles, showers, family rooms, a children's bathroom, sun beds, saunas and make up rooms. Units for disabled visitors. Kitchen with cookers, microwaves. Laundry facilities. Shop. Licensed restaurant. Heated pool (peak season). Games and TV rooms. Minigolf. Bicycle hire. Football field. Children's club. Boat excursions. Seal safaris. Internet and WiFi for hire. Off site: Golf on three courses at Strömstad.

Open: All year excl. 22 December - 6 January.

Directions

Daftö is signed 5 km. south of Strömstad on road 176. GPS: N58:54.256 E11:12.007

Charges 2007

Per pitch incl. electricity (max. 5 persons)	SEK 200 - 330
incl. water and drainage	SEK 200 - 340
tent incl. 2 persons	SEK 140 - 265

sw2740 Laxsjons Camping och Friluftsgard

S-660 10 Dals Långed (Västra Götalands Län)

Tel: **053 130 010**. Email: **office@laxjon.se**

In the beautiful Dalsland region, Laxsjöns is an all year round site, catering for winter sports enthusiasts as well as summer tourists and groups. On the shores of the lake, the site is in two main areas – one flat, near the entrance, with hardstandings and the other on attractive, sloping, grassy areas adjoining. In total there are 300 places for caravans or motorcaravans, all with electricity (10/16A), plus more for tents. Leisure facilities on the site include minigolf, trampolines and a playground. A restaurant is at the top of the site with a good range of dishes in high season.

Facilities

The main toilet block has hot showers (on payment), washbasins in cubicles, WCs and a hairdressing cubicle. With a further small block at the top of the site, the provision should be adequate. Facilities for disabled visitors. Laundry with drying rooms for bad weather. Cooking rooms for tenters. Restaurant (high season). Shop. Minigolf. Playground. Lake for swimming, Fishing and boating.

Open: All year (full services 22/6-15/8).

Directions

From Åmål take road no. 164 towards Bengtfors, then the 172 towards Billingsfors and Dals Långed. Site is signed about 5 km. south of Billinsfors, 1 km. down a good road. From the south, (Uddevalla) take road 172. From the west (Strömstad) take the 164 towards Bengtfors and 5 km. south of Billingsfors turn right towards Långed for 1 km. GPS: N58:57.172 E12:15.140

Charges 2007

Per pitch	SEK 130 - 175
electricity	SEK 35

SW2750 FirstCamp Årjäng

Sommarvik, S-672 91 Årjäng (Värmlands Län)

Tel: 057 312 060. Email: arjang@firstcamp.se

This is a good site in beautiful surroundings with some of the 350 pitches overlooking the clear waters of the Västra Silen lake in peaceful countryside. The numbered pitches are arranged in terraces on a hillside interspersed with pines and birches, with half set aside for static units and 20 for tents. The remaining touring pitches all have 10A electricity hook-ups and 40 also include water and drainage. The site also has 60 chalets for rent. This site makes an ideal base to explore this scenic region in summer or winter when skiing is an additional attraction. A large restaurant offers a full range of meals, soft drinks, beers, wines and takeaway meals. Close to reception, a heated swimming pool with a paddling pool, terraces and sun loungers has fine views down the lake. The pool and most activities on site attract daily charges. The lake with its sandy beach is popular and safe for children. There are plenty of activities available including canoeing, rowing boats, windsurfing, fishing, an attractive water featured minigolf, sauna, quizzes, guided walks and sightseeing trips. It is possible to ride trolleys around the area on disused railway tracks, go gold panning or slip into nearby Norway and visit Oslo.

Facilities

Five sanitary units provide shower cubicles (hot showers on payment), washbasins, toilets, family bathrooms, facilities for disabled persons and baby changing. All are clean and acceptable but may be stretched in high season. Campers kitchens. Laundry facilities. Motorcaravan services. All activities and amenities are open 1/6-31/8. Small shop 1/5-1/10. Bar, restaurant and takeaway 15/6-20/8. Good play areas. Bicycle hire. Internet access. 'Quick stop' pitches for overnight stays. Youth hostel and conference centre. Off site: Indoor pool complex 3 km. Riding 5 km. Golf 9 km.

Open: All year.

Directions

Site is well signed on road 172.3km. south of its junction with the E18 close to Årjäng.
GPS: N59:22.059 E12:08.377

Charges 2008

Per tent pitch	SEK 200
pitch with electricity and water	SEK 200 - 300

Camping Cheques accepted.

SW2755 Alevi Camping

Fastnäs 53, S-68051 Stöllet (Värmlands Län)

Tel: 056 386 050. Email: info@alevi-camping.com

Alevi Camping is a small, welcoming site with 60 large pitches, 5 cabins and 2 tepees for hire. Open all year, the site is situated on the bank of the river Klarälven, the longest river in Sweden. With its own beach this is a perfect place for swimming, fishing, canoeing and rafting. The site, which had its first season in 2006, offers large level pitches all with electricity (4/10A). The county of Värmland is famous for its lakes, rivers and forests. There, if you are lucky, you can see the 'big four' predators of Scandinavia – wolf, bear, wolverine and lynx. Further up the river, at Sysslebäck, you can build your own log raft for a slow journey down the river. The rafts are fully equipped with a tent and whatever you need for a few days on the water. The site owners are happy to help you to find the perfect activity for a pleasant stay.

Facilities

One new sanitary block with free hot water. Unisex toilets and showers. Washbasins, both vanity style and in cubicles. Facilities for babies and disabled visitors. Family room. Good campers' kitchen. Motorcaravan services. Reception with small shop, restaurant, takeaway. TV room. Canoes and bicycle hire. River beach. Barbecue area. Sauna. Playground. Fishing. Skiing in winter. Off site: Supermarket 10 minutes by car.

Open: All year.

Directions

Site is between Ekshärad and Stöllet on road no. 62. Follow signs. GPS: N60:17.116 E13:24.404

Charges 2007

Per unit incl. up to 5 persons	SEK 130 - 140
with private sanitary facility	SEK 210 - 230
electricity	SEK 35 - 65
dog	SEK 10

sw2760 Frykenbadens Camping

Frykenbaden, S-665 91 Kil (Värmlands Län)

Tel: 055 440 940. Email: frykenbaden@telia.com

Frykenbaden Camping is in a quiet wooded area on the southern shore of Lake Fryken, taking 200 units on grassy meadows surrounded by trees. One area nearer the lake is gently sloping, the other is flat with numbered pitches arranged in rows, all with electricity (10A). Reception, a good shop, restaurant and takeaway are located in a traditional Swedish house surrounded by lawns sloping down to the shore, with minigolf, a play barn and playground, with pet area also close by. Frykenbadens Camping is a quiet, relaxing place to stay, away from the busier and more famous lakes. Tables and benches are near the lake, where swimming and canoeing are possible. A good value restaurant is at the adjacent golf club which can be reached by a pleasant walk. Fryken is a long, narrow lake, said to be one of the deepest in Sweden, and it is a centre for angling. There are plenty of other activities in the area (golf, riding, skiing in winter) and Kil is not too far from the Norwegian border.

Facilities

The main sanitary block is of good quality and heated in cool weather with showers on payment, open washbasins, a laundry room and room for families or disabled people. A further small block has good facilities. Well equipped camper's kitchen. Shop. Snack bar, restaurant and takeaway. Minigolf. Play barn and playground. Lake swimming. Canoes and bicycles for hire. Off site: Golf 1 km. Go-karts, riding, jogging track 4 km.

Open: All year (full services 19/6-15/8).

Directions

Site is signed from the no. 61 Karlstad - Arvika road, then 4 km. towards lake following signs. GPS: N59:32.775 E13:20.479

Charges 2007

Per pitch	SEK 110 - 150
electricity	SEK 40

sw2780 Gustavsvik Camping

Sommarrovägen, S-702 30 Ørebro (Ørebro Län)

Tel: 019 196 950. Email: camping@gustavsvik.se

Gustavsvik is one of the most modern and most visited camping and leisure parks in Sweden. It is ideally situated almost half way between Oslo and Stockholm or Gothenburg and Stockholm, at the junction of the E18 and E20 roads. This large campsite provides 720 marked and numbered pitches partly shaded by birch and pine trees, 488 with electrical connections, 440 with cable TV and 56 with water and waste water drainage. There are also three partly shaded areas for tents. The leisure park includes adventure golf, a mini zoo, playgrounds, pools and a water slide and a swimming lake, plus a private fishing lake. It is also adjacent one of Europe's largest and most comprehensive swimming complexes. For those looking for shopping and other tourist attractions (for example, the old castle), the town centre of Ørebro is within walking distance. Gustavsvik's golf course is nearby the site and it not far to Marieberg shopping centre with an IKEA branch.

Facilities

Two excellent heated toilet blocks including washbasins with dividers, free hot showers, family rooms, facilities for disabled visitors and children. Make up rooms. Very well equipped kitchens with free hot water. Dining area. Washing machine and dryers. Motorcaravan service points. Shower room for pets. Well stocked shop. Restaurant and pub. Takeaway. TV room and playroom. Arcade with games room, internet room. Adventure golf. Football. Swimming pool with waterslide. Swimming lake. Fishing lake. Mini zoo. Bicycle hire. Off site: Pool complex adjacent. Golf. Ørebro city centre. Marieberg shopping centre. Vadköping (old town) and Karlslund manor house and gardens.

Open: 15 April - 6 November (full services 10/6-14/8).

Directions

Site is 1 km. south of Ørebro town centre. Follow signs from E18/E20 or main road 50/51.

Charges guide

Per pitch	SEK 190 - 305

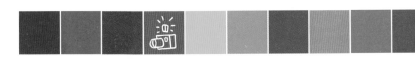

SW2800 Glyttinge Camping

Berggärdsvägen, S-584 37 Linköping (Østergötlands Län)

Tel: **013 174 928**

Only five minutes by car from the Ikea Shopping Mall and adjacent to a good swimming pool complex, Glyttinge is a most attractive site with a mix of terrain – some flat, some sloping and some woodland. A top quality site with enthusiastic and friendly management, it is maintained to a very high standard and flowers, trees and shrubs everywhere give it a cosy garden like atmosphere. There are 222 good size, mostly level pitches of which 120 have electricity (10A) and 35 are fully serviced. Children are well catered for – a wonderful, fenced play area plus tricycles, pedal cars, scooters and carts. There is also a wet weather playroom.

Facilities

The main, central toilet block (supplemented by additional smaller facilities at reception) is modern, well constructed and exceptionally well equipped and maintained. Separate facilities for disabled visitors. Baby rooms. Laundry. Solarium. Superb kitchen and dining/TV room. Small shop (15/6-15/8). Minigolf. Bicycle hire. Playground. Off site: Swimming pool complex adjacent (15/5-25/8). Riding and golf 3 km. Fishing 5 km.

Open: 27 April - 1 October.

Directions

Exit E4 Helsingborg - Stockholm road north of Linköping at signs for Ikea and site. Turn right at traffic lights and camp sign and follow signs to site. GPS: N58:26.282 E15:32.692

Charges guide

Per pitch	SEK 140 - 165
electricity	SEK 35

Low season discounts for pensioners.

SW2805 Camping Kolmården

S-618 34 Kolmården (Østergötlands Län)

Tel: **011 398 250**. Email: **kolmarden@firstcamp.se**

This is a family site, located on Bråviken Bay on the Baltic coast 160 km. south of Stockholm. Open all year, the site is just 4 km. from Kolmården Zoo, one of Sweden's most popular family attractions. There are 300 pitches of which 180 have electrical connections (10A). Some pitches have sea views and there is also a large beautiful wooded area for tents and 99 cabins of various standards for rent. A good range of amenities includes a 120 m. water slide and a children's playground. Adjacent to the site is a handicraft village and the Sjöstugans restaurant.

Facilities

Three sanitary blocks (two heated) provide a good supply of showers, washbasins and toilets. Baby rooms and facilities for disabled visitors. Good kitchen. Free hot water. Well equipped laundry rooms. Sauna. Motorcaravan services. Shop (1/5-15/9). Snack bar. Restaurant and bar. Takeaway. Playground. Water slide. Family entertainment (high season). Minigolf. WiFi. Chalets for rent. Off site: Riding 2 km. Golf 18 km.

Open: All year.

Directions

From the E4 motorway take Kolmården exit (no. 126) 23 km north of Norrköping. Follow signs for Kolmården and site is well signed. GPS: N58:39.566 E16:24.053

Charges 2007

Per pitch	SEK 145 - 195
electricity	SEK 45

SW2820 Skantzö Bad & Camping

S-737 27 Hallstahammar (Västmanlands Län)

Tel: **022 024 305**. Email: **skantzo@hallstahammar.se**

A very comfortable and pleasant municipal site just off the main E18 motorway from Oslo to Stockholm, this has 200 large marked and numbered pitches, 162 of these with electricity (10A). The terrain is flat and grassy, there is good shade in parts and the site is well fenced. There are 23 alpine style cabins for rent with window boxes of colourful flowers. Reception is very friendly. There is direct access to the towpath of the Strömsholms Kanal and nearby is the Kanal Museum. The site provides hire and transportation of canoes for longer canal tours.

Facilities

One sanitary block, maintained and equipped to a high standard, includes free hot showers (in cubicles with washbasin), facilities for disabled people and baby changing. Good kitchen. Good laundry facilities. Motorcaravan services. Barbecue grill area. Cafeteria and shop (18/5-19/8). Pool and slide (20/5-21/8). Minigolf. Tennis. Playground. Bicycle hire. Fishing. Canoe hire. Off site: Golf 6 km. Strömsholms Kanal.

Open: 1 May - 30 September.

Directions

Turn off E18 at Hallstahammar and follow road no. 252 to west of town centre and signs to campsite. GPS: N59:36.647 E16:12.925

Charges 2007

Per unit	SEK 130 - 160
electricity	SEK 40

SW2825 Camping Herrfallet

S-732 92 Arboga (Västmanlands Län)

Tel: **058 940 110**. Email: **reception@herrfallet.se**

Open all year, Herrfallets Camping is situated on a peninsula, a designated nature reserve, on Lake Hjälmaren, one of Sweden's large lakes. There is a 1 km. long sandy beach on the site and the atmosphere is friendly and 'green'. All the 135 touring pitches have electricity hook-ups (10A) and the area is neatly laid out overlooking the lake where you can hire boats, canoes, pedal boats and go fishing. Fishing is free. You can explore the beautiful, peaceful surroundings by bike which you hire at reception. There are 45 large cottages of an excellent standard and 5 are for 2 people.

Facilities

Two sanitary blocks, one basic for the summer season, one new with heating. Open washbasins, showers (charged). Provision for disabled visitors. Fully equipped kitchen and laundry facilities. Baby room. Motorcaravan service point. Sauna cottage with shower and relaxing room. Lapland hut for barbecues (charged). Shop (peak season). Restaurant and bar. Takeaway. Pedal car, pedal boat, bicycle, canoe and boat hire. Fishing (free). Minigolf. Fitness trail. Playground. Internet. Off site: Arboga (old town with medieval festival in July) 15 km. Golf 15 km.

Open: All year (full services 27/5-28/8).

Directions

Follow signs from the E20/E18. Turn off at Sätra exit towards Arboga and cross the river. Follow signs towards Herrfallet/Västermo. 15 km. from Arboga. GPS: N59:16.620 E15:54.180

Charges 2008

Per pitch	SEK 170
incl. electricity (10A)	SEK 200

SW2842 Bredäng Camping Stockholm

Stora Sällskapets väg, S-127 31 Skärholmen (Stockholms Län)

Tel: **089 770 71**. Email: **bredangcamping@telia.com**

Bredängs is a busy city site, with easy access to Stockholm city centre. Large and fairly level, with very little shade, there are 380 pitches, including 115 with hardstanding and 204 with electricity (10A), and a separate area for tents. Reception is open from 07.00-23.00 in the main season (12/6-20/8), reduced hours in low season, and English is spoken. A Stockholm card is available, or a three-day public transport card. Stockholm has many events and activities, you can take a circular tour on a free sightseeing bus, various boat and bus tours, or view the city from the Kaknäs Tower (155 m). The nearest Metro station is five minute walk, trains run about every ten minutes between 05.00 and 02.00, and the journey takes about twenty minutes. The local shopping centre is five minutes away and a two minute walk through the woods brings you to an attractive lake and beach.

Facilities

Four heated sanitary units of a high standard provide British style WCs, controllable hot showers, with some washbasins in cubicles. One has a baby room, a unit for disabled people and a first aid room. Cooking and dishwashing facilities are in three units around the site. Laundry facilities. Motorcaravan services and car wash. Well stocked shop and fully licensed restaurant (both 1/5-8/9). Sauna. Playground. Bicycle hire. Off site: Fishing 500 m.

Open: 15 April - 10 October.

Directions

Site is about 10 km. southwest of city centre. Turn off E4/E20 at Bredängs signpost and follow clearly marked site signs. GPS: N59:17.736 E17:55.389

Charges 2007

Per person	SEK 95 - 120
pitch	SEK 190 - 240
electricity	SEK 40
Discounts for pensioners in low season.	

SW2840 Stockholm Swecamp Flottsbro

S-141 22 Huddinge (Stockholms Län)

Tel: 085 353 2700. Email: info@flottsbro.se

Flottsbro is a neat, small site with good quality facilities and very good security system (including a night guard), located some 18 km. south of Stockholm. There are 80 large numbered pitches for caravans and motorhomes and a separate unmarked area for tents. Pitches are arranged on level terraces, 52 with electricity (10A), but the site itself is sloping and the restaurant is at the bottom with all the ski facilities and further good sanitary facilities. Campers have keys to the barrier and toilet blocks. The site has a small lakeside beach with grass area and a playground. The area is also good for walking, cycling and cross-country skiing.

Facilities

Two modern sanitary facilities include free showers, a suite for disabled people, baby facilities and a family bathroom. Excellent campers' kitchen with electric cookers and sinks with hot water. Washing machine, dryer (charged for) and sink. Shop (high season). Restaurant. Minigolf. Volleyball. Frisbee. Jogging track. Canoe hire. Playground. Off site: Large supermarket and rail station are 10 minutes by car from the site. Golf and riding 15 km. Stockholm 15 km.

Open: All year.

Directions

Turn off the E4 - E20 at Huddinge onto road no.259. After 2 km. turn right and follow signs to Flottsbro. GPS: N59:13.826 E17:53.291

Charges 2007

Per pitch	SEK 115 - 160
incl. electricity	SEK 180 - 220

SW2836 Mora Parkens Camping

Box 294, S-792 25 Mora (Dalarnas Län)

Tel: 025 027 600. Email: moraparken@mora.se

Mora, at the northern end of Lake Silijan is surrounded by small localities all steeped in history and culture. On the island of Sollerön, south of Mora, is evidence of a large Viking burial ground. Traditional handicrafts are still alive in the region. Mora is lively, friendly and attractive. The campsite which is good for family holidays is only 10 minutes walk from the town. The camping area is large, grassy, open and flat. It is bordered by clumps of trees and a stream. The staff are pleasant and helpful.Travel to Nusnäs, an old village with documents going back to the Middle Ages and see the production of the brightly coloured wooden horse. Every household should have two for luck. Winding country roads lead you through rich farmland to the pretty half timbered houses in Bergkarlås/Vattnås.

Facilities

Four fully equipped toilet blocks. Campers' kitchen. Laundry. Shop. Restaurant/bar. Sauna. Fishing. Minigolf. Playground. Canoe hire. Internet access. Off site: Swimming pools. Zorn Museum. Orsa Bear Park. Dalhalla (limestone quarry) musical stage. Nustriäs.

Open: All year.

Directions

Follow signs to centre of town. Campsite is clearly signed from the town centre and is next to Zorngården and Zorn museum.

Charges 2008

Per pitch incl. electricity	SEK 155 - 235
tent	SEK 85

Full services mid June - mid August.

Check real time availability and at-the-gate prices...

www.alanrogers.com

SW2845 Svegs Camping

Kyrkogränd 1, S-842 32 Sveg (Jämtlands Län)

Tel: **068 013 025**

On the 'Inlandsvägen' route through Sweden, the town centre is only a short walk from this neat, friendly site. Two supermarkets, a café and tourist information office are adjacent. The 80 pitches are in rows, on level grass, divided into bays by tall hedges, and with electricity (10/16A) available to 70. The site has boats, canoes and bicycles for hire, and the river frontage has a barbecue area with covered seating and fishing platforms. Alongside the river with its fountain, and running through the site is a pleasant well lit riverside walk.

Facilities

In the older style, sanitary facilities are functional rather than luxurious, providing stainless steel washing troughs, controllable hot showers with communal changing areas, and a unit for disabled visitors. Although a little short on numbers, facilities will probably suffice at most times as the site is rarely full. Kitchen and dining room with TV, four full cookers and sinks. Laundry facilities. TV room. Minigolf. Canoe, boat and bicycle hire. Fishing.

Open: All year.

Directions

Site is off road 45 behind the tourist information office in Sveg. Signposted.
GPS: N62:01.964 E14:21.869

Charges 2007

Per pitch	SEK 150
electricity	SEK 25

SW2850 Østersunds Camping

Krondikesvagen 95, S-831 46 Østersund (Jämtlands Län)

Tel: **063 144 615**. Email: **ostersundscamping@ostersund.se**

Østersund lies on Lake Storsjön, which is Sweden's Loch Ness, with 200 sightings of the monster dating back to 1635, and more recently captured on video in 1996. Also worthy of a visit is the island of Frösön where settlements can be traced back to pre-historic times. This large site has 254 pitches, electricity (10A) and TV socket available on 131, all served by tarmac roads. There are also 41 tarmac hardstandings available, and over 220 cottages, cabins and rooms for rent. Adjacent to the site are the municipal swimming pool complex with cafeteria (indoor and outdoor pools), a Scandic hotel with restaurant, minigolf and a Statoil filling station.

Facilities

Toilet facilities are in three units, two have controllable hot showers (on payment) with communal changing areas, suites for disabled people and baby changing. The third has four family bathrooms. Two kitchens, each with full cookers, hobs, fridge/freezers (all free of charge), and excellent dining rooms. Washing machines, dryers and free drying cabinet. Very good motorhome service point. Playground. Off site: Østersund, Frösön.

Open: All year.

Directions

Site is south of the town on the road towards Torvalla. Turn by Statoil station and site entrance is immediately on right. It is well signed from around the town. GPS: N63:09.565 E14:40.413

Charges 2008

Per pitch	SEK 135 - 170
electricity	SEK 40

SW2853 Snibbens Camping & Stugby och Vandrarhem

Hälledal 527, S-870 16 Ramvik (Västernorrlands Län)

Tel: **061 240 505**

Probably you will stop here for one night as you travel the E4 coast road and stay a week. It is a truly beautiful location in the area of 'The High Coast' listed as a World Heritage Site. During high season Snibbens is a busy, popular site but remains quiet and peaceful. Besides 30 bungalows for rent there are 50 touring places, each with a 16A electricity, set amongst delightful scenery on the shores of Lake Mörtsjön. The welcoming owners take you to your adequately sized grass pitch set amongst spacious trees.

Facilities

Excellent, spotlessly clean facilities include controllable showers and partitioned washbasins. Baby changing facilities. Two kitchens with hot plates, microwaves and a mini oven. Laundry room. Small shop (15/6-20/8). Rowing boats and pedaloes for hire. Minigolf. Free fishing for site guests. Youth hostel. Off site: Small supermarket 800 m. Golf 20 km.

Open: 30 April - 15 September.

Directions

Travelling north on the E4 and immediately prior to Höga Kusten bridge (one of the largest in Europe) take road 90 signed Kramfors. Site is directly off road 90 on left in 3 km, well signed. GPS: N62:47.943 E17:52.188

Charges 2007

Per pitch	SEK 140
incl. electricity	SEK 155

503

SW2855 Flogsta Camping

S-872 80 Kramfors (Västernorrlands Län)

Tel: 061 210 005. Email: flogsta@basterang.se

Kramfors lies just to the west of the E4, and travellers may well pass by over the new Höga Kusten bridge (one of the largest in Europe), and miss this friendly little site. This area of Ådalen and the High Coast, reaches as far as Ørnsköldsvik. The attractive garden-like campsite has 50 pitches, 21 with electrical connections (10A), which are arranged on level grassy terraces, separated by shrubs and trees into bays of 2-4 units. All overlook the heated outdoor public swimming pool complex and attractive minigolf course. The non-electric pitches are on an open terrace nearer reception.

Facilities

Sanitary facilities comprise nine bathrooms, each with British style WC, basin with hand dryer, shower. Laundry facilities. More WCs and showers are in the reception building with a free sauna. A new toilet block has a sauna and outside hot tub. A separate building houses a kitchen, with hot-plates, fridge/freezer and TV/dining room (all free). The reception building has a small shop and snack bar. Playground. Snowmobile hire. Off site: Fishing 10 km. Golf and riding 15 km.

Open: All year.

Directions

Signed from road 90 in the centre of Kramfors, site is to the west in a rural location beyond a housing estate and by the Flogsta Bad, a municipal swimming pool complex. GPS: N62:55.537 E17:45.385

Charges 2007

Per pitch	SEK 100 - 125

SW2857 Strömsund Swecamp

S-833 24 Strömsund (Jämtlands Län)

Tel: 067 016 410. Email: stromsund.turism@stromsund.se

A quiet waterside town on the north - south route 45 known as the Inlandsväen, Strömsund is a good place to begin a journey on the Wilderness Way. This is route 342 which heads northwest towards the mountains at Gäddede and the Norwegian border. Being on the confluence of many waterways, there is a wonderful feeling of space and freedom in Strömsund. The campsite is set on a gentle grassy slope backed by forest. Another part of the site, across the road, overlooks the lake. Cabins are set in circular groups of either six or seven. The site is owned by the town council.

Facilities

Excellent facilities include two toilet blocks, one on each side of the road. Both contain showers, toilets, washbasins with dividers and under-floor heating. Facilities for disabled visitors. Laundry. Large campers' kitchen with cooking rings, microwave and sinks. Motorcaravan service point. Bicycle, canoe, pedalo and boat hire. Play area. Off site: Municipal pool is next to the site.

Open: All year (full services mid June - mid August).

Directions

Site is 700 m. south of Strömsund on route 45. GPS: N63:50.787 E15:32.023

Charges guide

Per pitch	SEK 120
electricity	SEK 30 - 50

SW2860 First Camp Umeå

S-906 54 Umeå (Västerbotens Län)

Tel: 090 702 600. Email: umea@firstcamp.se

An ideal stop-over for those travelling the E4 coastal route, or a good base from which to explore the area, this campsite is 6 km. from the centre of this university city. It is almost adjacent to the Nydalsjön lake, which is ideal for fishing, windsurfing and bathing. There are 450 grassy pitches arranged in bays of 10-20 units, 320 with electricity (10/16A), and some are fully serviced. Outside the site, adjacent to the lake, are football pitches, an open air swimming pool, minigolf, mini-car driving school, beach volleyball and a mini-farm.

Facilities

The new large, heated, central sanitary unit includes controllable hot showers with communal changing areas. (Facilities stretched in high season). Kitchen. Large dining room. TV. Laundry facilities. Shop (25/5-21/8). Fully licensed restaurant. WiFi. Walk-on chess. Volleyball. Playgrounds. Bicycle hire. Rowing boat hire. Fishing in the lake. Canoes and pedal cars for hire. Adventure golf. Off site: Riding adjacent. Golf 18 km.

Open: All year (full services 25/5-12/8).

Directions

A camping sign on the E4 at a set of traffic lights 5km. north of the town directs you to the site. Direction also indicates Holmsund and Vassa. GPS: N63:50.596 E20:20.432

Charges 2007

Per pitch	SEK 160 - 220
incl. electricity	SEK 170 - 260
Camping Cheques accepted.	

SW2865 Camp Gielas

Järnvägsgatan 111, S-933 34 Arvidsjaur (Norrbottens Län)

Tel: **096 055 600**. Email: **gielas@arvidsjaur.se**

A modern municipal site with excellent sporting facilities on the outskirts of the town, Gielas is well shielded on all sides by trees, providing a very peaceful atmosphere. The 160 pitches, 81 with electricity (10A) and satellite TV connections, are level on sparse grass and accessed by tarmac roadways. The sauna and showers, sporting, gymnasium and Internet facilities at the sports hall are free to campers. Also on site is a snackbar. The lake on the site is suitable for boating, bathing and fishing. There is a swimming pool and a 9-hole golf course nearby, and hunting trips can be arranged.

Facilities

Two modern, heated sanitary units provide controllable hot showers and a unit for disabled visitors. Well equipped kitchens (free). Washing machine and dryer. The unit by the tent area also has facilities for disabled people and baby changing. Snack bar. Tennis courts. Minigolf. Children's playgrounds. Sauna. Sporting facilities. Boat and canoe hire. Pedal Cars. Lake swimming. Fishing. Winter golf course on snow on site. Off site: Golf 200 m. Bowling centre and riding 500 m. Bicycle hire 2 km.

Open: All year.

Directions

Site is on road 95 3 km. south of town centre. GPS: N65:34.955 E19:11.412

Charges 2007

Per pitch	SEK 150

SW2870 Jokkmokks Camping Center

Box 75, S-962 22 Jokkmokk (Norrbottens Län)

Tel: **097 112 370**. Email: **campingcenter@jokkmokk.com**

This attractive site is just 8 km. from the Arctic Circle. Large and well organised, the site is bordered on one side by the river and with woodland on the other, just 3 km. from the town centre. It has 170 level, grassy pitches, with an area for tents, plus 59 cabins for rent. Electricity (10A) is available to all touring pitches. The site has a heated open air pool complex open in summer (no lifeguard). There are opportunities for snow-mobiling, cross-country skiing in spring, or ice fishing in winter. Nearby attractions include the first hydro-electric power station at Porjus, built between 1910-15, with free tours in high season, Vuollerim, a reconstructed 60 year old settlement with excavations of the best preserved Ice Age village is 40 km. or try visiting for the famous Jokkmokk Winter Market (first Thurs-Sat February) or the less chilly Autumn Market (end of August).

Facilities

Heated sanitary buildings provide mostly open washbasins and controllable showers - some are curtained with a communal changing area, a few are in cubicles with divider and seat. A unit by reception has a baby bathroom, a fully equipped suite for disabled visitors, games room, plus a very well appointed kitchen and launderette. A further unit with WCs, basins, showers plus a steam sauna, is by the pool. Shop, restaurant and bar (in summer). Takeaway (high season). Swimming pools (25 x 10 m. main pool with water slide, two smaller pools and paddling pool). Sauna. Bicycle hire. Playground and adventure playground. Minigolf. Football field. Games machines. Free fishing. Off site: Riding 2 km.

Open: All year (for groups on request) or from 15 May.

Directions

Site is 3 km. from the centre of Jokkmokk on road 97. GPS: N66:35.698 E19:53.562

Charges guide

Per caravan or motorcaravan	SEK 120 - 150
hiker and small tent	SEK 70
car and small tent	SEK 90
electricity	SEK 30

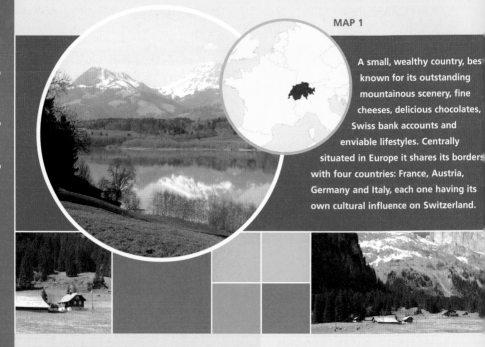

MAP 1

A small, wealthy country, best known for its outstanding mountainous scenery, fine cheeses, delicious chocolates, Swiss bank accounts and enviable lifestyles. Centrally situated in Europe it shares its borders with four countries: France, Austria, Germany and Italy, each one having its own cultural influence on Switzerland.

CAPITAL: BERN

Tourist Office

Switzerland Tourism
Swiss Centre, 10 Wardour Street
London W1D 6QF
Tel: 020 7292 1550 Fax: 020 7292 1599
Email: info.uk@switzerland.com
Internet: www.myswitzerland.com

The landscape of Switzerland boasts mountains, valleys, waterfalls and glaciers. The Bernese Oberland is probably the most visited area, with picturesque villages, lakes and awe inspiring peaks, including the towering Eiger, Mönch and Jungfrau. The highest Alps are those of Valais in the southwest where the small busy resort of Zermatt gives access to the Matterhorn. The southeast of Switzerland has densely forested mountain slopes and the wealthy and glamorous resort of St Moritz. Zurich in the north is a German speaking city with a wealth of sightseeing, particularly in the old town area with its 16th and 17th century houses. Geneva, Montreux and Lausanne on the northern shores of Lake Geneva make up the bulk of French Switzerland, with vineyards that border the lakes and medieval towns. The southernmost canton, Ticino, is home to the Italian speaking Swiss, with the Mediterranean style lakeside resorts of Lugano and Locarno.

Population

7.1 million

Climate

Mild and refreshing in the northern plateau. South of the Alps it is warmer, influenced by the Mediterranean. The Valais is noted for its dryness.

Language

German in central and eastern areas, French in the west and Italian in the south. Raeto-Romansch is spoken in the southeast. English is spoken by many.

Telephone

The country code is 00 41.

Money

Currency: Swiss franc
Banks: Mon-Fri 08.30-16.30. Some close for lunch.

Shops

Mon-Fri 08.00- 12.00 and 14.00- 18.00. Sat 08.00-16.00. Often closed Monday mornings.

Public Holidays

New Year; Good Fri; Easter Mon; Ascension; Whit Mon; National Day 1 Aug; Christmas 25 Dec. Other holidays are observed in individual Cantons.

Motoring

The road network is comprehensive and well planned. An annual road tax is levied on all cars using Swiss motorways and the 'Vignette' windscreen sticker must be purchased at the border (credit cards not accepted), or in advance from the Swiss National Tourist Office, plus a separate one for a towed caravan or trailer.

CH9430 Camping Lazy Rancho 4

Lehnweg 6, CH-3800 Interlaken (Bern)

Tel: 033 822 8716. Email: info@lazyrancho.ch

This super site is in a quiet location with fantastic views of the dramatic mountains of Eiger, Monch and Jungfrau. Neat, orderly and well maintained, the site is situated in a wide valley just 1 km. from Lake Thun and 4 km. from Interlaken. The English speaking owners lovingly care for the site and will endeavour to make you feel very welcome. Connected by tarmac roads, the 155 pitches, of which 90 are for touring units, are on well tended level grass (some with hardstanding, all with 10A electricity). 23 pitches also have water and waste water drainage. This is a quiet friendly site, popular with British visitors. The owners offer advice on day trips out, and how to get the best bargains which can be had on the railway.

Facilities

Two good sanitary blocks (one new, the other of an older design) are both heated with free hot showers, good facilities for disabled customers and a baby room. Laundry. Camper's kitchen with microwave, cooker, fridge and utensils. Motorcaravan service point. Well stocked shop. TV and games room. Play area. Small swimming pool. Off site: Cycle trails and way-marked footpaths. Riding 500 m. Golf and bicycle hire 1 km. Lake Thun for fishing 1.5 km. Boat launching 1.5 km. Interlaken (free regular bus service 400 m. from site) and leisure centre 2 km.

Open: 15 April - 15 October.

Directions

Site is on north side of Lake Thun. From road no. 8 (Thun - Interlaken) on south side of lake take exit 24 Interlaken West. Follow towards lake at roundabout then follow signs for campings. Lazy Rancho is Camp 4. The last 500 m. is a little narrow but no problem. GPS: N46:41.163 E07:49.838

Charges 2008

Per person	CHF 6,00 - 7,50
child (6-15 yrs)	CHF 3,50 - 4,50
pitch	CHF 10,00 - 32,00
electricity (10A)	CHF 4,00
dog	CHF 3,00

Payment accepted in euros.

CH9370 Camping Rendez-vous

CH-3718 Kandersteg (Bern)

Tel: 033 675 1534. Email: rendez-vous.camping@bluewin.ch

Camping Rendez-vous is an all year site located at an altitude of 1,200 m. just outside the delightful mountain village of Kandersteg. This site has been recommended by our Swiss agent and we plan to conduct a full inspection in 2008. There are 80 terraced touring pitches here and a further 20 pitches are occupied by chalets. The pitches are grassy and many have fine views over the surrounding mountain scenery. Although there are few amenities on site, Kandersteg is nearby and is an important mountain resort with a good selection of shops and restaurants, as well as a railway station and cable car service. Camping Rendez–vous is an excellent starting point for many of the area's superb walking and mountain biking opportunites, with over 500 km. of marked trails available. The site owners will be pleased to recommend routes. Adjacent to the site is the Oeschinensee chair lift which gives access to a summer toboggan run. During the winter, skiing and other winter sports are possible.

Facilities

Heated toilet block. Washing machines and dryers. Small shop. Restaurant at site entrance. Play area.
Off site: Kandersteg with a wide choice of restaurants, bars and shops 2 km. Oeschinensee chair lift. Railway station and cable cars. Many paths and cycle trails.

Open: All year.

Directions

From the north, take the N6 Bern - Spiez motorway and take the Kandersteg exit. Follow signs to Kandersteg (about 25 km.) and the site is well signed (to the left) in the village.

Charges 2007

Per person	CHF 6,30
child (to 16 yrs)	CHF 3,00
pitch	CHF 8,00 - 16,00
electricity per kWh	CHF 0,60

CH9330 TCS Camping Bettlereiche

CH-3770 Gwatt (Bern)

Tel: 033 336 4067. Email: camping.gwatt@bluewin.ch

Bettlereiche is an ideal site for those who wish to explore this part of the Bernese Oberland and who would enjoy staying on a small site in a quiet area, away from the larger sites and town atmosphere of Interlaken. There are 85 numbered, but unmarked pitches for tourists, most with 4A electricity available, and about the same number of static units. There are hard access roads but cars must be parked away from the pitches. Although there are some trees, there is little shade in the main camping area. Direct access to the lake is available for swimming and boating. The site has a cared for air and the friendly management speak good English. Part of the restaurant is reserved for young people. Some animation in high season.

Facilities

Single, modern, well constructed sanitary block, fully equipped with hot water provided for washbasins in cabins (cold otherwise). Facilities should be adequate in high season. Room for disabled visitors. Washing machine and dryer. Motorcaravan services. Well stocked shop. Restaurant. Lake swimming and boating.
Off site: Many cycle tracks.

Open: 1 April - 1st week in October.

Directions

From Berne-Thun-Interlaken autoroute, take exit Thun-Süd for Gwatt and follow signs for Gwatt. Site is signed near town centre to the left. GPS: N46:43.594 E07:37.671

Charges 2007

Per person	CHF 6,20 - 8,20
child (6-16 yrs)	CHF 3,10 - 4,10
caravan or motorcaravan and electricity	CHF 19,00 - 24,00

CH9380 Berg Camping Heiti

CH-3785 Gsteig bei Gstaad (Bern)

Tel: **033 755 11 97**. Email: **info@bergcamping.ch**

Bergcamping Heiti is a brand new site opened in June 2007 and is located 10 km. from the stylish resort of Gstaad. The site has been recommended by our Swiss agent and we plan to undertake a full inspection in 2008. Bergcamping Heiti is open all year and has 50 grassy pitches suitable for summer and winter use. There are also a number of traditional wooden chalets available for rent. The wash block is fully heated and has a drying room for skiers and walkers. For 2008, a new 'wellness' suite is planned and this will include a sauna, whirlpool and beauty salon. The site is situated at the foot of the Col du Pillon and a wide choice of walking and mountain biking routes are available. A little further afield, Les Diablerets offers the opportunity for both summer and winter skiing. The nearby village of Gsteig is five minutes by foot and has a good selection of shops and restaurants.

Facilities

Heated toilet blocks. Washing machines and dryers. Drying room. Small shop. Restaurant. Bar. Play area. Beach volleyball. Off site: Gsteig with a wide choice of shops, restaurants and bars 500 m. Gstaad 10 km. Many walking paths and cycle trails. Summer and winter skiing.

Open: All year.

Directions

From Gstaad, follow signs to Col du Pillon. Continue to Gsteig. Turn left here after the church and the site can be found 500m further to the left.

Charges 2007

Per person	CHF 4,30
child (0-15 yrs)	CHF 2,15
pitch	CHF 12,00 - 17,00
electricity	CHF 3,00

CH9055 TCS Camping Fanel

CH-3236 Gampelen (Bern)

Tel: **032 313 2333**. Email: **camping.gampelen@tcs.ch**

This Swiss Touring Club site is particularly suited to families with children. From the terrace of a well provisioned self service restaurant there is a view of the small swimming pool and the large grass area that leads to the gently shelving waters of the lake and a small wooden jetty. The site has 900 pitches (150 for tourists) which means that it could become quite busy at weekends and holidays. The level, grass pitches have electricity and some young trees provide shade. This quiet site is located in a protected nature area, a habitat for beavers, wild boar and foxes. There are over 200 species of birds and the woodpeckers can be quite noisy in the mornings! From the site there are walks through the nature reserve, cycle tracks for excursions and old towns, like Erlach, to visit. The site has its own harbour from which boats can be launched and where canoes and paddle boats can be rented.

Facilities

Three modern, well maintained toilet blocks with free showers and washbasins in cabins. Facilities for disabled people. Baby room. Laundry room with washing machines and dryers. Motorcaravan service point. Modern, well appointed self service restaurant with takeaway. Shop. Gas supplies. Internet access. Play area. Bicycle hire. Archery.

Open: 1 April - 1 October.

Directions

Site is on the northeast shore of Lake Neuchatel. From A1 exit 29 (Murten) or exit 30 (Kerzers) travel north towards Neuchatel as far as village of Gampelen where site is well signed. GPS: N47:00.407 E07:02.420

Charges 2007

Per person	CHF 7,00 - 8,00
child	CHF 3,50 - 4,00
pitch incl. electricity	CHF 20,50 - 34,00
dog	CHF 3,00 - 4,00

CH9420 Camping Manor Farm 1

CH-3800 Interlaken-Thunersee (Bern)

Tel: **033 822 2264**. Email: **manorfarm@swisscamps.ch**

Manor Farm has been popular with British visitors for many years, as this is one of the traditional touring areas of Switzerland. The flat terrain is divided entirely into 525 individual, numbered pitches which vary considerably both in size (60-100 sq.m.) and price with 10A electricity available and shade in some places. There are 144 equipped with electricity, water, drainage and 55 also have cable TV connections. Reservations are made although you should find space except perhaps in late July/early August, but the best places may then be taken. Around 30% of the pitches are taken by permanent or letting units and a tour operators presence. The site lies outside the town on the northern side of the Thuner See, with most of the site between road and lake but with one part on the far side of the road. Interlaken is rather a tourist town but the area is rich in scenery, with innumerable mountain excursions and walks available. The lakes and Jungfrau railway are near at hand. Manor Farm is efficiently and quite formally run, with good English spoken.

Facilities	Directions
Six separate toilet blocks are practical, heated and fully equipped. They include free hot water for baths. Twenty private units are for rent. Laundry facilities. Motorcaravan services. Gas supplies. Shop (1/4-15/10). Site-owned restaurant adjoining (1/3-30/11). Snack bar with takeaway (July/Aug). TV room. Playground and paddling pool. Minigolf. Bicycle hire. Sailing and windsurfing school. Lake swimming. Boat hire. Fishing. Daily activity and entertainment programme in high season. Excursions. Off site: Golf 500 m. (handicap card). Riding 3 km. Good area for cycling and walking. Free bus service to heated indoor and outdoor swimming pools (free entry).	Site is 3 km. west of Interlaken along the road running north of the Thunersee towards Thun. Follow signs for 'Camp 1'. From A8 (bypassing Interlaken) take exit 24 marked 'Gunten, Beatenberg', which is a spur road bringing you out close to site. GPS: N46:40.516 E07:48.550

Open: All year.

Charges 2008

Per person	CHF 5,00 - 10,00
child (6-15 yrs)	CHF 2,40 - 4,80
pitch with electricity	CHF 10,50 - 43,00
dog	CHF 2,00 - 4,00

Various discounts for longer stays.

CH9360 Camping Grassi

CH-3714 Frutigen (Bern)

Tel: **033 671 1149**. Email: **campinggrassi@bluewin.ch**

This is a small site with about half the pitches occupied by static caravans, used by their owners for weekends and holidays. The 70 or so places available for tourists are not marked out but it is said that the site is not allowed to become overcrowded. Most places are on level grass with two small terraces at the end of the site. There is little shade but the site is set in a river valley with trees on the hills which enclose the area. Electricity is available for all pitches but long leads may be required in parts. It would make a useful overnight stop en-route for Kandersteg and the railway station where cars can join the train for transportation through the Lotschberg Tunnel to the Rhône Valley and Simplon Pass, or for a longer stay to explore the Bernese Oberland.

Facilities	Directions
The well constructed, heated sanitary block is of good quality. Washing machine and dryer. Gas supplies. Motorcaravan services. Rest room with TV. Kiosk (1/6-31/8). Play area and play house. Mountain bike hire and tours. Fishing. Bicycle hire. WiFi. Off site: Shops and restaurants 10 minutes walk away in village. Riding 2 km. Outdoor and indoor pools, tennis and minigolf in Frutigen. Skiing and walking.	Take Kandersteg road from Spiez and leave at Frutigen Dorf exit from where site is signed. GPS: N46:34.925 E07:38.431

Open: All year.

Charges 2008

Per person	CHF 6,40
child (1-16 yrs)	CHF 1,50 - 3,20
pitch	CHF 8,00 - 14,00
dog	CHF 1,50

CH9460 Camping Jungfrau

CH-3822 Lauterbrunnen (Bern)

Tel: **033 856 2010**. Email: **info@camping-jungfrau.ch**

This friendly site has a very imposing situation in a steep valley with a fine view of the Jungfrau at the end. It is a popular site and, although you should usually find space, in season do not arrive too late. A fairly extensive area with grass pitches and hard surfaced access roads. All 391 pitches (250 for touring) have shade in parts, electrical connections (13A) and 50 have water and drainage also. About 30% of the pitches are taken by seasonal caravans and it is used by two tour operators. The von Allmen family own and run the site and provide a warm welcome (English is spoken). You can laze here amid real mountain scenery, though it does lose the sun a little early. There are naturally many more active things to do – mountain walks or climbing, trips up the Jungfrau railway or one of the mountain lifts or excursions by car.

Facilities

Three fully equipped modern sanitary blocks can be heated in winter and also provide facilities for disabled visitors. Baby baths. Laundry facilities. Motorcaravan services. Supermarket. Self-service restaurant with takeaway (May - end Oct). General room with tables and chairs, TV, jukebox, drink machines, amusements. Playgrounds and covered play area. Excursions and some entertainment in high season. Mountain bike hire. Internet point. ATM. Drying room. Ski store. Off site: Free bus to ski station (in winter only).

Open: All year.

Directions

Go through Lauterbrunnen and fork right at far end before road bends left, 100 m. before church. The final approach is not very wide.
GPS: N46:35.284 E07:54.646

Charges 2008

Per person	CHF 9,20 - 10,90
child (6-15 yrs)	CHF 4,40 - 5,10
pitch with electricity	
(plus meter in winter)	CHF 23,00 - 25,00
car	CHF 3,50
dog	CHF 3,00

Discounts for camping carnet and for stays over 3 nights outside high season.

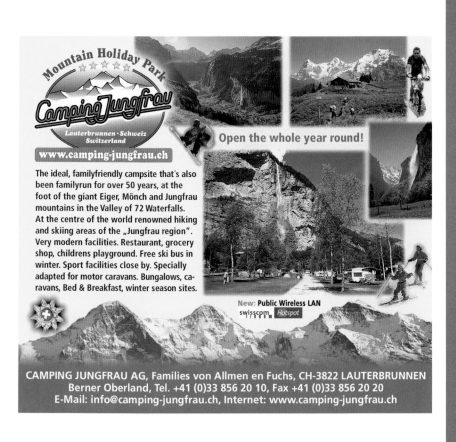

Mountain Holiday Park

Camping Jungfrau
Lauterbrunnen · Schweiz
Switzerland

www.camping-jungfrau.ch

Open the whole year round!

The ideal, familyfriendly campsite that´s also been familyrun for over 50 years, at the foot of the giant Eiger, Mönch and Jungfrau mountains in the Valley of 72 Waterfalls. At the centre of the world renowned hiking and skiing areas of the „Jungfrau region". Very modern facilities. Restaurant, grocery shop, childrens playground. Free ski bus in winter. Sport facilities close by. Specially adapted for motor caravans. Bungalows, caravans, Bed & Breakfast, winter season sites.

New: **Public Wireless LAN**
swisscom. *Hotspot*

CAMPING JUNGFRAU AG, Families von Allmen en Fuchs, CH-3822 LAUTERBRUNNEN
Berner Oberland, Tel. +41 (0)33 856 20 10, Fax +41 (0)33 856 20 20
E-Mail: info@camping-jungfrau.ch, Internet: www.camping-jungfrau.ch

CH9410 Camping Stuhlegg

Stueleggstr. 7, CH-3704 Krattigen (Bern)

Tel: 033 654 2723. Email: **campstuhlegg@bluewin.ch**

On the outskirts of the village of Krattigen, Camping Stuhlegg is a quiet and attractive site, located well above the lake and with beautiful, wide-ranging views over the lake to the mountains beyond. The 65 touring pitches are arranged on grassy terraced areas, some for motorcaravans having hardstanding. A few young trees provide shade. The friendly bar and bistro is also popular as a meeting point for the villagers, which gives a touch of local colour. This is a site where you can enjoy the fresh mountain air the scenery and relax. The site owner, Herr Schweizer, speaks excellent English. He is only too willing to advise on activities and excursions that can be undertaken in the region. In addition, the Krattigen guest information booklet is available in English and is a wealth of diverse information. Here you can discover where in the village good home Swiss cooking can be tried, what boat, train and bus excursions are available, museums to visit or where the William Tell play, in Swiss German, can be seen.

Facilities

Two modern sanitary facilities, the one near the entrance is heated, the other at the top of the site is for summer use and unheated. They contain all the usual facilities, showers operate with either coins or with tokens. Laundry room. Baby bath. Motorcaravan service point. Shop. Bar (all year) and bistro with takeaway (closed Nov). Swimming pool. TV room. Play area. Internet point. Off site: Plenty of footpaths in the immediate area. Bicycle hire 800 m. Riding, golf and fishing 4 km.

Open: All year.

Directions

Site is almost halfway between Spiez and Interlaken on the southern side of the Thunersee. Leave the A8 at exit 20 and follow signs for Krattigen. Site is signed at top of village to the right (north). GPS: N46:39.475 E07:43.076

Charges 2008

Per person	CHF 5,00 - 6,00
child	CHF 4,00 - 4,60
pitch	CHF 9,00 - 16,00
electricity	CHF 4,00

CH9440 Camping Jungfraublick

Gsteigstrasse 80, Matten, CH-3800 Interlaken (Bern)

Tel: 033 822 4414. Email: **info@jungfraublick.ch**

The Berner Oberland is one of the most scenic and well known areas of Switzerland with Interlaken probably the best known summer resort. Situated in the village of Matten, Jungfraublick is a delightful, medium sized site with splendid views up the Lauterbrunnen valley to the Jungfrau mountain. The 90 touring pitches 60-90 sq.m. with electricity connections (6A) are in regular rows on level, well cut grass. A few fruit trees adorn but do not offer much shade. The 30 static caravans are to one side of the tourist area and do not intrude. There is some traffic noise from the main road.

Facilities

Fully equipped sanitary facilities and provision for disabled visitors. Showers are on payment, as is hot water for dishwashing. Washing machines and dryers. Motorcaravan services. Shop for basics (from 1/6). Small swimming pool (12 x 8 m.) open mid June - end Aug. according to the weather. Heated rest room with TV and electronic games. Barbecues must be off the ground. Off site: Wilderswill train station 10 minutes walk. Bicycle hire 700 m. Town 1 km. Golf, riding and fishing 4 km.

Open: 1 May - 20 September.

Directions

Take the exit Nr. 25 from the N8 motorway, turn towards Interlaken. Site is within 500 m. on left. GPS: N46:40.345 E07:52.058

Charges 2008

Per person	CHF 5,80 - 6,80
child (4-16 yrs)	CHF 3,50 - 4,20
pitch acc. to size and season	CHF 6,00 - 30,00

CH9496 AlpenCamping

Brünigstrasse 47, CH-3860 Meiringen (Bern)

Tel: **033 971 3676**. Email: **info@alpencamping.ch**

Alpencamping is a small family site located close to Meiringen, an important winter sports resort and hiking centre in the summer. This all-year site in central Switzerland has been recommended by our Swiss agent and we plan to undertake a full inspection in 2008. There are just 27 touring pitches here. These are flat and grassy and all have electrical connections. A further 54 pitches are occupied by residential units. This is a simple site with few amenities but there is a centrally located wash block and a small shop for essentials. A larger supermarket is five minutes walk away. Meiringen is surrounded by stunning mountain scenery and there is great deal to see in the area. The dramatic Reichenbach Falls are just 10 minutes away, and are, of course, famous for the demise of Sherlock Holmes. Now, there is even a museum here, dedicated to the great detective! Even more dramatic are the many mountain walks in the area, many of which are easily accessible from the site.

Facilities

Heated toilet block. Washing machine and dryer. Small shop. Play area. Off site: Meiringen with a wide choice of shops, restaurants and bars 500 m. Reichenbach Falls. Brienzersee Lake. Many walking paths and cycle trails. Summer and winter skiing.

Open: All year excl. November.

Directions

From Bern take the A6 motorway towards Interlaken and Thun. At Interlaken, join the A8 towards Spiez. Continue on road 11 to Meiringen, from where the site is well signed.

Charges 2008

Per person	CHF 8,00
child (6-15 yrs)	CHF 4,50 - 5,00
pitch	CHF 7,00 - 18,00
electricity	CHF 3,50

CH9480 Camping Gletscherdorf

Gletscherdorf 31, CH-3818 Grindelwald (Bern)

Tel: **033 853 1429**. Email: **info@gletscherdorf.ch**

Set in a flat river valley on the edge of Grindelwald, one of Switzerland's well known winter and summer resorts, Gletscherdorf enjoys wonderful mountain views, particularly of the nearby north face of the Eiger. The site has 120 pitches, 60 for touring units. Most are marked and have electricity connections (10A), with a few others in an overflow field. There is a good community room with tables and chairs. This is, above all, a very quiet, friendly site for those who wish to enjoy the peaceful mountain air, walking, climbing and exploring with a mountain climbing school in Grindelwald.

Facilities

Excellent small, heated, fully equipped, sanitary block. Washing machines and dryer. Motorcaravan services. Gas supplies. Small shop for basic food items. Torches useful. Dogs are not accepted. Off site: Bicycle hire or golf 1 km. Indoor pool 1 km. Town shops and restaurants within walking distance.

Open: 1 May - 20 October.

Directions

To reach site, go into town and turn right at camp signs after town centre; approach road is quite narrow and steep down hill but there is an easier departure road. GPS: N46:37.264 E08:02.718

Charges 2008

Per person	CHF 7,50
child (6-15 yrs)	CHF 3,50
pitch	CHF 6,00 - 18,00

CH9450 TCS Camping Seeblick

Campingstrasse 14, CH-9450 Bonigen (Bern)

Tel: **033 822 1143**. Email: **camping.boenigen@tcs.ch**

This small, quiet site, bordered on two sides by Lake Brienz, is only 1.5 km. from the centre of Interlaken and the autoroute exit. It is therefore a useful site, not only to spend time on and enjoy the views, but also as an ideal base to tour this picturesque region, dominated by the Eiger and Jungfrau mountains. Almost all the 107 pitches are available for tourists. On level grassy ground and under tall trees, all have electricity. With magnificent views over the lake, gates give direct access to a footpath and to the lake shores. Interlaken is a tourist centre in the Berner Oberland, a region that has a great deal to offer, from sky diving to leisurely boat or train excursions. It pays to spend some time looking through the many tourist brochures available in reception and talking to the site manager Herr Krahenbühl to find activities and places to visit that particularly attract you. This is a region that has something for everyone.

Facilities

A well maintained, modern sanitary block has free showers and some washbasins in cabins. Facilities for disabled people. Baby room. Washing machine and dryer. Motorcaravan service point. Small shop sells gas and provides essentials. Informal bar and snack bar with takeaway food. Small solar heated swimming pool and paddling pool. Play area.

Open: 31 March - 1 October.

Directions

Site is beside the Brienzersee in the eastern suburbs of Interlaken. From A8 take exit 26 (Interlaken Ost) and follow signs for Bönigen and then site signs. GPS: N46:41.480 E07:53.610

Charges 2007

Per person	CHF 6,00 - 7,80
child	CHF 3,00 - 3,90
pitch incl. electricity	CHF 21,00 - 24,00
dog	CHF 3,00 - 4,00

CH9570 Camping Eienwäldli

Wasserfallstraße 108, CH-6390 Engelberg (Unterwalden)

Tel: **041 637 1949**. Email: **info@eienwaeldli.ch**

This super site has facilities which must make it one of the best in Switzerland. It is situated in a beautiful location 3,500 feet above sea level, surrounded by mountains on the edge of the delightful village of Engelberg. Half of the site is taken up by static caravans which are grouped together at one side. The camping area is in two parts – nearest the entrance are 57 hardstandings for caravans and motorcaravans, all with electricity (metered) and beyond this is a flat meadow for about 70 tents. The reception building houses the pool complex, shop, a café/bar and rooms and apartments to rent. There is also a restaurant opposite the entrance. The indoor pool has recently been most imaginatively rebuilt as a Felsenbad spa bath with adventure pool, steam and relaxing grottoes, Kneipp's cure, children's pool with water slides, solarium, Finnish sauna and eucalyptus steam bath (charged for). Being about 35 km. from Luzern by road and with a rail link, it makes a quiet, peaceful base from which to explore the Vierwaldstattersee region, walk in the mountains or just enjoy the scenery. The area is famous as a winter sports region and summer tourist resort.

Facilities

The excellent toilet block, heated in cool weather, has free hot water in washbasins (in cabins) and (on payment) showers. Washing machines and dryers. Shop. Café/bar. Small lounge. Indoor pool complex. Ski facilities. Playground. Torches useful. TV. Internet access. Golf. Off site: Golf driving range and 18-hole course near. Fishing and bicycle hire 1 km. Riding 2 km.

Open: All year.

Directions

From N2 Gotthard motorway, leave at exit 33 'Stans-Sud' and follow signs to Engelberg. Turn right at T-junction on edge of town and follow signs to 'Wasserfall' and site. GPS: N46:48.564 E08:25.420

Charges 2007

Per person	CHF 8,00
child (6-15 yrs)	CHF 4,00
pitch with electricity	
(plus meter)	CHF 14,00 - 16,50
dog	CHF 2,00

Credit cards accepted (surcharge).

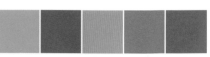

CH9500 Camping Hofstatt-Derfli

Hofstatt, CH-6085 Hasliberg Goldern (Bern)

Tel: 033 971 3707. Email: welcome@derfli.ch

This attractive new site has been created by a goldsmith and her husband. Small and family run, with 45 pitches, it is in a quiet location, over 1,000 metres high at the end of a small village in the Berner Oberland. One innovation is the one metre high mushrooms -; with their white dotted red tops they are difficult to miss. They provide the electrical supply points for the 35 touring pitches and site lighting. The grass pitches are level, some with gravel hardstanding for motorcaravans and the gently sloping site is partly surrounded by trees with mountain top views across the valley.

Facilities

Well maintained, all the year round, sanitary facilities are housed in the main building. Showers controllable and free, some washbasins in cabins. Facilities for disabled people. Baby areas. Kitchen to rent in community room. Laundry facilities. Motorcaravan service point, Small shop. Play area. Bicycle hire. Ski and snowboard room, ski lifts at 1.5 and 2 km. Off site: Shop and restaurant 300 m. in village. Lots of scenic walking in the region.

Open: 15 May - 31 October, 15 December - 30 April.

Directions

Site is 25 km. east-northeast of Interlaken. From the A8 exit 30 (Unterbach) follow signs for Luzern and Brünig Pass. At the top Brünig Pass follow signs for Hasliberg (you may spot a dwarf on a swing). Head towards Hasliberg Goldern where site is signed at bottom end of village on the right.
GPS: N46:43.231 E08:11.757

Charges 2008

Per person	CHF 7,00 - 8,00
pitch	CHF 8,00 - 18,00
electricity per kWh	CHF 0,50
No credit cards.	

CH9510 Camping Aaregg

Seestrasse 26, CH-3855 Brienz am See (Bern)

Tel: 033 951 1843. Email: mail@aaregg.ch

Brienz in the Bernese Oberland is a delightful little town on the lake of the same name and the centre of the Swiss wood carving industry. Camping Aaregg is an excellent site situated on the southern shores of the lake with splendid views across the water to the mountains. There are 60 static caravans occupying their own area and 240 tourist pitches, all with 10A electricity. Of these, 16 are larger with hardstandings, water and drainage also and many of these have good lake views. A surcharge is made for pitches fronting the lake. The trees and flowers make an attractive and peaceful environment.

Facilities

New very attractive sanitary facilities built and maintained to first class standards. Showers with washbasins. Washbasins (open style and in cubicles). Children's section. Family shower rooms. Baby changing room. Facilities for disabled visitors. Laundry facilities. Motorcaravan services. Pleasant restaurant with terrace and takeaway in season. Play area. English is spoken.

Open: 1 April - 31 October.

Directions

Site is on road B6 on the east of Brienz. Entrance between BP and Esso filling stations, well signed. From the Interlaken-Luzern motorway, take Brienz exit and turn towards Brienz, site then on the left.
GPS: N46:44.833 E08:02.833

Charges 2008

Per person	CHF 10,00
child (6-16 yrs)	CHF 5,00
pitch with electricity	CHF 14,00 - 24,00
Low season less 10%.	

CH9495 Camping Balmweid

Balmweidstrasse 22, CH-3860 Meiringen (Bern)

Tel: 033 971 5115. Email: Info@camping-meiringen.ch

This good, family run site is peaceful, just south of the village of Meiringen on the route to the Grimsel Pass and Susten Passes. With a backdrop of steep cliffs it has good views of the adjacent mountains and forest-covered slopes. It provides 180 pitches of which 120 are for tourers, 64 with 10A electricity. Whilst this is a good site on which to base a longer stay, it is also useful as an overnight stop en-route to the Grimsel Pass or for a rest having faced the challenges that the Pass has to offer.

Facilities

The excellent and well maintained heated sanitary block in the reception building has WCs, showers and washbasins. Facilities for disabled visitors. Dishwashing area. Washing machines and dryer. Motorcaravan service point. Restaurant and shop. TV Room. Playground. Covered communal grill area. Internet access.

Open: All year.

Directions

From Meiringen the site is well signed to the south. At roundabout turn left and then left again in about 200 m. From Bern and Interlaken just go straight on at the roundabout signed 'Grimsel'.

Charges 2008

Per person	CHF 7,00 - 8,00
child (3-16 yrs)	CHF 1,00 - 4,00

515

CH9110 TCS Camping Seeland

CH-6204 Sempach-Stadt (Luzern)

Tel: **041 460 1466**. Email: **camping.sempach@tcs.ch**

Lucerne is a very popular city in the centre of Switzerland and Camping Seeland makes a peaceful base from which to visit the town and explore the surrounding countryside or, being a short way from the main N2 Basel - Chiasso motorway, is a convenient night stop if passing through. This neat, tidy site has 200 grass pitches for tourists, all with electricity (6A), a few with gravel hardstanding on either side of hard roads under trees with further places on the perimeter in the open. There are about 235 static caravans. A small river runs through the site with a connecting covered bridge.

Facilities

Three good quality sanitary blocks have the usual facilities including excellent facilities for disabled visitors and a baby room. Washing machine and dryer. Motorcaravan service point. Excellent self-service bar/restaurant with terrace overlooking the play area, lake and surrounding hills. Shop. Children's paddling pool and playground. Fishing. Lakeside beach. Off site: Shops and restaurants in the village. Tennis courts, boat and bicycle hire, minigolf and golf club. Windsurfing school nearby.

Open: 31 March - 1 October.

Directions

From the N2 take exit 21 for Sempach and follow signs for Sempach and site.
GPS: N47:07.529 E08:11.397

Charges 2007

Per person	CHF 6,40 - 8,20
child (6-15 yrs)	CHF 3,20 - 4,10
caravan or motorcaravan incl. electricity	CHF 20,00 - 34,50

Camping Cheques accepted.

CH9115 TCS Camping Steinibachried

CH-6048 Horw-Luzern (Luzern)

Tel: **041 340 3558**. Email: **camping.horw@tcs.ch**

Situated in the southern suburbs of Luzern and with easy autoroute access, this site is a very convenient base for visiting what is quite deservedly a popular tourist area. The level, grassed site provides 100 touring pitches with electricity, separated into rows by trees and hedges. It is dominated by the Pilatus mountains, over 2,000 metres high. The peaks and mountain top restaurants offer fantastic views and can be reached by cable car on the steepest cog railway in the world from Alpnachstad. Access to the lake from the site is over a wooden walkway that passes through a small protected nature area.

Facilities

Single, well maintained toilet block to one end of tourist area. Showers are free, some washbasins in cabins. Facilities for disabled visitors. Baby room. Washing machine and dryer. Motorcaravan service point. Gas supplies. Small shop. Bar with terrace. Convenient self service restaurant with takeaway. New play area.

Open: 31 March - 1 October.

Directions

Site is 4 km. south of the centre of Luzern and borders the Vierwaldstatter See. Leave motorway 2 at exit 28 Luzern/Horw. Site signed at roundabout towards Horw-Sud. GPS: N47:00.711 E08:18.660

Charges 2007

Per person	CHF 6,00 - 8,00
child (6-15 yrs)	CHF 3,00 - 4,00
pitch with electricity	CHF 18,00 - 24,00

CH9130 Camping Vitznau

CH-6354 Vitznau (Luzern)

Tel: **041 397 1280**

Camping Vitznau is situated in the small village of the same name, above and overlooking Lake Luzern, with splendid views across the water to the mountains on the other side. It is a small, neat and tidy site very close to the delightful village on the narrow, winding, lakeside road. The 160 pitches for caravans or motorhomes (max length 8 m.) have 15A electricity available to most and all have fine views. They are on level, grassy terraces with hard wheel tracks for motorcaravans and separated by tarmac roads. There are separate places for tents.

Facilities

The single, well constructed sanitary block provides free hot showers (water heated by solar panels). Laundry and dishwashing facilities. Gas supplies. Motorcaravan services. Shop. General room for wet weather. Games room. Small heated swimming pool and children's splash pool (1/5-30/9). Off site: Village restaurants about five minutes walk. Fishing or bicycle hire within 1 km. Watersports near. Golf 15 km.

Open: 1 April - 31 October.

Directions

Site is signed from the centre of Vitznau.
GPS: N47:00.403 E08:29.174

Charges 2007

Per person	CHF 5,33 - 6,66
child (4-14 yrs)	CHF 5,33 - 6,66
pitch acc. to size and season	CHF 10,00 - 17,33
dog	CHF 2,00
electricity	CHF 2,67

CH9820 Camping Pradafenz

Girabadaweg 34, CH-7075 Churwalden (Graubünden)

Tel: 081 382 1921. Email: camping@pradafenz.ch

In the heart of the village of Churwalden, which is on the on the Chur - St Moritz road, Pradafenz makes a convenient night stop and being amidst the mountains, is also an excellent base for walking and exploring this scenic area. At first sight, this appears to be a site for static holiday caravans but three large rectangular terraces at the front take 50 touring units. This area has a hardstanding of concrete frets with grass growing through and 'super-pitch' facilities of electricity (10A), drainage, gas and TV sockets. A flat meadow is also available for tents or as an over-flow for caravans.

Facilities	Directions
New sanitary block is well appointed and heated. It includes some washbasins in cabins. Baby room. Another good, heated small block is in the tourist section. Washing machines, dryers and separate drying room. Motorcaravan services. Gas supplies. Small restaurant also selling basic provisions. Bicycle hire. Fishing. Torches useful. Off site: Restaurants and shops 300 m. in village. Municipal outdoor pool 500 m. Riding 3.5 km. Golf 5 km.	Churwalden is 10 km. south of Chur. From Chur take road towards Lenzerheide. It is initially a fairly long, steep climb with one tight hairpin. In centre of Churwalden turn right in front of the tourist office towards the site. GPS: N46:46.632 E09:32.500

Open: 1 June - 31 October, 15 December - 29 March.

Charges 2008

Per person	CHF 7,50
pitch	CHF 10,00 - 15,00
electricity	CHF 2,50 - 3,00

CH9830 Camping Sur En

CH-7554 Sur En/Sent (Graubünden)

Tel: 081 866 3544. Email: wb@bluewin.ch

Sur En is at the eastern end of the Engadine valley, about 10 km. from the Italian and Austrian borders. The area is, perhaps, better known as a skiing region, but has summer attractions as well. This level site is in an open valley with little shade. They say there is room for 120 touring units on the meadows where pitches are neither marked nor numbered; there are electricity connections for all (6A). As you approach on road 27 and spot the site way below under the shadow of a steeply rising, wooded mountain, the drop may appear daunting but, as you drive, it becomes reasonable.

Facilities	Directions
The modern, heated sanitary block is good with some extra facilities in the main building. Washing machine and dryer. Motorcaravan services. Shop and good restaurant (15/12-15/4 and 1/5-31/10) with covered terrace. Takeaway (high season). Pool (1/6-15/10). Bicycle hire. Fishing. Entertainment in July/Aug. A symposium for sculptors is held during the second week in July. Excursions arranged in high season. Off site: Golf 8 km. Bus service to Scuol for train to St Moritz.	Sur En is 28 km. east of Davos. It is signposted from the 27 road about halfway between Susch and Scuol. The road is a steady, winding descent. Cross covered timber bridge (3.8 m.) to site. GPS: N46:49.060 E10:21.570

Open: All year.

Charges 2007

Per person	CHF 5,00 - 5,80
child (6-16 yrs)	CHF 2,50 - 2,90
pitch	CHF 11,10 - 15,00
electricity	CHF 2,80

CH9850 TCS Camping Neue Ganda

CH-7302 Landquart (Graubünden)

Tel: 081 322 3955. Email: camping.landquart@tcs.ch

Situated close to the Klosters, Davos road and the nearby town of Landquart, this valley campsite provides a comfortable night-stop near the A13 motorway. The 80 touring pitches are not marked or separated but are all on level grass off a central tarmac road through the long, narrow wooded site. All pitches have 6/10A electricity. The many static caravans are mostly hidden from view situated in small alcoves. A modern, timber clad building at the entrance houses all the facilities – reception, community room and sanitary facilities. The restaurant/shop adjacent is open all the year.

Facilities	Directions
The toilet block is extremely well appointed and can be heated. Facilities for disabled visitors. Baby room. Washing machine and dryer. Drying room. Dog Shower. Motorcaravan services. Restaurant. Shop. Internet access. Off site: Rambling. Cycling tours. Tennis, riding and canoeing nearby. Fishing and riding 2 km.	From A13 take Landquart exit 14 and follow road to Davos. 800 m. after crossing large bridge, go down slip-road where site is signed on right. At the bottom turn left under road and follow signs right towards site. GPS: N46:58.140 E09:35.360

Open: 6 April - 23 October, 19 December - 20 March.

Charges 2007

Per person	CHF 5,40 - 6,60
pitch incl. electricity	CHF 19,60 - 21,80
Camping Cheques accepted.	

517

CH9855 Camping Cavresc

CH-7746 Le Prese (Graubünden)

Tel: 081 844 0797. Email: camping.cavresc@bleuwin.ch

Le Prese is on the Tirano to St Moritz road, south of the Bernina Pass. Camping Cavresc is on grassy meadows in the Valposchiano valley and, with its southern climate, peaceful ambience and beautiful views, is a very good, newly built site with ultramodern sanitary facilities. There are 36 flat, level pitches, all with 10A electricity and water, plus a large area for tents. There is no shade. If the campsite reception is unmanned, walk back into town, as the Sertori family who own the site also run the small well-stocked supermarket. Le Prese is close to Italy and the Poschiavo Lake.

Facilities

The excellent toilet block is very well maintained. Showers on payment. Facilities for disabled visitors. Washing machine and dryer. Motorcaravan services. Restaurant/bar. Small shop. Swimming pool (high season). There are plans for outdoor ice skating to be added. Off site: Le Prese 250 m. Windsurfing and sailing and of course skiing.

Open: All year.

Directions

Le Prese is 6 km. south of Poschiavo. Coming from Italy on road no. 29, the site is towards the southern end of the town. Turn right towards Pagnoncini and Cantone and site is on right in about 100 m. Go over a humpback bridge at the entrance. GPS: N46:17.330 E10:04.510

Charges 2007

Per person	CHF 10,00 - 12,00
pitch	CHF 6,00 - 15,00
electricity	CHF 4,00

CH9860 Camping Plauns

Morteratsch, CH-7504 Pontresina (Graubünden)

Tel: 081 842 6285. Email: plauns@bluewin.ch

This mountain site is in splendid scenery near St Moritz. Pontresina, at the mouth of the Bernina Pass road (B29), runs from Celerina in the Swiss Engadine to Titana in Italy. Camping Plauns, some 4 km. southeast of Pontresina, is situated in the floor of the valley between fir-clad mountains at 1,850 m. above sea level. There are about 250 pitches for tourists in summer, all with electricity, some in small clearings amongst tall trees, others in a larger open space. In winter the number is reduced to 40.

Facilities

Three fully equipped toilet blocks, one old and two new, modern and excellent, and can be heated in cool weather. Some washbasins in private cabins and showers on payment. Facilities for disabled visitors. Washing machines, dryers and drying room. Well stocked shop. Grill-snack bar for drinks or simple meals. TV room. Internet access. Bicycle hire. Playground. Torch useful. Off site: Restaurant 1 km.

Open: 1 June - 15 October, 15 December - 15 April.

Directions

Site is on B29, the road to Tirano and Bernina Pass, about 4 km. southeast of Pontresina - well signed. GPS: N46:27.420 E09:56.040

Charges 2007

Per person	CHF 10,40
child (6-15 yrs)	CHF 4,00 - 6,50
pitch	CHF 9,00 - 15,00
electricity (6-13A)	CHF 3,00 - 4,50
dog	CHF 3,00

CH9865 TCS Camping Fontanivas

Via Fontanivas 9, CH-7180 Disentis (Graubünden)

Tel: 081 947 4422. Email: camping.disentis@tcs.ch

Nestled in the Surselva valley with superb views of the surrounding mountains, this is an attractive site with its own lake. Surrounded by tall pine trees, the site is owned by the Touring Club of Switzerland, the Swiss version of the AA, and provides flat, level pitches, almost all with 13A electricity. There are plenty of opportunities for walks, nature trails and cycle rides, whilst the more adventurous can enjoy themselves canyoning, rafting, hang-gliding or mountain biking. The Medelser Rhine near Disentis is known to be the richest place in gold in the country.

Facilities

The excellent sanitary block is well maintained with free showers and hairdryers. Facilities for disabled visitors. Baby room. Washing machine and dryer. Motorcaravan services. Shop. Restaurant/bar. Play room. Bicycle hire. Fishing. Caravans and tent bungalows to rent. Off site: Disentis 2 km. Indoor pool.

Open: 27 April - 30 September.

Directions

The site is 2 km. south of Disentis. From Andermatt take the Oberalppass to Disentis. In town at T-junction turn right towards Lukmanier. Site is at bottom of hill on the left, past the droopy power cables. GPS: N46:41.814 E08:51.197

Charges 2007

Per person	CHF 6,20 - 7,20
pitch	CHF 14,80 - 18,80
electricity	CHF 4,50
Camping Cheques accepted.	

CH9160 TCS Camping Rheinwiesen

Haupt Strasse, CH-8246 Langwiesen (Schaffhausen)

Tel: 052 659 3300. Email: camping.schaffhausen@tcs.ch

Rheinwiesen is a friendly site in a very pleasant setting on the banks of the Rhine, with some tall trees, amongst which are some attractive willows. It is level and grassy, the first half quite open and the rest of the touring area wooded, with numbered pitches (mostly small – up to 70 sq.m.) many under tall trees. There are many day visitors in summer as the site is ideally placed for swimming, canoeing and diving in the Rhine. Dogs are not accepted at any time. Whilst here, you would not want to miss the impressive waterfalls at Schaffhausen, 150 m. wide and 25 m. high.

Facilities

For tourers, there is an old but clean building which might be under pressure at the busiest times. Washing machine and dryer. Two very deep, large waste collectors. Bar and snack bar with covered terrace for burgers etc. open daily. Bread to order, some essentials kept. Pool room also used as wet weather rest room. Two shallow paddling pools, with play area close by. Off site: Shop 500 m.

Open: 27 April - 29 September.

Directions

From Schaffhausen head east towards Kreuzlingen (road no. 14) for 2.5 km. Site is signed just before Langwiesen. Coming from the east, it is a tight turn into the site. GPS: N47:41.240 E08:39.350

Charges 2007

Per person	CHF 5,60 - 7,20
child (6-15 yrs)	CHF 2,80 - 3,60
pitch	CHF 14,00 - 17,00
electricity (4A)	CHF 3,00

Camping Cheques accepted.

CH9175 Camping Giessenpark

CH-7310 Bad Ragaz (St Gallen)

Tel: 081 302 3710. Email: giessenpark@bluewin.ch

The luxury spa resort of Bad Ragaz nestles in the Rhine valley and Giessenpark surrounds this site, which is located in a forest. There are 86 flat, level gravel pitches of which 52 are for touring, all with access to electricity (10A). The Rhine and the extensive park are within a minutes walk and add to the peaceful nature of the site. The local authority swimming pool is close to the site, which is open from mid May to mid September. There is also a children's pool in a very large play area about 200 m. from the site.

Facilities

Good, modern toilet is well maintained with free showers. Facilities for disabled visitors. Baby room. Sinks with hot water for laundry and dishwashing. Washing machine and dryer. Motorcaravan services. Shop (limited). Restaurant. Off site: Bad Ragaz 1 km. Golf and bicycle hire 1 km. Riding 3 km.

Open: All year.

Directions

From the A13 take Bad Ragaz exit and follow Bad Ragaz signs. In town, go over small bridge and turn right immediately, then right again after 300 m. following signs towards the site.

Charges 2008

Per person	CHF 10,10
pitch	CHF 8,00 - 10,00
with electricity	CHF 15,00

No credit cards.

CH9180 Camping Buchhorn

Philosophenweg 17, CH-9320 Arbon (Thurgau)

Tel: 071 446 6545. Email: info@camping-arbon.ch

This small site is directly beside Lake Bodensee in the town's parkland. The site has some shade but few of the touring pitches are by the water's edge. An overflow field used for tents is next door. There are many static caravans but said to be room for 100 tourists. Pitches are on a mixture of gravel and grass, on flat areas on either side of access roads, most with 6A electricity. Cars may have to parked elsewhere. A railway runs directly along one side. A single set of buildings provide all the site's amenities.

Facilities

Toilet facilities are clean and modern, and should just about suffice in high season. Washing machine, dryer and drying area. Fridge. Shop (basic supplies, drinks and snacks - all season). General room. Playground. Gates closed 12-14.00 hrs daily. Dogs are not accepted. Off site: Tennis 150 m. Town swimming lido 400 m. Watersports and steamer trips are available on the lake, walks and marked cycle tracks around it. Nature reserve.

Open: April - October.

Directions

On Arbon - Konstanz road 13. From the A1 take the Arbon West exit and head towards the town. Straight on at the lights and turn left just after the town sign. Turn left again and head towards the warehouses. Turn right and the site is straight ahead.

Charges 2007

Per person	CHF 8,00
child (6-16 yrs)	CHF 3,50

CH9185 Camping Fischerhaus

Promenadenstrasse 52, CH-8280 Kreuzlingen (Thurgau)

Tel: 071 688 4903. Email: camping.fischerhaus@bluewin.ch

Camping Fischerhaus is tucked behind the town's light industrial estate and next to Lake Constance. It provides 250 pitches of which 150 are for tourers, all with 10A electricity supply. The seasonal pitches are grouped together near reception and the lakeside, although from the site it is hardly visible. The touring pitches are grass, level and located towards the back of the site, a short walk from the main sanitary block. The town of Kreuzlingen is a short walk away along the banks of the lake past a marina.

Facilities

The main sanitary block, near reception, has WCs, showers and facilities for disabled visitors. The second block, near the area used by tourers, just has WCs. Good dishwashing area. Washing machines and dryer. Chemical disposal point. Small shop for basics. Restaurant and bar overlooking lake. Playground. Fishing. Dogs are not accepted. Off site: Swimming pool adjacent.

Open: 20 March - 26 October.

Directions

Site is at the east side of Kreuzlingen on the banks of Lake Constance. It is well signed from all directions as is the adjoining swimming pool. GPS: N47:38.824 E09:11.875

Charges 2008

Per person	CHF 9,00
child (6-16 yrs)	CHF 4,50

Camping Fischerhaus – an oasis of relaxation in a unique location.

Camping Fischerhaus Kreuzlingen

www.camping-fischerhaus.ch

Camping Fischerhaus, CH-8280 Kreuzlingen, Fon 0041 (0)71 688 49 03

CH9000 Camping Waldhort

Heideweg 16, CH-4153 Reinach bei Basel (Basel-Land)

Tel: 061 711 6429. Email: info@camping-waldhort.ch

This is a satisfactory site for night halts or for visits to Basel. Although there are almost twice as many static caravan pitches as spaces for tourists, this site, on the edge of a residential district, is within easy reach of the city by tram. It is flat, with 210 level pitches on grass with access from the tarmac road which circles round inside the site. Trees are now maturing to give some shade. All pitches have electricity (10A). Owned and run by the Camping and Caravanning Club of Basel, it is neat, tidy and orderly and there is usually space available.

Facilities

The good quality, fully equipped, central sanitary block includes facilities for babies and disabled people. Washing machine and dryer. Kitchen with gas rings. Fridge for ice packs. Motorcaravan services. Small shop with terrace for drinks. Children's playground with two small pools. Swimming pool and tennis next to site.

Open: 1 March - 25 October.

Directions

Take Basel - Delémont motorway spur, exit at 'Reinach-Nord' and follow camp signs. GPS: N47:29.954 E07:36.119

Charges 2008

Per person	CHF 9,00
child (6-14 yrs)	CHF 5,00
tent pitch	CHF 11,00
pitch incl. electricity	CHF 18,00

CH9890 Camping Campofelice

Via alle Brere 7, CH-6598 Tenero (Ticino)

Tel: **091 745 1417**

The largest site in Switzerland, it is bordered on the front by Lake Maggiore and on one side by the Verzasca estuary, where the site has its own harbour. Campofelice is divided into rows, with 1,030 individual pitches of average size on flat grass on either side of hard access roads. Mostly well shaded, all pitches have 10A electricity and some also have water, drainage and TV connections. Pitches near the lake cost more (these are not available for motorcaravans) and a special area is reserved for small tents. English is spoken at this good, if rather expensive site. Sporting facilities are good and there are cycle paths in the area, including into Locarno. The beach by the lake is sandy, long and wider than the usual lakeside ones. It shelves gently so that bathing is safe for children. Member of Leading Campings Group.

Facilities

The six heated toilet blocks are of excellent quality. Washing machines and dryers. Motorcaravan services. Gas supplies. Supermarket. Restaurant. Tennis. Minigolf. Bicycle hire. Playground. Doctor calls. Dogs are not accepted Off site: Fishing 500 m. Water skiing and windsurfing 1 km. Boat hire 5 km. Riding 6 km. Golf 8 km.

Open: 31 March - 27 October.

Directions

On the Bellinzona - Locarno road 13 take exit for Tenero. Site is signed at roundabout. GPS: N46:10.114 E08:51.355

Charges 2007

Per unit incl. 2 persons	CHF 44,00 - 84,00

Some pitches have min. stay regulations.

CH9880 Camping Lido Mappo

Via Mappo, CH-6598 Tenero (Ticino)

Tel: **091 745 1437**. Email: **camping@lidomappo.ch**

Lido Mappo lies on the lakeside at the northeast tip of Lake Maggiore, about 5 km. from Locarno, and has views of the surrounding mountains and hills across the lake. The site is attractively laid out in rows of individual, numbered pitches, half for tents and half for caravans and mostly split up by access roads or hedges. The pitches (418 for touring) vary in size, those by the lake costing more and most are well shaded. Electricity (10A) is available on all pitches. With helpful English speaking staff, this is a quiet site with its own narrow, mainly sandy beach.

Facilities

The five, recently renovated toilet blocks can be heated in cool weather and are well kept. They include individual washbasins, all in cabins for women and some for men. Facilities for disabled people. Baby room. Washing machines and dryers. Cooking facilities. Refrigerated compartments for hire. Motorcaravan services. Supermarket. Restaurant/bar. Takeaway. TV room. Large playground. Lake swimming. Fishing. First aid post. Dogs not allowed. Off site: Bicycle hire. Riding 3 km. Golf 5 km.

Open: 18 March - 23 October.

Directions

On Bellinzona - Locarno road 13 take exit for Tenero and site is signed at roundabout. GPS: N46:10.625 E08:50.570

Charges 2007

Per unit incl. 2 persons and electricity	CHF 35,00 - 53,00
lakeside pitch	CHF 45,00 - 79,00

Less 5% for stays over 10 days and 10% over 21 days.

CH9950 TCS Camping Piodella

CH-6933 Muzzano (Ticino)

Tel: **091 994 7788**. Email: **camping.muzzano@tcs.ch**

This modernised site, on the edge of Lake Lugano facing south down the lake must rank as one of the best in Switzerland. There are 265 numbered pitches (212 for touring units) all with 10A electricity and 26 with water connections. There is shade in the older part nearest the lake and young trees in the new area. Cars must be parked in the car park, not by your pitch. The site is a short way from the airport so there may be some aircraft noise. Well placed for exploring Lugano, southern Switzerland and northern Italy, or simply to enjoy the facilities of the site.

Facilities

The original refurbished toilet block and a splendid new one includes a baby room and a bathroom for disabled visitors, (heated in cool weather). Washing facilities. Motorcaravan services. Gas supplies. Shop. Bar/restaurant with pleasant terrace. Pools (May - mid Oct). Day and TV rooms. Playground. Two tennis courts. Marina. Off site: Bicycle hire 2 km. Riding 4 km. Golf 5 km.

Open: All year excl. 24 October - 10 December.

Directions

Piodella is on Bellinzona-Ponte Tresa road; take motorway exit 49 Lugano-Nord for Ponte Tresa and turn left at T-junction in Agno. Follow signs for Piodella or TCS at roundabout. Site is at south end of the airport. GPS: N45:59.755 E08:54.503

Charges 2007

Per person	CHF 7,80 - 9,80
pitch incl. electricity	CHF 24,00 - 44,60

CH9970 TCS Camping Parco al Sole

CH-6866 Meride (Ticino)

Tel: **091 646 4330**. Email: **camping.meride@tcs.ch**

Meride is a small village in the extreme south of Switzerland with the Italian border close on three sides. A little remote, Parco al Sole is on a slight slope 1 km. before the village, with mountain views. There is space for 64 small units, with electricity connections (10A) available for 40, and 16 static caravans. The pitches are not numbered or marked out and caravans are placed between tall trees or on an open space. When the site is busy, units could be crowded. Cars are parked by the entrance. Parco al Sole is better for a few days stay to explore the area rather than a single night stop.

Facilities

A good quality sanitary block with the usual facilities, free hot water and a baby room. 'Grotto Cafe' with a log fire during cool weather where drinks and simple meals are offered and limited basic food supplies can be obtained. Heated swimming pool (1/6-30/8) and paddling pool. Playground. Some animation is organised in high season. TV and videos (in café).

Open: 1 May - 25 September.

Directions

From N2 motorway take exit 52 for Mendrisio towards Stabio, Varese. Head to Rancate then Basazio, Arzo and Meride. Site signed. (Approx. 6 km. from motorway exit). Road to site is narrow. Any problems follow signs for camping Serpiano until village of Meride. GPS: N45:53.332 E08:56.930

Charges 2007

Per person	CHF 6,20 - 7,80
pitch incl. electricity	CHF 17,80 - 26,10

Camping Cheques accepted.

CH9520 Camping Du Botza

Route du Camping 1, CH-1963 Vétroz (Valais)

Tel: **027 346 1940**. Email: **info@botza.ch**

Situated in the Rhône Valley at a height of 460 m. and not far from the autoroute, this is a pleasant site with views of the surrounding mountains. It is set in a peaceful wooded location, even though it is close to an industrial zone. There are 125 individual touring pitches, ranging in size (60-130 sq.m.) all with 4A electricity, many with some shade and 25 with water and drainage. Considerable investment has taken place in making the site environmentally friendly with solar power used to heat the pool and sanitary blocks and a large recycling facility. English is spoken.

Facilities

Some private cabins in the heated sanitary block. Washing machines and dryers. Shop. Pizzeria. Swimming pool (15/5-1/9). Playground. Table tennis. Volleyball. Tennis court. Internet access. Off site: Many walks alongside small streams nearby. Good cycle track. Riding 2 km. Golf 8 km. The historic town of Sion is 8 km.

Open: All year.

Directions

From the A9/E62 between Sion and Martigny, take exit 25 Conthey/Vétroz and go south towards 'zone industrial', after 200 m. turn right to 'Camping 9.33 Botza' and follow signs. Site is 2.5 km. from autoroute exit. GPS: N46:12.210 E07:16.440

Charges 2007

Per person	CHF 3,40 - 5,50
child (6-16 yrs)	CHF 1,70 - 2,75
pitch	CHF 7,40 - 16,00
electricity	CHF 2,20 - 2,95

CH9600 Camping Rive-Bleue

Bouveret Plage, CH-1897 Bouveret (Valais)

Tel: **024 481 2161**. Email: **info@camping-rive-bleue.ch**

At the eastern end of Lac Léman with mountain views, the main feature of this site is the very pleasant lakeside lido only a short walk of 300 m. from the site and with free entry for campers. It has an 'Aquaparc' pool with a water toboggan and plenty of grassy sunbathing areas, a bathing area in lake, boating facilities with storage for sailboards, canoes, inflatables etc, sailing school, pedaloes for hire. The site has 220 marked pitches on well kept flat grass, half in the centre with 6A electricity, the other half round the perimeter.

Facilities

Two decent toilet blocks have washbasins with cold water in the old block, hot in the new, and preset free hot showers. Shop, restaurant by beach (both all season). Bicycle hire. Fishing. Covered area for cooking with electric rings and barbecue. Drying room. Motorcaravan services (Euro-relais; CHF 12).

Open: 1 April - 1 October.

Directions

From motorway 5, exit 16 (Villeneuve), south of Montreux, follow signs for Evian. Just after passing town sign for Le Bouveret, turn right, north, and follow Aquaparc and site signs. GPS: N46:23.194 E06:51.610

Charges 2007

Per person	CHF 8,10 - 9,90
child (6-16 yrs)	CHF 5,60 - 6,70
motorcaravan or caravan and car with electricity	CHF 14,30 - 17,50

CH9640 Camping de la Sarvaz

Route de Fully, CH-1913 Saillon (Valais)

Tel: **027 744 1389**. Email: **info@sarvaz.ch**

The Rhone valley in Valais with its terraced vineyards provides a beautiful setting for this site. Family owned and run, Camping de la Sarvaz provides excellent facilities and would be a good base for relaxing or for the more energetic visitor with walking, cycling, climbing or skiing in the area. The site adjoins a restaurant/bar. It has 41 level touring pitches all with electricity, 19 of which have water and drainage. Lovely mountain views surround the site and there are 5 chalets to rent. An inflatable pool is available from May to September. English is spoken.

Facilities

Modern, heated sanitary facilities are of very high standards, very well maintained. Free showers. Additional toilets on the first floor. Facilities for disabled people. Baby room. Washing machine and dryer. Motorcaravan services. Shop (all season). Restaurant/bar (all season, not Mondays and Tuesdays). Volleyball. Good play area. Internet access. Off site: Saillon 2 km. with Thermal centre and spa facilities.

Open: 4 February - 31 December.

Directions

From the A9 take exit 23 for Saxon/Saillon. Follow signs to Saillon then turn right towards the site, which is 3 km. from the autoroute exit. GPS: N46:09.593 E07:10.053

Charges 2007

Per person	CHF 8,00
child (6-16 yrs)	CHF 4,00
pitch	CHF 16,00
electricity	CHF 3,30 - 4,40

CH9655 TCS Camping les Neuvilles

Rue de Levant 68, CH-1920 Martigny (Valais)
Tel: 027 722 4544. Email: camping.martigny@tcs.ch

Easily accessible from the autoroute (A9) and close to the town centre, this site has a total of 225 pitches. There are 185 for touring units, all with electricity and most on level, grassy ground (some slope slightly). A number of trees provide some shade, although the site is fairly open allowing views of the surrounding mountains. Being close to the autoroute and located in an industrial area, the site can be quite noisy, especially noticeable during the night and mornings. With its ease of access and close proximity to shops, it makes a convenient night stop when travelling along the Rhône Valley.

Facilities

Two sanitary buildings, one close to the entrance the other at the far end. Showers are large and free, some washbasins in cabins, some with only cold water. Facilities for disabled people. Baby room. Cooking rings. Washing machines and dryers. Motorcaravan service point. Shop. Bar and snack bar. TV room. Play area and paddling pool. Bicycle hire. Off site: Entry to the municipal swimming pool is free. Riding 1 km. Fishing 3 km.

Open: 1 February - 15 November.

Directions

From A9 exit 22 (Martigny) follow signs for Expo. After leaving the autoroute, at first roundabout, site is signed. GPS: N46:05.822 E07:04.726

Charges 2007

Per person	CHF 6,80 - 7,80
child	CHF 3,40 - 3,90
pitch with electricity	CHF 18,70 - 24,20
dog	CHF 3,00 - 4,00

CH9660 Camping des Glaciers

CH-1944 La Fouly (Valais)
Tel: 027 783 1735. Email: camping.glaciers@st-bernard.ch

Camping des Glaciers at 1,600 m. above sea level is set amidst magnificent mountain scenery in a quiet, peaceful location in the beautiful Ferret Valley. The site offers some pitches in an open, undulating meadow and the rest are level, individual plots of varying size in small clearings, between bushes and shrubs or under tall pines. All of the 170 places have 25A electricity. The charming lady owner, Mme Darbellay, who has run the site for over 35 years, is fluent in six languages and always ready to welcome you to this peaceful haven and to give information on the locality.

Facilities

Three sanitary units of exceptional quality and heated when necessary. Hot water is free in all washbasins (some in cabins), showers and sinks. British style WCs. Washing machines and dryers in each block, one block has a drying room, another a baby room. Gas supplies. Motorcaravan services. Small shop. Recreation room with TV. Playground. Torches may be useful. Off site: Shop and restaurant 500 m. Bicycle hire 500 m. Riding 8 km.

Open: 15 May - 30 September.

Directions

Leave Martigny-Gd St Bernard road (no. 21) at Orsieres and follow signs (Ferret valley or La Fouly). Site is signed on right at end of La Fouly village. GPS: N45:56.008 E07:05.620

Charges 2007

Per person	CHF 6,50
child (2-12 yrs)	CHF 3,50
pitch with electricity	CHF 13,50 - 19,50

Less 10% in May, June and September.

CH9670 Camping de Molignon

CH-1984 Les Haudères (Valais)
Tel: 027 283 1240. Email: info@molignon@ch

De Molignon, surrounded by mountains, is a quiet, peaceful place 1,450 m. above sea level; although there may be some road noise, the rushing stream and the sound of cow bells are likely to be the only disturbing factor in summer. The 100 pitches for tourists (75 with 10A electricity) are on well tended, level terraces leading down to the river. Good English is spoken by the owner's son who is now running the site, who will be pleased to give information on all that is available from the site.

Facilities

Two fully equipped sanitary blocks, heated in cool weather, with free hot showers. Baby room. Washing machines and dryer. Kitchen for hikers. Motorcaravan services. Gas supplies. Shop for basic supplies (15/6-15/9). Restaurant. Heated swimming pool with cover for cool weather (6 x 12 m). Sitting room for games and reading. Playground. Guided walks, climbing, geological museum, winter skiing. Fishing. Off site: Tennis and hang-gliding near. Bicycle hire 1 km. Riding 15 km. Langlauf in winter.

Open: All year.

Directions

Follow signs southwards from Sion for the Val d'Herens through Evolène to Les Haudères where site is signed on the right at the beginning of the village. GPS: N46:05.670 E07:29.849

Charges 2007

Per person	CHF 6,70
child (4-16 yrs)	CHF 3,80
pitch with electricity	CHF 12,80 - 17,90
dog	CHF 3,00

Less 10% in low season.

524
Check real time availability and at-the-gate prices...
www.alanrogers.com

CH9680 TCS Camping Bois de Finges

CH-3960 Sierre (Valais)

Tel: 027 455 0284. Email: camping.sierre@tcs.ch

This site is situated in the middle of the 'Bois des Finges' pine forest on a rocky wooded hillside. It is attractive and well maintained with much to offer for the naturalist. With 100 pitches cut out of the hillside, some are difficult to access but the manager will help. They can take units of up to 7 m. but mainly smaller units and tents in some parts. All pitches are screened by trees and 62 have 4A electricity (long leads useful). Staff are welcoming and helpful but little English is spoken. This site would be useful for an overnight stop. There is road noise from a quarry opposite.

Facilities

Two very clean and well maintained wooden toilet blocks are fully equipped. Freezer, washing machine and dryer. Motorcaravan service point. Well stocked but limited shop and snack bar. Outdoor heated pool (6 x 12 m.) and paddling pool. Well appointed play area. Tennis. Table tennis. Bicycle hire. Barbecues are not permitted. Torches are useful. Off site: Sierre 1 km. Walking and hiking area. Fishing (licence required) 900 m. Golf and riding 3 km.

Open: 15 April - 3 October.

Directions

Leave motorway at exit 29, Sierre East. Follow sign for Sierre. Site is signed on the right (TCS) within 200 m. GPS: N46:17.633 E07:33.472

Charges 2007

Per person	CHF 6,00 - 7,00
child	CHF 3,00 - 3,50
pitch with electricity	CHF 16,90 - 23,70

Camping Cheques accepted.

CH9720 Camping Bella-Tola

Waldstrasse 57, CH-3952 Susten-Leuk (Valais)

Tel: 027 473 1491. Email: info@bella-tola.ch

An attractive site with good standards, Bella-Tola is on the hillside above Susten (east of Sierre) with good views over the Rhône valley. Extensive terracing has been carried out and most of the pitches are now terraced and flat. All of the 180 individually numbered pitches have electricity connections. The fullest season is 10/7-10/8, but they say that there is usually room somewhere. Used by tour operators (20%). Guests are asked to comply with environmental rules by sorting rubbish as directed.

Facilities

Three good quality modern sanitary blocks should be quite sufficient, with some washbasins in cabins. Free hot water in washbasins, showers and sinks for clothes and dishes, plus baby rooms. Facilities for disabled visitors. Washing machines, dryers and irons. Motorcaravan services. Shop. Newly renovated restaurant/bar. Takeaway (15/5-31/8). Heated swimming pool (9/5-21/9). General room with TV. Films and guided walks in July/Aug. Torches advised. WiFi (free). Off site: Riding and tennis. Golf 4 km.

Open: 26 April - 26 October.

Directions

Travelling eastwards from Sierre along main road, small site road is to the right (south) just after entering Susten (site signed). GPS: N46:17.937 E07:38.194

Charges 2008

Per person	CHF 6,67
child (2-16 yrs)	CHF 3,33 - 4,67
pitch acc. to type and season	CHF 10,00 - 17,33
electricity	CHF 2,40

Less 25% on person and pitch fees outside July/Aug.

CH9730 Camping Gemmi

Briannenstrasse 4, CH-3952 Susten-Leuk (Valais)

Tel: 027 473 1154. Email: info@campgemmi.ch

The Rhône Valley is a popular through route to Italy via the Simplon Pass and a holiday region in its own right. Gemmi is a delightful small, friendly site in a scenic location with 65 level pitches, all with 16A electricity, on well tended grass amidst a variety of trees, some of which offer shade. 40 pitches also have water and drainage. The pleasant, friendly owner speaks fluent English, maintains high standards and has established a campsite mainly for tourists with few resident static units. This site is probably more suitable for the mature camper.

Facilities

A modern sanitary block, partly heated, is of excellent quality and kept very clean. It includes some washbasins in cabins. Eight private bathrooms for hire on weekly basis. Washing machines and dryers. Motorcaravan services. Gas supplies. Well stocked shop. Small bar/restaurant where snacks and limited range of local specialities served. Terrace bar and snack restaurant. Playground. Tennis. Internet access. Off site: Golf 500 m. Riding 2 km. Fishing 6 km.

Open: 19 April - 18 October.

Directions

From east (Visp), turn left 1 km. after sign for Agarn Feithieren. From west (Sierre), turn right 2 km. after Susten at sign for Camping Torrent and Gemmi. GPS: N46:17.880 E07:39.544

Charges 2008

Per person	CHF 7,00 - 9,00
child	CHF 3,50 - 6,50
pitch with electricity	CHF 12,00 - 14,00
dog	CHF 2,00

CH9740 Camping Attermenzen

CH-3928 Randa (Valais)

Tel: **027 967 1379**. Email: **rest.camping@rhone.ch**

Randa, a picturesque Valais village, at 1,409 m. is a beautiful location for a campsite and ideal for those wishing to visit Zermatt only 10 km. away. Reception is open from mid June to mid September, otherwise call at the restaurant (closed on Tuesdays). Unmarked pitches are on an uneven field with some areas that are fairly level and 6A electricity is within easy reach. A paradise for walking, mountaineering, climbing and mountain biking and surrounded by famous 4,000 m. peaks, such as the Dom and Weisshorn, this site also offers modern facilities with a restaurant and bar next door.

Facilities

The sanitary block is of a good standard and well maintained with free showers. Washing machine. Shop (June-Sept). Gas supplies. Restaurant/bar. Takeaway. Off site: Zermatt 10 km.

Open: 1 May - 31 October.

Directions

From A9 at Visp turn right at roundabout (Zermatt). Go through the 3.3 km. long tunnel and follow road towards Zermatt. Go through Stalden and turn right at roundabout (Zermatt). Site is about 1 km. after Randa village on the left.
GPS: N46:05.080 E07:46.540

Charges 2008

Per person	CHF 6,00
pitch	CHF 9,00
electricity	CHF 4,00

CH9770 Camping Santa Monica

Kantonstrasse 56, CH-3942 Raron-Turtig (Valais)

Tel: **027 934 24 24**. Email: **info@santa-monica.ch**

We offer several different styles of campsite in the Rhône Valley including this pleasant, well tended site, that is open all year. About half of this site is occupied by static caravans and chalets, but these are to one side leaving two flat, open meadows for touring. The 270 level pitches (120 for touring units) all have electricity (16A) and are roughly defined by saplings. Being right beside the main road 9 (some road noise), makes this a good base either for a night stop or for exploring the area. With mountain views, across the valley, it has an air of peace.

Facilities

Two heated toilet blocks have free hot water in washbasins and sinks and on payment in the showers. Facilities for disabled visitors. Private cabins to rent. Motorcaravan services (Euro-Relais). Gas supplies. Bar, restaurant and shop (1/5-31/10). Small pool and child's pool (1/6-30/8). Playground and play house. Bicycle hire. Ski room. Walking country, cable cars near. Off site: Shops and restaurants near. Tennis next door. Riding 7 km.

Open: 1 January - 31 October.

Directions

On the south side of road 9 between Visp and Susten, signed. GPS: N46:18.172 E07:48.155

Charges 2008

Per person	CHF 5,50 - 6,50
child (6-16 yrs)	CHF 3,50 - 4,50
motorcaravan	CHF 9,50 - 15,00
tent	CHF 5,00 - 6,00
electricity	CHF 3,00
Special offers in low season.	

CH9775 Camping Schwimmbad Mühleye

CH-3930 Visp (Valais)

Tel: **027 946 2084**. Email: **info@camping-visp.ch**

Camping Mühleye is a popular family site located in the Valais, close to Brig, and has been recommended by our Swiss agent. We hope to undertake a full inspection here in 2008. The site has 148 grassy pitches, ranging in size from 50-150 sq.m. including a number of super pitches (with electricity, water and drainage). The town of Visp is just 800 m. away and the site is a useful base for exploring the region. On-site amenities include a large swimming pool with children's games. In high season, an entertainment and activity programme is organised and includes guided walks in the surrounding mountains.

Facilities

Restaurant, snack bar and takeaway meals. Supermarket. Swimming pool with water slide and children's games. Playground. Entertainment and activity programme in high season. Off site: Visp centre 800 m. Zermatt 36 km. Saas Fee 25 km. Riding. Cycling and walking trails. Golf.

Open: 21 March - 31 October.

Directions

Take the eastbound A9 motorway from Montreux to Sierre and continue to Visp on road 9. The site is located close to the town centre, well indicated.

Charges 2008

Per person	CHF 6,10 - 6,90
child (under 6 yrs)	CHF 3,20 - 3,90
pitch with electricity	CHF 10,30 - 17,30

CH9790 **Camping Augenstern**

Postfach 16, CH-3998 Reckingen (Valais)

Tel: **027 973 1395**. Email: **info@campingaugenstern.ch**

The village of Reckingen is about halfway between Brig and the Furka/Grimsel passes. You can still get the train with car and caravan, or motorcaravan from Oberwald to Andermatt to avoid the steep climbs and descents of the Furka Pass, but in doing so you will miss some unforgettable scenery. This family run site, at 1,326 m. provides 100 flat, level pitches for touring units, all with 10A electricity and not much shade. It provides an excellent base for walking, climbing or cycling as well as rafting on the Rhone in the summer or skiing in the winter.

Facilities

The toilet block is good and is well maintained. Showers on payment. Motorcaravan services. Restaurant/bar. Shop in high season. Bicycle hire. Off site: Large swimming pool complex 200 m. Reckingen 500 m. Riding 800 m.

Open: 16 May - 17 October, 15 December - 15 March.

Directions

From the no. 19 road turn south in Reckingen next to church. Go down hill, along one-way street and over railway (carefully!) and bridge. Over next bridge and right to end of lane past swimming pool. GPS: N46:27.900 E08:14.658

Charges 2008

Per person	CHF 7,50 - 9,50
child (0-12 yrs)	CHF 4,00 - 5,50
pitch	CHF 9,50 - 11,50
electricity	CHF 4,00 - 7,00

CH9040 **Camping des Pêches**

Route du Port, CH-2525 Le Landeron (Neuchâtel)

Tel: **032 751 2900**. Email: **info@camping-lelanderon.ch**

This recently constructed, touring campsite is on the side of Lake Biel and river Thienne, and close to the old town of Le Landeron. The site is divided into two sections, one side of the road for static caravans, and on the other is the modern campsite for tourists. The 220 pitches are all on level grass, numbered but not separated, a few with shade, all with electricity (10A) and many conveniently placed water points. All the facilities are exceptionally well maintained and in pristine condition during our visit throughout a busy holiday weekend.

Facilities

The spacious, modern sanitary block contains all the usual facilities including a food preparation area with six cooking rings, a large freezer and refrigerator. Payment for showers is by card. Baby room. Laundry facilities. Motorcaravan service point. Community room and small café in reception building. Playground. Bicycle hire. TV and general room. Treatment room. Card barrier. Off site: Fishing 300 m. Swimming pool 300 m. (16/5-1/9; charged). Golf and riding 7 km.

Open: 1 April - 15 October.

Directions

Le Landeron is signed from the Neuchâtel - Biel motorway, exit 19 and site is well signed from the town. GPS: N47:03.177 E07:04.184

Charges 2007

Per person	CHF 8,00
child (6-16 yrs)	CHF 4,00
unit incl. car and electricity	CHF 8,50 - 16,50

CH9300 Camping Le Bivouac

Route des Paccots 21, CH-1618 Châtel St Denis (Fribourg)

Tel: **021 948 7849**. Email: **info@le-bivouac.ch**

A pleasant little site in the mountains north of Montreux, Le Bivouac has its own small swimming pool and children's pool. Most of the best places here are taken by seasonal caravans (130) and there are now only about 30 pitches for tourists. Electrical connections (10A) are available and there are five water points. The site is also open for winter sports caravanning and all the sanitary facilities are heated. Entertainment is organised for adults and children in high season. This is a good centre for walking and excursions and there is a friendly welcome from the owner M. Fivaz.

Facilities

The good toilet facilities in the main building include preset, free hot water in washbasins, showers and sinks for laundry and dishes. Baby room. Gas supplies. Shop (1/7-31/8). Bar (1/6-30/9). Swimming pool (1/6-15/9). Room for general use adjoining. Fishing. Off site: Bicycle hire 3 km. Riding 10 km. Bus passes the gate.

Open: 1 April - 30 September.

Directions

From motorway 12/E27 Bern-Vevey take Châtel St Denis exit no. 2 and turn towards Les Paccots (about 1 km). Site is on left up hill.
GPS: N46:31.508 E06:55.097

Charges 2008

Per person	CHF 5,00 - 6,00
pitch	CHF 15,00
electricity	CHF 4,00

No credit cards. Less 10% on showing this guide. Euros are accepted.

CH9015 Camping Tariche

Tariche, Saint Ursanne, CH-2883 Montmelon (Jura)

Tel: **032 433 4619**. Email: **info@tariche.ch**

This lovely site is some 6 km. off the main road along a steep wooded valley, through which flows the Doub on its brief excursion through Switzerland from France. If you're looking for peace and tranquillity then this is a distinct possibility for a short or long stay. A very small friendly site, owned and managed by Vincent Gigandet, there are just 15 touring pitches. It is ideal for walking, fishing or for the more active, the possibility of kayaking along the Doub (the river is not suitable for swimming). Medieval St Ursanne, said to be the most beautiful village in the canton, is some 7 km.

Facilities

The modern, heated toilet block is of a high standard with free showers. Washing machine and dryer. Motorcaravan services. Good kitchen facilities include oven, hob and refrigerator. Restaurant with shaded terrace overlooking the play area so that adults can enjoy a drink and keep watch whilst enjoying the river views. Fishing. Off site: St Ursanne 7 km.

Open: 1 March - 31 October.

Directions

From A16 exit St Ursanne (at the end of the tunnel). Turn left towards town and at roundabout turn left and go past first campsite. After 5.6 km. site is on the left next to the restaurant.

Charges 2008

Per person	CHF 8,20
pitch	CHF 8,00 - 20,00
electricity	CHF 3,00

CH9240 Camping Le Petit Bois

CH-1110 Morges (Vaud)

Tel: **021 801 1270**. Email: **camping.morges@tes.ch**

This excellent TCS campsite is on the edge of Morges, a wine-growing centre with a 13th century castle, on Lake Geneva about 8 km. west of Lausanne. Flowers, shrubs and trees adorn the site and the neat, tidy lawns make a most pleasant environment. There are 170 grass pitches for tourists, all with 6A electricity and laid out in a regular pattern from wide hard access roads on which cars stand. There are eight larger pitches for motorcaravans with electricity, water and drainage. The friendly managers speak good English, and will advise on local attractions.

Facilities

Two well built, fully equipped, modern toilet blocks include hot water in half the washbasins and sinks and showers. Separate block with excellent baby room and cosmetics room. Facilities for disabled visitors. Washing machines, dryers and irons. Motorcaravan services. Restaurant and takeaway. Shop. Playground. Boules. Bicycle and scooter hire. Small general room. Internet point. Entertainment (high season). Picnic area. Fishing. Bicycle hire. Off site: Swimming pool adjacent. Small harbour. Town centre. Tennis.

Open: 23 March - 21 October.

Directions

Leave A1 autoroute (Lausanne - Geneva) at exit 15 (Morges-ouest). Turn towards town and signs for site. GPS: N46:30.274 E06:29.350

Charges 2007

Per person	CHF 6,00 - 7,40
child	CHF 3,00 - 3,70
pitch with electricity	CHF 23,10 - 32,30
dog	CHF 3,00 - 4,00

Camping Cheques accepted.

CH9270 Camping De Vidy

Chemin du Camping 3, CH-1007 Lausanne (Vaud)

Tel: 021 622 5000. Email: **info@campinglausannevidy.ch**

The ancient city of Lausanne spills down the hillside towards Lake Geneva until it meets the peaceful park in which this site is situated. The present owners have enhanced its neat and tidy appearance by planting many flowers and shrubs. Hard access roads separate the site into sections for tents, caravans and motorcaravans, with 10A electrical connections in all parts, except the tent areas. Pitches are on flat grass, numbered but not marked out, with 260 (of 350) for tourists. 20 are fully serviced and some large pitches near the lake are suitable for American type motorhomes. The lakeside bar/restaurant (also open to the public) provides entertainment in season in the various rooms so that the young and not so young can enjoy themselves without impinging on each other. Although only minutes from the city centre, only a gentle hum of traffic can be heard. A public footpath separates the site from the lakeside, but there is good access. The World HQ of the Olympic movement is adjacent in the pleasant park, which is also available for games and walking.

Facilities

Two excellent sanitary blocks, one heated, have mostly British, some Turkish style WCs, hot water in washbasins, sinks and showers with warm, pre-mixed water. Facilities for disabled people. A third small block has been added. Motorcaravan services (Euro-Relais). Gas supplies. Shop and self-service bar/restaurant (1/5-30/9). Takeaway (high season). Playground. Evening entertainment in high season. Internet point. Lake swimming. Fishing. Off site: Bus service into Lausanne. Boat excursions on the lake.

Open: All year.

Directions

Site is left of road to Geneva, 500 m. west of La Maladière. Take autobahn Lausanne-Süd, exit no. 3 La Maladière, and at this roundabout almost turn back on yourself following signs for CIO and camping. At traffic lights turn left, then on for site. Take care at La Maladière roundabout (large trolley buses).

Charges 2007

Per person	CHF 7,00
child (6-15 yrs)	CHF 5,00
pitch with electricity	CHF 13,00 - 22,00
dog	CHF 2,00

No credit cards.

CH9900 Camping Delta

Via Respini 7, CH-6600 Locarno (Ticino)

Tel: 091 751 6081. Email: **info@campingdelta.com**

Camping Delta is actually within the Locarno town limits, only some 800 m. from the centre, and it has a prime position right by the lake, with bathing direct from the site, and next to the municipal lido and sports field. Boats can be put on the lake and the site has some moorings on an estuary at one side. It has 300 pitches on flat ground of 60-100 sq.m. of which 255 are for touring units. They are marked out at the rear but have nothing between them. Delta is a well run and well situated site. Locarno is host to an International Film Festival, classical and jazz concerts and exhibitions.

Facilities

The single toilet block is very clean and should be adequate except perhaps at the busiest times. There are washbasins (some in cabins for women), showers and sinks. Washing machine and dryer. Motorcaravan services. Small supermarket. Restaurant/bar with limited menu. Fitness centre. Playgrounds. Baby sitting. Entertainment and excursions. Children animation programme in children. Fishing. Bicycle hire. Internet access. Kayaks and electric bikes for hire. Dogs are not accepted. Off site: Golf 500 m. Riding 3.5 km.

Open: 1 March - 31 October.

Directions

From central Locarno follow signs to Camping Delta, Lido or Stadio along the lake. Beware that approaching from south there are also Delta signs which lead you to Albergo Delta in quite the wrong place. GPS: N46:09.538 E08:48.133

Charges 2008

Per person	CHF 11,00 - 18,00
child (3-15 yrs)	CHF 6,00
pitch (depending on type)	CHF 21,00 - 57,00
electricity	CHF 5,00

Open All Year

The following sites are understood to accept caravanners and campers all year round. Please refer to the site's individual entry for details.

Andorra
AN7145 Valira
AN7143 Xixerella

Austria
AU0035 Alpin Seefeld
AU0055 Arlberg
AU0475 Brunner am See
AU0070 Hofer
AU0502 Im Thermenland
AU0515 Katschtal
AU0170 Kranebitten
AU0220 Krismer
AU0262 Oberwötzlhof
AU0045 Ötztal
AU0155 Prutz
AU0405 Ramsbacher
AU0440 Schluga
AU0065 Seehof
AU0102 Stadlerhof
AU0110 Tirol Camp
AU0100 Toni
AU0180 Woferlgut
AU0160 Zell am See
AU0090 Zillertal-Hell
AU0040 Zugspitze

Belgium
BE0590 De Gavers
BE0740 Eau Rouge
BE0732 Floreal La Roche
BE0555 Klein Strand
BE0670 La Clusure
BE0655 Lilse Bergen
BE0560 Lombarde
BE0580 Memling
BE0735 Petite Suisse
BE0700 Spa d'Or
BE0675 Spineuse
BE0725 Val de L'Aisne
BE0710 Vallée de Rabais
BE0530 Waux-Hall
BE0780 Wilhelm Tell

Croatia
CR6745 Bi-Village

Czech Republic
CZ4845 Busek Praha
CZ4795 Cisarska Louka
CZ4880 Roznov
CZ4850 Sokol Troja
CZ4815 Triocamp

Denmark
DK2015 Ådalens
DK2255 Feddet
DK2044 Hampen Sø
DK2140 Jesperhus
DK2020 Mogeltonder
DK2150 Solyst
DK2046 Trelde Næs
FI2970 Nallikari

Finland
FI2850 Rastila

France
FR47110 Cabri
FR77020 Chêne Gris
FR06080 Cigales
FR79020 Courte Vallée
FR86040 Futuriste
FR47150 Guillalmes
FR88040 Lac de Bouzey
FR65080 Lavedan
FR33090 Pressoir
FR88130 Vanne de Pierre

Germany
DE3415 Adam
DE3025 Alfsee
DE3685 Allweglehen
DE3452 Alte Sägemühle
DE3632 Altmühltal
DE3065 am Bärenbache
DE3255 Am Königsberg
DE3021 Am Stadtwaldsee
DE3847 Auensee
DE3436 Bankenhof
DE3710 Bayerischer Wald
DE3445 Belchenblick
DE3210 Biggesee
DE3432 Bonath
DE3697 Dreiqueller
DE3627 Ellwangen
DE3836 Erzgebirgsblick
DE3439 Freiburg
DE3650 Gitzenweiler
DE3215 Goldene Meile
DE3202 Grav-Insel
DE3455 Gugel's
DE3080 Hardausee
DE3254 Harfenmühle
DE3820 Havelberge
DE3490 Hegau
DE3411 Heidehof
DE3437 Hochschwarzwald
DE3256 Hunsrück
DE3440 Kirchzarten
DE3406 Kleinenzhof
DE3008 Klüthseecamp
DE3222 Moselbogen
DE3185 Münster
DE3450 Münstertal
DE3720 Naabtal
DE3610 Nürnberg
DE3855 Oberhof
DE3420 Oberrhein
DE3055 Prahljust
DE3010 Röders Park
DE3242 Schinderhannes
DE3002 Schlei-Karschau
DE3427 Schwarzwälder Hof
DE3275 Seepark
DE3180 Sonnenwiese
DE3850 Strandbad Aga
DE3070 Süd-See
DE3030 Tecklenburg
DE3280 Teichmann
DE3212 Wirfttal
DE3003 Wulfener Hals

Greece
GR8525 Chrissa
GR8330 Ionion Beach

Hungary
HU5210 Diófaház
HU5150 Fortuna
HU5300 Kek-Duna
(Dunafoldvar)

Italy
IT60420 Alba d'Oro
IT64030 Baciccia
IT68890 Costa Verde
IT64010 Dei Fiori
IT60530 Fusina
IT62080 Gamp
IT69230 Jonio
IT66670 La Finoria
IT67915 Le Foci
IT69300 Marinello
IT62000 Olympia
IT62420 Orta
IT69350 Rais Gerbi
IT62055 Rocchetta
IT69190 Scarabeo
IT62030 Sexten
IT66610 Toscana Village
IT64120 Valdeiva

Liechtenstein
FL7580 Mittagspitze

Luxembourg
LU7670 Ardennes
LU7850 Fuussekaul
LU7700 Gaalgebierg
LU7880 Trois Frontières
LU7770 Val d'Or

Netherlands
NL5985 Beerze Bulten
NL6520 BreeBronne
NL5600 Delftse Hout

NL5620	Duinrell
NL5910	Hertenwei
NL5540	Katjeskelder
NL5640	Kijkduinpark
NL5890	Klein Canada
NL5630	Koningshof
NL5790	Kuierpadtien
NL5760	Kuilart
NL6090	Lauwersoog
NL5500	Pannenschuur
NL6540	Rozenhof
NL6510	Schatberg
NL6930	Schoneveld
NL5735	Tempelhof
NL6425	Twee Bruggen
NL5960	Wielerbaan
NL5560	Wijde Blick

Norway

NO2515	Gjelten Bru
NO2510	Håneset
NO2432	Harstad
NO2400	Jolstraholmen
NO2375	Lærdal
NO2505	Magalaupe
NO2610	Neset
NO2320	Odda
NO2615	Olberg
NO2525	Østrea Æra
NO2460	Prinsen
NO2545	Rustberg
NO2475	Saltstraumen
NO2385	Sandvik
NO2590	Sandviken
NO2490	Skjerneset

Poland

PL3320	Auschwitz Centre
PL3170	Mazurski Eden
PL3300	Polana Sosny

Portugal

PO8210	Albufeira
PO8410	Armacao-Pera
PO8150	Caparica
PO8370	Cerdeira
PO8480	Foz do Arelho
PO8130	Guincho
PO8400	O Tamanco
PO8230	Olhao
PO8220	Quarteira
PO8030	Rio Alto
PO8100	S Pedro-Moel
PO8430	Sagres

PO8170	São Miguel
PO8202	Turiscampo
PO8200	Valverde

Romania

RO7190	Casa Alba
RO7090	De Oude Wilg
RO7040	International

Slovakia

SK4980	Levocská Dolina
SK4910	Turiec

Slovenia

SV4150	Kamne
SV4235	Klin
SV4100	Spik

Spain

ES85360	Ametlla
ES90910	Aranjuez
ES90240	As Cancelas
ES85590	Azahar
ES86830	Benisol
ES85800	Bonterra
ES87630	Cabo de Gata
ES88020	Cabopino
ES90860	Cáceres
ES85350	Cala d'Oques
ES81300	Calonge
ES86870	Cap Blanch
ES90890	Despenaperros
ES92900	El Balcon
ES90800	El Brillante
ES92000	El Escorial
ES90900	El Greco
ES87520	El Portus (Naturist)
ES86850	El Raco
ES90430	Errota el Molino
ES90470	Ezcaba
ES87540	Javea
ES80080	Joncar Mar
ES86150	Kiko
ES86250	Kiko Rural
ES87450	La Fuente
ES87530	La Manga
ES87420	La Marina
ES92850	Las Lomas
ES89400	Los Cantiles
ES87480	Los Madriles
ES88000	Marbella Playa
ES87430	Marjal
ES90870	Merida
ES90270	Monfrague

ES87550	Moraira
ES92100	Pico-Miel
ES84820	Pineda de Salou
ES86890	Playa del Torres
ES88650	Playa Las Dunas
ES85600	Playa Tropicana
ES85080	Poboleda
ES88590	Roche
ES90820	Sevilla
ES83900	Vilanova Park
ES86810	Villasol
ES90810	Villsom

Sweden

SW2755	Alevi
SW2855	Flogsta
SW2840	Flottsbro
SW2760	Frykenbaden
SW2865	Gielas
SW2715	Gröne Backe
SW2725	Hafsten
SW2825	Herrfallet
SW2720	Hökensås
SW2870	Jokkmokks
SW2805	Kolmårdens
SW2740	Laxsjons
SW2710	Lidköping
SW2705	Lisebergsbyn
SW2645	Mölle
SW2836	Mora Parkens
SW2850	Ostersunds
SW2665	Rosenlund
SW2650	Skånes
SW2750	Sommarvik
SW2857	Strömsund
SW2845	Svegs
SW2860	Umeå
SW2675	Västervik Swe

Switzerland

CH9495	Balmweid
CH9855	Cavresc
CH9270	De Vidy
CH9520	Du Botza
CH9570	Eienwäldli
CH9175	Giessenpark
CH9360	Grassi
CH9380	Heiti
CH9460	Jungfrau
CH9420	Manor Farm
CH9670	Molignon
CH9370	Rendez-vous
CH9410	Stuhlegg
CH9830	Sur En

Quick reference - dogs

Dogs

For the benefit of those who want to take their dogs with them or for people who do not like dogs at the sites they visit, we list here those sites that have indicated to us that they do not accept dogs. If you are, however, planning to take your dog we do advise you to check first – there may be limits on numbers, breeds, etc. or times of the year when they are excluded.

Never – these sites do not accept dogs at any time:

Austria
AU0090 Zillertal-Hell

Croatia
CR6731 Valalta (Naturist)
CR6736 Valdaliso

France
FR17010 Bois Soleil
FR46040 Moulin de Laborde
FR84020 Bélézy (Naturiste)
FR85210 Ecureuils

Germany
DE3005 Schnelsen Nord
DE3233 Holländischer Hof
DE3260 Bad Dürkheim

Hungary
HU5090 Füred
HU5380 Venus

Italy
IT60030 Pra' Delle Torri
IT60150 Il Tridente
IT60200 Union Lido
IT60210 Italy
IT60220 Portofelice
IT60320 Cavallino
IT60330 Malibu Beach
IT60340 Waikiki

IT60350 Mediterraneo
IT60360 Ca'Pasquali
IT60400 Garden Paradiso
IT60460 Miramare (Punta Sabbioni)
IT60550 Isamar
IT60560 Miramare (Chioggia)
IT60650 Tahiti
IT62560 Del Garda
IT62630 Bella Italia
IT63570 Cisano & San Vito
IT63580 Delle Rose
IT63590 Serenella
IT64010 Dei Fiori
IT66290 Tripesce
IT66450 Delle Piscine
IT66710 Argentario
IT66730 PuntAla
IT68190 Settebello
IT68200 Baia Domizia
IT68650 Riva di Ugento

Netherlands
NL5680 Noordduinen
NL5980 Roos
NL6285 Wildhoeve
NL6790 Kienehoef
NL6840 Vogelenzang
NL6925 Weltevreden
NL6960 Klepperstee
NL6980 Krabbeplaat

Portugal
PO8170 São Miguel

Romania
RO7040 International

Spain
ES80900 Cypsela
ES81010 Playa Brava
ES81030 El Maset
ES84810 Cambrils
ES85300 Playa Montroig
ES85400 Torre del Sol
ES85600 Playa Tropicana
ES86810 Villasol
ES87480 Los Madriles
ES90000 Playa Joyel
ES90860 Cáceres

Switzerland
CH9160 Rheinwiesen
CH9180 Buchhorn
CH9185 Fischerhaus
CH9480 Gletscherdorf
CH9880 Lido Mappo
CH9890 Campofelice
CH9900 Delta

Maybe – accepted but with certain restrictions:

Austria
AU0060 Natterer See
AU0227 Camp Grän
AU0232 Sonnenberg
AU0400 Arneitz

Belgium
BE0550 Nieuwpoort
BE0560 Lombarde
BE0565 Westende
BE0580 Memling
BE0595 Oudenaarde
BE0600 Groeneveld
BE0670 La Clusure

France
FR23010 Château de Poinsouze
FR35040 P'tit Bois
FR83200 Pêcheurs
FR85150 Yole

Germany
DE3232 Family Club
DE3440 Kirchzarten
DE3442 Herbolzheim
DE3465 Wirthshof

DE3686 Strandcamping
DE3820 Havelberge

Italy
IT60080 Sabbiadoro
IT62100 Steiner
IT62485 Conca d'Oro
IT62540 Lido
IT62610 Del Sole
IT66060 Europa
IT66310 Mareblu
IT66600 Maremma
IT66750 Cieloverde
IT66770 Baia Gabbiani
IT68130 Porticciolo
IT68890 Costa Verde
IT69230 Jonio
IT69300 Marinello
IT69350 Rais Gerbi
IT69960 Mariposa

Luxembourg
LU7770 Val d'Or

Netherlands
NL5560 Wijde Blick

NL5580 Veerhoeve
NL5600 Delftse Hout
NL5790 Kuierpadtien
NL5810 Luttenberg
NL6000 Vechtdalcamping
NL6140 Valkenhof
NL6470 Papillon
NL6510 Schatberg
NL6520 BreeBronne
NL6838 Krakeling
NL6950 Renesse

Portugal
PO8370 Cerdeira

Spain
ES80720 Les Medes
ES80800 Delfin Verde
ES81600 Cala Gogo
ES85590 Azahar
ES85800 Bonterra

Switzerland
CH9420 Manor Farm
CH9720 Bella-Tola

532

Travelling

When taking your car (and caravan, tent or trailer tent) or motorcaravan to the continent you do need to plan in advance and to find out as much as possible about driving in the countries you plan to visit. Whilst European harmonisation has eliminated many of the differences between one country and another, it is well worth reading the short notes we provide in the introduction to each country in this guide in addition to this more general summary.

Of course, the main difference from driving in the UK is that in mainland Europe you will need to drive on the right. Without taking extra time and care, especially at busy junctions and conversely when roads are empty, it is easy to forget to drive on the right. Remember that traffic approaching from the right usually has priority unless otherwise indicated by road markings and signs. Harmonisation also means that most (but not all) common road signs are the same in all countries.

Your vehicle

Book your vehicle in for a good service well before your intended departure date. This will lessen the chance of an expensive breakdown. Make sure your brakes are working efficiently and that your tyres have plenty of tread (3 mm. is recommended, particularly if you are undertaking a long journey).

Also make sure that your caravan or trailer is roadworthy and that its tyres are in good order and correctly inflated. Plan your packing and be careful not to overload your vehicle, caravan or trailer – this is unsafe and may well invalidate your insurance cover (it must not be more fully loaded than the kerb weight of the insured vehicle).

Check all the following:

- **GB sticker.** If you do not display a sticker, you may risk an on-the-spot fine as this identifier is compulsory in all countries. Euro-plates are an acceptable alternative within the EU (but not outside). Remember to attach another sticker (or Euro-plate) to caravans or trailers. Only GB stickers (not England, Scotland, Wales or N. Ireland) stickers are valid in the EU.

- **Headlights.** As you will be driving on the right you must adjust your headlights so that the dipped beam does not dazzle oncoming drivers. Converter kits are readily available for most vehicle, although if your car is fitted with high intensity headlights, you should check with your motor dealer. Check that any planned extra loading does not affect the beam height.

- **Seatbelts.** Rules for the fitting and wearing of seatbelts throughout Europe are   similar to those in the UK, but it is worth checking before you go. Rules for carrying children in the front of vehicles vary from country to country. It is best to plan not to do this if possible.

- **Door/wing mirrors.** To help with driving on the right, if your vehicle is not fitted with a mirror on the left hand side, we recommend you have one fitted.

- **Fuel.** Leaded and Lead Replacement petrol is increasingly difficult to find in Northern Europe.

Travelling continued

Compulsory additional equipment

The driving laws of the countries of Europe still vary in what you are required to carry in your vehicle, although the consequences of not carrying a required piece of equipment are almost always an on-the-spot fine.

To meet these requirements we suggest that you carry the following:

- Fire extinguisher
- Basic tool kit
- First aid kit
- Spare bulbs
- Two warning triangles – two are required in some countries at all times, and are compulsory in most countries when towing.
- High visibility vest – now compulsory in Spain, Italy and Austria (and likely to become compulsory throughout the EU) in case you need to walk on a motorway. In Spain we are told that you need a vest for every occupant of the car, and that they must be carried inside the car, not in the boot.

Insurance and Motoring Documents

Vehicle insurance

Contact your insurer well before you depart to check that your car insurance policy covers driving outside the UK. Most do, but many policies only provide minimum cover (so if you have an accident your insurance may only cover the cost of damage to the other person's property, with no cover for fire and theft).

To maintain the same level of cover abroad as you enjoy at home you need to tell your vehicle insurer. Some will automatically cover you abroad with no extra cost and no extra paperwork. Some will say you need a Green Card (which is neither green nor on card) but won't charge for it. Some will charge extra for the Green Card. Ideally you should contact your vehicle insurer 3-4 weeks before you set off, and confirm your conversation with them in writing.

Breakdown insurance

Arrange breakdown cover for your trip in good time so that if your vehicle breaks down or is involved in an accident it (and your caravan or trailer) can be repaired or returned to this country. This cover can usually be arranged as part of your travel insurance policy (see below) and this usually includes a Bail Bond for Spain.

Documents you must take with you

You may be asked to show your documents at any time so make sure that they are in order, up-to-date and easily accessible while you travel. These are what you need to take:

- Passports (you may also need a visa in some countries if you hold either a UK passport not issued in the UK or a passport that was issued outside the EU)
- Motor Insurance Certificate, including Green Card (or Continental Cover clause)
- DVLC Vehicle Registration Document plus, if not your own vehicle, the owner's written authority to drive.
- A full valid Driving Licence (not provisional). The new photo style licence is now mandatory in most European countries).

insure **4** campers.com

One call and you're covered

Travelling on the continent?
Holidaying on campsites?

Our policies provide exactly the right cover for holidays of this type

– at exceptionally low rates. Whatever you need, our policies are

tailored to suit self-drive campsite-based holidays.

- Are you covered if you're broken into on site?

- Is your caravan insurance excess reimbursed?

- If your vehicle breaks down will you be able to find
  someone to fix it?

- Can you get increased car hire limits when towing?
  (plus policies)

- Do you have access to a 24hr multi-lingual helpline?

Call us **NOW** for a no-obligation quote
01580 214006

Policies despatched within 24 hours

Travelling continued

Personal Holiday insurance

Even though you are just travelling within Europe you must take out travel insurance. Few EU countries pay the full cost of medical treatment even under reciprocal health service arrangements. The first part of a holiday insurance policy covers people. It will include the cost of doctor, ambulance and hospital treatment if needed. If needed the better companies will even pay for English language speaking doctors and nurses and will bring a sick or injured holidaymaker home by air ambulance.

The second part of a good policy covers things. If someone breaks into your motorhome and steals your passports and money, one phone call to the insurance company will have everything sorted out. If you manage to drive over your camera, it should be covered. NB – most policies have a maximum payment limit per item, do check that any valuables are adequately covered.

An important part of the insurance, often ignored, is cancellation (and curtailment) cover. Few things are as heartbreaking as having to cancel a holiday because a member of the family falls ill. Cancellation insurance can't take away the disappointment, but it makes sure you don't suffer financially as well. For this reason you should arrange your holiday insurance at least eight weeks before you set off.

Whichever insurance you choose we would advise reading very carefully the policies sold by the High Street travel trade. Whilst they may be good, they may not cover the specific needs of campers, caravanners and motorcaravanners.

Telephone **0870 405 4059** for a quote for our European Camping Holiday Insurance with cover arranged through Green Flag Motoring Assistance and Inter Group Assistance Services, one of the UK's largest assistance companies. Alternatively visit our website at **www.insure4campers.com**.

European Health Insurance Card (EHIC)

Important Changes since E111: Since September 2005 new European Health Insurance Cards have replaced the E111 forms .

Make sure you apply for your EHIC before travelling in Europe. Eligible travellers from the UK are entitled to receive free or reduced-cost medical care in many European countries on production of an EHIC. This free card is available by completing a form in the booklet 'Health Advice for Travellers' from local Post Offices. One should be completed for each family member. Alternatively visit www.dh.gov.uk/travellers and apply on-line. Please allow time to send your application off and have the EHIC returned to you.

The EHIC is valid in all European Community countries plus Iceland, Liechtenstein, Switzerland and Norway. If you or any of your dependants are suddenly taken ill or have an accident during a visit to any of these countries, free or reduced-cost emergency treatment is available - in most cases on production of a valid EHIC. Only state-provided emergency treatment is covered, and you will receive treatment on the same terms as nationals of the country you are visiting. Private treatment is generally not covered, and state-provided treatment may not cover all of the things that you would expect to receive free of charge from the NHS.

Remember an EHIC does not cover you for all the medical costs that you can incur or for repatriation - it is not an alternative to travel insurance. You will still need appropriate insurance to ensure you are fully covered for all eventualities.

Insurance Expertise from The Caravan Club!

All our insurance policies are designed with caravanners and motor caravanners in mind so, whether you're at home or away touring, you can rely on The Club to be sure you are fully covered.

Caravan Insurance

Our competitive policies offer comprehensive and flexible cover, based on over 35 years' experience operating the UK's largest Caravan insurance scheme.
Call us on 01342 336610 or get a quote & buy online at www.caravanclub.co.uk

UK Breakdown & Recovery

The Club's Mayday UK vehicle rescue is provided in conjunction with Green Flag and offers fast and reliable rescue and recovery, whether you're towing or not.
Call us on 0800 731 0112 or get a quote & buy online at www.caravanclub.co.uk

Car Insurance

Competitive Car insurance from a name you can trust, with a guarantee of a lower premium than your current insurer*.
Call us on 0800 028 4809

Home Insurance

Our Home insurance protects your buildings and/or contents against a wide range of risks and offers additional benefits.
Call us on 0800 028 4815

Pet Insurance

Be sure your pets are protected at home or when away touring in the UK or abroad, no matter how many trips you take.
Call us on 0800 015 1396

Motor Caravan Insurance

Another Club speciality, with wide cover at competitive rates and a guarantee to beat the renewal premium offered by your present insurer*.
Call us on 0800 028 4809

Overseas Holiday Insurance

When you travel abroad, take The Club's Red Pennant Holiday Insurance with you. Our own 24-hour emergency team helps you relax, knowing you're in experienced hands.
Call us on 01342 336633 or get a quote & buy online at www.caravanclub.co.uk

Club Credit Card & Personal Loan

Financial services to meet your needs.
Call us on 0800 373 191 (Credit Card) & 0800 032 5000 (Personal Loan)

THE
CARAVAN CLUB

To find out more, please call us stating reference AR07.
We look forward to hearing from you!

* Conditions apply

You're better off booking with The Club

As a member of Europe's Premier Club for touring caravanners, motor caravanners and trailer tenters, you'll enjoy an unrivalled range of services and benefits to ensure you make the most of your holiday.

- **Channel Crossing Booking Service** with special offers, discounts and 'Members Only' ferry rates. You could 'save' more than your membership fee on your first trip.

- **European Site Booking Service** for around 200 inspected sites.

- **Camping Cheque and ACSI Card** 'go as you please' schemes for freedom of choice.

- **Red Pennant Insurance** competitive, 'tailor-made' cover.

- **Inclusive Holidays,** touring information and much more....

- **Caravan Club Magazine** free monthly and full of useful information and great holiday ideas.

To make sure you get the best deal when you book, call or visit our website to join or request an information pack.

0800 328 6635
www.caravanclub.co.uk

Quote ref. AR2008

THE
CARAVAN
CLUB

How do I *arrive closer* to my holiday?

Sail direct to St Malo and avoid the busy roads of northern France.

We know a way

Take one of our direct routes to France or Spain from Portsmouth, Poole or Plymouth and arrive far closer to your holiday destination.

Our mile-saving routes are now better value than ever. And with excellent facilities and award-winning service all included as standard, you really can sit back, relax and enjoy great value for money.

brittanyferries.com
0871 244 1446

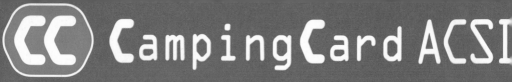

Europe by car
Best fares by far

* **Best value fares**
* **Up to 24 sailings per day**
* **Easy access to main European destinations**
* **Motorists only - no coach parties or foot passengers**

3 ISSUES FOR £1

Our practical titles are packed full of holiday tips, technical advice, reader reviews, superb photography…and much more! So subscribe to Practical Caravan or Practical Motorhome for just £1.

- **YOU** get your first 3 issues for £1
- **YOU** save 20% on the shop price after your trial ends
- **RISK-FREE** offer - you can cancel at any time
- **FREE** delivery, straight to your door!
- **EXCLUSIVE** subscriber offers and discounts

CALL 08456 777 812 NOW!
or visit **www.themagazineshop.com** quote code ALR08

Suncamp holidays

CAMPINGS · ACSI · INSPECTED

... on your way to a great journey!

▲ Completely furnished accommodation and camping pitches

▲ 243 camp sites in 13 countries!

▲ You never pay more than you would directly to the camp site

▲ Special offers in spring and autumn

Book now!

• www.suncampholidays.co.uk

• Call: 0845 - 2250931

kawan
VILLAGES CAMPINGS

NEW

83 Quality Campsites
'At-The-Gate' Prices

A New Concept

Kawan Villages offers 83 great family campsites in France and 7 other countries.

All are graded 3 or 4 star and all can be booked direct at the campsite's own 'at-the-gate' tariff. No surcharge, no premium, no hidden costs. You simply pay what you would pay at reception. Book on 01580 214017 for convenience and courteous, reliable service – at no extra cost!

High quality facilities, pleasant surroundings, great locations

Fully equipped mobile homes and chalets

Wonderful environment for children: safe, spacious, plenty to do

France

Spain

Portugal

Italy

Germany

Luxembourg

The Netherlands

Denmark

Sweden

FREE BROCHURE
01580 214017

www.**kawan-villages**.co.uk

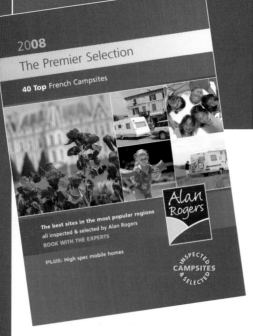

Belle France

Walking & Cycling Holidays

Discover the easy going alternative

It's all on-line
www.**bellefrance.co.uk**

Belle France offers leisurely holidays through the most beautiful and interesting parts of France.

On our walking and cycling holidays your luggage is moved for you whilst you find your own way, at your own pace with our detailed maps and notes.

Relax in the evening in charming family run hotels, offering a good standard of accommodation and a warm and friendly welcome.

Follow suggested routes, stopping where you choose and enjoy complete freedom.

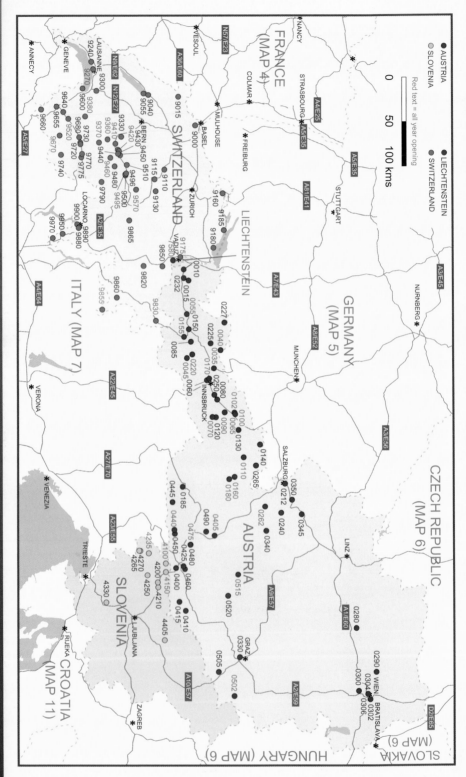

Please refer to the numerical index (page 565) for campsite page references

BELGIUM   NETHERLANDS
LUXEMBOURG

Red text = all year opening

0   50   100 kms

6030   6090   EMDEN ✱

GRONINGEN ✱   5770
6040
6120
6080   6130
A7/E22   A28/E232
6820   5710   6140
5760   6134   5790
5735   6160
5700   6190   6150
A7/E22
6004
NETHERLANDS   6000   5990
5980   5985
5810
6470
5720   6480
6870   ✱ AMSTERDAM   6285   A1/E30
6840   5670   ENSCHEDE ✱
5660
5680   5630   6830   6824
5620   6838   6832   5780
5640 ✱ DEN HAAG   5850   6310   6425
5600   A2/E35   5960   ✱ ARNHEM
5690   5870   GERMANY
6980   ✱ ROTTERDAM   6290   (MAP 5)
6960   6970   5950
5560   6950   5880
5540   5890   ESSEN ✱
6790
5570   5580   A58/E312   6560
6925   6920   6915   5900   EINDHOVEN ✱   6520
5510   ✱ VLISSINGEN   5910   6510
5500   6930   0660   5970   A61/E31
0650 0655   6515   DUSSELDORF ✱
0578   0780   KOLN ✱
OOSTENDE ✱   BRUGGE ✱   0580
0560 0565 0555   GENT ✱   A2/E314   6580
0520 0550 0610   6530
0600   A10/E17   0630   6540
0570   0595   BRUSSEL ✱   0640   LUIK ✱   AKEN
BELGIUM   0705   0700
LILLE ✱   0740
0530   ✱ CHARLEROI   0730
0725   A60/E42
ARRAS ✱   A2/E19   0735   7880
0770 0732   7780
0670   7670   7680
0720   7770
7850 7870   7650
N43/E44   7890   7640
0675   0711   7620   7610
AMIENS ✱   0712   0680
FRANCE   0715   LUXEMBOURG
(MAP 4)   0710   7660
7700
A1/E19

Please refer to the numerical index (page 565) for campsite page references

549

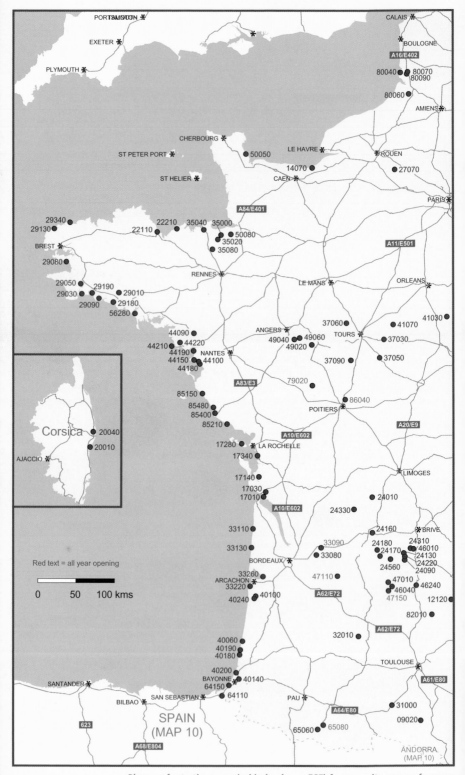

0   50   100 kms

Corsica

AJACCIO

SANTANDER

BILBAO   SAN SEBASTIAN

SPAIN
(MAP 10)

ANDORRA
(MAP 10)

Please refer to the numerical index (page 565) for campsite page references

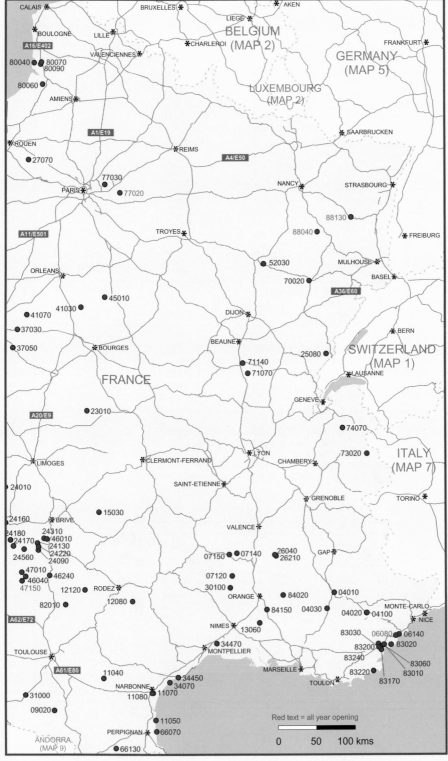

Red text = all year opening

0   50   100 kms

Please refer to the numerical index (page 565) for campsite page references

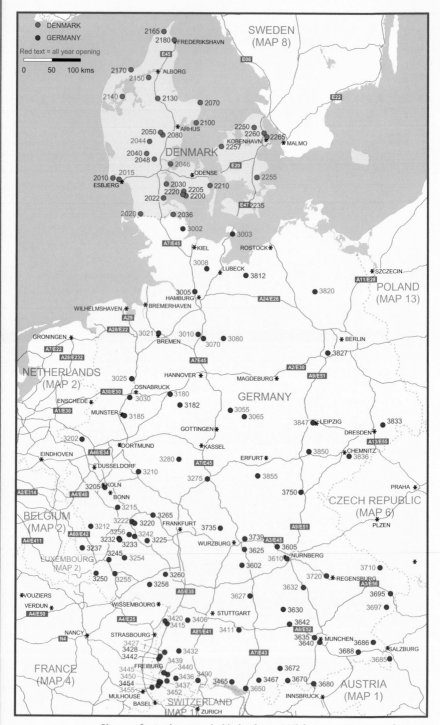

Please refer to the numerical index (page 565) for campsite page references

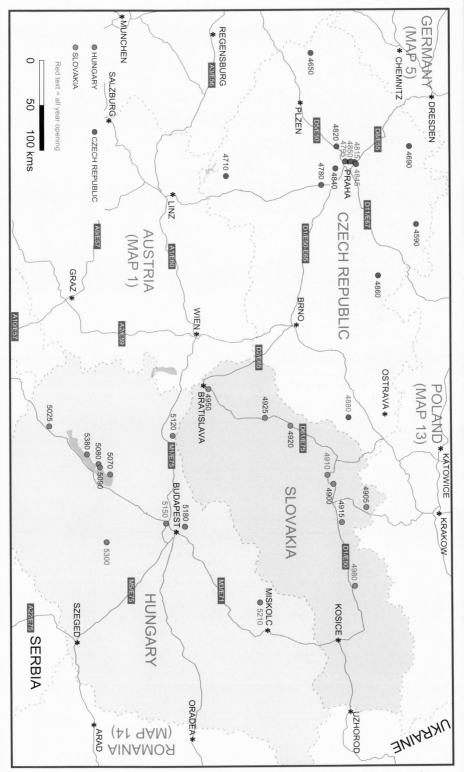

GERMANY
(MAP 5)

* DRESDEN

* CHEMNITZ

* MUNCHEN

* REGENSBURG

SALZBURG

* SLOVAKIA
* HUNGARY
* CZECH REPUBLIC

Red text = all year opening

0   50   100 kms

A3/E56

D5/E50

PLZEN

4650

4690

4590

4710

4820   4850   4795   4815   4845   PRAHA   4840   4780

D8/E55

D11/E67

D1/E50-E65

4860

CZECH REPUBLIC

BRNO *

POLAND
(MAP 13)

OSTRAVA *

4880

KATOWICE *

KRAKOW *

LINZ *

A1/E60

WIEN *

A9/E57

AUSTRIA
(MAP 1)

GRAZ *

A2/E59

A10/E57

D2/E65

BRATISLAVA *
4950

5120

M1/E75

BUDAPEST

4925

4920

D6/E75

4910

4900

4915

4905

4980

D1/E50

KOSICE *

SLOVAKIA

UZHOROD *

UKRAINE

5025

5380   5080   5070   5090

5150   5180

5300

M3/E71

MISKOLC *
5210

HUNGARY

M5/E75

SZEGED *

A22/E75

SERBIA

ROMANIA
(MAP 14)

ARAD *

ORADEA *

Please refer to the numerical index (page 565) for campsite page references

553

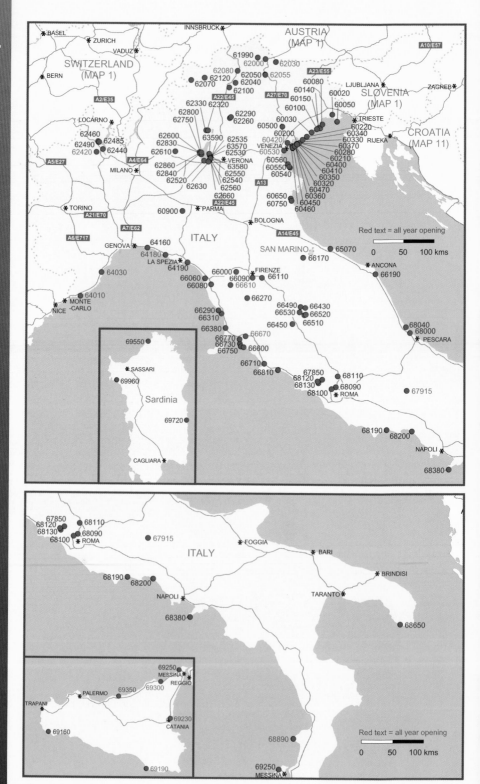

Please refer to the numerical index (page 565) for campsite page references

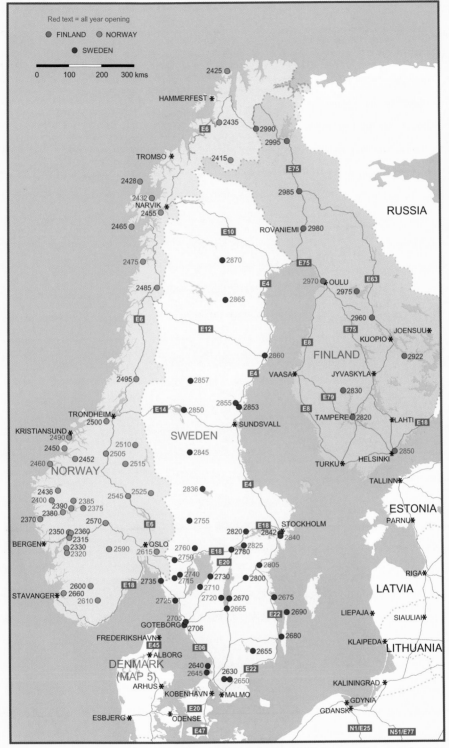

Red text = all year opening

FINLAND   NORWAY

SWEDEN

0   100   200   300 kms

2425

HAMMERFEST

E6   2435

2990

2995

TROMSO   2415

E75

2985

2428

2432   RUSSIA
NARVIK   2455

2465   E10

ROVANIEMI   2980

2475   E75

OULU   E63
2970   2975

2485   2870

2960
E4   E75
JOENSUU
2865   KUOPIO

2922
E8

E12   FINLAND

2860

2857   E4
VAASA   JYVASKYLA

2855   2853   E79
2850   2830
E14   SUNDSVALL   E8

TRONDHEIM   TAMPERE   2820
2500   SWEDEN   LAHTI   E18
KRISTIANSUND
2490   2845   2850
2450
2460   2452   HELSINKI
NORWAY   2515   TURKU
2505
2510   TALLINN

2836   E4

2436   ESTONIA
2400   2385   2525   PARNU
2390   2375   2545
2380   2755
2370   2570   2820   STOCKHOLM
2350   2315   E6   2842
2330   E18   2840
BERGEN   2320   OSLO   2825
2590   2615   2760   RIGA
2750   E18   2780
2805   LATVIA
2740   E20
2730
2735   2715   2800
E18   2710   2670   2675   LIEPAJA
2725   2720   2665   E22   2690   SIAULIAI
2600   2705   2680
STAVANGER   2660   GOTEBORG   KLAIPEDA   LITHUANIA
2610   2706
FREDERIKSHAVN   2655
E45
ALBORG   E06   2640   2630   E22
DENMARK   2645   2650   KALININGRAD
(MAP 5)
ARHUS   KOBENHAVN   MALMO
GDYNIA
E20   GDANSK
ESBJERG   ODENSE

E47   N1/E25   N51/E77

Please refer to the numerical index (page 565) for campsite page references

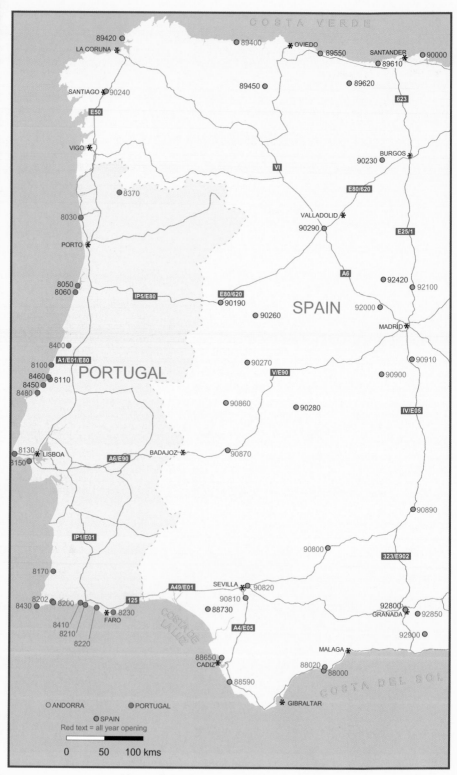

COSTA VERDE

89420
LA CORUNA
89400
OVIEDO
89550
SANTANDER
89610
90000

SANTIAGO
90240

89450
89620

623

E50

VIGO

VI

BURGOS
90230

8370

E80/620

8030

VALLADOLID
90290

PORTO

E25/1

A6

92420
92100

8050
8060

IP5/E80

E80/620
90190

90260

SPAIN

92000

MADRID

8400

90270

90910

8100
A1/E01/E80

PORTUGAL

V/E90

90900

8460
8450
8480

8110

90860

90280

IV/E05

8130
3150

LISBOA

A6/E90

BADAJOZ

90870

90890

IP1/E01

90800

323/E902

8170

A49/E01

SEVILLA

90820

8202
8430

8200

125

90810

88730

92800
GRANADA

92850

8410
8210

8230
FARO

COSTA DE LA LUZ

A4/E05

92900

8220

MALAGA

88650
CADIZ

88020

88000

88590

COSTA DEL SOL

○ ANDORRA   ● PORTUGAL

● SPAIN

Red text = all year opening

0   50   100 kms

GIBRALTAR

Please refer to the numerical index (page 565) for campsite page references

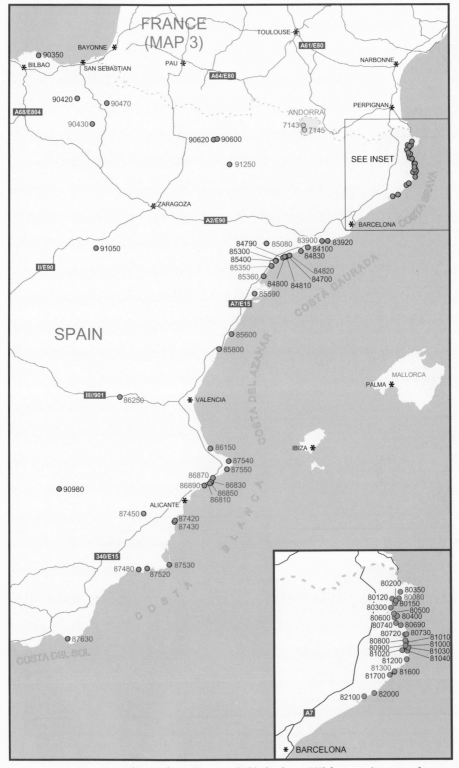

FRANCE
(MAP 3)

TOULOUSE ✱

90350 ●
BAYONNE ✱
A61/E80
BILBAO ✱
SAN SEBASTIAN ✱
PAU ✱
NARBONNE ✱
A64/E80
A68/E804
90420 ●
90470 ●
PERPIGNAN ✱
ANDORRA
90430 ●
7143 ● 7145
90620 ● ● 90600
SEE INSET
● 91250
91050 ●
BARCELONA ✱
II/E90
A2/E90
ZARAGOZA ✱
84790 ● 85080
83900 ● ● 83920
85300
84100
85400
84830
SPAIN
85350
84820
85360
84700
84800 84810
85590
A7/E15
COSTA DAURADA
● 85600
● 85800
MALLORCA
COSTA DEL AZAHAR
PALMA ✱
III//901
● 86250
VALENCIA ✱
● 86150
IBIZA ✱
● 87540
● 87550
86870
86890 ● 86830
90980 ●
86850
86810
ALICANTE ✱
87450 ●
● 87420
87430
COSTA BLANCA
340/E15
● 87530
87480 ● ●
87520
● 87630
COSTA DEL SOL

80200
80350
80120 80080
80300 80150
80500
80600 80400
80740 80690
80720 80730
80800 81010
80900 81000
81020 81030
81040
81200
81300 81600
81700
82100 ● ● 82000
A7
BARCELONA ✱

Please refer to the numerical index (page 565) for campsite page references

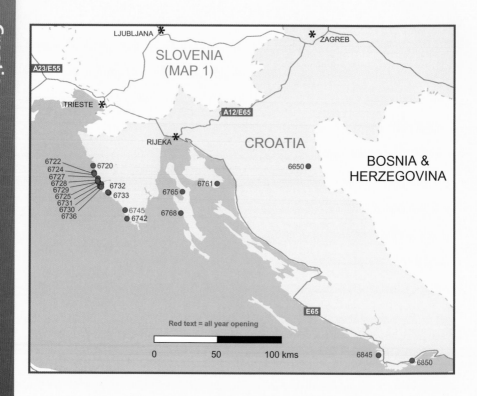

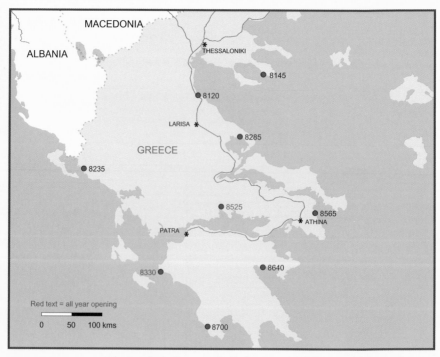

Please refer to the numerical index (page 565) for campsite page references

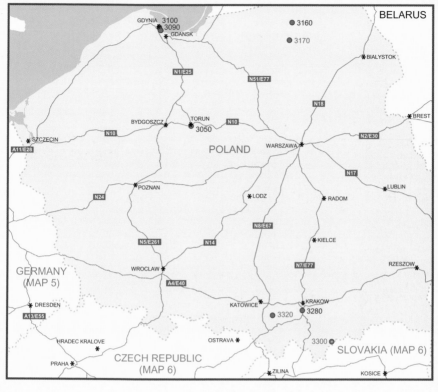

Please refer to the numerical index (page 565) for campsite page references

Index - town and village

Index - town and village

Index - campsite number

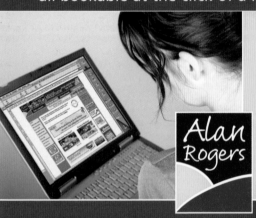

Index by Country and Campsite Name

Index - country and campsite name

Index - country and campsite name

Index by Country and Campsite Name continued

Acknowledgements

We would like to thank the following national and regional Tourist Boards for supplying photographs for use in this guide:

Andorra Tourist Office

Toerisme Vlaanderen

Croatian National Tourist Board

Danish Tourism Board

Bayern Tourismus

Hungarian Tourist Board

Italian Tourist Board

Liechtenstein Tourist Board

Luxembourg Tourist Office
Bourscheid Castle © Konrad Scheel
Vianden Castle overlooking the Old Town
© Marc Theis
Market town of Esch-sur-Sure © Marc Theis

Netherlands Tourist Board

Norwegian Tourist Board
North Cape Midnight Sun © Trym Ivar Bergsmo
Geirangerfjord © Per Eide
Sorlandet Lyngor © Niels Jorgensen

Portuguese National Tourism Office

Slovakia Travel

Turespana
L'Atmella de Mar © F. Ontanon
Broto © Oscar Masats

Costa Brava Girona Tourist Board

Sweden Travel & Travel Tourism Council

Switzerland Tourism

Widely regarded as the 'Bible' by site owners and readers alike, there is no better guide when it comes to forming an independent view of a campsite's quality. When you need to be confident in your choice of campsite, you need the Alan Rogers Guide.

✓ Sites only included on merit

✓ Sites cannot pay to be included

✓ Independently inspected, rigorously assessed

✓ Impartial reviews

✓ 40 years of expertise